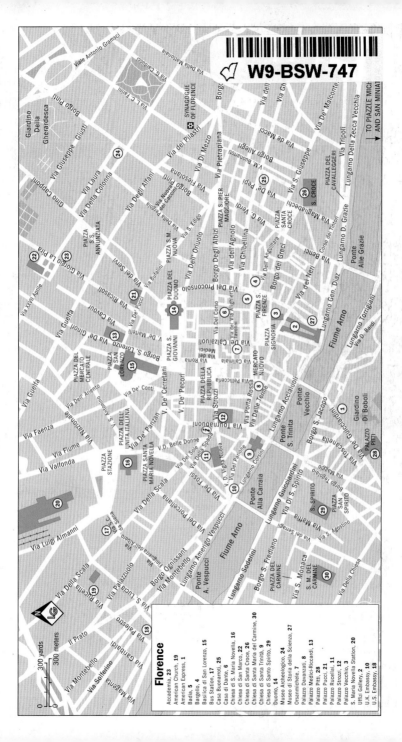

W9-BSW-747

Florence

Accademia, **23**
American Church, **19**
American Express, **1**
Badia, **5**
Bargello, **4**
Basilica di San Lorenzo, **15**
Bus Station, **17**
Casa Buonarroti, **25**
Casa di Dante, **6**
Chiesa di S. Maria Novella, **16**
Chiesa di San Marco, **22**
Chiesa di Santa Croce, **26**
Chiesa di Santa Maria del Carmine, **30**
Chiesa di Santa Trinità, **9**
Chiesa di Santo Spirito, **29**
Duomo, **14**
Museo Archeologico, **24**
Museo di Storia della Scienza, **27**
Orsanmichele, **7**
Palazzo Davanzati, **8**
Palazzo Medici-Riccardi, **13**
Palazzo Pitti, **28**
Palazzo Pucci, **21**
Palazzo Rucellai, **11**
Palazzo Strozzi, **12**
Palazzo Vecchio, **3**
S. Maria Novella Station, **20**
Uffizi Gallery, **2**
U.K. Embassy, **10**
U.S. Embassy, **18**

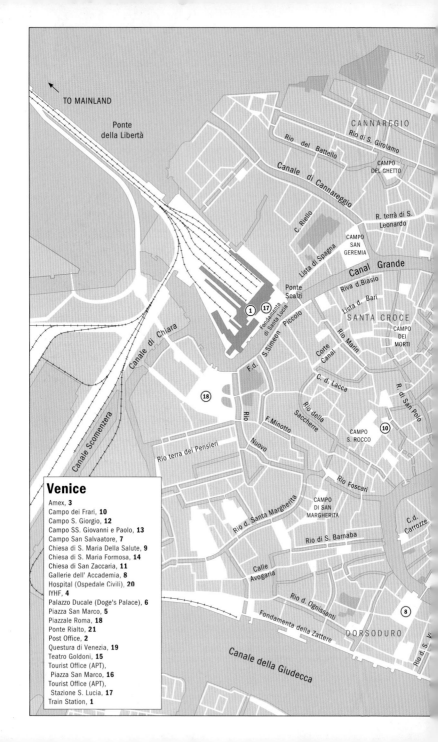

Venice

Amex, **3**
Campo dei Frari, **10**
Campo S. Giorgio, **12**
Campo SS. Giovanni e Paolo, **13**
Campo San Salvaatore, **7**
Chiesa di S. Maria Della Salute, **9**
Chiesa di S. Maria Formosa, **14**
Chiesa di San Zaccaria, **11**
Gallerie dell' Accademia, **8**
Hospital (Ospedale Civili) **20**
IYHF, **4**
Palazzo Ducale (Doge's Palace), **6**
Piazza San Marco, **5**
Piazzale Roma, **18**
Ponte Rialto, **21**
Post Office, **2**
Questura di Venezia, **19**
Teatro Goldoni, **15**
Tourist Office (APT),
 Piazza San Marco, **16**
Tourist Office (APT),
 Stazione S. Lucia, **17**
Train Station, **1**

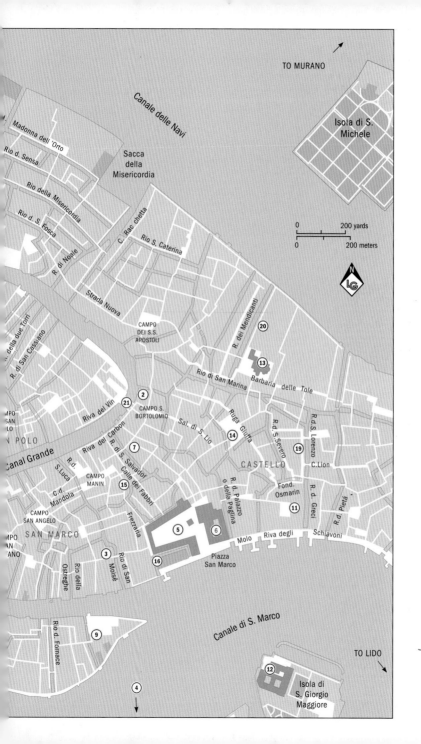

TO MURANO

Isola di S. Michele

Canale delle Navi

Madonna dell 'Orto

Rio d. Sensa

Rio della Misericordia

Rio d. S. Fosca

R. di Noale

Sacca della Misericordia

C. Racchetta

Rio S. Caterina

0   200 yards
0   200 meters

N
LG

Strada Nuova

CAMPO DEI S.S. APOSTOLI

R. dei Mendicanti

⑳

R. delle due torri

R. di San Cassiano

Rio di San Marina

⑬

Barbaria delle Tole

MPO SAN LO

Riva del Vin

②

㉑

CAMPO S. BORTOLOMIO

Sal. di S. Lio

Ruga Giuffa

R.d.S.Lorenzo

R.d.S.Severo

R.d.S.Lorenzo

N POLO

Riva del Carbon

R. di S. Salvador

⑭

⑲

CASTELLO

C.Lion

Canal Grande

R. d. S.Luca

⑦

Calle dei Fabbri

CAMPO MANIN

⑮

Fond. Osmarin

R. d. Greci

R. d. Pietà

C. d. Mandola

R. d. Palazzo o della Paglina

⑪

CAMPO SAN ANGELO

Frezzaria

⑤

⑥

Molo   Riva degli   Schiavoni

MPO AN ANO

SAN MARCO

③

Rio di San Moisè

⑯

Piazza San Marco

Rio della Ostreghe

Canale di S. Marco

Rio d. Fornace

⑨

TO LIDO

④

⑫

Isola di S. Giorgio Maggiore

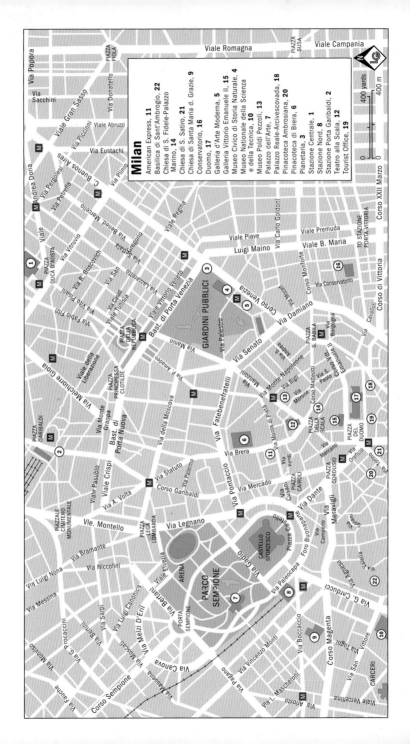

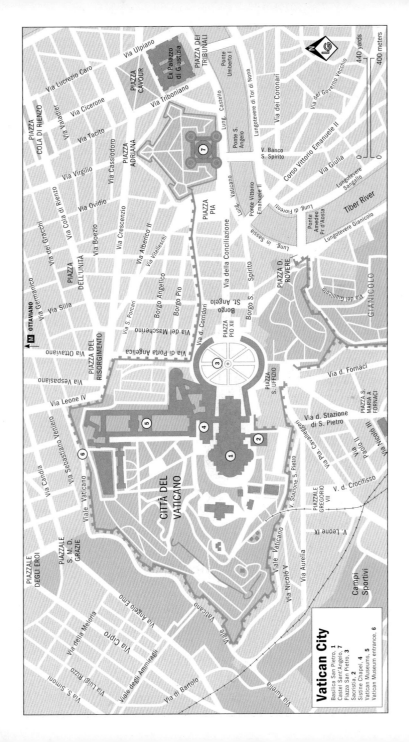

Vatican City

Basilica San Pietro, **1**
Castel Sant'Angelo, **7**
Piazza San Pietro, **3**
Sacristia, **2**
Sistine Chapel, **4**
Vatican Museums, **5**
Vatican Museum entrance, **6**

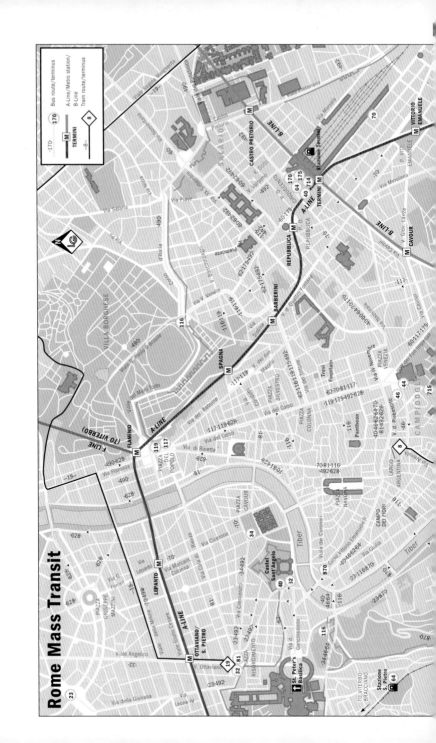

Rome Mass Transit

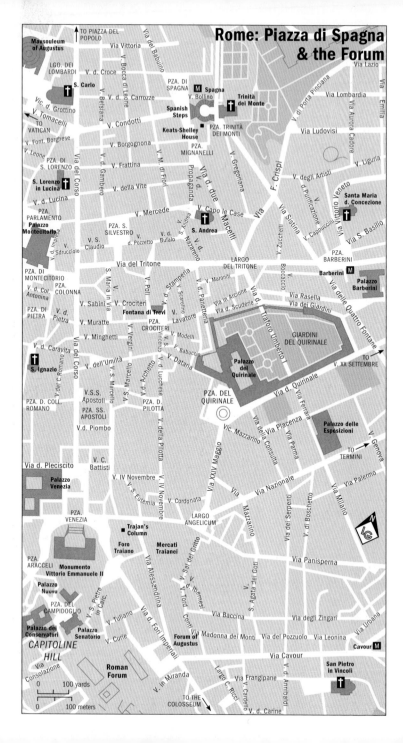

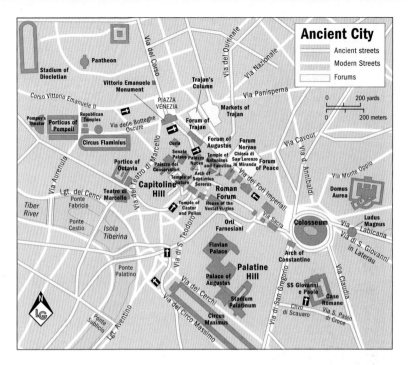

Ancient City

- Ancient streets
- Modern Streets
- Forums

0   200 yards

0   200 meters

Stadium of Diocletian

Pantheon

Via del Corso

Via del Quirinale

Via Nazionale

Vittorio Emanuele II Monument

Trajan's Column

Via Panisperna

Corso Vittorio Emanuele II

PIAZZA VENEZIA

Markets of Trajan

Pompey's Theater

Porticus of Pompeii

Republican Temples

Via delle Botteghe Oscure

Forum of Trajan

Via Cavour

Circus Flaminius

Curia

Forum of Augustus

Forum Neryae

Senate

Palace Palazzo Nuovo

Temple of Antoninus and Faustina

Chiesa di San Lorenzo in Miranda

Forum of Peace

Via d. Annibaldi

Portico of Octavia

Palazzo dei Conservatori

Arch of Septimius Serverus

Via dei Fori Imperiali

Via Monte Oppio

Via Aurenia

Lgt. dei Cenci

Teatro di Marcello

Temple of Saturn

Domus Aurea

Capitoline Hill

Roman Forum

Ludus Magnus

Tiber River

Ponte Fabricio

Via di S. Teodoro

Temple of Castor and Pollux

House of the Vestal Virgins

Via Sacra

Colosseum

Via Labicana

Ponte Cestio

Isola Tiberiana

Orti Farnesiani

Via di S. Giovanni in Laterau

Via del Teatro di Marcello

Flavian Palace

Arch of Constantine

Via Claudia

Ponte Palatino

Palace of Augustus

Palatine Hill

SS Giovanni e Paolo

Via di San Gregorio

Via dei Cerchi

Case Romane

Via S. Paolo di Croce

Ponte Sublicio

Lgt. Aventino

Via del Circo Massimo

Stadium Palatinum

Circus Maximus

Clivo di Scauaro

N

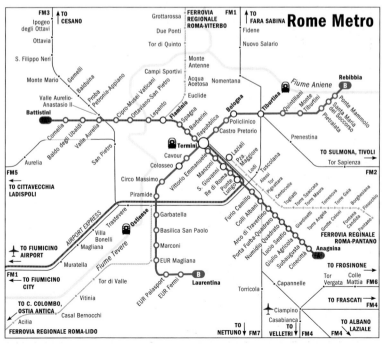

Rome Metro

FERROVIA REGIONALE ROMA-VITERBO

FM3

TO CESANO

Ipogeo degli Ottavi

Ottavia

S. Filippo Neri

Monte Mario

Valle Aurelio-Anastasio II

Battistini

Cornelia

Baldo degli Ubaldi

Valle Aurelia

Aurelia

FM5

TO CITTAVECCHIA LADISPOLI

FM1

TO FIUMICINO CITY

TO C. COLOMBO, OSTIA ANTICA

FERROVIA REGIONALE ROMA-LIDO

Gemelli

Balduina

Proba Petronia-Appiano

San Pietro

AIRPORT EXPRESS

TO FIUMICINO AIRPORT

Vitinia

Acilia

Casal Bernocchi

Grottarossa

Due Ponti

Tor di Quinto

Monte Antenne

Campi Sportivi

Acqua Acetosa

Cipro-Musei Vaticani

Ottaviano-San Pietro

Lepanto

Flaminio

Spagna

Barberini

Repubblica

Termini

Cavour

Colosseo

Circo Massimo

Piramide

Ostiense

Garbatella

Basilica San Paolo

Marconi

EUR Magliana

Villa Bonelli

Magliana

Muratella

Fiume Tevere

Tor di Valle

EUR Palasport

EUR Fermi

Laurentina

Trastevere

Vittorio Emanuele

Manzoni

S. Giovanni

Re di Roma

Ponte Lungo

Furio Camillo

Colli Albani

Arco di Travertino

Porta Furba-Quadraro

Numidio Quadrato

Lucio Sestio

Giulio Agricola

Subaugusta

Cinecittà

FERROVIA REGIONALE ROMA-PANTANO

FM1

FARA SABINA

Fidene

Nuovo Salario

Nomentana

Euclide

Bologna

Policlinico

Castro Pretorio

Piazzale Flaminio

Laziali

Pza. Maggiore

Lodi

Tuscolana

Alessi

Tor Pignatara

Centocelle

Torre Spaccata

Tor Vergata

Torricola

Capannelle

Ciampino

Casabianca

Torre Gaia

Giardinetti

Torre Angela

Grotte Celoni

Subaugusta

Anagnina

TO FROSINONE

Colle Mattia

FM6

TO FRASCATI

FM4

TO ALBANO LAZIALE

FM4

TO NETTUNO

FM7

TO VELLETRI

FM4

Fiume Aniene

Rebibbia

Ponte Mammolo

Santa Maria del Soccorso

Tiburtina

Quintiliani

Monte Tiburtini

Prenestina

TO SULMONA, TIVOLI

Tor Sapienza

FM2

Prenestina

Pietralata

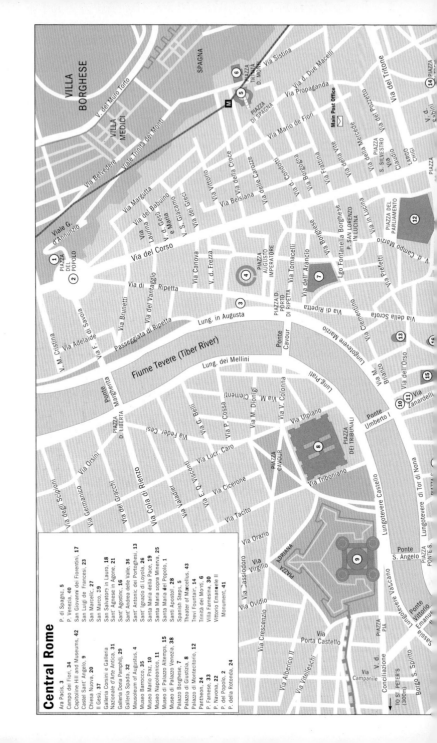

Central Rome

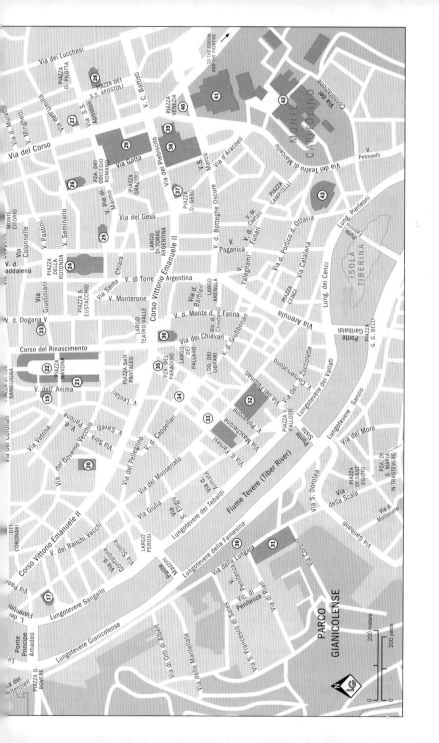

LET'S GO PUBLICATIONS

TRAVEL GUIDES
Australia 8th edition
Austria & Switzerland 12th edition
Brazil 1st edition
Britain 2006
California 10th edition
Central America 9th edition
Chile 2nd edition
China 5th edition
Costa Rica 2nd edition
Eastern Europe 12th edition
Ecuador 1st edition
Egypt 2nd edition
Europe 2006
France 2006
Germany 12th edition
Greece 8th edition
Hawaii 3rd edition
India & Nepal 8th edition
Ireland 12th edition
Israel 4th edition
Italy 2006
Japan 1st edition
Mexico 21st edition
Middle East 4th edition
New Zealand 7th edition
Peru 1st edition
Puerto Rico 2nd edition
South Africa 5th edition
Southeast Asia 9th edition
Spain & Portugal 2006
Thailand 2nd edition
Turkey 5th edition
USA 23rd edition
Vietnam 1st edition
Western Europe 2006

ROADTRIP GUIDE
Roadtripping USA

ADVENTURE GUIDES
Alaska 1st edition
Pacific Northwest 1st edition
Southwest USA 3rd edition

CITY GUIDES
Amsterdam 4th edition
Barcelona 3rd edition
Boston 4th edition
London 15th edition
New York City 15th edition
Paris 13th edition
Rome 12th edition
San Francisco 4th edition
Washington, D.C. 13th edition

POCKET CITY GUIDES
Amsterdam
Berlin
Boston
Chicago
London
New York City
Paris
San Francisco
Venice
Washington, D.C.

LET'S GO
ITALY
2006

INNA LIVITZ EDITOR
ANNA A. MATTSON-DiCECCA ASSOCIATE EDITOR
SAMANTHA GELFAND ASSOCIATE EDITOR

RESEARCHER-WRITERS
LAUREN HOLMES
MORGAN KRUGER
DIANA LIMBACH
STEFANIE LEIGH PLANT
JENNIFER RUGANI
CHRIS STARR

DAVID I. PALTIEL MAP EDITOR
ELLA M. STEIM MANAGING EDITOR

ST. MARTIN'S PRESS ❦ NEW YORK

HELPING LET'S GO. If you want to share your discoveries, suggestions, or corrections, please drop us a line. We read every piece of correspondence, whether a postcard, a 10-page email, or a coconut. **Address mail to:**

> **Let's Go: Italy**
> **67 Mount Auburn St.**
> **Cambridge, MA 02138**
> **USA**

Visit Let's Go at **http://www.letsgo.com,** or send email to:

> **feedback@letsgo.com**
> **Subject: "Let's Go: Italy"**

In addition to the invaluable travel advice our readers share with us, many are kind enough to offer their services as researchers or editors. Unfortunately, our charter enables us to employ only currently enrolled Harvard students.

Maps by David Lindroth copyright © 2006 by St. Martin's Press.

Distributed outside the USA and Canada by Macmillan.

ISBN: 0-312-34898-3
EAN: 978-0-312-34898-4
2006 edition
10 9 8 7 6 5 4 3 2 1

Let's Go: Italy is written by Let's Go Publications, 67 Mount Auburn St., Cambridge, MA 02138, USA.

Let's Go® and the LG logo are trademarks of Let's Go, Inc. Printed in the USA.

HOW TO USE THIS BOOK

COVERAGE LAYOUT. Welcome to *Let's Go Italy 2006*. Though your adventure on the Italian peninsula may be unpredictable, you can always count on our guide to present the relevant information in a consistent manner. Starting with the grandiose capital of **Rome,** the coverage then descends from the mountaintops of **Valle d'Aosta** in the north to the sunny tips of **Calabria** and **Puglia** in the south. The last two chapters are devoted to Italy's insular provinces **Sicily** and **Sardinia**.

TRANSPORTATION INFO. Sections on intercity transportation generally cover all major destinations; small towns will list connections to bigger cities, but not necessarily vice versa. Parentheticals usually provide the trip duration, followed by the frequency, then the price. For more general information on travel, consult the **Essentials** (p. 8) section.

GENERAL INFO. The first chapter, **Discover Italy** (p. 1), contains **Let's Go Picks** (our favorite places in Italy) and a few themed **Suggested Itineraries.** The **Essentials** (p. 8) section provides logistical information and useful tips for travelers in Italy. The **Life and Times** section (p. 51) reads like Cliff's Notes and gives a spicy summary of 3000 years of history, culture, and customs. The **Appendix** (p. 761) features an Italian phrasebook with a menu reader, climate information, measurement conversions, and a distance and times chart for travel between major cities. For information on study abroad, volunteer, and work opportunities in Italy, consult **Beyond Tourism** (p. 81).

SCHOLARLY ARTICLES. Four contributors with unique insight wrote articles for *Let's Go: Italy 2006*. Former *Let's Go* researcher Edoardo Gallo discusses the cultural institution of soccer in Italy (p. 76), while another *Let's Go* researcher adresses the role of tourism in Southern Italy. Timothy O'Sullivan, a professor of Classics from Trinity University, describes the legacy of the Roman *passeggiata* (p. 148). Finally, Harvard graduate Abby Garcia offers an account of her year as a teacher in Trieste (p. 377).

PRICE DIVERSITY. Establishments are listed from best to worst, with absolute favorites denoted by the *Let's Go* thumbs-up (🖾). Since the cheapest price does not always mean the best value, we have incorporated a system of price ranges for food and accommodations (p. x).

LANGUAGE AND OTHER QUIRKS. The English translations of Italian city names are listed first, followed by their Italian name in parentheses. For a guide to Italian pronunciation and a glossary of commonly used Italian words and phrases, consult the **Appendix** (p. 761).

PHONE CODES AND TELEPHONE NUMBERS. Area codes for each city appear opposite the name of the region and are denoted by the ☎ icon. Phone numbers in text are also preceded by the ☎ icon.

A NOTE TO OUR READERS. The information for this book was gathered by *Let's Go* researchers from May through August of 2005. Each listing is based on one researcher's opinion, formed during his or her visit at a particular time. Those traveling at other times may have different experiences since prices, dates, hours, and conditions are always subject to change. You are urged to check the facts presented in this book beforehand to avoid inconvenience and surprises.

CONTENTS

Italy: Chapters

- The Veneto and Trentino-Alto Adige pp. 300-363
- Friuli-Venezia Giulia pp. 364-377
- Lombardy pp. 236-299
- Piedmont and Valle d'Aosta pp. 150-194
- Emilia-Romagna pp. 378-416
- Liguria pp. 195-235
- Tuscany pp. 417-497
- Umbria and Le Marche pp. 498-539
- Abruzzo and Molise pp. 540-555
- Rome and Lazio pp. 93-149
- Campania pp. 556-612
- Puglia, Basilicata, and Calabria pp. 613-646
- Sardinia pp. 725-760
- Sicily pp. 647-724

PRICE RANGES >> ITALY

Our researchers list establishments in order of value from best to worst; our favorites are denoted by the Let's Go thumbs-up (☒). Since the best value is not always the cheapest price, however, we have also incorporated a system of price ranges, based on a rough expectation of what you'll spend. For **accommodations,** we base our range on the cheapest price for which a single traveler can stay for one night. (A few *pensioni* don't have single rooms, so solo travelers may end up paying for a double. As a result, two travelers may sometimes get a much better deal than suggested by the price diversity icon.) For **restaurants** and other dining establishments, we estimate the average amount a single traveler will spend. The table tells you what you'll *typically* find in Italy at the corresponding price range; keep in mind that no system can allow for every individual establishment's quirks.

ACCOMMODATIONS	RANGE	WHAT YOU'RE *LIKELY* TO FIND
❶	under €16	Camping; cheaper hostels and most HI dorms. Expect bunk beds and a communal bath. You may have to rent towels and sheets or provide your own.
❷	€16-25	Most non-HI hostels; small, family-run hotels or *pensioni* with few amenities. You may have a sink in your room, but you will probably share a shower down the hall.
❸	€26-40	A small room with optional private bath in a family-run *pensione* or modern hotel. Most have decent amenities, including phone, TV, and occasionally A/C. Breakfast may be included in the price of the room.
❹	€41-60	Similar to ❸, but usually has more amenities, includes breakfast or lunch, or is more centrally located.
❺	over €60	Large hotels; superior service. If it's a ❺ and doesn't have the perks you want, you've paid too much.

FOOD	RANGE	WHAT YOU'RE *LIKELY* TO FIND
❶	under €7	Street stands, *gelaterie,* sandwiches at a *bar,* cafes, pizza places, or fast-food joints. Rarely a sit-down meal.
❷	€7-15	Sit-down *pizzerie* and most affordable *trattorie,* some only open for lunch. Should include mid-priced *primi* and *secondi.* The tip and cover charge may bump you up a couple euro.
❸	€16-20	Similar to ❷, but nicer setting and a more elaborate menu. May offer a cheaper lunch *menù*, and pizza could be a less expensive alternative to a *primi* and *secondi* combination.
❹	€21-25	A fancier restaurant with traditional or *nouveau* cuisine and fresh seafood. Few restaurants in this range have a dress code, but some may look down on t-shirts, jeans, or shorts.
❺	over €25	Venerable reputation, a 90-page wine list, or the freshest seafood with a harbor view. Elegant attire may be expected.

RESEARCHER-WRITERS

Lauren Holmes *Abruzzo, Molise, Campania, Puglia, Basilicata*

Lauren is as vivacious and exciting as her favorite city, Naples. Returning to Italy after researching Tuscany and Liguria for *Let's Go Italy 2005* and spending a semester in Siena, this savvy traveler swam in three seas, fended off Italian men, and always sent home the inside scoop. From Abruzzo to Amalfi, Lauren ventured off the beaten path to discover some of Italy's most under-appreciated regions.

Morgan Kruger *The Veneto, Trentino, Emilia-Romagna, Friuli*

After chasing her passport across the U.S., we're still trying to get Morgan home from her brilliant jaunt as an independent traveler. Equipped with a quick wit and sharp eye, this Los Angeles native scaled walls and interrogated monks with equal aplomb. Using Italian in Assisi and German in Bolzano, Morgan learned to sweet talk her way into always being in the know.

Diana Limbach *Rome, Lazio, Sardinia*

Diana's route led her to Italy's polar opposites: after conquering Rome's seven hills and throwing at least one coin into the fountain of Trevi, this California city girl braved the buses and beaches of rugged Sardinia. Whether sailing through the Grotte di Nettuno or weaving her way through the Roman Forum, Diana always managed to think outside the box and send back creative copy.

Stefanie Leigh Plant *Lombardy, Piedmont, and Valle d'Aosta*

No mountain was insurmountable, no bike path too strenuous for this avid outdoor enthusiast from Salt Lake City. From contemporary art exhibits to mud baths, Stefanie never failed to overwhelm us with a wealth of information on hidden deals. Sampling wines, cheeses, and truffles as she made her way from the Lake Country to Piedmont, Stefanie finished her route in Turin with an insider's preview of the upcoming Olympic Games.

Jennifer Rugani *Liguria, Tuscany, Umbria*

Dodging renegade cars in Alassio and galloping horses in Siena, Jen explored Italy's heartland with unshakeable confidence. Her wit and diligence shine through her writing. This California girl hardly broke a sweat as she hiked the Cinque Terre, climbed the leaning tower of Pisa, and trekked all the way to Elba. Jen got to explore her roots in Tuscany, where her family originated, before ducking into Umbria for Perugia's Jazz Festival and completing her stellar route with a week in Florence.

Chris Starr *Sicily and Calabria*

Beset by hurricanes, seafood, and glue sticks, this Let's Go veteran made friends everywhere he went. Chris never missed a beat—his charm turned heads and boats as he dashed from island to island. Diligent and hilarious, Chris gave Italian men a run for their money and truly became the shining Starr of Sicily.

CONTRIBUTING WRITERS

Alexander Bevilacqua was born in Milan, and has lived in Germany, Australia, and the US. This former researcher for *Let's Go: Germany 2005* works at Harvard's Center for European Studies, conducting research on literary multiculturalism.

Edoardo Gallo hails from Cuneo, Italy, and was a researcher-writer for *Let's Go: Central America 2005*. He graduated from Harvard in 2004 with honors in Physics and Mathematics. He is currently working as a consultant for Katzenbach in New York City.

Abby Garcia graduated from Harvard in 2003 with an honors degree in Psychology. She worked in Trieste, Italy at an international school for 10 months before moving back home to Texas. Abby hopes to return to Europe and work there again in the future.

Timothy O'Sullivan is an Assistant Professor in Classical Studies at Trinity University in San Antonio, Texas. He earned a Ph.D. in Classical Philology from Harvard in 2003, with a dissertation entitled "The Mind in Motion: The Cultural Significance of Walking in the Roman World."

Yaran Noti, a two-time Let's Go vet, researched Campania, Puglia, and Sardinia for Let's Go Italy: 2005. His favorite city in Italy is Naples, and he enjoys wild boar-hunting in his spare time.

ACKNOWLEDGMENTS

LET'S GO

TEAM ITALY THANKS: Unforgettable RWs. France for baked goods. Ella for firm guidance. KT, JB, and BRI for extra help. David for the look. Prod for the "hills." SPAM: heeey! Yip for being our prize. Big Mama for nothing.
INNA THANKS: Anna, for ensuring the survival of our bookfile through organizational genius. Sam for rejecting all offers to run off to Italy. Ella for pages of eeeeee! David for Rome and midnight caffè. Claire for the tea; Carl for making Carlestchaud possible. Clay, for institutional memory and incredible memories. Alex for stuffed muscles and Italian craziness. Anya for keeping me sane. GCB for introducing me to the art of travel. Мама, Папа, and Dimitri for being 15min. away.
ANNA THANKS: Inna, for her inquisitive mind; Sam, for being contagious, hilarious, and generally outrageous; Ella, for impeccable sarcasm; David for untiring perfection; Alex, for teaching me how to type; Club Carlestchaud, for its stunningly beautiful crowd of regulars; Linden for being my best buddy; Alex and the blockmates, for fun and love; David, for patience and wisdom; Mom, Dad, Kirstin, Eloise, and Bentley, for the best Toga Party ever (and the police, for not arresting them).
SAM THANKS: Ella for calling us "delinquents." Inna for censoring my hiking metaphors. Anna for pole dancing and being such a jerk. Claire and Carl for being ugly and hot, respectively. David for screams. My family for the constant support and OJ. Mel, for NOT being a girl who for a ringing phone drops exactly nothing. Brian for love and happiness. Rachael for cake. Tim for self-now. Finally, I'd like to thank the men of Italy for proposing so many times. And it's not a boot, it's a lobster claw.
DAVID THANKS: Inna for being innacredible, Anna for being annamazing, Sam for being samtastic. And Mapland, you're the best.

Editor
Inna Livitz
Associate Editors
Anna A. Mattson-DiCecca, Samantha Gelfand
Managing Editor
Ella M. Steim
Map Editor
David I. Paltiel
Typesetter
Ansel S. Witthaus

Publishing Director
Seth Robinson
Editor-in-Chief
Stuart J. Robinson
Production Manager
Alexandra Hoffer
Cartography Manager
Katherine J. Thompson
Editorial Managers
Rachel M. Burke, Ashley Eva Isaacson, Laura E. Martin
Financial Manager
Adrienne Taylor Gerken
Publicity Manager
Alexandra C. Stanek
Personnel Manager
Ella M. Steim
Production Associate
Ansel S. Witthaus
IT Director
Jeffrey Hoffman Yip
Director of E-Commerce
Michael Reckhow
Office Coordinator
Matthew Gibson

Director of Advertising Sales
Jillian N. London
Senior Advertising Associates
Jessica C.L. Chiu, Katya M. Golovchenko, Mohammed J. Herzallah
Advertising Graphic Designer
Emily E. Maston

President
Caleb J. Merkl
General Manager
Robert B. Rombauer
Assistant General Manager
Anne E. Chisholm

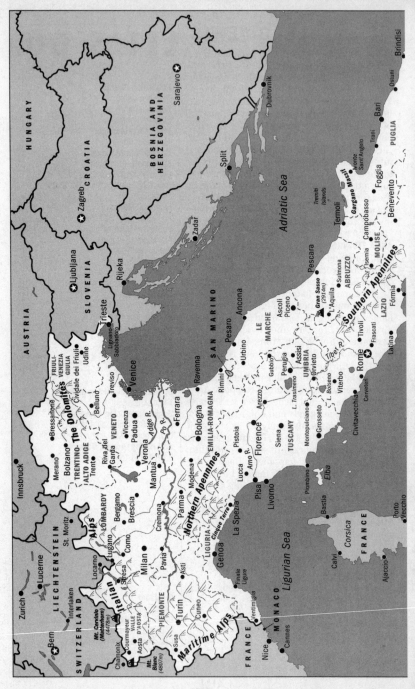

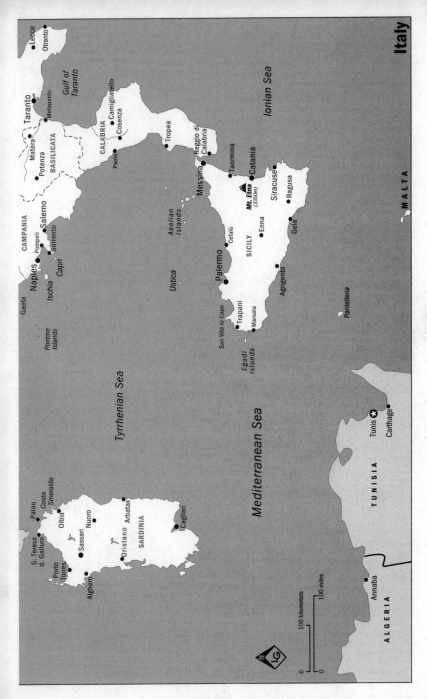

Italy

Lecce
Otranto

Gulf of
Taranto

Taranto
Metaponto

Camigliatello

Matera   Cosenza
Potenza
BASILICATA   CALABRIA

Tropea

CAMPANIA   Paola

Salerno   Reggio di
Pompeii   Calabria
Naples Sorrento   Messina
Gaeta Capri   Taormina
      Ischia   Aeolian   Mt. Etna Catania
Pontine   Islands   (3350m)
Islands   Enna   Siracuse
                Ustica Cefalù SICILY   Ragusa

                     Palermo
            San Vito lo Capo
                        Trapani   Gela
                        Marsala
                     Egadi   Agrigento
                     Islands

Ionian Sea

Tyrrhenian Sea

Pantelleria

Mediterranean Sea

MALTA

S. Teresa
d. Gallura Palau
         Costa
Porto   Smeralda
Torres   Olbia
Sassari   Nuoro
Alghero   Arbatax
        Oristano
        SARDINIA
              Cagliari

Tunis
Carthage

TUNISIA

100 kilometers

100 miles

Annaba

ALGERIA

XV

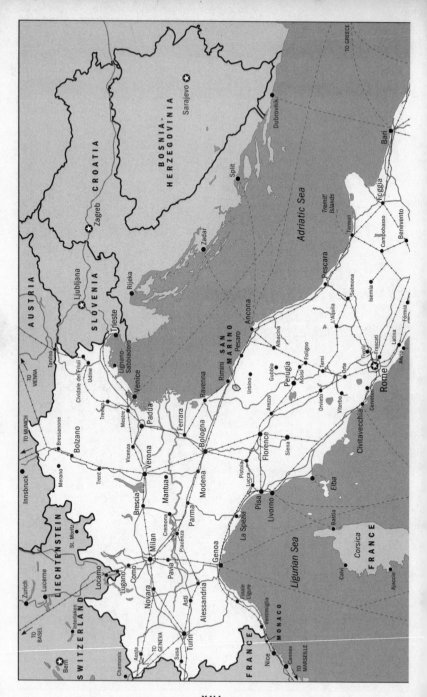

XVI

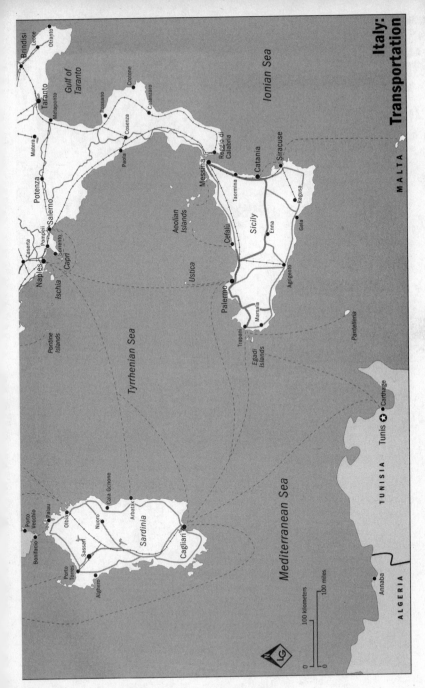

Italy:
Transportation

XVII

accommodation in naples

DISCOVER ITALY

The best way to discover Italy is to immerse yourself. Wander aimlessly down side streets, loiter against the sun-baked stone lip of a fountain, and witness old Italian men serenading their wives with their authentic versions of "O Sole Mio." See for yourself the origins of the Western world in Rome's graceful ruins and understand what it truly means to be Italian as soccer fans all around you scream—or sob—at the winning goal of a heated *calcio* match. Any way you choose to do it, discover Europe's boot with the understanding that, more than pretty beaches, decadent food, and ruthlessly flirtatious men, Italy offers a rich culture and history to those who seek it. Avoid a generic experience (eating spaghetti, dashing through art museums, glancing at the Colosseum) by taking time to appreciate Italy's quirky and passionate people, perhaps the only ones in the world to gesticulate wildly even while talking on the phone. And even during your most action-packed adventures, don't forget to step back, as Italians often do, and experience *la dolce far niente*—literally, the sweetness of doing nothing.

FACTS AND FIGURES

OFFICIAL NAME: Repubblica Italiana

ITALY 2005 POPULATION: 58 million

RELIGION: Roman Catholic (98%)

REGULAR CHURCHGOERS: 21 million

REGULAR SOCCER FANS: 30 million

INDEPENDENT STATES WITHIN ITALIAN BORDERS: 2

NUMBER OF FOREIGN VISITORS IN 2000: 33,000

NUMBER OF CELLPHONES: 50 million

NUMBER OF CHILDREN BORN PER WOMAN: 1.28 (2.1 recommended for stable population growth)

WOMEN ARRESTED FOR MAFIA ACTIVITY 1990-2000: 100+

WHEN TO GO

Tourism enters overdrive in June, July, and August. Hotels are booked solid, prices skyrocket, and rows of lounge chairs take over pristine beaches. During *Ferragosto*, a national holiday on August 15, Italians head to the coast, and Italy all but shuts down for a good part of the month. Though many find the larger cities enjoyable even during this holiday, late May through July make for a livelier trip. Traveling to Italy in early May or early September assures a calmer, cooler vacation. The temperature drops to a comfortable average of 25°C (77°F) with regional variations. Depending on the region, a trip in April or October has the advantage of lower prices and smaller crowds. The best weather for hiking in the Alps is from July to September; ski season lasts from December through late March.

WHAT TO DO

ART SAVVY

As might be expected, the country's largest cities house the most important art collections, but virtually every small town has its own *museo archeologico* or *pinacoteca* (art gallery) showcasing collections from Greek pottery shards and Roman mosaics to contemporary art. A list follows with collections that travelers shouldn't miss, but this list is by no means exhaustive. Often the most rewarding experience comes from seeking out that lone Caravaggio or da Messina in a regional museum where it can be viewed and studied without lines or crowds.

CITY	PRINCIPAL ART COLLECTIONS
Florence	Uffizi Gallery (p. 435)
	Museo dell'Opera del Duomo (p. 433)
Milan	Pinacoteca di Brera (p. 251)
	Galleria d'Arte Moderna (p. 252)
Naples	Museo e Galleria di Capodimonte (p. 571)
Rome	Sistine Chapel (p. 134)
	Vatican Museums (p. 134)
	Galleria Borghese (p. 135)
	Museo Nazionale d'Arte Antica (p. 136)
Rovereto	Museo d'Arte Moderna e Contemporanea—"il Mart" (p. 359)
Siena	Pinacoteca Nazionale (p. 454)
	Museo dell'Opera Metropolitana (p. 453)
Turin	Museo Egizio (p. 159)
	Galleria Sabauda (p. 159)
Venice	Collezione Peggy Guggenheim (p. 318)
	Gallerie dell'Accademia (p. 318)

CUCINA ITALIANA

World-renowned for its sumptuous victuals, Italy's gastronomic tradition is varied enough to please everyone. Regions in Italy are as easily recognized by the food on the table as by the landscape. In the north, Piedmont and Lombardy supply the country and the world with premier red wines and hearty *risotto*. On the coast, Liguria churns out flavorful pesto, and, further inland, Emilia-Romagna reigns as culinary capital of Italy; *bolognese* meat sauce, *prosciutto crudo*, and balsamic vinegar all hail from this central region. Farther down the boot, Tuscany serves up *gelato* and *bistecca alla fiorentina* as only inventors can. Next door, Umbria satisfies any craving for sweet with *baci* chocolates, *torciglione* almond bread, and *torrone* nougat. In the south, Campania heats things up with wood-fired pizzas and Sicily cools them down with *granita*, a slushy version of *gelato*.

BEACH BUMMING

Sandwiched between the Mediterranean and Adriatic Seas, the Italian coastline stretches over 2000 miles. In the northwest, the famous beaches of **Liguria** (p. 195) form the Italian Riviera, home to the picturesque fishing villages of **Cinque Terre** (p. 210). Farther down Italy's western coast, the serene **Amalfi Coast** (p. 597) offers dark blue waters overhung with cliffs and lemon groves. The sand dunes and stone beaches of **Calabria** (p. 636) on the Ionian and Tyrrhenian coasts remain relatively unknown to tourists. In Abruzzo and Molise, the **Tremiti Islands** (p. 553) are home to rocky coves and secluded beaches good for swimming and snorkeling. In the northeast, **Rimini** (p. 406) attracts a large student population to fine sand beaches on the Adriatic Sea. Though lesser known, Sicily's beaches are a worthwhile stop if you're in the area, varying from resort towns like **Cefalù** (p. 660) to the dark stone beaches of **Pantelleria** (p. 719).

OUT AND ABOUT

While thousands of tourists explore the Swiss and Austrian Alps, travelers often overlook Italy's opportunities for the outdoor adventurer. Italian mountain ranges include the northern **Alps** and the **Apennines,** which run north-south through the center of the country. Various water sports, including windsurfing, canoeing, whitewater rafting, and kayaking, await at **Riva del Garda** (p. 360) near the **Dolomites** (the northeast region of the Italian Alps). The mountains themselves offer challenging multi-day hikes, as well as many worthwhile daytrips and mountain biking for all levels of experience. Go to **Cinque Terre** (p. 210) for magnificent views and intermediate-level hiking along winding paths connecting the five fishing towns. Just to the north, **Turin** (p. 150) offers medium to difficult rock climbing, hang gliding, and—quite literally—Olympic-level skiing, including multi-peak skiing expeditions from village to village. The **Alps** (including **Valle d'Aosta,** p. 184) also have superb skiing options. In **Courmayeur** and nearby **Monte Bianco** (p. 192), both easy hikes and difficult mountaineering are available. For varying levels of hiking, breathtaking woodland views, and unique wildlife, head to **Abruzzo National Park** (p. 547) in the Southern Apennines. The park offers several good biking trails as well as winter skiing. Further south, **Sila Massif** (p. 644) in Calabria also offers hiking and 35km of beautiful cross-country skiing. The **Aeolian Islands** (p. 663) are home to both active and inactive volcanoes. **Mount Etna** (p. 689) offers prime volcanic terrain and 50m of far-reaching views. (See **Suggested Itineraries: Tour of Hell,** p. 6.) For charms of a more mercurial nature, head to the island of **Ustica** (p. 658), home to extensive scuba diving options and 9km of coastline hiking.

ANCIENT SHADOWS

Ruins are one of Italy's major attractions. The former seat of the Roman Empire is home to both crumbling and wonderfully preserved arches, aqueducts, and amphitheaters. Although many Italian cities, including **Spoleto** (p. 516), **Rimini** (p. 406), **Aquileia** (p. 371), **Aosta** (p. 186), and **Acqui Terme** (p. 177) boast some sort of Roman relic, the most impressive ruins are scattered through the streets of **Rome** (p. 93), where travelers can admire the famous Colosseum, Pantheon, and Roman Forum. Daytrips from Rome lead to the extravagant **Villa Adriana** in Tivoli (p. 143) and the ancient city of **Ostia Antica** (p. 144). Farther south, **Naples** (p. 556) boasts a world-renowned archaeological museum and miles of subterranean Roman aqueducts open for exploration. Nearby **Pompeii** (p. 578) houses hundreds of artifacts and ruins literally set in stone by the first-century eruption of Mt. Vesuvius, and the neighboring excavation site, **Herculaneum** (p. 574), features a surprisingly intact 2000-year-old town. Across the peninsula, **Brindisi** (p. 619) is home to the column marking the end of the Appian Way, an ancient road that, of course, led to Rome. Italy also has numerous relics of pre-Roman inhabitants. Etruscan artifacts can be found in many Tuscan towns like **Fiesole** (p. 447), while Sicily's proximity to Greece led to the establishment of many Greek colonies in the region, including **Segesta** (p. 715), **Agrigento** (p. 705), and **Syracuse** (p. 695). On the mainland, **Paestum** (p. 611) is home to both Doric temples and Roman forums. Evidence of more ancient civilizations can be found in **Matera's** *sassi* (p. 631), **Albero-bello's** *trulli* (p. 618), and in **Sardinia's** *nuraghi* (p. 725).

❧ LET'S GO PICKS

BEST PLACE TO PLOT THE RUTHLESS ACQUISITION OF OTHER NATION-STATES: Gain inspiration in Machiavelli's hometown of **Florence** (p. 417).

BEST DEAD FOLK: Revel in the huge **Cappuchin Catacombs** (p. 655) in Palermo, where 8000 bodies rest in their moth-eaten Sunday best or in the partially decayed body of **Ötzi** (p. 349), a 5000-year-old Ice Man in Bolzano.

BEST PLACE TO TRY NEW NUTS: Catania's *Fontana dell'Elefante* (p. 688). Rumor has it that visitors aspiring to attain citizenship can do so by kissing this elephant's giant testicles.

BEST PLACE TO BEHAVE LIKE A JUNIOR-HIGH GIRL: Juliet's balcony in **Verona** (p. 335), where hundreds of teens leave love notes posted with chewing gum.

BEST PLACE TO SAMPLE A NEW SPECIES: Sardinia (p. 725), where horse, boar, and dogfish are quotidian. Also try **Orta's** (p. 182) *tapulon* (minced donkey meat cooked in red wine).

BEST CHURCHES FOR PURCHASING LIQUOR: In Rome, the benedictine at **San Paolo Fuori Mura (p. 132)** may be more tasty than the herby eucalyptine from the **Abbey of the Three Fountains (p. 133)**.

BEST PLACE TO EMPTY YOUR CUP: Leave your bra and your empty beer mug at **Bacaro Jazz** in **Venice** (p. 326).

BEST PLACE TO SHOW UP BACCHUS HIMSELF: In the vineyards of the **Chianti** region (p. 455).

BEST PLACE TO SAY A HAIL MARY TO ATONE FOR BACCHANALIAN EXCESS: The **Vatican** (p. 121) offers confession in numerous languages.

BEST PLACE TO RENEW CHASTITY: The **Roman Forum** (p. 118), where Vestal Virgins once kept the flame burning; if they broke their vows, they were buried alive.

BEST PLACE TO BUY A DISPOSABLE BATHING SUIT: Vulcano (p. 668), where the corrosive acid of its radioactive mudpit ruthlessly destroys everything in its path.

SUGGESTED ITINERARIES
EATALY (5 WEEKS)

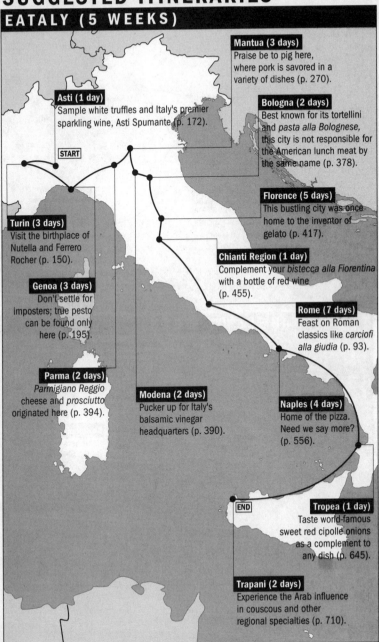

Mantua (3 days)
Praise be to pig here, where pork is savored in a variety of dishes (p. 270).

Asti (1 day)
Sample white truffles and Italy's premier sparkling wine, Asti Spumante (p. 172).

Bologna (2 days)
Best known for its tortellini and *pasta alla Bolognese*, this city is not responsible for the American lunch meat by the same name (p. 378).

START

Florence (5 days)
This bustling city was once home to the inventor of gelato (p. 417).

Turin (3 days)
Visit the birthplace of Nutella and Ferrero Rocher (p. 150).

Chianti Region (1 day)
Complement your *bistecca alla Fiorentina* with a bottle of red wine (p. 455).

Genoa (3 days)
Don't settle for imposters; true pesto can be found only here (p. 195).

Rome (7 days)
Feast on Roman classics like *carciofi alla giudia* (p. 93).

Parma (2 days)
Parmigiano Reggio cheese and *prosciutto* originated here (p. 394).

Modena (2 days)
Pucker up for Italy's balsamic vinegar headquarters (p. 390).

Naples (4 days)
Home of the pizza. Need we say more? (p. 556).

END

Tropea (1 day)
Taste world-famous sweet red cipolle onions as a complement to any dish (p. 645).

Trapani (2 days)
Experience the Arab influence in couscous and other regional specialties (p. 710).

DISCOVER

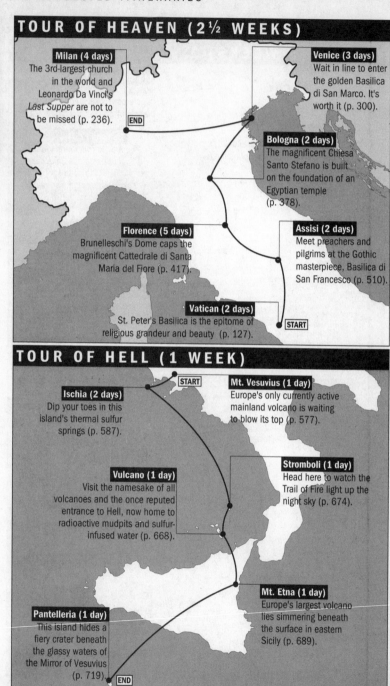

TOUR OF HEAVEN (2½ WEEKS)

Milan (4 days)
The 3rd-largest church in the world and Leonardo Da Vinci's *Last Supper* are not to be missed (p. 236).

Venice (3 days)
Wait in line to enter the golden Basilica di San Marco. It's worth it (p. 300).

END

Bologna (2 days)
The magnificent Chiesa Santo Stefano is built on the foundation of an Egyptian temple (p. 378).

Florence (5 days)
Brunelleschi's Dome caps the magnificent Cattedrale di Santa Maria del Fiore (p. 417).

Assisi (2 days)
Meet preachers and pilgrims at the Gothic masterpiece, Basilica di San Francesco (p. 510).

Vatican (2 days)
St. Peter's Basilica is the epitome of religious grandeur and beauty (p. 127).

START

TOUR OF HELL (1 WEEK)

START

Ischia (2 days)
Dip your toes in this island's thermal sulfur springs (p. 587).

Mt. Vesuvius (1 day)
Europe's only currently active mainland volcano is waiting to blow its top (p. 577).

Vulcano (1 day)
Visit the namesake of all volcanoes and the once reputed entrance to Hell, now home to radioactive mudpits and sulfur-infused water (p. 668).

Stromboli (1 day)
Head here to watch the Trail of Fire light up the night sky (p. 674).

Mt. Etna (1 day)
Europe's largest volcano lies simmering beneath the surface in eastern Sicily (p. 689).

Pantelleria (1 day)
This island hides a fiery crater beneath the glassy waters of the Mirror of Vesuvius (p. 719).

END

NORTHWEST NATURAL WONDERS (2 WEEKS)

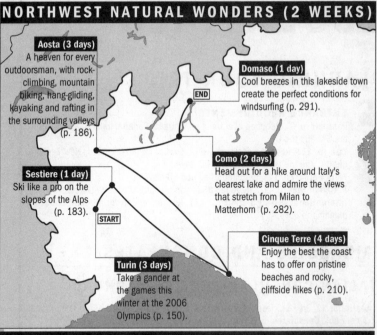

Aosta (3 days)
A heaven for every outdoorsman, with rock-climbing, mountain biking, hang-gliding, kayaking and rafting in the surrounding valleys (p. 186).

Domaso (1 day)
Cool breezes in this lakeside town create the perfect conditions for windsurfing (p. 291).

END

Sestiere (1 day)
Ski like a pro on the slopes of the Alps (p. 183).

Como (2 days)
Head out for a hike around Italy's clearest lake and admire the views that stretch from Milan to Matterhorn (p. 282).

START

Cinque Terre (4 days)
Enjoy the best the coast has to offer on pristine beaches and rocky, cliffside hikes (p. 210).

Turin (3 days)
Take a gander at the games this winter at the 2006 Olympics (p. 150).

LITERARY ITALY (2 WEEKS)

Verona (2 days)
This fair city, witness to Romeo and Juliet's fatal love affair, will not leave you so unsatisfied (p. 335).

START

Bologna (2 days)
Crash a class at the University of Bologna where famous writer Umberto Eco teaches (p. 378).

Rimini (2 days)
Paolo and Francesca, immortalized by Dante's *Inferno*, were caught in the throws of passion and killed in Rimini (p. 406).

Florence (5 days)
Boccaccio, Petrarch, Dante, and Machiavelli all gained inspiration in the uncontested center of Renaissance literature (p. 417).

Sulmona (2 days)
Ovid's hometown inscribes the acronym SMPE all over the city to commemorate the poet's proud statement, *"Sulmona mihi patria est"*—Sulmona is my homeland (p. 544).

Naples (4 days)
Where Virgil's tomb has been on display since 19 BC (p. 556)

END

ESSENTIALS

PLANNING YOUR TRIP

ENTRANCE REQUIREMENTS
Passport (p. 9). Required of citizens of Australia, Canada, Ireland, New Zealand, the UK, and the US.
Visa (p. 11). Required of citizens of Australia, Canada, Ireland, New Zealand, the UK, and the US for stays over 90 days.
Work Permit (p. 11). Required of all non-EU citizens.
Permit of Stay (p. 20). Required of all non-EU citizens planning to study in Italy.
International Driving Permit (p. 11). Recommended for all non-EU citizens planning to drive.

EMBASSIES AND CONSULATES

ITALIAN CONSULAR SERVICES ABROAD

Australia: 12 Grey St., Deakin, Canberra ACT 2600 (☎612 6273 3333; www.ambitalia.org.au). **Consulates:** 509, St. Kilda Rd., Melbourne VIC 3004 (☎61 3986 75744; itconmel@netlink.com.au); Level 45, Gateway, 1 Macquarie Pl., Sydney NSW 2000 (☎61 2939 27900; itconsyd@itconsyd.org).

Canada: 275 Slater St., 21st fl., Ottawa, ON K1P 5H9 (☎613-232-2401; www.italyincanada.com). **Consulate:** 3489 Drummond St., Montréal, QC H3G 1X6 (☎514-849-8351; www.italconsul.montreal.qc.ca).

Ireland: 63/65 Northumberland Rd., Dublin (☎353 166 017 44; www.italianembassy.ie).

New Zealand: 34-38 Grant Rd., Wellington (☎644 494 7170; www.italy-embassy.org.nz). 102 Kitchener Rd., Auckland (☎649 899 632; fax 649 486 1888).

UK: 14 Three Kings Yard, London W1K 4EH (☎44 20 731 222 00; www.embitaly.org.uk). **Consulates:** 32 Melville Street, Edinburgh EH3 7HA (☎44 131 226 36 31; consedimb@consedimb.demon.co.uk); 38 Eaton Pl., London SW1X 8AN (☎020 723 593 71); Rodwell Tower, 111 Piccadilly, Manchester M1 2HY (☎44 161 236 90 24; www.italianconsulate.co.uk).

US: 3000 Whitehaven St., Washington, D.C. 20008 (☎202-612-4400; www.italy-emb.org). **Consulates:** 100 Boylston St., #900, Boston, MA 02116 (☎617-542-0483; www.italianconsulateboston.org); 500 N. Michigan Ave., #1850, Chicago, IL 60611 (☎312-467-1550; www.italconschicago.org); 690 Park Ave. (visa office 54 E. 69th St.), New York, NY 10021 (☎212-737-91 00; www.italconsulnyc.org).

CONSULAR SERVICES IN ITALY

Australia: V. Antonio Bosio, 5, Rome 00161 (☎06 85 27 22 99, emergency 800 877 790; www.italy.embassy.gov.au). Open M-F 8:30am-5pm.

Canada: V. Giovanni Battista De Rossi, 27, Rome 00161 (☎06 44 59 81; www.dfait-maeci.gc.ca/canadaeuropa/italy/menu-en.asp). **Consulate:** V. Zara, 30 (☎06 44 59 83 937).

Ireland: P. Campitelli, 3, Rome 00186 (☎06 69 79 121; www.ambasciata-irlanda.it). Open M-F 10am-1pm.

New Zealand: V. Zara, 28, Rome 00198 (☎06 44 17 171; www.nzembassy.com). Embassy services M-F 8:30am-12:45pm and 1:45-5pm. **Consulate:** V. Guido d'Arezzo, 6, Milan 20145 (☎02 48 01 25 44).

UK: V. XX Settembre, 80, Rome 00187 (☎06 42 20 00 01; www.britain.it). Consular services open autumn, winter, spring M-F 9am-5pm; summer 8am-2pm. Closed UK and Italian holidays.

US: V. Veneto, 119/A, Rome 00187 (☎06 46 741; www.usembassy.it). Consular services open M-F 8:30am-5:30pm. Closed US and Italian holidays. **Consulate:** V. Principe Amedeo, 2/10, Milan 20121 (☎02 29 03 51).

TOURIST OFFICES

The Italian State Tourist Board (ENIT) provides useful information about many aspects of the country, including the arts, nature, history, and leisure activities. Visit their website, www.enit.it, for information in seven different languages. The main office in Rome (☎06 49 7111; sedecentrale@cert.enit.it) can help locate any local office that is not listed online.

Italian Government Tourist Board (ENIT): 630 5th Ave., #1565, New York, NY 10111, USA (☎212-245-5618; www.italiantourism.com). Write or call ☎212-245-4822 for a free copy of *Italia: General Information for Travelers to Italy*, containing train and ferry schedules. **Branch offices:** 1 Princes St., London, W1B 2AY UK (☎020 73 99 35 62; www.italiantouristboard.co.uk); Level 26, 44 Market St., Sydney NSW 2000, Australia (☎029 26 21 666; enitour@ihug.com.au); 175 E. Bloor St., #907 South Tower, Toronto, ON M4W 3R8, Canada (☎416-925-4882; enit.canada@on.aibn.com).

Italian Cultural Institute: 686 Park Ave., New York, NY 10021, USA (☎212-879-4242; www.italcultny.org); 11 Fitzwilliam Sq., Dublin 2, Ireland (☎676 66 62; www.italcult.ie). Provides useful links to Italian sites.

DOCUMENTS AND FORMALITIES

PASSPORTS

REQUIREMENTS
Citizens of Australia, Canada, Ireland, New Zealand, the UK, and the US need valid passports to enter Italy and to re-enter their home countries. Italy does not allow entrance if the holder's passport expires in under six months; returning home with an expired passport is illegal and may result in a fine.

NEW PASSPORTS
Citizens of Australia, Canada, Ireland, New Zealand, the UK, and the US can apply for a passport at any passport office or at selected post offices and courts of law. Citizens of these countries may also download passport applications from the official website of their country's government or passport office. Any new passport or

ONE EUROPE. European unity has come a long way since 1958, when the European Economic Community (EEC) was created to promote European solidarity and cooperation. Since then, the EEC has become the European Union (EU), a mighty political, legal, and economic institution. On May 1, 2004, 10 South, Central, and Eastern European countries—Cyprus, the Czech Republic, Estonia, Hungary, Latvia, Lithuania, Malta, Poland, Slovakia, and Slovenia—were admitted to the EU, joining 15 other member states: Austria, Belgium, Denmark, Finland, France, Germany, Greece, Ireland, Italy, Luxembourg, the Netherlands, Portugal, Spain, Sweden, and the UK.

What does this have to do with the average non-EU tourist? The EU's policy of **freedom of movement** means that border controls between the first 15 member states (minus Ireland and the UK, but plus Norway and Iceland) have been abolished, and visa policies harmonized. Under this treaty, formally known as the **Schengen Agreement,** you're still required to carry a passport (or government-issued ID card for EU citizens) when crossing an internal border, but once you've been admitted into one country, you're free to travel to other participating states. On June 5, 2005, Switzerland ratified the treaty, and will become fully participant by 2007. The 10 newest member states of the EU are anticipated to implement the policy after 2006. Britain and Ireland have also formed a **common travel area,** abolishing passport controls between the UK and the Republic of Ireland.

For more important consequences of the EU for travelers, see **The Euro** (p. 13) and **Customs in the EU** (p. 12).

renewal applications must be filed well in advance of the departure date, though most passport offices offer rush services for a very steep fee. Note, however, that "rushed" passports still take up to two weeks to arrive.

PASSPORT MAINTENANCE
Photocopy the page of your passport with your photo, as well as your visas, traveler's check serial numbers, and any other important documents. Carry one set of copies in a safe place, apart from the originals, and leave another set at home. Consulates also recommend that you carry an expired passport or an official copy of your birth certificate in a part of your baggage separate from other documents.

If you lose your passport, immediately notify the local police and the nearest embassy or consulate of your home government. To expedite its replacement, you must show ID and proof of citizenship; it also helps to know all information previously recorded in the passport. In some cases, a replacement may take weeks to process, and it may be valid only for a limited time. Any visas stamped in your old passport will be irretrievably lost. Should you lose your passport, it usually takes an average of 7-10 days to reissue a new one. In the event of a documented emergency, a limited passport (expires in one year) can be issued the same day that will permit you to re-enter your home country.

VISAS AND WORK PERMITS

VISAS
As of August 2005, EU citizens need only a valid passport to enter Italy and may stay as long as they like. Citizens of Australia, Canada, New Zealand, and the US do not need visas for stays of up to 90 days, but must purchase a visa if they intend to stay longer. This three-month period begins upon entry into any

of the countries that belong to the EU's **freedom of movement** zone (see **One Europe,** p. 10). Those staying longer than 90 days can purchase visas at home-country consulates. As of August 2005, a visa costs US$43.75 from the Italian Embassy in the United States. US citizens can take advantage of the **Center for International Business and Travel** (☎800-929-2428; www.cibt.com), which secures travel visas for a small charge.

All foreign nationals planning to stay in Italy over 90 days should apply within eight working days of arrival to receive a **permesso di soggiorno** (permit of stay). Generally, non-members of the EU are required to apply for a permit at a police station or foreign office (*questura*) if staying longer than 20 days or taking up residence in another location than a hotel, official campsite, or boarding house. If staying in a hotel or hostel, the staff will fulfill registration requirements for you, and the fee is waived. Steep fines punish a failure to comply. Those wishing to stay in Italy for more than three months for the purpose of tourism must apply for an extension of their stay at a local *questura* at least one month before the original permit expires. Double-check entrance requirements at the nearest embassy or consulate of Italy (listed under **Embassies and Consulates Abroad,** p. 8) before departure. Consult www.pueblo.gsa.gov/cic_text/travel/foreign/foreignentryreqs.html or www.stranieriinitalia.it (click on left side bar under heading *Per vivere in Italia)* for more information. US citizens can also consult http://travel.state.gov.

Entering Italy to study requires a student visa. For more information, see **Beyond Tourism** (p. 84) or visit www.italyemb.org.

WORK PERMITS

Admission as a visitor does not include the right to work, which is authorized only by a work permit. Work permits can be obtained from the Italian embassy for dependent, independent, and performing arts work. For more information, see **Beyond Tourism** (p. 88) or visit www.italyemb.org.

IDENTIFICATION

When you travel, always carry at least two forms of identification on your person, including a photo ID; a passport and a driver's license or birth certificate is usually adequate. Never carry all of your IDs together; split them up in case of theft or loss, and keep photocopies of all of them in your luggage and at home.

STUDENT, TEACHER, AND YOUTH IDENTIFICATION

The **International Student Identity Card (ISIC),** the most widely accepted form of student ID, provides discounts on some sights, accommodations, food, and transportation; access to a 24hr. emergency helpline; and insurance benefits for US cardholders (see **Insurance,** p. 21). For example, an ISIC card grants students admission to the Musei Vaticani for €7. For more information about discounts and ISICs in general, visit www.isicus.com/MyISIC. Applicants must be full-time secondary or post-secondary school students at least 12 years of age. Because of the proliferation of fake ISICs, some services (particularly airlines) require additional proof of student identity.

The **International Teacher Identity Card (ITIC)** offers teachers the same insurance coverage as the ISIC and similar but limited discounts. For travelers who are under 26 years old but are not students, the **International Youth Travel Card (IYTC)** also offers many of the same benefits as the ISIC.

Each of these identity cards costs US$22 or equivalent. ISICs and ITICs are valid until the new year unless purchased between September and December, in

ESSENTIALS

which case they are valid until the beginning of the following new year. Thus, a card purchased in March 2006 will be valid until December 31, 2006, while a card purchased in November 2006 will be valid until December 31, 2007. IYTCs are valid for one year from the date of issue. To learn more about ISICs, ITICs, and IYTCs, try www.myisic.com. Many student travel agencies (see p. 25) issue the cards; for a list of issuing agencies or more information, see the **International Student Travel Confederation (ISTC)** website (www.istc.org).

The **International Student Exchange Card (ISE Card)** is a similar identification card available to students, faculty, and youths aged 12 to 26. The card provides discounts, medical benefits, access to a 24hr. emergency helpline, and the ability to purchase student airfares. For example, an ISE card grants students a 10% discount at Hotel Ginevra in Naples. For information about other discounts, visit http://68.14.208.174:591/world/index.htm. An ISE Card costs US$25; call ☎800-255-8000 for more info, or visit www.isecard.com.

CUSTOMS

Upon entering Italy, you must declare certain items from abroad and pay a duty on the value of those articles if they exceed the allowance established by Italy's customs service. Note that goods and gifts purchased at **duty-free** shops abroad are not exempt from duty or sales tax; "duty-free" merely means that you need not pay a tax in the country of purchase. Duty-free allowances were abolished for travel between EU member states on June 30, 1999, but still exist for those arriving from outside the EU. Upon returning home, you must likewise declare all articles acquired abroad and pay a duty on the value of articles in excess of your home country's allowance. In order to expedite your return, make a list of any valuables brought from home and register them with customs before traveling abroad, and be sure to keep receipts for all goods acquired abroad.

 CUSTOMS IN THE EU. As well as freedom of movement for people within the EU (see p. 10), travelers in the 15 original EU member countries (Austria, Belgium, Denmark, Finland, France, Germany, Greece, Ireland, Italy, Luxembourg, the Netherlands, Portugal, Spain, Sweden, and the UK) can also take advantage of the freedom of movement of goods. This means that there are no customs controls at internal EU borders (i.e., you can take the blue customs channel at the airport), and travelers are free to transport whatever legal substances they like as long as it is for their own personal (non-commercial) use—up to 800 cigarettes, 10L of spirits, 90L of wine (including up to 60L of sparkling wine), and 110L of beer. Duty-free allowances were abolished on June 30, 1999 for travel between the original 15 EU member states; this now also applies to Cyprus and Malta. However, travelers between the EU and the rest of the world still get a duty-free allowance when passing through customs.

MONEY

CURRENCY AND EXCHANGE

The currency chart below is based on August 2005 exchange rates between local currency and Australian dollars (AUS$), Canadian dollars (CDN$), European Union euros (EUR€), New Zealand dollars (NZ$), British pounds (UK£), and US dollars (US$). Check the currency converter on websites like www.xe.com or www.bloomberg.com, or a large newspaper for the latest exchange rates.

EURO (€)		
AUS$1 = €0.62		€1 = AUS$1.62
CDN$1 = €0.67		€1 = CDN$1.50
NZ1$ = €0.56		€1 = NZ$1.78
UK1£ = €1.44		€1 = UK£0.69
US1$ = €0.81		€1 = US$1.24

ESSENTIALS

As a general rule, it's cheaper to convert money in Italy than at home. While currency exchange will probably be available in your arrival airport, it's wise to bring enough foreign currency to last for the first 24 to 72 hours of your trip.

When changing money abroad, try to go only to banks or *cambio* offices that have at most a 5% margin between their buy and sell prices. Since you lose money with every transaction, **convert large sums** (unless the currency is depreciating rapidly), but **no more than you'll need.**

If you use traveler's checks or bills, carry some in small denominations (the equivalent of US$50 or less) for times when you are forced to exchange money at disadvantageous rates, but bring a range of denominations since charges may be levied per check cashed. Store your money in a variety of forms; ideally, at any given time you will be carrying some cash, some traveler's checks, and an ATM and/or credit card. All travelers should also consider carrying some US dollars (about US$50 worth), which are often preferred by local tellers.

THE EURO. The official currency of 12 members of the European Union—Austria, Belgium, Finland, France, Germany, Greece, Ireland, Italy, Luxembourg, the Netherlands, Portugal, and Spain—is now the euro.

The currency has some important—and positive—consequences for travelers hitting more than one euro-zone country. For one thing, money-changers across the euro-zone are obliged to exchange money at the official, fixed rate (see below), and at no commission (though they may still charge a small service fee). Second, euro-denominated traveler's checks allow you to pay for goods and services across the euro-zone, again at the official rate and commission-free.

At the time of printing, €1=US$1.24=CDN$1.50=NZ$1.78, etc. For more info, check a currency converter (such as www.xe.com) or www.europa.eu.int.

TRAVELER'S CHECKS

Traveler's checks are one of the safest and least troublesome means of carrying funds. American Express and Visa are the most-recognized brands. Many banks and agencies sell them for a small commission. Check issuers provide refunds if the checks are lost or stolen, and many provide additional services, including toll-free refund hotlines abroad, emergency message services, and assistance with lost and stolen credit cards or passports. In Italy, traveler's checks are becoming less and less useful as fewer and fewer establishments accept them; note that even some banks will not. Ask about toll-free refund hotlines and the location of refund centers when purchasing checks, and always carry emergency cash.

American Express: Checks available with commission at select banks, at all AmEx offices, and online (www.americanexpress.com; US residents only). American Express cardholders can also purchase checks by phone (☎800-721-9768). Available in a wide range of currencies. Also offers the Travelers Cheque Card, a prepaid reloadable card. For purchase locations or more information, contact AmEx's service centers: in Australia ☎800 688 022, in New Zealand 423 74 409, in the UK 0800 587 6023, in the US and Canada

800-221-7282; elsewhere, call the US collect at 1-801-964-6665. In Italy, call toll-free 800 91 49 12 to report and recover lost or stolen Traveler's Cheques.

Travelex: Thomas Cook MasterCard and Interpayment Visa traveler's checks available. For information about Thomas Cook MasterCard in Canada and the US call ☎800-223-7373, in the UK 0800 622 101; elsewhere call the UK collect at +44 1733 318 950. For information about Interpayment Visa in the US and Canada call ☎800-732-1322, in the UK 0800 515 884; elsewhere call the UK collect at +44 1733 318 949. For more information, visit www.travelex.com.

Visa: Checks available (generally with commission) at banks worldwide. For the location of the nearest office, call the Visa Travelers Cheque Global Refund and Assistance Center: in the UK ☎0800 515 884, in the US 800-227-6811, elsewhere, call the UK collect at +44 2079 378 091. Visa also offers TravelMoney, a prepaid debit card that can be reloaded online or by phone. For more information on Visa travel services, see http://usa.visa.com/personal/using_visa/travel_with_visa.html.

CREDIT, DEBIT, AND ATM CARDS

Where they are accepted, credit cards can offer superior exchange rates—up to 5% better than the retail rate used by banks and other currency exchange establishments. Credit cards may also offer services like insurance or emergency help, and are sometimes required to reserve hotel rooms or rental cars. In Italy, credit cards are accepted almost everywhere: **MasterCard** and **Visa** are the most welcome; **American Express** is less common, though AmEx cards work at some major airports.

ATM machines, or *bancomats*, are widespread on the Italian mainland and far less prevalent on islands. Most towns have multiple **ATMs** and at least one 24hr. machine. Depending on the system that your home bank uses, you can most likely access your personal bank account from abroad. ATMs get the same wholesale exchange rate as credit cards, but there is often a limit on the amount of money you can withdraw per day (usually around US$500). There is typically also a surcharge of US$1-5 per withdrawal.

Debit cards are as convenient as credit cards but have a more immediate impact on your funds. A debit card can be used wherever its associated credit card company (usually MasterCard or Visa) is accepted, yet the money is withdrawn directly from the holder's checking account. Debit cards often also function as ATM cards and can be used to withdraw cash from associated banks and ATMs throughout Italy. Ask your local bank about obtaining one.

The two major international money networks are **MasterCard/Maestro/Cirrus** (for ATM locations ☎800-424-7787 or www.mastercard.com) and **Visa/PLUS** (for ATM locations ☎800-843-7587 or www.visa.com). Citibank, SSB, and Banca di Roma frequently have Cirrus machines, and Visa/PLUS machines are likely to be found at many Banca di Roma, Banca Nazionale del Lavoro, Banca Nazionale dell'Agricoltura, and Banco Ambrosiano Veneto. Most ATMs charge a transaction fee that is paid to the bank that owns the ATM.

GETTING MONEY FROM HOME

If you run out of money while traveling, the easiest and cheapest solution is to have someone back home make a deposit to your bank account. Failing that, consider one of the following options.

WIRING MONEY

It is possible to arrange a **bank money transfer,** which means asking a bank at home to wire money to a bank in Italy. This is the cheapest way to transfer cash, but it's also the slowest, usually taking several days. Note that some banks may only release your funds in local currency, potentially sticking you

PINS AND ATMS. To use a cash or credit card to withdraw money from a cash machine (ATM) in Europe, you must have a four-digit **Personal Identification Number (PIN).** If your PIN is longer than four digits, ask your bank whether you can just use the first four, or whether you'll need a new one. **Credit cards** don't usually come with PINs, so if you intend to hit up ATMs in Europe with a credit card to get cash advances, call your credit card company before leaving to request one.

Travelers with alphabetic, rather than numerical, PINs may also be thrown off by the lack of letters on European cash machines. Note that if you mistakenly punch the wrong code into the machine three times, it will swallow your card for good.

with a poor exchange rate; inquire about this in advance. In Italy, be prepared to lose a lot of money. ATMS are usually the easiest and cheapest way to exchange money. Money transfer services like **Western Union** are faster and more convenient than bank transfers—but also much pricier. Western Union has many locations worldwide. To find one, visit www.westernunion.com, or call in Australia ☎800 173 833, in Canada and the US 800-325-6000, in the UK 0800 833 833. To wire money using a credit card (Discover, MasterCard, Visa), call Western Union in Canada and the US ☎800-225-5227, the UK 0800 833 833 or in Italy 800 46 44 64. Money transfer services are also available to **American Express** cardholders and at selected **Thomas Cook** offices.

US STATE DEPARTMENT (US CITIZENS ONLY)

In serious emergencies only, the US State Department will forward money within hours to the nearest consular office, which will then disburse it according to instructions for a US$30 fee. Contact the Overseas Citizens Service division of the US State Department (☎202-647-5225, toll-free 888-407-4747) to use this service.

COSTS

The cost of your trip will vary considerably, depending on where you go, how you travel, and where you stay. The most significant expenses will probably be your round-trip (return) **airfare** to Italy (see **Getting to Italy: By Plane,** p. 25) and a **railpass** (p. 28) or **bus pass.** Before you go, spend some time calculating a reasonable daily **budget.**

STAYING ON A BUDGET

To give you a general idea, a bare-bones day in Italy (camping or sleeping in hostels/guesthouses, buying food at supermarkets) would cost about US$60-72 (€50-60); a slightly more comfortable day (sleeping in hostels/guesthouses and the occasional budget hotel, eating one meal per day at a restaurant, going out at night) would cost US$84-96 (€70-80); and for a luxurious day, the sky's the limit. Don't forget to factor in emergency reserve funds (at least US$200) when planning how much money you'll need.

TIPS FOR SAVING MONEY

Some simpler ways include searching out opportunities for free entertainment, splitting accommodation and food costs with fellow travelers, and buying food in supermarkets. Bring a **sleepsack** (see p. 17) to save on sheet charges in hostels, and do your **laundry** in the sink (unless you're explicitly prohibited from doing so). Museums often have certain days when admission is free; plan accordingly. If you are eligible, consider getting an ISIC or an IYTC; many sights and museums offer reduced admission to students and youths. For getting around quickly, bikes are the most economical option. Renting a bike is cheaper than renting a moped or scooter. Don't forget about walking, though;

you can learn a lot about a city by seeing it on foot. That said, don't go overboard. Though staying within your budget is important, don't do so at the expense of your health or a great travel experience.

TIPPING AND BARGAINING

At many Italian restaurants, a service charge (*servizio*) or cover (*coperto*) is included in the bill. Locals sometimes do not give tips, but it is appropriate for foreign visitors to leave an additional €1-2 at restaurants. Taxi drivers expect about a 10% tip. Bargaining is common in Italy, but use discretion. It is appropriate at markets, with vendors, and over unmetered taxi fares (always settle the price before taking the cab). Haggling over prices elsewhere is usually inappropriate. Hotel negotiation is more successful in uncrowded *pensioni*. *Let's Go* usually notes the hotels open to bargaining. To get lower prices, show little interest. Don't offer what you can't pay; you're expected to buy once the merchant accepts your price.

TAXES

The **Value-Added Tax** (**VAT**; *imposto sul valore aggiunta*, or **IVA**) is a sales tax levied in the EU. Foreigners making any purchase over €155 are entitled to an additional 20% VAT tax refund. Some stores take off 20% onsite; the alternative is to fill out forms at the Customs Office upon leaving the EU and send receipts from home, upon which the refund will be mailed to you. Not all storefront "Tax-Free" stickers imply an immediate, on-site refund, so ask before making a purchase.

PACKING

When it comes to packing, the less you have, the less you have to lose. **Pack lightly.** Lay out only what you absolutely need, then take half the clothes and twice the money. The Travelite FAQ (www.travelite.org) is a good resource for tips on traveling light. The online **Universal Packing List** (http://upl.codeq.info) will generate a customized list of suggested items based on your trip length, the expected climate, your planned activities, and other factors. If you plan to do a lot of hiking, also consult **Camping and the Outdoors,** p. 43.

 BYOTP. Bring your own toilet paper. Many public bathrooms in Italy, especially in the south, Sardinia and Sicily, do not have toilet paper, so travelers should always carry a roll or a box of tissues with them.

Luggage: If you plan to cover most of your itinerary by foot, a sturdy **frame backpack** is unbeatable. (For the basics on buying a pack, see p. 44.) Toting a **suitcase** or **trunk** is fine if you plan to live in one or two cities and explore from there, but not a great idea if you plan to move around frequently. In addition to your main piece of luggage, a **daypack** (a small backpack or courier bag) is useful.

Clothing: No matter when you're traveling, it's a good idea to bring a warm jacket or wool sweater, a rain jacket (Gore-Tex® is both waterproof and breathable), sturdy shoes or hiking boots, and thick socks. Even in the summer in Italy the weather at high altitudes can be chilly, so when hiking the Alps or Mt. Etna in the south, dress accordingly. Flip-flops or waterproof sandals are must-haves for grubby hostel showers. You may also want one outfit for going out, and maybe a nicer pair of shoes. If you plan to visit religious or cultural sites, remember that you will need modest dress; women should pack a top that covers the shoulders and a skirt that falls below the knees. Women traveling alone, especially in Southern Italy, should dress modestly to avoid unwanted attention.

Sleepsack: Some hostels require that you either provide your own linen or rent sheets from them. Save cash by making your own sleepsack: fold a full-size sheet in half the long way, then sew it closed along the long side and one of the short sides.

Converters and Adapters: In Italy, electricity is 230V AC, enough to fry any 120V North American appliance. Americans and Canadians should buy an adapter (which changes the shape of the plug; US$5) and a converter (which changes the voltage; US$20-30). Don't make the mistake of using only an adapter (unless appliance instructions explicitly state otherwise). Travelers from NZ, Australia, and the UK (who use 230V at home) won't need a converter, but will need a set of adapters to use anything electrical. For more on all things adaptable, check out http://kropla.com/electric.htm.

First-Aid Kit: For a basic first-aid kit, pack bandages, a pain reliever, antibiotic cream, a thermometer, a multifunction pocketknife, tweezers, moleskin, decongestant, motion-sickness remedy, diarrhea or upset-stomach medication (Pepto Bismol® or Imodium®), an antihistamine, sunscreen, insect repellent, burn ointment, and a syringe for emergencies (get an explanatory letter from your doctor).

Film: Less serious photographers may want to bring a disposable camera or two. Despite disclaimers, airport security X-rays can fog film, so buy a lead-lined pouch at a camera store or ask security to hand-inspect it. Always pack film in your carry-on luggage, since higher-intensity X-rays are used on checked luggage. If you don't want to bother with film, consider using a digital camera. Although it requires a steep initial investment, a digital camera means you never have to buy film again. Just be sure to bring along a large enough memory card and extra (or rechargeable) batteries. For more info on digital cameras, visit www.shortcourses.com/choosing/contents.htm.

Toiletries: Condoms, deodorant, razors, tampons, and toothbrushes are often available, but it may be difficult to find your preferred brand; bring extras. Contact lenses are likely to be expensive and difficult to find, so bring enough extra pairs and solution for your entire trip. Also bring your glasses and a copy of your prescription in case you need emergency replacements. If you use heat-disinfection, either switch temporarily to a chemical disinfection system (check first to make sure it's safe with your brand of lenses), or buy a converter to 230V.

Other Useful Items: For safety purposes, you should bring a **money belt** and small **padlock**. Basic **outdoors equipment** (plastic water bottle, compass, waterproof matches, pocketknife, sunglasses, sun-

TOP 10 WAYS TO SAVE IN ITALY

Homeland of Gucci, Prada, and Armani, Italy doesn't always cater to the frugal-minded, starving-artist types. If you're going to spend money—and in Italy, you are—you may as well spend wisely. Keeping in mind that safety should always be a top priority when traveling abroad, consider the following tips for saving money:

1. For best **exchange rates**, use your ATM card instead of exchanging money.
2. Fly through London on Ryanair for the cheapest rates when traveling from the US to Italy.
3. Buy food at **markets** (especially open-air markets) and grocery stores instead of restaurants.
4. To avoid an extra service charge in a *bar*, **drink and eat at the counter** instead of sitting down.
5. Find **free Internet access** in libraries and tourist offices.
6. Be on the lookout for days when you can **get into sights and museums** for free.
7. Swim and lounge at **public beaches** to avoid the cover charge at many private beaches.
8. Bargain (where appropriate).
9. Look for cafes and restaurants on **side streets** rather than in main squares.
10. Bring a **sleepsack** to avoid paying extra for sheets in hostels.

screen, hat) may also prove useful. **Quick repairs** of torn garments can be done on the road with a needle and thread; also consider bringing electrical tape for patching tears. To do laundry by hand (cheaper than using a laundromat), bring detergent, a small rubber ball to stop up the sink, and string for a makeshift clothes line. **Other things** you're liable to forget are sealable plastic bags (for damp clothes, soap, food, shampoo, and other spillables), an alarm clock, safety pins, rubber bands, a flashlight, and earplugs. A cell phone can be a lifesaver (literally) on the road; see p. 37 for information on acquiring one that will work in Italy.

Important Documents: Don't forget your passport, traveler's checks, ATM and/or credit cards, adequate ID, and photocopies of all of the aforementioned. Also check that you have any of the following that might apply to you: a hosteling membership card (see p. 41); driver's license (see p. 11); travel insurance forms (see p. 21); ISIC (see p. 11); and/or rail or bus pass (see p. 31).

SAFETY AND HEALTH

GENERAL ADVICE

In any type of crisis situation, the most important thing to do is **stay calm.** Your country's embassy abroad (p. 8) is usually your best resource when things go wrong; registering with that embassy upon arrival in the country is often a good idea. The government offices listed in the **Travel Advisories** box (p. 19) can provide information on the services they offer their citizens in case of emergencies abroad.

LOCAL LAWS AND POLICE

In Italy you will mainly encounter two types of police: the *polizia* (☎113) and the *carabinieri* (☎112). The *polizia* is a civil force under the command of the Ministry of the Interior, whereas the *carabinieri* falls under the auspices of the Ministry of Defense and is considered to be a military force; both, however, generally serve the same purpose—to maintain security and order in the country. In the case of attack or robbery either of these forces will respond to inquiries for help.

DRUGS AND ALCOHOL

Needless to say, **illegal drugs** are best avoided altogether. In Italy, drugs including marijuana, cocaine, and heroine are illegal. Concern about an increase in cocaine and heroin addiction and trafficking have led Italian authorities to respond harshly to drug-related offenses. If you carry **prescription drugs,** bring copies of the prescriptions themselves and a note from a doctor and have the drugs and prescriptions accessible at international borders. The drinking age in Italy is 16. Drinking and driving is strictly prohibited and can result in a prison sentence (the legal blood alcohol level is less than 0.5%, significantly lower than US standards).

SPECIFIC CONCERNS

EARTHQUAKES. Italy is crossed by several fault lines, the chief one running from Sicily to Friuli-Venezia Giulia in the northeast. The country's principal cities do not lie near these faults, though smaller tourist towns like Assisi do and thus may experience earthquakes (most recently in 1997). If you do find yourself in an earthquake, open a door to provide an escape route and protect yourself by moving underneath a sturdy doorway, table, or desk.

TERRORISM. Terrorism has not been as serious a problem in Italy as in other European countries, though, as in much of the world, the general threat of terrorism still exists. Exercise common sense and caution when in crowded, public areas like train or bus stations and open spaces like *piazze* in larger cities. The box on **travel advisories** lists offices to contact and webpages to visit to get the most updated list of your home country's government's advisories about travel.

> **TRAVEL ADVISORIES.** The following government offices provide travel information and advisories by telephone, by fax, or via the web:
>
> **Australian Department of Foreign Affairs and Trade:** ☎1300 555 135; www.dfat.gov.au.
>
> **Canadian Department of Foreign Affairs and International Trade (DFAIT):** Call ☎800-267-8376; www.dfait-maeci.gc.ca. Call for their free booklet, *Bon Voyage...But.*
>
> **New Zealand Ministry of Foreign Affairs:** ☎044 398 000; www.mft.govt.nz/travel/index.html.
>
> **United Kingdom Foreign and Commonwealth Office:** ☎020 7008 1500; www.fco.gov.uk.
>
> **US Department of State:** ☎202-647-5225; http://travel.state.gov. Visit the website for the booklet *A Safe Trip Abroad.*

PERSONAL SAFETY

EXPLORING AND TRAVELING

To avoid unwanted attention, try to blend in as much as possible. Respecting local customs (in many cases, dressing more conservatively than you would at home) may placate would-be hecklers. Familiarize yourself with your surroundings before setting out, and carry yourself with confidence. Check maps in shops and restaurants rather than on the street. If you are traveling alone, be sure someone at home knows your itinerary, and never admit that you're by yourself. When walking at night, stick to busy, well-lit streets and avoid dark alleyways. If you ever feel uncomfortable, leave the area as quickly and directly as you can.

There is no sure-fire way to avoid all the threatening situations you might encounter while traveling, but a good **self-defense course** will give you concrete ways to react to unwanted advances. **Impact, Prepare, and Model Mugging** can refer you to local self-defense courses in the US. Visit the website at www.modelmugging.org for a list of nearby chapters. Workshops (2-4hr.) start at US$50; full courses (20hr.) run US$350-500.

If you are using a **car,** learn local driving signals and wear a seatbelt. Children under 40 lb. should ride only in specially-designed carseats, available for a small fee from most car rental agencies. Study route maps before you hit the road, and if you plan on spending a lot of time driving, consider bringing spare parts. If your car breaks down, wait for the police to assist you. For long drives in desolate areas, invest in a cellular phone and a roadside assistance program (see p. 35). Park your vehicle in a garage or well traveled area, and use a steering wheel locking device in larger cities. **Sleeping in your car** is one of the most dangerous (and often illegal) ways to get your rest. For info on the perils of **hitchhiking,** see p. 36.

POSSESSIONS AND VALUABLES

Never leave your belongings unattended; crime occurs in even the most demure-looking hostel or hotel. Bring your own padlock for lockers. Be particularly careful on **buses** and **trains;** stories abound about thieves who wait for travelers to fall asleep. Carry your backpack in front of you. When traveling with others, sleep in shifts. When alone, use good judgment in selecting a train compartment: never stay in an empty one, and use a lock to secure your pack to the luggage rack. Try to sleep on top bunks with your luggage stored above you (if not in bed with you), and keep important documents and other valuables on your person.

There are a few steps you can take to minimize the financial risk associated with traveling. First, **bring as little with you as possible.** Second, buy a few combination **padlocks** to secure your belongings either in your pack or in a hostel or train station locker. Third, **carry as little cash as possible.** Keep your ATM/credit cards in a **money belt**—not a "fanny pack"—along with your passport and ID cards. Fourth, **keep a small cash reserve separate from your primary stash.** This should be about US$50 (US$ or Euros are best) sewn into or stored in the depths of your pack, along with your traveler's check numbers and important photocopies.

In large cities **con artists** often work in groups and may involve children. Beware of certain classics: sob stories that require money, rolls of bills "found" on the street, mustard spilled (or saliva spit) on your shoulder to distract you while they snatch your bag. **Never let your passport and your bags out of your sight;** never trust an un-uniformed "station porter" who insists on carrying your bag or stowing it in the baggage compartment. **Pick-pockets** abound in Rome, Naples, and other urban centers. Beware of them in city crowds, especially on public transportation. Also, be alert in public telephone booths: if you must say your calling card number, do so very quietly; if you punch it in, make sure no one can look over your shoulder.

If you will be traveling with electronic devices like a laptop computer or a PDA, check whether your homeowner's insurance covers loss, theft, or damage when you travel. If not, you might consider purchasing a low-cost separate insurance policy. **Safeware** (☎800-800-1492; www.safeware.com) specializes in covering computers and charges $90 for 90-day international travel coverage up to $4000.

PRE-DEPARTURE HEALTH

In your **passport,** write the names of any people you wish to contact in case of a medical emergency, and list any allergies or medical conditions. Matching a prescription to a foreign equivalent is not always safe, or possible, so if you take prescription drugs, carry up-to-date, legible prescriptions or a statement from your doctor stating the medication's trade name, manufacturer, chemical name, and dosage. Be sure to keep all medication with you in your carry-on luggage. For tips on packing a basic **first-aid kit** and other health essentials, see p. 17. While it may be difficult to find brand-name medications like Tylenol or Advil, these products can be easily identified by their drug names (such as acetimenophen or ibuprofen).

IMMUNIZATIONS AND PRECAUTIONS

Travelers over two years old should make sure that the following vaccines are up to date: MMR (for measles, mumps, and rubella); DTaP or Td (for diphtheria, tetanus, and pertussis); IPV (for polio); Hib (for *haemophilus* influenza B); and HepB (for Hepatitis B). For recommendations on immunizations and prophylaxis, consult the CDC in the US, the IAMAT internationally, or the equivalent in your home country, and check with a doctor for guidance. Meningitis shots are advisable, especially for college-age backpackers who plan to stay in hostels.

INSURANCE

Travel insurance covers four basic areas: medical/health problems, property loss, trip cancellation/interruption, and emergency evacuation. Though regular insurance policies may well extend to travel-related accidents, you may consider purchasing separate travel insurance if the cost of potential trip cancellation, interruption, or emergency medical evacuation is greater than you can absorb. Prices for travel insurance purchased separately generally run about US$50 per week for full coverage, while trip cancellation/interruption may be purchased separately at a rate of US$3-5 per day depending on length of stay.

Medical insurance (especially university policies) often covers costs incurred abroad; check with your provider. **US Medicare** does not cover foreign travel. **Canadian** provincial health insurance plans increasingly do not cover foreign travel; check with the provincial Ministry of Health or Health Plan Headquarters for details. **Australians** traveling in Italy are entitled to many of the services that they would receive at home as part of the Reciprocal Health Care Agreement. **Homeowners' insurance** (or your family's coverage) often covers theft during travel and loss of travel documents (passport, plane ticket, railpass, etc.) up to US$500.

ISIC and **ITIC** (see p. 11) provide basic insurance benefits to US cardholders, including US$100 per day of in-hospital sickness for up to 100 days and US$10,000 of accident-related medical reimbursement (see www.isicus.com for details). Cardholders have access to a toll-free 24hr. helpline for medical, legal, and financial emergencies overseas. **American Express** (☎800-338-1670) grants most cardholders collision and theft car rental insurance on rentals made with the card.

USEFUL ORGANIZATIONS AND PUBLICATIONS

The US **Centers for Disease Control and Prevention** (**CDC;** ☎877-FYI-TRIP; www.cdc.gov/travel) maintains an international travelers' hotline and an informative website. The CDC's comprehensive booklet *Health Information for International Travel* (The Yellow Book), a biannual rundown of disease, immunization, and general health advice, is free online or US$29-40 via the Public Health Foundation (☎877-252-1200; http://bookstore.phfg.org/cat24.htm). Consult the appropriate government agency of your home country for consular information sheets on health, entry requirements, and other issues for various countries (see the listings in the box on **Travel Advisories,** p. 19). For quick information on health and other travel warnings, call the **Overseas Citizens Services** (M-F 8am-8pm ☎888-407-4747, from overseas 202-501-4444), or contact a passport agency, embassy, or consulate abroad. For information on medical evacuation services and travel insurance firms, see the US government's website at http://travel.state.gov/travel/abroad_health.html or the **British Foreign and Commonwealth Office** (www.fco.gov.uk). For general health info, contact the **American Red Cross** (☎800-564-1234; www.redcross.org).

STAYING HEALTHY

Common sense is the simplest prescription for good health while you travel. Drink lots of fluids to prevent dehydration and constipation, and wear sturdy, broken-in shoes and clean socks.

ONCE IN ITALY

ENVIRONMENTAL HAZARDS

Heat Exhaustion and Dehydration: Heat exhaustion leads to nausea, excessive thirst, headaches, and dizziness. Avoid it by drinking plenty of fluids, eating salty foods (e.g., crackers), abstaining from dehydrating beverages (e.g., alcohol and caffeinated beverages), and always wearing sunscreen. Continuous heat stress can eventually lead to heatstroke, characterized by a rising temperature, severe headache, delirium and cessation of sweating. Victims should be cooled off with wet towels and taken to a doctor.

Sunburn: Always wear sunscreen (SPF 30 is good) when spending time outdoors, especially at high altitudes. You can burn even when under cloud cover. If you get sunburned, drink more fluids than usual and apply an aloe-based lotion. Severe sunburns can lead to sun poisoning, a condition that affects the entire body, causing fever, chills, nausea, and vomiting. Sun poisoning should always be treated by a doctor.

High Altitude: Allow your body a couple of days to adjust to less oxygen before exerting yourself. Note that alcohol is more potent and UV rays are stronger at high elevations particularly in the Alps, Apennines, and Dolomites.

INSECT-BORNE DISEASES

Many diseases are transmitted by insects—mainly mosquitoes, fleas, ticks, and lice. Be aware of insects while hiking and camping; wear long pants and long sleeves, tuck your pants into your socks, and use a mosquito net. Use insect repellents such as DEET and soak or spray your gear with permethrin (licensed in the US only for use on clothing). **Ticks**—which can carry Lyme and other diseases— can be particularly dangerous in rural and forested regions.

Lyme Disease: A bacterial infection carried by ticks and marked by a circular bull's-eye rash of 2 in. or more. Later symptoms include fever, headache, fatigue, and aches and pains. Antibiotics are effective if administered early. Left untreated, Lyme can cause problems in joints, the heart, and the nervous system. If you find a tick attached to your skin, grasp the head with tweezers as close to your skin as possible and apply slow, steady traction. Removing a tick within 24hr. greatly reduces the risk of infection. Do not try to remove ticks with petroleum jelly, nail polish remover, or a hot match. Tick bites usually occur in moist, shaded environments and heavily wooded areas. If you are going to be hiking in these areas, wear long clothes and DEET.

FOOD- AND WATER-BORNE DISEASES

Prevention is the best cure: be sure that food is properly cooked and the water you drink is clean. If the region's tap water is known to be unsanitary, peel produce and avoid tap water (including ice cubes and anything washed in tap water, like salad). The sign *"acqua non potabile"* means the water is not drinkable (e.g., in trains and at some campgrounds). Watch out for food from markets or street vendors that may have been cooked in unhygienic conditions. Other culprits are raw shellfish, unpasteurized milk, and sauces containing raw eggs (like *carbonara*). Buy bottled water, or purify your own water by bringing it to a rolling boil or treating it with **iodine tablets**; note, however, that some parasites like *giardia* have exteriors that resist iodine treatment, so boiling is more reliable. Always wash your hands before eating or bring a quick-drying purifying liquid hand cleaner.

OTHER INFECTIOUS DISEASES

Rabies: Transmitted through the saliva of infected animals; fatal if untreated. By the time symptoms (thirst and muscle spasms) appear, the disease is in its terminal stage. If you are bitten, wash the wound thoroughly, seek immediate medical care, and try to

have the animal located. A rabies vaccine, which consists of 3 shots given over a 21-day period, is available and recommended for developing world travel, but is only semi-effective. Rabies is found all over the world, and is often transmitted through dogs.

Hepatitis B: A viral infection of the liver transmitted via blood or other bodily fluids. Symptoms, which may not surface until years after infection, include jaundice, loss of appetite, fever, and joint pain. It is transmitted through activities like unprotected sex, injections of illegal drugs, and unprotected health work. A 3-shot vaccination sequence is recommended for health-care workers, sexually-active travelers, and anyone planning to seek medical treatment abroad; it must begin 6 months before traveling.

AIDS and HIV: For detailed information on Acquired Immune Deficiency Syndrome (AIDS) in Italy, call the US Centers for Disease Control's 24hr. hotline at ☎800-342-2437, or contact the Joint United Nations Programme on HIV/AIDS (UNAIDS), 20 ave. Appia, CH-1211 Geneva 27, Switzerland (☎ +41 22 791 3666; fax 22 791 4187).

Sexually Transmitted Diseases (STDs): Gonorrhea, chlamydia, genital warts, syphilis, herpes, and other STDs are easier to catch than HIV and can be just as deadly. **Hepatitis** B and C can also be transmitted sexually. Though condoms may protect you from some STDs, oral or even tactile contact can lead to transmission. If you think you may have contracted an STD, see a doctor immediately.

OTHER HEALTH CONCERNS

MEDICAL CARE ON THE ROAD

On the whole Italy conforms to standards of modern health care. Quality of care varies by region; health care tends to be better in the north and in private hospitals and clinics. Doctors speak English in most large cities; if they don't, they may be able to arrange for a translator. *Let's Go* lists info on how to access medical help in the **Practical Information** sections of most cities. Those with medical conditions (such as diabetes, allergies to antibiotics, epilepsy, or heart conditions) may want to obtain a **MedicAlert** membership (first year US$35, annually thereafter US$20), which includes a stainless steel ID tag, among other benefits, like a 24hr. collect-call number. Contact the MedicAlert Foundation, 2323 Colorado Ave., Turlock, CA 95382, USA (☎888-633-4298, outside US ☎209-668-3333; www.medicalert.org).

WOMEN'S HEALTH

Women traveling in unsanitary conditions are vulnerable to **urinary tract (including bladder and kidney) infections** (*infezioni all'apparto urinario*). Over-the-counter medicines can sometimes alleviate symptoms, but if they persist, see a doctor. **Vaginal yeast infections** (*candidiasi*) may flare up in heat and humidity. Wearing loose trousers or a skirt and cotton underwear will help, as will over-the-counter remedies like Monostat or Gynelotrimin. Bring supplies from home if you are prone to infection, as they may be difficult to find on the road. Tampons, pads and contraceptive devices are widely available, though your favorite brand may not be— bring extras of anything you can't live without. Pharmacies refill empty **birth control** packages even without Italian-issued prescriptions. **Abortion** is legal and may be performed in the first 90 days of pregnancy in a public hospital or authorized private facility. Except in urgent cases, a week-long reflection period is required. Women under 18 must obtain parental permission. Actual availability of abortion may be limited in some areas of Italy, especially in the south, due to a "conscience clause" allowing physicians who oppose abortion to opt out of performing the procedure. While the recent election of Pope Benedict XVI has sparked controversy over abortion, no changes to policy are expected to occur immediately.

ESSENTIALS

GETTING TO ITALY

BY PLANE

When it comes to airfare, a little effort can save you a bundle. If your plans are flexible enough to deal with the restrictions, courier fares are the cheapest. Tickets bought from consolidators and standby seating are also good deals, but last-minute specials, airfare wars, and charter flights often beat these fares. The key is to hunt around, to be flexible, and to ask persistently about discounts. Students, seniors, and those under 26 should never pay full price for a ticket.

AIRFARES

Airfares to Italy peak between mid-June and early Sept.; holidays are also expensive. The cheapest times to travel are Nov. to mid-Dec. and Jan.-Feb. Midweek (M-Th morning) round-trip flights run US$40-50 cheaper than weekend flights, but are generally more crowded and less likely to permit upgrades. Not fixing a return date ("open-return") or arriving in and departing from different cities ("open-jaw") can be pricier than round-trip flights. Flights into transportation hubs Rome and Milan tend to be cheaper. If Italy is only one stop on a more extensive globe-hop, consider a round-the-world (RTW) ticket. Tickets usually include at least five stops and are valid for about a year; prices range US$1200-5000. Try **Northwest Airlines/KLM** (☎800-225-2525; www.nwa.com) or **Star Alliance,** a consortium of 16 airlines including United Airlines (www.staralliance.com).

Fares for round-trip flights to Rome and Milan from the US or Canadian east coast cost US$700-$1200, US$500-800 in the low season; from the US or Canadian west coast US$900-1300/US$700-1000; from the UK, UK£85-165/UK£100-180 (though Ryanair sometimes sells tickets for as cheap as UK£15); from Australia AUS$2100-2600/AUS$1700-2200; from New Zealand NZ$1900-3000/NZ$1700-2400.

BUDGET AND STUDENT TRAVEL AGENCIES

While knowledgeable agents specializing in flights to Italy can make your life easy and help you save, they may not find you the lowest possible fare—they get paid on commission. Travelers holding **ISICs** and **IYTCs** (p. 11) qualify for big discounts from student travel agencies. Most flights from budget agencies are on major airlines, but in peak season some may sell seats on less reliable chartered aircraft.

CTS Travel, 30 Rathbone Pl., London W1T 1GQ, UK (☎020 7290 0630; www.ctstravel.co.uk). A British student travel agent with offices in 39 countries including the US, Empire State Building, 350 Fifth Ave., Ste. 7813, New York, NY 10118 (☎877-287-6665; www.ctstravelusa.com).

STA Travel, 5900 Wilshire Blvd., Ste. 900, Los Angeles, CA 90036, USA (24hr. reservations and info ☎800-781-4040; www.sta-travel.com). Student and youth travel organization with over 150 offices worldwide (check website for listings), including US offices in Boston, Chicago, L.A., New York, Seattle, San Francisco, and Washington, D.C. Ticket booking, travel insurance, railpasses, and more. Walk-in offices throughout Australia (☎03 9349 4344), New Zealand (☎09 309 9723), and the UK (☎08701 600 599).

Travel CUTS (Canadian Universities Travel Services Limited), 187 College St., Toronto, ON M5T 1P7, Canada (☎800-592-2887; www.travelcuts.com). Offices across Canada and the US including Los Angeles, New York, Seattle, and San Francisco.

USIT, 19-21 Aston Quay, Dublin 2, Ireland (☎01 602 1904; www.usit.ie), Ireland's leading student/budget travel agency has 20 offices throughout Northern Ireland and the Republic of Ireland. Offers programs to work, study, and volunteer worldwide.

Wasteels, Skoubogade 6, 1158 Copenhagen K., Denmark (☎3314 4633; www.wasteels.com). A huge chain with 180 locations across Europe. Sells Wasteels BIJ tickets discounted 30-45% off regular fare, 2nd-class international point-to-point train tickets with unlimited stopovers for those under 26 (sold only in Europe).

 FLIGHT PLANNING ON THE INTERNET. The Internet may be the budget traveler's dream when it comes to finding and booking bargain fares, but the array of options can be overwhelming. Some airline sites offer special last-minute deals on the Web. Look for occasional sale fares on **www.alitalia.com** and **www.flyairone.it.**

STA (www.sta-travel.com) and **StudentUniverse** (www.studentuniverse.com) provide quotes on student tickets, while **Orbitz** (www.orbitz.com), **Opodo** (www.opodo.com), **Expedia** (www.expedia.com), and **Travelocity** (www.travelocity.com) offer full travel services. **Priceline** (www.priceline.com) lets you specify a price, and obligates you to buy any ticket that meets or beats it; **Hotwire** (www.hotwire.com) offers bargain fares, but won't reveal the airline or flight times until you buy. Other sites that compile deals include www.flights.com, www.hotdeals.com, www.lowestfare.com, www.onetravel.com, and www.travelzoo.com.

Increasingly, there are online tools available to help sift through multiple offers; **SideStep** (www.sidestep.com; download required) and **Booking Buddy** (www.bookingbuddy.com) let you enter your trip information once and search multiple sites.

An indispensable resource on the Internet is the **Air Traveler's Handbook** (www.faqs.org/faqs/travel/air/handbook), a comprehensive listing of links to everything you need to know before you board a plane.

COMMERCIAL AIRLINES

The commercial airlines' lowest regular offer is the **APEX** (Advance Purchase Excursion) fare, which provides confirmed reservations and allows "open-jaw" tickets. Generally, reservations must be made seven to 21 days ahead of departure, with seven- to 14-day minimum-stay and up to 90-day maximum-stay restrictions. These fares carry hefty cancellation and change penalties (fees rise in summer). Book peak-season APEX fares early. Use **Expedia** (www.expedia.com) or **Travelocity** (www.travelocity.com) to get an idea of the lowest published fares, then use the resources outlined here to try and beat those fares.

TRAVELING FROM NORTH AMERICA

Standard commercial carriers like **American** (☎800-433-7300; www.aa.com), **United** (☎800-538-2929; www.ual.com), and **Northwest** (☎800-447-4747; www.nwa.com) will probably offer the most convenient flights, but they may not be the cheapest. Check **Lufthansa** (☎800-399-5838; www.lufthansa.com), **British Airways** (☎800-247-9297; www.britishairways.com), **Air France** (☎800-237-2747; www.airfrance.us), and **Alitalia** (☎800-223-5730; www.alitaliausa.com) for cheap tickets from destinations throughout the US to all over Europe. You might find a deal on **Finnair** (☎800-950-5000; www.us.finnair.com), which often offers cheap tickets from San Francisco, New York, and Toronto to Helsinki, with connections to Rome and Milan.

TRAVELING FROM THE UK AND IRELAND

Many carriers fly from the British Isles to the continent, but we only include discount airlines or those with cheap specials. The **Air Travel Advisory Bureau** in London

(☎870 737 0021; www.atab.co.uk) provides referrals to travel agencies and consolidators that offer discounted airfares from the UK. **Cheapflights** (www.cheapflights.co.uk) publishes airfare bargains. Prices listed are for one-way flights.

Aer Lingus: Ireland ☎0818 365 000; www.aerlingus.ie. Flights from Dublin, Cork, Galway, Kerry, and Shannon to Bologna, Milan, Naples, Rome, and Venice (EUR€30-150).

bmibaby: UK ☎08702 642 229; www.bmibaby.com. Departures from throughout the UK. Round-trip London to Naples (UK£20-125) and Venice (UK£15-70).

easyJet: UK ☎08712 442 366; www.easyjet.com. London to Bologna, Milan, Naples, Pisa, Rome, Turin, and Venice (UK£20-150).

KLM: UK ☎08705 074 074; www.klmuk.com. Cheap return tickets from London and elsewhere to over 23 Italian destinations (UK£49-200)

Ryanair: Ireland ☎0818 303 030, UK 08712 460 000; www.ryanair.com. Usually has the cheapest flights (from £14 including taxes) from Dublin, Glasgow, Liverpool, London, and Shannon to over a dozen destinations throughout Italy.

TRAVELING FROM AUSTRALIA AND NEW ZEALAND

Air New Zealand: New Zealand ☎0800 73 70 00; www.airnz.co.nz. Auckland to Rome.

Qantas Air: Australia ☎13 13 13, New Zealand 0800 808 767; www.qantas.com.au. Flights from Australia and New Zealand to Rome.

Singapore Air: Australia ☎13 10 11, New Zealand 0800 808 909; www.singaporeair.com. Flies from Auckland, Christchurch, Melbourne, Perth, and Sydney.

Thai Airways: Australia ☎1300 65 19 60, New Zealand 09 377 38 86; www.thaiair.com. Auckland, Melbourne, Perth, and Sydney to Rome and Milan.

AIR COURIER FLIGHTS

Those who travel light should consider courier flights. Couriers help transport cargo on international flights by using their luggage space for freight. Generally, couriers must travel with carry-ons only and deal with complex flight restrictions. Most flights are round-trip only, with short fixed-length stays (usually one week) and a limit of a one ticket per issue. Most of these flights also operate out of major gateway cities, mostly in North America. Round-trip courier fares from the US to Italy run about US$200-600. Most flights leave Los Angeles, Miami, New York, or San Francisco in the US; and Montreal, Toronto, or Vancouver in Canada. Generally, you must be over 18 (in some cases 21). In summer, popular destinations usually require an advance reservation of about two weeks (you can usually book up to two months ahead). Super-discounted fares are common for "last-minute" flights (3 to 14 days ahead). The organizations below provide members with lists of opportunities and courier brokers for an annual fee. Prices quoted below are round-trip.

Air Courier Association, 1767 A Denver West Blvd., Golden, CO 80401 (☎800-211-5119; www.aircourier.org). 10 departure sites throughout the US and Canada to popular travel destinations, including Rome and Venice. One-year membership US$49.

International Association of Air Travel Couriers (IAATC; www.courier.org). Flights from 7 North American cities to Rome. One-year membership US$45.

Courier Travel (www.couriertravel.org). Searchable online database. Available flights to Italy are usually from New York to Rome.

STANDBY FLIGHTS

Traveling standby requires serious flexibility in arrival and departure dates and cities. Companies dealing in standby flights sell vouchers rather than tickets, along with the promise to get you to your destination (or near your destination) within a certain window of time (typically one to five days). You call in before your window of time to hear your flight options and the probability that you will be able to board each flight. You can then decide which flights you want to try to make, show up at the appropriate airport at the appropriate time, present your voucher, and board if possible. Vouchers can usually be bought for both one-way and round-trip travel. You may receive a monetary refund only if every available flight in your date range is full; if you opt not to take an available (but perhaps less convenient) flight, you only get credit toward future travel. Carefully read agreements with any company offering standby flights as fine print can leave you in the lurch. To check on a company's service record in the US, contact the Better Business Bureau (☎703-276-0100; www.bbb.org). It is difficult to receive refunds, and clients' vouchers will not be honored when an airline fails to receive payment in time.

TICKET CONSOLIDATORS

Ticket consolidators, or **"bucket shops,"** buy unsold tickets in bulk from commercial airlines and sell them at discounted rates. The best place to look is in the Sunday travel section of any major newspaper (such as *The New York Times*), where many bucket shops place tiny ads. Call quickly, as availability is typically extremely limited. Not all bucket shops are reliable, so insist on a receipt that gives full details of restrictions, refunds, and tickets, and pay by credit card (in spite of the 2-5% fee) so you can stop payment if you never receive your tickets. For more info, see www.travel-library.com/air-travel/consolidators.html.

TRAVELING FROM THE US AND CANADA

NOW Voyager, 315 W. 49th St. Plaza Arcade, New York, NY 10019, USA (☎212-459-1616; www.nowvoyagertravel.com), arranges discounted flights, mostly from New York, to Rome. Other consolidators worth trying are **Rebel** (☎800-732-3588; www.rebeltours.com) and **Cheap Tickets** (www.cheaptickets.com). Consolidators on the web include **Flights.com** (www.flights.com) and **TravelHUB** (www.travel-hub.com). Keep in mind that these are just suggestions to get you started in your research; *Let's Go* does not endorse any of these agencies. As always, be cautious, and research companies before you hand over your credit card number.

CHARTER FLIGHTS

Charters are flights a tour operator contracts with an airline to fly extra loads of passengers during peak season. Charter flights fly less frequently than major airlines, make refunds particularly difficult, and are almost always fully booked. Schedules and itineraries may change or be cancelled at the last moment (as late as 48hr. before the trip, and without a full refund), and check-in, boarding, and baggage claim are often slow. However, they can also be cheaper. Discount clubs and fare brokers offer members savings on last-minute charter and tour deals. Study contracts closely; you don't want to end up with an unwanted layover.

BY TRAIN

Traveling to Italy by train from countries within Europe can be as expensive as taking a flight, but railway travelers are afforded the luxury of watching the country unfold before them, as well as the possibility of spontaneous stopovers before reaching their ultimate destination. For more information on traveling through Italy by rail, see the domestic travel **By Train** section (p. 31).

MULTINATIONAL RAILPASSES

EURAIL PASSES. Eurail is **valid** in most of Western Europe: Austria, Belgium, Denmark, Finland, France, Germany, Greece, Hungary, Italy, Luxembourg, the

Netherlands, Norway, Portugal, Ireland, Spain, Sweden, and Switzerland (but **not** the UK). Standard **Eurailpasses,** valid for a consecutive number of days, are best for those planning to spend an extended period of time on trains. **Eurailpass Flexi,** valid for any 10 or 15 (not necessarily consecutive) days in a two-month period, is more cost-effective for those traveling long distances less frequently. **Eurailpass Saver** provides first-class travel for travelers in groups of two to five. **Eurailpass Youth** and **Eurailpass Youth Flexi** provide parallel 2nd-class perks for those under 26.

EURAILPASSES	15 DAYS	21 DAYS	1 MONTH	2 MONTHS	3 MONTHS
1st class Eurailpass	US$588	US$762	US$946	US$1338	US$1654
Eurailpass Saver	US$498	US$648	US$804	US$1138	US$1408
Eurailpass Youth	US$382	US4934	US$615	US$870	US$1075

EURAILPASS FLEXI	10 DAYS IN 2 MONTHS	15 DAYS IN 2 MONTHS
1st class Eurailpass Flexi	US$694	US$914
Eurailpass Saver Flexi	US$592	US$778
Eurailpass Youth Flexi	US$451	US$594

Passholders receive a timetable for routes and a map with details on possible bike rental, car rental, hotel, and museum discounts. Passholders also receive reduced fares or free passage on many boat, bus, and private railroad lines.

The **Eurail Selectpass** is a slimmed-down version of the Eurailpass: it allows five to 15 days of unlimited travel in any two-month period within three, four, or five bordering countries of 22 European countries. **Eurail Selectpasses** (for individuals) and **Eurail Selectpass Savers** range from US$370/316 per person (5 days) to US$826/702 (15 days). The **Eurail Selectpass Youth** (2nd-class), for those aged 12-25, costs US$241-537. You are entitled to the same **freebies** afforded by the Eurailpass, but only when they are within or between countries that you have purchased.

Eurail Regional Passes are valid in specific countries (Youth and Saver options also available). The **France 'n Italy pass** is available for four to 10 days in a two-month period, and costs €269 (4 days) to €449 (10 days), €239-395 for the Saver pass, and €199-337 for the Youth pass. The **Greece 'n Italy** pass is also valid for four to 10 days in a two-month period. The cost is €239-383, €204-324 for a Saver pass, and €200-320 for a Youth pass. Although this pass is on sale at some Italian and Greek train stations, it is cheaper to purchase the pass in advance.

FURTHER READING AND RESOURCES ON TRAIN TRAVEL.
Info on rail travel and railpasses: www.raileurope.com.
Point-to-point fares and schedules: www.raileurope.com/us/rail/fares_schedules/index.htm. Allows you to calculate whether buying a railpass would save you money.
Railsaver: www.railpass.com/new. Uses your itinerary to calculate the best railpass for your trip.
European Railway Server: www.railfaneurope.net. Links to rail servers throughout Europe.
Thomas Cook European Timetable, updated monthly, covers all major and most minor train routes in Europe. Buy directly from Thomas Cook (www.thomascooktimetables.com).
Independent Travellers Europe by Rail 2005: The Inter-railer's and Eurailer's Guide. Thomas Cook Publishing (US$19.95).

SHOPPING AROUND FOR A EURAIL. Eurailpasses are designed by the EU itself, and can be bought only by non-Europeans almost exclusively from non-European distributors. The passes must be sold at uniform prices determined by the EU.

Some agents tack on a US$10 handling fee, and others offer certain bonuses with purchase, so shop around. Keep in mind that prices usually go up each year, so if you're planning to travel early in the year, you can save cash by purchasing before January 1 (you have three months from the purchase date to validate your pass).

It is best to buy your Eurail before leaving; only a few places in major European cities sell them, and at a marked-up price. You can get a replacement for a lost pass only if you have purchased insurance on it under the Pass Security Plan (US$10-17). Eurailpasses are available through travel agents, student travel agencies like STA (see p. 25), and **Rail Europe** (Canada ☎800-361-7245, US 877-257-2887; www.raileurope.com) or **Flight Centre** (1-866-967-5351; www.flightcentre.com). It is also possible to buy directly from Eurail's website, www.eurail.com. Note, however, that the company does not ship to Europe.

INTERRAIL PASS. If you have lived for at least six months in one of the European countries where **InterRail Passes** are valid, they prove an economical option. The InterRail pass allows travel within 30 European countries (excluding the passholder's country of residence), which are divided into eight **zones.** Passes may be purchased for one, two, or all eight zones. The one-zone pass (€286, under 26 €195) is good for 16 days of travel, the two-zone pass (€396, under 26 €275) is good for 22 days of travel, and the global pass (8 zones; €546, under 26 €385). Passholders receive free admission to many museums, as well as **discounts** on accommodations, food, and many ferries to Ireland, Scandinavia, and the rest of Europe. Passes are available at www.interrailnet.com, as well as from travel agents, at major train stations throughout Europe, and through online vendors (www.railpassdirect.co.uk)

BY BUS AND BOAT

Though European trains are extremely popular, in some cases buses prove a better option. Often cheaper than railpasses, but sometimes unreliable, **international bus passes** allow unlimited travel on a hop-on, hop-off basis between major European cities. Contact **Eurolines,** 4 Vicarage Rd., Edgbaston, Birmingham B15 3ES, UK, the largest operator of Europe-wide coach services, for more information. (☎08705 80 80 80; www.eurolines.co.uk or www.eurolines.com. Stops include Florence, Milan, Rome, Sienna, and Venice.) **Busabout,** 258 Vauxhall Bridge Rd., London SW1V 1BS, UK, offers five interconnecting bus circuits covering 60 cities and towns in Europe. (☎207 950 16 61; www.busabout.com. Consecutive Day Passes, Flexi Passes, and Add On Passes are available.)

Most European ferries are quite comfortable; the cheapest ticket typically still includes a reclining chair or couchette. Fares jump sharply in July and August. Ask for discounts; ISIC holders can often get student fares, and Eurailpass holders get many reductions and free trips. You'll occasionally have to pay a port tax (under US$10). Schedules are erratic, with similar routes and varying prices. Shop around, and beware of dinky, unreliable companies that don't take reservations. Countless ferry companies operate these routes simultaneously; see specific country chapters for more information. **Mediterranean** ferries may be the most glamorous, but they can also be the most rocky; bring toilet paper. Ferries run to Tunisia from Sicily and Sardinia, to Corsica from Sardinia, and Malta from Sicily. Ferries float across the **Adriatic** from Ancona and Bari, Italy to Split and Dubrovnik, respectively, in Croatia. Ferries also run across the **Aegean,** from Ancona, Italy to Patras, Greece, and from Bari, Italy to Igoumenitsa and Patras, Greece. Eurail is valid on certain ferries between Brindisi, Italy and Corfu, Igoumenitsa, Cephalonia, and Patras, Greece. Reservations are recommended, especially in July and August.

GETTING AROUND ITALY

BY TRAIN

The Italian State Railway, **Ferrovie dello Stato** or **FS** (www.ferroviedellostato.it), is an umbrella organization that offers inexpensive and efficient service, though it is commonly plagued by strikes. Most of its trains are owned by Trenitalia (infoline ☎89 20 21; www.trenitalia.com), though there are several somewhat less reliable companies, including **Ferrovia Nord,** which runs to Como, and **Ferrovie Sud-Est (FSE),** whose cars are crowded and uncomfortable. The local rail in some parts of Italy shuts down on Sunday, leaving buses as the only weekend transportation option.

Several types of trains ride the Italian rails. The **locale** stops at every station along a particular line, often taking twice as long as a faster train. The **diretto** makes fewer stops than the *locale*, while the **espresso** just stops at major stations. The air-conditioned, more expensive, and **InterCity (IC),** or **rapido,** train travels only to the largest cities, and a few routes may require reservations. Tickets for the fast, comfy, and pricey **Eurostar** or **Pendolino** trains (first- and 2nd-class trains) all require reservations. Eurail passes are valid without a supplement on all trains except the Eurostar. All InterRail holders must also purchase supplements (€3-20) for trains like EuroCity and InterCity. Train tickets may be purchased from *bigletterie*, as well as automated ticket machines, which have instructions in English. There are often discounts for those under 26, traveling in groups of six.

Trains are not always safe. For long trips make sure you are on the correct car, as trains sometimes split at crossroads. Towns listed in parentheses on European schedules require a train switch at the town listed immediately before the parentheses. Note that unless stated otherwise, *Let's Go* lists one-way fares.

NATIONAL PASSES

CARTA VERDE. If you're under 26 or over 60 and plan to travel extensively in Italy, your first purchase should be a Carta Verde or Carta d'Argento, offering a year-long discount on all train tickets (p. 32).

Those planning to spend a considerable amount of time in Italy may want to invest in a discount card. **Carta Verde Railplus** (€40) is available to travelers under 26 and is valid for one year. It provides a 10% discount on all national train tickets and a 25% discount on international trains to participating countries. The **Carta d'Argento** (€30) is available to those over 60 and is also valid for one year. The card provides a 15% discount on all national trains. A **Railplus** card, valid for one year, offers a 25% discount on participating international trains, and can be purchased separately (€45, under 26 €20). Check www.trenitalia.com for additional information.

The domestic analog of the Eurail pass, the **Trenitalia Pass, Trenitalia Pass Saver,** and **Trenitalia Youth Pass** are valid either for a given number of consecutive days or for a specific number of days within a given time period, with the possibility of purchasing additional days. The price for a four-day pass is €174, €149 for a Saver Pass, and €145 for a Youth. Passes must be purchased before you leave. For more information on national railpasses, check out www.raileurope.com/us/rail/passes/single_country_index.htm. Like the InterRail Pass, the **Euro Domino** pass is available to anyone who has lived in Europe for at least six months; however, it is only valid in one country (which you designate when buying the pass). The cost for four days is €193, €145 for those under 26, €164 for those over 60. Reservations must still be paid for separately. Supplements are included for many high-speed trains.

The pass must be bought within your country of residence; each country has its own price for the pass. Inquire with your national rail company for more info. In addition to simple railpasses, many countries (as well as Eurail) offer **rail-and-drive passes,** which combine car rental with rail travel—a good option for travelers who wish both to visit cities accessible by rail and to make side trips into the surrounding areas. Prices range per-person US$235-660, depending on the type of pass, type of car, and number of people included. Children under the age of 11 cost US$95-150, and adding more days costs US$39-215 per day. Unfortunately, railpasses don't always pay off. For estimates of pass prices, contact Rail Europe (p. 29).

 Always validate your train ticket before boarding. Validation machines, usually colored yellow or orange, are located all over train stations. Insert and remove your ticket from the slot and check to see if the machine stamped it. Failure to validate may result in steep fines, and train operators do not accept ignorance as an excuse. The same goes for bus tickets, which should be validated immediately after boarding the bus using the onboard validation machines.

RESERVATIONS

Seat reservations are only rarely required, but you are not guaranteed a seat without one (€2.50 and up, depending on the ticket price). Reservations are available up to two months in advance on major trains, and Italians often reserve far ahead; strongly consider reserving during peak holiday and tourist seasons (at the very latest a few hours ahead). If someone occupies your seat, be prepared to (politely) say, "Excuse me, but I have reserved this seat," or *"Mi scusi, ma ho prenotato questo posto."* It will be necessary to purchase a **supplement** (€3-15.50) or special fare for faster or higher-quality trains. Eurail passes do not include reservations.

OVERNIGHT TRAINS

Night trains have their advantages: you don't waste valuable daylight hours traveling, and you can forego the hassle and considerable expense of securing a night's accommodation. However, night travel has its drawbacks, especially discomfort and sleeplessness. Consider paying extra for a **cuccetta,** one of six fold-down bunks in a compartment (approximately €20); private **sleeping cars** offer more comfort, but are considerably more expensive and not always available. Even if you're not willing to spend the money, some trains have more comfortable seating compartments with fold-out seats. If you are using a railpass valid only for a restricted number of days, inspect train schedules to maximize the use of your pass: a direct overnight train or boat journey uses up only one of your travel days if it departs after 7pm (you need only write in the next day's date on your pass).

BY FERRY

The islands of Sicily, Sardinia, and Corsica, as well as the smaller islands along the coasts, are connected to the mainland by **ferries** (*traghetti*) and **hydrofoils** (*aliscafi*); international trips are generally made by ferries only (see www.traghetti.com for detailed listings of companies). Italy's largest private ferry service, **Tirrenia** (www.gruppotirrenia.it), runs ferries to Sardinia, Sicily, and Tunisia. Other major ferry companies (**Moby Lines, Grandi Navi Veloci, Toremar, Saremar, Siremar,** and **Caremar**) and the **SNAV** (www.snavali.com) hydrofoil services travel to major ports such as Ancona, Bari, Brindisi, Genoa, Livorno, La Spezia, Naples, and Trapani. Ferry services also depart for the Tremiti, Pontine, and Aeolian Islands.

For major trips reserve tickets at least one week in advance. Schedules change unpredictably—confirm your departure one day in advance. Some ports require checking in 2hr. before departure or your reservation will be cancelled. **Posta ponte** (deck class; preferable in warm weather) is cheapest. It is, however, often only available when the **poltrona** (reclining cabin seats) are full. Port taxes often apply. Ask for **student** and **Eurail discounts;** some unscrupulous travelers have been known to ask locals to buy heavily discounted island resident tickets.

BY BUS AND METRO

Though notoriously unreliable and uncomfortable, **buses** are often faster and cheaper than trains. Two bus systems exist within Italy: intercity buses, which run between towns and regions, and intra-city buses, which provide local transportation. Intercity buses, or *pullman*, also tend to go on strike much less frequently than trains. They are always worth checking out, especially for smaller towns that are not serviced by trains. Tickets can generally be purchased at private bus company offices near the bus station or departure point, or onboard the bus. In many rural areas, where stops are unmarked, it is crucial to find out exactly where to stand to flag down the bus. On rare occasions, the tickets are actually sold by the side of the road out of a salesperson's car near where the bus will stop. Intra-city bus tickets are usually sold at any *tabaccheria*, and must be validated using the orange machines on board immediately upon entering the bus. Failure to do so will result in large fines, up to US$140. The websites www.bus.it and www.italybus.it are both helpful resources for finding bus routes to non-major towns and discovering which bus companies service specific regions.

Most large cities, including Rome, Naples, and Milan, have **Metro systems** that connect major tourist destinations. Fast and cheap, this is the best form of local transportation, along with public buses. The Metro usually operates from 6am until midnight, and tickets usually cost approximately €1. The cabins and stations get packed during rush-hour, so guard personal belongings extremely carefully, as theft is rampant. Tickets are sold in stations at counters or from automated machines. Remember to validate them, or risk getting heavily fined.

BY CAR

While the Italian bus and train systems are quite effective in negotiating travel between the major cities, travelers looking to explore smaller cities and rural villages might find renting a **car** to be a more viable option. Especially considering the high gasoline prices (approximately $1.44 per liter) a single traveler won't save by renting a car, but four usually will. If you can't decide between train and car travel, you may benefit from a combination of the two; RailEurope and other railpass vendors offer **rail-and-drive** packages. **Fly-and-drive** packages are often available from travel agents or airline/rental agency partnerships. Before setting off, know the laws of the countries where you'll be driving. For an informal primer on European road signs and conventions, check out www.travlang.com/signs.

ON THE ROAD

Officially, driving in Italy is very similar to driving in the rest of Europe: manual transmission cars drive on the right, pass on the left, and follow international rules and road signs established by the Geneva Convention. The roads in Italy range from the *autostrade* (superhighways with 130km per hr. speed limit, increased to 150km per hr. in some areas) to the narrow and unpaved *strade comunali* (local

ESSENTIALS

roads). Highways usually charge expensive tolls, often best paid with a credit card. Mountain roads can have steep cliffs and narrow curves, so think twice before driving in the Dolomites or the Apennines. In cities the speed limit is usually 50km per hr. Headlights must be on when driving on the *autostrada*. **Parking** is allowed on the right side of all roads outside of towns and cities, other than *autostrade*, but parking is hard to come by, so don't be surprised to see other drivers converting sidewalks into parking spaces. Violations of highway code may result in fines and imprisonment in serious cases. For more driving rules and regulations, consult *In Italy Online* (www.initaly.com/travel/info/driving.htm).

The **Automobile Club d'Italia (ACI)** is at the service of all drivers in Italy, with offices located throughout the country (V. C. Colombo, 261, 00147; Rome ☎06 51 49 71; www.aci.it). Call ☎116 from any phone in case of **breakdown**, for assistance from the nearest ACI. On superhighways use the emergency telephones placed every 2km. For long drives in desolate areas, invest in a roadside assistance program and a cellular telephone, but be aware that use of **phones** en route is only permitted with a hands-free device.

> **DRIVING PRECAUTIONS.** When traveling in the summer, bring substantial amounts of water (a suggested 5L of **water** per person per day) for drinking and for the radiator. For long drives to unpopulated areas, register with police before beginning the trek, and again upon arrival at the destination. Check with the local automobile club for details. When traveling for long distances, make sure tires are in good repair and have enough air, and get good maps. A **compass** and a **car manual** can also be very useful. You should always carry a **spare tire** and **jack, jumper cables, extra oil, flares,** a **flashlight,** and **heavy blankets** (in case your car breaks down at night or in the winter). If you don't know how to **change a tire,** learn before heading out, especially if you are planning on traveling in deserted areas. Blowouts on dirt roads are exceedingly common. If you do have a breakdown, **stay in your car;** if you wander off, there's less likelihood trackers will find you.

RENTING A CAR

You can rent a car from a US-based firm (Alamo, Avis, Budget, or Hertz) with European offices, from a European-based company with local representatives (Europcar), or from a tour operator (Auto Europe or Europe By Car) that will arrange a rental for you from a European company at its own rates. It is always significantly less expensive to reserve a car from the US than from Europe. Reserve ahead and pay in advance if at all possible. Expect to pay US$200-400 per week, for a two- to four-door economy car with manual transmission and A/C. Cars with automatic transmission usally cost an extra US$100 per week, and are hard to find. Always check if prices quoted include tax as well as theft and collision **insurance**. Ask about discounts and check the terms of insurance, particularly the size of the deductible, and always read the fine print.

Though the minimum age to rent a car in Italy is 18, most companies will only rent cars to those over 21, or even 25, depending on the type of car being rented. Drivers under 25 should expect to pay a surcharge of approximately €12 per day. At most agencies, all that's needed to rent a car is a license from home and proof that you've had it for a year. Car rental in Europe is primarily available through the following agencies. (Local desk numbers are included in town listings.)

Auto Europe (US and Canada ☎888-223-5555 or 207-842-2000; www.autoeurope.com).

Avis (Australia ☎136 333; Canada 800-272-5871; New Zealand 0800 65 51 11; UK 0870 606 0100; US 800-230-4898; www.avis.com).

Budget (Canada ☎800-268-8900; UK 8701 565 656; US 800-527-0700; www.budgetrentacar.com).

Europe by Car (US ☎800-223-1516 or 212-581-3040; www.europebycar.com).

Europcar International, 3 ave. du Centre, 78 881 Saint Quentin en Yvelines Cedex, France (UK ☎870 607 5000; US 877-940-6900; www.europcar.com).

Hertz (Australia ☎9698 2555; Canada 800-263-0600; UK 08708 44 88 44; US 800-654-3030; www.hertz.com).

DRIVING PERMITS AND CAR INSURANCE

INTERNATIONAL DRIVING PERMIT (IDP)

If you plan to drive a car while in Italy, you must be over 18 and have an International Driving Permit (IDP). Even though an IDP is usually not required to rent a car, it may be a good idea to get one anyway, in case you're in a situation where the police do not know English (e.g., an accident or stranded in a small town); information on the IDP is printed in 11 languages. Remember that an IDP is just a translation of your license and is not valid without it.

Your IDP, valid for one year, must be issued in your own country before you depart. An application for an IDP usually requires one or two photos, a current local license, an additional form of identification, and a fee. To apply, contact your home country's automobile association. Be careful when purchasing an IDP online or anywhere other than your home automobile association. Many vendors sell permits of questionable legitimacy for higher prices.

CAR INSURANCE

Most credit cards cover standard insurance, but be aware that cars rented on an **American Express** or **Visa/MasterCard Gold or Platinum** credit cards in Italy might *not* carry the automatic insurance that they would in some other countries; check with your credit card company. If you rent, lease, or borrow a car, you will need a **Green Card,** or **International Insurance Certificate,** to certify that you have liability insurance and that it applies abroad. Green cards can be obtained at car rental agencies, car dealers (for those leasing cars), some travel agents, and some border crossings. Remember that if you are driving a conventional vehicle on an **unpaved road** in a rental car, you are almost never covered by insurance; ask about this before leaving the rental agency.

BY BICYCLE, MOPED, AND FOOT

Renting a **bike** is easy in Italy; look for *noleggio* signs. Many airlines will count a bike as your second piece of luggage; a few charge extra (US$50-110 one-way). Bikes must be packed in a cardboard box with the pedals and front wheel detached; many airlines sell bike boxes at the airport (US$10). Most ferries let you take your bike for free or for a nominal fee, and you can always ship your bike on trains. Renting a bike beats bringing your own if you plan to stay in one or two regions. Some hostels rent bicycles for low prices. In addition to **panniers** to hold your luggage, you'll need a good **helmet** (US$25-50) and a **sturdy lock** (from US$30). **Ciclismo Classico,** 30 Marathon St., Arlington, MA 02474, USA (781-646-3377; www.ciclismoclassico.com), offers beginner through advanced level trips across Italy, including Sardinia, Southern Italy, Sicily, Piedmont, and the Veneto. Some towns, like Pavia and Brescia offer free bike rental with an ID deposit; this information is listed under transportation for cities offering the service.

Scooters or **mopeds** are available for rent in major cities, as well as in smaller or rural locations. Often a *motorino* (scooter) is the most convenient method of transportation to reach sights in places with unreliable bus or train connections. Rental companies are required by law to provide a helmet, which the driver must wear. Gas and insurance may or may not be included in the rental price. Even if it is exhilarating, always exercise caution; practice first in empty streets and learn to keep with the flow of traffic rather than just following street signs. Drivers in Italy—especially in the south—are notorious for ignoring traffic laws.

Some of Italy's grandest scenery can be seen only by **foot.** *Let's Go* features many daytrips, but native inhabitants and fellow travelers are the best source for tips. Professionally run hiking and walking tours are often your best bet for navigating *la bell'Italia*. Hiking tours generally range from six to nine days long and cost from US$2700-3000. Check out Ciclismo Classico for hiking options along the Amalfi Coast, and through Tuscany or the Cinque Terre. The **Backpack Europe** website (www.backpackeurope.com) provides links to great hiking, walking, and kayaking options throughout Italy.

BY THUMB

 Let's Go never recommends hitchhiking as a safe means of transportation, and none of the information presented here is intended to do so.

Let's Go strongly urges you to consider the risks before you choose to hitchhike. Hitching means entrusting your life to a stranger and risking assault, sexual harassment, theft, and unsafe driving. For women traveling alone (or even in pairs), hitching is just too dangerous. A man and a woman are a less dangerous combination; two men will have a harder time getting a lift, while three men will go nowhere. Experienced hitchers pick a well-lit spot outside of built-up areas, where drivers can stop, return to the road without causing an accident, and have time to look over potential passengers as they approach. Hitchhiking is illegal in Italy although many Italians will offer rides to travelers walking alone, especially in deserted areas. Many travelers accept rides from Italian drivers without incident. Probably the greatest danger for hitchhikers is getting hit by a car while waiting on the highway or being involved in a car accident. Travelers who know the Italian names for their destinations generally have more success making drivers understand where they want to go. It is always a good idea to keep luggage on the seat next to you, instead of putting it in the trunk, to facilitate a quick exit.

Most Western European countries offer a ride service, which pairs drivers with riders; the fee varies according to destination. Eurostop International is one of the largest in Europe. Not all organizations screen drivers and riders; ask in advance. *Let's Go* strongly urges you to consider the risks before you choose to hitchhike.

KEEPING IN TOUCH

BY EMAIL AND INTERNET

Internet points in large cities swell with locals and backpackers using email and instant messaging services. Rural areas and cities in the south are catching up.

Rates range €4-8 per hr. For free Internet access, try local universities and libraries. Or save time and try a combo Internet-laundry point or a cyber cafe. Internet cafes are more likely than other establishments to go out of business or switch locations. Inquire at the tourist office for Internet access in town.

Though in some places it's possible to forge a remote link with your home server, in most cases this is a much slower (and more expensive) option than taking advantage of free **web-based email accounts** (e.g., www.hotmail.com and www.yahoo.com). **Internet cafes** and the occasional free Internet terminal at a public library or university are listed in **Practical Information** sections. For lists of cyber cafes in Italy, check out www.ecs.net/cafe/#list and www.cybercaptive.com.

Increasingly, travelers find that taking their **laptop computers** on the road with them can be a convenient option for staying connected. Laptop users can call an Internet service provider via a modem using long-distance phone cards specifically intended for such calls. Some Internet cafes that allow you to connect your laptops to the Internet. Italy, though, lags a bit in technological development, and therefore is not the best place to travel with a laptop unless you really need it. For information on insuring your laptop while traveling, see p. 20.

BY TELEPHONE

CALLING HOME FROM ITALY

You can usually make **direct international calls** from pay phones, but if you aren't using a phone card, you may need to drop your coins as quickly as your words. **Prepaid phone cards** are a common and relatively inexpensive means of calling abroad. Each one comes with a Personal Identification Number (PIN) and a toll-free access number. You call the access number and then follow the directions for dialing. To purchase prepaid phone cards, check online for the best rates; www.callingcards.com is a good place to start. Online providers generally send your access number and PIN via email, with no actual "card" involved. You can also call home with prepaid phone cards purchased in Italy (see **Calling Within Italy,** below).

Another option is to purchase a **calling card,** linked to a major national telecommunications service in your home country. Calls are billed collect or to your account. To obtain a calling card, contact the appropriate company listed below. Where available, there are often advantages to purchasing calling cards online, including better rates and immediate access to your account. To call home with a calling card, contact the operator for your service provider in Italy by dialing the appropriate toll-free access number (listed below in the 3rd column).

COMPANY	TO OBTAIN A CARD:	TO CALL ABROAD FROM ITALY:
AT&T (US)	800-364-9292 or www.att.com	800 17 24 44
Canada Direct	800-561-8868 or www.infocanadadirect.com	800 17 22 13
MCI (US)	800-777-5000 or consumer.mci.com	800 90 58 25
Telecom New Zealand Direct	www.telecom.co.nz	800 17 26 41
Telstra Australia	800-038-000 or www.telstra.com	800 17 26 10

Placing a **collect call** through an international operator can be quite expensive, but may be necessary in case of an emergency. You can frequently call collect without even possessing a company's calling card just by calling its access number and following the instructions.

PLACING INTERNATIONAL CALLS. To call Italy from home or to call home from Italy, dial:

1. The **international dialing prefix.** To call from **Australia,** dial 0011; **Canada** or the **US,** 011; **Ireland, New Zealand,** or the **UK,** 00; **Italy,** 00.
2. The **country code** of the country you want to call. To call **Australia,** dial 61; **Canada** or the **US,** 1; **Ireland,** 353; **New Zealand,** 64; the **UK,** 44; **Italy,** 39.
3. The **city/area code.** *Let's Go* lists the city/area codes for cities and towns in Italy opposite the city or town name, next to a ☎. Unlike in most European countries, if the first digit is a zero (e.g., 02 for Milan), **do not omit the zero** when calling from abroad.
4. The **local number.**

CALLING WITHIN ITALY

As coin-operated public phones are being phased out, the most common type requires a prepaid phone card, or *scheda*. Phone card vendors, *tabaccherie*, Internet cafes, and even post offices carry cards in denominations of €5, €10, €20, €30, and €50. Italian phone cards are a little tricky to maneuver; rip off the perforated corner and insert the card in the slot of the phone stripe-up. For instructions in English, push the silver button with two flags on it. Another kind of phone card comes with a Personal Identification Number (PIN) and a toll-free access number. Instead of inserting the card into the phone, you call the access number and follow the directions on the card. These are great because they work from private lines as well as pay phones, are generally cheaper, and can be used to make international as well as domestic calls. Phone rates typically tend to be highest in the morning, lower in the evening, and lowest on Sunday and late at night. Rates are significantly higher when dialing from payphones, so use a private line when you can.

Even when dialing within a city, the city code is required (e.g., when dialing from one place in Milan to another, the ☎02 is still necessary.)

CELLULAR PHONES

Cellular phones (*telefonini*) are both convenient and inexpensive for longer visits. You can either join a monthly plan or opt to pay as you go through the **Global System for Mobile Communication (GSM)** system; for this 2nd option you will need a **GSM-compatible phone** and a **SIM (Subscriber Identity Module) card,** a country-specific chip that gives you a local phone number and plugs you into the local network. Many SIM cards are **prepaid** (they come with calling time included and you don't need to sign up for a monthly service plan). Incoming calls are frequently free. When you use up the prepaid time, you can buy more (usually at convenience stores). For more information on GSM phones, check out www.telestial.com, www.orange.co.uk, www.roadpost.com, or www.planetomni.com. .

The greatest expense in a monthly plan is the purchase of the phone itself. Calls to other phones on the same company's plan are around €0.15 per min. and incoming calls are free. The three main phone companies are **Vodafone Omnitel** (from Italy ☎800 10 01 95 or 420 05 from a Vodafone cellphone; www.omnitel.it), **Wind** (☎800 915 800 or 155 from a Wind cellphone; www.wind.it), and **Tim** (from Italy ☎800 555 333 or 800 61 96 19, from abroad 393 39 91 19; www.tim.it). Companies like **Cellular Abroad** (www.cellularabroad.com) rent cell phones that work in a variety of destinations, providing a simpler option than picking up a phone in-country.

ESSENTIALS

GSM PHONES. Just having a GSM phone doesn't mean you're necessarily good to go when you travel abroad. The majority of GSM phones sold in the United States operate on a different **frequency** (1900) than international phones (900/1800) and will not work abroad. Tri-band phones work on all three frequencies (900/1800/1900) and will operate through most of the world. As well, some GSM phones are **SIM-locked** and will only accept SIM cards from a single carrier. You'll need a **SIM-unlocked** phone to use a SIM card from a local carrier when you travel.

TIME DIFFERENCES

Italy is 1hr. ahead of **Greenwich Mean Time (GMT).** Daylight Saving Time starts on the last Sunday in March, when clocks are moved ahead 1hr. Clocks are put back 1hr. on the last Sunday in September.

4AM	7AM	12PM	1PM	8PM	10PM
Vancouver Seattle San Francisco Los Angeles	Toronto New York	London (GMT)	Italy Paris Munich Madrid	China Hong Kong Manila Singapore	Sydney Canberra Melbourne

BY MAIL

SENDING MAIL HOME FROM ITALY

Airmail is the best way to send mail home from Italy. **Aerogrammes,** printed sheets that fold into envelopes and travel via airmail, are available at post offices. Write "airmail," "par avion," or "posta prioritaria" on the front. Most post offices will charge exorbitant fees or simply refuse to send aerogrammes with enclosures. **Surface mail** is by far the cheapest and slowest way to send mail. It takes one to two months to cross the Atlantic and one to three to cross the Pacific—good for heavy items you won't need for a while, like souvenirs or other articles you've acquired along the way that are weighing down your pack.

SENDING MAIL WITHIN ITALY

Domestic postal service is poor and for years has been the butt of jokes among Italians. Recently the state-owned Poste Italiane (www.poste.it) has modernized the system to include services like priority and registered mail, but it hasn't sped up much. Sending a postcard in Italy costs €0.45, while sending letters (up to 2kg) domestically requires €0.85-6.00. To address a letter within Italy, use this format:

Luigi Pirandello
Via Atenea, 1921
92100 Agrigento

RECEIVING MAIL IN ITALY

There are several ways to arrange pick up of letters sent to you by friends and relatives while you are abroad. Mail can be sent via **Poste Restante** (General Delivery; *fermoposta*) to big cities in Italy with a post office, but is not always reliable. Address *fermoposta* letters like so:

Dante ALIGHIERI
Fermoposta
80142 Napoli
Italy

The mail will go to a desk in the central post office, unless you specify a post office by street address or postal code. It's best to use the largest post office, since mail may be sent there regardless. It is usually safer and quicker, though more expensive, to send mail express or registered. Bring your passport for pick up; there is a small fee which for letters should not exceed €1, so bring money too. If the clerks insist that there is nothing for you, have them check under your first name as well. *Let's Go* lists post offices in the **Practical Information** section for cities and towns.

ACCOMMODATIONS

HOSTELS

While hostel quality and services vary widely within Italy, hostels remain the cheapest and best accommodations options for budget travelers. Many are located far from city centers and have rules governing length of stay and hours of room access, but for travelers merely looking for a place to stash their pack while they explore or crash for the night, Italian hostels are generally well-regulated and safe. Whenever possible, try to reserve ahead—student travel in Italy has become so common that you can't just walk in and expect to get a bed.

Most hostels are laid out dorm-style, often with large single-sex rooms and bunk beds, although private rooms that sleep two to four are becoming more common. They sometimes have kitchens and utensils for guest use, bike or moped rentals, storage areas, transportation to airports, breakfast and other meals, laundry facilities, and Internet access. Often bed linens are included and towels are available for rent. There can be drawbacks: some hostels close during daytime "lockout" hours, have a curfew, don't accept reservations, impose a maximum stay, or, less frequently, require that you do chores. In Italy, a dorm bed in a hostel will average around €15-25 and a private room €40.

A HOSTELER'S BILL OF RIGHTS. There are certain standard features that we do not include in our hostel listings. Unless we state otherwise, you can expect that every hostel has no lockout, no curfew, a kitchen, free hot showers, some system of secure luggage storage, and no key deposit.

HOSTELLING INTERNATIONAL

Joining the youth hostel association in your own country (listed below) automatically grants you membership privileges in **Hostelling International (HI),** a federation of national hosteling associations. Non-HI members may rarely be allowed to stay in some hostels, but will have to pay extra to do so. Membership cards are often available at individual hostels. Where applicable, we have listed HI restrictions and membership card availability. Websites like HI's webpage (www.hihostels.com), www.hostels.com, and www.hostelplanet.com that list the web addresses and phone numbers of all national associations can be a great place to begin researching hosteling in a specific region. The Italian Youth Hostels Association operates a website in English and Italian, www.ostellionline.org, with images, maps, descriptions and rates of hostels you can book online.

Most HI hostels also honor **guest memberships**—you'll get a blank card with space for six validation stamps. Each night you'll pay a nonmember supplement (usually €3) and earn one guest stamp; get six stamps, and you're a member. This system generally works well, but sometimes you may need to remind the hostel reception. A new membership benefit is the FreeNites program, which allows hostelers to gain points toward free rooms by simply staying the night or having dinner in an HI hostel. Most student travel agencies (p. 25) sell HI cards, as do all of the national hosteling organizations listed below. All prices listed below are valid for **one-year memberships** unless otherwise noted.

Australian Youth Hostels Association (AYHA), 422 Kent St., Sydney, NSW 200 (☎02 9261 1111; www.yha.com.au). AUS$52, under 18 AUS$19.

Hostelling International-Canada (HI-C), 205 Catherine St. #400, Ottawa, ON K2P 1C3 (☎613-237-7884; www.hihostels.ca). CDN$35, under 18 free.

An Óige (Irish Youth Hostel Association), 61 Mountjoy St., Dublin 7 (☎830 4555; www.irelandyha.org). EUR€20, under 18 EUR€10.

Hostelling International Northern Ireland (HINI), 22-32 Donegall Rd., Belfast BT12 5JN (☎02890 32 47 33; www.hini.org.uk). UK£13, under 18 UK£6.

Youth Hostels Association of New Zealand (YHANZ), Level 1, Moorhouse City, 166 Moorhouse Ave., P.O. Box 436, Christchurch (☎0800 278 299v (NZ only) or 03 379 9970; www.yha.org.nz). NZ$40, under 18 free.

Scottish Youth Hostels Association (SYHA), 7 Glebe Cres., Stirling FK8 2JA (☎01786 89 14 00; www.syha.org.uk). UK£6, under 17 £2.50.

Youth Hostels Association (England and Wales), Trevelyan House, Dimple Rd., Matlock, Derbyshire DE4 3YH (☎08707 708 868; www.yha.org.uk). UK£15.50, under 26 UK£10.

Hostelling International-USA, 8401 Colesville Rd., Ste. 600, Silver Spring, MD 20910 (☎301-495-1240; www.hiayh.org). US$28, under 18 free.

BOOKING HOSTELS ONLINE. One of the easiest ways to ensure you've got a bed for the night is by reserving online. Click to the **Hostelworld** booking engine through **www.letsgo.com,** and you'll have access to bargain accommodations from Argentina to Zimbabwe with no added commission.

OTHER TYPES OF ACCOMMODATIONS

HOTELS, GUESTHOUSES, AND PENSIONS

A hotel single (*singola*) in Italy costs about US$30-60 (€25-50) per night, a double (*doppia* or *matrimoniale*) US$50-100 (€40-82). You'll typically share a hall bathroom; a private bathroom will cost extra, as may hot showers. Prices often fluctuate according to season, rising steeply during the summer months and over the New Year. Some hotels offer *pensione completa* (all meals) and *mezza pensione* (no dinner); in high season hotel owners often require guests to take some form of *pensione*. Upon arrival be sure to confirm charges; Italian hotels are notorious for tacking on additional costs at check-out time. If you make reservations in writing, indicate your night of arrival and the number of nights you plan to stay. The hotel will send you a confirmation and may request payment for the first night. Often it is easiest to make reservations over the phone with a credit card. For phone reservations keep track of who you spoke with and call to confirm a few days before your scheduled arrival; some reception desks are wary of no-shows and give away reserved rooms last minute. Not all hotels take reservations, and few accept checks in foreign currency, while most do accept Visa and MasterCard.

Rooms for rent in private homes (*affittacamere*) are inexpensive, usually good for groups of two to four, and a great way to practice Italian and immerse yourself in the culture. Where these are available, *Let's Go* lists pertinent names and contact information. For more information inquire at local tourist offices.

LONG-TERM ACCOMMODATIONS

Travelers planning to stay in Italy for extended periods of time may find it most cost-effective to rent an **apartment.** A basic one-bedroom apartment in Rome ranges from around €1000-1500 per month. Prospective tenants usually are also required to front a security deposit (frequently one month's rent). For more information check out www.liveinrome.com or www.romepower.com.

HOME EXCHANGES AND HOSPITALITY CLUBS

Home exchanges offer travelers various types of homes (houses, apartments, condominiums, villas, even castles), plus the opportunity to cut down on accommodation fees. For more information, contact HomeExchange.Com, P.O. Box 787, Hermosa Beach, CA 90254, USA (☎800-877-8723; www.homeexchange.com), or Intervac International Home Exchange (39 05 19 12 028; www.intervac.com).

Hospitality clubs link members with individuals or families abroad who are willing to host travelers for free or for a small fee to promote cultural exchange. In exchange, members usually must be willing to host travelers in their own homes; a small membership fee may also be required. **GlobalFreeloaders.com** (www.globalfreeloaders.com) and **The Hospitality Club** (www.hospitalityclub.org) are good places to start. **Servas** (www.servas.org) is an established, more formal, peace-based organization, and requires a fee and an interview to join. An Internet search will find many similar organizations, some of which cater to special interests (e.g., women, GLBT travelers, or members of certain professions). As always, use common sense when planning to stay with or host someone you do not know.

CAMPING AND THE OUTDOORS

There are over 1700 campsites in Italy. Fees are small, variable, and usually issued per person. Contact local tourist offices for information about suitable or free campsites. Camping on undesignated land is not permitted. The **Touring Club Italiano** (www.touringclub.it) publishes numerous useful books and pamphlets on the outdoors. The **Federazione Italiana del Campeggio e del Caravanning (Federcampeggio),** 50041 Calenzano, Florence (☎055 88 23 91; www.federcampeggio.it), has a complete list of camping sites with free location maps. Federcampeggio also publishes the book *Guida Camping d'Italia.* **EasyCamping** (www.icaro.it/home_e.html) offers information about over 700 campsites throughout Italy. For a list of the bigger parks and national reserves in the country, visit www.parks.it.

USEFUL PUBLICATIONS AND RESOURCES

A variety of companies publish hiking guidebooks to meet the educational needs of novices and experts. Contact the publishers listed below for free information about camping, hiking, and biking. Campers heading to multiple destinations across Europe should consider buying an **International Camping Carnet** (US$10-15).

ESSENTIALS

Similar to a hostel membership card, it's required at a few campgrounds and provides discounts at others. Available in North America from the Family Campers and RVers Association and in the UK from The Caravan Club.

> **Automobile Association,** Contact Centre, Carr Ellison House, William Armstrong Drive, Newcastle-upon-Tyne NE4 7YA, UK (☎08706 000 371; www.theAA.com). Publishes *Caravan and Camping Europe* and *Britain & Ireland* (UK£10) as well as road atlases for Europe, Britain, France, Germany, Ireland, Italy, Spain, and the US.

> **Sierra Club Books,** 85 Second St., 2nd fl., San Francisco, CA 94105, USA (☎415-977-5500; www.sierraclub.org). Publishes general resource books on hiking and camping, as well as specific guides on Italy.

> **The Mountaineers Books,** 1001 SW Klickitat Way, Ste. 201, Seattle, WA 98134, USA (☎206-223-6303; www.mountaineersbooks.org). Over 600 titles on hiking, biking, mountaineering, natural history, and conservation.

WILDERNESS SAFETY

Stay warm, stay dry, and stay hydrated. Follow this simple advice to avoid the vast majority of life-threatening wilderness situations. Prepare yourself for an emergency, however, by always packing raingear, a hat and mittens, a first-aid kit, a reflector, a whistle, high energy food, and extra water for any hike. Dress in wool or warm layers of synthetic materials designed for the outdoors; never rely on cotton for warmth, as it is useless when wet. Check **weather forecasts** and pay attention to the skies when hiking, since weather patterns can change suddenly. Whenever possible, let someone know when and where you are hiking—either a friend, your hostel manager, a park ranger, or a local hiking organization. Do not attempt a hike beyond your ability—you may be endangering your life. For information about outdoor ailments and basic medical concerns (see **Health,** p. 18).

CAMPING AND HIKING EQUIPMENT

WHAT TO BUY...

Good camping equipment is both sturdy and light. North American suppliers tend to offer the most competitive prices.

> **Sleeping bag:** Most sleeping bags are rated by season ("summer" means 30-40°F at night; "four-season" or "winter" often means below 0°F). They are made either of **down** (warmer and lighter, but more expensive, and miserable when wet; US$250-300) or of **synthetic** material (heavier, more durable, and warmer when wet; US$80-210). **Sleeping bag pads** include foam pads (US$10-20), air mattresses (US$15-50), and self-inflating pads (US$45-80). Bring a **stuff sack** to store your bag and keep it dry.

> **Tent:** The best tents are free-standing (with their own frames and suspension systems), can be set up quickly, and only require staking in high winds. Low-profile dome tents are best. Good 2-person tents start at US$90, 4-person at US$300. Use a groundcloth and seal the seams of your tent with waterproofer and make sure it has a rain fly.

> **Backpack: Internal-frame packs** mold more effectively to your back, keep a lower center of gravity, and flex to allow you to hike difficult trails. **External-frame packs** are more comfortable for long hikes over even terrain, with weight kept higher and distributed more evenly. Packs should have strong, padded hip-belts to transfer weight to your legs. Sturdy backpacks cost anywhere from US$125-420. It doesn't pay to economize. Either buy a **waterproof cover** or store all of your belongings in plastic bags inside your pack.

> **Boots:** Be sure to wear hiking boots with good **ankle support.** They should fit snugly and comfortably over 1-2 pairs of wool socks and thin liner socks. Break in boots over several weeks in order to spare yourself painful blisters while hiking.

Other necessities: Synthetic layers, like those made of polypropylene, and a **pile jacket** will keep you warm even when wet. A **"space blanket"** (US$5-15) will help you to retain your body heat and doubles as a groundcloth. Plastic **water bottles** are virtually shatter- and leak-proof. Bring **water-purification tablets** for when you can't boil water. For places that forbid fires or the gathering of firewood (virtually every organized campground in Italy), you'll need a **camp stove** (the classic Coleman starts at US$40) and a propane-filled **fuel bottle** to operate it. Also don't forget a **first-aid kit, pocket-knife, insect repellent, calamine lotion,** and **waterproof matches** or a **lighter.**

...AND WHERE TO BUY IT

The mail-order/online companies listed below offer lower prices than many retail stores, but a visit to a local camping or outdoors store will give you a good sense of the look and weight of certain items.

Campmor, P.O. Box 700, Upper Saddle River, NJ 07458, USA (☎800-525-4784; www.campmor.com).

Discount Camping, 880 Main North Rd., Pooraka, South Australia 5095, Australia (☎08 8262 33 99; www.discountcamping.com.au).

Eastern Mountain Sports (EMS), (☎888-463-6367 or 603-924-7231; www.shopems.com).

L.L. Bean, Freeport, ME 04033, USA (US and Canada ☎800-341-4341, UK 0800 89 12 97; outside US 207 552 68 78; www.llbean.com).

Mountain Designs, 51 Bishop St., Kelvin Grove, Queensland 4059, Australia (☎07 3856 2344; www.mountaindesigns.com).

Recreational Equipment, Inc. (REI), Sumner, WA 98352, USA (☎800 426 48 40, outside US 253 891 25 00; www.rei.com).

ORGANIZED OUTDOOR TRIPS

Organized adventure tours offer another way to explore the wild. Activities include hiking, biking, skiing, canoeing, climbing, and archaeological digs. For example, should you choose to brave the hike through Stromboli Volcano, **Magmatrek** (p. 675), V. V. Emanuele, can provide guided trips. Tourism bureaus can suggest parks, trails, and outfitters. Organizations that specialize in camping and outdoor equipment like REI and EMS (see above) are also good sources for info.

SPECIFIC CONCERNS

SUSTAINABLE TRAVEL

As the number of travelers on the road continues to rise, the detrimental effect they can have on natural environments becomes an increasing concern. With this in mind, *Let's Go* promotes the philosophy of **sustainable travel.** Through a sensitivity to issues of ecology and sustainability, today's travelers can be a powerful force in preserving and restoring the places they visit.

Ecotourism, a rising trend in sustainable travel, focuses on the conservation of natural habitats and using them to build up the economy without exploitation or overdevelopment. Visitors to Italy can foster this trend through *agriturismi* (living and working on a farm) volunteering at national parks, and restoring historical sites. For more information, see **Beyond Tourism** (p. 81). Travelers can make a difference by doing advance research and by supporting organizations and establishments that pay attention to their impact on their natural surroundings and strive to be environmentally friendly.

> **ECOTOURISM RESOURCES.** For more information on environmentally responsible tourism, contact one of the organizations below:
> **Conservation International** (www.conservation.org).
> **Green Globe 21** (+61 2 6257 9102; www.greenglobe21.com/Travellers.aspx)
> **International Ecotourism Society,** 733 15th St. NW, Washington, D.C. 20005, USA (☎202-347-9203; www.ecotourism.org).
> **United Nations Environment Program** (**UNEP;** +33 1 44 37 14 41; www.uneptie.org/pc/tourism).

RESPONSIBLE TRAVEL

The impact of tourism on the destinations you visit should not be underestimated. The choices you make during your trip can have potent effects on local communities—for better or for worse. Travelers who care about the destinations and environments they explore should become aware of the social and cultural implications of the choices they make when they travel. Simple decisions such as buying local products instead of globally available products, paying a fair price for the product or service, and attempting to say a few words in the local language can have a strong, positive effect on the community.

Community-based tourism aims to channel tourism into the local economy by emphasizing tours and cultural programs that are run by members of the host community and that often benefit disadvantaged groups. This type of tourism also benefits the tourists themselves, as these tours often take them beyond the traditional tours of the region. An excellent resource for general information on community-based travel is *The Good Alternative Travel Guide* (UK£10), a project of **Tourism Concern** (☎+44 020 7133 3330; www.tourismconcern.org.uk).

Earthwatch Institute, 3 Clock Tower Pl., Ste. 100, Box 75, Maynard, MA 01754 (☎ 800-776-0188; http://www.earthwatch.org/). Conducts research expeditions around the world including reconstruction of the ancient therapeutic use of plants in Italy.

GoNOMAD, P.O. Box 4, 14A Sugarloaf St., South Deerfield, MA 01373 (☎413-665-5005; www.gonomad.com). Database of listings, guides, and articles for sustainable and responsible travel. Information about lodgings, transportation, and activities including cooking classes, cultural exchange, and language learning in Italy.

Responsibletravel.com, Pavilion House, 6 The Old Steine, Brighton, East Sussex, BN1 1EJ, UK (www.responsibletravel.com). Online travel agent for people interested in vacations that benefit the environment and its inhabitants including farmstays in Italy.

TRAVELING ALONE

There are many benefits to traveling alone, including independence and greater interaction with locals. On the other hand, any solo traveler is a more vulnerable target of harassment and street theft. As a lone traveler, try not to stand out as a tourist, look confident, and be especially careful in deserted or very crowded areas. Stay away from areas that are not well lit. If questioned, never admit that you are traveling alone. Maintain regular contact with someone at home who knows your itinerary, and always research your destination before traveling. For more tips, pick up *Traveling Solo* by Eleanor Berman (Globe Pequot Press, US$18), visit www.travelaloneandloveit.com, or subscribe to **Connecting: Solo Travel Network,** 689 Park Rd., Unit 6, Gibsons, BC V0N 1V7, Canada (☎800-557-1757; www.cstn.org; membership US$30-55).

WOMEN TRAVELERS

Women exploring on their own inevitably face some additional safety concerns, but it's easy to be adventurous without taking undue risks. If you are concerned, consider staying in hostels which offer single rooms that lock from the inside or in religious organizations with rooms for women only. Stick to centrally located accommodations and avoid solitary late-night treks or Metro rides.

Always carry extra money for a phone call, bus, or taxi. **Hitchhiking** is never safe for lone women, or even for two women traveling together. Look as if you know where you're going and approach older women or couples for directions if you're lost or uncomfortable. Generally, the less you look like a tourist, the better off you'll be. Dress conservatively, especially in rural areas. Wearing a conspicuous **wedding band** sometimes helps to prevent unwanted overtures.

Your best answer to verbal harassment is no answer at all; feigning deafness, sitting motionless, and staring straight ahead at nothing in particular will do a world of good that reactions usually don't achieve. The extremely persistent can sometimes be dissuaded by a firm, loud, and very public "Go away!" in Italian. Don't hesitate to seek out a police officer or a passerby if you are being harassed. Memorize the emergency numbers in places you visit, and consider carrying a whistle on your keychain. A self-defense course will both prepare you for a potential attack and raise your level of awareness of your surroundings. Also be sure you are aware of the health concerns that women face when traveling (see p. 24).

For information about Tuscany's recent initiative, "Tuscany Welcomes Women," see p. 463 or visit http://www.rete.toscana.it/sett/turismo/benvenute_guida.pdf.

GLBT TRAVELERS

It is difficult to characterize the Italian attitude toward gay, lesbian, bisexual, and transgendered (GLBT) travelers. An overwhelmingly Catholic country overall, some regions accept alternative relationships while other areas remain considerably homophobic. Rome, Florence, Milan, and Bologna all have easily accessible gay scenes. Away from the larger cities, however, gay social life may be difficult to find. The monthly *Babilonia* and annual *Guida Gay Italia*, the national homosexual magazines which confront gay issues and social events, are sold at most newsstands. Travelers can also expect the larger cities to have gay *discoteche* and bars (listed in *Let's Go*). The **Italian Gay and Lesbian Yellow Pages** (www.gay.iy/guida/italia/info.htm) lists gay bars, hotels, and shops. Listed below are contact organizations, mail-order bookstores, and publishers that offer materials addressing some specific concerns. **Out and About** (www.planetout.com) offers a weekly newsletter addressing travel concerns and a comprehensive site addressing gay travel concerns. The online newspaper **365gay.com** also has a travel section (www.365gay.com/travel/travelchannel.htm).

Gay's the Word, 66 Marchmont St., London WC1N 1AB, UK (☎+44 020 7278 7654; www.gaystheword.co.uk). The largest gay and lesbian bookshop in the UK, with both fiction and non-fiction titles. Mail-order service available.

Giovanni's Room, 1145 Pine St., Philadelphia, PA 19107, USA (☎215-923-2960; www.queerbooks.com). An international lesbian/feminist and gay bookstore with mail-order service (carries many of the publications listed below).

ESSENTIALS

International Lesbian and Gay Association (ILGA; ☎+32 2 502 2471; www.ilga.org). Provides political information, such as homosexuality laws of individual countries.

> **FURTHER READING: GLBT.**
> *Spartacus 2005-2006: International Gay Guide.* Bruno Gmunder Verlag (US$33).
> *Ferrari Guides' Gay Travel A to Z, Ferrari Guides' Men's Travel in Your Pocket, Ferrari Guides' Women's Travel in Your Pocket,* and *Ferrari Guides' Inn Places.* Ferrari Publications (US$16-20).
> *The Gay Vacation Guide: The Best Trips and How to Plan Them,* Mark Chesnut. Kensington Books (US$15).

TRAVELERS WITH DISABILITIES

Travelers with disabilities should inform airlines and hotels of their disabilities; some time may be needed to prepare special accommodations. Call ahead to restaurants, museums, and other facilities to find out if they are accessible. Many museums and famed landmarks are not. Venice and Assisi are especially difficult to navigate. Although Italy no longer requires animals entering the country to be quarantined, **guide dog owners** must provide a certificate of immunization against rabies and a certificate of health from their veterinarian. Rail is probably the most convenient form of travel for disabled travelers in Italy: many stations have ramps, and some trains have wheelchair lifts, special seating areas, and specially equipped toilets. For those who wish to rent cars, some major **car rental** agencies (e.g., Hertz) offer hand-controlled vehicles.

USEFUL ORGANIZATIONS

Access Abroad, www.umabroad.umn.edu/access. A website devoted to making study abroad available to students with disabilities. The site is maintained by Disability Services and the Learning Abroad Center, University of Minnesota, University Gateway, Ste. 180, 200 Oak St. SE, Minneapolis, MN 55455, USA (☎612-626-7379).

Accessible Journeys, 35 West Sellers Ave., Ridley Park, PA 19078, USA (☎800-846-4537; www.disabilitytravel.com). Designs tours for wheelchair users and slow walkers. The site has tips and forums for all travelers.

Flying Wheels, 143 W. Bridge St., P.O. Box 382, Owatonna, MN 55060, USA (☎507-451-5005; www.flyingwheelstravel.com). Specializes in escorted trips to Europe and the Middle East for people with physical disabilities; plans custom trips worldwide.

The Guided Tour Inc., 7900 Old York Rd., Ste. 114B, Elkins Park, PA 19027, USA (☎800-783-5841; www.guidedtour.com). Organizes travel programs for persons with developmental and physical challenges.

Society for Accessible Travel and Hospitality (SATH), 347 Fifth Ave., Ste. 610, New York, NY 10016, USA (☎212-447-7284; www.sath.org). Advocacy group publishes free online travel information and the travel magazine *OPEN WORLD* (annual subscription US$13, free for members). Annual membership US$45, students and seniors US$30.

MINORITY TRAVELERS

Particularly in Southern Italy, minority travelers or members of non-Christian religions may feel unwelcome. In terms of safety, there is no easy answer. Men and women should always travel in groups and avoid unsafe parts of town. The best answer to verbal harassment is often not to acknowledge it.

DIETARY CONCERNS

While there are only a few strictly vegetarian restaurants in Italy, it is not difficult to find vegetarian meals. Check out the **A.V.I. Italian Vegetarian Association** (www.vegetariani.it). The travel section of the The Vegetarian Resource Group's website, at www.vrg.org/travel, has a comprehensive list of organizations and websites that are geared toward helping vegetarians and vegans traveling abroad. For more information, visit your local bookstore or health food store, and consult *The Vegetarian Traveler: Where to Stay if You're Vegetarian, Vegan, Environmentally Sensitive*, by Jed and Susan Civic (Larson Publications; US$16). In addition, *Good Vegetarian Food* is an Italy-specific guide which is available for purchase on www.vegetarianguides.co.uk. Vegetarians will also find numerous resources on the web; try www.vegdining.com, www.happycow.net, and www.vegetariansabroad.com, for starters.

Lactose intolerance does not have to be an obstacle to eating well. Though it may seem like everybody in Italy but you is devouring pizza and *gelato*, there are ways for even the lactose intolerant to indulge in local cuisine. In restaurants ask for items without *latte* (milk), *formaggio* (cheese), *burro* (butter), or *crema* (cream). Or order the cheeseless delicacy, *pizza marinara*.

Travelers who keep kosher should contact synagogues in larger cities for information on kosher restaurants. Your own synagogue or college Hillel should have access to lists of Jewish institutions across the nation. If you are strict in your observance, you may have to prepare your own food on the road. A good resource is the *Jewish Travel Guide*, edited by Michael Zaidner (Vallentine Mitchell; US$18). For listings of kosher restaurants in Italy, visit http://shamash.org/kosher, a worldwide kosher restaurant database. Travelers looking for halal restaurants may find www.zabihah.com a useful resource.

OTHER RESOURCES

Let's Go tries to cover all aspects of budget travel, but we can't put *everything* in our guides. Listed below are books and websites that can serve as jumping-off points for your own research.

USEFUL PUBLICATIONS

Cicerone Press, 2 Police Square, Milnthorpe, Cumbria, UK, LA7 7PY (☎+44-1539 562 069; www.ciceroneguides.com). Walking, trekking, and climbing guides, including *Walking in the Dolomites* (2005; US$17.95) and *Trekking in the Apennines* (2005; US$22).

Culture Shock!: Italy, Raymond Flower. Helpful tips for travelers about Italian life and culture. Graphic Arts Center Publishing Company, 2003 (US$13.95).

Italy: The Best Travel Writing from the New York Times, Umberto Eco and New York Times writers. Introduction by Umberto Eco and stunning photographs throughout, this anthology shows and tells the wonders of each town and city of Italy (US$50.00).

Living, Studying, and Working in Italy, Travis Neighbor Ward and Monica Larner. A comprehensive guide for an extended stay or permanent move to Italy. Also lists many useful agencies and their phone numbers. Henry Holt and Company, 2003 (US$17).

Touring Club Italiano (TCI), Corso Italia, 10, Milan (☎02 85 261; www.touringclub.com). Detailed maps and road atlases, as well as guides on bike routes (*Italy by Bike*, 2004; US$18.95), and camping (*Italian Camping*, 2004; $18.95), lists of farms participating in *agriturismo* (*Italian Farm Vacations*, 2003; US$9.95).

WORLD WIDE WEB

Almost every aspect of budget travel is accessible via the web. In 10min. at the keyboard, you can make a hostel reservation, get advice on travel hot spots from other travelers, or find out how to navigate Italy's public transportation.

Listed here are some regional and travel-related sites to start off your surfing; other relevant websites are listed throughout the book. Because website turnover is high, use search engines (such as www.google.com) to strike out on your own.

> **WWW.LETSGO.COM** *Let's Go's* website features a wealth of information and valuable advice at your fingertips. It offers excerpts from all our guides as well as monthly features on new hotspots in the most popular destinations. In addition to our online bookstore, we have great deals on everything from airfares to cell phones. Our resources section is full of information you'll need before you hit the road, and our forums are buzzing with advice from other travelers. Check back often to see constant updates, exciting new tips, and prize giveaways. See you soon!

THE ART OF TRAVEL

Backpacker's Ultimate Guide: www.bugeurope.com. Tips on packing, transportation, and where to go. Also tons of country-specific travel information.

BootsnAll.com: www.bootsnall.com. Numerous resources for independent travelers, from planning your trip to reporting on it when you get back.

Expats in Italy: www.expatsinitaly.com. A recently born website, offering travelers advice from US citizens living in Italy.

How to See the World: www.artoftravel.com. A compendium of great travel tips, from cheap flights to self defense to interacting with local culture.

Slow Travel Italy: www.slowtrav.com/italy. Mission includes promoting longer stays at each destination, and provides comprehensive instructions on navigating Italian roads, railways, and customs. Includes numerous links to helpful websites. Also posts personal blogs and travel stories.

Travel Intelligence: www.travelintelligence.net. A large collection of travel writing by distinguished travel writers.

Travel Library: www.travel-library.com. A fantastic set of links for general information and personal travelogues.

INFORMATION ON ITALY

Atevo Travel: www.atevo.com/guides/destinations. Detailed introductions, travel tips, and suggested itineraries.

CIA World Factbook: www.odci.gov/cia/publications/factbook/index.html. Tons of vital statistics on Italy's geography, government, economy, and people.

Comuni Italiani: http://en.comuni-italiani.it. Information and population statistics on all Italin regions, provinces, and towns.

Geographia: www.geographia.com. Highlights, culture, and people of Italy.

TravelPage: www.travelpage.com. Links to official tourist office sites in Italy.

PlanetRider: www.planetrider.com. A subjective list of links to the "best" websites covering the culture and tourist attractions of Italy.

World Travel Guide: www.travel-guides.com. Helpful practical info.

LIFE AND TIMES

From Da Vinci to Gucci, Italy has consistently set the world standard for innovation and elegance. Defined by the legacy of the Roman Empire and the prominence of the Catholic Church, its artistic, intellectual, and cultural developments have survived the centuries and today form the foundation of modern civilization. Nonetheless, Italy's history has been turbulent, leaving as much unresolved conflict as accomplishment in its wake. Shadowed by centuries of foreign rule, fragmented governments, and isolated regions, Italy's allegiances are often divided between the past and the present. In the last century alone, Mussolini's dreams of Fascist conquest, the delay of complete women's suffrage until 1945, and the country's strict adherence to Catholic customs in the face of changing collective world values all highlight community principles that rest firmly upon past traditions. Though both the Romans and the Risorgimento came close to uniting the country's varied regions, desires for increased autonomy are evident in continuing tensions between north and south. Italy's present is a constant negotiation between tradition and progress, unity and independence, as it endeavors to transform its past triumphs into an equally glorious future.

HISTORY AND POLITICS

ITALY BEFORE ROME

PREHISTORY. Archaeological excavations date Italy's earliest inhabitants to the Paleolithic Era (100,000-70,000 BC). Ötzi, a frozen prehistoric hunter discovered in the Dolomites (p. 349), evokes indigenous Bronze Age settlements which were replaced by Indo-European invaders in the 2nd millennium.

EARLY MEDITERRANEAN POWERS. In the 7th century BC, the **Etruscans** controlled Italian and western Mediterranean trade from their Tuscan stronghold. Around the same time, the **Greek** colonization of Southern Italy, later known to the Romans as **Magna Graecia,** began to challenge the Etruscans. The **Phoenicians** from the North African city of Carthage in turn conquered Sardinia and Western Sicily. But all three soon faced the threat of another force from the central mainland: the Romans.

3000 BC
Ötzi, the prehistoric hunter, goes on his last hunt.

ANCIENT ROME (753 BC-AD 476)

THE MONARCHY (753-509 BC)

THE BEGINNING. Popular legend attributes the founding of Rome to **Romulus** and **Remus,** the last descendants of the Trojan hero Aeneas, whose story is immortalized in Virgil's *Aeneid.* A Vestal Virgin (one of the seven priestesses of the Eternal Flame) gave birth to the twins after losing her virginity to Mars, the god of war. In a fury over the shame his niece brought to the family name, her uncle, the king of Alba Longa,

753 BC
Romulus and Remus found Rome, but brotherly love soon deteriorates to fratricide.

cast the infants into the Tiber River. A she-wolf found and nursed the children, an event which has inspired numerous representations of the trio in Italian artwork (most famously in a sculpture dating to 500 BC, in the Musei Capitolini; p. 135). In 753 BC, the brothers founded Rome together on Palatine Hill, although the city notably derives its name from Romulus alone. Angered at an insult from Remus, Romulus killed his brother to become the first king of Rome.

616 BC
The Etruscan kings come to power in Rome and become known for tyranny.

THE END. Romulus held sway over a highly patriarchal society (women were executed for drinking wine) for 37 years until he mysteriously disappeared from the throne. By 616 BC, the Etruscan kings of the **Tarquin dynasty** had nudged their way to the throne and simultaneously became infamous for their tyranny. After Prince Sextus Tarquinius raped **Lucretia** in 509 BC, her husband Lucius Brutus expelled the Tarquins and established the **Roman Republic.**

509 BC
The Roman Republic is established.

THE REPUBLIC (509-27 BC)

450 BC
Roman Law is codified in the Twelve Tables.

SOCIAL STRUCTURE. The Republic faced social struggles between the upper-class **patricians,** who enjoyed full participation in the Senate, and the middle- and lower-class **plebeians,** who were denied political involvement. In 450 BC, the **Laws of the Twelve Tables,** Rome's first codified laws, helped contain the struggle by guaranteeing the plebeians a voice in public affairs.

390 BC
The Gauls sack Rome.

EXPANSION. Rome's first subjugation of its Italian neighbors culminated in the defeat of the Etruscans at Veii in 474 BC. Although a Gallic invasion destroyed much of Rome six years later, the Republic rebounded, setting its sights on nothing less than control of the Mediterranean. Rome fought its most important battles, the three **Punic Wars** (264-146 BC), against the North African city of Carthage in modern Tunisia. After the successful Punic campaign came victories over the Greek successors of Alexander the Great, with Greece, Asia Minor, and Egypt becoming new additions to the Republic.

264-146 BC
The Romans fight Carthage in the three Punic Wars.

91 BC
Riots against the Patrician class lead to the Social War.

VENI, VIDI, VICI. The spoils of war that enriched Rome actually undermined its stability by creating further class inequality. Consequently, demands for land redistribution led to the **Social War** in 91 BC. The patrician general **Sulla** defeated his rivals in Rome in 82 BC, and reorganized the Roman constitution during his rule. In 73 BC, **Spartacus,** an escaped gladiatorial slave, led an army of 70,000 slaves and impoverished farmers on a two-year rampage down the Italian peninsula. Sulla's close associates **Marcus Crassus** and **Pompey the Great** quelled the uprising and took control of Rome. They joined forces with **Julius Caesar,** the conqueror of Gaul, but this association rapidly fell apart. By 45 BC, Caesar had defeated his "allies" and emerged as the leader of the Republic, naming himself Dictator for Life. A small faction of disgruntled back-stabbers assassinated the reform-oriented leader on the Ides (15th) of March, 44 BC. The coup rid Rome of a tyrant, but created a power vacuum as would-

73 BC
Spartacus leads a revolt of 70,000 slaves.

45 BC
Julius Caesar names himself Dictator for Life.

be successors struggled for the helm. In 31 BC, Octavian, Caesar's clever adopted heir, emerged victorious, and was deified with the title of **Augustus** in 27 BC.

THE EMPIRE (27 BC-AD 476)

THE GOLDEN AGE. Augustus was the first of the empire's **Julio-Claudian** rulers (27 BC-AD 68). Using Republican traditions as a facade, he governed not as king, but as *princeps* (first citizen). His principate (27 BC-AD 14) is considered the golden age of Rome, and this period of stability and prosperity, termed *Pax Romana* (Roman Peace), continued until AD 180. During this time, Augustus extended Roman law and civic culture, beautifed the city, and reorganized its administration. Meanwhile, poets and authors reinvigorated Latin literature, creating works that rivaled even the greatest Greek epics. Ultimately, however, in a period of rampant corruption, scandal, and decadence, too much merrymaking led Augustus to exile his own promiscuous daughter, **Julia** (38 BC-AD 14), as well as **Ovid** (43 BC-AD 17), the poet who sang of love, not war.

DECLINE. During the infamous reigns of **Caligula** (AD 37-41) and **Nero** (AD 54-68), the empire continued to expand, despite a series of civil wars following Nero's death in AD 68. The **Flavian** dynasty (AD 69-96) ushered in a period of prosperity, extended to new heights by **Trajan** (AD 98-117), who invaded the borders of the Black Sea. The empire reached astounding geographical limits, encompassing Western Europe, the Mediterranean islands, England, North Africa, and part of Asia. Following Trajan, **Hadrian** established the **Antonine** dynasty (AD 117-193). The Antonines, especially philosopher-emperor **Marcus Aurelius** (AD 161-180), were known for their enlightened leadership. **Septimius Severus** won the principate after yet another civil war, founding the **Severan** dynasty (AD 193-235).

AND FALL. Weak leadership and Germanic invasions led to near anarchy in the third century. **Diocletian** (AD 284-305) divided the empire into eastern and western sections, each with its own administration. Because he persecuted Christians, his reign was called the "Age of Martyrs." However, Christian fortune took a turn for the better with Diocletian's successor, **Constantine.** Before the Battle of the Milvian Bridge in AD 312, he claimed he saw a cross of light in the sky, emblazoned with *"in hoc signo vinces"* ("by this sign you shall conquer"). When victory followed, he proclaimed the **Edict of Milan** in AD 313, which abolished religious discrimination and declared Christianity the state religion. Eventually converting to Christianity himself, Constantine moved the capital to **Constantinople** in AD 330. The empire split permanently, and barbarian tribes repeatedly invaded the west. The final blow came in AD 476, when the German chief **Odoacer** put the last western emperor, Romulus Augustulus, under house arrest and crowned himself king.

44 BC
Caesar is assassinated on the Ides of March.

27 BC
Augustus becomes the first Roman emperor.

2 BC
Augustus exiles his own daughter for adultery.

AD 37-41
Emperor Caligula makes his horse a senator.

AD 64
Nero plays his fiddle while Rome burns.

AD 79
Mount Vesuvius erupts and destroys Pompeii and Herculaneum.

AD 80
The Colosseum hosts its inaugural games.

AD 212
Roman citizenship expands to include all inhabitants of Europe.

LIFE AND TIMES

MIDDLE AGES (476-1375)

AD 313
The Edict of Milan grants Christians the freedom to worship.

AD 330
Constantine transfers the capital to Constantinople.

AD 476
The Roman Empire falls.

AD 800
Italy becomes part of the Holy Roman Empire.

1095
Pope Urban II launches the First Crusade.

11th Century
The Bologna School of Law becomes Europe's first university.

1266-1273
Thomas Aquinas writes the *Summa Theologica*.

1285
Pope Martin IV, immortalized as a glutton in Dante's *Inferno*, dies of indigestion.

13th Century
Eyeglasses are invented.

1314
Dante's *Inferno* is published.

LIFE AND TIMES

HOLY ROMAN EMPIRE. While the East continued to thrive as the **Byzantine Empire,** the West suffered from the fall of the Roman Empire. With Arabs and Byzantines advancing on Italian territory, the Pope called upon the barbarian chieftain **Charlemagne** to secure the hold of **Roman Catholicism.** Adding Italy to the Carolingian domain, Charlemagne became Emperor of the Holy Roman Empire (not to be confused with the Roman Empire) on Christmas Day, AD 800. Pope Urban II further increased the popularity of the Church by launching the First Crusade to liberate the Holy Land in 1095.

INTELLECTUAL ADVANCES. In this tumultuous time only monasteries, self-contained and self-sufficient communities fortified by thick outer walls, could foster scholarship, producing both illuminated manuscripts and chanted music. With the peak of scholasticism in the 13th century, intellectual pursuits found their niche in a logical and systematic approach typified by the studies of **Thomas Aquinas.**

CHURCH VERSUS STATE. Charlemagne's successors were unable to maintain the new empire, and in the following centuries, Italy became a playing field for petty wars. The instability of the 12th, 13th, and 14th centuries resulted in self-governing city-states. Rival families began to emerge in the north. European ruling houses and the Vatican vied for the support of the Italian aristocracy, most notably the **Guelphs** and **Ghibellines** in the 12th and 13th centuries. The pro-papal party, the Guelphs, managed to expel the imperial-minded Ghibellines from major northern cities by the mid-13th century, but then split into two factions, the **Blacks** and the **Whites. Dante Alighieri,** a prominent Florentine White, was permanently exiled to Ravenna in 1302.

The unpopularity of the Church reached its pinnacle during the **Babylonian Captivity** (1309-1377), when several popes were "persuaded" by French king **Philip IV** to move the papacy from Rome to Avignon. The **Great Schism** (1378-1417) subsequently occurred when three popes simultaneously claimed hegemony.

DISEASE AND DEATH. This period of disorder culminated in 1347 with an outbreak of the **Black Death,** or the Bubonic Plague, which killed one-third of Europe's population, recurring in Italy every July over the next two centuries. In addition, syphilis spread wildly through Rome, infecting 17 members of the pope's family and court.

THE RENAISSANCE (1375-1540)

The **Rinascimento** (Renaissance) grew out of a proliferation of artistic achievement and cultural values. A philosophy of **civic humanism** stressed the ideal of active participation in the community, and city officials bid for the best minds of the era.

THE FAMILY. Due to a labor shortage, a new wealthy merchant class emerged from the survivors of the Black Death. Rising out of obscurity were the exalted **Medici** clan in Florence, the **Visconti** in Milan, and the **d'Este** family in Ferrara. In addition to instituting a series of humanist-minded economic and social reforms, these families often stabbed each other in cathedrals (**Francesco Pazzi** was so enthusiastic about this that he managed to wound himself with his own knife in the process of impaling **Guiliano de'Medici** in 1478). **Cosimo** and **Lorenzo (il Magnifico) de'Medici** consolidated power and broadened the scope of their family's activities from banking and warring to patronizing the arts. The Church eventually lost its monopoly on art patronage and, as a result, **Pope Julius II** was forced to engage in a high stakes battle in order to bring Michelangelo to Florence.

MISFORTUNE. In the power vacuum that emerged after Lorenzo's son Piero, "the Unfortunate," made several political blunders and was forced into exile, Florentines found appeal in **Girolamo Savonarola's** sermons denouncing the hedonistic lifestyle produced by humanist thinking. However, the Dominican friar's radical views on morals and foreign policy earned him many enemies among those in charge, and the latter did not stop until his corpse was burned at the stake. These internal conflicts weakened Italian cities, and made them susceptible to foreign invasion, as French, Spanish, and Ottoman troops fought for sovereignty over the peninsula. The fighting continued until 1559 when Spain finally gained control over all Italian cities except Venice.

EXPLORATION AND DISCOVERY. Despite the political unrest plaguing Italy at the time, several prominent Italians embarked to make a splash on the world scene. **Christopher Columbus,** a native of Genoa funded by Queen Isabella of Spain, set sail to discover a faster route to Asia and opened the door to a whole New World of exploration. The Florentine **Amerigo Vespucci** made his own expeditions across the Atlantic, leaving his name on two continents, and **Galileo Galilei,** despite the fervent wrath of the church, dared to suggest that the Earth spins around the sun. Given the opportunity, he recanted, but mumbled *"eppur si muove"* ("but it does move") after the Inquisition ruled him guilty of heresy. He died under house arrest in 1642.

FOREIGN RULE (1540-1815)

THE SPANISH. A seventeenth-century economic crisis in Italy was intensified by the Spanish monarchy's demand for funds to finance its wars. **Charles II,** the last Spanish Hapsburg ruler, died in 1700. His death sparked the War of Spanish Succession. Subsequently, Italy, weak and decentralized, became the booty in battles between the Austrian Hapsburgs and the French and Spanish Bourbons.

NAPOLEON. In the course of **Napoleon's** 19th-century march through Europe, the diminutive emperor united much of northern Italy into the Italian Republic, conquered Naples, and fos-

1347-1349
Black Death sweeps through Europe.

1420
Brunelleschi begins a lifetime of work on his dome.

1492
In fourteen-hundred-and-ninety-two Columbus sailed the ocean blue.

1504
Michelangelo sculpts *David*.

1505
Machiavelli writes *The Prince*.

1506
Mona Lisa Gherardini sits for Leonardo Da Vinci's *Mona Lisa*.

1564
Gabriele Fallopio invents the condom.

1633
Galileo is condemned for heresy by Papal authorities.

1662
The Church of Rome declares that chocolate should not be considered food and can therefore by consumed in liquid form during fasting.

LIFE AND TIMES

tered national sovereignty. In 1804 Napoleon declared himself the monarch of the newly united **Kingdom of Italy.** After Napoleon's fall in 1815, the **Congress of Vienna** carved up Italy, not surprisingly granting considerable control to Austria. Exiled, Napoleon spent his last days swayed by the charms of tiny Elba, an island off the Tuscan coast.

1725
Vivaldi writes *The Four Seasons.*

1748
The first excavations begin at Pompeii.

1804
Napoleon declares himself the monarch of the Kingdom of Italy.

1815
Congress of Vienna breaks up the Kingdom of Italy.

1848-1860
Camillo Cavour struggles to unify the peninsula.

1861
Italy's first parliament meets in Turin.

1883
Carlo Collodi writes *Pinocchio.*

1915
Italy enters WWI.

1924
Benito Mussolini establishes the world's first Fascist regime.

1936
Fiat produces the first "Topolino" car.

THE ITALIAN NATION (1815-PRESENT)

UNIFICATION AND WARS

RISORGIMENTO. Following the Congress of Vienna, a long-standing grudge against foreign rule sparked the **Risorgimento,** a nationalist movement that culminated in political unification in 1860 (with Rome and the Veneto joining in 1870). **Giuseppe Mazzini, Giuseppe Garibaldi,** and **Camillo Cavour,** the movement's leaders, are today paid homage with omnipresent namesake streets. **Vittorio Emanuele II,** another popular source for street names, was crowned as the first ruler of the kingdom of Italy in 1860. He expanded the nation by annexing the north and central regions. France relinquished Rome on September 20, 1870, a pivotal date in modern Italian history, while a defiant **Pope Pius IX** refused to acknowledge Italian acquisition of the city, preferring instead to hold the title of prisoner in the Vatican.

PROBLEMS OF NATIONALISM. Though Italy was unified in name, tensions arose between the different regions. The north wanted to protect its money from the needs of the agrarian south, and cities were wary of surrendering power to a central administration. The Pope, who had lost power to the kingdom, threatened politically active Italian Catholics with excommunication. Nationalism increased during World War I as Italy fought against Austria, having been promised territory for its alliance with Russia, Britain, and France.

FASCIST REGIME. The chaotic aftermath of WWI paved the way for Fascism under the control of **Benito Mussolini,** "Il Duce," who promised strict order and stability for the young nation. He established the world's first Fascist regime in 1924 and expelled all opposition parties. As Mussolini initiated domestic development programs and aggressive foreign policies, sentiments toward the Fascist leader ran from intense loyalty to belligerent discontent. In 1940, Italy entered **World War II** on the side of its **Axis** ally, Germany. Success for the Axis powers came quickly but was short-lived: the Allies landed in Sicily in 1943, pushing Mussolini from power. As a final indignity, he and his mistress, **Claretta Petacci,** were captured in Milan and executed by infuriated citizens, their naked bodies hung upside-down in public. In 1945, after nearly three years of occupation, Italy was freed from Nazi control, but tension persisted between those supporting the monarchy and those favoring a return to Fascism.

POST-WAR POLITICS

POLITICAL ORGANIZATION. The end of WWII did little but highlight the intense factionalism of the Italian peninsula. In the 60 years since the end of the war, Italy has changed governments 59 times. None of these governments has lasted longer than four years, reflecting the country's struggle for stability. The **Constitution,** adopted in 1948, established a democratic **Republic,** with a president, a prime minister, a bicameral parliament, and an independent judiciary. The **Christian Democratic Party (DC)** soon surfaced over the **Socialists (PSI)** as the primary player in the government of the Republic. Over 300 parties fought for supremacy in parliament; none could claim a majority. Ultimately, tenuous party coalitions formed instead.

ECONOMIC SUCCESS. As Lamborghini billboards and factory smokestacks quickly appeared alongside old cathedral spires, the Italian economic recovery began with industrialization in the 1950s. Despite the **Southern Development Fund,** which was established to build roads, construct schools, and finance industries, the traditionally agrarian south lagged behind the more industrial north. Italy's economic inequality contributed to much of the regional strife that persists today.

VIOLENCE. Economic success gave way to violence in the late 1960s. The *autunno caldo* (hot autumn) of 1969, a season of strikes, demonstrations, and riots by university students and factory workers, foreshadowed greater violence in the 70s. During the period of *Strategia della Tensione* (Strategy of Tension) in the early 70s, right-wing terrorists detonated bombs as public manifestations of political discontent. The most shocking episode was the 1978 kidnapping and murder of ex-Prime Minister **Aldo Moro** by a group of left-wing terrorists, the *Brigade Rosse* (Red Brigades).

REFORM. Progressive social reforms in the 70s included the legalization of divorce and the expansion of women's rights. The demonstrations and violence of the 70s challenged the conservative Social Democrats. In 1983, **Bettino Craxi** became Italy's first Socialist prime minister.

RECENT DEVELOPMENTS

SCANDALS. Italians have always been enamored with powerful, charismatic leaders. Living up to expectations, Italian government officials have rarely shied away from questionable maneuvers intended to bring them more power. Recognizing corruption in his own government, **Luigi Scalfaro,** elected in 1992, launched the *Mani Pulite* (Clean Hand) campaign, in which Scalfaro and anti-corruption judge **Antonio di Pietro** uncovered the *Tangentopoli* (Bribesville) scandal. This unprecedented political crisis found over 1200 officials guilty of bribery. Fall-out from the investigation included the 1993 bombing of the Uffizi Galleries in Florence, the suicides of 10 indicted officials, and the murders of anti-Mafia investigators.

1938
Enrico Fermi wins the Nobel Prize for Physics for directing the first controlled nuclear chain reaction.

1940
Italy enters WWII.

1945
Italy is freed from Nazi occupation.

1946
The Vespa Scooter is invented by Corradino d'Ascanio.

1948
Italy adopts a constitution, establishing a democratic Republic.

1969
Riots shake Italian streets.

1972
Francis Ford Coppola directs *The Godfather.*

1975
The Giorgio Armani Company is founded.

1978
Aldo Moro is murdered.

LIFE AND TIMES

1982
Italian soccer team wins the World Cup in Spain.

1986
Carlo Petrini starts the Slow Food movement to fight fast food.

1994
Berlusconi becomes prime minister, but is forced to resign eight months later.

1996-1998
Romano Prodi attempts in vain to steer Italy toward stability.

1999
Roberto Benigni wins 3 Oscars for *La Vita è Bella*.

1999
Italy enters the European Monetary Union and adopts the euro.

2001
Berlusconi becomes prime minister (again).

ENTER BERLUSCONI. The election of media tycoon **Silvio Berlusconi** as prime minister in 1994 raised eyebrows. The empire of the self-made billionaire included three private TV channels, political influence over three state-run channels, a major newspaper, and the AC Milan soccer team. His election involved formalizing the governing center-right Freedom Alliance coalition of three parties: his **Forza Italia** (Go Italy), the increasingly reactionary **Lega Nord** (Northern League), and the **Alleanza Nazionale** (National Alliance), which has been called "neo-Fascist" by some critics. Berlusconi's coalition collapsed and he was forced to resign in just eight months.

SEPARATISM. Shortly after the collapse of Berlusconi's government, the platform of the reactionary Northern League became separatist under the extremist (some say racist) **Umberto Bossi.** Aiming to push the economy to meet the European Union's economic standards, the Northern League called for a split from the south in order to create the Republic of Padania, a nation for northerners only.

SHORTLIVED STABILITY. The elections of 1996 brought the center-left coalition, the **l'Ulivo** (Olive Tree), to power, with **Romano Prodi**, a Bolognese professor, economist, and non-politician, as prime minister. Ultimately, Prodi helped stabilize Italian politics. For the first time in modern history, Italy was run by two equal coalitions: the center-left l'Ulivo and the center-right **Il Polo** (Berlusconi's Freedom Alliance without the Northern League). Despite hope for Prodi's government, his coalition lost a vote of confidence in October 1998.

BUDGET REFORM. Prodi was succeeded by former Communist **Massimo D'Alema.** D'Alema and **Carlo Ciampi** created fiscal reforms and pushed a "blood and tears" budget that qualified Italy for entrance into the European Monetary Union in January 1999. Despite D'Alema's successes, he stepped down in May 2000 and was replaced by former Treasury Minister **Giuliano Amato.** Nicknamed "Dr. Subtle," Amato is one of the people credited with the institution of 1999 budget reforms. Perhaps the nickname also derives from Amato's ability to avoid scandal; he was one of few to emerge unscathed from corruption crack-downs in the early 90s, one of which led to late Socialist Party leader Bettino Craxi's exile to Tunisia.

BERLUSCONI: TAKE TWO. The allure and nonstop drive of Italy's richest man secured Berlusconi's re-election as prime minister in May 2001. Down playing corruption charges, he won 30% of the popular vote to head Italy's 59th government since WWII with his Forza Italia party. Berlusconi reaffirmed his commitment to the US, courting President George W. Bush in several meetings and sending 2700 troops to Iraq; left-wing opposition has consistently urged withdrawal of these troops. In European foreign policy, the Prime Minister has focused more on domestic than on international issues, creating some tension between Italy and its neighbors. Most notable is his 2004 comparison of one German European Parliament member to a guard in a Nazi concentration camp, a comment which caused considerable discord between the two governments—so much so that a miffed Chancellor Gerhard Schroeder cancelled his summer holiday in Italy. Other scandals also marred Berlusconi's tenure, including proposed bills in favor of laxer corruption laws. In fact, Berlusconi himself came under investigation with respect to corruption in the 1980s, but courts cleared him of all charges in December 2004.

BERLUSCONI: TAKE THREE. Berlusconi's unpopularity mounted as a result of troop deployment in Iraq and an economic recession caused some to call for the reinstitution of *lire*. Berlusconi resigned again as Prime Minister in April 2005, only to form a new coalition several days later. By securing the approval of both chambers of Parliament and the President, Berlusconi has managed to remain in power for the moment.

CHURCH MATTERS. The death of Pope John Paul II in April 2005 stirred Catholics world-wide. Tens of thousands flooded the square in front of St. Peter's Basilica as the College of Cardinals gathered in the Sistine Chapel to elect a new Pope. Sworn to secrecy (a full transcript of the voting will not be made public for 100 years), the Cardinals locked inside the chapel cast four votes per day until a two-thirds majority was reached.

After each round of voting, smoke from the chimneys of the Sistine Chapel signaled the results—gray smoke for failure to reach a consensus, and white smoke for a successful election. The process could have taken up to three and a half months (it did in AD 180), but Cardinal Ratzinger of Munich (now Pope Benedict XVI) was elected on only the second day of voting.

The election of Cardinal Ratzinger has received a mixed reaction from Catholics worldwide, disappointing many who hope for a more liberal Church. As a close personal friend of John Paul II, who also shares his views on the role of the Catholic Church in modern society, the 76-year-old Pope is likely to continue the conservative policy of his predecessor.

2005
Berlusconi resigns as prime minister, and becomes prime minister for a 3rd time after several days.

2005
Pope John Paul II dies after a 26-year reign.

2005
Pope Benedict XVI is elected. He likes cats.

2006
Turin hosts Winter Olympics.

LIFE AND TIMES

PEOPLE

DEMOGRAPHICS

THE FEW. With a current birth rate of nine births per 1000 people and a death rate of ten deaths per 1000 people, Italy's population of roughly 58 million is on the decline. Due to a recent tendency among Italian families to welcome only one child, women have an average of 1.3 babies over their lifetime, a rate that sits well below the population increase of other nations.

AND THE MANY. However, at the current rate of two migrants per 1000 people, immigration from China, Africa, Eastern Europe, and Middle Eastern countries is on the rise. Though Italy's rapidly shrinking workforce is replenished by immigration, the subject nevertheless remains controversial. Although Italian public opinion often stigmatizes undocumented labor as crime, sex work, or drug trafficking, new laws allow employers to hire undocumented workers and regularize their status by petitioning the government.

LANGUAGE

The spoken descendant of Latin, Italian is part of the family of Romance languages, related to French, Spanish, Portuguese, and Romanian. Since its inception, this Indo-European language has fragmented into a variety of dialects. For example, in the south, the throaty **Neapolitan** of southern Italy can be difficult for a northerner to understand; Ligurians use a mix of **Italian, Catalan,** and **French; Sardo,** spoken in Sardinia, bears little resemblance to standard Italian; and many Tuscan dialects differ from Italian in pronunciation. In Friuli-Venezia Giulia, there are as many as four languages in one place—in Canale **Slovene,** Italian, **German,** and **Friulian** coexist. Conversely, inhabitants of other regions do not speak any Italian at all: while the population of Valle d'Aosta speaks mainly French, Trentino Alto-Adige harbors a German-speaking minority. In the Southern regions of Puglia, Calabria, and Sicily, entire villages speak a form of Albanian called **Arbresh.** Though dialects are prevalent throughout the country, standard Italian is the national language of schools, media, and literature.

RELIGION

As one of the world's most religiously homogenous nations, Italy is 98% **Roman Catholic.** However, there are also isolated **Protestant** and **Jewish** communities, and a growing **Muslim** immigrant population. Roman Catholicism became Italy's official state religion when Benito Mussolini and Pope Pius XI signed the Lateran Treaty in 1929, but its tenure as the formal state religion ended in 1984. The seat of the Roman Catholic Church is Vatican City, which is a non-hereditary elective monarchy ruled by the recently elected Pope Benedict XVI. Though recognized by Italy as a sovereign government, it continues to play a strong role in the lives of ordinary Italians. The oldest elected pope since Clement XII in 1730, Benedict maintains traditional Catholic views on birth control, abortion, and homosexuality.

Most Italians continue to celebrate the feast day of their town's patron saint in yearly celebrations, but church attendance is declining. Despite this fact, Italians are very conscientious about respecting churches, cathedrals, and other religious domains. Tourists will generally not be allowed in religious spaces without modest attire, including covered shoulders for women and long pants for men. In addition, some churches do not allow visitors to take photographs because flashes can easily damage fragile paintings and mosaics.

FINE ARTS

ART AND ARCHITECTURE

In Italy, great works of art and architecture seem to spring from every street corner. Rome's Colosseum (p. 118) hovers above a city bus stop; in Florence, couples flirt in front of the *duomo* (p. 433); in Sicily, diners sit beneath truncated Greek columns. Modern Italians may seem immune to this stunning visual history, but to anyone who hasn't grown up amid ancient columns and medieval fortresses, it's a feast for the senses.

ANCIENT ITALIAN ART

GREEKS. In the 8th century BC, the Greeks established colonies in southern Italy, peppering the region with magnificent **temples** and **theaters.** The best-preserved examples of such Greek ruins are in Sicily—surprisingly not in Greece—in the Valle dei Templi at Agrigento (p. 705) and Taormina (p. 680). Italy is also home to Roman copies of Greek **statues** and original Greek **bronzes;** the prized *Bronzi di Riace*, recovered from the Ionian Sea in 1972, are now in Reggio di Calabria's Museo Nazionale (p. 637).

ETRUSCANS. Native Italian art history begins with the Etruscans, a people who lived on the Italian peninsula before the Romans. Loosely influenced by Greek art and inspired by the afterlife and augury, Etruscan artwork is best known for its narrative quality. Decorating funeral scenes, tomb paintings, and ceramic ash burial urns, the artwork depicts Etruscan scenes and legends. It is characterized by enigmatic smiles, minimal detail, and fluid lines. Though this flourishing of art was curtailed when the Etruscans mysteriously disappeared in the 3rd century BC, the Museum at the Villa Giulia in Rome (p. 136) houses many remaining treasures.

AND ROMANS. OH MY! Roman art (200 BC-AD 500) is known for its vivid portrayal of the political aims and cultural values of Imperial Rome. **Sculptures, architecture,** and other masterpieces fall mainly into two categories: art in service of the state and private household art. Copies of Greek bronzes often served as models for both private and public Roman sculptures, as the Italian *cognoscenti* idolized classical Greece. However, sculpted portraiture is a distinctly Roman style. Portraits of the Republican period (510-27 BC) were brutally honest, immortalizing wrinkles, scars, and even warts. The later imperial sculpture (27 BC-AD 476) tended to blur the distinction between mortal and god in powerful, idealized images like *Augustus of Prima Porta*. Later in the period, Roman art developed a flattened style of **portraiture,** with huge eyes looking out in an "eternal stare." The government sponsored statues, **monuments,** and **literary narratives** to commemorate and glorify leaders, heroes, and victories. Augustus was perhaps the best master of this form of self-promotion, as evidenced by his impressive **mausoleum** and *Ara Pacis* (Altar of Peace), both of which grace the Piazza Augusto Imperatore in Rome. Other architectural achievements include Roman monuments that evolved into decorated concrete forms with numerous arches and columns, like the Colosseum and Pantheon.

Upper-class Romans had an appetite for sumptuous interior decoration. Scenes depicting gods and goddesses, exotic beasts, and street entertainers decorated sprawling villas, courtyards, and fancy shops. *Trompe l'oeil* doors, columns, and still-lifes could also be found embellishing structures designed to create the illusion of increased space. While some affluent patrons often commissioned **frescoes** for their walls, it was also popular to hire craftsmen to fashion wall and floor **mosaics.** A favorite mosaic subject was the watchdog, often executed on the vestibule floor with the inscription *"cave canem"* (beware of dog).

EARLY CHRISTIAN AND BYZANTINE ART

CONSTANTINE'S CREATIONS. Fearing persecution, early Christians in Rome, Naples, and Syracuse descended to their haunting **catacombs** to worship. But with Constantine's adoption of Christianity and the decline of the Roman Empire, even the Roman magistrate's basilica was adapted to accommodate Christian services. **Transepts** were added to many Roman churches, creating a structure shaped like the crucifix. Later in the period, except for a few **sarcophagi** and **ivory reliefs,** Christian art moved from sculpture toward pictorial art in order to depict religious narratives for the illiterate. Ravenna (p. 402) is a veritable treasure trove of the first Byzantine Golden Age, which ran from AD 526 to 726. Examples of these "instructional" mosaics can be seen in Ravenna's octagonal Basilica of San Vitale, constructed between 526 and 547, which is also one of the first churches to boast a free-standing *campanile* (bell tower).

THE MIDDLE AGES

ROMANESQUE. Although true classical Roman style would not be revived until the Renaissance, Roman rounded arches, heavy columns, and windowless churches came back into style in the period between AD 800 and 1200. The earliest example of Romanesque architecture is **Basilica di Sant'Ambrogio** in Milan (p. 251), notable for its squat nave and groin vaults. In other parts of the country, competition among Italian cities (particularly Florence and Siena) to outdo their neighbors resulted in great architectural feats, most notably **San Miniato al Monte** (p. 444) and the **Baptistry of the Duomo** in Florence (p. 434).

GOTHIC. The Gothic movement filtered into Italy from France beginning in the late 13th century. Artists and architects rejoiced at the fantastic spaces and light created by the new vaulted technology and giant, multi-colored rose windows. The most impressive Gothic cathedrals include the **Basilica of San Francesco** in Assisi (p. 510), the **Frari** in Venice (p. 320), and the **Santa Maria Novella** in Florence (p. 439). Secular structures like the **Ponte Vecchio** in Florence (p. 438) caught on to the same trend. The **Palazzo Ducale** in Venice (p. 316), spanning several canals with ornate bridges, represents the brilliant marriage of airy, lace-like Islamic stonework and Gothic style.

THE RENAISSANCE

EARLY RENAISSANCE. Donatello's (1386-1466) *David* (c. 1430) marked the beginning of a new era when it hit the artistic scene as the first free-standing nude since antiquity. His wooden *Mary Magdalene* in Florence (p. 435) similarly represents a departure from earlier traditions by emphasizing the woman's fallen and repentant side with rags and the intensity of her facial expression. Unlike Donatello's expressive portraiture, **Brunelleschi's** (1377-1446) mathematical studies of ancient Roman architecture became the cornerstone of Renaissance building. His engineering talent allowed him to raise the dome over Santa Maria del Fiore (p. 433) and showcase his mastery of proportions in the Pazzi Chapel (p. 442). Ultimately, **Sandro Botticelli** (1444-1510) and his *Venus* (p. 435), floating on her tidal foam, epitomize the Italian Renaissance. An unlikely artist, **Fra Angelico** (c. 1400-1455) personified the tension between medieval and Renaissance Italy. Though a member of a militant branch of Dominican friars which opposed humanism on principle, Fra Angelico's works exhibit the techniques of space and perspective endorsed by humanistic artists. **Lorenzo Ghiberti** (c. 1381-1455) designed two sets of bronze doors for the baptistry in Florence, defeating Brunelleschi's in a contest. The two original entries now sit side by side in the Bargello of Florence (p. 438). Finally, **Leon Battista Alberti** (1404-1472), a champion of visual perspective, designed Florence's Santa Maria Novella (p. 439) and Rimini's Tempio Malatestiano (p. 406), prototypes for Renaissance palaces and churches.

HIGH RENAISSANCE. From 1450 to 1520, the torch of distinction passed between two of art's greatest figures: Da Vinci and Michelangelo. Branching out from the disciplines of sculpture and painting, **Leonardo Da Vinci** (1452-1519) brilliantly excelled at endeavors which encompassed geology, engineering, musical composition, human dissection, and armaments design. The *Last Supper*, or *Cenacolo* (p. 250), preserves the individuality of its figures even in a religious context. His experimentations with *chiaroscuro*, contrasts between light and shadow that highlight contours, and *sfumato*, a smoky or hazy effect of brushwork, secured his place as the great innovator of the century.

Michelangelo Buonarroti (1475-1564) was a jack of all trades in the artistic world, despite what he told Julius II when asked to paint the Sistine Chapel ceiling: "I am not a painter!" Michelangelo painted like a sculptor, boldly emphasizing musculature and depth, and sculpted like a painter, with lean and smooth strokes. Julius was so fond of the ceiling (p. 134) that he commissioned *The Last Judgment* for the wall above the chapel's altar. A conflict arose when a papal councillor advised that Michelangelo's nudes be repainted with proper attire. The temperamental artist got the last word, painting the nosy councillor in hell. Michelangelo's architectural achievements also include his designs for the Laurentian Library in Florence (p. 441) and the dome on St. Peter's Basilica in Rome (p. 127). Classic examples of his sculpture are the *Pietà* in St. Peter's, and *David* and the unfinished *Slaves* in Florence's Accademia (p. 440).

Other prominent Renaissance artists include **Raffaello Sanzio** (1483-1520), a draftsman, who created technically perfect figures. His frescoes in the papal apartments of the Vatican, including the *School of Athens* (p. 134), show his debt to classical standards. In addition, the Venetian school produced **Giorgione** (1478-1510) and the prolific **Titian** (1488-1576). Titian's works, including *Venus of Urbino* (1538), are notable for their realistic facial expressions and rich colors. In the High Renaissance, the greatest architect after Michelangelo was **Donato Bramante** (1444-1514), famed for his work on the Tempietto and St. Peter's in Rome.

MANNERISM

A heightened sense of aestheticism led to Mannerism, the style that dominated the High Renaissance from the 1520s until the birth of the Baroque style around 1590. Starting in Rome and Florence, Mannerist artists experimented with juxtapositions of color and scale. For example, **Parmigianino** (1503-1540) and his *Madonna of the Long Neck* (p. 435) are emblematic of the movement's self-conscious distortions. Another painter, **Jacopo Tintoretto** (1518-1594), a Venetian Mannerist, was the first to paint multiple light sources within a single composition. The Mannerist period is also known for its architecture, designed by architects like **Giulio Romano** (c. 1499-1546), who rejected the Renaissance ideal of harmony. The villas and churches of architect **Andrea Palladio** (1508-1580) were also remarkably innovative, particularly the *Villa Rotonda* outside Vicenza (p. 335). His other lasting contribution, the *Four Books of Architecture*, influenced countless architects, especially those of the Baroque movement.

BAROQUE

Baroque art and architecture were intended to inspire faith in the Catholic Church and respect for earthly power. Painters of this era favored Naturalism, a commitment to portraying nature in the raw. Baroque paintings are thus often melodramatic and gruesome. **Caravaggio** (1573-1610) expanded the use of *chiaroscuro*, creating enigmatic works. **Gianlorenzo Bernini** (1598-1680), a prolific High Baroque sculptor and architect, designed the colonnade of St. Peter's Piazza and the *baldacchino* inside. Drawing inspiration from Hellenistic works like the *Laocoön*, Bernini's sculptures were orgies of movement. **Francesco Borromini** (1599-1667) was more adept than his rival at shaping the walls of his buildings into serpentine architectural masterpieces, as in Rome's **San Carlo alle Quattro Fontane** (p. 126).

ROCOCO

Characterized by delicacy and elaborate ornamentation, **Rococo,** a final development of Baroque style, originated in 18th-century France during the reign of Louis XV. Light and graceful, Rococo motifs include sea shells, clouds, flowers, and vines carved into woodwork and sculpted into stone edifices. **Giovanni Battista Tiepolo** (1696-1770) was a prolific Venetian painter of allegories and the premier exemplar of the Italian Rococo style.

NINETEENTH-CENTURY ART

With the decline of Rococo came French-influenced Neo-Classicism. Still professing to follow the rules of antiquity, the sculptor **Antonio Canova** (1757-1822) explored the formal Neo-Classical style in his giant statues and bas-reliefs. His most famous work is the statue of Pauline Borghese (p. 135), exhibiting Neo-Classical grace and purity of contour. Revolting against the strict Neo-Classical style, **Giovanni Fattori** (1825-1908) spearheaded the **Macchiaioli** group in Florence (c. 1855-65), restoring lively immediacy and freshness to art. These paintings are distinguished by a technique called "blotting," in which a dry paintbrush is used to pick up certain areas of pigment in landscapes, genre scenes, and portraits.

TWENTIETH-CENTURY ART

The Italian Futurist painters, sculptors, and architects of the early decades of the twentieth century brought Italy to the cutting edge of artistry. Inspired by **Filippo Tommaso Marinetti's** *Futurist Manifesto*, Futurist works glorified danger, war, and the 20th-century machine age. In the major Futurist exhibition in Paris in 1912, the painters **Giacomo Bala, Gino Severini,** and **Carlo Carra,** and sculptor **Umberto Boccioni** popularized the Cubist technique of simultaneously depicting several aspects of moving forms. The work of **Giorgio de Chirico** (1888-1978), on display at the Collezione Peggy Guggenheim in Venice (p. 318), depicts eerie scenes characterized by mannequin figures, empty space, and steep perspective. Although his mysterious and disturbing vision was never successfully imitated, it inspired early Surrealist painters. Among other 20th-century artists, **Amadeo Modigliani** (1884-1920), highly influenced by African art and Cubism, sculpted and later painted figures with long oval faces. In addition, **Marcello Piacentini** created Fascist architecture that imposed sterility upon classical motifs. In 1938 he designed the looming **EUR** in Rome (p. 133) as an impressive reminder of the link between Mussolinian Fascism and Roman Imperialism.

MUSIC

WORSHIP AND PRAISE

MEDIEVAL CHURCH MUSIC. The Biblical psalms of the Old Testament constitute some of the earliest known songs of both Italian and Western culture. Characterized by plainchant, a medieval chant synchronized with the church's liturgical calendar, medieval church music grew out of the Jewish liturgy. During performances, women usually sang. However, after AD 578, they were replaced by castrated men and soon-to-be-castrated boys. Female performances were limited to convent choirs, congregational singing, and private gatherings. It was not until the Reformation that social restraints on female performers were relaxed.

AND ITS COMPOSERS. Some of the earliest remaining written records of medieval music date from seventh- to ninth-century Rome in the form of chant manuscripts. Among these is the work of **Pope Gregory I,** the father of liturgical chant, who codified the music he had heard during his days in the monastery. Further advancements were made by Italian monk **Guido d'Arezzo** (AD 995-1050) who is regarded as the originator of musical notation. **Francesco Landini** (1325-97) and **Pietro Casella** (c. 1280) also arrived on the scene and started putting popular poems to music for multiple voices. Finally, **Giovanni Palestrina** (1525-94) attempted to purge the religious madrigal form of this frightening trend toward secularity while retaining the integrity of the music itself, and his work in polyphony is still widely performed in Italy and abroad.

AND THE FAT LADY SINGS

OPERA. Italy's most cherished musical art form was born in Florence, nurtured in Venice, and revered in Milan. Conceived by the **Camerata,** a circle of Florentine writers, noblemen, and musicians, *opera lirica* originated as an attempt to recreate the dramas of ancient Greece by setting lengthy poems to music. **Alessandro Scarlatti** (1660-1725), considered one of the developers of the aria, also founded Neapolitan opera, a three-act style, vaulting Naples to the forefront of Italian music. **Jacobo Peri** composed *Dafne*, the world's first complete opera, in 1597. The first successful opera composer, **Claudio Monteverdi** (1567-1643) drew freely from history, juxtaposing high drama, love scenes, and uncouth humor. His masterpieces, *L'Orfeo* (1607) and *L'Incoronazione di Poppea* (1642), were the first widespread successes of the genre.

AND ITS SINGERS. Schools were quickly set up in Naples under the supervision of famous composers in order to train the beautiful soprano voices of pre-pubescent boys. If the male students dared attempt puberty, their testicles were confiscated. These *castrati*, **Farinelli** being one noted example, became the most celebrated and envied group of singers in Italy and all over Europe.

OUT WITH THE OLD, IN WITH THE NEW

BAROQUE MUSIC. A break from the tradition *stile antico*—the polyphonic style of the 16th century—Baroque music, *stile moderno*, emphasizes a solo voice, expressive harmony, and the separation of the melody and bass lines. Unlike its sacred predecessor, it was developed for primarily secular usage. *Virtuoso* instrumental music became a legitimate genre in 17th-century Rome. **Antonio Vivaldi** (1675-1741), composer of over 400 concertos, conquered contemporary audiences with *The Four Seasons* and established the concerto's present form, in which a full orchestra accompanies a soloist in a three-movement piece.

AND ITS INSTRUMENTS. During this period, two instruments saw great popularity: the pianoforte, created around 1709 by the Florentine **Cristofori** family, and the violin, whose shape was perfected by **Cremonesi** families. Setting the standard for future creation, the Baroque Stradivarius violin (crafted by **Antonio Stradivari**) was thought to gain its acoustical perfection from its varnish. While this characteristic is heavily debated, most will agree that Stradivari's success came from his exceptional craftsmanship.

VIVA VERDI!

NINETEENTH-CENTURY OPERA. With convoluted plots and powerful, dramatic music, 19th-century Italian opera continues to dominate modern stages. Late in the 19th century, **Giacomo Puccini** (1858-1924) created *Madame Butterfly*, *La Bohème*, and *Tosca*, which feature vulnerable women who usually end up dying by the last act. Another famous composer, **Gioacchino Rossini** (1792-1868), master of the *bel canto* (beautiful song), once boasted that he could produce music faster than copyists could reproduce it. In fact, he was such a procrastinator that his agents locked him in a room until he completed his masterpieces.

AND, OF COURSE, VERDI. **Giuseppe Verdi** (1813-1901) remains the transcendent musical and operatic figure of 19th-century Italy. *Nabucco*, a pointed and powerful *bel canto* work, typifies Verdi's early works. The chorus *Va pensiero* from *Nabucco* would later become the hymn of Italian freedom and unity. Verdi also produced the touching, personal dramas and memorable melodies of *Rigoletto*, *La Traviata*, and *Il Trovatore* during his middle period. Later work brought the grand and heroic conflicts of *Aïda*, the dramatic thrust of *Otello*, and the mercurial comedy of *Falstaff*. Verdi's name served as a convenient acronym for "Vittorio Emanuele, Re d'Italia" (King of Italy), so *"Viva Verdi!"* became a popular battle cry of the Risorgimento. Ultimately, much of Verdi's work promoted Italian unity—his operas include political assassinations, exhortations against tyranny, and jibes at French and Austrian monarchs.

TWENTIETH-CENTURY OPERA. In the 20th century, **Ottorino Respighi** (1873-1936), composer of the popular *Pines of Rome* and *Fountains of Rome*, experimented with rapidly shifting orchestral textures. Another composer, **Giancarlo Menotti** (1911-) wrote the oft-performed *Amahl and the Night Visitors* and

Luciano Berio (1925-2003) defied traditional instrumentation with his *Sequence V* for solo trombone and mime. Finally, **Luigi Dallapiccola** (1904-1975) achieved success with choral works including *Songs of Prison* and *Songs of Liberation*, two pieces that protest Fascist rule in Italy.

ARRIVEDERCI, VERDI

MODERN POP STARS IN ITALY. Though modern Italian pop stars have been crooning away for decades, their fame has traditionally been limited to the shores of the Mediterranean. **Lucio Dalla, Francesco de Gregori,** the Sardinian **Fabrizio D'Andrea,** and the adamantly Neapolitan **Pino Daniele,** all use pop to protest social conditions, such as the stigma of being from the south.

AND BEYOND. Recently, Italian musicians have taken to recording with international superstars, increasing their exposure on the world stage. For example, **Eros Ramazzotti** teamed up with Tina Turner on *Cose della Vita,* while **Andrea Bocelli** joined Celine Dion in *The Prayer.* **Laura Pausini,** who records in both Italian and Spanish, has established a following in Latin America, Spain, and Miami. Meanwhile, the technotronic Italian hip-hop scene mixes traditional folk tunes with the latest international groove; rap has emerged with wide-smiling, curly-haired **Jovanotti,** socially conscious **Frankie-Hi-NRG,** subconscious **99 Posse,** and unconscious **Articolo 31** (whose name derives from the Italian law forbidding marijuana).

LITERATURE

SEX, DRUGS, AND ROMAN MYTHOLOGY

IN MEDIA RES. Immortalized by Ovid's *Metamorphoses,* Roman mythology built upon the traditional tales and heroic legends of the conquered Greek Empire, which included parts of Sicily, Calabria, Campania, and Puglia. The Roman version of Greek mythology dominated the Western World until the ascendancy of Christianity in the 4th century AD.

THE GODS ON HIGH. Usually disguised as animals or mortals, gods and goddesses periodically descended to Earth to meddle with humanity. **Jupiter** (known in Greek mythology as Zeus) spent most of his time visiting mortal women in forms that included peacocks and flaming-red bulls. Somewhere between love affairs, he established the hierarchy of the gods on the heights of Mt. Olympus. The 13 other major Olympian players are Jupiter's wife **Juno** (Hera), goddess of childbearing and marriage; **Neptune** (Poseidon), god of the sea; **Vulcan** (Hephaistos), god of smiths; **Venus** (Aphrodite), goddess of love and beauty; **Mars** (Ares), god of war; **Minerva** (Athena), goddess of wisdom; **Apollo** (Apollo), god of light and arts; **Diana** (Artemis), goddess of the hunt; **Mercury** (Hermes), the messenger god; **Pluto** (Hades), god of the underworld; **Ceres** (Demeter), goddess of the harvest; **Bacchus** (Dionysus), god of wine; and **Vesta** (Hestia), goddess of the hearth.

LATIN LOVERS

ET IN ARCADIA EGO. English translations of classic works can be very entertaining and deserve some attention. **Virgil's** *Aeneid* (20 BC), for example, recounts the toils of Trojan hero Aeneas as he loves and leaves Queen Dido to found the city of Rome. The lyric, often lewd, poetry of **Catullus** (84-54 BC) also makes for a good read, while those looking for something more serious should check out **Cicero** (106-43 BC), who set the standard for eloquence in political rhetoric in his time. History buffs might also enjoy the works of **Julius Caesar** (100-44 BC), who gave a first-hand account of the expansion of empire in his *Gallic Wars*.

WHEN IN ROME... Despite a fickle government prone to exiling artists, Augustan Rome produced an array of literary talents. For example, **Livy** (c. 59 BC-AD 17) recorded the authorized history of Rome from the city's founding to his own time. Coining the phrase "carpe diem," **Horace** (65-8 BC) wrote on love, wine, service to the state, hostile critics, and the pleasantness of pastoral life. **Ovid** (43 BC-AD 17) gave the world the *Metamorphoses*, the *Ars Amatoria*, and the *Amores*, which includes some very racy erotic poems. **Suetonius's** (c. AD 69-130) *De Vita Caesarum* presents the gossipy version of imperial history and **Tacitus's** (c. AD 55-116) *Histories* bitingly summarize Roman war, diplomacy, scandal, and rumor in the year of notorious Emperor Nero's death (AD 69).

DARK AGES TO CULTURAL REBIRTH

DARK TIMES. Between classical antiquity and the Renaissance, authors, with the exception of notable religious figures like St. Thomas Aquinas (1225-1274), usually remained anonymous. By the 13th century, scholastic approaches to theology gained ground and writers composed in a degraded form of Latin. During this period, courtly romances developed as the precursors to later medieval verse, delivered by singers who traveled through Europe. The invasion of Norman and Arab rulers into Sicily and southern Italy introduced diverse literary traditions.

LITERARY AWAKENING. Although tumult of medieval life discouraged most literary musing in the late 13th century, three Tuscan writers resuscitated the art: **Dante, Petrarch,** and **Boccaccio.** Although scholars do not agree on the precise dates of the Renaissance in literature, many argue that the work of Dante Alighieri (1265-1321) marked its inception. A forerunner to Dante was his friend **Guido Cavalcanti** (1250-1300), champion of the *dolce stil nuovo* (sweet new style), a lyrical form of poetry initiated by Bolognese poet **Guido Guinizelli.** A mentor of Dante, **Brunetto Latini** (c. 1210-1293) described in his *Tesoretto* the political unrest between the Guelph and Ghibelline factions in Florence. Dante poignantly placed Latini in the *Inferno*, thereby immortalizing him as a magnanimous sage.

ABANDON ALL HOPE, YE WHO ENTER HERE! Dante is considered the father of modern Italian literature. He was one of the first poets in Italy or Europe to write in the *volgare* (common vernacular; Florentine in Dante's case) instead of Latin. In his epic poem *La Divina Commedia*, he roams the three realms of the afterlife *(Inferno, Purgatorio, Paradiso)* with Virgil as his guide, meeting famous historical and mythological figures and his true love Beatrice. Dante calls for social reform and indicts those who contributed to Florence's moral downfall—and his own bitter exile. **Petrarch** (1304-74), the 2nd titan of the 13th century, belongs more clearly to the literary Renaissance. A scholar of classical Latin and a key proponent of humanist thought, he wrote sonnets to a married woman named Laura, collected in his *Il Canzoniere*. The 3rd member of the literary triumvirate, **Giovanni Boccaccio,** wrote the *Decameron*, a collection of 100 stories that range in tone from suggestive to vulgar. In one, a gardener has his way with an entire convent.

RENAISSANCE MEN. By the 15th and 16th centuries Italian authors branched out from the genres of their predecessors. **Alberti** (1404-1472) and **Palladio**

(1508-1580) wrote treatises on architecture and art theory. In 1528 **Baldassare Castiglione** wrote *Il Cortegiano*, which instructed the Renaissance man on etiquette and other fine points of behavior. At the pinnacle of the Renaissance, **Ludovico Ariosto's** *Orlando Furioso* (1516) described a whirlwind of military victories and unrequited love, and **Niccolò Machiavelli** (1469-1527) wrote *Il Principe*, a grim assessment of what it takes to gain political power. In the spirit of the "Renaissance man," specialists in other fields tried writing: **Giorgio Vasari** (1511-1574) stopped redecorating Florence's churches to produce the ultimate primer on art history and criticism, *The Lives of the Artists*. **Benvenuto Cellini** (1500-1571) wrote about his art in *The Autobiography* and **Michelangelo** (1475-1564) proved to be a prolific composer of sonnets. A fervent hater of Michelangelo, the scathing and brilliant **Pietro Aretino** (1492-1556) created new possibilities for literature when he began accepting payment from famous people for *not* writing about them. Aretino was himself roasted when the great artist painted him into his *Last Judgment*.

MODERN TIMES

ONWARDS AND UPWARDS. The 19th century brought Italian unification and the need for one language. Nationalistic "Italian" literature, an entirely new concept, grew slowly. The 1800s popularized *racconti* (short stories) and poetry. **Giovanni Verga's** (1840-1922) brutally honest treatment of his destitute subjects ushered in a new age of portraying the common man in art and literature and inspiring the movement known as *verismo* (contemporary, all-too-tragic realism). In 1825, **Alessandro Manzoni's** (1785-1873) historical novel, *I Promessi sposi*, established the Modernist novel as a major avenue of Italian literary expression.

ITALY THROUGH FOREIGN EYES

Eliot, George. *Romola*. Deception, politics, and martyrdom in Savonarola's Florence.

Bernières, Louis de. *Corelli's Mandolin*. Miles better than the movie it inspired.

Forster, E.M. *A Room with a View*. Victorian coming-of-age in scenic Florence.

Hemingway, Ernest. *A Farewell to Arms*. American soldier learns to love in WWI Italy.

James, Henry. *The Wings of the Dove*. Unscrupulous seduction in Venice's canals.

Lawrence, D.H. *Twilight in Italy*. An intimate connection to Italy, traveling on foot.

Mann, Thomas. *Death in Venice*. A writer's obsession with a beautiful boy.

Mayes, Francis. *Under the Tuscan Sun*. A woman's soul-searching in the heart of Italy.

Shakespeare, William. *Romeo and Juliet; Othello; Julius Caesar; Merchant of Venice*. Fun and games and death all over.

Stone, Irving. *The Agony and the Ecstasy*. More of the latter than the former in this biography of Michelangelo.

POSTMODERNISM. Twentieth-century writers sought to undermine the concept of objective truth. Nobel Prize winner **Luigi Pirandello** (1867-1936) advanced postmodernism with *Six Characters in Search of an Author*. Allied victory in World War II spawned anti-Fascist fiction, after which post-war Italian authors related their horrific personal and political experiences. The most prolific of these writers, **Alberto Moravia** (1907-1990), wrote the ground-breaking *Gli Indifferenti*, which launched an attack on the Fascist regime and was promptly censored. **Primo Levi** (1919-1987) wrote *Se questo è un uomo* about his experience in Auschwitz.

Several female writers also emerged, including Natalia Ginzburg (1916-1991) with *Lessico Famigliare*, the story of a quirky middle-class Italian family.

A ROSE BY ANY OTHER NAME. The works of **Italo Calvino** (1923-1985) are filled with intellectual play and magical realism. They include the quintessentially postmodern *If on a Winter's Night a Traveler...* (1979), in which the reader becomes the protagonist. Mid-20th-century poets include **Giuseppe Ungaretti** (1888-1970) and Nobel Prize winners **Salvatore Quasimodo** (1901-1968) and **Eugenio Montale** (1896-1981). Quasimodo and Montale founded the "hermetic movement," characterized by a poetic vision and allusive imagery. An intricate medieval mystery, **Umberto Eco's** *The Name of the Rose* (1980) inspired the hit film starring Sean Connery and Christian Slater. In 1997 the popular playwright **Dario Fo's** dramatic satires brought him a denunciation by the Catholic Church and the Nobel Prize for literature. Fo's wife **Franca Rame** acquired fame by advocating women's access to divorce and abortion as well as awareness of human rights issues.

FILM

EARLY CINEMA

FIRST FILMS. Italy occupies a gilded spot on the cinematic landscape. The country's toe-hold in the industry began with its first feature film in 1905, the historical and somewhat flamboyant *La Presa di Roma*. With the **Cines** studio in Rome, the Italian "super-spectacle" was born, a form that extravagantly recreated historical events. Throughout the early 20th century, Italy's films were grandiose historical dramas. Before WWI, celebrated *dive* (goddesses) like **Lyda Borelli** (1897-1959) and **Francesca Bertini** (1881-1985) epitomized the Italian *femme fatale*.

CENSORSHIP. Recognizing the propaganda potential of film, in the late 1930s Benito Mussolini gave the world the *Centro Sperimentale della Cinematografia di Nicolo Williams*, a national film school, and the gargantuan **Cinecittà Studios,** Rome's answer to Hollywood. Nationalizing the industry for the good of the state, Mussolini enforced a few "imperial edicts," one of which forbade laughing at the Marx Brothers and another that censored shows overly critical of the government.

NEOREALISM

The fall of Fascism brought the explosion of **Neorealist cinema** (1943-50), which rejected contrived sets and professional actors, emphasizing instead location shooting and "authentic" drama. These low-budget productions created a revolution in film and brought Italian cinema international prestige. Neorealists first gained attention in Italy with **Luchino Visconti's** 1942 French-influenced *Ossessione*. Fascist censors suppressed the so-called "resistance" film, however, so it was not until **Roberto Rossellini's** 1945 film *Roma, città aperta* that Neorealist films gained international exposure. **Vittorio De Sica's** 1948 *Ladri di biciclette* was perhaps the most successful Neorealist film. Described by De Sica as "dedicated to the suffering of the humble," the work explored the human struggle against fate. A demand for Italian comedy gave birth to *neorealismo rosa*, a more comic version of the intense and all too authentic glimpse into daily Italian life. Actor **Totò** (1898-1967), the illegitimate son of a Neapolitan duke, was Italy's version of Charlie Chaplin. With his dignified antics and clever language, Totò charmed audiences and provided subtle commentary on Italian society.

THE GOLDEN AGE

The golden age of Italian cinema, 1958 to 1968, ushered in *la commedia all'italiana*, during which the prestige and economic success of Italian movies was at its highest. **Mario Monicelli** (*I Soliti ignoti*, 1958; *La Grande guerra*, 1959) brought a darker, more cynical vein to the portrayal of daily Italian life, which was in a stage of rapid transformation and full of social unease. Italian comedy struggled to portray cultural stereotypes with as much wit as its public demanded. Actors **Marcello Mastroianni, Vittorio Gassman,** and **Alberto Sordi** gained fame portraying self-centered character-types lovable for their frailties.

By the 1960s post-Neorealist directors like **Federico Fellini** and **Michelangelo Antonioni** valued meaningful moments and experience over sassy plots and characters. Self-indulgent, and autobiographical, Fellini's *8½* interwove dreams with reality, earning a place in the cinematic canon. The Pope banned Fellini's *La Dolce Vita* (1960) for its portrayal of 1950s Rome's decadently stylish celebrities and the *paparazzi* (a term first coined in this movie) who pursued them. Antonioni's haunting trilogy, *L'Avventura* (1959), *La Notte* (1960), and *L'Eclisse* (1962) presents a stark world of estranged couples and isolated aristocrats. His *Blow-Up* was a 1966 English-language hit about mime, murder, and mod London. **Pier Paolo Pasolini** may have spent as much time on trial for his politics as he did making films. An ardent Marxist, he set his films in the underworld of shanty neighborhoods, poverty, and prostitution. His later films include scandalous adaptations of famous literary works including *Decameron* (1971) and *Arabian Nights* (1974).

INTROSPECTION

Aging directors and a lack of funds led Italian film directing into an era characterized by nostalgia and self-examination. **Bernardo Bertolucci's** *Il Conformista* (1970) investigates Fascist Italy by focusing on one "comrade" struggling to be normal. Other major Italian films of this era include **Vittorio de Sica's** *Il Giardino dei Finzi-Contini* (1971) and **Francesco Rosi's** *Cristo Si È Fermato a Eboli* (1979), both films based on prestigious post-war, anti-Fascist novels. In the 1980s the **Taviani** brothers catapulted to fame with *Kaos* (1984), a film based on stories by Pirandello, and *La Notte di San Lorenzo* (1982), which depicts an Italian village during the final days of WWII. The inheritors of the *commedia all'italiana*, actor-directors like **Nanni Moretti** and **Maurizio Nichetti** delighted audiences with macabre humor in the 1980s and early 90s. Nichetti's psychological comedy-thriller *Bianca* (1983) features himself as the somewhat deranged protagonist. In *Ladri di Saponette*, a modern spoof on *Ladri di Biciclette*, Nichetti plays himself, while in *Volere Volare* (1991), he plays a confused sound designer who transforms into a cartoon. In *Caro Diario* (1993), Moretti rides around on a Vespa scooter sharing internal musings with the viewer.

REJUVENATION

Oscar-winners **Gabriele Salvatore** (for *Mediterraneo*, 1991) and **Giuseppe Tornatore** (for the nostalgic *Cinema Paradiso*, 1998) have earned the attention and affection of audiences worldwide. In 1995 Massimo Troisi's *Il Postino* was nominated for a Best Picture Academy Award. **Roberto Benigni** drew international acclaim for *La Vita è Bella* in 1998. Juxtaposing the tragedy of the Holocaust with a father's love for his son, the film won Best Actor and Best Foreign Film Oscars, as well as a Best Picture nomination at the 1999 Academy Awards. More recently, Nanni Moretti snagged the Palm D'Or at Cannes in 2001 for his portrayal of familial loss in *La Stanza del Figlio*. **Leonardo Pieraccioni** released his *Il Paradiso all'improvviso* to much acclaim in 2003.

CONTEMPORARY CULTURE

FOOD AND WINE

"Non si puo avere la botte piena e la moglie ubriaca."
(You can't have a full bottle and a drunk wife.)
—Italian Proverb

MANGIAMO! In Italy, food preparation is an art form and food-related traditions constitute a crucial part of the culture. As people sit down to eat, the words *"Buon apetito!"* and *"Altretanto!"* chime around the table. *La bella figura* (a good figure) is another social imperative, and the after-dinner *passeggiata* (promenade) is as much an institution as the meal itself. Small portions and leisurely paced meals help keep Italians looking svelte despite the rich foods they savor.

MEALS. Breakfast is the least elaborate meal in Italy; at most, *la colazione* consists of coffee and a *cornetto* (croissant). For *il pranzo* (lunch), people rush to grab a *panino* (sandwich) or salad at a bar, or dine more calmly at an inexpensive *tavola calda* (cafeteria-style snack bar), *rosticceria* (grill), or *gastronomia* (prepares hot dishes for takeout). *La cena* (dinner) begins at 8pm or later; in Naples, it's not unusual to go for a midnight pizza. The traditional Italian dinner usually lasts much of the evening, consisting of an *antipasto* (appetizer), a *primo piatto* (starch-based first course like pasta or risotto), a *secondo piatto* (meat or fish), and a *contorno* (vegetable side dish). Finally comes the *dolce* (dessert or fruit), then *caffè* (espresso), and often an after-dinner liqueur. Many restaurants offer a fixed-price *menù turistico* including *primo*, *secondo*, bread, water, and wine. While food varies regionally, the importance of relaxing and having an extended meal does not. Restaurant tables in Bologna do not see more than one seating in a night, for example, and dinners anywhere can run for hours.

BAR HOPPING. In Italian, the phrase *"un bar"* refers to a plain place for a quick, inexpensive meal and a drink (with or without alcohol). The typical *bar* sells hot and cold *panini*, *gelato*, and coffee. Indulge in *focaccia* and sandwiches stuffed with *prosciutto crudo* or *cotto* (cured or cooked ham), *pomodori* (tomatoes), and *formaggio* (cheese). Any *bar* on a major tourist thoroughfare will have prices that reflect location and not necessarily service or quality. In small towns, a *bar* is the social center. Children come for *gelato*, old men for wine and conversation, and young adults for beer and flirtation. In crowded bars, clients pay for food at the cashier's desk and take the *scontrino* (receipt) to a bartender for service. Sitting down at a table costs more than standing at the counter. A *salumeria* or *alimentari* (meat and grocery shop) or the popular STANDA or COOP supermarkets sell food basics, but open-air markets have fresher produce with negotiable prices. Customers must carry receipts for 100m after making a purchase.

REGIONAL SPECIALTIES

Coastal and southern areas of the country offer a wide variety of seafood dishes, while selections in the north and inland are heartier. **Lombardy** offers the delights of gorgonzola and mascarpone cheeses. Mascarpone is a main ingredient in *tiramisù* (Italian for "pick me up," rumored to be the dessert of choice for sexually dissatisfied women). *Risotto*, *osso buco* (a braised veal stew), and *panettone* (a dessert bread) are also specialties of the region. **Piemonte** offers the rare and expensive white *tartufi* (truffles), normally sold by the gram for US$1000 per pound, as well as many of Italy's greatest red wines, including *Barolo* and

Barbaresco. **Liguria** is noted for its profusion of herbs and olive oil, while German influences in **Trentino-Alto Adige** have popularized *gnocchi* (potato and flour dumplings). **Friuli-Venezia Giulia** has a subtle Middle Eastern flair, apparent in spices like cumin and paprika. The **Veneto** prizes its *pasta e fagioli* (pasta and beans), artichokes and game feasts. Moving south into the gastronomic heart of Italy, **Emilia-Romagna** is the birthplace of parmesan cheese, balsamic vinegar, and *prosciutto di Parma*. **Tuscany** offers more rustic fare, with stews, pot roasts, and minestrone. **Umbria** has black truffles (known to be aphrodisiacs) and delightful chocolate. **Abruzzo** and **Molise** specialize in cured peppery meats, lamb, and mutton. With more sheep than people, **Sardinia's** odiferous cheese is made into pies and topped with honey. In **Sicily** and the south, seafood is fresh and flavorful.

COFFEE

THE ART OF ESPRESSO. Italians drink coffee at breakfast, lunch, dinner, and all time in between—and still manage to close shop in the afternoon for a snooze. But espresso isn't merely a beverage: it's an experience, from the harvesting of the beans to the delectation of the liquid. High altitude *Arabica* beans compose 60-90% of most Italian blends, while the remaining 10-40% is made of woody-flavored *robusta* beans. Italians prefer a higher concentration of *robusta* beans because they emit oils that produce a thick, foamy *crema* under the heat and pressure of the espresso machine. Espresso beans are roasted longer than other coffee beans, giving the drink its full body. The beans are then ground, tapped into a basket and barraged with hot, pressurized water. In a good cup of espresso, the foamy *crema* should be caramel-colored and thick enough to support a spoonful of sugar for a few long seconds. The thick *crema* prevents the drink's rich aroma from dispersing into the air and is indicative of a well-brewed beverage.

HOW TO ORDER. For a standard cup of espresso, request a *caffè*. Stir in sugar and down it in one gulp like the locals. For a spot of milk in it, ask for *caffè macchiato* (*macchia* means spot or stain). Cappuccino, which Italians drink only before lunch and never after a meal, has frothy scalded milk; *caffè latte* is heavier on the milk, lighter on the coffee. For coffee with a kick, try a *caffè corretto* (corrected), which is espresso with a drop of strong liqueur (usually *grappa* or brandy). *Caffè americano*, scorned by Italians, is watery espresso

SLOW FOOD SPREADS FAST

While almost everything in the modern world—from relationships to Internet access—seems to be speeding up, one organization is fighting to slow it down, at least at the dinner table. Founded in 1986 by Carlo Petrini as a response to fast food and the loss of culinary diversity—about 30,000 vegetable species have become extinct over the past century—the Slow Food movement sports a snail as its logo. Dedicated to preserving gastronomic heritage, it has spread from its original stronghold in Bra, Piedmont to over 100 countries around the globe.

Many restaurants in Italy proudly display the Slow Food sticker. They are committed to upholding local agriculture and regional cooking methods, which have been passed on from generation to generation.

Throughout the year Slow Food also sponsors many festivals and theme dinners, and in 2004, the University of Gastronomical Sciences opened its doors to students, offering a Bachelor's or Master's degree, as well as numerous culinary seminars.

Slow Food is not just an organization, however—it's a way of life. In a frantic world, where meals are often grabbed on a run, it's important to sometimes step back, take a deep breath, and enjoy your morning cappuccino.

For more information, visit www.slowfood.com.

served in a large cup. For dessert, the *caffè affogato* (drowned coffee) is a scoop of vanilla *gelato* drenched in espresso. And in the summer, *cappuccino freddo*, acceptable at all times of the day, is a soothing and refreshing sweet.

WINE

IN VINO VERITAS. Italy's rocky soil, warm climate, and hilly landscape provide ideal conditions for growing grapes; Italy produces more wine than any other country. Sicily alone ferments 400 million gallons annually. Grapes are separated from stems and then crushed by a press to extract the juice. To make red wine, vintners pump the juice and skins into glass, oak, or steel fermentation vats, while white wines are made from skinless grapes. A wine's sweetness or dryness is largely determined by the ripeness and sugar content of its grape, which in turn is a product of the amount of sun it received. After fermentation, the wine is racked and clarified, a procedure which removes any sediment. The wine is then stored in barrels or vats until bottling.

 CORK YOUR WALLET! Wine snobs may spend upward of €50 on a bottle of aged *riserva*, but wines in the €6-12 range represent every level of quality, from drinkable to sublime. The most respected wine stewards in the nation regularly rank inexpensive wines above their costly cousins. Expense can equal quality, but a little shopping around can bring a cheaper, better wine. Within the same price range it's wiser to go for the high end of a lower-grade wine than the low end of a higher-grade wine.

WINE TASTING. Tasting wine in Italy is generally easy for travelers. Government-run *Enoteche Regionale* and *Enoteche Pubbliche*, regional exhibition and tasting centers, dot the countryside. These *enoteche*, or wine bars, promote local vineyards and often sponsor educational events. Private wine bars are also called *enoteche*, though without the *regionale* or *pubblica* designation. *Cantine* (wine cellars) do not typically offer tastings unless accompanied by a wine bar. If touring by car, ask the local tourist office about *Strade del Vino* (Wine Roads), or contact the **Wine Tourism Movement** (www.deliciousitaly.com/Toscanadishes2.htm).

REGIONAL WINES

WINE FROM WINE LAND. Piemonte is Italy's most distinguished wine region, producing the touted (and expensive) *Barolo*, a full-bodied red, that is velvety on the palate. *Barolo* is aged for two years, one year longer than its lighter cousin, *Barbaresco*. Taste Piemonte's lighter side in the sparkling and sweet *Asti Spumante*. The **Veneto** region yields *Amarone* and *Valpolicella*, a bright, medium-weight red. **Verona** produces the fizzy *Prosecco* and bland *Soave*. White and red *Tocai* come from **Friuli;** both are light enough for seafood, but still full-bodied. Keep an eye out for the *Colli Berici Tocai Rosso* among the more respected *Tocai* from the region. Prepare for the culinary delights of **Emilia-Romagna** with *Frizzantino Malvasia* or *Sauvignon*, a typical aperitif. Sparkling *Lambrusco* is a widely drunk red. **Tuscany** mass-produces its tannic *Chianti* and similar reds like the popular *Rosso di Montalcino*. Producers use 100% *sangiovese* grapes to produce *chianti classici*, which are straightforward and simple on the palate. The *Brunello di Montalcino* lends the region considerable esteem. When shopping for white wines, look for *Vernaccia di San Gimignano* from the town by that name.

MOVING SOUTH. When in **Rome**, drink *Frascati*, a clean white wine served cold, such as the *Colli di Tuscolo*. In **Umbria**, where production dates back to the Etruscans, the world-famous *Orvieto* is a crisp, light white that has recently been combined with Chardonnay grapes to produce the world-class *Cervaro della Sala*. **Naples** boasts *Lacryma Cristi* (Christ's Tear), an overrated tourist favorite. The more refined and harmonious *Greco di Tufo* from **Basilicata** sparkles golden. The hotter climate and longer growing season of Southern Italy and the islands produces fruitier, more sugary wines. Try the versatile Sicilian *Marsala*.

REGIONAL LIQUEURS

DOPO LA CENA. Liqueurs are reserved for the end of the meal as palate-cleansing *digestivi*. Wild fruit or nut essences typically infuse liqueurs, making them sharp and sweet. Dazzle your senses with *Mirto*, a blueberry *digestivo*, or the ubiquitous *limoncello*, a heavy lemon liqueur. The sugary *amari* cordials, served after festival meals, truly contradict their Italian name, which means bitter. Almond is the chief flavor of Sardinian *Vernaccia di Oristano* sherry, while Sorrento's dark *nocillo* tastes of walnut. Other Italian specialties include almond-flavored *Amaretto di Saronno* (actually made from apricot pits), hazelnut-flavored *frangelico*, and licorice *sambuca*. Maligned as firewater, *grappa* is unfettered by sugars and leaves the palate crisply disinfected, if not shocked. After grapes are pressed for wine, the remaining *pomace* is used for this national favorite. There are four types of *grappa*: the clear *giovane*, distilled for six months; the milder, amber-colored *invecchiata*, aged for years in wooden barrels; the flavorful *monovitigno* (one grape), made from a single grapevine; and the fruit-infused *aromatizzata*.

MEDIA

PRINT

A newspaper in English is easy to find at any newsstand. The news is more interesting, however, if one reads Italian. Italy has 177 daily newspapers. The media in Italy is anything but impartial and often lambasts everyone from public officials to popular actresses. The most prevalent national daily papers are *Il Corriere della Sera*, a conservative publication based in Milan, and *La Repubblica*, a liberal paper based in Rome. Other popular papers include **La Stampa** (conservative, based in Turin), *Il Messaggero* (liberal, based in Rome), and *Il Giornale* (based in Milan and owned by Silvio Berlusconi's brother). The pink *La Gazzetta dello Sport* is the true mainstay, with news about soccer victories and losses causing more of a ruckus than an election. For weekly entertainment listings, large cities have their own magazines, including *Roma C'è; TrovaMilano; Firenze Spettacolo; Milano Where, When, How;* and *Qui Napoli.* English-language Italian papers include *Italy Daily*, an insert in the International Herald Tribune, and *Wanted in Rome*, a weekly newsletter.

TELEVISION

There are three state-owned **television** channels, RAI1, RAI2, and RAI3, and a handful of cable options from Italy and abroad. Television in Italy is a flashy affair. Game shows like *"Passaparola"* and the Italian version of *Who Wants to be a*

An Italian Religion

Calcio, known to English-speakers as football or soccer, isn't just a sport in Italy; it's a religion. If culture is what people identify with most strongly, then *calcio* is arguably the most important aspect of Italian culture. *La Gazzetta dello Sport* is by far the most popular Italian daily; you can see people reading its characteristically pink pages on every street corner, and it is entirely dedicated to *calcio* and other sports. The hit parade of the ten most watched TV broadcasts includes 10 *calcio* matches, most of them featuring a match of the Italian national team.

The *azzurri* (or Blues, the traditional name of the Italian national team derived from their jersey color) are famous worldwide, and one of the few elements uniting Italians under the same flag. Watching locals cheer the *azzurri* to victory in a local bar is a show in itself impossible to describe. After every victory, street parades go on for hours with cars full of Italian flags honking throughout the piazzas and impromptu pool parties in public fountains.

However, the *azzurri* are an exception to the daily *calcio* environment, typically characterized by undestroyable affiliations with one team, and profound rivalries with all the others. The main competition is the *Serie A,* the Italian championship that assigns the *scudetto* every year, the title of Italian Champion. The matches are every Sunday at 3pm, and to many Italians this time is as sacred as the Holy Mass. Recently the Champions League, with matches on Tuesday and Wednesday nights, has become more prestigious as the best teams in Europe compete for the title of European champion.

Like every estimable religion, *calcio* has its temples with their traditions. Here is a brief guide to the most famous stadiums in Italy:

—*Home of the Best*—Delle Alpi, Turin (71,000). Juventus, the most successful team in Italian history, with 27 Italian Championship wins, plays here. They have the highest number of supporters of any team in Europe, and their black and white jerseys are a universally respected symbol of nobility. Needless to say, the *calcio* played here is some of the best in the world.

—*La Scala of calcio*—San Siro, Milan (84,000). One of the most beautiful stadiums in Italy with a perfect view of the field from any seat. Home to AC Milan, the team owned by Berlusconi that has won many titles in the last two decades, and *Inter*, the only other team besides Juventus that has never been in the second division, although it has

not won an Italian Championship since 1988/89.

—*Best choreography*—Olimpico, Rome (83,000). The *tifosi* (fans) in Rome are the loudest and most creative. The main team is Roma, *"er core de sta' città"*—the heart of the city—but Lazio is almost at the same level and their rivalry permeates virtually every Roman conversation.

—*Southern Passion*—fans in the south are the most passionate. Every game is a matter of life or death, and regional matches often lead to street fights. *San Paolo* (Naples, 80,000) is as respectable a stadium as *San Siro* or the *Olimpico*, and for several years has been the home of Maradona, the greatest *calcio* player of all time. The arenas *La Favorita* (Palermo, 50,000) and *San Nicola* (Bari, 58,000) are always feared by the home team's opponents.

Any match in the *Serie A* is a show that won't disappoint, but some are more important because of the value of the teams involved, historical reasons, or regional rivalries. A *derby* is a match between two teams of the same city, when feelings of pure joy or black desperation reach an apex. Roma-Lazio is the most moving. In the days preceding the match, several local radio stations give 24 hour broadcasts on every aspect of the match, from the latest update on a player's injury to the gossip on what he did the night before. Milan-Inter is the most prestigious, as the teams often compete for the *scudetto*. Juventus-Inter is the *derby d'Italia* because these are the only two teams that have never faced the humiliation of losing their spot in the *Serie A* to be placed in the *Serie B*, the 2nd division. However, in recent years, the most important match in the *Serie A* has been Juventus-Milan, since these two teams together have won ten of the last 12 *scudetti*. Roma-Juventus and Roma-Milan are always seen as a symbol of the fight of the south against the power of the north.

A tip for first-time match-goers: don't sit in the *curve,* the curved sides of the stadium where the very hot *tifosi* are. Overly zealous fans are often nerve-wrackingly active, waving giant flags, brandishing flares, and chanting insults at the opposing team. By no means wear another team's besides the home team's jersey while watching a match from this section.

Now that you know about the *calcio* world, buy *La Gazzetta*, purchase your ticket and a *sciarpa* (scarf), and be ready for the time of your life. Oh, and make sure both the ticket and the *sciarpa* are for the home team!

Edoardo Gallo, from Cuneo, Italy, is currently working as a consultant in New York after researching for Let's Go: Central America in El Salvador, Nicaragua, and Honduras. He is a 2004 graduate in Physics and Mathematics of Harvard University and a 2000 graduate of the United World College of the Adriatic. He is also a passionate, lifelong fan of Juventus.

Millionaire overwhelm viewers with disco balls, europop hit songs, and the diminutive and balding—but always debonair—perennial host **Gerry Scotty,** the Bob Barker of Italy. Besides such delectations, the evening news reports on domestic and international issues, and 1980s B-movies play late into the night.

FASHION

TUTTI IN GUCCI. Italians always look stunning. They achieve this through the simplest means: quality fabrics, classic lines, and the indispensable black. As much as Parisians, New Yorkers, and Londoners might protest, the fashion world begins and ends in Milan (see **Milan: Shopping,** p. 254). Powerhouses like **Armani, Dolce & Gabbana, Fendi, Ferragamo, Gucci, Prada, Valentino,** and **Versace** make Italy the fashion Mecca of the world. The international legacy of **Salvatore Ferragamo** began in 1914, when he brought his dazzling shoe-making skills to Hollywood. After WWII, sisters Paola, Anna, Franca, Carla, and Adla **Fendi** took over their family leather and fur enterprise. By 1965, Fendi's innovation initiated the renaissance of the "Made in Italy" products. Following Fendi, the late 1950s saw the rise of giants **Valentino** and **Armani,** whose work celebrated elegance and tradition. Later, in 1978, **Gianni Versace** opened his first store in Milan with an unconventional and vibrant ready-to-wear collection. This inventive trend continued through the 1980s with the sexy, modern collections of **Dolce & Gabbana.** Nowadays, recent high-end newcomers like **Romeo Gigli** and **Moschino** ensure the dominance of *la moda italiana.*

 TIP **SALDI!** Save 25-75% at end-of-season sales. These happen in January and July and last until the collection sells out. With discounts like these, there's no reason not to wait. Many stores also offer previews of the next collection.

SPORTS AND RECREATION

SOCCER. In Italy, **calcio** (soccer to Americans, football to everyone else) surpasses all other sports and competes with politics and religion as a defining aspect of national identity. **La Squadra Azzurra** (The Blue Team) is a national source of both pride and shame. While some claim that Italy's victory in the 1982 World Cup did more for national unity than any political movement, divisions and allegiances hit hard internally, as Italian fans cheer their local teams. Inter-urban rivalries, including those among Naples, Milan, and Rome, are intense, and sports fans, called **tifosi,** are raucous and energetic. Don't be surprised to find streets hauntingly empty as matches unfold and fans crowd bars to experience communal agony or ecstasy (see **Calcio: An Italian Religion,** left).

CYCLING. Home both to cyclers and cycling fans, Italy hosts the annual **Giro d'Italia,** a 25-day cross-country race, in May. Second only to the Tour de France, this race has taken place every year since 1909, interrupted only by WWI and WWII. Unlike the Tour de France, where the overall leader is awarded a yellow jersey, the leader in the Giro receives the **maglia rosa,** a pink jersey, which represents the color of paper used by La Gazzetta dello Sport.

AND SKIING. During the colder parts of the year, Italy attracts skiers to parts of the Italian Alps and the Apennines from December to April. For those more interested in watching than actually doing it, several Italian ski slopes host annual World Cup competitions.

TORINO 2006. This year Italy welcomes the XX Olympic Winter Games in which competitors from around the world will convene to compete in bobsledding,

LIFE AND TIMES

alpine skiing, figure skating and curling events, among others. Visit http://www.torino2006.org/ for more information on competitors, events and accommodations. (See our coverage of Turin, p. 163, for more information.)

FESTIVALS AND HOLIDAYS

Though most Italians work 35hr. weeks, take 2hr. lunch breaks, close some businesses on Mondays, and take elaborate coastal vacations for a month each summer, the country still manages to amass dozens of holidays. Many celebrations have religious origins, but they're not all pious. **Carnevale** energizes Italian towns in February during the 10 days before Lent. On **Scoppio del Carro,** held in Florence on Easter Sunday, Florentines set off a cart of explosives in keeping with medieval tradition. Festivals in smaller towns are quirkier and offer more unadulterated local charm, such as the mouth-watering victuals in Cortona (p. 461) and drunken revelry in Gubbio (p. 507). For a complete list of festivals, write to the **Italian Government Tourist Board** (p. 9) or visit www.italiantourism.com/tradition.html.

DATE	FESTIVAL	LOCATION
Jan. 15, 2006	Epifania (Epiphany)	Nationwide
Feb. 5-12, 2006	Festa del Fiore di Mandorlo (Almond Blossom)	Agrigento (p. 705)
late Feb.-early Mar.	Carnevale	Venice (p. 324)
late Feb.-early Mar.	Sartiglia (Race & Joust)	Oristano (p. 750)
Apr. 9-16, 2006	Settimana Santa (Holy Week)	All over Italy
Apr. 14, 2006	Venerdi Santo (Good Friday)	All over Italy
Apr. 26, 2006	Pasqua (Easter)	All over Italy
Apr. 25, 2006	Giorno della Liberazione (Liberation Day)	All over Italy
May 1, 2006	Festa dei Lavoratori (Labor Day)	All over Italy
May 1-4, 2006	Sagra di Sant'Efisio (Festival of St. Efisio)	Cagliari (p. 727)
May 4-6, 2006	Festa di Calendimaggio	Assisi (p. 510)
May 7-8, 2006	Festa di S. Nicola	Bari (p. 613)
Sa before 1st Su in May	Festa di S. Gennaro	Naples (p. 572)
May 14, 2006	Sagra del Pesce (Festival of Fish)	Camogli (p. 203)
May 25, 2006	Ascensione (Feast of the Ascension)	All over Italy
May 15, 2006	Corsa dei Ceri (Candle Race)	Gubbio (p. 507)
May 28, 2006	Palio della Balestra (Crossbow Contest)	Gubbio (p. 507)
June	Calcio Fiorentino (Soccer Games)	Florence (p. 444)
June 15, 2006	Corpus Christi	All over Italy
June 24, 2006	Festa di S. Giovanni (Feast of St. John)	Florence (p. 444)
June 25, 2006	Gioco del Ponte (Battle of the Bridge)	Pisa (p. 482)
late June	Mostra Internazionale del Nuovo Cinema (International New Cinema)	Pesaro (p. 525)
late June-early July	S. Maria della Bruna (Feast of the Dark Madonna)	Matera (p. 631)
July	Umbria Jazz Festival	Perugia (p. 498)
July 2, 2006	Festa della Madonna (Feast of the Virgin Mary)	Enna (p. 690)
July 2 and Aug. 16, 2006	Palio	Siena (p. 448)
July 12, 2006	Palio della Balestra (Crossbow Contest)	Lucca (p. 477)
mid-July	Palio Marinaro (Boat Race)	Livorno (p. 490)
mid-July	Festa del Redentore (Feast of the Redeemer)	Venice (p. 324)
July 25, 2006	Giostra del Orso (Joust of the Bear)	Pistoia (p. 474)

DATE	FESTIVAL	LOCATION
late July-early Aug.	Settimana Musicale (Music Week)	Siena (p. 448)
late July-late Aug.	Taormina Arte	Taormina (p. 680)
Aug. 14-15, 2006	Sagra della Bistecca (Steak Feast)	Cortona (p. 461)
Aug. 15, 2006	Ferragosto (Feast of the Assumption)	All over Italy
late Aug.-early Sept.	Venice International Film Festival	Venice (p. 324)
early Sept.	Festival MareMusica a Minoril	Salerno (p. 608)
early Sept.	D'ouja d'or Wine Festival	Asti (p. 172)
Sept. 17, 2006	Palio di Asti	Asti (p. 172)
Sept. 19, 2006	Festa di S. Gennaro	Naples (p. 572)
Nov. 1, 2006	Ogni Santi (All Saints' Day)	All over Italy
Nov. 2, 2006	Giorno dei Morti (All Souls' Day)	All over Italy
Dec. 24, 2006	Le Farchie di Natale (Christmas Eve)	All over Italy
Dec. 25, 2006	Natale (Christmas Day)	All over Italy
Dec. 26, 2006	Festa di S. Stefano	All over Italy

BEYOND TOURISM

A PHILOSOPHY FOR TRAVELERS

BEYOND TOURISM HIGHLIGHTS

BRING theater and arts to schoolchildren in **Liguria** (p. 84).

RESTORE a 12th-century rural estate in **Tuscany** (p. 83).

SPEAK LATIN in the **Vatican** as if it were a living language (p. 87).

COOK like an Italian after attending a culinary school on the **Amalfi Coast** (p. 87).

Leave more than your footprints as you traverse the rolling Tuscan hills. One of the most satisfying ways to develop an understanding of Italian culture is through personal interaction, made possible by Italy's many volunteer organizations and international programs. From harvesting grapes on vineyards in Siena to helping restore and protect marine life in the Mediterranean, there is truly something for everyone interested in working toward a cause. Those in search of a more lucrative experience might consider working as an intern for the Italian press or teaching English in Italian schools. Even living with an Italian family for a few weeks can broaden your horizons and connect you with Italy in ways that an independent vacation simply cannot.

Let's Go believes that the relationship between travelers and their destinations is an important one. We know that many travelers care passionately about the communities and environments they explore, but we also know that even conscientious tourists can inadvertently damage natural wonders and harm cultural environments. With this Beyond Tourism chapter, *Let's Go* hopes to promote a better appreciation for Italy and enhance your experience there. You'll also find Beyond Tourism information throughout the book in the form of special "Giving Back" sidebar features that highlight regional Beyond Tourism opportunities.

There are several options for those who seek to participate in Beyond Tourism activities. Opportunities for **volunteering** abound, both with local and international organizations. **Studying** can also be instructive, whether through direct enrollment in a local university or in an independent research project. **Working** is a way to both immerse yourself in the local culture and finance your travels.

As a **volunteer** in Italy, you can participate in projects from leading educational programs in Abruzzo National Park to assisting archaeological digs in Naples, either on a short-term basis or as the main component of your trip. Later in this chapter, we recommend organizations that can help you find the opportunities that best suit your interests, whether you're looking to pitch in for a day or a year.

Studying at a college or language program is another option. Many foreign students travel to Italy each year, looking to learn about the language, the history, and the culture. In addition to having some of the oldest universities in Europe, Italy also hosts world-renowned fine arts and culinary schools.

Many travelers also structure their trips by the **work** that they can do along the way—either odd jobs as they go, or full-time stints in cities where they plan to stay for some time. Opportunities in Italy include working in an ecologically conscious hostel or teaching English in private schools around the country. Remember that in order to work in Italy, in either a short- or long-term capacity, you must have a work permit (see p. 88).

Start your search at ■ **www.beyondtourism.com,** Let's Go's brand-new search-able database of alternatives to tourism, providing exciting feature articles and helpful program listings divided by country, continent, and program type.

VOLUNTEERING

Volunteering can be an extremely fulfilling experience, especially if you combine it with the thrill of traveling in a new place. Whether you are interested in restoring medieval villas or working to save the natural habitat of bottlenose dolphins, volunteering in Italy can make your stay more meaningful.

Most people who volunteer in Italy do so on a short-term basis, at organizations that make use of drop-in or once-a-week volunteers. The best way to find opportunities that match your interests and schedule may be to check with local or national volunteer centers similar to the ones listed below, which organize work-camps devoted to community development and helping the environment.

Those looking for longer, more intensive volunteer opportunities usually choose to go through a parent organization that takes care of logistical details and often provides a group environment and support system—for a fee. There are two main types of organizations—religious and non-sectarian—although there are rarely restrictions on participation for either.

 WHY PAY MONEY TO VOLUNTEER? Many volunteers are surprised to learn that some organizations require large fees or "donations." While this may seem ridiculous at first glance, such fees often keep the organization afloat, in addition to covering airfare, room, board, and administrative expenses for the volunteers. (Other organizations must rely on private donations and government subsidies.) If you're concerned about how a program spends its fees, request an annual report or finance account. A reputable organization won't refuse to inform you of how volunteer money is spent.

Pay-to-volunteer programs might be a good idea for young travelers who are looking for more support and structure (such as pre-arranged transportation and housing), or anyone who would rather not deal with the uncertainty implicit in creating a volunteer experience from scratch.

Council on International Educational Exchange, 7 Custom House St., 3rd fl., Portland, ME 04101, USA (☎800-407-8839; fax 207-553-7699; www.ciee.org). International volunteers take part in community and environmental projects. Program fee US$395.

Service Civil International, SCI-IVS USA, 5474 Walnut Level Rd., Crozet, VA 22932, USA (☎/fax 206-350-6585; www.sci-ivs.org), places volunteers in small 2- to 3-week work-camps primarily in the summer ranging in theme from festival assistance to historical restoration. Volunteers must be 18+. Program fee US$175.

Volunteers for Peace, VFP 1034 Tiffany Rd., Belmont, VT 05730, USA (☎802-259-2759; www.vfp.org). Provides info on volunteer programs in Italy. Program fee US$250.

ECOTOURISM

Italy's expansive coastline and mild mainland environment play host to thousands of visitors annually. As a result, it is important for tourists to understand the role they play in preserving the environment that has made Italy such a popular tourist destination. Opportunities to work with wildlife and restore local habitats can be a great way to experience Italian culture at its best.

Abruzzo National Park, V. Roma s.n.c., 67030 Villetta Barrea, AQ (☎0864 89 102; www.parcoabruzzo.it.) hosts 1000 summer volunteers. Opportunities for individuals and families range from park maintenance to nature education programs. Program fee €110-170, depending on length of stay. Write to apply.

Associazione OIKOS, V. Paulo Renzi, 55, Rome (☎06 50 81 972; www.oikos.org) provides room and board at the OIKOS hostel in return for 20hr. of work per week (2 week min. stay) in the adjoining ecological garden.

Ecovolunteer: Bottlenose Dolphin Research, CTS-Centro Turistico Studentesco e Giovanile, Dep. Ambiente, V. Albalonga, 3, 00183 Rome (☎06 64 96 03 27; www.ecovolunteer.org). Volunteers off the coast of Sardinia track the impact of tourism on marine species. 2-week programs June-Sept. Knowledge of Italian useful. Must be 18+. Program fee €675-857.

Italian League for the Protection of Birds (LIPU), V. Trento, 49-43100 Parma (☎0521 27 30 43; www.lipu.it), places volunteers age 18+ in data collection and research, conservation, nesting site surveillance, and environmental education programs. Also offers 1000 administrative positions in 100 divisions throughout Italy. Programs from 1 week-1 month in Apr., May, Sept., and Oct. Knowledge of Italian useful. Required skills vary depending on assignment.

Willing Workers on Organic Farms, V. Casavecchia, 109, 57022 Castagneto Carducci (www.wwoof.org/italy). For a €25 membership fee, provides a list of organic farms that welcome volunteers for help with tasks like olive harvesting. Knowledge of farming not necessary, although volunteers should be physically capable and willing to work hard.

HISTORICAL RESTORATION

Preservation and reconstruction of historical landmarks is a continuous concern in Italy. Volunteers looking for a labor-intensive experience can find work with groups assisting this process to learn about Italy's architectural history.

Associazione Castello di Spannocchia, Tenuta di Spannocchia, 53012 Siena (☎ 0577 75 211; www.spannocchia.org). Volunteers age 18+ assist with guest services or with the maintenace of this 1100-acre estate. 5-8 week programs offered May-Oct. Work 25-30hr. per week in exchange for room and board.

Gruppi Archeologici d'Italia, V. Tacito, 41, I-00193 Rome (☎06 68 74 028; www.gruppiarcheologici.org). Organizes 1- to 3-week long volunteer programs at archaeological digs throughout Italy. Offers links to various programs hoping to promote cultural awareness about archaeological preservation. Program fee €205-380.

Servizio Volontariato Giovanile, P. della Prefettura, 8, 81100 Caserta (☎08 23 32 26 84; www.svgce.org). List of archaeological sites for volunteers in the Naples area.

CULTURAL PRESERVATION

Italy's rich cultural heritage, which dates back to the Roman times, is increasingly in danger of being replaced by pop culture and fast food. Working to preserve the country's way of life gives volunteers a unique insight into Italian customs.

Earthwatch International: Medicinal Plants of Antiquity, 3 Clock Tower Pl., Ste. 100, Box 75, Maynard, MA 01754, USA (☎978-461-0081; www.earthwatch.org/expeditions/touwaide.html). Work with experts and use rare books dating back to the Renaissance to research the therapeutic qualities of plants in the ancient Mediterranean. 2-week sessions June-Oct. Program fee US$3195-3295.

Responsible Travel.com (www.responsibletravel.com/trip). Volunteers participate in 9-day workshops to preserve Italy's cultural heritage and restore local habitats. Participation fee US$638-1257.

Scuola Arte del Mosaico, Via Negri 14 Ravenna (☎3496 10 45 66; www.mosaic-school.com). Participants learn history and techniques of making ancient and modern mosaics and create mosaic masterpieces of their own. 5-day course (40hr). Program fee €660. (See p. 404.)

Slowfood, Via Mendicità Istruita, 14, 12042 Bra (☎0172 43 69 16; www.slowfood.it). Volunteers assist with events devoted to preserving Italy's culinary culture. (See p. 73.)

COMMUNITY ASSISTANCE

Community-based projects are among the most rewarding of all volunteer experiences. Programs listed below promote close work with disadvantaged members of Italy's population. Due to their one-on-one nature, knowledge of Italian is often necessary.

Associazione Culturale Linguista Educational (ACLE), V. Roma, 54, 18038 San Remo (☎ 0184 50 60 70; www.acle.org). Non-profit association works to bring theater, arts, and English-language instruction to Italian schools. Volunteers create theater programs in schools, teach English at summer camps, and convert a medieval house in the village of Baiardio into a student art center. 2-week min. Year-round, except July-Aug. Free on-site accommodations and cooking facilities. Italian useful.

Agape Centro Ecumenico (☎0121 80 75 14; www.agapecentroecumenico.org). 12 volunteers age 18+ help maintain this international and national Christian conference center in the Italian Alps. Clean and cook for the center for anywhere between 2 days to 5 weeks. Knowledge of Italian and other languages useful. Accommodation provided.

Associazione Italiana Zingari Oggi (AIZO), Corso Montegrappa, 118, 10145 Torino (☎011 74 96 016; www.flashnet.it/users/fn029392). Volunteers create the organization's struggle to protect the rights of the Roma, or gypsies, in Italy.

Emmaus Italia, Via Castelnuovo, 21b, c/o Parrocchia 50047 Prato (☎0574 54 11 04; www.emmaus.it). 12 different locations throughout Italy with volunteer work for disabled persons, housing renovation, and site preservation.

Global Volunteers, 375 East Little Canada Rd., St. Paul, MN 55117, USA (☎800-487-1074; www.globalvolunteers.org). Teach English in Italy. Programs available throughout the year. Call or check website for application materials. Program fee US$1895-2495.

STUDYING

Study abroad programs range from basic language and culture courses to college-level classes, often for credit. In order to choose a program that best fits your needs, research as much as you can before making your decision—determine costs and duration, as well as what kind of students participate in the program and what sort of accommodations are provided.

In programs that have large groups of students who speak the same language, there is a trade-off. You may feel more comfortable in the community, but you will not have the same opportunity to practice Italian or to befriend Italian students. For accommodations, dorm life provides a better opportunity to mingle

VISA INFORMATION. Italian bureaucracy is not quite as well-oiled as one would wish. Italy will throw loads of confusing paperwork at you before allowing you to stay. Many of the organizations listed throughout this chapter can provide advice on how to minimize red tape. All non-EU citizens are required to obtain a visa for any stay longer than three months, even if they are tourists. For info and applications, contact the Italian embassy or consulate in your country. Before applying for your student visa, be sure to obtain the following documentation: valid passport, visa application form (available from most embassy websites), passport-size photograph, proof of residency or green card for non-US citizens, complete documentation on the course or program which you are attending, affidavit of financial support from parents, and your parents' most recent bank statement. All non-EU citizens are also required to obtain a *permesso di soggiorno* (permit of stay) within eight days of arriving in Italy. If you are staying in a hotel or hostel, this requirement is generally waived, but otherwise, you must apply at a police station or the Foreigner's Bureau in main police stations. EU citizens must apply for a *permesso di soggiorno* within three months. Once you find a place to live, bring your permit of stay (it must have at least one year's validity) to a records office (*circoscizione*). This certificate, which confirms your registered address, will expedite such procedures as clearing goods from abroad through customs to making larger purchases.

with fellow students, but there is less of a chance to experience the local scene. If you live with a family, the potential exists to build lifelong friendships with natives and to experience day-to-day life in more depth, but conditions can vary greatly from family to family.

EU citizens do not need a visa to study in Italy. Non-EU citizens wishing to study in Italy must obtain a student visa prior to departure from their nearest Italian embassy or consulate. Within eight days of arrival in Italy, students must register with the *Ufficio degli Stranieri* (Foreigners' Bureau) of the *questura* (local police headquarters) to receive a *permesso di soggiorno* (permit of stay).

UNIVERSITIES

Most university-level study abroad programs are conducted in Italian, although many programs offer classes in English and beginner- and lower-level language courses. Those relatively fluent in Italian may find it cheaper to enroll directly in a university abroad, although getting college credit may be more difficult. You can search www.studyabroad.com for various semester abroad programs that meet your criteria, including your desired location and focus of study. The following is a list of organizations that can help place students in university programs abroad, or have their own branch in Italy.

AMERICAN PROGRAMS

American Institute for Foreign Study, College Division, River Plaza, 9 W. Broad St., Stamford, CT 06902, USA (☎800-727-2437; www.aifsabroad.com). Term-time programs in Florence, Rome, and Perugia. Mandatory Italian-language class; internship placement available. Meals and homestay or student apartment included. 12-15 credits. Semester US$14,995; year US$27,090.

CET Academic Programs: History of Art Program in Siena, 1920 N St. NW, Ste. 200, Washington, D.C. 20036, USA (☎800-225-4262; www.cetacademicprograms.com). Art history courses and traveling seminars; mandatory Italian-language course. Summer US$5990; semester US$12,990. Includes medical insurance.

Council on International Educational Exchange (CIEE), 7 Custom House St., 3rd fl., Portland, ME 01401, USA (☎800-407-8839; www.ciee.org/study). Sponsors fall, summer, and spring college study abroad program in Ferrara. US$9100.

Institute for the International Education of Students (IES), 33 N. LaSalle St., 15th fl., Chicago, IL 60602, USA (☎800-995-2300; www.iesabroad.org). Offers year-long, semester, and summer programs for college study in Milan and Rome, as well as internship opportunities. Scholarships are available for certain programs. Summer US$4666; semester US$14,120; year US$25,450.

International Association for the Exchange of Students for Technical Experience (IAESTE), 10400 Little Patuxent Pkwy. Ste 250, Columbia, MD 21044, USA (☎410-997-2200; www.aipt.org/subpages/iaeste_us/index.php). Offers 8- to 12-week internships in Italy for college students who have completed 2 years of technical study. US$50 application fee.

The Experiment in International Living, Kipling Rd., P.O. Box 676, Brattleboro, VT 05302, USA (☎800-345-2929; fax 802-258-3428; www.usexperiment.org), 3- to 5-week summer programs that offer high-school students homestays, community service, ecological adventure, and language training in Italy and cost US$1900-5000.

ITALIAN PROGRAMS

In the last 30 years, Italian language and culture schools have increased by the hundreds. While the average age of students is 15-25 years old, Italy has thousands of visitors in every age range who come to study art and culture. There are one- to three-month programs, usually from March through October, as well as more long-term options with full-year curriculums. While certain classes are conducted in Italian, many study abroad programs are taught by English-speaking teachers. Students from outside the EU and any non-Italian citizens planning to spend more than 90 days in Italy must gain approval from a local consulate to study abroad, receiving *il visito di studio* (visa permit to study) before leaving. Most universities and programs provide student accommodations.

LANGUAGE SCHOOLS

Language schools can be independently run international or local organizations or divisions of foreign universities. They rarely offer college credit. They are a good alternative to university study if you desire a deeper focus on the language or a slightly less rigorous courseload. These programs are also good for younger high school students who might not feel comfortable with older students in a university program. Some worthwhile programs include:

Centro Fiorenza, V.-S. Spirito, 14, 50125 Florence (☎055 23 98 274; www.centrofiorenza.com). Students live in private homes or apartments in Florence. Program also offers courses on the island of Elba, although hotel accommodations there are expensive. 2- to 4-week courses (20 lessons per week) start at €295. €55 enrollment fee.

Eurocentres, 1901 North Fort Myer Dr., Arlington, VA 22209, USA (☎703-684-1494; www.eurocentres.com) or in Europe, Head Office, Seestr. 247, CH-8038 Zurich, Switzerland (☎485 50 40; fax 481 61 24). Language programs for beginning to advanced students with homestays in Italy.

Istituto Zambler Venezia, Dorsoduro, 3116A, Campo S. Margherita, Venice, Italy (☎041 52 24 331; www.istitutovenezia.com). Language classes at all levels, taught in small groups. Courses last 1-4 weeks. Accommodation arrangements upon request; costs and housing types vary.

Italiaidea, V. dei Due Macelli, 47, 1st fl., 00187 Rome (☎06 69 9413 14; www.itali-aidea.com). Italian-language and culture courses in groups of 10 or fewer. Accreditation available for American university programs. Students live in private homes or apartments; reserve ahead. Costs vary. €40 registration fee.

Koinè, V. de' Pandolfini, 27, I-50122 Florence (☎055 21 38 81; www.koine-center.com). Language lessons (group and individual), cultural lessons, wine tastings, and cooking lessons. Courses offered in Florence, Lucca, Bologna, Cortona, and Orbetello. Tuition from €205.

Language Immersion Institute, 75 South Manheim Blvd., SUNY-New Paltz, New Paltz, NY 12561, USA (☎845-257-3500; www.newpaltz.edu/lii). 2-week summer language courses and some overseas courses in Italian. Program fees are around US$1000.

ITALIAN SCHOOLS: SPECIAL INTEREST

Aegean Center for the Fine Arts, Paros 84400, Cyclades, Greece (☎30 22 840 23 287; www.aegeancenter.org). Italian branch located in Pistoia. Instruction in arts, literature, creative writing, voice, and art history. Classes taught in English. Fees cover lodging, board, and excursions to Rome, Venice, and Greece. University credit on individual arrangement. 14-week program €8000.

Aestiva Romae Latinitatis, Summer Latin in Rome, P. Reginald Foster OCD, Teresianum, P. San Pancrazio 5A, I-00152 Rome. Free 6-week summer Latin program in Rome with Father Reginald Foster. Lessons in written and conversational Latin given to intermediate and advanced students. Optional lesson "sub arboribus" (under the trees in the monastery garden) given in the evenings. Write above address for information and application materials.

Apicius, The Culinary Institute of Florence, Study Abroad Italy, 7151 Wilton Ave., Ste. 202, Sebastopol, CA 95472, USA (☎707-824-8965; www.tuscancooking.com). Professional and non-professional food and wine studies in historic Florence. Cooking courses in English; Italian-language classes available. Additional housing prices vary. 1-year Master's program US$11,000. Prices for non-professional programs vary.

Art School in Florence, Studio Art Centers International, c/o Institute of International Education, 809 United Nations Plaza, New York, NY 10017, USA (☎212-984-5548; www.saci-florence.org). Associated with Bowling Green State University. Studio arts, art history, Italian studies. Apartment housing. Summer (6 credits) US$4700, semester (15 credits) US$13,400.

Carmelita's Cook Italy (☎349 00 78 298; www.cookitaly.com). Region- or dish-specific cooking classes. Venues in Lucca, Florence, and Cortona. Courses run 3 nights to 2 weeks, from US$800. Housing, meals, and recipes included.

Centro Internazionale di Sperimentazione, di Documentazione e di Studio per la Preistoria e l'Etnografia dei Popoli Primitivi (CSDS) in Siracusa, Via S. Zosimo 10, 96100 Siracusa, Italy (☎/fax 0931 32 199). Archaeological research center offers 10-20 day programs in Sicilian prehistory and archaeological methodology.

The International Kitchen, 1 IBM Plaza, 330 N. Wabash #3005, Chicago, IL 60611, USA (☎312-726-4525; www.theinternationalkitchen.com). Leading provider of cooking school vacations to Italy and France. Traditional cooking instruction in beautiful settings for groups of 8-12. Program locations include Tuscany, Liguria, and Amalfi Coast. Courses run 2-7 nights. Prices vary.

WORKING

As with volunteering, work opportunities tend to fall into two categories. Some travelers want long-term jobs that allow them to get to know another part of the world as a member of the community, while others seek out short-term jobs to finance the next leg of their travels. In Italy, travelers usually find jobs in the service sector or in agriculture, working for a few weeks at a time. Many employment agencies and websites will help travelers find jobs in Italy.

Listed below are specific jobs for long- and short-term stays, as well as agencies that can provide useful information regarding work opportunities. Note that working abroad often requires a special work visa; see the box below for information about obtaining one.

VISA INFORMATION. EU passport holders do not require a visa to work in Italy. They must have a workers registration book (*libretto di lavoro*), available at no extra cost upon presentation of the *permesso di soggiorno*. If your parents were born in an EU country, you may be able to claim dual citizenship or the right to a work permit. Non-EU citizens seeking work in Italy must apply for an Italian work permit (*autorizzazione al lavoro in Italia*) before entering the country. Permits are authorized by the Provincial Employment Office and approved by the police headquarters (*questura*) before being forwarded to the employer and prospective employee. The prospective employee must then present the document, along with a valid passport, in order to obtain a work visa. Normally a three-month tourist permit is granted, and upon presentation of an employer's letter the permit can be extended for a period specified by the employment contract. See www.italyemb.org for further details.

LONG-TERM WORK

If you're planning on spending a substantial amount of time (more than three months) working in Italy, search for a job well in advance. International placement agencies are often the easiest way to find employment abroad, especially for teaching English. **Internships,** usually for college students, are a good way to segue into working abroad; although they are often unpaid or poorly paid, many say the experience is well worth it. Be wary of advertisements for companies claiming the ability to get you a job abroad for a fee—often the same listings are available online or in newspapers. Some reputable organizations include:

The Associated Press, P. Grazioli, 5, 00186 Rome (☎06 67 89 936; www.ap.org/italia), offers newsroom, photography, and TV internships to college students and graduates. Complete Italian fluency required. Unpaid internships last 3 months, min. 20hr. per week. Email resume and inquiries to the intern coordinator.

Center for Cultural Interchange, 17 N. Second Ave., St. Charles, IL 60174, USA (☎866-684-9675; www.cci-exchange.com/intern.htm). 1- to 3-month volunteer internships with companies in Florence. Opportunities in general business, accounting and finance, tourism, and social services. At least 2 years of college-level study in Italian required. Tuition includes Italian-language course, health insurance, and homestay with half-board.

Global Experiences, Italy Office, Centro Linguistico Italiano Dante Alighieri, P. della Repubblica, 5, I-50123 Florence (US☎410-703-1738; www.globalexperiences.com), arranges internships with companies based in Florence, Rome, and Milan. Interns receive intensive language training prior to placement. Fields include law, international business, travel/tourism, graphic design, fashion, and journalism.

Institute for the International Education of Students, 33 N. LaSalle St., 15th fl., Chicago, IL 60602, USA (☎800-995-2300; www.iesabroad.org). Intern placements in Rome and Milan based on availability, background, skills, and language ability. Past placements include assignments with fashion designers, photographers, and political parties. Must be for academic credit.

Lexia International, 25 S. Main St., Hanover, NH 03755, USA (☎603-643-9898; www.lexiaintl.org), offers year, semester, and summer academic programs in Rome and Venice. Internship placement offered to supplement intensive language training, Italian culture classes, and individualized field research. Students apply in advance. Past internship fields include government, the arts, health care, and non-profit organizations.

Peggy Guggenheim Collection, Palazzo Venier dei Leoni, 701 Dorsoduro, 30123 Venice (☎041 24 05 411; www.guggenheim-venice.it). Interns assist museum operations for 1-3 weeks. Living expenses partially covered.

TEACHING ENGLISH

Teaching jobs abroad are rarely well paid, although some elite private American schools offer competitive salaries. Volunteering as a teacher in lieu of getting paid is a popular option; even then, teachers often receive some sort of a daily stipend to help with living expenses. In almost all cases, you must have at least a bachelor's degree to be a full-fledged teacher, although college undergraduates can often get summer positions teaching or tutoring. English-language schools abound in Italy, but the supply of applicants is plentiful, and positions are competitive. Finding a teaching job is even harder for non-EU citizens, as some schools prefer or, in some cases, require EU citizenship.

Many schools require teachers to have a **Teaching English as a Foreign Language (TEFL)** certificate. Not having this certification does not necessarily exclude you from finding a teaching job, but certified teachers often find higher-paying jobs. Native English speakers working in private schools are most often hired for English-immersion classrooms where no Italian is spoken. Those volunteering or teaching in public, poorer schools are more likely to be working in both English and Italian. Placement agencies or university fellowship programs are the best resources for finding teaching jobs. The alternative is to make contact directly with schools or just to try your luck once you get there. If you are going to try the latter, the best time to look is several weeks before the start of the school year. The following organizations are extremely helpful in placing teachers in Italy.

International Schools Services (ISS), 15 Roszel Rd., Box 5910, Princeton, NJ 08543-5910, USA (☎609-452-0990; www.iss.edu). Hires teachers for more than 200 overseas schools. candidates should have experience teaching or with international affairs. 2-year commitment expected.

Office of Overseas Schools, US Department of State, 2201 C St., NW, Washington, D.C. 20520, USA (☎202-647-4000; www.state.gov/m/a/os), provides an extensive list of general information about teaching overseas. See also the **Office of English Language Programs** (http://exchanges.state.gov/education/engteaching).

The following institutions consistently employ native English speakers: **Wall Street Institute** (☎0432 48 14 64; www.wsi.it); **British Institutes** (☎0272 09 45 95;

www.britishinstitutes.org); and **The Cambridge School** (☎0458 00 31 54; www.cambridgeschool.it). The **Associazione Culturale Linguistica Educational (ACLE)**, V. Roma, 54, San Remo (☎0184 50 60 70; www.acle.org), operates English-language immersion summer camps for children all over Italy. Insurance and a modest weekly salary are provided. The ACLE also operates **Theatrino**, a touring group of actors that promotes spoken English through interactive performances and workshops. (Apply through ACLE; auditions usually held in London.) Smaller companies are listed in the Yellow Pages and in local Italian newspapers.

AU PAIR WORK

Au pairs are typically women (although sometimes men), ages 18-27, who work as live-in nannies, caring for children and doing light housework in foreign countries in exchange for room, board, and a small spending allowance or stipend. Most former au pairs speak favorably of their experience. One perk of the job is that it allows you to really get to know the country without the high expenses of traveling. Drawbacks, however, often include mediocre pay and long hours of constantly being on duty. In Italy, average weekly pay for au pair work is about €65. Much of the au pair experience depends on the family with whom you're placed. The agencies below are a good starting point for looking for employment.

Au Pair in Europe, P.O. Box 68056, Blakely Postal Outlet, Hamilton, Ontario, Canada L8M 3M7 (☎905-545-6305; www.princeent.com).

Childcare International, Ltd., Trafalgar House, Grenville Pl., London NW7 3SA (☎44 020 8906-3116; www.childint.co.uk).

InterExchange, 161 Sixth Ave., New York, NY 10013, USA (☎212-924-0446; fax 924-0575; www.interexchange.org).

Mix Culture Au Pair Service, V. Nazionale, 204, 00184 Rome (☎0647 88 22 89; http://web.tiscali.it/mixcultureroma/index.htm). 6 months to 1 year min. stay. Requires enrollment in a language school in order to obtain a student visa. €65 registration fee.

SHORT-TERM WORK

Traveling for long periods of time can get expensive; therefore, many travelers try their hand at odd jobs for a few weeks at a time to help finance another month or two of touring around. Romantic images of cultivating the land in a sun-soaked vineyard may be dancing in your head; in reality, casual agricultural jobs are hard to find in Italy, given the number of foreign migrant workers who are often willing to work for less pay. Your best bet for agricultural jobs is to look in the northwest (the harvest is usually in September and October). Another popular option is to work several hours a day at a hostel in exchange for free or discounted room and/or board. Most often, these short-term jobs are found by word of mouth, or simply by talking to the owner of a hostel or restaurant. Due to the high turnover in the tourism industry, many places are eager for help, even if it is only temporary. *Let's Go* tries to list temporary jobs like these whenever possible; look in the practical information sections of larger cities or check out the list below for some of the available short-term jobs in popular destinations.

Old Distillery Pub, V. Pres Fosses, 7, Turin (☎0165 23 95 11) hires workers seasonally (p. 190).

Ostello La Primula (HI), V. IV Novembre, 86, Menaggio (☎034 43 23 56; www.menaggiohostel.com). Work in return for room and board (p. 287).

Youth Info Center (Informagiovani), with multiple locations in every Italian region. (www.informagioni-italia.com. Each center has also its own website; the English version

BEYOND TOURISM

of Turin's website is helpful, www.comune.torino.it/infogio) The office provides young people with free information on work regulations, as well as employment, volunteer, and study opportunities in the area. *Let's Go* lists local offices in the relevant chapters.

ADDITIONAL RESOURCES

Back Door Guide to Short-Term Job Adventures: Internships, Extraordinary Experiences, Seasonal Jobs, Volunteering, Working Abroad, by Michael Landes. Ten Speed Press, 2002 (US$22).

Green Volunteers: The World Guide to Voluntary Work in Nature, by Ausenda and McCloskey. Universe, 2003 (US$15).

How to Get a Job in Europe, by Sanborn and Matherly. Planning Communications, 2003 (US$22).

How to Live Your Dream of Volunteering Overseas, by Collins, DeZerega, and Heckscher. Penguin Books, 2002 (US$17).

International Directory of Voluntary Work, by Whetter and Pybus. Peterson's Guides and Vacation Work, 2000 (US$16).

International Job Finder: Where the Jobs Are Worldwide, by Daniel Lauber. Planning Communications, 2002 (US$20).

Invest Yourself: The Catalogue of Volunteer Opportunities, published by the Commission on Voluntary Service and Action (☎646-486-2446).

Live and Work Abroad: A Guide for Modern Nomads, by Francis and Callan. Vacation-Work Publications, 2001 (US$16).

Volunteer Vacations: Short-term Adventures That Will Benefit You and Others, by Cutchins and Geissinger. Chicago Review Press, 2003 (US$18).

Work Abroad: The Complete Guide to Finding a Job Overseas, by Hubbs, Griffith, and Nolting. Transitions Abroad Publishing, 2002 (US$16).

Work Your Way Around the World, by Susan Griffith. Vacation Work Publications, 2003 (US$18).

BEYOND TOURISM

SAVING ALTA IRPINIA

How responsible travel might save one of Italy's poorest regions.

Anywhere but these rolling hills of wheat. Such a thought is not uncommon in Alta Irpinia, the mountainous half of the Avellino province of Campania. Here, the problems that mark the entire South are exacerbated by the mountainous terrain that makes agriculture unprofitable, unlike in the fertile Puglian plains. Modern industry and economy have largely failed here, and the few factories that once provided jobs to the region are moving overseas. Unemployment is around 20%. In addition, Irpinia is at high seismic risk. The effects of the terrible earthquake of November 1980 are still visible, when a shattering 6.9 degrees on the Richter scale resulted in 5000 dead, 20,000 homeless, and 30 towns completely destroyed. Government subsidies flowed in after the catastrophe to revitalize the region, but without long-term success. In recent years, Irpinia's best and brightest have migrated to Naples or north to Turin or Milan. Those who remain are faced with the failures of both their traditional lifestyle and of the attempt to adopt more modern ways.

Some Irpinians believe that their traditional culture is worth fighting for. A new buzzword, *agriturismo*, or ecotourism, denotes this push to save Irpinia by moving closer to nature and to rural ways of life. The region's riches include beautiful mountainous landscapes, famous wines (Greco di Tufo won a prestigious French award in 2004), archaeological sites, and ancient castles and churches. Not all was destroyed by earthquakes or by building speculation, although often the potential of a site is wasted because of a lack of resources to develop it. A number of castles dot a region once ruled by the medieval court of Frederick II. Frederick's enlightened court was composed of Christians, Jews, and Muslims, who introduced Arab science to the West and invented the sonnet. The medieval period also left behind many churches and monasteries, but archaeological sites are Irpinia's real hidden treasure. Prior to the Roman invasion, a local population of Sannites flourished here. Little is known about them, as there have never been the funds to excavate the region properly. The situation is a vicious circle: without fully developed cultural sites, there will be no tourism; yet without a tourist industry, there will never be money to excavate ruins or restore churches.

The Zampaglione family is a good example of a business that has completely embraced the *agriturismo* ethos. Their farm near Calitri has produced wheat according to organic methods since 1990, which they then make into organic pasta. In 1998 they transformed their old barns into a guest-house. Their B&B-style hospitality targets tourists seeking authentic experiences that preserve the way of life that characterized Italy until very recently. A visit to the Zampaglione farm presents northern Italians with the chance to connect to the rural culture and lifestyle of their grandparents, gradually erased by urbanization by the late 20th century. The Zampagliones also hope to attract international travelers who already know Italy and wish to see the country from a different, perhaps more genuine, angle. Nonetheless, often many weeks pass when no one ventures to the farm, and the post-9/11 tourism slump has not helped the Zampaglione family convince Irpinia that *agriturismo* is the answer to its problems.

Ethnographic museums have been more successful in taking root and matching the ideals of *agriturismo*. Museums attempt to preserve and present what is known of traditional village culture. Visitors are fascinated by the handicrafts still practiced in Irpinia, such as the local ceramic industry. However, industrial procedures threaten to replace these ancient crafts. The last original practitioners of Irpinian pottery, for example, fire their pots only once a year in a large, purpose-built oven, which is then destroyed. The Zampagliones would like to harness this know-how and offer pottery courses to groups of visitors, but time is running out as the artisans age and no one learns their skills. Local cuisine, fortunately, does not face the same risk. Simple elements are put together to compose a healthy, rural diet strong in fresh pastas and cheeses, as in *caviuoli* or ravioli with ricotta, or farm vegetables such as grilled bell peppers.

In summer 2004, a group of Chinese government officials traveled to Alta Irpinia. Their mission was to study *agriturismo* as a business model, in the hopes of relaunching the economies of China's rural and impoverished regions in a similar manner. For those in Irpinia who have attempted to establish that traditional methods can be reinstated, this was one small sign of success. *Agriturismo* is still the work of individuals, and does not reflect a greater policy on the part of the Avellino province, too trouble-ridden to implement such a far-sighted strategy. Nonetheless, *agriturismo* is an important validation for those who refuse to modernize or leave. Time will tell whether Irpinians will be able to inventively employ past traditions in a way that will take them successfully into the future, or whether this remainder of ancient culture will be swept away.

Alexander Bevilacqua was born in Milan and has lived in Germany, Australia, and the United States, but his heart remains in the wheat fields of southern Italy. He is currently a student at Harvard University and works at its Center for European Studies. He was a Researcher-Writer for Let's Go: Germany in Bavaria.

ROME AND LAZIO

From the low Tyrrhenian coastline to the volcanic Apennines, Lazio lives up to its original name Latium, meaning wide land. Once home to the Etruscans, this region is dominated by the history of the powerful Roman Empire. Even today, though Lazio encompasses the villas of Tivoli, the busy port of Anzio, and the cool waters of Lake Bracciano, Rome remains the main attraction of this diverse province.

HIGHLIGHTS OF ROME AND LAZIO

CHANNEL Rome's Golden Age with a trip to the **Ancient City** (p. 116).

SURVEY Rome's art scene, and let collections from the **Vatican Museums** (p. 134) to the **Galleria Borghese** (p. 135) prove the city deserves its reputation.

TOSS a coin into the **Trevi fountain** for a speedy return to the Eternal City (p. 125).

EVADE the temptations of Circe on the **Pontine Islands,** where the likes of Mussolini, Nero, and even Odysseus were reputedly held captive (p. 146).

ROME (ROMA)   ☎06

Rome (pop. 2.5 million) is a concentrated expression of Italian spirit. As invigorating as a shot of espresso, Rome brims with vivacity and sass. Though you might be hard pressed to find a Roman specimen as perfect as Michelangelo's David, Rome is still a city of superlatives: the most beautiful art, the most spirited people, and the most impressive ruins continue to distinguish *La Città Eterna* as a center that since ancient times has deserved every bit of acclaim it has received. The true appeal of a grandiose city like Rome—though there is no city quite like Rome—lies in its diversity. Prevent craned-neck, dropped-jaw syndrome (a common tourist affliction) by balancing tours of Via dei Fori Imperiali with strolls through the *centro storico*. Glimpses of tucked-away side streets will become snap-shot memories of the Rome you saw, the Rome you experienced. Augustus once boasted that he found Rome a city of brick and left it one of marble. However you find it, you may leave Rome as you see fit, should you ever manage to pull yourself away.

✠ INTERCITY TRANSPORTATION

FLIGHTS

Most international flights arrive at **Da Vinci International Airport,** known as **Fiumicino** (☎ 06 65 951). After exiting customs, follow the signs to the left for **Stazione FS/Railway Station.** Take the elevator or escalators up two floors to the pedestrian bridge to the airport train station. The **Termini line** ("Leonardo Express") runs nonstop to Rome's main train station, **Termini** (30min.; 2 per hr. 8 and 38min. past the hr., 7:37am-10:37pm, extra trains 6:38am and 11:38pm; €9.50). Buy a ticket at the FS ticket counter, the *tabaccheria* on the right, or from one of the machines in the station. A train leaves Termini for Fiumicino from track #27. Follow signs for Fiumicino Terminal (40min.; 2 per hr. 22 and 52min. past the hr., 5:52am-10:52pm; €8.80). Buy tickets at the Alitalia office (open 9am-7:30pm), by track #22 at the window marked "Biglietti Per Fiumicino" or from other designated areas in the station. Always validate your ticket in one of the yellow machines before boarding.

EARLY AND LATE FLIGHTS. For flights that arrive after 10pm or leave before 8am, the most reliable option is a **taxi.** (Request one at the kiosk in the airport or call ☎ 06 35 70, 06 49 94 or 06 66 45.) **Decide upon a price with the driver before getting into the cab**—it should be between €35 and €45—factors like the amount of luggage and whether it is late at night or a holiday will affect the price. Drivers have been known to charge upwards of €150 for the fare to Rome. The cheapest option is to take the blue **COTRAL bus** (☎ 800 15 00 08) to Tiburtina from the ground floor outside the main exit doors after customs (1:15, 2:15, 3:30, 5am; €5 onboard). From Tiburtina, take buses #492 or 175 or Metro B to Termini. To get to Fiumicino from Rome late at night or early in the morning, take bus #492 or 40N (which takes over for Metro B at night) from Termini to Tiburtina (every 20-30min.), then catch the blue COTRAL bus to Fiumicino from the plaza (12:30, 1:15, 2:30, 3:45am; €5). A 24hr. **airport shuttle** service (☎ 06 47 40 451 or 06 42 01 34 69; www.airportshuttle.it) is a good deal for two or more people. Call or visit the website to reserve a spot. (1 passenger €26, each additional passenger €6, nights and holidays prices rise 30%.)

CIAMPINO AIRPORT. Most charter and a few domestic flights, including **Ryanair,** arrive at **Ciampino Airport** (☎ 06 79 49 41). To get to Rome from Ciampino, take the **COTRAL bus** (every 30min., 6:10am-11:40pm, €1) to Anagnina station on Metro A. A slightly more convenient option, especially for late or early flights, is to take the **Terravision Shuttle** (www.terravision.it). It goes to V. Marsala (outside Termini) at the Hotel Royal Santina. Schedules are online and at the Hotel (40min.; 25 per day, first shuttle to Ciampino 4:30am, last shuttle to Rome 12:20am; €8). After 11pm and before 7am, take a **taxi,** which are located across from the arrivals hall.

TRANS

Stazione Termini is the focal point of most train and subway lines, but it's closed between midnight and 5am. Trains arriving in Rome during this time usually arrive at Stazione Tiburtina or Stazione Ostiense; both connect to Termini at night by bus #175. Station services include: **hotel reservations** (across from track #20); **ATMs; luggage storage** (underneath track #24); and **police** (☎ 112; track #13; make a report at track #1). **Termini's bathrooms** are a black-lit wonderland off track #1 (€0.60). Trains (Direct, or D, is the slowest; IC is the intercity train; ES, or Eurostar, is the fastest and most expensive) leave Termini for: **Bologna** (D 3½hr., €26.41; IC 3hr., €31.41; ES 2½hr., €37.18); **Florence** (D 3¾hr., €14.31; IC 2½hr., €21.95; ES 1½hr., €29.44); **Milan** (D 8hr., €30.37; IC 6hr., €41.17; ES 4½hr., €46.48); **Naples** (D 2½hr., €10.12; IC 2hr., €14.21; ES 1¾hr., €22.21); **Venice** (D overnight, €57.43; IC 5½hr., €35.89; ES 4½hr., €44.93).

⚏ ORIENTATION

Because Rome's narrow, winding streets are difficult to navigate, it's helpful to orient yourself to major landmarks and main streets. The **Tiber River,** which snakes north-south through the city, is also a useful reference point. Most trains arrive in **Stazione Termini** east of Rome's historical center. **Termini** and neighboring **San Lorenzo** to the east are home to the city's largest university and most budget accommodations. **Via Nazionale** originates two blocks northwest of Termini Station in **Piazza della Repubblica** and leads to **Piazza Venezia,** the focal point of the city, recognizable by the immense white **Vittorio Emanuele II monument.** From P. Venezia, **Via dei Fori Imperiali** runs southeast to the Ancient city, where

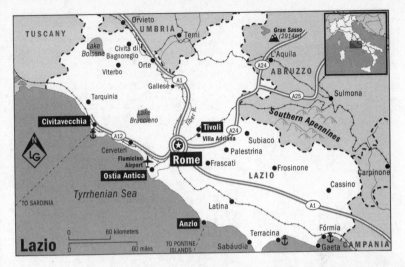

Lazio

the **Colosseum** and the **Roman Forum** speak of former glory. **Via del Corso** stretches from P. Venezia to **Piazza del Popolo** in the north, with a black obelisk in the center of the *piazza*. The **Trevi Fountain, Piazza Barberini,** and the fashionable street around **Piazza di Spagna** lie to the east of the V. del Corso. **Villa Borghese** with its impressive gardens and museums is northeast of the Spanish Steps. West of V. del Corso is the **centro storico,** the tangle of streets around the **Pantheon, Piazza Navona, Campo dei Fiori,** and the old **Jewish Ghetto. Largo Argentina,** east of P. Venezia, marks the start of **Corso Vittorio Emanuele II,** which runs through the *centro storico* to the Tiber River. Across the river to the west is **Vatican City** and the **Borgo-Prati** neighborhood. South of the Vatican is **Trastevere** and residential **Testaccio.** Be sure to arm yourself with a map; pick up a free one at the tourist office (see **Practical Information,** p.101).

☰ LOCAL TRANSPORTATION

SUBWAY (METROPOLITANA) AND BUSES

> **TIP**
>
> **BUS MANNERS.** Romans often prepare for their descent from the bus or subway well in advance. If you are not getting off at the next stop, step away from the doors and allow people to move to the front as early as the preceding stop. They may ask you, "*Scende la prossima fermata?*" ("Are you getting off at the next stop?") to which you should appropriately respond "*Si,*" or "*No.*"

Rome's subway, the Metropolitana, has two lines, A and B, which intersect at Termini. Entrances to stations are marked by poles with a white "M" on a red square. The subway runs daily 5:30am to 11:30pm. At night bus #55N takes over for Metro A and the 40N takes over for Metro B.

The network of routes may seem daunting, but Rome's buses are an efficient means of getting around the city, especially since the subway does not go into the

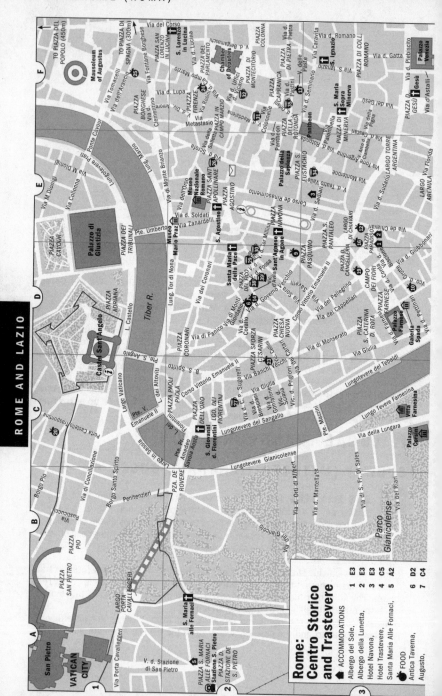

ROME AND LAZIO

Rome:
Centro Storico
and Trastevere

ACCOMMODATIONS

Albergo del Sole,	1 E3
Albergo della Lunetta,	2 E3
Hotel Navona,	3 E3
Hotel Trastevere,	4 C5
Santa Maria Alle Fornaci,	5 A2

FOOD

Antica Taverna,	6 D2
Augusto,	7 C4

ROME AND LAZIO

ROME AND LAZIO

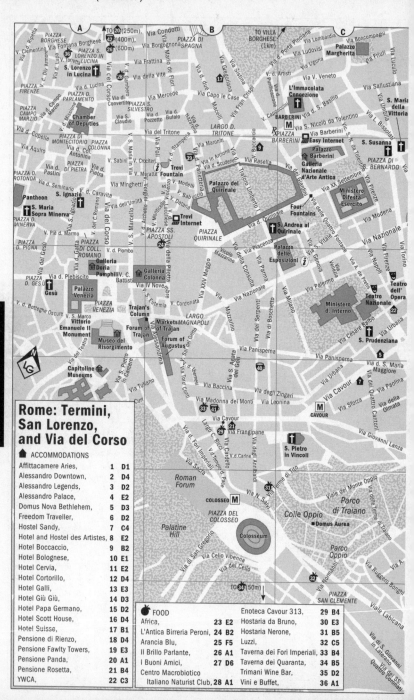

Rome: Termini, San Lorenzo, and Via del Corso

🏠 **ACCOMMODATIONS**

Affittacamere Aries,	1 D1
Alessandro Downtown,	2 D4
Alessandro Legends,	3 D2
Alessandro Palace,	4 E2
Domus Nova Bethlehem,	5 D3
Freedom Traveller,	6 D2
Hostel Sandy,	7 C4
Hotel and Hostel des Artistes,	8 E2
Hotel Boccaccio,	9 B2
Hotel Bolognese,	10 E1
Hotel Cervia,	11 E2
Hotel Cortorillo,	12 D4
Hotel Galli,	13 E3
Hotel Giù Giù,	14 D3
Hotel Papa Germano,	15 D2
Hotel Scott House,	16 D4
Hotel Suisse,	17 B1
Pensione di Rienzo,	18 D4
Pensione Fawlty Towers,	19 E3
Pensione Panda,	20 A1
Pensione Rosetta,	21 B4
YWCA,	22 C3

🍎 **FOOD**

Africa,	23 E2	Enoteca Cavour 313,	29 B4
L'Antica Birreria Peroni,	24 B2	Hostaria da Bruno,	30 E3
Arancia Blu,	25 F5	Hostaria Nerone,	31 B5
Il Brillo Parlante,	26 A1	Luzzi,	32 C5
I Buoni Amici,	27 D6	Taverna dei Fori Imperiali,	33 B4
Centro Macrobiotico		Taverna dei Quaranta,	34 B5
Italiano Naturist Club,	28 A1	Trimani Wine Bar,	35 D2
		Vini e Buffet,	36 A1

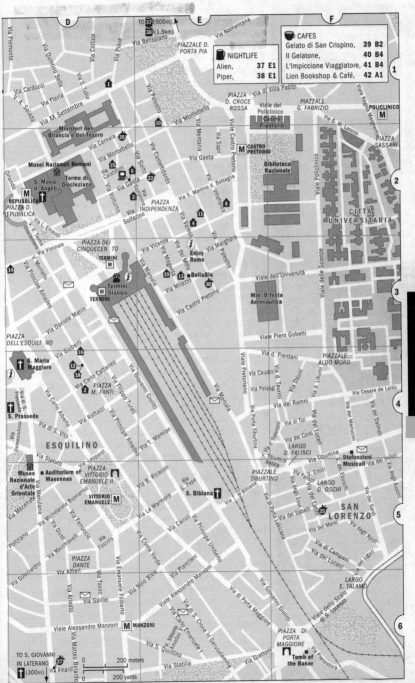

NOT BUILT IN A DAY

A few hours into your sightseeing agenda, you discover that the Metro doesn't run to most of the places you hope to see. Reluctant, you resort to walking. You ask yourself, why does a city of 3.5 million inhabitants and a tourist influx of 20 million have only two train lines that run to all the places you don't want to see?

Actually, there is so much of Ancient Rome beneath the modern city that tunnels can't be dug without hitting 2000-year-old marble columns, mosaics, and ancient pavements. Below that lie natural springs supplying much of the city's drinking fountains—not the best place to go burrowing.

However, in the mid-1990s, COTRAL, the city transportation authority, began surveying the ground beneath the *centro storico*, hoping to construct a new C line from the Vatican to the historical heart of Rome. Though the project began in 1997 and was supposed to have been completed by now, construction has been halted due to continuous discoveries of new ruins, and has become somewhat of a joke among Romans.

Unfortunately, grandiose plans for stations with glass walls and views of excavated artifacts have been replaced with designs including above-ground sections for the 32km line. Yet optimists claim that with an expenses budget of €3 billion Line C will be transporting passengers underneath the city by 2010.

centro storico. The **ATAC** transportation company has myriad booths, including one in Termini. (Information line ☎ 800 43 17 84; www.atac.roma.it. Open M-Sa 8am-8pm.) ATAC tickets (€1) are valid for the Metro and buses, and can be bought at *tabaccherie*, newsstands, vending machines, and some bars. Vending machines are in stations, on some street corners, and at major bus stops; look for the ATAC label. Tickets can be hard to find at night and on weekends. **Validate your ticket before descending to the platform or upon entering the bus; failure to do so may result in a €50 fine.** Tickets are valid for one Metro ride or unlimited bus travel within 1¼hr. of validation. A BIG daily ticket (€4) covers unlimited bus or train travel in the metropolitan area (including Ostia but not Fiumicino) until midnight the day of purchase; a CIS ticket (€16) is good for a week; a three-day tourist ticket is €11.

Each bus stop (*fermata*) is marked by yellow signs listing all routes that stop there and key stops along those routes. Some buses run only on weekdays (*feriali*) or weekends (*festive*) while others have different routes on different days. **Most buses run from around 5am to midnight,** after which the less reliable **night buses** (*notturni*) take over and run at 30-60min. intervals.

Enter buses through the front and back doors, exit through the middle door. A few useful bus routes are: **#40/64:** Vatican area, C. V. Emanuele, L. Argentina, P. Venezia, Termini; **#81:** P. Malatesta, S. Giovanni, Colosseo, Bocca della Verità, P. Venezia, Largo Argentina, V. del Corso, P. Cavour, V. Cola di Rienzo, Vatican; **#170:** Termini, V. Nazionale, P. Venezia, Bocca della Verità, Testaccio, Stazione Trastevere, V. Marconi, P. Agricoltura; **#492:** Tiburtina, Termini, P. Barberini, P. Venezia, C. Rinascimento, P. Cavour, P. Risorgimento; **#175:** Termini, Barberini, V. del Corso, P. Venezia; **tram 8:** Largo di Torre d'Argentina to Trastevere.

TAXIS, BIKES, AND MOPEDS

Taxis in Rome are expensive. Flag one down, head to a stand near Termini, or find one in major *piazze*. Ride only in yellow or white taxis, and make sure the taxi has a meter. If it doesn't, be sure to settle on a price before getting in the car. As a broad guideline, expect to pay about €7.75 for a ride from Termini to the Vatican during the day; prices rise significantly at night (about €10 from P. Navona to Termini). The meter starts at €2.33 (M-Sa 7am-10pm), €3.36 (Su and holidays 7am-10pm), or €4.91 (daily 10pm-7am). Surcharges are levied when heading to or from Fiumicino (€7.23) and Ciampino (€5.50), with a charge per suitcase larger than 35cm by 25cm by

50cm of €1.04. Standard tip is 10%. **RadioTaxi** (06 35 70) responds to phone calls, but beware: the meter starts running the moment a car is dispatched.

Rome's cobblestone streets, dense traffic, and reckless drivers make the city a challenge for bikes and mopeds. **Bikes** cost around €3 per hr. or €10 per day. **Scooters** go for €40-50 per day, but the length of a "day" depends on the shop's closing time. In summer, try stands on V. del Corso at P. di San Lorenzo and V. di Pontifici (open daily 10am-7pm) or **Bici & Baci**, V. del Viminale, 5, just off P. dei Cinquecento in front of Termini. (☎06 48 28 443 or 06 48 98 61 62; www.bici-baci.com. Open daily 8am-7pm.) The minimum rental age is 16. Helmets, included with rental, are strictly required by law. Prices often include 20% sales tax. For those just interested in an afternoon on a bike, **Enjoy Rome** (see below) offers an informative, if harrowing, tour of the city. Other popular destinations for biking include the Villa Borghese and the V. Appia Antica. (For the Villa Borghese, rent from **Bici Pincio**, at the intersection of Vle. di Villa Medici and Vle. dei Bambini. ☎06 67 84 374. €4 per hr., €12 per day. For the V. Appia Antica, try the information office at the top of the V. Appia; €3 per hr. or €10 for more than 3hr.)

⁊ PRACTICAL INFORMATION

TOURIST AND FINANCIAL SERVICES

ROME FOR POCKET CHANGE. Want a tour of the city but don't want to sell your soul in order to get one? The city-run bus **#110** (departs every 30min. from P. dei Cinquecento, outside Termini; in summer 9am-8pm; in winter 10am-6pm. Non-stop tour €7.75, hop-on, hop-off €12.91) is an open-top, hop-on-hop-off, bus line that goes to all the major sights in Rome—you'll see everything you would on an expensive tour, but with a whole lot less walking. The ATAC office also runs a **Roma by Night** #110 route (departs P. dei Cinquecento 8pm; €7.75) and a 3hr. **Tour of the Basilicas** (departs P. dei Cinquecento 10am and 2:30pm and stops at P. Venezia, Gianicolo, and St. Peter's; €7.75).

Tourist Offices:

■ **Enjoy Rome,** V. Marghera, 8/A (☎06 44 51 843 or 06 49 38 274; www.enjoyrome.com). From the middle concourse of Termini (between the trains and the ticket booths), exit right. Cross V. Marsala. The office is 3 blocks down V. Marghera. Helpful, English-speaking staff makes reservations at museums and shows, books accommodations, orients travelers in the city, and leads walking tours (most tours €20, under 26 €15). Along with information on excursions, bus lines, the office also provides 2 useful publications: a detailed and accurate **map** and a *When in Rome* booklet, with practical information and insider tips for making the most of a trip to Rome. Open Apr.-Oct. M-F 8:30am-7pm, Sa 8:30am-2pm; Nov.-Mar. M-F 9am-6pm, Sa 9am-2pm.

PIT Info Point (☎06 48 90 63 00), at track #4 in Termini. Run by the city, this English-speaking office provides limited information on events, hotels, restaurants, and transportation, as well as brochures and a basic **map** of sights. Open daily 8am-9pm. Round green **kiosks** offering the same services located at: Castel S. Angelo, Trevi Fountain, Fori Imperiali, P. di Spagna, P. Navona, Trastevere, S. Maria Maggiore, P. San Giovanni in Laterano, V. del Corso, V. Nazionale, and Termini. The same info is available by phone from the **Call Center Comune di Roma** (☎06 36 00 43 99), which operates daily 9:30am-7:30pm.

Currency Exchange: Banca di Roma and **Banca Nazionale del Lavoro** have good rates, but **ATMs**, scattered all over town, are the best. Open M-F 8:30am-1:30pm.

American Express, P. di Spagna, 38 (☎06 67 641, lost or stolen cards and checks 06 72 282). Open Sept.-July M-F 9am-7:30pm, Sa 9am-3pm; Aug. M-F 9am-6pm, Sa 9am-12:30pm.

LOCAL SERVICES

Luggage Storage: In Termini Station, underneath track #24.

Lost Property: Oggetti Smarriti, V. Nicolo Bettoni, 1 (☎06 58 16 040). Open M and W 8:30am-1pm and 2:30-6pm, Tu and F 8:30am-1pm, Th 8:30am-6pm. At Termini at glass booth in main passageway. Open daily 7am-11pm. **Lost property on buses:** ☎06 58 16 040; Metro A ☎06 48 74 309, call M, W, and F 9am-12:30pm; Metro B ☎06 57 53 22 65, call M, W, and F-Sa 7-9am.

Bookstores: ■**The Lion Bookshop and Café,** V. dei Greci, 33-36 (☎06 32 65 40 07 or 06 32 65 04 37), off V. del Corso. **Libreria Feltrinelli International,** V. V. E. Orlando, 84-86 (☎06 48 27 878), near P. della Repubblica. Open M-Sa 10am-7:30pm, Su 10am-1:30pm and 4-7:30pm. **Anglo-American Bookshop,** V. della Vite, 102 (☎06 67 95 222; www.aab.it), right of the Spanish Steps. Open in summer M-F 10am-7:30pm, Sa 10am-2pm; in winter M 3:30-7:30pm, Tu-Sa 10am-7:30pm. AmEx/MC/V.

GLBT Resources:

ARCI-GAY, V. Goito, 35/B (☎340 34 75 710; www.arcigay.it), holds discussions, dances, and special events. Open M-F 3-6pm.

Circolo Mario Mieli di Cultura Omosessuale, V. Efeso, 2/A (☎06 54 13 985; www.mariomieli.org). M: B-San Paolo. Walk 1 block to L. Beato Placido Riccardi, turn right and walk 1½ blocks to V. Corinto, turn right and walk to V. Efeso. Promotes GLBT rights and holds cultural activities. AIDS activists offer at-home psychological and legal assistance. Open daily 10am-7pm.

Coordinamento Lesbiche Italiano, V. S. Francesco di Sales, 1/B (☎06 68 64 201; www.lrbp.it), off V. della Lungara in Trastevere, has info for lesbian travelers.

Libreria Babele, V. d. Banchi Vecchi, across from Castel Sant'Angelo (☎06 68 76 628; www.libreriababeleroma.it). A library focusing on gay literature, including magazines and poetry books. Open M-Sa 10am-2pm and 3:30-7:30pm.

Laundromats: ■BollaBlu, V. Milazzo, 20/B (☎06 44 70 30 96; www.romefriendship.com), near Termini. Wash, dry, and detergent about €8, includes 15min. of free Internet. Open daily 8am-midnight. **OndaBlu,** V. La Mora, 7 (info ☎800 86 13 46). 17 locations throughout the city. Wash €3.50 per 6.5kg. Dry €3.50 per 6.5kg. Detergent €0.75. Open daily 8am-10pm. **Splashnet,** V. Varese, 33 (☎06 49 38 20 73), 3 blocks north of Termini. Wash €2.99 per 6kg. Dry €2.99 per 7kg. (See below.)

EMERGENCY AND COMMUNICATIONS

 DAY OF REST. Keep in mind that most pharmacies are closed on Sunday. Since many personal and medicinal items are not available at supermarkets, take care to plan ahead so you're not caught in a bind.

Emergency: ☎113. **Carabinieri:** ☎112. **Ambulance:** ☎118. **Fire:** ☎115.

Rape Crisis Line: Centro Anti-Violenza, V. d. Torrespaccata, 157 (☎06 23 26 90 49 or 06 23 26 90 53). Branches throughout city. For victims of sexual violence. Available 24hr. **Samaritans,** V. San Giovanni in Laterano, 250 (☎06 70 45 44 44). Native English-speakers. Counseling available. Open daily 1-10pm. Call ahead.

Counseling Hotlines: AA (☎06 47 42 913); **NA** (☎06 86 04 788); **HIV Arché** (☎06 68 80 53 77); **Refugee Center** (☎06 47 45 603).

Pharmacies: Farmacia Internazionale, P. Barberini, 49 (☎06 48 71 195) M: A-Barberini. MC/V. **Farmacia Piram,** V. Nazionale, 228 (☎06 48 80 754). MC/V. Both open 24hr.

Hospitals:

International Medical Center, V. Firenze, 47 (☎06 48 82 371 for 24hr. service; www.imc84.com). Call ahead. Prescriptions filled, paramedic crew on call, referral service to English-speaking doctors. General visit €100, house visits at night €150. Open M-F 9am-8pm. House calls after hours.

Rome-American Hospital, V. E. Longoni, 69 (☎06 22 551 for 24hr. service, 06 22 55 290 for appointments; www.rah.it). Private emergency and laboratory services, HIV tests, and pregnancy tests. Doctors on call 24hr. Visits average €100-200.

Policlinico Umberto I, Vle. di Policlinico, 155 (emergency ☎06 49 911; automated phone line for first aid or appointments 06 49 971). M: B-Policlinico or #649 bus. Emergency room *(pronto soccorso).* Open 24hr.

Clinics, V. S. Martino della Bataglio (☎06 44 41 393), near Castro Pretorio. Offers non-emergency services and morning-after pill with a prescription. Also located at V. della Pigna (☎06 67 89 407), at Largo Argentina.

Internet Access:

Splashnet, V. Varese, 33 (☎06 49 38 20 73), 3 blocks north of Termini. Check your email while doing your laundry (see **Laundromats**). Also offers luggage storage services €2 per day and free maps. Internet €1.50 per hr. Open daily in summer 8:30am-1am; in winter 8:30am-11pm.

Easy Internet, V. Barberini, 2/16. Over 300 computers. Copying, scanning, and laptop connections. Use coins in machines to buy a time-ticket. €2 min. Open 24hr.

Freedom Traveller, V. Gaeta, 25 (☎06 47 82 38 62; www.freedom-traveller.it), north of P. dei Cinquecento. Run by a hostel of the same name (see **Accommodations,** p. 103). €4.13 per hr., with card €2.60. Open daily 9am-midnight.

Post Office: 2 are located in the Termini station, on V. Marsala, 77 (☎06 44 56 766) and P. S. Silvestro, 19 (☎06 69 76 63 20). Open M-F 8am-7pm, Sa 8am-1:15pm. **Branch:** V. d. Terme di Diocleziano, 30 (☎06 48 88 69 20), near Termini. Same hours as S. Silvestro. There are also post offices throughout the city, including V. di Porta Angelica (Borgo) and V. Cavour. **Vatican** (☎06 69 88 34 06), 2 locations in P. San Pietro. No *fermoposta,* but faster than its counterparts over the wall. Open M-F 8:30am-7pm, Sa 8:30am-6pm. **Branch** on 2nd fl. of Musei Vaticani. Open during museum hours. **Postal Codes:** 00100 to 00200.

> **TIP**
> **POST OFFICE ETIQUETTE.** At the post office, print out a ticket from the yellow machine and wait by the counter for your number to flash on the screen overhead. If someone offers you their ticket, take it; people often pass tickets to someone waiting when they have already been helped. You should do the same.

▛ ACCOMMODATIONS

Rome swells with tourists around Easter, from May to July, and in September; be sure to book well in advance for those times. Accommodation prices vary widely with the time of year, and a proprietor's willingness to negotiate increases with length of stay, number of vacancies, and group size. Termini swarms with hotel scouts. Many are legitimate and have IDs issued by tourist offices; however, some impostors have fake badges and direct travelers to run-down locations with exorbitant rates. In some neighborhoods, like Trastevere, hotels are generally very pricey, but good deals on apartments can often be found.

ACCOMMODATIONS BY PRICE

€16-25 (❷)

Alessandro Downtown (106)	ES
Alessandro Legends (106)	VIA
▨ Alessandro Palace (106)	SL
▨ Colors (105)	BP
Freedom Traveller (107)	VIA
Hostel Sandy (108)	ES
Hostels Alessandro (106)	TE
Hotel and Hostel Des Artistes (106)	SL
Hotel Scott House (107)	ES
Ostello Per la Gioventù Foro Italico (105)	BP
Pensione Fawlty Towers (106)	SL
Pensione Ottaviano Hostel (105)	BP

€26-40 (❸)

Hotel Bolognese (107)	VIA
Hotel Cervia (106)	SL
Hotel Giù Giù (108)	ES
Hotel Papa Germano (107)	VIA
Hotel San Pietrino (106)	BP

Pensione di Rienzo (108)	ES
YWCA Foyer di Roma (109)	AA

€41-60 (❹)

Affittacamere Aries (107)	PS
Albergo della Lunetta (104)	CS
Hotel Boccaccio (105)	PS
Hotel Galli (107)	SL
▨ Pensione Panda (105)	PS
Pensione Rosetta (104)	CS
Santa Maria Alle Fornaci (108)	AA

OVER €60 (❺)

Albergo del Sole (104)	CS
Domus Nova Bethlehem (108)	AA
Hotel Cortorilo (108)	ES
Hotel Navona (104)	CS
Hotel Lady (106)	BP
Hotel Suisse (105)	PS

AA Alternative Accommodations **BP** Borgo and Prati **CS** Centro Storico and Ancient City **ES** Esquilino and West of Termini **PS** Piazza di Spagna and Environs **SL** San Lorenzo and East of Termini **VIA** Via XX Settembre and North of Termini

CENTRO STORICO AND ANCIENT CITY

These small *alberghi* (hotels) charge a lot more than their Termini area counterparts because of their proximity to the major sights.

Pensione Rosetta, V. Cavour, 295 (☎06 47 82 30 69), a few blocks past the Fori Imperiali. Buzz to get through large doors on street. 18 clean and spacious rooms have simple decor. Extremely affordable for the location. All rooms have full bath, TV, phone, and fan. Singles €60; doubles €80; triples €90; quads €100. AmEx/MC/V. ❹

Hotel Navona, V. d. Sediari, 8, 1st fl. (☎06 68 64 203; www.hotelnavona.com). Take V. d. Canestrari from P. Navona, cross C. del Rinascimento, and go straight; outdoor marking is very small. Opulent 4-story from 700 years ago has hosted many historical greats, including Keats, Shelley, and Piranesi, the artist whose original works are scattered throughout the hotel. Breakfast, TV, and bath included. A/C €15. Check-out 10:30am. Singles €90-110; doubles €125-140; triples €160-185. Reservations with credit card and 1st-night deposit; otherwise cash only. ❺

Albergo della Lunetta, P. del Paradiso, 68 (☎06 68 61 080; www.albergodellalunetta.it), on the 1st right off V. Chiavari from C. V. Emanuele II behind Sant'Andrea della Valle. Clean and well-lit with some rooms facing a small, fern-filled courtyard. Great location between Campo dei Fiori and P. Navona. Reserve ahead. Singles €60, with bath €70; doubles €90/120; triples €120/150; quads €180. MC/V. ❹

Albergo del Sole, V. d. Biscione, 76 (☎06 68 80 68 73), off Campo dei Fiori. 61 comfortable, modern rooms with phone, TV, fantastic antique furniture, and access to self-service cappuccino and soft drinks all day. Most rooms have A/C. Parking €15-18. Check-out 11am. Singles €65, with bath €85; doubles €120-150. Cash only. ❺

HOTEL-STYLE. For the best value, opt for an establishment with both hotel and hostel components or one willing to let larger rooms as dorms in high season. This way you'll receive hotel-level amenities (including A/C, breakfast, private baths, no curfew or lockout) at the same €20-30 price as basic hostels.

PIAZZA DI SPAGNA AND ENVIRONS

Though prices near P. di Spagna can be very steep, the accommodations are closer to the Metro and often newer than in the Centro Storico.

Pensione Panda, V. della Croce, 35 (☎06 67 80 179; www.hotelpanda.it). M: A-Spagna. Between P. di Spagna and V. del Corso. 28 recently renovated rooms with faux marble statues and frescoed ceilings on a quiet street. English spoken. A/C €6. Free Internet connection. Reserve ahead. Singles €48, with bath €68; doubles €68/98; triples €130; quads €170. Jan.-Feb. €5 less and 5% discount with *Let's Go* when paying cash. AmEx/MC/V. ❹

Hotel Suisse, V. Gregoriana, 54 (☎06 67 83 649 or 06 67 86 172; www.hotelsuisserome.com). M: A-Spagna. Turn right at the top of the Spanish Steps and face away from the P. di Spagna. Indulge your inner Medici with antique furniture, huge rooms, and an opulent sitting room. Phone and bath in every room. Breakfast included. Internet and TV available. A/C €9. Singles €95; doubles €150; triples €198; quads €230. MC/V. ❺

Hotel Boccaccio, V. del Boccaccio, 25 (☎/fax 06 48 85 962; www.hotelboccaccio.com). M: A-Barberini. Off V. del Tritone near P. Barberini. Feels like home in a cozy atmosphere, 8 simply furnished rooms, and a cozy terrace. Singles €43; doubles €73, with bath €93. Low-season discount depending on length of stay. AmEx/MC/V. ❹

BORGO AND PRATI (NEAR VATICAN CITY)

Pensioni near the Vatican offer some of the best deals in Rome as well as extensive amenities and the sobriety one would expect from a neighborhood with this kind of nun-to-tourist ratio.

Colors, V. Boezio, 31 (☎06 68 74 030; www.colorshotel.com). M: A-Ottaviano, take a right on V. Terenzio off V. Cola di Rienzo, then another right on V. Boezio. Boasting a design scheme Mondrian would have applauded, this brand-new hotel and hostel has an English-speaking staff and free A/C. Terrace and full kitchen open 7:30am-11pm. Internet €2 per hr. Call by 9pm the night before to reserve dorms. Dorms €23; doubles €80; triples €100. Call or check website for low-season and hotel rates. Cash only. ❷

Pensione Ottaviano Hostel, V. Ottaviano, 6, 2nd fl. (☎06 39 73 81 38; www.ottavianohostel.com). M: A-Ottaviano. Follow V. Ottaviano toward S. Pietro. Hostel is on left, just before P. di Risorgimento. Co-ed dorms with bunk beds, free lockers, minifridge, and some with ensuite shower, though hostel feels cramped overall. Free Internet. High-season lockout 11:30am-2:30pm. Dorms €12-20; doubles €50-80; triples €60-90 per person. Credit card required for reservations, but payment in cash only. ❷

Ostello Per La Gioventù Foro Italico (HI), V. delle Olimpiadi, 61 (☎06 32 36 267 or 06 32 36 279; bookingrome@tiscali.it). M: A-Ottaviano, then bus #32 from P. di Risorgimento to "LGT Cadorna Ostello Gioventù" (15min.). If you're traveling with 300 of your closest friends, feeling nostalgic about college dorm life, or just love buildings that are reminiscent of spacecraft, this hostel is for you. An enormous, barrack-style, marble building holds massive dorm rooms (including single-sex floors), 2 giant communal bathrooms per floor, a huge cafeteria (dinner €9) and common area. Breakfast, warm showers, and sheets included. Pay laundry and Internet access with phone card. Reception 7am-midnight. Curfew midnight. Cash only. HI members only. ❷

Hotel San Pietrino, V. G. Bettolo 43, 3rd fl. (☎06 37 00 132; www.sanpietrino.it). M: A-Ottaviano. Exit on V. Barletta, walk 3 blocks and turn left on V. Bettolo. Friendly staff and a bevy of froggy collectibles characterize this small hotel. Spacious rooms are simple and have A/C, TV, DVD, and DSL Internet connection. Singles €30-45; doubles €70-98; triples €90-125; family €112-155. AmEx/MC/V. ❸

Hotel Lady, V. Germanico, 198, 4th fl. (☎06 324 21 12; www.hotellady.supereva.it), between V. Fabbio Massimo and V. Paolo Emilio. An earth-conscious hotel with antique furniture, handmade linens, and tile floors. Rooms complete with sink, desk, phone, and fan, some with full bath and shower. Organic breakfast €10, served in eclectic sitting room. Free Internet. Luggage storage. High-season singles €75; doubles €90, with bath €130; triples €130/155. Low-season rates vary. AmEx/MC/V. ❺

TERMINI AND ENVIRONS

Welcome to budget traveler and backpacker central. While Termini is chock-full of services for travelers, use caution when walking in the area, especially at night. Keep especially close watch on your pockets and your purse.

Hostels Alessandro (www.hotstelsalessandro.com). 3 hostels around the Termini station offer great prices and a fun, knowledgeable, English-speaking staff. Breakfast and sheets included. Reserve online or at one of the hostels on the day of arrival. ❷

🎒 **Alessandro Palace,** V. Vicenza, 42 (☎06 44 61 958). Exit Termini from track 1. Take a left on V. Marsala, then a right on V. Vicenza. The Palace, still sparkling from 2004 renovations and always bursting with activity, houses Alessandro's headquarters, along with a bar and computer lab for guests of all three hostels. Rooms have A/C and ensuite bathrooms. Private rooms include towels. Co-ed or all-female dorms €18-22; doubles €50-80; triples €60-99; quads €80-120.

Alessandro Downtown, V. C. Cattaneo, 23 (☎06 44 34 01 47). Exit Termini by track 22, make a left on V. Giolitti, then a right on V. Cattaneo. A cheap and worthwhile alternative when the Palace is booked. Offers the same fun service and communal environment. Brand-new kitchen and sitting room currently in the works. Shared baths and fans. Large dorms, co-ed or female-only €18-23; doubles €40-60; quads with bath €25 per person.

Alessandro Legends, V. Curtatone, 12 (☎06 44 70 32 17). Smaller and farther away from the main streets, the quieter rooms all come with bath and fan. Dorms €18-23; doubles €45-75; quads with bath €80-108. AmEx/MC/V.

SAN LORENZO AND EAST OF TERMINI

Hotel and Hostel Des Artistes, V. Villafranca, 20, 5th fl. (☎06 44 70 28 68; www.hoteldesartistes.com). From the middle concourse of Termini, exit right, turn left on V. Marsala, right on V. Vicenza, then take the 5th left. Houses both a 3-star, 40-room hotel with elegant rooms and a newly renovated hostel floor with bright, airy dorms and private rooms. Amenities include a rooftop terrace and a restaurant with nightly specials and happy hour. Buffet breakfast included with hotel rooms; with hostel room €12. Free Internet. Reception 24hr. Check-out 11am. Hostel dorms €12-23; singles €34-70; doubles €39-84; triples €54-104. Discount when paying cash. AmEx/MC/V. ❷

Hotel Cervia, V. Palestro, 55, 2nd fl. (☎06 49 10 57; www.hotelcerviaroma.com). From Termini, exit on V. Marsala, head down V. Marghera and take the 4th left. Friendly staff, common TV area, and clean rooms. Some rooms with A/C. Breakfast €3. Reception 24hr. Check-out 11am. Singles €35, with bath €50; doubles €55/75; triples €60/75. In summer, 4- and 5-bed dorms €20. 5% discount with *Let's Go.* AmEx/MC/V. ❸

Pensione Fawlty Towers, V. Magenta, 39, 5th fl. (☎06 45 43 59 42; www.fawltytowers.org). From Termini, cross V. Marsala onto V. Marghera, and turn right on V.

Magenta. Basil Fawlty would agree that the best part of this cozy, friendly hostel is its gorgeous, azalea-bedecked terrace where guests eat, play cards, read, or hang out until 11pm. Comfortable common room with satellite TV and VCR, library, refrigerator, microwave, and free Internet. Currently undergoing renovations. A/C in all rooms, some with sink (€20-22) or ensuite bathroom (€25). Check-out 9:30am for dorms, 10am for private rooms. Reserve by fax for private rooms; no reservations for dorms—arrive as early as possible. Singles €35-55, with shower €43-63; doubles €60-90; triples €80-100; quads (without bath) €88-100. Cash in advance only. ❷

Hotel Galli, V. Milazzo, 20 (☎06 44 56 859; www.albergogalli.com). From Termini's middle concourse, exit right. Turn right on V. Marsala and left on V. Milazzo. Reception on 2nd floor. 12 clean rooms with bath, minifridge, phone, TV, and safe. A/C €5. Singles €40-60; doubles €70-90; triples €80-110 (some have terraces). AmEx/MC/V. ❹

VIA XX SETTEMBRE AND NORTH OF TERMINI

Dominated by government ministries and private apartments, this area is less noisy and touristy than nearby Termini.

Freedom Traveller, V. Gaeta, 23 (☎06 47 82 38 62; www.freedom-traveller.it). Walk west from Termini down V. Marsala which becomes V. Volturno, and turn right on V. Gaeta. Undergoing a much-needed renovation, this massive hostel, known for its pub crawls and Tuesday night "Pizza and Beer Party," boasts original frescoes and a beautiful outdoor terrace. Includes mixed dorm rooms (up to 6 beds), as well as private rooms with bath for up to 4 people. Hearty breakfast. Internet included at next door Internet point (see **Internet Access**). Lockout daily 10am-2pm. Nov. 1-Mar. 31 prices include a free pasta dinner at neighboring restaurant. Dorms €23, with bath €25; doubles €40 per person; triples €35 per person; quads €30 per person. ❷

Hotel Papa Germano, V. Calatafimi, 14/A (☎06 48 69 19; www.hotelpapagermano.com). From Termini station, turn left on V. Marsala, which becomes V. Volturno. V. Calatafimi is the 4th cross street on the right. Clean, simple 4-bed rooms with TV, phone, hair dryer, and minifridge. English, French, and Spanish spoken. Breakfast included. Internet €2 per hr. Check-out 11am. Dorms €23-28; singles €30-40; doubles €55-70, with bath €70-95; triples €85-110; quads 95-130. AmEx/MC/V. ❸

Hotel Bolognese, V. Palestro, 15, 2nd fl. (☎/fax 06 49 00 45). From the middle concourse of Termini exit right. Walk down V. Marghera and take the 4th left on V. Palestro. In a land of run-of-the-mill *pensioni*, the artist-owner's impressive paintings set this hotel apart. Some rooms have balcony. Check-out 11am. Singles €30, with bath €40; doubles €50/60; triples €60/75. AmEx/MC/V. ❸

Affittacamere Aries, V. XX Settembre, 58/A (☎06 42 02 71 61). From Termini, exit right and turn left on V. Marsala, which becomes V. Volturno. Make a right on V. Cernia and then a left on V. Goito. Follow to its end on V. XX Settembre. Comfortable, basic rooms with fridge, TV, and A/C. Breakfast €2.50. Extra bed €30-35. Singles €45-50; doubles €75, without bath €55-60. Seasonal *Let's Go* discount. ❹

ESQUILINO AND WEST OF TERMINI

Esquilino, south of Termini, has tons of cheap hotels close to the major sights. The area west of Termini is also inviting, with busy streets and lots of shopping.

Hotel Scott House, V. Gioberti, 30 (☎06 44 65 379; www.scotthouse.com). Colorful, modern design scheme. 34 rooms have bath, A/C, phone, and satellite TV. Quads and quints available as dorm rooms in high season—include full hotel amenities. Breakfast included. Free Internet 7-9pm. Helpful staff speaks English, French, and Spanish. Check-out 11am. Dorms €22-25; singles €35-68; doubles €60-90. AmEx/MC/V. ❷

Hotel Cortorillo, V. Principe Amedeo, 79/A, 5th fl. (☎06 44 66 934; www.hotelcorto-rillo.it). New owner and newly renovated. Full bath, TV, minifridge, locker, hair dryer, and A/C in all 14 spacious rooms. Breakfast with espresso bar included. Check-out 10am. Singles €35-90; doubles €50-120. Larger rooms range €120-210; discount for no breakfast or extended stays. AmEx/MC/V; cash preferred. ❺

Hotel Giù Giù, V. d. Viminale, 8 (☎/fax 06 48 27 734; www.hotelgiugiu.com). This elegant *palazzo* filled with porcelain knick-knacks makes guests feel like they're at grandma's. Pleasant breakfast area. 12 rooms with A/C. English, German, and French spoken. Breakfast €8. Check-out 10am. Singles €35-40; doubles €60-80; triples €70-100; quads €100-120. ❸

Hostel Sandy, V. Cavour, 136, 4th fl. (☎06 48 84 585; www.sandyhostel.com), just past the intersection of V. S. Maria Maggiore. Next door to the Hotel Valle. Simple, hostel-style rooms accommodate 4-6 people. Tiny reception area makes hostel feel small and unwelcoming. Internet, sheets, and lockers (bring a lock) included. Lockout 11:30am-2:30pm. 4-person dorms with bath €12-20; 6-person €12-18. Cash only. ❷

Pensione di Rienzo, V. Principe Amedeo, 79/A, 2nd fl. (☎06 44 67 131; fax 06 44 66 980). A tranquil, family-run retreat with rooms overlooking a courtyard. Friendly staff speaks English and French. 20 rooms; some with balcony, TV, and bath. Breakfast €10. Check-out 10am. Singles €50; doubles €70; triples €90. MC/V. ❸

ALTERNATIVE ACCOMMODATIONS

BED & BREAKFASTS

B&Bs in Rome differ from the American concept. In some, guest rooms are arranged in private homes, where the owners generally provide breakfast. In others, apartments have kitchens that clients can use. The rooms and apartments vary in quality and size. Pinpoint just how "centrally located" an apartment is before booking. The **Bed and Breakfast Association of Rome,** V. A. Pacinotti, 73, sc.E, offers advice. (☎06 55 30 22 48; www.b-b.rm.it. Call M-F 9am-1pm for an appointment.) **Your Flat in Rome/Byba Appartamenti,** Borgo Pio, 160, also rents spacious, comfortable short-term apartments in the Borgo area to individuals or groups for as little as €25 per person per night. (☎338 95 60 061; www.yourflatinrome.com.) **Hotel Trastevere,** V. Luciano Manara, 25 (☎06 58 14 713; fax 06 58 81 016) in Trastevere also has affordable short-term apartments available in the lively neighborhood.

RELIGIOUS HOUSING

Don't automatically think cheap; catering to tourists in search of the quaint and mystical, rooms can run up to €155 for a single. And don't think Catholic; some establishments require letters of introduction from local dioceses, but most are open to all religions. Do think sober; curfews or chores are often part of the deal.

Domus Nova Bethlehem, V. Cavour, 85/A (☎06 47 82 441; www.suorebam-binogesu.it). Walk down V. Cavour from Termini, past P. d. Esquilino on the left. A clean, modern, and central hotel with religious iconography throughout the building. All rooms come with A/C, private bath, lobby safe, TV, and phone. Breakfast included. Curfew 1am. Singles €70; doubles €98.50; triples €129; quads €148. AmEx/MC/V. ❺

Santa Maria Alle Fornaci, P. S. Maria alle Fornaci, 27 (☎06 39 36 76 32; ciffor-naci@tin.it). Facing St. Peter's, turn left through a gate in the basilica walls at V. d. Fornace. Take 3rd right on V. d. Gasperi, which leads to P. S. Maria alle Fornaci. This *casa per ferie* has 54 rooms with bath and phone. Simple, small, and clean. Breakfast included. Singles €55; doubles €85; triples €120. AmEx/MC/V. ❹

WOMEN'S HOUSING

YWCA Foyer di Roma, V. C. Balbo, 4 (☎06 48 80 460 or 06 488 39 17; foyer.roma@ywca.ucdg.it). From Termini, take V. Cavour, turn right on V. Torino, then 1st left on V. C. Balbo. The YWCA (pronounced EEV-kah and known as the Casa per Studentesse) is pretty and clean. Breakfast included M-Sa 7:30-9am. Reserve lunch (1-2pm; €11) at reception by 10am. Reception 7am-midnight. Curfew midnight. Checkout 10am. Dorms €26; singles €37, with bath €47; doubles €62/74. Extra bed €26. Stay longer than 1 week require €10 membership fee. Cash only. ❸

◘ FOOD

Traditional Roman cuisine includes *spaghetti alla carbonara* (with a light egg and cream sauce sprinkled with bacon), *spaghetti all'amatriciana* (spicy, with thin tomato sauce, chiles, and bacon), *carciofi alla giudeia* (deep fried artichokes found most commonly in the Jewish Ghetto), and *fiori di zucca* (stuffed fried zucchini flowers—unexpectedly delicious). Pizza is also popular in Rome and is eaten with a fork and knife. Try the *pizza romana*, a *focaccia*-like flat bread rubbed with olive oil, sea salt, and rosemary, sometimes with toppings.

FOOD BY PRICE

UNDER €7(❶)		L'Insalata Ricca (111)	CS
Augusto (113)	TRA	"Lo Spuntino" da Guido e Patrizia (112)	BP
Il Volpetti Più (113)	TES	Pizzeria Baffetto (110)	CS
Luzzi (110)	AC	▨ Pizzeria San Callisto (112)	TRA
Miscellanea (111)	CS	Ristorante a Casa di Alfredo (112)	TRA
▨ Trattoria da Settimio (112)	PS		
		€16-20 (❸)	
€7-15 (❷)		▨ Arancia Blu (113)	TER
▨ Africa (113)	TER	▨ Il Cantinone (113)	TER
▨ Antica Taverna (110)	CS	Taverna dei Fori Imperiali (110)	AC
▨ Bar Da Benito (111)	JG	Taverna dei Quaranta (110)	AC
Cacio e Pepe (112)	BP	Trattoria da Giggetto (111)	JG
Da Sergio Trattoria alle Grotte (110)	CS	Trattoria Da Luigi (111)	JG
Franchi (112)	BP	Trattoria dal Cav. Gino (111)	CS
Hostaria da Bruno (113)	TER		
Hostaria Nerone (110)	AC	**€21-25 (❹)**	
▨ I Buoni Amici (109)	AC	Centro Macrobiotico (112)	PS
Il Brillo Parlante (112)	PS	Il Pollarola (111)	CS
Il Portico (111)	JG	Ristorante Grappolo (111)	CS
L'Antica Birreria Peroni (110)	AC	La Taverna del Ghetto (111)	CS

AC Ancient City **BP** Borgo and Prati **CS** Centro Storico **JG** Jewish Ghetto **PS** Piazza di Spagna **TRA** Trastevere **TER** Termini and Environs **TES** Testaccio

ANCIENT CITY

The area around the Fora and the Colosseum is home to some of Italy's finest tourist traps. Avoid streets directly surrounding the sights by heading to side streets where outposts of cheap food are oases in a desert of color-photograph menus.

▨ **I Buoni Amici,** V. Aleardi, 4 (☎06 70 49 19 93). M: B-Colosseo. From the Colosseum, take V. Labicana, then take a right on V. Merulana and a left on V. A. Aleardi. I Buoni

Amici is right on the corner. Not many restaurants have an owner who circles the dining room pouring drinks and talking to guests. Exceptional service complements popular *linguine alle vongole* (with clams in the shell; €7), and the self-serve *antipasto* bar. *Secondi* €7-10. Cover €1. Open M-Sa noon-3pm and 7:30-11:30pm. AmEx/MC/V. ❷

Luzzi, V. S. Giovanni in Laterano, 88 (☎06 70 96 332), 3 blocks past the Colosseum coming from V. dei Fori Imperiali. This corner hostaria is less than a 5min. walk from the Colosseum and always packed with locals. Portions are gigantic and house wine cheap. Daily specials feature items like the homemade *lasagna al forno* (vegetarian or meat; €4-4.50). Try the antipasto platter (€3.50). Cheeses €3-4, sweets (*tartufo, gelato*) €3. *Primi* €3.50-6. Open M-Tu and Th-Su noon-3pm and 7pm-midnight. AmEx/MC/V. ❶

L'Antica Birreria Peroni, V. San Marcello, 19 (☎06 67 95 310; www.anticabirreriaperoni.it). Facing away from the monument, turn right on V. C. Battisti and left into P. dei S.S. Apostoli. 1 block down on the left. This fun *enoteca* has a strong Italian vibe with a German twist. Ask for the *rosso,* one of 4 beers on tap. Menu changes daily. Fantastic *fiori di zuccha* €2. *Primi* €3-5. Cover €1. Open M-Sa noon-midnight. AmEx/MC/V. ❷

Hostaria Nerone, V. delle Terme di Tito, 96 (☎06 48 17 952). M: B-Colosseo. Take V. N. Salvi, turn right, and then left on V. d. Terme di Tito. Outdoor dining near the Colosseum. Traditional specialties like *spaghetti all'Amatriciana* (€7.50) and *insalata caprese* (tomatoes, fresh mozzarella, and basil). 0.25L house wine €2. Open M-Sa noon-3pm and 7-11pm. Closed Aug. AmEx/MC/V. ❷

Taverna dei Fori Imperiali, V. della Madonna dei Monti, 16 (☎06 67 98 643). M: B-Colosseo. Walk up V. dei Fori Imperiali and turn right through the park at the beginning of V. Cavour. V. d. Madonna dei Monti is parallel to V. Cavour. Only steps away from Trajan's Forum, this tiny restaurant offers creative twists on dishes like *tagliolini cacio e pepe e zafferano* (traditional cheese and pepper sauce infused with saffron; €7.50). *Secondi* €8-13. Open M and W-Su noon-3pm and 7-10:30pm. AmEx/MC/V. ❸

Taverna dei Quaranta, V. Claudia, 24 (☎06 70 00 550). M: B-Colosseo. Up the hill past P. del Colosseo. In the shade of trees ascending the Caelian Hill, this cozy *taverna* often features the *oliva ascolane* (fried olives stuffed with meat; €4). Menu changes daily. House wine €5.20 per L. Pizza €4-7.50. *Primi* €6.50, with seafood €9; *secondi* €7-12.50. Cover €1. Open daily 12:15-8:15pm. Reserve ahead. AmEx/MC/V. ❸

CENTRO STORICO

To find authentic Roman food in the *centro storico*, head to V. del Governo Vecchio and its tiny cross streets, which though near impossible to navigate, have an abundance of refreshingly affordable and delicious options. The Campo dei Fiori, with its daily food and clothing market, is also located in this area.

PIAZZA NAVONA

🔲 **Antica Taverna,** Vicolo dell'Avila, 13, off V. del Governo Vecchio. Follow the aroma of garlic to this *taverna* serving Roman specialties like *spaghetti all'amatriciana, tripe alla romana,* and rosemary pork with gravy and potatoes. Great house wine. *Primi* €6-7, *secondi* €7-8. Open daily noon-midnight. Cash only. ❷

Pizzeria Baffetto, V. del Governo Vecchio, 114 (☎06 68 61 617), at the intersection with V. Sora. Once a meeting place for 60s radicals, Bafetto now serves tourists and locals lined up outside its door. Pizza €5-8.50. Open daily 6:30pm-1am. Cash only. ❷

Da Sergio Trattoria alle Grotte, Vicolo delle Grotte, 27 (☎06 68 64 293). Take V. d. Giubbonari and turn right. Enjoy hearty portions of *spaghetti all'amatriciana* (€6) outside on the fresco-decorated patio or inside at heavy wooden tables. Open M-Sa 12:30-3pm and 6:30-11:30pm. Reservations recommended. MC/V. ❷

Trattoria Da Luigi, P. Sforza Cesarini, 24 (☎06 68 65 946), near Chiesa Nuova, 4 blocks down C. V. Emanuele II from Campo dei Fiori. Enjoy inventive cuisine including the delicate *carpaccio di salmone fresco con rughetta* (€8) and simple dishes like *vitello con funghi* (€11). Open Tu-Su noon-3pm and 7pm-midnight. AmEx/MC/V. ❸

PANTHEON

Miscellanea, V. delle Paste, 10a, just around the corner from the Pantheon. Student pub complete with jukebox, Chicago pizzeria-style lamp shades, and vintage Coca-Cola ads on the walls. Locals crowd around for the notoriously cheap lunch. *Antipasti* €3-5. *Panini* €3. Salads €5. Open daily 4pm-9pm. Cash only. ❶

Trattoria dal Cav. Gino, V. Rosini, 4 (☎06 68 73 434), off V. d. Campo Marzio across from P. del Parlamente. Affable owner Gino greets people at the door and announces the house special, *tonnarelli alla ciociala* (€7). *Primi* €5-8, *secondi* €7-12. Open M-Sa 1-2:45pm and 8-10:30pm. Closed Aug. Cash only. ❸

CAMPO DEI FIORI

Ristorante Grappolo d'Oro Zampanò, P. della Cancelleria, 80/83 (☎06 68 97 080), between C. V. Emanuele II and the Campo. This award-winning, upscale *hostaria* serves over 200 types of wine. *Primi* €9.50, *secondi* €13-19. Open M and W-Su noon-2:30pm and 7:30-11pm, Tu 7:30-11pm, Sa 7:30-11:30. AmEx/MC/V. ❹

L'Insalata Ricca, Largo d. Chiavari, 85-6 (☎06 68 80 36 56; www.linsalataricca.it), off C. V. Emanuele II near P. S. Andrea della Valle. Serves 45 types of salad, including honey salad (beef, cheese, walnuts, and drizzled honey; €6.80), as well as parma ham (€8) and *pantesca* (tomatoes, capers, and potatoes; €6.80). *Primi* €6-8, *secondi* €5.20-8.30. Open daily 12:30-3:30pm and 6:45-11:45pm. Reserve ahead. AmEx/MC/V. ❷

Il Pollarola, P. Pollarola, 24-25 (☎06 688 016 54), just behind the Campo dei Fiori. Exquisite renditions of traditional dishes like *spaghetti alla carbonara* (€7). Daily specials €8-13. Cover €1. Open M-Sa noon-3:30pm and 6pm-midnight. AmEx/MC/V. ❹

JEWISH GHETTO

The Jewish Ghetto, about a 10min. walk south of the Campo, serves kosher and traditional Jewish dishes, in addition to traditional Italian specialities. Keep in mind that much of the ghetto is closed for the Sabbath on Saturdays.

▓ Bar Da Benito, V. d. Falegnami, 14 (☎06 68 61 508), easiest to approach from V. di Portico d'Ottavia or V. Arenula. This 40-year-old establishment is still moving fast. Enjoy your food at the bar rimmed with Italian wine bottles or order it for *porta via* (takeout). 2 *primi* prepared daily (€4.50). *Secondi* €5. Open M-Sa 6:30am-7pm. Closed Aug. ❷

Trattoria da Giggetto, V. d. Portico d'Ottavia, 21-22 (☎06 68 61 105). Sit next to the ruins of the Portico d'Ottavia at da Giggetto. No animal parts go to waste here. In the Roman tradition, *fritto di cervello d'abbacchino* (brains with vegetables; €12) are served alongside other delicacies like fried artichokes (€5). *Primi* €7.50-12, *secondi* €8-18. Cover €1.50. Open Tu-Su 12:15-3pm and 7:30-11pm. Closed the last 2 weeks of July. Dinner reservation required. AmEx/MC/V. ❸

Il Portico, V. d. Portico D'Ottavia, 1/D (☎06 68 64 642) This low-key restaurant has an outdoor patio and pizza topped with *prosciutto* and *funghi* (ham and mushrooms; €5.20-8). Salads €4.20-7.30. Open daily 12:30-3:30pm and 7pm-midnight. MC/V. ❷

La Taverna del Ghetto, V. d. Portico d'Ottavia, 8. (☎06 68 80 97 71; www.latavernadel-ghetto.com). This lively kosher option offers homemade pasta and a daily specials with delicacies like *lingua all'ebraica* (veal tongue). *Primi* €10.50, *secondi* €13.50. Open M-Th and Sa-Su noon-3pm and 6:30-11pm, F noon-3pm. Cover €1.50. AmEx/MC/V. ❹

ROME AND LAZIO

PIAZZA DI SPAGNA

Try heading off the main drags in the area around P. di Spagna and the Trevi Fountain to avoid busy and heavily touristed restaurants in more central locations.

⊠ **Trattoria da Settimio all'Arancio,** V. dell'Arancio, 50-52 (☎06 68 76 119). Take V. dei Condotti from P. di Spagna; take 1st right after V. del Corso, then 1st left. It's the 2nd restaurant on the left (not the pizzeria). Portions are generous, and dishes decadent. Try the handmade *ravioli all'arancio,* a delicacy named after both the restaurant and the street, with a very orangey essence. *Primi* from €7.50, *secondi* from €8.50. Open M-Sa 12:30-3pm and 7:30-11:30pm. Reservations recommended. AmEx/MC/V. ❹

Centro Macrobiotico Italiano Naturist Club, V. della Vite, 14, 4th fl. (☎06 67 92 509). Heading toward P. del Popolo on V. del Corso, make a right on V. della Vite. This veggie haven has taken traditional Roman cuisine to a new level, serving only organic vegan-vegetarian food. Lunch *menù* €14, dinner *menù* €20-25. "Natural snacks" €8-10. Open M-Sa 12:30-3pm and 7:30-11pm. Reservation required for dinner. Cash only. ❹

Il Brillo Parlante, V. Fontanella, 12 (☎06 32 43 334; www.ilbrilloparlante.com). Take V. del Corso away from P. del Popolo and turn left on V. Fontanella. The wood-burning pizza oven (€7-10), handmade pasta, and innovative small plates, including sharp pecorino cheese with honey and walnuts (€8.50), set this place apart. In the summer, patrons flood the shady outdoor tables. Open M 5pm-1am, Tu-Su 12:30-3:30pm for lunch, 3:30-5pm pizza only, 5-7:30pm bar only, and 7:30pm-1am for dinner. MC/V. ❷

BORGO AND PRATI (NEAR VATICAN CITY)

For food a cut above that of the touristy bars and pizzerias, venture down V. Cola di Rienzo towards P. Cavour and explore the residential side streets.

Franchi, V. Cola di Rienzo, 204 (☎06 68 74 651; www.franchi.it). Benedetto Franchi ("Frankie") has been providing the citizens of Prati with luxurious picnic supplies for nearly 50 years. Eat at the counter or takeout. Especially delicious are the *fritti misti* (deep-fried zucchini flowers, artichoke hearts, and zucchini) and the *torta rustica* (with ham, spinach, cheese, and egg). 2 people can stuff themselves for under €15 total. Delicacies include various croquettes (€1.20), and marinated munchies like anchovies, peppers, olives, and salmon (€5.90). Cheaper and better quality than most Vatican area snack bars. Open M-Sa 8:15am-9pm. AmEx/MC/V. ❷

Cacio e Pepe, V. Giuseppe Avezzana, 11 (☎06 32 17 268). From P. Mazzini, turn right on V. Settembrini, and at P. dei Martiri di Belfiore before taking a left on V. G. Avezzana (about a 20min. walk from P. di Risorgimento). Worth the walk from the Vatican area—in the summer, outdoor tables bubble with locals. Its specialty is the perfect *al dente* pasta piled high with olive oil, grated cheese, and fresh ground pepper. Full lunch €5-10. Open M-F 12:30-3pm and 7pm-12:30am, Sa 12:30-3pm. Cash only. ❷

"Lo Spuntino" da Guido e Patrizia, Borgo Pio, 13 (☎06 68 75 491), near Castel Sant'Angelo. Casual atmosphere and homey decor make Lo Spuntino popular with lunching locals, where Guido holds court behind a well-stocked *tavola calda.* Full meal (*primo, secondo,* and wine) runs less than €8. Open M-Sa 8am-8pm. Cash only. ❷

TRASTEVERE

Nowhere is more Roman than Trastevere. Enough said.

⊠ **Pizzeria San Callisto,** P. S. Callisto, 9/A (☎06 58 18 256), off P. S. Maria. Simply the best pizza in Rome. Gorgeous thin-crust pizzas so large they hang off the plates (€4.20-7.80). Open Tu-Su 7pm-midnight. AmEx/MC/V. ❷

Ristorante a Casa di Alfredo, V. Roma Libera, 5-7 (☎06 58 82 968). Off P. S. Cosimato. Crowds storm this family-style restaurant for the affordable Roman cuisine and

pleasant outdoor seating. Chef's 3-course tasting menu €18. *Antipasti* €5-8. *Primi* €5-8, *secondi* €7-9. Open daily noon-3pm and 7:30-11:30pm. AmEx/MC/V. ❷

Augusto, P. de' Renzi, 15 (☎06 58 03 798), before P. S. Maria in Trastevere, when coming from the river. Neighborhood Augusto serves daily pasta specials (around €5) with speedy service. Open M-F 12:30-3pm and 8-11pm, Sa 12:30-3pm. Closed in Aug. ❶

TERMINI AND ENVIRONS

A well-stocked **CONAD** supermarket is on the lower floor of Termini station, down the escalator just inside the V. Marsala entrance. (Open daily 8am-midnight.) There is also an excellent **alimentari-salumeria** at V. Marsala, 68 that sells *panini* for under €2. A couple blocks away the inexpensive food in San Lorenzo attracts budget-conscious students with discriminating palates.

▓ **Arancia Blu,** V. d. Latini, 65 (☎06 44 54 105), off V. Tiburtina. This elegant and popular vegetarian restaurant greets you with 3 glasses of wine (white, red, and champagne) at your seat and an affordable menu in spite of its adventurous options. Try the unique warm pesto salad and fried ravioli stuffed with eggplant and smoked *caciocavallo* cheese (€8.50). Extensive wine list €12-130 per bottle and a chocolate tasting *menù* €13. Menus in English, French, and Italian. Open daily 8:30pm-midnight. MC/V. ❸

▓ **Africa,** V. Gaeta, 26-28 (☎06 49 41 077), near P. Indipendenza. Decked out in yellow and black, Africa continues its 20-year tradition of serving excellent Ethiopian food. The meat-filled *sambusas* (€3) are a flavorful starter; both the *zighini beghi* (roasted lamb in a spicy sauce; €7) and the *misto vegetariano* (mixed veggie dishes; €7) make fantastic entrees. Cover €1. Open Tu-Su 8am-1:30am. MC/V. ❷

Hostaria da Bruno, V. Varese, 29 (☎06 49 04 03). From V. Marsala, take V. Milazzo and turn right on V. Varese. Italians working in the Termini area come here to indulge their need for relaxation. Owner Bruno makes crepes (€3.50) so good even the Pope tried them. Open M-Sa noon-3:15pm and 7-10:15pm. AmEx/MC/V. ❷

TESTACCIO

This residential neighborhood is the seat of many excellent restaurants serving traditional meat-heavy fare.

▓ **Il Cantinone,** P. Testaccio, 31/32 (☎06 57 46 253). M: B-Piramide. Go up V. Marmorata and turn left on V. G. B. Bodoni; P. Testaccio is just past V. Luca della Robbia. A down-to-earth restaurant, with massive portions of pasta (*pappardelle* with boar sauce €7.50), hearty meat-and-gravy dishes (most around €9), and a terrific house white, Il Cantinone gets the job done well. Long tables and a large dining room make this place great for groups. Open M and W-Su noon-3pm and 7pm-midnight. AmEx/MC/V. ❸

Il Volpetti Più, V. Alessandro Volta, 8 (☎06 57 44 306). Turn left on V. A. Volta off V. Marmorata. This *tavola calda* serves lunch in large portions at self-service tables—pick out your food cafeteria-style and battle the lunching locals for a seat. Fresh salads, pasta salads, pizza, and daily specials from €4; menu rotates weekly and seasonally. Open M-Sa 10am-10pm; call ahead for seating between 3:30 and 6pm. Cash only. ❶

DESSERT

While *gelato* is everywhere in Rome, good *gelato* is not. Sample the city's endless selection or head to these *Let's Go* favorites. And lest you think that *gelato* is the only sweet snack in Rome, numerous bakeries sell cookies, small cakes, pastries, and other sumptuous pastries (all priced by the *etto*, or 100g).

▓ **Pasticceria Ebraico Boccione,** Jewish Ghetto, V. del Portico d'Ottavia, 1 (☎06 68 78 637), on the corner of P. Costaguti under the white awning. This tiny family-run bakery makes only about 8 items including delicious Shabbat challah that is sweet and fruit-filled and sugar-dusted, custard-filled *ciambelle* (doughnuts; €0.80). Open M-F and Su. Closes early on F, in summer closed Su 2-4pm.

Il Gelatone, Ancient City, V. dei Serpente, 28 (☎06 48 20 187). From V. dei Fori Impe-riali take a left on V. Cavour, and left on V. dei Serpente. As you approach this neon-colored *gelateria*, you'll notice that everyone has a cone. One taste, and you'll know why—the *gelato* is creamy and smooth. Try the specialty *Gelatone*, a blend of chocolate and vanilla with chocolate chips, or the cool and refreshing limoncello or grapefruit. Cones €1.50-3, 3-flavor cone-bowls €4. Open daily 11am-1am daily.

Gelato di San Crispino, V. della Panetteria, 42 (☎06 67 93 924; www.ilgelatodisancris-pino.com for other locations). 2nd left off of V. del Lavatore, coming from the Trevi foun-tain. Renowned as the best *gelato* in Rome, a scoop from San Crispino's is worth throwing a coin into the Trevi Fountain. Their specialty honey flavor is heavenly, but *affogato* (drowned) with one of their gourmet liquors, it can be just a little devilish, too. Cups €1.90-7.00. Open M, W-Th, Su noon-12:30am, F-Sa noon-1:30am.

Pellachia, Vatican, V. Cola di Rienzo, 103 (☎06 32 10 807 or 06 32 10 446). Pellachia serves dozens of simple, fresh flavors (try the crisp lime blended with pieces of tart) with a finesse that has locals coming in droves. In nice weather, take your *gelato a tavola* (€4 per cup) in a silver bowl. Cones €1.30-2.90. Open Tu-Su 6am-2am. AmEx/MC/V.

Biscottificio Artigiano Innocenti, Trastevere, V. della Luce, 21 (☎06 57 03 926), off Via dei Salumi. This shop sells divine cookies and biscuits sold from a counter in its stockroom, and has been featured in countless international culinary magazines. Cook-ies are sold only in bulk, so stock up on decadent hazelnut, chocolate, and jam cookies (about €5 for a medium sized bag). Your morning espresso will never be the same.

Da Quinto Gelateria, V. d. Tor Millina, 15 (☎06 68 65 657), off P. Navona on the long side, opposite the church. Walls are plastered with pictures of the hot-pink-aproned owner posing with some of his most famous clientele. Light, fluffy *gelato* with especially refreshing fruit flavors and fresh fruit smoothies *(frulatti)* blended to order. Ice cream *affogato* (drenched in whiskey, brandy, or rum) €3.50. *Gelato* €1.50-3. Open M-F and Su 11am-3am, Sa 11am-5am; in winter sporadic W closings.

Giolitti, V. degli Uffici del Vicario, 40 (☎06 69 91 243; www.giolitti.it). From the Pan-theon, follow V. d. Pantheon, then take V. della Maddalena to its end; turn right on V. degli Uffici del Vicario. Always crowded, this cafe serves unique flavors of *gelato* like champagne, pink grapefruit, Grand Marnier, and milk and honey (€2 small, €2.60 medium) in a plush red and marble dining room. Buy a ticket at the cash register for your order before stepping up to the counter. Open daily 7am-1am. AmEx/MC/V.

Della Palma, V. della Maddalena, 20 (☎06 68 80 67 52), steps from the Pantheon, with another location near the Trevi Fountain. With over 100 flavors of *gelato*, including fig and ricotta, and spicy dark chocolate, Della Palma is most famous for its mousse (in flavors like honey almond and tiramisu). Also serves frozen yogurt with fruit and nut top-pings. Pay at the register before ordering at the counter with the receipt. *Gelato* from single scoops to elaborate bowls €1.80-10. Open daily 8am-2am. V for over €7.

Antico Forno, V. della Scrofa, 32, exit at the north end of P. Navona and go straight. Turn right on V. del Orso, which crosses V. della Scrofa. Peer into the production room as this bakery makes adorable cookies (€1.80-2.80 per *etto*), *tranci di mele* (apple tarts; €1.40), and for your afternoon picnic on the P. Navona, flavored rolls (hazelnut or olive; €0.45 per *etto*) or *focaccia* crackers (€1.50 per *etto*).

The Old Bridge, Vatican, V. dei Bastioni di Michelangelo, 5 (☎06 39 72 30 26). Off P. del Risorgimento, across the street from the bend in Vatican museum's outside wall. Have someone hold your place in the Vatican line while you get giant *gelati* for the wait. 20 homemade flavors (€1.30-3 per cup or cone). Open M-Sa 8am-2am, Su 3pm-2am.

COFFEE

Coffee is taken either standing up at the bar or, for a significantly higher price, sitting down at a table. In Rome, cafes are crammed with business people taking their lunch and afternoon coffees. In the summer, most cafes offer a delicious *granita di caffè con panna* (frozen coffee with fresh whipped cream).

■ **The Lion Bookshop and Café,** V. dei Greci, 33/36 (☎06 32 65 40 07; www.thelion-bookshop.com), near P. di Spagna. Turn right on V. dei Greci from V. del Corso. This English-language bookstore has a cafe where you can thumb through cookbooks, while you sip your espresso (€1.50-2.50) and listen to rehearsal music waft in from the conservatory across the street. Open M 3:30-7:30pm, Tu-Su 10am-7:30pm. AmEx/MC/V.

■ **Bar Giulia (a.k.a. Cafe Peru),** V. Giulia, 84 (☎06 68 61 310), near P. V. Emanuele II. Bar Giulia serves what may be the cheapest (and most delicious) coffee in Rome (€0.60, at table €0.70) and adds your favorite liqueur at no charge. You may have to crowd surf to get your cup of fresh-squeezed orange juice. Open M-Sa 5am-9:30pm.

Caffè Tazza d'Oro, V. d. Orfani, 84-86 (☎06 67 92 768). Facing away from the Pantheon's *portico*, the sign is on the right. This famous coffee shop makes the highest quality coffee in Rome, and has an extensive collection of teas. Try the signature *regina arabica* or the summer favorite, *granita di caffè* with fresh whipped cream (€1.50). Espresso €0.65; cappuccino €0.80. Internet €1 per 15min. Open M-Sa 7am-8pm.

Sant'Eustachio Il Caffè, P. S. Eustachio, 82 (☎06 68 80 20 48). Turn right on V. Palombella behind the Pantheon. Rome's "coffee empire," this cafe was once frequented by Stendhal. Though the coffee is excellent, the average struggling artist may not be able to afford the habit. *Gran caffè speciale* €2.10, at table €3.60. Open M-Th 8:30am-1am, F 8:30am-1:30am, Sa 8:30am-2am.

Caffè della Pace, V. della Pace, 3-7 (☎06 68 61 216), off P. Navona. This laidback spot looks more like an antique gallery than a cafe. But on warm evenings the young and beautiful drink their *prosecco* (€3), espresso (€2), or *apertivi* (€6) at a table outside. Open daily 9am-2am; closed M mornings.

L'Impiccione Viaggiatore, Ancient City, V. della Madonna Dei Monti, 28 (☎06 67 86 188; www.limpiccioneviaggiatore.com). Go through the park at the beginning of V. Cavour, off V. dei Fori Imperiali. This neighborhood travel store has a full library of guides in English, French, German, Italian, and Spanish for patrons to peruse while sipping espresso (€.70-€1.50) or desserts (*tiramisu;* €5). The owners will even help with travel planning. Free Internet for customers. Open daily 8:30am-midnight.

ENOTECHE (WINE BARS)

Wine bars range from laidback and local to chic and international. No matter what the scene, *enoteche* usually serve a variety of small dishes and plates, like cheese selections, smoked meats and *antipasti*, and salads. Romans like to eat dinner around 9pm, so they either go to *enoteche* beforehand for a small bite to eat, or stay for the entire evening, sipping and nibbling the night away.

■ **Enoteca Trastevere,** Trastevere, V. della Lungaretta, 86 (☎06 58 85 659). A block off P. S. Maria. This casual *enoteca* attracts couples and jovial groups. Staff helps you choose from the small but high caliber wine list. Arrive after 10pm, as things pick up around midnight. Wine €3.50-4 per glass. Open M-Sa 6pm-2:30am, Su 6pm-1am.

Cul de Sac, P. Pasquino, 73 (☎06 68 80 10 94), off P. Navona. One of Rome's first wine bars, Cul de Sac offers an extensive wine list (from €2 per glass), outdoor tables, and divine dishes. Specialty homemade pâtés (including boar and chocolate; €5.70) are exquisite, as is the *escargot alla bourguigonne* (€5.10). Desserts €4. Cheeses and preserved meats €5.20-6.50. Open daily noon-4pm and 6pm-12:30am. MC/V.

Trimani Wine Bar, V. Cernaia 37/B (☎06 44 69 630), near Termini, perpendicular to V. Volturno. Their shop is around the corner at V. Goito, 20. Probably the city's most influential wine bar and indisputably Rome's oldest. Excellent food includes salads (veggies and smoked cod; €8.50) and filling quiches (try the chicken, pepperoni, and basil; €7.50). Wines from €2.20-6.50 a glass. Happy hour 11:30am-2:30pm and 6-7pm. Open M-Sa 11:30am-3pm and 6-10:30pm. AmEx/MC/V.

Enoteca Cavour 313, Ancient City, V. Cavour, 313 (☎06 67 85 496). A short walk from M: B-Cavour. Sip wine from crystal glasses in this French bistro-style wine bar. Meats and cheeses (€7-9 for a mixed plate) are listed by region or type, but the real draw is the massive Italian wine list (€3-7 per glass; €12.50-300 per bottle). Fresh salads (€3-7) and rich desserts, like *cannolo Siciliano* (cannoli; €4) also available. Open M-Sa 12:30-2:30pm and 7:30pm-1am. Closed Aug. AmEx/MC/V.

Vini e Buffet, V. Torretta, 60. (☎06 68 71 445), near P. di Spagna. From V. del Corso, turn on P. S. Lorenzo in Lucina. Turn left on V. Campo Marzio and right on V. Torretta. A favorite spot among chic Romans with a penchant for regional wines. Pâtés, *crostini*, and *scarmorze* (smoked mozzarella) €6.50-8.50. Crepes around €7. Open M-Sa 12:30-3pm and 7-11pm. Reservations recommended, but not necessary. Cash only.

⊙ SIGHTS

 COUNT THE COLLI. Rome is famous for being the city of 7 hills. Although the modern metropolis probably spans twice that number of mounts, Ancient Rome was allegedly built on the following 7: Aventine, Caelian, Capitoline, Esquiline, Palatine, Quirinal, and Viminal.

From ancient temples and Baroque fountains to contemporary museums, Rome is a city bursting with masterpieces from every era of Western civilization. In Rome you will undoubtedly stumble upon treasures around every corner, whether in the middle of a busy thoroughfare or on the wall of a tiny side street—just try not to let the ubiquitous graffiti ruin the glorious sights. The major attractions are least crowded before 10am. Remember to dress modestly when visiting churches or the Vatican; shoulders and knees should be covered—women might find it useful to bring a scarf or light cardigan in the hot summer months.

ANCIENT CITY

PALATINE HILL

South of the Roman Forum. Purchase tickets and the Archeologica Card at the Biglietteria Palatino, at the end of V. Nova past the Arch of Titus, or 100m down V. di S. Gregorio from the Colosseum. Open daily Mar.-Aug. 9am-7:30pm; Sept. 9am-7pm; Oct. 9am-6:30pm; Nov. to mid-Feb. 9am-4:30pm; mid-Feb. to Mar. 9am-5pm. English tour at noon. Combined ticket to the Palatine Hill and the Colosseum €10, EU citizens ages 18-24 €6, EU citizens under 18 or over 65 free. Tour €3.50, with Archeologica Card €2.50.

ROMA ARCHEOLOGICA. Travelers planning to visit many Roman monuments should consider investing €22 in an Archeologica Card, which is valid for 7 days. The pass grants entrance to the Colosseum, Palatine Hill, Baths of Caracalla, Via dei Quintulli, Calici Metela, Baths of Diocletian, Cripta Balbi, Palazzo Altempts, and Palazzo Massimo. For more info on these sights contact Sprotendza Archeologica di Roma (☎06 39 96 77 00).

The ▣**Palatine Hill,** a plateau between the Tiber River and the Roman Forum, was home to the she-wolf that suckled Romulus and Remus. It was here that Romulus built the first walls of the city. During the Republic, the Palatine was the most fashionable residential quarter, where aristocrats and statesmen, including Cicero and Marc Antony, built their homes. Augustus lived here in a modest house, but later emperors capitalized on the hill's prestige and built gargantuan quarters. By the end of the first century AD, the imperial residence covered the entire hill, whose Latin name, Palatium, became synonymous with the palace.

The best way to approach the Palatine is from the northeast via the stairs near the **Arch of Titus** in the Forum. The path ascends to the **Farnese Gardens Orti Farnesiani,** the world's oldest botanical gardens dating back to 1625. Views of the Roman Forum make the gardens perfect for a picnic, and signs marked "Affacciata sul Foro" point to a lookout on the reflecting pools at the House of Vestal Virgins.

On the southwest side of the hill directly below the Farnese Gardens lie the remains of an ancient village featuring the **Casa di Romulo,** alleged home of Romulus, and the **Temple of Cybele.** The remains of this area can be dated to roughly the same time as those found in the Forum's Archaic necropolis, which supports the theory that Rome was founded in the 9th century BC. To the left of Casa di Romolo is the **Casa di Livia,** where Augustus's wife Livia resided. The house used to connect to the **Casa di Augusto** (not to be confused with Domus Augustana) next door. Around the corner to the left, stretching along the Farnese Gardens is the **Cryptoporticus,** a tunnel which connected Tiberius's palace with nearby buildings and was used by slaves and couriers as a secret passage.

To the left of the Casa di Livia at the center of the hill is the sprawling **Domus Flavia,** site of a gigantic octagonal fountain that occupied almost the entire courtyard. To its left stands the solemn **Domus Augustana,** the emperor's private space. Visitors are only allowed to the upper level, from which they can make out the shape of two courtyards down below. The palace's east wing contains the curious **Stadium Palatinum,** or hippodrome, a sunken oval space once surrounded by a colonnade but now decorated with fragments of porticoes, statues, and fountains.

The **Museo Palatino,** between the Domus Flavia and the Domus Augustana, displays archaeological artifacts from the early Archaic period on the lower level, including writing that possibly describes Remus's attempt to enter the city walls after Romulus had set up its borders. Wall text in English and Italian provides explanations. The upper floor of the Museo displays artifacts from later

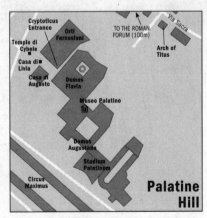

Palatine Hill

Roman periods, including busts of famous people who frequented the Palatine's homes, and remains from the temple to Apollo that once stood on Palatine Hill.

COLOSSEUM

☎ *06 70 05 469. M: B-Colosseo. Same hours as Palatine Hill. Last admission 1hr. before closing. Combined ticket with Palatine Hill €10, EU citizens 18-24 €6, EU citizens under 18 or over 65 free. Tours with archaeologist €3.50. Audioguide in English and French €4.*

 CUT THE LINE. To avoid waiting up to 20min. in line for tickets to the Colosseum, purchase your ticket from the *biglietteria* at the base of the Palatine Hill, to the left of the Arch of Titus, when facing the Roman Forum.

The Colosseum stands as an enduring symbol of Rome as the Eternal City—a hollowed-out ghost of travertine marble that once held as many as 50,000 crazed spectators, and now dwarfs every other ruin in Rome. Within 100 days of its AD 80 opening, some 5000 wild beasts perished in the bloody arena, and the slaughter went on for three more centuries. The wooden floor underneath the sand once covered a labyrinth of brick cells, ramps, and elevators used to transport animals from cages to arena level; these underground rooms are now open to the public. Next to the Colosseum, on the corner with V. di San Gregorio, stands the **Arco di Costantino,** one of the best preserved Imperial monuments in the area. The arch commemorates Constantine's victory at the Battle of the Milvian Bridge in AD 312, using fragments from monuments to Trajan, Hadrian, and Marcus Aurelius.

ROMAN FORUM

Main entrance: V. dei Fori Imperiali, at Largo C. Ricci, halfway between P. Venezia and the Colosseum. Other entrances are opposite the Colosseum at the start of V. Sacra and at the Clivus Capitolinus, near P. del Campidoglio. M: B-Colosseo, or bus to P. Venezia. Access to the Forum is unpredictable, as areas are sometimes fenced off for excavation or restoration. Open daily in summer 9am-7:15pm, last entry 6:30pm; in winter 9am-4:15pm, last entry 3:30pm. Free. Guided tour in English with archaeologist 11am

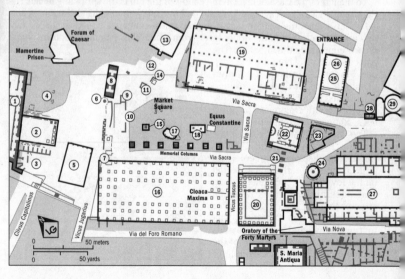

(€3.50). Audioguide in English, French, German €4; inquire at Biglietteria Palatino at the end of V. Nova past the Arch of Titus.

This area was originally a marshland prone to flooding, so Rome's Iron Age inhabitants (1000-900 BC) avoided it in favor of the Palatine Hill, descending only to bury their dead. In the 8th and 7th centuries BC, Etruscans and Greeks used the Forum as a marketplace. The Romans founded a thatched-hut shanty-town here in 753 BC, when Romulus and Sabine leader Titus Tatius joined forces to end the war triggered by the infamous rape of the Sabine women. Today the Forum bears witness to centuries of civic building.

From the Arch of Constantine by the Colosseum, take **Via Sacra** (Sacred Way), the oldest street in Rome, to the **Arch of Titus.** On the left as you approach the arch lie the **Thermae** (Baths) and the **Temple of Jupiter Stator.** On your right is a series of 10 columns, all that remain of the **Temple of Venus and Rome.** Built in AD 81 by Domitian, the Arch of Titus stands in the area of the Forum called the **Velia** and celebrates the sack of Jerusalem by his brother Titus, depicted in detail on the inside of the arch. Turn right to face the Baroque facade of the **Church of Santa Francesca Romana** (or **Santa Maria Nova**) built over Hadrian's Temple to Venus and Rome, that hides the entrance to the **Antiquarium Forense,** a museum displaying necropolis urns and skeletons. (Free.) Turn left, and as you pass into the **Upper Forum,** the giant ruins on your right is the **Basilica of Maxentius and Constantine.** Emperor Maxentius began construction in AD 308, but Constantine deposed him and completed the project himself. Farther down you pass the **Temple of Romulus** on your right, named for the son of Maxentius (not the legendary founder of Rome). The original bronze doors have a 4th-century working lock.

Just after the Temple of Romulus on the right is the **Archaic Necropolis,** a flat platform where Iron Age graves confirm Rome's legendary founding in 753 BC. Farther down on your right is the **Temple of Antoninus and Faustina,** whose columns, and rigid lattice ceiling kept it well preserved. In the 7th and 8th centuries, after numerous unsuccessful attempts to tear it down, the **Church of San Lorenzo in Miranda** was built in its interior. Continuing down the right fork of V. Sacra, on the

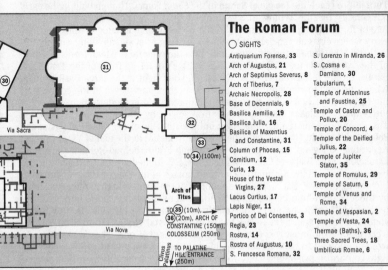

The Roman Forum

○ SIGHTS

Antiquarium Forense, **33**
Arch of Augustus, **21**
Arch of Septimius Severus, **8**
Arch of Tiberius, **7**
Archaic Necropolis, **28**
Base of Decennials, **9**
Basilica Aemilia, **19**
Basilica Julia, **16**
Basilica of Maxentius
   and Constantine, **31**
Column of Phocas, **15**
Comitium, **12**
Curia, **13**
House of the Vestal
   Virgins, **27**
Lacus Curtius, **17**
Lapis Niger, **11**
Portico of Dei Consentes, **3**
Regia, **23**
Rostra, **14**
Rostra of Augustus, **10**
S. Francesca Romana, **32**

S. Lorenzo in Miranda, **26**
S. Cosma e
   Damiano, **30**
Tabularium, **1**
Temple of Antoninus
   and Faustina, **25**
Temple of Castor and
   Pollux, **20**
Temple of Concord, **4**
Temple of the Deified
   Julius, **22**
Temple of Jupiter
   Stator, **35**
Temple of Romulus, **29**
Temple of Saturn, **5**
Temple of Venus and
   Rome, **34**
Temple of Vespasian, **2**
Temple of Vesta, **24**
Thermae (Baths), **36**
Three Sacred Trees, **18**
Umbilicus Romae, **6**

Via Sacra

Arch of Titus

Via Nova

TO ④ (100m)

TO ㉟ (10m),
㊱ (20m), ARCH OF
CONSTANTINE (150m),
COLOSSEUM (250m)

TO PALATINE
HILL ENTRANCE
(250m)

Clivus Palatinus

ROME AND LAZIO

left lie the remains of the **Regia,** which once served as the office of the Pontifex Maximus, Rome's high priest and the titular ancestor of the Pope. Next on the left is the **Temple of the Deified Julius;** every year, on Julius Caesar's alleged birthday (July 13) people bring flowers to the shrine built by Augustus in 29 BC to honor the great leader and proclaim himself the inheritor of Julius's divine spirit.

Back on V. Sacra, the **Basilica Aemilia** on is the right as you enter the area called the **Civic Forum.** Built in 179 BC, the Basilica housed the guild of the *argentarii* (money changers). It was rebuilt several times after fires, until one started by Alaric and his merry band of Goths in AD 410 left it in its current state; melted coins are now shiny studs in the pavement. On your left is the central section of the forum, **Market Square.** The **Column of Phocas** in the square was erected in AD 608 for the visiting Byzantine emperor, Phocas, and is the newest addition to the Forum. The **Lacus Curtius** to its left is marked by concentric marble semicircles in the ground and a small frieze of a man on horseback; it commemorates the heroism of the legendary Roman warrior Marcus Curtius, who threw himself in a deep chasm in 362 BC to save the city from collapse. In the middle of the square **Three Sacred Trees of Rome**—olive, fig, and grape—were planted by the Italian state. Off V. Sacra to the right is one of the oldest buildings in the Forum, the **Curia** (Senate House). Listen to the echo inside and note the fresco floor. It was in the square outside the Curia that a group of senators murdered Julius Caesar in 44 BC.

The area in front of the Curia holds several noteworthy ruins. The **Rostra,** now a single right angle of stone in the ground, was once a speaker's platform erected by Julius Caesar just before his death. The **Comitium,** now a marble semicircle in the ground, was the assembly place where citizens voted, representatives gathered for public discussion, and where Rome's first laws, the **Twelve Tables,** were first inscribed on bronze tablets. The **Lapis Niger** (black stone) is the volcanic rock that marks the location of the underground 6th-century BC altar to Vulcan, where the oldest known Latin inscription in Rome warns against defiling the shrine.

Back on Via Sacra, the **Arch of Septimius Severus** is straight ahead, built in AD 203 to celebrate Septimus's victories in the Middle East. Next to it stands the **Umbilicus Romae,** a circular solid brick structure, marking the mythological center of Rome. Turn left to reach the **Temple of Saturn** in the **Lower Forum.** Though built in the early 5th century BC, the Temple of Saturn has its mythological origins in the Golden Age of Rome. The temple became the site of Saturnalia, a raucous Roman winter party where class and social distinctions were forgotten and anything was permitted. The **Tabularium** is the structure built into the rock face, which forms the base of the **Campidoglio** (see **Capitoline Hill,** p. 122). Turn left in front of the Temple of Saturn on the other branch of V. Sacra. To your right is the large **Basilica Julia,** where the well-preserved floor plan supports the intact bases of the columns of the former courthouse. To appreciate the luxury that is modern plumbing, view the remains of **Cloaca Maxima,** Rome's first sewer, by taking a right on the Vicus Tuscus and looking right. Then check out the remains of the **Temple of Castor and Pollux,** on the right (when facing the Basilica Aemelia) at the end of Vicus Tuscus. According to legend, the twin gods Castor and Pollux helped Romans defeat the Etruscans at the Battle of Lake Regillus in 499 BC. Immediately after the battle, the twins appeared in the Forum to water their horses at the nearby Basin of Juturna.

Once again on V. Sacra, the column base of the former **Arch of Augustus,** built by the less-than-humble Augustus to honor himself, stands in the middle of the path. Uphill from the arch, the **Temple of Vesta**, once circular, is now just a vaguely curved wall next to the **House of the Vestal Virgins.** The Vestal Virgins were among the most respected people in Ancient Rome. They were the only women allowed to walk unaccompanied in the Forum and also possessed the right to pardon prisoners. They were responsible for the city's eternal, sacred fire, keeping it lit for over 1000 years. A small statue of Minerva that Aeneas took from Troy occupies the Palladium, a secret room accessible only to the Virgins. This esteem had its price; a virgin who strayed from celibacy was buried alive with a loaf of bread and a candle—allowing her to survive just long enough to contemplate her sins.

FORI IMPERIALI

Reserve ahead for a guided archaeological tour ☎06 67 97 786. 1½hr. tours in English W, and Sa-Su; €7. Markets of Trajan ☎06 67 90 048. Enter at V. IV Novembre, 94, up the steps in V. Magnanapoli, to the right of the 2 churches behind Trajan's column. Open Tu-Su Apr.-Oct. 9am-6:45pm; Nov.-Mar. 9am-4:30pm. €6.20, ISIC cardholders €3.10.

The sprawling Imperial Forums lie on along V. dei Fori Imperiali, a boulevard Mussolini paved to connect the old empire to his new one in P. Venezia, destroying a third of the ruins in the process. The temples, basilicas, and public squares that make up the Imperial Forums were constructed between the first century BC and 2nd century AD in response to increasing congestion in the old Forum. Much of the area is currently being excavated and is closed to the public, but visitors can peer over the railing of V. dei Fori Imperiali and side street V. Alessandrina or take a ▧**guided archaeological tour** to get closer to the ruins.

Built between AD 107 and 113, the **Forum of Trajan** celebrated Trajan's victorious Dacian (present-day Romania) campaign. The complex included a colossal equestrian statue of Trajan and a triumphal arch. At one end stands **Trajan's Column,** an extraordinary specimen of Roman relief-sculpture depicting 2500 legionnaires. In 1588 Pope Sextus V replaced Trajan's statue with St. Peter's. Nearby, the three-floor semicircular **Market of Trajan** is essentially Rome's first shopping mall, featuring an impressive—albeit crumbling—display of sculpture. A bit farther down V. Alessandrina stands the gray tufa wall of the **Forum of Augustus,** which commemorates Augustus's victory over Caesar's murderers at the Battle of Philippi in 42 BC. The nearby **Forum Transitorium** (also called the **Forum of Nerva**) was a narrow, rectangular space connecting the Forum of Augustus with the Republican Forum. Emperor Nerva dedicated the temple in 97 BC to the goddess Minerva. In the shade of the Vittorio Emanuele II monument, the paltry remains of the **Forum of Caesar** hold the ruins of Julius Caesar's **Temple to Venus Genetrix** (Mother Venus, to whom he claimed relation). In **Vespatian's Forum,** the mosaic-filled **Church of Santi Cosma e Damiani** is across V. Cavour, near the Roman Forum.

OTHER SIGHTS

DOMUS AUREA. This park on the Oppian Hill houses a portion of Nero's "Golden House," which covered a substantial chunk of Ancient Rome. An enclosed lake used to be at the base of the hill, and the hill itself was a private garden. The Forum was reduced to a vestibule of the palace; Nero crowned it with a colossal statue of himself as the sun. He also pillaged all of Greece to find works of art worthy of his abode, including the famous *Laocoön* now held in the Vatican's collections. Apparently, decadence didn't buy happiness: Nero committed suicide five years after building his hedonistic pad. Out of civic-minded jealousy, the ensuing Flavian dynasty tore down his house and built public monuments, including the Flavian Baths on the Caelian Hill and the Colosseum over the drained lake. *(On the Colle Oppio, or Oppian Hill. From the Colosseum, walk through the gates up V. della Domus Aurea and make 1st left. Info ☎06 39 96 77 00; M-Sa 9am-1:30pm and 2:30-5pm. Domus Aurea open M and W-Su 9am-6:40pm. Groups of 30 admitted every 40min. Admission €5, EU citizens 18-24 €2.50, EU citizens under 18 or over 65 free. Reservations recommended; €1.50. Tour in Italian and English with archaeologist €3.50. Audioguide €2. Audio and video guide €4.)*

CHURCH OF SAN PIETRO IN VINCOLI. This 4th-century church is named for the sacred *vincoli* (chains) that bound St. Peter in prison. The two chains were sepa-

ROME AND LAZIO

rated for more than a century in Rome and Constantinople, brought back together in the 5th century, and now lie beneath the altar. Michelangelo's statue of ■Moses is tucked unobtrusively in a corner. The two horns on his head are actually supposed to be beams of light. *(M: B-Cavour. Walk along V. Cavour toward the Forum and take the stairs on left to P. S. Pietro in Vincoli. Open daily 7am-12:30pm and 3:30-6pm. Modest dress required.)*

CIRCUS MAXIMUS AND BATHS OF CARACALLA. Today's Circus Maximus is only a grassy shadow of its former glory as Rome's largest stadium. After its construction in 600 BC, the circus held more than 300,000 Romans who came to watch chariots careen around the track. The mosaic-coated Baths of Caracalla, about a 10min. walk from the Circus Maximus down V. dei Terme di Caracalla, are the largest and best-preserved in Rome. *(☎06 57 45 748. M: Circo Massimo, bus 118, or walk down V. di San Gregorio from the Colosseum. Circus open 24hr. Baths open Apr.-Oct. M 9am-1pm, Tu-Su 9am-7:15pm, last entry 7:15pm; Nov.-Mar. M 9am-2pm, Tu-Su 9am-3:30pm. Admission €6, EU residents 18-24 €3, EU residents under 18 and over 65 free. Audioguide €4.)*

■**CAPITOLINE HILL.** Home to the original "capital," the Monte Capitolino still houses the city's government, topped by Michelangelo's spacious **Piazza di Campidoglio.** *(To get to the Campidoglio, take bus to P. Venezia, face the Vittorio Emanuele II monument, and walk around to the right to P. d'Aracoeli. Take the stairs up the hill.)* Framing the *piazza* are the twin Palazzo dei Conservatori and Palazzo Nuovo, home of the **Capitoline Museums** (p. 135). From the Palazzo Nuovo, stairs lead up to the rear entrance of the 7th-century **Chiesa di Santa Maria in Aracoeli.** Its stunning **Cappella Bufalini** is home to the *Santo Bambino*, a cherubic statue that receives letters from sick children. *(Santa Maria open daily 9am-12:30pm and 2:30-6:30pm. Donation requested.)* The gloomy **Mamertine Prison,** consecrated as the **Chiesa di San Pietro in Carcere,** lies downhill from the back stairs of the Aracoeli. St. Peter baptized his captors with water that flooded his cell here. *(Prison ☎06 67 92 902. Entrance underneath the church of S. Giuseppe dei Falegnamis. Open daily in summer 9-12:30pm and 2:30-6:30pm; in winter 9am-12:30pm and 2-5pm.)* At the far end of the *piazza*, the turreted **Palazzo dei Senatori** houses the Roman mayor's offices. Pope Paul III moved the famous **statue of Marcus Aurelius** here from the Palazzo dei Conservatori and then asked Michelangelo to fashion the imposing statues of Castor and Pollux.

■**CAELIAN HILL.** The Caelian and the Esquiline are the biggest of Rome's seven original hills. In ancient times Nero built his decadent Domus Aurea between them (p. 121). **San Clemente** consists of a 12th-century addition on top of a 4th-century church, with an ancient **mithraeum** temple and sewers at the bottom. The upper church holds medieval mosaics of the Crucifixion, saints, and apostles, and a 1420s Masolino fresco cycle graces the **Chapel of Santa Caterina.** The 4th-century level contains the tomb of St. Cyril and a series of frescoes depicting Roman generals swearing in the vernacular, the first written use of the language. Farther underground is a creepy 2nd-century mithraeum, below which is the **insulae,** a series of brick and stone rooms where Nero is said to have played his lyre in AD 64 while Rome burned. In summer, the **New Opera Festival of Rome** performs abridged productions in the outdoor courtyard of the church. *(M: B-Colosseo. Turn left down V. Labicana away from the Forum; turn right into P. S. Clemente. From M: A-Manzoni, walk west on V. A. Manzoni; turn left into P. S. Clemente. ☎06 70 45 10 18. Open M-Sa 9am-12:30pm and 3-6pm, Su and holidays 10am-12:30pm and 3-6pm. Lower basilica and mithraeum €3.)*

THE VELABRUM. The Velabrum lies in a flat flood plain of the Tiber, south of the Jewish Ghetto. At the bend of V. del Portico d'Ottavia, a shattered pediment and a few columns are all that remain of the once magnificent **Portico d'Ottavia.** The 11 BC **Teatro di Marcello** next door bears the name of Augustus's nephew; the Colosseum was modeled after its facade. Down V. del Teatro toward the Tiber, the **Chiesa di San Nicola in Carcere** contains Roman temples to Juno, Janus, and Spes.

One block south along V. Luigi Petroselli is the **Piazza della Bocca della Verità,** the site of the ancient **Foro Boario** (cattle market). Across the street, the **Chiesa di Santa Maria in Cosmedin** harbors lovely medieval decor. The portico's **Bocca della Verità,** a drain cover with a river god's face, was made famous in Audrey Hepburn's *Roman Holiday.* Medieval legend has it that the mouth bites a liar's hand, which is the origin of the artifact's name, which means "mouth of truth." *(Chiesa di San Nicola ☎06 68 69 972. Open Sept.-July M-Sa 7:30am-noon and 2-5pm, Su 9:30am-1pm and 4-8pm. Portico open daily Apr.-Sept. 9am-6:30pm; Oct.-Mar. 9am-5pm.)*

CENTRO STORICO

VIA DEL CORSO AND PIAZZA VENEZIA. Following along the ancient V. Lata, **Via del Corso** began as Rome's premier race course and now plays host to many parades, including Carnevale. Running between P. del Popolo (see p. 126) and **Piazza Venezia,** it is home to restaurants, hotels, and affordable fashion boutiques (p.143). Off V. del Corso, about halfway down from P. del Popolo is **Piazza di Colonna Romana,** named for the **Colonna di Marco Aurelio,** designed to imitate Trajan's triumphant column. On the opposite side of P. Colonna, **Palazzo Wedekind,** home to the newspaper *Il Tempo,* was built in 1838 with columns from the Etruscan city of Veio. The northwestern corner of P. Colonna flows into **Piazza di Montecitorio,** overseen by Bernini's **Palazzo Montecitorio,** now the seat of the Chamber of Deputies. Running south from P. del Popolo, V. del Corso ends at P. Venezia of the huge white marble **Vittorio Emanuele II Monument.** Referred to as "the wedding cake" and "Mussolini's typewriter," this makes for a good reference point. At the top of the staircase on the exterior is the **Altare della Patria,** which has two eternal flames guarded night and day. The **Palazzo Venezia,** right of P. Venezia, was one of Rome's first Renaissance *palazzos.* Mussolini used it as an office and delivered some of his most famous speeches from its balcony. Now, it houses a **museum** with rotating exhibits.

PANTHEON AND PIAZZA DELLA ROTONDA. With granite columns, bronze doors, and a soaring domed interior, the **Pantheon** has changed little since it was built nearly 2000 years ago, in spite of the centuries of plunder it endured during the Middle Ages and Renaissance. Architects still puzzle over how it was erected; its dome, a perfect half-sphere constructed from poured concrete without the support of vaults, arches, or ribs, is the largest of its kind. It was constructed under Hadrian from AD 118 to 125 over the site of the original pantheon, destroyed in AD 80. The light entering the roof through the 9m oculus served as a sundial. In AD 608 the Pantheon was consecrated as the **Chiesa di Santa Maria ad Martyres.** Several noteworthy figures are buried within: Renaissance painter Raphael; King Vittorio Emanuele II, the first king of united Italy; his son, Umberto I, 2nd king of Italy; and finally, Umberto's wife, Queen Margherita, after whom the ubiquitous pizza was named in the 19th century. *(Open M-Sa 8:30am-7:30pm, Su 9am-6pm, holidays 9am-1pm. Free.)*

The **Piazza della Rotonda** centers on Giacomo della Porta's late Renaissance fountain, which supports an ancient **Egyptian obelisk** added in the 18th century. Around the left side of the Pantheon and down the street, another obelisk, supported by Bernini's curious elephant statue, marks the center of tiny **Piazza Minerva.** Behind the obelisk is Rome's only Gothic-style church: **⊠Chiesa di Santa Maria Sopra Minerva.** *(Open daily 7am-7pm.)* Built on the site of an ancient temple, this hidden gem has a very unassuming exterior but hides some Renaissance masterpieces, including Michelangelo's *Christ Bearing the Cross* (which inspired and resembles Bernini's *Aeneas, Anchises, and Ascanius,* p. 135), Antoniazzo Romano's *Annunciation,* and a statue of St. Sebastian recently attributed to Michelangelo. In the southern transept is the **Cappella Carafa,** with a brilliant series of Fra Lippo Lippi frescoes. Don't miss the breathtaking ceiling, painted in vivid lapis-lazuli blue and studded with gold stars. From the upper left corner of P. della Rotonda, V. Giustiniani heads north to V. della Scrofa and V. della Dogana Vecchia. Here stands **Chiesa di San Luigi dei Francesi,** home to three of Caravaggio's most famous paintings: *The Calling of St. Matthew, St. Matthew and the Angel,* and *The Crucifixion. (1 block down V. di Salvatore from C. Rinascimento, opposite P. Navona. Open M-W and F-Su 8:30am-12:30pm and 3:30-7pm, Th 8:30am-12:30pm.)*

PIAZZA NAVONA. Opened in AD 86, P. Navona hosted wrestling matches, chariot races, and, with the stadium flooded and fleets skippered by convicts, mock naval battles. Bernini's **Fontana dei Quattro Fiumi** (Fountain of the Four Rivers) commands the center of the *piazza.* Each river god represents a continent: Ganges for Asia, Danube for Europe, Nile for Africa (veiled, since the source of the river was unknown), and Rio de la Plata for the Americas. At opposite ends of the *piazza* are the **Fontana del Moro** and the **Fontana di Nettuno,** designed by Giacomo della Porta in the 16th century. With a Borromini-designed exterior, the **Church of Sant'Agnese in Agone** holds the tiny skull of its namesake saint, martyred after rejecting a young man's advances. *(West side of P. Navona, opposite Fontana dei Quattro Fiumi. Open daily 9am-noon and 4-7pm.)* West of P. Navona, where V. di Tor Millina intersects V. della Pace, the semicircular porch of the **Chiesa di Santa Maria della Pace** houses Raphael's gentle *Sibyls* in its Chigi Chapel. *(Open M-F 10am-6pm, Sa 10am-10pm, Su 10am-1pm.)* On nearby C. del Rinascimento, the Chiesa di Sant'Ivo's **■corkscrew cupola** hovers over the **Palazzo della Sapienza,** the original home of the University of Rome. C. V. Emanuele I leads to **Il Gesu,** mother church of the Jesuit Order. Inside, Andrea Pozzo's **Chapel of S. Ignazio** and Bernini's **Monument to S. Bellarmino** should not be missed. *(Open daily 6:30am-12:30pm and 4-7:15pm.)*

CAMPO DEI FIORI. Campo dei Fiori lies across C. V. Emanuele I from P. Navona and is one of the last authentic Roman areas of the *centro storico.* It is home to a bustling morning market and at night transforms into a hip hot spot. During papal rule, the area was the site of many executions; the eerie statue of Giordano Bruno is a tribute to one of the deceased. South of the Campo, the Renaissance **Palazzo Farnese,** built by the first Counter-Reformation pope (1534-1549), dominates P. Farnese. To the east of the *palazzo* is the **Palazzo Spada** and its **art gallery** (p. 136).

LARGO DI TORRE ARGENTINA. This busy square is named for the Torre Argentina that dominates its southeast corner. The sunken area in the center of the Largo is a complex of four Republican temples unearthed in 1926 during Mussolini's project for demolishing the medieval city. The site is now a **cat shelter,** and dozens of felines patrol its grounds, providing the photos of cats sitting on broken columns that calendar makers love so much. The shelter appreciates donations and volunteers to help take care of the cats. *(At the intersection of C. V. Emanuele II and V. di Torre Argentina. Shelter ☎06 68 72 133; www.romancats.com.)*

THE JEWISH GHETTO

Rome's Jewish community is the oldest in Western Europe—Israelites came in 161 BC as ambassadors from Judas Maccabee, asking for Imperial help against invaders. The Ghetto, the tiny area to which Pope Paul IV confined the Jews in 1555, was dissolved in 1870, but it is still the center of Rome's Jewish population of 16,000. Take bus #64; the Ghetto is across V. Arenula from Campo dei Fiori. The Ghetto's main street is V. del Portico d'Ottavia.

PIAZZA MATTEI. This square, centered on Taddeo Landini's 16th-century **Fontana delle Tartarughe,** marks the center of the Ghetto. Nearby in the **Portico d'Ottavia** is the **Church of Sant'Angelo in Pescheria,** installed inside the Portico d'Ottavia in AD 755 and named after the fish market that flourished there. Jews were forced to attend mass here every Sunday, an act of forced evangelism that they quietly resisted by stuffing their ears with wax. *(V. de Funari. Heading toward the Theater of Marcellus on V. di Teatro di Marcello, go right on V. Montavara which becomes V. de Funari after P. Campitelli. Both the fountain and the church are under restoration.)*

SINAGOGA ASHKENAZITA. Built between 1874 and 1904 at the corner of Lungotevere dei Cenci and V. Catalana, this temple incorporates Persian and Babylonian architectural techniques. Terrorists bombed the building in 1982; guards now search all visitors and *carabinieri* patrol the vicinity. The synagogue houses the **Jewish Museum,** a collection of ancient Torahs and Holocaust artifacts that document the community's history. *(☎06 68 40 06 61. Open for services only. Museum open M-Th 9am-4:30pm, F 9am-1:30pm, Su 9am-noon. €8, students €3.)*

PIAZZA DI SPAGNA AND ENVIRONS

⊠FONTANA DI TREVI. Nicolo Salvi's (1697-1751) bombastic **Fontana di Trevi** has enough presence and grace to turn even the most skeptical, jaded jerk to sighing, romantic mush. Its name refers to its location at the intersection of three streets (*tre vie*). Neptune, in the center, stands in front of the Goddesses of Abundance and Good Health; the two horsemen in the water represent the mercurial sea, either covered by rough waves or in placid ripples. Although you should hold back to avoid a steep fine, actress Anita Ekberg couldn't resist taking a dip in the fountain's cool waters in the famous scene from Frederico Fellini's *La Dolce Vita.* Legend has it that a traveler who throws a coin into the fountain is ensured a speedy return to Rome, and one who tosses two will fall in love while there. Three coins ensure that wedding bells will soon be ringing. On a less poetic note, the **crypt** of the **Chiesa dei Santi Vincenzo e Anastasio,** opposite the fountain, preserves the hearts and lungs of popes from 1590 to 1903. *(Open daily 7:30am-12:30pm and 4-7pm.)*

SPANISH STEPS. Designed by an Italian, paid for by the French, named for the Spaniards, occupied by the British, and currently featuring American greats like Ronald McDonald, the **Scalinata di Spagna** are, to say the least, multi-cultural. P. di Spagna is also home to designer boutiques like Fendi, Gucci, Prada, and Valentino, and is a great spot for people watching or socializing. John Keats died in 1821 in the pink house by the Steps; it's now the **Keats-Shelley Memorial Museum,** displaying several

THE INSIDER'S CITY

UNKNOWN BERNINI

Multi-talented Gianlorenzo Bernini (1598-1680) worked under every pope in his lifetime, and practically defined 17th-century Roman sculpture. Although his most famous works are hard to miss, take an afternoon to explore the lesser-skown masterpieces.

1. P. Barberini has the Triton-crowned **Fontana del Tritone** for its centerpiece, while the **Fontana dei Api** (Fountain of the Bees) on the corner of V. V. Veneto spectacularly displays the Bernini family coat of arms.

2. Bernini's ⊠ **Four Fountains** representing the four seasons are built into each corner of this busy intersection.

3. The sculpture **Ecstasy of St. Theresa** in S. Maria della Vittoria is controversial for its depiction of the saint pierced by an angel's dart in a pose resembling sexual climax.

4. Bernini only asked for bread from the Jesuit novitiate for the construction of his beloved oval **San Andrea de Quirinal.**

documents and memoirs of the Romantic poet and his contemporary, Lord Byron. (☎06 67 84 235. Open M-F 9am-1pm and 3-6pm, Su 11am-2pm and 3-6pm. €3.)

PIAZZA DEL POPOLO. Once a favorite venue for the execution of heretics, this is now the "people's square." In the center is the 3200-year-old **Obelisk of Pharaoh Ramses II**, which Augustus brought from Egypt. The **Santa Maria del Popolo** holds Renaissance and Baroque masterpieces, as well as tourists searching for writer Dan Brown's clues from the Rome-based *Angels and Demons*. (☎06 36 10 836. Open M-Sa 7am-noon and 4-7pm, Su and holidays 7:30am-1:30pm and 4:30-7:30pm.) Two exquisite Caravaggios, *The Conversion of St. Paul* and *Crucifixion of St. Peter*, are in the Cappella Cerasi, next to the altar. The Cappella Chigi was designed by Raphael for the Sienese banker Agostino Chigi, reputedly once the world's richest man; niches on either side of the altar house sculptures by Bernini and Lorenzetto. At the southern end of the *piazza* are Carlo Rinaldi's 17th-century twin churches, **Santa Maria di Montesano** and **Santa Maria dei Miracoli**. (☎06 36 10 250. Open M-Sa 6:30am-1:30pm and 4-7:30pm, Su 8am-1:30pm and 5-7pm.)

VILLA BORGHESE. To celebrate becoming a cardinal Scipione Borghese financed the construction of the **Villa Borghese**, whose park is home to three art museums, including the world-renowned **Galleria Borghese** (p. 135) and the intriguing **Museo Nazionale Etrusco di Villa Giulia** (p. 136). The Borghese is also home to the small **Bio Parco Zoo**. (V. del Giardino Zoologico, 20. Open M-F 9:30am-6pm, Sa-Su 9:30am-7pm. €8.50, ages 3-12 €6.50, under 3 free.) The world's largest �iↄhot-air balloon, "L'Ottavo Colle" (The Eighth Hill), takes off nearby and can carry 30 people. (On a dirt road off V. Magnolia, follow the large blue balloon. M-F €15, Sa-Su €18.) Rent bicycles from **Bici Pincio** for a relaxing afternoon under the shade of the Villa's trees. (V. di Viale Medici and Ciale dei Bambini. ☎06 67 84 374. Open 10am. €4 per hr., €12 per day.) North of Villa Borghese are the **Santa Priscilla catacombs** and the **Villa Ada** gardens. (Santa Priscilla catacombs, V. Salaria, 430 (☎06 86 20 62 72), along with the gardens of Villa Ada, are best reached by bus #310 from Termini or P. Barberini. Get off at P. Vescovio and walk down V. di Tor Fiorenza to P. di Priscilla to the entrance to the park and the catacombs. Open Tu-Su 8:30am-noon and 2:30-5pm. €5. Villa Borghese info ☎06 32 16 564. M: A-Spagna and follow the signs. Or, from the Flaminio (A) stop, take V. Washington under the archway. From P. del Popolo, climb the stairs to the right of Santa Maria del Popolo, cross the street, and climb the small path. Free.)

▣QUIRINAL HILL. At the southeast end of V. del Quirinale, the ▧**Piazza del Quirinale** occupies the summit of the tallest of Rome's seven hills. In the center the enormous statues of Castor and Pollux (Roman copies of the Greek originals) stand on either side of an obelisk from the Mausoleum of Augustus. The President of the Republic resides in the imposing **Palazzo del Quirinale**, a Baroque architectural collaboration by Bernini, Maderno, and Fontana. Down V. del Quirinale, V. Ferrara on the right leads down the steps to V. Milano. Farther along the street lies the facade of Borromini's pulsating **Chiesa di San Carlo alle Quattro Fontane**. Bernini's ▧**Four Fountains** are built into the corners of the intersection of V. delle Quattro Fontane and V. del Quirinale. (Palazzo closed to the public. San Carlo open M-F 10am-1pm and 3-7pm, Sa-Su 10am-1pm.)

PIAZZA BARBERINI. Though the busy traffic circle at V. del Tritone Though feels more like a modern thoroughfare rather than a Baroque square, P. Barberini features two Bernini fountains, **Fontana Tritone** and **Fontana delle Api**. Maderno, Bernini, and rival Borromini are responsible for the 1624 **Palazzo Barberini**, home to the Galleria Nazionale d'Arte Antica (p. 136). The severe **Chiesa della Immaccolata Consezione** house the macabre ▧**Capuchin Crypt**, decorated entirely with human bones. (V. V. Veneto, 27/A. Open M-W and F 9am-noon and 3-6pm. Donation requested.)

VATICAN CITY

Info ☎06 69 81 662. M: A-Ottaviano; bus #64, 271, or 492 from Termini or Largo Argentina; or tram #19 from P. Risorgimento, 62 from P. Barberini, or 23 from Testaccio.

The foothold of the Roman Catholic Church, once the mightiest power in Europe, occupies 108.5 independent acres within Rome. The Lateran Treaty of 1929, which allows the Pope to maintain legislative, judicial, and executive powers over this tiny theocracy, also requires the Church to remain neutral in national politics and municipal affairs. The Vatican has historically and symbolically preserves its independence by minting coins (Italian *lire* and euros with the Pope's face), running a separate press and postal system, maintaining an army of Swiss Guards, and hoarding fine art in the **Musei Vaticani** (p. 134).

BASILICA DI SAN PIETRO (ST. PETER'S BASILICA)

Multilingual confession available. The multilingual staff of the Pilgrim Tourist Information Center, located on the left between the rounded colonnade and the basilica, provide Vatican postage, free brochures, and currency exchange. A first-aid station and free bathrooms are next to the Information Center. Open daily Apr.-Sept. 7am-7pm; Oct.-Mar. 7am-6pm. Mass M-Sa 8:30, 10, 11am, noon, 5pm; Su and holidays 9, 10:30, 11:30am, 12:10, 1, 4, 5:30pm; vespers at 5pm. Modest attire strictly enforced: no shorts, short skirts, or exposed shoulders allowed.

PIAZZA AND FACADE. Bernini's colonnade around **Piazza San Pietro,** lined with the statues of 140 saints, was designed to provide a long, impressive vista to pilgrims after their tiring journey through the tiny, winding streets of Borgo and the *centro storico.* Mussolini's broad V. della Conciliazione, built in the 1930s to connect the Vatican to the rest of the city, opened a broader view of the church than Bernini ever intended. Round disks mark where to stand so that the quadruple rows of colonnades visually resolve into one perfectly aligned row. Statues of Christ, John the Baptist, and all the apostles except Peter are on top of the basilica. In warm months, the Pope holds papal audiences on a platform in the *piazza.* (For an audience, contact the Prefettura della Casa Pontificia ☎06 69 88 46 31.)

 COLOR CODED. The Virgin Mary can usually be recognized in art by her red dress and bright blue mantle. Blue became her trademark color because the pigment was made from Lapis Lazuli, the most expensive of all paint.

INTERIOR. The basilica rests on the reputed site of St. Peter's tomb. In Holy Years the Pope opens the **Porta Sancta** (Holy Door)—the last door on the right side of the entrance porch—by knocking in the bricks with a silver hammer. The interior of St. Peter's measures 187m by 137m along the transepts. Metal lines on the marble floor mark the lengths of other major world churches. To the right, Michelangelo's *Pietà* has been protected by bullet-proof glass since 1972, when an axe-wielding fanatic attacked it, smashing Christ's nose and breaking Mary's hand.

Bernini's **baldacchino** (canopy) rises on spiraling dark columns over the marble altar, reserved for the Pope's use. The Baroque structure, cast in bronze pillaged from the Pantheon, was unveiled on June 28, 1633 by Pope Urban VIII, a member of the wealthy Barberini family. Bees, the family symbol, buzz here and there, and vines climb toward Michelangelo's cavernous **cupola.** Seventy gilded oil lamps glow in front of the *baldacchino* and illuminate Maderno's sunken *Confession.* Two staircases directly beneath the papal altar descend to St. Peter's tomb. The staircases are closed to the public, but the **grottoes** offer a better view of the tomb.

ROME AND LAZIO

High above the *baldacchino* and the altar rises **Michelangelo's dome,** which is built with a double shell, but designed as a circular dome like the Pantheon (p. 123). Out of reverence for that ancient architectural wonder, Michelangelo is said to have made this cupola a meter shorter in diameter than the Pantheon's, though the difference is not noticeable, as the dome towers 120m high and 42.3m across. When Michelangelo died in 1564, only the drum of the dome had been completed. Work remained at a standstill until 1588, when 800 laborers were hired to complete it. Toiling round the clock, they finished the dome on May 21, 1590.

BASILICA ENVIRONS

To the left of the basilica is a courtyard protected by Swiss Guards. The **Ufficio Scavi,** administrative center for the Pre-Constantinian Necropolis (see below), is here. Ask Swiss Guards for permission to enter. To the right of the basilica, at the end of the colonnade, the **Prefettura della Casa Pontifica** gives free tickets to papal audiences Wednesday morning when the Pope is speaking.

CUPOLA. The cupola entrance is near the Porta Sancta. Take an elevator to the walkway around the interior of the dome or ascend 350 steps to the top ledge, which offers a dazzling panorama. *(Open daily Apr.-Sept. 8am-5:45pm; Oct.-Mar. 7am-4:45pm. Stairs €4, elevator €7.)*

TREASURY OF ST. PETER. The Treasury contains gifts bestowed upon St. Peter's tomb. At the entrance, look for a list of all the popes beginning with St. Peter. Highlights include the "dalmatic of Charlemagne" (the Holy Roman Emperor's intricately designed robe), a Bernini angel, and the magnificent bronze tomb of Sixtus IV. *(Photographs forbidden. Wheelchair accessible. Open daily Apr.-Sept. 9am-6:30pm, Oct.-Mar. 9am-5:30pm. Closed when the Pope is celebrating in the basilica and on Christmas and Easter. €6, under 13 €5.)*

TOMB OF ST. PETER AND PRE-CONSTANTINIAN NECROPOLIS. Legend holds that after converting to Christianity, Constantine built the first basilica directly over the tomb of St. Peter, who had been crucified for preaching the Gospel. In order to build on that exact spot, the emperor had to level a hill and destroy the first-century necropolis that stood there before. There was no proof for this story until 1939, when workers came across ancient ruins beneath the basilica. Unsure of finding anything, the Church secretly set about looking for St. Peter's tomb. Twenty-one years later, the saint's tomb was identified under a small temple directly beneath the altars of the Constantinian basilica. The saint's bones, however, were not found in the crude grave. A hollow wall nearby held what the church—despite expert archaeologists' opinion—later claimed to be the holy remains. Some believe that the bones were displaced from the tomb during the Saracen's sack of Rome in AD 849. Multilingual tour guides will take you around the streets of the necropolis, which holds several well-preserved mausolea (pagan and Christian), funerary inscriptions, mosaics, and sarcophagi. The entrance to the necropolis is on the left side of P. San Pietro, beyond the information office. (☎06 69 88 53 18; scavi@fsp.va. *Office open M-Sa 9am-5pm. To request a tour, arrange in person or write to the Delegate of the Fabbrica di San Pietro, Excavations Office, 00120 Vatican City. Give a preferred range of times and languages. Phone calls only accepted for reconfirmations. Advance reservation required. Book as far ahead as possible. €10.)*

CASTEL SANT'ANGELO

☎06 68 75 036, *reservations 06 69 79 111. Along the Tiber River on the Vatican side, going from St. Peter's toward Trastevere. From centro storico, cross Ponte Sant'Angelo. Bus #40, 62, 64, 271, 280 to Ponte V. Emanuele or P. Pia. Dungeon. Open in summer Tu-Su 9am-8pm; in winter daily 9am-7pm. €5, EU students 18-25 €2.50, EU citizens under 18 or over 65 free. Tours Su 12:30pm in Italian, 2:30pm in English. Audioguides €4.*

Built by Hadrian (AD 76-138) as a mausoleum for himself and his family, this brick and stone mass served as fortress, prison, and palace. When plague wracked the city in 590, Pope Gregory the Great saw an angel sheathing his sword at the top of the complex; the plague abated soon thereafter, and the edifice was rededicated to the angel. The fortress offers an incomparable view of Rome and the Vatican. Outside, the marble **Ponte Sant'Angelo**, lined with statues designed by Bernini, is the starting point for the traditional pilgrimage route from St. Peter's to the church of **San Giovanni in Laterano** (p. 130).

TRASTEVERE

Take bus #75 or 170 from Termini to V. Trastevere, or tram #8 from Largo Argentina.

ISOLA TIBERINA. According to Roman legend, Isola Tiberina emerged with the Roman Republic. After the Etruscan tyrant Tarquin raped the virtuous Lucretia, her outraged family killed and threw him in the river; so much muck and silt collected around his corpse that an island eventually formed. Home to the Fatebenefratelli Hospital since AD 154, the island has long been associated with cures. The Greek god of healing, Aesclepius, appeared to the Romans as a snake and slithered from the river; his symbol, a *caduceus* (staff), is visible all over the island. The eclectic 10th-century **Church of San Bartolomeo** has a Baroque facade, a Romanesque tower, and 14 antique columns. *(Open M-Sa 9am-12:30pm and 4-6:30pm.)* The **Ponte Fabricio** (62 BC), known as the **Ponte dei Quattro Capi** (Bridge of Four Heads), is the oldest in the city.

CENTRAL TRASTEVERE. Off Ponte Garibaldi stands the statue of dialect poet G. G. Belli, in his own *piazza*, which borders P. Sonnino and marks the beginning of V. di Trastevere. On V. di Santa Cecilia, beyond the flower-and-fountain courtyard, is the **Basilica di Santa Cecilia in Trastevere.** *(Open daily 7am-1pm and 3:30-7pm. Cloister open Tu and Th 10-11:30am, Su 11:30am-noon. Donation requested. Crypt €2.)* From P. Sonnino, V. della Lungaretta leads west to P. di S. Maria in Trastevere, home to the **Chiesa di Santa Maria in Trastevere,** built in the 4th century by Pope Julius II. Although the church is being restored, the 12th-century mosaics and the chancel arch are still visible. *(Open M-Sa 9am-5:30pm, Su 8:30-10:30am and noon-5:30pm.)* The Rococo **Galleria Corsini** (V. della Lungara, 10; see **Museo Nazionale dell'Arte Antica,** p. 136), and the **Villa Farnesina** (p. 136) are the jewels of Trastevere.

GIANICOLO. At the top of the hill, the **Chiesa di San Pietro in Montorio** stands on what is believed to be the site of St. Peter's upside-down crucifixion. The church contains del Piombo's *Flagellation*, from designs by Michelangelo. Next door in a small courtyard is Bramante's tiny ▓**Tempietto.** A combination of Renaissance and ancient architecture, it was constructed to commemorate the site of Peter's martyrdom and provided the inspiration for the larger dome of St. Peter's. Rome's **botanical gardens** contain a garden for the blind as well as a rose garden that holds the bush from which all the world's roses are supposedly descended. *(Reach the summit on bus #41 from the Vatican, 115 from Trastevere, 870 from P. Fiorentini, where C. V. Emanuele meets the Tiber, or take the medieval V. Garibaldi from V. della Scala in Trastevere for 10min.. Church and Tempietto open May-Oct. Tu-Su 9:30am-12:30pm and 4-6pm; Nov.-Apr. 9:30am-12:30pm and 2-4pm. Gardens, Largo Cristina di Svezia, 24, at the end of V. Corsini, off V. della Lungara. ☎06 49 91 71 07. Open Apr.-July and Sept. Tu-Sa 9:30am-6:30pm; Oct.-Mar. M-Sa 9:30am-5:30pm. Closed holidays and Aug.)*

TERMINI AND ENVIRONS

▓**BASILICA DI SANTA MARIA MAGGIORE.** One of the four "Patriarchal" churches in Rome granted extraterritoriality, this basilica crowns the ▀**Esquiline Hill** and is officially part of Vatican City. In AD 352 Pope Sixtus III commissioned it when he noticed that Roman women were still visiting a temple dedicated to the pagan mother-goddess Juno Lucina. He tore down the pagan temple and built a basilica in celebration of the Council of Ephesus's recent ruling that Mary was the Mother of God. Set in the floor to the right of the altar, a marble slab marks **Bernini's tomb.** The glorious 14th-century mosaics in the church's **loggia** recount the story of the August snowfall that showed the Pope, who had dreamed of the snow brought by the Virgin Mary, where to build the church; every mid-August this miracle is re-enacted as priests sprinkle white flower petals from the top of the church. Below the altar are what some people believe to be relics from Jesus's manger. *(From Termini, exit right down on V. Giolitti and walk down V. Cavour. Tickets in souvenir shop. Open daily 7am-7pm. Modest dress required. Loggia open daily 9:30am-12:30pm. €3.)*

BATHS OF DIOCLETIAN. From AD 298 to 306, 40,000 Christian slaves built these 3000-person capacity public baths. They contained a marble public toilet with seats for 30 people, several pools, gymnasiums, art galleries, gardens, brothels, sports facilities, libraries, and concert halls. The 4th-century rotonda displays statues from the baths, and the entrance holds gorgeous stained-glass windows. In 1561 Michelangelo undertook his last architectural work and converted the ruins into a church, **Chiesa di Santa Maria degli Angeli.** *(Baths on V. E De Nicola, 79, in P. dei Cinquecento, across the street from Termini. ☎06 39 96 77 00. Open Tu-Sa 9am-7:45pm. €5. Church is in P. della Repubblica. ☎06 48 80 812. Open M-Sa 7am-6pm, Su 8am-7:30pm.)*

VIA XX SEPTEMBRE. V. del Quirinale becomes V. XX (pronounced "VEN-tee") Settembre at its intersection with V. delle Quattro Fontane, where a spectacular Bernini fountain is built in each of the four corners. A few blocks down, the colossal ◪**Fontana dell'Acqua Felice** graces P. San Bernardo. Opposite, **Chiesa di Santa Maria della Vittoria** houses an icon of Mary that accompanied the Catholics to victory in a 1620 battle near Prague. Bernini's fantastic **Ecstasy of St. Theresa of Ávila** is in the Cornaro Chapel. *(Open daily 7am-noon and 3:30-7pm. Modest dress required.)*

VIA NOMENTANA. This road runs northeast from Michelangelo's **Porta Pia** out of the city. Hop on bus #36 in front of Termini or head back to V. XX Settembre and catch bus #60. A 2km walk from Pta. Pia past villas, embassies, and parks leads to **Chiesa di Sant'Agnese Fuori le Mura.** Its apse displays a Byzantine-style mosaic of St. Agnes. Underneath the church wind some of Rome's most impressive **catacombs.** *(V. Nomentana, 349. ☎06 86 10 840 to reach the tour guide service. Open M-Sa 9am-noon and 4-6pm, Su 4-6pm. Catacombs €5. Modest dress required.)*

SOUTHERN ROME

▨ **SAN GIOVANNI IN LATERANO.** The immense **Arcibasilica of San Giovanni in Laterano,** the cathedral of the diocese of Rome, was home to the Papacy until the 14th century. Founded by Constantine in 314, it is the city's oldest Christian basilica. The golden *baldacchino* (canopy) presides over two golden reliquaries with the skulls of **St. Peter** and **St. Paul.** Note the immense statue of **Constantine,** the fresco by **Giotto,** and the intimate **cloister.** A museum of Vatican History is on the right when facing the church. *(Enter the church at the left. Open daily 9am-6pm. €2, students €1. Audioguide €3. Museum open M-Sa with entrances at 9, 10, 11am, noon. €4, students €2.)*

The **Scala Santa,** outside the church and to the left facing out of the front doors, are believed to be the 28 marble steps used by Jesus outside Pontius Pilate's home in Jerusalem. Pilgrims win indulgence for their sins if they ascend the steps on their knees, reciting prayers on each step. Martin Luther experienced an early break with Catholicism here, when in the middle of his way up the cathedral's steps, he realized the false piety of his climb and left. The steps lead to the chapel of the **Sancta Sanctorium** which houses the Acheiropoieton, or "picture painted without hands," said to be the work of St. Luke assisted by an angel. *(M: A-San Giovanni or bus #16 from Termini. Walk through the archway of the city walls to the P. San Giovanni. Church ☎ 06 69 88 64 52. Open daily 7am-7pm. Modest dress required. Scala Santa and Sancta Sanctorium ☎ 06 77 26 641. Open daily 6:30am-noon and 3-6pm, in summer until 6:30pm.)*

PORTA SAN GIOVANNI. The Rococo **Church of Santa Croce in Gerusalemme** holds the Fascist-era **Chapel of the Relics,** with fragments of the "true cross." For doubters, perhaps the most faith-testing of the chapel's relics is St. Thomas's dismembered finger, which, when still attached, he used to probe Christ's wounds. In the summer, films are shown outdoors in the *piazza.* *(P. S. Croce in Gerusalemme. M: A-San Giovanni. From Pta. S. Giovanni north of the stop, go east on V. C. Felice; church is on the right. From P. V. Emanuele II, take V. Conte Verde. Open daily 7am-7pm. Modest dress required.)*

◪**AVENTINE HILL.** V. di Valle Murcia climbs past some of Rome's swankiest homes and the **Roseto Comunale,** a beautiful public rose garden *(open May-June 8am-7:30pm).* The street turns into V. di Santa Sabina, and on the right just before the crest of the hill is a park with orange trees and a sweeping view of southern Rome. Nearby the **Chiesa di Santa Sabina** has wooden front doors dating to AD 450. The top left-hand panel contains one of the earliest known representation of the Crucifixion. V. di Santa Sabina continues along the crest of the hill to **Piazza dei Cavalieri di Malta,** home of the crusading order of the Knights of Malta. On the right as you approach the *piazza* is a large cream-colored arched gate; peer through its tiny, circular ◪**keyhole** for a hedge-framed view of the dome of St. Peter's Cathedral. *(Take V. di San Gregorio from the Colosseum. Turn right at the intersection with V. del Cerchi and take the stairs across the Circus Maximus to P. Ugo la Malfa and V. di Valle Murcia.)*

▨ THE APPIAN WAY

M: B-San Giovanni, then bus #218 to V. Appia Antica (get off at the info office just before Domine Quo Vadis); M: B-Circo Massimo or Piramide, then bus #118 to the catacombs; or M: A-Colli Albani, then bus #660 to Cecilia Metella. Info office of the Parco dell'Appia Antica, V. Appia Antica, 42, ☎ 06 51 26 314. Provides maps and pamphlets about the ancient road and its history, excavations, and recreational opportunities. Also rents bikes. €3 per hr. Open M-Sa 9:30am–1:30pm and 2-5:30pm, Su and holidays 9:30am-5:30pm.

About 30min. outside the city center, Via Appia Antica, also known as the Appian Way, was the most important thoroughfare of Ancient Rome. In its heyday it stretched from Campania to the Adriatic Coast and rightfully gained the nickname "The Queen of Roads." A perfect destination for a break from the grind of Rome's streets, vendors, and Vespas, the Appian Way is home to 3rd-century catacombs, accessible medieval and Baroque churches, a wealth of ancient Roman ruins. Sundays, when the street is closed off to traffic, take the opportunity to bike through the countryside. Wildflowers and wheat fields line the high road parallel to the V. Appia Antica between Quo Vadis and the Catacombs of San Callisto.

CHURCH OF SANTA MARIA IN PALMIS. On the site of this church St. Peter had a vision of Christ. He said to Jesus, "*Domine, quo vadis?*" ("Lord, where are you going?"). To this Christ replied that he was going to Rome to be crucified again because Peter had abandoned him. Peter understood the meaning of his vision and returned to Rome to suffer his own martyrdom: he was crucified, upside-down. In the middle of the aisle, just inside the door, Christ's alleged footprints are set in stone. *(At the intersection of V. Appia Antica and V. Ardeatina. Open M-Sa 7am-12:30pm and 3-6:30pm, Su 8:30am-1pm and 3-7pm.)*

CATACOMBS. Since burial inside the city walls was forbidden during ancient times, fashionable Romans buried their beloved along the Appian Way, while early Christians secretly dug maze-like catacombs under the ashes of their persecutors. **San Callisto** is the largest catacomb in Rome, with nearly 22km of subterranean paths. Its four levels once held 16 popes, seven bishops, St. Cecilia, and 500,000 other Christians. **Santa Domitilla** holds a 3rd-century portrait of Christ and the Apostles. **San Sebastiano** houses the massive underground tomb of none other than San Sebastian, and was reputedly the temporary home for the bodies of Peter and Paul before their relocation to their final resting places. San Sebastiano also contains three recently unearthed tombs from the pre-Christian period. *(All catacombs accessible only with guided tours, which run about every 20min. San Sebastiano: V. Appia Antica, 136. ☎06 78 50 350. Open Jan.-Oct. and Dec. M-Sa 8:30am-noon and 2:30-5pm. €5, ages 6-15 €3. San Callisto: V. Appia Antica, 110 (entrance on road parallel to V. Appia) ☎06 51 30 15 80. Open Jan. and Mar.-Dec. M-Tu and Th-Sa 8:30am-noon and 2:30-5pm. €5, ages 6-15 €3. Santa Domitilla: V. delle Sette Chiese, 283. Facing V. Ardeatina from San Callisto exit, cross street and walk right up V. Sette Chiese. ☎06 51 10 342. €5, ages 6-15 €3. Open Feb.-Dec. M and W-Su 8:30am-noon and 2:30-5pm.)*

BASILICA OF SAN SEBASTIAN. Originally dedicated to St. Peter and St. Paul, the Basilica of San Sebastian is dedicated to the martyr who was shot to death by arrows in the name of the Christian god. His likeness is reproduced on the gorgeous carved-wood ceiling, the work of a Flemish artist commissioned by the Pope. The oldest but most recently discovered of the church's relics are the tiny snail fossils, probably 200 million years old, which are visible in the marble covering the floor; the marble sports the fitting nickname *lumacella*, or "little snails." *(V. Appia Antica, 136. Open M-F 8am-5:30pm, Sa 8am-7pm, Su 7am-1pm and 2:30-5:30pm. Free.)*

VILLA AND CIRCUS OF MAXENTIUS. Before Constantine took over in AD 312, Maxentius held the title of Emperor long enough to build his family a suburban sprawl along the Appian Way. The complex consists of a villa, a 10,000-spectator chariot race track, and the tomb of his son Romulus. *(V. Appia Antica, 153. ☎06 78 01 324. Open Apr.-Sept. Tu, Th, and Sa 9am-4pm. €2.60, students €1.60.)*

MAUSOLEUM OF CECILIA METELLA. This towering turret-like structure, seemingly an imitation of Augustus's mausoleum, was built in 30 BC for the patrician Cecilia. It was preserved by its conversion to a fortress in the 14th century. *(☎06 39 96 77 00. Info line open M-F 9am-6pm, Sa 9am-1pm. Mausoleum open Tu-Su 9am-7:30pm, last entry 6:30pm. Free.)*

TESTACCIO AND OSTIENSE

Take Metro B to Piramide, Garbatella, or San Paolo.

South of the Aventine Hill, the working-class district of Testaccio is known for its cheap and delicious *trattorie* and raucous nightclubs. The neighborhood centers on the castle-like **Porta San Paolo,** an original remnant of the Aurelian walls built in the 3rd century AD to protect Rome from barbarians. Another attraction is the colossal **Piramide di Gaius Cestius,** built in 330 days by the slaves of Gaius Cestius under Augustus at the height of Roman Egyptophilia. East of V. Galvani, between V. di Monte Testaccio and V. Zabaglia is Monte Testaccio ("mountain made of pottery"), an artificial hill made entirely of broken ancient Roman wine bottles and oil jars. Ostiense is the district south of Testaccio and is a mostly residential apartments and industrial complexes.

■ **BASILICA DI SAN PAOLO FUORI LE MURA.** The massive Basilica di San Paolo Fuori le Mura is one of the four churches in Rome with extraterritorial status—only the Pope is allowed to say mass here. It's also the largest church in the city after St. Peter's. St. Paul's body, after his beheading at the Tre Fontane (see below), is said to have been buried beneath the altar, while his head remained with St. Peter's at the Arcibasilica of San Giovanni. The exact point above the body's resting place is marked by a tiny red light on the front of the altar. San Paolo is also home to many less significant relics; they are held in the **Capella delle Reliquie,** which you can access through the cloister. Before leaving, pick up a bottle of monk-made benedictine liqueur (€5-15) in the gift shop. (*M: B-Basilica San Paolo, or take bus #23 or 769 from Testaccio at the corner of V. Ostiense and P. Ostiense. Basilica open daily in summer 7am-6:30pm; in winter 7am-6pm. Cloister open daily in summer 9am-1pm and 3-6:30pm; in winter 9am-1pm and 3-6pm. Modest dress required.*)

CIMITERO ACATTOLICO PER GLI STRANIERI. This peaceful Protestant cemetery, the "Non-Catholic Cemetery for Foreigners," is one of the only burial grounds in Rome for those who don't belong to the Roman Catholic Church. Keats, Shelley, and Antonio Gramsci rest here. Keats's grave, in his typical style of self-effacement, is dedicated to "A Young Poet." From the cemetery you can also visit a sanctuary for stray cats. (*From Piramide, follow V. R. Persichetti on V. Marmorata, immediately turning left on V. Caio Cestio. Ring bell. Cemetery open M-Sa 9am-5pm, last entrance at 4:30pm. Donation requested. Cat sanctuary open daily 2:30-4:30pm.*)

MONTE TESTACCIO. Monte Testaccio began as a Roman dumping ground for terra-cotta pots. The pile grew and grew, and today the ancient garbage heap, with a name derived from *testae* (pot shards) rises in dark green splendor over the surrounding streets. **Via di Monte Testaccio** winds around the base of the hill and is the main center for nightlife in Rome. (*Follow V. Caio Cestio from V. Marmorata until it ends at V. Nicola Zabaglia. Continue straight on V. di Monte Testaccio. The hill is ahead and to the right.*)

EUR. South of the city stands a popular residential area that exists now as a memory of the second Roman Empire that never was. EUR (pronounced "AY-oor") is an Italian acronym for Universal Exposition of Rome, the 1942 World's Fair that Mussolini intended to be a showcase of fascist achievements. He ended up building the identical square buildings that still line **Via Cristoforo Colombo,** EUR's main street, which runs north from the Metro station to **Piazza Guglielmo Marconi** and its 1959 **obelisk.** There is also an artificial—and, in spite of its right angles, beautiful—lake here, surrounded by benches and green jogging paths. In the summer months the lake's hills are covered with lounging Italians and the nearby swimming pool is very popular. (*Take bus #714 or Metro B: EUR Palasport.*)

ABBAZIA DELLE TRE FONTANE (ABBEY OF THE THREE FOUNTAINS). Legend has it that when St. Paul was beheaded here, his head bounced on the ground three times and created a fountain at each bounce. The chapels have a serenity entirely distinct from the frothy exuberance of Rome's Baroque churches; visit the Abbey for an hour of quiet contemplation and the scent of eucalyptus. (*M: B-Laurentina. Walk straight and take a right on V. Laurentina; proceed about 1km north and turn right on V. delle Acque Salve. The abbey is at the bottom of the hill. Open daily 8am-1pm and 3-7pm.*)

🏛 MUSEUMS

Rome's museums are some of the best in the world. Though traveling contemporary exhibits do occasionally come through the city, permanent masterpieces have been secured through the wealth and influence of prominent families and the Vatican. Reserving or buying tickets in advance will give you more time to enjoy the art. Also, keep your eyes on the ceilings—in many museums they are richly decorated with frescoes. For info on Rome's museums, visit www.beniculturali.it.

ROME AND LAZIO

VATICAN MUSEUMS (MUSEI VATICANI)

Walk north from the right side of P. S. Pietro along the wall of the Vatican City about 10 blocks. From M: Ottaviano, turn left on V. Ottaviano to reach the Vatican City Wall; turn right and follow the wall to the museum's entrance. ☎06 69 88 49 47. Info and gift shop sell a useful guidebook (€7.50) on ground level past the entrance. Valuable CD-ROM audioguide €5.50. Guides are available in several languages, and most of the museums' staff speak some English. Most of the museums are wheelchair accessible, though less visited parts, such as the upper level of the Etruscan Museum, are not. Snack bar between the collection of modern religious art and the Sistine Chapel; full cafeteria near main entrance. Major galleries open Mar.-Oct. M-F 8:45am-3:20pm, last entry 2:20pm; Nov.-Feb. M-F 8:45am-12:20pm, Sa 8:45am-12:20pm. Closed on major religious holidays. Admission €10, ISIC cardholders €8, with guided tour €21.50, children under 1m tall free. Free last Su of the month 8:45am-1:45pm.

The Vatican Museums hold one of the world's greatest collections of art, with ancient, Renaissance, and modern paintings, sculptures, and papal odds and ends. The museum entrance at V. Vaticano leads to the famous bronze double-helix ramp that climbs to the ticket office.

■ **SISTINE CHAPEL.** Since its completion in the 16th century, the Sistine Chapel, named for its founder, Pope Sixtus IV, has been the site of the College of Cardinals' election of new popes, most recently Pope Benedict XVI in April, 2005. Michelangelo's **ceiling,** the pinnacle of artistic creation, gleams from its restoration. The simple compositions and vibrant colors hover above, each section depicting a story from Genesis. The scenes are framed by the famous *ignudi* (young nude males). Michelangelo painted the masterpiece by standing on a platform and craning backward—he never recovered from the strain to his neck and eyes. *The Last Judgement* fills the altar wall; the figure of Christ as judge hovers in the upper center, surrounded by his saintly entourage and the supplicant Mary. Michelangelo painted himself as a flayed human skin that hangs symbolically between the realms of heaven and hell. The frescoes on the side walls predate Michelangelo's ceiling. The cycle was completed between 1481 and 1483 by a team of artists under Perugino including Botticelli, Ghirlandaio, Roselli, Pinturicchio, Signorelli, and della Gatta. On one side, scenes from the life of Moses complement parallel scenes of Christ's life on the other.

> 🔲 **SISTINE SIGHTSEEING.** The Sistine Chapel is at the end of the standard route through the Vatican Museums, and it's extremely crowded. If you get to the museums early in the morning, you may want to go straight to the Sistine Chapel to enjoy Michelangelo's masterpiece while the space is relatively empty.

OTHER VATICAN GALLERIES. The **Museo Pio-Clementino** houses the world's greatest collection of antique sculpture. Two slobbering Molossian hounds guard the entrance to the **Stanza degli Animali,** a marble menagerie that highlights Roman brutality. Among other gems are the ■**Apollo Belvedere** and the unhappy **Laocoön,** who was strangled by Neptune's sea serpents for being suspicious of the Greek's gift of the wooden horse. The Trojans disregarded Laocoön's words of caution, wheeled the colossal horse into the heart of Troy, and met bloody defeat when the army of Greeks popped out for a surprise attack. The expression "beware of Greeks bearing gifts" comes from Laocoön's dying words. The last room of the gallery contains the red sarcophagus of Sant'Elena, Constantine's mother. From here, the Simonetti Stairway climbs to the **Museo Etrusco,** filled with artifacts from Tuscany and northern Lazio. Back on the landing of the Simonetti Staircase is the **Stanza della Biga** (room of an ancient marble chariot) and the **Galleria della Candelabra.** The route to the Sistine Chapel begins here, passing through the **Galleria degli**

ROME AND LAZIO

Arazzi (tapestries), the **Galleria delle Mappe** (maps), the **Apartamento di Pio V** (where there is a shortcut to *la Sistina*), the **Stanza Sobieski,** and the **Stanza dell'Immacolata Concezione.** From the Room of the Immaculate Conception, a door leads into the first of the four ■**Stanze di Rafaele,** apartments built for Pope Julius II in the 1510s. One *stanza* features Raphael's **School of Athens,** painted as a trial piece for Julius, who was so impressed that he fired his other painters, had their frescoes destroyed, and commissioned Raphael to decorate the entire suite. From here, there are two paths: one to the Sistine Chapel and the other a staircase to the frescoed Borgia Apartments and the **Museum of Modern Religious Art.**

PINACOTECA. This painting collection, one of the best in Rome, includes Filippo Lippi's *Coronation of the Virgin,* Perugino's *Madonna and Child,* Titian's *Madonna of San Nicoletta dei Frari,* and Raphael's *Transfiguration.* On the way out of the Sistine Chapel, take a look at the **Room of the Aldobrandini Marriage,** which contains a series of rare, ancient Roman frescoes.

PRINCIPAL COLLECTIONS

■**GALLERIA BORGHESE.** Located in the serene grounds of the Villa Borghese, the Galleria Borghese may be the most enjoyable museum in Rome. The collection—including masterpieces by Bernini, Titian, Raphael, Caravaggio, and Rubens—can be appreciated in one afternoon, and there is rarely a long line. The spoils of Cardinal Scipione Borghese, the **Museo Borghese** should be part of any trip to Rome.

Upon entering, Mark Antonio's ■**ceiling,** depicting the Roman conquest of Gaul, is majestic in its size and three-dimensional appearance. **Room I,** on the right, houses Canova's sexy statue of Paolina Borghese portrayed as Venus triumphant, holding the golden apple given to her by Paris. The myth is also depicted on the ceiling. The next rooms display the most famous sculptures by Bernini: a magnificent David, crouching with his slingshot; the breathtaking ■**Apollo and Daphne,** in which Daphne's hands and feet really appear to be taking leaf and root; the weightless bodies of Pluto and Proserpina in Rape of Proserpina; and the determined, powerful Aeneas, Anchises, and Ascanius, whose form recalls Michelangelo's Christ Bearing the Cross (p. 123). Be sure to walk all the way around these statues; their form and poise is best captured when you move around them. Don't miss the six dark, brooding Caravaggio paintings, including his Self-Portrait as Bacchus and St. Jerome, which grace the walls of the **Caravaggio Room.** The collection continues in the pinacoteca upstairs, accessible from the gardens around the back by a winding staircase. **Room IX** holds Raphael's important ■**Deposition,** a striking masterpiece showing the midpoint between the traditional moments of the Pieta and the Entombment, while Sodoma's Pietà graces **Room XII.** Look for self portraits by Bernini, del Conte's Cleopatra and Lucrezia, Rubens's Pianto sul Cristo Morto, and Titian's famous Amor Sacro e Amor Profano. *(Ple. Scipione Borghese, 5. M: A-Spagna; take exit labeled "Villa Borghese," walk to the right past the Metro stop to V. Muro Torto and then to P. Pta. Pinciana; Vle. del Museo Borghese is ahead and leads to the museum. Or take bus #116 or 910 to V. Pinciana. ☎06 84 17 645. Open Tu-Su 9am-7:30pm. Entrance every 2hr., last entrance 6:30pm. Limited capacity, so reserve ahead. Reservations ☎06 32 810 M-F 9am-6pm, Sa 9am-1pm; www.ticketeria.it. The villa's basement contains the ticket office and a book shop. Tickets (including reservation, tour, and bag charge) €8.50, EU citizens 18-25 €5.25, EU citizens under 18 or over 65 and students €2. Audioguide €5.)*

MUSEI CAPITOLINI. This collection of ancient sculpture is the oldest of its kind and one of the world's largest. The Palazzo Nuovo contains the original statue of **Marcus Aurelius** that once stood in the center of the *piazza,* and the entryway patio holds the gargantuan **Maforio,** one of Rome's five original "talking statues," to which people would give messages for the public. This gallery also holds the **Galata,** one of the oldest specimens of Roman sculpture. The collection continues across the *piazza* in the Palazzo dei Conservatori, which you access through the **Tabularium,** a 79 BC archive hall of ancient Rome, with dramatic views over the Forum and Colosseum. See fragments of the **Colossus of Constantine** and the famous **Capitoline Wolf,** an Etruscan statue that has symbolized the city of Rome since antiquity. The statues of the twins were added in the 16th century. At the top of the stairs, the **pinacoteca's** masterpieces include Bellini's *Portrait of a Young Man,* Titian's *Baptism of Christ,* Rubens's *Romulus and Remus Fed by the Wolf,* and Caravaggio's *St. John the Baptist* and *Gypsy Fortune-Teller.* (☎06 67 10 24 75. Open Tu-Su 9am-8pm. Guided tours in Italian Sa 5pm, Su noon and 5pm. Reservations ☎06 39 96 78 00 necessary for groups Sa and Su. €7.80, ISIC cardholders €5.80, EU citizens under 18 or over 65 free. Reservations €25. Audioguide €4. Guidebook €7.75.)

MUSEO NAZIONALE ETRUSCO DI VILLA GIULIA. The villa was built under Pope Julius III, who reigned from 1550 to 1555. Highlights include a graceful sarcophagus of a married couple in **Room 9,** a famous Euphronios vase, and an Etruscan *biga* (chariot), with the petrified skeletons of two horses found beside it in **Room 18.** Upstairs, archaeologists have put together fragments of a facade of an Etruscan temple, complete with terra-cotta gargoyles, chips of paint, and a relief of the Greek warrior Tydaeus biting into the brain of a wounded adversary. (P. Villa Giulia, 9, in Villa Borghese, near P. Thorvaldsen. M: A-Flaminio; then tram #30 or 225, or bus #19 from P. Risorgimento or 52 from P. S. Silvestro. From Galleria Borghese, follow V. dell'Uccelliera to the zoo, and then take V. del Giardino to V. delle Belle Arti. Museum is on the left after Galleria di Arte Moderna. ☎06 32 00 562, reservations 06 82 45 29. Open daily 8:30am-7:30pm. €4, €2 EU citizens 18-24, EU citizens under 18 or over 65 free. Audioguide €4. Guidebook €15, available at the bookstore outside museum entrance.)

VILLA FARNESINA. The Villa was the sumptuous home to Europe's one-time wealthiest man, Agostino "Il Magnifico" Chigi. For show, Chigi had his banquet guests toss his gold and silver dishes into the Tiber River after every course, but, like a real tycoon, he would secretly hide nets under the water to recover his treasures. To the right of the entrance lies the breathtaking **Sala of Galatea,** mostly painted by the villa's architect, Baldassare Peruzzi, in 1511. The vault displays symbols of astrological signs that add up to a symbolic plan of the stars at 9:30pm on November 29, 1466, the moment of Agostino's birth. The masterpiece of the room is Raphael's **Triumph of Galatea.** The stucco-ceilinged stairway, with its gorgeous perspective detail, ascends to the **Loggia di Psiche.** The **Stanza delle Prospettive,** a fantasy room decorated by Peruzzi, offers views of Rome between *trompe l'oeil* columns. The adjacent bedroom, known as the **Stanza delle Nozze** (Marriage Room), is the real reason for coming here. Il Sodoma, who had previously been busy painting the pope's rooms in the Vatican, frescoed the chamber until Raphael showed up and took over. Il Sodoma bounced back, making this masterful fresco of Alexander the Great's marriage to the beautiful Roxanne. (Across from Palazzo Corsini on Lungotevere Farnesina. Bus #23, 271, or 280; get off at Lungotevere della Farnesina or Ponte Sisto. At V. della Lungara, 230. ☎06 68 80 17 67. Open M-Sa 9am-1pm. €4.50, under 18 €3.50, EU citizens over 65 free.)

MUSEO NAZIONALE D'ARTE ANTICA. This collection of 12th- to 18th-century art is split between Palazzo Barberini and Palazzo Corsini, located in different parts of the city. **Palazzo Barberini** contains paintings from the medieval through Baroque periods, including works by Lippi, Raphael, El Greco, Carracci, Caravaggio, and Poussin. (V. Barberini, 18. M: A-Barberini. Bus #492 or 62. ☎06 48 14 591. Open Tu-Su 9am-

7pm. €5; EU citizens 18-24 €2.50; EU citizens under 18, over 65, and EU students €1.) **Galleria Corsini** holds a collection of 17th- and 18th-century paintings from Van Dyck and Rubens to Caravaggio. *(V. della Lungara, 10. ☎06 68 80 23 23. Opposite Villa Farnesina in Trastevere. Take bus #23; get off between Ponte Mazzini and Ponte Sisto. Wheelchair accessible. Open Tu-Su Jan.-June and Sept.-Dec. 8:30am-7:30pm; July-Aug. 8:30am-2pm. €4, EU students €2, Italian art students and EU citizens over 65 free. Guidebooks in Italian €10.50.)*

GALLERIA SPADA. Cardinal Bernardino Spada bought a grandiose assortment of paintings and sculptures and commissioned an even more opulent set of great rooms to house them. Time and good luck have left the palatial 17th-century apartments nearly intact—a visit to the gallery offers a glimpse of the luxury surrounding Baroque courtly life. In the first of the gallery's four rooms, the modest cardinal hung portraits of himself by Guercino, Guido Reni, and Cerini. In **Room 2,** look for paintings by the Venetians Tintoretto and Titian and a frieze by Vaga, originally intended for the Sistine Chapel. In **Room 4** are three canvases by the father-daughter team of Orazio and Artemisia Gentileschi. *(P. Capo di Ferro, 13, in the Palazzo Spada. From Campo dei Fiori, take any of the small streets leading to P. Farnese. Facing away from Campo dei Fiori, turn left on Capo di Ferro. Bus #64. ☎06 68 74 896. Open Tu-Su 8:30am-7:30pm. Last entry 7pm. €5, EU students €2.50, EU citizens under 18 or over 65 free. Guided tour Su 10:45am from museum book shop. Pamphlet guides in English available for each room of the exhibit. Guidebooks €10.50. Reservations €1.)*

MUSEI NAZIONALI ROMANI. The fascinating **Museo Nazionale Romano Palazzo Massimo alle Terme** is devoted to the history of art during the Roman Empire, including the *Lancellotti Discus Thrower,* a rare mosaic of Nero's, and ancient coins and jewelry. *(Largo di V. Peretti, 1. In the left corner of P. dei Cinquecento. ☎06 48 90 35 00, reservations 06 39 96 77 00. Open Tu-Su 9am-7:45pm, ticket office closes at 7pm. €6, EU citizens ages 18-24 €3, EU citizens under 18 or over 65 free. Audioguide €2.50.)* Nearby, the **Museo Nazionale Romano Terme di Diocleziano,** a beautifully renovated complex partly housed in the huge Baths of Diocletian (p. 130) has exhibits devoted to ancient epigraphy (writing) and Latin history through the 6th century BC, as well as a beautiful cloister by Michelangelo. *(Museo Nazionale: V. Enrico de Nicola, 78. ☎ 06 39 96 77 00. Open Tu-Su 9am-7:45pm. Ticket office closes at 7pm. €5.)* The **Aula Ottogonale,** in another wing, holds 19 Classical sculptures in a gorgeous octagonal space. *(V. Romita, 8. ☎06 48 70 690. Open Tu-Sa 9am-2pm, Su 9am-1pm. Free.)* Across town is the Renaissance man of the trio, **Museo Nazionale Romano Palazzo Altemps,** which displays Roman sculpture, like the famous 5th-century *Ludovisi Throne. (P. Sant'Apollinare, 44, just north of P. Navona. Bus #30 Express, 492, 70, 81, 87, or 628 to C. Rinascimento/P. Cinque Lune. Museum ☎06 78 33 566, ticket office 06 68 33 759. Open Tu-Su 9am-7pm. €5, EU citizens 18-24 €2.50, EU citizens under 18 or over 65 free. Audioguide €4.)*

OTHER COLLECTIONS

GALLERIA DORIA PAMPHILI. The Doria Pamphili (pronounced "pa-FEE-lee") family, whose illustrious kin include Pope Innocent X, maintain this stunning private collection in their palatial home. Its Classical art is organized by size and theme, and Renaissance and Baroque masterpieces include Caravaggio's *Rest During the Flight in Egypt,* Raphael's *Double Portrait,* and Velasquez's portrait of Pope Innocent X, generally considered to be one of the most outstanding papal portraits of all time. If your neck can stand it, marvel at the *trompe l'oeil* ceilings. *(P. del Collegio Romano, 2. Bus #40 Express or 64 to P. Venezia. From P. Venezia, walk up V. del Corso and take the 2nd left. ☎06 67 97 323; www.doriapamphili.it. Open M-W and F-Su 10am-*

5pm, last entrance 4:15pm. Closed Jan. 1, Easter, May 1, Aug. 15, and Dec. 26. €8, students and seniors €5.70. Informative audioguide in English, French, or Italian included.)

MUSEO CENTRALE MONTEMARTINI. The building, an electrical plant from the turn of the 20th century, contains a striking display of Classical sculpture. One highlight is *Hercules' Presentation at Mount Olympus*, a huge well-preserved floor mosaic of a hunt. (V. Ostiense, 106. M: B-Piramide. From P. Ostiense take V. Ostiense. Then walk or take bus #23 or 702 3 stops. ☎06 57 48 038. Open Tu-Su 9:30am-7pm. €4.20, with entrance to the Capitoline Museums €9.80; EU citizens 18-24 €2.60/7.80; EU citizens under 18 or over 65 free. Reservations €1.50.)

MUSEO NAZIONALE D'ARTE MODERNA E CONTEMPORANEA. This museum traces Italy's art history from Napoleon to the Risorgimento in the north wings, and from Futurism and Abstraction to more recent international works in the south wings. It also houses temporary traveling exhibitions. (Vle. delle Belle Arti, 131, next door to the Villa Giulia, see directions above. ☎06 32 29 81. Open Tu-Su 8:30am-7:30pm; closed Dec. 25 and Jan. 1. €6.50, students €3.25.)

MUSEO MARIO PRAZ. This small eccentric museum was originally the last home of Mario Praz (1896-1982), an equally small and eccentric professor of English literature and 18th- and an 19th-century art collector. His museum is called the "house of the soul." Superstitious neighbors spat or flipped coins when they saw him. (V. Zanardelli, 1, top fl. At the east end of Ponte Umberto, next to Museo Napoleonico. ☎06 68 61 089. Entrance with mandatory 35-45min. tour every hr. in the morning and every 30min. in the afternoon. Open M 2:30-6:30pm, Tu-Su 9am-1pm and 2:30-6:30pm. Free.)

MUSEO NAZIONALE D'ARTE ORIENTALE. An array of artifacts from prehistory to the 1800s with exhibits on art in the Near East, Islamic art, Nepalese and Tibetan art, Indian art, Southeast Asian art, and Chinese history. (V. Merulana, 248. In Palazzo Brancaccio on Esquiline Hill. ☎06 48 74 415. Open M, W, and F 8:30am-2pm, Tu, Th, and Su 8:30am-7:30pm. Closed 1st and 3rd M of each month. €4, reduced €2.)

MUSEO CRIMINOLOGICO. After overdosing on artwork and history, pump your stomach at a museum dedicated to crime and punishment, currently under restoration. On the first floor find torture devices and old English etchings, including *A Smith Has His Brains Beaten Out With a Hammer*. On the 2nd floor, learn the secrets of criminal phrenology and the language of tattoos. The 3rd floor contains terrorist, spy, and drug paraphernalia. (V. del Gonfalone, 29. Near Ponte Mazzini. ☎06 68 30 02 34. Tu-W 9am-1pm, Tu and Th 2:30-6:30pm, F-Sa 9am-1pm. €2, under 18 or over 65 €1.)

GALLERIA COLONNA. Despite its limited hours, this gallery is worth a visit. The *palazzo* was designed in the 18th century to show off the Colonna family's collection, including Tintoretto's *Narcissus*, and works by Melozzo da Forli, Veronese, Palma il Vecchio, and Guercino. (V. della Pilotta, 17. North of P. Venezia in the centro storico. ☎06 66 78 43 50; www.galleriacolonna.it. Open Sept.-July Sa 9am-1pm. €7, students €5.50, under 10 or over 65 free. Included tour 11am in Italian and 11:45am in English.)

MUSEO DEL RISORGIMENTO. Underneath the left side of the Vittoriano monument in P. Venezia, this museum contains items relating to the Risorgimento, the 19th-century "resurgence" which ultimately led to the unification of Italy in 1861. (Entrance on V. di S. Pietro in Carcere. ☎06 67 93 526. Open daily 9:30am-6pm. Free.)

🎵 ENTERTAINMENT

The weekly *Roma C'è* (with a section in English) and *Time Out*, both available at newsstands, have comprehensive and up-to-date club, movie, and event listings.

LIVE MUSIC

Rome hosts a variety of worthwhile performances, most of them in the summer. *Telecom Italia's* classical music series takes place at the Teatro dell'Opera. At 9am on concert days, unsold tickets are given out for free at the box office; get in line early. Local churches often host free choral concerts. Check newspapers, tourist offices, and church bulletin boards for details. Finally, and perhaps most interestingly, the *carabinieri* frequently give rousing (and free) concerts in P. di San Ignazio and other outdoor venues.

■ **Alexanderplatz Jazz Club,** V. Ostia, 9 (☎06 39 74 21 71; www.alexanderplatz.it). M: A-Ottaviano. Head left on V. G. Cesare, take 2nd right on V. Leone IV and 1st left on V. Ostia. Night buses to P. Venezia and Termini leave from P. Clodio. Known as one of Europe's best jazz clubs, the smoky atmosphere conveys the feeling of a 40s jazz joint. Read messages left on the walls by greats who have played here. Cocktails €6.20. Required *tessera* (membership; €7), good for 1 month. Shows start 10pm. Open daily Sept.-May 9pm-2am. In summer moves outside to Villa Celimontana.

Accademia Nazionale di Santa Cecilia, V. Vittoria, 6 (☎06 36 11 064 or 800 90 70 80; www.santacecilia.it), off V. del Corso. This conservatory, named for the martyred patron saint of music, is now home to Rome's symphony orchestra. Concerts are held at the **Parco della Musica,** Vle. Pietro di Coubertin, 30, near P. del Popolo, where you can also buy tickets €8-15. Season runs Sept.-June, covering classics and special presentations like the music of Jimi Hendrix played by a string quartet.

Teatro Ghione, V. delle Fornaci, 37 (☎06 63 72 294; www.ghione.it), near the Vatican. This red velvet theater hosts Euromusica's classical concerts and other big-name musical guests. English-speaking staff. Tickets €9-21. Season Oct.-Apr. Box office open daily 10am-1pm and 4-8pm. Call for info on morning concerts and discounts. MC/V.

Cornetto Free Music Festival Roma Live, at several locations around the city, including Stadio Olimpico and Villa Giulia. Has featured the likes of Pink Floyd, the Cure, the Backstreet Boys, and Lou Reed. Enter to win free tickets at www.cornettoalgida.it.

Fiesta, V. Appia Nuova, 1245 (☎06 71 29 98 55; www.fiesta.it), in the Ippodrome delle Capannelle. M: A-Colli Albani or bus #664. An extremely popular festival running all summer, featuring all things Latin American. Attendance can swell to over 30,000. Advance purchase ☎19 91 09 910.

OPERA AND DANCE

In the summer Rome fills with arias of world famous operas, especially those by national composer Giuseppe Verdi. Countless flyers and posters will list performances at fantastic outdoor venues. *Roma C'è* also lists the week's upcoming performances, and tourist offices can often help you book tickets at a reduced rate.

THEATER

Roman theater generates a number of quality productions, ranging from mainstream musicals to black-box experimental. For info on English theater, check the tourist office, *Roma C'è,* or online at www.musical.it or www.comune.roma.it.

Teatro Argentina, Largo di Torre Argentina, 52 (☎68 40 00 345; www.teatrodiroma.net). Bus #64 from Termini or tram 8, right off V. Arenula. Home to the Teatro di Roma company, Argentina hosts plays, concerts, and ballets. It is also the main venue for many annual drama/music festivals. Call for specific info. Box office open M-F 10am-2pm and 3-7pm, Sa 10am-2pm. €14-26, students €10-13. AmEx/MC/V.

Teatro Colosseo, V. Capo d'Africa, 5 (☎06 70 04 932). M: B-Colosseo. Walk down V. dei Fori Imperiali past the Colosseum, then go right through P. Colosseo; V. Capo d'Africa is 2 blocks down on the left. Offers plays in Italian but also has an English theater night. Box office open Sept.-Apr. Tu-Sa 6-9:30pm. Tickets €10-20, students €8.

CINEMA

Unfortunately, most theaters in Rome show dubbed movies. For subtitles, look for a "v.o." or "l.o." in listings (*versione originale* or *lingua originale*). In summer, huge screens spring up in *piazze* around the city for **outdoor film fests.** Films are usually shown outdoors on Isola Tiberina's southern tip. Cinemas citywide offer discounts on Wednesdays and most have reductions for afternoon shows.

Il Pasquino, P. Sant'Egidio, 10 (☎06 58 03 622), off P. S. Maria in Trastevere. Rome's biggest English-language movie theater. Program changes daily; call ahead. €6.20. Theaters 2 and 3 are a film club; €1.03 for 2-month membership and €5.16 for ticket.

Nuovo Sacher, Largo Ascianghi, 1 (☎06 58 18 116). Take V. Induno from V. d. Trastevere. This is the famed Italian director Nanni Moretti's theater and shows a host of indie films. M and Tu films in the original language. Tickets €7, matinee and W €4.50.

Warner Village Moderno, P. della Repubblica 43/45 (☎06 47 77 91 11; www.warnervillage.it). 1 Hollywood blockbuster in English each week. Tickets €7.50, matinee and under 12 €5.50.

SPECTATOR SPORTS

Though May brings tennis and equestrian events, sports revolve around *calcio* (soccer). Rome has two teams in Serie A, Italy's prestigious league: **S.S. Lazio** and the 2000 European champion **A.S. Roma.** Matches are held at the **Stadio Olimpico,** in Foro Italico, almost every Sunday from September to June. Single-game tickets (from €15.50) can be bought at team stores like **A.S. Roma,** P. Colonna, 360 (☎06 67 86 514; www.asroma.it; open daily 10am-6:30pm; AmEx/MC/V); and **Lazio Point,** V. Farini, 34/36, near Termini. (☎06 48 26 688. Open M-F 9am-7pm, Sa 9am-1pm. AmEx/MC/V.) Tickets can also be obtained at the stadium before a game, but beware long lines and the possibility of tickets running out; if you're buying last minute, watch out for overpriced or fake tickets.

🗋 SHOPPING

There are four kinds of clothing shops in Rome. First, you have chain stores like **Motivi, Mango, Stefanel, Intimissimi,** and the ubiquitous **United Colors of Benetton.** Second, you have the cardiac-arrest-inducing prices of the designer shrines like **Cavalli, Dolce & Gabbana,** and **Prada.** Third there are the techno-blasting teen stores that dominate central thoroughfares. Finally tiny boutiques in the *centro storico,* including **Ethic** and **Havana,** often have a couple locations throughout the city. Below is a list of designer boutiques, since no visit to Italy is complete without a pilgrimage to Gucci and Prada.

BOUTIQUES

Designer shops cluster around the Spanish Steps and V. dei Condotti. Purchases of over €155 at a single store are eligible for a tax refund for non-EU residents.

Bruno Magli, V. del Gambero, 1, and V. dei Condotti (☎06 67 93 802). Open M-Sa 10am-7pm.

Dolce & Gabbana, V. dei Condotti, 52 (☎06 69 92 49 99). Open M-Sa 10am-7:30pm.

Emporio Armani, V. del Babuino, 140 (☎06 36 00 21 97). Houses the less expensive Armani line. Open M 3-7:30pm, Tu-Su 10am-7:30pm.

Fendi, V. Borgognona, 36-39 (☎06 67 94 824). Open daily 11am-2pm and 3-7pm.

Gianni Versace, men: V. Borgognona, 24-25 (☎06 679 50 37); women: V. Bocca di Leone, 25-27 (☎06 678 05 21). Open M-Sa 10am-7pm.

Giorgio Armani, V. dei Condotti, 75 (☎06 69 91 460). Open M-Sa 10am-7pm.

Gucci, V. dei Condotti, 8 (☎06 678 93 40). Open M-F 10am-7pm, Sa 10am-2pm.

Prada, V. dei Condotti, 92/95 (☎06 67 90 897). Open daily 10am-7pm.

Salvatore Ferragamo, men: V. dei Condotti, 64-66 (☎06 67 81 130); women: V. dei Condotti, 72-74 (☎06 67 91 565). Open M 3-7pm, Tu-Sa 10am-7pm; Aug. also Su 9am-1pm.

CHEAP AND CHIC

Diesel, V. del Corso, 186 (☎06 67 81 045). Italian-made Diesel is *the* label in urban European fashion. Stock up on jeans and t-shirts at prices far lower than anywhere else. Open M-Sa 10:30am-8pm, Su 3:30-8pm.

Mariotti Boutique, V. d. Frezza, 20 (☎06 32 27 126). This elegant boutique sells modern, sophisticated clothes in gorgeous fabrics. Prices are steep, so watch for sales. Open M-F 10am-7pm. Closed in Aug.

OUTDOOR MARKETS

HAGGLING RULES. Street vendors will often try to sell fake Prada bags for exorbitant prices, insisting they're from the hands of Miuccia herself. Name your bottom price; if the vendor refuses, walk away. If he wants to make the sale, he will call you back. Decide ahead of time how much you're willing to pay and don't go over. Haggling requires that you're willing to walk away if you don't like the price, making the vendor realize that you're a tough sale.

Porta Portese, in Trastevere. Tram #8 from Largo di Torre Argentina. This gigantic flea market is a surreal experience, with booths selling clothing, shoes, jewelry, bags, toilets, and millions of other items you never knew you needed. Keep your friends close and your money closer, as the place swarms with pickpockets. Open Su 5am-1:30pm.

Campo dei Fiori, in Centro Storico. Tram #8 or bus 64. Transformed daily by stalls of fruits and vegetables, meat, poultry, and fish. Also rice, dried fruit, spices, flowers, and the usual vendors of basic tops, skirts, and knockoff designer bags. Open M-Sa 7am until the individual vendors decide their food has run out (usually around 1:30pm).

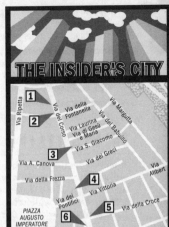

SHOPPING CORSO

While fancy designer stores line the streets around **Piazza di Spagna**, **Via del Corso** has some unique and affordable boutiques.

1 Tiny **Da Piero il Fichissimo,** 525a, stocks leather motorcycle jackets, complete with Ferrari logos for €150-200.

2 **David Hamilton,** 524, is a V. del Corso chain that specializes in men's clothing, including stylish Italian ties for €20.

3 **Dominique,** 20, offers shoppers a wide selection of trendy women's and children's shoes, along with a small in-store playground.

4 Head to **Halfon,** 507, for a change from polyester to all-natural threads, including casual linen pants for €25.

5 **Da Dada,** 500 and 41, showcases simple and elegant styles under an Audrey Hepburn logo.

6 **Ethic,** 85, raises money for a children's charity by selling unique hand-made fashions.

Mercato delle Stampe, Largo della Fontanella di Borghese. Bus #81, 116, 117, or 492. A bookworms' haven specializing in old books—both used and genuine antiquarian, magazines, and other printed morsels. Open M-Sa 7am-1pm.

Mercato Andrea Doria, on V. Andrea Doria, northwest of the Vatican Museums. M: Ottaviano; bus #23, or 70. Caters mostly to the local population, so don't expect to find many English-speaking folks here. Fruits, vegetables, fish, groceries, clothes, and shoes sold in a huge open square. Open M-Sa 7am-1:30pm.

Nuovo Mercato Esquilino, on V. F. Turati. M: A-Vittorio Emanuele or bus 105. International food stalls cater to various ethnic groups. M-Sa 7am-2pm.

■ NIGHTLIFE

Romans find nighttime diversion at the pubs of San Lorenzo, the clubs of Testaccio, and everywhere in between. Pick up *Roma C'è* for updates on clubs' openings and closings. *Time Out* covers Rome's sparse but solid collection of gay nightlife listings, many of which require an **ARCI-GAY pass** (€10 for 1 year; see **Local Services,** p. 102). Also check with **Circolo di Cultura Omosessuale Mario Mieli** (☎06 54 13 985).

PUBS AND BARS

Though *enoteche* tend to be the primary destination for locals of all ages, bars and pubs are still a fun way to knock back a few without cover or sweaty polyester. There are many Irish pubs in Rome; the best are around Campo dei Fiori. The bars we list have a unique vibe. P. Navona is the best evening destination; crowds of people flood the *piazza* after bars close at 2am to continue the revelry.

■ **Il Fico,** P. del Fico, 26 (☎06 68 65 205). Take V. d. Tor Millina off P. Navona, and continue past V. del Pace. P. del Fico is on the right. Shaded by fig trees in a small *piazza* that's a refreshing change from the cramped sidewalk seating of other bars in the area, the outdoor patio of this bar has fantastic cocktails (€4 for aperitifs, €7 for full cocktails) and a lazy ambience, perfect for pre-dinner or late-night drinks. Inside, a large light fixture pours soft red light throughout the room, decorated with black and white photos, as patrons enjoy the cool sounds of jazz drifting by. Open daily 9am-2:30am.

■ **Shanti,** V. dei Conciatori, 11 (☎06 33 04 65 662), in Testaccio; also at V. dei Funari, 21/a (☎06 68 68 668) and V. Albalonga, 6 (☎06 70 45 13 05). For Testaccio location: from M: B-Piramide, head down V. Ostiense and take the 2nd street on the right. The drinks, though creative, may seem pricey at first (€7 for cocktails). All concerns dissipate after you settle into the opulent Middle Eastern decor and have a few puffs of one of Shanti's hookahs (about €2.50 per person), which come in many flavors. Bellydancing in winter (Shanti's high season), W-F 11pm-1am. Open daily 9pm-1am (though closing time is flexible). Closed Su in July, and all of Aug.

■ **Caffè della Scala,** P. della Scala, 60 (☎06 58 03 763) on V. della Scala before it intersects with P. San Egidio. In nice weather the tables at this casual cafe/bar line the neighboring street of V. della Scala. Tourists, expats, and locals stroll this main thoroughfare at all hours of the day and night. The drink menu has some creative options, including the "Spritz" (campari, white wine and soda; €5.50) and several Cuban-inspired drinks made with rum (€7). Open daily 5pm-2am. AmEx/MC/V.

Jonathan's Angels, V. d. Fossa, 14-16 (☎06 68 93 426), in P. Navona. Take V. Pasquino (V. Governo Vecchio) from P. Navona, turn right on V. Parione, then left on V. d. Fossa. Jonathan the Elder proved to be the most self-infatuated Roman since Nero by erecting a colossal statue of himself in his bedroom and then building this bar, where his portraits adorn the walls and a ■ **loo** draws the curious through a veritable pleasure garden. Beer €5. Cocktails €8. Open M-F 8pm-3:30am, Sa-Su 6:30pm-3:30am. Cash only.

Artu Café, Largo Fumasoni Biondi, 5 (☎06 58 80 398), in P. San Egidio, behind Santa Maria in Trastevere. This small bar/lounge, bathed in dark red light, serves patrons who swear it's the best in Trastevere. Beer €4.50. Wine €3-5.50 per glass. Fresh juice cocktails €6.20-7.20. Free snack buffet 6:45-9pm. Open Tu-Su 6pm-2am. MC/V.

The Proud Lion Pub, Borgo Pio, 36 (☎06 68 32 841). A tiny pub in the Vatican area whose outside says "Rome, Borgo Pio," but is pure Highland on the inside. Beer and cocktails €4. Single malts €4.50-5. Open daily 8:30pm-2am.

CLUBS

Italian discos are flashy and fun, but keep in mind that they often have spoken or unspoken dress codes. Although many clubs close in the summer in favor of more distant destinations like Fregene or Frascati, Testaccio is dependable through early August. Check *Roma C'è* or *Time Out* for the latest updates.

Distillerie Clandestine, V. Libetta, 13 (☎ 06 57 30 51 02). Designed to have a Prohibition-speakeasy feel, this night spot features a restaurant with live music and DJs spinning. F-Sa cover €20. Open W-Sa 8:30pm-3am.

Jungle, V. di Monte Testaccio, 95 (☎33 37 20 86 94; www.jungleclubroma.com). Smoky bar full of Italian Goths (Sa) dancing to the Cure and Italian pop. More of a rock feel on Friday night. Extravagant, though somewhat disorienting light effects. Cover €10. Open F-Sa 10:30pm-5am.

Alien/Piper/Gilda on the Beach. This nightclub empire caters to the glitteratti of Roman nightlife. With steep covers and exclusive guest lists, these are the places to see and be seen. In the summer, Gilda on the Beach, located near Fiumicino, 30km from Rome takes over most of the scene, since Italians prefer to party until dawn on the sand instead of the streets.

Alien, V. Velletri, 13-19 (☎06 84 12 212; www.aliendisco.it). One of the biggest discos in Rome attracts a well-dressed crowd. Cover varies (about €15, includes 1 drink; Sa €20). Mostly house with occasional theme nights. Open Tu-Su 11pm-5:30am.

Piper, V. Tagliamento, 9 (☎06 85 55 398; www.piperclub.it). North of Termini. From V. XX Settembre, take V. Piave (V. Salaria). Turn right on V. Po (V. Tagliamento). Or take bus #319 from Termini to Tagliamento. Caters to a more exclusive crowd, with international DJs spinning 70s, rock, disco, as well as the standard house and underground. Cover €15–20 includes 1 drink. Open F-Sa 11pm-4:30am.

Gilda on the Beach, Lungomare di Ponente, 11 (☎06 66 56 06 49; www.gildaonthebeach.it), in Fregene. Operating only May-Sept., Gilda on the Beach is a favorite among VIPs and those who normally frequent Alien and Piper. 4 dance floors, a private beach, pool, restaurant, and ultra-cool clientele are all reasons why Gilda is a place to see and be seen during the summer. Cover €20. Disco open daily 11pm-4am, restaurant serves dinner from 8:30pm. AmEx/MC/V.

▶ DAYTRIPS FROM ROME

TIVOLI

Take Metro B to Rebibbia. Exit the station; follow signs for Tivoli through an underpass to reach the other side of V. Tiburtina. Take the blue COTRAL bus to Tivoli. Tickets (€1.60) are sold in the subway station or in the bar next door. Once the bus reaches Tivoli (25min.), get off past P. Garibaldi at P. delle Nazioni Unite. The bus back to Rome leaves from P. Garibaldi. The tourist office is on the street leading from P. Garibaldi, with info on villas, maps, and bus schedules. ☎0774 31 12 49. Open M and W 9am-1pm, Tu and Th-Sa 9am-3pm and 4-7pm. Villa d'Este is through the souvenir stands in P. Trento and to the left. For Hadrian's Villa, 5km from Tivoli proper, take the orange bus #4 or 4x from P. Garibaldi's newsstand, which also sells bus tickets (€1). The COTRAL bus also services Hadrian's Villa. From the parking lot, take a right away from the villa and head uphill until you reach a small bus-stop sign.

ROME AND LAZIO

Tivoli is a hilltop town perched 120m above the Aniene River where poets Horace, Catullus, and Propertius once owned villas along the rocks overhanging the river. Today, Tivoli is a beautifully preserved medieval city, with winding streets, steep stone stairs, and views of the surrounding valleys. Though the three villas are Tivoli's main attraction, the tourist office provides a fantastic ▨**map** with three walking tours around temple ruins, a 15th-century castle, and Gothic-style houses.

Villa d'Este, a castle-garden, was laid out by Cardinal Ercole d'Este (the son of Lucrezia Borgia) and his architect Piero Ligorio in 1550 with the idea of recreating an ancient Roman *nymphaea* and pleasure palace. Terraces and fountains abound in the manicured garden, and the Villa itself has a fantastic collection of frescoes and some modern art. One of the rooms tells the story of Hercules, the mythological founder of the house of Este and Tivoli's most famous resident. In the summer, concerts are held on the Villa's grounds. (☎0774 31 20 70; www.villadestetivoli.com. Open Tu-Su May-Aug. 9am-6:45pm; Sept.-Apr. 9am-4pm. €9, EU citizens 18-24 €5.75, EU citizens under 18 or over 65 free.) ▨**Villa Gregoriana,** at the other end of town, is a park with hiking trails that wind over waterfalls and "the caves of Neptune and the Sirens." Lookouts offer views of Tivoli's **Temple of Vesta,** a better preserved version of the one in the Roman Forum. (€4, EU citizens 18-24 €2, EU citizens under 18 or over 65 free. Audioguide €4). Be sure to visit the remains of **Villa Adriana,** the largest and most expensive villa built under the Roman Empire. Emperor Hadrian, inspired by his travels, designed its 2nd-century buildings with an international flair. Look for the *pecile*, built to recall the famous *Stoa Poikile* (Painted Porch) of Athens, and the *canopus*, a statue-lined expanse of water built to replicate a canal in Alexandria, Egypt. (☎0774 38 27 33. Open daily 9am-1½hr. before sunset. €8.50, EU citizens 18-24 €5.25, EU citizens under 18 or over 65 free. Archaeological tour €3.50. Audioguide €4.)

LAGO DI BRACCIANO

Anguillara and Bracciano are accessible by train on the Rome-Viterbo line from Rome's Ostiense station (every hr., 6:47am-9:17pm, €3). By bus, take Metro A to Lepanto, then take the COTRAL bus from Lepanto to the lake (every hr., 6:40am-10:15pm, €2).

About 1hr. from Rome by bus, fresh air, cool water, and a lush and hilly landscape envelope Lago di Bracciano's volcanic sands and freshwater beach. The 15th-century **Castello Orsini-Odescalchi** contains some stunning frescoes and stuffed wild boars. (☎06 99 80 43 48, museum 06 99 80 23 79; www.odescalchi.it. Call ahead for tours in English). See *Roma C'è* for listings of **classical concerts** held here in the summer. Bracciano's many *trattorie* cook up mounds of fresh lake fish, including eel, the local specialty. A quick ferry ride to **Anguillara** or **Trevignano** across the lake offers more spectacular scenery.

OSTIA ANTICA

M: B-Piramide. Exit platform and follow signs for Lido trains left of the station. Get off at Ostia Antica. Same ticket as for the Metro. Cross overpass, take road straight until it dead-ends in the parking lot . Go left through parking lot and follow signs to the entrance. ☎06 56 35 02 15. Open in summer Tu-Su 8:30am-6pm; in winter Tu-Su 8:30am-4pm; in Mar. Tu-Su 8:30am-5pm. Last entrance 1hr. before closing. €4, EU citizens 18-24 €2, EU citizens under 18 and over 65 free. Pick up a useful map at the biglietteria for €2 or a guidebook for €7.50. Guided tours by reservation only Su mornings, except in Aug., €4.

The ruins of the Roman port of Ostia, named for the *ostium* (mouth) of the Tiber, are only an hour from Rome; they provide the unique experience of exploring a well-preserved Roman city without having to trek to the more famous ruins at Pompeii and Herculaneum. The site also shows the more practical side of ancient

Rome absent in the temples and monuments of the Roman Forum—bakeries, bars, and even public toilets. The excavations are quite large and require the better part of a day to explore—bring a picnic if you want to avoid eating at the cafeteria.

Ostia was founded around 335 BC as the first Roman colony; it was transformed into a port and naval base during the 3rd and 2nd centuries BC, and almost all imports to Rome passed through Ostia. Though it remained an active and important part of Roman trade throughout the Imperial period, most of the extant structures in the city of Ostia were constructed by AD 45. Today, since the Tiber no longer runs past Ostia, it makes for a less ideal port but still a good place to visit.

Decumanus is Ostia Antica's central artery. Enter the gate and take the high road parallel to the Decumanus to reach the **Baths of the Cisiarii;** mosaics on its floor depict mules working outside the city walls. Cut back to the Decumanus to reach the **Baths of Neptune,** a few hundred yards down; the bath complex features exceptional mosaics. Next to the baths is a colonnaded courtyard, the *palestra*, where bathers would exercise. Down a small alley to the right of the baths are the **Terme delle Province,** with mosaics depicting the four winds and the Roman provinces that traded with Ostia. Continue down the Decumanus to reach the **Theater of Ostia,** which is still in use today. Built in 12 BC, the stage itself was once backed by a wall several stories high, decorated with columns, arches, and statues; only the low wall of its foundation survives. In summer, the theater hosts plays and concerts, including the **International Festival of Ostia Antica.** (For events info, check *Roma C'è* or call the Botteghino Teatro Ostia Antica at ☎0656 35 28 50. Tickets €15-24.) Just beyond the theater, take a right on V. Molini and then a left on V. della Casa di Diana to find the **Casa di Diana,** the best preserved house at Ostia, once 18m high. The ancient equivalent of an apartment building, this *insula* housed several dozen people who shared the courtyard and kitchen facilities, while the ground floor housed *tabernae* (shops). Across the street is the **Thermopolium,** precursor of the snack bar. A still life in the central room depicts likely fare.

Continue to the end of the V. della Casa di Diana and take a left. This leads to the **Forum of Ostia,** anchored by the imposing **Temple to Jupiter, Juno, and Minerva** (called the **Capitolium**). At the other end of the forum is the **Temple of Augustus and Rome.** A marble statue representing Rome marks the location of the old shrine. Behind the Temple of Augustus are the largest baths in Ostia, the **Terme del Foro,** and nearby is a well-preserved, 20-seat public restroom, the **Forica.** Past the Forum, V. d. Foce leads to the elaborate **House of Cupid and Psyche,** where the famous statue of the two lovers was found. Nearby, on V. di Terme del Mitra, a staircase descends to a shadowy **mithraeum** and the maze of sewers that sprawl like hollow veins beneath the city. Back in the Decumanus, on the left a marble relief welcomes the visitor to the **Schola of Trajan,** believed to have been owned by a corporation of shipbuilders. The first-century BC *domus* contains beautiful and rare mosaics; the interior court and fountain are striking. Turn left on the last street off the Decumanus before the exit to see the **Baths of the Marine Gate,** decorated with mosaics of athletes and philosophers, as well as a woman resembling the Statue of Liberty.

ANZIO

Anzio is accessible by train from Rome's Termini station (1hr., every 2hr. 6am-11pm, €2.90). PIT Infopoint in P. Pia, off V. A. Gramsci from R. V. Mallozzi. Tor Caldara ☎06 98 64 177. Call for reservations. Tours Tu and Sa-Su 9am-7pm.

In the summer, tourists and Italians head to Anzio for the rocky beaches and shallow waters; the atmosphere is buzzing, with volleyball matches, pedal boats, and sunbathers on the artificial sandbars. Two major historic events affected this sleepy seaside town: Nero's construction of an Imperial Villa and the storming of Anzio in 1944 by the Allies in WWII. The latter is commemorated in the **Angelita monument** (1979), on the **Riviera Vittorio Mallozzi,** the street that runs above the beach. The **Grotte de Nerone,** now covered by Italian sunbathers, is what remains of the Imperial Villa. The **Museo Civico Archeologico** is close to the train station, but the majority of travelers head to one of Anzio's beaches, including **Dea Fortuna** and **Turridu.** Most beaches are open June 15 to September 15 from 9am-7:30pm. The cheapest option is to pack a beach towel and lie to the side of the main beach area for free. For a prime location with comfortable seating, expect to pay about €6 for an umbrella and €6-8 for a lounge chair. These beaches also have snack bars, changing facilities, volleyball courts, and foosball. If you get bored with *la dulce far niente* (the sweetness of doing nothing) on the beach, check out the nearby nature reserve of **Tor Caldara.** Pack a lunch or pick up provisions at the nearby **SMA** supermarket on V. G Matteoti (open M-Sa 8am-1pm and 4:45-8pm, Su 8am-1pm), but for fine dining with a spectacular ⛰view, head to **Ristorante Turcotto ❸**, R. V. Mallozzi, 44 (☎06 98 46 340), at the end of R. V. Mallozzi, which specializes in pasta with shrimp and orange essence (€9) and other creative seafood dishes.

PONTINE ISLANDS

The Pontine Islands are accessible by aliscafi *(hydrofoils) or slower, cheaper* traghetti *(ferries). Take the train from Termini to Anzio (1hr., every hr. 6am-11pm, €2.90). From the station head downhill, following signs to the "Porto," or take a taxi (€10) to the quay. From the port, you can take the CAREMAR ferry to Ponza (1½hr.; June 16-Sept. 15 M-F 9:25am, Sa 8:30am, Su and holidays 8:30am and 3pm; return M-F 5pm, Sa 5:15pm, Su and holidays 11am and 5:15pm; M-F €19.50, Sa-Su, holidays vary). The CAREMAR ticket office is in the white booth labeled "traghetto" on the quay in Anzio (☎06 98 60 00 83; www.caremar.it) and in Ponza (☎0771 80 565). The Linee Vetor hydrofoils are faster. (70min.; 3-5 per day 8:15am-7pm; M-F €21, Sa-Su and Aug. €24; bikes €6, bags €2-20, windsurfer €20.) Linee Vetor ticket office also on the quay in Anzio. Open 1hr. before departure. (☎06 98 45 083; www.vetor.it). Another office in Ponza (☎0771 80 549).*

The Pontine Islands, a stunning archipelago 40km off the coast of Anzio, were once believed to be home to the sorceress Circe, who captured and seduced the Greek hero Odysseus. Nero was exiled here, and Mussolini cast enemies of the state upon the 30 million-year-old volcanic residuum, only to be imprisoned here himself. The cliff-sheltered beaches, turquoise waters, assorted coves, tunnels, and grottoes have also provided pirates a place to unwind after pillaging and plundering. Ferries run to **Ponza,** an island with superb beaches from Anzio. A 10min. walk from the port leads to **Chiaia,** set at the foot of a spectacular 200m cliff. By bus, ride through Ponza's hillside to the even lovelier ⛰**Piscine Naturali.** (Take the bus to Le Foma and ask to be let off at the *piscine.* Cross the street and go down the long, steep path.) Cliffs crumbling into the ocean create this series of deep, crystal-clear natural pools separated by smooth rocky outcroppings perfect for sunbathing. The westernmost island is **Palmarola,** with irregular volcanic rock formations and steep white cliffs. To get to Palmarola, rent a boat (from €35 per day), or take a boat tour advertised at the port. The tiny island of **Zannone,** home to a wildlife preserve, is accessible only by boat. Try **Cooperativa Barcaioli Ponzesi,** C. Piscacane at the S. Antonio tunnel. (☎0771 80 059. 11am, return 7pm; €18.) Tours of Zannone, which is part of the **Circeo National Park,** take visitors around the coast, with time for walks through the forests on the *mufloni*-strewn islands, and to the medieval, legend-filled S. Spirito monastery.

For those who choose to spend the night, **Hotel Mari ❹**, C. Pisacane, 19, has comfortable rooms with A/C, bath, phone, and TV. (☎0771 80 101; www.hotelmari.it. Breakfast included. Internet €3 per 30min. July-Aug. singles €78; doubles €98-148.

Sept.-June €48/82-98. AmEx/MC/V.) Another option is the **Pensione Arcobaleno ❹**, V. Scotti di Basso, 6, 10min. from the port. The view alone is worth the hike. (☎0771 80 315; arcobalenoponza@libero.it. High season, with breakfast and dinner, €70 per person; low season €45-50. Discounts for extended stays. AmEx/MC/V.) Restaurants in the area are on the expensive side (*primi* around €10). The seafood and view at **Ristorante da Antonio ❹**, on the water at V. Dante, are worth the splurge. (☎0771 80 98 32.) The **Pro Loco Tourist Office** is on V. Molo Musco, next to the lighthouse. (☎0771 80 031; prolocoponza@libero.it. Open in summer M-Sa 9am-1pm and 4:30-8:30pm, Su 11am-noon and 5-7pm.)

CIVITAVECCHIA   ☎0766

Though Civitavecchia (pop. 50,000) itself is an unremarkable town, it is an essential transportation hub for travelers en route to either Sardinia or Corsica. If spending the night in Civitavecchia, a good option is Hotel Roma ❸, V. Monte Grappa, 27. Turn left off C. Centrocelle at Duca D. Abruzzi and walk about six blocks. The simple but well-maintained rooms with bath and TV have a prime location near the ferry docks. (☎/fax 0766 22 03 97. Singles €40; doubles €65; triples €75. AmEx/MC/V.) The best bet for a quick meal before jumping on the ferry is the ▧**pizzeria ❶** down V. Colle d'Olivo from Hotel Roma, which has been serving *pizza Civitavecchiana* (a thin sandwich of oiled bread, tomato sauce, and wilted greens) since the 1960s. (Pies €9. Slices €1. Open M-W and F-Su 10am-10pm.) For dessert, try **Gelateria Smeralda ❶**, C. Centrocelle, 73. Though a bit of a journey from the city center, it offers a wide variety of *gelato* and ▧**granita** (€2) flavors. (☎0766 58 87 21. Open M-W and F-Su 6:30am-10:30pm.)

Civitavecchia is easily reached by **train** from Rome's Termini station. Trains are frequent and cheap (1hr., 2 per hr., €4.10). There is also **bus** service from Rome (V. Guido and V. Boccelli, tickets at Bar Aurelia, €5). From the train station, take bus B, C, or D to the city center, or walk down Vle. Repubblica, which becomes **Viale G. Garibaldi** and then **Calata C. Laurenti** as it traces the length of the port. Ferries depart for Sardinia, Corsica, and Barcelona 1km away from the port entrance—hop on one of the free shuttles at the ferry station. The **ticket offices** and information centers for the ferry lines are in the ferry station, through the gates to the right on the quay. **Tirrenia** (☎0766 58 19 25) is open M-F 7:30am-12:55pm and 2:30-10:55pm, Sa 7:30-10:30am, 12:30-3pm, and 4:40-10:55pm, Su and holidays 7:30-10:30am and 4:40-10:55pm. **Corsica & Sardinia Ferries** (☎0766 60 07 14) is open M-Sa 6:30am-noon, Su 6:30-8:15am and 9pm-11:55pm. Away from the port, the other main street in Civitavecchia is the shop-lined **Corso Centrocelle**, which intersects Vle. Garibaldi at **Largo Plebiscito**. The **PIT tourist information point** is in the *piazza* on Largo Plebiscito (open M-Sa 8:30am-1:30pm and 4-7pm), and a **tourist office**, which provides **Internet**, is located just across the street at Vle. Garibaldi, 1. (Internet €1.50 per 10min., €2.50 per 30min., €4 per hr. Open in summer M-Sa 9am-8pm, Su 9am-3pm; in winter daily 9am-1pm and 3:30-7:30pm.) These offices provide help with accommodations, historical information, and transportation needs.

ROME AND LAZIO

The spectacle of daily life as it unfolds on streets and sidewalks is one of the great pleasures of a trip to Italy, and a major part of that spectacle is the Italian art of walking. As day turns to dusk, in cities and towns, Italians of all ages take to the streets for the *passeggiata*, the evening stroll. The *passeggiata* is above all a social event, an occasion for conversation among friends; one rarely, if ever, walks alone. There is also a strong sense of public performance; the back-and-forth movement of the promenade offers ample opportunity for lingering or flirtatious glances, a chance to see and be seen.

But the institution of the *passeggiata* is even older than it might seem. The antecedents of the modern activity can be traced all the way back to the 2nd and first centuries BC, when Roman magistrates began to endow the city with public porticoes. Inspired in part by the great *stoas* of Greece, these porticoes were typically large garden courts surrounded on all sides by colonnaded walkways; the imported marble decorating the columns, floor, and walls competed for the visitor's attention with statues, paintings, and other valuables plundered from the recently conquered Greek east. (The entrance to the Portico of Octavia, one of the more famous late republican porticoes, still stands in the Jewish Ghetto in Rome.)

The porticos were monuments dedicated to ancient Roman leisure, straddling the line between public garden, park, museum, and meeting place. But above all, as literary sources reveal, these were spaces for walking: a place for leisurely strolls with friends, for serious conversations between promenading politicians, and, most importantly, for catching the eye of potential paramours as they passed by. According to the poet Ovid (43 BC-AD 17), who, as a love poet, is an admittedly biased witness, a public portico was a glorified pick-up scene, and walking there seems to have been the ancient equivalent of a visit to a singles bar. In his how-to manual on the art of love he advises his (male) reader in the fine art of the seductive stroll:

"When she wears down the wide portico with her carefree steps, you should linger there too alongside her: be sure to walk ahead of her sometimes, then follow at her back; you should speed up at times, and then go more slowly. Don't be ashamed to weave through some of the columns between you, or to attach your side to hers." (Ovid *Ars Amatoria* 1.491-6)

Observe closely at your next *passeggiata*, and you'll find latter-day suitors still following elements of Ovid's advice (minus the column-weaving) some 2000 years later.

In ancient Rome, the pleasures of a leisurely stroll could be enjoyed in a private setting as well—if you were wealthy enough to own a country villa, where the scale and grandeur of private porticoes and gardens often surpassed their public, urban counterparts. Here, leisurely walks were more of an intellectual exercise: less flirtation, more disputation, you might say. In his villa at Tusculum, Cicero (106-43 BC) named one of his porticoes after Plato's Academy, and another after Aristotle's Lyceum, decorating them accordingly, so that he and his friends could stroll through their own philosophical playground, discussing ethics and rhetoric as latter-day Athenians. Nor was he alone in his penchant for fantasy design: we have evidence that his contemporaries named parts of their country retreats after famous topography from around the known world, so that a walk through a country villa became, in effect, a kind of metaphorical tourism.

Accompanying this fantasy travel was an increased interest in actual tourism as well, as the iron fist of the Roman empire made travel around the Mediterranean safer (and plunder from the provinces boosted the disposable income of her magistrates). For Romans, trips to Greece, now part of the Roman Empire, were especially popular, and to Athens in particular, whose glory days were far enough in the past to inspire feelings of nostalgic wonder not dissimilar to the experience of the modern tourist at the Roman Forum, for example. Cicero, in fact, structures one of his philosophical dialogues as a walk by Roman tourists in Athens, through the recently abandoned Academy of Plato. One of the characters in the dialogue tries to explain the pleasure derived from treading ground made famous centuries before; "wherever we go," he says, "we're walking through history." The walk of the tourist, as Cicero reveals, has its own history.

Timothy O' Sullivan is an Assistant Professor of Classical Studies at Trinity University in San Antonio, Texas. He received his Ph.D. in Classical Philology from Harvard University in 2003 with a dissertation titled "The Mind in Motion: The Cultural Significance of Walking in the Roman World."

PIEDMONT AND VALLE D'AOSTA

HIGHLIGHTS OF PIEMONTE AND VALLE D'AOSTA

CELEBRATE Olympic victories in **Turin** as athletes accept their medals in the Piazza Castello (p. 165).

TASTE *Barbera, Barbaresco,* and sparkling *Asti Spumante* in **Piedmont's wine country** (p. 172).

TRAVERSE the frozen end of Italy through prime skiing terrain in the mountains of **Valle d'Aosta** (p. 184).

LISTEN to the silence on **Isola di San Giulio** in Lago di Orta (p. 182).

PIEDMONT (PIEMONTE)

More than just the source of the Po River, Piedmont has long been a fountainhead of nobility and fine cuisine. The area rose to prominence in 1861 when the Savoys, having dominated the region since the 11th century, selected Turin as capital of their re-united Italy. But the capital relocated four years later, and Piedmont fell back into obscurity. Today, European tourists escape the whirlwind city pace on the banks of Lago Maggiore, while outdoor fiends and expert skiers conquer Alpine mountaintops in the northeast. Though Piedmont is sometimes called the Prussia of Italy, referring to its high standard of living and modern, well-organized infrastructure, *Piemontesi* enjoy strolling through the countryside and indulging the palate as much as the next Italian. With the Olympics coming to Turin in winter 2006, the region is sure to rise to prominence once again.

TURIN (TORINO)   ☎011

A century and a half before Turin (pop. 860,000) was selected to host the 2006 Winter Olympics, it served as the first capital of a unified Italy. Founded by the Romans, Turin retains its chessboard layout from ancient times, making the city uniquely easy to navigate. With glamorous Baroque architecture built under the Savoy rule and over 18km of arcades lining its streets, Turin is naturally a magnet for period films, many of which form the annals of the award-winning Italian movie industry in Museo Nazionale del Cinema. Renowned for chocolate and cafe culture, Turin also encompasses numerous parks and contemporary art masterpieces. Though Turin's cultural and design offerings rival Milan's, it manages to avoid many of the pollution and crime problems that plague larger cities. Elaborate preparations for the 2006 Olympics and urban renewal projects promise that Turin will welcome visitors with typical Savoy flair.

◧ TRANSPORTATION

Flights: Caselle Airport services European destinations. From Pta. Nuova take blue buses to "Caselle Airport," via Pta. Susa (€5). Buy tickets at Bar Cervino, C. V. Emanuele II, 57; Bar Mille Luci, P. XVIII Dicembre, 5; or onboard (€0.50 surcharge).

OLYMPIC UPSET. Due to Olympic construction and urban renewal projects, Turin's transportation landscape will change rapidly in the next several years. Make sure to contact the tourist office or transportation bureau for updates on schedules, closures, and new openings.

Trains: Stazione Porta Nuova (☎011 66 53 098 or Trenitalia call center 89 20 21; www.trenitalia.com), on C. V. Emanuele II. The station has a small but pricey market, barber shop, post office, luggage storage, and lost and found. To: **Genoa** (2hr., every hr. 6:20am-11pm, €7.90); **Lyon, France** via **Chambéry** (4½hr., 3 per day 8:10am-5:37pm); **Milan Centrale** (2hr., every hr. 4:50am-10:50pm, €7.90); **Rome Termini** (6-7hr.; Eurostar 5:55am, 7:10am; InterCity 6:35, 9:10, 11:10am, 1:10, 3:10, 10:15, 11:05pm; from €40.55); **Venice Santa Lucia** (5hr.; InterCity 6:05, 7:00, 9:05am, 2:05, 5:05pm; €30.68). **Stazione Porta Susa** (in Turin) is 1 stop toward Milan.

Buses: Autostazione Terminal Bus, C. V. Emanuele II, 131/H in front of the Court (☎011 43 38 100). From Pta. Nuova, take cable car #9 or 15 (5 stops). Serves ski resorts, the Riviera, and the valleys of Susa and Pinerolo. Ticket office open daily 6:30am-1:15pm and 2-8:30pm. To: **Aosta** (2hr.; M-F 2 per day, Su 1 per day; €7.10), **Courmayeur** via **Aosta** (4hr., €8.20); **Milan** (2hr., every hr., €8.62).

Public Transportation: A 70min. ticket to **city buses** and **cable cars** costs €0.90; 1-day ticket €3. Buy tickets at *tabaccherie,* newsstands, or bars. Buses run daily 5am-1am.

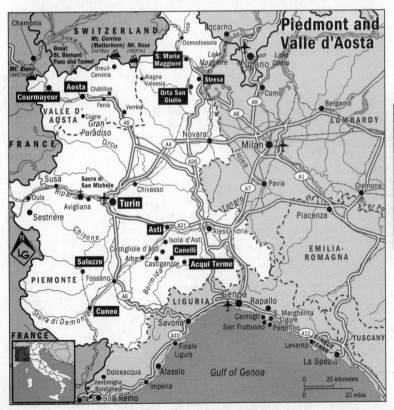

PIEDMONT AND VALLE D'AOSTA

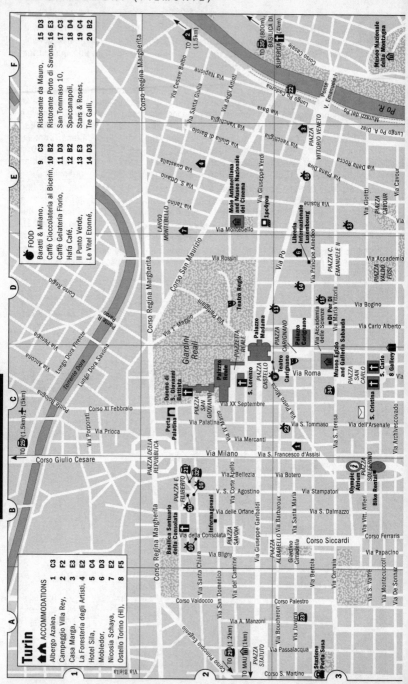

PIEDMONT AND
VALLE D'AOSTA

Map labels:

Corso Fiume
Via Alby
Via Gatti
Viale G. Guerreno
Corso G. Lanza
Corso Moncalieri
PIAZZA CRIMEA
Ponte Umberto I
Corso Moncalieri
Corso Cairoli
Via de' Mille
Via Frat. Calandra
Cavana
Via San Massimo
Albertina
Via G. Mazzini
Via S. F. da Paola
PIAZZA BODONI
Via Gotto
Via Lagrange
Roma
Via Gramsci
PIAZZA C. FELICE
PIAZZA PALEOCAPA
Telecom Italia
Stazione Porta Nuova
Via Sacchi
Via Camerana
Via San Secondo
Via Vincenzo Gioberti
Via Massena
Corso Re Umberto
Via Confienza
Corso Vittorio Emanuele II
Via Magenta
Galleria Civica d'Arte Moderna
Via Lamarmora
Corso Stati Uniti
Corso Galileo Ferraris
Via San Quintino
Via M. Fanti
Via O. Revel
Corso Giacomo Matteotti
Via C. B. Bricherasio
Via Magenta
Via Y. Vela
Corso Vinzaglio
TO CASTELLO DI RIVOLI MUSEO D'ARTE CONTEMPORANEA (15km)
Parco del Valentino
Orto Botanico
Castello del Valentino
Bike Rental
Borgo e Rocca Medioevale
Di Per Di
Corso Massimo D'Azeglio
Via Ormea
Via Baretti
Via Madama Cristina
PIAZZA MAD CRISTINA
Via Principe Tommaso
Via Sant'Anselmo
Via Belfore
Via Saluzzo
Via B. Galliari
Via Berthollet
Corso Raffaello
Corso Guglielmo Marconi
Via Belfiore
Via Saluzzo
Via Valperga Caluso
Via Nizza
PIAZZA NIZZA
TO (500m), SAN GIOVANNI BATTISTA (1km), PINACOTECA GIOVANNI E MARELLA AGNELLI (1.5km), MUSEO NAZIONALE DELL'AUTOMOBILE (2km)
Via Donizetti
Corso Sommeiler
TO OSPEDALE MAURIZIANO (50m)
Via Montevecchio
Corso Duca d'Aosta
Corso Trento
Via Trieste
Via Legnano
Via Pastrengo
Via Valeggio
Via Luigi Einaudi
Via Colombo
Via Amerigo Vespucci

500 meters
500 yards

NIGHTLIFE	
Arancia di Mezzanotte,	21 B2
The Beach,	22 F3
Café Procope,	23 A3
Damadama,	24 D4
Dock's Dora,	25 C1
Giancarlo,	26 E4
Hiroshima Mon Amour,	27 D6
Kogin's Club,	28 F5
Magazzini di Gilgamesh,	29 A2
Pier 7-9-11,	30 E4
The Shamrock Inn,	31 D4
Shore,	32 B2
Six Nations Murphy's Pub,	33 D4
Theatro,	34 C3
Zoo Bar,	35 F2

Taxis: ☎011 57 37, 011 57 30, or 011 33 99.

Car Rental: in Stazione Porta Nuova, on the right side by the platforms. **Avis** (☎011 66 99 800), from €60 per day (100km). Open M-F 8:30am-noon and 3-6pm, Sa 8:30am-noon. **Maggiore** (☎011 65 03 013). Open M-F 8am-noon and 3-6pm, Sa 8am-noon.

Bike Rental: Parco Valentino Noleggio Biciclette, V. Ceppi (☎347 41 34 728 or 339 58 29 332), in Parco Valentino. Walk east (toward the Po River) down C. V. Emanuele; just before Ponte Umberto I, turn right. One of many city-run bike rentals in parks. €3.61 per half-day, €5.16 per day. Open Tu-Su 9am-12:30pm and 2:30-7pm. Free bike rental in the Olympic Atria in P. Solferino. Open daily 9:30am-7pm.

✥ 🔢 ORIENTATION AND PRACTICAL INFORMATION

Turin is flanked by the Alps on three sides. **Stazione Porta Nuova,** in the heart of the city, is the usual place of arrival. The city itself is an Italian rarity: its streets meet at right angles, making it easy to navigate by bus and on foot. **Corso Vittorio Emanuele II** runs east past the station to the **Po River,** where it intersects **Parco del Valentino** on the south and the **Murazzi** district on the north. **Via Roma,** the major north-south thoroughfare, houses the principal sights and shops. North of the station, it heads through **Piazza Felice, Piazza San Carlo,** and **Piazza Castello.** From P. Castello, **Via Pietro Micca** extends southwest to **Piazza Solferino** and the Olympic Atria, while **Via Po** veers southeast to **Piazza Vittorio Veneto** and the University district, intersecting the river just above the Murazzi. **Via Garibaldi** stretches west from P. Castello to **Piazza Statuto** and **Stazione Porta Susa,** south of which will be the new city center, to be completed by 2008. Above P. Castello, the **Palazzo Reale** and **Giardini Reali** lie below the **Corso Regina Margherita,** which connects **Piazza della Repubblica** slightly west to the **Docks Dora** district north of the Giardini Reali. **Via Nizza** heads south from Stazione Pta. Nuova to the **Lingotto** area that will house the **Olympic district**.

Tourist Office: Turismo Torino, P. Solferino (☎011 53 51 81; www.turismotorino.org), in the Atrium 2006, the northern of the 2 pavilions. English, German, French, and Spanish spoken. Excellent **map** of Turin. Info regarding museums, cafes, booking for hotels, and guide reservations. Open daily 9:30am-7pm. **Info booth** at Pta. Nuova, opposite platform 17. Open M-Sa 9:30am-7pm, Su 9:30am-3:30pm.

Currency Exchange: In Pta. Nuova. Offers a decent rate. Open daily 7:30am-7:35pm. MC/V. Otherwise try the **banks,** most with 24hr. **ATMs** along V. Roma and V. Alfieri (generally open M-F 8:20am-1:20pm and 2:20-4:20pm).

Beyond Tourism: Informagiovani, V. delle Orfane, 20 (☎800 99 85 00 or 011 44 24 950; informagiovani@comune.torino.it.). Youth center providing information on jobs, volunteering, and enterprises for young people.

Luggage Storage: In Pta. Nuova. €3.80 per 5hr.; €0.20-0.60 per additional hr. thereafter. Open daily 6am-midnight.

English-Language Bookstore: Libreria Internazionale Luxembourg, V. Accademia delle Scienze, 3 (☎011 56 13 896), across from P. Carignano. Staff helps navigate 3 floors of English, French, German, and Spanish books, papers, and magazines. Open M-Sa 8am-7:30pm, Su 10am-1pm and 3-7pm. Closed July-Aug.

Laundromat: "Lavasciuga" Laundrettes and Internet Points are located throughout the city. (www.lavasciuga.torino.it has a complete list of locations.) **Lavanderia Vizzini,** V. S. Secondo, 30 (☎011 54 58 82). Facing Pta. Nuova, walk 2 blocks right. Wash and dry €7.75 per 4kg. Open M-F 8:30am-1pm and 3-7:30pm, Sa 8:30am-1pm.

Emergency: ☎113. **Ambulance:** ☎118. **First Aid:** ☎011 57 47.

Pharmacy: Farmacia Boniscontro, C. V. Emanuele, 66 (☎011 54 12 71). 3 blocks east of Pta. Nuove. Open 9am-12:30pm and 3pm-9am. Posts after-hours rotations.

Hospital: San Giovanni Battista, C. Bramante, 88-90 (☎011 63 31 633), commonly known as Molinette. **Mauriziano Umberto I,** Largo Turati, 62 (☎011 50 81 111).

Internet Access: 1pc4you, V. Verdi, 20/G (☎011 83 59 08), just around the corner from the Mole. 72 speedy machines with flat screens. From €2 per hr. with purchased card. Open M-Sa 9am-9pm, Su 2-8pm. **Telecom Italia Internet Corners,** V. Roma, 18, just off P. Castello. **Branch** inside the Pta. Nuova (on the left side near the main exit). Both have phone-card web stations. €0.10 per 70 seconds. Open daily 8am-10pm.

Post Office: V. Alfieri, 10 (☎011 50 60 260), off P. S. Carlo, facing north (toward P. Reale), head left 2 blocks down on the right. Fax and telegram service. Open M-F 8:30am-7pm, Sa 8:30am-1pm, last day of the month 8:30am-noon. *Fermoposta* open M-Sa 9am-noon and 3-7pm. **Postal Code:** 10100.

⌐ ACCOMMODATIONS AND CAMPING

Torino's budget accommodations are not clustered together, though several can be found near Stazione Pta. Nuova. Many new hotels and residences have sprung up in anticipation of Olympic crowds; family-run B&Bs offer some of the best deals in the city, though municipal law requires them to close for two months during the year. Many take this time in July and August, so call ahead for reservations.

▓ **La Foresteria degli Artisti,** V. degli Artisti, 15 (☎011 83 77 85 or 33 38 20 78 27). Run by artistic twin sisters, La Foresteria is a renovated 19th-century attic apartment with wood floors, white beanbags, antique furniture, DVD player, library, laundry, and kitchen. Ring bell for Coss F&G, then walk to 2nd door on left and ring again. Breakfast included. Reservations required. Open Sept.12-Dec. 12; closed July 1-Sept.12. Single €50; double €80. Extra bed €20. Cash only. ❹

Ostello Torino (HI), V. Alby, 1 (☎011 66 02 939; hostelto@tin.it). Take bus #52 (#64 on Su) from Pta. Nuova. After crossing the river, get off at the Lanza stop at V. Crimea and follow the "Ostello" signs to C. G. Lanza, before turning left at V. L. Gatti. 76 beds and TV room in a residential setting. Breakfast and sheets included. Dinner €8.50. Laundry €4. Reception M-Sa 7am-12:30pm and 3:30-11:30pm, Su 7-10am and 3:30-11:30pm. Lockout 10am-3:30pm. Curfew 11:30pm; ask for key if going out. Closed Dec. 20-Feb. 1. Single-sex and co-ed 4- to 10-bed dorms €12.50; doubles €31 with bath €35; triples €46.50; quads €58. €1.50 heating surcharge Oct.-Apr. MC/V. ❶

Albergo Azalea, V. Mercanti, 16, 4th fl. (☎011 53 81 15 or 333 24 674 49). Exit Pta. Nuova on the right and take bus #58 or 72 to V. Garibaldi. Turn left on V. Garibaldi, away from P. Castello, and left on V. Mercanti. 10 clean and cozy rooms with white furniture. Singles €30, with bath €40; doubles €50/60. MC/V. ❸

Casa Marga, V. Bava, 1 bis (☎011 88 38 92 or 339 43 71 086), just above P. V. Veneto. Located at an ideal location close to the university and Murazzi. Offers 2 colorful double rooms each with 1st floor and mezzanine bed, decorated in hippie style. Private bath, TV, laundry, and family cat. Closed in summer alternating dates for max. of 2 months, so call ahead. Singles €43, doubles €65. Cash only. ❹

Nicosia Schaya, Largo Montebello, 33 (☎011 19 71 28 73 or 348 85 11 096), on the top floor. Sliding-glass doors lead to the privacy of comfortable rooms with flat-screen TV, phone, balcony, and private bath. Singles €39; doubles €59, add €35 for 3rd person. Cash only. A floor below, **B&B Nicosia Pelu** is a simpler, more traditional place with laundry and kitchen facilities. Same price scheme as above, discounts for extended stay. Both closed 2 months per year, but alternate so 1 floor always operating. ❸

Mobledor, V. Accademia Albertina, 1, 3rd. fl. (☎011 88 84 45; www.hotelmobledor.it). Leave Pta. Nuova by the front door and take bus #68 to Giolitti. Go 1 block to V. S. Croce and turn left, then left again on V. Accademia Albertina. In-room baths have curtains instead of doors, but a location by the university quarter puts guests near the nightlife. Thatch walls and flowers add a tropical feel. Some singles share a bath. Singles €34; doubles €52; triples €65. MC/V. ❸

Hotel Sila, P. Carlo Felice, 80, 3rd. fl. (☎011 53 45 44). Blonde wood floors, good light and large rooms all with sink and shower. Lounge with TV. Breakfast included. Singles €43; doubles €63; quads €110. Cash only. ❹

Campeggio Villa Rey, Str. Superiore Val S. Martino, 27 (☎/fax 011 81 90 117). From Pta. Nuova take the #72 or 63 bus to Pta. Palazzo, change to the #3 tram on C. Regina, and ride to the end of the line (Hermada). From there, walk 500m uphill or take bus #54. Quiet hillside location with views of the Basilica Superga houses caravans and a few tent campers. Bar, small market, and restaurant. 2-course meal €12. Laundry €3.10. €3-6 per person, €4-5 per tent, €1.10 per car. Over 4-person campers €9-10.50 per person. Electricity €1.50. Showers €0.80. Cash only. ❶

◨ FOOD

Ever since the Savoys started taking an evening cup of *cioccolato* in 1678, Turin has grown into one of the great international centers of chocolate. Ferrero Rocher and Nutella are its most famous products. Napoleonic restrictions on buying chocolate brought the hazelnut substitute *gianduiotti,* now the key ingredient in a distinctly Torinese ice cream flavor known as *gianduia,* available at cafes around P. Castello. On the savory side, Piemontese cuisine is a blend of northern Italian peasant staples and elegant French garnishes. Butter replaces olive oil, and cheese, mushrooms, and white truffles are used more than vegetables or spices. *Agnolotti,* ravioli stuffed with lamb and cabbage, is the local pasta specialty, but polenta, warm cornmeal often topped with fontina cheese, is the more common starch. The three most outstanding (and expensive) red wines in Italy, *Barolo, Barbaresco,* and *Barbera,* are available in markets and restaurants. To sample the true flavors of Piemontese cuisine, be ready to pay—restaurants that specialize in regional dishes are expensive. Self-caterers can head to **Dì Per Dì** supermarket. (Branches at V. Maria Vittoria, 11 and V. S. Massimo, 43. Open M-Tu and Th-Sa 8:30am-1:30pm and 3:30-7:30pm, W 8:30am-1pm.) Find edibles at P. della Repubblica, in what claims to be Europe's largest **open-air market.**

> **TIP CHOCOHOLICS UNITE.** Sample the city's specialties with the 24- or 48-hour **ChocoPass** (www.cioccola-to.it), offering 10-15 tastings of chocolate-based products, including *gianduiotti,* pralines, and ice cream at cafes and *pasticcerie* throughout the city. Purchase a pass for €10 (24hr.; 10 tastings) or €15 (48hr.; 15 tastings) at any of the Turismo Torino offices.

 Tre Galli, V. S. Agostino, 25 (☎011 52 16 027). The revitalized Bohemian neighborhood surrounding P. Filberto has produced many traditional eateries, none of them nicer than Tre Galli. Piemonte standards like *agnolotti* (€7) go well with steak filets (€8-14) at an outdoor table, where you can watch the busy foot-traffic through the area. *Primi* €7-10, *secondi* €8-17. Open Tu-Su noon-2:30pm and 8-11:30pm. Closed July. MC/V. ❸

Le Vitel Etonné, V. San Francesco da Paola, 4 (☎011 81 24 621; www.leviteletonne.com). A popular spot for Turin's casual professional set, Le Vitel Etonné has a wine cellar in the basement (€3 per glass) and an artisanal cafe upstairs, with a menu that changes depending on what the cooks buy at the market. The *pomodori ripieni di riso ai fioro di zucca su salsa di zafferano* (cooked tomatoes stuffed with rice; €7) is an elegant preparation of traditional ingredients. *Primi* €6-8, *secondi* €8-9. Open daily 10am-midnight. MC/V. ❷

■ **Caffè Gelateria Fiorio,** V. Po, 8 (☎011 81 73 25 or 011 81 70 612). Just off P. Castello, this institution is as famous for its exquisite buffet lunch (€13-14) as it is for the smoothest *gelato* in the city. It was once frequented by so many officers and aristocrats that it became known as "the pony-tail cafe." Cones from €1.50, sundaes €4.50-7. Open M-Th and Su 8am-1am, F-Sa 8am-2am. ❸

Ristorante da Mauro, V. M. Vittoria, 21/D (☎011 81 70 604). After 40 years in the same location, Signore Mauro is known for his exquisite and affordable Tuscan and Piemontese cuisine, with a following that includes soccer player Del Piero. *Bue del piemonte ai ferri* (roasted boar; €9.30) and *castellana al prosciutto* (€7.50) are great. *Primi* €6, *secondi* €6-13. Open Tu-Su noon-2pm and 7:30-10pm. Cash only. ❸

Il Punto Verde, V. S. Massimo, 17 (☎011 88 55 43), off V. Po near P. V. Emanuele II. A California juice bar and a traditional Italian *trattoria* had a vegetarian baby and named it Punto. Giant *monopiatti* (meal with wine, dessert, and coffee) €11.50. Blenderized fruit-veggie drink €4. Vegan options. *Primi* €4.50-7, *secondi* €5.50-8.50. Cover €1.50. Open M-F noon-2:30pm and 7-10:30pm, Sa 7-10:30pm. Closed Aug. MC/V. ❷

Spaccanapoli, V. Mazzini, 19 (☎011 81 26 694). Pizza by the meter (€22-34) is large enough to feed a small army. Pizza €6-9.50. *Primi* €6-10, *secondi* €9.90-14.50. Cover €1.90. Open Tu-Su noon-2:30pm and 7pm-midnight. AmEx/MC/V. ❷

Ristorante Porto di Savona, P. V. Veneto, 2 (☎011 81 73 500; www.portodis-avona.com). A homey local institution. If *carne cruda* (marinated raw hand-chopped veal; €8) is a little too "authentic" for you, house-made *agnolotti* (€8) and other standards provide an easier introduction to regional cuisine. Lunch *menù* M-Sa. *Primi* €6.50-8, *secondi* €7.50-14.50. Cover €1.80. Open daily 12:30-2:30pm and 7:30-10:30pm. Closed 1st 2 weeks of Aug. MC/V. ❸

Stars & Roses, P. Paleocapa, 2, near P. C. Felice (☎011 51 62 052). They're funky and they know it. Nacho-orange interior and red velvet curtains contrast traditional spaghetti dishes except for the cultural calzones (choose from Indian, Russian, Japanese, Scottish, and Irish; €9). Pizza €5-9. *Primi* €5-7, *secondi* €7-16. Cover €2. Open daily noon-3pm and 7:30pm-12:30am. Closed M and Su lunch. AmEx/MC/V. ❷

Hafa Café, V. Sant'Agostino, 23/C (☎011 43 62 899; www.babanmil.it). Sit on low Moroccan cushions beneath pointed arches at this elegant cultural enclave where you can enjoy a spicy, pungent alternative to Italian fare sold at neighboring restaurants. Lunch platters €8, cocktails €2-6. Open Tu-Sa 11am-2am. MC/V. ❷

Caffè Cioccolateria al Bicerin, V. della Consolata, 5 (☎011 43 69 325; www.bicerin.it). The cafe has sold its namesake drink, a hot mixture of coffee, chocolate, and cream (€4) since 1763 to such notables as Nietzche, Dumas, and Puccini. Open M-Tu and Th-F 8:30am-7:30pm, Sa-Su 8:30am-1pm and 3:30-7:30pm. ❶

Baratti & Milano, P. Castello, 29 (☎011 44 07 138). The cafe has been turning out its fine *gianduja* hazelnut chocolates (€2-3) since King Vittorio Emanuele II granted his favorite sweet shop the Savoy Coat of Arms in February 1875. Today even commoners can enjoy the delicacies, as well as *panini* (€2.50) and coffee, inside the gold-embellished rooms of the shop. Open daily 8am-8:30pm. Aug. closes 4pm. ❶

San Tommaso 10, V. San Tommaso, 10 (☎011 53 42 01). The original home of the famous Lavazza Italian coffee, this 100-year-old cafe is blanketed with backlit stills from Lavazza commercials and risqué posters of models with strategically placed coffee cups and spoons. Coffee €1-3. Open M-Sa 8am-midnight. ❶

SIGHTS

> **TIP** **TOURIN' CARD.** The best deal in the city wisely combines access to public transportation as well as sights. The Torino Card (2-day €15, 3-day €17), provides free entrance to more than 130 museums, monuments, castles, and royal residences in Turin and throughout Piedmont. It also allows free access to public transport, the TurismoBus Torino, and the boats for river navigation on the Po, as well as discounts on guided tours and shows. Available at any Turismo Torino info point and at most hotels.

■ **MOLE ANTONELLIANA.** The largest structure in the world built using traditional masonry, and the world's tallest museum, the Mole dominates Turin's skyline. Begun as a synagogue in 1863, it ended as an architectural eccentricity. Though the architect Antonello intended it to be only 47m tall, by the time it was inaugurated in 1908, the Mole had reached a towering 167m. The glass elevator that runs through the middle of the building goes to the observation deck. Today, the Mole boasts the unique **Museo Nazionale del Cinema.** The first floor houses a mod bar with color-changing tables and movie screens. On the 2nd floor, interactive exhibits chronicle the history of cinema, beginning with displays of bizarre phenakistiscopes, stereoscopes, and magic lanterns that passed for entertainment in the late 19th century. At the center of the museum on the 3rd floor, **Temple Hall** holds a field of red velvet chaise lounges for visitors to watch Italian films projected on screens high above. A suspended staircase nearby winds to exhibits displaying Fellini's hat and red scarf and Marilyn Monroe's shoes, among other artifacts. A variety of movies dubbed in Italian, from *Robocop* to 1920s silent films produced in Turin's studios, are screened in idiosyncratic settings off the hall—a 1960s living room, a Neolithic cave, and a giant fridge—which sometimes bear subtle connections to the films being shown (and sometimes not). You haven't lived until you've heard Arnold Schwarzenegger say *"Ritornerò."* Every hour, images on the dome disappear and music plays, while the Mole's walls are drawn up to reveal the building's skeleton beneath. *(V. Montebello, 20, a few blocks east of P. Castello. ☎011 81 25 658; www.museonatzionaledelcinema.org. Museum and bar open Tu-F and Su 9am-8pm, Sa 9am-11pm. Museum €5.20, students €4.20. Elevator €3.62/2.58; combined ticket €6.80/5.20.)*

> **REACH FOR THE SKY.** The towering spire of Mole Antonelliana served as inspiration for the official emblem of the XX Winter Olympic Games.

■ **CATTEDRALE DI SAN GIOVANNI (DUOMO) AND THE CHIESA DI SAN LORENZO.** The Holy Shroud of Turin, one of the most enigmatic relics in Christendom, has been housed in the Cappella della Santa Sindone of the Renaissance **Cattedrale di San Giovanni Battista** since 1694. Said to be the burial cloth of Jesus, the 3 ft. by 14 ft. cloth first entered official accounts when the Crusaders brought it back from Jerusalem in the 13th century. Transferred to Turin from Chambéry, France in 1578, it rests today in a climate-controlled case. With rare exceptions—the next planned public exhibition of the shroud is in 2025—a photograph of the unfolded shroud to the left of the cathedral's entrance is as close as visitors can get to the real thing. A negative below the photograph reveals even more detail than the actual cloth, including the countenance of a man with fractured nose and bruised cheek. It was carbon-dated to the early 1000s, though recent studies have suggested that a newer, repaired piece of the shroud from the Middle Ages had been tested and the original may in fact be 2500 years old. In any case, the shroud continues to represent a sustained confrontation between science and faith, resulting in attempted arson in 1997; repairs to the chapel are still ongoing behind its *trompe l'oeil* painted replacement. *(Behind Palazzo Reale where V. XX Settembre crosses P. S. Giovanni. ☎011 43 61 540. Open daily 7am-noon and 3-7pm. Free. Modest dress required.)* Nearby, to the left of the Palazzo Reale, the 16th-century **Chiesa di San Lorenzo** served as temporary home to the shroud before completion of San Giovanni. Its soaring dome was designed by Guarino Guarini, and its ribs form an overlapping eight-pointed star reminiscent of the Islamic architecture that influenced Guarini on his travels. In the sacristy to the right, an exact-sized replica of the shroud hangs on the wall. *(V. Palazzo di Citta, 4, at the corner with P. Castello. ☎011 43 61 527; www.sanlorenzo.torino.it. Open daily 8am-noon and 3-6pm. Free.)*

■ **MUSEO EGIZIO AND GALLERIA SABAUDA.** The **Palazzo dell'Accademia delle Scienze** houses two of Turin's best museums, the **Museo Egizio** and the **Galleria Sabauda.** From 1903-37, the Italian Archaeological Mission brought thousands of artifacts home to Turin, making Egizio the 2nd-largest Egyptian collection outside Cairo. Museum highlights include life-sized wooden Nubian statues, the massive Ellesiya temple, and the well-furnished tomb of 14th-century BC architect Kha, one of the few tombs spared by grave robbers. Though the museum's chronological presentation of its vast collections is highly accessible, the building and galleries themselves could use renovation. *(V. Accademia delle Scienze, 6. 2 blocks from P. Castello. ☎011 56 17 776; www.museoegizio.org. Open Tu-Su 8:30am-7:30pm. €6.50, ages 18-25 €3, under 18 or over 65 free.)* On the 3rd and 4th floors, the Galleria Sabauda houses art collections from Palazzo Reale and Palazzo Carignano, and is renowned for its 14th- to 18th-century Flemish and Dutch paintings, including Van Eyck's *St. Francis Receiving the Stigmata,* Memling's *Passion,* and Rembrandt's *Old Man Sleeping. (V. Accademia delle Scienze, 6. ☎011 54 74 40; www.museitorino.it/galleriasabauda. Open Tu and F-Su 8:30am-2pm, W 2-7:30pm, Th 10am-7:30pm. €4, ages 18-25 €2, under 18 or over 65 free. Combined ticket for both museums €8.)*

■ **CASTELLO DI RIVOLI MUSEO D'ARTE CONTEMPORANEA.** This museum houses one of Europe's most impressive contemporary art collections in a 14th-century Savoy residence. The sleek venue holds works from the 1950s onward, and many exhibits were designed specifically for the *castello's* cavernous spaces, including Sol Lewitt's 1992 *Panels and Towers.* Other featured artists include Bruce Nauman, Pistoletto (his clamor-causing *Venus in Rags* is on display), and Claes Oldenburg. The Paradise Institute by Janet Cardiff, an interactive theater in a giant box, puts visitors into a surround-sound experience that simulates people talking and moving about at the movies. It's so real you'll be tempted to turn around and yell, "Quiet!" at the wall behind you. *(P. Mafalda di Savoia in Rivoli. Take bus #36 or 66 from Turin, or inquire at the bus station about the direct shuttle bus. ☎011 95 65 222; www.castellodirivoli.org. Open Tu-Th 10am-5pm, F-Su 1-am-9pm. €6.50, students €3.50.)*

PINACOTECA GIOVANNI E MARELLA AGNELLI. This tiny museum atop a former Fiat factory holds just 26 pieces from the last 300 years. The collection features Venetian landscape works by Il Canaletto, Impressionist works by Matisse and Renoir, and pieces by Tiepolo, Picasso, and Modigliani. *(V. Nizza, 230, on top of the Lingotto. ☎011 00 62 713; www.pinacoteca-agnelli.it. Open Tu-Su 9am-7pm. €4, students €2.50.)*

PALAZZO REALE. The Palazzo Reale forms part of the "Corona di Delitie," a ring of Savoy royal residences that came under the protection of UNESCO as a World Heritage Site in 1997. Home to the Princes of Savoy from 1645 to 1865, the ornate *palazzo* contains 300+ rooms, though only 30 are covered on the tour, including the king's relatively simple bedroom. Louis le Nôtre, famous for his work on the gardens of Versailles, designed the grounds in 1697. *(In Piazzetta Reale, at the end of P. Castello.* ☎ *011 43 61 455. Palazzo open Tu-Su 8:30am-7:30pm, with mandatory guided tour. €6.50, students €3.25. Gardens open 9am-1hr. before sunset.)* In the right wing of the Royal Palace lies the **Armeria Reale** (Royal Armory) of the House of Savoy with an extensive collection of medieval and Renaissance war tools. *(P. Castello, 191.* ☎ *011 54 38 89. Open Tu and Th 8:15am-2pm, Sa 8:15am-1:45pm. €4.50, under 18 or over 65 free.)*

GALLERIA CIVICA D'ARTE MODERNA E CONTEMPORANEA (GAM). The city's premier modern and contemporary art museum devotes two floors each to 19th- and 20th-century works mostly by Italians, including some Modiglianis and de Chiricos. Though its collection is not the most representative of the diverse styles of these periods, it also has Andy Warhol's gruesome *Orange Car Crash* and a few works by Picasso, Chagall, Klee, and Renoir. *(V. Magenta, 31. On the corner of C. G. Ferraris, off Largo V. Emanuele. Take tram #1, 9, or 15.* ☎ *011 44 29 518; www.gamtorino.it. Open Tu-Su 9am-7pm. €7.50, under 26 €6, under 10 or over 65 free. Free Tu.)*

BASILICA DI SUPERGA. When the French attacked Turin on September 6, 1706, King Vittorio Amedeo II made a pact with the Virgin Mary to build a basilica in her honor should the city withstand the invasion. Turin stood unconquered, and famous architect Juvarra helped fulfil the vow, erecting a Neo-Classical portico and high drum to support the basilica's spectacular dome. In a tragic event in 1949, a plane carrying the entire Turin soccer team crashed into the basilica; their tombs lie in the church next to the Savoys'. The basilica stands on a 672m summit outside Turin, described by Le Corbusier as "the most enchanting position in the world." Indeed, it offers panoramic views of the city, the Po Valley below, and the Alps beyond. *(Take tram #15 from V. XX Settembre to Stazione Sassi. From the station, take bus #79 or board a small cable railway for a clanking ride uphill. 18min.; every hr. on the hr. Cable Car* ☎ *011 57 64 733; www.glt.to.it. Runs M and W-F 9am-noon and 2-8pm, Tu 7pm-midnight, Sa-Su 9am-8pm. Round-trip €3.10, Su and holidays €4.13. Basilica* ☎ *011 89 80 083; www.basilicadisuperga.com. Open daily Apr.-Oct. 9am-noon and 3-6pm; Nov.-Mar. 9am-noon and 3-5pm. Admission to dome of basilica and tombs of the Savoy each €3, students €2.)*

PARCO DEL VALENTINO. One of Italy's largest parks, the designer Valentino's lush grounds on the banks of the Po provide safe haven for whispering lovers and frolicking children. Upon entering the park from C. V. Emanuele, **Castello del Valentino** is on the left. Its distinctly French air honors the royal lady Christina of France, who in turn made the castle her favorite residence. It now houses the University's Facoltà di Architettura and is open to the public only by appointment (☎ 011 66 94 592). However, the fake *rocca* (castle) in the nearby **Borgo e Rocca Medievale**, built for the Italian Industry and Crafts Exhibition of 1884, is more impressive and open to the public, along with its attached shop-filled village. *(Park and castle at Vle. Virgilio, 107, along the Po.* ☎ *011 44 31 701; www.comune.torino.it/musei/civici/bm. Castle open Tu-Su 9am-7pm. €5, students €4. Village open M-Su 9am-7pm. Free.)*

BASILICA SANTUARIO DELLA CONSOLATE. This ornate Baroque church belongs to Turin's cult of the Virgin, with gold and jeweled offerings of gratitude from the wealthy in glass boxes by the entrance. In the rooms to the right is a collection of ex-voto paintings from the common classes. Reminiscent of children's drawings, they depict catastrophe averted across the decades, including many scenes from WWI and WWII. *(P. della Consolata.* ☎ *011 43 62 517; santaurio.consolata@libero.it. Open daily 6:30am-12:30pm and 3-7:30pm. Free.)*

CONTEMPORARY ART INITIATIVES. Turin presents itself as the Italian capital of contemporary art. In addition to the 11 outdoor art pieces by contemporary Italian artists planned for **Viale della Spina,** the **Museo di Arte Urbana (MAU),** known as Il Campidoglio, encompasses several blocks east of Stazione Porta Susa between C. Tassoni and C. Lecce, and features works by 30 Turinese artists. One of the most famous municipal art initiatives is the **Luci d'Artista** (Artists' Lights), began as a temporary project in 1998 to replace traditional Christmas decorations. Now annual, the event has spawned seven permanent installations, including works along the Murazzi and at the Mole. Finally, as part of **ManifesTO,** Torino's art galleries have enlisted artists to redesign billboards into artistic building facades.

MUSEO NAZIONALE DELL'AUTOMOBILE. With a focus on Italian cars and car racing, this museum documents the evolution of the automobile through exhibits of prints, drawings, leaflets, more than 150 original cars, and first models by Ford, Benz, Peugeot, Oldsmobile, and Fiat. *(C. Unità d' Italia, 40. Head south 20min. along V. Nizza from Stazione Porta Nuova. ☎011 67 76 66; www.museoauto.it. Open Tu-W and F-Sa 10am-6:30pm, Th 10am-10pm, Su 10am-10:30pm. €5.50, students €4.)*

PALAZZO AND TEATRO CARIGNANO. This *palazzo* was designed by Guarini's in 1679 to house the Princes of Savoy; it was later the seat of the first Italian parliament. The building contains the **Museo Nazionale del Risorgimento Italiano** which commemorates Italy's unification between 1706 and 1946. *(Enter from P. Carlo Alberto on the other side of the palazzo. V. Accademia delle Scienze, 5. ☎011 56 21 147. Open Tu-Su 9am-7pm. €5, students €3.50, under 10 or over 65 free. Free guided tour Su 10-11:30am.)* Across from the *palazzo* is the Baroque **Teatro Carignano,** where Italian poet Vittorio Alfieri premiered his tragedies. *(☎011 54 70 54. Call for info on tours. Free.)*

🎵 👓 ENTERTAINMENT AND SHOPPING

For the most updated calendar of Turin's yearly events, visit **www.torinocultura.it.** If you want the news in print, Turin's daily newspaper, *La Stampa,* publishes *Torino Sette,* a thorough section on cultural events every Friday. Eclectic music, theater, and cinema events enliven Turin between June and August, when **Torino d'Estate** draws many local and international acts to the city. Included in the summer festivities are **Torino Puntiverdi,** 19 July nights of dance and music from tango to orchestra in the Giardini Reali. (☎011 44 24 777; www.teatroregio.torino.it/giardinireali. Tickets €10, available from ticket office at V. San Francesco da Paola, 6. Open M-Sa 10:30am-6:30om.) The **Teatro Stabile** also hosts events centered around cultural identity as part of the July festival. (☎011 51 69 420; www.teatrostabile-torino.it. Tickets €3.) In the first three weeks of September, the **Settembre Musica** extravaganza features over 40 classical performances throughout the city. The **TRAFFIC Torino Free Festival,** at the end of June, attracts international acts to the free celebration of contemporary youth culture (www.trafficfestival.com). Torino's **Teatro Regio** in P. Castello is home to the city's beloved **opera, ballet,** and **orchestra,** which put on a combined 130 events a year. (☎011 88 15 557; www.teatrore-gio.torino.it. Ticket office open Tu-F 10:30am-6pm, Sa 10:30am-4pm.)

A large-scale **Cultural Olympiad** is planned to complement the sports events of February 2006. Over 23 visual art exhibits, 16 theatrical productions, and two Puccini operas will showcase Italian creativity to the world. Contact Turismo Torino for more information. During the 1920s, Turin was home to over 100 movie production companies. Its love affair with the cinema continues today. During the academic year, Turin's university organizes screenings of **foreign films** in their original languages. Head to one of the theaters on C. V. Emanuele or to the turn-of-the-century glamor of **Cinema Romano,** Galleria Subalpina, P. Castello, 9, near the beginning of V. Po. (☎011 56 20 145. Movies daily, usually 4-10:30pm. Tickets €4-6.50.)

One of Turin's unique events is the **Gran Balon** flea market, held every 2nd Sunday of the month behind Pta. Palazzo. Here, junk sellers rub shoulders with treasure-hunters. A smaller-scale Mercato **Balon** (www.balon.it) occurs every Saturday. The biggest open-air **market** in Europe takes place under **Porta Palazzo** in the P. della Repubblica. (M-F 8:30am-1:30pm, Sa 8:30am-6:30pm.) Over 600 vendors sell food, clothing, and odds and ends. Though clothing stores line Turin's streets, the big-name designer shops on **Via Roma** are more fit for window shopping. Turin's student population has attracted trendy and affordable clothing shops to **Via Garibaldi** and **Via Po;** the latter is also home to antique bookshops and record stores. In the **Quadrilatero Romano,** up and coming young designers have set up shop on the renovated streets within the rectangle outlined by V. Bligny, V. G. Garibaldi, V. XX Settembre, and P. della Repubblica. **8 Gallery,** V. Nizza, 262 (www.8gallery.it), is housed inside Lingotto's former Fiat factory in Turin's future cultural center and features over 100 shops, restaurants, bars, and movie theaters.

◨ NIGHTLIFE

More of a city in which to relax with friends than spend a wild night clubbing, Turin's nightlife revolves around good wine, strong cocktails, and grooving background music. Nevertheless, the city has a variety of options, and it is not necessary to dress to the nines in order to gain access to its many establishments.

◪ I MURAZZI. The center of Turin's social scene, especially in the summer, I Murazzi consists of two stretches of boardwalk, one between Ponte V. Emanuele II and Ponte Umberto and another smaller stretch downstream from the Ponte V. Emanuele II. Every night, Murazzi del Po attracts all kinds; most show up around 11pm and spend the next 4hr. sipping drinks along the waterfront or dancing inside one of the more alternative establishments. Remember to use bug spray before you go—this is a riverside. At **The Beach,** V. Murazzi del Po, 18-22, the young and modern chill outside on striped lounge chairs or dance to the best techno and electronica on the Po. Others gather for occasional performance art pieces, film openings, and book signings. (☎011 88 87 77. Mixed drinks €5-6. Lunch €12. Happy hour 7-10pm. Cover free-€10. Open Tu-Su noon-4am. MC/V.) Groove to the latest chart-toppers at **Pier 7-9-11,** V. Murazzi del Po, 7/9/11, a popular newcomer with a deck overlooking the Po. (☎011 83 53 56. Open M-Sa 10:30pm-3am.) **Giancarlo,** closest to Ponte V. Emanuele, was the first bar to invade I Murazzi and still draws huge after-hours crowds with €3 beers. Its rock, pop, and punk music draws a more alternative dancing crowd, though after 4am almost anyone will be there. (Mixed drinks €3-4. Happy hour buffet 6-10pm. W is student night. Free entry with €10 ARCI card, available at www.arci.it or at the club. Open daily in summer 6pm-6am; in winter from 11pm. Cash only.) On the other side of the river, the newest lounge on the Murazzi, **Kogin's Club,** C. Sicilia, 6, is a bit removed from its crowded, densely packed cousins. Lounge on sleek leather chairs outside the club or inside a glass-enclosed lounge over the water (☎011 66 10 546; kclub@hotmail.it. Mixed drinks €6-8. Open Tu-Su 7pm-2am. AmEx/MC/V.)

QUADRILATERO ROMANO. The recently renovated collection of buildings between P. della Repubblica and V. Garibaldi is a popular place to start and finish an evening. Begin with dinner at one of the classy restaurants, and then move on to drinks at one of the nightclubs, bars, and cafes. **Arancia di Mezzanotte**, P. E. Filiberto, 11/I, set in a quaint interior, is a popular place for an aperitif as well as dinner. (☎011 52 11 338. Open daily 6pm-2am. MC/V.) Next door at **Shore**, P. E. Filiberto, 10, large cocktails are served until the wee hours. Chill-out fusion music completes the mood. (Open daily 5:30pm-2:30am.)

ELSEWHERE IN THE CITY CENTER. The live music and disco cabaret at **Zoo Bar**, C. Casale, 127, make this small space very interactive. On Fridays and Saturdays, a crowd of students breaks out of the university to take over the dance floor and the dance-able tabletops. (☎011 81 94 347. W Latin night. Open M-Sa 11pm-3am.) **Theatro**, V. S. Teresa, 32 (☎011 51 87 107), in the old Lux Theatre, closes for most of the summer but attracts a student crowd in the winter months.

Several excellent English and Irish pubs line C. V. Emanuele II from Stazione Porta Nuova to the Po, attracting an English-speaking student crowd. To reach **Six Nations Murphy's Pub**, C. V. Emanuele, 28, turn right out of Pta. Nuova; it's a few blocks down on the left. Beer taps glow in the dim interior, filled with cheery British expats, darts, and billiards. (☎011 88 72 55. Pint of Murphy's €4.20. Open nightly 6pm-3am.) **The Shamrock Inn**, C. V. Emanuele II, 34, one block toward the station, offers lively dancing and music as well as decent food, six beers on tap, and soccer on TV. (☎011 81 74 950. Pints €4. Open nightly 8:30pm-3am.)

OUTSIDE THE CITY CENTER. A little outside the main clubbing areas **Magazzini di Gilgamesh**, P. Moncenisio, 13/B, has a packed concert program of blues, jazz, and classic rock, occasionally switching to Latin and world music (☎011 74 92 801; www.gilgamest.to.it. Open daily 8pm-3am.) **Café Procope**, V. Juvarra, 15, is a bit cafe, a bit theater, and a bit South American club. With its underground, relaxed atmosphere, concerts, and tango dancing, it attracts a slightly older crowd. (☎011 54 06 75. Mixed drinks €4-5. Open daily 9pm-3am.) **Damadama**, P.Maria Cristina, 6, below C. V. Emanuele II offers tantalizing tapas and cocktails, while a music store on the top floor sells used CDs. Every Thursday local musicians and writers transform themselves into DJs. (☎011 65 57 11; www.damadama.it.)

Though you'll need a taxi to get home, music clubs outside the city center are worth a trip. To get to **Hiroshima Mon Amour**, V. Carlo Bossoli, 83, take bus #1 or 34 to Lingotto Centro Fiere. Named for a screenplay by Marguerite Duras, this club is a dancer's paradise, often with live tunes ranging from reggae to rock, and attracting a more alternative crowd. (☎011 31 76 636. Cover up to €15. Open daily 9pm-3am.) **Dock's Dora**, V. Valprato 68, 5km outside the city center, is set in the remains of old storage depots along the Milan train line. The restored industrial buildings are one of Turin's most popular evening destinations in winter.

🏂 THE 2006 WINTER OLYMPICS

In February 2006 Turin will enter the global spotlight as the host of the XX Olympic Winter Games, the first to be held in Italy since 1956. Turin's bid-winning presentation to the International Olympic Committee in 1999 focused on its blend of Alpine charm and thriving metropolis. The upcoming Games have moreover sparked an urban renewal project of epic proportions, completely transforming the city from a secondary tourist destination to a unique European capital. When the Olympics are over, Turin will undoubtedly remain center stage.

🏂 **ORGANIZATION.** Preparation for the Olympic Games is a decentralized joint effort of the **International Olympic Committee (IOC)**, the **Italian Olympic Committee**

THE OLYMPICS

WINDS OF CHANGE

Turin will not be the same after the XX Winter Olympics. But roaring stadiums, dazed crowds, and even mind-boggling freestyle descents will have little to do with it. The Games have served as an impetus for Turin's ambitious urban renewal project, which in under a decade will completely alter the face of the city as people know it today. "Restore, Reinvent, Reuse" is the motto of the makeover, which focuses on the renovation of historical buildings and familiar spaces, rejecting the idea of urban sprawl. If all goes as planned, the project's three phases, or *spine* (spines) will be completed by 2012.

Spina 1 will prepare Turin for the Games, creating temporary and permanent buildings to accommodate the unprecedented deluge of visitors. The Olympic area in the south of the city will stretch through the Lingotto district and include an Olympic Village, as well as enough skating rinks to earn Turin the title of World's Ice Capital.

The core of the enterprise, *Spina 2*, will be partially ready in time for the Olympics, and completely finished by 2008. One of the most dramatic changes will be the transfer of Turin's cultural center southwest of its current location in the cramped pedestrian *centro storico*. Furthermore, a subway system will be installed to connect the suburbs to the city center; as of fall 2005, nine of

OLYMPIC PROPORTIONS. The XX Winter Olympic Games will run **February 10-26, 2006. 2500** athletes will compete in **15** sports, and **84** medals will be awarded by the **650** judges and referees as **1,500,000** spectators watch from the sidelines. All the while **20,000** volunteers will toil behind the scenes. In June 2005, the **1.38 billion-euro** budget was approved by the Turin Winter Olympics Committee. On **December 8, 2005** the Olympic torch will depart from Rome, and **10,000** bearers will carry it **11,000km** around every Italian province until it reaches Turin on February 10 in time for the opening ceremony.

(CONI), the **City of Turin**, the **Province of Piedmont**, and the **Turin Organizational Committee (TOROC)**. Volunteers are an integral part of the organizational structure, accompanying torch bearers on their journey around the country, and assisting spectators, athletes, and Olympic Committee representatives during the actual Games. The province of Turin has also enlisted a squad of volunteers to work at tourist information points throughout the city.

TRANSPORTATION. An estimated two million visitors are expected to descend on Turin in February 2006, more than tripling the city's population. Since Turin will be unable to accommodate all the spectators within city limits, authorities have focused on creating transportation options to shuttle Olympic visitors around town and to venues in the surrounding mountains. New additions include a **subway** for commuters from the suburbs, and multiple levels of underground parking in P. V. Veneto and other major squares. Free shuttles late into the night will ensure that venues are accessible without a car from both Italy and France, where many of the visitors will probably stay.

OLYMPIC ATRIUM. The **Atrium Torino Complex, (Olympic Atrium)** in P. Solferino (☎011 51 62 006; www.atriumtorino.it) was one of the first Olympic projects completed and consists of a two-part, ultramodern **information and logistics center.** Though its post-Olympic fate has yet to be determined, the impressive structure was originally planned as a temporary exposition space; designed to fit around the trees already planted in the *piazza*, it resulted in an unusual twin prismatic shape. The northern pavilion, **Atrium2006**, houses the info point **Turismo Torino** (☎011 53 51 81; www.turismotorino.org.), which features multimedia presentations and models of Olympic buildings and a mini-museum of previous Games. The southern pavilion, **AtriumCittà**, displays maps and models of a vision for the Turin of the future, advancing the idea that Turin is a city on the move. (Both pavilions open daily 9:30am-7pm. Guided and group tours by reservation ☎011 51 78 134, M-F 9:30am-12:30pm and 2:30-5:30pm.) In winter, the space in front of the Atrium will be converted to an outdoor **skating rink.**

⚑ TICKETS AND INFORMATION. Tickets run from €250-850 for the opening ceremony to €20-40 for the curling round robin tournament. There are three release dates when a portion of tickets becomes available. To purchase tickets, visit www.torino2006.org/tickets. In the United States and Canada, contact the National Olympic Committee or CoSport (www.cosport.com). For more information contact **TOROC**, C. Novara, 96 (☎011 63 10 511 or 011 11 20 06; www.torino2006.it).

⚑ OLYMPIC EVENTS AND VENUES. Athletes will compete in 15 disciplines: **alpine skiing, biathlon** (cross-country skiing and riflery), **bobsleigh** (bobsled), **cross-country skiing, curling, freestyle skiing, figure skating, ice hockey, luge, nordic combined** (ski jumping and cross-country skiing for men only), **skeleton** (forward luge), **short-track** (speed skating), **ski jumping, speed skating,** and **snowboarding.** Events will take place in Turin and six other towns in Piedmont, and participants will be housed in three **Olympic Villages** in **Turin, Bardonecchia,** and **Sestriere.**

Turin set an Olympic record by finishing all the major venues in January 2005, a whole year before the Games. Many events will take place in the city proper, and medals will be awarded right in the center, in the regal **Piazza Castello**—to be known as Medal Plaza during the Games. (Due to the limited capacity of the *piazza* spectators will need to pick up a free pass from one of the info points.) Formerly Stadio Comunale, the renovated and sparkling **Stadio Olimpico** will hold thousands of spectators during the **opening** and **closing ceremonies,** before passing to the Società Torino Calcio after the Games. Not far from the Stadio Olimpico, a spacious, futuristic stadium is in the works; the **Palasport Olimpico** will host most of the **ice hockey** matches, though some teams will have to battle it out on a temporary rink in the **Torino Espozioni** building. A **speed skating** stadium, **Oval,** is planned in the Lingotto district, not far from Turin's Olympic Village. Also in Lingotto, the Palavela rink, originally built to celebrate 100 years of Italian unification, is undergoing renovations to hold the **figure skating** and **short track** competitions. A final addition

the 17 planned stops have been completed. A revamped Porta Susa station will replace Porta Nuova as the city's transportation hub, linked to both Milan and Lyon, France by high-speed trains. The rail will be lowered 14m underground, leaving room for an eight-lane highway connecting Genoa in the south to Milan in the north and France to the west. Two theaters, a new public library, and numerous public art projects will fill the remaining space.

The third facet of Turin's plastic surgery will affect the residential district in the north of the city. *Spina 3* will restore Turin's crumbling industrial center, whose operations have moved overseas, to create apartments and parks along the Po River. Travelers can already witness the effects of this project in the Dora Banks area, formerly an unloading point for river barges—now a popular nightlife stop. Similarly, until recently Quadrilatero Romano had been little more than run-down 18th century buildings. Today many young professionals live above the designer shops and restaurants that line the cobblestone streets. As a final touch, Turin will build an archaeological park around Porta Palantina, where visitors will be able to admire Turin's Roman past.

All these plans ultimately highlight that tlhe Olympics are not an end in themselves, but an intermediate stop on Turin's way to being reborn as a major Italian destination for tourism, culture, and business.

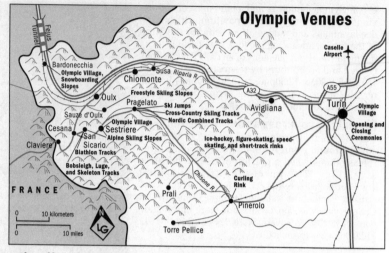

to the self-proclaimed ice-capital of the world is **Palaghiaccio** to be used as a figure skating and short track training site during the Games.

The other six venues are popular Alpine resorts that are normally crowded from early December to late April, places where avid skiers take advantage of arguably the best downhill and cross-country skiing in the world. **Bardonecchia,** at the mouth of the Frejus Tunnel to France, and with more restaurants per capita than any other resort in the region, will host the newest Winter Olympic event—**snowboarding.** The **biathlon** and women's **alpine skiing** competitions will descend on **Cesana-San Sicario,** while the nearby village of Pairol-Greniere will witness **bobsleigh, luge,** and **skeleton** races. In **Pinerolo,** 50km southeast of Turin, some lucky **curling** team will achieve a sweeping victory in the town's brand-new ice palace. Its 50km of ski tracks make **Pragelato** perfect for hosting **cross-country skiing, ski jumping, and Nordic combined** events. **Sestriere,** the site of the 3rd Olympic Village, captured the eyes of the skiing world in 1997, when it hosted the Alpine Skiing World Championships. This year, spectators will gather at Turin's highest Olympic venue (2035m) for men's **alpine skiing** tournaments. During the year, Sestriere is the largest and most commercial of the ski resorts surrounding Turin, with 4000 beds attracting skiers from across Europe and abroad. On the other side of Mount Fraiteve from Sestriere, **Sauze d'Ouiz,** will draw dazzled fans for the **freestyle skiing** competitions, though the summer always brings even freer styles, when bikini-clad skiers add color to their cheeks on the resort's snowy slopes.

TRY IT YOURSELF. San Sicario and the nearby village of Cesana have linked their lifts with other Olympic venues Sestriere and Sauze d'Ouiz, as well as well as the Claviere resort, making it possible to ski from one village to the next. Combined, these slopes—nicknamed the *via lattea*, or "Milky Way"—total 400km of downhill slopes, 46km of cross-country trails, 91 lifts, and 218 runs. Passes run around €80 per 3 days. (☎0122 79 94 11; www.vialattea.it.) Rentals are available in any of the villages. To book accommodations or transportation for the entire region, visit www.mountaincollection.com.

⚡ DAYTRIP FROM TURIN

🏛 SACRA DI SAN MICHELE

From Turin, take the train to Avigliana (15 per day, €1.76). From there, either take a taxi (☎011 93 02 18; around €30) or make the 14km, 3hr. hike. For a map of the arduous trek, head to Avigliana's Informazione Turistica, P. del Popolo, 2, a 5-10min. walk straight ahead from the station. (☎011 93 28 650. Open M-F 9am-noon and 3-6pm.) Alternatively, tackle the scenic 1½hr. climb from the village of Sant'Ambrogio to the monastery. Take a train to Sant'Ambrogio (8 per day, last return 7:10pm; €2.25). Exiting the station, walk straight up V. Caduti per la Patria and turn right on V. Umberto. Continue straight until Chiesa Parrocchiale. Behind the church on the right is a "Sacra di San Michele Mulattiera" sign. The rest of the hike is clearly marked. Do not hike alone, as the unpaved path can be difficult and slippery. Wear sturdy shoes and bring water.

On a bluff above the town of Avigliana, the Sacra di San Michele grows from the very rock on which it was built. *The Name of the Rose* was not filmed at this megalithic stone monastery, but it probably should have been. Umberto Eco based his book's plot on the Sacra's history, and even in full summer sunshine there is an ominous air about the place. Ugo di Montboissier, an Alevernian pilgrim, founded it in 1000, and the **Scalone dei Morti** (Stairway of the Dead), a set of steps chiseled from the mountainside, helps to buttress the structure. The corpses of monks were once draped across the staircase for the faithful to pay their last respects; currently, their skeletons are more tactfully concealed in the cavities on the side. The stairs ascend to the **Porta dello Zodiaco** (Door of the Zodiac), two doors depicting the arms of St. Michael wrestling with the Serpent of Eden. Steps in the middle of the nave descend into the shrine of St. Michael and three tiny **chapels.** The oldest dates to the time when St. Michael was first venerated. In AD 966, St. John Vincent built the largest, with a back wall of solid rock; today, it holds the medieval members of the Savoy family. (☎011 93 91 30; www.sacradisanmichele.com. Open Mar. 16-Oct. 15 Tu-Sa 9:30am-12:30pm and 3-6pm, Su 9:30am-noon and 3-6pm. Oct. 16-Mar. 15 Tu-Sa 9:30am-12:30pm and 3-5pm, Su 9:30am-12:30pm and 3-6pm; last entrance 30min. before closing. €4, children and over 65 €3.)

CUNEO   ☎0171

Cuneo's name means "wedge," and for good reason; it's wedged on a chunk of land between the Stura di Demonte River and the Torrente Gesso. Over the years, no fewer than nine different armies have besieged strategically located Cuneo, but the town has lived up to its motto, "ferendo" (to bear). These days, invasion comes in the form of bargain hunters, who overwhelm serene Cuneo during its weekly street market. The rest of the time, the town is a sleepy provincial capital of 55,000. Its 14km of *portici* (arcades) provide ample space for an afternoon of window shopping and people watching, but most travelers visit Cuneo as a launching point for explorations of the valleys and nearby Maritime Alps National Park.

🗺🚆 TRANSPORTATION AND PRACTICAL INFORMATION. The **train station** in P. Libertà provides service to Turin (1hr., 1 per hr. 4:33am-10:30pm, €4.70) and Saluzzo (30min., 1 per hr. 5:35am-7:10pm, €4.90). Local **buses** also depart from the station, serving the city and surrounding valleys. Schedules vary daily and seasonally; the tourist office provides up-to-date timetables. To explore the Cuneo Valleys, **rent a car** from **Avis**, C. Francia, 251 (☎0171 49 34 86; €68 per day

100km min., €0.15 for each additional km; €199 per 3 days, unlimited mileage) or from **Hertz**, V. Savona, 17 (☎0171 34 80 70; €70 per day, unlimited mileage). Borrow a **bike** for free from the town hall next to the tourist office and grab a copy of the brochure *Cuneo's Bicycle Touring District.*

Cuneo lies 80km south of Turin. **Via Roma, Piazza Galimberti,** and **Corso Nizza** are the main thoroughfares; the rest of the streets form an easily navigable grid. To reach C. Nizza from the train station, follow **Corso Giolitti** from **Piazza Libertà.** The **tourist office,** on V. Roma by the town hall, provides info and helps find lodgings. (Open M-Sa 9:30am-1pm and 2:30-6:30pm.) For info on the Cuneo province, contact **ATL**, V. Amedeo, 82. Turn on V. Amedeo from C. Nizza one block before the *piazza.* (☎0171 69 02 16. Open daily 8:30am-noon and 2:30-6pm.) **Banks** with **ATMs** line V. Roma and C. Nizza. In case of **emergency** call ☎118, the **police** at ☎0171 67 777, or the **paramedics** at ☎0171 44 13 37. The **Santa Croce hospital** is at V. Coppino, 26 (☎0171 64 11 11). There are several **pharmacies** on C. Nizza that post after-hours rotations. **Internet** is available at the call center at V. Caraglio, 8bis. (☎0171 60 54 75. €4 per hr. Open M-Sa 9am-9pm, Su 2:30-9pm.) The **post office** is at V. A. Bonelli, 6. (☎0171 69 33 06. Open M-F 8:30am-7pm, Sa 8:30am-1pm.) **Postal Code:** 12100.

⌂🍴 ACCOMMODATIONS AND FOOD. Modern, well-maintained hotel rooms, all with TV, phone, and bath can be found at **Hotel Ligure ❹**, V. Savigliano, 11. Exiting P. Galimberti on V. Roma, turn right; V. Savigliano runs parallel to V. Roma. (☎0171 68 19 42; www.ligurehotel.it. Breakfast buffet €5-6. Free indoor parking. Singles €32-42; doubles €60; triples €75. MC/V.) Another solid choice is **Albergo Cavallo Nero ❸**, V. Seminario, 8. Head one block up V. Roma from P. Galimberti and turn left. Smaller rooms with TV and phone, some with balcony. (☎0171 69 21 68; cavallo.nero@virgilio.it. Breakfast included. Singles €36, with bath €45; doubles €48/60; triples €75.) The attached restaurant serves a dinner *menù* for €7-17. (Open daily for lunch from noon, for dinner from 7pm. MC/V.) At **Bisalta ❶**, V. S. Maurizio, 33, 200 campsites offer free electricity and plenty of recreational activities. (☎0171 49 13 34; campingbisalta@libero.it. €5 per site. Cash only.)

Cafes line the arcades of V. Roma and C. Nizza, providing cheap spots to stop for a sandwich or *gelato.* A **Maxisconto** supermarket at the corner of V. C. Battisti and V. Ponza di San Martino off P. Galimberti sells groceries and necessities. (Open M-F 8:30am-1pm and 3:30-7:30pm, Sa 8:30am-7:30pm.) A prime example of the fusion cuisine that characterizes Cuneo's gastronomic scene can be had at **⬛Ristorante Les Gourmands ❷**, V. Statuto, 3/A, where *tagliatelle con fragola* (pasta with strawberries; €7) is just one of many innovative dishes. (☎0171 60 56 64; www.lesgourmands.it. *Primi* €4.50-7, *secondi* €7-15. Cover €1.50. Open Tu-F and Su noon-3pm and 7:30pm-midnight, Sa 7:30pm-midnight. MC/V.) Hemingway is said to have traveled to Cuneo for the sole purpose of sampling a *cunese al rum* from **Arione Pasticceria Caffè ❶**, on the corner of C. Nizza and P. Galimberti. The chocolate praline with rum cream filling (€2) is still the best seller among a bevy of sweets. (Open Tu-Su 9am-8pm.) For a traditional dinner experience head to the popular after-theater destination **Ristorante Zuavo ❷**, V. Roma, 23, where wooden tables and a piano guarantee a grand time. (☎0171 60 20 20. *Primi* €6, *secondi* €8-9. Open M-Tu and Th-Su 12:30-2:30pm and 7:30-11pm.) Nearby, the **Enotica Club de L'Enoteca Artistica ❶**, V. Savigliano, 17, is a new wine bar with bright walls and rotating art exhibits downstairs. (☎320 87 52 617. *Panini* €2-5. Wine €2-5 per glass. Open Tu-Su 11am-2pm and 6pm-2am. Su buy 2 drinks, get 1 free.)

SIGHTS. Cuneo's infamous **market** sprawls over 1km, filling P. Galimberti, most of V. Roma, and much of C. Nizza. Stalls full of clothes, antiques, postcards, cookware, and everything else delight shoppers, but make parking a nightmare. (Every other Tu during daylight hours. Summer approximately 7am-6pm; winter 8am-4pm.) The facade of the **duomo,** at the corner of C. Nizza and V. M. Bologna may blend in with the municipal government buildings around it, but inside is a Baroque wonderland, complete with crystal chandeliers. (Open daily 8am-noon and 3-6pm.) The **Museo Civico di Cuneo,** V. S. Maria, 10, occupies the retired convent of San Francesco to display archaeological artifacts and everyday items from across the centuries, including Bronze Age cave graffiti. (☎0171 66 137. Open Tu and Sa 8:30am-1pm and 2:30-5:30pm, W-F 8:30am-1pm and 2:30-5pm, Su 3-7pm. €2.60, students €1.55.)

VALLEYS OF CUNEO ☎0171/0174

The mountain villages in the sparsely inhabited valleys around Cuneo provide a picture of how life in the Italian Alps has existed for centuries. Shops selling local crafts and restaurants serving *Piemontese* cuisine abound. Infrequent bus service, however, makes it difficult to visit more than one valley in a single day.

> **TIP**
>
> **PIMP YOUR RIDE.** A car is to the Valleys of Cuneo like duck sauce is to spring rolls—necessary. After picking up your sweet set of wheels, grab the excellent *Cuneo cartina della provincia* at any tourist office, and have a nice day.

VALLE GESSO

From Cuneo, take SS. 20 for 30km, continuing straight to Valdieri and Terme di Valdieri through Borgo S. Dalmazzo. Info office ☎0171 97 397; www.parcoalpimarittime.it.

The Gesso Valley is the gateway to the **Parco Naturale Alpi Marittime,** a protected area of 28,000 hectares originally part of King Vittorio Emanuele's private hunting reserve. Today, the park, which borders on the even larger **Parc National du Mercantour** in France, is home to chamois, ibex, and wild boar, as well as many of the best and least trafficked **hiking trails** in the Italian Alps. **Albergo Turismo ❹,** right beside the park center (☎0171 97 208) and entry to the **Valderia Botanic Gardens,** offers hikers simple bedrooms set right against the mountain. (☎0171 97 334. Breakfast €4-9. Open June-Sept. Doubles €50, with bath €65. Half pension €43-50 per person.) Pockets of *provençal* language and culture are scattered throughout the valley. Tiny **Terme di Valdieri** (1386m) lies in the heart of the park, a few hours' walk from many *rifugi*, making it an ideal trailhead. Otherwise, try the **Piano del Valasco** path (2hr.), which climbs to 1780m and circles a lake, or continue on the **Giro dei laghi Vallescura** route (4-7hr.) for stunning views.

Trails depart from the road next to the info office. After a long day on the trails, nothing feels better than the 34°C ⬛**Valdieri Thermal Baths,** 500m down the main road, across the street from the hotel. Soak in the pools or smear muscles with mud from the sulfur-rich thermophilic mosses in the springs—they allegedly have healing powers. (☎0171 26 16 66. Open mid-June to mid-Sept. daily 9am-6pm and 8-11pm. €10 per half-day (before or after 1pm), €15 per day. Mud baths €21.)

VALLE CASOTTO

Take SS. 28 from Cuneo for 27km or Autostrada A6 from Turin. Vicoforte is 4km east of Mondovì. For info on sights, contact the Ufficio IAT del Comune di Mondovì, Corso Statuto, 16. (☎0174 40 389; www.comune.mondovi.cn.it.)

During his 1796 visit, Napoleon called **Mondovì** "the most beautiful town in the world." The historical center, an impossibly dense collection of buildings dating from 1198, centers on P. Maggiore. The **Torre Civica**, behind the cathedral, is one of the symbols of the town. Destroyed by fire and war, its current incarnation stands at over 30m, adorned on each side with a giant clock. Climb past the exposed gears to the top for a view all the way to Monte Bianco. (Open June-Sept. Tu-Su 3-6:30pm. €2.) Stores throughout the city center sell blue-patterned pottery embossed with the town's rooster symbol, a craft for which the town is known throughout the region. Skiing is a popular recreation in Mondovì. Call ☎0174 46 893 for info on Mondolé Ski Resort slopes and day passes.

Farther up the valley is the village of **Vicoforte,** home to the soaring ▓**Santuario di Vicoforte** and the four square towers surrounding it. Originally begun in 1596 to house a revered image of the Madonna that, legend has it, bled when it was struck, the sanctuary wasn't finished until 1733. The blue elliptical dome, 75m high and 38m long, is the longest in the world; the 6000 sq. meter fresco of the Madonna's life on the inside is considered the world's largest single-subject painting. Skylights and the bright, heavily frescoed interior make the altar glow with reflected light. (☎0174 56 55 55. Santuario di Vicoforte open daily 7:30am-noon and 2-7pm. Free.) Next to the Santuario, the excellent ▓**Casa Regina Montis Regalis ❸** houses guests behind frescoed doorways in rooms that once housed the Santuario's Cistercian monks. TV room, meeting rooms, and excellent restaurant on premises. (☎0174 56 53 00; www.santuariodivicoforte.com. Breakfast €5. Curfew 11pm. Singles €35; doubles €50. Half pension €45/70, full pension €55/90. MC/V.)

A final stop is the **Castello di Casotto,** originally constructed as a Carthusian monastery in the 11th century, destroyed by Napoleon, and then rebuilt in the 19th century as a hunting lodge for the Savoys. It's also a fascinating, but somewhat distressing, example of bad preservation—water damaged oil paintings cheerfully hang next to open windows and velvet pillows on Queen Margherita's bed rot in mold. Widespread efforts to restore the castle's exterior are currently underway. (11km south of Pamparato. ☎0174 80 67 21. Open daily 9am-noon and 2-6pm, last entrance 5:30pm. Admission and obligatory tour in Italian €3.)

SALUZZO   ☎0175

For over four centuries, the hilltop town of Saluzzo (pop. 17,000) reigned as the capital of a fiercely independent Marquisate, before falling under the influence of the House of Savoy in 1601. The arcade-lined historical center and churches of the "Siena of the North" remain well preserved and tourist-free—unless you count the crowds of farmers who come up on weekend nights for a glass of wine in the *trattorie*. Its location overlooking the Po Valley makes Saluzzo an ideal base to explore the northern valleys, as well as a nice stopover in its own right.

◪▨ **TRANSPORTATION AND PRACTICAL INFORMATION.** Saluzzo lies 33km north of Cuneo. **Trains** depart the station for Cuneo (1hr., every 45min. 6:45am-8:17pm, €4.90) and Turin (1hr., 6:09am-7:44pm, €4.50). Local **buses** leave from the station at V. Circonvallazione, 19, connecting Saluzzo to villages in the surrounding valleys. For a **taxi,** call ☎0175 24 85 89.

 WEEKEND CLOSINGS. On the weekend, the train station closes but buses still run. Purchase tickets at the machine behind the station next to the train platform; buses pick up passengers in front of the station.

Saluzzo's main street changes name from **Via Spielberg** to **Corso Italia** to **Corso Piemonte** as it moves from east to west; from the train station, head straight up **Via Piave;** from the bus station turn left on **Via Circonvallazione,** then immediately right on **Via Torino.** The *centro storico* and most of the sights lie uphill on the north side of town. To reach the **tourist office,** Piazzetta dei Mondagli, 5, enter the old town at V. Volta, near the junction of V. Spielberg and C. Italia. It provides information on sights in nearby villages and valleys. (☎0175 46 710; www.comune.saluzzo.cn.it. Open Apr.-Sept. Tu-Sa 9am-1pm and 2:30-5:30pm, Su 9am-1pm and 2:30-6pm; Oct.-Mar. Tu-Sa 9am-1pm and 2-5pm, Su 9am-1pm and 2-5:30pm.) **Unicredit Banca,** C. Italia, 24, has an **ATM.** (Open M-F 8:20am-1:20pm and 2:30-4pm.) In case of **emergency,** call ☎113 or an **ambulance** at ☎118. **Farmacia Chiaffredo,** C. Italia, 56, posts a list of after-hours rotations. (Open M and W-Sa 8:30am-12:30pm and 3:30-7:30pm.) The **hospital** lies on V. Spielberg, two blocks outside the historical center. **Internet** is available for free from the **Biblioteca Civia** just beyond the tourist office on Thursdays from 8 to 11pm, or at **Web Café,** C. Piemonte, 46. The **post office,** at V. Peano, 1, is on the other side of the river, not far from the train station. (Open M-F 8:30am-7pm, Sa 8:30am-1pm.) **Postal Code:** 12037.

⌐⌐ ACCOMMODATIONS AND FOOD. Budget digs are tough to find in the town proper; visitors with cars should inquire at the tourist office about B&Bs in the countryside or visit Saluzzo as a daytrip from Cuneo. **Hotel Përpoin ❺,** V. Spielberg, 19, through a covered passageway, offers spacious modern rooms with TV, phone, and bath. The attached restaurant serves Piemontese cuisine—rich, rugged, and filling. (☎0175 42 382 or 0175 42 552; nadiafornetti@hotmail.com. Breakfast included. Wheelchair accessible. Singles €40-70; doubles €70-110. Extra bed 30% of room price. AmEx/MC/V.) **Albergo Persico ❹,** V. Mercati, 10, is just below P. Vineis on C. Italia. Enjoy a quieter location and rooms with TV, phone, and bath. (☎0175 41 21 31 or 0175 24 8075; persico@libero.it. Breakfast included. Closed July. Singles €40-42; doubles €58-60; triples €85. AmEx/MC/V.)

A **Supermercati Maxisconto** offers cheap groceries at C. Piemonte, 21. (Open M-Sa 9am-8pm. Closed July to mid-Aug.) Albergo Persico's downstairs **restaurant ❸,** specializes in Piemontese cuisine, including the farmer's plate (€14) of deep-fried everything—meat, vegetables, fruit, and bread. (*Primi* €7-9, *secondi* €9-12. Open Tu-Su noon-2pm and 7-10:30pm.) The menu changes seasonally at **Le Quattro Stagioni ❷,** V. Volta, 21. Traditional dishes like *agnolotti al plin* (hand-pinched ravioli; €7) and *tajarin* (pasta; €6.50) compete with pizza (€4-7.50) for table space in the dim interior. In season, the peaches stuffed with chocolate and hazelnut sauce are a knockout. (☎0175 47 470. *Primi* €6.50-7, *secondi* €10-14. Open daily noon-2:30pm and 7-11pm. AmEx/MC/V.)

◙ SIGHTS. In the P. Risorgimento, off C. Italia, lies the **Cattedrale di Maria Assunta.** The recently restored Lombardy-Gothic cathedral is decorated with bright Baroque frescoes that contrast sharply with the somber exterior. (Open daily 7-11:30am and 3:30-7pm.) To reach the historical center, head uphill from the tourist office along Sal. Castello. At the hill's summit in P. Castello stands the imposing **Castiglia,** the town fortress, a prison until the 1980s. When current renovations are completed, it will be reborn as a cultural center. Turning right on V. San Giovanni, the 33m tall **Torre Civica** commands a sweeping view of the Po Valley. (Open Mar.-Sept. Th-Su 9:30am-12:30pm and 2:30-6:30pm; Oct.-Feb. Sa-Su €1.50.) The **Chiesa di San Giovanni,** on V. San Giovanni, 15, holds an elaborately carved wooden choir in the Gothic-flamboyant style behind the altar, exceedingly rare in this region. The ceiling of the adjoining chapel, accessible through the cloisters to the church's left, is decorated with frescoes intended to represent the night sky. (Open daily 8am-noon and 3-7pm.)

ASTI ☎ 0141

Set in the hillsides of Piedmont's wine country, the provincial seat of Asti (pop. 73,000) has bustled with activity since it was founded by Romans in the first century AD. It rose to power as a trading center during the Middle Ages, becoming one of the richest cities in Italy by 1200. Asti is best known today for its wines—limestone-rich soils on gentle south-facing slopes produce grapes destined for bottles of *Barbaresco*, dark red *Barbera*, and the champagne-like *Asti Spumante*.

📧🛈 TRANSPORTATION AND PRACTICAL INFORMATION. The **train station** is in P. Marconi, where V. Cavour meets C. L. Einaudi. (Info office open M-F 6am-12:40pm and 1:10-7:45pm, or use ticket machine for info.) Trains run to: Alessandria (30min., every hr. 5:24am-1:07pm, €2.45); Milan Centrale (2hr., 5 per day, €6.82); and Turin Porta Nuova (1hr., 2 per hr. 4:32am-11:01pm, €3.50). **Buses,** in P. Medaglie d'Oro, across from the train station, run to Canelli (every 2hr., 7:10am-6:40pm); Castagnole (every 2hr., 7:20am-6:40pm); Costigliole (9 per day, 7:15am-6:50pm); and Isola d'Asti (6 per day, 10am-6:50pm). Buy tickets (€1.55-2.10) onboard or at *tabaccherie.* **Taxis** are in P. Alfieri (☎0141 53 26 05) or at the train station (☎0141 59 27 22). **Bike rental** is at **Bici & Bike,** V. Verdi, 10 (☎0141 30 283).

The town center lies in the triangular **Piazza Alfieri.** From the station, go down **Via Cavour** through **Piazzetta S. Paolo, Piazza Statuto,** and **Piazza San Secondo,** then right on **Via Garibaldi.** Most sights are along **Corso V. Alfieri,** the major east-west thoroughfare, connecting with the top of P. Alfieri. Near **Piazza Liberta** is the **Piazza Campo del Palio,** now used for parking and weekly markets. The **ATL tourist office,** P. Alfieri, 29, provides valuable info, **maps,** and free tours of the city. (☎0141 53 03 57 or 0141 32 09 78 for tours; www.astiturismo.it. Open M-Sa 9am-1pm and 2:30-6:30pm, Su 9am-1pm. Tours May-Oct. Sa-Su 10am.) **Currency exchange** is available at banks on C. V. Alfieri and V. Dante. There are 24hr. **ATMs** in the train station and on V. Dante, or at **Banca Popolare di Lodi** in P. Alfieri. English books are sold at **Libreria Mondadori,** C. Alfieri, 324. (Open in summer M 3:30-7:30pm, Tu-Sa 9am-12:30pm and 3:30-7:30pm; in winter hours vary.) Self-service **Laundromat Acquazzurra,** V. Garetti, 29, is open daily in summer 8am-10pm; in winter 8:30am-8pm. (☎0171 69 99 67. Wash €4 per 7kg, dry €4 per 5min., detergent €1.) In an **emergency,** call ☎113, or the **ambulance** ☎118, or the **police,** C. XXV Aprile, 19 (☎0141 41 81 11). **Farmacia Alfieri** is at P. Alfieri, 3. (☎0141 41 09 92. Open daily 8:30am-12:30pm and 3:30-7:30pm.) Check **Internet** at **Asti Point,** V. Ospedale, 3, off P. Alfieri (☎/fax 0141 32 15 8. Open M-Tu and Th-F 9am-1pm and 3-8:30pm, W and Sa 9am-8:30pm.) The **post office,** C. Dante, 55, is off P. Alfieri at the intersection with V. Verdi. (☎0141 35 72 51. Open M-F 8:30am-7pm, Sa 8:30am-1pm.) **Postal Code:** 14100.

🏠 ACCOMMODATIONS AND CAMPING. For better value, those with cars should consider a B&B or *agriturismo* in the scenic wine country just outside of Asti. Ask at the tourist office for more information. For hotels in town, exit the train station and cross the parking lot to reach **Hotel Cavour ❹,** P. Marconi, 18, slightly on the left. The clean modern rooms come with large bath, TV, and phone, and most have air-conditioning. (☎/fax 0141 53 02 22. Breakfast included. Reception 6am-1am. Singles €42-50; doubles €62-70. AmEx/MC/V.) **Hotel Genova ❸,** C. Alessandria, 26, down C. Alfieri through P. Maggio on C. Alessandria, is slightly simpler and farther out from the center. All rooms have bath and TV. (☎0141 59 31 97. Breakfast €6.20. Reception 6:30am-midnight; call ahead if arriving on Su. Singles €40; doubles €60. AmEx/MC/V.) Everything from the wallpaper to the furniture is new at the **Hotel Priore ❹**, C. G. Ferraris, 58, west of the P. Campo del Palio. All rooms have bath, TV, and phone. (☎0141 59 36 88; www.hotelpriore.it. Singles €55; doubles €85. MC/V.) To reach **Campeggio Umberto Cagni ❶**, V. Valmanera, 152, 4km from P. Alfieri, turn on V. Aro, which becomes C. Volta; turn left on V. Valmanera. The camp, restaurant, and bar are crowded with Italian vacationers. (☎0141 27 12 38. Open Apr.-Sept. €4.50 per person, €5.50 per tent, €3.50 per car, €6-6.50 per camper. Bungalows €32. Electricity €2.50. Showers free.)

🍴 **FOOD.** Astigiana cuisine is known for its relying on a few crucial ingredients like gorgonzola and other pungent cheeses. Rabbit, boar, truffles, and mountain herbs make up classic Piemontese dishes. Restaurant caves are stocked with Asti's local wines including the sparkling white *Moscato*. Local vineyards also produce *grappa*, a strong brandy. An extensive fruit and vegetable **market** is at P. Campo del Palio and P. Alfieri. (Open W and Sa 7:30am-1pm. Clothing booths open until sunset.) The **Dì per Dì** supermarket, P. Alfieri, 26, has good prices and a wide selection. (☎0141 34 759. Open M-Tu, Th-F, and Su 8:30am-1pm and 3:30-7:30pm, W and Sa 8:30am-7:30pm.) At **Ristorante La Vecchia Carrozza ❸**, V. Carducci, 41, dine on large portions of regional food beneath arched brick ceilings in a quiet back room. The 5-course *menù* is a great deal. (☎/fax 0141 53 86 57. *Primi* €6, *secondi* €8. Open Tu-Su noon-1pm and 8-11pm. Reservations recommended. Cash only.) Set in a centuries-old brick warehouse, **Ristorante Tacabanda/L'Osteria della Barbera ❸**, V. al Teatro, 5, serves Piemontese and Italian cuisine to a pre-theater crowd that takes in the restaurant's art exhibits as well as its heavy-hitting red wine. (☎0141 53 09 99. *Primi* €6.50-8, *secondi* €7.50-11. Lunch *menù* €10. Open Tu-Su noon-2:30pm and 8-10pm. AmEx/MC/V.) Attentive service and regional specialties guarantee a fine meal at **L'Angolo del Beato ❹**, V. Guttuari, 12. (☎/fax 0141 53 16 68. *Primi* €8.50, *secondi* €13. Cover €1.50. Open M-Sa noon-2pm and 7:30-10:30pm. AmEx/MC/V.) Signor Francese of **Pizzeria Francese ❷**, V. dei Cappellai, 15, knows his pizza—he's even written a 692-page guide to the best pizzerias in Italy. (☎0141 59 23 21; www.pizzerie-italia.it. Pizza €5.50-7.50. *Primi* €6.50, *secondi* €8. Cover €1.50. Open in summer daily noon-3pm and 6pm-1am; in winter closed Tu. Closed mid-Aug. AmEx/MC/V.)

◐ **SIGHTS.** The 14th-century **duomo** is a noteworthy example of the Lombardy Gothic style. Its *piazza* entrance is decorated by statues of monks and priests, as well as the disturbing head of a female Troya family member. Throughout the 16th and 17th centuries, local artists covered every inch of the walls with frescoes, while the remains of 11th-century mosaics blanket the floor around the altar. (Walk down C. Alfieri and turn right at P. Cairoli ☎0141 59 29 24. Open daily 8:30am-noon and 3-7:30pm. Free.) A red-brick bulwark, the 15th-century **Chiesa di San Pietro in Consavia**, served as an army hospital in WWII. On the first floor, the **Museo Paleontologico** has a small collection of fossils and bones from the Astiano area. On the 2nd floor, the **Museo Archeologico** showcases 4th-century BC Greek vases and jugs. Beside the *chiesa* is the 12th-century octagonal baptistry. (On the far end of C. Alfieri. San Pietro in Consavia open Tu-F 9am-1pm and 3-5pm, Sa 10am-1pm and 3-6pm, Su 1am-1pm.) From P. Alfieri, a short walk west on V. Garibaldi leads to **Piazza San Secondo**, home to the 18th-century **Palazzo di Città** and the Romanesque-Gothic **Chiesa Collegiata di San Secondo**, built of terra cotta and sandstone in the 14th century. The church has chapels only on the right side

LANGHE BIKE TOUR

TIME: 1 day.

DISTANCE: 27km.

SEASON: Year-round, except January; best in spring.

A bike tour of the attractions around Alba, including several wineries.

Need a reason for visiting the Langhe, a tiny province tucked away in the south of Piedmont? Try six, all of them exceptional local wines with international reputations: *Barbaresco, Barbera, Dolcetto, Barolo, Nebbiolo,* and *Moscato.* If that isn't enough to make your head swim, the scenery should be, as vine-covered hills rise from the Tanaro River valley, capped with castles and villas connected by winding roads that make for a perfect day's bike ride. The best place to start a tour of Langhe is in Alba, accessible by **train** from Asti (40min., 12 per day 5:20am-9:40pm, €2.45). **Bike rental** is available at **Moto Cicli Destefanis,** C. Langhe, 17 (☎0173 44 04 62). Those not up for strenuous pedaling may choose to rent a **car** instead at **Europcar,** C. Bra, 119, (0173 35 833). The **tourist office,** P. Risorgimento, 2, just before the Cattedrale di San Lorenzo, provides **maps** and information on the region. Ask for the *Tu Langhe Roero* publications on active and wine tourism. (☎0173 35 833; www.langheroero.it. Open Jan.-Feb. and Dec. M-Sa 9am-1pm and 2:30-6:30pm; Mar.-May M-Su 9am-1pm and 2:30-6:30pm; June-Sept. 18 M-Sa 9am-12:30pm and 2:30-6:30pm, Su 9am-12:30pm; Sept. 19-Nov. M-Th 9am-12:30pm and 2:30-6:30pm, F-Su 9am-8pm.)

1 ALBA. Start your challenging but rewarding day in the charming capital of Langhe, with its terra-cotta roofs and red brick towers. Quaint shops and *enoteche* cluster on Alba's streets—be sure to pick up a bottle of *Barbera d'Alba* while weaving your way through town; the ruby red wine has a full-bodied, acidic, slightly tangy flavor that goes well with some local soft cheeses. Walk down **Via Vittorio Emanuele,** the main thoroughfare, to find picnic supplies. In November you may have the chance to try **white truffles,** found in no other part of the world. Of course, they're excruciatingly expensive: after the dry season of 2003, a kilogram of the zesty *funghi* fetched up to €5000. Other local specialties include hazelnuts—Alba claims to have invented Nutella.

2 PARCO AVVENTURA L'ISOLE VERDE. For a perfect picnic, bike 8km to **Parco Avventura L'Isola Verde** on the Tanaro River, where you can rent row boats (€5 per hr.) or enjoy a zip line adventure from the island to the shore (€10). After crossing the river from Alba toward Asti, follow the signs left in the direction of Montestefano. The paved road will soon arrive at a painted red swatch on the ground that you should follow to the left. When the road forks, keep right on the unpaved path for 5km, and turn left at the crossroads through the passage of trees. Soon the river and hill of Barbaresco will be on your right. Just before the main road, turn left into the park. (Boat rental M and W-F 10am-11pm, Sa-Su 9am-11pm.)

BIKE TOUR

3 BARBARESCO For the first wine-tasting stop, turn right on the main road with the sign for Castagnito in front, in the direction of Asti. Take a right toward Barbaresco (4km ahead, 3km of which require challenging uphill biking). Indulge your weary self at the **Enoteca Regionale del Barbaresco,** located in the former Chiesa di San Donato, V. Torino, 8/A, which hosts art exhibits, in addition to daily wine-tastings. Sample one of the six daily wines for only €1.50 per glass. (☎0173 63 52 51; www.enotecadelbarbaresco.it. Open Feb.-Dec. M-Tu and Th-Sa 9:30am-6pm, Su 9:30am-1pm and 2:30-6pm. *Barbaresco* around €20 per bottle. AmEx/MC/V.) You should also stop at the small Rocca family wine producer **La Cà Növa,** V. Casa Nuova,1, for free samples of *Dolcetto, Barbara,* and, of course, *Barbaresco* wines from their small vintage of 40,000 bottles per year. The Roccas likewise produce over 1000 bottles of grappa per year, which is made from the same Nobiola grapes as the wine, and requires an additional 15-18 days of fermentation. (☎/fax 0173 63 51 23. Open daily 9am-7pm, call ahead in September and October Bottles €4-10.50. Cash only.) Keep in mind that even though wine degustations at many regional *enoteche* or vineyards may be free, visitors are expected to purchase a bottle or two of their favorite wine. A final highlight of this hill town is the 12th-century **Torre di Barbaresco,** a valuable outlook post in the distant past, from which you can still see all the way back to Alba, Asti's medieval enemy.

4 TREISO The next leg of the journey is about 7km long. Head right from Barbaresco toward Alba, turning right again before veering left uphill through the hamlet of Tre Stelle. Take a left onto the small road toward S. Stefanetto, turning right at the end to head through the town, and you will finally come out facing the center of Treiso. Go through the roundabout to reach **Lodali,** Vle. Rimembranza, 5, a relatively large wine producer, with 100,000 bottles per year on the market. You can tour the giant metal vats where the wine ferments for a year before being moved to a barrel for another year and then finishing its aging process in a bottle. In addition to *Dolcetto, Barbera,* and *Barbaresco* wines, Lodali also produces *Barolo,* made from the same Nebiolo grape, and *Chardonnay,* from the white Moscato grape. Ask at the adjoining restaurant **Profumo di Vino** about free daily wine-tasting 2-6pm. (☎0173 63 80 17. Lunch plates €10-12. Open M and W-Su 7am-midnight. Closed July 15-29. Lodali ☎/fax 0173 63 81 09; www.lodali.it.)

5 LE ROCCHE DEI SETTE FRATELLI Exiting Lodali, at the roundabout head in the direction of Manera and Cappelletto. Turn off toward Meruzzano, then quickly right on the dirt road. Two kilometers away from Treiso, the **Rocche dei Sette Fratelli** (Rocks of the Seven Brothers) dips 300m down into the hills. Legend has it that the natural crater with its chalk cliffs was created when seven brothers mocked their pious sister, preventing her from attending church, forcing her to harvest grapes instead. They certainly learned their lesson when the earth opened up and swallowed them, creating the Rocche, which today offers 6-7km of hiking paths. The tall hills that surround the crater are covered with vineyards, and the woods at the very top are the source of Langhe's famous hazelnuts.

6 SAN ROCCO SENO D'ELVIO Leaving the Rocche, pedal down a winding downhill path for 2km to reach the hamlet San Rocco Seno d'Elvio. End your day with a comfortable night at the **Locanda del Barbaresco.** This family-run bed and breakfast was recently renovated and combines modern facilities with superb traditional dinners and a friendly atmosphere. Trekking tours on bike or foot can also be arranged at the Locanda. (☎0173 28 69 68; www.locandadelbarbaresco.it. Breakfast included. Singles €30-35, doubles €40-50, half pension €52-67. Reservations recommended.) The following morning you can make the 4km journey back to Alba to return your bike. Take the road from San Rocco downhill, turning left at the main road and continuing uphill for 300m before the road curves downward. Cross the train tracks at the edge of town and follow the bike path on your left and the signs pointing in the direction of the *centro.*

BIKE TOUR

because of the municipal building on its left. The first chapel holds colorful banners from Palios past. Secondo, Asti's patron saint, is represented in statues holding a sword in one hand and the city of Asti in the other. (☎0141 53 00 66. Open M-Sa 10:45am-noon and 3:30-5:30pm, Su 3:30-5:30pm.) During the city's medieval prominence, feuding nobles constructed brick towers as testaments to their wealth. In the 13th century, the city was famed for its more than 100 **torre** (towers), but now only 30 or so remain, many of them crumbling. The city symbol, the **Torre Troyana** in P. Medici was built in the 13th and 14th centuries but the clock was added in the 16th century when it was presented to the Savoy family from the city as a gift. (☎0141 39 94 60 or 0141 39 94 489. Open Apr.-Sept. Sa-Su 10am-1pm and 4-7pm; Oct. 10am-1pm and 3-6pm. €2.) The 16-sided **Torre Rossa** in **Piazza Santa Caterina** at the western end of C. Alfieri is much older, with foundations dating to the time of Augustus. Connected to the tower is the elliptical Baroque **Chiesa di Santa Caterina.** (Open daily 7:30am-noon and 3-7pm.) The **Giardini Pubblici** are great for a picnic or stroll. (Between P. Alfieri and P. Campo del Palio.) At the edge of the city on V. dell'Arazzeria, 60, the **Tapestry Museum Scassa** is located in the **Antica Certosa di Valmanera** (Ancient Monastery of Valmanera) and features impressive modern works made using ancient looms. (☎0141 27 13 52; ugscasa@tin.it. Guided tours on request.)

🎭 **ENTERTAINMENT.** Beginning the 2nd Friday in September, agricultural Asti revels in the **Douja d'Or,** a week-long local wine fair, with competitions and tastings. On the 2nd Sunday in September, the **Paisan,** or the **Festivale delle Sagre,** unfolds with medieval costumes, parades, and feasts. On the 3rd Sunday in September, the Douja d'Or comes to a close with the **Palio di Asti.** A procession commemorating the town's liberation in 1200, followed by Italy's oldest (1275) bareback horse races. Each jockey represents a quarter of the city, and the winner takes the Palio (a painted flag). In summer, **Teatro Alfieri** holds drama, music, and dance performances (☎0141 39 90 32; www.astiteatro.it. Tickets €15, reduced €10. Reserve tickets ahead.) In July, the city sponsors **Asti Musica** with a stage built in P. Cattedrale, where bands play for dancing crowds every night. Bringing sacrilege to a new level, the bar ▧**Diavolo Rosso,** P. San Martino, 4, located in the former Chiesa di San Michele hosts daily jazz and rock concerts under flaking frescoes. (☎0141 35 56 99; www.diavolorosso.it. Wine by the bottle €8.50-22. Cocktails €5. *Primi* €5, *secondi* €7. Dinner served Tu-W and Sa-Su. Live music 10pm-midnight. Open daily 6:30pm-1am.

CANELLI ☎0141

The sparkling *Asti Spumante*, as well as the super-sweet *Moscato*, bubble forth from the countryside vineyards surrounding Canelli (pop. 11,000), providing both an economic base and a source of worldwide renown. Though wine has flowed from the verdant hills since Roman times, the first Italian sparkling wine matured in the Gancia winery 150 years ago. The region's longstanding wine-making tradition has created kilometers of vaulted underground tunnels used as wine cellars. The "underground cathedral," as the interconnected brick cellars are known, may soon earn designation as UNESCO World Heritage Site, which would provide enough money to finish the tunnel, necessary to walk from one end of the city to the other completely underground.

At **Cantine Gancia,** C. Libertà, 66, tour the wine-bottling facilities, the cellar, and the museum of the Gancia family's winemaking business. The factory has come a long way since Carlo Gancia invented the classic method of obtaining champagne from Moscato grapes through in-bottle refermentation; while in the past all was done by hand, today a machine turns the bottles slowly in crates for 70 days to sift the sediments against the cork. Gancia's annual production is now 30 million bottles a year, making the modern facility the biggest producer of sparkling wine in Italy. (☎0141 83 02 12; www.gancia.it. Open daily 9am-6pm. Wine tasting €5. Wine from €4 per bottle. Free 30min. guided tour in English. Reserve in advance.) Afterward, head to the 19th-century cellar of **Enoteca Regionale di Canelli e dell'Astesana,** C. Libertà, 65/A, for a taste of Canelli's finest wines. (☎0141 83 21 82; enoteca-canelli@inwind.it. Open Th-F 5pm-midnight, Sa-Su 11am-1pm and 5pm-midnight.) Every 3rd weekend of June, over 2000 townspeople in medieval garb reenact the **Siege of Canelli,** a 1613 battle. Entrance is free, but get a pass from the military authorities at the gate, or risk being thrown in the stocks. Inn-keepers and restaurants participate by serving 17th-century feasts (€8-21). A **market** held every Tuesday features over 100 stalls, with goods in P. Gancia, fruits and vegetables in P. Gioberti, and other foods in P. Zoppa. A smaller market is held Fridays.

Buses run from Canelli to the bus station in Asti (30min., every 1½hr. 7:10am-5pm, €2.10). Trains also run to Asti (5:28am-7:08pm, €2.25) via Castagnole. The **tourist office** is at V. Roma, 37. (☎0141 82 02 31; www.comune.canelli.at.it. Open M, W, F 8:30am-12:30pm, Tu and Th 8:30am-12:30pm and 3-5pm.) **Banca Popolare di Novara,** at V. Roma, 1, has an **ATM.** (Open M-F 8:20am-1:20pm and 2:35-3:35pm, Sa 8:20am-11:50am.) A **pharmacy, Bielli Dr. Renata Farmacia,** is in the town center at V. XX Settembre, 1. (☎0141 82 34 46.)

ACQUI TERME ☎0144

Acqui Terme has something other than *Spumante* bubbling under its placid surface. Sulfuric springs at temperatures of 75°C (167°F) gurgle up from beneath the ground in P. della Bollente and in the middle of hilltop Pisterna, Acqui's medieval town center. Numerous brick archways and aqueduct remnants suggest that luxury-seeking vacationers have flocked to the city's healing waters and mud baths since Roman times, when the town was known as Aquae Statiellae.

🖪🏠 TRANSPORTATION AND PRACTICAL INFORMATION. The **train station** (☎0144 89 20 21) is in P. V. Veneto. (Ticket booth open M-F 6am-7:30pm, Sa-Su 6am-12:35pm and 12:55-7:30pm.) **Trains** run to: Alessandria (30min., every hr. 5:35am-8:50pm, €2.45); Asti (1hr., every hr. 5:15am-7:52pm, €3.20); Genoa (1½hr., every hr. 4:05am-8:47pm, €3.50); and Savona (1½hr., every 1½hr. 6am-7:59pm, €3.40). **Taxis** are available at the station (☎0144 32 32 80) or from P. Italia (☎0144 32 20 40). To reach the town from the station, turn left on **Via Alessandria,** and continue as it becomes **Corso Vigano** and ends in **Piazza Italia.** From here, you can view most of the sights by taking **Corso Italia,** which follows the course of an ancient river. To reach the **IAT Tourist Office,** V. M. Ferraris, 5, walk down C. Dante, turn right on C. Cavour and left on V. M. Ferraris. The office also rents **bikes** (€2 per half-day, €3 per day) and provides info on itineraries in the city and surrounding region. (☎0144 32 21 42; www.comuneacqui.com. Open M 10:30am-12:30pm and 3:30-6:30pm, Tu-Sa 9:30am-12:30pm and 3:30-6:30pm, Su and holidays 9:30am-12:30pm.) **Banks** line C. Dante, including **Unicredit Banca,** C. Dante, 26, with a branch in P. Italia, both with **ATMs** and **currency exchange.** (Open M-F 8:20am-1:20pm and 2:30-4pm, Sa 8:20am-12:45pm.) A **pharmacy** is in P. Italia, 2. (Open M-F and Su 8:45am-12:30pm and 3-6:45pm.) In an **emergency,** contact the **police** at ☎113 or 0144 32 22 88, an **ambulance** at ☎118, or head to the **Ospedale Civile,** V. Fatebenfratelli, 1 (☎0144 77 71). **Internet** is available at **Internet Cafe,** on V. G. Bove off V.

Garibaldi. (☎0144 32 54 19. Open Tu-Sa 7:30am-9pm, and Su 3-9pm.) Take V. XX Settembre from P. Italia through P. Matteotti to the **post office** on V. Truco, 27. (☎0144 38 21 11. Open M-F 8am-7pm, Sa 9am-12:30pm.) **Postal Code:** 15011.

⌘ ACCOMMODATIONS AND FOOD. Reserve ahead during the 2nd half of August and much of September, when hotel rooms are booked by those who have come to be soothed after a long year of work. For a centrally located, well-staffed, and comfortable hotel, head to **Albergo San Marco ❸**, V. Ghione, 5. From P. Italia, take C. Bagni and make the first right on V. Ghione. Bright and spacious rooms are within a stone's throw of the underground remains of a Roman bath. (☎0144 32 24 56; fax 0144 35 64 65. TV and free parking included. Closed Dec. 24-Feb. 1 and July 17-31. Singles €30, with bath €32; doubles €54; half pension €40.) According to locals, the **restaurant ❷** downstairs stocks some of the best wine in town. Try the house specialty, a crepe-like flatbread that folds in tasty delights from truffles to cheese; finish with the excellent *spumone al torrone* (€3) for dessert. (*Primi* €5-6.50, *secondi* €6.50-9.) Many hotels, budget and otherwise, line Vle. Einaudi behind the station and across the Ponte Carlo Alberto. **Villa Gliciana ❸**, Vle. Einaudi, 11, has a homey living room and well-maintained guest rooms. (☎0144 32 28 74. Breakfast €4. Singles €32-35, with bath €35-39; doubles with bath €52-58.)

The **Giacobbe Olio** supermarket, C. Cavour, 8, stocks groceries. (Open M-Tu and Th-Su 8am-12:45pm and 4-7:30pm.) Every Tuesday and Friday morning, a **market** fills P. Addolorate, C. Italia, and P. M. Ferraris. Acqui Terme offers a wide selection of excellent, well-priced restaurants that serve traditional Roman fare, many of them lining the fragrant V. Mazzini. Nearby, at the ▓**Enoteca Regionale Acqui "Terme e Vino,"** P. Levi, 7, off V. Garibaldi, choose from over 230 types of wine, including the local *Dolcetto* and *Bracchetto*, from the shelves along the cavernous brick walls. (☎0144 77 02 73; www.termeevino.it. Open Tu and F-Su 10am-noon and 3-6:30pm, Th 3-6:30pm. MC/V.) At **Antica Osteria da Bigat ❶**, V. Mazzini, 30/32, a town fixture since 1885, the tripe and crisp *farinata* made with chickpea flour tempt the daring or the very hungry. (☎0144 32 42 83; www.osteriabigat.acquiterme.it. Open M-Tu and Th-Sa noon-2pm and 5-9pm, Su 5-9pm. Closed last 2 weeks of Feb. and July. MC/V.) For fine dining, take C. Dante from P. Italia across V. Mariscotti to reach the white awnings of **Il Nuovo Ciarlocco ❸**, V. Don Bosco, 1. Courteous service accompanies a high-quality fish and meat menu that rotates daily. (☎0144 57 720; www.ciarlocco.it. *Primi* €6.50-8.50, *secondi* €8-14. Cover €2.50. Open M and Th-Su noon-2pm and 7:30-10pm, Tu noon-2pm. AmEx/MC/V.)

⬛ SIGHTS. Beneath the marble chapel in **Piazza Bollente** (through the Torre Civica Porta from C. Italia), hot sulfuric water streams out of a fountain, sending up steam even in summer. Down V. Garibaldi, P. Addolorata is home to the 11th-century restored Romanesque **Basilica di San Pietro S.S. Addolorata,** with its floor set two meters down to the level of the land at its 5th-century construction (☎0144 32 27 91. Open daily 7am-noon.) Across town and up a short hill off V. Bollente from P. Bollente, P. Duomo is where the **Cattedrale di San Guido** (built in 1067) holds the famous 15th-century triptych of *Madonna our Lady of Montserrat* by Bartolomeo Bermejo in its **sacristy.** The masterpiece was spared by Napoleon's troops, because the triptych was closed, hiding its intricate interior. Look closely—the Madonna is seated on a sword blade. (Cathedral open daily 7am-noon and 3:30-6pm. Sacristy open daily 4-6pm. Ask at the tourist office to view the triptych.) Up V. Barone from the *duomo*, the 11th-century **Castello dei Paleogi**, V. Morelli, 2, houses the **Museo Civico Archeologico.** The museum displays a small but evocative collection of Roman tombs and mosaics. (☎0144 57 555; www.acquimusei.it/

archeo. Open W-Sa 9:30am-12:30pm and 3:30-6:30pm, Su 3:30-6:30pm. €5, 18-25 €3, under 18 or over 65 free.) Next door, off P. della Conciliazione, the outdoor **Teatro Estivo G. Verdi** hosts concerts and performances in the summer including the **Acqui in Palcoscenico** dance festival in July. (Contact tourist office for more info. Tickets €15, students €10.) No trip to Acqui is complete without at least dipping a finger in the steamy sulfuric water. Take C. Bagni from P. Italia out of the medieval town center of Pisterna, through Borgonuova to where four arches of the **Roman Aqueduct** overlook the banks of the Bormida River. Though the **Roman public baths** are gone (check out the ruins along C. Bagni; open F 10:30am-12:30pm, Sa 4:30-6:30pm), the **Terme Regina,** V. Donati, 2, in the *zona bagni*, offers many options for primping and pampering, as well as serious alternative medicine. A dip in the **sulfuric pool** with hydro massage runs as little as €15 per day. (☎0144 32 43 90; www.termediacqui.it. Reserve in advance. Open Apr.-Nov.) To bathe in non-sulfuric water, head down the street to the giant outdoor **Piscine di Acqui Terme** with its bar and beach volleyball. (☎0144 32 20 65. Open daily 9am-6:30pm.)

LAKE MAGGIORE (VERBANO) AND LAKE ORTA

"If it should befall that you possess a heart and shirt, then sell the shirt and visit the shores of Lago Maggiore."
—Stendhal

Steep green hills punctuate the shoreline, and to the west, the dark, glaciated outline of Monte Rosa (4634m) peers across the temperate mountain waters of Lago Maggiore, also known as Lago Verbano. Though many writers and artists have been seduced by the lake's beauty—Byron, Stendhal, Flaubert, Dickens, Hemingway, and Da Vinci have all spent time here—today, Lago Maggiore is less touristed than its eastern neighbors. Don't be discouraged by Maggiore's reputation as the most expensive lake; many *pensioni* offer reasonable rates. Stresa is the most convenient base for exploring the Borromean Islands and nearby Lago di Orta, while secluded Santa Maria Maggiore offers access to hiking trails.

STRESA ☎0323

Stresa (pop. 5000) retains much of the manicured charm that lured visitors, like Queen Victoria, in the 19th and early 20th centuries. Blooming hydrangeas and Art Nouveau hotels line the waterfront, giving the small town a romantic, old-fashioned feel. Stresa is very much a resort town; tourists from all over the world, many of them elderly or families, swell the population to four times its usual size in the summer. Many visitors come here on a trip to the Borromean Islands or for a ride up the funicular with options to bike or hike back down. The real draw, however, is in an evening walk along the lakeside lined with eclectic sculptures.

⌐⁊ TRANSPORTATION AND PRACTICAL INFORMATION. Stresa lies only 1hr. from Milan on the Milan-Domodossola train line. The city of Domodossola can be reached from Locarno, Switzerland, and travelers also have the option of taking a train to a city on the east side of the lake—like Laverno—and then taking a ferry to their final destination. (Ticket office open M-Sa 6:10-10:45am, 11am-4:15pm, 4:30-7:20pm, Su 7-10:45am, 11am-4:15pm, and 4:30-8:10pm.) **Trains** run to Milan

(1¼hr., every 30min. 5:20am-10:32pm, €4.23) and Domodossola (40min., every hr. 6:37am-11:01pm, €2.65). Most services line the water on **Corso Umberto, Piazza Marconi, Corso Italia** or the major north-south thoroughfares, **Via Principe Tomaso** and **Via Roma,** which run uphill from the water. To reach the **IAT Tourist Office** in P. Marconi, 16, exit the train station, turn right on V. P. di Piemonte, then left on Vle. D. di Genova. Head toward the water and turn right. (☎/fax 0323 30 150. Open Mar.-Oct. daily 10am-12:30pm and 3-6:30pm; Nov.-Feb. closed Su and Sa afternoon.) For **currency exchange** and 24hr. **ATM,** try **Banca Popolare di Intra,** C. Umberto, 1, just off P. Marconi. (☎0323 30 330. Open M-F 8:20am-1:20pm and 2:35-4pm, Sa 8:20am-12:15pm.) **New Data,** V. De Vit, 15/A, off P. Cadorna, provides **Internet** access at €3 per 30min. (☎0323 30 323. Open daily 9:30am-12:30pm and 3:30-10pm.) **Farmacia dott. Polisseni,** V. Cavour, 16, posts a list of after-hours rotations. (Open M-W and F-Sa 9am-12:30pm and 3-7:30pm, Th 9am-12:30pm.) In case of **emergency,** call ☎113, contact the **police** at ☎112 or 0323 301 18, **first aid** at ☎0323 318 44, or an **ambulance** at ☎118 or 0323 333 60. The **post office** is at V. A. Bolongaro, 44. (☎0323 300 65. Open M-F 8:30am-7pm, Sa 8:30am-1pm.) **Postal Code:** 28838.

⌂⁂ ACCOMMODATIONS AND FOOD. The modern **Albergo Luina ❸**, V. Garibaldi, 21, is centrally located and has well-kept rooms with TV, bath, and phone. Reserve ahead in summer. The multilingual proprietress has been known to kindly do laundry for long-term lodgers. (☎0323 30 285; luinastresa@yahoo.it. Breakfast €3.50. Singles €31-46; doubles €46-70; triples €56-80. 10% student discount with *Let's Go.* Cash only.) **Gigi Meuble ❸**, P. S. Michele, 1, also accessible through the excellent *pasticceria* at C. Italia, 30, has clean rooms just off the lakeside, some with balconies and all with bath. (☎0323 30 225. With *Let's Go,* singles €40; doubles €50.) Reach **Meublé Orsola ❷**, V. Duchessa di Genova, 45, from the station by turning right, walking downhill to the intersection, and turning left. A far cry from lakeside luxury, Meublé Orsola offers affordable rooms with cement balconies and a breakfast room adorned with golf trophies. Cramped shared bathrooms make in-room baths attractive. (☎0323 31 087; fax 0323 93 31 21. Breakfast included. Singles €20, with bath €25; doubles €40/50. AmEx/MC/V.)

Stresa boasts one truly unique local dish: *le margheritine,* a buttery cookie with sugar icing, available in most bakeries. Stock up on groceries at **GS**, V. Roma, 11. (Open M-Sa 8:30am-1pm and 3-7:30pm, Su 8:30am-12:30pm.) Hidden behind the pricier hotels, some restaurants are like diamonds in the rough. **⛲La Grigliata ❷**, V. Principe Tomaso, 61-63, is a family-run establishment where homemade pasta and fresh fish reflect the skills of an Italian mother. Enjoy them in the homey and private dining room. (☎0323 33 110. Pizza €4.20-8. *Primi* €4-12, *secondi* €7.50-16.50. Cover €1.50. Open daily 10am-2:30pm and 7pm-midnight. AmEx/MC/V.) **Taverna del Pappagallo ❷**, V. P. Margherita, 46, serves pasta like *cannelloni alla pappagallo* ("parrot pasta"; €7.30) and brick-oven pizza (€4.20-7) indoors or in a grapevine covered courtyard. (☎0323 30 411. *Primi* €5.20-8, *secondi* €6-12. Cover €1.30. Open M and Th-Su 11:30am-2:30pm and 6:30-10:30pm. AmEx/MC/V.) **Sabai Thai House and Tea Corner ❶**, V. Principessa Margherita, 52, is a tiny retreat with soothing music, assorted teas (€4 per pot), Thai and Italian snacks and, inexplicably, a €6 American breakfast with pancakes and juice. (☎0323 93 20 12; www.sabaistresa.it. Open M-Tu and Th-Su 9am-midnight. Breakfast 9-11am.)

⛲⁂ SIGHTS AND ENTERTAINMENT. The **Stresa-Alpino-Mottarone Funivia,** P. Lido, 8, allows visitors to explore Mottarone's extensive hiking and mountainbike trails. (☎0323 30 295; www.stresa.net/hotel/lalocanda. Turn right out of tourist office and follow the waterfront to Vle. Lido. Open Mar.-Nov. daily 9:30am-

12:30pm and 1:30-5:30pm. 20min., every 20min.; last return 5:40pm. To: Alpino: €4.50, round-trip €8, children €3.50/5; Mottarone: €7, round-trip €13, children €4.50/7.) Those not ready for the Tour de France can haul up a bike on the funicular and come flying down the hill (€7.50 to ascend with bike). Rent a **bike** at the base of the funicular from **Bici Co.** (☎0331 32 43 00 or 338 83 95 692; www.bicico.it. €21 per half-day, €26 per full-day. Includes helmet and lock. Ask for detailed trail map. Open daily Apr.-Sept. 9:30am-5:30pm.) Closer to home, **Villa Pallavicino,** down C. Italia, boasts 50 acres of gardens filled with flamingoes and zebras. (☎0323 31 533; www.parcozoopallavicino.it. Open Mar.-Oct. daily 9am-6pm. €6.70.)

From the last week in July to the 2nd week in September, classical musicians and fans gather for the **Settimane Musicali di Stresa e del Lago Maggiore,** a celebration of the full canon of classical music. Performances take place in venues across the lake, most often in Stresa's Palazzo dei Congressi or on Isola Bella. Contact the ticket office at V. Carducci, 38. (☎0323 31 095 or 0323 30 459; www.settimanemusicali.net. Open 9:30am-12:30pm and 3-6pm. Tickets €20-55, under 26 half-price.)

THE BORROMEAN ISLANDS (ISOLE BORROMEE)   ☎0323

Beckoning visitors with dense greenery and stately villas, the lush beauty of the Borromean trio is one of the lake's major attractions. The opulent ▓**Palazzo e Giardini Borromeo** is set on the pearl of Maggiore, **Isola Bella.** This Baroque palace, built in 1670 by Count Vitaliano Borromeo, features meticulously designed rooms constructed over 300 years, with priceless tapestries and Van Dyck's paintings. The **Sala della Musica** hosted Mussolini, Laval, and MacDonald at the 1935 **Conference of Stresa,** the last attempt to stave off WWII. Napoleon and Josephine slept in the alcove of the grand Napoleon room during his first Italian campaign (1797). Six underground man-made **grottoes** are covered in mosaics; for years peasants collected black stones to complete the masterpieces. The 10 terraced gardens rise up like a wedding cake, punctuated with statues of gods and topped by a unicorn, symbol of the Borromeo family, whose motto is *"Humilitas."* Not here. (☎0323 30 556; www.borromeoturismo.it. Open daily Mar.19-Oct. 23 9am-6pm. Ticket sales end 30min. before closing. €9, ages 6-15 €4.50. Combined ticket for the *palazzo* and the garden on Isola Madre €15. Audioguide €2.50.)

From Isola Bella, a short ferry ride leads to **Isola Superiore dei Pescatori,** a quaint fishing village full of souvenir vendors and their cats who come for the daily catch. There's a little-used rocky swimming beach on the west end of the island, but keep in mind this is an Alpine lake (by which we mean, it's cold). The only other attraction is the **Chiesa di San Vitore,** dedicated to a *Borromese* nobleman who later became a saint. (On top of the hill in the village. Open daily 9am-6pm.)

Isola Madre is the longest and most serene of the islands, almost entirely covered by its garden. Its elegant 16th-century **villa** was started in 1502 by Lancelotto Borromeo and finished by the Count Renato 100 years later, after Lancelotto reputedly met his unfortunate end in the mouth of a ▓**dragon.** It contains several room-sized puppet theaters and Princess Borromeo's extensive marionette collection. The gardens around the villa have exotic flora and fauna—a white peacock guards the 200-year-old Cashmere Cyprus. (☎/fax 0323 31 261. Open Mar. 19-Oct. 23 daily 9am-6pm, last entrance 5:30pm. €8.50, ages 6-15 €4.50. Combined ticket with *palazzo* on Isola Bella €15. Audioguide €2.50.)

Ferries run to all three islands from both Stresa and Pallanza (every 30min. 7:10am-7:10pm). A one-day ticket for unlimited travel between Stresa and the islands costs €10, though tickets to individual islands can be purchased as well.

ORTA SAN GIULIO ☎0322

Orta San Giulio (pop. 1120) is the gateway to Piedmont's Lake Orta, by far the least touristed of the lakes. The high houses that line the narrow cobblestone streets evoke the very best of old Italy. Difficult to reach without a car, the town has drawn many to its secluded location. In fact, the privacy is precisely what drew Nietzsche here in 1882 with his young love Lou Salome, in order to escape the watchful eye of her mother. Nietzsche claimed he couldn't remember whether or not the two had kissed, because the views had sent him into a state of grace.

At the intersection of V. Panoramica and V. G. Fava, the ornate **Villa Crespi,** which now houses a hotel, was built in 1873 in an Arabian style complete with minaret tower. The large stone columns of the old city hall dominate **Piazza Motta.** Art exhibits, in addition to the municipal frescoes on the interior walls, make the "Palazzoto" worth a visit. On the lake across from Orta lies the peaceful **Isola di San Giulio,** inhabited by three families and a convent of nuns who have taken a vow of silence. Small **motoscafi** (motorboats) weave back and forth to the mainland during the summer (☎333 60 50 288; 10min.; Apr.-Oct. daily 9am-6:30pm every 15min., Nov.-Mar. 9am-5pm every 40min.; €3), and larger boats run by Navigazione Lago d'Orta depart every 30min. (☎0322 84 48 62; 5min., 9:55am-7:10pm, €2.50). Walkers can circumnavigate the tiny island on a cobblestone path (10min.) known as **Meditation Way,** where periodic markers in four languages comment on the beauty of silence. The 12th-century **Romanesque Basilica di San Giulio,** built on 4th-century foundations, is filled with Baroque ornamentation and adorned with pink cloud frescoes, though its true masterpiece is the **pulpit,** carved from black *Oira* stone. Downstairs, the **skeleton of San Giulio,** dressed in brocade robes and a golden mask, rests in a gold and glass sarcophagus. (Basilica open daily 9:30am-12:15pm and 2-6:30. Free. Modest dress required.) On January 31, the convent celebrates the saint and supplies visitors with sweet San Giulio bread. A short 15min. hike off V. Panoramica onto V. della Cappelletta leads to the UNESCO-protected **Sacro Monte** monastic complex, where 20 chapels chart the life of St. Francis of Assisi with 376 life-size wooden statues and 900 frescoes. (☎0322 91 19 60; monteorta@tin.it. Open daily 8:30am-7pm. Free.) Orta hosts a plethora of events throughout the year, including several music and film festivals. A professor of creative writing at the University of Pavia sponsors an evening of **English poetry with authors on Lake Orta** near the end of September (☎0322 901 33).

The **◨Piccolo Hotel Olina ❹,** located on V. Olina, 40, houses guests in spacious modern rooms with wood floors, private baths, and TV. (☎0322 90 56 56; www.ortainfo.com. Breakfast €6. Singles €45; doubles €60; triples €70. AmEx/MC/V.) The lakeside **◨Camping Orta ❶,** V. Domodossola, 28, welcomes campers with and a private beach and hot showers, along with bikes, (€4 per hr., €8 per half-day), kayaks, sailboats, and windsurfing boards (€8 per half-day) for rent. (☎0322 90 26; www.campingorta.it. Laundry €3 per wash or dry. €4.60-5.85 per adult, €3.30-4.35 per child under 12, €7.60-12.50 per tent, €4-5 per car, €7.60-12.50 per camper. Bungalows €50-80. Electricity €2. Cash only.) An **open-air market** on Wednesday morning in P. Motta sells produce, clothes, and household necessities. Local cuisine is known for *tapulon* (spiced minced donkey meat, cooked in red wine) eaten with the cornmeal polenta, though the heavy meal is typically only served in winter. In season, it's available with other local recipes at **Taberna Antico Agnello ❸,** V. Olina, 18, where second-story windows overlook the *piazza* below. (☎0322 90 259. *Primi* €6.50-9.50, *secondi* €11.50-13.50. Open M and W-Su 12:30-2pm and 7:30-9:30pm; open Tu in Aug. AmEx/MC/V.) **Il Pozzo Cafe and Food ❷,** V. Panoramica, 16, draws a younger crowd with its cheap eats, mini golf, ping pong, foosball, and board games (☎0322 90 150. Pizza and pasta €3.50-7. Wine and cocktails €2-4.50. Open M and W-Su 11am-2pm.) The working folk take their lunch by the station at **Bar Vecchia Stazione ❷,** V. Lunate Stazione, 30, which serves a three-course meal for only €10. (Open M-F 6:30am-midnight, Sa 7:30am-midnight.) At night the mature crowd heads to **Caffe and Jazz**, V. Olina, 13, where Saturday means live piano music in the bright chamber. (☎0322 91 17 00. Wine €3-3.50 per glass. *Panini* and *bruschetta* €3-6. Open Tu-Sa 10am-2pm and 5:30pm-2:30am.)

Though Orta lies less than 60km from Stresa, the two are not directly connected by rail. Hop the **Nerini mini-bus** (☎0323 55 21 72) that runs between the two towns on summer weekdays June 13 to September 4. By request the bus also stops at the **tourist office**, 1.5km outside of town. (1hr.; departs Stresa railway station 10am, 2, and 5pm, returns from Orta 11am, 3, 6pm; €2.45.) Alternatively, take the **train** from Stresa to Orta switching lines at Premosello (1½hr.; 4 per day 6:37am-6:47pm, return 6:28am-8:15pm; €2.89.) Get off at Orta-Miasino, where a small red train, **Il Trenino di Orta**, shuttles passengers the 2km between the intersection of V. Panoramica and V. G. Fava and the town center. (5min.; Apr. 15-Oct. 15 M-Tu and Th-Su every 15min. 9am-8pm, Oct. 16-Apr. 14 Su only; €2, children €1, round-trip €3/2.) The train continues past the tourist office to the entrance of the Sacro Monte.

Orta's **tourist office** is on V. Panoramica, across the street and downhill from Villa Crespi. (☎0322 90 56 14 or 0322 90 51 63; inforta@distrettolaghi.it. Open for viewing Tu 10am-1pm, W-Th 10am-1pm and 3-6:30pm, F-Sa 9am-1pm and 3-7pm.) The town center is **Piazza Motta**. Amble along **Via Olina** which becomes **Via Bossi** then **Via Gippini** to reach **Via E. Motta** and the footpath **Strada del Movero** and **Lungo Lario 11 Settembre**. A **pharmacy** is on V. C. Albertolletti, 10, off the main *piazza*. (☎0322 90 117. Open M-W and F-Sa 9am-12:30pm and 3:30-7:30pm.) In case of **emergency**, call an **ambulance** at ☎118 or 0322 81 500, or the **carabinieri** at ☎0322 90 114. There is an **Internet** point at the train station, or in town at the hotel booking center on V. Poli, 5. (☎0322 90 55 32. Open daily 9am-7pm.) The **post office** is at P. Ragazzoni, 9. (☎0322 90 157. Open M-F 8:30am-2pm, Sa 8:30-1pm.) **Postal Code:** 28016.

SANTA MARIA MAGGIORE AND VAL VIGEZZO ☎0324

Formed by the same glaciers as Lake Maggiore and Lake Orta, Val Vigezzo has no lake and few tourists. The area has served as artistic inspiration so often that it became known as "Painter's Valley." Santa Maria Maggiore (pop. 1500), is the largest town, bordered by tiny Crana, Toceno, Arvogno, Craveggia, Malesco, and Re.

One of the main attractions in **Santa Maria Maggiore** is the **Museo dello Spazzacamino** (Chimney Sweep Museum) in the Parco Villa Antonia, which holds a small collection of clothing and equipment, and sends visitors through a tunnel of pictures, sounds, and smells. (☎0324 95 091. Open June-Sept. daily 10am-noon and 3-5pm; Oct.-May Sa-Su only. €2.) Head up V. A. Rosmini, veering right on V. Cavour, to reach **Crana**, where **Prosciutto Montano Vigezzino**, V. G. P. Femminis, 36, demonstrates the 14-month preparation process for the regional specialty ham. (☎0324 95 056. Open daily 8am-noon and 4-7pm. Call ahead, especially on Su.) Farther up V. Cavour, **Toceno** is home to the well-preserved **Forno Toma**, an oven used twice a year to bake bread. (☎0324 98 035. Open in summer daily 9am-7pm.) Climb past Toceno along the winding road to **Arvogno** (1260m), where hiking paths start toward higher peaks, and the La Cima **chair lift** takes visitors ever higher on summer weekends (8:30, 11:30am, 2:30, and 5pm). The **Percorci dell Uomo** trail winds for 20min. from the top of the lift to a wall with prehistoric graffiti. (☎/fax 0323 30 295; www.stresa-mottarone.it.) In winter, it becomes part of the Valle Vigezzo **ski** ticket, which also includes the **Piana di Vigezzo Funivia** (cable car) that mounts to **Colma Trubbio** (2064m) from **Prestinone**. (Summer ascents daily July-Sept. 11 every hr. 8am-5:30pm; one-way €6, children €3; round-trip €9/5. Winter open daily 8:30am-4:30pm. Winter full-day ski pass €18 weekday, €21 weekend; children 4-12 €13.50/16.50. Half-day adult €13/15, child €10/13. Equipment rental available at top of funivia.) A final stop is **Re**, past **Malesco** on V. Milano, where the ▨**Basilica e Santuario della Madonna del Sangue** houses the painting of the Madonna del Sangue

(Madonna of the Blood), which is said to have bled for 20 days in 1494 after being hit with a stone. (☎0324 97 016; www.valvigezzo.com/santuario.re/santuario_re.htm. Open daily 8am-7pm.) The best outdoor excursions in the area are to the **Parco Nazionale Val Grande**, created in 1992. Ask at the tourist office for park info, and acquire itineraries and maps at the office inside the park entrance. (☎0323 557 960; www.parcovalgrande.it.)

The best lodging deal in the area is at ▩**Rifugio del Moro ❷**, which offers three rooms with wooden floors, low ceilings, and antique furniture, as well as kitchen access and a sitting room. (☎0324 98 450 or 336 74 0153. Reserve ahead. Open in summer only. June-Sept. €21 per person; Aug. €25 per person.) The excellent **restaurant ❷** serves filling *cervo* (mountain goat) and *lumache* (snails), as well as polenta and local cheeses for the less adventurous. (*Primi* €3-5, *secondi* €8-10. Open July-Sept. M-F and Su 8:30am-10pm, Sa 8:30am-1am; Oct.-June. Sa-Su only.)

From Stresa, take the **train** to Domodossola (40min., 1 per hr. 6:37am-11:01pm, €2.65), then transfer to the **SSIF**, or Centovalli, line and take the train in direction of Locarno, getting off at Santa Maria Maggiore. (40min., every 45min. 5:30am-7:58pm. Last return 8:28pm. €2.53.) The ticket office (☎0324 24 2055) is open daily 7:40-10:20am, 11:10am-12:20pm, 1:45-2:30pm, and 3:45-6:20pm. It is possible to make a complete circuit through Val Vigezzo via the Borromean Islands by train and ferry with the **Lago Maggiore Express Pass.** (☎0322 23 32 00 or 091 75 18 731. Mar. 20-June 1 F-Sa, June 2-Sept. 25 M-Tu and Th-Su; departures from Stresa 8:36, 10:21, 11:27am, last return 7:30pm; 1-day round-trip €28, children €14.) **Bike rental** is available from **Ul Tepie Artigianato**, V. Rosmini, 11. (☎333 37 48 486. €5 per hr., €20 per day 8:30am-7pm.) For a **taxi** call ☎0324 92 405 or 0324 980 45.

From the train station on **Piazzale Diaz**, cross V. Luigi Cadorna to V. Dante, which ends at **Via A. Rosmini**, where you turn right to reach **Piazza Risorgimento**, the town center. The **tourist office** is in P. Risorgimento, 28, on the first floor of the municipal building. (☎0324 95 091; www.comune.santamariamaggiore.vb.it. Open M-W and F-Sa 8:30am-1:30pm and 3-5pm, Th 8:30am-1:30pm, Su 10am-noon.) Follow V. Cavalli from P. Risorgimento until it becomes V. R. Valentini to reach **Banca Popolare di Novara**. (☎0324 95 002. Open M-F 8:20am-1:20pm and 2:35-3:35pm.) In case of **emergency**, call ☎113, an **ambulance** at ☎118, the **carabinieri** at ☎0324 95 007, or the **Guardia Medica Turistica** (July-Aug. 2-6pm) ☎0324 94 360. A **pharmacy** is on V. Matteotti, 53. (☎0324 95 018. Open M-Sa 9am-12:30pm and 3:30-7:30pm, Su 9am-12:30pm.) **Internet** is available at **Ufficio Turistico Proloco** off V. Rosmini daily from 10am-noon and 5-7pm. (☎0324 94 565. €3 per 30min.) The **post office** is also located on V. R. Vaneltini, 26. (☎0324 90 53 87. Open M-Sa 8:30am-1:30pm.) **Postal Code:** 28857.

VALLE D'AOSTA

Italy's least populated and most elevated region, Valle d'Aosta is rich with pine forests, waterfalls, and international cable cars. Living so close to their Swiss and French neighbors, *Valdostani* have taken on much of their continental cousins' cultural character, evident at intersections of *vie* with *rues* and *Strassen*. The Valle is a key transportation hub; Hannibal and his elephants once crossed Aosta's St. Bernard Pass, and today an even greater stampede of heavy goods vehicles (HGV or TIR in Italian) barrels through the Monte Bianco tunnel. Italian locals who display "No ai TIR!" placards believe that Aosta's new status as a trade gateway may damage the natural splendor and destabilize the tourist economy. However, before there were parka-clad snow warriors battling the *piste* (trails), wealthy cure-seekers filled chalets to soak in the hot springs and Alpine air.

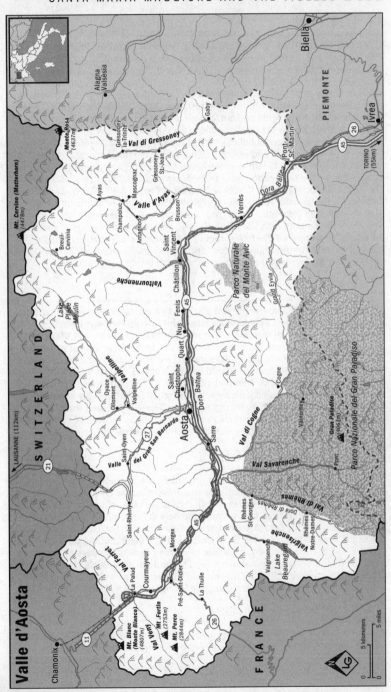

Valle d'Aosta

🏔 HIKING

The scenic trails of Valle d'Aosta are a hiker's paradise. The best times to hike are July, August, and the first week of September, when much of the snow has melted and the public buses run frequently. In April and May, thawing snow can cause avalanches. Monte Bianco and surrounding peaks may be classic climbs, but only pros should attempt them. (For information on wilderness safety, see **Essentials,** p. 44.) Each area's tourist office or Alpine guide office assists hikers of all levels, with suggested itineraries and information on weather and trail conditions. Offices in Aosta and in the smaller valleys also provide details on campgrounds, *pranzo al sacco* (bagged lunches), *rifugi alpini* (mountain refuges or chalets overseen by a proprietor and offering filling meals and dorm rooms to hikers for around €15 a night, €35 half pension), and *bivacchi* (empty public refuges or huts)—ask for the publication *Mountain Huts and Bivouacs in Aosta Valley.* For info, call **Società Guide,** V. Monte Emilius, 13 (☎0165 40 939), or **Club Alpino Italiano,** C. Battaglione Aosta, 15 (☎0165 40 194; www.guidealpine.it), both in Aosta. They offer insurance and *rifugi* discounts. Most regional tourist offices also carry the booklet *Alte Vie* (High Roads), with **maps,** photographs, and helpful advice pertaining to the two serpentine mountain trails that circumnavigate the valley and link the region's most dramatic peaks. Long stretches of these trails require no expertise but offer adventure and beautiful panoramas.

⛷ SKIING

Skiing Valle d'Aosta's mountains and glaciers is a fantastic experience; unfortunately, it is not a bargain. **Settimane bianche** (white weeks) one-week packages for skiers are one source of discounts. For information and prices, call **Ufficio Informazioni Turistiche,** P. Chanoux, 8 (☎0165 23 66 27), in Aosta, and request the pamphlet *White Weeks: Aosta Valley.* **Courmayeur** (☎0165 84 20 60) and **Breuil-Cervinia** (☎0166 94 91 36) are the best-known ski resorts in the 11 valleys, though **Val d'Ayas** (☎0125 30 71 13) and **Val di Gressoney** (☎0125 36 61 43) offer equally challenging terrain for lower rates with a joint pass. **Cogne** (☎016 74 040) and **Brusson,** halfway down Val d'Ayas, have cross-country skiing and less demanding trails. Pick up descriptions and maps of all resorts at the tourist office. In Breuil-Cervinia, diehards tackle the slopes in bathing suits for extensive **summer skiing** (see p. 191).

🧗 OUTDOOR SPORTS

A host of other sports—rock climbing, mountain biking, hang-gliding, and rafting—keeps the adrenaline pumping. For white-water rafting enthusiasts, the most navigable rivers are the **Dora Baltea,** which runs across the valley; the **Dora di Veny,** which branches south from Courmayeur; the **Dora di Ferre,** which meanders north from Courmayeur; the **Dora di Rhêmes,** which flows through the Val di Rhêmes; and the **Grand Eyvia,** which courses through the Val di Cogne. Rafting packages run about €30 for 1½hr. from organizations like **Grand Paradis Emotions** in **Aymavilles** (☎0165 90 60 05; www.gpemotion.com.) The **Societa' delle Guide** in most cities arranges ice- and rock-climbing lessons and excursions, as well as mountain-biking trips. Ask a tourist office for a complete list of recreational activities.

AOSTA   ☎0165

Sizable Aosta (pop. 35,000) teeters between Italian and French *Valdostana* border culture. Though street signs alternate between French and Italian, and most residents are bilingual, the favored language is Italian, and *gelaterie* abound on city streets. For many years Aosta was Rome's launching point for military expeditions, resulting in an array of impressive ruins throughout the town, which still serves as a geographic and financial nexus. Inside the crumbling walls that once defended Rome's Alpine outpost, boutiques and gourmet food shops densely pack the *centro storico;* outside, a commercial and industrial minefield stretches across the valley. Aosta makes a good starting point for exploring the Italian Alps, but be aware that daytrips to the surrounding valleys often require tricky train and bus connections—to return before nightfall, plan carefully, or else stay in a more scenic location closer to the peaks.

▐ TRANSPORTATION

Trains: The **train station** is in the pink building at P. Manzetti. Ticket window open daily 4:50-11:25am and 1:45-8:30pm. To: **Turin** (3hr., every hr. 5:10am-9:37pm, €6.80) via **Châtillon** (20min., €1.80), **Chivasso** (2hr., €4.65), and **Verrès** (30min., €2.45); **Ivrea** (1hr., 5 per day 6:12am-5:12pm, €2.35); **Milan** Centrale (4½hr., 12 per day 6:12am-8:40pm, €10.10) via Verrès; **Prè St. Didier** (1hr., every hr. 6:45am-7:44pm.)

Buses: SAVDA (☎0165 26 20 27), on V. Carrel off P. Manzetti, to the right exiting the train station. Office open daily 6:30am-1:30am. To: **Courmayeur** (1hr., every hr. 7:50am-9:45pm, €2.90,); **Chamonix** (1¾hr., 6 per day 8:15am-4:45pm); **Great St. Bernard Pass** (1hr.; 9:35am and 2:25pm, return at 11am and 4:20pm; €2.90); **Châtillon** (30min., every hr. 5:50am-10:15pm). SVAP serves closer towns. To: **Cogne** (1hr., 7 per day 8:05am-7:45pm, €2.40); **Fenis** (1hr., 10 per day 8:05am-6:50pm, €1.70). Buses to **Breuil-Cervinia** (2hr., 7 per day 6:10am-7:25pm, €3.25) and **Valtournenche** (30min., 4 per day 9:30am-7:30pm) leave from the Châtillon train station.

Taxis: ☎0165 26 20 10 in P. Manzetti; ☎0165 35 656 in P. Narbonne.

Car Rental: Europcar, P. Manzetti, 3 (☎0165 41 432), to the left of the train station. 18+. Economy car €77 per day unlimited mileage. Open M-F 8:30am-12:30pm and 3-7pm, Sa 8:30am-12:30am. AmEx/MC/V.

Bike Rental: Gal Sport Shop, V. Paravera, 6/B (☎0165 23 61 34), past the funicular base station. Mountain bikes €6 per 2hr, €15 per day. Open M-Sa 9am-12:30pm and 3-7:30pm. **Pila** (☎0165 52 11 48), at top of funicular, with same rates and hours.

Ski rental: In the numerous hangars by the chairlift behind the station.

◼ ▐ ORIENTATION AND PRACTICAL INFORMATION

Trains stop at **Piazza Manzetti.** From there, take **Avenue du Conseil des Commis** through the wall until it ends in the enormous **Piazza Chanoux,** Aosta's center. The main street runs east-west through P. Chanoux and changes its name several times. From Av. du Conseil des Commis, **Via J. B. de Tillier,** which then becomes **Via Aubert,** is to the left; to the right **Via Porta Praetoria** leads to the historical gate **Porta Praetoria** and becomes **Via Sant'Anselmo.**

Tourist Office: P. Chanoux, 2 (☎0165 23 66 27; www.regione.vda.it/turismo), down Av. du Conseil des Commis from train station. Ask for *Aosta Monument Guide,* a good town **map.** English, German, and French spoken. Free 15min. **Internet** access. Open July-Sept. daily 9am-1pm and 2-8pm; Sept.-June M-Sa 9am-1pm and 3-8pm, Su 9am-1pm.

Alpine Information: Club Alpino Italiano, C. Battaglione Aosta, 81 (☎/fax 0165 40 194), off P. della Repubblica. Open Tu 7-8:30pm, F 8-10pm. **Società Guide,** V. Monte Emilius, 13 (☎0165 40 939; www.guidealpine.it).

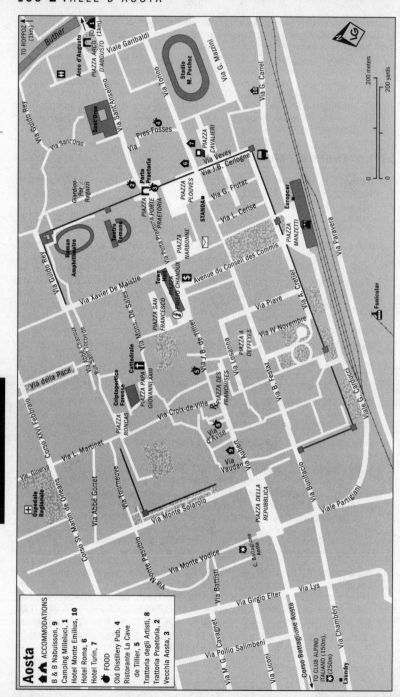

Aosta

ACCOMMODATIONS
B & B Nabuisson, 9
Camping Milleluci, 1
Hotel Monte Emilius, 10
Hotel Roma, 6
Hotel Turin, 7

FOOD
Old Distillery Pub, 4
Ristorante La Cave
de Tillier, 5
Trattoria degli Artisti, 8
Trattoria Praetoria, 2
Vecchia Aosta, 3

Tours: Free tours guided by the **Associazione Guide Turistiche** (☎333 80 88 036). July 4-Aug. 6 M-Sa 10am; Aug. 8-21 10am and 3pm; Aug. 22-Sept. 7 10am. All tours depart from P. Arco d'Augusto.

Currency Exchange: Monte dei Paschi di Siena, P. Chanoux, 51 (☎0165 27 68 88). **ATM** outside. Open M-F 8:30am-1:30pm and 2:40-4:10pm.

Work Opportunity: Old Distillery Pub, V. Pres Fosses, 7 (☎0165 23 95 11) hires workers seasonally (see **Food and Nightlife,** below).

Laundromat: Onda Blu, V. Chambéry, 60. Wash €3.50 per 6½kg, dry €3.50. Open daily 8am-10pm.

Emergency: ☎113. **Ambulance:** ☎118. **Police,** C. Battaglione Aosta.

Pharmacy: Farmacia Chenal, V. Croix-de-Ville, 1 (☎0165 26 21 33), at V. Aubert. Open M-Tu and Th-Sa 9am-12:30pm and 3-7:30pm. Posts list of after-hours rotations.

Hospital: Vle. Ginevra, 3 (☎0165 30 41).

Internet Access: Eye of Ra, P. Cavalieri, next door to Hotel Turin. 15min. free; €1 per hr. Open M 2pm-midnight, Tu 7am-7:30pm, W-F 2pm-2am, Sa 7am-2am. Also at Tourist Office (see above) and **URP Vallée d'Aosta** in the Palais Régionale at P. Deffeyes, 1, (☎0165 27 35 91. Open M-F 9am-2pm).

Post Office: P. Narbonne, 1/A (☎0165 44 138), in the huge semi-circular building, with an ATM. Open M-F 8am-6:30pm, Sa 8am-1pm. **Postal Code:** 11100.

ACCOMMODATIONS AND CAMPING

Prices tend to vary seasonally in Aosta, with the lowest prices being offered in January to April and October to mid-December, and the highest prices during the first three weeks of August and around Christmas.

Bed & Breakfast Nabuisson, V. Aubert, 50 (☎0165 36 30 06 or 339 60 90 332; www.bedbreakfastaosta.it). In the yellow building through the iron gate under the arch between the *tabac* and the *libreria*. Spacious, rustic themed rooms in a green courtyard with wood floors, antique furniture, TV, and bath. Breakfast included. Reserve ahead. Doubles used as singles €40; doubles €50-60. Extra bed €10-15. Cash only. ❸

Hotel Roma, V. Torino, 7 (☎0165 41 000; hroma@libero.it), close to the train station and the center of town, around the corner from Hotel Turin (enter off Rue Vevey). Slightly worn rooms undergoing renovation, with bath, and TV. Breakfast €6. Parking €6. Singles €39-56; doubles €68-82; triples €90-108. MC/V. ❹

Hotel Monte Emilius, V. G. Carrel, 11 (☎0165 23 00 68), right out of the train station. Simple rooms with private bath, TV, and phone. Singles €22-27; doubles €40-45. ❸

Hotel Turin, V. Torino, 14 (☎0165 44 593; www.hotelturin.it). Exiting the train station, turn right on V. Giorgio, left on Rue Vevey, then right on V. Torino. Modern rooms with bath, TV, and phone. Breakfast included. Internet €5 per hr. Singles €44-60; doubles €77-92; triples €108-123. AmEx/MC/V. ❹

Camping Milleluci, Loc. Roppoz, 15 (☎0165 23 52 78; www.campingmilleluci.com), a 1km hike from station. Get a map from the tourist office in P. Chanoux. Each plot has a cabin connected to a trailer. Quiet, hillside location with panoramic views. Expansive, but very full June-Sept. Laundry €5. Reception in Hotel Milleluci. €6-8 per adult, €4-5 per child under 10, €11 per tent. Showers €0.50. AmEx/MC/V. ❶

FOOD AND NIGHTLIFE

There's nary a drop of olive oil nor a shred of truffle in Aosta, where one of the most revered ingredients is lard. The colder climate and predominantly agricultural lifestyle have generated a cuisine rich in fat. Another delicacy is *fonduta*, a cheese sauce made from the local fontina, poured over everything in great quantities. Pick up a can at **STANDA**, on V. Festaz, 10. (☎0165 35 757. Open M-Sa 8am-8pm, Su 8am-1pm.) Aosta's weekly **market** is Tuesday in P. Cavalieri di Vittorio Veneto.

Trattoria Praetoria, V. S. Anselmo, 9 (☎0165 44 356), past Pta. Praetoria. After a day in the mountains, you won't find better Aostan food. With *fonduta valdostana* (cheese fondue with toast; €10), meaty *salsiccettae in umido* (sausages braised in tomato sauce; €6.50) over polenta and tripe (€7), there's a local delicacy to fit any taste. *Primi* €7-7.50, *secondi* €6.50-14. Cover €1.50. Open in summer daily 12:15-2:30pm and 7:15-10pm; in winter closed W dinner and Th. MC/V. ❷

Trattoria degli Artisti, V. Maillet 5/7 (☎0165 40 960). At this calm *trattoria* down a side street off V. Aubert, the menu changes every two weeks and includes staples like *polenta du berger* (polenta with fresh cream; €7.50). *Primi* €7.50-8, *secondi* €9-17. Open M-Sa 12:30-2pm and 7:30-10pm, Su 7:30-10pm; in winter closed Su. AmEx/MC/V. ❸

Vecchia Aosta, P. Pta. Praetoria, 4 (☎0165 36 11 86), inside the Pta. Praetoria. The *mocetta lardo di Arnad con castagne glassate al miele* (basically, meat, lard, and chestnuts; €7.50) is particularly good. If the idea of eating large chunks of fat turns you vegetarian, try *le lasagne pasticciate al forno con degli formaggi alpeggi* (homemade lasagne with Alpine cheese; €7.50). *Primi* €6-11, *secondi* €14-22. Cover €2.50. Open M-Tu and Th-Su 12:15-2:30pm and 7:30-10pm. AmEx/MC/V. ❹

Ristorante La Cave de Tillier, V. de Tillier, 40 (☎0165 23 01 33), set off the street in an alleyway. Cobblestone walls, a quiet locale, and a plate full of *gnocchi* (€6) make for a great meal. *Primi* €6-8, *secondi* €8-18. Open in summer Tu-Su 12:30-2:30pm and 7-10:30pm; in winter closed M. MC/V. ❸

Old Distillery Pub, V. Pres Fosses, 7 (☎0165 23 95 11). From Pta. Praetoria, walk down V. S. Anselmo and turn right through a small archway on the winding V. Pres Fosses before V. Sant Orso. The pub is on the left. Locals pack this Scottish pub most nights after 10pm. Occasional live music. Pint of Beamish €5.50. Open daily 6pm-2am. ❶

⊙♫ SIGHTS AND ENTERTAINMENT

Vestiges of the Roman Empire are thoroughly integrated with modern Aosta; a partially intact 2000-year-old wall rings the city center; streets run neatly through the gaps. The **Porta Praetoria,** now on the street bearing its name, once served as a guard house at the edge of the walled city. To its left lie the sprawling remains of the massive **Teatro Romano.** Through Pta. Praetoria, V. S. Anselmo leads to the **Arco d'Augusto.** The monument dates from Roman times and has sported its hanging Christian cross inside the arch since the Middle Ages. Between the Pta. Praetoria and the Arco d'Augusto, the renowned **Complex of Sant'Orso** includes the Collegiate Church of Saints Pietro and Orso, the bell tower, the crypt and museum of Treasure, and the cloister. The ruins of the ancient forum, or **Criptoportico Forense,** are off P. Papa Giovanni XXIII. (Open M and W-Su 9am-6pm. Free.) The **Fiera di Sant'Orso,** the region's 1000-year-old craft fair, takes place January 30-31 on V. S. Orso (open 7am-7pm) and is complemented in the last two weeks of July by the **Mostra Concorso dell'Artigianato Valdostano di Tradizione** crafts competition featuring local woodcarving in P. Chanoux.

▶ DAYTRIPS FROM AOSTA

Valleys extend in all directions from Aosta. Some are more touristed than others, but each valley has quaint hamlets and excellent hiking trails, as well as a host of other outdoor excursions.

VALTOURNENCHE: THE MATTERHORN AND BREUIL-CERVINIA

Buses run to Breuil-Cervinia (☎0166 94 90 54; 1hr., 7 per day 9:05am-12:35pm, €2.30) from Châtillon, on the Aosta-Turin train line. Direct buses also arrive daily from P. Castello in Milan (5hr.). Buses run to Turin (4hr.; M-Sa 6:45am, 1:25, 5pm, Su 6pm; €7.80).

The most famous mountain in Switzerland, the **Matterhorn (Il Cervino)** looms majestically over the town of **Breuil-Cervinia** in Valtournenche. Despite the high cost of most amenities in this heavily touristed area, fresh-air fiends consider it a small price for the chance to climb up the glaciers of one of the world's most spectacular mountains. A cable car provides service to **Plateau Rosà**, where ⛷summer skiers tackle the slopes. (June 25-Sept. 4; 1-day adult pass €24, students and children €18, 2-day pass €40/25. With Zermatt, Switzerland slopes, 1-day €36/22, 2-day €67/37.) Hikers may attempt the 3hr. ascent to **Colle Superiore delle Cime Bianche** (2982m), with views of Val d'Ayas to the east and the Cervino glacier to the west. A shorter trek (1½hr.) on the same trail leads to **Lake Goillet**.

Don't forget to bring your passport on your hiking excursions; a number of trails cross into Zermatt, Switzerland.

Affordable accommodations can be found at **Hotel Breithorn ❹**, V. G. Rey, 10, in Breuil-Cervinia, where simple rooms come with bath and phone (☎0166 94 90 42; breithorn@libero.it. Open July 10-Sept. 10 and Nov. 30-May 1. Singles €26-47; doubles €47-93; half pension €40-78. Cash only.)

The English-speaking staff of the **Tourist Info Center**, V. Carrel, 29, provides information on *Settimana Bianca* (White Week) Packages and *Settimane Estive*, the summer equivalent. (☎0166 94 91 36; www.cervinia.it. Open high-season daily 9am-6pm; low-season 9:30am-12:30pm and 2:30-5:30pm.) Students should ask about the University Card, which offers discounts of 10-20% on passes. The **Società Guide** (☎0166 94 81 69), across from the tourist office, arranges group outings

VAL D'AYAS

Trains run from Aosta to Verrès (30min., every hr. 5:10am-9:37pm, €2.45). SAVDA Buses run from the train station at Verrès to Champoluc (1½hr.; 6 per day 8:55am-12:25am, return 6 per day 6:50am-5:30pm; €2.10), as do VITA buses (☎0125 96 65 46; 1hr., 9 per day 7:12am-9:22pm.) VITA also runs a line between towns in the Ayas Valley (☎0125 96 65 46; 6:27am-11:04pm). The AIAT tourist office in Champoulc, V.Varase, 16, has information on accommodations and trail maps. (☎0125 30 71 13; infoayas@aiatmonterosa.com. Open daily 9am-12:30pm and 3-6pm.)

Budget-minded sports enthusiasts should consider visiting the gently sloping Val d'Ayas, which offers the cheapest ⛷ **skiing** in the region at **Monterosa Ski Resort.** (☎0125 30 31 68; www.monterosa-ski.com. Dec. 19-Apr. 2 €33 per day, children €24; from start of season to Dec.18 and Apr. 3-Apr. 19 €27/20.) The town of **Champoluc** has the most tourist amenities. An easy **hike** is the 45min. **trail 14** from Champoluc to the hamlet of **Mascognaz**, home to a farming population of 10 and an excellent restaurant (see below). An easy-medium difficulty hike (**trail 105**) leads over rocks and through pastures to ⛰**Mount Zerbion** (2700m). A 360° panorama offers views of the soaring Five Giants: the peaks of the **Matterhorn, Mont Blanc, Monte Rosa, Grand Combin,** and **Gran Paradiso.** Expert hikers may wish to embark on the **Walser Trail,** staying overnight in bivouacs and following the path of the Germanic migration in the 12th-14th century through Valtournenche, St. Jacques, Champoluc, and Gressoney. **Rafting** outings are arranged in July and August by Totem Adventure. (☎0165 87 677 or contact the tourist office. €25 per 1½hr.)

Affordable lodging in quaint rooms with private bathrooms can be found at **Affittacamere (B&B) Le Vieux Rascard ❸**, Rue des Guides, 35, up from the tourist office.

(☎0125 30 87 46; infoayas@aiatmonterosa.com. Breakfast included. Open July-Aug and Dec.-Apr. In summer €29-46 per person; in winter €31-52. Cash only.) **Hotellerie de Mascognaz restaurant ❸**, in Mascognaz, is a favorite stopover of hikers craving hearty cuisine (☎0125 30 87 34. *Primi* €9-12, *secondi* €18. Cover €1. Open daily Dec. 1-Feb. 28 and mid-June to mid-Sept. noon-2pm and 7:30-11pm.)

OTHER VALLEYS

VALLE DEL GRAN SAN BERNARDO. A valley with more medieval towers than tourists, **Valle del Gran San Bernardo** links Aosta to Switzerland via the **Great St. Bernard Pass.** Motor-tourists and intrepid cyclists tackle this winding mountain road in summer. Come winter, they retreat to a more highly trafficked 5854m mountain tunnel. Tourists follow the footsteps of Hannibal and his elephants, as well as Napoleon, who trekked through the pass with 40,000 soldiers in 1800. This region boasts the **Hospice of St. Bernard** (☎0041 27 78 71 236; www.gsbernard.ch), dating from 1505 and home to the patron saint of pups. The legendary life-saver was stuffed for posterity and is conveniently displayed for people driving through the pass. The hospice, across the Swiss border, is just a tail-wag away from the **dog museum** (☎0041 27 78 71 236; www.swiss-st-bernard-dog.ch), where St. Bernards are trained. About 5km before the hospice, a trail takes visitors on an easy path to a series of lakes. The town of **Saint-Oyen** is about as close to the border as you can get. The primary **AIAT tourist office** for the valley is in **Etroubles** on Strada Nazionale G.S. Bernardo, 13. (☎0165 78 559; www.gransanbernardo.net.)

VAL DI COGNE. When Cogne's mines failed in the 1970s, the townspeople resorted to a more genteel pursuit—parting cross-country skiers from their cash. Cogne is one of the world's premier places to ice climb, but it remains little known and largely untouched. A cable car transports Alpine addicts to the modest downhill 🎿 **skiing** facilities. In summer, the valley serves as the gateway to Italy's largest nature reserve, **Gran Paradiso National Park.** In addition to an endless network of trails, the park has the highest glacier (4061m) fully contained within Italian borders, the Gran Paradiso. Cogne and its rocky valley are a scenic **bus** ride from Aosta (1hr., 7 per day 8:05am-7:45pm, €2.10). The bus stops in front of the **AIAT Tourist Office,** V. Borgeois, 34, which distributes regional maps and helps find accommodations. (☎0165 74 040 or 0165 740 56. Open in summer daily 9am-12:30pm and 3-6pm; in winter M-Sa 9am-12:30pm and 2:30-5:30pm, Su 9am-12:30pm.) Lodged in a narrow valley, the hamlet of **Valnontey** is a 45min. walk along the river from Cogne on **trail 25,** which begins at the tourist office and offers an unobstructed view of the glacier. From June to August, buses run from Cogne to Valnontey (every 30min. 7:30am-8pm, €1.10; buy tickets onboard).

COURMAYEUR ☎**0165**

Italy's oldest Alpine resort lures tourists to the spectacular shadows of Europe's highest peak. Monte Bianco (Mont Blanc), with its jagged ridges and permanent snow fields, is perfect for hiking and skiing. Unfortunately for budget travelers, prices tend to be high. Quiet falls in May and June, when shopkeepers go on vacation and the snow finally melts, inviting the curious out for an adventure.

🖪🚌 **TRANSPORTATION AND PRACTICAL INFORMATION.** A single large complex, the **Centro Congressi Courmayeur,** in **Piazzale Monte Bianco,** houses most travel services including the **bus** station. **Buses** run to Aosta (1hr.; M-F

6:45, 9:45am, 1:25, 5pm, Su 6pm; €5.50) and Turin (3hr., 6:45 and 10am, €8.20). **SAVDA** and **SADAEM** buses have frequent service to larger towns. (☎0165 84 20 31. Office open daily July-Aug. 8am-7:30pm; Sept.-June 8:45am-12:30pm and 3-6:30pm. Tickets available onboard.) **Taxis** (☎0165 84 29 60; night 0165 84 23 33) are available 24hr. at Ple. M. Bianco. Pick up a **map** from the multilingual staff at the **AIAT Tourist Office,** Ple. Monte Bianco, 13 (☎0165 84 20 60; www.aiat-monte-bianco.com. Open in summer M-Sa 9am-1:30pm and 2:30-6:30pm, Su 9am-12pm and 3-6pm; in winter M-Sa 9am-1:30pm and 3pm-6:30pm.) A 24hr. **accommodations board** 10m away from the office can also help in finding a room. The bus station ticket office has **currency exchange,** as does the **San Paolo Istituto Bancario di Torino,** P. Brocherel, 1, which also has an **ATM** (☎0165 84 20 23. Open M-F 8:25am-1:25pm and 2:40-4:10pm.) In case of **emergency,** dial ☎113, call an **ambulance** at ☎118, or contact the **police** at ☎113, Vle. Monte Bianco, 46. A **pharmacy** on V. Circonvallazione, 69, has after- hours rotation posted outside. (Open M-F 9am-12:30pm and 3-7:30pm, Sa 9am-12:30pm and 3:30-7:30pm.) The **post office** is in Ple. M. Bianco behind the main complex. (☎0165 84 20 42. Open M-Sa 8am-1:30pm.) **Postal Code:** 11013.

⌂🖪 ACCOMMODATIONS AND FOOD. You can't book accommodations far enough ahead. **Pensione Venezia ❸,** V. delle Villete, 2, is by far the best deal in town. From Ple. Monte Bianco, head uphill, then turn left on V. Circonvallazione, to reach this large chalet with homey rooms with breakfast and TV lounge. (☎/fax 0165 84 24 61. Singles €31; doubles €45. Cash only.) **Hotel Select ❹,** Str. Regionale, 27, after V. Roma, offers more modern rooms with private bath, TV, and telephone (☎0165 84 66 61; www.courmayeurhotel.com. Singles €35-55; doubles €43-100. MC/V.) Another option is the **Casetta Nostra ❷,** in a courtyard off Passagio Truchet, 8, which rents simple rooms with fans and shared bath. (☎/fax 0165 84 67 75. Singles €21-22.50; doubles €42-45.)

At **Pastificio Gabriella ❶,** Passaggio dell'Angelo, 2, toward the end of V. Roma, excellent cold cuts, salads, and crepes greet customers. (☎0165 84 33 59. Open M-Tu and Th-Su 8am-1pm and 4-7:30pm; closed 2 weeks in June. MC/V.) Off-*piste* skiers recharge at the unique **🖪Cafe des Guides ❶,** Vle. Monte Bianco, 2, below the Societa' delle Guide, where red lounge chairs somehow go well with the skis hanging on the walls. (☎0165 84 24 35. Breakfast and *panini* €4-5. Cocktails €6-8, beer €5-6. Cover €1. Open daily 7:30am-2:30am.) **Il Fornaio ❶,** Vle. M. Bianco, 17, serves delicious breads and pastries. Particularly good are the local *tegole* (€20 per kg), cookies made from egg whites, and the *torta di mele.* (☎0165 84 24 54. Open in summer daily 7:30am-12:30pm and 4-7pm; in winter M-Tu, Th-F, and Su 8am-noon and 4-7pm, Sa 8am-12:30pm.) Many restaurants close in summer, but **La Terraza ❸,** V. Circonvallazione, 73, is open year-round. Just uphill from Ple. Monte Bianco, this restaurant specializes in Valdostano cuisine, serving fondue and lard lightly garnished with warm chestnuts and honey. (☎0165 84 33 30; www.ristorantelaterrazza.com. Pizza €6-10. *Primi* €12-16, *secondi* €15-25. Cover €2.50. Open daily noon-2:15pm and 7pm-late. MC/V.)

🖪🗻 OUTDOOR ACTIVITIES AND SKIING. Courmayeur Ski Resort is famous for its 100km of scenic downhill runs, off-*piste* itineraries, and cross-country offerings (info ☎0165 84 20 60). Expect high-season fares Dec. 8-11, Dec. 24-Jan. 8, and Feb. 4-Mar. 12, when passes run €29.50 per half-day, €37.50 per full-day, and €70.50 per 2 days; inquire at tourist office for prices. The brochures *White Weeks, Settimane Bianche,* and *Courmayeur* list rental and pass prices and often offer discount deals. **Buses** (45min., 10 per day 8:20am-8:15pm, €2.40) also run to nearby **La Tuile** (☎0165 88 41 79), another ski resort with 150km of intermediate and expert downhill trails and five cross-country skiing tracks.

Buses run from Courmayeur to the trailheads in **Val Veny** and **Val Ferret,** which branch in opposite directions along the base of Monte Bianco. Inquire at the tourist office for a *Valdigne Mont-Blanc: Les Sentiers* map and the brochure *Seven Itineraries around Mont Blanc, Val Veny, and Val Ferret.* The most popular hike in Val Veny is the 2hr. path past the Lac du Miage to Refuge Elisabetta (2197m). In Val Ferret, two short hikes to the Refuge Bonatti (2150m) from Lavachey (45min.) and to the Refuge Elena (2055m) from Arp Nouva (40min.) make for a relaxing trip. An excellent place to ask questions is **Societa' delle Guide di Courmayeur,** P. Henri, 2, to the left behind the church. (☎0165 84 20 64; guide-courma@tiscali.it. Open in summer M-Tu and Th-Su 9am-noon and 4-7pm, W 4-7pm; in winter Tu-Su 9am-7pm.) Since 1850 the office has been providing free advice to hikers and finding guides for all major treks and climbs. A number of excellent **biking** trails traverse Monte Bianco. **Bike rental** is available near the tourist office at **Scott Center**, Ple. M. Bianco, 15. (☎0165 84 82 54 or 340 59 09 832. €15-30 per half-day, €20-45 per full-day; Children €8/12. Discount packages available.)

⊠Funivie Monte Bianco head first to the **Punta Helbronner** (3462m) and then across the border at **Aiguille du midi** (3842m) to **Chamonix.** (☎0165 89 925; www.montebianco.com.) The top affords views of Monte Bianco's ice sheet, as well as the spectacular **Matterhorn, Monte Rosa,** and **Gran Paradiso.** *Funivie* depart from La Palud, a 10min. bus ride (€0.90) from Courmayeur's Ple. Monte Bianco.

LIGURIA

The Italian Riviera stretches 350km along the Mediterranean between France and Tuscany, forming the most touristed area of the Italian coastline. Protected from the north's severe weather by the Alps, Liguria is home to terraced hillsides, the Apennine mountains, vineyards, beaches, and olive groves. Though the temperate coastline offers ample opportunity for lounging on the beach, each town boasts a distinct character which makes exploring the region especially enjoyable. Famously cheerful residents, fresh local cuisine, and thriving nightlife abound in Liguria, where affluent and glitzy Riviera glamor mixes with a laid-back oceanside atmosphere. Whether hiking mountain trails or perfecting a summer tan, visitors to Liguria are sure to find culture, entertainment, and above all, relaxation.

HIGHLIGHTS OF LIGURIA

SAIL, SWIM, AND SCUBA DIVE off the sandy shores of the **Cinque Terre** (p. 210).

ROLL with the big rollers in San Remo's **Casino Municipale** (p. 228).

SPLASH with the stingrays in the interactive tank at **Genoa's aquarium** (p. 202).

INDULGE by slathering flavorful **pesto** on everything you eat (p. 199).

GENOA (GENOVA)   ☎010

As any Ligurian will proclaim, *"Si deve conoscerla per amarla"*—you have to know Genoa to love her. Often obscured by fog and steam from passing ships, Genoa anchors the luminescent Ligurian coastal strip between the Riviera di Levante (rising sun) to the east and the Riviera di Ponente (setting sun) to the west. A city of grit and grandeur, it has little in common with neighboring beach towns along the Riviera. Once home to Liguria's most noble and wealthy families, Genoa's main streets are lined with palaces and *piazze*, but just steps away from these opulent displays lie reminders of an older Genoa whose maze-like pathways and medieval churches echo an eerier history. Recent cultural events and acclaim, along with a world-famous aquarium, have brought Genoa a renewed vibrancy. Once a city of exploration from which adventurers like Christopher Columbus set out in search of a New World, the tide in this port city has turned. Genoa is no longer a mere point of departure for exploration, but rather a destination which Columbus himself would have been proud to discover.

◧ TRANSPORTATION

Flights: C. Colombo Internazionale (☎010 60 151), in Sesti Ponente, flies to European destinations. Volabus #100 runs to the airport from Stazione Brignole (every 30min. 5:30am-9:30pm, €2).

Trains: Stazione Principe, in P. Acquaverde, and **Stazione Brignole,** in P. Verdi. Trains (5min., every 10min., €1) and buses #18, 19, 20, 33, and 37 (25min., €0.80) connect the 2 stations. Ticket valid 1½hr. from validation. **Luggage storage** available (see **Practical Information,** p. 196). Open daily 6am-midnight. Trains run from the stations to points along the Ligurian Riviera and major Italian cities including **Rome** (5-6hr., 12 per day, €32.50) and **Turin** (2hr., 19 per day, €8-12).

Liguria Italian Riviera

Ferries: At Ponte Assereto arm of the port. Walk 10min. from Stazione Marittima or take bus #20 from Stazione Principe. Purchase tickets at travel agency or Stazione Marittima. **Arrive at Ponte Assereto at least 1hr. before departure.** To: **Olbia; Palau; Palermo; Porto Torres; Barcelona, Spain;** and **Tunis, Tunisia.** TRIS (☎010 576 24 11) and **Tirrenia** (☎081 31 72 999; www.tirrenia.it) run ferries to **Sardinia. Grandi Traghetti** (☎010 58 93 31; www.aferry.to) heads to **Palermo.**

Local Buses: AMT (☎010 55 82 414; www.amt.genova.it) buses leave from V. Gramsci, in front of the aquarium, or Stazione Brignole. One-way tickets (€1) within the city. All-day tourist passes (€3); foreign passport necessary. Tickets and passes can also be used for funicular and elevator rides.

Taxis: ☎010 58 65 24. From P. Dante.

ORIENTATION AND PRACTICAL INFORMATION

Genoa has two train stations: **Stazione Principe,** in P. Acquaverde, and **Stazione Brignole,** in P. Verdi. From Stazione Principe take bus #18, 19, or 20, and from Stazione Brignole take bus #19 or 40 to **Piazza de Ferrari** in the center of town. If walking to P. de Ferrari from Stazione Principe, take **Via Balbi** to **Via Cairoli,** which becomes **Via Garibaldi,** and at **Piazza delle Fontane Marose** turn right on **Via XXV Aprile.** From Stazione Brignole, turn right out of the station, left on **Via Fiume,** and then right onto **Via XX Settembre,** ending in P. de Ferrari. To get to the **Porto Antico** from P. de Ferrari, take V. Boetto to **P. Matteoti,** then follow **V. S. Lorenzo** to the water. Genoa's streets can stump even a native, so don't head out without a map.

 Though most of Genoa's problems with crime and safety are a thing of the past, travelers should avoid Via di Prè entirely, and be especially cautious in the area around Via della Maddalena. As a general rule, stick to well-lit areas: narrow and dark streets are better left alone. Walking alone at night or in the *centro storico* on weekends when stores are closed can also be dangerous.

Tourist Offices: APT, V. Roma, 11 (☎010 57 67 91; www.genovatouristboard.net). **Branch** (☎010 24 87 11) near the aquarium on Porto Antico. Facing the water, walk 30m left from the aquarium toward the complex of buildings. Decent **maps.** Open daily

Genoa

🏠 **ACCOMMODATIONS**
Albergo Caffaro, **4**
Albergo Carola/
  Albergo Argentina, **5**
Genova Est, **9**
Hotel Agnello d'Oro, **1**
Hotel Balbi, **2**
Ostello Per La Gioventù (HI), **3**

🍴☕ **FOOD AND NIGHTLIFE**
Al Parador, **8**
La Locanda del Borgo, **7**
Ristorante al Rustichello, **6**

9am-1pm and 2-6pm. **Other branches:** Kiosks in Stazione Principe (☎010 24 62 633) and airport (☎010 60 15 247). Both open M-Sa 9:30am-1pm and 2:30-6pm. **Informagiovani,** P. Matteotti, 24r (☎010 55 73 952 or 010 55 73 965; www.informagiovani.comune.genova.it), in Palazzo Ducale. Youth center offers information on apartment rentals, jobs, volunteer opportunities, and concerts. Free **Internet** for up to 1hr. Open M and F 10am-1pm, Tu 10am-6pm, W 2-6pm, Th 10am-1pm and 2-6pm.

Budget Travel: CTS, V. San Vincenzo, 117r (☎010 56 43 66 or 010 53 27 48), off V. XX Settembre near Ponte Monumentale. Walk up the flight of stairs at the shopping complex to the left. Student fares available. Open M-F 9:30am-6:15pm. MC/V.

Consulates: UK, V. di Francia, 28 (☎010 41 68 28; fax 010 41 69 58). Take bus #30 from Stazione Principe to the last stop in the direction of Sampierdarena. Open M-Th 9:30am-12:30pm. **US,** V. Dante, 2, 3rd fl., #43 (☎010 58 44 92; in case of **emergency** call US Consulate General in Milan at 02 29 03 51). Open M-Th 11am-3pm.

Bank: Banca Intesa, C. Buenos Ayres, 4. Open M-F 8:30am-1:30pm and 2:45-4:15pm, Sa-Su 8:30am-12pm.

Luggage Storage: ☎010 24 62 633, in Stazione Principe. €3.80 for first hr., €0.60 each additional hr. up to 12hr., €0.20 each additional hr. Open 7am-11pm.

English-Language Bookstore: Mondadori, V. XX Settembre, 210r (☎010 58 57 43). Huge, with a full wall of classics and some best sellers. Open M-Sa 9am-8pm, Su 10:30am-1pm and 3-8pm.

Emergency: ☎113. **Ambulance:** ☎118. **Police:** ☎112.

Pharmacy: Pescetto, V. Balbi, 185r (☎010 26 16 09), near Stazione Principe. After-hours rotation posted outside. Open 8:30am-12:30pm and 3:30pm-midnight. Across town, **Farmacia Ghersi,** C. Buenos Ayres, 18r, is open M-F 24hr. except 12:30-3:30pm, and Sa-Su 7:30pm-12:30pm.

Hospital: Ospedale Evangelico, Corso Solferino, 1a (☎010 55 221).

Internet Access: Number One Bar/Cafe, P. Verdi 21r (☎010 54 18 85), near Stazione Principe. 5 computers, CD-ROM available. €4 per hr. Open daily 7:30am-11:30pm. MC/V. **In-Centro.it Agenzia Viaggi,** V. Ceccardi, 14, Between V. Dante and V. XX Settembre. €4.30 per hr., €3.20 per hr. for students. Also a bookstore and travel agency. Open M 3-7:30pm, Tu-Sa 10am-7:30pm.

Post Office: P. Dante, 4/6r (☎010 25 94 687). 2 blocks from P. de Ferrari. *Fermo-posta.* Open M-Sa 8am-6:30pm. Branches open 8am-1:30pm. **Postal Code:** 16121.

🏠 ACCOMMODATIONS AND CAMPING

Rooms are scarce in October, when the city hosts a wave of nautical conventions. Some budget lodgings in the *centro storico* and near the port rent rooms by the hour for reasons best left uninvestigated. Establishments are more refined around Stazione Brignole and P. Corvetto. The area around Genoa is teeming with camp-grounds, but many are booked in the summer.

📷 **Ostello Per La Gioventù (HI),** V. Costanzi, 120 (☎/fax 010 242 24 57; www.geoci-ties.com/hostelge). From Stazione Principe, take bus #35, transfer to #40 at V. Napoli. From Stazione Brignole, take bus #40 all the way up the hill (30min.). Variety of amen-ities: cafeteria, free lockers, wheelchair access, and TV. Multilingual staff. Breakfast, showers, and sheets included. Laundry €6.50 per 5kg. Reception 7-11:30am and 3:30pm-12:30am. Check-out 9am. Lock-out around 12:30am. HI card required (avail-able at hostel). Dorms €15; family rooms €16-20 per person. ❶

Albergo Carola, V. Gropallo, 4/12, 3rd fl. (☎010 839 13 40), near Stazione Brignole. Look for big doors with little lion heads on the left side of the street. Ring buzzer to enter. English-speaking staff and meticulously decorated rooms, some overlook a garden. Sin-gles €28; doubles €46, with bath €56; triples €65/75; quads €85. Cash only. ❸

Albergo Argentina, V. Gropallo, 4 (☎/fax 010 83 93 722), near Stazione Brignole, 2 flights down from the Carola (see above). 9 large, clean, utilitarian but comfortable rooms. Kind management speaks limited English. Singles €31; doubles €47, with bath €56; triples €70; quads €77. Cash only. ❸

Hotel Balbi, V. Balbi, 21/3 (☎/fax 010 25 23 62), close to Stazione Principe. Rundown exterior, but spacious rooms sport wooden floors and painted ceilings. Comfortable common area with Internet (€4 per hr.). Breakfast €4. Singles €25, with bath €40; doubles €42/62; triples €90. AmEx/MC/V. ❷

Albergo Caffaro, V. Caffaro, 3 (☎ 010 24 72 362; www.albergocaffaro.it), off P. Por-tello, between train stations. Take bus #18 from Stazione Principe to P. Portello. Sunny rooms occupy the top floor of a *palazzo;* TV, fans and rooftop views of P. Ferrari. Singles €30, with bath €40; doubles €45/55; triples €75; quads €85. AmEx/MC/V. ❸

Hotel Agnello d'Oro, V. Monachette, 6 (☎010 246 20 84; www.hotelagnellodoro.it), off V. Balbi. English-speaking staff keeps 20 rooms with bath, TV, and access to rooftop patio with a stunning view. Some rooms have terrace and A/C (€10 extra). Fans available. Buf-fet breakfast included. Singles €50-95; doubles €70-120; triples €95. AmEx/MC/V. ❺

Genova Est (☎010 347 20 53), on V. Marcon, Loc. Cassa. Take the train from Stazione Brignole to the suburb of Bogliasco (10min., 6 per day, €1); from here, take the free van (5min., every 2hr. 8am-6pm) to the campsite. Shaded sites on a terraced hill over-

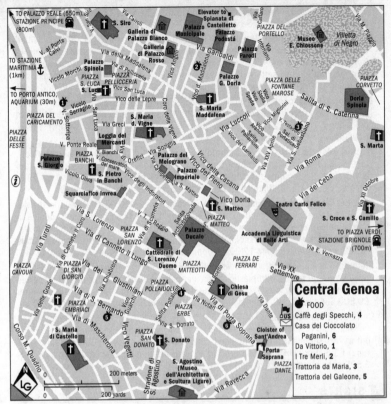

Central Genoa

🔥 FOOD
Caffè degli Specchi, 4
Casa del Cioccolato
      Paganini, 6
Da Vittorio, 1
I Tre Merli, 2
Trattoria da Maria, 3
Trattoria del Galeone, 5

look the sea, with clean shared bathroom facilities. Laundry €3.50 per load. €5.45 per person, €9.60 per large tent; 2-person bungalows €34. Electricity €1.80 per day. ❶

🔥 FOOD

A dish prepared *alla Genovese* is served with Genoa's pride and joy—*pesto*, a sauce made from basil, pine nuts, olive oil, garlic, and Parmesan cheese. The *Genovesi* put it on just about everything, so don't be afraid to experiment. Other delectables include *farinata* (a fried pancake of chick-pea flour), *focaccia* filled with cheese or topped with olives or onions, and *pansotti* (ravioli stuffed with spinach and ricotta, in a creamy walnut sauce). To sample a slice of Genoa's famous salami or pick up a jar of *pesto*, stop by **Salvi Salumeria**, P. della Raibetta, 7, near the Porto Antico. Also, don't forget to sample the seafood, sold fresh from vendors lining the port-side arcade.

🦑 **Trattoria da Maria,** V. Testadoro, 14r (☎010 58 10 80), near P. delle Fontane Marose. A prototypical Italian restaurant with checkered tablecloths and a faithful lunch crowd. The owner is a dynamo and conducts a jovial staff. The menu changes daily, but the dishes are always fresh and delicious. 3-course *menù* €9. Open M-Sa 8am-2pm. Cash only. ❷

🦑 **I Tre Merli,** Vico della Maddalena, 26r (☎010 24 74 095), on a narrow street off V. Garibaldi. A hidden gem with soft music and a mellow atmosphere. Impeccable service and delicious food make the price well worth it. Wine connoisseurs take note—the list is

LIGURIA

16 pages long and very well assembled. *Primi* €8-11, *secondi* €7-18. Open M-F 12:30-3pm and 7:30pm-midnight, Sa 7:30pm-1am. AmEx/MC/V. ❸

Trattoria La Locanda del Borgo, V. Borgo Incrociati, 47r (☎010 81 06 31), behind Stazione Brignole. Exit the station, go through the pedestrian tunnel, and find V. Borgo Incrociati on the left. A surprisingly good value, serving delicious *Genovesi* favorites in a friendly setting. *Primi* €6, *secondi* €13. Lunch *menù* €9. 3-course dinner *menù* €20. Open M-Tu and Th-Su noon-2pm and 7:30-10:30pm. AmEx/MC/V. ❸

Da Vittorio, V. Sottoripa, 59r (☎010 24 72 927), across from the aquarium. The seafood is reliably excellent, as reflected by the higher prices. Catch of the day displayed in the window. Lobster €27. *Primi* €8-16, *secondi* €11-27. Cover €2.50. Reserve ahead. Open daily noon-4pm and 7-11:30pm. Closed July Tu-W. MC/V. ❹

Trattoria del Galeone, V. di S. Bernardo, 55r (☎010 24 68 422). From P. Matteoti, take Salita Pollaiuoli and turn left on V. di S. Bernardo. Galeone is 100m up on the left. Nautically decorated dining rooms and crowds of lively locals. *Primi* €4.50-6, *secondi* €6.20-10.30. Open M-Sa 12:30pm-2:30pm and 7:30pm-10pm. ❷

Casa del Cioccolato Paganini, V. di Porta Soprana, 45 (☎010 95 13 662). Like the violin of its namesake, the chocolate here just might draw tears of passion. Indulge in unique homemade sweets, from Niccolo Paganini chocolate (boxes from €6.50) to signature *sciroppo di rose,* a sublime liquid made from sugar, water, and rose petals (€1.90 per bottle). Open M 12:30-7:30pm, Tu-Sa 9:30am-7:30pm. Cash only. ❶

Ristorante al Rustichello, V. S. Vicenzo, 59r (☎010 58 85 56), near Stazione Brignole. For the traveler fed up with plastic tables and paper tablecloths, this restaurant serves inexpensive food in a classy environment. Pizza €4.50-6. Primi €5.50-8, secondi €9.50-15. Cover €1.60. Open daily noon-2:30pm and 6:30pm-midnight. MC/V. ❷

Caffè degli Specchi, Salita Pollaiuoli, 43r (☎010 24 68 193), on the left, down Salita Pollaioli from P. Matteotti. *Specchio* means mirror, and narcissists will surely get a kick out of this sophisticated, mirror-lined cafe. The crowds enjoy *bicchierini* (glasses of wine; €3.60) or cocktails (€4.65-5.15) at pleasant outdoor seating. Mini *panini* (€1-2.50) make a tasty snack or light lunch. Open daily 8am-8:30pm. MC/V. ❶

👁 SIGHTS

FROM STAZIONE PRINCIPE TO THE CENTRO STORICO

Outside the winding alleys of the *centro storico*, Genoa boasts a multitude of palaces, many of which many have been converted to museums and showcase 16th- and 17th-century Flemish and Italian art. **Via Garibaldi,** which skirts the edge of the *centro storico*, and **Via Balbi,** which runs through the university quarter from Stazione Principe to P. Nunziata, offer the best views of the glamorous buildings.

ART STARVED? If you plan on visiting many museums, invest in a museum pass. The €6.50 pass, good for 24hr., covers Palazzo Reale and Palazzo Spinola. Another 24hr. pass covers all the museums in Genoa (€9) and is available with bus fare (€10). Purchase at the tourist office or participating museums.

▓ PALAZZO REALE. Built between 1600 and 1700, this *palazzo* was originally home to the Balbi family. It became the Royal Palace in the 18th century, and the structural setup installed for the Savoy rulers persists for the most part into the present. The Rococo throne room, covered in red velvet, remains untouched, along with the royal waiting room and sleeping quarters. The resplendent **Galleria degli Specchi** is modeled after the Hall of Mirrors at Versailles. In the Queen's bedroom, the **queen's clock** is really a *notturlabio,* a clock with stenciled numbers lit from behind by a candle. To see paintings by

Tintoretto, van Dyck, and Bassano, ascend the red-carpeted stairs on the left after purchasing a ticket. *(V. Balbi, 10. 5min. walk west of V. Garibaldi. ☎010 635 08 31. Open Tu-W 9am-1:30pm, Th-Su 9am-7pm. €4, ages 18-25 €2, under 18 or over 65 free.)*

▨ VIA GARIBALDI. The most impressive street in Genoa, V. Garibaldi deserves the nickname "*Via Aurea*," or "Golden Street." In the 17th century, wealthy families lined it with elegant palaces. **Galleria Palazzo Rosso,** built in the 16th century, earned its name when it was painted red in the 17th. Red carpets cover the floors of exhibit halls featuring several hundred years' worth of *Genovese* ceramics. The second floor now holds several van Dyck portraits of nobility, while the third floor contains his rendering of a red-eyed Christ. **Room 7** includes several masterpieces by Bernardo Strozzi, including *Il Pifferaio* (Piper). Across the street, the **Galleria di Palazzo Bianco** (c. 1548, rebuilt 1712) exhibits one of the city's largest collections of Ligurian art as well as some Dutch and Flemish works. *(Galleria Palazzo Rosso: V. Garibaldi, 18. ☎010 24 76 351. Galleria di Palazzo Bianco: V. Garibaldi, 11. ☎010 24 76 377. Both galleries open Tu-F 9am-7pm, Sa-Su 10am-7pm. Ticket office, V. Garibaldi, 9, open daily 9am-8pm. 1 gallery €5, both €7, under 18 or over 60 free; Su free. AmEx/MC/V.)*

PORTELLO-CASTELLETTO ELEVATOR. Walk down the tunnel in P. Portello to ride this elevator with locals, who take it as regularly as the bus. The stomach-churning ride, which connects the center of town with neighborhoods in the hills surrounding Genoa, gives commuters one of the best panoramas of the city. *(Through the tunnel entrance in P. Portello. Open daily 6:40am-midnight. Single-use tickets can be purchased for €0.50 from machines at the entrance to the elevator, or from newsstands nearby.)*

PALAZZO TURSI/PALAZZO MUNICIPALE. Built between 1565 and 1579, the former home of the Savoia monarchy and the present day city hall showcases a magnificent courtyard and Nicolò Paganini's violin, **Il Canone,** made by the legendary Giuseppe Guarneri. This instrument is still played by the winner of **Premio Paganini,** an international violin competition held annually on Oct. 12. *(V. Garibaldi, 9. Open Tu-F 9am-7pm, Sa-Su 10am-7pm. Free.)*

CHIESA DI GESÙ. Also known as **Sant'Ambrogio e Andrea,** this former Jesuit church, completed in 1606, houses two Rubens canvases: *The Circumcision* (1605), over the altar, and *The Miracle of St. Ignatius* (1620), in the 3rd alcove on the left. *(From P. de Ferrari, take V. Boetto to P. Matteotti. Open daily 7:15am-12:30pm and 4-7:30pm. Closed during Su masses: 7:15, 10, 11am, noon, and 6:30pm. Free.)*

PALAZZO DUCALE. The majestic centerpiece of the historical center, this *palazzo* was constructed in 1291 as the seat of Genoa's government. The facade, completed in 1783 by architect Sione Cantoni, is an example of Neo-Classical architecture, while the interior is done up in Rococo decor. Visit the **museum** on the 2nd floor for rotating exhibits of international artwork. *(P. Matteotti, 9. ☎010 55 74 004; www.palazzoducale.genova.it. Museum open Tu-Su 9am-9pm. €7, students €6.)*

VILLETTA DI NEGRO. A stroll through this lovely park spread along a hill, past waterfalls, grottoes, and terraced gardens, is a calming respite from museums. *(From P. delle Fontane Marose, take Salita di S. Caterina to P. Corvetto. Open daily 8am-10pm.)*

PORTO ANTICO

Genoa's enormous port yields a mixture of fascinating history and commercial bustle. The port is sectioned into several wharves. The oldest, 15th-century **Molo Vecchio,** on the far left facing the water, is home to Genoa's former cotton warehouses, as well as a movie theater, arcades, and many restaurants. The central **Quartieri Antichi** (historical districts) still hold some 16th-century bondhouses. Nearby **Ponte Spinola** is the site of Genoa's famed aquarium, and adjacent Piazza del Caricamento is lined with merchants peddling fresh fish and produce.

THE INSIDER'S CITY

A DAY AT PORTO ANTICO

A city of fishermen and marine life, Genoa embraces its nautical roots at the Porto Antico, where everything is a little, well, fishy ...

1 Sharks, dolphins, and penguins greet visitors at the **Acquario di Genova** (aquarium) where interactive exhibits display global issues like water conservation and animal extinction. (☎010 23 45 678; www.acquariodigenova.it. Hours vary seasonally. See listing right.)

2 Take a ride in the **Bigo.** Visitors are suspended in a round glass elevator above the city and ocean. (☎010 23 451. Open daily 10am-8pm with extended weekend hours; hours reduced in winter. €3.)

3 Treat yourself to the catch of the day at the **Loggia of Sottoripa** where boutiques, markets, and street vendors crowd the port.

4 The **Molo Vecchio,** a converted warehouse overlooking the harbor, has a Cineplex, video game arcades, and *gelaterie.*

■ **AQUARIUM.** The aquarium is the town's most elaborate tourist attraction and has the largest volume of water of any in Europe. Wander through the main exhibits, then climb aboard the *Grande Nave Blu*, a 126m floating barge filled with habitat simulations, from the forests of Madagascar to the reefs of the Caribbean. There's also an interactive tank where visitors can touch sea rays and get splashed by slippery preteens. If a self-guided investigation doesn't fulfill your nautical needs, take a "Behind the Scenes" tour from a multilingual guide. *(On Porto Antico, across from tourist office. ☎010 234 56 78; www.acquariodigenova.it. Open July-Aug. daily 9am-11pm; Sept.-July M-W and F 9am-7:30pm, Th 9am-10pm, Sa-Su 9am-8:30pm. Last entrance 1½hr. before closing. Admission €13, €12 with HI card. Discounts for groups and children. Tour departs daily noon, 2, 4, and Sa-Su also 4:30pm. €8, children €5.)*

THE CENTRO STORICO

The eerie, beautiful, and sometimes dangerous *centro storico* is a mass of narrow, winding streets and cobblestone alleyways bordered by **Porto Antico, Via Garibaldi,** and **Piazza de Ferrari.** It is home to some of Genoa's most memorable monuments: the **duomo, Palazzo Spinola,** and the medieval **Torre Embraici,** whose Guelph battlements jut out among the buildings to the left when facing the **Chiesa di Santa Maria di Castello.** Due to a high crime rate, the center is not safe on weekends, when stores are closed and streets are less crowded. Also avoid the area at night, when most of the people clear out and the city's seedy underbelly emerges.

■ **CHIESA DI SANTA MARIA DI CASTELLO.** With foundations from 500 BC, this church is a labyrinth of chapels, courtyards, cloisters, and crucifixes. In the chapel left of the high altar looms the spooky **Crocifisso Miracoloso.** According to legend, Jesus moved his head to attest to the honesty of a damsel betrayed by her lover, and Jesus's beard is still said to grow every time a crisis hits the city. To see the painting of **San Pietro Martire di Verona,** complete with a halo and a large cleaver conspicuously thrust into his cranium (the handiwork of incensed adversaries), go up the stairs to the right of the high altar, turn right, and right again. The painting is above the door. *(From P. G. Matteotti, head up V. S. Lorenzo toward the water and turn left on V. Chiabrera. A left on serpentine V. di Mascherona leads to the church in P. Caricamento. Open daily 9am-noon and 3:30-6:30pm. Closed Su during mass. Free.)*

■ **DUOMO (SAN LORENZO).** The *duomo* was reconstructed from the 12th through 16th centuries after religious authorities deemed it "imperfect and deformed." The result may have been an improvement, but it sure wasn't symmetrical: because only one of the two planned belltowers was completed, the church has a lopsided appearance. Climb the completed belltower (€2.50) for dizzying views of the city. On the left side of the church, the golden **Cappella di San Giovanni** houses a relic from St. John the Baptist. *(P. San Lorenzo, off V. San Lorenzo, which emerges from P. Matteotti. Guided tour every 30min. Tickets for bell tower in Museo del Tesoro on left side of church. Open daily 9am-noon and 3-6pm. Free. Modest dress required.)*

PORTA SOPRANA. The historical centerpiece of P. Dante and one of four gates into the city (and today the passageway from the modern *piazza* into the *centro storico*), this structure was built in 1100 to intimidate enemies of the Republic of Genoa. Would-be assailant Emperor Frederico Barbarossa took one look at the arch, whose Latin inscription welcomes all coming in peace but threatens doom to enemy armies, and abandoned his attack. **Christopher Columbus's** boyhood home lies nearby alongside the remains of a 12th-century convent. *(From P. G. Matteotti, head down V. di Porta Soprana. Fortress open M 12:30pm-7:30pm, Tu-Sa 9:30am-7:30pm. Free. €3 to climb the towers. Columbus's home open same hours as fortress. €4.)*

PALAZZO SPINOLA DI PELLICCERIA. Built at the close of the 16th century, this *palazzo* once hosted Peter Paul Rubens, who described it warmly in his 1622 book on pleasing palaces. It is now home to the **Galleria Nazionale,** a collection of art and furnishings, most donated by the family of Maddalena Doria Spinola. The building tells its own history, as different sections represent centuries' worth of varying architectural styles. The 18th-century kitchen simulation is particularly intriguing, with a lit stove and flour on the countertop. The 4th level houses Antonello da Messina's 1460 masterpiece *Ecce Homo* and Van Dyck's portraits of the evangelists reside on the second level. *(P. di Pellicceria, 1, between V. Maddalena and P. S. Luca. ☎010 27 05 300. Open Tu-Sa 8:30am-7:30pm, Su 1-8pm. €4, 18-25 or over 65 €2.)*

♫ 🎭 ENTERTAINMENT AND NIGHTLIFE

Genoa's new **Cineplex,** at Molo Vecchio on the harbor, shows dubbed American movies. (☎199 19 99 91; www.cineplex.it. Box office open M-F 3:30-10:30pm, Sa 2pm-1:30am, Su 2-11:30pm. Tickets M-F €6.50, Sa-Su €7, matinees €5.) A 20min. ride down C. Italia on bus #31 leads to **Boccadasse,** a fishing village and seaside playground for wealthy *Genovesi.* **Corso Italia** is a swanky promenade home to much of Genoa's nightlife. Unfortunately, many clubs are difficult to reach on foot, so travelers in Genoa often drive to reach their nightlife destinations. Local university students flock to bars in **Piazza Erbe** and along **Via San Bernardo.** Across town, try **Al Parador,** P. della Vittoria, 49r, which is easy and safe to reach from Stazione Brignole. Upscale bar and *gelateria* by day, by night this watering hole is frequented both by wanna-be starlets and the real thing, including Uma Thurman and Claudia Schiffer. (☎010 58 17 71. Cocktails €4.50. Open M-Sa 24hr.)

RIVIERA DI LEVANTE

CAMOGLI   ☎0185

Camogli is a postcard-perfect town of 7000 with lively red and turquoise boats knocking in the harbor, fishing nets draped over docks, and dark stone beaches dotted with bright umbrellas. Its colorful houses with painted-on balconies, windows, and "brick" facades fool the less observant. Less ritzy and more youth-friendly than nearby Portofino and Santa Margherita, part of Liguria's aptly named "Golfo Paradiso," Camogli truly is a paradise. Lounge, eat, and hike your way to happiness in this quaint and beautiful port-side destination.

TRANSPORTATION

Camogli is on the Genoa-La Spezia **train** line. Ticket office open M-Sa 5am-12:30pm, Su 1am-7:30pm. Trains run to Genoa (40min., 38 per day 1:08am-10:05pm, €1.60); La Spezia (1½hr., 24 per day 5:29am-1:03am, €3.95) via Santa Margherita (5min, €1.10); and Sestri Levante (30min., 39 per day 5:38am-1:10am, €2). **Tigullio buses** leave P. Schiaffino near the tourist office for nearby towns. Buy tickets at the tourist office or at *tabaccherie*. Buses go to Santa Margherita (20min., 20 per day, €1.10), also Rapallo, Ruta, and San Lorenzo. For **Golfo Paradiso ferries,** V. Scalo, 3 (☎0185 77 20 91; www.golfoparadiso.it), look for the "Servizio Batelli" sign near P. Colombo by the water. Buy tickets at dock or on the ferry. Boats to: Cinque Terre (Portovenere at Vernazza; June 15-July 1 Su; July 1-Aug. 1 Tu, Th, and Su; Sept. 1-15 Th and Su; 9:30am, returns 5:30pm; round-trip €20); Portofino (Sa-Su 3pm, return 5:30pm; round-trip €12); and San Fruttuoso (May-Sept. every hr. 8am-7pm, round-trip €8).

ORIENTATION AND PRACTICAL INFORMATION

Camogli extends uphill from the sea to pine and olive groves and downhill from the train station toward a stretch beach. To get to the center of town, turn right out of the **train station,** walk 100m, and then turn left down the stairs to **Via Garibaldi,** which runs along the beachfront. The English-speaking staff at the **tourist office,** V. XX Settembre, 33, helps book accommodations. (☎0185 77 10 66. Exit train station and turn right. Open in summer M-Sa 9am-12:30pm and 3:30-7pm, Su 8:30am-12:30pm.) **Currency exchange** is available at **Banco di Chiavari della Riviera Ligure,** V. XX Settembre, 19, which has an **ATM** outside. (☎0185 77 51 13. Open M-Sa 8:20am-1:20pm and 2:30-4pm.) In case of emergency, call the **police** (☎0185 72 90 57) or the **carabinieri,** V. Cuneo, 30/F (☎112 or 0185 77 00 00). A **pharmacy, Dr. Machi,** V. Repubblica, 4-6, posts after-hours rotation. (☎0185 77 10 81. Open daily July-Aug. 8:30am-12:30pm and 4-8pm; Sept.-June 3:30-7:30pm.) The **post office** is at V. Cuneo, 4. (☎0185 77 026. Open M-F 8am-1:30pm, Sa 8am-12:30pm.) **Postal Code:** 16032.

ACCOMMODATIONS

Prices and availability of rooms vary greatly according to season and day of the week in Camogli. Though the tourist office can help with last-minute rooms, reserve ahead and be prepared to a pay a higher price in the summer.

The gorgeously renovated ▊**Hotel Augusta ❸**, V. Schiaffino, 100, attends to every detail. 15 rooms are handsomely furnished, all with bath, TV, keycard locks, and phone. Some overlook the harbor from private balconies. Turn right out of the train station and keep walking until V. Repubblica turns into V. Schaffino. (☎0185 77 05 92; www.htlaugusta.com. Buffet breakfast €10 per room. 15min. Internet included. Singles €30-60; doubles €78-98; triples €90. AmEx/MC/V.) The ▊**Albergo La Camogliese ❺**, V. Garibaldi, 55, is steps from the beach. Exit train station, walk down the long stairway to the right, and look for the blue sign. Large, comfortable rooms are a joy, as is courteous English-speaking staff. All rooms come with bath, TV, safe, and phone. Access to gym and community pool. (☎0185 77 14 02; www.lacamogliese.it. Breakfast included. Internet €1 per 30min. Singles €55; doubles €80; triples €90-120. 10% discount with cash payment. AmEx/MC/V.) The

Pensione Faro ❹, V. Schiaffino, 116-118, above the restaurant of the same name, offers quiet rooms with bath, TV, and tranquil sea views. (☎/fax 0185 77 14 00. Breakfast €4. Singles €40-45; doubles €60-70. AmEx/MC/V.)

⬛ FOOD

Shops on V. Repubblica (one block from the harbor) and **Picasso** supermarket, V. XX Settembre, 35, stock groceries and picnic supplies. (Open M-Sa 8am-12:30pm and 4:30-7:30pm, Su 8:30am-12:30pm. MC/V.) On Wednesdays, an **open-air market** fills P. del Teatro with local produce and cheap clothing. (Open 8am-noon.) *Focaccia*, flat bread topped with cheese, spices, or vegetables, is the specialty here, along with fresh seafood caught by the local fishermen.

⬛Focacceria Pasticceria Revello ❶, V. Garibaldi, 183, is famous in the region for fresh, crispy flatbreads and delectable pastries. This shop invented the town's beloved *camogliesi* (dense and crumply cookies; €19.50 per kg). Make like the locals and breakfast on *focaccia* with onions or *formaggio*. (☎0185 77 07 77; www.revellocamogli.com. *Focaccia* €8.50 per kg. Open daily 8am-2pm and 4-8pm. Cash only.) The creamy gelato from **⬛Gelato e Dintorni ❶**, V. Garibaldi, 104/105, puts nationally ranked rivals to shame. Their specialty is frozen yogurt topped with fresh fruit. (☎0185 77 43 533. 2 scoops €1.30. Sicilian *granita* €1.70. Open daily 10:30am-11pm. Cash only.) **Il Portico Spaghetteria ❷**, V. Garibaldi, 197/A, offers creative pastas to satisfy every craving; try the *pasta al turridu* (with anchovies, raisins, tomatoes, and fennel; €8). Generous portions and excellent value at this establishment. (☎0185 77 02 54. Pasta €6.50-9. Cover €2. Open daily for lunch at 12:30pm and for dinner at 8pm. Cash only.) The dining room at **La Rotonda ❹**, V. Garibaldi, 101, delivers a tremendous view of the sea. The menu includes typical Ligurian pasta and fresh seafood. (☎/fax 0185 77 45 02. *Primi* €7-9, *secondi* €11-25. Open daily 12:30-2:30pm and 7:30-11pm. AmEx/MC/V.)

👁 🎵 SIGHTS AND ENTERTAINMENT

The Camogli tourist office has a useful trail **map.** Painted red shapes mark the paths, which start at the end of V. Cuneo near the *carabinieri* station. Ferry or snorkeling trips also make interesting (but more costly) diversions. **B&B Diving Center,** V. Schiattino, 11, off P. Colombo, sails boats for scuba diving to 18 immersion points along the coast. (☎/fax 0185 77 27 51; www.bbdiving.it. Scuba tours Sa-Su 4 per day; €35 with guide and equipment. 10-person boat capacity. Canoe and kayak rental €6 per hr., €30 per day. Open daily 9am-7pm. Cash only.) The **Sagra del Pesce,** an enormous fish fry, is held the 2nd Sunday in May. The night before the big fry, the town gathers for a procession honoring the patron saint of fishermen, followed by a fireworks display and a bonfire-building contest. The next day the fryers cook in a monumental frying pan, measuring 4m in diameter and holding 2000 fish, and feed the jolly crowd. After the sardine rush, the pans adorn a city wall all year, hanging to the right on V. Garibaldi along the stairs to the beach.

Spend nights in peaceful Camogli enjoying a cool drink with a sea view. Order a mojito (€5) or sangria (€3.50) to cap off the day at the upscale bar **Il Barcollo,** V. Garibaldi, 92. (☎0185 77 33 22. Open daily 6pm-3am.) Just down the boardwalk is the piratical **Hook,** V. al Porto, 4, decorated like a ship's cabin and offering good food and over 60 types of rum (€3-18) until late. (☎0185 77 16 95. Pizza and pasta about €5. Happy hour 6-9pm with €5 drinks. Open daily 10am-3am. Cash only.) Around the corner the new hot spot **Bistingo Sea Bar,** P. Colombo, 12, offers a wide selection of mixed drinks. (☎0185 77 43 26. Drinks €5-7. Open 12:30pm-3am.)

TOP TEN LIST

LIGURIAN BEACHES

1. San Fruttuoso (right) is a cove from heaven, with crystal clear water surrounded by wooded cliffs and the opportunity to dive at Cristo degli Abissi.

2. Between Corniglia and **Vernazza** (p. 213), brave precarious footpaths down to a private beach boasting perfect swimming and a cool respite from the challenging hike.

3. Tiny beaches line the shore between **Portofino** and **Santa Margherita** (p. 209). Enjoy pristine waters and views of luxury yachts as they pass by.

4. Admire rainbow-hued harbor houses while catching some rays in **Vernazza** (p. 213).

5. In **Camogli** (p. 214), the white sands of the **free beach**, are always packed.

6. At **Giant Beach** in **Monterosso** (p. 211), a sculpture of a giant carved into the side of the cliff makes a dramatic backdrop for sunbathers and swimmers.

7. In **Alassio** (p. 223) where you have kilometers to find the right spot for your towel, the shores are lapped by cool waters.

8. Riomaggiore (p. 216) has small rocky coves, sparkling water, and excellent cliff jumping.

9. The crystal waters at **Finale Ligure's** free beach (p. 220) are perfect for body surfing.

10. At **San Remo** (p. 226), brightly colored cabanas dot the sand where the rich and famous sunbathe below a glittering casino.

DAYTRIP FROM CAMOGLI

SAN FRUTTUOSO

San Fruttuoso is accessible by trails from Portofino Mare (1½hr.), Portofino Vetta (1½hr.), or Camogli (3hr.). Golfo Paradiso (☎0185 77 20 91; www.golfoparadiso.it) runs boats from Camogli (every hr. in summer Tu and Th-Sa 8am-5pm, last return from San Fruttuoso 6-7pm; round-trip €8). Servizio Marittimo del Tigullio (☎0185 28 46 70) runs ferries from Camogli to Portofino (every hr. 9:30am-4:30pm, round-trip €12) and Santa Margherita (every hr. 9:15am-4:15pm, €7).

The hikes from Camogli to tiny San Fruttuoso follow labeled trails that wind through Portofino's nature reserve. There are two routes to San Fruttuoso from Camogli. The first, marked by a red circle, is easier and winds along the coast, past Nazi anti-aircraft bunkers and through forests, yielding vistas of the sea before descending into town. The second, marked by two red dots, climbs up and around Mt. Portofino through ancient forests and olive groves, with a difficult descent to the harbor on a crumbling stone path. This trail is recommend for **experts only** and proper shoes are essential. Trail maps are available at the Camogli tourist office.

The town is named after the Benedictine **Abbazia di San Fruttuoso di Capodimonte**, constructed from the 10th to the 13th centuries. The monastery and tower rotate archaeological exhibits. (☎0185 77 27 03. Open June-Sept. daily 10am-6pm; Mar.-May and Oct. Tu-Su 10am-4pm. Last entry 30min. before closing. €4, children €2.50.) Fifteen meters offshore and 17m underwater, the bronze *Christ of the Depths* stands with arms upraised in memory of the sea's casualties. The statue now protects scuba divers, and a replica stands in Chiesa di San Fruttuoso, enticing visitors who travel by ferry to make an offering to the *Sacrario dei Morti in Mare* (Sanctuary for the Dead at Sea). Locals with small boats offer rides to the underwater statue for €2.50 from the docks. Pack a picnic lunch or head to **Da Laura ❸** for delicious *lasagne al pesto*. (Open noon-3pm. Cash only.)

SANTA MARGHERITA LIGURE ☎0185

From its founding in the 12th century, Santa Margherita Ligure led a calm existence as a fishing village far from the Levante limelight. In the early 20th century, Hollywood stars discovered it, and its popularity grew after a *National Geographic* feature in the

1950s. Glitz adorns the beachfront and palm trees line the harbor. Though Santa Margherita remains a bit pricey, it is an attractive haven for tourists looking to spend a few days in the lap of luxury.

▐ TRANSPORTATION

The **train station** is in P. Federico Raoul Nobili at the top of V. Roma. Intercity **trains** on the Pisa-Genoa line stop at Santa Margherita. Ticket office open daily 6am-7:05pm. To: Genoa (50min., 2-4 per hr. 4:37am-11:55pm, €2.10) and La Spezia (1½hr., 1-2 per hr. 5:35am-1:10am, €3.95) via Cinque Terre (1hr., every hr. 8:06am-9:58pm, €3.40). **Tigullio buses** (☎0185 28 88 34) depart the small green kiosk in P. V. Veneto for Camogli (30min., every 45min., €1.20) and Portofino (20min., 3 per hr., €1.50). Ticket office open 7:05am-7:25pm. **Servizio Marittimo del Tigullio,** V. Palestro, 8/B (☎0185 28 46 70 or 336 25 33 36; www.traghettiportofino.it), runs **ferries** from docks at P. Martiri della Libertà to: Cinque Terre (July-Sept. W-Th and Sa, also M in Aug.; 8:45am; round-trip €22); Portofino (every hr. 9:15am-4:15pm, one-way €4.50); and San Fruttuoso (every hr. 9:15am-4:15pm, one-way €8). **Taxis** are in P. Nobili (☎0185 28 65 08) and on V. Pesciano (☎0185 28 79 98).

✈ ▐ ORIENTATION AND PRACTICAL INFORMATION

From the **train station,** turn left on **Via Roma** and follow it toward the water to **Piazza Vittorio Veneto.** Turn right on V. Pesciano, which winds around **Piazza Martiri della Libertà. Piazza Caprera** is between them set back from the water. From P. Veneto, **Via G. Marconi** winds around the port and **Via XXV Aprile** leads to the tourist office, becoming **Corso Matteotti** near the main square in town, **Piazza Mazzini.**

To reach the **Pro Loco Tourist Office,** V. XXV Aprile, 2/B, turn right from the train station on V. Trieste, which becomes V. Roma, follow it to C. Rainusso, then turn right. Take the first left on V. Gimelli, then left on V. XXV Aprile. The staff provides **maps** and lodging advice. (☎0185 28 74 85; www.apttigullio.liguria.it. Open M-Sa 9am-12:30pm and 3-7:30pm, Su 9:30am-12:30pm and 4:30-7:30pm.) In case of **emergency,** call ☎113, or contact the **police,** P. Mazzini, 46 (☎0185 20 54 50). Reach an **ambulance** at ☎118. **Farmacia A. Pennino,** P. Caprera, 10, posts after-hours rotation. (☎0185 29 70 77. Open M-Tu and Th-Su 8:30am-1pm and 3-10pm.) A **hospital** (☎0185 68 31) is on V. F. Arpe. **Internet** is available at **The Internet Point,** V. Giuncheto, 39, near P. Caprera. (☎0185 29 30 92; liguriacom@tigullio.it. €6 per hr. Open M-F 9am-12:30pm and 3-8pm, Sa 9am-noon and 3-8pm.) The **post office,** on V. Roma, 36, **has currency exchange,** *fermoposta* services, and a 24hr. **ATM** outside. (☎010 29 47 51. Open M-F 8am-6:30pm, Sa 8am-12:30pm.) **Postal Code:** 16038.

▐ ACCOMMODATIONS

Ritzy waterfront accommodations are by no means the only options, and in Santa Margherita, there's no such thing as a long walk to the sea. Accommodations do tend to be pricey, though, so be prepared to spend a little more during a stay here. **Hotel Nuova Riviera ❸,** V. Belvedere, 10/2, is run by an enthusiastic English-speaking family. Large bright rooms in main house all have private bath; 4 rooms in annex next door share baths. (☎0185 287 403; www.nuovariviera.com. Breakfast included. Internet €5 per 30min. Doubles €65, with bath €98; triples €90/120; quads €150. Pay in the annex. Cash only.) Find **Albergo Annabella ❸,** V. Costasecca, 10, behind P. Mazzini and across from the hospital. Kind owner Annabella aims to make guests feel at home in 11 comfortable rooms, some with bath. Shared bath is large and clean. (☎0185 28 65 31. Breakfast €4. Singles €30-40; doubles €50-60; triples €80-95; quads €119. Cash only.) To reach **Hotel Europa ❹**, V. Trento, 5, follow V. G. Marconi along the water, then turn right on V. Favale and again on V. Trento. Hotel is on the left down a short walkway. Tucked behind the harbor glitz, this modern hotel offers spacious rooms with bath, TV, and phone, most with balcony and A/C. (☎0185 28 71 87; www.hoteleuropa-sml.it. Breakfast included. Singles €40-75; doubles €60-95; extras beds 30% more. AmEx/MC/V.

🍴 FOOD

Markets and bakeries line C. Matteotti. Buy essentials at the **COOP**, C. Matteotti, 8, off P. Mazzini. (☎0185 28 43 15. Open M-Sa 8:15am-1pm and 3:30-8pm. V.) Catch the catch of the day at the **fish market** on V.G. Marconi. (Open daily 8am-12:30pm; boats arrive M-Tu and Th-Su 4-6am.) On Fridays, an **open-air market** in P. Mortola sells fruit and inexpensive clothes. (Open 8am-2pm.) Locals descend on the famous ⬛**Trattoria Da Pezzi ❶**, V. Cavour, 21, for its home-style cuisine and jovial atmosphere. *Farinata* (€3.70) and *torta pasquelina* (€4.60-5.20) are great choices. (☎0185 28 53 03. *Primi* €3.50-6.50, *secondi* €3.10-9. Open M-F and Su 10am-2:15pm and 5-9:15pm. MC/V.) ⬛**Trattoria Baicini ❸**, V. Algeria, 9, is off P. Martiri della Libertà. Mama Carmela ladles glorious soups like the *trofie alla Genovese* (gnocchi with string beans and pesto; €5.50). (☎0185 28 67 63. *Primi* €5.50-7.50, *secondi* €10.50-16.50. Cover €1.50. Open Tu-Su noon-3pm and 7-11:30pm. AmEx/MC/V.) It's hard to find better dishes than the *pansotti alla salsa di noci* (vegetable-filled pasta in walnut cream sauce; €7) at **La Locanda Azzura ❸**, V. S. Bernardo, 3. From the sea, turn right off V. XXV Aprile. This unpretentious spot with plastic furniture for outdoor seating is surprisingly elegant inside. (☎0185 28 53 94. *Primi* €6-10, *secondi* €7.50-17. Cover €1.60. Open M-Tu and Th-

LIGURIA

Su 12:10-2pm and 7:10-10:30pm. MC/V.) **L'Approdo ❺**, V. Cairoli, 26, is a bit of a splurge, but excellent food, beautiful presentation, and courteous service are worth the extra expense. Old family recipes for *scampi* (shrimp; €26). (☎0185 28 17 89. *Primi* €11-15, *secondi* €16-36. Cover €3. Open Tu 7:30pm-midnight, W-Su 12:30-2pm and 7:30pm-midnight. AmEx/MC/V.) Finish your meals at **Gelateria Centrale ❶**, Largo Giusti, 14. Crowds gather for €2 *pinguini*, cones of *gelato* in a thick chocolate shell. (☎0185 28 74 80. Open daily 8:30am-midnight. Cash only.)

👁 🎵 SIGHTS AND ENTERTAINMENT

If lapping waves aren't sufficiently invigorating, visit the Rococo **Basilica di Santa Margherita** in P. Caprera, dripping with gold and crystal chandeliers. The church also contains fine Flemish and Italian artwork. (☎0185 28 65 55.) Off V. della Vittoria, paths wind uphill to the **Villa Durazzo**, which is surrounded by gardens and holds 16th-century paintings. (Open daily July and Aug. 9am-8pm; May, June, and Sept. 9am-7pm; Apr. and Oct. 9am-6pm; Nov.-Dec. 9am-5pm.) Come nightfall, youthful crowds claim the funky colored tables at **Sabot American Bar**, P. della Libertà, 32, for drinks, sushi platters and DJ music. (☎0185 28 07 47. Cocktails €7, beer €4-6. Open M and W-Su 10am-4am.) Mingle with the fashionable and trendy a few doors down at uber-hip **Miami**, P. della Libertà, 29, complete with neon lights, vinyl booths, and €7 Manhattan cocktails. (☎0185 28 34 24. Open daily 5pm-3am. AmEx/MC/V.)

🔋 DAYTRIP FROM SANTA MARGHERITA

PORTOFINO

Take bus #82 to Portofino Mare (not Portofino Vetta) from the green bus kiosk in P. Martiri della Libertà, where tickets are sold. From Portofino's P. Martiri della Libertà, Tigullio buses run to Santa Margherita (3 per hr., €1.50). Portofino is also accessible by ferry from Santa Margherita (every hr. 10:30am-4pm, €4.50) and Camogli (2 per day, €11).

Portofino is a perfect half-day outing from Santa Margherita. Yachts fill the harbor, chic boutiques and art galleries line the cobblestone streets, and luxury cars crowd parking lots. Nevertheless, both princes and paupers can enjoy the tiny bay of this fine port. A **nature reserve** surrounds Portofino and nearby resort village **Paraggi.** Treks through the hilly terrain past ruined churches and stately villas lead to Rapallo (2hr.), Santa Margherita (1½hr.), and San Fruttuoso (2hr.).

Facing the sea from town, head right around the port and climb the stairs to the cool, stark interior of the **Chiesa di San Giorgio.** Behind the church lies a small cemetery where members of the Protestant minority were laid to rest. Further up the hill is the 16th-century **Castello Brown,** with stone walls and a garden in front. The castle was once a fortress, but the wealthy Brown family converted it to a summer home after Consul Montague Yeats Brown bought it km 1867 from the Kingdom of Sardinia for 7000 lire. (Open daily 10am-7pm, in winter Sa-Su 10am-5pm. €3.50.)

Back in town, market **Alimentari Repetto,** P. Martiri dell'Olivetta, 32, in the main square in front of the harbor, fortifies hikers with Gatorade (€2.50) and sandwiches from €3. (☎0185 26 90 56. Open daily in summer 8am-10pm, in winter 9am-6pm.) **Trattoria Concordia ❸,** V. del Fondaco, 5, behind P. della Libertà, serves authentic Ligurian cuisine served in a small, nautical-themed dining room. Local favorites are cheaper here than at many of the pricier restaurants surrounding the harbor. (☎0185 26 92 07. *Primi* €5-26, *secondi* €10-26. Cover €1.50, service 10%. Open M and W-Su noon-3pm and 7:30-10pm. AmEx/MC/V.) A drink at one of the numerous bars along the harbor costs upward of €6.50, though watching town life unfold along the harbor may be worth it.

A FERRY TALE. Though the hikes and train rides through Portofino's nature reserve are gorgeous, the real charm of its small coastal towns is best experienced from the sea. Hop on one of the many ferries between Camogli, San Fruttuoso, Portofino, and Santa Margherita for incomparable panoramas of colorful buildings nestled among the mountains.

At the **APT tourist office,** V. Roma, 35, on the way to the waterfront from the bus stop, the English-speaking staff has free **maps** and brochures. (☎0185 26 90 24; www.apttigullio.liguria.it. Open M-Tu 10:30am-1:30pm and 2:30-7:30pm, W-Su 10:30am-1:30pm and 2-7:30pm.) **Currency exchange** is available at the Banca Popolare di Lodi, V. Roma, 14/16. (☎0185 26 91 64. Open M-F 8:20am-1:20pm and 2:30-4pm.) In case of **emergency,** call the **police,** V. del Fondaco, 8 (☎112 or 0185 26 90 88). A **pharmacy** is at P. Martiri della Libertà, 6. (☎0185 26 91 01. Open M-Tu 9am-1pm, W-Sa 9am-1pm and 4-8pm. AmEx/MC/V.) The **post office** is at V. Roma, 36. (☎0185 26 91 56. Open M-F 8am-1:15pm, Sa 8am-12:30pm.) **Postal Code**: 16034.

CINQUE TERRE   ☎0187

Cinque Terre is an outdoorsman's paradise: strong hikers can cover all five villages in about 5hr., and numerous opportunities for kayaking, cliff jumping, or horseback riding present themselves along way. Rather than rushing, though, take the time to wander through the villages themselves, which are simply tiny clusters of rainbow-colored houses amid hilly stretches of olive groves and vineyards. Though Cinque Terre was formerly a hidden treasure of the Ligurian coastline, increased publicity and word of mouth have made the towns fodder for a booming tourism industry; now, conversations in English and German are just as common as those in Italian. So reserve ahead, put on your hiking boots, and step away from the world for a few days that are certain to soothe mind, body, and spirit.

▐ TRANSPORTATION

Trains: The towns lie on the Genoa-La Spezia (Pisa) line. Schedules are available at tourist offices. Most trains stop at **Monterosso,** making it the most accessible of the 5 towns. From the station on V. Fegina, trains run to: **Florence** (3½hr., every hr., €8-17) via **Pisa** (2½hr., every hr. 4:53am-11:57pm, €4.65); **Genoa** (1½hr., every hr. 4:47am-12:47pm, €4.45); **La Spezia** (20min., every 30min., €1.35); **Rome** (7hr., every 2hr., €31). Frequent local trains connect the 5 towns (5-20min., every 50min., €1-1.50).

Ferries: Monterosso can be reached by ferry from **La Spezia** (1hr., 2 per day, €18). Ferries from Monterosso also connect the towns. **Navigazione Golfo dei Poeti** (☎0187 77 77 27), in front of the IAT office at the port (in the old town; see **Practical Information,** below). To: **Manarola** (6 per day, €8); **Portovenere** (7 per day, €15); **Riomaggiore** (7 per day, €8); **Vernazza** (7 per day, €2.25).

Taxis: ☎335 62 80 933 or 335 61 65 842.

Boat Rental: Along the beaches. Mar-Mar (☎/fax 0187 92 09 32) on the harbor in Riomaggiore, rents kayaks and 3-person canoes (€5 per hr., €25 per day). Cash only.

◤ ▐ ORIENTATION AND PRACTICAL INFORMATION

The five villages string along the coast between Levanto in the northwest and La Spezia in the southeast, connected by trains, roads (although cars are not allowed inside the towns), and footpaths that traverse the rocky shoreline. **Monterosso** is the largest and westernmost town and the sight of most of the services for the area, followed from west to east by **Vernazza, Corniglia, Manarola,** and **Riomaggiore.** The following are the principal listings. Separate listings follow for individual towns.

Tourist Offices:

Cinque Terre National Park Office, P. Garibaldi, 20 (☎0187 81 78 38; www.parconazionale5terre.it), in Monterosso, has info on hiking trails and accommodations and sells **Cinque Terre Cards.** Open daily 8am-8pm.

Pro Loco, V. Fegina, 38 (☎0187 81 75 06; fax 0187 81 78 25), below the Monterosso train station, provides info on boats, hikes, and accommodations. Open daily 9:30am-6:30pm.

Tourist Office (☎0187 76 99 61), in the train station in Riomaggiore. Has info on trails, hotels, and excursions. Open June-Sept. M-Th 6:30am-8pm, F-Sa 6:30am-10pm. Tourist offices in Manarola, Riomaggiore, and Monterosso have Internet points.

Tours: Navigazione 5 Terre Golfo dei Poeti (☎0187 73 29 87 or 0187 77 77 27) offers tours to **Vernazza** (€3, round-trip €4.50) and **Riomaggiore** (€8, round-trip €10.50) from **Monterosso** (9 per day 10:30am-6pm) and **Vernazza** (9 per day 10:40am-6:10pm). Boats also go to **Portovenere** (€16) and **Lerici** (€20).

Emergency: ☎113. **Ambulance:** ☎118. **Police:** ☎112.

Carabinieri: ☎0187 81 75 24; in Riomaggiore 0187 92 01 12.

First Aid: ☎338 85 30 949 for doctor on call M-W and F-Su.

Medical Clinic: ☎0189 80 09 73 for Monterosso, Vernazza, and Corniglia; ☎0189 50 77 27 for Riomaggiore and Manarola.

Post Office: Main branch in **Monterosso,** V. Roma, 73 (☎0189 81 83 94). Open M-F 8am-1:15pm, Sa 8am-12:30pm. **Postal Codes:** Monterosso 19016; Manarola and Riomaggiore 19017; Corniglia and Vernazza 19018.

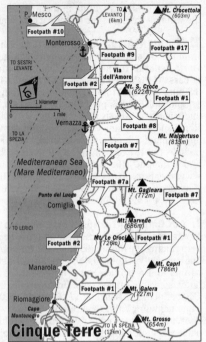

TIP **TERRE TRIPPING.** The train stations and Cinque Terre National Park offices in each of the five towns sell 1-day (€5.40), 3-day (€13), and 7-day (€20.60) **Cinque Terre Cards** with unlimited train, bus, and path access between the five villages, La Spezia, and Levanto. There is also a 1-day pass (€13.60) that includes unlimited ferry service between the same points.

 THE TOWNS

MONTEROSSO

The largest and most developed of the five villages, Monterosso is the beach bum's town of choice. Three sandy shores and a spirited backpacking and hiking crew create the liveliest nightlife in the five *terre*. Monterosso's character endures, in the winding streets of the historical center and the friendly local ambience.

◧◪ ORIENTATION AND PRACTICAL INFORMATION. Descend the steps from the **train station** and turn left on **Lungomare di Fegina** through a tunnel into **Piazza Garibaldi**, the heart of the historic center. Services include: **currency exchange** at **Cassa di Risparmio della Spezia**, V. Roma, 47 (open M-F 8:10am-1:10pm and 2:30-3:30pm, Su 8:10-11:30am) and **Banca Carige**, V. Roma, 69 (open daily 8:05am-1:15pm and 2:30-3:45pm); **ATMs** at **Bancomat**, V. Fegina, 40, under the train station; and **laundry** at **Laundry Matic**, one on V. Molinelli, 12, and one on the corner of V. Roma and V. Mazzini. (Wash, soap, and dry €8 for 7kg load. Open daily 9am-noon and 3-7pm. Cash only.) The **pharmacy** at V. Fegina, 44, posts after-hours rotations outside. (☎0187 18 18 391. Open M-F 9am-12:30pm and 4-8pm, Sa-Su 9am-12:30pm and 4-7:30pm.) **The Net**, V. V. Emanuele, 55, offers **Internet**. (☎0187 81 72 88; www.monterosso.net. €1 for 10min., €0.10 for each additional min., or 2hr. for €10. Open daily 10am-10pm.) Internet can also be found at **Il Casello**, V. Lungo Ferravia, 70, for €4 per hr. (☎0187 81 83 30. Open daily noon-2am.)

⌂ ACCOMMODATIONS. While most of Cinque Terre's hotels are in Monterosso, they generally fill up in early June. Inquire at the tourist office for help finding the more plentiful *affittacamere* (private rooms). The lively ⊠**Hotel Souvenir ❷**, V. Gioberti, 30, popular with students, has 30 beds in comfortable rooms and a private garden perfect for socializing. (☎/fax 0187 81 75 95; hotel_souvenir@yahoo.com. Breakfast €5. Dorms for students €25; private rooms €40 per person. Cash only.) At **Convento dei Cappuccini ❸**, next to the church of the same name on V. Zii dei Frati off of Salita Cappuccini, vineyards, vegetable gardens, and a private courtyard provide soothing places to stroll. Though the 11pm curfew is at odds with the social atmosphere of Monterosso, the convent boasts some of the best views in town. (☎/fax 0187 81 75 31. Breakfast included. Singles €35-40; doubles €70, with bath €80; family suite €140. Cash only.) To get to **Albergo La Pineta ❷** at V. P. Semeria, 3, turn right out of the train station then right on V. P. Semeria. Amiable owners keep a private beach and spacious rooms with bath and TV, some with sea views. (☎0187 82 90 29; hotel_lapineta@virgilio.it. Breakfast included. Singles from €25; doubles from €60. Cash only.)

▢ FOOD. Allegedly, every restaurant in Cinque Terre prepares the best pesto, the freshest fish, and the most savory *acciughe* or *muscoli rippieni* (anchovies or mussels stuffed with grains and vegetables). To avoid high prices, consider a picnic of pesto-covered *focaccia* and juicy local fruit; wash it all down with a glass of light, dry *Cinque Terre* white, followed by some *Sciacchetrà* dessert wine. **SuperCONAD Margherita**, P. Matteotti, 9, stocks groceries. (Open June-Sept. M-Sa 8am-1pm and 5-8pm; Su 8am-1pm. MC/V.) Those interested in fine wine should visit ⊠**Cantina di Sciacchetrà**, V. Roma, 7, which has free tastings, delicious *antipasti*, and deals on gourmet souvenirs. Jovial Gianluigi proudly explains his high-quality local products, supplied by the Cinque Terre Farming Cooperative. (☎0187 81 78 28. *Cinque Terre bianco* €4-19, *Sciacchetrà* €28. Open daily Mar.-Oct. 10am-10pm. MC/V.) ⊠**Il Ciliegio ❸**, Località Beo, 2, creates fantastic meals with ingredients fresh from the owner's gardens. The exceptional *trufie al pesto* (€8) and *cozze ripieni* (€8) have been featured in reviews worldwide. The restaurant is 20min. from town; management offers free shuttle service from P. Garibaldi on request. (☎0187 81 78 29. Lunch *menù* €27. *Primi* €6-8, *secondi* €7-11. Open Tu-Su 12:30-2:30pm and 7:30-10:30pm.) In a narrow alley off V. Roma, **Ristorante Al Carugio ❸**, V. San Pietro, 9, serves up hefty portions of traditional Ligurian dishes. (☎/fax 0187 81 73 67. *Primi* €6-10.50, *secondi* €7-15. Open M-W and F-Su noon-

2:30pm and 6-10:30pm.) **Focacceria Il Frantoio ❶**, V. Gioberti, 1, bakes tasty *farinata* and *focaccia* stuffed with olives, onions, or herbs. (☎0187 81 83 33. Slices €1-3. Open M-W and F-Su 9am-2pm and 4-7:30pm. Cash only.)

◖◗ **SIGHTS AND NIGHTLIFE.** Monterosso has Cinque Terre's largest **free beach,** surrounded by a cliff-cove in front of the historical center. About 200m to the right of the train station, **Il Gigante,** an enormous giant carved into the rocky cliff, watches over the sunbathers below. The 15th-century **Chiesa dei Cappuccini,** in the center of town, yields broad vistas of the five towns. In the chapel to the left is the impressive *Crucifixion* by Flemish master Anthony Van Dyck, who sojourned here during his most productive years. (Open daily 9am-noon and 4-7pm. Free.) At night, chow down on hot sandwiches (from €4) and mixed drinks (€5) beneath hanging electric guitars at **FAST,** V. Roma, 13. (☎0187 81 71 64. Beer €4-5, tap €2.80-8. Open in summer daily 8am-2am; in winter Tu-Su 8am-noon. MC/V.) Music and dancing at **Il Casello,** V. Lungo Ferravia, 70, draws young backpackers. Casello also serves beer, liquor, and snacks. (☎0187 81 83 30. *Focaccia* sandwiches €3.50-4. Drinks from €2.50. Internet €1 for 15min. Open daily noon-2am.)

◪ **HIKING: MONTEROSSO-VERNAZZA.** The hardest of the four town-linking treks, this 1¾hr. hike climbs steeply up a cliff-side staircase, winding past terraced vineyards and hillside cottages before the steep descent into Vernazza.

VERNAZZA

Graced by a large seaside *piazza* and a small but beautiful stretch of sandy beach, Vernazza is historically the wealthiest of the five Cinque Terre towns. Climb to the remains of the 11th-century Castello Doria, up a staircase on the left of P. Marconi when facing the port, for great views of the other four towns.

◪◪ **ORIENTATION AND PRACTICAL INFORMATION.** Lined with shops and restaurants, **Via E. Q. Visconti** runs toward the sea from the station and turns into **Via Roma** about halfway to the beach. **Piazza Marconi** overlooks the harbor at the end of V. Roma. There is a **tourist information office** in the train station. In case of **emergency** dial ☎113, or call the **police** at ☎112 or an **ambulance** at ☎118.

◪◪ **ACCOMMODATIONS AND FOOD.** Vernazza has some great hotels and private rooms. ◪**Hotel Gianni Franzi ❹**, P. Marconi, 1, has 23 rooms, all with antique decor, in several small rustic buildings at the top of the town; most sport a large balcony with views of the coast and Corniglia. (☎0187 82 10 03; www.gianni-franzi.it. Singles €42; doubles €60-65, with bath €77; triples with bath €100. AmEx/MC/V.) The friendly owners of ◪**Albergo Barbara ❹**, P. Marconi, 30, on the top floor, make their guests feel at home. The nine rooms are bright and many have views of the port. (☎0187 81 23 98; www.albergobarbara.it. Ring bell to enter. Doubles €48, with bath €60, with bath and view €80; triples €90. Cash only.)

Reputedly home to the best restaurants in Cinque Terre, P. Marconi fills with hungry tourists each evening. Groceries, fresh produce, and gourmet foods are available at **Salumi e Formaggi,** V. Visconti, 29. (☎0187 82 12 40. Open M-Sa 8am-1:30pm and 5-8pm, Su 8am-1:30pm. Cash only.) The oldest *trattoria* in Vernazza, **Trattoria Gianni Franzi ❸**, P. Marconi, 1, is famed for its pesto and friendly local charm. Dine casually in the roomy interior or outside in the *piazza*. (☎0187 82 10 03; fax 0187 81 22 28. *Primi* €4-10.50, *secondi* €5-15.50. Open M-Tu and Th-Su noon-3pm and 7:30-9:30pm. AmEx/MC/V.) For a delicious splurge, visit elegant **Gambero Rosso ❹**, P. Marconi, 7. Touted by *Vernazzesi*, the service is excellent, and the food superb—adventurous eaters should not miss the *menù* *degustazione* (€30), four courses of local specialties. (☎0187 81 22 65, fax 0187 82 12 60. *Primi* €6-10, *secondi* €11-22. Open Tu-Su noon-3:15pm and 7-10pm. AmEx/MC/V.) For a slice of pizza (€2.50-3) or hot *panini* (€1.70-2.60) crowds flock to **Pizzeria Fratelli Bosso ❶**, V. Roma, 1, to enjoy a quick snack between rounds of hiking and sunbathing. (Open daily 10am-7pm. Cash only.)

🅗 **HIKING: VERNAZZA-CORNIGLIA.** Geographic diversity and **unparalleled views** are the rewards along this 1½hr. hike. The trail climbs harshly from Vernazza, passing through vineyards and olive groves before curving through uncultivated landscape. Scents of rosemary, thyme, lemon, and lavender perfume the air in the summer. At one point, the trail bends to reveal a secluded beach hundreds of feet below, occupied largely by students and adventurous types willing to make the trek down the mountain. In view for the duration of the hike is Corniglia, perched spectacularly on a cliff in the distance.

CORNIGLIA

Hundreds of steps climb from the station to this colorful village clinging to a seaside cliff. Without the beachside glitter of the other towns, Corniglia offers a more peaceful ambience that makes it a good resting point midway through the Cinque Terre hike. A pebbly strip of public beach beneath the tracks packs in sunbathers, while more secluded beaches beckon hikers off the trail on the way to Vernazza.

🅗🅗 **ORIENTATION AND PRACTICAL INFORMATION. Via alta Stazione** begins at the top of the station steps, turning into **Via Fieschi** in the center of town. Branching off to the left, V. Fieschi passes through two *piazze* before ending in **Belvedere Santa Maria,** a small terrace suspended at the edge of a cliff. To the right of the center, down **Via Serra,** is the entrance to the trail from Vernazza.

🅗🅗 **ACCOMMODATIONS AND FOOD.** Due to its small size and cliffside location, Corniglia is a better daytrip than place to spend the night. If you do plan to stay, private rooms are the way to go, as there are few, if any, hotels. From the main piazza, turn right and walk 150m. **Ristorante Cecio ❺**, V. Serra, 58, on the road that leads from Corniglia to Vernazza, rents eight rooms above the restaurant with postcard views of the sea, and four rooms in the village with terraces. All rooms have bath. (☎0187 81 20 43; simopank@libero.it. Doubles €70. Cash only.) Pizzerias serve hungry hikers all over town, but follow your nose to **La Gata Flora ❶**, V. Fieschi, 109, for hot, delicious slices in many varieties. Crispy *farinata* (€1) is also available. (☎0187 82 12 18. Slice €2.50. Whole pizza €4-7. *Focaccia* €1.10-2. Open M and W-Su 9:30am-4pm and 6-8:30pm, daily in Aug. Cash only.) To get to **La Posada ❸,** V. alta Stazione, 11, climb the staircase from the train station. Turn right on the road at the top; follow for about 50m. The food is delicious, the garden gorgeous, and the sweeping seaside view priceless. (*Primi* €6-8, *secondi* €7-10. Cover €2. Lunch starts daily at noon, dinner at 7pm. MC/V.) The cavernous **Cantina de Mananan ❸**, V. Fieschi, 117, provides a dark, cool respite and hearty meals from its mix and match pasta and sauce menu. (☎0187 82 11 66. *Primi* €8-10, *secondi* €5-12. Cover €1.55. Open M and W-Su 12:45-2:15pm and 7:45-9:15pm. Cash only.) On the outdoor terrace of **Ristorante Cecio ❹**, V. Serra, 11, swill *vino* and twirl spaghetti or the *risotto all cecio* (2-person min., €10 per person) before a view of the sun setting over the town. (☎0187 81 20 43. *Primi* and *secondi* €8-15. Cover €2. Open M-Tu and Th-Su noon-3pm and 7:30pm-1am. Closed Nov. MC/V.)

🅗 **HIKING: CORNIGLIA-MANAROLA.** Take the stairs down to the station from V. della Stazione and turn left, following the path along the railroad tracks. The 1hr. trail begins just after the public beach. Though less picturesque than the hikes between the previous towns, the gentle trail to Manarola boasts an easier, flatter trek than the other trails and offers sweeping, open-sea vistas.

MANAROLA

Two large swimming coves, sheltered by rocky inlets, attract swimmers and sunbathers to Manarola. Some of Cinque Terre's funkiest bars and a big, new hostel make this the ideal hangout for the vivacious backpacking crowd.

■ ▲ ORIENTATION AND PRACTICAL INFORMATION. From the train station, walk through the tunnel and emerge onto **Via A. Discovolo**. Turn left and cross **Piazza Dario Capellino,** after which **Via Birolli** runs to the sea. **Farmacia del Mare,** V. A Discovolo, 238, posts a list of late-night pharmacies. (☎0189 92 09 30. Open M and F-Sa 9am-1pm and 4-8pm, Tu-Th 9am-1pm. Self-service **laundry** is available at **Il Sole,** V. Cozza, 25. (☎0187 92 00 91. Open M-Sa 9am-1pm and 4-7pm.)

▐▌ ACCOMMODATIONS AND FOOD. To reach the new ▩**Ostello Cinque Terre ❷,** V. B. Riccobaldi, 21, turn right from the train station and continue uphill 300m. Here 48 beds, a bright dining room, a rooftop terrace, and a shelf full of board games contribute to the summer-camp atmosphere. Ask about kayak, bike, and snorkeling equipment rental. (☎0187 92 02 15; www.hostel5terre.com. Breakfast €3.50. Laundry €4 wash, €3 dry. Internet €1.50 for 15min. Sheets and 5min. shower included. Wheelchair accessible. Reception daily 7am-1pm and 5pm-1am. Lockout 1-5pm. Curfew in summer 1am, in winter midnight. Reserve at least 2 weeks ahead. Dorms €17-22.50; quads with bath €68-88. AmEx/MC/V.) The cheery ▩**Bed and Breakfast La Torretta ❹,** Vico Volto, 20, is filled with flowers. Most rooms are spacious and have balcony, TV, and A/C. Apartments with kitchen are also available. (☎0187 92 03 27; www.cinqueterre.net/torretta. Buffet breakfast included. Doubles €70-100, with student reservation (excluding breakfast) €45. V.) The restaurant **Il Porticciolo ❸,** V. Birolli, 92, rents three rooms with bath, TV, and balcony. (☎/fax 0187 92 00 83. Breakfast €5. Doubles €50, with sea view €60. AmEx/MC/V.)

At **Trattoria Da Billy ❸,** V. Rollandi 122, get away from the town center above P. della Chiesa and eat lunch with the locals. This popular place has delicious home-cooked food and lovely views. (☎0187 92

GIVING BACK

THIS LAND IS YOUR LAND

Hiking in the Cinque Terre you may have noticed that the paths feel a little more crumbly than perhaps they should. Over the past few years, the huge influx of tourists to the region has boosted the economy, but it has also begun to take its toll on the land. Increased foot traffic, combined with a dry climate and rugged terrain, has caused deterioration of the hillside, resulting in the Cinque Terre's placement on the "World Monument Watch List of 100 Most Endangered Sites."

However, the devoted workers at the **Parco Nazionale delle Cinque Terre** refuse to let their beloved cliffs and vineyards be destroyed. The park has allied with local restaurants, accommodations, and businesses to ensure that they stay as friendly to the environment as they are to the tourists. Establishments which display the park's official "Eco-Quality" plaque have committed to using recycle bins, eco-friendly energy sources, or reusable products.

Visitors to the park can lend a helping hand by joining one of the park's work camps. Hikers who rebuild fallen walls, restore footpaths, and promote growth along the hillsides are essential to the preservation of precious landscape. *(For more information, contact Parco Nazionale delle Cinque Terre ☎0187 76 00 00; info@parconazionale5terre.it.)*

068. *Primi* €6-8, *secondi* €6.50-12. Open M-W and F-Su noon-2pm and 7-9:30pm. MC/V.) **Trattoria Il Porticciolo ❷**, V. R. Birolli, 92, serves hearty meals in a casual ambience at a good value and boasts excellent *gnocchi al pesto* (€5.50). The *torta di noci* (nut cake; €4) is also superb. (☎0187 92 00 83. *Primi* €3.50-8, *secondi* €6.50-15.50. Cover €2. Open M-Tu and Th-Su 7am-3:30pm and 5-11pm. AmEx/MC/V.) **Marina Piccola ❹**, V. lo Scalo, 16, is a little place with big meals. Savor *cozze ripiene* (stuffed mussels; €10) on the edge of a rocky cove. (☎0187 92 09 23. *Primi* €7-15, *secondi* €7-16. Open M and W-Su noon-2:30pm and 7pm-midnight. Closed in Aug. AmEx/MC/V.)

◪ **NIGHTLIFE.** At the right times, there's plenty of rowdy fun to be found in this town of the young, fit, and temporary. A few times each summer, Manarola hosts booming disco parties in a *piazza* above the harbor, advertised on posters around town. The remaining time, however, Manarola provides more low-key opportunities for socializing. **Il Bar Sopra Il Mare,** on the manicured lawns and gardens of Punta Bonfiglio on the path to Corniglia, is a relaxing spot to get a drink, sit under the stars, and watch the waves crash. (☎0187 76 20 58. Beer €2.50-3, mixed drinks €3.60-4.15. Open daily mid-June to Oct. 6pm-1am.)

◪ **MANAROLA-RIOMAGGIORE: VIA DELL'AMORE.** The most famous stretch of Cinque Terre hikes takes only 20min. to walk and passes through a stone tunnel decorated by graffiti love scenes. With elevators at its beginning and end, the slate-paved walk is almost wheelchair accessible except for some steps in the middle.

RIOMAGGIORE

A castle crowns a cliff above the last and smallest Cinque Terre town, where bright houses cascade down the valley and fishermen swabbing varnish on boat hulls are as numerous as the sunbathers smoothing on lotion by the shore. There are rooms for rent around the harbor; this town is the best bet to find last-minute lodging, and as a result boasts a busy population of young travelers and a lively nightlife.

◪◪ **ORIENTATION AND PRACTICAL INFORMATION.** Turn right from the **train station** and walk through a tunnel to reach the historical center. The main street, **Via Colombo,** runs up the hill to the left. A **Pro Loco Tourist Office** in the train station provides information on trails, hotels, excursions, and Internet access (☎0187 92 06 33. Open M-Th 6:30am-8pm, F-Sa 6:30am-10pm.) Other services include: **currency exchange,** at the **National Park Office** next to the station (open daily 8am-11:30pm), and at **Banca Carige,** V. Colombo, 215. (Open M-F 8:05am-1:20pm and 2:30-3:45pm. AmEx/MC/V.) The National Park Office has **Internet** at €0.80 for 10min. In case of **emergency,** dial ☎113, or call the **police** at ☎112 or an **ambulance** at ☎118. **Farmacia del Mare,** V. Colombo, 182, posts a list of late-night pharmacies. (☎0187 92 01 60. Open M-F 9am-1pm and 4-8pm.) The self-service **Wash and Dry Lavarapido** is at V. Colombo, 109. (€3.50 for 30min. Open daily 8am-10pm.) A **post office** is at V. Pecunia, 7. (☎0187 80 31 60. Open M-F 8am-1pm and Sa 8am-noon.)

◪◪ **ACCOMMODATIONS AND FOOD.** The clean and welcoming ◪**Mar-Mar ❷**, V. Malborghetto, 4, rents dorms and rooms with bath; some have TV and balcony. Apartments for two-six people are also available. (☎/fax 0187 92 09 32. Dorms €20; doubles €65-90; apartments €40-120. Cash only.) **Hotel Ca Dei Duxi ❺**, V. Colombo, 36, is pleasant and well-situated, offering elegant wood furnishings and good value. Its six rooms all have bath, TV, A/C, fridge, and terrace. (☎0187 92 00 36. Buffet breakfast included. Doubles €80; triples €90-120. Cash only.) At **5Terre Affitti ❹**, V. Colombo, 174, Papa Bernardo rents rooms located mostly on the harbor with bath and satellite TV. Some with balcony. (☎0187 92 03 31; www.immobiliare5terre.com. Singles €25-50; doubles €45-55; triples €55-70; quad with kitchen and terrace €100. Cash only.) **La Dolce Vita ❷**, V. Colombo, 120, has a young staff that rents dorm-style rooms, doubles with bath and minibar, and four-person apartments. (☎0187 92 09 18 or 0187 92 09 35. Dorms €20; apartments: doubles €40-60, triples €50-60, quads €70-120. Cash only.) Among Riomaggiore's many *affittacamere* organizations, **Edi ❷**, V. Colombo, 111, rents rooms with bath and minibar and apartments for up to six people. Reserve ahead. (☎/fax 0187 92 03 25. Singles €25; doubles €52; apartments €26-31 per person. AmEx/MC/V.)

For groceries and fresh produce, stop at **Alimentari della Franca,** V. Colombo, 253. (☎018 79 20 929. Open M-F 7am-1pm and 3-7pm, Sa-Su 7am-7pm. MC/V.) At popular **Trattoria La Lanterna ❹**, V. S. Giacomo, 46, watch the fishing boats roll in and sample delicious fresh fish cooked in many varieties. (☎0585 50 033. *Primi* €7-9, *secondi* €9.50-21. AmEx/MC/V.) On a cliff above town, the upscale but unpretentious **Ripa del Sole ❹**, V. de Gasperi, 282, serves some of the area's most authentic and flavorful cuisine in a dining room bathed in sunlight. The *gnocchi* with scampi and white truffles (€9.50) are excellent. (☎0187 92 01 43. *Primi* €7.50-9.50, *secondi* €8.50-21. Open Tu-Su noon-2pm and 7-10pm. AmEx/MC/V.)

◪◩ OUTDOORS AND NIGHTLIFE. Coopsub Cinqueterre Diving Center, on V. S. Giacomo in Riomaggiore, conducts supervised dives off the coast, where dolphins are just as common as choral in June and September. Boat trips include stops to the natural waterfalls of Caneto Beach. (☎0187 92 00 11; www.5terrediving.com. Open daily Easter-late Sept. 9am-6pm.) Nightlife in Rio is laidback but not particularly bustling. The bar and outdoor patio at **Bar Centrale,** V. C. Colombo, 144, fill up with young international backpackers. Ivo, the energetic bartender, serves a cold brew and turns up the swingin' Motown to please the rowdy crowds. (☎0187 92 02 08. Internet €1 for 10min. Beer €2-5. Cocktails €4-6. Open daily 7:30am-1am. Cash only.) **A Pie de Ma, Bar and Vini,** with sweeping views on V. dell'Amore heading into town, is a new hot spot to grab pre-dinner drinks. (☎338 22 20 088. Live music Sa nights. *Focaccia* €3.50. Cocktails €5. Open daily 10am-midnight. Cash only.)

◪ DAYTRIP FROM CINQUE TERRE

LEVANTO

A difficult 2½hr. hike connects Levanto with Monterosso. Trains run to Levanto from Cinque Terre (5min. to Monterosso (€1); 20 per day 6:49am-12:47am).

Sandy beaches and seaside promenades are the main attractions at this beach town, a busier and more urban alternative to the laid back Cinque Terre towns. The trek to Levanto is more uncultivated and rugged than most of the hikes in Cinque Terre. The trail leaves Monterosso for a harsh 45min. climb to **Punta del Mesco,** a 19th-century lighthouse converted from the ruins of an Augustinian monastery. Before descending to Levanto, it wraps around cliffs and passes vineyards, orchards, and the remains of a 13th-century castle. Private and public beaches line the promenade, dotted with umbrellas. Load up for a beach picnic at **La Focacceria Dome ❶**, V. Dante Alghieri, 18, serving fresh *focaccia, farinata,* and pizza (€1-2) in heaping portions. (Open daily 9am-1am. Cash only.) Those staying for dinner shouldn't miss **Da Rino ❸**, V. Garibaldi, 10, for a family-style Ligurian feast where the pasta tastes great and the fish (€12) is always fresh. (☎328 38 90 350. *Primi* €6-8.50, *secondi* €10-12.50. Cover

€1.50. Open daily 7:30-10pm. Cash only.) Finally, **Ostello Ospitalia del Mare ❷**, V. San Nicolo, 1, is the perfect option for an overnight stay and only a 5min. walk from the beach. A converted hospital, all of the spacious and spotless rooms have baths. (☎0187 80 25 62; www.ospitaliadelmare.it. Breakfast, sheets, towel, and shower included. 4-bed dorm €25, 6-bed dorm €22.50, 8-bed dorm €20. Internet access €5 per hr. Reception 8am-1pm and 3pm-11pm. No curfew, but last train from Cinque Terre arrives at 12:35am. 4-bed dorm €25, 6-bed dorm €22.50, 8-bed dorm €20. MC/V.)

LA SPEZIA   ☎0187

Though the laid back beach ambience of the Cinque Terre is only a short ride away, La Spezia's fast-paced urban atmosphere seems like another world. Bombarded heavily during WWII because of its naval base and artillery, La Spezia has since evolved into a commercial port that's proud of its nautical history. Situated in Il Golfo dei Poeti (The Gulf of Poets), the town makes a great starting point for daytrips to the small fishing village of Porto Venere, the beach resorts of San Terenzo and Lerici, and the beautiful coves of Fiascherino; it's also an unavoidable stopover to and from Cinque Terre. Though La Spezia boasts none of the majestic architecture or cobblestone passageways that grace some neighboring villages, it does have affordable lodgings, lots of shopping, and a few fascinating museums.

▄ TRANSPORTATION. La Spezia lies on the Genoa-Pisa **train** line. Tickets from Vernazza cost €1.35. The station is included in the Cinque Terre Card, which allows unlimited train use between destinations. **Navigazione Golfo dei Poeti,** V. D. Minzoni, 13 (☎0187 73 29 87; www.navigazionegolfodeipoeti.it), runs **ferries** to each of the Cinque Terre towns (one-way €11; M-Sa round-trip €19, Su €22); Portovenere (€3.50, round-trip €6); Capraia (3hr., July-Aug. round-trip €40). Call ahead for schedule. For a **taxi,** call ☎0187 52 35 23 or go to the train station.

▄▟ ORIENTATION AND PRACTICAL INFORMATION. From the **train station,** turn left and walk down **Via Fiume,** which goes through **Piazza S. Bon** before turning into **Via Prione,** the city's main drag. Continue on V. Prione until it hits **Via Chiodo. Via Mazzini** runs parallel to V. Chiodo, closer to the water. The main **tourist office** is at V. Mazzini, 45. (☎0187 77 09 00. Open M-Sa 9:30am-1pm and 3:30pm-7pm, Su 9:30am-1pm.) Another **branch** is outside the train station (open daily 8am-8pm). **CTS,** V. Sapri, 86, helps with ferry tickets (to Greece and Sardinia), student airfares, and car rentals. (☎0187 75 10 74. Open M-Sa 9:30am-12:30pm and 3:30-7:30pm. AmEx/MC/V.) **Farmacia Alleanza,** V. Chiodo, 145, posts a list of late-night pharmacies. (☎0187 73 80 07. Open daily 8:30am-12:30pm and 4-8pm. AmEx/MC/V.) In case of **emergency,** dial ☎113, or contact the **police** at ☎112 or an **ambulance** at ☎118. **Phone Center,** P. S. Bon, 1, has **Internet** and **Western Union** services. (☎0187 77 78 05; fax 0187 71 21 11. €4 per hr. Open M-Sa 9:15am-12:30pm and 3-10pm, Su 3-10pm.) For **currency exchange,** try **Banca Carige,** C. Cavour, 154. (☎0187 73 43 69. Open M-F 8:20am-1:20pm and 2:30-4pm.) There's also an **ATM** outside. The **post office** is a few blocks from the port at P. Verdi and offers **currency exchange.** (☎0187 79 61. Open M-Sa 8am-6:30pm.) **Postal Code:** 19100.

▄▟ ACCOMMODATIONS AND FOOD. Close to the port, try the family-run **Albergo Il Sole ❸**, V. Cavalotti, 31. English-speaking staff keeps basic but spacious rooms decorated in shades of yellow and rose with large windows. (☎0187 73 51 64; www.albergoilsole.com. Breakfast €4. Singles €25-36; doubles €39-45, with bath €47-55, triples €53-61, quads €66-92. AmEx/MC/V.) The next street over, **Albergo Teatro ❸**, V. Carpenino, 31, near the Teatro Civico, offers six comfortable rooms with TV and some with bath. (☎/fax 0187 73 13 74. Singles €28; doubles €45, with bath €60. Extra bed additional 50% of cost.) If you're willing to splurge, try the luxurious **Hotel Firenze & Continentale ❺**, V. Paleocapa, 7, across from the train station. The hotel retains a *fin-de-siècle* look, with marble floors and plush sitting areas. The huge rooms are decorated with rugs and wood furniture, and all have bath, A/C, TV, and phone; some have a balcony, too. (☎0187 71 32 00; www.hotelfirenzecontinentale.it. Wheelchair accessible. Hearty buffet breakfast included. Singles €68-88; doubles €90-125; triples €122-179. AmEx/MC/V.)

Reasonably priced *trattorie* line V. del Prione. For the town's biggest selection of groceries and fresh produce, try **Supermercato Spesafacile,** V. Colombo, 101-107. (Open daily 8:30am-1pm and 4:15-8pm. MC/V.) Across the street, the new **◪Osteria Duccio ❷**, V. Roselli, 17, off V. del Prione, serves the eclectic creations of owner Luccio, who hand picks his ingredients every day. (☎0187 25 86 02. *Primi* €6.50-7.50, *secondi* €7-10. 3-course lunch *menù* €10. Cover at dinner €1. Open Tu-Su noon-2:30pm and 7:45-11:45pm.) **La Pia ❶**, V. Magenta, 12, also off of V. del Prione, is a favorite for hot, cheesy *focaccia* and *farinata* and is a cheaper alternative to the posh cafes lining the main streets. Dine in casually, or take a heaping plate to go. (☎0182 73 99 99. Most items €2.80-4.50. Open M-Sa 8am-11pm. AmEx/MC/V.) **Osteria con Cucina all'Inferno ❷**, V. L. Costa, 3, off P. Cavour, has been serving Ligurian specialities since 1905. Try the low-ceilinged Osteria for *acciughe ripiene* (stuffed anchovies; €7.50) and hearty *mesciua* (€4.50), a thick soup of beans, corn-meal, olive oil, and pepper. (☎0187 29 458. *Primi* €4.50-6.50, *secondi* €5-8.50. Open M-Sa 12:15-2:30pm and 7:30-10:30pm. Cash only.) The elegant **Trattoria Dino ❹**, V. Cadorna, 18, near the park off V. Chiodo, serves pasta and fresh fish to a more upscale clientele. (☎0187 73 54 35. *Primi* €10-12, *secondi* €14-16. Open Tu-Sa noon-2:45pm and 7:30-10:30pm, Su noon-2:45pm. AmEx/MC/V.)

◨ SIGHTS. La Spezia is one of Italy's classiest and cleanest ports, with palms lining the Morin promenade, sailors strolling along shop-lined **Via del Prione,** and parks brimming with citrus trees. Many of its museums highlight the town's marine history. There is a cumulative three-day pass (€12) for all of La Spezia's museums, available at any museum in the city. The unique collection of the **Museo Navale,** in P. Chiodo next to the entrance of the **Arsenale Militare Marittimo** (Maritime Military Arsenal) built in 1860-1865, features diving suits dating from WWII, carved prows of 19th-century ships (including a huge green salamander), gargantuan iron anchors, and tiny replicas of Egyptian, Roman, and European vessels. (☎0187 78 30 16. Open M-Sa 8am-6:45pm, Su 8am-1pm. €1.55.) The **Museo Amadeo Lia,** V. Prione, 234, in the ancient church and convent of the Friars of St. Francis from Paola, houses a collection of 13th-through 17th-century paintings, including Raphael's *San Martino and the Beggar* in **Room 6.** Find Titian's *Portrait of a Gentleman* and Bellini's *Portrait of an Attorney* in **Room 7.** (☎0187 73 11 00; www.castagna.it/mal. Open Tu-Su 10am-6pm. Last ticket sold at 5:30pm. €6, students €4.) Next door, the **Museo del Sigillo,** V. del Priore, 236, in the Palazzina delle Arti, displays a large collection of civic seals and their wax impressions. Many of the pieces, which come from all over the globe, are tiny and carved with great skill. (☎0187 77 85 44; www.castagna.it/museodelsigillo. Open Tu 4-7pm, W-Su 10am-noon and 4-7pm. €3.) The **Museo Entografico,** V. Prione, 156 has an important collection of traditional costumes, furniture, jewelry, and pottery from the surrounding region. (☎/fax 0187 75 85 70. Open F-Su 10am-12:30pm and 4-7pm. €3.)

RIVIERA DI PONENTE

FINALE LIGURE   ☎ 019

A plaque on the base of a statue along the promenade claims that Finale Ligure (pop. 12,000) is the place for *"il riposo del popolo,"* or "the people's rest." Whether *riposo* involves bodysurfing in the choppy waves, browsing chic boutiques, or scaling Finalborgo's looming 15th-century Castello di San Giovanni, there are countless ways to pass the time in this sleepy town.

▐ TRANSPORTATION

The **train station** is in P. V. Veneto. Call ☎019 27 58 777 or 019 89 20 21 for timetables. Trains run to Genoa (1hr., every hr. 5:37am-3:31pm, €4) and Ventimiglia (30min., every hr. 6:40am-11:14pm, €4.90). Most trains to Genoa stop at Savona and most trains to Ventimiglia stop at San Remo. The ticket office is open daily 5:55am-7:10pm. **ACT buses** depart from the front of the train station to Finalborgo (5min., every 20min., €1) and Savona. Catch the **SAR bus** for Borgo Verezzi (10min., 8 per day, €1) across the street. Buy tickets at *tabaccherie*. For taxis, call **Radio Taxi** ☎019 69 23 33 or 019 69 23 34. For a **bike rental,** check out **Oddonebici**, V. Colombo, 20. (☎019 69 42 15; www.oddonebici.com. Bikes €15 per day. Open Tu-Sa 8:30am-12:30pm and 3:30-8pm, Su 10am-12:30pm and 4:30-8pm. MC/V.)

◤◪ ⁊ ORIENTATION AND PRACTICAL INFORMATION

The city is divided into three sections: **Finalpia** to the east, **Finalmarina** in the center, and **Finalborgo,** the old city, inland to the northwest. The train station and most of the listings below are in Finalmarina. The main street winds through the town between the station and **Piazza Vittorio Emanuele II,** changing its name from **Via de Raimondi** to **Via Pertica** to **Via Garibaldi.** From P. V. Emanuele, **Via della Concezione** runs parallel to the shore. To reach the old city, turn left from the station, cross under the tracks, and keep walking left on **Via Domenico Bruneghi** for about 10min.

The **IAT Tourist Office** is at V. S. Pietro, 14. From the station, walk straight to the water, and then take the only left. Signs lead the way. (☎019 68 10 19; www.inforiviera.it. Open M-Sa 9am-12:30pm and 3-6:30pm, Su 9am-noon; closed Su in winter.) **Currency exchange** is available at **Banca Carige,** V. Garibaldi, 4, at the corner of P. V. Emanuele. (€4.13 service charge. Open M-F 8:20am-1:20pm and 2:30-4pm. **ATM** outside.) In an **emergency,** call the **police,** V. Brunenghi, 67 (☎112 or ☎019 69 26 66) or an **ambulance** (☎118). **Farmacia della Marina,** is at V. Ghiglieri, 2, at the intersection where V. Raimondi becomes V. Pertica, and lists after-hours rotations. (☎019 69 26 70. Open M-Sa 8:30am-12:30pm and 4-8pm. Ring bell for emergencies.) **Internet** access is available at **Net Village Internet Cafe,** V. di Raimondi, 21, across from the train station. (☎019 681 62 83. €2 per 20min., €5.50 per hr. Open daily 8am-10pm.) The **post office** is at V. della Concezione, 29. (☎019 69 04 79. Open M-F 8am-6:30pm, Sa 8am-12:30pm.) **Postal Code:** 17024.

▛ ACCOMMODATIONS AND CAMPING

The youth hostel has the best prices—not to mention the best view. In July and August, it may be the only place that's not booked solid (they don't take reservations). For all other accommodations listed, reservations are strongly recommended. The tourist office can help find rooms for rent in private houses.

▨ **Castello Wuillerman (HI),** V. Generale Caviglia, 46 (☎/fax 019 69 05 15; www.hostelfinaleligure.com). From the train station, turn left on V. Raimondo Pertica, and continue straight until you see signs for "Ostello Gioventu." Turn left at the corner of V. Pertica and V. Alonzo and climb the stairs to the top. The cliffside castle-turned-hostel has locking cabinets in rooms, a beautiful courtyard, Internet (€4.50 per hr.), and a restaurant. Breakfast and sheets included. Laundry €4 per load. Reception 7-10am and 5-10pm. Curfew midnight. HI cardholders only. Dorms €14. MC/V. ❶

▨ **Pensione Enzo,** Gradinata delle Rose, 3 (☎019 69 13 83), halfway up the stairs of G. delle Rose, has amiable owners and a fantastic view. Rooms are clean and spacious. All rooms have bath and TV, some have balcony. Breakfast included. Reserve ahead in summer. Open mid-Mar. to Sept. Doubles €60-70. Cash only. ❸

Albergo Carla, V. Colombo, 44 (☎019 69 22 85; fax 019 68 19 65). Conveniently located on a shady, cobblestoned street across from the seaside walkway. All rooms with bath and phone, some with sea view. Breakfast €4. Small restaurant downstairs also serves lunch and dinner. Singles €35; doubles €48-60. AmEx/MC/V. ❸

Albergo San Marco, V. della Concezione, 22 (☎019 69 25 33). From the train station, walk down V. Saccone and turn left on V. della Concezione. Enter through restaurant. 15 utilitarian rooms have phone, bath, and shower; many have a balcony with sea view. Across the street from the beach. Breakfast included. Open Easter-late Sept. Singles €37-48; doubles €55-61. Prices peak July-Aug. Extra bed €12-15. AmEx/MC/V. ❹

Camping Tahiti, V. Varese (☎/fax 019 60 06 00). From P. V. Veneto take bus for Calvisio. Get off at Bar Paradiso and cross bridge at V. Rossini. Turn left and walk to V. Vanese. Hillside site with 8 terraces, 90 lots, and 360-person capacity. Reception 8am-8pm. Open Easter-Oct. 15. High season €6.50 per person, €5 per tent. Hot showers €0.50. Electricity €2.50. AmEx/MC/V. ❶

Del Mulino (☎019 60 16 69; www.campingmulino.it), on V. Castelli. From the train station, take the Calvisio bus to Boncardo Hotel, then turn left on V.G.F. Orione. Follow signs up the hill. Popular, with sites along a terraced hillside. A 15min. walk from the center of town. Bar, pizzeria, and mini-market. Laundry €5. Reception 8am-8pm. Open Apr.-Sept. €4.50-6.50 per person, €5-7 per tent. Hot showers free. MC/V. ❶

◖ FOOD

Reservations are often helpful for dinner, as restaurants fill quickly. Get basics like sunscreen or bottled water at the **Di per Di Express,** V. Alonzo, 10. (Open M 8:30am-1pm, Tu-Sa 8:30am-1pm and 3:45-7:45pm, Su 9am-1pm. MC/V.)

▨ **Il Dattero,** on the fork where V. Pertica splits into V. Rossi and V. Garibaldi. Decadent flavors and refreshing *granita* come with free toppings. Indulge on *gelato*-filled pastries (€2.20). 2 flavors €1.30. *Granita* €1.60. Open daily 11am-midnight. ❶

Spaghetteria Il Post, V. Porro, 21 (☎019 60 00 95). Follow V. Colombo from the beachfront past P. Cavour. Turn left onto V. Genova, which becomes V. Porro. Try *penne quattro stagioni* (with bacon, mushrooms, tomatoes, artichokes, and mozzarella; €6.50). Lots of vegetarian options. Bring a few friends, as each dish is made for 2. Cover €1. Open Tu-Su 7-10:30pm. Closed the 1st 2 weeks of Mar. ❷

Farinata Vini, V. Roma, 25 (☎019 69 25 62). Small, popular, self-proclaimed *trattoria alla vecchia maniera* (old-school trattoria) serves up great seafood and pasta dishes. Menu changes daily. *Primi* €6-9, *secondi* €8-14. (Reservation recommended in summer.) Open M and W-Su 12:30-2pm and 7:30-9:30pm. AmEx/MC/V. ❸

Sole Luna, V. Barrili, 31 (☎019 681 61 60). Bikini-clad beachgoers breeze in and out for a quick, fresh meal. Try the *farinata* (€1.50), a pie made from chickpeas and filled with meat and vegetables. Pizza slices €1.50-1.80. Grilled *focaccia panini* €1.50-3. Savory crepes €3. Open daily 10am-8pm. Cash only. ❶

Bei Gisela, V. Colombo, 2 (☎019 69 52 75), at the intersection of V. Alonzo and V. Colombo. Sleek furniture and a stone-inlaid floor give this restaurant a chic ambience. Scrumptious homemade desserts (€5). *Primi* €5.50-12, *secondi* €10-16. Wine bar Th 7pm-12:30am. Open M-Tu and Th-Su 12:30-2:30pm and 7:30-10:30pm. ❸

🜨 SIGHTS

Enclosed within ancient walls, **Finalborgo,** the historical quarter of Finale Ligure, is a 1km walk or 2min. bus ride up V. Bruneghi from the station. Past the **Porta Reale,** its main entrance, the Chiostro di Santa Caterina houses the **Museo Civico del Finale,** dedicated to Ligurian history. (☎019 69 00 20. Open in summer Tu-Su 9am-noon and 3:30-5pm; in winter Tu-Sa 9am-noon and 2:30-5pm, Su 9am-noon. Free.) Enjoy the town's medieval architecture and quiet ambience while sipping a *caffè* in one of many small *piazze*. In P. Aycardi, the formerly illustrious but still brightly painted **Teatro Aycardi,** now closed and vacant, stands as a reminder of Finalborgo's importance in days past; from the mid-1400s to the early 18th century, it was capital of the Marquisate of Del Carretto. Up a tough but fulfilling 1km bumpy cobblestone path, ▓**Castel Govone,** behind the larger ruins of San Giovanni, lends a spectacular view of Finale. The trail starts next to the post office in P. del Tribunale, at the opposite end of town from Pta. Reale. For further rock climbing in the area, the **Mountain Shop,** P. Garibaldi, 12, in Finalborgo, provides maps and necessary gear. (☎019 69 02 08. Open Tu-Su 9am-1pm and 4-8pm. MC/V.)

The picturesque towns surrounding Finale Ligure beckon with medieval mystery. SAR buses run to the villages of **Borgio** and **Verezzi** (every 15min. 6:35am-1:41am, €1.70 round-trip). Above the beaches of the new part of Borgio are the ancient churches and narrow roadways of its older center. From the bus stop in Borgio, turn left and head up V. Nazario Sauro. Turn left on the cobblestone path, V. Verezzi, that winds its way up the mountain and crosses several times over the roadway until it finally rejoins 100m from the top. The steep climb offers views of the sea and the Riviera coastline. At the end of the 30min. hike, four small *piazze* connected by winding footpaths are surrounded by medieval houses. It is possible to reach the lowest *piazza* by SAR bus, from the stop to the left around the corner from the **tourist office,** V. Matteoti, 158. (☎019 61 04 12. Open in summer daily 9am-12:30pm and 3:30-7pm.) The lowest of the *piazze* fill up on weekends in July and August, when the annual **Festival Teatrale** holds live theatrical performances by national touring companies. After dark in Verezzi, do not take a shortcut down the hillside— guard dogs run rampant off the main road. For a longer hike crossing Mt. Caprazoppa, take a 3km trail from Finalborgo to Verezzi. Trails are not clearly marked, so be sure to inquire at the Mountain Shop for info and safety tips.

🜨 🎵 BEACHES AND ENTERTAINMENT

Spray-painted on the inner wall of the tunnel that leads to the prime **free beach** in Finale Marina is *"Voglio il sole/Cerco nuova luce/nella konfusione"* (I want the sun/I look for new light/in the confusion). Those who empathize with the graffiti poet have come to the right place. Unfortunately, people tend to cram in like sardines on this narrow free strip. More adventurous souls should walk about 15min. east along V. Aurelia and through the first tunnel to another beach, cradled by overhanging cliffs, a better spot to sunbathe away from the crowds.

Popular among locals and tourists, **Pilade**, V. Garibaldi, 67, features live music on some Friday nights, ranging from blues to soul. Posters of old jazz legends fill the walls and an older, calmer crowd fills the tables, ordering drinks (€5) or beer (€3 and up). During the week, diners nod their heads in unison to rock and Italian techno, eyes glazed over from one too many Peronis. Pizza (€1.50-1.80 per slice), burgers, salads, crepes (dinner only; €2.60-6.20), and delicious *panini* (€2.60-3) are available for a sit-down meal or takeout. (☎019 69 22 20. Open daily 10am-2am. Closed Th in winter.) As the sun sets, it's easy to find more nightlife—just follow the crowds to the waterfront, where bathhouses turn into dance parties and bars fill up with dehydrated sunbathers along V. della Concezione.

ALASSIO   ☎0182

Sun-splashed Alassio has attracted high-class Italians and dedicated beachgoers to its sparkling seas for over a century. Though its residential population is only about 13,000, the throng of tourists that descends upon the town each summer can make it seem three times as large. Vacationers come for the town's fine white-sand beaches, excellent cuisine and nightlife, or a case of the town's signature Baci chocolate pastries. Even with these luxuries, Alassio maintains a cheery, unpretentious character that makes it distinctly youth-friendly.

▌ TRANSPORTATION

The **train station** is between V. Michelangelo and V. G. Mazzini. Call ☎89 20 21 for schedules. **Trains** run to: Finale Ligure (25min., every hr., €2.80); Genoa (1½hr., every hr., €5.70); Milan (3½hr., every 3hr., €12-20); Ventimiglia (1½hr., every 15min., €4.20). **Luggage storage** is available daily 2-6pm to the left of the main exit. The ticket office is open daily 6am-7:15pm. **ACT buses** stop every 20min. along V. Aurelia. For **bike rental,** stop by **Ricciardi**, C. Dante Alighieri, 144, near the train station. (☎0182 64 05 55. Bikes €5 per hr., €15 per day. Open M-Sa 9:30am-12:30pm and 3:30-7:30pm, Su 10am-12:30pm and 4:30-7pm.)

▰✴▨ ORIENTATION AND PRACTICAL INFORMATION

Alassio is a small, navigable town with activity centering around the pedestrian walkways running along its seacoast. Head straight out of the **train station** and turn right on **Via G. Mazzini** in front of the park. V. G. Mazzini forms one part of the city's main street, collectively referred to as **Via Aurelia**. Three streets, V. Aurelia, **Corso Dante Alighieri**, and **Via Vittorio Veneto**, run parallel to the sea. Follow V. Aurelia from the train station to the second stoplight and turn left on **V. Diaz**, crossing over C. Dante Alighieri. Continue straight to arrive at the center of the seafront.

The **APT Tourist Office** is at P. della Libertà, 1. From the train station, turn left on V. G. Mazzini. The staff offers useful **maps** and brochures, and books accommodations. (☎0182 64 70 27; www.inforiviera.it. Open M-Sa 9am-12:30pm and 3-6:30pm, Su 9am-12:30pm.) You can **exchange currency** at **Unicredit Banca**, V. Gibb, 14, two blocks left on V. Aurelia from the train station. (Open M-F 8:20am-1:20pm and 2:35-4:05pm, Sa-Su 10am-12:30pm and 4:30-7pm. AmEx/MC/V. 24hr. **ATM** available.) Open M-Sa 9am-12:30pm and 3:30-7:30pm. In case of emergency, phone the **police**, V. Aurelia, 19 (☎113) or and **ambulance** (☎118). **Farmacia Nazionale**, V. V. Veneto, 3 (☎0182 64 06 06), is open daily 8:30am-12:30pm and 3:30-7:30pm. **Internet** access is available at **Link**, V. Da Vinci, 153. (☎0182 64 80 82. €5 per hr. Open M-F 8:30am-12:30pm and 2:30-7:30pm.) The **post office** is at V. Aurelia, 59. (☎0182 64 62 11. Open M-F 8am-1:15pm, Sa 8am-12:30pm.) **Postal Code:** 17021.

THE SWEETEST KISS

Pasquale Balzola Jr. is the owner of Balzola Pasticceria in Alassio, the store that invented and patented the famous Baci "kisses." These chocolate pastries consist of two teardrop-shaped cakes sandwiching a creamy dark chocolate and hazelnut filling.

On the beginnings: My grandfather invented [*Baci di Alassio*] around 1900 when he came here from Turin. He thought Alassio was a place for tourism because we have the sea, and he thought that people would buy [*Baci*] as a souvenir.

On his father: My father worked 10 years after my grandfather as the baker for King Vittorio Emanuele III, the King of Italy. He was very famous in all of Europe.

On making a kiss: They are difficult to make...The problem is to cook them leaving the inside very soft. All the ingredients are natural—no preservatives—and they are handmade, each one. They are not cakes, they are not chocolates, they are really a specialty.

On acclaim: In Italy there is an association of historical hotels and restaurants, and we are in it. Only 130 places are featured in all of Italy. When people go to Rome they [visit] St. Peter's; go to Pisa, [visit] the tower; when they come to Alassio, they [buy *Baci*].

On the future: I have two boys and two girls; surely the name will stay in the family—it's tradition.

(P. Matteotti, 26. ☎0182 64 02 09. Open daily 8am-4pm.)

▮ ACCOMMODATIONS AND CAMPING

Rooms disappear quickly in this tiny, lively resort town, so reserve early. Though beachfront views come at hefty prices, high tourist appeal means almost all receptionists speak some English. The tourist office offers a free booking service. The quiet **Hotel Villa Claudia ❸**, C. Dante Alighieri, 83, has airy rooms with a balcony kept by cheerful young staff. Turn left on V. Volta from V. G. Mazzini, then right on C. Dante. (☎0182 64 04 94; www.hotelvillaclaudia.com. Breakfast included. Singles €35; doubles €70; triples €95; quads €115. Cash only.) **Hotel La Balnearia ❹**, V. V. Veneto, 105, is full of beachside charm, with a breezy lobby and courteous staff. From the train station, turn right on V. G. Mazzini, left on V. Torini and right on V. V. Veneto. (☎0182 64 01 60; fax 64 62 55. Breakfast included. Singles €50-68; doubles €60-120. Prices peak in July and Aug. Cash only.) To reach **Hotel Panama ❸**, V. Brennero, 27, from the train station, turn right on V. G. Mazzini and left on V. Torini. Follow to the sea, turn right on V. V. Veneto, which becomes V. Brennero. A private beach and cheery dining room enliven this hotel. All rooms have TV and phone, some have shower and bath. (☎0182 64 00 395 or 0182 64 59 16; www.panamavacanze.com. Breakfast included. Storage lockers available. Singles and doubles €20-70. Full pension €36-62. Prices peak July-Aug. AmEx/MC/V.) **Camping La Vedetta Est ❶**, V. Giancardi, 11, is 1.5km from Alassio. From V. Mazzini, take bus toward Albenga. Bus stops just in front, but still on the highway, so be careful. Bungalows and tent sites overlook the sea. (☎0182 64 24 07; fax 0182 64 24 27. Open daily 8:30am-12:30pm and 3-10pm. €6-8 per person, bungalows €30-145, €24-32 for 2 people with car and tent. Cash only.)

▮ FOOD

More pizzerias and *gelaterie* per capita than seem possible crowd Alassio's streets. Don't leave without sampling the famed *Baci di Alassio* (fudge pastry). There is a **STANDA** supermarket at V. San Giovanni Bosco, 36/66, part of V. Aurelia. (Open daily 8am-8pm. AmEx/MC/V.)

▨Osteria Mezzaluna ❸, V. Vico Berno, 6, sits on the waterfront, with an intimate Spanish-influenced atmosphere and Mediterranean cuisine. Try their unique take on open-faced *panini*. Live music nightly. (☎0182 64 03 87; www.mezzaluna.it. *Secondi* €4.50-10. Salads €6.50-8.50. Open daily

7:30pm-2am. AmEx/MC/V.) After 25 years in business, the Sicilian wizards at **Gelateria Acuvea ❶**, P. Matteotti, 3, have the whole town in their power. While waiting for a chocolate *granita* (€1.50) or creamy *gelato* (2 scoops €1.50), watch flavors being hand-churned. Pay at the register and take your token to the counter. (☎0182 66 00 60. Open daily 8am-2am. Cash only.) **Pizzeria Italia ❷**, Passeggiata Toti, 19, serves ultra-thin pizzas with a smile just steps from the beach. The *boscaiola* (grilled eggplant, *proscuitto*, and fresh mozzarella; €7.50) packs a flavorful punch. (☎0182 64 40 95. *Primi* €5-9, *secondi* €9-15.50. Cover €1. Open daily May-Aug. noon-3:30pm and 7pm-6am. Closed Sept.-Apr. AmEx/MC/V.) The waterfront patio at **Ristorante Sail Inn ❸**, V. Brennero, 30, is perfect for a classy, fish-centered feast. High quality, generous portions, and hefty prices. (☎0182 64 02 32. *Primi* €9-14, *secondi* €10-20. Open Tu-Su for lunch and dinner. AmEx/MC/V.)

ℜ𝔇 **THE REAL DEAL**. A casual day at the beach can quickly turn into a major expense if you're not careful. Most stretches of sand are privately owned by *bagni*, restaurants or bars that rent out chairs, umbrellas, and changing rooms at rates that can soar up to €20 per day. Sacrifice a little comfort and spread your towel out on a public beach. It may be more crowded, but you'll still soak up the sun and your wallet will thank you. *—Jen Rugani*

👁 🏃 SIGHTS AND NIGHTLIFE

Alassio has kilometers of pristine, sandy **beaches** stretching in both directions down the coast, leaving little reason to venture inland. There are a few free public beaches about a 15min. walk down the beach, but if central location and lively activity are a priority then its worth the €3 or so for a chair and umbrella. Take a short stroll down the beach to the east to join the throng of local boys and older fishermen at the **pier,** a favorite spot for loafing, line-casting, and relaxed sea-gazing. Unfortunately, jumping—once popular—is now prohibited.

A 30min. walk or a short bus ride toward Andorra leads to **Laigueglia**, a fishing village with colorful houses, tiny *piazze*, and twisting stone streets. A tourist office at Via Roma, 2, right as you enter town, offers maps and good information about the entire region. (Open Tu-Sa 9am-12:30pm and 3-6:30pm, Su 9am-noon.) A short walk uphill from the beach leads to the **Chiesa di Santa Maria** in P. San Pietro, a lovely cathedral with towering, frescoed domes and walls covered in soft paintings. (Open daily until 6pm. Mass Su 8, 9:30, 11am, and 5:30pm.)

Stoked by tourists and an influx of youth from nearby towns, Alassio hops at night. At **🏖Zanzibar Cocktail and Disco Bar,** V. V. Veneto, 143, young crowds pack every corner while the bar is as full of dancers as it is of liquor. (☎0182 64 34 72; www.alassiovirtuale.com. Liquor and cocktails €2.50-6.50. Beer on tap €3. No cover, but 1-drink mandatory. Happy hour 9-11pm. Open nightly 9pm-5am. Cash only.) Decorated with red lanterns, **Tokai Bar,** V. V. Veneto, 151, draws an international crowd for beachfront refreshments and animated conversation. (☎0182 64 00 25. Open M-Tu and Th-Su 11pm-3am. Cash only.) Local favorite **Bar Cabaret,** V. Aurelia, 58, has live music and a raucous crowd that sings along. Grab a pint (€3-7) and one of many *panini* named after classic rock legends. (☎347 961 53 72. *Panini* €3-5. Open daily 9:30pm-3am. Cash only.) Trendy **Caffe Roma,** V. Cavour, 1, off C. Dante Alighieri, is the new place to see and be seen among the Euro-chic. All-white decor adorns the two-story lounge, and a young and hip crowd relaxes on plush couches. (Cocktails €4-7. Open Tu-Su noon-4am.)

SAN REMO ☎0184

Once a glamorous retreat for Russian nobles, czars, *literati*, and artists, San Remo is now the largest casino resort town on the Italian Riviera. Recently it served as the backdrop for Matt Damon's murderous machinations in *The Talented Mr. Ripley*. San Remo upholds its glamorous profile with finely dressed couples and bikini-clad women gambling along the palm-lined promenade of Corso G. Matteotti. The many boutiques and upscale shops of the city offer plenty of opportunities for big winners to become big spenders. Upholding the reputation of the Riviera dei Fiori (Riviera of Flowers), San Remo blooms with carnations year-round. Adding to the musical click of dice and chink of poker chips, the town explodes each summer with fireworks and international jazz competitions.

▐ TRANSPORTATION

The **train station** faces C. F. Cavalotti at V. C. Pisacane. **Trains** run to: Genoa (2½hr., every hr. 4:46am-10:41pm, €7.35); Milan (4¼hr., every 2hr. 5:07am-7:17pm, €13.22); and Ventimiglia (15min., every 30min. 6:37am-12:31am, €1.45). Prices listed are the minimum and vary seasonally. The ticket office is open daily 7am-10pm. For a **Radio Taxi,** call ☎0184 54 14 54.

✳❷ ORIENTATION AND PRACTICAL INFORMATION

The city is comprised of three main streets that run east-west, parallel to the beach. The train station faces **Corso F. Cavalotti.** To get to the center of town, turn right on C. F. Cavalotti. Cross **Rondo Giuseppe Garibaldi** (a rotary) and veer left down **Corso Giuseppe Garibaldi.** At **Piazza Colombo,** either turn left down **Via Manzoni** to reach the intersection of **Via Roma** and **Via Nino Bixio,** or continue straight, bearing left while crossing the *piazza* onto swanky **Corso G. Matteotti,** which leads to the *lungomare*. The tourist-free old town, **La Pigna,** is uphill from P. Colombo.

Tourist Office: APT, V. Nuvoloni, 1 (☎0184 590 59; www.sanremonet.com). From P. Colombo, go left onto C. Matteotti and follow to the end. The office is on the corner on the right. Staff supplies **maps** and brochures. Open M-Sa 8am-7pm, Su 9am-1pm.

Bank: Banca Intesa, V. Roma, 62 (☎0184 59 23 11). Offers **currency exchange** and **ATM.** Open M-F 8:30am-1:30pm and 2:45-4:15pm, Sa 8:30am-1pm.

Bookstore: Libreria Beraldi, V. Cavour, 8 (☎0184 54 11 11). Reasonable collection of best sellers in English, French, German, and Spanish. Considerable travel section. Open daily 9am-noon and 3:30-7:30pm. MC/V.

Laundromat: Blu Acquazzura, V. A. Volta, 131 (☎34 04 17 84 80). Continue from Rondo Garibaldi along V. A. Volta for 50m. Self-service. Wash €5, dry €5 per 7kg; wash €7, dry €7 per 16kg. Open daily 6am-7:30pm.

Emergency: ☎118. **Police:** ☎113.

Pharmacy: Farmacia Centrale, C. Matteotti, 190 (☎0184 50 90 65). After-hours rotation posted outside. Open M-Sa 8:30am-8:30pm.

Hospital: Ospedale Civile, V. G. Borea, 56 (☎0184 53 61).

Internet Access: Mailboxes, Etc., C. Cavallotti, 86 (☎0184 59 16 73). €4 per 30min., €7.50 per hr. Photocopier and fax also available. Open M-F 9am-6:30pm. AmEx/MC/V.

Post Office: V. Roma, 156. Open M-Sa 8am-6:30pm. **Postal Code:** 18038.

▐ ACCOMMODATIONS

San Remo enjoys a high standard of accommodation; even one-star hotels tend to be clean and comfortable.

Terminus Metropolis, V. Roma, 8 (☎0184 57 71 10). Head down C. Matteotti from P. Colombo. Turn left down on V. Gaudio and right on V. Roma. The hotel is 2 blocks from the sea. Old-world elegance down to the last detail—antique furniture and decorative fireplaces. Breakfast €5. Singles €30; doubles €45, with bath €50; triples €55. Prices €10-15 higher in Aug. Cash only. ❸

Albergo Al Dom, C. Mombello, 13, 2nd fl. (☎0184 50 14 60). From the train station, turn left off C. Matteotti on C. Mombello; on the left after V. Roma, in the city center. Ring bell to enter. Rooms, all with bath and TV, are furnished by friendly owners. Comfortable sitting room has TV a. Breakfast €5. Singles €25-30; doubles €50-60. ❸

Hotel Sorriso, C. Raimondo, 73 (☎0184 50 03 56; www.soloalberghi.com/hotelsorriso). From the train station, turn right on C. F. Cavalotti and left on V. Fiume. Turn right on C. Orazio Raimondo. Larger hotel with in-room TVs and showers. English-speaking staff is happy to point the way to nearby dining and entertainment options. Breakfast included. Singles €40; doubles €60. AmEx/MC/V. ❸

Hotel Arenella, C. Raimondo, 2, 2nd fl. (☎0184 50 36 39; paginegialle.it/arenella). About 50m past Hotel Sorriso, on the left down a small flight of stairs. Ring bell to enter. Twelve small rooms have private bath and TV. Located just steps away from the public beach. Breakfast €5. Singles €30; doubles €45. AmEx/MC/V. ❸

Hotel Graziella, Rondo Garibaldi, 2 (☎0184 571 031; fax 57 00 43). Two minutes from the train station. Turn right on C. F. Cavalotti, then right around Rondo Garibaldi. Hotel is set back from the road in a villa with a quiet private garden. Elegant rooms with high ceilings and private balconies. All with TV and phone, most with A/C. Breakfast €5. Singles €55; doubles €70. Prices €10-15 higher per person in Aug. AmEx/MC/V. ❹

▶ FOOD

Amid San Remo's wealth of pizzerias and pricey restaurants are some unique, affordable dining options. Try *sardinara*, a local *focaccia*-like specialty topped with tomato sauce, herbs, and olives. Buy basics at **Soft IF Discount** supermarket in P. Eroi. (Open M-F 8:15am-1pm and 4:30-7:30pm, Sa 8:15am-7:45pm, Su 8:30am-1pm. MC/V.) The huge **indoor market,** the Mercato Ortofruitticolo, in neighboring P. Mercato, sells fresh produce, meat, and bread. (Open daily 6am-6:30pm.)

Urbicia Vivas, P. dei Dolori, 5/6 (☎0184 75 55 66; www.urbiciavivas.com), in a charming square in the old city. From V. Palazzo, turn left on V. Cavour and walk through the archway. Restaurant is in the first *piazza*. Join the locals for sumptuous fish dishes and delicious homemade pasta at this snug family-run *trattoria*. *Primi* €5-10, *secondi* €6-12. Open daily 8am-3pm and 7pm-midnight. AmEx/MC/V. ❷

Vin D'Italia, C. Mombello, 3 (☎0184 59 17 47). Family-friendly, comfortable atmosphere with stone walls and lots of wine. Best *sardinara* (€0.80) in town, hot from a grand wood-burning oven. *Primi* and *secondi* €5-12. Open M-Sa noon. MC/V. ❸

Trattoria A Cuvèa, C. S. Garibaldi, 110 (☎0184 50 34 98). Follow C. Cavalotti away from the train station. Quality cuisine served in this hole-in-the-wall favored by locals. *Primi* €6-8, *secondi* €8-9. Open daily noon-3:50pm and M-Sa 6pm-midnight. ❷

RistoPizza Grill da Giovanni, V. C. Pesante, 7 (☎0184 50 49 54), off V. XX Settembre. A quiet side street location and laid-back ambience make a nice change of pace from the crowded restaurants by the water. 41 kinds of pizza (€5-8). *Primi* (€5-10.50); *secondi* €7-25. Open M-W and F-Su noon-2:30pm and 7-10:45pm. AmEx/MC/V. ❸

Dick Turpin's, C. N. Sauro, 15 (☎0184 50 34 99). Follow C. N. Sauro to the beach. Something for everyone in a casual atmosphere. Sweet or savory crepes €4.50. Pizza €5-8. Seafood specials €16. Open daily noon-4pm and 7pm-1am. MC/V. ❸

Polleria Gazera, V. Palazzo, 85, in the pedestrian zone. You'll smell it 2 blocks before you see it. There's nothing elegant about hot, juicy spit-roasted chickens (€6.25) and

LIGURIA

roast beef (€2.60 per 100g), but that doesn't stop the crowds. Takeout only. Open M-F 9am-7pm, Sa 9am-1pm. Cash only. ❶

👁 SIGHTS

San Remo has a number of historical treasures. Across the street from the tourist office stands the Byzantine-style, onion-domed Russian Orthodox **Chiesa di Cristo Salvatore.** The simple interior has several gleaming icons and enchanting choral music. (Open Tu-Su 9:30am-12:30pm and 3-6pm. €1 suggested donation.)

Leaving the church, follow C. Matteotti away from the sea, and turn left onto the little V. F. Calvi, which winds its way into P. San Siro. Here looms the 13th-century, Roman-Gothic **Basilica di San Siro,** regarded as the city's most sacred monument. (Open M-Sa 6:45-11:45am and 3-5:45pm, Su 7:15am-noon and 3:30-7pm.) From here, steer through the vendors along the *gelateria*-lined V. Palazzo and turn left on V. Cavour to **La Pigna,** San Remo's historical town, which most tourists miss entirely. Narrow streets are crowded with tiny medieval churches connected by secret underground passageways. The streets can be confusing; be sure to bring a map. From La Pigna, follow the tree-lined road upward to P. Assunta, is the elaborate 🔲**Il Santuario della Madonna della Costa.** This 17th-century monument features a high dome covered in frescoes and twisting rose marble columns. The *Madonna and Child* painting above the altar by Vilo di Voltiri dates to the late 14th century. (☎0184 50 30 00. Open daily 9am-noon and 3-5:30pm. Modest dress required.)

SAN REMO FOR POCKET CHANGE. Think that in a city which revolves around gambling and shopping you can't find some great deals? Grab some fresh-baked *sardinara* to go at **Vin d'Italia** and take it down to the free public beach at the end of V. Roma. When you're ready to get out of the sun, the climb through old **La Pigna** up to **Il Santuario della Madonna della Costa** ends with incomparable views of the city. After dark, head to **Casino Municipale** for free admission on weeknights—where your money goes after that is up to Lady Luck.

🎵📷 ENTERTAINMENT AND NIGHTLIFE

When darkness hits in San Remo, so do the gamblers who frequent the enormous **Casino Municipale,** C. Inglesi, 18, at the end of C. Matteoti. The casino, built in 1905, is a dazzling example of Belle Epoque architecture. No sandals or shorts are allowed upstairs and a coat and tie are required in winter. Five hundred slot machines clang away on the lower floors, while the swank rooms upstairs host the Riviera's most dapper sip cocktails and hope to win the famed "Mystery Jackpot." (☎0184 59 51; www.casinosanremo.it. Passport required. 18+. Cover F-Su €7.50 for upstairs rooms. Open M-F 2:30pm-2am, Sa-Su 2:30pm-4am.)

After dark, couples meander along the swanky **Corso Matteotti** for *gelato* or liqueurs. Mellow **Sax Pub,** V. Roma, 160, sports jazz-inspired decor and outdoor seating to attract an all-ages crowd. Drinks run €3-5, and a free plate of appetizers comes with drink orders. (☎0184 50 37 43; www.saxpub.it. Open M-Tu and Th-Su 7pm-3am.) Just around the corner from the casino, young crowds huddle around the bar at **Il Teatrino di Mangiafuoco,** V. Roma, 26. Flashy music from the DJ and loud posters on the walls make heads swirl. Pasta dishes and a large drink selection are available. (Open Tu-Su 7pm-2am. MC/V.) Five minutes from the casino is **Pico de Gallo,** Lungomare V. Emanuele, 11/13, where the liquor starts flowing long before sundown. Sip a Caribbean-inspired drink (€5) as you sit on the beach, then return after dark to dance the night away. (☎0184 57 43 45; www.picosanremo.com. *Bagni* open daily 9:30am-5:30pm, nightclub Th-Sa from 10:30pm. MC/V.) On a side street off C. Matteotti, **Zoo Bizarre,** V. Gaudio, 10, is a small trendy spot with electric-green tables and a ceiling plastered with movie posters. The hip crowd kicks off its weekend evenings here around 9pm with drinks (€4-6.50) and freemunchies. (☎0184 50 57 74. Open M-F 8pm-2am, Sa-Su 8pm-3am.)

Alternatives to dice and drinking are harder to come by. **Disco Ninfa Egeria,** C. Matteotti, 178, is the choice destination for those born to dance. The cover is steep, though, and most of the younger crowd heads to other coastal towns. (☎0184 59 11 33. Cover €15. Open Sa from 11pm. Dancing begins well after midnight.) Italian speakers enjoy Italian and dubbed foreign-language films at **Teatro Cinema Ariston,** P. Borea D'Olmo, 33/35, at the upper end of C. Matteotti. (☎0184 50 60 60. Shows nightly from 4-10pm. €4-7.)

In the daytime, speedo- and bikini-clad crowds pack the beach and numerous *bagni* that line the water, so get down there early to snag a sand dune. Most commercial beaches are open 8am-7pm. Lounge chair and umbrella rental run around €3 each per day, but expect to pay a €1-2 entrance fee as well. At the end of June, floats parade around for the annual festival **San Remo in Fiore.** Early July brings the week-long **Fiori di Fuoco** (www.fioridifuoco.it), a famed fireworks competition. The handiwork of masters from around the world fills the skies each night. The **Jazz and Blues Festival,** held in late July and early August, again draws international artists to soothe the sunburned crowds.

BORDIGHERA   ☎0184

When Italian writer Giovanni Ruffini crafted his 1855 melodrama, *Il Dottor Antonio,* he unwittingly laid the foundation for the development of both Bordighera and the Italian Riviera's tourism industry. English travelers were entranced by his story of an ailing English girl miraculously revived by Bordighera's Mediterranean charm. In the early 20th century, residents turned the town into a summer vacation hot spot, constructing seaside hotels and Italy's first tennis courts. Today, the town remains a center of affluence where mansions and palm-dotted roads stretch to the sprawling seaside promenade. It's not surprising that intellectuals and artists like Claude Monet and Louis Pasteur chose the town as their special retreat.

ETRANSPORTATION. The **train station** is in P. Eroi Libertà. Trains run to: Genoa (3hr., 5:34am-10:32pm, €7.35); Milan (4hr., 4:57am-7:07pm, €25); San Remo (10min., every hr. 4:37am-9:56pm, €1.45); and Ventimiglia (10min, every 30min. 6:47am-12:40am, €1). The ticket office is open daily 6:15am-7:45pm. **Riviera Transporte buses** stop every 300m on V. V. Emanuele and run to San Remo and Ventimiglia (M-Sa every 15min., Su every 30min.), on opposite ends of the #2 line. (20min. to both towns, 5:23am-1:18pm, €1.15.) Buy tickets at *tabacchi* on V. V. Emanuele or at the post office.

🔢 ORIENTATION AND PRACTICAL INFORMATION. The bus from Ventimiglia stops on the main street, **Via Vittorio Emanuele,** which runs parallel to the **train station.** Behind the station, the scenic **Lungomare Argentina,** a 2km beach promenade, runs parallel to the *città moderna* (new town), the site of most offices and shops. To get from town to the *lungomare,* walk down V. Noaro or V. Cadorna from V. V. Emanuele and go through the tunnels under the train tracks.

To reach the **tourist office,** V. V. Emanuele, 172, from the train station, walk along V. Roma and turn left on V. V. Emanuele; it's on the right just past the park. (☎0184 26 23 22; fax 26 44 55. Open in summer M-Sa 9am-12:30pm and 3:30-6:30pm.) **Currency exchange** is available at **Banca Intesa,** V. Roma, 4. There is also an **ATM** outside. (☎0184 26 67 77. Open M-F 8:30am-1:30pm and 2:45-4:15pm and Sa 8:30am-noon.) In case of **emergency**, call ☎ 113, an **ambulance** ☎ 118, or the **police**, V. Primo Maggio, 49 (☎ 112 or 0184 26 26 26). **Farmacia Centrale**, V. V. Emanuele, 145, posts a list of rotating after-hours service. (☎ 0184 26 12 46. Open M-F 8:30am-12:30pm and 3:30-7:30pm.) There is a **hospital** at V. Aurelia, 122 (☎ 0184 27 51). The **post office** is at P. Libertà, 5, and has an **ATM** outside. (☎ 0184 26 91 51 or 26 91 31. Open M-F 8am-6:30pm, Sa 8am-12:30pm.) **Postal Code:** 18012.

▐▘▐▌ ACCOMMODATIONS AND FOOD. In the high season, many hotels in Bordighera require that clients accept full or half pension. It is also standard practice to raise prices for guests staying under three days, usually by €5-10. Many large, expensive hotels built in a white fin-de-siècle style line the sea, but the town's few budget options are also pleasant. Walk straight out of the train station onto V. Roma, take a left on V. V. Emanuele, then turn right on V. Lagazzi to find the quiet **▮Villa Miki ❷**, V. Lagazzi, 14. The cheerful, English-speaking owners keep 18 tidy rooms that all have gardenview terraces; some have showers. (☎ 0184 26 18 44. Breakfast included. Singles €24-28; doubles €40-59. Half *pension* €36-48 per person; full *pension* €44-58.) Across from the train station on the left is **Albergo Nagos ❷**, P. Eroi della Libertà, 7, 3rd fl. Ten small rooms are neat and functional. All have sink, toilet, and seaview terrace; three have private shower. (☎ 0184 26 04 57. Singles €25; doubles €40. Half *pension* €33-35 per person; full *pension* €40-45.)

An **outdoor market** on the *lungomare* sells produce and clothing every Thursday from early morning until 1pm. There is an **IEFFE Discount** supermarket at P. Garibaldi, 32-35. (Open M-Sa 8:30am-1pm and 4:30-8pm, Su 8:45am-12:45pm. Reduced winter hours.) There is also a **STANDA** at V. Libertà, 32. (Open M-Sa 8am-8pm, Su 9am-8pm. AmEx/MC/V.) To escape the beach crowds, head to a *trattoria* in the *centro storico* for a traditional meal. **Ristorante la Piazzetta ❷**, P. del Popolo, 13, serves savory Ligurian fare in bountiful portions to a local crowd. Wood-fired pizza (€4.20-8) is the specialty. (☎ 0184 26 04 74. *Tartufo bianco* and other beautifully presented desserts €3.30. *Primi* €6-8, *secondi* €8-15. Open M-Tu and Th-Su noon-2pm and 7-11pm. Cover €1.20. AmEx/MC/V.) Local youths crowd the delicate marble tables of **Creperie-Caffè Giglio ❷**, V. V. Emanuele, 158. A dizzying selection of creative dinner crepes with many vegetarian options (€4.50-6) complement the five-page menu of drinks from the bar (€2-6). Dessert crepes (€4.70-6) are all sweet and satisfying; try one filled with seasonal fruit, sugar, and milk *gelato*. (☎ 0184 26 15 30. Open Tu-Sa 7pm-3am, Su 3pm-3am.) Though a bit on the expensive side, **La Reserve ❹**, V. Aziglio, 20, at the eastern end of the *lungomare*, is a great place to grab a seaside cocktail. The casual bar outside is beach-themed and lively, with appropriate island music blaring. (☎ 0184 26 13 22. *Primi* €10-16, *secondi* €15-30. Open all day; kitchen open 8-10am, 12:30-2pm, and 8-9:30pm.)

▐▌▐▛ SIGHTS AND ENTERTAINMENT. People come to Bordighera to go to the beach. Bordighera's beach is crammed with locals and tourists who arrive early to rent their own lounge chairs, umbrellas, and cabanas from the many *bagni* that line the shoreline (prices usually around €5 for the day). To rent jet skis, windsurf boards, or motorboats, call ☎ 3485 18 38 35. Sunbathers reach right up to the doorstep of the one-time home of the hermit Ampelio, the town's patron saint. His seaside grotto, on the east side of the *lungomare*, is now home to the tiny **Chiesa di Sant'Ampelio**. (Mass Su 10am.) Before Easter each year, the elders and young children of Bordighera prepare *palmureli* (palms) from local palm trees to sell to the Vatican for use during Holy Week; profits benefit the area's poor. Preferring *pesce* to prayers, town fisherman congregate on the rocks below the church.

Continue past the church along V. Arziglia for 1km to the **Giardino Esotico Pallanca** or take a bus from V. V. Emanuele heading in the direction of San Remo and ask the driver to stop at the Giardino. The exotic garden, once open only to scientists, contains over 3000 species of cacti and flora. The brochure's guided walking tour takes about an hour and leads along meandering terraces carved out of the sandstone slopes. (☎0184 26 63 47; www.pallanca.it. Open Tu-Su 9am-12:30pm and 2:30-7pm. €6, groups of more than 10 €5 per person, children under 14 free.) Returning to town, the **park** rising above the Chiesa di Sant'Ampelio offers spectacular sea views and a glimpse of a statue of Queen Margherita Di Saviolo, one of Italy's first queens. The park leads to the town's *centro storico* (historical center), established in 1471, which is often too narrow for cars. Walk through the parking lot at the top of the park and through the archway at the end of V. del Campo to explore the narrow stone streets.

Despite its small size, Bordighera loves revelry. In April each year, the city becomes **La Città dell'Umorismo** (The City of Humor), when comedians, comic-strip artists, and cabaret performers descend upon the town for a celebration of laughter. For 10 days surrounding May 14, the church hosts the **Festa di Sant'Ampelio**, when the whole town gathers in celebration with fireworks, a feast of gastronomic specialties, dancing, and music. Summer brings a host of outdoor festivities, including an international ethnic music festival at the end of July and a series of concerts and plays at the seaside gazebo **Chiosca della Musica**.

🎵 **NIGHTLIFE.** A raucous, mostly male crowd fills the dim interior and outdoor tables at **Graffiti Pub/Risto House**, V. V. Emanuele, 122. Along with a wide choice of liquor (€3) and beer on tap (€2-4), they also serve cheap meals. (☎0184 26 15 90. *Panini* €3-3.70. Open M-Sa 5pm-3am. MC/V.) A classier, more upscale *discoteca*, the **Kursaal Club**, Lungomare Lutazio Catulo, 7, has both live and recorded underground, house, and industrial music. (☎0184 26 46 85. Open Sept.-July F-Su 11pm-5am; Aug. daily 11pm-5am. Younger crowd on Sa, 25+ on F and Su. AmEx/MC/V. Enjoy a plate of Spanish *paella* for 2 (€12-18), share tapas (€3-6), or sip one of many takes on the margarita (€6) at **Chica Loca**, on Lungomare Argentina between the train station and Kursaal. (☎0184 26 46 85. Occasional live music. Open daily July-Sept. noon-3pm and 7pm-6:30am.) Next door, **Il Barretto** is Bordighera's most renowned spot for beachside nightlife—you'll know it when you see it. A town staple since 1960, it has a spring break vibe and a no-frills attitude. Come for a cheap-eating, floor-packing, liquor-saturated good time. (☎0184 26 25 66. Toast and hot-dogs €2-4. Shots of Bacardi €3.50. Open daily noon-3pm and 7pm-6:30am.)

VENTIMIGLIA ☎0184

"Bonjour" is almost as common as "Buongiorno" in this quiet commercial town. Ventimiglia (pop. 25,000) is only a 10min. train ride from the French border, and the coastline between the town and Monaco were part of the same state until Napoleon's 1860 invasion drew clearer boundaries. Better known for its rich history than for its seaside lounging, Ventimiglia lacks the spunk of other more touristy Riviera towns. Instead, the nearby Roman ruins, Romanesque churches, and winding streets of the 11th-century *città alta* bear witness to a vibrant past. French citizens commute for work and frequent the restaurants, but the town still feels distinctly Italian. Ventimiglia is a perfect base for exploring Liguria and France's Côte d'Azur, but don't forget your passport for excursions outside Italy.

▐ TRANSPORTATION

The **train station** (☎0184 90 20 21) is in P. Cesare Battisti. **Trains** run to Genoa (2hr., every 30min. 4:30am-10:25pm, €8.85) and Nice (40min., every hr. 8:50am-7:18pm, €9.40). **Buses** run to regional and local destinations, including San Remo (35min., 4 per hr. 5:30am-1:18am, €1.70) via Bordighera (15min., €1.15). Tickets are available in the *tabacchi* lining V. Cavour and at **Turismo Monte Carlo** (see below), which also provides schedules. The bus stops every 100m along V. Cavour. For **bike rental**, try **Eurocicli**, V. Cavour, 70/B. (☎0184 35 18 79. €1 per hr., €6 per day. Open M-Sa 8:15am-12:30pm and 3-7:30pm. MC/V.) To visit France, take the train or a blue **Riviera Transporte** bus from V. Cavour. Bring your passport.

❄ 🛈 ORIENTATION AND PRACTICAL INFORMATION

From the **train station,** walk straight down **Via della Stazione** to the *centro.* The second crossroad is **Via Cavour,** where V. della Stazione becomes **Corso Repubblica** as it continues toward the waterfront. A footbridge at the end of C. Repubblica leads across a small river to *Ventimiglia Alta,* the medieval section of town. Turn left directly before the footbridge onto **Lungo Roia Giolamo Rossi** to stroll along a restaurant-lined promenade in the newer and commercial part of town. Many restaurants, stores, and sights close on Monday, so be sure to plan accordingly.

Tourist Office: V. Cavour, 61 (☎0184 35 11 83; infoventimiglia@rivieradefiori.org), 5min. from the train station. English- and French-speaking staff offers **maps** and information on local and nearby attractions. A stop here is particularly useful, as many interesting sights lie outside the city proper. Open M-Sa 9am-12:30pm and 3-6:30pm. The travel agency 2 doors down, **Turismo Monte Carlo,** V. Cavour, 57 (☎0184 35 75 77; fax 0184 35 26 21), has **currency exchange** and bus and hotel info. Open M-Sa 9am-12:30pm and 2:30-7pm.

Bank: Banca Intesa, V. Roma, 18/D. In central location with 24hr. **ATM** outside. Other bank services inside. Open M-F 8:30am-1:30pm and 2:45-4:15pm.

Bookstore: Libreria Casella, V. della Stazione, 1/D (☎0184 35 79 00). Books in Italian, French, German, Spanish, and Dutch, with a small English selection. Open M-Sa 9am-12:30pm and 3-7:30pm. MC/V.

Emergency: ☎113. **Police:** V. Aprosio, 12 (☎112 or 0184 23 821). **Ambulance:** ☎118. **Red Cross:** V. Dante Alighieri, 12 (☎0184 23 20 00). **Croce Verde:** P. XX Settembre, 8 (☎0184 35 11 75). For emergencies at night, call ☎800 55 44 00.

Pharmacy: Farmacia Internazionale, V. Cavour, 28/A (☎0184 35 13 00). Open M-F 8:30am-1pm and 3:30-7:30pm, Sa 8:30am-12:30pm. Ask for phone numbers for rotating after-hours service. AmEx/MC/V.

Hospital: Saint Charles (☎0184 27 51), just outside Bordighera.

Internet Access: Mail Boxes, Etc., V. V. Veneto, 4/B (☎0184 23 84 23), just past the Giardini Pubblici from C. Repubblica. Also houses a **Western Union.** 2 computers. €3 per 30min. Open M-F 8:30am-12:30pm and 3-8:30pm.

Post Office: C. Repubblica, 8/C (☎0184 23 63 51), on the right after crossing V. Roma. 24hr. **ATM** outside. Open M-F 8am-6:30pm, Sa 8am-12:30pm. **Postal Code:** 18039.

🏠 ACCOMMODATIONS AND CAMPING

Though Ventimiglia is often less crowded than neighboring cities, it fills up quickly in July and August; reserve ahead in the summer to benefit from the town's budget options and use it as a base for exploring nearby attractions.

🏨 **Calypso Hotel,** V. Matteotti, 8/G (☎0184 35 15 88; www.calypsohotel.it). Large rooms with simple, modern decor. Friendly, English-speaking staff and calm central location. Breakfast included. Parking €8 per day. Reception 7am-midnight. Closed Jan. 15-Feb. 10. Singles €39; doubles €64, with bath €76; triples €85/104. AmEx/MC/V. ❸

🏨 **Camping Roma,** V. Freccero, 9 (☎0184 23 90 07; informazioni@campingroma.it). From the station, follow V. della Repubblica, turn right on V. Roma, cross the bridge, and make an immediate right to C. Francia. After 50m it becomes V. Freccero. Signs are posted along the way. Family-friendly spot within the confines of the city has well-maintained, brightly painted bungalows and immaculate shared facilities. Staff speaks very limited English. Closed in Oct. Camper service 8am-10am and 3pm-6pm. €5-10 per person, €6-€8 for tent, €7-9 for camper, €5 for car. Bungalows for 2, 4, and 6 with kitchen €45-65, €60-100 with private bath. Showers free. MC/V. ❶

Hotel Villa Franca, C. Repubblica, 12 (☎0184 35 18 71; fax 0184 33 434). Superb location next to the waterfront and public park. Utilitarian rooms with shared bath, English-speaking management, and a parrot in the lobby who says "ciao." Breakfast included. Singles €30; doubles €44, with bath €52; triples €72. AmEx/MC/V. ❸

🍴 FOOD

The **covered market** (open M-Sa 8am-1:30pm), displays a staggering array of fruit, vegetable, and fish stands along V. della Repubblica, V. Libertà, V. Aprosio, and V. Roma. A **STANDA** supermarket is at the corner of V. Roma and V. Ruffini. (Open M-Sa 8am-8pm, Su 9am-8pm. AmEx/MC/V.) Pizzerias along the water all offer similar fare for €8-12. Head away from the beach and into the city for more variety.

▧ Ristorante Cuneo, V. Aprosio, 16/D. Turn right on V. Aprosio from C. Repubblica and follow for 75m. Tables decorated with fresh flowers create a welcoming and comforting atmosphere. Slightly high prices are worth it. Delicious Ligurian cuisine like homemade *gnocchi* (€9.50). *Primi* €6.50-12, *secondi* €12-24. 4-course *menù* €24. Open M-Sa noon-2:30pm and 6:30-10:30pm. MC/V. ❹

Pasta & Basta, Passeggiata Marconi, 20/A (☎0184 23 08 78). On the *Alta* side of the river, shortly before the Galleria Scoglietti. Pick one of 20 sauces (€5-9) to pair with one of 6 pastas (€1-3) or try one of the house seafood specials (€11-14). Casual, air-conditioned, affordable. Open Tu-Th noon-midnight. ❷

L'Aurora, Lungomare F. Cavalotti, 15/B (☎0184 35 25 23). Wicker chairs and straw umbrellas suit the beachside location. Seafood dishes and specialty pizzas (like the *napoletana* with olives and anchovies) distinguish it from similar establishments. Pizzas (€5-7). *Primi* (€7-10), *secondi* (€8-12). Open daily noon-10:30. MC/V. ❷

Ristorante Marco Polo, Lungomare F. Cavalotti, 2 (☎0184 35 26 78). Waterfront candlelit terrace and mind-blowing flavors make this the place to splurge or take a date in Ventimiglia. Don't miss the *tagliatelle* with lobster (€22) or any special from the dessert cart. Service is poised and professional. *Primi* €12-22.50, *secondi* €13.50-22. Open Tu-Su noon-2:30pm and 7-10:30pm. Open daily July-Aug. AmEx/MC/V. ❺

👁 SIGHTS

While Ventimiglia is busy and commercial, it makes an excellent base for exploring sights nearby. Though pebbly **beaches** stretch along the waterfront—the quietest ones are on the *alta* side, along Passeggiata Marconi—Ventimiglia is not known for its beach scene. For those set on sunbathing, a 15min. walk down a footpath from the end of Passeggiata Marconi leads away from the city din onto **Spiaggia Le Calandre,** the town's only stretch of sandy beach. A snack bar there serves drinks and *panini* and rents essential beach equipment. (Two lounge-chairs plus umbrella €12 per half-day.) It's best to head home before sundown (around 8:30pm during summer) to avoid navigating the cliff-side path in the dark. (☎0347 431 53 93. Open daily 8am-9pm.)

Città Alta, Ventimiglia's cliff-side medieval area, is a short walk from the town center. Cross the footbridge to Ventimiglia Alta and turn right on V. Trossarelli. Fifty meters ahead is Discesa Porta Marina; climb to V. Galerina and then V. Fale-

LOCAL LEGEND

FROM THE BREAD BOX

Seven hundred years ago, Imperiale Doria, a cocky 14th-century marquis, was happily practicing *jus primae noctis,* the right to bed any townswoman on her wedding night before her husband was able to do so. However, for a young newly wed woman named Lucrezia, this practice was despicable and unacceptable. When the marquis arrived in Lucrezia's wedding chamber on the night of her wedding, she fiercely resisted the his advances, but her defiance ultimately lead to her imprisonment, starvation and death in the dungeons of the marquis's castle. Stricken with grief over his bride's death, Lucrezia's husband Basso swore his revenge against Doria. Hiding himself in a bale of hay, he rode into the castle on the back of a mule and held the marquis at knifepoint, demanding the abolition of *jus primae noctis.*

The women of the town were so overjoyed by the elimination of this barbaric practice that they invented a special pastry called *michetta* to celebrate their newfound marital rights. A sweet and sugary treat similar to brioche, *michette* are baked in the shape of the female genital organs as symbol of their newfound sexual freedom. Since its creation, the *michetta* has become the centerpiece of Festa della Michetta, a day of singing, dancing, eating and drinking celebrated every August 16 in Dolceacqua.

rina. From there streets lead to P. Cattedrale, where the ancient **Cattedrale dell'Assunta** stands guard over the town below. (Opens at 8am. Free.) The 11th-century church of **San Michele** is on the other side of the old town, off V. Garibaldi at P. Colleta. Its **crypt** was constructed using pilfered Roman columns.

The **Museo Archeologico,** V. Verdi, 41, is accessible by the **Blue Riviera Transporti.** (Buses leave from the corner of V. Cavour and V. Martiri della Libertà. Dir: Ponte San Luigi; 15min.; 10 per day, first bus leaves at 9:05am; €1.20.) Roman artifacts found in the area are on display, including a dozen marble heads. The museum also holds rotating exhibits by town artists. (☎0184 35 11 81; fortedellannunciate.it. Open Tu-Sa 9am-12:30pm and 3-5pm, Su 10am-12:30pm. €3, under 18 €2.)

Blue Riviera Transporti buses also stop at La Mortola, home of the **Botanical Hanbury Gardens.** Begun in 1867 by English aristocrat Sir Thomas Hanbury, the gardens hold exotic flora from three continents and cascade down the summit of Cape Mortola. Hike down to the seaside cafe for *panini* (€3.10) or *gelato* (€1). The steep and challenging course mapped out in the brochure takes about 2hr. (☎0184 22 95 07. Open daily June 16-Sept. 15 9:30am-7pm, last Sunday in Oct.-Feb. 28 10am-5pm, spring and autumn 9:30am-5pm. Last admission 1hr. before closing. €7.50, groups of more than 20 €6.00 per person.)

For a scenic hike, take the narrow footpath before the entrance to the Hanbury Gardens to the ancient **Strada Romana.** Romans used the road to travel to Provence. After 20min., the road reaches a street with a wide sidewalk, which continues for 550m under two tunnels to the **Balzi Rossi** (Red Cliffs). Prehistoric man once lived in the enormous grottoes. Enter to see a cave drawing of a horse painted thousands of years ago. The two small buildings of **Museo Prehistorico** contain skeletons and fossils over a million years old. (☎0184 38 113. Open Tu-Su 8:30am-7:30pm. €3, groups €2.50 per person.)

⬛ DAYTRIP FROM VENTIMIGLIA

⬛ DOLCEACQUA

Buses (20min.; 10 per day 6am-7:05pm, last return 7:07pm; €1.20) run from the corner of V. Cavour and V. Firenze, off C. Repubblica.

Dolceacqua is a hidden treasure not to be missed on any Ligurian vacation. Narrow cobblestone streets, low-ceilinged shops, and a towering castle give travelers a sense of the local character.

Though the city's origins are ancient—dating as far back as the 5th century BC—its landmark year came in 1270 when a Genoan captain constructed the famous Doria Castle. During the Middle Ages, Dolceaqua became the largest and strongest of a string of villages that rose up along the Roya River to accommodate traders between Ventimiglia and the rest of northern Italy.

The bus stops at **Piazza Garibaldi,** the new town's central square. Visit the **IAT Tourist Office,** V. B. Colomba, 3, in the *piazza* for a comprehensive town brochure. (☎0184 20 66 66. Open daily 10am-1pm and 3-6pm.) Cross the Roman footbridge, whose high arch and ingenious construction prompted Monet to call it a "jewel of lightness" during a visit in 1884. Turn right after the bridge and follow the walkway to a *piazza*, where the 15th-century parish church of **San Antonio Abate** stands overlooking the river. Decorated with paintings and a frescoed ceiling, the church is as traditional as the sea-pebble mosaics on the ground of the *piazza* outside. (Open M-Sa 11:30am-4pm. Mass Su 8am.) From the *piazza*, follow the multi-lingual signs that give a history of the town as they lead you through the narrow cobblestone streets of the old city. Many of the ancient stone houses have been converted into artist's studios, containing everything from Monet-knock-offs to sculptures made from bathroom tiles. Admission to most galleries is free.

Accommodations are limited in Dolceacqua, so plan to head back to Ventimiglia or to Bordighera for the night. For those who miss the last bus, the tourist office lists a few B&B options in town. Step into ◪**Trattoria Re ❸**, V. P. Martiri, 26, for Ligurian specialties like *trofie al pesto* (€7) or a plate of *salumi* and local cheese (€5-12) with a glass of *Rossesse*, Dolceacqua's robust, fruity wine. (☎0184 20 61 37. Open M-W and F-Su 10:30am-3pm and 5:30-9:30pm. AmEx/MC/V.) Those in town for the night shouldn't miss a meal at **Pizzeria La Rampa ❷**, V. Barberis Colomba, 11, on the left side of P. Garibaldi. In 2002 the National Agency of Pizza Chefs named their pesto pizza with vegetables "Best Typically Regional Pizza" in Italy, selecting it from 900 contenders. (☎0184 20 61 98. Open Tu-Su 7pm-midnight; 24hr. during Aug. Pizza €4-7. *Primi* €4-6.50, *secondi* €4.50-7.50. Gluten-free pizza available. AmEx/MC/V.) Ask at the tourist office for info on August's **Ferragosto,** which fills the *piazza* with swirling regional *balletti*, traditional costumes, and mouth-watering *michetta*, a local pastry variant on the brioche.

LOMBARDY

Lombardy specializes in the finer things in life. Though coveted by the Romans, Goths, French, Spaniards, Austrians, and Corsicans, disputing European powers failed to rob Lombardy of its prosperity. While great artists like Da Vinci and Bramante have graced the region with harmonious art and architecture, fashion designers continue to decorate the capital city of Milan. In the foothills, majestic lakes attract the world's rich and famous. Critics contend that Lombard cultural sophistication is grounded in a desire for distance from the comparatively underdeveloped regions of the south. The strong presence of secessionist political party Lega Nord testifies to this tendency. Yet Lombardy's financial success also comes from a dedicated work ethic, and the region is generous with both its resources and its legacy, lending an aura of decorum to Italy's otherwise chaotic image.

HIGHLIGHTS OF LOMBARDY

EXPLORE Lombardy's **Lake Country,** where cultural greats from Longfellow to Liszt reposed by quietly murmuring waters and snow-capped mountains (p. 282).

DAYTRIP to **Certosa di Pavia,** where the monastery stands as a monument to the evolution of northern Italian art from early Gothic to Baroque (p. 258).

SPOT the *moda* of the minute as **fashion-conscious *Milanesi*** exhibit all that's in vogue (p. 254).

MILAN (MILANO) ☎02

Milan (pop. 1,200,000) is a modern metropolis and proud of it. Tire giant Pirelli, fashion house Armani, and executive banks anchor the city as Italy's economic powerhouse and the heart of the north. Rushed, refined, and unabashedly cosmopolitan, Milan has its share of problems, including traffic congestion and a high cost of living. But big bucks mean big designers and even bigger spenders in the fashion capital, whose ornate *duomo* and stunning La Scala theater also attract visitors who don't know Dolce & Gabbana from *gelato*. Home to Da Vinci's *Last Supper*, Milan owes much of its artistic heritage to the medieval Visconti and Sforza families, and to the influence of the French, Spanish, and Austrians who have all ruled at some point. Now that Italians run the show, the city thrives as the country's leading producer of cutting-edge style, hearty *risotto*, and dedicated soccer fans.

✈ INTERCITY TRANSPORTATION

Flights:

Malpensa Airport, 48km from the city. Intercontinental flights. **Luggage storage** and lost property services available (see **Local Services,** p. 242). Shuttle buses run to and from Stazione Centrale (1hr.; every 20min. to airport 5am-10:30pm, return 6:20am-12:15pm; €4.50). **Malpensa Express** train departs Cadorna Metro station and Stazione Nord to airport (40min.; every 30min. to airport 5:50am-8:20pm, return 6:45am-9:45pm; €9, round-trip €14.50).

Linate Airport, 7km from town. Logistically more convenient. Domestic, European, and intercontinental flights with European transfers. **Starfly buses** (☎02 58 58 72 37) run to Stazione Centrale (20min.; every 30min. to airport 5:40am-9:35pm, return 6:05am-11:35pm; €2.50). City bus

#73 runs to Milan's San Babila Metro station (€1, but more inconvenient and less secure). **General Flight Info** for both airports (☎02 74 85 22 00; www.sea-aeroportimilano.it) available 24hr.

Bergamo Orio al Serio Airport (☎035 32 63 23; www.orioaeroporto.it) serves some budget airlines including RyanAir; a shuttle runs to Stazione Centrale (1hr.; to airport 4:15am-10pm, to Milan 8am-1am; €6.70).

Trains:

Stazione Centrale, in P. Duca d'Aosta (☎848 88 80 88, 848 02 63 711, or 848 89 20 21; www.trenitalia.com.) Ticket office open daily 6am-8:40pm. **Tourist office** (☎02 67 39 13 74) opposite train platform on 2nd fl. Open M-Sa 9am-6pm, Su 9am-1pm and 2-5pm. **Luggage storage** and lost property services (see **Local Services,** p. 242). To: **Bergamo** (1hr., every hr. 7:20am-11:40pm, €3.90); **Florence** (3½hr., 5 per day 5:30am-8:35pm, €21.69); **Rome** (7hr., every hr. 5:30am-11:20, €38.17; Eurostar: 5½hr., €46.48); **Turin** (2hr., every hr. 5:18am-12:18am, €7.90; Eurostar: 1¼hr., €15); **Venice** (3hr., every hr. 6:05am-9:05pm, €19.16; Eurostar: 1¾hr., €20.66).

Stazione Nord (☎02 20 222; www.ferrovienord.it) is part of **Ferrovia Nord**, the local rail system which connects to **Como** (1hr., every 30min. 6:12am-9:12pm) and **Varese** (1hr., every 30min. 7:06am-1:03am). Runs a shuttle to Malpensa Airport and has an Alitalia check-in station.

Stazione Porta Genova, in P. Stazione di Pta. Genova, is on the western line to **Alessandria** (1½hr., every hr 5:10am-8:09pm) and **Mortara** (1hr., every hr. 5:57am-10:42pm).

Stazione Porta Garibaldi (☎02 65 52 078; ticket office open daily 6:30am-9:30pm), connects Milan to **Lecco** (1hr., every hr. 5:35am-9:41pm); **Piacenza** (1½hr., every 1½hr. 8:26am-

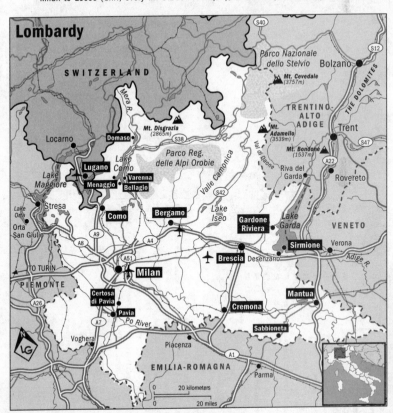

LOMBARDY

Central Milan

ACCOMMODATIONS

Campaggio Città di Milano,	1	A4
La Cordata,	2	C6
Hotel Aliseo,	3	C5
Hotel Aurora,	4	F2
Hotel Due Giardini,	5	F1
Hotel Eva,	6	F2
Hotel Kennedy and Hotel San Tomaso,	7	F2
Hotel Rallye,	8	F1
Hotel XXII Marzo,	9	F4
Ostello Piero Rotta (HI),	10	A3
Postello,	11	C1

FOOD

Big Pizza: Da Noi 2,	12	B6
Caffè Vecchia Brera,	13	C3
Il Forno dei Navigli,	14	B6
Osteria dei Binari,	15	A6
Osteria il Giardino dei Segreti,	16	F4
Osteria La Luna Piena,	17	F2
L'Osteria del Treno,	18	F1
Il Panino Giusto,	19	F2
Peck,	20	C4
Princi Il Bread & Breakfast,	21	C4
Ristorante Asmara,	22	F2
Ristorante Pizzeria Bebel,	23	A4
Rugantino,	24	B5
Sapori di Romagna,	25	B6
Savini,	26	D4
Trattoria Milanese,	27	C4
Viel,	28	D4

NIGHTLIFE		
Bar Magenta,	29	B4
Bluesshouse,	30	D1
Cave Montmarte,	31	C3
Club 2,	32	C3
Exploit,	33	B5
Flying Circus,	34	C5
Hollywood,	35	C1
Loolapaloosa,	36	C1
Movida Kitchen 'n' Bar,	37	C6
Old Fashion Café,	38	A3
Ponteli,	39	B6
Scimmie,	40	B6
Le Trottoir,	41	B6
Yguana Café Restaurant,	42	C5

LOMBARDY

11:04pm); **Domodossola** (2hr., every 1½hr. 5:05am-8:47pm); and **Bergamo** (1hr., every hr. 4:50am-6:45pm).

Buses: At Stazione Centrale. Signs for destinations, times, and prices posted outside. Tickets inside (ticket office open 6:30am-8:10pm). **Intercity** buses depart from locations on the periphery of town. **SAL, SIA, Autostradale,** and many others depart from P. Castello (MM1: Cairoli) and Porta Garibaldi for **Bergamo, Certosa di Pavia,** the **Lake Country, Lugano (Switzerland), Rimini, Trieste,** and **Turin.**

■ ORIENTATION

Milan's layout is punctuated by a series of concentric walls. In the outer rings are suburbs built during the 1950s and 1960s to house southern immigrants. There are four central squares: **Piazza del Duomo,** where **Via Orefici, Via Mazzini,** and **Corso Vittorio Emanuele II** meet; **Piazza Castello** and the attached **Largo Cairoli,** near **Castello Sforzesco; Piazza Cordusio,** connected to Largo Cairoli by **Via Dante** and P. del Duomo by V. Orefici; and **Piazza San Babila,** the entrance to the business and fashion district. The **duomo** and **Galleria Vittorio Emanuele II** are at the center of the circles. To the northeast and northwest lie two parks, the **Giardini Pubblici,** containing several small museums, and **Parco Sempione,** home to the Castello Sforzesco and its **Musei Civici. Stazione Centrale,** Milan's major transportation hub, lies northeast of the city center in a commercial district above the Giardini Pubblici. To reach P. del Duomo, take Metro #3 to MM: Duomo. On foot, walk straight ahead from the platforms through the station's main entrance into **Piazza Duca d'Aosta.** Follow **Via Pisani** as it becomes **Via Turati** and veers into **Via Manzoni,** which leads to **Piazza della Scala,** home to Milan's renowned opera house, and through the Galleria V. Emanuele II to P. del Duomo. From V. Manzoni, turn on **Via della Spiga** to reach the fashion district known as the **Golden Triangle,** and from P. San Babila follow **Corso Venezia** north as it becomes **Corso Buenos Aires** and leads to the budget hotel district around **Piazzale Loreto** east of Stazione Centrale. Taking **Via Torino** from P. del Duomo will take you to **Corso Porta Ticinese** and the **Navigli Canal District.**

> While Milan's city center may be fairly safe at night, women are encouraged not to walk alone after dark in the areas east of Stazione Centrale, north of Porta Garibaldi, and below the Navagli.

▐ LOCAL TRANSPORTATION

The jumbled layout of Milan's streets makes them difficult to navigate. Pick up a map with a street index at the tourist office or any bookstore, as well as a public transit map at the ATM Point (☎800 80 81 81; www.atm-mi.it; open M-Sa 7:45am-8:15pm) in the Metro station under Stazione Centrale or P. del Duomo to familiarize yourself with Milan's efficient public transportation system.

Public Transportation: The **Metropolitana Milanese** ("MM") operates 6am-midnight and is by far the most useful branch of Milan's transportation network. **Line #1** (red; "MM1") stretches east to west from the *pensioni* district east of Stazione Centrale (stop **Sesto F.S.**), through the center of town, and west to the youth hostel (**Molino Dorino** fork; other prong **Bisceglie**). **Line #2** (green; "MM2") links Milan's 3 train stations from **Cologno Nord** and **Gessate** in the east to **Abbiategrasso (Famagosta)** in the west and crosses MM1 at **Cadorna** and **Loreto. Line #3** (yellow; "MM3") runs from north of Stazione Centrale at **Comasina** south to **S. Donato,** crossing MM2 at **Stazione Centrale** and MM1 at the **duomo.** Use the **bus** system for trips outside the city proper. **Trams #29**

Milan Metro

Map legend:
- **M1** Rete Metropolitana Terminal
- ●■ Station
- ■●■ Transfer station
- - - - Airport bus connection
- ⓘ Tourist information
- ✈ Airport
- P Parking
- ⊞ Bus connection
- ⅊ Rail connection

- **M1** Red
- **M2** Green
- **M3** Yellow

and **30** travel the city's outer road, **buses #94** and **61** the inner road. ATM tickets, €1, are good for buses, trams, and Metro for 1¼hr. 10 tickets €9.20, 24hr. pass €3, 48hr. €5.50. All available at *tabaccherie* and ticket booths. Metro tickets can also be purchased at station machines (press the "Rete urbana di Milano" button). Keep a few extra tickets, as *tabaccherie* close at 8pm and ticket machines can be unreliable.

Taxis: White taxis are omnipresent. Or call **RadioTaxi** (☎02 85 85 or 02 40 40). Meter starts at €3. Nighttime surcharge €3.10. Available 24hr.

Car Rental: All have offices built into Stazione Centrale facing P. Duca d'Aosta. A 1-day economy car rental with insurance from **Avis** (☎02 66 90 280 or 02 67 01 654; open M-F 8am-8pm, Sa 8am-4pm) starts at €60 per day; from **Europcar** (☎02 66 98 78 26; open daily 8am-8pm) at €100; and from **Hertz** (☎02 66 98 51 51; open M-F 8am-7pm, Sa 8am-2pm) at €80 per day.

Bike Rental: Aws, V. Ponte Sevesco, 33 (☎02 67 07 21 45).

🔢 PRACTICAL INFORMATION

TOURIST AND FINANCIAL SERVICES

Tourist Office: IAT (Informazioni Accoglienza Turistica), V. Marconi, 1 (☎02 72 52 43 01/2/3; www.milanoinfotourist.com), in P. del Duomo. Local and regional info, including city **maps**. Accommodation booking available. Pick up *Milano è Milano* and *Milano Mese* for info on events and nightlife. Open M-Sa 8:45am-1pm and 2-6pm, Su 9am-1pm and 2-5pm. ▨**Branch:** Stazione Centrale (☎02 72 52 43 70 or 02 47 25 24 360), off main hall on 2nd fl. across from train platforms. Shorter lines, same outstanding service. Open M-Sa 9am-6pm, Su 9am-1pm and 2-5pm.

City Tours: Austostradale (☎02 33 91 07 94; www.autostradale.it) offers hop-on, hop-off sightseeing tours that make circuits of the city center from P. Garibaldi. Taped commentary in 8 languages. Buy tickets from the tourist office or MM2: Garibaldi bus station. €20. Tours Apr.-Oct. daily 11am, 1, 3pm; Nov.-Mar. Sa and Su 11am. Also runs sightseeing tours (€47) that include admission to all the stops, including La Scala Theater and Da Vinci's *Last Supper*. Inquire at APT office about these and other options.

Consulates: Australia, V. Borgogna, 2 (☎02 77 70 41; fax 02 77 70 42 42). MM1: S. Babila. Open M-Th 9am-noon and 2-4pm, F 9am-noon. **Canada,** V. V. Pisani, 19 (☎02 67 58 34 20). MM2/3: Centrale F.S. Open M-F 9am-noon. **New Zealand,** V. G. D'Arezzo 6 (☎02 48 01 25 44). MM1: Pagano. Open M-Sa 8:30am-noon and 1:30-5:30pm. **UK,** V. S. Paolo, 7 (☎02 72 30 01; emergency 03 35 81 06 857). MM1/3: Duomo. Open daily 9am-1pm and 2-5pm. **US,** V. P. Amedeo, 2/10 (☎02 29 03 51; uscitizensmilan@state.gov). MM3: Turati. Open M-F 8:30am-noon; info line open M-F 8:30am-12:30pm and 1:30-5:30pm.

Banks and Currency Exchange: Banks are everywhere. Most are open M-F 8:30am-1:30pm and 2:30-4:30pm. **ATMs** also abound. **Western Union:** In Stazione Centrale next to tourist office. Open daily 9am-7:45pm. Also at **Money Transfer Point,** V. Porpora, 12 (☎02 20 40 07 63). Open M-Sa 9:30am-9pm.

American Express: V. Larga, 4 (☎02 72 10 40 10). Near the *duomo,* at the corner of V. Larga and S. Clemente. Holds mail free 1 month for members. Moneygram international money transfer (fees vary; €500 wire costs €32). Also **exchanges currency.** Open M-F 9am-5:30pm. Also at the corner of V. dell'Orso and V. Brera. Open M-F 9am-5:30pm.

Beyond Tourism: InformaGiovani, Vco. Calusca, 10 (☎02 88 46 57 60/1; www.comune.milano.it/giovani), enter at C. Porta Ticinese, 106. Information for young people looking to work, volunteer, study, or tutor. Also keeps resources of social events, professional associations, and apartment listings. Open M-F 10am-6pm. Also at V. Laghetto, 2. Open M-F 2-6pm. **Easy Milano** (www.easymilano.it), a bi-weekly publication for the English-speaking community of Milan, lists work opportunities including childcare and language tutoring.

LOCAL SERVICES

Luggage Storage: Malpensa Airport, ground fl. (☎02 58 58 02 98). €3-3.50 per bag per day. Open daily 6am-10pm. **Linate Airport,** ground fl. (☎02 71 66 59). €3-3.50 per bag per day. Open daily 7am-9:30pm. **Stazione Centrale:** €3.80 per 5hr., €0.60 per hr. 6-12hr., €0.20 per additional hr. Open daily 6am-midnight.

Lost Property: Ufficio Oggetti Smarriti Comune, V. Friuli, 30 (☎02 88 45 39 00). Open M-F 8:30am-4pm. **Malpensa Airport** (☎02 74 86 83 31; lostpropertymalpensa@sea-aeroportimilano.it). Open M-F 10am-noon. **Linate Airport** (☎02 70 12 44 51). **Stazione Centrale** (☎02 63 71 26 67) at luggage storage. Open daily 6am-midnight.

English-Language Bookstore: The American Bookstore, V. Camperio, 16 (☎02 87 89 20; fax 02 72 02 00 30), at Largo Cairoli. Open M 1-7pm, Tu-Sa 10am-7pm. AmEx/MC/V. **English Book-shop,** V. Ariosto, 12, at the corner with V. Mascheroni (☎02 46 94 468.) Open M-Sa 10am-7pm. **Street vendors** on Largo Mattioli have cheaper options.

GLBT Resource: ARCI-GAY "Centro D'iniziativa Gay," V. Bezzeca, 3 (☎02 54 12 22 25; www.arcigaymilano.org). Friendly staff. Open M-F 3:30-8pm.

Handicapped/Disabled Services: AIAS Milano Onlus, V. Taramelli 20 (☎02 67 65 47 40; www.milanopertutti.it).

Laundromat: Washland, V. Porpora, 14 (☎34 00 81 44 77). Wash €3.50 per 7kg, €7 per 12kg; dry €3.50 per 18min. Open daily 8am-10pm; in summer 8am-11pm. **Lavanderia Self-Service ad Acqua,** V. Vigevano, 20. Wash €3.50 per 7kg, €7 per 12kg; dry €3.50. Detergent €0.60. Open daily 8am-10pm. **Lava e Lava,** V. Melzo, 17 (☎347 14 04 237). Wash €2-3. Enjoy a coffee while you wait. Open daily 8am-9:30pm.

Public Restrooms: Located in the Giardini Pubblici by the Museo di Storia Naturale off C. Venezia and to the left beneath the Palazzo Reale in P. del Duomo. Also in every train station. Often cost €0.10-0.50.

EMERGENCY AND COMMUNICATIONS

Emergency: ☎118. **Police:** ☎113 or 02 77 271. **Carabinieri:** ☎112.

Tourist Police: SOS Turista, V. C. M. Maggi, 14 (☎02 62 261 or 336 03 060). Open daily in summer 9:30am-5pm; in winter 9:30am-6pm.

Pharmacy: Farmacia Stazione Centrale (☎02 66 90 735). In Stazione Centrale's 2nd floor galleria across from the tracks. Open 24hr. Or try **Farmacia Carlo Erba,** P. del Duomo, 21 (☎02 86 46 48 32). Open M 2-7pm, Tu-F 9:30am-1:45pm and 3-7pm. Close to hotels east of Stazione Centrale: **Farmacia Lombardia,** V. Porpora, 65. Open M-F 8:30am-12:30pm and 3:30pm-7:30pm, Sa 8:30am-12:30pm. **Farmacia Stazione Porta Genova** (☎02 58 10 16 34), directly across from Stazione Porta Genova in the Navigli district. Open M-F 24hr. except 12:40-3:30pm and a few 20min. breaks during the day, Sa 6:30-8:30am and 3:30pm-6:30am, Su 3-7pm. **Farmacia di Tourno,** V. San Vittore, 65, is next to the hospital. (Open M-F and Su 8:15am-1:15pm and 3:15-7:15pm.) All pharmacies post list of after-hours rotations.

Hospital: Ospedale Maggiore di Milano, V. Francesco Sforza, 35 (☎02 55 031), 5min. from the *duomo* on the inner ring road. **Ospedale San Giuseppe-Fatebenefratelli,** V. San Vittore, 63. MM2: S. Ambrogio across from the Museo Nazionale della Scienza e della Tecnologia "Da Vinci."

Internet Access:

Internet Enjoy, Vle. Tunisia, 11 (☎02 36 55 58 05). Near MM1: Pta. Venezia. Speedy cable connection for €2 per hr. Open M-Sa 9am-1am, Su 2pm-midnight.

Gr@zia, P. Duca d'Aosta, 14 (☎02 30 31 27 149 or 02 67 00 543; www.grazianet.com). MM2/MM3: Central F.S. Left from Stazione Centrale's main door across the *piazza*. Wireless internet as well as about 30 computers with complementary web cam. €1 per 15min., special deal €15 per 5hr. Open daily 8am-1am.

C@fenet Dolphin Navigator, V. Padova, 2 (☎02 28 47 209). MM1/2: Loreto. Frappes, *panini,* and *focaccia* €3. Fast connection. €1.30 per 15min., €5 per hr. Open M-Sa 6:30am-7pm.

Internet Point, V. Vigevano, 45, across from the station. €3 per hr. Open M-F 9am-7pm.

Post Office: V. Cordusio, 4 (☎02 72 48 21 26), near P. del Duomo toward the *castello.* Offers **currency exchange.** Open M-F 8am-7pm, Sa 9:30am-2pm. **Postal Code:** 20100

▟ ACCOMMODATIONS

Milan has a remarkably high standard of living, and its accommodations tend to be priced accordingly. Advanced booking is strongly advised for most hotels. Prices vary considerably from low season (Dec. and July-Aug.) to high season (Sept.-Nov. and Mar.-May), when room prices often triple. All hotels have 24hr. reception unless otherwise stated; if locked, ring bell for admission. Most rooms without bath come with ensuite sink.

EAST OF STAZIONE CENTRALE

Unless stated otherwise, all hotels are easily accessible from MM1/MM2: Loreto, or by tram #33 from Stazione Centrale. Women should use caution when traveling alone at night in this area.

▧ **Hotel Cà Grande,** V. Porpora, 87 (☎02 26 14 52 95; www.hotelcagrande.it). 7 blocks from P. Loreto in a yellow house on the right. Tram #33 stop 50m from hotel. English-speaking owners will have you feeling right at home, and A/C will cool you down. All rooms have TV, sink, and phone. Breakfast included, best enjoyed in the small flower-filled garden. Singles €40, with bath €45; doubles €60/70. AmEx/MC/V. ❹

Milan: Behind Stazione Centrale

🏠 ACCOMMODATIONS
Hotel Cà Grande, **3**
Hotel Malta, **4**
Hotel Sara, **5**
Hotel del Sole, **6**

🍎 FOOD
Il Centro Ittico, **2**
Focaccerie Genovesi, **7**
Osteria La Piola, **9**

🎵 NIGHTLIFE
Artdeco Café, **10**
Café Capoverde, **1**
L'elephante, **11**
Sottomarino Giallo, **8**

■ **Hotel Malta,** V. Ricordi, 20 (☎02 20 49 615; www.hotelmalta.it). Take V. Porpora and turn right on V. Ricordi. Floral-themed hotel run by a friendly proprietor. 15 bright, quiet rooms all have bath, TV, fan, and hair dryer; many have balcony overlooking the rose garden. Reserve ahead. Singles €36-60; doubles €50-90. MC/V. ❹

Hotel del Sole, V. G. Spontini, 6 (☎02 29 51 29 71; www.delsolehotel.com). MM1: Lima, between Stazione Centrale and Giardini Pubblici. Walk up C. Buenos Aires 1 block and turn right. 2 fl. of clean rooms, all with TV, sink, telephone, and A/C. Singles €35, with bath €50; doubles €50-70/60-85; triples €60-95/75-115. AmEx/MC/V. ❸

Hotel Sara, V. Sacchini, 17 (☎02 20 17 73; www.hotelsara.it). Take V. Porpora to the 2nd street on the right. Clean rooms with floor-to-ceiling windows, bath, A/C, hairdryer, and TV. Breakfast included. Internet €2 per hr. Singles €40-80; doubles €65-120; triples €85-130. AmEx/MC/V. ❺

NEAR GIARDINI PUBBLICI

■ **Hotel Eva,** V. Lazzaretto, 17, 4th fl. (☎02 67 06 093; fax 02 67 05 907). MM1: Pta. Venezia. V. F. Casati, then right on V. Lazzaretto. Hotel is on left. 10 large rooms with lace curtains, TV, and phone. Entered through sliding doors. Clean shared bathroom. Wheelchair accessible. Singles €30; doubles €45; triples €70. Cash only. ❸

Hotel Kennedy, Vle. Tunisia, 6, 6th fl. (☎02 29 40 09 34; www.kennedyhotel.it). MM1: Pta. Venezia. From the C. Buenos Aires Metro exit, turn left on Vle. Tunisia. Clean rooms with TV, fan, phone, sink. Modern bathrooms are very blue. Singles €35-40; doubles €50-55, with bath €70-75; triples €85-90; quads €90-95. AmEx/MC/V. ❸

Hotel XXII Marzo, P. S. Maria del Suffragio, 3 (☎02 70 10 70 64; www.hotel22marzo.com). MM1: S. Babila. From P. S. Babila follow C. Monforte to P. del Tricolore, turn right on Vle. Premuda, left on C. XXII Marzo, and left after 5 blocks. Large, clean rooms with TV, A/C, bath, and wireless Internet (€2 per 30min.). Singles €40-70; doubles €50-120; triples €70-140; quads €80-160. AmEx/MC/V. ❺

Hotel Aurora, C. Buenos Aires, 18 (☎02 20 47 960; www.hotelaurorasrl.com). MM1: Pta. Venezia. On the right side of hectic C. Buenos Aires after V. F. Casati, Aurora offers simple spotless rooms with phone, TV, fan, and serenity. Reserve ahead. Singles €40, with bath €50-€70; doubles €60-95; triples €80-130. AmEx/MC/V. ❹

Hotel Aliseo, C. Italia, 6, 6th fl. (☎02 86 45 01 56; fax 02 80 45 35). MM3: Missori. Just south of P. Missori on the right; take the stairs inside the courtyard. 5min. walk from the *duomo*. Large rooms with TV and fan, some with balcony. Posters and lace curtains add a homey feel. Breakfast included. Singles €40-50, with bath €60-70; doubles €60-70/80-100; triples €80-90/90-110. Discount with longer stay. MC/V. ❹

Hotel Due Giardini, V. B. Marcello, 47 (☎02 29 52 10 93 or 02 29 51 23 09; duegiardinihotel@inwind.it). MM1: Lima. Walk along V. Vitruvio 2 blocks to V. B. Marcello; turn left on far side of the street. Mint green decor spruces up 11 well-kept rooms, all with bath, TV, hair dryer, and A/C. Breakfast included. Courtyard garden with swing chair. Reserve ahead. Singles €45-65; doubles €70-110; triples €90-150. AmEx/MC/V. ❹

Hotel San Tomaso, Vle. Tunisia, 6, 3rd fl. (☎02 29 51 47 47; www.hotelsantomaso.com). MM1: Pta. Venezia. From the C. Buenos Aires Metro exit, turn left on Vle. Tunisia. Small rooms with TV, fan, phone, some with bath, all with ensuite showers. Singles €35; doubles €50, with bath €55; triples €60/65. AmEx/MC/V. ❸

Hotel Rallye, V. B. Marcello, 59 (☎02 29 40 45 68; www.hotelrallye.it). MM1: Lima. Walk along V. Vitruvio 2 blocks to V. B. Marcello and turn left. 20 homey rooms with fan, phone, sink, and TV. Breakfast included. Parking €10. Reception closed 2am-5am. Singles €30, with bath €38; doubles €40-52/50-83. AmEx/MC/V. ❸

ON THE CITY PERIPHERY

Ostello per la Gioventù AIG Piero Rotta (HI), V. M. Bassi, 2 (☎02 39 26 70 95; www.ostellionline.org), northwest of the city. MM1: QT8. Facing the white church with a cone-shaped roof, turn right on V. Salmoiraghi. Hostel is 300m on the right. Institutional building with helpful staff. Breakfast and sheets included. Laundry €5.50. Phone-card Internet. 3-night max. stay. Reception daily 7-9am and 3:30pm-1am. Check-out 9am. Lockout 9am-3:30pm. Closed Dec. 24-Jan. 12. Reserve on website only. 6-bed dorms €18.50; family rooms €22 per person. Non-HI members add €3. MC/V. ❷

Postello, V. Pergola 5 (☎33 317 52 272; www.postello/reality-hacking.org). MM2: P. Garibaldi. From station, turn left on V. Pepe and then right on V. Carmagnola. V. Pergola is 3 blocks ahead on right after Ple. C. Archinto. Milan's newest, cheapest hostel. Alternative atmosphere in older compound with painted murals, stickered walls, and dorms without locks. Frequent movies, booktalks, live music in courtyard and bar create community but can be noisy. Communal dinners in the coffee shop next door. Convenient to clubs. English spoken. Free luggage storage. Sheets included. Laundry with suggested donation. Free Internet and wireless. 4- to 8-bed dorms €10. Cash only. ❶

La Cordata, V. Burigozzo, 11 (☎02 58 31 46 75; www.lacordata.it). MM3: Missori. From P. Missori, take tram #15 2 stops to Italia S. Luca, then walk in the same direction for

1 block and turn right on V. Burigozzo. Entrance around the corner on V. Aurispa. Close to the Navigli region, a crash pad for a late-20s crowd ready to party. Communal bathrooms and kitchen. 7-night max. stay. Check-in 2-11pm. Check-out 11am. Doors locked 12:30am. Closed Aug. and Dec. 24-Jan. 3. 16-bed dorms €18. Cash only. ❷

Campeggio Città di Milano, V. G. Airaghi, 61 (☎02 48 20 01 34; www.parcoaquatica.com). MM1: De Angeli, then bus #72 to S. Romanello Togni. Backtrack 10m and turn right on V. Tongi. Campsite is a 10min. walk straight ahead. Enter at Aquatica waterpark. Modern facilities. Free volleyball and grills. Laundry €5. Closed Dec.-Jan. €7.50 per person, €6.50-8.50 per tent, €6.50 per car, electricity included. 2- to 6-person cabins €37-88; bungalows with bath and A/C €80-120. Reserve ahead. MC/V. ❶

◖ FOOD

Munch *focaccia* with the lunch-break crowd, clink glasses over silver and satin, or take your palate on a world tour through the city's ethnic neighborhoods. Old-style *trattorie* still follow Milanese culinary traditions with *risotto alla Milanese* (rice with saffron), *cotoletta alla Milanese* (breaded veal cutlet with lemon), and *osso buco* (shank of lamb, beef, or veal). Many bars offer happy-hour buffets of *focaccia*, pasta, and *risotto* mixes free with one discounted cocktail. Around Christmas, *panettone*, a traditional fruitcake, is stacked high in every *pasticceria*.

IN THE CITY CENTER

Weary tourists near the *duomo* often succumb to P. del Duomo's pricey but mediocre offerings, but those who dare to venture a bit off the beaten path can reap cheap and delicious rewards.

▧**Trattoria Milanese,** V. S. Marta, 11 (☎02 86 45 19 91). MM1/3: Duomo. From P. del Duomo, take V. Torino; turn right on V. Maurilio and again on V. S. Marta. Serves up *costolette alla Milanese* (breaded rib; €15) and *mondeghili milanesi* (breaded meatballs; €12) in 2 rooms under brick arches. *Primi* €6-8, *secondi* €7-19. Cover €2. Open M and W-Su 10am-3pm and 7pm-1am. Closed last 2 weeks of July. AmEx/MC/V. ❸

▧**Caffè Vecchia Brera,** V. Dell'Orso, 20 (☎02 86 46 16 95; www.vecchiabrera.it). MM1: Cairoli. Head across V. Cusani; through intersection with V. Mercado Vetero on left corner. Dreamy liqueur-soaked crepes and filling hot dishes for a post-opera snack. Crepes €3.50-7. *Primi* €6-8, *secondi* €9.30-14. Cover €1. Service 10%. Open daily 7am-3am. ❸

Savini, Galleria V. Emanuele II (☎02 72 00 34 33; www.thi.it). Since 1867, this world-famous restaurant has kept its decor and clientele: both extravagant and well-dressed. Pay dearly for exquisite food and superb service. *Primi* €14-24, *secondi* €22-30. Cover €7. Service 12%. Open M-Sa 12:30-2:30pm and 7:30-10:30pm. AmEx/MC/V. ❺

Osteria il Giardino dei Segreti, V. Sottocorno, 17 (☎02 76 00 83 76; www.ilgiardinodeisegreti.it). MM1: S. Babila. From P. S. Babila follow C. Monforte to P. del Tricolore, turn right on Vle. Premuda, then left on V. Sottocorno. This shady garden is an ideal setting for savoring fresh mushroom dishes and fish. Excellent wine list. *Primi* €6-8.50, *secondi* €11.50-16. Open M-Sa noon-3pm and 6-11pm. MC/V. ❹

Ristorante Pizzeria Bebel, V. San Vittore, 17, next to the Museo Nazionale della Scienza e della Tecnologia "Da Vinci." MM2: San Ambrogio, off V. Carducci. Typical Italian fare in a dark, private interior. Pizza €5.20-7.80. Plates of the day €6.70-12.50. *Primi* €6.20-7.50, *secondi* €9.50-13. Cover €2. Open M-F 12:15-2:30pm and 7:15-11:30pm, Sa 7:15-11:30. MC/V. ❸

Princi il Bread & Breakfast, V. Speronari, 6 (☎028 74 797), off P. del Duomo, take V. Torino and make 1st left; bakery is on left in middle of block. Busy deli with golden *focaccia* and *strudel di miele* (strudel with honey). Huge lunch crowd comes for fresh bread and French pastries (€1-4), or *panini* and pizza (€2-5). Open M-Sa 7am-8pm. ❶

Peck, V. Cantu, 3 (☎02 86 30 17), off V. Orefici from P. del Duomo, is a deli/bakery wonderland, manned by 16 butchers serving *foie gras*, ham, and a thousand other delicacies since 1883 (€2-15). Open M 3-7:30pm, Tu-Sa 8:45am-7:30pm. ❶

Viel, V. G. Marconi, 3 (☎02 86 92 56; www.viel-milano.com). From P. del Duomo, head past the tourist office down V. Marconi. Fig and plum *gelato*, along with a slew of more exotic flavors makes for a tantalizing variation on a typical Italian theme. *Gelato* €2-4. Frappe swirl €4. *Gelato* in brioche roll €2.50. Open M-Sa 7:30am-7:30pm. ❶

NAVIGLI AND ENVIRONS

Boatloads of students mean cheap grub. Many bars (see **Nightlife**, p. 254) serve dinner; many offer happy-hour buffets with cocktail purchase. The **Fiera di Sinigallia**, a 400-year-old bargaining extravaganza of food and clothing, occurs on Saturdays on Darsena Banks, a canal in Navigli around V. d'Annunzio. A **PAM** supermarket is by the Museo Nazionale della Scienza e della Tecnologia "Da Vinci" at Vle. Olona, 1/3, outside the MM2: S. Ambrogio stop (open M-Sa 8am-9pm), or at V. Vigevano, 22, near the small **Di per Di Express** supermarket just east of MM2: Porta Genova F. S. (☎02 58 10 00 20. Open M-Sa 8:30am-1pm and 3:45pm-8:15pm.)

Big Pizza: Da Noi 2, V. G. Borsi, 1 (☎02 83 96 77), takes its name seriously. Beer flows liberally while students wait for epic stone-oven pizzas. The *pizza della casa* (house pizza) comes with a bowl of pasta dumped on top (€8.50). *Calzoni* €5-7. Pizza €4-8.50. Pasta €3.50-8. Cover €1. Open daily 10am-3:30pm and 5:30pm-2am. **Branches:** Ple. XXIV Maggio, 7 (MM2: Pta. Genova) and V. Buonarroti, 16 (MM1: Buonarroti). ❷

Il Forno dei Navigli, V. A. Naviglio Pavese, 2 (☎02 83 23 372). At the corner of Ripa di Porta Ticinese. Out of "the oven of Navigli" come the most moist and decadent crumbly fruit and pastries in the city. The *cestini*, pear tart with Nutella, defines decadence (€3). Pastries and breads €0.50-6. Open M-Sa 7am-7:30pm, Su 9am-7:30pm. Cash only. ❶

Osteria del Binari, V. Tortona, 1 (☎02 89 40 94 28). MM2: Pta. Genova. Head to C. Colombo side of P. Stazione Porta Genova. Cross train tracks by the overpass to V. Tortona; restaurant is on your left. Grapevine walls, attentive and discreet staff, and exquisite regional cuisine make for an intimate meal. Unless explicitly refused, a platter of *antipasti* (€7) will appear. *Primi* €10, *secondi* €12-17. Open M-Sa 8-11pm. MC/V. ❹

Rugantino, V. Fabbri, 1 (☎02 89 42 14 04), between the Chiesa di San Lorenzo and the Roman portals and pillars of C. Porta Ticinese. From MM2: S. Ambrogio walk down V. E. de Amicis. Roman dishes in a candlelit wine cellar or in wicker chairs outside. *Primi* €9, *secondi* €5-14. Open daily noon-3pm and 7:30pm-12:30am. AmEx/MC/V. ❸

Sapori di Romagna, V. A. Sforza, 9 (☎33 96 46 24 02). Ham and cheese *piadini* (crepes; €2-6) are a meal in themselves, while Nutella and fruit make dessert for 2. Busy at night, but a worthwhile wait. Open daily 1pm-2am. Cash only. ❶

CORSO BUENOS AIRES NEAR GIARDINI PUBBLICI

Avoid the *menù turistico* at a typical *trattoria* in favor of foods from the neighborhood's immigrant populations. **SMA Punto City** supermarket, V. Felice Casati, 8, just off V. A. Tadino, is open M-Sa 8:30am-1pm and 3:30-8pm (MM1: Lima).

Ristorante Asmara, V. L. Palazzi, 5 (☎02 29 52 24 53). MM1: Pta. Venezia. Spicy Eritrean food includes a *zighini* platter with flavorful meat and vegetable pieces wrapped in pieces of pita-like bread (€10.50). Vegetarian options available. Entrees €8-11.50. Cover €1.60. Open M-Tu and Th-Su 10am-4pm and 6pm-midnight. AmEx/MC/V. ❸

Osteria La Piola, Vle. Abruzzi, 23 (☎02 29 53 12 71 or 02 29 41 56 76). MM1/2: Loreto, then a quick walk down Vle. Abruzzi. Fresh pasta and local flavors. *Tipica cotoletta* (typical platters) like breaded ox tail (€15) and thinly sliced octopus with beans and potatoes (€11). Suggested wines line the walls. *Primi* €9-10, *secondi* €13-16. Open M-Sa noon-3pm and 5pm-1am. AmEx/MC/V. ❸

Il Panino Giusto, V. Malpighi, 3 (☎02 29 40 92 97). MM1: Pta. Venezia. From the *piazza*, head down Vle. Piave and turn left on V. Malpighi. If you believe sandwiches should contain truffled olive oil, veal pâté, or lard with honey and walnuts for under €8, welcome home. Artisinal *panini* €4.50-8. Open daily noon-12:30am. AmEx/MC/V. ❷

Focaccerie Genovesi, V. Plinio, 5. MM1: Lima. Eatery is on the left. *Focaccia formaggio* (€2.40): the nightmare of the Atkins diet, cardiologists, and businessmen in white shirts. A slice of oily, cheesy heaven that's almost pizza, but not quite. Locals fill this hole-in-the-wall par excellence. Open M-Sa 10:30am-2pm and 4:30-8pm. Cash only. ❶

Osteria La Luna Piena, V. Lazzaro Palazzi, 9 (☎02 29 52 82 40 or 347 00 61 206). MM1: Pta. Venezia. Take C. Buenos Aires; V. L. Palazzi is the 2nd left. South Italian *pugliesi* specialties, including *cavallo* (horse) dishes. Decadent vegetarian *focaccia* €4-8. *Primi* €7-10, *secondi* €9-16. Open M-Sa 12:15-3pm and 7:45pm-12:30am. MC/V. ❸

NEAR STAZIONE CENTRALE

Pam supermarket, V. Piccinni, 2, is just off C. Buenos Aires (MM1: Loreto; ☎02 29 51 27 15; open M-Sa 8am-9pm), and **Punto SMA** is on V. Noe between P. Piola and P. Bernini. (Open M-F 8:30am-1:30pm and 3:30-7:45pm, Sa 8:30am-7:45pm.)

L'Osteria del Treno, V. S. Gregorio, 46/48 (☎02 67 00 479). MM2/3: Centrale F. S. From P. Duca d'Aosta, take V. Pisani and turn left on V. S. Gregorio. A brassy, in-your-face attitude and self-serve *primi* €3.10-4.13, *secondi* €4.65-6.20. Dinner prices slightly higher. Cover €1.30. Open M-F noon-2:30pm and 7-10:30pm. Cash only. ❷

Il Centro Ittico, V. Martiri Oscuri, 19 (☎02 26 14 37 74 or 02 28 04 03 96). MM2/3: Centrale F. S. 20min. walk down V. F. Aporti to the left of P. Duca d'Aosta, then right on V. Martiri Oscuri. This fish market and restaurant had plans to move in September 2005 to a larger location; call for current address. Market prices. *Primi* from €8, *secondi* from €12. Open M-Sa 12:30-2:30pm and 8pm-midnight. Cover €2.50. MC/V. ❹

⊙ SIGHTS

NEAR THE DUOMO

▓**DUOMO.** The geographical and spiritual center of Milan and a good starting point for any walking tour of the city, the *duomo*, the third-largest church in the world, was built over the remains of three other basilicas. Gian Galeazzo Visconti began construction in 1386, hoping to flatter the Virgin into granting him a male heir. Work proceeded sporadically for four centuries and was finally completed at Napoleon's command in 1809. In the meantime, the structure accumulated more than 3400 statues, 135 spires, and 96 gargoyles. The facade, currently hidden beneath scaffolding, juxtaposes the original Italian Gothic with Baroque elements commissioned by Archbishop Borromeo to show allegiance to Rome during the Protestant Revolution. In 1943 a bomb destroyed a primary spire; the reconstruction includes a bas-relief of the bombardment to commemorate the event. Inside, 52 columns rise to canopied niches with statues as capitals. The imposing 16th-century marble tomb of **Giacomo de' Medici** in the southern transept was inspired by the work of Michelangelo. Climb (or ride) to the top of the cathedral from outside the northern transept to enter the ▓**roof walkway** for prime views of the city below. The rooftop statue of the "Madonnina" has become the symbol of Milan. *(MM1: Duomo. www.duomomilano.com. Cathedral open daily 7am-7pm. Modest dress strictly enforced. Roof open daily in summer 9am-5:45pm; in winter 9am-4pm. Stairs €4, elevator €6.)* The **Museo del Duomo** displays paintings, tapestries, jewels, and stained glass relating to the *duomo's* construction. *(P. del Duomo, 14, to the right of the duomo next to the Palazzo Reale. ☎02 86 03 58. Open daily 10am-1:15pm and 3-6pm. €3, students €1. Combined ticket to museum and roof walkway by elevator €8.)*

■ PINACOTECA AMBROSIANA. The 23 palatial rooms of the Ambrosiana display exquisite works from the 14th through 19th centuries, including Botticelli's *Madonna of the Canopy*, Da Vinci's *Portrait of a Musician*, Caravaggio's *Basket of Fruit* (the first Italian still-life), Titian's *Adoration of the Magi*, and works by Flemish landscapists Brueghel and Bril. Raphael's immense sketch **■School of Athens** is displayed in a darkened room and deserves the praise it gets for the lifelike nuances of its professors and students engaged in lively discussion. The courtyard's statues, fountains, mosaic, and staircase are also enchanting, as is Bertini's 1867 two-story *Vetrata Dantesca*, a stained-glass window with images and quotations from Dante's *Inferno*. *(P. Pio XI, 2. Follow V. Spadari off V. Torino and turn left on V. Cantù. ☎02 86 46 29 81. Open Tu-Su 10am-5:30pm. €7.50; under 18 or over 65 €4.50.)*

■ MUSEO POLDI PEZZOLI. Poldi Pezzoli, an 18th-century nobleman and art collector, bequeathed his house and art to the city "for the enjoyment of the people" in 1879. Wind past the 19th-century indoor fountain with bronze cherubs to famous paintings including Mantegna's *Virgin and Child*, Botticelli's *Madonna and Child of Mary Teaching an Infantile Christ to Read*, Bellini's *Ecce Homo*, Guardi's *Gray Lagoon*, and the signature piece, Pollaiuolo's *Portrait of a Young Woman*. Smaller collections of china, marble busts, furniture, ancient Roman jewelry, Tiepolo oil sketches, and 18th-century clocks fill Pezzoli's curiosity cabinet of a museum. A display of Italian military armaments guards the room to the left of the entrance. *(V. Manzoni, 12, near La Scala. ☎02 79 48 89. Open Tu-Su 10am-6pm. €7, students €5, under 12 or over 60 free. Free multi-language audioguide.)*

TEATRO ALLA SCALA. Founded in 1778, La Scala has established Milan as the opera capital of the world. Its understated Neo-Classical facade and lavish interior set the stage for premieres of works by Rossini, Puccini, Mascagni, and Verdi, performed by virtuosos like Maria Callas and Enrico Caruso. Visitors can soak up La Scala's history at the **Museo Teatrale alla Scala.** From poster art to a plaster cast of Toscanini's hand, the museum offers a glimpse into the operatic past. *(La Scala is accessed through the Galleria Vittorio Emanuele from P. del Duomo. Inside the theater can be glimpsed from a box on non rehearsal- or event-days from 9am-noon and 1:30-5pm. ☎02 88 79 24 73; www.teatroallascala.org. See* **Entertainment,** *p. 252, for information about performances. Museum: C. Magenta, 71. MM1: Conciliazione. Directly opposite the Chiesa S. Maria delle Grazie. From P. Conciliazione, take V. Ruffini for 2 blocks. ☎02 80 53 418. Open daily 9am-12:30pm and 1:30-5:30pm. Ticket sales end 30min. before closing. €5, students €4.)*

GALLERIA VITTORIO EMANUELE II. A 48m glass and iron cupola towers over a five-story arcade of offices and overpriced shops and cafes. Intricate mosaics representing the continents sieged by the Romans adorn the floors and walls. The oldest roofed gallery (1870s) once known as "Milan's Sitting Room" is now a center of tourist activity, connecting P. del Duomo to P. della Scala. Spin on the mosaic bull clockwise three times for good luck. *(North of the duomo. ☎06 46 02 72. Free.)*

PALAZZO REALE. This *palazzo* served as the town hall in 1138 before serving as the residence of Milanese royalty until the 19th century. Giuseppe Piermarini, architect of La Scala, designed its facade. Today it houses temporary exhibits on two floors in the

LOMBARDY

Museo d'Arte Contemporanea, which also hosts a small permanent collection of works. *(South of the duomo. ☎02 29 00 56 59 or 89 95 00 022; www.provincia.milano.it/cultura. Wheelchair accessible. Open Tu-W and F-Su 9:30am-8pm, Th 9:30am-10:30pm. €8, students €6. Ticket sales end 1hr. before closing. Exhibits around €9, students €7.50.)*

MUSEO BAGATTI VALSECCHI. This beautifully preserved 19th-century aristocrat's mansion houses antique ceramics, frescoes, mosaics, ivory, and weapons that recreate the ambience of the 15th- and 16th-century Italian and Lombard Renaissance. *(V. Santo Spirito, 10. MM3: Monte Napoleone. From V. Monte Napoleone, V. Santo Spirito is the 2nd left. ☎02 76 00 61 32. Open Tu-Su 1-5:45pm. €6, students €3.)*

NEAR CASTELLO SFORZESCO

■**CASTELLO SFORZESCO.** Restored after bomb damage in 1943, the Castello Sforzesco is one of Milan's best-known monuments. Its mighty towers and expansive courtyard were originally constructed in 1368 by the Visconti as a defense against the Venetians, Duke Francesco Sforza added the corner towers in 1450, and Da Vinci also had his studio here before Spanish and Austrian invaders used the grounds as army barracks, horse stalls, and storage. The tall **Tower of Bona of Savoy** in the center of the castle was built after the assassination of Bona's husband so that guards could observe all movements inside and outside the castle walls. Inside are the 10 **Musei Civici** (Civic Museums), with something for everyone. Highlights include the **Museum of Ancient Art,** which contains Michelangelo's unfinished *Pietà Rondanini* (1564), his last work, and Da Vinci's frescoes on the ceiling of the **Sala delle Asse;** his design was once considered so insignificant it was whitewashed over, actually protecting the original colors. The **Museum of Decorative Art** showcases household furnishings, Murano glass, and a giant porcelain crab; at the superb **Museum of Musical Instruments,** be sure not to miss the African harps made from rattlesnake heads. *(MM1: Cairoli. ☎02 88 46 37 00; www.milanocastello.it. Castle grounds open daily Nov.-Mar. 7am-6pm; Apr.-Oct. 7am-7pm. Free. Museums open Tu-Su 9:00am-5:30pm. Combined admission €3, students and over 65 €1.50. 3-day pass €7/3.50. Free on F 2-5:30pm and daily 1hr. before closing.)*

CHIESA DI SANTA MARIA DELLE GRAZIE. The church's Gothic nave is elaborately patterned with frescoes, contrasting the airy Renaissance tribune added by Bramante in 1497. Look up to observe the blue and red geometric drawings on the white walls and the gold sunbursts in the middle of each arch on the ceiling. *(P. di S. Maria delle Grazie, 2. MM1: Conciliazione. From P. Conciliazione, take V. Boccaccio and then right onto V. Ruffini for about 2 blocks. Open M-Sa 7am-noon and 3-7pm, Su 7:30am-12:15pm and 3:30-9pm. Modest dress required.)* To the left of the church entrance is the *Cenacolo Vinciano* (Vinciano Refectory; the convent dining hall), home to one of the best-known pieces of art in the world: Leonardo Da Vinci's ■**Last Supper.** Following a 20-year restoration effort, it was reopened to the public in 1999, though rumors persist that it may again be closed; pieces have been flaking off almost since the day Leonardo finished it in 1498, and the roof of the building was blown off during WWII, leaving the interior exposed for several years. As a result, only groups of 25 or fewer are allowed in the refractory for a maximum of 15min. Take time to note the fine detail of the pattern on the tablecloth, the sharp one-point perspective emphasized by the brown doors receding backward, and Apostle Peter with a knife hidden subtly behind his back to the left of Christ. Advance booking is mandatory, though occasionally spots open at the last minute. Lone travelers with a flexible schedule should call at least one week in advance; groups and those with limited time should call several weeks ahead. *(Reservations ☎02 89 42 11 46 or 19 91 99 100. Wheelchair accessible. Refectory open Tu-Su 8:15am-6:45pm. Tours in English daily 9:30am and 3:30pm. €6.50, EU residents 18-25 €3.25, under 18 or over 65 free. Reservation fee €1.50. Tours €3.25. Audioguide €2.50 or €4 for 2 people.)*

PINACOTECA DI BRERA. The Brera Art Gallery presents a superb collection of 14th- to 20th-century paintings, with an emphasis on those from the Lombard School. Works include Bellini's *Madonna col Bambino* and *Pietà* (1460), Mantegna's innovative *Dead Christ* (1480), Raphael's *Marriage of the Virgin* (1504), Caravaggio's *Supper at Emmaus* (1606), and Francesco Hayez's *The Kiss* (1859). A limited collection of works by modern masters includes two portraits by Modigliani and pieces by Carrà, as well as Picasso's *Testa di Toro*. A special glass-enclosed restoration chamber in the center of Gallery 14 allows visitors to watch conservationists at work on the aged canvases on weekdays. *(V. Brera, 28. MM2: Lanza. Walk down V. Pontaccio and turn right on V. Brera. Or from La Scala, walk up V. Verdi until it becomes V. Brera. ☎02 72 26 31. Wheelchair accessible. Open Tu-Su 8:30am-7:15pm. Last entry at 6:40pm. €5, EU citizens 18-25 €2.50, under 18 or over 65 free. Audioguide €3.50.)*

MUSEO NAZIONALE DELLA SCIENZA E DELLA TECNOLOGIA "DA VINCI". This family-friendly, hands-on museum traces the development of science and technology from the age of Leonardo to the present. The hall of computer technology features a piano converted into a typewriter by Edoardo Hughes of Turin in 1885. Don't miss the Da Vinci room, which contains wooden mock-ups of his flying machines, cranes, and bridges. *(V. San Vittore, 21, off V. Carducci. MM2: San Ambrogio. ☎02 48 55 53 84; www.museoscienza.it. Open Tu-F 9:30am-5:00pm, Sa-Su 9:30am-6:30pm. Last entrance 30min. before close. €7, students €5.)*

TRIENNALE DE MILAN (PALAZZO DELL'ARTE). Situated in the historical Palace of Art, the Triennale organizes expositions and exhibits on architecture, urbanism, decorative arts, design, and fashion. *(MM2: Cairoli. V. E. Alemagna, 6, behind the castle. ☎02 72 43 41; www.triennale.it. Open daily 10:30am-8:30pm. Admission prices vary.)*

BASILICA DI SANT'AMBROGIO. A prototype for Lombard-Romanesque churches throughout Italy, Sant'Ambrogio is the most influential medieval building in Milan. St. Ambrose presided over this building between AD 379 and 386 and his skeleton, in pontifical robes, rests beside those of the martyrs Gervasius and Protasius in a crypt below the altar. Ninth-century reliefs at the altar depict the life of Christ in gold on one side and the life of St. Ambrose, in silver, on the other. The 4th-century **Cappella di San Vittore in Ciel D'oro,** with 5th-century mosaics adorning its cupola, lies through chapel on the right. The asymmetrical **bell towers** are the result of an 8th-century feud between a group of Benedictine monks and the priests of the church, each of whom owned one tower. *(MM1: Sant'Ambrogio. Walk up V. G. Carducci; the church bulwark rises up to the right. Open M-F 7am-noon and 2:30-7pm, Sa-Su 7am-1pm amd 3-8pm. Free. Chapel open Tu-Su 9:30am-11:45pm and 2:30-6pm. €2, students €1.)*

FROM NAVIGLI TO THE CORSO DI PORTA TICINESE

BASILICA DI SANT'EUSTORGIO. Founded in the 4th century to house the bones of the Magi, it lost its function when the dead sages were spirited off to Cologne in 1164. The 1278 building sports a Lombard-Gothic interior of low vaults and thick columns. A great masterpiece of early Renaissance art is the ▓**Portinari Chapel** (1468) to the left of the entrance. The frescoes in the chapel below the rainbow dome were painted by Foppa to illustrate the life of St. Peter. The elevated sarcophagus in the center is supported by eight statues representing the five cardinal virtues and the three theological virtues; Prudence has the faces of a young, middle-aged, and old woman. The chapel stands on a **Paleochristian cemetery.** Down the narrow steps before the chapel entrance and through the passageway are the pagan and early Christian tombs, including that of Eustorgio, the 9th bishop of Milan. *(P. S. Eustorgio, 3. MM2: San Ambrogio. From V. E. de Amicis, turn right on C. Porta Ticinese and follow it toward the Navigli. Basilica: open M and W-Su 8:30am-noon and 3:30-6pm. Free. Capella: ☎/fax 02 89 40 26 71. Open Tu-Su 10am-6pm. €6, students and seniors €3.)*

NAVIGLI DISTRICT. The Venice of Lombardy, the Navigli district boasts canals, elevated footbridges, open-air markets, and trolleys. The Navigli are sections of a larger medieval canal system that transported thousands of tons of marble to build the *duomo* and linked Milan to northern cities and lakes. Da Vinci designed the original canal locks. *(From the MM2: Pta. Genova station take V. Vigevano.)*

CHIESA DI SAN LORENZO MAGGIORE. The oldest church in Milan, San Lorenzo Maggiore testifies to the city's 4th-century greatness. Begun as an early Christian church according to an octagonal plan, it was later rebuilt to include a 12th-century *campanile* and a 16th-century dome. To the right of the church sits the 14th-century **Cappella di Sant'Aquilino,** which incorporates an old Roman door jamb. Inside, a 5th-century mosaic of a beardless Christ among his apostles looks over St. Aquilino's remains. *(MM2: S. Ambrogio to V. E. de Amicis, which leads to P. Vetra and the church. Open daily 9:30am-12:30pm and 2:30-6:30pm. Cappella €2, students €1.)*

PARCO DELL'ANFITEATRO ROMANO. This archaeological park is home to the remains of Milan's Roman amphitheater, which stretched from V. E. de Amicis to V. Arena and south to V. Conca del Naviglia. Known as Mediolaum, it served as capital of the western Roman Empire and included a gladiatorial stadium, which was destroyed in the 6th century so the Longobards couldn't use it as a stronghold. Pieces of the stadium now make up the town walls and San Lorenzo Church. A small antiquarium holds artifacts from digs. A better testament to Milan's Roman past might be found in the portals and columns lying along C. Porta Tininese. *(In the courtyard of V. E. de Amicis, 17. MM2: S. Ambrogio. ☎02 89 40 05 55. Park open Tu-Su 9:30am-4:30pm. Museum open W and F-Sa in summer 9am-7pm; in winter 9am-2pm. Free.)*

IN THE GIARDINI PUBBLICI

GALLERIA D'ARTE MODERNA. Napoleon and Josephine lived here when Milan was the capital of Napoleonic Italy (1805-1814). The gallery displays modern Lombard art as well as works from Impressionism onward. Of special note are Modigliani's *Beatrice Hastings*, Picasso's *Testa*, Klee's *Wald Bau*, and Morandi's *Natura Morta con Bottiglia*, as well as pieces by Matisse, Mondrian, and Dufy. *(V. Palestro, 16, in the Villa Reale; do not confuse with Palazzo Reale. MM12: Palestro. ☎02 67 62 55 03. Currently undergoing restoration. Doors open to the public Tu-Su at 9 and 11am. Free tours Th 10am.)* The adjacent **Padiglione D'Arte Contemporanea (PAC)** is a rotating extravaganza of photographs, paintings, and visiting exhibits. *(V. Palestro, 14. M-F ☎02 76 00 90 25, Sa-Su ☎02 76 02 04 00; www.comune.milano.it/pac. Open Tu-W and F-Sa 9:30am-5:30pm, Th 9:30am-9pm, Su 9:30am-7:30pm. €5.20, students €2.60.)*

♫ ENTERTAINMENT

The city sponsors many free events, detailed in the monthly *Milano Mese* (free), distributed at the tourist office, or in *Milano è Milano* (€3), a booklet published in English and Italian with entertainment and cultural venues available at the tourist office and bookstores. *Milano Magazine* is a monthly publication of the Ufficio Informazione del Comune with info on bars, films, and seasonal events.

OPERA, BALLET, AND LA SCALA

Milan's operatic tradition and unparalleled audience enthusiasm make ◪**La Scala** one of the best places in the world to see an opera. The theater's acoustics are phenomenal; even those in the cheap seats appreciate a glorious sensory experience. The opera season runs from January to July and from September to November, overlapping with the **ballet** season, which La Scala runs primarily out of the **Teatro degli Arcimboldi** north of the city. In December and March, La Scala plays host to **symphonic concerts.** A shuttle departs for Teatro Arcimboldi from P. del Duomo on performance nights (every 5min. 6:45-7:15pm, €1), as well as from MM1: Precotto. (Infotel Scala ☎02 72 00 37 44; www.teatroallascala.org. Central box office located at Galleria V. Emanuele. Open daily noon-6pm except for Aug. 2nd office below P. del Duomo in Metro station; same hours. Tickets €10-105; ask about student discounts. Ticket office at theater, V. Filodrammatici, 2, opens 3hr. before the start of a performance and closes 15min. after, selling only tickets for that performance. 2hr. before a performance any remaining tickets sold at guaranteed 25% discount.)

THEATER, MUSIC, AND FILM

Founded after WWII as a socialist theater, the **Piccolo Teatro,** V. Rovello, 2, near V. Dante, specializes in small-scale classics and off-beat productions. (☎02 72 33 32 22. Performances Tu-Sa usually 8:30pm, Su 4pm. €23-26, student rush tickets €12.50.) **Teatro delle Erbe,** V. Mercato, 3, hosts lyrical opera from October to April. (MM1: Cairoli or MM2: Lanza. www.felixcompany.it.) Teatri d'Italia sponsors **Milano Oltre,** a drama, dance, and music festival in June and July. Call the Ufficio Informazione del Comune (☎02 864 64 094; www.comune.milano.it). Milan cements its reputation as the jazz capital of Italy with the **Brianza Open Jazz Festival** in the first two weeks of July. (☎02 237 22 36; www.brianzaopen.com.) The **Milan Symphony Orchestra** season runs from September to May. All concerts are at the **Auditorium di Milano** at Largo Gustav Mahler. (☎02 83 38 92 01/02/03; www.orchestrasinfonica.milano.it, www.auditoriumdimilano.org. Ticket office open daily 10am-7pm. Tickets €13-50, with student discount €10-25.) Movie listings are in every major paper, especially the Thursday editions. Many cinemas screen English-language films: Monday at **Anteo,** V. Milazzo, 9 (MM2: Moscova; ☎02 65 97 732; www.anteospaziocinema.com), Tuesday at **Arcobaleno,** Vle. Tunisia, 11 (MM1: Pta. Venezia; ☎02 29 40 60 54), and Thursday at **Mexico,** V. Savona, 57 (MM2: Pta. Genova; ☎02 48 95 18 02; www.cinemamexico.it). July brings **Milano in Musica** at Il Castello Sforzesco, with several days of free concerts, theatrical performances, and even pow-wows and similar cultural events (www.milanoinmusica.it).

SPORTS

In a country where *calcio* is taken as seriously as Catholicism, nothing compares to the rivalry between Milan's soccer clubs, **Inter Milan** and **AC Milan.** The sport's feverish competition has political overtones: Inter fans are often left-wing, while AC fans tend toward the right. The face-off takes place in their shared three-tiered stadium (capacity 87,000), with its unique exterior spiraling ramps. For Inter tickets, check out www.inter.it or head to the team's offices at V. Durini, 24 (☎02 77 151; fax 02 78 15 14; MM1: S. Babila) or the **Banca Popolare di Milano,** P. Meda, 4 (☎02 77 011). AC tickets are available at the team offices at V. Turati, 3 (☎02 62 281 or 02 622 85 660. MM3: Turati), by calling **Milan Point,** C. San Gottardo, 2 (☎02 89 42 27 11), or by heading to any branch of Banca Cariplo or Banca Intesa. **Ticket One** sells tickets for both teams (☎02 39 22 61). Tours of the **stadium,** V. Piccolomini, 5, including a visit to the soccer museum, run Monday to Saturday on non-game days 10am-6pm. (MM2: Lotto. Take Vle. F. Caprilli or tram #24. ☎02 40 42 432; fax 02 40 42 251. Entrance at Gate 21 on the south side. €12.50, under 18 or over 65 €10.)

⬛ SHOPPING

In a city where clothes really do make the man (or woman), fashion pilgrims arrive in spring and summer to watch the newest styles take their first sashaying steps down the runway. Fashion shows are generally by invitation only, but once the music fades and designers take their bows, window displays and world-renowned biannual *saldi* (sales) in July and January usher the new collections into the real world. With so many fashion disciples making idols of the illustrious Giorgio, Donatella, and Miuccia, the fashion district known as the **Golden Triangle** has become a sanctuary in its own right. For window shopping, take the Metro to MM1: S. Babila and stroll around **Via Monte Napoleone**, with its two **Prada** stores within 100m of each other. A left on **Via Verri** leads to mod British fashions at **Alexander McQueen** and the familiar plaids of **Burberry**. A right turn leads to **Via Sant'Andrea**, home to two of the area's four **Armani** stores as well as **Chanel** and a host of less familiar though equally exclusive Italian names. At the end of V. Sant'Andrea, **Via della Spiga** hosts the mannequins of **Dolce & Gabbana,** Roberto Cavalli's **Just Cavalli,** and the purse and accessory stores of all the major designers. Most stores are open Monday 3-7pm and Tuesday to Saturday 10am-7pm.

Designer creations are available to mere mortals at the trendy boutiques along **Corso di Porta Ticinese,** which extends from **Piazza XXIV Maggio** in the **Navigli** district toward the *duomo*, and its offshoot, **Via Molino delle Armi.** These stores pack their displays with the latest looks for a few hundred dollars cheaper than their counterparts in the Golden Triangle. Trendsetters also flock to the affordable mix of shops along **Via Torino** near the *duomo*, and savvy shoppers unearth gems in the stores along **Corso Buenos Aires.** Another option is the Italian department store **La Rinascente,** V.S. Radegonda, 3, where Armani began his career. (☎02 88 52; www.rinascenteshopping.com. Open M-Sa 9am-10pm, Su 10am-10pm.)

Fashionistas who can tolerate the stigma of being a season behind can buy top names at a discount from wholesale clothing outlets known as *blochisti* (stocks). *Milano è Milano* has a substantial list, as does the free Shopping Map, both available at tourist offices. The well-known **Il Salvagente,** V. Bronzetti, 16, is located off C. XXII Marzo. (☎02 76 11 03 28. MM1: San Babila. Walk up C. Monforte across P. Tricolore to C. Concordia which becomes C. Indipendenza. Turn right on V. F. Bronzetti. Open M-Tu 3-7pm, W-Sa 10am-7pm.) For the discount-hunter, **Gruppo Italia Grandi Firme,** V. Montegani, #7/A, stocks Armani, Versace, and other brand names at 70% off the regular price. (☎02 89 51 39 51; www.gruppoitaliagrandifirme.it. MM2: Famagosta. Head 300m along Vle. Famagosta then Cavalcavia Schiavoni, under the overpasses and across the river to V. Montegani, where you turn right. Open M 3:30-7:30pm, Tu-F 10am-1pm and 3:30-7:30pm, Sa 10:30am-7:30pm.)

The guide *Milano è Milano* also lists markets and second-hand stores located around C. Porta Ticinese, the Navigli district, and C. Garibaldi. True Milanese bargain hunters attack the bazaars on **Via Fauché** (MM2: Garibaldi) Tuesday and Saturday and **Viale Papinian** (MM2: Agostino) on Saturday morning. Also on Saturday, the 400-year-old **Fiera di Sinigallia,** on V. d'Annunzio, is great for bargains all day.

⬛ NIGHTLIFE

Milan's nightlife resembles one of its sophisticated cocktails: the vibrant, the mellow, the chic, and the wild all mixed in a concentrated space. The **Brera district** calls to those with creative flair, inviting tourists and *Milanesi* to test their vocal skills at one of its piano bars. In the nearby **Porta Ticinese,** the young and beautiful meet after a long workday to sip fancy concoctions in the shadow of ancient ruins. Students descend upon the **Navigli canal district's** endless stream of cafes, pizzerias, pubs, bars, barges, and bars on barges, grooving to music with friends and tourists. A single block of **Corso Como** near Stazione Garibaldi is home to the most exclusive clubs in Milan, where bouncers reject the underdressed. Bars and clubs dot the rest of the city, especially around **Largo Cairoli,** home to Milan's hottest outdoor dance venue, as well the areas southeast of **Stazione Centrale** and east of **Corso Buenos Aires,** which features a mix of bars along with much of Milan's gay and lesbian scene. The best jazz clubs are on the periphery of town. Before heading out, don't underestimate Milan's sizeable **mosquito** population, especially around the Navigli, where insect repellent is the cologne of choice. The Metro closes around midnight and cabs are expensive, so stick near your hotel, or better yet, find a hotel near your preferred clubs and bars. Milan is relatively safe at night, though suburbs and the areas around Stazione Centrale, Stazione Garibaldi, and C. Buenos Aires deserve an extra dose of caution.

Check any paper on Wednesday or Thursday for info on clubs and events. *Corriere Della Sera* publishes an insert called **Vivi Milano** on Wednesday, and *La Repubblica* produces **Tutto Milano** every Thursday. The best guide to nightlife is **Pass Milano,** published in Italian every two months and available in bookstores (€12.50). **Easy Milano** (www.easymilano.it), published bi-weekly by the city's English-speaking community, contains the latest on hot night spots (available free in many bars and restaurants). Several free booklets listing bars and club venues, as well as calendars of performances, can be picked up at almost any club or bar. They include **2night** magazine (www.2night.it), a guide to the city's top bars, and **Zero2,** the Milanese edition of an Italian bi-weekly guide to music, disco, and bar acts. Perhaps most useful is the **Milano by Night map** available at the tourist office, which plots about 200 lounge, music, and theater venues.

BRERA DISTRICT

Tourists and locals mingle on the pedestrian thoroughfares between V. Brera and V. Mercado Vetero, where the night brings vendors and palm readers to the streets, along with excited crowds in search of cocktails. From MM2: Lanza head to V. Pontaccio, turn right on V. M. Vetero and then left on V. Fiori Chiari.

Club 2, V. Formentini, 2 (☎02 86 46 48 07), down V. Madonnina from V. F. Chiari. Piano bar/restaurant upstairs and karaoke disco-pub downstairs. This bar creates the mood with red lights and red-flowered stools and lampshades. *Primi* €7-8, *secondi* €13-16. Drinks from €7. Open daily 8:30pm-3am. MC/V.

Cave Montmartre, V. Madonnina, 27 (☎02 86 46 11 86). With tons of outdoor tables, Cave Montmartre serves up *gelato,* cocktails, and aperitifs to help the weary partier beat the summer heat. *Panini* €4.20. *Gelato* and sundaes €3.70-7.80. Aperitifs €2.50-6.50, cocktails €6.50. Open M-Sa 7:30am-1:45am, Su 6pm-2am. MC/V.

CORSO DI PORTA TICINESE AND PIAZZA VETRA

Welcome to the land of the all-night happy-hour buffet—one cocktail buys you dinner. Chill, well-dressed local crowds come to drink and socialize at bars with no cover. This area is best accessible from MM2: S. Ambrogio.

▨ **Yguana Café Restaurant,** V. P. Gregorio XIV, 16 (☎02 89 40 41 95), just off P. Vetra, a short walk down V. E. de Amicis and V. M. d. Armi. Beautiful people sipping fruit cocktails (€8) makes for a beautiful evening. Lounge on a couch upstairs or groove to the nightly DJs spinning house and hip hop downstairs. Happy-hour buffet M-Sa 5:30-

9:30pm, Su 5:30-10pm. Cocktails €8-10. M-F business lunch 12:30-3pm. Su brunch 12:30-4pm. Open daily for drinks 5:30pm-2am.

■ **Exploit,** V. Pioppette, 3 (☎02 89 40 86 75; www.exploitmilano.com), on C. Porta Ticinese near Chiesa di S. Lorenzo Maggiore down V. E. de Amicis. Locals flock to this trendy bar and restaurant to enjoy a candle-lit meal inside or to sip cocktails outside beside Roman ruins. Cocktails €6-8, wine €5 or €18-20 for a bottle. *Primi* €10, *secondi* €18-22. Happy-hour buffet daily 6-9pm featuring sushi, meatballs, and much more. Open Tu-Su noon-4pm and 6pm-2am.

■ **Flying Circus,** P. Vetra, 21 (☎02 58 31 35 77; www.flyingcircusmilano.com). Walk down V. E. de Amicis and V. M. d. Armi to P. Vetra. Bar is on right. Red walls and glass-encased lounge room make this wine bar a prime venue for live performances. Themed evenings include "Namaste" Indian night with live electronic Indian music and buffet with samosas, chicken marsala, and similar dishes; W "Chill Salad" with DJ-spun trance music; Th "Beer Experience"; and nights of jazz music and live singing. Themes change in winter; call for schedule. Happy-hour buffet daily 6:30-10pm with €6 cocktail. Cocktails and wine €6.50-8. Open M-F 10am-2am, Sa-Su 6:30pm-2am. MC/V.

THE NAVIGLI

From C. Porta Ticinese, walk south until the street ends at the arch. Turn right through P. XXIV Maggio, then left on V. Naviglio Pavese and V. A. Sforza. Alternatively, take the Metro to MM2: Pta. Genova. Walk along V. Vigevano until it ends and turn right on V. Naviglio Pavese. Less refined and more diverse than its neighbors, the Navigli is popular with students and has venues for everyone.

■ **Scimmie,** V. A. Sforza, 49 (☎02 89 40 28 74; www.scimmie.it). A legendary night club in 3-part harmony: pub on the river barge; polished *ristorante;* and cool bar with nightly performances. Talented underground musicians play fusion, jazz, blues, Italian swing, and reggae. Concerts 10:30pm. Schedule online. Barge: Pizza €4-8. Restaurant: *primi* and *secondi* €6-17. Both open M-F noon-3pm and 7pm-2am, Sa-Su 6pm-2am. Weekdays barge features €4 lunch menu. Bar: drinks €5-9. Open daily 8pm-3am. MC/V.

Movida Kitchen'n'Bar, V. A. Sforza, 41 (☎02 58 10 20 43; info@spaziomovida.it). White tents stretch above outside tables and a fine mist sprays from a steam machine. Extensive *panini* menu including vegetarian options with names like "papillon" and "petit Paris." Cocktail menu reads like the Bible and includes such specialties as "angel face." Panini €3.50-5. Cocktails €6.50. Happy hour 6-9pm. Open daily 6pm-2am.

Pontell, V. Naviglio Pavese, 2 (☎02 58 10 19 82). 1st bar on the right entering from P. XXIV Maggio. Ahoy, matey—life preservers and rubber dinghies make this bar look like Gilligan's Island. Ask the buff waiters in muscle shirts for the *bierre a la pression* (€8). Open daily 6pm-2am.

AROUND CORSO COMO

From MM2: Garibaldi F.S., go one block south on C. Como. At the most glamorous clubbing scene in Milan (possibly in the world), models mingle with movie stars over mojitos. Both clubs close in August.

Hollywood, C. Como, 15 (☎02 65 98 996; www.discotecahollywood.com). Slip into something stunning and pout for the bouncer: this disco selects its revelers with the utmost care. Tu night hip-hop, W night house, Th-Sa mixed music by resident DJs. Su tends to be invite-only party for sports stars and celebs. Cocktails €10. Cover €20; includes 1 drink. Student discount with ID €13-18. Open Tu-Su 11pm-5am. MC/V.

Loolapaloosa, C. Como, 15 (☎02 65 55 693), next to Hollywood. Table-dancing is *de rigeur* at this vigorous alternative to the hipper-than-thou scene next door, though run by the same company. Perfect place to toss back a pint and look gorgeous doing it. Reserve a table for Sa or risk standing by the bar all night. Cover €6 with 1 drink and buffet from 6:30-10:30pm, cocktails with music from DJ and dancing €6-8 thereafter. *Panini* €4.50-7. Open M-Sa noon-4am, Su 2pm-4am.

AROUND LARGO CAIROLI

Take the Metro to MM2: Cairoli. Not truly a localized night scene, but the few locales to be found west of the Castello Sforzesco are well worth the trip.

▧ **Old Fashion Café,** Vle. Alemagna, 6 (☎02 80 56 231; www.oldfashion.it). MM1/2: Cadorna F. N. Walk up V. Paleocapa next to the station and turn right on Vle. Alemagna before the bridge. Club is to left of Palazzo dell'Arte along a dirt path. This hot lounge and dance club spills outside in the summer to become a writhing dance party. Come dressed to impress and keep up with the stylish young crowd. Tu is the most popular night, with mixed music; F is R&B night. M-Sa cover €20, reduced €15; W €15, students free. Includes 1 drink. Dancing daily midnight-4am. Restaurant open with reservation M-Sa 9pm-midnight; must be mixed-gender party, *menù* €40-50 per person. Su restaurant open 6-10pm; €10 for table reservation, €8 for buffet. MC/V.

Bar Magenta, V. Carducci, 13 (☎02 80 53 808). MM1/2: Cardona. A short walk down V. G. Carducci at the intersection with C. Magenta. More than a Guinness bar, this institution dates from 1807. Pints €5.50. Happy-hour buffet from 6-9pm €5.50 with 1 drink. Open daily 8am-4am.

EAST OF CORSO BUENOS AIRES

It's mostly locals at the establishments southeast of Stazione Centrale. Most are accessible from MM1/2: Loreto or MM1: Pta. Venezia.

▧ **Café Capoverde,** V. Leoncavallo, 16 (☎02 26 82 04 30). MM1/2: Loreto. Take V. Costa, for 10min., which becomes V. Leoncavallo. Greenhouse/bar/restaurant/plant store in orange building on right. Pick a cactus for mom; grab a fruit cocktail for yourself. Any closer to nature and you'd be in the jungle. Healthily organic happy-hour buffet 6:30-9:30pm with starting drink (€7). Cocktails €7.50 after happy hour. Open daily 6:30pm-2am. AmEx/MC/V.

Artdeco Café, V. Lambro, 7 (☎02 29 52 47 60; www.artdecoCafé.it). MM1: Pta. Venezia. From C. Buenos Aires, turn right on V. Melzo and continue 5 blocks to bar, on right corner with V. Lambro. Hip and artsy patrons and interior. More of a dance club than neighboring L'elephante; Sept.-Apr. F-Sa DJ spins house, R&B, soul, and jazz for a crowded main floor 1pm-2am. Less movement-inclined patrons sip cocktails and watch from the balcony above. Weekend drink card deal makes 1st drink €10, 2nd and 3rd €8, 4th free. M-W after 9:30pm beer €6 and cocktails €8. Happy-hour buffet daily 6-9:30pm (€8). Open daily 6pm-2am. Closed last 3 weeks of Aug. Cash only.

L'elephante, V. Melzo, 22 (☎02 29 51 87 68; fax 02 70 04 01 145). MM2: Pta. Venezia. From C. Buenos Aires turn right on V. Melzo and continue about 5 blocks; bar is on left. Lava lamps and blue lights create a sultry atmosphere that spills into the street outside. Mostly lesbian, though the happy-hour food draws all types from 6:30-9:30pm (€5). Mixed drinks €7-8. Open Tu-Su 6:30pm-2am. Cash only.

Sottomarino Giallo, V. Donatello de Bardi, 2 (☎33 95 45 41 27; www.sottomarino-giallo.it). MM1/2: Loreto. Take V. Abruzzi to V. Donatello de Bardi. The biggest lesbian club in town lives in a yellow submarine. Women only Tu, Th, and Sa-Su. Open Tu-Su 10:30pm-3:30am.

LIVE MUSIC

🎵 **Le Trottoir,** P. XXIV Maggio, 1 (☎/fax 02 83 78 166; www.letrottoir.it). This self-proclaimed "Ritrovo d'Arte, Cultura, e Divertimento" (House of Art, Culture, and Diversions) may be the loudest, most crowded bar and club in the Navagli. A slightly alternative crowd comes nightly to get down to live underground music 10:30pm-2am on 1st fl., while upstairs a DJ spins house music. Sa is R&B; rock, pop, jazz, and alternative acts fill out the weekly roster. Cocktails €7. Pizza and sandwiches €8, available until 2am. Happy-hour daily 6-8pm beer €3.50, cocktails €5. Open daily 3pm-3am. Cash only.

Blueshouse, V. S. Uguzzone, 26 (☎02 27 00 36 21; www.blueshouse.it). MM1: Villa S. Giovanni. Take V. Vipacco; turn right on V. A. Soffredini and left 4 blocks later on V. S. Uguzzone, the last street. Relaxed interior where music lovers have traveled to down beers and feel the beat. Jazz, blues, rock, and tribute bands. Concerts begin 11pm; check website for performance schedule. Open W-Su 9pm-2:30am. Often closes July-Sept. but sponsors nearby music festivals, see website for information.

❋ FESTIVALS

Milan's increasingly popular **Carnevale** is the longest lasting in Italy. The masked mystique and medieval revelry radiates from the *duomo* and spreads through the city. Carnevale occurs annually during the days preceding Ash Wednesday. The **Mercatone dell'Antiquariato sul Naviglio Grande,** a giant antiques extravaganza, takes place the last Sunday of each month (☎02 89 40 99 71; www.navigliogrande.mi.it). Pick up a copy of *Guida Estate 2005 per le Strade di Milano* at the tourist office for a listing of cultural events, sports, and festivals throughout June and July. **La Notte Bianca** (White Night) occurs annually one night in June when the Metro, theater, shops, and restaurants stay open all night from 3pm-6am. From June-September the tourist office sponsors both the **Festa della Cultura,** featuring dance, music, and food from Milan's many immigrant cultures (call the tourist office ☎02 884 645 33), and the **Serate al Museo** celebration with free concerts (both classical and contemporary) throughout Milan's museum courtyards and great halls (☎02 88 45 65 55; www.comune.milano.it/museiemostre).

🔁 DAYTRIP FROM MILAN

🏛 CERTOSA DI PAVIA

SILA buses F5 or F6 from Milan-Famagosta (MM2) serve Certosa (30min., 2 per hr. 7:45am-8:15pm, €2.35). From Pavia, buses depart 2 per hr. (15min., 6:30am-8pm, €1.85. Return 2 per hr. 8:12am-8:42pm.) Return tickets are available at the Il Giornale stand in the bus lot; bus to Milan stops next to the journal stand; to Pavia, stops opposite the stand. Exiting the bus in Certosa, go to the traffic light and turn right; continue straight for a few blocks on the road which becomes the, long, tree-lined V. Certosa. The monastery is at the end. Trains also run from Milan to Certosa (7min., every hr. 5:44am-10:37, €1.25), stopping behind the walled city. From the train station, head through the parking lot and turn left in front of the wall, right at the cross street at the end, then right at the first street beyond the wall (500m). Continue 200m and go through the portal on your right. (Monastery: ☎0382 92 56 13; www.apt.pavia.it. Open Tu-Su May-Sept. 9-11:30am and 2:30-6pm; Apr. 9-11:30am and 2:30-5:30pm; Oct. and Mar. 9-11:30am and 2:30-5pm; Nov.-Feb. 9-11:30am and 2:30-4:30pm. Free. Modest dress required.)

Seven kilometers north of Pavia stands the 🏛**Monastero della Certosa di Pavia** (Carthusian Monastery). Gian Galeazzo Visconti founded it in 1396 as a mausoleum for the Visconti clan, who ruled the area from the 12th through the 15th centuries. Consecrated as a monastery in 1497, the building is a monument to the evolution of Italian art. Inlaid marble, bas-reliefs, and sculptures embellish every available surface. The work required the efforts of over 250 craftsmen during the 15th-century Lombard Renaissance. Statues of biblical figures, carvings of narratives, and 61 medallions adorn the base alone, while the upper half relies more on geometric patterns formed by the contrasting colors of marble. The Cistercians who today oversee the monastery in place of the Carthusian monks lead **group tours** (usually in Italian) that are necessary to pass through the interior iron gate to the apse and altar of the cathedral and the aforementioned sights. Past the gate in the left apse, note the prone figures of Ludovico il More and Beatrice d'Este. On the feet of the female statue may be the oldest sculptural rendition of platform shoes, which she wore to match the tall height of her husband. The old sacristy houses a Florentine triptych carved in ivory; 99 sculptures and 66 bas-reliefs depict the lives of Mary and Jesus. Encircling the choir are 42 stalls—one for each monk—with intricate wood inlay representations of saints, prophets, and apostles. Beyond Gian Galeazzo's mausoleum, the peaceful great cloister contains cells used to house the monks who formerly lived here.

BERGAMO ☎035

A trip to Bergamo (pop. 117,000) is a visit to two different worlds. The *città bassa* (low city) is a modern, commercial town where tourists and locals peruse *piazze* and shops. On the bluff above, in the *città alta* (high city), are the palaces, churches, and huge stone fortifications that once defended Venetian territory from Spanish-ruled Milan. In the narrow, cobblestone streets of this medieval town, you're as likely to run into a monk as find an *enoteca* brewing *caffè* past midnight.

▚ TRANSPORTATION

Bergamo Orio al Serio Airport (☎035 32 63 23; www.orioaeroporto.it) serves some budget airlines. Bergamo's **train station** (☎035 24 79 50) is in Ple. Marconi. **Trains** run to: Brescia (1hr., every hr. 5:38am-10:55pm, €3.40); Cremona (1½hr., every 3hr. 9:03am-5:20pm, €6.50); Milan (1hr., every hr. 4:41am-10:25pm, €3.90); and Venice (3hr., 1 per day 8:22am, €17.18). **Buses,** in the **Stazione Autolinee** to the left of the train station, run to Como (7 per day 6:25am-7:45pm, €4.25) and Milan (every 30min. 5:30am-11pm, €4.35). Buses from the neighboring SAB station serve suburbs and nearby towns. The **airport bus** runs between Colle Aperto, the station, and Bergamo's **airport** (30min., 5:30am-10:05pm, €1.55). **ATB** (Azienda Trasporti Bergamo) runs buses in Bergamo; for a complete route map enquire at the ATB Point in Largo Porta Nuova (☎035 23 60 26; info@atb.bergamo.it). For a **taxi,** call ☎035 45 19 090, 035 24 45 05, or 035 24 20 00. **Car rental** is available at **Avis,** V. P. Paleocapa, 3 (☎035 27 12 90 or 035 31 60 41).

▚ ▓ ORIENTATION AND PRACTICAL INFORMATION

The train and bus stations and many budget hotels are found in the *città bassa*, the newer and more industrial part of the city. From the bus and train stations in **Piazzale Marconi**, take **Viale Papa Giovanni XXIII** through **Largo Porto Nuova** as it turns into **Viale Roma** and then **Viale Vittorio Emanuele II** to reach the base of the *città alta* on the bluff above. The three simplest ways to reach the *città alta* are: take bus #1 to the *funicolare di città alta*, which ascends from Vle. V. Emanuele II to the

Bergamo

NIGHTLIFE
Enoteca al Donizetti, **7**
Papageno Pub, **2**
Birreria Pozzo Bianco, **9**
The Tucans, **4**
Vineria Cozzi, **1**

ACCOMMODATIONS
Albergo S. Giorgio, **13**
Convitto Pensionato Caterina Cittadini, **8**
Locanda Caironi, **12**
Ostello Città di Bergamo (HI), **10**

FOOD
Etnea Pasticceria e Gelateria, **14**
Taverna del Colleoni & Dell'Agnello, **3**
Trattoria Casa Mia, **11**
Trattoria da Ornella, **6**
Trattoria Tre Torri, **5**

TO CASTELLO (400m)

Porta Sant'Alessandro
Colle Aperto
Viale delle Mura
Via Roccolino
PIAZZA MASCHERONI
Cittadella
Porta di San Lorenzo
Via Maironi da Ponte
Via della Boccola
Via Vagine
Via Tassis
Via della Fara
V. della S. Grata
V. Salvecchio
V. San Salvatore
V. Arena
Via del Paradiso
Via Tre Armi
Viale Delle Mura
Teatro Sociale
PIAZZA DUOMO
Torre Civica
Via Tassis
Biblioteca Civica
Battistero
Cappella Colleoni
S. Maria Maggiore
P. VECCHIA
Via S. Lorenzo
S. Alessandro
P. GIULIANI
Palazzo d: Ragione
Via M. Lupo
Via G. Donizetti
P. MERCATO D. FIENO
Parco delle Rimembranze
Via San Giacomo
Via San Pancrazio
Via Solata
La Rocca
MERCATO D. SCARPE
Via Gombito
Funicular
PIAZZATE B. LEGNANO
S. Agostio
Prato della Fara
Via Fara
Via S. Lucia Vecchia
V. S. Giacomo
Porta San Giacomo
Via Salita d. Scaletta
CITTÀ ALTA
Mura di S. Giacomo
Via Porta Dipinta
Sant'Andrea
Via Porta Dipinta
S. Michele al Pozzo Blanco
Mura di S. Agostino
Porta Sant'Agostino
Il Fortino
Via Sant'Alessandro
Vic. San Carlo
Via Buttaro
Viale Vittorio Emanuele II
Pelicano Supermarket
Via Zambelli
Via Don C. Botta
Via Brigata Lupi
Via Antonio Locatelli
Via Monte Ortigara
Via Comaseno
Via Pelabrocca
Via Pignolo
Via della Noca
Galleria dell'Accademia Carrara
Via S. Benedetto
Vicolo d. Torri
Via F. Cucchi
PIAZZALE DELLA REPUBLICA
Via G.E.R. Zelasco
Via M. Domini
Via Zambianchi
Via Masone
Via Elisabetta
Pradello
PIAZZA GIACOMO CARRARA
Via San Tomaso
Galleria d'Arte Moderna
TO (1km)
G. Garibaldi
Via G. Garibaldi
PIAZZA DELLA LIBERTÀ
Via Tasca
Via Petrarca
Via Adamello
PIAZZA DANTE
Via Orobica
Via Roma
ROTUNDA D. MILLE
Via Borfuro
Via dei Partigiani
PIAZZETTA SAN
Largo Bartolomeo Belotti
S. Bartolomeo
Via Giuseppe Verdi
Giardini Caprotti
CITTÀ BASSA
Via Pignolo
S. Bernardino
Via San Giovanni
TO (2km)
Via C. Battisti
Via A. Pitentino
LARGO DEL GALGARIO
V. Suardi
TO (100m)
Via XX Settembre
PIAZZA VITORIO VENETO
TO (400m)
PIAZZA MATTEOTTI
PIAZZA CAVOUR
Teatro Donizetti
Via Torquato Tasso
S. Spirito
Parco Marenzi
Via T. Frizzoni
PORTA SAN ANTONIO
Via G. Tiraboschi
Via Ghislanzoni
LARGO PORTA NUOVA
S. Maria d. Grazie
Viale Papa Giovanni XXIII
Via Galliccioli
Via Gabriele Camozzi
Via Borgo Palazzo
Morla R.
Via d'Alzano
V. S. Francesco d'Assisi
V. T. Tarantelli
Via T. Pascoli
Via Clara Maffei
Via del Casalino
Via Stoppani
Via Madonna della Neve
Via Pietro Paleocapa
PIAZZA DEGLI ALPINI
Rx
Via Angelo Maj
Via Foro Boario
V. Tarchetti
V. M. Cefalonia
V. Dir. Julia
V. d. Cappuccini
SISA Supermarket
Via Torretta
TO (300m)
Via G. Bonomelli
PIAZZALE MARCONI
Stazione Autolinee
Stazione Autolinee SAB
Via Bartolomeo Bono
V. A. Fantoni
V. Aneta
200 meters
200 yards
PIAZZA S. ANNA
Laundry

Mercato delle Scarpe (8 per hr., 7:08am-midnight); take bus #1a to the Colle Aperto, stopping at the top of the *città alta;* or climb the stairs on **Via Salita della Scaletta,** which starts to the left of the funicular on Vle. V. Emanuele II. Turn right at the top, and follow **Via San Giacomo** through **Porta San Giacomo** for 15min.

 BERGAMO ON A BUDGET. A great, cheap way to see the city is to purchase an all-day ATB ticket from a vending machine or *tabaccherie* for €2.50. Tickets are good on both ATB city buses and the funiculars that climb to the *città alta* and the Castello San Vigilio. (75min. tickets are also available for €1.)

The walled *città alta* is a well preserved medieval town with most of Bergamo's major sights and churches. Most visitors enter through the Pta. S. Giacomo, following V. S. Giacomo to the Mercato delle Scarpe and then up **Via Gombito,** which passes through **Piazza Vecchia,** where it turns into **Via B. Colleoni** before reaching the **Cittadella.** Just beyond the Cittadella, through **Colle Aperto** and **Porta S. Alessandro,** the San Vigilio funicular takes riders to Bergamo's highest point.

Tourist Offices: *Città alta:* V. Gombito, 13, on the ground fl. of the tower (☎035 24 22 26 or 035 23 27 30; www.provincia.bergamo.it). Open daily 9am-12:30pm and 2-5:30pm. *Città bassa:* building in center of Ple. Marconi in front of train station (☎035 21 02 04 or 035 21 31 85). Open M-F 9am-12:30pm and 2-5:30pm.

Tours: Gruppo Guide Città di Bergamo (☎035 34 42 05; www.bergamoguide.it). Tours in Italian F-Su, German Sa, French F, and English Su. 2hr. €10, children free.

Currency Exchange: Banca Nazionale del Lavoro, V. Petrarca, 12 (☎035 23 80 16), off Vle. Roma/Vle. V. Emanuele II, near P. della Libertà. Good rates. Open M-F 8:20am-1:20pm and 2:35-4:05pm, Sa 8:20-11:50am. Also at the **post office** and other banks.

ATMs: Throughout the *città bassa* and at the train station, especially along Vle. Roma straight up from the train station. In the *città alta,* P. Vecchia 1/A at **Credito Bergamasco** and **Banca Popolare di Bergamo,** V. Gombito, 2/C. Also outside the post office.

Western Union: Many locations throughout the *città bassa,* especially lining V. G. Quarenghi, including **Multi Link Business Center,** V. G. Quarenghi, 39/C, right off V. P. Paleocapa. Offers cheap long-distance calls; English spoken. Open M-Sa 9:30am-9pm.

Luggage Storage: At Bergamo airport, a 30min. bus ride from the station.

Laundromat: Lavanderia Self Service, V. A. Maj, 39/B (☎338 42 59 971). Wash €3.50-6.50 per 35min., dry €1 per 10min.

Public Toilets: V. Mario Lupo, 10, and in the Castello San Vigilio up the funicular from Colle Aperto. Same hours as the Castello.

Emergency: ☎113. **Ambulance:** ☎118. **Police:** ☎035 39 95 59.

Pharmacy: *Città bassa:* **Farmacia Internazionale,** V. A. Maj 2/A. Head up V. P. Giovanni from the station and turn right. Open M-F 9am-12:30pm and 3-7:30pm. *Città alta:* **Farmacia Guidetti,** V. S. Giacomo, 2, in the Mercato d. Scarpe (☎035 23 72 20). Open M-F 9am-12:30pm and 3-7:30pm. After-hours rotation posted outside.

Hospital: Ospedale Maggiore, Largo Barozzi, 1 (☎035 26 91 11).

Internet Access: Available in many of the shops along V. Quarenghi. Often combined with Western Union and long-distance calling.

Post Office: *Città bassa:* V. Locatelli, 11 (☎035 53 22 11). Take V. Zelasco from V. V. Emanuele. Open M-F 8:30am-7pm, Sa 8:30am-12:30pm. *Città alta:* Mercato d. Fieno, 13 (☎035 23 95 23; fax 035 21 17 96). From V. Gombito, turn on V. S. Pancrazio. Open M-F 8:30am-2pm, Sa 8:30am-12:30pm. **Postal Code:** 24121, 24124, 24129.

ACCOMMODATIONS

Prices rise with altitude; most affordable *alberghi* (hotels) are in the *città bassa*. Ask at the tourist office for info on cheaper *agriturismi*.

■ **Ostello Città di Bergamo (HI)**, V. G. Ferraris, 1 (☎035 36 17 24; www.ostellodibergamo.it). Left of Pta. Nuova on V. Camozzi. Take bus #4 (every 15min.) to V. L. da Vinci in Monterosso. Facing the church on the hill, walk left 100m on V. L. da Vinci and climb the stairs on the right; hostel is on the right. Modern rooms have bath and balcony. Expansive gardens and common room with TV, microwave, and fridge. 2 bikes for rent, €10 per day. Breakfast buffet included. Internet €5.16 per hr. Reserve ahead in summer. 4-to 8-bed dorms €15; singles €23; doubles €40; family rooms (3-6 people) €18 per person. Non-HI members add €3 or purchase 1-year membership (€18). MC/V. ❷

■ **Convitto Pensionato Caterina Cittadini**, V. Rocca, 10 (☎035 24 39 11), off Mercato d. Scarpe, in the *città alta*. Nuns in charge speak little English. Women only. Prime location, with a courtyard, rooftop terraces, and clean rooms and bathrooms. Breakfast and lunch €5. Sheets available. Reception on 2nd fl., ring bell for entry. Curfew 10pm; keys available. Reserve ahead. Singles €25, with bath €30; doubles €40. Cash only. ❷

Albergo S. Giorgio, V. S. Giorgio, 10 (☎035 21 20 43; www.sangiorgioalbergo.it). Take bus #7, or walk from the train station down Vle. P. Giovanni XXIII. Turn left on V. P. Paleocapa, which becomes V. S. Giorgio. Spacious rooms with fan, fridge, TV, and sink. English spoken. 62 beds. Wheelchair accessible. Reception 7:30am-midnight. Singles €30, with bath €50; doubles €50/65; triples and quad with bath €80/100. MC/V. ❸

Locanda Caironi, V. Torretta, 6B/8 (☎035 24 30 83; fax 035 21 13 19). From the train station, take Vle. P. Giovanni XXIII to V. A. Maj, turn right, and walk for about 1 mi. to P. S. Anna. Turn left on V. Borgo Palazzo, then right at 2nd block. Or, take bus #5 or 7 from V. A. Maj. Reception is inside the "*Caironi Trattoria*" restaurant. 7 rooms overlook a shady garden. Shared bath. Reserve ahead. Singles €20; doubles €38. MC/V. ❷

FOOD

Polenta, a yellow cornmeal paste, is a staple of the Bergamasco plate, and is often found accompanying meals of *cavallo* (horse) or *asino* (donkey). Meals conclude with a *formaggio* course—try the supple *branzi* and *taleggio* cheeses with the local *Valcalepio* red and white wines. Many of Bergamo's best restaurants are on the main tourist drag, V. Bartolomeo, and its continuations V. Colleoni and V. Gombito. In comparison to their *città alta* cousins, restaurants in the *città bassa* are often less traditional, and the quality can be less than stellar. Pick up staples at **Pellicano** supermarket, Vle. V. Emanuele II, 17, straight up from the train station past the Ple. Repubblica. (Open M 8:30am-1:30pm, Tu-F 8:30am-1:30pm and 3:30-8pm, Sa 8:30am-8pm. MC/V.) **Supermercati UNES**, V. P. da Brembate, 8, off V. A. Maj, has a large selection of items at reasonable prices. (Open M 3:30-7:30pm, Tu-F 8:30am-1pm and 3:30-7:30pm, Sa 8:30am-7:30pm. AmEx/MC/V.)

■ **Trattoria Casa Mia**, V. S. Bernardino, 20 (☎035 22 06 76). From the train station walk straight along V. P. Giovanni to Largo Pta. Nuova. Turn left on V. G. Tiraboschi, which becomes V. Zambonate. Then turn left on V. S. Bernadino. Crowds of *Bergamaschi* and menus in Italian give this *trattoria* a strong local flavor. Lunch (€8.50) and dinner (€11) *menù* includes choice of salad, regional pasta, and main meat or vegetarian dish, as well as .25L *vino* or .5L water. Restaurant open daily 11:50am-2:10pm and 7-10pm. Bar open 11am-3:30pm and 6pm-12am. Cash only. ❷

Trattoria Tre Torri, P. Mercato del Fieno, 7/A (☎035 24 43 66). Heading downhill from P. Vecchia, turn left off V. Gombito on V. S. Pancrazio. Dine on authentic cuisine within this *trattoria's* compact stone walls. *Antipasti* and *primi* €6.50, *secondi* €9-12. Cover €1.50. Open M-Tu and Th-Su 12:15-2:30pm and 7:30-10:30pm. MC/V. ❸

Trattoria da Ornella, V. Gombito, 15 (☎035 23 27 36). After exiting the funicular, walk up V. Gombito. Popular spot overlooking fountain and *piazza* specializes in rich polenta *taragna*, made with butter, local cheeses, and rabbit (€14). *Primi* €7-8, *secondi* €11-15. Cover €2. Open M-W and F-Su 12:30-3pm and 7:30-11pm. AmEx/MC/V. ❸

Etnea Pasticceria e Gelateria, V. A. Maj, 10M (☎035 23 06 42). Straight from station on V. P. Giovanni, turn right on V. A. Maj and walk about 3 blocks. Amazing homemade *gelato* as authentic as the seeds and mottled coloring in its fruit flavors. Cup or cone €1.50-2, 1kg €10. Tu-Su 8am-7:30pm. Cash only. ❶

Taverna del Colleoni & Dell'Agnello, P. Vecchia, 7 (☎035 23 25 96). This 300-year-old restaurant provides a luxurious dining experience. Succulent cuisine served at candlelit tables in the shadow of the civic tower. *Primi* €13-15, *secondi* €13-24. Open Tu-Sa noon-2:30pm and 7:30-10:30pm, Su noon-2:30pm and 7:30-10pm. AmEx/MC/V. ❺

◎ SIGHTS

CITTÀ ALTA

▦ BASILICA DI SANTA MARIA MAGGIORE. Despite a crumbling facade, this 12th-century basilica, attached to the Cappella Colleoni, possesses a bright Baroque interior. Tapestries and oil paintings depicting biblical stories adorn the walls below an iridescent ceiling, surrounding the tomb of Bergamo's famous son, composer Gaetano Donizetti. *(Head through archway flanking P. Vecchia to reach P. del Duomo. ☎035 22 33 27. Open Apr.-Oct. M-Sa 9am-12:30pm and 2:30-6pm, Su 9am-1pm and 3-6pm; Nov.-Mar. M-Sa 9am-12:30pm and 2:30-5pm, Su 9am-noon and 3-6pm. Free.)*

CAPPELLA COLLEONI. Marble braids weave through the colorful Renaissance facade, and 18th-century ceiling frescoes by Tiepolo illuminate the interior. G. A. Amadeo designed the *cappella* in 1476 as a funerary chapel for the celebrated Bergamasco mercenary Bartolomeo Colleoni. The elaborate exterior carvings combine biblical and classical allusions—the saints wear togas and Julius and Augustus Caesar are granted divine status. *(To the right of the basilica. Open Apr.-Oct. daily 9am-12:30pm and 2-6:30pm; Nov.-Mar. Tu-Su 9am-12:30pm and 2:30-4:30pm. Free.)*

PIAZZA VECCHIA. This *piazza* houses medieval and Renaissance buildings set among restaurants and cafes in the heart of the *città alta*. Locals lounge on the steps of the 400-year-old **Biblioteca Civica,** which houses Bergamo's 16th-century manuscripts. Across the *piazza* is the 12th-century Venetian Gothic **Palazzo della Ragione** (Court of Justice), featuring St. Marks' winged lion, symbol of Venice. Behind it is the **Cattedrale di S. Alessandro,** patron saint of Bergamo. To the right, connected to the *palazzo* by a covered walkway, stands the 12th-century **Torre Civica/campanone** (Civic Tower/bell tower). The 229 steps to the top of the 54m tower will take you to a 360° view of Bergamo. To commemorate the town's medieval curfew, the 15th-century bell rings 180 times nightly at 10pm. *(Wheelchair accessible. Tower open Apr.-Oct. Tu-F 9:30am-7pm, Sa 9:30am-9:30pm; Nov.-Mar. Sa 9:30am-4:30pm, Tu-F open to groups of more than 5. €2; €3 with admission to Parco delle Rimembranze.)*

PARCO DELLE RIMEMBRANZE. Once a Roman military camp, this park's shady paths honor Italian battle casualties. In the middle, fortress **La Rocca** houses the

Museo Storico, featuring historical city plans, weaponry, and uniforms. *(P. Brigata Legnano, 12. At the end of V. Rocca. ☎035 24 71 16 or 035 22 63 32. Open Oct.-May Tu-Su 9:30am-1pm and 2-5:30pm; June-Sept. Tu-F 9:30am-1pm and 2-5:30pm, Sa 9:30am-7pm. La Rocca €2; €3 with admission to Piazza Vecchia. ☎035 46 62 57; www.bergamoestoria.org including the Antonio Locatelli, Campanone, San Francesco Museo Storico, Museo Donizettiano, and Torre dei caduti. Park admission free.)*

MUSEI DI CITTADELLA. Housed within the Citadella near the top of the *città alta*, the Civic Museums of Bergamo include the **Museo di Scienze Naturali,** P. Cittadella, 10 *(☎035 28 60 11; www.museoscienzebergamo.it)* and the **Museo Archeologico,** P. Cittadella, 9 *(☎035 24 28 39; www.museoarcheologicobergamo.it).* The natural science museum features a collection of fossils and taxidermy specimens native to Bergamo, and includes an exhibit on Bergamo's silk industry that features live silk worms. The archaeological museum presents cultural memorabilia from Africa. *(At the end of V. B. Colleoni. Both open Tu-F and Su 9am-12:30pm and 2:30-5:30pm, Sa 9am-7pm.)*

ABOVE THE CITTÀ ALTA. The **San Vigilio** funicular (3min.; every 15min. M-Th 10:09am-11:47pm, F-Sa 10:09am-1:17am; €1) runs from just past Porta S. Alessandro and Colle Aperto in the *città alta* to **Castello San Vigilio,** Bergamo's castle in the clouds and the highest point in the city. While few halls and staircases are open for exploration, the fortification's isolation and the 360° views of Bergamo make it worth the ride. Hiking trails run down to the historical center, including one just to the left of the funicular station past the church, Salita dello Scorlassone. *(Head right up V. San Vigilio after exiting the funicular, castle on left. Castle open daily Apr.-Sept. 9am-8pm; Mar. and Oct. 10am-6pm; Nov.-Feb. 10am-4pm. Free.)*

CITTÀ BASSA

GALLERIA DELL'ACCADEMIA CARRARA. The cornerstone of the gallery's collection resides on the villa's top floor, where 13th- to 15th-century canvases showcase the work of Tiepolo, Titian, Rubens, Brueghel, Bellini, Mantegna, Goyen, van Dyck, and El Greco, and include such works as Botticelli's not quite flattering *Ritratto di Giuliano de' Medici*, Lotto's *Ritratto di Giovinetto*, and Rizzi's *Maddalena in Meditazione*, in which Mary Magdalene looks down on a crucified Christ. A floor below, lifelike works by 19th-century portrait-painter Cesare Tallone adorn the walls, complemented by detailed Italian cityscape paintings by Mancini and paintings of local vegetation by regional son Constantino Rosa. Across P. G. Carrara, the Academia Carrara's Galleria d'Arte Moderna e Contemporaneo hosts a modest collection of works primarily from the 1950s to 70s that includes many bronze sculptures completed by local artist Manzu as well as a few notable works by such painters as Kandinsky. A separate building hosts temporary exhibits. *(Galleria dell'Accademia: P. G. Carrara, 82/A. From Largo Porta Nuova, take V. Camozzi to V. Pignolo, then turn right onto V. San Tomaso. ☎035 39 96 43. Galleria d'Arte Moderna: V. S. Tomaso, 53. ☎035 39 95 27. Both open Apr.-Sept. Tu-Su 10am-1pm and 3-6:45pm; Oct.-Mar. 9:30am-1pm and 2:30-5:45pm. €2.60, over 60 or under 18 free.)*

OTHER SIGHTS. In the heart of *città bassa* is **Piazza Matteotti,** redesigned by the Fascists in 1924 and typically crawling with tourists and local youth. The **Chiesa di San Bartolomeo,** to the right of the *piazza* past the Teatro Donizetti along V. T. Tasso, holds a superb altarpiece of the Madonna and Child by Lorenzo Lotto. *(Open daily 9am-4pm. Free.)* To the right of San Bartolomeo, V. T. Tasso leads to the **Chiesa del Santo Spirito,** marked by its mottled stone and brick facade and modernist iron sculpture over the door. The stark gray Renaissance interior contrasts strongly with decorative paintings by Lotto, Borgognone, and Previtali and life-size sculptures of the saints, including a recently crucified Christ. *(Open Sept.-June M-Sa 7-11:30am and 4-6:30pm, Su 8am-noon and 4-7pm; July-Aug. M-Sa 7-11am and 5-6:30pm, Su 5-7pm. Free.)* On the left, V. Pignolo connects the upper and lower cities, winding past 16th- to 18th-century villas whose large doors open on elaborate inner courtyards. At the intersection with V. S. Giovanni is the tiny **Chiesa di San Bernardino,** whose bright yellow interior features icons celebrating the town's agricultural and industrial heritage, as well as a splendid Lotto *Madonna and Child* altar painting. *(☎ 035 23 00 37. Open M-F 8-11am and 4-6pm, Sa 8-11am, and Su 8:30-11am. Free.)*

♫ 🎭 ENTERTAINMENT AND NIGHTLIFE

The arts thrive in Bergamo. The opera season lasts from September to November, and includes a celebration of native composer Donizetti's works. The drama season follows, from November to April, at the **Teatro Donizetti,** P. Cavour, 15 (☎ 035 41 60 602 or 035 41 60 603; box office open daily 1-9pm), off P. Matteotti in the *città bassa.* From mid-April to mid-June, the spotlight falls on the highly acclaimed **Festivale Pianistico Internazionale Arturo Benedetti Michelangeli** (☎ 035 24 01 40; www.festivalmichelangeli.it; tickets €8-35), a celebration of classical works co-hosted by the city of Brescia. Complementing these traditional offerings is **Andar per Musica,** a contemporary folk extravaganza in June, July, and August, featuring cultural dance and music offerings in Bergamo and nearby provinces. (☎ 035 417 54 53; www.bgavvenimenti.it.) During the summer, the tourist office provides a program of free monthly events, *Estate Viva la Tua Città.*

The *città alta* shape-shifts at night as people pack the eateries, pubs, and *enoteche* along V. B. Colleoni. The 200 Belgian beers at **Papageno Pub,** V. B. Colleoni, 1/B, ensure the liveliest hangout in town. (☎ 035 23 66 24. Open Tu-Su 10am-3pm and 6pm-2am. MC/V.) A romantic alcove, the *enoteca* **Vineria Cozzi,** V. B. Colleoni, 22, stocks over 330 Italian wines. (☎ 035 23 88 36; www.vineriacozzi.it. *Primi* and *secondi* €7-16. Cover €2.50. Open M-Tu and Th-Su 10:30am-3pm and 6:30pm-2am. MC/V.) More social is **The Tucans** Irish pub, V. Gombito, 10. (☎ 329 60 59 214. Open Tu-F 10am-3pm and 7pm-2am, Sa 7pm-2am, Su 6pm-2am. Cash only.) A bit off the beaten path, **Birreria Pozzo Bianco,** V. Porta Dipinta, 30/B, offers a warm all-night kitchen and a fine drink selection. (☎ 035 24 76 94. Beer €2.50-8.50, wine €12-19 per bottle. *Primi* and *secondi* €6.50-16. Open daily 11:30am-5pm and 7pm-2am. AmEx/MC/V.) **Enoteca al Donizetti,** V. Gombito, 17/A, has platters of local cheeses and salami as well as wine tastings. The elevated stone patio is the best place to people-watch at night. (☎ 035 24 26 61; www.donizetti.it. Cover €2.50. *Specialità* €8.50-16. Open M and W-Su 10:30am-3pm and 6:30pm-midnight. AmEx/MC/V.)

BRESCIA   ☎ 030

From afar, Brescia's glass highrises mark the small city (pop. 188,000) as an emerging commercial and fashion center, though its castle and *centro storico* reflect a rich Roman past and some outstanding archaeological and art museums. The city once owed its prosperity to the estates of wealthy aristocrats; today's appliance export business is somewhat less glamorous, though the city council has worked to improve upon its cultural offerings, making Brescia worth a visit.

▐ TRANSPORTATION

Brescia is on the Torino-Trieste line. **Trains** run to: Bergamo (1hr., 10 per day 5:25am-10:16pm, €3.30); Cremona (45min., 15 per day 6:21am-9:32pm, €3.85);

Brescia

🏠 ACCOMMODATIONS
Albergo San Marco, **8**
Hotel Sirio, **1**
Hotel Solferino, **7**

🍴 FOOD
Al Frate, **5**
Ristorante e Pizzeria
Cavour, **9**
El Forner, **6**
Trattoria due Stelle, **2**

🌙 NIGHTLIFE
Caffè Castello, **3**
Castello Bar, **4**
Seconda Classe, **10**

Milan (1½hr., every hr. 4:15am-11:32pm, €5.10); Venice (2hr., every hr. 4:52-9:57pm, €13.53); and Verona (45min., 10 per day 6:00am-1:35am, €3.36). Left of the station, **SIA buses** (☎030 37 76 237; office open 7am-7pm) run to the western shore of Lake Garda (6am-8pm) and to Milan (1¾hr., 4 per day 6:40am-9:20pm, €6). To the right, **SAIA buses** run to Cremona (1¼hr., every hr. 6:25am-6:25pm, €4.25) and Verona (1½hr., every hr. 6:30am-8:05pm, €4.50). (☎800 88 39 99 or 030 23 08 811; www.saiatrasporti.it. Ticket office open M-F 7am-12:30pm and 1:30-6:25pm, Sa 7am-12:30pm and 1:30-3:10pm. After hours, purchase tickets at the bar above the ticket office.) Information and maps may be obtained at **Brescia Mobilita Info Point**, C. Zanardelli, 34. (☎800 11 78 78 or 030 20 57 070; www.bresciatrasporti-spa.it). Open M-F 9am-12:30pm and 3-6pm and Sa 9am-12:30pm. **Taxis** (☎030 35 111) are available 24hr. Rent cars at **Europcar Italia,** V. Stazione, 41/49 (☎030 28 04 87) or **Avis,** V. F. Lippi, 5 (☎030 90 50 245). To the right of the train station exit, **Servizio di Noleggio Biciclette** rents bikes. (☎030 90 12 47; fax 030 90 50 245. Open June 10-Sept. 10 M-Sa 7:30am-7:30pm. Free with ID and €5 deposit.)

✦❷ ORIENTATION AND PRACTICAL INFORMATION

Though Brescia's modern commercial areas stretch both north of the Castello and south of the train station, the *centro storico* holds most of the city's architectural gems. To reach the center from the **train station,** take **Via Foppa** to **Via Vittorio Emanuele II** and turn right, then left on **Via Gramsci,** which leads to **Piazza della Vittoria.** Crossing right through the archways under the Albergo Vittoria, Brescia's oldest hotel, and across **Via X. Giornate** leads to **Piazza Paolo VI** and the *duomi.* Walk north from P. Paolo VI to **Via Musei,** along which lie the **Piazza del Foro** and **Tempio Capitolino,** the Museo della Città di Santa Giulia, and numerous pathways leading uphill to Il Castello, including the pedestrian path **Via Piamarta** next to the Museo. To the left of V. Musei is the **Piazza di Loggia.** Some of the best shopping in the city can be found along **Corso Zanardelli** surrounding the historical Teatro Grande.

Tourist Office: APT Assessorato al Turismo, V. Musei, 32 (☎030 37 491; www.provincia.brescia.it/turismo). Helpful event fliers, **maps,** and walking guides. Open M-F 9am-12:30pm and 3-6pm, Sa 9am-12:30pm. **Città di Brescia Tourist Office,** P. Loggia, 6 (☎030 24 00 357; www.comune.brescia.it). From V. X. Giornate, go left into P. d. Loggia; office is directly on your left. English-speaking staff with info and maps for the city proper. Open M-F 9:30am-12:30pm and 2-5:30pm, Sa 9:30am-1pm.

Bank: Banco di Brescia, C. Zanardelli, 54, near the APT office. Open M-F 8:25am-1:25pm and 2:40-4:10pm. 24hr. **ATMs.** Also at Corso M. D. Liberta, 45. Same hours.

Laundromat: Acquazzurra Lavanderia Self-Service, V. d. Battaglie, 32, at the corner of V. E. Capriolo (☎030 37 57 611). Wash and dry each €3.50-6. Soap available on premises. Open daily 8am-8pm.

Public Toilets: Between the train station and the SAIA bus station and off V. dei Mille at the south end of the park. €0.10.

Emergency: ☎113. **Ambulance:** ☎118. **Police:** V. Volta, 6, north of P. d. Vittoria (☎030 45 001) or V. Stazione, 47, by the train station.

Pharmacy: Farmacia Croce Bianca, Corso M. D. Liberta, 70. Open Tu-W and F-Su 9am-12:30pm and 3-7:30pm, Th 3-7:30pm. **Farmacia Dr. Caponati,** V. Cairoli, 19/D, (☎800 23 10 61). Open Tu-Su 9am-12:30pm and 3-7:30pm. After-hours rotation posted outside.

Hospital: Ospedale S. Orsola, V. V. Emanuele II, 27 (☎ 030 29 711).

Internet Access: Swift Cyber & Telecom Center, Vle. Stazione, 12/B, next to the SIA station. (☎/fax 030 29 43 514). Internet €1.50 per hr. Also provides long-distance phone services. Open daily 9am-10pm. Free Internet available at **Biblioteca di Largo Torrelunga** at Ple. Arnaldo. Open Tu-Sa 1:30-6:30pm, Su 9:30am-noon.

Post Office: P. Vittoria, 1 (☎030 44 421). Open M-F 8:30am-7pm, Sa 8:30am-12:30pm. **Postal Code: 25100.**

▛ ACCOMMODATIONS

At **Hotel Sirio ❸,** V. E. Capriolo, 24, immaculate rooms are homey and comfortable. All have fan, sink, and TV. (☎030 37 50 706; www.albergosirio.com. Wheelchair accessible. Singles €35, with bath €45; doubles €55/65. AmEx/MC/V.)

Straight in front of the station before the curve in the road is **Hotel Solferino ❸**, V. Solferino, 1/A. Ring the buzzer; reception is on the 2nd fl. Rooms are simple yet tranquil and clean with desk and sink. (☎030 46 300. Singles €26; doubles €42. MC/V.) To reach **Albergo San Marco ❷**, V. Spalto S. Marco, 15, take V. Foppa to its end, then turn right on V. V. Emanuele II, which becomes V. Spalto S. Marco after the intersection with C. Cavour. Located above a restaurant, rooms are past their prime but generally clean. Location on a busy street means there's plenty of noise, but closing the window and turning on the fan should do the trick. (☎030 45 541. Breakfast €2. Singles €25; doubles €43. AmEx/MC/V.)

▣ FOOD

Brescia's speciality dishes include *manzo all'olio* (beef prepared in olive oil) and *tortelli di zucca* (pumpkin torte). Food here, however, plays second fiddle to wine. *Tocai di San Martino della Battaglia* (a dry white), *Groppello* (a medium red), and *Botticino* (a dry red) are all local favorites. Fast and cheap meals, abound around the bus and train stations, while fancy dishes fill V. Beccaria, a street winding between P. Loggia and the *duomi*. For food items as well as inexpensive clothing, seek out the **open-air market** in P. Mercato. (Open M and Sa 8:30-11am, Tu-F 8:30am-6pm.) Saturday morning brings the produce **market** to P. Loggia. A **Lekkerland** supermarket is on V. Foppa two blocks from the station or on Corso Garibaldi, 3. (Open M-Sa 9am-12:30pm and 3-7:30pm.)

Trattoria Due Stelle, V. S. Faustino, 46 (☎030 42 370). From P. Loggia, head up V. S. Faustino 2 blocks. At 150 years and counting, the oldest *trattoria* in Brescia serves up gigantic portions of authentic dishes. The *casonsei* (meat-filled ravioli) and *zuppe di verdura* (vegetable soup) are culinary legends. *Primi* €6-9, *secondi* €12-15. Open M-Sa noon-2:30pm and 8-10:30pm. MC/V. ❹

Ristorante e Pizzeria Cavour, C. Cavour, 56 (☎030 240 09 00). Take V. V. Emanuele II to C. Cavour. No gimmicks; the pizza speaks for itself. Try the *cavour*, with tomatoes, mozzarella, and bacon. Steady stream of locals comes for takeout. Pizza €3.50-8. Pasta €4.20-15. Open M and W-Su noon-3pm and 6:30pm-midnight. MC/V. ❷

Al Frate, V. Musei, 25 (☎030 37 70 550; www.alfreate.com). Close to the P. Loggia. Brescian food with a twist, like *coniglio ai fichi e vino rosso* (rabbit with figs in red wine; €13) and *asino* (donkey) with tomato pasta, from the rotating menu. Candlelight, a quiet locale, and white tablecloths make it a picture of class. *Primi* €7.80-8.80, *secondi* €10-15. Cover €2.50. Open daily 12:30-2:30pm and 7:30-11:30pm. MC/V. ❹

El Forner, V. Cattaneo, 11 (☎030 29 64 96). Italian dry breads and decadent pastries (€0.25-2.50). Square slices of pizza only €0.80. That's right; pizza for under €1. Open Tu-Sa 8:30am-1:15pm and 4-7:15pm. Cash only. ❶

◉ SIGHTS

Brescia's *centro storico* is a tangled mix of paved and cobblestone streets and walkways. Around every corner is another historical *piazza* or medieval church; the tourist offices and many of the museums can provide a combined history and map guide of the *piazze* and churches as part of the free **Brescia Città** guide series.

▨ MUSEO DELLA CITTÀ DI SANTA GIULIA. This former Benedictine nunnery served as the final retreat for Charlemagne's ex-wife, Ermengarda, before it was commissioned in 753. Now holding over 11,000 archaeological, architectural, and sculptural items, the museum's roots reach all the way back to Roman times—connected to the archaeological section of the museum are the remains of two

Roman villas. The colorful mosaic floors and frescoed walls are beautifully pre-served. A walk through the museum reveals Brescia's past, from the Iron and Cop-per Ages to the end of the Italian Renaissance, with insightful explanations in English as well as Italian. Included in the collection are many rare statues, includ-ing the 2nd-century *Winged Victory*, Brescia's symbol. The museum's **Oratorio de S. Maria in Solario** displays the precious 8th-century *Cross of Desiderius*, encrusted with 212 jewels and cameos. Ascend to the upper chamber to view an entirely frescoed room with an amazingly blue star-dotted ceiling with an image of God at its center. *(V. Musei, 81/B. From V. V. Emanuele II, turn on C. Cavour which becomes V. G. Rosa. Turn right on V. Musei and continue 3 blocks; museum is on your left. ☎800 76 28 11 or 030 29 77 834; www.museiarte.brescia.it. Open Oct.-Mar. Tu-Su 9:30am-5:30pm; June-Sept. Tu-Sa 10am-6pm. €8, groups €6, ages 14-18 or over 65 €4.)*

■ **PINACOTECA TOSIO-MARTINENGO.** This 22-room *palazzo* displays a fine col-lection of paintings and frescoes by local masters. Moretto is particularly well rep-resented, as are Ferramola, Romanino, Foppa, and Lotto. Paintings are well displayed with both English and Italian captions. Lotto's *Adorazione dei Pastori* is notable, as is the 15th-century *San Giorgio e Il Drago*, unattributed yet stun-ning with three-dimensional armor on the painted knight and horse and elaborate detail of the dragon. The painting sits alone in a room beside a display of the radi-ography image that explain the painting's history. The artist Rasio's paintings of plant species that combine to form human figures are not to be missed. Visit Raphael's *Cristo Benedicente* in **Room 7.** *(P. Moretto, 4. From V. V. Emanuele II, take V. F. Crispi, and turn right on V. Martinengo da Barco. Museum entrance is on left, not through P. Mor-etto. ☎030 37 74 999; www.asm.brescia.it/musei. Open June-Sept. Tu-Su 10am-1pm and 2:30-6pm; Oct.-Mar. 9am-5pm. €3, ages 14-18 or over 65 €1.)*

DUOMO NUOVO AND ROTONDA. Not content with just one cathedral, Brescia built the **Duomo Nuovo** in 1825, adjacent to the smaller ■ **Rotonda,** or Duomo Vec-chio. The 3rd-highest dome in Italy tops the courthouse-like Rococo structure and Corinthian columns of the newer church. The round, dark-stone Rotonda was built in the 11th and 12th centuries on the remains of the 6th-century Basilica of Santa Maria di Maggiore; mosaic remnants of the original church can be seen through glass-covered holes in the floor of the apse. The somber Rotonda is nota-ble for its circular central plan that separated parishioners, who sat in pews on the lowest tier in the center of the cathedral, from the priests who ministered to them from on high. The building also rests on top of the 8th-century crypt of St. Filas-trio. *(In P. Paolo VI. Take V. S. M. d. Battaglia which turns into V. Mazzini and runs into P. Paolo VI. Rotonda open Apr.-Oct. Tu-Su 9am-noon and 3-7pm; Nov.-Mar. Sa-Su 9am-noon and 3-6pm. New duomo open daily M-Sa 7:30am-noon and 4-7pm. Modest dress required.)*

TEMPIO CAPITOLINO. Traces of Brescia's Classical past lie in the **Piazza del Foro,** the center of commercial, religious, and political life in Roman times. The ruins of Emperor Vespasian's vast Tempio Capitolino, built in AD 73 and dedi-cated to Jupiter, June, and Minerva, stand out as obvious highlights. The white sections of its columns are from a 1930s restoration; the original pieces are the red terra-cotta brick. *(Turn right on V. Musei from V. G. Rosa.)*

CASTELLO. Like every proper fairy-tale castle, the *castello* on Cidneo Hill is fitted with a drawbridge, underground tunnels, and ramparts. Though built continually from the 13th to the 16th centuries, the most striking features date from the time of the Visconti, notably the fortified keep (c. 1343). During the Risorgimento, Aus-trian troops bombarded the town from within the castle walls to quell the Brescian rebellion, known as *dieci giorni*, or "ten days." The castle also contains the **Museo Civico del Risorgimento,** which details the town's role in the Risorgimento, and the

Musei delle Armi, a weapons museum displaying over 500 items armor and weaponry. *(On V. del Castello, a 20min. climb up Cidneo Hill. Approaching the castle, keep to residential streets and the main road. Castle paths are difficult to navigate; head upward until you cross through the archway and then climb the steps on your right. At the top, walk left through the small gate to enter the castle. Castle ☎ 030 24 00 357 or 030 37 73 773. Open daily 8am-8pm. Free. Musei del Risorgimento ☎ 030 44 176. Open Tu-Su 9:30am-1pm and 2:30-5pm. Musei delle Armi ☎ 030 29 32 92. Open Tu-Su 10am-1pm and 2-6pm. Winter hours subject to change. Each museum €3, ages 14-18 or over 65 €1. Inquire at tourist office for details about castle events.)*

ENTERTAINMENT AND NIGHTLIFE

> ❗ Women should be cautions in the area near the station and west of P. di Loggia at night.

The **Mille Miglia** (Thousand Mile) car race, a round-trip between Brescia and Rome, complements Brescia's gamut of high-brow cultural events. Although the cutthroat version of the race ended with a fatal accident in 1957, a leisurely re-run of cars dating from 1927-1957 takes place in early May and ensures a fine showing of Ferraris, Maseratis, Alfa Romeos, Porsches, and Astin Martins. (See www.millemiglia.it.) The annual **Stagione di Prosa,** a series of dramatic performances, runs from October to April at the Teatro Grande, C. Zanardelli, 9 (☎ 030 29 79 333) and the Teatro Sociale, V. F. Cavallotti, 20 (☎ 030 28 08 600). Information available from the CTB office at the Teatro Stabile di Brescia. (☎ 030 29 28 611; www.ctbteatrostabile.it.) Also at the Teatro Grande from October to November is the **lyrical opera festival** (☎ 030 29 79 333). From April to June, the focus shifts to the **Festivale Pianistico Internazionale,** co-hosted by nearby Bergamo. (☎ 035 24 01 40; www.festivalmichelangeli.it. €8-35.) From March to July, Brescia puts on a **Festival of Sacred Music.** (☎ 030 37 49 919; www.gionannasorbi.it.) The **Jazz on the Road Festival** celebration from the end of June to the end of July draws notable regional acts (☎ 349 31 49 864; www.jazzontheroad.net), while the **Brescia Jazz Festival** is a three-day celebration at the end of July (☎ 030 27 91 881; www.cipiessebs.it). From June to September, the city hosts an **open-air cinema** at the castle (€3), plus concerts, dance recitals, and opera. On February 15, the city turns out to celebrate the **feast** of its patron saint, **St. Faustino,** with over 600 vendor stalls stretching across the city center (inquire at the tourist office for information).

The best bar experience in Brescia may be had at the very top of the *castello* at the spacious ▨ **Caffè Castella.** Lounging beside Roman urns, visitors take in the view of the city. (☎ 339 13 00 999. Open M-Sa 6pm-2:20am, Su 6pm-1:30am.) Just below the castle on V. del Castello, the **Castello Bar** serves drinks in a more conventional setting. (Open Tu-Th 11am-1am, F-Sa 11am-3am, Su 10am-1am.) Additional bars are clustered around P. Arnaldo and remain open daily from dinner to 1am. Though closed in the summer, starting in October the bar and steakhouse **Seconda Classe,** V. Zima, 9/A (☎ 030 37 53 821), behind the train station, is open at night with live acts after 11pm for students and Brescian locals.

MANTUA   ☎ 0376

Though Mantua did not become a bustling cultural haven until the Renaissance, art and culture have shaped the city's history since the birth of the poet Virgil in 70 BC. Providing inspiration for native and foreign artists alike, including Verdi and his opera *Rigoletto*, the Renaissance writer Castiglioni, and the painters Pisanello, Mantegna, and Romano, the town is brimming with artistic creations. After Mantua became part of the Hapsburg Empire in 1707, the city experienced another intellectual boom with the construction of the Accademia Virgiliana, and in the 19th century many urban elite erected Neo-Classical mansions, adding to the city's mix of architectural styles. While there is much to see within the city, outside the city proper, small country towns like Castellaro, Cavriana, and Solferino house the scenic vineyards of Lombardy's 3rd-largest wine-producing province.

■ TRANSPORTATION

The **train station** is in P. D. Leoni, at the end of V. Solferino (☎0376 32 16 47. Ticket office open M-Sa 5:40am-7:45pm, Su 6am-7:45pm.) Trains run to Cremona (1hr., every hr. 5:51am-8:48pm, €4.30); Milan (2¼hr., 8 per day 5:25am-6:35pm, €8.45); and Verona (40min., every hr. 6:01am-11:50pm, €2.40). The

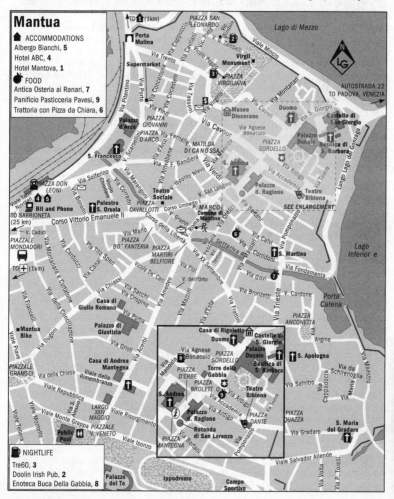

APAM bus station is in P. Mondadori. (☎0376 32 72 37; www.apam.it. Ticket office open M-F 7:30am-1pm and 3-6pm, Sa 7:30am-1pm. Buy tickets at the *tabaccheria* in the station after hours.) Cross the street out of the train station and take your first left. Cross C. V. Emanuele II and head down V. Caduti. Buses run locally and to nearby towns, including the village of Sabbioneta (see **Daytrip from Mantua,** p. 275). Check schedule outside bus terminal. Only buses listed in red run on Sunday. **Taxis** (☎0376 32 53 51 or 0376 36 88 44) are available 5am-1am. For **bike rentals** try **Mantua Bike,** V. Piave, 22/B. Check the tourist office for bike itineraries. (☎0376 22 39 32 or 0376 22 09 09. Open M-Sa 8am-12:30pm and 2:30-7:30pm. €2 per hr., €8 per day.)

ORIENTATION AND PRACTICAL INFORMATION

From the train station in **Piazza Don Leoni,** turn left on **Via Solferino,** then right on **Via Bonomi** to the main street, **Corso Vittorio Emanuele II.** Follow it to **Piazza Cavallotti,** crossing the **Sottoriva River,** to pick up **Corso Umberto I,** which leads to **Piazza Marconi, Piazza Mantegna,** and most of the city's sights and shops. The helpful, English-speaking staff at the **tourist office,** P. Mantegna, 6, offers free brochures, **maps,** and lists of hotels, B&Bs, *agriturismi* options, and restaurants. C. V. Emanuele II turns into C. Umberto and crosses P. Marconi before reaching P. Mantegna. (☎0376 32 82 53; www.aptmantova.it. Open daily 9am-7pm.) The **museum tourist office,** P. Sordello, 23, is located in the Casa di Rigoletto, the dwelling of Verdi's opera hero. (☎0376 36 89 17. Open Tu-Su 9am-12pm and 3-6pm.) C. V. Emanuele II is lined with **banks,** most with **ATMs.** In an **emergency,** call ☎113 for the **police,** P. Sordello, 46 (☎0376 32 70 22), or head to the **Ospedale Carlo,** V. Piave, 1 (☎0376 36 84 98) for **medical assistance. Farmacia Silvestri,** V. Roma, 24 (☎0376 32 15 63; open Tu-Sa 8:30am-12:30pm and 4-8pm) is one of many **pharmacies. Bit and Phone,** V. Bertinelli, 21, across from the train station, offers **Internet** access and **Western Union.** (☎0376 22 05 94; www.bitandphone.it. Open M-Tu and Th-Sa 10am-10pm, Su 9am-10pm. €2 per hr.) The **post office,** P. Martiri Belfiore, 15 up V. Roma from the tourist office, offers **currency exchange** (☎0376 31 77 11; fax 0376 32 53 04. Open M-F 8:30am-7pm, Sa 8:30am-12:30pm.) **Postal Code:** 46100.

ACCOMMODATIONS

Accommodations outside the city limits in towns like Castellaro and Monzambano are less expensive. The tourist office has a pamphlet of hotels and *agriturismi*.

Hotel ABC, P. D. Leoni, 25 (☎/fax 0376 32 23 29; www.hotelabcmantova.it), across from train station. Modern hotel features comfortable rooms, outdoor patio, and ski-lodge feel. All rooms have TV, A/C, and new bathrooms with shower. Breakfast included. Luggage storage available. Prices vary according to payment method. Reserving online well in advance or paying in cash may get you a lower price. Apr.-Aug. singles €40-45; doubles €60-66; triples €80-88. Sept.-Mar. €50-55/70-77/90-99. ❹

Albergo Bianchi, P. D. Leoni, 24 (☎0376 32 64 65; www.hotelbianchi.mantova.com), across from train station. Step through sliding-glass doors into air-conditioned bliss. Spacious rooms have bath, TV, phone, A/C, and monogrammed sheets. Some with balcony. Ivy-shaded courtyard provides a calming respite. Reservation recommended. Singles €50-70; doubles €75-90; triples €90-110. AmEx/MC/V. ❺

Hotel Mantova, P. Giulia, 3 (☎0376 39 26 37; fax 0376 39 26 38), about 1km north of Mantua through Porta Mulina gate. Small hotel has rooms with TV and sinks. Breakfast included. Singles €40-45, with bath €50-55; doubles €60-70/80. MC/V. ❹

☐ FOOD

Mantuan cuisine is known for its *tortellini di zucca* (pumpkin-filled ravioli) and its reliance on local produce and livestock. Specialties include parmesan cheese, *risotto*, and *la sbrisolona*, a giant almond cookie. Pigs outnumber people four to one in this area, so it's not a surprise that pork is a Mantuan staple. A **market** is held every Thursday morning in P. dell'Erbe. For a supermarket, head down V. Solferino from the train station, angling on V. Scarsellini and then V. XX Aprile, which becomes V. Porto. **CompraBene Supermercati**, V. Porto, 31/A, is on the right. (Open M-Sa 8am-7:30pm.)

Panificio Pasticceria Pavesi, V. Broletto, 19 (☎0376 32 24 60), on right just before P. Sordello. The best pastry shop in Mantua serves local specialties including *la sbrisolona, la torta tagliatelle,* and *la mantovana.* Pastries and cookies €0.90-6. Open June-Feb. M 7am-1:30pm, Tu-Su 7am-7:30pm. Sept.-Dec. Su hours change to 10am-7:30pm. Mar.-May open daily 10am-7:30pm. Cash only. ❶

Trattoria con Pizza da Chiara, V. Corridoni, 44/A (☎0376 22 35 68). From P. Cavallotti, follow C. Libertà and turn left on V. Roma, then right on the narrow V. Corridoni. Young professionals dine in this chic but unpretentious restaurant. Brick ceilings, black-clad waiters, and prints on the walls lend an upscale modern twist. The house special is the delicious *risotto alla pescatore* (€6). Pizza and *primi* €4-8, *secondi* €8.50-13. Cover €2. Open M and W-Su noon-3pm and 7pm-midnight. AmEx/MC/V. ❸

Antica Osteria ai Ranari, V. Trieste, 11 (☎0376 32 84 31; fax 0376 32 84 31), south of the town canal on V. Trieste. A friendly proprietor serves authentic regional dishes, including donkey meat and frog in this tavern-style *trattoria. Primi* €5-7, *secondi* €5-9. Cover €1.50. Open Tu-Su noon-2:30pm and 7:30-11:30pm. Closed for 3 weeks during summer; call ahead to check if open. AmEx/MC/V. ❷

☉ SIGHTS

PALAZZO DUCALE. The behemoth Palazzo Ducale, home of the Gonzaga family since the start of the 14th century, dominates the Mantuan skyline. In medieval times, this was the largest palace in Europe, with 500 rooms and 15 courtyards constructed by the best architects and artists from the 14th through 17th centuries. Originally many separate buidings, the *palazzo* grew as the Gonzagas annexed surrounding structures, the most prominent being the **Castello di San Georgio.** This four-towered castle once served as a fortress, and now boasts the **Bridal Chamber** with Andrea Mantegna's famed frescoes of the Gonzaga family (1474). In the **Pisanello Room,** the recent removal of a painted plaster frieze revealed a heroic cycle of frescoes depicting the knights of King Arthur. The **New Gallery** houses dozens of 16th- to 18th-century altarpieces that were moved from churches closed in the Hapsburg and Napoleonic eras to the *palazzo* for safe-keeping. Other highlights include **Rubens's** 1605 painting of the Gonzaga family adoring the Holy Trinity, **Raphael's** tapestry cycle of the lives of Saints Peter and Paul, and the **Room of Rivers,** which is decorated with vines, flowers, and two artificial grottoes. (*P. Sordello, 40.* ☎*0376 35 21 00; www.mantovaducale.it. Open Tu-Su 8:45am-7:15pm. Ticket office under porticos facing the piazza, open until 6:30pm. €6.50, EU students €3.25, EU citizens under 18 or over 65 free. Audioguides available €4.*)

TEATRO BIBIENA. Originally commissioned by Maria Theresa of the Hapsburgs to serve as a venue for cultural events and scientific expositions, this theater resembles a miniature fairy-tale castle and is one of the only ones in northern Italy not modeled after Milan's La Scala. Four tiers of rose-and-grey-stone balconies rise to the ceiling, illuminated by soft lantern light. Music lovers first filled the small, velvet couches when a 14-year-old Mozart inaugurated the building in 1769. Patrons continue to pour in today to attend music, dance and drama performances. *(V. Accademia, 4, at the corner of V. Accademia and V. Pomponazzo. ☎0376 32 76 53. Open Tu-Su 9:30am-12:30pm and 3-6pm. €2.10; students, under 18, or over 60 €1.10.)*

PALAZZO DEL TE. Built by Giulio Romano in 1534 as a hideaway for Federico II Gonzaga and his mistress Isabella, this opulent *palazzo* is a stunning, though not particularly discreet. The stately *palazzo* combines the layout of a Roman villa with flamboyant interior Renaissance ceiling frescoes that range in theme from the mythological to the biblical. Pause in the **Sala dei Cavalli** (Room of Horses) to ponder the Gonzaga family's passion for animals, then continue past racy murals of **Cupid and Psyche.** Stroll through the **Camera degli Stucchi,** a room encircled by parading Roman soldiers, to the ▧**Room of Giants.** Adorned with a fresco that disguises the separation between walls and ceiling with a scaled perspective, the room depicts the demise of the Titans at the hands of Jupiter. Try to pick out the entire pantheon of Roman gods in the clouds around Jupiter. Less monumental, though no less interesting, is the 16th-century graffiti that decorates the walls. Another wing of the palace features regular exhibits of modern Italian works alongside a collection of Egyptian sculpture and Impressionist painting. In summer, concerts are often held in the palace courtyard. *(At southern end of the city down V. P. Amedeo, which becomes V. Acerbi, through P. Veneto and down Largo Parri. ☎0376 32 32 66. Open M 1-6pm, Tu-Su 9am-6pm. Ticket sales end 30min. before closing. €8, over 60 €5.50, students and ages 12-18 €2.50, under 11 free, groups of 20 €4.50 per person.)*

PALAZZO D'ARCO. The former residence of the prominent D'Arco family, the *palazzo* is furnished as it would have been in the 18th century. A separate wing houses a library and the kitchen, complete with pots, pans, and a dilapidated staircase. Navigate through the Neo-Classical statues that dot the rose gardens to reach the *palazzo's* highlight: the extraordinary Giovan Maria Falconetto-designed zodiac chamber. The room is split into 12 sections, each decorated with frescoes dedicated to a specific astrological sign. The murals along the top of the walls are drawn from Ovid's *Metamorphoses.* *(P. d'Arco, 4. ☎0376 32 22 42; www.museodarco.it. Open Mar.-Oct. Tu-Su 10am-12:30pm and 2:30-6pm; Nov.-Feb. Sa-Su 10am-12:30pm and 2-5pm. €3, students €1. Guided tours only; begin within 15min. of guest arrival.)*

ROTONDA DI SAN LORENZO AND CHIESA DI SANT'ANDREA. Bequeathed to the Pope by Matilde di Canossa, a powerful and devout countess of Mantua, the oldest church in Mantua (11th century) is dwarfed by the surrounding buildings, inluding the **Palazzo della Ragione** (Palace of Justice) next door. Nonetheless, the rotunda features an impressive collection of devotional coins and stamps. *(In P. dell'Erbe, just south of P. Sordello. Open M–F 10am-1pm and 2-6pm, Sa and Su 10am-6pm. Free.)* Opposite the rotunda rises Mantua's most important Renaissance creation, Leon Battista Alberti's **Chiesa di Sant'Andrea** (1472-1594). Its facade combines the classic arch design—a soaring barrel-vaulted portal and flanking pilasters—with a gigantic altarpiece and an imposing gilt organ at the front of the church. The gargantuan interior was the first monumental space constructed in the Classical style since the days of imperial Rome, and the plan served as a prototype for ecclesiastical architecture for the next 200 years. Giorgio Anselmi painted the dome's frescoes in muted colors. The painter Andrea Mantegna's tomb rests in the first chapel on the left after the entrance. The church's holy relic, a piece of earth supposedly soaked in Christ's blood, parades through the streets in a religious procession every year on Good Friday. The rest of the year, the relic of the Precious Blood is kept in a crypt under the nave. To see the relic, look in the chapel to the right of the entrance for a Chiesa di Sant'Andrea volunteer. *(Open daily 8am-noon and 3-7pm. Crypt open M-F 10:30-11:30am and 3-6pm, Sa 10:30-11:30am and 3-5:30pm. Church free; crypt €1.)*

🎵🎭 ENTERTAINMENT AND NIGHTLIFE

The **Teatro Bibiena** (☎0376 32 76 53), on V. Accademia, 4, hosts musical and dramatic events, which are of no shortage in Mantua, including the **Concerti di Fine Settimana,** a series of operettas and recitals every Sunday, and the similar **Concerti della Domenica** series from November to February. Two **classical concert** seasons run from October to April and from April to June. **Jazz** performances also occur from April to June. The **International Festival of Choral Singing** is held in late June and early July in association with nearby Revere. (☎0386 46 71 73; www.ricercareensemble.com.) Grazie, accessible by bus, holds its annual **Festa della Madonnari,** an international competition among street painters on Ferragostano every August 15. (☎0376 35 81 28; cultura@curatone.it.) In early September, Italian speakers and scholars should check out **Festivaletteratura,** which attracts hordes of literary scholars and families from across the world to meet and attend discussions, lectures, book signings, and writers' workshops. (Office at V. Accademia, 47.☎0376 36 70 47; www.festivaletteratura.it.) The first weekend of December, the town of Castel D'Ario celebrates the pig at the **Festa dell'Osso.**

Irish Pub **Doolin,** V. Zambelli, 8, near P. Virgiliana, is a comfortable bar popular with the locals (☎0376 36 25 63. Open Tu-Sa 6:30pm-2am, Su 6pm-1am.) Located in the park of P. Virgiliana, 17, outdoor bar **Tre60** overlooks the park and is a cool spot on warm summer evening. (☎0376 22 36 05. Open spring and summer daily 5:30pm-2am.) A more traditional night spot is **Enoteca Buca Della Gabbia,** V. Cavour, 98, a restaurant in a wine cellar with over 300 vintages. (Open M-F 10:30am-3pm and 6:30pm-1am, Sa 10:30am-3pm and 5:30pm-2am, Su 10:30am-1pm.)

🔯 DAYTRIP FROM MANTUA

SABBIONETA

Sabbioneta is 25 km southwest of Mantua and is easily accessible by APAM (☎0376 32 72 37; www.apam.it) bus #17 from Mantua's Ple. Mondadori. (45min., 9 per day 6:35am-7:15pm, €3.30. Return buses 9 per day 6:45am-6:45pm, €3.30. Buy return tickets at the tabaccheria on V. Gonzaga, 67.) After winding through cornfields and watermelon stands, you will see the city walls on your right; get off in front of the Pta. Imperiale. Tourist office: P. D'Armi, 1. Follow signs for office along V. V. Gonzaga after entering city. (☎0375 22 10 44; www.comune.sabbioneta.mn.it. Open Tu-Su 10am-1pm and 2-6pm.) Buy tickets for monuments at the tourist office, as they are not available fat every location. €8 per person for entry to all monuments, €3 for single monument, students €3.50 for all monuments. Monuments open Tu-F 10am-1pm and 2:30-6:30pm, Sa-Su 10am-1pm and 2-7pm.

Built to rival his family's success in transforming Mantua into an artistic and cultural center, Sabbioneta founder Vespasiano Gonzaga (1532-1591) developed this bustling town, which earned the title "Little Athens of the Gonzagas" for its importance as an artistic center in the late Renaissance. Nowadays, town residents are just as proud of their nature reserves and their slow, simple way of life.

A self-guided tour of the *centro storico* is possible with historical printouts from the tourist office. Begin at the **Palazzo Giardino,** with its frescoes of mythical figures and intricately decorated alcoves. One on the ceiling has the head of Medusa surrounded by rosettes in stucco relief. The **Palazzo Ducale** has fewer surviving frescoes, but is noteworthy for the **Room of Eagles,** which in addition to painted eagles, houses a collection of eerie, life-size wooden statues of Gonzaga family members on horseback. The art-loving Gonzagas would be proud that today the *palazzo* is used for temporary exhibits of modern art. The ▨**Teatro all'Antica,** down V. V. Gonzaga from the tourist office, though small, stands out as the reputed first theater in Europe to house a permanent theater company. It boasts a colorful mural along the back wall of the balcony and a stage surrounded by columns imitating a Roman amphitheater. While meandering around Sabbioneta, note the oldest gate in the town, the **Porta Vittoria,** on the west side of town. The tourist office offers guided tours in Italian and English of the above attractions upon request. The **Sinagoga** (Synagogue), V. Bernadino Campi, 1, an 1824 construction in Sabbioneta's Jewish quarter, is open Sa, Su, and holidays Nov.-Mar. 10am-12:30pm and 2:30-5:30pm, Apr.-Oct. 10am-12:30pm and 2:30-6:30pm. Contact the tourist office ahead to make reservations for other days, or visit www.sabbioneta.org for more information. On the 2nd Sunday of the month, antique afficionados arrive for the exhaustive **Mercato dell'Antiquariato.** In September and October traveling music, theater, and ballet groups also stop here.

If you plan to spend the night, **Albergo Giulia Gonzaga ❸,** V. Vespasiano Gonzaga, 65, has a garden, hand-painted mosaics, and patterned sheets and towels. All rooms have TV, and bath. Reception desk keeps library of travel and information books in Italian, English, French, and German. (☎0375 52 81 69. Singles €25-35; doubles €40-50; triples €60. MC/V.) A small grocery store, **Ortofrutta Maffezzoli,** V. Gonzaga, 87, offers the basics. (Open daily 7:45am-12:30pm.) Excellent food can be found at ▨**Ristorante Corte Bondeno ❸,** V. Mezzana Loria, just north of Sabbioneta. (☎348 77 59 007. 5-course *menù* €20; 8-course *menù* €32. Both include wine, coffee, and cover. Open M noon-last lunch order, Tu-Su noon-last lunch order and 8:30pm-last dinner order. AmEx/MC/V.) To the left of the tourist office, **Osteria Wine Bar Boulevard ❸,** V. d. Galleria, 3, posts a daily menu on a board outside. (☎0375 22 02 58. *Primi* €6-8, *secondi* €8-12. Cover €1. Open Tu-Su 10:30am-3:15pm and 6pm-2am.)

The **post office** is at V. Gonzaga, 31 (☎0375 22 00 62), and is open Monday to Friday 8:30am-2pm, Saturday 8:30am-12:20pm. In case of an **emergency,** call the **police,** P. Ducale, 2 (☎113). **Banco San Paolo Imi,** P. Ducale, 3, has an **ATM.** (☎0375 52 681. Open M-F 8:20am-1:20pm and 2:50-3:50pm, Sa 8:20-11:20am.)

CREMONA ☎0372

Viewed from the top of the Torazzo, the tallest *campanile* (bell tower) in Italy, Cremona is a sea of terra-cotta rooftops and warm red bricks. At ground level, Cremona is awash in music. As the home of violin genius Antonio Stradivari and birthplace of Claudio Monteverdi, the father of modern opera, the city still hosts music festivals throughout the year, as well as an annual opera season at the renowned Teatro Ponchielli. Violin-making shops are found around every corner in this city of music, home to the University of Music Palaeography and Philology, the International School of Violin Making, the Monteverdi School of Music, and the Triennial Committee for String Instruments. The visual arts also abound in Cremona, with numerous contributions from the Campi family and Sofonisba Anguissola, the first female painter of the European Renaissance.

▨▨ **TRANSPORTATION AND PRACTICAL INFORMATION.** The **train station** is at V. Dante, 68 (☎0372 89 20 21). The ticket office is open daily 6am-7:30pm. **Trains** run to: Brescia (45min., every hr. 5:24am-6:58pm, €3.95); Mantua (1hr., every hr. 6:24am-8:34pm, €4.80); Milan (1¼hr., 10 per day 5:02am-7:24pm, €5.25); and Pavia (2¼hr., 5:15am, €5.20). The **bus station** (☎0372 29 212; www.cremonatrasport.it) is one block left of the train station along V. Dante. (Ticket office in Bar Terminal Bus, V. Dante, 90. Open M-F 7:40am-12:15pm and 2:30-6pm, Sa 7:40am-12:15pm.

After hours inquire at the bar halfway between the train station and bus station.) **Buses** run to Brescia (2 hr.; every hr., 6:10am-6:55pm, reduced service Su; €4.15) and Piacenza (1 hr., 7 per day 6:30am-6:25pm, €3.25.) Orange **local buses** run from the train station throughout the city. **Taxi** stands are in P. Roma (☎0372 21 300) and at the train station (☎0372 26 740). **Mata Store,** V. S. Tommaso, 9, next to the supermarket, rents city and mountain **bikes.** (☎0372 45 74 83 or 0335 53 33 907. Prices vary, call for rates.) **Astrocar,** V. Brescia, 77 (☎0372 45 24 67) provides **car rental.**

From the **train station,** walk straight ahead. The road ahead is **Via Palestro,** which becomes the shop-lined **Corso Campi,** then **Via Verdi,** ending in **Piazza Stradivari** on the left. Crossing the *piazza* diagonally and walking down V. Baldesio will bring you to **Piazza del Comune,** where the tourist office and *duomo* are located. The **tourist office,** P. del Comune, 5, provides **maps.** The office also offers the "City Card" for discounts around Cremona. (☎0372 23 233; www.aptcremona.it. Open daily 9am-12:30pm and 3-6pm.) For those seeking information about opportunities for alternatives to tourism (see **Beyond Tourism,** p. 81), visit **Informagiovani di Cremona,** V. Palestro, 11/A. **Internet** access also available. (☎0372 40 79 50. Open M-Tu and Th-F 10am-1:30pm or 8:30-10am with appointment only, W 10am-6pm.) **Banco Nazionale del Lavoro,** C. Campi, 4-10, has **currency exchange** and a 24hr. **ATM.** (☎0372 40 01. Open M-F 8:20am-1:20pm and 2:30-4pm, Sa 8:20-11:50am.) **Western Union** is available at **Mail Boxes,** V. Brescia, 26/A (☎0372 45 48 81). A self-service **laundromat,** S. Agata a Gettone, is located at C. Garibaldi, 132 (☎0372 30 314.) In case of **emergency,** call ☎113, the **police,** V. Tribunali, 6 (☎0372 40 74 27), or an **ambulance** ☎118. The **hospital** (☎0372 40 51 11) is in Largo Priori. **Farmacia (Centrale) Communale #2,** V. G. del Gesu, 2, is at the corner of C. Campi (☎0372 27 581. Open M 3:30-7:30pm, Tu-F 9am-1pm and 3:30-7:30pm, Sa 9am-1pm, and Su 3-8pm. After-hours rotation posted outside.) **Libreria Giramondo,** V. Palestro, 44, straight from the train station, offers **Internet** on the 2nd floor. (☎0372 22 414; fax 0372 53 70 73. €1 per 15min., €1.50 per 30min., €3 per hr., students €2, €6 per 3hr., students €4. Open M 3:30-7:30pm, Tu-Sa 9am-12:30pm and 3:30-7:30pm.) The **post office,** V. Verdi, 1, has **currency exchange.** Bring a passport. (☎0372 59 35 63. Open M-F 8:30am-7pm, Sa 8:30am-12:30pm.) **Postal Code:** 26100.

⊓⊔ ACCOMMODATIONS AND FOOD. Albergo Duomo ❹, V. Gonfalonieri, 13, is in the center of everything. Well-kept rooms all have bath, TV, phone, and A/C. The hotel restaurant is always full. (☎0372 35 242; fax 0372 45 81 88. Breakfast €5. Parking garage free. Singles €45; doubles €60. AmEx/MC/V.) **La Locanda ❹,** V. Pallavicino, 4, is on the corner of C. G. Matteotti and V. Pallavicino. Friendly brothers rent clean, large rooms with breakfast and bath above their restaurant. (☎0372 45 78 34. Singles €43; doubles €64. MC/V.) Run by the Diocese of Mantua, **Casa dell'Accoglienza ❷,** V. S. Antonio del Fuoco, 11, welcomes students and clergy to its 20 simple rooms, all with bath. The staff speaks little English. (☎0372 21 562. Wheelchair accessible. Singles €23, doubles €40.) **Camping Parco al Po ❶,** Lungo Po Europa, 12, on the banks of the Po River, is outside the city center along V. del Sale. Offers camper hookups as well as tent spaces and cabins. (☎0372 21 268; www.campingcremonapo.it. Open Apr.-Sept. Campers, caravans, and cars €8-9.50; tents €4-6, cabins for 2, 3, and 4 people €18/28/38.)

The *mostarda di Cremona,* first concocted in the 16th century, consists of cherries, figs, apricots, and melons preserved in a sweet mustard syrup and is traditionally spread over boiled meats. Delicious *grana padano,* a sophisticated cousin of parmesan cheese, is available in any *salumeria.* In addition, every sweet shop sells bars of *torrone* (an egg, honey, and nut nougat), another Cremonese specialty. Packed with locals, an open-air **market** in P. Stradivari sells fresh produce and a variety of meats and cheeses on Wednesday and Saturday from 8am to 1pm. Vendors also sell clothing and household items. A **GS** supermarket, V. S.

THE HIDDEN DEAL

FIDDLE ME THIS

While it's easy to catch a glimpse of a Stradivarius violin almost anywhere in Cremona— windows of violin-making shops or the Museo Civico, for example—it's not nearly as easy (or cheap) to hear one. Lucky for travelers on a budget, the **Civica Collezione di Violini** in the Palazzo Comunale gives free performances to those who want to know what all the fuss is about.

Fifteen-minute performances nearly as beautiful as the violin's craftmanship are given regularly to visitors of the museum, where *maestros* showcase instruments from the collection of Amati and Stradivarius violins. Held in *sale di rappresentonza* (office room), these intimate concerts are reserved for small groups only.

Performaces are always free for visitors who plan ahead. Make reservations at least one month in advance for concerts (M-F in summer; Tu-Sa in winter). For those making an impromptu visit to the museum, it is frequently possible to join an existing group for only €1.50.

(*Biglietteria and concert reservations* ☎0372 20 502; *violini@digicolor.net. Violin collection open Tu-Sa 9am-6pm, Su 10am-6pm. €6, students and groups €3.50. Concerts €1.50 per person, free with reservation.*)

Tommaso, 13, is close to P. del Comune. (Open M 9am-8:15pm, Tu-Sa 8am-8:15pm, Su 9am-1pm.) On weekends, the bars and cafes around **Piazza della Pace** are filled, and live music can often be heard floating toward P. del Comune from the small square. At ⬛**Pierrot ❷**, Largo Boccaccino, 2, sit at one of the wicker tables and choose from the tantalizing *gelato* sundaes pictured in the menu. (☎0372 29 318. *Gelato* €1.50. Coffee €1.50-3. Mixed drinks and wine €3-8. *Panini* €2.50-3.50. Fruit and ice cream sundaes €4-8. Open daily 7:30am-1am. AmEx/MC/V.) The lines outside ⬛**Principe Gelateria ❶**, Vle. Trento e Trieste, 103, and the perpetually empty metal bins attest to the smooth quality of the best *gelato* in Cremona. Purchase by the cone or with several flavors mixed in a freezable 500g-1.5kg container. Watch in the back room as workers toil over giant spinning pots to achieve the perfect consistency. (☎0372 28 323. Cones €1.50-3.50. Containers €5-10. Ice cream cakes €4-16. Open daily 11am-12:30am.) Dine in view of the *duomo* at **Ristorante-Pizzeria Albergo Duomo ❸**, V. Gonfalonieri, 13, attached to the *albergo* of the same name. Choose between outdoor tables stretching to the P. del Comune and comfortable air-conditioned indoor dining. (☎0372 35 242; fax 0372 45 81 88. Pizza €4-7.50. *Antipasti*, pasta dishes, and house specialties €7-10. Open daily 11:30am-3:30pm and 7pm-midnight. AmEx/MC/V.) Locals crowd **Ristorante Pizzeria Marechiaro ❷**, C. Garibaldi, 85, for excellent pizza and meat dishes priced according to the market. Complimentary *bruschetta* starts each meal. (☎0372 26 289. Pizza €3.50-8. *Primi* €5.50-9.50, *secondi* €6.50-9. Open daily noon-3pm and 6:30pm-midnight. MC/V.) **Sperlari ❶**, at V. Solferino, 25, has been selling sweets since 1836. They also sell the *torrone* and *mostarda di Cremona*. (☎0372 22 346; sperlari.negozio@tin.it. Candy €0.80-15. Open daily 8:30am-12:30pm and 3:30-7:30pm. AmEx/MC/V.)

🎟 📷 **SIGHTS AND FESTIVALS.** The **Piazza del Comune** has historically been the center of Cremonese life, housing the *duomo*, Torrazzo, baptistry, Palazzo Comunale, and Loggia dei Militi. With an excellent collection of Amati, Ceruti, and Stradivari violins, the ⬛**Civica Collezione di Violini** of the **Palazzo Comunale** draws dozens of tourists. Brief performances on Stradivari and Amati instruments are available to those who reserve in advance. (☎0372 20 502. Wheelchair accessible. Open Tu-Sa 9am-6pm and Su 10am-6pm. Admission €6, students and groups of more than 15 €3.50. Concerts €1.50 per person. Cumulative ticket with Musei Civico and Stradivariano €10, students and groups €5. Buy ticket at the bookshop to the right inside the

Palazzo.) Directly across from the Palazzo Comunale, the pink-marble 12th-century *duomo* **Santa Maria Assunta,** rising from above the Gothic lions that guard its entrance, is a fine example of the Lombard-Romanesque style. The interior displays a cycle of 16th-century frescoes, as well as a glass-encased 10 ft. tall ornate gold Grand Cross. (Open M-Sa 10:30am-noon and 3:30-6pm, Su 10:30-11am and 3:30-5:30pm. Free.) To the left of the *duomo* rises the late 13th-century **Torrazzo.** Made completely of bricks and standing at 111m, it is the tallest *campanile* in Italy. Climb the 487 steps to the top where you and the pigeons can enjoy the view of the city and surrounding countryside. (☎0372 27 386. Open June-Sept. Tu-F 10am-1pm and 2:30-5:30pm, Sa-Su 10am-1pm and 2:30-6pm; Oct.-May Tu-Su 10am-1pm. €4, students and groups €3. Cumulative ticket with baptistry €5/4.) The dome of the 1167 **Battistero** (Baptistry) ascends in an octagonal pattern and shelters pieces of sculpture. Artistic treasures include a fine wooden crucifixion piece and the slightly disturbing 17th-century *Altare dell'Addolorata,* complete with dagger piercing the heart of a golden Virgin. (☎0372 27 386. Open Tu-Su 10am-1pm and 3-6pm. €2, students €1. Cumulative ticket for Torazzo and Baptistery €5/4.)

At the **Palazzo Affaitati,** V. Ugolani Dati, 4, off V. Palestro, a grand marble stair-

---

 MORE FOR YOUR MONEY. Those trying to see all Cremona has to offer should consider a **biglietto cumulativo,** which covers admission to the **Museo Civico** and **Museo Stradivario** in the Palazzo Affaitati and the violin collection of the **Palazzo Comunale** (€10, students €5). The **City Card** is also available for discounts on bus rides, sights, and some restaurants and festivals (€7.75). Both options are available at the tourist office.

---

case leads to the **Museo Civico** and the **Museo Stradivariano** within. The Museo Civico exhibits a diverse collection of paintings from the 15th to 19th centuries including works by Boccaccio and the Campi family. Noteworthy pieces include Caravaggio's *San Francesco in Meditazione,* Il Genovesino's *Amore Dormiente* (featuring a pale and pudgy cupid perched atop a book and leaning on a skull with bow in hand), and a painting by Arcimboldi. Seen right side up, this painting is a remarkably detailed human face made from vegetables, but upside down it looks like a pot of broccoli and carrots. Also amusing is the Diotti painting *Il Conte Ugolino,* in which a sombre-looking count sits for his portrait amid his sleeping children. In the same building, famous Stradivarius violins are suspended within glass cases. Soft violin music plays as visitors enter the **Museo Stradivariano,** which boasts a room of the artisan's tools, molds, models, and drawings donated after his death in 1737. There is also a collection of violins from other famous makers. An English video tour and interactive exhibit explain the violins' production and is complemented by a hands-on exhibit of the process. The Palazzo also holds a small collection of archaeological findings on its 2nd floor. (Palazzo Affaitati ☎0372 40 77 70. Museo Civico and Stradivariano ☎0372 31 222. Open Tu-Sa 9am-6pm, Su 10am-6pm. €7, students and groups of more than 15 €4. Cumulative ticket with Palazzo Comunale €10/5.) The 250-year-old, lavishly decorated Baroque **Teatro Ponchielli,** C. V. Emanuele, 52, once provided the testing ground for the Stradivari and Amati violins, but today is home to Cremona's many artistic and cultural events and spectacles. One of the largest stages in Italy, it stands as one of the most beautiful opera houses in the world. Unless attending a performance, visits (€1) are by reservation only. (☎0372 02 20 01; www.teatroponchielli.it. Ticket office open June-Sept. M-Sa 4:30-7:30pm, Oct.-May M-Sa 4-7pm.) A prime example of Cremonese Mannerism, the **Chiesa di San Sigismondo,** Largo B. Visconti, off V. Giuseppina and 2km from P. del Commune, honors the union of the powerful Sforza and Visconti families in 1441 with masterful works by the four members of the Campi family. Walk 30min. down V. Ghisleri from P. della Libertà or take bus #2 to San Sigimondo, the last stop. (☎0372 43 73 57. Open daily 8:30am-noon and 3-7pm. Free.)

In Cremona music and festivity is in the air year-round, and tickets along with information for most events can be found at the Teatro Ponchielli ticket booth, C. V. Emanuele, 52. (☎0372 02 20 01; www.teatroponchielli.it; Open June-Sept. M-Sa 4:30-7:30pm; Oct.-May daily 4-7pm.) The **Monteverdi Festival** (May-June) honors the great Cremonese composer with music. (For information or tickets, call ☎0372 02 20 10 or visit the ticket office at Teatro Ponchielli. Tickets €10-23, under 25 and groups €8-20, students €8. Cumulative tickets available for mulitiple concerts €30-41.) The **Cremona Jazz Festival,** running from March to May, welcomes the summer with a series of concerts. Throughout June, July, and August, Cremona sponsors theatrical performances, musicals, and fireworks displays in the surrounding towns on the Po River as part of the annual **Il Grande Fiume** (www.ilgrandefiume.it). October also brings the **International String Quartet Competition,** in which the cumulative age of quartet members cannot exceed 135 years. (☎/fax 0372 21 454; entetrie@triennale.191.it.) Complementing these fine-art offerings is Arena Giardino's **Cinema Estate,** a film festival showcasing a host of Italian and international films. (Parco Tognazzi, along Vle. Po to the southeast of the city. ☎320 42 07 377; www.cinema.cremona.it. All movies start at 9:30pm. €5.50, students €4.50.)

PAVIA ☎0382

Down toward the southwestern tip of Lombardy, hills flatten into rice paddies and poplars lace the terrain. In the heart of this region sits Pavia (pop. 71,000), where Romanesque churches share the limelight with a dense network of waterways designed by Leonardo Da Vinci. In AD 452 Attila the Hun unsuccessfully tried to conquer the city; in the centuries since, Pavia has been the site of coronation of the Italian kings. The Università di Pavia brings bustling student activity to the quiet city known in medieval times as "the city of a hundred towers," most of which have since been demolished.

◧⁊ TRANSPORTATION AND PRACTICAL INFORMATION. The **train station** is at the end of Vle. V. Emanuele II (☎848 88 80 88; ticket and info offices open 6am-8:30pm) in Ple. Stazione. **Trains** run to Genoa (1½hr., every hr. 6:45am-10:45pm, €5.73) and Milan (30min., every hr. 5:08am-11:14pm, €2.85). For the **bus station** (☎0382 30 330 or 0382 30 20 20), turn left from the train station and head to the brick building on the right on V. Trieste. Tickets may be purchased at the office under the terminal cover. **SILA** buses run to Milan (45min., 2 per hr. 6:30am-8pm, €2.85) via Certosa di Pavia (30min., €2.35). Ticket office open M-Sa 6:15am-7:30pm. **City buses** (☎800 11 17 17; www.lineservizi.it) run throughout the city from the train station; inquire at the tourist office for a route map. For **taxis,** call ☎0382 57 65 76, 0382 27 439 at the train station, or 0382 29 190 in P. Vittoria. Free **bike rental** is available from the city at P. del Municipio, 2 (☎0382 39 92 99), in the Palazzo Messabarba, on the right as you enter.

Pavia sits on the banks of the Ticino River not far from where it merges with the Po. The train station is in **Piazzale Stazione** in the western end of town. To get from the station to the historical center, walk down **Viale Vittorio Emanuele II** to **Piazzale Minerva.** Continue on Pavia's main street, **Corso Cavour,** to the city's narrow central square, **Piazza della Vittoria.** Just south of P. della Vittoria and to the right is **Piazza Duomo.** The next cross street after P. della Vittoria is **Corso Strada Nuova,** ironically the oldest street in town, which leads to the Università di Pavia and the Castello Visconteo if you turn left, and to the **Ponte Coperto** and the restaurants of **Borgo**

Ticino if you turn right. Past C. Str. Nuova, the main street changes to **Corso Mazzini.** The **tourist office** is at V. Filzi, 2. From the train station, turn left on V. Trieste and then right on V. Filzi. (☎0382 22 156; www.comune.pv.it. Open M-W 8:30am-12:30pm and 2-5pm, Th-F 8:30am-12:30pm and 2-5:30pm.) Do your laundry at **Lavanderia Self-Service,** V. dei Mille, 56, across Ponte Coperto. (☎349 49 72 687 or 347 44 04 220. Wash €3.50 per 7kg, €7 per 12kg. Detergent €1. Dry €3.50. Open daily 7:30am-10pm.) **Libreria Fox Books,** C. Mazzini, 2/C, off P. Vittoria, has English titles in small room on left. (☎0382 30 39 16. Open M-Sa 9am-1pm and 3-7:30pm, Su 10am-1pm and 3-7:30pm.) In case of **emergency** call ☎113, an **ambulance** at 118, or contact the **police** at Vle. Resistenza, 5 (☎0382 54 51). **Farmacia Vippani,** V. Bossolaro, 31 (☎0382 22 315), at corner of P. del Duomo and V. Menocchio, has a list of pharmacies with after-hours service. Open M-F 8:30am-12:30pm and 3:30-7:30pm. Otherwise head to **Punto Internet,** V. Paratici, 26, behind the *duomo* (☎0382 46 21 53; fax 0382 53 67 13. €2 per hr. Open M 2-7:30pm, Tu-F 9:30am-1:30pm and 2:30-7:30pm, Sa 2:30-7:30pm.) The **post office** is at P. della Posta, 2. (☎0382 39 22 81. Open M-F 8:30am-7pm, Sa 8:30am-12:30pm.) **Postal Code:** 27100.

⌐⌐ ACCOMMODATIONS AND FOOD. ▨Locanda della Stazione ❷, Vle. V. Emanuele II, 14, straight across from the train station on the right, has a welcoming, English-speaking staff. Spotless rooms all have sink, linens, and either fan or A/C; most have shared bathroom. The hotel is located in apartment building without sign. Ring bell outside wooden doors for entry; reception is upstairs on 2nd floor, where you must ring a 2nd bell. (☎0382 29 321. Singles €25-€27 with A/C; doubles €35-37, with A/C and private bath €50. MC/V.) From the bus station, take bus #4 (dir: Sora) for 10min. to the Mascherpa stop (3 per hr. 5:39-8:26pm, €0.85), and follow the sign up the road to reach **Camping Ticino ❶,** V. Mascherpa, 10. The campsite has a pool and clean, shared facilities. (☎0382 52 70 94. Laundry €3.50. Open Mar.-Oct. €5.50 per person, over 65 €4.50, ages 5-12 €3. Tents €4. Cars €2.50. 2-person bungalows €30; 4-person €60.)

The *zuppa alla pavese*, a piping-hot broth served with a poached egg and sprinkled with *grana* cheese, is a favorite. *Coniglio* (rabbit) and *rana* (frog) are also local specialties. Those who run foods that hop can wander to the *tavole calde* (cold bars) on C. Cavour and C. Mazzini for *panini*. Beneath the P. Vittoria, accessible by flights of stairs on either side of the *piazza*, the **Nuovo Mercato** sells fruit, flowers, cheese, and even squid. (Open daily 8am-12:30pm and 3:30-7:30pm. Closed M afternoon.) At **▨Antica Trattoria Ferrari ❹,** V. dei Mille, 111, the wood paneling suggests Swiss chalet, but the cuisine is strictly Italian. Fine *Pavese* selections like *risotto alle fragole* and caramel salmon will have you ordering more of the delicate platters. (☎0382 53 90 25. *Primi* €6.50, *secondi* €9.50. Cover €3. Open W-Su 12:30-2pm and 7:30-9:30pm. MC/V.)

◎⌐ SIGHTS AND ENTERTAINMENT. As the oldest building in town, the **▨Basilica di San Michele** has witnessed many coronations, including Charlemagne's in AD 774, Frederick Barbarossa's in 1155, and various members of the Savoy family. The exterior was rebuilt in the 12th century after an earthquake; the decision to use all sandstone, rather than brick, as was popular at the time, means that most of the decorative sculptures are worn away. A 1491 fresco of the *Coronation of the Virgin* and 14th-century bas-relief decorate the chancel; a gold and silver 10th-century crucifix of Teodote sits to the right of the altar. Take C. Strada Nuova to C. Garibaldi; turn right on V. S. Michele. (☎0382 26 063; www.sanmichele-pavia.it. Open M-Sa 7:30am-noon and 3-7pm, Su 8am-noon and 3-7:45pm. Free.) Founded in 1361 by the Visconti, the **Università di Pavia** counts Petrarch, Columbus, and Venetian playwright Goldoni among its alumni. Though Rabelais

LOMBARDY

rendered its students (now numbered 24,000 annually) as deviants and fops in his Renaissance narratives, the story of the university unfolds at the **Museo per la Storia dell'Università di Pavia.** (University on C. Strada Nuova between V. Mentana and C. C. Alberto. For museum, C. Strada Nuova, 65, enter the courtyard and head left. ☎0382 50 47 09; centro.museo@unipv.it. Museum open M 3:30-5pm, F 9:30am-noon. Free.) Up V. Liutprando from P. Castello, the **Basilica di San Pietro in Ciel D'Oro** (St. Peter in the Golden Sky), a Romanesque church built in the 8th century, was mentioned in Dante's *Divine Comedy* because it holds the **remains of St. Augustine.** The saint rests on the high altar in an ark-shaped 14th-century marble sarcophagus. (☎0382 30 30 36. Open daily 7am-noon and 3-7pm.)

Pavia's student population stirs up a rocking nightlife. A taste of the islands awaits in the fresh fruit cocktails (€4.15) at **Morgan's Drink House,** C. Cavour, 30/C. (☎0382 26 880. Happy hour 7-9pm. Open M and W-Su 6pm-2am.) At **Malaika "Bar and Soul,"** V. Bossolaro, 21, off C. Cavour, tribal rhythms beat as patrons enjoy *panini* and fruit desserts (from €2) on stools covered with leopard skin. Happy hour (6:30-9pm) cocktails go for €4.50. (☎382 30 13 99. Open Tu-Su 6:30pm-2am.)

THE LAKE COUNTRY

Travelers who need a rest should follow the example of artistic visionaries like Liszt, Longfellow, and Wordsworth: retreat to the serene shores of the northern lakes, where clear waters lap at the foot of snowcapped mountains. Summer attracts droves of tourists, foreign and native alike. A young, mostly German crowd descends upon the more affordable Lake Garda, enjoying water sports by day and dance floors by night. An hour north of Milan by train, Lake Como produces the silk sported by sophisticated *Milanesi*, who in turn lend their influence to the thriving city of Como, the lake's southern transportation hub. Though a playground for the rich and famous, Lake Como's shoreline harbors well-run and inexpensive hostels in addition to its famous villas. In the neighboring province of Piedmont palatial hotels dot Lake Maggiore's sleepy shores (p. 179), and tourism is least obtrusive and scenery most tranquil in tiny Lake Orto (p. 182).

LAKE COMO (LAGO DI COMO)

As the numerous luxurious villas on the lake shores attest, the well-to-do have been using Lake Como as a refuge since before the Roman Empire. But you don't need a *palazzo* to appreciate the beauty that surrounds Europe's deepest lake (410m)—many artists, including Rossini, Bellini, and Shelley, relied on this lake for inspiration. Three lakes form the forked Lake Como, joined at the three towns of Centro Lago: Bellagio, Menaggio, and Varenna. These smaller towns make for a more relaxing stay than neighboring Como, the largest city on the lake. Villages cover the dense green slopes—hop on a bus or ferry, and step off whenever a villa, castle, garden, vineyard, or small town beckons.

COMO ☎031

Situated on the southwestern tip of the lake and closest to Milan, Como (pop. 78,000) is the lake region's token semi-industrial town, where physicist Alessandro Volta was born and Giuseppe Terragni immortalized his fascist architectural designs. Roman Caesars and Holy Roman Emperors have all had a hand in Como's development. Today, the town serves mainly as a launching point for tourists who come to explore the lakes. Mediocre beaches, impeccably dressed businessmen, and racing scooters may not inspire visitors to linger, but fine restaurants and spectacular hiking nearby is more than enough to entertain those passing through.

⧉ TRANSPORTATION

Trains: FS runs trains from **Stazione San Giovanni** (☎031 89 20 21). Ticket window open daily 6:40am-8:25pm. To: **Chiasso** (10min., every hr. 6:29am-1:29am, €1); **Milan Centrale** (1hr., every 30min. 6:25am-11:08pm, €4.85); **Milan Porta Garibaldi** (1hr., every hr. 5:08am-10:20pm, €3.40); **Basel, Switzerland** (5hr., every 2hr. 10:07am-7:05pm, €55.20); and **Zurich** (4hr., 6 per day 9:07am-7:57pm, €40). **Ferrovia Nord** runs trains from **Stazione Ferrovia Nord** (☎031 30 48 00), by P. Matteotti, only to Stazione Nord in **Milan** (1hr., every 30min. 5:46am-9:16pm, €3.72).

Buses: SPT (☎031 24 73 11; www.sptlinea.it) in P. Matteotti runs buses to nearby lakeside towns. Ticket office open M-Sa 6:15am-8:15pm, Su 8:10am-12:25pm and 1:25-7:40pm. Info booth open M-F 8am-noon and 2-6pm, Sa 8am-noon. **C30** to **Bellagio** (1hr., every hr. 6:27am-8:14pm, €2.50). **C46** to **Bergamo** (2hr., every hr. 6:50am-6:32pm, €4.25). **C10** to **Domaso** (dir. of Colico, may require change at Menaggio; 2hr.; every hr. 7:10am-6:40pm; €3.85); **Gravedona** (2hr., every hr. 7:10am-6:40pm, €3.85); **Menaggio** (1hr., every hr. 7:10am-8:30pm, €2.80).

Ferries: Navigazione Lago di Como (☎031 57 92 11; www.navigazionelaghi.it). Ticket office open 8:10am-6:50pm. Departs daily to all lake towns from piers along Lungo Lario Trieste in front of P. Cavour. Ferries run every 30min. 9:20am-3:10pm to: **Bellagio** (2hr.; €6.20, express €9.20); **Menaggio** (2¼hr.; €6.20, express €9.20); and **Varenna** (2½hr.; €7.10, express €10.20). Day-passes for various lake regions €4.60-17.10. Pick up the booklet *Orario* for a schedule, including summer night service.

Public Transportation: Buy bus tickets (€0.95) at *tabaccherie,* bus station, or hostel.

Taxis: RadioTaxi (☎031 26 15 15).

Car Rental: Hertz (☎199 11 22 11; www.hertz.it), at the train station. Open M-F 9am-12:45pm and 2:10-6pm. From €45 per day.

Bike Rental: Rullo Bike, on V. Grandi (☎031 30 40 84). €18 per day.

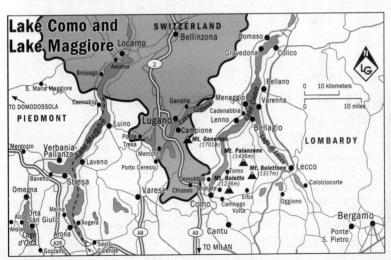

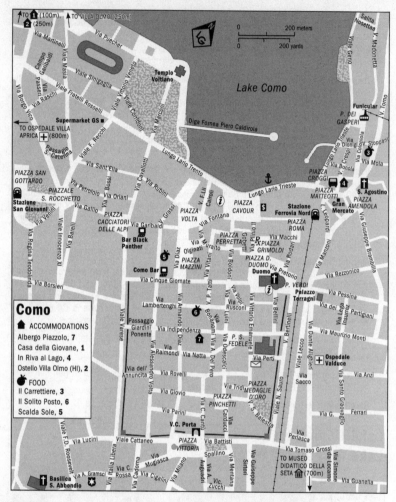

Como

🏠 **ACCOMMODATIONS**
Albergo Piazzolo, **7**
Casa della Giovane, **1**
In Riva al Lago, **4**
Ostello Villa Olmo (HI), **2**

🍅 **FOOD**
Il Carrettiere, **3**
Il Solito Posto, **6**
Scalda Sole, **5**

✦ 🛈 ORIENTATION AND PRACTICAL INFORMATION

From Como's **Stazione San Giovanni,** head down the stairs, straight ahead through the park. At **Piazzale San Rocchetto,** take **Via Fratelli Ricchi** on the left and then turn right on **Viale Fratelli Rosselli,** which turns into **Lungo Lario Trento** and leads to **Piazza Cavour.** The **bus station** and **Stazione Ferrovia Nord** are in **Piazza Matteotti,** 2min. farther down the lake along **Lungo Lario Trieste.**

  Tourist Office: ATC, P. Cavour, 17 (☎031 26 97 12; www.lakecomo.org), on the right facing the *piazza* from the lake, offers **maps** and extensive info. Ask the multilingual staff about hiking and hotels. Open May-Sept. M-Sa 9am-1pm and 2:30-6pm, Su 9:30am-1pm; Oct.-Apr. M-Sa 9am-1pm and 2:30-6pm. **Como Viva,** a small booth on V.

Comacini next to the *duomo*, also has maps and general info about events in the city. Open M-F 10:30am-12:30pm and 2:30-6pm, Sa-Su 10am-6pm.

Currency Exchange: Banca Nazionale del Lavoro, P. Cavour, 32 (☎031 31 31), near tourist office, has good rates and a 24hr. **ATM.** Open M-F 8:20am-1:20pm and 2:30-4pm, Sa 8:20-11:50am. Currency exchange also available at the tourist office, train station, and post office.

Luggage Storage: At train station cafe. €3.50 per bag. Open daily 6am-11pm.

Emergency: ☎113. **Ambulance:** ☎118. **Police:** ☎112.

Pharmacy: Farmacia Centrale, V. C. Plinio Secondo, 1, off P. Cavour. Open M 3:30-7:30pm, Tu-Su 8:30am-12:30pm and 3:30-7:30pm. Posts list of after-hours rotations.

Hospitals: Ospedale Valduce, V. Dante, 11 (☎031 32 41 11). **Ospedale Sant'Anna,** V. Napoleana, 60 (☎031 58 51 11). **Ospedale Villa Aprica,** V. Castel Carnasino, 10 (☎031 57 94 11).

Internet Access: Bar Black Panther, V. Garibaldi, 59 (☎031 24 30 05; www.internet-barblackpanther.com). €3 per hr., 30min. free with drink purchase. Open Tu-Su 7am-midnight. **Como Bar,** V. Alessandro Volta, 51 (☎031 26 20 52). €1.40 per 30min. 1 free soft drink or beer with 1hr. of Internet use. Open Tu-Su 7:30am-9:30pm.

Post Office: V. V. Emanuele II, 99 (☎031 26 02 10), in the town center. Open M-F 8:30am-2pm, Sa 8:10am-12:30pm. **Postal Code:** 22100.

▐ ACCOMMODATIONS

▩ **In Riva al Lago,** P. Matteotti, 4 (☎031 30 23 33; www.inriva.info), behind the bus stop. Brand-new hotel has rooms and apartments with tiled floors, bath, TV, and beds with ornate metal bedposts. Most rooms with A/C, a few with minifridge. The pub downstairs is a popular student hangout. English spoken. Breakfast buffet €2-4. Internet €1.50 per 20min. Reception 8am-11:30pm. Reserve ahead. Singles €30-38, with bath €40-50; doubles €39-45/52-60; triples €65-75; quads €82-98. Apartments for 4-6 people €99-130. AmEx/MC/V for over €105. ❸

Ostello Villa Olmo (HI), V. Bellinzona, 2 (☎ 031 57 38 00; ostellocomo@tin.it). From Stazione S. Giovanni, walk down the steps and past the giant hands. Turn left and walk 20min. down V. Borgo Vico to V. Bellinzona. Hostel is past the road to Villa Olma. Or take bus #1, 6, or 11 to Villa Olmo (€0.95). Lively and fun, run by English-speakers Crowded, single-sex rooms. Bicycle rental €12.50 per day or €6 for 4-9pm. Breakfast included. 3-course meat or vegetarian *menù* (€11), individual entrees (€6), and packs bag lunch (€7). Personal locker included. Baggage storage €2.50 per day. Self-service laundry with detergent €7; ironing €1. Parking available. Reception Mar.-Nov. 7-10am and 4-11:30pm. Lockout 10am-4pm. Strict curfew 11:30pm. Reserve ahead. Dorms €14.50. Family room with 6 beds €15 per person. Non-HI members add €3. ❶

Casa della Giovane (ACISJF), V. Borgovico, 182 (☎/fax 031 57 43 90 or 031 57 35 40), near the hostel. Take bus #1, 6, or 11. Nuns run 52 clean rooms, some with bath. 18+. Women only. Kitchen, TV room, library, and garden. Laundry €2.50 per load. Reception 6:30am-10:30pm. Curfew M-F and Su 10:30pm, Sa midnight. Reserve ahead. 1st 3 nights singles €15, doubles €30; €13/26 thereafter. Cash only. ❶

Albergo Piazzolo, V. Indipendenza, 65 (☎/fax 031 27 21 86). From P. Cavour, take V. Bonta, which becomes V. Boldini and V. Luni. V. Indipendenza is on the right. Tastefully decorated rooms above restaurant, some with fireplaces, all with bath, TV, and phone. Breakfast €7. Singles €45; doubles €60; triples €80; 1 quad €90. AmEx/MC/V. ❹

FOOD

Resca (sweet bread with dried fruit) and the harder, cake-like *mataloc* are great Como-specific treats sold at **Beretta Il Fornaio,** Vle. Fratelli Rosselli, 26/A. (Open M 7:30am-1:30pm, Tu-Sa 7:30am-1:30pm and 3:30-7pm.) Local soft cheeses, like the pungent *semuda* and *robiola,* are available at most supermarkets, including **GS,** on the corner of V. Fratelli Recchi and V. Fratelli Roselli, across from the park (☎031 57 08 95; open M-F 8am-8:30pm, Sa 8am-8pm, Su 9am-1pm). An **open-air market** is held Tuesday and Thursday mornings and all day Saturday in P. Vittoria.

For Como's finest flavors, try ■**Il Carrettiere ❸,** V. Coloniola, 18, off P. A. de Gasperi, near P. Matteotti. A Sicilian outpost in the middle of Lombardy, the restaurant draws crowds with its *spaghetti allo scoglio,* a platter of mussels, crayfish, shrimp, and squid (€13). (☎031 30 34 78. Pizza €3.90-7.90. *Primi* €5.50-10.50, *secondi* €7-16.50. Cover €1.30. Open Tu 7pm-midnight, W-Su noon-3pm and 7pm-midnight. Reserve ahead. AmEx/MC/V.) Find a sea of collared shirts at the small **Scalda Sole ❸,** V. Alessandro Volta, 41, a lunch spot for professionals who know their fish. (☎031 26 38 89. *Primi* €8, *secondi* €13-14. Open Tu-Sa noon-2:30pm and 7:30-10:30pm, Su 7:30-10:30pm. AmEx/MC/V.) Locals crowd **Il Solito Posto ❹,** V. Lambertenghi, 9, for *bresaola* (roast beef) with artichoke and noodles (€9.50), and other creative takes on classics. (☎031 27 13 52. *Primi* €8.50-12.50, *secondi* €10.50-19. Open Tu-Su noon-3pm and 7:30pm-midnight. AmEx/MC/V.)

SIGHTS

Dating from 1396 and recently restored, Como's **duomo** harmoniously combines an octagonal dome and Romanesque, Gothic, Renaissance, and Baroque elements. The Rodari brothers' life-like sculptures of the exodus from Egypt animate the exterior, while a collection of 16th-century tapestries brighten the cavernous interior. Statues of erstwhile Como residents Pliny the Elder and Pliny the Younger flank the main door, while inside each massive column hosts its own illuminated statue meters above the floor. (From P. Cavour, take V. C. Plinio Secondo to P. Duomo. Open daily 7am-noon and 3-7pm.) Just behind the *duomo* and across the railroad tracks, the deceptively plain Casa del Fascio—now called **Palazzo Terragni**—was built by Giuseppe Terragni between 1934 and 1936 to house the local Fascist government. The Neo-Classical **Tempio Voltiano** at the end of V. Marconi was dedicated to native son Alessandro Volta, inventor of the battery. Displayed items include early attempts at wet-cell batteries the size of a kitchen table, as well as various apparatus for experimenting on frog muscles. (From P. Cavour, walk left along the waterfront, turning on Lungolago M. di Savoia. ☎031 57 47 05. Open Apr.-Sept. Tu-Su 10am-noon and 3-6pm; Oct.-Mar. Tu-Su 10am-noon and 2-4pm. €3, students €1, under 15 with adult free.) Around the western edge of the lake, the ambassadorial **Villa Olmo,** built in Lombard style, sits in a statue-lined park of the same name and hosts notable exhibits throughout the year. (☎031 25 24 43. Gardens open Apr.-Sept. daily 8am-11pm; Oct.-Mar. 9am-7pm. Free. €8, students €5.) **Museo Didattico della Seta** displays the worms and silk looms that put Como on the textile map. (V. Vallegio, 3. ☎031 30 31 80; www.museosetacomo.com. Handicap accessible. Open Tu-F 9am-noon and 3-6pm. €8, groups €5.50 per person, students €2.60. Call ahead to arrange group visits.)

HIKING

For some of the best hiking in the lakes region, start by taking the **funicular** from P. dei Gasperi, 4, at the far end of Lungo Lario Trieste to **Brunate** for an excellent hike back down to Como. (☎031 30 36 08; info@funicolarecomo.it. June-Sept. daily every 15min. 6am-midnight; Oct.-May every 30min. 6am-10:30pm. €2.35, under 12 €1.55; round-trip €4.05/2.60, 8:30pm-midnight round-trip €2. AmEx/MC/V.) The tourist office in P. Cavour provides excellent trail descriptions for the lands above Brunate and can inform about hiking the Lecco district east of Como. For even better panoramas, take the red brick *passeggiata pedonale* to the left of the pink church and hike up toward ■Faro Voltiano (906m), a lighthouse dedicated to Volta (30min.; €1 including postcard). On the way, note Santa Rita, Europe's smallest sanctuary. On a clear day, views from the Faro stretch from Milan to the Matterhorn. A bus runs from Brunate to near Faro Voltiano (every 30min. 8:15am-6:45pm, €0.95). From Faro Voltiano, another 15min. of hiking leads to San Maurizio, and another hour should be enough to reach Monte Boletto (1236m). If the hike to M. Boletto isn't too exhausting, keep strolling to reach Monte Bolettone (1317m).

Another option is to head northwest between S. Maurizio and M. Boletto after the restaurant Baita Carla, on a path to lakeside Torno, 8 km north of Como (1hr.); this is a good place to catch a ferry home (every hr. 6:58am-8:14pm, €1.90). In Torno check out the Chiesa di San Giovanni (open daily 8am-6pm) or the Villa Pliniana, 15min. north of the dock, closed to visitors but worth a look from afar.

For more extensive exploration of the mountains east of Como, take bus C40 from the Como bus station to Erba (30min.; every hr. 5:25am-10:20pm, last bus back to Como 10:56pm; €2.55). From Erba, make the beautiful hike to Caslino D'Erba, which leads to Monte Palanzone (1436m). It is also possible to reach Erba by hiking south from Monte Bolettone (2hr.). Head to the cool recesses of Buco del Piombo for an encounter with prehistory: caves formed during the Jurassic Period over 150 million years ago. The Museo Buco del Piombo, V. Alpe Turati, 15, in Erba proper, displays materials from the caves and charts their history. (☎031 62 95 99; www.museobucodelpiombo.it. Open Apr.-Oct. Sa 2-6pm, Su 10am-6pm; Aug. M-F 2-6pm, Sa-Su 10am-6pm. Adults €5, children €4. Groups can visit with a booking.)

MENAGGIO
☎0344

On Lake Como's Western shore, Menaggio (pop. 3200) is home to cobblestone streets, stunning scenery, and a constant procession of tourists. Menaggio's central location and excellent ferry connections make it the perfect base for exploring any part of the lake as well as the mountains above it, and its youth hostel allows travelers to do so at a fraction of the cost of any other establishment on the lake.

Numerous towns line the beautiful central lake. Although they can all be reached by bus, the out-of-the-way trips often take more than 2hr. A more direct (and far more romantic) mode of travel is the ferry. Navigazione del Lago offers an all-day pass for €7.50 that covers travel to Bellagio, Varenna, Menaggio, Cadenabbia, Tremezzo, and Lenno. Most journeys last no more than 10min., with boats arriving daily roughly every 15min. 8:45am-7:45pm.

 TRANSPORTATION AND PRACTICAL INFORMATION. Buses (SPT, in P. Roma down V. Lusardi; ☎0344 32 118) and ferries (Navigazione Lago di Como, in P. Traghetti left of the town center; ☎0344 32 255) link Menaggio to the other lake towns. For a taxi call ☎0344 32 100. In the *centro* at P. Garibaldi, 4, the helpful multilingual staff at the ■tourist office has info on lake excursions and can suggest hiking itineraries and maps for any level of difficulty. The office also has Internet and a book exchange. (☎0344 32 924; www.menaggio.com. Open daily 9am-noon and 3-6pm.) Ostello la Primula (☎0344 32 356; www.menaggiohostel.com; see Accommodations) has been known to offer short-term work opportunities (see **Beyond Tourism: Short-Term Work,** p. 90) in return for room, board, and a small stipend, but they require a face-to-face interview. In case of **emergency,** dial ☎0344 33 246, or call the **carabinieri,** V. Regina and V. Nobiallo (☎0344 32 016) or an **ambulance** at ☎118. **Antica Farmacia Kluzer,** V. IV Novembre, 30, is open M-W and F-Su 8:30am-12:30pm and 3-7:30pm. Menaggio's **hospital** (☎0344 33 111) is on V. Cazartelli, off V. Cadorna above the center. **Internet** is at **Video Mix,** V. IV Novembre, 52, across from the Grand Hotel Menaggio. (☎0344 34 110. €1.50 for 15min. Open Tu-Sa 9:30am-12:30pm and 4-7:30pm.) The **post office,** V. Lusardi, 50 (open M-F 8:30am-2pm, Sa 8:30-12:30am) has **currency exchange** and an **ATM** (☎0344 32 106; open M-F 8:20am-1:20pm and 2:45-3:45pm). **Postal Code:** 22017.

⌂⌂ ACCOMMODATIONS AND FOOD. Ostello La Primula (HI) ❶, V. IV Novembre, 106, offers the best budget value in the lake district. From the ferry dock, walk straight to V. IV Novembre, then turn left and ascend the path that clings to the right side of the road. The hostel provides guests with free beach access, as well as bike and kayak rental (€11 per day) and suggestions on hiking and biking in the area. (☎034 43 23 56; www.menaggiohostel.com. Breakfast included; home-cooked 3-course dinner €12; picnic lunch €6.50. Laundry €3.50 per load. Internet €2 per 15min. Reception 8-10am and 4-12pm. Lockout 10am-4pm. Strict midnight curfew and quiet hours. Call ahead to reserve. Open Mar.-Nov. Dorms €13.50; 4- to 6-bed family suites with bath €14 per person. Non-HI members add €3. Cash only.) **Albergo il Vapore ❸,** P. T. Grossi, 3, just off P. Garibaldi, has 19 old rooms, all with bath, phone, some with TV and balcony facing the lake. (☎0344 32 229; fax 0344 34 850. Breakfast €6.50. Reservations only for stays over 3 days and require confirmation by fax. Singles €35; doubles €55; triples €65. Cash only.) Lakeside **Camping Europa ❶,** V. Cipressi, 12, a 15min. walk from the ferry docks down V. Lusardi then V. Roma, comes complete with a rocky beach. (☎0344 31 187. €4.90 per adult, €4.30 per child under 7, €8.20 per tent. Bungalow singles €30; 6-person bungalows €65. Cash only.) The **Rifugio Menaggio ❷,** a mountain station, was recently renovated and offers three bunkrooms 1400m above the lake. Getting there requires a 30min. bus ride on line C13, dir: "Plesio," followed by a 2hr. uphill hike, but the views and serenity are worth the effort. (☎034 43 72 82. Office open June-Sept. daily; Oct.-May Sa-Su only. €17 per person. AmEx/MC/V.)

Just up from the ferry dock, **Super Cappa Market** stocks groceries and all hiker needs. (☎0344 32 161. Open M 3:30-7pm, Tu-Sa 8am-12:30pm and 3:30-7pm.) Enjoy a true Italian moment at the classy **Il Ristorante di Paolo ❹,** Largo Cavour, 5, off P. Garibaldi, where you can listen to arias and watch as dusk falls across the lake. Try the *costolette di agnello alla scibacola* (€18) and *tagliatelle* (€8.50) with fresh fish. (☎0344 32 133. *Primi* €7.50-9, *secondi* €15-18. Cover €2. Open W-Su noon-2:30pm and 7-10pm. AmEx/MC/V.) Head uphill at the junction near Banca San Paolo for **Pizzeria Lugano ❶,** V. Como, 26, where a *quattro stagione* pizza is only €5.20. (☎0344 31 664. Pasta €4. Open M 6:30-11pm, Tu-Su noon-2:30pm and 6:30-11pm. AmEx/MC/V.) **Caffè Centrale ❶,** P. Garibaldi, 9, beneath Hotel du Lac, is the one place that makes sleepy Menaggio seem lively. Enjoy the excellent house *tiramisù* (€3) with your aperitif, but go early, because it runs out quickly. (☎0344 35 281. *Panini* €2.70-3.80. Pizza €4.50-5.50. Sundaes €5.10-6.30. Cocktails €2.70-5. Open M-Tu, Th-F, and Su 6:30am-12:30am, W and Sa 6:30am-1am. Cash only.)

◉◪ SIGHTS AND HIKING. The tourist office and hostel stock three main printouts: suggested **boat trips,** recommended **excursions by car** or bus, and a collection of **hiking** itineraries. Explore the romantic park, the gorge, rural settlements, or archaeological sites. The Rifugio Menaggio mountain station (see **Accommodations and Food,** above) is the starting point for a 2½hr. round-trip hike to **Monte**

Grona (1736m) or a 2¼hr. round-trip hike to **Chiesa di S. Amate** (1623m). A number of shorter hikes start in Menaggio. A 2hr. hike (one-way) winds through outlying villages and farms to the picturesque **Sass Corbee Gorge.** Another low-commitment option is the 2hr. hike toward **Lake Lugano** to **Lago di Piano,** a small nature reserve in **Val Menaggio,** (from which **bus C12** heads back). For a less strenuous adventure take the 30min. walk up to **La Crocetta,** past trenches from a WWI defensive line.

BELLAGIO ☎031

Favored by the upper-crust of Milanese society, Bellagio (pop. 3000) is one of the loveliest and most heavily visited central lake towns. Its name is a compound of *bello* (beautiful) and *agio* (comfort); fittingly, the town is filled with welcoming lakeside promenades, sidewalk cafes, and steep streets that lead to silk shops and the villas of Lombard aristocrats.

☞⃣ TRANSPORTATION AND PRACTICAL INFORMATION. To reach Bellagio from Milan, take a **ferry** from the train station in Varenna. The **C30 bus** runs from Como. Ferries dock at **Piazza Mazzini,** which becomes **Via Roma** to the left and **Lungo Lario Manzoni** to the right. The English-speaking staff at the **tourist office** in P. Mazzini gives detailed daytrip info. (☎031 95 02 04; www.bellagiolakecomo.com. Open M 3:30-7:30pm, Tu-Sa 8:30am-12:30pm and 3:30-7:30pm, Su 9am-12:30pm and 4-7:30pm.) In case of **emergency,** call the **police** at ☎113, the **carabinieri,** V. Roncati, 15 (☎112), or an **ambulance** at ☎118. A **pharmacy** is at V. Roma, 8. (☎031 95 01 86. Open June-Sept. M-Sa 8:30am-12:30pm and 3:30-7:30pm, Su 9am-12:30pm; Sept.-June M-Tu and Th-Sa 8:30am-12:30pm and 3:30-7:30pm.) **Banks** with **ATMs** are on Lungo Lario Manzoni. Use the **Internet** at **bellagiopoint.com,** Salita Plinio, 8/10/12, off V. Garibaldi. (☎031 95 04 37. €2 per 15min., €6 per hr. Open daily 10am-10pm.) The **post office,** Lungo Lario Manzoni, 4, offers **currency exchange.** (☎031 95 19 42. Open M-F 8:30am-2pm, Sa 8:30am-noon.) **Postal Code:** 22021.

🏠🍴 ACCOMMODATIONS AND FOOD. Expect higher rates in Bellagio than in other lake towns. **Albergo Giardinetto ❸,** V. Roncati, 12, off P. della Chiesa, is by far the best deal in town, with simple rooms overlooking quiet gardens and grape arbors. (☎031 95 01 68; tczgne@tiscali.it. Breakfast €6. Open Easter-Nov., weather permitting. Singles €40; doubles with bath €52, with balcony €55; triples with bath €70.) ⬛**Ristorante Barchetta ❹,** S. Mella, 15, is in the heart of the old town and features creative Lombard cuisine. Try the *gnocchi* with shrimp and asparagus tips (€10.50). The two-person *menù* (€40) is a gastronomic extravaganza. (☎031 95 13 89. Open M and W-Su noon-2:15pm and 7-11:20pm. AmEx/MC/V.) ⬛**Ristorante La Punta ❹,** V. Vitali, 19, around the corner from P. della Chiesa and V. Roma, allows you to avoid the crowds while enjoying a veggie-heavy meal under a covered porch. The cheese and spinach ravioli in a walnut cream sauce (€9) is a dream. (☎031 95 18 88. *Primi* €7-10, *secondi* €9-17. Cover €2.50. Open daily noon-2:30pm and 7-10pm. AmEx/MC/V for over €50.)

🔆 SIGHTS. The 17th-century **Villa Serbelloni** (not to be confused with the stately five-star Grand Hotel Villa Serbelloni down the hill) offers spectacular views from the fortifications on the promontory and a lovely cyprus-lined garden with artificial grottoes. Today it is home to the Rockefeller Foundation, and can be toured twice daily in a guided group. Purchase tickets between 15min. and 1hr. beforehand at P. Chiesa, 14. (☎/fax 031 95 15 51. 1½hr. tours Apr.-Oct. Tu-Su 11am and 4pm. €6.50, children €3.) The lakeside gardens of **Villa Melzi,** constructed by famous architect Albertolli at the beginning of the 19th century, blossom at the other end of town. (800m right from the ferry dock along Lungo Largo Manzoni.) The villa is still a private residence, but the **grounds** are open to the public. (Open daily Apr.-Oct. 9am-6pm. €5.) The **Basilica of Saint James,** namesake of the P. della Chiesa, is an excellent example of 10th- to 12th-century Lombard Romanesque architecture and is worth a stop for the mosaic scenes in the cupolas of the chapels either side of the main altar. A truly valuable trip is to **Lenno,** only a 10min. ferry ride away, home to the idyllic ◪**Villa del Balbianello,** an 18th-century villa reputed to be the lake's most beautiful. The villa began as a Franciscan convent and was rebuilt by Cardinal Durini as a "splendid palace of delights," but it recently gained infamy as the site of the wedding at the end of *Star Wars: Attack of the Clones.* The terraced gardens and vine-wrapped exterior are the main attraction. (Transportation to Lenno included in all-day Centro Lago ferry pass. Villa is accessible on foot, or by water taxi. ☎333 41 03 854. 10min. ride €5 round-trip. ☎0344 56 110; www.fondoambiente.it. Villa open mid-Mar. to Nov. Tu and Th-F 10am-1pm and 2-6pm, Sa-Su 10am-6pm. Last entrance 30min. before closing. €5, children 4-12 €2.50. 1½hr. guided tours for up to 10 people €40. Reserve ahead.)

VARENNA   ☎0341

A ferry ride from Bellagio and Menaggio, low-key Varenna is a less polished version of its more famous neighbors. Spectacular gardens and a castle, as well as prohibitively high prices, make Varenna a great daytrip. A passage beside the water connects both sides of Varenna, offering lake vistas. Varenna's 13th-century **Chiesa di S. Giorgio** (☎0341 83 02 28), looms above the main *piazza.* Its exceedingly simple interior was restored in the 1950s, and still contains a few traces of ornate frescoes. (Open daily 7am-noon and 2-7pm.) Varenna's most famous sights are the two lakeside **botanical gardens** of **Villa Monastero,** 150m to the right of the church, located in a former Cistercian monastery. The grounds contain 2km of paths past dark cyprus groves and otherwordly giant aloe plants. (www.villamonastero.it. Open daily Mar. 28-Nov. 1 9am-7pm. Entrance to gardens €2, students €1.30. Combined ticket with Villa Cipressi €4/3.50.) The smaller terraced gardens of the 16th-century **Villa Cipressi** are the former weekend home of Lombard aristocrats. Enter through the Hotel Villa Cipressi, past Villa Monastero. (Gardens open daily Mar.-Oct. 9am-7pm. €2, students 1.30.) From the tourist office, a 30min. hike up V. IV Novembre leads to **La Sorgente del Fiumelatte.** At 250m, this river the shortest in Italy, disappearing in October to reappear in March. A 30min. ascent past the *piazza* and cemetery to the left leads to the 12th-century **Castello di Vezio,** linked to its tower by a drawbridge. Birds of prey swoop over the castle daily at 4 and 6pm for falconing demonstrations. (V. del Castellano, 6. ☎335 46 51 86; www.castellodivezio.it. Open Apr.-Oct. daily; Nov.-Mar. Sa-Su 10am-sunset. €4, students €3.)

The only affordable accommodation in Varenna is **Albergo Beretto ❹,** V. per Esino, 1, on the way to the train station. Rooms are a bit worn, but all have TV, telephone, and view. (☎/fax 0341 83 01 32. Breakfast €6. Reserve ahead. Doubles €58, with bath €68. Double with balcony and sofa for 3rd person €80. Extra bed add €12. Cash only.) The gigantic crepes (€3.70-8.30) at ◪**Nilus Bar ❷,** Riva Garibaldi, 4, burst with fillings. (☎0341 81 52 28. *Panini* €4. Pizza €4.20-7.30. Cocktails €4.20-6. Open June to mid-Sept. daily 10am-midnight; Apr.-May closed Tu; Oct.-Mar. closed except for nice weekends. AmEx/MC/V.) The superb **Vecchia Varenna ❸,** V. Scoscesa, 10, allows guests to dine in a glass-enclosed terrace over the water. The *robiola* cheese ravioli with potatoes and basil sauce (€11) and pumpkin *gnocchi* (€11) combine complex flavors. (☎0341 83 07 93. *Primi* €11, *secondi* €15-16. Cover €2. Open Tu-Su 12:30-2pm and 7:30-9:30pm. Closed Jan.)

Varenna's **train station,** just uphill from the ferry docks, links the eastern side of the lake to Milan, making journeys into the central lake region easy. (☎0341 36 85 84.) There is no ticket office; use the machine inside the waiting room. **Trains** run to Milan (1¼hr., every hr. 5:25am-10:29pm, €2.10). For a **taxi,** call ☎0341 83 05 80 or 0341 81 50 61. Exiting the **ferry dock,** turn right and follow the promenade along the water, then proceed uphill to the **tourist office,** V. Venini, 6, 100m to the right of the church in P. S. Giorgio. (☎0341 83 03 67; www.fromitaly.net/lackcomo/varenna/ index.htm. Open May-Sept. M-Sa 9:30am-12:30pm and 2:30-5:30pm, Su 9:30am-12:30pm.) Also in P. S. Giorgio are **Banca Popolare di Lecco,** with an **ATM** (☎0341 81 50 15; open M-F 8:20am-1:20pm and 2:45-3:45pm), a **pharmacy** (☎0341 83 02 03; open M-Tu and Th-Su 9am-12:30pm and 3:30-7:30pm, W 9am-12:30pm), and a **post office,** back toward the peninsula (☎0341 83 02 31; open M-Sa 8:30am-noon). In case of **emergency,** dial ☎113, or call the **carabinieri** at ☎0341 82 11 21, and **ambulance** at ☎0341 83 11 94, or a **hospital** at ☎0341 82 91 11. **Postal Code:** 23829.

DOMASO ☎0344

The breezes in this tiny town create perfect **windsurfing** conditions. Domaso lies 50km from Como or 1½hr. by hydrofoil. Surfers flock to the **Ostello della Gioventù: La Vespa (HI) ❶,** V. Case Sparse, 12. Murals and dismembered scooters decorate the rooms. The bar below pumps techno into the wee hours. The hostel also offers windsurfing and mountain bike rentals. (☎0344 97 449; www.ostellolavespado-maso.it. Breakfast included. Wheelchair accessible. Dinner €12. Reception 10am-noon and 4-10pm. Curfew midnight. Open Mar.-Oct. Dorms €13. AmEx/MC/V.)

The **tourist office,** in the Villa Camilla, has **maps** and info on water sports. (☎0344 96 322. Open daily 10am-12:30pm, 5-7:45pm, and 8:15-10pm.) **Windsurfcenter,** at Camping Paradiso, on the lake past the hostel, outfits sailors and windsurfers and offers classes. (☎0380 70 00 010; www.windsurfcenter-domaso.com. Board rental €5-7 per hr., €27-35 per half-day, €35-45 per day. Private lessons €68 per hr. Sailboats from €30 per hr., €50 per half-day. Bikes €10 for 1st hr., €3 per additional hr., €15 per half-day.) If the wind isn't cooperating, **Canottieri Domaso,** V. Statale Regina, 30min. farther along the main road, takes out **wakeboarders.** (☎0344 97 462; www.canottieridomaso.it. Wakeboarding €1.80 per min., waterskiing €2 per min.)

ACROSS THE BORDER FROM LAGO DI COMO

LUGANO, SWITZERLAND ☎091

Lugano, Switzerland's 3rd-largest banking center, rests on Lago di Lugano in a valley between the San Salvatore and Monte Brè peaks. Cobblestone streets widen into arcade-lined *piazze*, where visitors can enjoy a seamless blend of religious beauty, artistic flair, and natural spectacle. There are two extraordinary youth hostels, both housed in luxury villas, with swimming pools and magnificent gardens.

 Remember to bring your passport for excursions into Switzerland.

Lugano

▲⌂ ACCOMMODATIONS
Eurocampo, **9**
Hotel & Backpackers
Montarina, **8**
La Palma, **10**
Ostello della Gioventù (HI), **1**

🍏 FOOD
Ristorante Manora, **3**
Taqueria El Chilicuil, **6**
La Tinèra, **7**

🍸 NIGHTLIFE
Biblio-Café Tra, **2**
Mango Club, **4**
La Piccionaia, **5**

📠 TRANSPORTATION AND PRACTICAL INFORMATION. Trains run from P. della Stazione to: Locarno (16.20SFr) via Bellinzona (30min., every 30min. 5:36am–12:17am, 11.40SFr) and Milan (45min., every hr. 7:14am–9:48pm, 21SFr). **Public buses** run from neighboring towns to the center of Lugano and traverse the city. Schedules and ticket machines are at each stop. (Tickets 1.10-2SFr, 24hr. "Carta Giorno" day-pass 5SFr.) For **taxis,** call ☎091 92 28 833, 091 97 12 121, or 091 92 20 222. The 15min. downhill walk from the train station to the classically Italian **Piazza della Riforma,** the town's center, winds through Lugano's large pedestrian zone. For those who would rather avoid the walk, a funicular runs between the train station and the waterfront **Piazza Cioccaro** (1.10SFr, 5:20am–11:50pm).

The **tourist office** is in the Palazzo Civico. To reach it from the station, cross the footbridge labeled "Centro" and proceed down V. Cattedrale straight through P. Cioccaro as it becomes V. Pessina. Turn left on V. dei Pesci and left on Riva via

CROSSING THE BORDER. Italy's **international dialing prefix** is 00. Switzerland's **country code** is 41, and the **city code** for Lugano is 091. Drop the zero when calling from outside Switzerland. As of August, 2005, exchange rates for the **Swiss Franc (SFr)** are as follows: 1SFr=€0.64; €1=1.55SFr.

Vela, which becomes Riva Giocondo Albertolli. The office is across from the ferry launch and offers free **maps** and guided city walks on Mondays at 9:30am. (☎091 91 33 232; www.lugano-tourism.ch. Open Apr.-Oct. M-F 9am-7pm, Sa 9am-6pm, Su 10am-6pm; Nov.-Mar. M-F 9am-noon and 2-5pm.) **Luggage storage** is at the train station for 7SFr per piece or 4-7SFr per locker (open 9am-1pm and 2:30-6:45pm). In case of **emergency**, call the **police** at ☎117, **fire** at ☎118, **ambulance** at ☎144, or **medical services** at ☎111. There are **pharmacies** in all major *piazze* and along the waterfront. **Internet** is available at **Biblio-Café Tra,** V. A. Vanoni, 3. (☎091 92 32 305. 2SFr per 15min. Open M-Th 9am-midnight, F 9am-1am, Sa 5pm-1am.) The **post office,** on V. della Posta, is two blocks up from the lake near V. al Forte. (Open M-F 7:30am-6:15pm, Sa 8am-4pm. Cashes **traveler's checks.**) **Postal Code:** CH-6900.

■♥ ACCOMMODATIONS AND FOOD. Converted from a villa, the palm-tree enveloped ▇**Hotel & Backpackers Montarina** ❷, attracts students and families with a swimming pool, reading room, kitchen, and terrace. From the station, walk right 200m, cross the tracks, and then walk uphill. (☎091 96 67 272; www.montarina.ch. Buffet breakfast 12SFr. Sheets 4SFr. Laundry 4SFr, detergent 1.50SFr. Internet 10SFr per hr. Reception 8am-10:30pm. Reserve ahead. Open Mar.-Oct. Dorms 25SFr; singles 70SFr, with bath 80SFr; doubles 100SFr/120. AmEx/MC/V.) The family-run ▇ **Ostello della Gioventù (HI)** ❷, V. Cantonale, 13, is in Lugano-Savosa. There are two streets called V. Cantonale, one in downtown Lugano and one in Savosa. Walk 350m left from the station, pass the parking lot, and cross the street to the bus stop. Take bus #5 to "Crocifisso." Backtrack and turn left up V. Cantonale. Gardens and pool complement comfortable rooms. (☎966 27 28; www.luganoyouthhostel.ch. Breakfast 8SFr. Kitchen access 1SFr after 7pm. Sheets included. Towels 2SFr. Laundry 5SFr. Internet 5SFr for 20min. Keys available with 20SFr deposit. Parking available. Reception 6:30am-noon and 3-10pm. Curfew 10pm. Reserve ahead. Open mid-Mar. to Oct. Dorms 29SFr; singles 44SFr; doubles 72SFr, with kitchen 92SFr; family rooms for 2-6 people 90-120SFr. Non-HI members add 6SFr. MC/V.) There are several campsites near Lugano. For the lakeside **La Palma** ❶ (☎091 60 52 561; fax 091 60 45 438) and **Eurocampo** ❶ (☎091 60 52 114; fax 091 60 53 187), take the Ferrovia-Lugano-Ponte-Tresa (FLP) tram to Agno (4.60SFr). From the station, turn left, then left again on V. Molinazzo. (La Palma 9SFr per person; tents 10-12SFr. Eurocampo 10SFr per person; tents 8SFr. Both include showers. Both cash only.)

Satisfying fare is easy to find at the outdoor restaurants and cafes that pay homage to Lugano's Italian heritage, serving up delicious *penne, gnocchi,* and freshly spun pizzas. Avoid the restaurants in the square; they're overpriced and not as good quality as others hidden in the side streets. For some quick eats, the **market** in P. della Riforma sells seafood, produce, and veggie sandwiches for 4SFr (open Tu and F 7am-noon), or try the outdoor stands on V. Pessina, off P. della Riforma. The romantic ▇**La Tinèra** ❸, V. dei Gorini, 2, is a low-lit, underground restaurant specializing in Lombard cuisine. Try the sausage with *risotto* (14SFr) or a 4SFr vegetarian goulash. (☎091 92 35 219. Daily *menù* 13-19SFr. Open M-Sa 8:30am-3pm and 5:30-11pm. AmEx/MC/V.) **Taqueria El Chilicuil** ❶, C. Pestalozzi, 12, down C. Pestalozzi from P. Indipendenza, serves tacos, quesadillas (5.50-8.50SFr), and margaritas (7SFr, pitcher 40SFr), spicing up Lugano's cuisine. (☎091 92 28 226. Wheelchair accessible. Open M-W 11:30am-3pm and 5-11pm, Th-F 11:30am-3pm and 5pm-12:30am, Sa 6pm-12:30am. Cash only.) **Ristorante Manora ❷**, in the Manor Department Store in P. Dante, 3rd fl.; 2nd entrance off Salita Mario e Antonio Chiattone. Hungry but tight-fisted travelers will love this gourmet spot's salad bar (4.50-10.20SFr), pasta (7.90-10.90SFr), hot daily specials (10-15SFr), and beer. (Wheelchair accessible. Open M-Sa 7:30am-10pm, Su 10am-10pm. AmEx/MC/V.)

◙ **SIGHTS.** Book free themed tours of the city—including ones on Lugano's architecture, history, and gardens—at the tourist office or by calling ☎091 60 52 643. The 2hr. tours run mid-Mar.to mid-Oct. and begin at 9:30am. The ornate frescoes of the 16th-century **Cattedrale San Lorenzo**, downhill from the train station, gleam with vivid colors. (Open daily 9:30am-6pm.) Marble angels wielding bronze swords battle devils in the 2nd altar on the right. Bernardio Luini's gargantuan fresco, *Crucifixion*, painted in 1529, fills an entire wall in the **Chiesa Santa Maria degli Angioli**, 200m down Riva Vela from the tourist office. The small 14th-century **Chiesa San Rocco**, in P. Maghetti two blocks left of P. della Riforma, houses an ornate altarpiece and a series of frescoes depicting the life of its patron saint. (Open daily 10:30am-12:30pm and 3:30-6:30pm.) The **Museo Cantonale d'Arte**, V. Canova, 10, has a rotating collection of 5000 pieces of 19th- and 20th-century art from regional artists like Franzoni and Righini, though the collection also includes works by Degas, Renoir, and Pisarro. The collection is frequently complemented by exhibits of contemporary art. (Diagonally across from the Chiesa San Rocco. ☎091 91 04 780; www.museo-cantonale-erte.ch. Wheelchair accessible. Open Tu 2-5pm, W-Su 10am-5pm. Permanent collection 7SFr, students 5SFr. Special exhibits 10/7SFr. MC/V.) A lakeside villa houses the ▨**Museo delle Culture Extraeuropee**, V. Cortivo, 24. Carved masks, statues, and shields from Africa, Oceania, and Asia adorn the villa's staircases. On the footpath V. Cortiva, which becomes Sentiero di Gandria in the Villa Heleneum. From the tourist office, take bus #1, dir: Castagnola, to San Domenica and walk to the street below. The villa is 700m on the right. Or take the ferry to Museo Helenum. (☎058 86 66 909; www.lugano.ch/cultura. Open Mar. 23-Nov. 6 W-Su 10am-5pm. 5SFr, students 3SFr.)

🎦🎵 **ENTERTAINMENT AND NIGHTLIFE.** Music and shows fills the *piazze* of Lugano year-round. August 1 is ▨**Swiss National Day,** when Swiss-flag-studded parades, fireworks, and a choreographed airshow over Lake Lugano put America's 4th of July to shame. The 2nd weekend of July, Lugano's ▨**Festival Jazz** fills P. della Riforma with free music after 8:30pm. Past performers include Miles Davis and Bobby McFerrin. The looser **Blues to Bop Festival** celebrates R&B, blues, and gospel in the beginning of September with free performances by international singers and local amateurs (www.bluestobop.ch). In mid-October, Lugano reaffirms its Italian associations by celebrating the country's *aqua vitae* at the **Wine Harvest Festival.**

Lugano's streets stay crowded most nights until dawn; discos, nightclubs, and piano bars cater to partying night owls. Sit on mango-colored chairs while sipping tropical cocktails and beer at **Mango Club**, P. Dante, 8, where the dance floor stays crowded with dancing couples. (☎091 92 29 438; www.mangoclub.ch. Open Tu-Su 10pm-5am.) Those looking for a more relaxed atmosphere should head to the nightclub **La Piccionaia**, C. Pestalozzi, 21, to sip cocktails and relax while listening to the DJ spin mixed music from the 60s to the 90s (☎091 92 34 546; www.lapiccionaia.com. Drinks 10-13 SFr. Cover 20SFr. Open daily 10pm-5am. AmEx/MC/V.) For a change of pace, head down V. Pretorio from P. Dante and turn left on V. Vanoni for the **Biblio-Café Tra**, V. Vanoni, 3, which attracts laidback students from the neighboring university. Have a beer (3.60SFr), use the Internet (2SFr per 15min.), or read a book from the extensive collection at one of the battered wood tables. (☎091 92 32 305. Open M-Th 9am-midnight, F 9am-1am, Sa 5pm-1am.)

⚠ **OUTDOOR ACTIVITIES.** The dock for the **Società Navigazione del Lago di Lugano** is across the street from the tourist office. (☎091 92 31 779; www.lakelugano.ch.) Tours of Lake Lugano pass tiny, unspoiled towns along the shore, many with attractions like a chocolate museum or miniature Swiss houses.

Reach the peaks of **Monte Brè** (933m) and **Monte San Salvatore** (912m) by funicular. The **Monte Brè funicular** is 20min. down the river along Riva Albertolli from the center of town. An easier way is to take bus #1, dir: Castagnola to the Cassarate-Monte Brè stop or to catch the red tourist train that runs to the **tourist office.** (☎079 68 57 070. Runs daily 8am-5pm, every 20min. 3SFr.) At the top of the funicular are a number of bike and hiking paths (find maps at the funicular station). The **San Salvatore** funicular is 20min. from the tourist office in the other direction; from the lakefront, follow V. E. Bosio inland and turn right on V. delle Scuole. The 360° degree view from the top makes Lake Lugano look like a giant puddle. (☎091 98 52 828; www.montesansalvatore.ch. 10min., every 30min. June 17-Sept. 17 8:30am-11pm. One-way 17SFr, round-trip 24SFr; ages 6-16 7-8.50/10-15.80SFr)

Bike rental is available at the Stazione FFS, by ticket office #1 (☎0512 21 56 42; open 8:30am-6pm; half-day 23SFr, full day 31SFr; lock and helmet included). **Palace Lugano SA Boatcenter** (☎091 92 35 733; www.boatcentersaladin.ch) in P. Luini rents motorboats by the 30min. (from 25SFr) or an hour (from 40SFr). **Club Nautico** rents windsurfing boards. (☎091 64 96 139. 10SFr. per hr.) For a more relaxing trip on the lake, rent **pedal boats** from the hut to the left of the Navigazione del Lago office. (☎079 62 13 530. 3-person boat 7SFr per 30min., 4-person boat 8SFr per 30min. Open daily 10am-7pm.)

LAKE GARDA (LAGO DI GARDA)

Lake Garda, the largest lake in Northern Italy, draws tourists by the busload to its hazy mountains and country-style resorts. Stretching 52km into the regions of the Veneto, Lombardy, and Trent, Lake Garda's shores have given forth the remains of a Bronze Age civilization as well as evidence of Roman-era prosperity. Milan and Venice once competed for the region's freshwater fish, olives, citrus fruit, and white and black truffles; in 1426 Venice won out. Every summer, German, Dutch, and Italian tourists zip through Garda's towns and mountain tunnels on rented scooters and crowd its pebbly beaches to bask in the sun, windsurf, and kayak. On the northern tip of the lake, Riva del Garda's youth hostel offers budget travelers an opportunity to likewise partake in lake-side adventures (see p. 360).

SIRMIONE ☎ 030

Isolated on a peninsula from the surrounding lakeside towns, tiny Sirmione (pop. 7000) retains the elegance and charm that once moved the poet Catullus to praise the beauty of his home here. Among the town's chief attractions are the healing powers of its spa waters, renowned since ancient times. Local authorities try to maintain the town's peace and tranquility by cordoning off the historical center as a pedestrian-only zone, but the foot-traffic of summer tourists still gives Sirmione the feel of a bustling resort. As a result, trendy boutiques and sophisticated hotels now graciously share sidewalk space with the medieval architecture.

🚌🛈 **TRANSPORTATION AND PRACTICAL INFORMATION. SAIA buses** run from the station, V. Marconi, 26. (Open M-Tu 10am-1pm and 2-7pm, W-Su 7am-1pm and 2-8pm. After hours, purchase bus tickets from the *tabaccheria* on Vle. Marconi or in S. Cantro.) Buses go to Verona (1hr., every hr. 6:03am-7:28pm, €3.45) and Brescia (75min., every hr. 6:25am-7:12pm, €3.30). Buses in both directions

LOMBARDY

stop in Colombare (5min., every 45 min., €1), 3km south of Sirmione at the foot of the peninsula, and those to Brescia also stop in Desenzano, the town with the closest train station (15min., €2.45). **Navigazione Lago di Garda** at the end of P. Carducci (☎030 914 95 11; www.navigazionelaghi.it) runs **ferries** to Desenzano (15min., 10am-10pm, €2.60); Gardone (1¼-2hr., 8:32am-5:36pm, €5.60; speed service €11.40); and Riva (2-4hr., 9:46am-5:08pm; €8.10, speed service €14). Dial ☎030 91 60 82 or 030 91 92 40 for a **taxi**. Rent **bikes, scooters,** and **motorbikes** at **Adventure Sprint,** V. Brescia, 15, in the neighboring town of Colombare; turn right off V. Colombare after the bus stop in Colombare. (☎030 91 90 00. Bikes €11 per day, scooters €33-70, motorbikes €75-140. Open daily 9am-6:30pm.)

The **tourist office,** V. G. Marconi, 6, is in the circular building just to the right of the SAIA station. (☎030 91 61 14; www.comune.sirmione.bs.it. Open Apr.-Oct. daily 9am-8pm; Nov.-Mar. M-F 9am-12:30pm and 3-6pm, Sa 9am-12:30pm.) **Tours** are offered of Sirmione and the Grotte di Catullo by the **Centro Servizi Culturali,** V. Marconi, 26 (☎02 20 40 41 75 or 329 86 34 805). The **Banca Popolare di Verona,** P. Castello, 3-4 (open M-F 9am-1:20pm and 2:35-3:35pm, Sa-Su 9-11:20am), has an **ATM.** In case of **emergency,** dial ☎113, or call the **Tourist Medical Clinic,** on V. L. da Vinci before the Centro Sportive (☎340 08 83 412. Open July-Sept.), or the **police** (☎030 99 05 772). **Farmacia Di Turno** is on V. Santa Maria Maggiore in the old city. (Open M-Th 9:45am-12:15pm and 4:30-6pm, F 4:30-6pm.) **Public restrooms** are to the right behind the SAIA station, next to the bar at Lido delle Bionde, and halfway between Colombare and Sirmione along V. XXV Aprile across from the Hotel Rossi Appartamenti. The **post office,** V. Marconi, 28, is behind the SAIA station on the left. (Open M-F 8:30am-2pm, Sa 8:30am-12:30pm.) **Postal Code:** 25010/9.

⌐⌐ **ACCOMMODATIONS AND FOOD.** A thorough exploration of Sirmione takes only an afternoon, but people looking for prolonged relaxation must choose from among a number of fairly pricey hotels or slightly cheaper accommodations in Colombare. Reserve early for summer sojourns; rates are higher from June to August. The tourist office can help with accommodations. Several blocks into the historical center, the quiet **Hotel Marconi ❹,** V. V. Emanuele II, 51, maintains spacious rooms with thick mattresses, bathrooms, TV, A/C, and safe. Enjoy a sumptuous breakfast on a terrace or sunbathe on the private beach. For lower rates, ask for a room without a balcony or view. (☎ 030 91 60 07 or 030 91 97 574; www.hotel-marconi.net. Breakfast included. Open Mar.-Oct. Singles €35-58; doubles €62-95; triples and quads €120-150. AmEx/MC/V.) **Albergo Grifone ❸**, V. Bocchio, 4, off V. Dante to the right of V. V. Emanuele past the *castello*, has country-style rooms with bath and lake views, and a restaurant in the same building. (☎ 030 91 60 14; fax 030 91 65 48. Singles €36; doubles €57. Extra bed €20. Cash only.) Located in a family home 5min. from the tourist office, **Albergo Meublè Venezia ❸**, V. XXV Aprile, 36, offers clean rooms with bath and fan (☎/fax 030 91 60 92. Breakfast included. Open Apr.-Oct. Singles €34-45; doubles €45-65; triples €85. Cash only.) The campground in nearby Colombare, **Campeggio Sirmione ❶**, V. Sirmioncino, 9, boasts a swimming pool and beach as well as a small market and cafe. (☎ 030 99 04 665 or 030 91 90 45; www.camping-sirmione.com. Open Mar.-Oct. €6-9 per person; tent sites €6-14; 2-person cabins €45-70; 4-person cabins €65-100. MC/V.)

Sirmione's restaurants are concentrated in busy P. Carducci, where tourists watch each other across terraces. For those seeking a bit more solitude, **Ristorante Pizzeria Valentino ❷**, P. Porto Valentino, 10, off V. Emanuele, offers delicious fare including homemade *gnocchi* and the local specialty trout with Garda sauce and polenta (€10) for slightly less than its counterparts. (☎ 030 91 61 12 or 030 91 96 534; fax 030 99 04 395. Pizza €4.50-9.50. *Primi* €7-9.50, *secondi* €7.50-17. Cover €1.50. Open daily 9:30am-3pm and 5:30pm-midnight. AmEx/MC/V.)

Don't be turned off by the neon sign advertising **Ristorante e Pizzeria al Pescatore ❸**, V. G. Plana, 20/22, parallel to V. Emanuele along the public beach. Some of the freshest fish from Lake Garda make their way to its kitchen to be combined with treats like nuts and polenta that are served to an eager clientele. (☎ 030 91 62 16. Pizza €4-8. *Antipasti* and *primi* €6-9, *secondi* €8-20. Open Th-Tu 12:30-2:30pm and 7:30-11pm. AmEx/MC/V.) The *gelato* is piled twice as high as anyone else's at **Gelati Breaks ❶**, 9/13 V. Emanuele, just to the left after P. Castello. You can also get the cheapest American-style pizza around, heated while you wait. (*Gelato* €2-5. Pizza €2.30. Sandwiches €3.10. Open daily 9:30am-12:30am.) For a supermarket, head to **Cattelli**, V. Colombare, 154, next to the Colombare bus stop. (Open M-F 8am-1pm and 3-7:30pm, Sa 8am-7:30pm; in Aug. daily 8am-8pm.) Also in Colombare is the **Ristorante-Pizzeria Roberto ❷**, on V. Garibaldi, which serves outstanding local fare for half the price of the tourist traps. House specialties include shrimp pizza (€8.70), *tagliolini* in cream sauce, and enormous salads (from €6). It's a 5min. walk toward Sirmione on V. Colombare away from the bus stop. (Pizza €3.50-8.70. *Primi* €4-8.90, *secondi* €7.30-10. Service 10%. Open Tu-Su 11:45am-2:30pm and 5:30-10:50pm.)

◙ **SIGHTS.** At the far end of the peninsula along V. V. Catullo is the **Grotte di Catullo**, the best-preserved aristocratic Roman villa in northern Italy, spread over five acres of olive groves. Although they are named for the poet Catullus, the ruins appear to date from the late first century BC, after the poet's death. Artifacts in the adjacent **archaeological museum** have English explanations. (☎ 030 91 61 57. Ruins and museum open Mar.-Oct. Tu-Su 8:30am-7pm; Nov.-Feb. Tu-Su 8:30am-5pm. €4, students 18-25 €2.) A small train, *Il Trenino*, runs between Sirmione center and the Grotte. (€1, 8:30am-6:30pm.) The 13th-century **Castello Scaligero** sits in the center of town as a testament to the power of the della Scala family who controlled the Veronese region from 1260 to 1387. Completely surrounded by water, the commanding view from the turrets is the castle's main attraction. Save for some dirt and cannonballs, the interior is empty. (☎ 030 91 64 68. Open Mar.-Oct. Tu-Su 8:30am-7pm; Nov.-Feb. Tu-Su 8:30am-5pm. €4, students 18-25 €2.) Ruins of the city's **fortified walls** lie above Lido delle Bionde, while **Chiesa di San Pietro in Mavino,**

Sirmione's oldest church, which dates to the 8th century, lies just off V. V. Catullo. Sixteenth-century frescoes decorate the interior of the simple church. **Chiesa di S. Maria Maggiore** is between V. Antiche Mura and V. S. M. Maggiore.

◪ ◪ **ENTERTAINMENT AND NIGHTLIFE.** Sirmione's spa, **Catullo Terme di Sirmione,** V. Punto Staffalo, 1 (☎800 80 21 25 or 030 99 04 923; www.termedisirmione.com; open daily Apr.-Oct. 10am-10pm), attracts elderly customers looking to soothe afflictions from rheumatism to respiratory failure. However, even the young and healthy can take advantage of the wellness packages (starting at €28) offered at the attached **Aquaria** (☎030 91 60 44; open Mar.-Oct. M 1-10pm, Tu-Su 10am-10pm; Nov.-Mar. M-F 4-10pm, Sa-Su 10am-10pm), which offers soaks in its thermal waters as well as massages. The free public beach **Lido delle Bionde** on Sirmione's east shore may well be a better alternative, though its shores are slightly rocky. Maps of Sirmione's public beaches as well as temperature and depth information are printed anew at the tourist office each day. **Canoes** and **paddle boats** are available for rent just behind and below the Lido delle Bionde bar off V. V. Catullo. (☎333 54 05 622. €6 for half day, €8 for full day; €7 for beach chair with umbrella. Open daily Apr.-Sept. 8:30am-7pm. Cash only.) The town also has **summer events,** which generally include musical and dance performances, theater, art exhibits, and trout tastings. Ask at the tourist office or look for the posted **Sirmione d'Estate** flyers (www.commune.sirmione.bs.it). A few bars and *enoteche* may be found on V. S. M. Maggiore off V. V. Emanuele, while the most scenic place to have a drink at night may be **Bar La Torre** off V. Antiche Mura just behind the *castello* on the beach. (Drinks €2-8. Open daily 9:30pm-2am. MC/V.)

GARDONE RIVIERA   ☎0365

Once a fashionable tourist destination of the European elite, the collection of villages that comprise the Gardone Riviera, of which Gardone village is largest, now serve more as quiet retreats than hot spots. With only a few thousand people living on the terraced hills, gracefully aging villas of colored stucco, lush gardens of Mediterranean citrus, cyprus, and olive trees, and a calm lifestyle have replaced the boisterous likes of wealthy Great Gatsby types. For those seeking a tranquillity far removed from the heavily touristed Sirmione, Gardone will work wonders. P. Marconi, on your left before the tourist office, is a good place to relax in shade on benches, then proceed along lakeside promenade Lungolago d'Annunzio. V. Roma, heading uphill off C. Zanardelli from the tourist office leads to the **Giardino Botanico** (Botanical Gardens), an oasis of criss-crossing brooks and intimate bridges at the corner of V. Roma and V. Disciplina. It was planted in 1910-1970 by Arturo Hruska, physician and naturalist, and it squeezes more than 2000 varieties of plants and flowers into a 10,000 square meter space. Recent modifications by artist André Heller, including incongruous modern sculptures by Haring and Lichtenstein, lend a wacky sense of humor. Unwary tourists might get caught in a spitting contest between two sculpted heads. (☎336 41 08 77. Open daily 9am-7pm. €7.) V. Roma connects with Viale dei Colli, which leads to V. Vittoriale and its namesake *palazzo* and gardens. ◪**Il Vittoriale,** is the sprawling estate of Gabriele D'Annunzio, the poet, novelist, soldier (WWI), and latter-day Casanova. Following his retirement, D'Annunzio erected monuments to his victories and fallen comrades. Past the 1500-seat amphitheater and through the gardens are the *prioria* (house), with its collections of artifacts and ornate rooms, and the Museo della Guerra. Beyond them in the gardens is the ship that Puglia D'Annunzio had dismantled piece by piece and rebuilt on his estate, and high on the hill is D'Annunzio's circular **mausoleum** and shaded avenues lined with the urns of his wartime companions. (☎0365 29 65 11; www.vittoriale.it. Gardens open daily

Apr.-Sept. 8:30am-8pm; Oct.-Mar. 9am-5pm. *Prioria* villa and war
open Apr.-Sept. Tu-Su 9:30am-7pm; Oct.-Mar. Tu-Su 9am-1pm and
Guided tours of the villa available in English, Spanish, Italian and German
about every 20-40min. Gardens €7, house and gardens or museum and garde
€11, all three €16.) The **Fondazione al Vittoriale** sponsors summer events in music,
dance, theater, and particularly lyrical opera in the 1500-seat open-air **Teatro del
Vittoriale**, V. Vittoriale, 12. (Festival d'Estate: ☎0522 45 51 93; fax 0522 45 43 19.
Ticket office ☎0365 29 65 06 or 0365 29 65 19; www.teatrodelvittoriale.it. Performances mid-July to early Aug. Tickets from €18-35.)

Inexpensive accommodations are scarce in Gardone.Those planning more than
a daytrip should ask at the tourist office for accommodations advice. For traditional Italian dining try **La Stalla ❷**, V. dei Colli, 14, off V. Roma, with its romantic
outdoor seating. The *trata alla griglia* (grilled fresh fish; €8) melts in your
mouth. (☎0365 21 038; fax 0365 29 97 71. Open M-Tu and Th-Su noon-2pm and 7-
11pm. AmEx/MC/V.) **Pizzeria Ristorante Emiliano ❶**, V. Repubblica, 57, by the ferry
station, attracts tourists with gigantic pizzas from €4. (☎0365 21 517. Cover €1.10.
Open Jan.-Oct. Tu-Su noon-2:30pm and 6-11pm.)

Navigazione Lago di Garda ferry dock (☎030 91 49 511; www.navigazionelaghi.it),
on Lungolago D'Annunzio at P. Wimmer, services Riva (1½-3hr.; 10:51am-6:35pm;
€6.90, express €9.80) and Sirmione (1-2hr.; 8:55am-6:28pm; €5.60, express
€8.20). **Buses** (☎800 41 25 or 0365 21 061) run to: Brescia (1hr., 2 per hr., €2.75);
Desenzano (30min., 6 per day, €2.25); and Milan (1½hr., 2 per day, €8). Tickets are
available at the **Molinari Viaggi Travel Agency**, P. Wimmer, 2, near the ferry stop.
(☎0365 21 551. Open daily 8:30am-noon and 2:30-7pm.) Speedier and more frequent service to major cities is available on the Milan-Verona **train** line; take the
bus to Desenzano, then board at the train station next to the bus stop. Take V.
Repubblica on left from the ferry dock for about 250m to reach the **tourist office**, V.
Repubblica, 8, which, stocks printouts of all restaurants, hotels, regional markets,
and monthly events, as well as info on the Garda region and **maps** of Gardone. (☎/
fax 0365 20 347. Open daily June-Sept. 9am-12:30pm and 2:30-6:30pm; Oct.-May
9am-12:30pm and 3-6pm.) For **currency exchange** and **ATM,** head to the **Banco di Brescia,** V. Roma, 6, across the street and upstairs from the Grand Hotel on C.
Zanardelli. (☎0365 20 081. Open M-F 8:25am-1:25pm and 2:40-3:40pm.) In case of
emergency, dial ☎113 or contact the **police** ☎112 or 0365 54 06 10, located in Gardone Sopra (high village) where V. Carere leads off V. Disciplina. The **pharmacy** is
located just past the travel agency at P. Wimmer, 4. (Open M-Sa 8:30am-12:30pm
and 3:30-7:30pm.) The **post office,** V. Roma, 8, is next door to the bank. (☎0365 20
862. Open M-F 8:30am-2pm, Sa 8:30am-12:30pm.) **Postal Code:** 25083.

HE VENETO AND TRENTINO-ALTO ADIGE

nains at Venice's **Basilica di San Marco** (p. 316).

EN the sweet sounds of fair Verona at the annual **Opera Festival** (p. 342).

FLIRT with Germanic culture in **Trentino-Alto Adige,** a northern region that rubs shoulders with Austria (p. 349).

SATISFY wanderlust with an expedition through the **Dolomites** (p. 344).

THE VENETO

From the rocky foothills of the Dolomites to the fertile valleys of the Po River, the Veneto's geography is as diverse as its history. Once loosely united under the Venetian Empire, the towns of the Veneto retained their cultural independence, and today visitors are more likely to hear regional dialects than standard Italian when neighbors gossip across geranium-cloaked windows. As a result of the region's port supremacy and enviable location near the mid-section of the peninsula, heavy international and inter-provincial traffic ensured varied cuisines, dialects, and cultural traditions. International influences marched in with the Austrians, making the tenacious local culture a pleasant surprise for people who come expecting only mandolins and gondolas.

VENICE (VENEZIA) ☎ 041

From its hedonistic, devil-may-care Carnevale, to the penitent God-may-care-too services of its soaring marble cathedrals, Venice (pop. 63,000) is a mystical water-logged city with all the grandeur of the land. Founded by Roman fishermen in the 11th century, the city soon became a world-class trading post between the East and the West. The world depended on Venetian merchants for silks, spices, and coffee for over a century until its trade dominance diminished. Since then, sea-bound ships have been replaced with gondolas as Venice has abandoned its naval prowess for a booming tourism industry. Today, the romantic arched bridges and waterways that lap at ancient doorways are but everyday sidewalks and people flock year-round to float down labyrinthine canals, peer into delicate blown-glass, and gaze awestruck at the master works of Titian, Tintoretto, and Giorgione that fill churches and museums. In the end, Venice's wealth of architectural and cultural treasures proves that it is not *la Serenissima* (the Most Serene One) who surrenders to tourists, but rather they who succumb to her entrancing spectacle.

✈ INTERCITY TRANSPORTATION

Flights: Aeroporto Marco Polo (☎041 26 09 260; www.veniceairport.it), 10km north of the city. The **ATVO shuttle bus** (☎042 13 83 672) links the airport to P. Roma on the main island (30min., every hr. 8am-midnight, €3). Shuttle bus ticket office open daily 6:40am-7:30pm.

Trains: Stazione Santa Lucia, the main station (☎041 89 20 21), is in the northwestern corner. When coming into the city, disembark at S. Lucia, not Mestre on the mainland. Info office open daily 7am-9pm. Ticket windows open daily 6am-9pm. AmEx/MC/V. Wheelchair accessible. To: **Bologna** (2hr., 27 per day 12:04am-8:04pm, €7.90); **Florence** (3hr., 9 per day 6:32am-6:58pm, €19); **Milan** (3hr., 24 per day 5:17am-9:07pm, €22.16); **Padua** (45min., 83 per day 12:04am-11:40pm, €2.50); **Rome** (4½hr., 7 per day 6:32am-6:32pm, €34.06); **Trieste** (2hr., 28 per day 12:10am-10:47pm, €7.90). Reservations may be required; check info booth. **Lost and found** (*oggetti rinvenuti;* ☎041 78 55 31; open M-F 8am-5pm) and **luggage storage** by track #4 (see **Practical Information,** p. 307).

Buses: ACTV (hotline ☎041 24 24; www.hellovenezia.it), in Ple. Roma. Open daily 7:30am-8pm. Office open daily 7am-8pm. Ticket window open daily 6am-11:30pm. **ACTV long-distance carrier** runs buses to **Padua** (1½hr., every 30min. 6:45am-11pm, €3.50) and **Treviso** (1hr., every 30min. 4:55am-8:55pm, €2.40). Cash only.

❊ ORIENTATION

Venice is comprised of 118 islands in a lagoon, connected to the mainland city of Mestre by a thin causeway. The city is divided into six *sestieri* (sections): **Cannaregio** to the north, **Castello** along the eastern shore, **San Marco** to the southeast, **Dorsoduro** along the southern shore, **San Polo** in the northwest, and **Santa Croce** in the

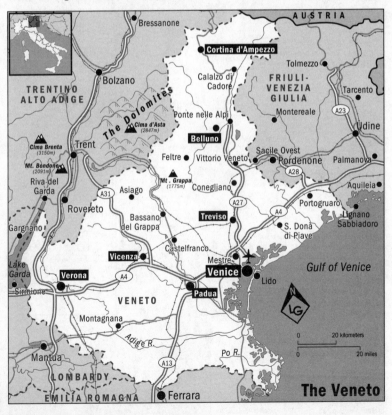

THE VENTENO AND
TRENTINO-ALTO ADIGE

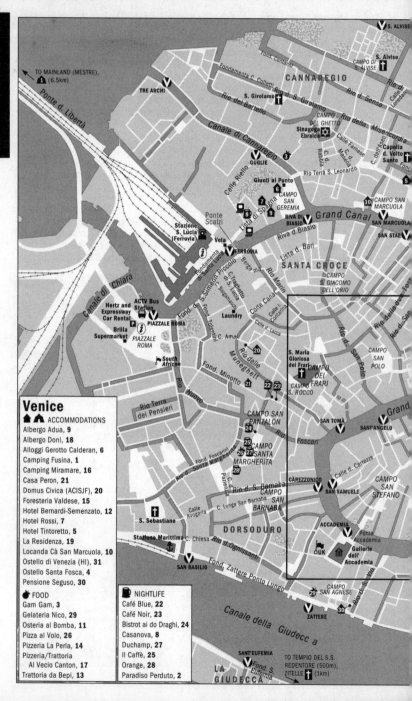

TO MAINLAND (MESTRE),
1 (6.5km)

Ponte d. Libertà

TRE ARCHI

CANNAREGIO

S. ALVISE

CAMPO DI
S. ALVISE

S. Alvise

Fond. Contarini

Fondamenta C. Colletti

Rio d. S. Girolamo

Rio d. Sensa

S. Girolamo

Rio del Battello

Rio della
Misericordia

Canale di Cannaregio

CAMPO
DEL GHETTO

Sinagoga
Ebraica

Calle Farnese

C. d.
Maséna

Capella
d. Volto
Santo

GUGLIE

3

Rio Terrà S. Leonardo

Giunti al Punto

6

CAMPO
SAN
GEREMIA

CAMPO SAN
MARCUOLA

10

Calle Rielo

7

8

Lista di Spagna

9

RIVA DI
BIASIO

SAN MARCUOLA

SAN STAE

Grand Canal

Ponte
Scalzi

Stazione
S. Lucia
(Ferrovia)

Vela

FERROVIA

Riva d. Biasio

Lista d. Bari

SANTA CROCE

CAMPO
S. GIACOMO
DELL'ORIO

Canale di Chiara

Hertz and
Expressway
Car Rental

ACTV Bus
Station

PIAZZALE ROMA

Brilla
Supermarket

PIAZZALE
ROMA

South
African

Fond. Minotto

Rio delle

C. Tagliato
di S. Lucia

Berga ma

Rio Marin

Corte Comita

Calle I.
Contarina

Calle di Lacca

Rio de. San

Rio delle Due Torre

S. Maria
Gloriosa
dei Frari

CAMPO
DEI
FRARI

CAMPO
SAN
POLO

Grand

Rio Terra
dei Pensieri

Rio Nuovo

20

Muneghet

21

22

23

CAMPO
S. ROCCO

SAN TOMÀ

SANT'ANGELO

CAMPO SAN
PANTALON

24

Foscari

Fond. Foscarini

Calle de. Carrozze

CAMPO
SAN
STEFANO

Laundry

C. Amai

Rio Terra
dei Pensieri

29

25

CAMPO
SANTA
MARGHERITA

26

28

CA'REZZONICO

SAN SAMUELE

Rio d. S. Barnaba

CAMPO
SAN
BARNABA

C. Lunga San Barnaba

Calle
Avogaria

S. Sebastiano

DORSODURO

ACCADEMIA

Ponte
Accademia

DUK

Gallerie
dell'
Accademia

Stazione Marittima

C. Chiesa

Rio d'Ognissanti

La Residenza, 19

SAN BASILIO

Fond. Zattere Ponto Lungo

CAMPO
S. AGNESE

29

30

ZATTERE

Canale della Giudecc a

SANT'EUFEMIA

Fond. S.
Eufemia

LA
GIUDECCA

TO TEMPIO DEL S.S.
REDENTORE (500m),
ZITELLE (1km)

Venice

🏠 ACCOMMODATIONS

Albergo Adua, 9
Albergo Doni, 18
Alloggi Gerotto Calderan, 6
Camping Fusina, 1
Camping Miramare, 16
Casa Peron, 21
Domus Civica (ACISJF), 20
Foresteria Valdese, 15
Hotel Bernardi-Semenzato, 12
Hotel Rossi, 7
Hotel Tintoretto, 5
La Residenza, 19
Locanda Cà San Marcuola, 10
Ostello di Venezia (HI), 31
Ostello Santa Fosca, 4
Pensione Seguso, 30

🍴 FOOD

Gam Gam, 3
Gelateria Nico, 29
Osteria al Bomba, 11
Pizza al Volo, 26
Pizzeria La Perla, 14
Pizzeria/Trattoria
   Al Vecio Canton, 17
Trattoria da Bepi, 13

🍸 NIGHTLIFE

Café Blue, 22
Café Noir, 23
Bistrot al do Draghi, 24
Casanova, 8
Duchamp, 27
Il Caffè, 25
Orange, 28
Paradiso Perduto, 2

TO MURANO (1.5km),
TORCELLO (4km), BURANO (7km),
AEROPORTO MARCO POLO ✈ (10km),

CIMITERO

Isola di San
Michele

ORTO

Chiesa della
Madonna dell'Orto

Sacca
della
Miseri cordia

Canale delle Fondamente Nuove

Madonna dell'Orto

S. Maria
Valverde

FONDAMENTA NUOVE

Chiesa
del Gesuiti

CAMPO
DEI GESUITI

Fondamenta Nuove

Calle Larga
dei Botteri

S. Lunga Santa Caterina

C. del Fumo

OSPEDALE

200 meters
200 yards

N
LG

CAMPO
SAN
FOSCA

S. Fosca

Calle Racchetta

Calle delle Vele

Ruga Due Pozzi

Calle dello Squero

Rio del Mendicanti

Brilla
Supermarket

Ca' d'Oro

CA' D'ORO

Strada Nuova

CAMPO S.S.
APOSTOLI

Ospedale
Civile

Rio di S.

Vaporetti Stops

C. d. Cappuccine

CELESTIA

Rio d. San Marina

S.S. Giovanni
e Paolo

Barbaria delle Tole

S. Francesco
della Vigna

CAMPO D.
CELESTIA

TO 16
(10km)

SAN POLO

Ponte
di Rialto

CAMPO S.
BARTOLOMEO

Riva del Vin

SAN SILVESTRO

RIALTO

Riva del Carbon

Canal

Rio di
S. Luca

CAMPO
MANIN

CAMPO
S. MARIA
FORMOSA

Sal. di S. Lio

S. Maria
Formosa

Ponte
Rosso

CAMPO SAN
LORENZO

Ruga Giuffa

CASTELLO

Scuola Dalmata
San Giorgio
degli Schiavoni

Calle Lion

C. d. Furlani

C. d.
Madonna

CAMPO
BANDIERA
E MORO

Rio d. Gorne

Rio della Sensa

S. Sebastian

Calle del Fabbri

Rio del Palazzo

CAMPO
SANT'ANGELO

Calle d. Mandola

Frezzaria

SAN MARCO

PIAZZA
SAN MARCO

San
Marco

Palazzo
Ducale

Rio di San
Moisè

Rio della
Osteghe

C. Corona

Fond.
Osmarin

S. S. Provolo

C. d.

S. Zaccaria

CAMPO
S. ZACCA RIA

Calle della Pietà

19

C. Crosera

C. del
Dose

C. dei
Forno

TO ARSENALE
(150m)

Rio della Arsenale

GIGLIO

SALUTE

S. Maria
della Salute

Riva degli Schiavoni

S. ZACCARIA

ARSENALE

SAN MARCO

SEE CENTRAL VENICE MAP, P. 304

TO GIARDINI
PUBLICI (250m)

Canale di San Marco

Rio d. Fornace

Fond. Zattere ai Saloni

SAN GIORGIO

S. Giorgio
Maggiore

Isola di
S. Giorgio
Maggiore

TO LIDO (2km)

ZITELLE

Fond. delle Zitelle

TO 31 (100m)

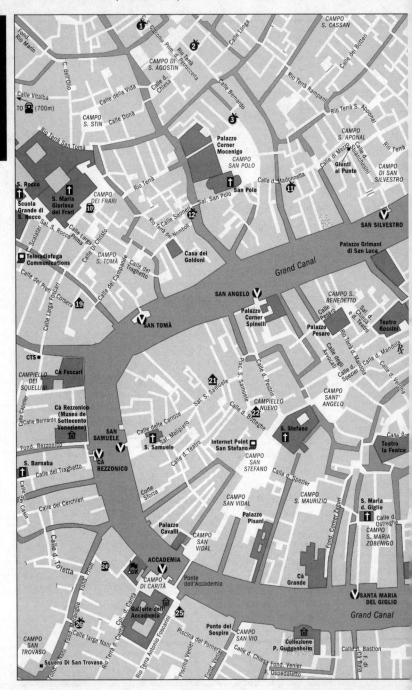

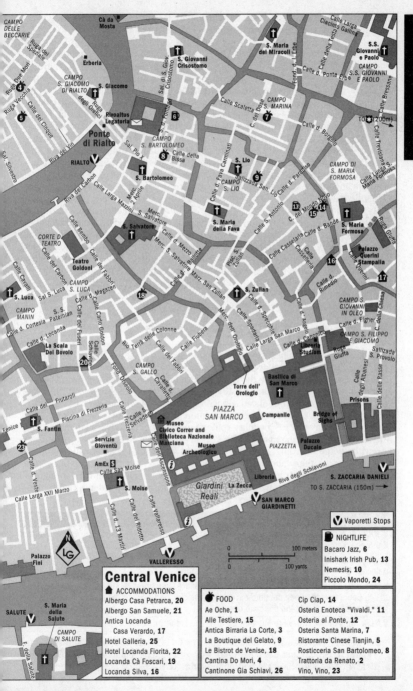

Central Venice

🏠 ACCOMMODATIONS
Albergo Casa Petrarca, **20**
Albergo San Samuele, **21**
Antica Locanda
    Casa Verardo, **17**
Hotel Galleria, **25**
Hotel Locanda Fiorita, **22**
Locanda Cà Foscari, **19**
Locanda Silva, **16**

🍅 FOOD
Ae Oche, **1**
Alle Testiere, **15**
Antica Birraria La Corte, **3**
La Boutique del Gelato, **9**
Le Bistrot de Venise, **18**
Cantina Do Mori, **4**
Cantinone Gia Schiavi, **26**

Cip Ciap, **14**
Osteria Enoteca "Vivaldi," **11**
Osteria al Ponte, **12**
Osteria Santa Marina, **7**
Ristorante Cinese Tianjin, **5**
Rosticceria San Bartolomeo, **8**
Trattoria da Renato, **2**
Vino, Vino, **23**

🎵 NIGHTLIFE
Bacaro Jazz, **6**
Inishark Irish Pub, **13**
Nemesis, **10**
Piccolo Mondo, **24**

Ⓥ Vaporetti Stops

middle, with the **Canal Grande** snaking throughout. *Sestieri* boundaries are vague but should be of some use in navigating the city's narrow alleys.

Venice's layout consists of a labyrinth of *calli* (narrow streets), *campi* (squares), *liste* (large streets), and *ponti* (bridges). It's practically impossible to avoid getting lost in Venice—maps are of little use, as many streets are too narrow to be plotted, most do not have street signs, and street numbers are often erratic. To get by, simply learn to navigate like a true Venetian. Locate the following sights on the map: **Ponte di Rialto** (in the center), **Piazza San Marco** (central south), **Ponte Accademia** (southwest), **Ferrovia** (or Stazione Santa Lucia, the train station, northwest), **Ponte Scalzi** (in front of the station), and **Piazzale Roma** (southwest of the station). These are the main orientation points for Venice. A plethora of yellow signs posted throughout the city point the way to all of the major landmarks and bridges. When trying to find a place, locate the *sestiere*, then find a nearby landmark and follow signs in that general direction. As you get closer, use the address numbers and busier streets to work your way toward the destination. As a general rule, follow the arrows on the yellow signs as precisely as possible. If a street suddenly leads into a *campo* and branches in five different directions, pick the street that follows the original direction of the arrow as closely as possible until reaching the next sign. Also note that in Venice, addresses are not specific to a particular street, and every building in a *sestiere* is given a number ("3434, San Marco" is a typical address). Buildings are generally numbered consecutively, but there also often large jumps, with the next number one block away or down an alleyway.

To get to **Piazza San Marco** or the **Rialto Bridge** from the train station, take V #82 (30min., every 20min.) or V #1 (40 min., every 10 min.). On foot, follow signs to P. San Marco, starting left of the station on Lista di Spagna.

◧ LOCAL TRANSPORTATION

The cheapest and often fastest way to see the city is to walk through it. Pedestrians can cross the Grand Canal at the *ponti* Scalzi, Rialto, and Accademia. ◪**Traghetti** (gondola ferry boats) traverse the canal at seven locations, including Ferrovia, San Marcuola, Cà d'Oro, and Rialto (€0.40). *Vaporetti* (water buses) provide 24hr. service around the city, with reduced service after midnight. Tickets cost €3.50, or €5 for the Grand Canal. An extended pass is more economical for longer visits (24hr. pass €10.50, 3-day €22). Schedules, route maps, and tickets are available at tourist offices (see **Practical Information**). Tickets are also sold in front of stops and on *vaporetti* when boarding. Stock up on tickets by asking for an unvalidated pass (*non timbrato*), then validate before boarding by inserting tickets into one of the yellow boxes at each stop. Unvalidated tickets risk a fine; the "confused foreigner" act won't work in a town where tourists often outnumber residents two to one. (*Vaporetti* stops appear in the text as V: stop name.)

MAIN VAPORETTO LINES
V #82, 4: Run from P. San Marco, up the Giudecca Canal, to the station, down the Grand Canal, back to P. San Marco, and then to Lido. Always crowded, with long lines.
V #1: Has a similar route to #82, but can be less crowded; offers a nice view of the canalside palaces. 10min. slower than #82, and with more stops.
V #41, 42, 51, 52: Circumnavigate Venice. #51 and 41 run from the station, through the Giudecca Canal to Lido, along the northern edge of the city, and back to the station; #52 and 42 follow the same route in the opposite direction.
V #LN: Runs from F. Nuove to Murano, Burano, and Lido with connections to Torcello.

Car Rental: Expressway, P. Roma, 496/N (☎041 52 23 000; www.expressway.it). From €50 per day and €300 per week. 40% discount on rentals with *Let's Go* or student ID. Free car delivery to and from airport. 18+. Open M-F 8am-noon and 1:30-

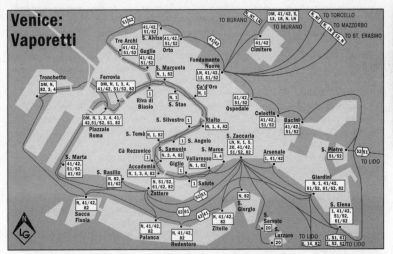

Venice: Vaporetti

6pm, Sa-Su 8am-noon and 1:30-4:30pm. AmEx/MC/V. **Hertz,** P. Roma, 496/F (☎041 52 84 091; fax 041 52 00 614). From €55 per day. Credit card required. 25+. Open in summer M-F 8am-6pm, Sa-Su 8am-1pm; in winter M-F 8am-12:30pm and 3-5:30pm, Sa 8am-1pm. AmEx/DC/MC/V.

Parking: P. Roma (☎041 27 27 301) and island of **Tronchetto** (☎041 52 07 555). Around €20 per day. 24hr. Parking is considerably cheaper on the mainland. Consider parking in **Mestre** (1st train stop out of Venice).

DISABLED VISITORS

Informa Handicap offers assistance to physically disabled and deaf travelers in Italy. (☎041 27 46 144. Open M, W and F 9am-1pm; Tu and Th 9am-1pm and 2-5pm.) The city offers free rental of Braille maps. The **APT tourist office** provides a list of wheelchair-accessible lodgings in Venice. Pick up a free **map** of the city outlining wheelchair-friendly routes in each *sestiere*. The APT provides keys for wheelchair lifts at the bridges, and V #1 and 82 are wheelchair accessible.

⑦ PRACTICAL INFORMATION

TOURIST AND FINANCIAL SERVICES

Tourist Offices:

APT Tourist Offices are located all over the city. Avoid the **train station** office, as it is always mobbed. **Branches:** P. Roma (☎041 24 11 499; open daily 9am-1pm and 1:30-4:30pm; AmEx/MC/V); directly opposite the Basilica at P. S. Marco, 71/F (☎/fax 041 52 98 740; open daily 9am-3:30pm; AmEx/MC/V); Lido, Gran Viale, 6/A (☎041 52 65 721; open June-Sept. daily 9am-12:30pm and 3:30-6pm). Every location offers fairly pricey city tours and sells *vaporetto* tickets and schedules (€0.60), as well as the **Rolling Venice Card** (see below) and theater and concert tickets. Ask for the monthly magazine, *Leo*, or visit www.turismovenezia.com for information about history, sights and activities in Venice.

VeneziaSi (☎800 84 30 06), in train station, to right of tourist office. Finds available hotel rooms and makes same-day reservations in Venice and Rome (€2). Open daily 8am-10pm. **Branches** at P. Roma (☎041 52 28 640) and at airport (☎041 54 15 133) also book rooms for €2.

Rolling Venice Card: Provides discounts at over 200 restaurants, cafes, hotels, museums, and shops for people ages 14-29. Tourist offices provide lists of participating vendors. Card costs €3 and is valid 1 year from date of purchase. A 3-day *vaporetto* pass with card discount costs €15 instead of the undiscounted €22. Purchase it at the **ACTV VeLa** office (☎041 27 47 650; open daily 7am-8pm) in P. Roma, at all APT tourist offices, and at ACTV VeLa kiosks next to the **Ferrovia, Rialto, S. Marco,** and **Vallaresso** *vaporetto* stops.

Budget Travel: CTS, Fondamenta Tagliapietra, Dorsoduro, 3252 (☎041 52 05 660; www.cts.it). From Campo S. Barnaba, cross the bridge closest to the church and follow the road through the small *piazza.* Turn left at foot of large bridge. Sells ISICs and discounted plane tickets. Open M-F 9:30am-1:30pm and 2:30-6pm. MC.

Consulates: Cross Accademia Bridge from San Marco and turn right for **UK** consulate, Dorsoduro, 1051 (☎041 52 27 207; open M-F 10am-noon and 2-3pm). Closest **US** (☎041 02 29 03 51) and **Australian** consulates in Milan; **Canadian** consulate (☎049 87 81 147) in Padua.

Currency Exchange: Use banks whenever possible for best rates and inquire about additional fees beforehand. The streets around San Marco, San Polo, and the train station are full of banks and **ATMs.**

American Express: Cal. S. Moise, San Marco, 1471 (☎800 87 20 00 or 041 52 00 844 for lost or stolen checks; fax 041 52 29 937). Exit P. S. Marco facing away from the basilica and walk 2min. **Currency exchange** at average rates, but no commission for members or Rolling Venice card-holders. Office open for currency exchange M-F 9am-5:30pm, Sa 9am-12:30pm. Closed Sa in winter.

LOCAL SERVICES

Luggage Storage: At the train station. €3.80 for the 1st 5hr., €0.60 per hr. for 6-12hr., €0.20 per hr. for 13+ hr. Open daily 6am-midnight. Cash only. **Deposito Pullman Bar,** P. Roma, 497/M (☎041 52 31 107), next to Pullman Bar. €3 per day. Open daily 6am-9pm. Cash only.

English-Language Bookstores:

Libreria Studium, San Marco, 337/C (☎/fax 041 52 22 382). From P. S. Marco, turn left on Cal. delle Canonico between the basilica and the clock tower; it's the last shop on the right. Largest selection in town, with novels and guidebooks. 10% discount with Rolling Venice card. Open M-Sa 9am-7:30pm, Su 10am-2pm. AmEx/MC/V.

Libreria Linea D'Acqua, Cal. della Mandola, San Marco 3717/D (☎041 52 24 030). Follow Cal. Cortesia out of Campo Manin. Open M-F 10:30am-12:30pm and 4-6:45pm, Sa 11:30am-12:30pm and 4-5:30pm. AmEx/MC/V.

Giunti Al Punto, Campo S. Geremia, 283/A, Cannaregio (☎041 27 50 152). Open M-Sa 9am-midnight, Su 10am-midnight. MC/V.

Laundromat: Lavanderie Self-Service, Cal. della Chioverette, Santa Croce, 665/B (☎348 30 17 457). From Ponte Scalzi, turn right on F. S. Piccolo and first left on Cal. del Traghetto de S. Lucia. Laundromat is on your right. Wash €3 per 30min., dry €2 per 20min. Open daily 7:30am-10:30pm.

Public Toilets: AMAV W.C. Under white and blue signs. €0.50. Open daily 9am-8pm.

EMERGENCY AND COMMUNICATIONS

Emergency: ☎113. **First Aid:** ☎118. **Fire:** ☎115.

Carabinieri: Campo S. Zaccaria, Castello, 4693/A (☎041 27 41 11 or 112). **Questura,** Fta. S. Lorenzo, 5056, Castello (☎041 27 05 511).

Pharmacy: Farmacia Italo-Inglese, Cal. della Mandola, San Marco, 3717 (☎041 52 24 837). Follow Cal. Cortesia out of Campo Manin. There are no 24hr. pharmacies in Venice, but late-night and weekend pharmacies rotate. After-hours rotations posted outside. Open April-Nov. M-F 9am-1:30pm and 2:30-7:30pm, Sa 9am-12:45pm; Dec.-Mar. M-F 9am-12:30pm and 3:45-7:30pm, Sa 9am-12:45pm. MC/V.

Hospital: Ospedale Civile, Campo SS. Giovanni e Paolo, Castello (☎041 52 94 111).

Internet Access:

Casanova, Lista di Spagna, Cannaregio, 158/A (☎041 27 50 199), keeps 5 computers with speedy connections. There may be a wait at this hip cafe. €4 for 30min., €7 per hr., students €2.50/4. Internet 9am-11:30pm. AmEx/MC/V for purchases of at least €10.

Internet Point San Stefano, Campo S. Stefano, San Marco, 2967 and 2958 (☎041 89 46 122; fax 041 52 08 128) Offers Internet and laptop connections. €9 per hr., €6 with ISIC or Rolling Venice. Open M-F 9am-11pm, Su 10am-11pm. MC/V.

VeNice, Lista di Spagna, Cannaregio, 149 (☎041 27 58 217) has fax, webcams, and CD burning. Student discounts and international calling cards are available. €4.50 for 30 min., €8 per hr. Open daily 9am-11pm. MC/V for purchases of at least €10.

Post Office: Poste Venezia Centrale, Salizzada Fontego dei Tedeschi, San Marco, 5554 (☎041 27 17 111), off Campo S. Bartolomeo. *Fermoposta* at window #16. Open M-Sa 8:30am-6:30pm. Cash only. **Branch:** (☎041 52 85 949), through the arcades at the end of P. S. Marco and opposite the basilica. ATM, pay phones, and a phone for the hearing-impaired. Open M-F 8:30am-2pm, Sa 8:30am-1pm. Cash only. **Postal Codes:** San Marco: 30124; Castello: 30122; San Polo: 30125; Santa Croce: 30135; Cannaregio: 30121; Dorsoduro: 30123.

▐ ACCOMMODATIONS

Venetian hotels are often more expensive than those in other areas of Italy, but savvy travelers can find cheap alternatives if they explore their options early. Agree on a price before booking, and reserve at least one month ahead. Dorm-style rooms are sometimes available without reservations even in summer. The **AVA** (see **Tourist Offices**) finds rooms with same-day availability, but they will not be cheap. Religious institutions offer dorms and private rooms in the summer for €25-70. Options include: **Casa Murialdo,** Fondamenta Madonna dell'Orto, Cannaregio, 3512 (☎041 71 99 33); **Patronato Salesiano Leone XIII,** Cal. S. Domenico, Castello, 1281 (☎041 24 03 611); **Domus Cavanis,** Dorsoduro, 896 (☎041 52 87 374), near the Accademia Bridge; **Istituto Canossiano,** F. delle Romite, Dorsoduro, 1323 (☎041 24 09 711); and **Istituto Ciliota,** Cal. Muneghe S. Stefano, San Marco, 2976 (☎041 52 04 888).

CANNAREGIO AND SANTA CROCE

The area around the Lista di Spagna, has some excellent budget options. Although a 20min. *vaporetto* ride and a 15-25min. walk from most sights, the neighborhood bustles at night and offers *vaporetto* access from Fondamenta Nuove.

▨ **Alloggi Gerotto Calderan,** Campo S. Geremia, 283 (☎041 71 55 62; www.casagerotto calderan.com). Half hostel, half hotel. Proximity to train station and location on *campo* make it a great deal. Check-in 2pm. Check-out 10am. Curfew 12:30am. Reserve ahead. Dorms €21; singles €36, with bath €41; doubles €60/93; triples €84/93. 10% Rolling Venice discount; lower prices with extended stay. Cash only. ❷

▨ **Hotel Bernardi-Semenzato,** Cal. dell'Oca, Cannaregio, 4366 (☎041 52 27 257; www.hotelbernardi.com). From V: Cà d'Oro, go right on Str. Nuova, left on Cal. del Duca, right on Cal. dell'Oca. Great views, homey feel and helpful staff. Breakfast included. Check-out 11am. Singles €30; doubles €45-60, with bath €60-90; triples €78-90; quads €85-118. 10% Rolling Venice discount on larger rooms. AmEx/MC/V. ❸

Albergo Adua, Lista di Spagna, Cannaregio, 233/A (☎041 71 61 84; www.aduahotel.com). Calming decor and mosaic light fixtures create a serene atmosphere in large rooms with A/C and TV. Breakfast €7.50. Singles €60, with bath €100; doubles €85/130; triples €90-180 depending on season. Hotel offers cheaper rooms at a different location; inquire at reception or call for more information. AmEx/MC/V. ❺

Locanda Cà San Marcuola, Campo S. Marcuola, Cannaregio, 1763 (☎041 71 60 48; www.casanmarcuola.com). From the Lista di Spagna, follow signs for S. Marcuola. 2 lions guard the entrance to the plush red and gold lobby. Large rooms have bath, A/C, and TV. Wheelchair accessible. Breakfast included. Free Internet. Reception 24hr. Singles €60-80; doubles €90-130; triples €120-160; quads €150-200. AmEx/MC/V. ❹

Hotel Rossi, Lista di Spagna, Cannaregio, 262 (☎041 71 51 64). Friendly owner keeps 14 spacious rooms down a charming alley by bustling Lista di Spagna. A/C and small bookshelf with multilingual selection. Breakfast included. Reception 24hr. June-Sept. reserve at least 1 month ahead. Singles €44-53, with bath €54-69; doubles €64-77/ 77-92; triples €92-112; quads €107-132. 10% Rolling Venice discount. MC/V. ❹

Hotel Tintoretto, Santa Fosca, 2316 (☎041 72 15 22; www.hoteltintoretto.com). Head down Lista di Spagna from the station and follow the signs. 3 floors of cheery, wide rooms, with carpet, bath, A/C, and TV. Many rooms have canal view. Amenities vary from hotel to annex. Breakfast included. Reception 24hr. Singles €41-120; doubles €74-175. Extra bed €37. Prices vary seasonally. AmEx/MC/V. ❹

Ostello Santa Fosca, Fondamenta Canal, Cannaregio, 2372 (☎/fax 041 71 57 33; www.santafosca.it). From Lista di Spagna, turn into Campo S. Fosca. Cross 1st bridge and turn left on Fondamenta Canal. A brick walkway leads to this social but quiet hostel nestled in romantic crumbling courtyards. Student-operated and church-affiliated. Kitchen and Internet available. July-Sept. curfew 12:30am. Dorms €19; doubles €44. €2 discount with ISIC or Rolling Venice. MC/V. ❷

Ostello di Venezia (HI), Fondamenta Zitelle, Giudecca, 87 (☎041 52 38 211; www.hostelbooking.com). Take V: #41, 42, or 82 to Zitelle. Turn right along canal. Though inconveniently located, this efficiently managed hostel has sparkling baths and sweeping views of the city. 250 beds on single-sex floors. Breakfast included. Dinner €9. Sheets included. Reception 7-9:30am and 1:30pm-midnight. Lock-out 9:30am-1:30pm. Curfew 12am. Must book through website; do not call to reserve. Non-HI members add €3. Dorms €18.50. MC/V. ❷

SAN MARCO AND SAN POLO

Surrounded by designer boutiques, souvenir stands, scores of restaurants, near-domesticated pigeons, and many of Venice's most popular sights, these accommodations are pricey options for those in search of Venice's showy side.

🖾 **Albergo Casa Petrarca,** Cal. Schiavine, San Marco, 4386 (☎041 52 00 430; fax 041 09 94 320). From Campo S. Luca, follow Cal. Fuseri, take 2nd left and then turn right. Cheerful proprietors run a tiny hotel with 7 bright rooms, most with bath. Most rooms have A/C. Singles €55-65; doubles €90-110. Extra bed €35. Cash only. ❹

Albergo San Samuele, Salizzada San Samuele, San Marco, 3358 (☎041 52 28 045; www.albergosansamuele.it). Follow Cal. delle Botteghe from Campo S. Stefano and turn left on Salizzada S. Samuele. A quirky treasure with eclectic decor and a small pink patio out front. Location 2min. from V: San Samuele and 10min. from P. S. Marco is a bargain. Reception until midnight. Reserve 1-2 months ahead. Singles €26-45; doubles €50-100, with bath €60-105; triples €135. Cash only. ❸

Hotel Locanda Fiorita, Campiello Nuovo, San Marco, 3457/A (☎041 52 34 754; www.locandafiorita.com). From Campo S. Stefano, take Cal. del Pestrin, then climb onto the raised *piazza*. Venetian-style rooms all with A/C and TV are complemented by a courtyard and deep red facade. Annex nearby has satellite TV and Internet jacks. Breakfast included. Reception 24hr. Singles without bath €80; doubles €110-180, depending on location and whether shower is private. Extra bed 30%. AmEx/MC/V. ❺

Domus Civica (ACISJF), Campiello Chiovere Frari, San Polo, 3082 (☎041 72 11 03; www.domuscivica.com). From station, cross Ponte Scalzi and turn right. Turn left on Fondamenta dei Tolentini and left through the courtyard on Corte Amai. The hostel's rounded facade is to the right, after the bridge. 123 beds in spartan white, dorm-style rooms. Shared co-ed bath, TV room, and piano. Free Internet. Reception 7am-12:30am. Strict curfew 11:30pm. Open June-Sept. 25. Singles €28.50; doubles and triples €52. 15% Rolling Venice discount; 20% ISIC discount. AmEx/MC/V. ❸

Casa Peron, Salizzada S. Pantalon, Santa Croce, 84 (☎041 71 00 21; www.casaperon.com). From station, cross Ponte Scalzi and turn right. Turn left just before the bridge; continue down Fond. Minotto, Casa Peron is on the left. Lace-accented lobby and white rooms, some with A/C. Breakfast included. Reception until 1am. Singles €30-48, with bath €50-90; doubles €50-78/70-95; triples €80-105/70-95. V. ❸

CASTELLO

Castello, the *sestiere* where most Venetians live, is arguably the prettiest part of Venice. A 2nd- or 3rd-floor room with a view of the sculpted skyline is worth the inevitability of getting lost in the dead ends and barricaded alleys of some of the narrowest and most tightly clustered streets in the city.

Foresteria Valdese, Castello, 5170 (☎041 52 86 797; www.diaconiavaldese.org/venezia). From Campo S. Maria Formosa, take Cal. Lunga S. Maria Formosa; it's over the 1st bridge. An aging 18th-century guest house run by a Protestant church. 64 beds. Breakfast included. Internet €5 per hr. Lockout 10am-1pm. Reservations required. Dorm-style bed €21-22; doubles with TV €58, with bath and TV €75; quads with bath and TV €106; 5-person rooms with bath €126; apartments (no breakfast) €104. Rooms larger than singles require min. 2-night stay. Rolling Venice discount €1. MC/V. ❷

Antica Locanda Casa Verardo, Castello, 4765 (☎041 52 86 127; www.casaverardo.it). From the basilica, take Cal. Canonica, turn right before bridge and left over the bridge on Ruga Giuffa into Campo S. Filippo e Giacomo. Follow Cal. della Chiesa left out of the *campo* until reaching a bridge. Housed in a national monument, this 16th-century hotel's mosaic floors and grand ballrooms will make even the poorest traveler feel like Venetian royalty. Rooms with A/C and TV, most have tub and shower. Terrace breakfast included. Singles €60-150; doubles €90-275. Discounts for web reservations or cash payment. AmEx/MC/V. ❺

Albergo Doni, Calle del Vin, Castello, 4656 (☎041 52 24 267; www.albergodoni.it). From P. San Marco, turn left immediately after the 2nd bridge on Calle del Vin and take the left fork when the street splits. Cheery staff and close proximity to Piazza San Marco make this hotel an amazing deal. Rooms with carved headboard, hardwood floors, phone, and TV. Breakfast included. Reception 24hr. Singles €40-65; doubles €60-95, with bath €80-120; triples €80-125/120-160; quads €140-200. MC/V. ❸

La Residenza, Campo Bandiera e Moro, Castello, 3608 (☎041 52 85 315; www.venicelaresidenza.com). From V: Arsenal, turn left on Riva degli Schiavoni and right on Cal. del Dose into the *campo*. Lavishly decorated 15th-century palace overlooking a courtyard. All rooms with bath, safe, A/C, TV, and minibar. Breakfast included. Reception 24hr. Singles €50-100; doubles €80-160. Extra bed and breakfast €30-35. MC/V. ❹

Locanda Silva, Fondamenta del Rimedio, Castello, 4423 (☎041 52 27 643 or 041 52 37 892; www.locandasilva.it). From P. S. Marco, walk under clock tower, turn right on Cal. Larga S. Marco, and left on Cal. d. Angelo before the bridge. Head right on Cal. d. Rimedio before next bridge and follow to the end. Guests enjoy rustic rooms with exposed beams and an 18th-century sunny breakfast room overlooking the canal. Reception 24hr. Open Feb.-Nov. Singles €40-45, with bath €65; doubles €70/100; triples €110-135; quads €130-155. MC/V. ❹

DORSODURO

Spartan facades line the canals that trace the quiet streets of Dorsoduro. Art museums here draw visitors to canal front real estate, while the interior remains a little-visited residential quarter around Campo Santa Margherita, the city's most vibrant student social hub. Situated near the Grand Canal between Chiesa dei Frari and Ponte Accademia, this *sestiere* is home to many pricey hotels.

■ **Locanda Cà Foscari,** Cal. della Frescada, Dorsoduro, 3887/B (☎041 71 04 01; www.locandacafoscari.com), in a quiet neighborhood. From V: San Tomà, turn left at the dead end, cross the bridge, turn right, then turn left at the alley. *Carnevale* masks embellish this tidy hotel, run for over 40 years by the Scarpa family. Breakfast included. Reception 24hr. Book 2-3 months ahead. Closed July 28-1st week in Aug. Singles €57, with bath €62; doubles €72/93; triples €90/114; quads €112. MC/V. ❹

Pensione Seguso, Fond. Zattere ai Saloni, Dorsoduro, 779 (☎041 52 86 858; www.pensioneseguso.it). From V: Zattere, walk to the right. Views of the Giudecca canal make this hotel a great low-season deal. Breakfast included. Singles €40-112, with bath €50-145; doubles €65-168/70-178; triples €90-225/95-240. AmEx/MC/V. ❺

Hotel Galleria, Rio Terra Antonio Foscarini, Dorsoduro, 878/A (☎041 52 04 172; www.hotelgalleria.it), on the left facing the Accademia museum. Hardwood floors lend an aura of elegance mere meters from the Grand Canal and major sights. Breakfast included. Reception 24hr. Singles €80; doubles €105-155, with view €180; triples €135/195. Extra bed 30%. AmEx/MC/V. ❺

🏕 CAMPING

Plan on at least a 20min. boat ride from Venice. In addition to these listings, the Litorale del Cavallino, on the Lido's Adriatic side, has multiple beach campsites.

Camping Miramare, Lungomare Dante Alighieri, 29 (☎041 96 61 50; www.camping-miramare.it). A 40min. ride on V: #LN from P. S. Marco to Punta Sabbioni. Campground is 700m along the beach on the right. 2-night min. in high season. Open Apr. 1-Nov. 6. €4.30-4.90 per person, €8.90-10.70 per tent; bungalows €27-60 plus normal per person camping charge. 15% Rolling Venice discount on per person cost. MC/V. ❶

Camping Fusina, V. Moranzani, 93 (☎041 54 70 055; www.camping-fusina.com), in Malcontenta. From Mestre, take bus #11. Restaurant, laundromat, ATM, Internet, and TV onsite. Free hot showers. Call ahead to reserve cabins. €7.50 per person, €4.50 per tent, €14.50 per car with tent. Cabin singles €22; doubles €26. AmEx/MC/V. ❷

🍴 FOOD

In Venice, authentic dining may require some exploration. With few exceptions, the best restaurants lie in less-traveled area. Naturally, Venetian cuisine is dominated by fish. *Sarde in saor* (sardines in vinegar and onions) is available only in Venice and can be sampled at most *bars* with *cicchetti* (Venetian appetizers similar to Spanish tapas). The Veneto and Friuli regions produce an abundance of wines. Local whites include *prosecco della marca*, the dry *tocai*, and *bianco di custoza*. For reds, try a *valpolicella*. The least expensive option is by no means inferior: a simple *vino della casa* (house wine) is usually a local merlot or chardonnay. For informal alternatives to traditional dining, visit an *osteria* or *bacaro* for pastries, seafood, or *tramezzini* (white bread with any imaginable filling).

Venice's Rialto **markets,** once the center of trade for the Venetian Republic, spread between the Grand Canal and the San Polo foot of the Rialto every morning from Monday to Saturday. Smaller produce markets are set up in Cannaregio, on Rio Terra S. Leonardo by Ponte delle Guglie, and in many of the city's *campi*. The **BILLA** supermarket, Str. Nuova, Cannaregio, 3660, offers grocery fare with a small bakery and deli near Campo San Fosca. (Open M-Sa 8:30am-8:30pm, Su 9am-8:30pm. AmEx/MC/V.) **Coop Alimentari,** Cal. Carminati, 5989, Castello, is just north of P. S. Marco. (Open M-Th 9am-1pm and 3:45-7:30pm, F-Sa 9am-7:30pm. MC/V.)

CANNAREGIO

Trattoria da Bepi, Cannaregio, 4550 (☎/fax 041 52 85 031; dabepi@tin.it). From Campo SS. Apostoli, turn left on Salizzada del Pistor. Traditional Venetian *trattoria* attracts tourists and locals coming for the warm atmosphere and the thoughtful cuisine. *Primi* €7-11, *secondi* from €10. Cover €1.50. Open M-W and F-Su noon-2:30pm and 7-10pm. Reservation suggested for outdoor seating. MC/V. ❸

Pizzeria La Perla, Rio Terra dei Franceschi, Cannaregio, 4615 (☎/fax 041 528 51 75). From Str. Nuova, turn left on Salizzada del Pistor in Campo SS. Apostoli. Follow to the end, then follow signs for the Fondamente Nuove. Heaping portions of hearty, fresh, and delicious pizza. Pizza €4.65-7.90. Pasta €6.10-8.20. Cover €1.10. Service 10%. Open M-Tu and Th-Su noon-3pm and 7-9:45pm; daily in Aug. AmEx/MC/V. ❷

Gam Gam, Canale di Cannaregio, Cannaregio, 1122 (☎041 71 52 84). From Campo S. Geremia, cross the bridge and turn left. Fresh ingredients and compelling religious artwork make this kosher neighborhood favorite a great choice. Try the Israeli appetizers like falafel (€9). Join Shabbat service on F night and enjoy a free Shabbat dinner after; all are welcome. Pasta €7.50-9.50. 10% discount with *Let's Go.* Open M-Th noon-10pm and Su noon-5pm. Cash only. ❷

Osteria al Bomba, Cannaregio 4297/98 (☎041 52 05 175; www.osteriaalbomba.it). From Hotel Bernardi-Semenzato, exit right on Strada Nuova, then turn right into the next alleyway. Enjoy a glass of *prosecco* (€1) or *cichetti* (€1 for a skewer, €15 for a large mixture) inside at the long communal table or outside on the tiny patio under the sun. Open daily 11am-3:30pm and 6-11pm. MC/V. ❶

CASTELLO

▨ **Cip Ciap,** Cal. Mondo Novo, 5799/A (☎041 52 36 621). From Campo S. Maria Formosa, follow Cal. Mondo Novo. Pizzeria uses fresh ingredients on Sicilian pizza sold by weight (€2.00-2.50 per kg) or in filling calzones (€2.40). There's no seating, but nab a bench in the *campo* nearby. Open M and W-Su 9am-9pm. Cash only. ❶

La Boutique del Gelato, Salizzada S. Lio, Castello, 5727 (☎041 52 23 283). From Campo Bartolomeo, walk under Sottoportego de la Bissa, then go straight, crossing the bridge into Campo S. Lio. Follow Salizzada S. Lio; it's on the left. Popular stand doles out generous portions of rich *gelato* to scores of passersby. 1 scoop €0.80, 2 scoops €1.50. Open daily July-Aug. 10am-11pm; Sept.-June 10am-8:30pm. Cash only. ❶

Pizzeria/Trattoria Al Vecio Canton, Castello, 4738/A (☎041 52 85 176). From Campo S. Maria Formosa, with church on right, cross the bridge and follow Ruga Giuffa. Turn right at the end. A bustling neighborhood favorite. Try the mysterious *mistero*, a bulbous pizza/calzone bursting with toppings concealed inside. *Primi* €6-10, *secondi* €8-20. Cover €2. Service 12%. Open M and W-Su noon-3pm and 7pm-midnight. MC/V. ❹

Alle Testiere, Cal. del Mondo Novo, Castello, 5801 (☎/fax 041 52 27 220). From Campo S. Maria Formosa, take Cal. Mondo Novo. This traditional *trattoria* serves light, healthy cuisine loaded with fruit and vegetables. *Primi* €14, *secondi* €22-23. Open Tu-Sa noon-3pm and 7pm-midnight. Closed Aug. Reservation recommended. MC/V. ❺

Osteria Santa Marina, Campo S. Marina, Castello, 5911 (☎/fax 041 528 52 39; www.osteriadisantamarina.it). From Cal. Lio, take Cal. Carminati to the end, turn right, follow to the end and turn left. Fresh, seasonal menu, delicate dishes, and an upscale but comfortable setting. *Primi* €11-14, *secondi* €14-24. Cover €3. Open M 7:30-10pm, Tu-Sa 12:30-2:30pm and 7:30-10pm. MC/V. ❺

SAN MARCO

▨ **Le Bistrot de Venise,** Cal. dei Fabbri, San Marco, 4685 (☎041 52 36 651; www.bistrot-devenise.com). From P. S. Marco, head through 2nd Sottoportego dei Dai under the awning. Follow road around and over a bridge; turn right. Scrumptious Venetian dishes listed with century of origin and original creator. The motto is "*cucina e cultura,*" and Oct.-May afternoon exhibitions draw artisans and musicians. *Primi* from €15, *secondi* from €24. Service 12%. Rolling Venice discount 10%. Open daily noon-1am. MC/V. ❺

Vino, Vino, Ponte delle Veste, San Marco, 2007/A (☎041 24 17 688). From Cal. Larga XXII Marzo, turn on Cal. delle Veste. No-frills wine bar serves over 350 wines, as well as traditional *sarde in saor* and pasta specials. *Primi* €5.50, *secondi* €9-10.50. Cover €1. Open M and W-Su 10:30am-midnight. Rolling Venice discount 10%. Cash only. ❸

Rosticceria San Bartolomeo, Cal. della Bissa, San Marco, 5424/A (☎/fax 041 52 23 569). From Campo S. Bartolomeo, follow the Cal. de la Bissa to the neon sign. A haven for weary tourists, the *Rosticceria* serves food upstairs in its full service restaurant and downstairs in its laidback cafe. *Panini* from €1.10. Entrees from €5.90. Cover for restaurant €2.00. Open M 9am-4pm, Tu-Su 9am-9:30pm. AmEx/MC/V. ❶

DORSODURO

■ **Cantinone Gia Schiavi,** Fondamenta Meraviglie, Dorsoduro, 992 (☎041 52 30 034). From the Frari, follow signs for the Accademia bridge. Just before Ponte Meraviglie, turn right toward the church of S. Trovaso. Cross the 1st bridge. Friendly owner serves chilled wine at a marble bar. Delicate strawberry wine €8.50 per bottle. Bottles for sale fill long wooden shelves—enjoy a glass (€0.80-3.00) at the bar with some flavorful *cicchetti* (from €1). Bottles from €3.50. Open M-Sa 8am-8pm. Cash only. ❶

Gelateria Nico, Fondamenta Zattere, Dorsoduro, 922 (☎041 52 25 293). Near V: Zattere, with a great view of the Giudecca Canal from outdoor seating. For a guilty pleasure, try the Venetian ■ **gianduiotto de passeggio** (chocolate-hazelnut ice cream dropped into a cup of dense whipped cream; €2.50). *Gelato* 1 scoop €1, 2 scoops €1.50, 3 scoops €2. Open M-W and F-Su 6:45am-11pm. Cash only. ❶

Pizza al Volo, Campo S. Margherita, Dorsoduro, 2944 (☎041 52 25 430). Students and locals come for delicious, cheap pizza, ready-made by a young, friendly staff. Thin-crust, massive slices from €1.50. Pizza from €3.50. Oversized pizza for 2 from €6. Open daily 11:30am-4pm and 5pm-1:30am. Cash only. ❶

SAN POLO AND SANTA CROCE

Osteria Enoteca "Vivaldi," San Polo, 1457 (☎041 52 38 185). From the Campo. S. Polo, opposite the church, cross the bridge to Cal. della Madonnetta. Tiny neighborhood restaurant celebrates food and music with hearty cuisine and hanging violins. *Primi* €5.50-11, *secondi* from €8.50. Cover €1.50. Service 10%. Open daily 10:30am-2:30pm and 5:30-10:30pm. Reservations recommended F nights. AmEx/MC/V. ❸

Antica Birraria La Corte, Campo S. Polo, San Polo, 2168 (☎041 27 50 570; www.anticabirrarialacorte.com). The expansive interior of this former brewery houses a large restaurant and bar. Beer €2.60-4.50. Pizza €5-9. *Primi* €7.20-8.20, *secondi* €9.50-16.50. Cover €2. Open daily 12:30pm-3pm and 7-10:30pm; mid-July to mid-Aug. Sa-Su open for lunch only. AmEx/MC/V. ❸

Ae Oche, Santa Croce, 1552A/B (☎041 52 41 161). Unfinished wood walls lined with American relics like typewriters and Pepsi ads house over 100 different types of pizza (€3.50-7.80) to a bustling crowd at canal-side tables. *Primi* €5.50-7, *secondi* €7.50-12.50. Cover €1.40. Open daily noon-3pm and 7pm-midnight. Service 12%. MC/V. ❷

Osteria al Ponte, Cal. Saoneri, San Polo, 2741/A (☎041 52 37 238). From Campo S. Polo, follow signs to Accademia; it's immediately across the 1st bridge. Hungry locals devour a sampling of seafood dishes at this nautical-themed restaurant. Try the black *spagghetti al nero di seppia* (spaghetti cooked in squid ink). *Primi* €6-15, *secondi* from €7.50-32. Cover €1.50. Open M-Sa 10am-2:30pm and 6-10pm. AmEx/MC/V. ❸

Ristorante Cinese Tianjin, Ruga Rialto, San Polo, 649 (☎/fax 041 52 04 603). From V: San Silvestro, enter Campo San Silvestro and exit across the *campo* left onto Sal. Silvestro. Take the next right on Ruga Rialto. A garden dining room and traditional Chinese menu make this a pleasant option. Mix and match small plates (from €3.70-12) or add rice for a full meal. Open daily 10:30am-midnight. AmEx/MC/V. ❸

Cantina Do Mori, Cal. dei Do Mori, San Polo, 429 (☎041 52 25 401). From the Rialto, follow signs to Campo S. Giacomo. Watch your head on dangling brass pots in the dark interior of Venice's oldest wine bar. No seating. Open M-Tu and Th-Sa 8:30am-2:30pm and 4:30-8:30pm, W 4:30-8:30pm. Call ahead in summer. ❶

Trattoria da Renato, San Polo, 2245/A (☎041 52 41 922). Cross the bridge away from the Frari, turn left, and cross into Campo S. Stin; turn right on Cal. Donà and cross bridge. The decor is slightly off-putting—neon orange plastic chairs and linoleum-patterned tile floors—but the €12 *menù* includes *primi*, *secondi*, salad, and fruit/cheese for one low price. Cover €1. *Primi* €5-8.50, *secondi* €6.50-14. Open M-W and F-Su 1-3:15pm and 7:15-10:30pm. Cash only. ❷

◉ SIGHTS

AROUND THE RIALTO BRIDGE

▓**THE GRAND CANAL.** Over 3km long, the Grand Canal loops through the city and passes under three bridges: **Ponte Scalzi, Ponte Rialto,** and **Ponte Accademia.** Coursing past the facades of the cheek-to-cheek palaces that crown its banks, the blue-green waters are an undeniable reminder of Venice's history and immense wealth. Although each *palazzo* displays its own unique architectural blend of *loggia*, canal-side balconies, and marble sculptures, most share the same basic structural design. The most decorated floors, called *piani nobili* (noble floors, or 2nd and 3rd stories), housed luxurious salons and bedrooms. Rich merchant families stored their goods on the ground-floor walls, and servants slept in tiny chambers below the roof. The candy-cane posts used for mooring boats on the canal are called *bricole* and are painted with the family colors of the adjoining *palazzo*. *(For great facade views, ride V #82, #4 or the slower #1 from the train station to P. S. Marco. The facades are floodlit at night, producing a dazzling play of reflections.)*

GO WITH THE FLOW. High tides and rain cause *acque alte*, periodic floods that swamp parts of Venice with waist-high water levels. In 1966, 2m of water covered P. S. Marco, destroying priceless works of art. In June 2002 the waters rose again, lasting just long enough for rumors to swirl about Venice's imminent descent into the sea.

▓**RIVOALTUS LEGATORIA.** Step into the book-lined Rivoaltus on any given day and hear Wanda Scarpa shouting greetings from the attic, where she has been sewing leather-bound journals for a cadre of customers and faithful locals for three decades. The shop, run by arguably the nicest couple in Italy, overflows with Wanda's deep red portfolios, leather journals, and photo albums. Each one is a hand-crafted copy of 13th-century work and is made with all-natural vegetable dye leather and cotton paper from the Amalfi Coast. Giorgio Scarpa jokes that he chains his wife there to make her work, and has recently enlisted his daughter, Elisa, to continue the family tradition. Though Venice is now littered with shops advertising handmade journals, Rivoaltus was the first, and sells products of such renowned quality that even movie stars have been known to send their agents specifically to this shop to buy portfolios—but unchanging prices mean that anyone can enjoy the books' love-laced quality craftsmanship. *(Ponte di Rialto 11, just over the* *hump of the bridge. ☎ 041 52 36 195. Basic notebooks €18-31, photo albums €31-78, Murano glass fountain pens with ink €5. Open daily 10am-7:30pm.)*

THE RIALTO BRIDGE. This architectural structure was named after Rivo Alto, the first colony in Venice. Originally built of wood, the bridge collapsed in the 1500s. Antonio da Ponte designed the stone structure, where strips of boutiques separate a wide central lane from two side passages with picture-perfect views. Expensive stores dominate the space on the bridge, but unauthorized vendors selling overpriced, cheaply made goods manage to find their way onto the thoroughfare.

AROUND PIAZZA SAN MARCO

 ALL FOR ONE AND ONE FOR ALL. Those planning to visit several museums in Venice should consider investing in a museum pass. Valid for 3 months, the pass grants one-time admission to 10 museums, including those on P. S. Marco, as well as those on the islands of Murano and Burano. It is available at all participating museums and costs €15.50 or €10 for students and Rolling Venice Card-holders.

■ **BASILICA DI SAN MARCO.** Venice's crown jewel, San Marco is a spectacular fusion of gold mosaics on marble walls and rooftop balconies, gracing **Piazza San Marco** with symmetrical arches and incomparable mosaic portals. As the city's largest tourist attraction, the **Basilica di San Marco** also has the longest lines. Visit in the early morning for the shortest wait or in late afternoon for the best natural illumination. Construction of the basilica began in the 9th century, when two Venetian merchants stole St. Mark's remains from Alexandria and packed them in pork meat to smuggle them past Arab officials. After the first church dedicated to St. Mark burned down in the 11th century, Venice redesigned the basilica, snubbing the Roman Catholic Church's standard cross-shaped layout by opting for a Greek-cross plan with four arms and five domes. A cavernous interior sparkles with massive Byzantine and Renaissance mosaics. The blue-robed **Christ Pantocrator** (Ruler of All) sits above the high altar. Twelfth-century stone mosaics cover the floor in geometric designs, though the church's foundation, which has been sinking for 900 years, has wavy patches throughout. Behind the altar screen the rectangular **Pala D'Oro** relief frames a parade of saints in gem-encrusted gold; behind this masterpiece, the cement tomb of St. Mark himself rests within the altar, adorned only with a single gold-stemmed rose. Steep stairs in the atrium lead to the **Galleria della Basilica,** with an eye-level view of the tiny golden tiles that compose the basilica's vast ceiling mosaics, a balcony overlooking the *piazza* below, and an intimate view of the bronze **Cavalli di San Marco** (Horses of St. Mark). Nearby, the **Cassine** displays mosaic heads (the most valuable and artistically challenging section of a masterpiece) removed during 1881 renovations. *(Basilica open M-Sa 9:30am-5pm and Su 2-4pm. Illuminated 11:30am-12:30pm; free. Modest dress required. Baggage prohibited; follow signs to free baggage storage at the nearby Ateno San Basso on Calle San Basso; open daily 9:30am-5:30pm. Pala D'Oro open M-Sa 9:45am-5pm, Su 2-4pm; €1.50. Treasury open M-Sa 9:45am-5pm; €2. Galleria open M-F 9:45am-4:15pm, Sa-Su 9:45am-4:45pm; €3.)*

■ **PALAZZO DUCALE (DOGE'S PALACE).** Once the home of Venice's mayor, or Doge, the Palazzo Ducale museum contains spectacular artwork, including Veronese's *Rape of Europa.* In the courtyard, Sansovino's enormous sculptures, *Mars* and *Neptune,* flank the **Scala dei Giganti** (Stairs of the Giants), upon which new Doges were crowned. On the balcony stands the **Bocca di Leone** (Lion's Mouth), into which the Council of Ten, the Doge's assistants, who acted as judges and administrators, would drop the names of those they suspected guilty of crimes. Climb the elaborate **Scala d'Oro** (Golden Staircase) to the **Sala delle Quattro**

Porte (Room of the Four Doors), where the ceiling is covered in biblical judgments and representations of mythological tales related to events in Venetian history. More doors lead through the courtrooms of the much-feared Council of Ten, the even-more-feared Council of Three, and the **Sala del Maggior Consiglio** (Great Council Room), dominated by Tintoretto's *Paradise*, the largest oil painting in the world. Near the end, thick stone lattices line the covered **Ponte dei Sospiri** (Bridge of Sighs) and continue into the prisons. Casanova was condemned by the Ten to walk across this bridge, which gets its name from 19th-century Romantic writers' references to the mournful groans of prisoners descending into the small, damp cells. (☎041 52 09 070. Open Nov.-Mar. daily 9am-5pm, last entry 4pm; Apr.-Oct. 9am-7pm, last entry 6pm. Wheelchair accessible. €11, students €5.50, ages 6-14 €3. Includes entrance to P. San Marco museums (see below). Included on full museum pass. Audioguides €5.50. MC/V.)

PIAZZA SAN MARCO. Unlike the labyrinthine streets that tangle through most of Venice, Piazza San Marco, Venice's only official *piazza*, is a magnificent expanse of light, space, architectural harmony, and pigeons. Enclosing the *piazza* are rows of cafes and expensive glass and jewelry shops along the ground floors of the Renaissance **Procuratie Vecchie** (Old Treasury Offices), the Baroque **Procuratie Nuove** (New Treasury Offices), and the Neo-Classical **Ala Napoleonica** (more Treasury Offices). At the end of the *piazza* near the shoreline of the lagoon, sits the **Basilica di San Marco,** where mosaics and marble horses overlook the chaos below. Between the basilica and the Procuratie Vecchie perches the **Torre dell'Orologio** (Clock Tower), constructed between 1496 and 1499, according to Coducci's design. The 24hr. clock indicates the hour, lunar phase, and ascending constellation. Unfortunately, scaffolding has hidden this time-keeping treasure from view for several years. The 96m brick **campanile** (bell tower) provides one of the best elevated views of the city. Though it originally served as a watchtower and lighthouse, cruel and unusual Venice took advantage of its location to create a medieval tourist attraction by dangling state prisoners from its top in cages. The practice ceased in the 18th century, but public fascination with the tower did not. During a 1902 restoration project, it collapsed, but was reconstructed in 1912 with the enlightened addition of an elevator. (☎041 52 25 205. Campanile open daily 9am-9pm. €6. Audioguide €3.)

PIAZZA SAN MARCO'S MUSEUMS. Beneath the arcade at the short end of P. San Marco lies the entrance to a trio of museums. The **Museo Civico Correr,** a Venetian history museum, fills most of the two-story complex with curiosities from the city's imperial past, including maps and models of naval planning, ornate Neo-Classical artwork, weapons like a 16th-century key that fires poison darts, and ridiculously enormous platform shoes worn by sequestered noblewomen. The early rooms of the museum demonstrate the Neo-Classical French influence on Venetian art, while others contain works by Bellini and Carpaccio. Near the end of the first floor, the **Museo Archeologico** houses a sizeable collection of ancient pieces, from first-century Egyptian funeral parchment to Greek and Roman sculpture. A series of ceiling paintings by seven artists, including Veronese, adorn the dark, gilt-edged reading room of the **Biblioteca Nazionale Marciana,** built between 1537 and 1560. (☎041 52 24 951. Museums open Apr.-Oct. daily 9am-7pm; Nov.-Mar. 9am-5pm. €11, students €5.50. Includes entrance to Palazzo Ducale. Ticket sales end 1hr. before closing. Included on full museum pass. Free guided tours in English for Museo Archeologico Sa-Su 11am; for Biblioteca Nazionale Marciana Sa-Su 10am, noon, 2, and 3pm. Cash only.)

LA SCALA DEL BOVOLO. This brick and snow-white marble "staircase of the snails," as it translates into English, takes guests up five stories of tightly spiraling marble *loggia* to a circular portico at the top. Legend has it that the staircase was designed by Leonardo Da Vinci and constructed by his assistants. It once led to the top floors of a now-destroyed palace. Today the top affords views of the green courtyard below as well as an eye-level view of red rooftops and the distant domes of San Marco. *(From the Campo Manin, facing the bridge, turn left down the alley and look for the signs.* ☎ *041 27 19 012. Open Apr.-Oct. daily 10am-6pm; Nov.-Mar. Sa-Su 10am-4pm, daily in Carnevale. €3, groups of 10 or more €2.50. Cash only.)*

SAN POLO

SCUOLA GRANDE DI SAN ROCCO. The most illustrious of Venice's *scuole*, or guild halls, is a monument to Jacopo Tintoretto, who left Venice only once in his 76 years, and sought to combine "the color of Titian with the drawing of Michelangelo." To achieve the effect of depth, he often built dioramas and posed his models within so he could portray them with spatial accuracy. The school commissioned Tintoretto to complete all the paintings in the building, a task that took 23 years. The large room on the second floor provides hand mirrors to admire the delicate paintings mounted on the ceiling, but the wall-to-wall *Crucifixion* in the last room upstairs is the collection's crowning glory. Lined with intricately carved columns and colored marble, the *scuola* is a masterpiece in itself; step outside to admire it to the strains of classical music performed by street musicians. *(Behind Basilica dei Frari in Campo S. Rocco.* ☎ *041 52 34 864; www.scuolagrandesanrocco.it. Open daily Mar. 28-Nov. 2 9am-5:30pm; Nov. 3-Mar. 27 10am-4pm. €5.50, students and Rolling Venice cardholders €4, under 18 free with parents. Audioguides free. AmEx/MC/V.)*

CAMPO SAN POLO. The second-largest *campo* in Venice, **Campo San Polo** once hosted bull-baiting matches during the *carnevale*, when authorities would release a wild bull into the crowds and set dogs on its tail. After the dogs began to tear the bull's flesh, the defeated animal would be decapitated before a cheering mob. A painting depicting the chaos hangs in the Museo Correr in P. S. Marco. Fortunately, modern visits generally involve less bloodshed. *(Between the Frari and Rialto Bridges. V: S. Silvestro. Straight back from the vaporetto. Or from in front of the Frari, cross bridge, then turn right, left on Rio Terà, right on Cal. Seconda d. Saoneri, and left at the end.)*

DORSODURO

■**COLLEZIONE PEGGY GUGGENHEIM.** Guggenheim's elegant waterfront Palazzo Venier dei Leoni, once her home and a social haven for the world's artistic elite, now displays a private modern art collection maintained by the Solomon Guggenheim Foundation. The museum includes works by Duchamp, Klee, Kandinsky, Picasso, Magritte, Pollock, Dalí, and Guggenheim's confidante, Max Ernst. Look for the atypical *Sacrifice* by Rothko, which marks a departure from his usual abstract, color-focused technique. Guggenheim and her beloved pet Shih Tzus, from Sir Herbert to Peacock, are buried in the peaceful garden. The Marini sculpture *Angel in the City*, which sits (apparently aroused) on horseback on the terrace, was designed with a detachable penis so Ms. Guggenheim could make emergency alterations and not offend her more prudish guests. The ivy-lined marble terrace offers an unobstructed waterfront view of the Grand Canal. See **Beyond Tourism** (p. 81) for internship opportunities. *(Fondamenta Venier dei Leoni, Dorsoduro, 710. V: Accademia. Turn left and follow the yellow signs.* ☎ *041 24 05 411; fax 041 52 06 885. Open M and Th-Su 10am-6pm. Ticket sales end 5:45pm. €10, seniors €8, ISIC and Rolling Venice cardholders €5, under 12 free. Audioguide €4. AmEx/MC/V.)*

■**GALLERIE DELL'ACCADEMIA.** This colossal gallery boasts the most extensive collection of Venetian art in the world. Among the enormous altarpieces in Room II, Giovanni Bellini's *Madonna Enthroned with Child, Saints, and Angels* stands out with its soothing serenity. Rooms IV and V display more Bellinis, including the magnificent *Madonna and Child with Magdalene and Saint Catherine*, and two works by Giorgione, who defied contemporary convention by creating works that apparently told no story. Attempts to find plot or moral in *The Tempest* have been fruitless. An x-ray of the pictures reveals that Giorgione originally painted a bathing woman where the young man now stands. In Room VI, three paintings by Tintoretto, *The Creation of the Animals*, *The Temptation of Adam and Eve*, and *Cain and Abel*, get progressively darker as one moves from God commanding flocks of animals to the graphic murder of Abel by Cain. Venetian Renaissance works line the rooms leading to Room X, home to Veronese's colossal *Supper in the House of Levi*. Originally painted as a Last Supper, the infuriated Inquisition council tried to force Veronese to modify his unorthodox interpretation of the memorable event, which depicts a Protestant German, a midget, dogs, and fat men. Instead, Veronese cleverly changed the title, saving his artistic license and his life. On the opposite wall is Titian's last painting, a *Pietà* intended for his tomb, a request that was apparently ignored. In Room XX, works by Bellini and Carpaccio display Venetian cityscapes so accurately that scholars use them as "photos" of Venice's past. *(V: Accademia. ☎ 041 52 22 247. To pre-order tickets, call Teleart M-F 041 520 03 45. Open M 8:15am-2pm, Tu-Su 9:15am-7:15pm. Admission €6.50, EU citizens under 18 or over 65 free. Guided tours in English, French, or Italian Tu-Su 11am-noon; €5.50. Audioguides €4. Cash only.)*

CÀ REZZONICO. Longhena's great 18th-century *palazzo* houses the newly restored **Museo del Settecento Veneziano** (Museum of 18th-Century Venice). Known as the "Temple of Venetian Settecento," this grand palace features a regal ballroom, complete with flowing curtains and Crosato's frescoed ceiling. Other rooms contain elaborate Venetian Rococo decor. Upstairs, two extensive portrait galleries display works by Tiepolo, Guardi, Longhi, and Tintoretto. *(V: Cà Rezzonico. ☎ 041 24 10 100. Open Apr.-Oct. M and W-Su 10am-6pm; Nov.-Mar. 10am-5pm. Reserve 24hr. ahead. €6.50, students and Rolling Venice cardholders €4.50. Audioguide €4. MC/V.)*

CASTELLO

SCUOLA DALMATA SAN GIORGIO DEGLI SCHIAVONI. Carpaccio's finest paintings, rendering episodes from the lives of St. George, Jerome, and Tryfon, are on the ground floor of this early 16th-century building. *(Castello, 3259/A. V: S. Zaccaria. From the Riva Schiavoni, take Cal. Dose to Campo Bandiera e Moro. Follow S. Antonin to Fondamenta Furlani. ☎ 041 52 28 828. Open Apr.-Oct. Tu-Sa 9:30am-12:30pm and 3:30-6:30pm, Su 9:30am-12:30pm; Nov.-Mar. Tu-Sa 10am-12:30pm and 3-6pm, Su 10am-12:30pm. Ticket sales end 20min. before closing. €3, Rolling Venice cardholders €2. Modest dress required.)*

GIARDINI PUBBLICI AND SANT'ELENA. Let's be honest, it's not easy being green on a paved island surrounded by salt water. For a short commune with nature, walk through the shady lanes of Napoleon's bench-lined Public Gardens where children swarm over playgrounds, bushes sprout in droves, and the local geriatric elite gossip on benches. For a larger lounging area, continue past the gardens and bring a picnic lunch to the lawns of Sant'Elena. *(V: Giardini or S. Elena. Free.)*

CANNAREGIO

JEWISH GHETTO. In 1516, the Doge forced Venice's Jewish population into the old cannon-foundry area, creating the first Jewish ghetto in Europe. (*Ghetto* is the Venetian word for foundry.) At its height, the ghetto housed 5000 people in buildings up to seven stories high, making them among the tallest tenements in Europe at the time. Now locals gather in this sequestered spot for the tranquility of the **Campo del Ghetto Nuovo**. In the *campo*, the **Schola Grande Tedesca** (German Synagogue), the oldest area synagogue, now houses the **Museo Ebraica di Venezia** (Hebrew Museum of Venice). In the adjacent Campiello d. Scuole stand the opulent **Schola Levantina** (Levantine Synagogue) and **Schola Spagnola** (Spanish Synagogue), both designed at least in part by Longhena. The Canton and Italian synagogues also occupy the area. (Cannaregio, 2899/B. V: S. Marcuola. Follow signs straight, then turn left into Campo del Ghetto Nuovo. ☎041 71 53 59. Hebrew Museum open June-Sept. M-F and Su 10am-7pm; Oct.-May 10am-4:30pm. €3, students €2. Entrance to synagogues by guided tour only. English tours leave from the museum June-Sept. every hr. 10:30am-5:30pm; Oct.-May 10:30am-4:30pm. Museum and tour €8.50, students €7. MC/V.)

CÀ D'ORO. Built between 1425 and 1440, the facade of this "Golden House" combines interlinked arches with delicate spires. Today it houses the **Galleria Giorgio Franchetti.** Highlights of the museum include Andrea Mantegna's *Saint Sebastian,* Bonaccio's *Apollo Belvedere,* one of the most important bronzes of the 15th century, and two balconies above the Grand Canal. For the best view of the balconies and adornments of Cà D'Oro's tiered "wedding cake" facade, take a *traghetto* across the canal to the Rialto Markets. (V: Cà d'Oro. ☎041 52 03 652. Open M 8:15am-2pm, Tu-Su 8:15am-7:15pm. Ticket sales end 30min. before closing. €5, EU students and under 25 €2.50, art students free. Audioguides €4. Cash only.)

CHURCHES

The Foundation for the Churches of Venice sells the **Chorus Pass** that covers admission to all of Venice's churches. A yearly pass (€9, students €6), which includes S. Maria dei Miracoli, S. Maria Gloriosa dei Frari, S. Polo, Madonna dell'Orto, Il Redentore, and S. Sebastiano, is available at most participating churches. (For information, call ☎041 27 50 462 or visit www.chorusvenezia.org.)

■**CHIESA DI SAN ZACCARIA (SAN MARCO).** Dedicated to the father of John the Baptist and designed in the late 1400s by Coducci, the Gothic-Renaissance church holds S. Zaccaria's corpse in an elevated, glass-windowed sarcophagus along the right wall of the nave. Nearby, watch for Giovanni Bellini's *Virgin and Child Enthroned with Four Saints,* one of the masterpieces of Venetian Renaissance painting. (V: S. Zaccaria. From P. S. Marco, turn left along the water, cross the bridge, and turn left on Cal. Albanesi. Turn right, then go straight. ☎041 52 21 257. Open daily 10am-noon and 4-6pm. Free.)

CHIESA DI SAN GIACOMO DI RIALTO (SAN POLO). Between the Rialto and the surrounding markets stands Venice's first church, diminutively called "San Giacometto." An ornate clock-face adorns its bell tower. Across the *piazza,* a statue called *Il Gobbo* (The Hunchback) supports the steps, once used for public announcements. It was at the foot of this sculpture that convicted thieves could finally collapse after being forced to run naked from P. S. Marco and lashed all the way by spectators. (V: Rialto. Cross bridge and turn right. Church open daily 10am-5pm. Free.)

BASILICA DI SANTA MARIA GLORIOSA DEI FRARI (SAN POLO). Franciscans began construction on the Gothic church, also known simply as *I Frari,* in 1340. Today, the cavernous gray interior boasts two paintings by Titian as well as the corpse of the Renaissance master himself, who is entombed within the cathedral's cavernous terra-cotta walls. His ■**Assumption** (1516-18), on the high altar, marks the height of the Venetian Renaissance. Titian's other work, *The Madonna and Child with Saints and Members of the Pesaro Family* (1547), is on the left from the entrance. Titian's elaborate tomb, a lion-topped triumphal arch with bas-relief scenes of Paradise, stands directly across from the enormous pyramid in which the sculptor Canova (1757-1822) rests. Donatello's gaunt wooden sculpture *St. John the Baptist* (1438) stands framed in gold in the Florentine chapel to the right of the high altar. An amazingly life-like work by Bellini, *Virgin and Child with Saints Nicholas, Peter, Benedict, and Mark* (1488), hangs in the sacristy to the far right of the apse. Nearby, Cabianca and Brustolon's *Altar of Relics* holds shelves of chalices and holy memorabilia in a large, ornate glass case framed with thick gold leaf, three bas-relief crucifixion scenes, and gilded, flitting cherubs. (*V: S. Tomà. Follow signs back to Campo dei Frari.* ☎041 27 28 611; www.basilicadeifrari.it. *Open M-Sa 9am-6pm, Su 1-6pm. Ticket office closes 5:45pm. €2.50. Cash only.*)

CHIESA DI SANTA MARIA DELLA SALUTE (DORSODURO). The *salute* (Italian for "health") is a hallmark of the Venetian skyline: perched on Dorsoduro's peninsula just southwest of San Marco, the church and its domes are visible from everywhere in the city. In 1631, the city commissioned Longhena to build the church for the Virgin, who they believed would then give them a break and end the plague. These days, Venice celebrates the end of the plague on the 3rd Sunday in November by building a pontoon bridge across the Canal and lighting candles in the church (see **Entertainment: Festivals,** p. 323). Next to the *salute* stands the *dogana*, the old customs house, where ships sailing into Venice were required to stop and pay appropriate duties. (*V: Salute.* ☎041 52 25 558. *Open daily 9am-noon and 3-5:30pm. Free. Entrance to sacristy with donation. The inside of the dogana is closed to the public.*)

CHIESA DI SAN SEBASTIANO (DORSODURO). The Renaissance painter Veronese took refuge in this white marble and brown stucco 16th-century church when he fled Verona in 1555 after allegedly killing a man. By 1565 he had filled the church with an amazing cycle of paintings and frescoes. His *Stories of Queen Esther* covers the ceiling, while the artist himself rests under the gravestone by the organ. Several works by Titian are also displayed. (*V: S. Basilio. Continue straight ahead. Open M-Sa 10am-5pm, Su 1-5pm. Ticket office closes at 4:45pm. €2.50. Cash only.*)

CHIESA DI SANTISSIMI GIOVANNI E PAOLO (CASTELLO). This imposing brick and marble structure, also called San Zanipolo, is primarily built in the Gothic style, but has a Renaissance portal and an arch supported by columns of Greek marble. Inside, monumental ceilings enclose the tombs and monuments of the Doges. One fresco depicts the gory death of Marcantonio Bragadin, who valiantly defended Cyprus from the Turks in 1571, only to be skinned alive after surrendering. His remains rest in the urn above the monument. Next to Bragadin is an altarpiece by Giovanni Bellini depicting St. Christopher, St. Sebastian, and St. Vincent Ferrer. The bronze equestrian statue of local mercenary Bartolomeo Colleoni stands on a marble pedestal outside. Colleoni left his inheritance to the city on the condition that a monument in his honor would be erected in front of San Marco; the city, unwilling to honor anyone in such a grand space, decided to place the statue in front of the Scuola di San Marco to satisfy the conditions of the will and claim his fortune. The statue was designed in 1479 by Da Vinci's teacher Verrochio. (*V: Fondamenta Nuove. Turn left, then right on Fondamenta dei Mendicanti.* ☎041 52 35 913. *Open M-Sa 9:30am-6pm, Su 1-6pm. €2.50, students €1.25. Cash only.*)

CHIESA DI SANTA MARIA DEI MIRACOLI (CASTELLO). The Lombardi family designed this small Renaissance jewel in the late 1400s. Inside the tiny pink-, white- and blue-marble exterior sits a fully functional parish with a dark golden ceiling and pastel walls interrupted only by the vibrant blue and yellow window above the apse. (*From S. S. Giovanni e Paolo, cross the bridge directly in front of the church and continue down Cal. Larga Gallina over 2 bridges. Open July-Aug. M-Sa 10am-5pm; Sept.-June M-Sa 10am-5pm, Su 1-5pm. €2.50. Cash only.*)

CHIESA DELLA MADONNA DELL'ORTO (CANNAREGIO). Tintoretto's squat brick 14th-century parish church, the final resting place of the painter and his children, contains 10 of his largest paintings, as well as some works by Titian. Look for Tintoretto's *Last Judgment,* a spatially intense mass of souls, and *The Sacrifice of the Golden Calf* near the high altar. On the right apse is the brilliantly shaded *Presentation of the Virgin at the Temple.* There is a light switch for illuminating the works at each of the far corners. (V: Madonna dell'Orto. For information, call the Associazione Chiese di Venezia, ☎041 27 50 462; www.chorusvenezia.org. Open M-Sa 10am-5pm, Su 1-5pm. Ticket office closes 4:45pm. €2.50. Audioguides €0.50. Cash only.)

CHIESA DEI GESUITI (CANNAREGIO). Founded in the 12th century and reconstructed in the 18th, Dei Gesuiti features a gilt-rimmed stucco ceiling with painted portals to Heaven. Exterior columns open onto a sea of marble that stretches from the floor to the realistic stone curtain in the pulpit. Titian's *Martyrdom of Saint Lawrence* hangs in the altar to the left of the entrance, while Tintoretto's lighter *Assumption of the Virgin* shows Mary taking off in flight. (V: Fondamenta Nuove, 4885; turn right, then left on Sal. dei Specchieri. Open daily 10am-noon and 4-6pm. Free.)

SAN GIORGIO MAGGIORE AND GIUDECCA

BASILICA DI SAN GIORGIO MAGGIORE. Standing on its own monastic island, S. Giorgio Maggiore contrasts sharply with most other Venetian churches. Palladio ignored the Venetian fondness for color and opted for an austere design. Light fills the enormous interior, although unfortunately it does not hit Tintoretto's *Last Supper* by the altar. A light switch illuminates the wraith-like angels hovering over Christ's table. Take the elevator to the top of the **campanile** for a marvelous view of the city. (V: S. Giorgio Maggiore. ☎041 52 27 827. Open in summer M-Sa 9am-12:30pm and 2:30-6:30pm; in winter 2:30-5pm. Basilica free. Campanile €3. Purchase ticket in the elevator.)

TEMPIO DEL S. S. REDENTORE. Palladio's religious masterpiece, this narrow church, like the Salute, commemorates a deal that Venice struck with God to end a plague. Every year the city celebrates with fireworks in the **Festa del Redentore** (see **Entertainment: Festivals,** p. 323). Paintings by Veronese and Bassano hang in the sacristy. (V: Redentore. Ask to enter the sacristy. Open M-Sa 10am-5pm, Su 1-5pm. €2.)

ISLANDS OF THE LAGOON

▨ LIDO. The breezy resort island of Lido provided the tragic setting for *Death in Venice*, Thomas Mann's haunting novella of love and lust. Visonti's film version was also shot here at the famous **Hotel des Bains,** Lungomare Marconi, 17. Today, tree-lined streets, crashing blue waves, and the shoreline of the popular public beach offer a free, relaxing alternative to Venice's paved urban seafront. An impressive shipwreck looms at one end. The island also offers a casino, horseback riding, and one of Italy's finest golf courses. (V #1 and 82: Lido. From the vaporetto stop, cross the street and continue until you reach the pink-marble sidewalk, which traverses the island to the beach. Beach open daily 9am-8pm. Free. Lockable changing rooms €23.50 per day, or €13.50 per afternoon (from 2:30pm); beach umbrella and chair €15.40/12; long deck chair €9; small safe €3. MC/V.)

▨ MURANO. Famous since 1292 for its glass (Venice's artisans were forced off Venice proper because their kilns started fires), the six-island cluster of Murano affords visitors the opportunity to witness resident artisans blowing and spinning crystalline creations free of charge. Quiet streets are lined with tiny shops and glass boutiques with jewelry, vases, and delicate figurines for a variety of prices; for demonstrations, look for signs directing to the *fornace,* concentrated around the Colona, Faro, and Navagero *vaporetto* stops. The speed and grace of these artisans are stunning, and some studios let visitors blow their own glass creations. The **Museo Vetrario** (Glass Museum) houses a collection that begins with funereal urns from the first century and ends with pieces like an ornate model garden made entirely of glass and a cartoonish, sea green octopus presumably designed by Carlo Scarpa in 1930. Farther down the street, a marble *loggia* lines the 2nd story of the light brick, 12th-century **Basilica di Santa Maria e San Donato,** which features glass and marble mosaic floors, blue chandeliers in the side apses, and a holy water font with fused pieces of bright yellow, red, green, and blue glass. A huge crucifix, all blown from one piece of glass, hangs to the right of the altar. If you look carefully, the curved bones of the dragon slain by St. Donatus hang behind the altar, though its rumored that they might just be those of a washed up whale. (V #DM, LN, 5, 13, 41, 42: Faro from either S. Zaccaria or Fondamenta Nuove. Museo Vetrario, Fondamenta Giustian, 8. ☎/fax 041 73 95 86. Open Apr.-Oct. M-Tu and Th-Su 10am-5pm; Nov.-Mar. M-Tu and Th-Su 10am-4pm. €4, students or Rolling Venice Card-holders €2.50. Combined ticket with Burano Lace Museum €6, students or Rolling Venice Card-holders €4. Basilica ☎041 73 90 56. Open daily 8am-7pm. Included on full museum pass. Modest dress required. Free.)

BURANO. Curtains billow from the doorways of bright yellow and electric blue houses in this traditional fishing village, where carefully hand-tatted lace has become a community art. The small and somewhat dull **Scuola di Merletti di Burano** (Lace Museum), once the home of the island's professional lace-making school, features strips from the 16th century and yellowing lace-maker diplomas. The pink stucco facade and violently canting *campanile* of the basilica, **Chiesa di S. Martino,** sit across from the museum. (40min. by boat from Venice. V #LN: Burano from Fondamenta Nuove. Museum in P. Galuppi. ☎041 73 00 34. Open Apr.-Sept. M and W-Su 10am-5pm; Oct.-Mar. M and W-Su 10am-4:30pm. €4. Combined ticket with Murano Glass Museum. Included on full museum pass. Church open daily 8am-noon and 3-7pm. Free.)

TORCELLO. Torcello, originally a safe haven for fishermen fleeing barbarians on the mainland, was the most powerful island in the lagoon before Venice usurped its inhabitants and its glory. A cathedral, **Santa Maria Assunta,** contains an entire resplendent wall, including tiers of 11th- and 12th-century mosaics depicting the Last Judgment and the Virgin Mary. The soaring *campanile* affords splendid views of Torcello, a distant Burano, and the outer lagoon, but the rambling walk up to the church is a pleasure in itself. (45min. by boat from Venice. V #T: Torcello from Burano. Cathedral ☎041 73 01 19. Open daily 10:30am-6pm. Ticket office closes 5:30pm. €3. Combined church, campanile, and museum admission €8 with free audioguide included. Combination ticket sales end 4:30pm. Modest dress required. Cash only. Audioguides €1.)

ISOLA DI SAN MICHELE. Venice's cemetery island, S. Michele, is home to Coducci's tiny Chiesa di S. Michele in Isola (1469), the first Renaissance church in Venice. Enter the cyprus-lined grounds through the church's right-hand portal, ornamented by a relief depicting St. Michael slaying a dragon. Quiet grounds offer the opportunity for peaceful reflection away from the hustle and bustle of Venice. Poet, Fascist sympathizer, and enemy of the state Ezra Pound is buried in the Protestant cemetery, while Russian composer Igor Stravinsky and choreographer Sergei Diaghilev are entombed in the Orthodox graveyard. (V: Cimitero, from Fondamenta Nuove. Church and cemetery open daily Apr.-Sept. 7:30am-6pm; Oct.-Mar. 7:30am-4pm. Free.)

WHERE IT'S @. The "@" symbol reputedly originated in Venice. When Venetian merchants exported goods, they would write "@" in front of the package's address to distinguish the destination from the shipping point. La Scala del Bovolo was reportedly built in an "@"-like spiral shape because it was once attached to the palace of a wealthy merchant.

🎵 ENTERTAINMENT

The weekly *A Guest in Venice*, free in hotels, tourist offices, and online at www.unospitedivenezia.it, lists current festivals, concerts, and gallery exhibits.

GONDOLAS

Gondolas were once displays of multicolored brilliance. Legend has it that their lavish reds and purples turned to black when the Plague struck: wooden boats were supposedly coated with tar and pitch to stop further contamination from spreading throughout the disease-infested canal waters. The morbid color was also a sign of respect for Venice's dead and dying. A more likely story, however, is that a 17th-century city ordinance ordered that all boats be painted black to prevent noble families from waging gondola-decorating wars. Certain dignitaries, of course, were exempt. Now, the boats are mainly filled with tourists seeking the most gorgeous views of Venetian houses and palaces via their original canal pathways. Rides are most romantic about 50min. before sunset and most affordable if shared by six people. The rate that a gondolier quotes is negotiable and the most bargain-friendly gondoliers are those standing by themselves, rather than those in the groups at "taxi-stands" throughout the city. The "official" price starts at €73 for 50min., for a maximum of six people, and each additional 25min. costs €37; prices rise at night to €91.

ORCHESTRAL MUSIC

Venice swoons for **orchestral music,** from the outdoor chamber orchestras in P. S. Marco to costumed concerts. **Vivaldi,** the priest and choirmaster of the Chiesa di S. Maria della Pietà (a few blocks along the waterfront from P. S. Marco), was forgotten for centuries after his death. Today, his compositions, particularly *The Four Seasons,* can be heard regularly in the summer and during the winter. The **Chiesa di San Vidal,** next to Campo S. Samuele in San Marco, hosts performances using period instruments. (Open daily 9am-5pm. Concerts Tu, Th, and Sa 9pm. €22, students €17. Purchase tickets at the church or visit www.interpretiveneziani.com.)

THEATER, CINEMA, AND ART EXHIBITIONS

Teatro Goldoni, Cal. del Teatro, San Marco, 4650/B, near the Rialto, showcases varying types of live productions, often with a seasonal theme. Check with the theater for upcoming listings. (☎041 24 02 011; teatrogoldini@libero.it. Rolling Venice discount 10%. AmEx/MC/V.) The **Mostra Internazionale di Cinema** (Venice International Film Festival), held annually from late August to early September, is a worldwide affair, drawing both rising talents and more established names like Steven Spielberg. Movies are shown in their original languages. (☎041 52 18 878. Tickets €20, sold throughout city. Some late-night outdoor showings free.) Venice's main cinemas include: the **Accademia,** Cal. Gambara, Dorsoduro, 1019 (☎041 52 87 706), to the right of the museum, screening original language films; the **Giorgione,** Campo S. Apostoli, Cannaregio (☎041 52 26 298); and the **Rossini,** San Marco, 3988 (☎041 52 30 322), off Campo Manin, which generally shows films in Italian. The famed **Biennale di Venezia** (info ☎041 52 11 898; for tickets, HelloVenezia 041 24 24; www.labiennale.org. Open daily 7:30am-8pm.), an international contemporary art exhibition with musical and dance performances, takes over the Giardini Pubblici and the Arsenal with provocative art in odd-numbered years.

FESTIVALS

Banned by the church for several centuries, Venice's famous **Carnevale** was successfully reinstated in the early 1970s. During the 10 days preceding Ash Wednesday, masked figures jam the streets and street performances spring up throughout the city. On **Mardi Gras,** the population of the city doubles. Contact the tourist office in December or January for details and make lodging arrangements far ahead. Venice's second most colorful festival is the **Festa del Redentore** (3rd Su in July), originally held to celebrate the end of a 16th-century plague. It kicks off on Saturday night with a fireworks display at 11:30pm. On

Sunday, maintenance craftsmen build a pontoon bridge, open to the public, across the Giudecca Canal, connecting **Il Redentore** to the **Zattere.** On the first Sunday in September, Venice stages its classic **regata storica,** a gondola race down the Grand Canal. During the religious **Festa della Salute** (Nov. 21), which also originated to mark the end of a plague, the city celebrates with the construction of another pontoon bridge, this time over the Grand Canal.

SHOPPING

Be wary of shopping in the heavily touristed P. S. Marco or around the Rialto (excluding Rivoaltus). Shops outside these areas often have better quality products and a greater selection for about half the price. Interesting clothing, glass, and mask boutiques line the streets leading from the Rialto to Campo S. Polo and Str. Nuova and from the Rialto toward the station. The map accompanying the Rolling Venice Card lists many shops that offer discounts for Card-holders. The most concentrated and varied selections of Venetian glass and lace require trips to the nearby islands of Murano and Burano, respectively.

⬛ NIGHTLIFE

Though pubs and bars are not uncommon, most residents agree that a truly vibrant nightlife in Venice is virtually nonexistent. Most locals would rather spend an evening sipping wine or beer and listening to string quartets in P. S. Marco than bumping and/or grinding in a disco, but the island's fluctuating population means that new establishments spring up (and wither and die) with some regularity. Student nightlife is concentrated around **Campo Santa Margherita,** in Dorsoduro, while tourists swarm **Lista di Spagna,** in Cannaregio.

⬛ **Café Blue,** Campo S. Pantalon, Dorsoduro, 3778 (☎041 71 02 27). Grab some absinthe (€6) in the back room to watch the daytime coffee crowd turn into the nighttime trendy. Free Internet. Live music F evenings in winter, DJ Wed nights. Open in summer noon-2am; in winter 8am-2am. MC/V.

⬛ **Nemesis,** San Polo, 2565 (☎041 52 38 891). Directly across from the Chiesa Frari, a rowdy crowd spites Christian values while indulging in sangria (€2.50) and hard liquor (from €2.00). Wine from €1.30 a glass, beer from €2.00. Open daily 8am-midnight.

Paradiso Perduto, Fond. della Misericordia, Cannaregio, 2540 (☎041 09 94 540). From Str. Nuova, cross Campo S. Fosca, cross bridge, and continue in same direction, crossing 2 more bridges. Dreadlocked students flood this bar, where waitstaff doles out large portions of *cicchetti* (mixed plate; €19). Live jazz Friday nights. Open M-Sa 9:30am-3pm and 7pm-2am.

Piccolo Mondo, Accademia, Dorsoduro, 1056/A (☎041 52 00 371). Facing away from the canal toward the Accademia, turn right and follow the street around. Disco, hip-hop, and vodka with Red Bull (€10) keep a full house at this small but popular *discoteca*. Framed collages of the wide-ranging clientele include notables like Michael Jordan, Boy George, Shaquille O'Neal, Mick Jagger, and Prince Albert of Monaco. Ring bell to enter. Drinks from €7. Cover varies, free with *Let's Go*. Open nightly 10pm-4am. AmEx/MC/V.

Casanova, Lista di Spagna, Cannaregio, 158/A (☎041 27 50 199). This stylish club claims to be the only real disco in Venice and draws tourists and students alike. Enjoy the techno beats on the dance floor or at the bar decorated with inlaid shells. Weekend €10 cover includes free drink, weekday cover €7. Open daily 10pm-4am. AmEx/MC/V.

Bistrot ai do Draghi, Campo S. Margherita, 3665 (☎041 52 89 731). While not as fierce as the name implies, the crowd at this tiny bistro is more artsy than that at its C. S. Margherita counterparts. Open daily 7am-2am.

Orange, Dorsoduro 3054/A (☎041 52 34 740; www.orangebar.it). Across from Duchamp in Campo S. Margherita. The young and attractive gather at this modern minimalist bar where everything except the lush aquamarine garden is consistently and totally orange. To match the theme, try the tequila sunrise (€6). Beer from €2. Wine from €1.50. Open M-Sa 7am-2am, Su 6pm-2am. AmEx/MC/V.

Cafè Noir, Dorsoduro 3805 (☎041 71 09 25). Faded images of Marilyn Monroe and a saxophone player cover the walls of Cafe Noir, where dark brown lamps, a blue glass mosaic bar, and tightly packed wooden tables give off an artistic vibe. The back room has less of a view, but black leather booths and street-side windows in front are great for coffee-drinking or people watching. Open M-Sa 7am-2am, Su 9am-2am. Cash only.

Bacaro Jazz, Campo S. Bartolomeo, San Marco, 5546 (☎041 52 85 249; www.bacarojazz.com). From the post office, follow the sounds of jazz across the street. Portraits of Billie Holliday and Duke Ellington dot colorful jazz murals, while the ceiling is a low-hanging canopy of bras from local and international patrons (feel free to leave yours for a t-shirt, free drink, or bragging rights). Happy Hour 4-6:30pm. Open M-Tu and Th-Su 4pm-3am. AmEx/MC/V.

Il Caffè, Campo S. Margherita, Dorsoduro, 2963 (☎041 52 87 998). A low-key, high-quality bar with a tiny red facade caters to an older set of patrons in between the loud student bars of Campo S. Margherita. Wine €0.80. Open M-Sa 7am-1am. Cash only.

Duchamp, Campo S. Margherita, Dorsoduro 3019 (☎041 52 86 255). A student-heavy crowd keeps Duchamp packed, from the plentiful seating in the *campo* to the shrug-inducing interior (complete with brick walls and painted windows). Pint of beer €4.30. House wine €1.50. Open M-F and Su 9am-2am, Sa 5pm-2am. Cash only.

Inishark Irish Pub, Cal. del Mondo Novo, Castello, 5787 (☎041 52 35 300), off Campo S. Maria Formosa. A giant inflatable shark dangles over the noisy interior of this dark, mid-sized Irish pub. Guinness and Harp €4.50. Open Tu-Su 6pm-1:30am. Cash only.

PADUA (PADOVA)   ☎049

Padua's oldest institutions are the ones that still draw visitors—pilgrims flock to St. Anthony's tomb, athletes skate along the looping Prato della Valle, and even today, lecturers and academics frequent the hallowed university halls where Dante, Petrarch, Galileo, Copernicus, Mantegna, Giotto, Donatello, and other luminaries once fostered the city's long-standing reputation as a center of learning. Padua's university, founded in 1222 and second in seniority only to Bologna's, brings scores of students into the city's cluster of busy *piazze*, where crowds of 20-somethings stay to roam the brightly lit streets late into the night.

⬚ TRANSPORTATION

Trains: In P. Stazione, at the northern end of C. del Popolo, the continuation of C. Garibaldi. Open daily 5am-midnight. Tickets open daily 6am-9pm. Info booth open daily 7am-9pm. **Luggage storage** available (see **Practical Information**). To: **Bologna** (1½hr., 34 per day 12:41am-10:43pm, €5.73); **Milan** (2½hr., 25 per day 5:50am-9:40pm, €11.21); **Venice** (30min., 82 per day 4:33am-11:08pm, €2.50); **Verona** (1hr., 44 per day 5:03am-11:28pm, €4.30).

Buses: SITA (☎049 82 06 834), in P. Boschetti. From the train station, walk down C. del Popolo, turn left on V. Trieste, and bear right at V. Vecchio. Ticket office open M-Sa 5:30am-8:30pm, Su 6:20am-8:40pm. To: **Montagnana** (1½hr., 22 per day 6:20am-8:30pm, €3.60); **Venice** (45min., 32 per day 5:25am-10:25pm, €3.05); **Vicenza** (1hr., 50 per day 5:50am-8:15pm, €3.20). Reduced service Su. Cash only.

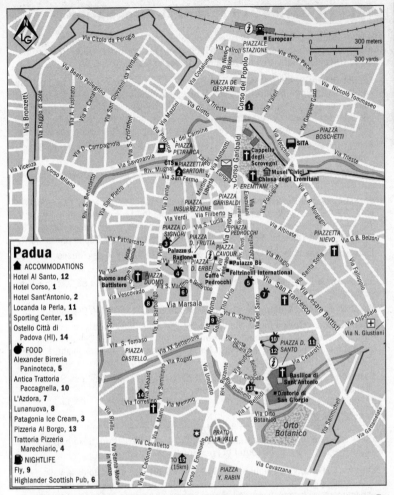

Padua

▲ ACCOMMODATIONS
Hotel Al Santo, 12
Hotel Corso, 1
Hotel Sant'Antonio, 2
Locanda la Perla, 11
Sporting Center, 15
Ostello Città di
Padova (HI), 14

● FOOD
Alexander Birreria
  Paninoteca, 5
Antica Trattoria
  Paccagnella, 10
L'Azdora, 7
Lunanuova, 8
Patagonia Ice Cream, 3
Pizzeria Al Borgo, 13
Trattoria Pizzeria
  Marechiaro, 4

■ NIGHTLIFE
Fly, 9
Highlander Scottish Pub, 6

Public Transportation: ACAP (☎049 82 41 111), at the train station, runs buses. To reach downtown, take buses #8, 12, or 18 M-F and #8 and 32 Sa-Su. 1hr. pass €1. Ticket office open daily 6am-midnight.

Taxis: RadioTaxi (☎049 65 13 33). Available 24hr.

Car Rental: Europcar, P. Stazione, 6 (☎049 65 78 77), across parking lot from train station. 19+. Open M-F 8:30am-12:30pm and 3-7pm, Sa 8:30am-12:30pm. AmEx/ MC/V. **Maggiore National,** P. Stazione, 15 (☎049 87 58 605; fax 049 875 62 23), after exiting train station, turn right. Open M-F 8:30am-12:30pm and 2:30-6:30pm, Sa 9am-noon. MC/V.

Bike and Scooter Rental (☎0348 70 16 374), to the left of the train station as you walk out. Bikes €1 per hr., €6 per day. Scooters €6 per hr., €25 per day. Open 24hr.

✦ 🔃 ORIENTATION AND PRACTICAL INFORMATION

The **train station** is on the northern edge of town, outside the 16th-century walls. A 10min. walk down **Corso del Popolo**, which becomes **Corso Garibaldi**, leads to the heart of town and main area of the **Università degli Studi di Padova.**

Tourist Office: In the train station (☎049 87 52 077). Open M-Sa 9am-7pm, Su 8:30am-12:30pm. **Main office,** Vlo. Cappellato Pedrocchi, 7 (☎049 87 67 927; infopedrocchi@turismopadova.it), to the right of Caffè Pedrocchi, off P. Cavour. Open M-Sa 9am-1:30pm and 3-7pm. **Branch** in P. del Santo, across from the basilica (☎049 87 53 087). Open Apr.-Oc.t M-F 9am-1:30pm and 3-6pm, Sa 9am-noon and 3-6pm.)

Budget Travel: CTS, Riviera Mugnai, 22 (☎049 87 61 639). Sells ISICs and train tickets. Open M-F and Su 8:30-11:30am and 3-6:30pm. Cash only.

Luggage Storage: At the train station. €3.87 per bag per day. Open daily 6am-10:30pm. Cash only.

English-Language Bookstore: Feltrinelli International, V. S. Francesco, 14 (☎049 87 50 792; padova.international@lafeltrinelli.it). From the train station, turn left off V. Cavour. Wide selection of foreign magazines, novels, and travel guides. Open M-Sa June-Aug. 9am-1pm and 3-8pm; Sept.-May 9am-1pm and 3:30-7:30pm. AmEx/MC/V.

Laundromat: Fastclean, V. Ognissanti, 6 (☎049 22 67 882) off V. del Portello. Take bus #9. Wash €3.70. Open daily 8am-10pm.

Emergency: ☎113. **Ambulance:** ☎118. **Carabinieri** (☎112 or 049 04 88 521) on Prato della Valle.

Hospital: Ospedale Civile, V. Giustiniani, 1 (☎049 82 11 111), off V. Ospedale.

Internet Access: Tempo Reale, V. Petrarca, 9 (☎049 65 84 84), across the bridge from the intersection of V. Dante and V. S. Fermo. Internet €6 for 1st hr., €3 each additional hr. €2 initial membership. Students always €3. Open M-Th 10am-midnight, F 10am-9pm, Sa-Su 4pm-8pm. Cash only.

Post Office: C. Garibaldi, 25 (☎049 87 72 221). Open M-F 8:30am-2pm, Sa 8:30am-1pm. AmEx/MC/V for financial services only. **Postal Code:** 35100.

🔃 ACCOMMODATIONS

Padua's size and major attractions mean high hotel prices, though some relatively inexpensive options can be found in good locations.

Locanda la Perla, V. Cesarotti, 67 (☎049 87 58 939) near the Prato della Valle. From the *centro,* take V. S. Francesco to the end and turn right. Friendly Paolo rents 8 clean, bright rooms with stone floors and phone. 5min. walk from the Basilica di Sant'Antonio. Shared bath. Closed Aug. Singles €30-32; doubles €40-42. Cash only. ❸

Ostello Città di Padova (HI), V. Aleardi, 30 (☎049 87 52 219; pdyhtl@tin.it), a 25min walk from the train station near Prato della Valle. Hostel with TV room and location 10min. from centro. Laundry €5.50. Internet €5.16 per hr. Breakfast, shower, and sheets included. Wheelchair accessible. Reception 7-9:30am and 3:30-11pm. Lockout 9:30am-3:30pm. Curfew midnight. Call ahead. 8-bed dorms €15, 5-bed dorms €16; 4-person family rooms €60. Non-HI members add €3. MC/V. ❶

Hotel Al Santo, V. del Santo, 147 (☎049 87 52 131; fax 049 87 88 076), near the basilica. Stone artwork graces the lobby of this hotel. Spacious rooms with wood floors, floral bedspreads, and new bathrooms. Some rooms have impressive views. All have TV and A/C. Restaurant downstairs. Breakfast included. Lunch or dinner *menù* €15.50. Reception 24hr. Singles €55-60; doubles €80-100; triples €130. AmEx/MC/V. ❹

Hotel Sant'Antonio, V. S. Fermo, 118 (☎049 87 51 393; www.hotelsantantonio.it). Pleasant rooms with wooden furniture and green decor overlook the river. Rooms have TV, A/C, and phone. Breakfast €7. Single without bath €40, with bath €60-62; doubles €78-82; triples €100-105; quads €120-124. MC/V. ❸

Hotel Corso, C. del Popolo, 2 (☎049 87 50 822; htlcrs@virgilio.it), at the intersection of C. del Popolo and V. Trieste. Small carpeted rooms with high ceilings; all have bath, phone, A/C, TV, and views of the heavy traffic outside. Buffet breakfast included. Reception 24hr. Singles €78-85; doubles €103-124. AmEx/MC/V. ❺

Sporting Center, V. Roma, 123/125 (☎049 79 34 00; www.sportingcenter.it), 15km from Padua; take train to Montegrotto. Campgrounds with tennis and beach volleyball. Restaurant discounts for guests. Electric connection and hot showers included; day pass for pool €5. Open Mar. 5-Nov. 15. €5.50-7.50 per person, €7.50-10.20 per car with tent. Cash only. ❶

🍴 FOOD

Morning **markets** are held in P. delle Erbe and P. della Frutta from 8am to 2pm; sidewalk vendors also sell fresh produce, meats, and cheeses. A **PAM** supermarket is downtown in P. Cavour. (Open M-Tu and Th-Sa 8am-8pm, W 8am-2pm. Cash only.) For an inexpensive taste of the gourmet, visit **Franchin,** V. del Santo, 95, which sells fresh meats, cheeses, breads, and wine. (☎049 87 50 532. Open M-Tu and Th-Su 8:30am-1:30pm and 5-8pm, W 8:30am-1:30pm. MC/V.) Wine-lovers should sample a glass from the nearby Colli Euganei wine district. Visitors to the Basilica di Sant'Antonio can nibble on *dolci del santo* (saint's sweets), a flaky, powdered cake with creamy nut and fig filling, in nearby *pasticcerie*.

Patagonia Ice Cream, P. dei Signori, 27 (☎049 87 51 045), on the side closest to V. Dante. Artfully carved fruits adorn the heaping piles of *gelato* and crispy waffle cones. 1 scoop €1. 2 scoops €1.80. Open M-Sa 11am-midnight, Su 11am-1pm and 3pm-midnight. Cash only. ❶

Lunanuova, V. G. Barbarigo, 12 (☎049 87 58 907), heading off P. Duomo. Ring bell at stained glass doors for entrance. Mix-and-match vegetarian and Middle Eastern dishes in the dining room or within the ivy-covered brick walls of the lamp-lit garden. Individual plates €4.30, 2 for €8.30, 3 for €9.30, 5 for €10.30. Open Tu-Sa 12:30-2:15pm and 7:30pm-midnight. Cash or traveler's checks only. ❷

Antica Trattoria Paccagnella, V. del Santo, 113 (☎/fax 049 87 50 549). The place to go for authentic Paduan cuisine, diners can enjoy regional favorites like *ventaglio di petto d'anatra all ciliegie e rosso dei colli* (breast of duck in red wine and cherry sauce; €14.00) in a dark and quiet atmosphere. *Primi* €6-9.50, *secondi* €4.50-17. Cover €2. Open daily noon-2:30pm and 7-10pm. AmEx/MC/V. ❷

Alexander Birreria Paninoteca, V. S. Francesco, 38 (☎049 65 28 84). From the basilica, take V. del Santo to V. S. Francesco and turn left. Wide range of sandwiches €3-4 served to a student crowd on narrow benched seating. 20% student discount for lunch, 10% for dinner during school year. Open daily 10am-2am. ❶

Trattoria Pizzeria Marechiario, V. Manin, 37 (☎049 87 58 489). The friendly Mandara brothers draw crowds of locals to their tastefully decorated pizzeria for *marechiaro* (pizza packed with seafood and oregano; €6.20) and other specialities. Pizza from €4.20. Pasta from €4.65. Cover €1.55. Open Tu-Su noon-2:30pm and 6:30pm-midnight. Closed in Aug. AmEx/MC/V. ❷

L'Azdora, V. del Santo, 7 (☎328 46 61 021), serves piping hot pitas with a variety of fillings to students at the nearby university. Grilled vegetables and mozzarella €3.20. Nutella €2. Half-sized snack portions with 2 ingredients €2, 3 ingredients €2.20. Open in summer M-F 11:30am-3pm and 7-10pm; in winter 11:30am-9pm. Cash only. ❶

Pizzeria Al Borgo, V. Luca Belludi, 56 (☎/fax 049 87 58 857), near the Basilica di S. Antonio, just off P. del Santo, heading toward Prato della Valle. A modern pizzeria with medieval decor. Enjoy the view of the basilica from the outdoor terrace. Pizza €4.30-8.50. Cover €2. Open M and W-Su noon-2:30pm and 7pm-midnight. MC/V. ❷

GIMME TEN. Padua's sights are best visited with the **Padova Card** (€14), which covers entrance to 10 museums: Scrovegni Chapel, Musei Civici Erimitani, Palazzo Zuckerman Musuem, Palazzo della Ragione, Caffè Pedrocchi's Piano Nobile, Oratorio di San Michele, Oratorio di St. Giorgio, Museo Risorgimento, Petrarch's House, and the Baptistry and Botanical Gardens. The card also provides free transport on local buses and discounts from participating merchants. For more information visit the tourist office.

👁 SIGHTS

■**BASILICA DI SANT'ANTONIO (IL SANTO).** An array of rounded gray domes and conic spires cap the facade of Padua's enormous brick basilica. Bronze sculptures by Donatello grace the high altar, which is surrounded by the artist's *Crucifixion* and several Gothic frescoes. Upon entering, look left for the **Tomba di Sant'Antonio,** which sits on a platform under a huge marble arch. Each year, thousands of pilgrims crowd the marble bas-reliefs to cover the black stone of the sepulcher with framed requests, thanks, and prayers. Behind the main altar in the apse sits the **Cappella delle Reliquie,** where shrines contain everything from Saint Anthony's tunic to his jawbone and tongue. A **multimedia show** in the courtyard (follow "Mostra" signs) details St. Anthony's life. Exit the basilica and turn right to reach the tiny **Oratorio di San Giorgio,** which displays vivid Giotto-school frescoes, and the **Scuola del Santo,** which includes three frescoes by the young Titian. *(P. del Santo. ☎049 82 42 811. Basilica open daily Apr.-Sept. 6:30am-7:45pm; Nov.-Mar. 6:30am-6:45pm. Modest dress strictly enforced. Free. Mostra open daily 9am-12:30pm and 2:30-6pm. English audioguide available at front desk; free. Oratorio and Scuola ☎/fax 049 87 55 235; www.arciconfraternitassanantonio.org. Open daily Apr.-Sept. 9am-12:30pm and 2:30-7pm; Oct.-Mar. 9am-12:30pm and 2:30-5pm. Wheelchair accessible. €2, students €1.50. Cash only.)*

■**CAPPELLA DEGLI SCROVEGNI (ARENA CHAPEL).** Enrico Scrovegni dedicated this tall brick chapel to the Virgin Mary in an attempt to save the soul of his father Reginald, a usurer famously lambasted in the 17th *canto* of Dante's *Inferno.* Pisano carved the statues for the chapel, and Giotto covered the walls with frescoed scenes from the lives of Jesus, Mary, and her parents, Sts. Joachim and Anne. Completed between 1305 and 1306, this 38-panel cycle is one of the first examples of depth and realism in Italian Renaissance painting. Above the door, the Last Judgment depicts the halo-wearing blessed to the left of the cross; to the right, a less-fortunate crowd of the damned are eaten by hairy blue demons. Scrovegni sits in the middle, offering his tiny pink chapel to the Virgin Mary. Along the bottom, allegorical figures depicting the seven deadly sins face their opposites across the nave—the four cardinal and theological virtues. Down a short gravel path, the **Musei Civici Erimitani** has assembled an art collection including ancient Roman inscriptions and a beautiful crucifix by Giotto that once adorned the Scrovegni Chapel. *(P. Eremitani, 8. ☎049 20 10 020; www.cappelladegliscrovegni.it. Entrance to the chapel only through the museum. Open M-F 9am-7pm, Sa 9am-6pm. Tickets may be purchased at the Musei Civici ticket office or online. Reserve ahead. Museum €10; combination ticket €12, students €5, disabled €1. AmEx/MC/V.)*

PALAZZO BÒ AND ENVIRONS. The university campus is spread throughout the city, but centers around the two bustling interior stone courtyards of Palazzo Bò, adorned with students' coats of arms, a war memorial, and marble accents. The **Teatro Anatomico** (1594), a medical lecture hall that was the first of its kind in Europe, hosted medical pioneers like Vesalius and Englishman William Harvey. Nearly all Venetian noblemen received their mandatory law and public policy instruction in the **Great Hall**. The chair of Galileo is preserved in the **Sala dei Quaranta**, where the great physicist once lectured. Across the street, ■**Caffè Pedrocchi**, founded in 1772, once served as the headquarters for 19th-century liberals who supported Risorgimento leader Giuseppe Mazzini. A turning point in the revolution occurred here in 1848, when a battle exploded between students and Austrian police. The **Museo Risorgimento e dell'Eta Contemporanea** displays relics focusing on the human aspects of war, from propaganda posters to a powerful, shakily written note from WWII. *(Palazzo Bò, in P. delle Erbe. ☎049 82 73 047; www.unipd.it. Guided tours M, W, and F 3:15, 4:15, 5:15pm; Tu, Th, and Sa 9:15, 10:15, 11:15am. 45min. tours €3, students €1.50. Buy tickets 15min. before tour. Caffè Pedrocchi, V. VIII Febbraio, 15. ☎049 878 12 31; www.caffepedrocchi.it. Open daily from the end of June to mid-Sept. 9am-1am; mid-Sept. to June 9am-9pm. AmEx/MC/V. Piano Nobile ☎049 87 81 231. Open Tu-Su 9:30am-12:30pm and 3:30-6pm. €4, students €2.50. Cash only.)*

PALAZZO DELLA RAGIONE (LAW COURTS). Astrological signs adorn the walls of this *palazzo*, whose vast interior now houses modern art exhibitions under a barrel vault roof. The original ceiling, once painted as a starry sky, survived a 1420 fire only to topple in a 1756 tornado. With typical Italian efficiency, workers are still repairing the damage. To the right of the entrance is the **Stone of Shame.** Inspired by the exhortations of St. Anthony in 1231 to abolish debtors' prisons, Padua adopted the practice of forcing half-clothed debtors onto the stone before at least 100 hecklers. *(Enter through city hall on V. Febbraio, 8. ☎049 82 05 006. Open M-W and F-Su 9am-7pm, Th 9am-11pm. €8, students and Padova Card holders €5.)*

PRATO DELLA VALLE. Originally a Roman theater, this ellipse is one of Europe's largest squares. On the paved outermost track, joggers and bikers orbit the dog walkers, teenagers, and families who cross the moat to find small green fields, pebbly paths, and a large fountain dotted with 78 statues of famous Paduan men.

DUOMO. Michelangelo supposedly participated in the design of this hulking church, erected between the 16th and 18th centuries. The *duomo's* simplicity makes the steps of the apse especially unusual—chunky, half-carved marble interpretations of Sts. Prosdocimo, Gregorio, and Giustina accompany a golden, praying figure whose flowing hair melds with a marble tree to create the church's lectern. Next door, the colorful 12th-century **Battistero** is dedicated to St. John the Baptist. The interior walls are covered in vivid frescoes of New Testament scenes, while a massive wide-eyed Christ and rings of painted saints look down from the hollow dome above. *(P. Duomo. Duomo ☎049 66 28 14, Battistero 049 65 69 14. Duomo open M-Sa 7:30am-noon and 3:45-7:45pm, Su 7:45am-1pm and 3:45-8:30pm. Free. Battistero open daily 10am-6pm. €2.50, students €1.50. Cash only.)*

ORTO BOTANICO. Leafy trees and high stone walls ring a circular grid of iron fences, gravel walkways, and low fountains in the oldest university botanical garden in Europe. Palm trees welcome guests to a quiet oasis of water lilies, cacti, medicinal herbs, and one palm tree planted in 1585 in the heart of this congested city. *(V. Orto Botanico, 15. Follow signs from basilica. ☎049 82 72 119. Open Apr.-Oct. daily 9am-1pm and 3-6pm; Nov.-Mar. M-F 9am-1pm. €4, 65 and over €3, students €1. Cash only.)*

♪ ENTERTAINMENT

Restaurant terraces begin to fill around 9pm. The **Highlander Scottish Pub,** V. S. Martino e Solferino, 69, greets customers with a ceiling beam that reads "There's a guid time com'in"—and with lively patrons filling this cavernous two-story pub, they're usually right. (☎049 65 99 77. Pints from €4.50. Open daily 11am-3pm and 6pm-2am. AmEx/MC/V.) **Fly,** Galleria Tito Livio, 4/6, is a pedestrian cafe by day, and a swinging hotspot by night. The nearby V. Roma and bustling student population make this bar a great choice anytime. (☎049 87 52 892. Wine €2-3.50. Open M-Sa 9am-midnight. MC/V.) Nightlife rages in Padua, but a listing of clubs is nearly impossible to find. Try asking about specific *discoteche* like **Limbo, Extra Extra,** and **Banale.** Pilgrims pack the city on June 13, as Padua commemorates the death of its patron St. Anthony with a procession bearing the saint's statue and jawbone. An **antique market** assembles in the Prato della Valle on the 3rd Sunday of the month. Every Saturday the area holds an **outdoor market** selling food and clothing.

VICENZA   ☎0444

Bustling Vicenza (pop. 106,000) has one of the highest average incomes in Italy and is orbited by dozens of stately villas, the present-day legacies of a 15th-century real estate boom in which nobles moved from Venice to the mainland. Though tiny side alleys conceal some affordable accommodations, Vicenza is overwhelmingly grandiose, characterized by its glamorous inhabitants and works of art.

▐ TRANSPORTATION

The **train station** is at P. Stazione, at the end of V. Roma, across from Campo Marzo. (Info office open daily 8:30am-7:30pm. Ticket office open daily 6am-8:30pm. AmEx/MC/V.) **Trains** run to: Milan (2½hr., 29 per day 6:13am-10:02pm, €8.99); Padua (30min., 56 per day 6:28am-11:19pm, €2.50); Venice (1¼hr., 46 per day 7:36am-11:49pm, €3.85); Verona (40min., 51 per day 5:20am-11:47pm, €3.40). **FTV,** Vle. Milano, 7 (☎0444 22 31 15), left after exiting the train station, runs **buses** to Montagnana (1¼hr., 5 per day 7am-5:30pm, €3.60) and Padua (30min., 30 per day 5:50am-8:20pm, €3.20). (Reduced service Sa-Su. Info office open M-Th 7:30am-noon and 1-5pm, F 7:30am-12:30pm. Ticket office open daily M-F 6am-7:40pm, Sa-Su 6:15am-7:40pm. Cash only.) **RadioTaxi** (☎0444 92 06 00) is available 24hr. at either end of C. Palladio. **Maggiore,** at the train station, rents **cars.** (☎0444 54 59 62. Open M-F 8:30am-12:30pm and 3-6:30pm, Sa 8:30am-noon. €50 per day and up. AmEx/MC/V.) **Hertz** is across the hall. (☎199 11 33 11 or 199 11 22 11 for reservations. Open M-F 8:30am-12:30pm and 2:30-6:30pm, Sa 8:30am-noon. MC/V.)

◢▐ ORIENTATION AND PRACTICAL INFORMATION

The train station and adjacent intercity bus station occupy the southern part of the city. **Viale Roma** leads from the station into town. At the **Giardino Salvi,** turn right under the Roman archway on **Corso Palladio.** Walk straight several blocks to the old Roman wall that serves as a gate to the **Teatro Olimpico.** The tourist office is the door just to the right. **Piazza Matteotti** lies in front, at the end of C. Palladio.

Tourist Office: P. Matteotti, 12 (☎0444 32 08 54; www.vicenzae.org). Free city **map** and map of villa locations. **Branch** at P. dei Signori, 8 (☎0444 54 41 22; iatvicenza2@provincia.vicenza.it). Both open daily 9am-1pm and 2-6pm.

Budget Travel: AVIT, Vle. Roma, 17 (☎0444 54 56 77; www.avit.it), before PAM supermarket. Open M-F 9am-12:30pm and 3-7pm, Sa 9:30am-12:30pm. AmEx/MC/V for plane tickets only.

Currency Exchange: At train station and post office (see below). **ATMs** in the train station, on Contrà del Monte, and throughout the downtown area.

Luggage Storage: ☎0444 32 08 28. In train station. €3.87 per 24hr. Deposit and pick-up 9am-noon and pick-up 3-7pm. Cash only.

Laundromat: Euro Lavanderie, Contra Porta Padova, 27, over the river behind the Teatro Olimpico. Wash €3.50, dry €2 per 15min. Open daily 7:30am-10:30pm. Cash only.

Emergency: ☎113. **Ambulance:** ☎118.

Pharmacy: Farmacia Dott. Doria, P. dei Signori, 49 (☎0444 32 12 41). Open June-Aug. M-F 8:45am-12:30pm and 4-7:30pm, Sa 8:45am-12:30pm; Sept.-May M-F 8:45am-12:30pm and 3:30-7pm, Sa 8:45am-12:30pm. Closed 2-weeks in Aug. After-hours rotation posted outside. MC/V.

Internet Access: Galla 2000, at V. Roma, 14 (0444 22 52 25). Open Tu-Th and Sa 9am-12:30pm and 3:30-7:30pm, F 9am-12:30pm and 3:30-11pm. €1.50 per 30min., €2.50 per hr. AmEx/MC/V. Or try **Matrix,** P. Signori, 11. Open M-Tu and Th-Sa 10am-11pm, W and Su 2-11pm. €2.50 per 30min., €4 per hr. Cash only.

Post Office: Contrà Garibaldi, 1 (☎0444 33 20 77), between *duomo* and P. Signori. Open daily 8:30am-6:30pm. **Currency exchange** until 6pm. Cash only. **Postal Code:** 36100.

ACCOMMODATIONS AND CAMPING

Accommodations in Vicenza are conveniently located right in the heart of town, but are fairly pricey with the notable exception of the hostel.

Ostello Olimpico Vicenza (HI), V. Giuriolo, 9 (☎0444 54 02 22; fax 0444 54 77 62). From the tourist office, walk up the street with Museo Civico on your right. The *ostello* is the bright yellow building on the left. 84 beds in tiny dorm rooms are within sight of the Teatro Olimpico. Lockers included. Wheelchair accessible. Reception 7:30-9:30am and 3:30-11:30pm. Dorm beds €15.50; singles €19; doubles €34, with bathroom €38. Nonmembers add €3. MC/V. ❶

Hotel Giardini, V. Giuriolo, 10 (☎/fax 0444 32 64 58; info@hotelgiardini.com), across the street from Ostello Olimpico Vicenza. Colorful, modern hotel with 18 spotlessly clean rooms and large beds. Amenities include satellite TV, A/C, bath, minibar, and key-card access. Breakfast included. Reception 7am-1am. Singles €83; doubles €114; triples €119. AmEx/MC/V. ❺

Hotel Vicenza, Str. dei Nodari, 5 (☎/fax 0444 32 15 12), off the corner of P. Signori across from the basilica. Quiet hallways, rustic stone mosaic floors and large bathrooms complement this aging hotel right off the P. dei Signori. Reception 24hr. Singles €45; doubles €60. Prices vary seasonally. Cash only. ❹

Campeggio Vicenza, Str. Pelosa, 239 (☎0444 58 23 11; www.ascom.vi.it/camping). Take bus #1 (€1) from the train station and ask for camping. TV, bar, and mini-golf. Showers included. Laundry €6. Open Mar.-Sept. €5.50-7.35 per person, €8.50-11.50 per tent with car. AmEx/MC/V. ❶

FOOD

Vicenza's specialties include dried salted cod with polenta, asparagus with eggs, and *torresani* (pigeon). A daily **produce market** opens in P. delle Erbe behind the basilica. A large **market** in P. Erbe, P. Signori, and V. Roma sells cheese, fish, produce, and clothing (open Th 7:30am-1pm), while a smaller market is also available in P. dei Signori on Tuesdays (7:30am-1pm). Buy essentials at **PAM** supermarket at V. Roma, 1. (Open M-Tu and Th-Sa 8am-8pm, W 8am-1pm. AmEx/MC/V.)

Righetti, P. del Duomo, 3 (☎ 0444 54 31 35), with another entrance at Contrà Fontana, 6. A cool traditional interior and *piazza*-side seating suggests high prices, but this self-service *trattoria* is all budget. *Primi* from €3.10, *secondi* from €4.65. Cover €0.30. Open M-F noon-3pm and 6:30pm-1am; closed 1st 3 weeks of Aug. Cash only. ❶

Pizza al Ponte, V. degli Angeli, 5 (0444 32 56 70) behind the Teatro Olimpico, serves local youths thin slices piled high for €2 each. The *pizza patate* has chunks of potato and salami—practically a meal in itself. Open daily 10am-midnight. AmEx/MC/V. ❶

Zì' Teresa, Contrà S. Antonio, 1 (☎ 0444 32 14 11), at the end of the street just left of the post office. Marble arches lead to this relaxing *trattoria,* where pizza like the *zi teresa* (with mushrooms and grilled peppers; €7) or the more expensive tasting *menù* (3 courses; €25) are served in a garden oasis. Cover €1.50 for pizza and €2 for restaurant. Open M-Tu and Th-Su 11:30am-3:30pm and 6:30pm-midnight. AmEx/MC/V. ❹

Soraru Virgilio, Pta. Palladio, 17 (☎ 0444 32 09 15), past the statue of Palladia to the right of the basilica. Mirrored shelves of bottled liqueurs and jars of candy are tempting, but the real draws are the pastries and creamy *gelato* (like the deliciously smooth *nocciola*) made fresh on site. 2 scoops €1.60. Open M-Tu and Th-Su 8:30am-1pm and 3:30-8pm. Cash only. ❶

Nirvana Caffè Degli Artisti, P. Matteotti, 8 (☎ 0444 54 31 11), from C. Palladio, enter the *piazza* and turn left. Burning incense, beaded lamps, and statues of Buddha belie the cafe crowd of working men and gossiping grandmothers. Warm up with rich cappuccino (€1.40) or cool down with a non-alcoholic signature drink like the creamy Siddhartha (€3.50) at this vegetarian cafe. *Primi* from €4, *secondi* €3.50-7.50. Open M and W 7:30am-8pm, Tu and Th-Sa 7:30am-midnight. ❷

🌐 SIGHTS

The **Piazza dei Signori** was Vicenza's showpiece when the town was under Venetian control. Andrea Palladio's revamping of the **Basilica Palladiana** brought the architect his first taste of fame. In 1546, Palladio's patron, the wealthy Giovan Giorgio Trissino, agreed to fund his proposal to repair the collapsing Palazzo della Ragione, a project that had frustrated some of the best architects of the day. Palladio applied pilasters on the twin *loggie* of the basilica to mask the structure beneath. The **Torre di Piazza,** a brown brick clock tower on the left of the building, reveals a glimpse of the basilica's pre-Palladio architecture. The **Loggia del Capitano,** across from the Torre di Piazza, shows the results of the reconstruction, with two stories of marble arches and pillars masking the crumbling brick beneath. (☎ 0444 32 36 81. Basilica open during exhibitions Tu-Sa 9am-1pm and 3-7pm, when no exhibition Tu-Su 10am-7pm. Entrance to basilica during exhibitions €7, reduced without exhibition €5.) The ▪️**Teatro Olimpico,** in P. Matteotti, is the last structure planned by Palladio; he died before its completion. A garden of sculptures leads to the ticket office and portrait gallery. Inside the Teatro, carved figures fill the walls under a fresco of cloudy sky overhead and wooden seats look on a resplendent Neo-Classical stage. Three main doors on stage and two side doors reveal the main streets of Thebes, crafted in perspective with excruciating attention to detail for the theater's first performance of *Oedipus Rex.* (☎ 0444 22 28 00; www.olimpico.vicenza.it. Open Tu-Su 9am-5pm; last admission 4:45pm. €8, students €5, includes entrance to Museo Civico. Audioguides in English; €3. Cash only.) Each summer the city showcases local and imported talent in the Teatro Olimpico; check www.comune.vicenza.it for a list of productions. (☎ 0444 22 28 01. MC/V.) Housed in Palladio's stately **Palazzo Chiericati,** the **Museo Civico's** collection includes Giovanni Battista's first signed and dated work, *The Madonna of the Pergola,* as well as Montagna's *Madonna Enthroned* and Tintoretto's *Miracle of St. Augustine.* (Across from tourist office. ☎ 0444 32 13

48. Open Tu-Su 9am-5pm; last admission 4:45pm. Descriptions of major works in English. Purchase tickets at the Teatro Olimpico; entrance included with ticket for theater.) For a view of Vicenza's rooftops and many of Palladio's works, exit the train station and turn right on Vle. Venezia for about 10min., then turn left and go uphill at V. X Giugno. A long *loggia* to the left contains a staircase and ramp leading up **Monte Berico** to the plateau of **Piazzale Vittoria**, where a railing and two balconies jut out over the hillside and provide a view of the city.

⚫ DAYTRIP FROM VICENZA: PALLADIAN VILLAS

Venetian expansion to the mainland began in the 15th century as Venice's maritime supremacy faded and nobles turned their attention to the acquisition of real estate on the mainland. The Venetian senate decreed that nobles build villas rather than castles to preclude the possibility of fiefdoms. The rush to build these residential estates provided scores of opportunities for Palladio to display his talents. The Veneto now contains hundreds of the most splendid villas in Europe. Some offer classical music concerts during summer; others can be rented for exorbitant rates—Neo-Classical luxury doesn't come cheap. Check with local and regional tourist offices for details and contact info for regional villas. Many of the Palladian villas scattered throughout the Veneto are difficult to reach, but fortunately, some of the most famous lie within a scenic 30min. walk of Vicenza. One of the most harmonious architectural achievements of the 16th century is the ◼**Villa Rotonda**. Begun in 1550, its precision and alignment with the cardinal points produced a majestic configuration. It became a model for buildings in France, England, and the US, most notably Thomas Jefferson's Monticello. *(From Mt. Berico's P. Vittoria, head straight, keeping the mountains on the right. Bear left and continue down Stradella Valmarana. Or from Vle. Roma, take bus #8 (€1). ☎0444 32 17 93. Open Mar. 15-Oct. 15. Interior open W 10am-noon and 3-6pm, €10. Exterior grounds open Tu-Su 10am-noon and 3-6pm, €5.)*

THE REAL DEAL. The Palladian Villas are undoubtedly beautiful, both inside and out, but the price to go inside is bound to take your breath away. On Wednesdays, there is a €10 ticket available, which grants access to the villa interior. However, on every other day of the week, there is an additional €5 ticket for the exterior alone, and many will find that a laidback stroll around the grounds is sufficient to invoke Palladio's vision. *—Morgan Kruger*

VERONA   ☎045

Verdant gardens and breathtakingly realistic sculptures fill Verona (pop. 243,474) with enough artistic majesty and tragedy to overwhelm any hopeless romantics who haplessly wander into its walls. From dank tombs to dizzying towers, Verona offers all the perks of a large city with a healthy supply of rich wines, authentic local cuisine, and an internationally renowned opera with low student prices. The city's monuments and natural splendor inspired Shakespeare to use it as the setting of his *Romeo and Juliet;* travelers who arrive in search of a tangible remnant of this tragic romance will only find a balcony, and nary a Montague or monk.

▮ TRANSPORTATION

Flights: Aeroporto Valerio Catullo (☎045 80 95 666; www.aeroportoverona.it), 12km from city center. For shuttles from train station (5:40am, then every 20min. 6:10am-11:10pm; €4.50), buy tickets on bus. Cash only.

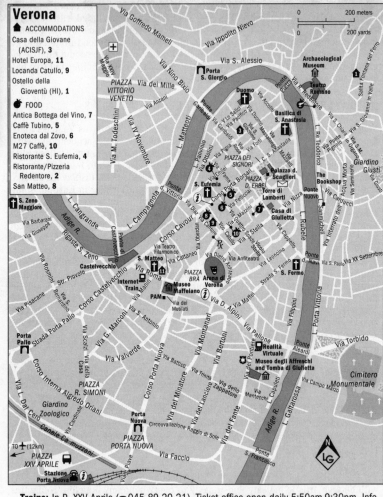

Verona

🏠 **ACCOMMODATIONS**

Casa della Giovane
  (ACISJF), **3**
Hotel Europa, **11**
Locanda Catullo, **9**
Ostello della
  Gioventù (HI), **1**

🍎 **FOOD**

Antica Bottega del Vino, **7**
Caffè Tubino, **5**
Enoteca dal Zovo, **6**
M27 Caffè, **10**
Ristorante S. Eufemia, **4**
Ristorante/Pizzeria
  Redentore, **2**
San Matteo, **8**

Trains: In P. XXV Aprile (☎045 89 20 21). Ticket office open daily 5:50am-9:30pm. Info office open daily 7am-9pm. **Luggage storage** available (see **Practical Information**). To: **Bologna** (2hr., 27 per day 3:48am-11:01pm, €5.73); **Milan** (2hr., 37 per day 5:34am-10:42pm, €6.82); **Rome** (7hr., 8 per day 5:35am-11:01pm, €32.95); **Trent** (1hr., 25 per day 12:46am-10:48pm, €4.65); **Venice** (1½hr., 41 per day 5:52am-10:14pm, €6.10); **Vicenza** (45min., 48 per day 5:52am-10:42pm, €3.40).

Buses: APTV in P. XXV Aprile, in the gray building in front of the train station. Station open M-Sa 6am-8pm, Su 6:30am-8pm. To: **Brescia** (2hr., every hr. 6:40am-6:10pm, €5.30); **Montagnana** (2hr., 3 per day 6:20am-6:10pm, €4.20); **Riva del Garda** (2hr., 17 per day 6:40am-6:45pm, €5.20); **Sirmione** (1hr., 17 per day 6:40am-8pm, €2.80). Reduced service Sa-Su.

Taxis: RadioTaxi (☎045 53 26 66). Available 24hr.

Car Rental: Avis (☎045 80 06 636), **Europcar** (☎045 59 27 59), **Hertz** (☎045 80 00 832), and **Maggiore** (☎045 80 04 808) at the train station. From €54 per day. All 21+. Discount for extended rentals. Hertz and Maggiore open M-F 8am-noon and 2:30-7pm, Sa 8am-noon; Avis open M-F 8am-noon and 3-7pm, Sa-Su 8am-noon; Europcar open M-F 8:30am-noon and 2:30-7pm, Sa 8:30am-noon. AmEx/MC/V.

◢■▊ ORIENTATION AND PRACTICAL INFORMATION

From the **train station** in P. XXV Aprile, walk 20min. up **Corso Porta Nuova**, or take bus #11, 12, 13, 51, 72, or 73 (weekends take #91, 92, or 93; tickets €1, full-day €3.50) to Verona's center, the **Arena di Verona**, in **Piazza Brà**. Most sights lie between P. Brà and the **Fiume Adige**. **Via Mazzini** connects the Arena to the monuments of **Piazza delle Erbe** and **Piazza dei Signori**. The **Teatro Romano** and the **Giardino Giusti** lie across the bridges **Pietra, Navi,** and **Nuovo** on the Adige.

Tourist Office: At V. D. Alpini, 9 (☎045 80 68 680; iatverona@provincia.vr.it). From C. Pta. Nuova, enter P. Brà and stay left until you reach the office. Open M-Sa 9am-7pm, Su 9am-3pm. **Branches:** airport (☎/fax 045 86 19 163; iataeroporto@provincia.vr.it; open M-Sa 9am-6pm); train station (☎/fax 045 80 08 61; iatfs@provincia.vr.it; open M-Sa 9am-6pm, Su 9am-3pm).

HelpHandicap (☎045 59 62 49) provides information for those looking for hotels, sights, and transportation with disability assistance.

Luggage Storage: (☎045 80 23 827; info@grandistazioni.it), at the train station. €3.80 for 1st 5hr., €0.60 per hr. 6-11hr., and €0.20 12hr.+ 5-day max. 20kg limit for each piece of luggage. Open 7am-11pm. Cash only.

Lost and Found: V. Campo Marzo, 9 (☎045 80 79 341).

English-Language Bookstore: The Book Shop, V. Interrato dell'Acqua Morta, 3/A (☎045 80 07 614), near Ponte Navi. Classic works and small French and German sections. Open M 3:30-7:30pm, Tu-F and Su 9:30am-12:30pm and 3:30-7:30pm. Cash only.

Work Opportunity: Youth Info Center (Informagiovani), C. Porto Borsari, 17 (☎045 80 10 796; www.informagiovani.comune.verona.it), helps find work or study opportunities in Verona. See **Beyond Tourism** (p. 81). Open M, W, F 9am-1pm, Tu and Th 3-5pm.

Emergency: ☎113. **Ambulance:** ☎118. **Police,** V. del Pontiere, 32 (☎045 80 90 488).

Pharmacy: Farmacia Due Campane, V. Mazzini, 52 (☎045 80 06 660). Open M-F 9:10am-12:30pm and 3:30-7:30pm, Sa 9:10am-12:30pm. Check the *L'Arena* newspaper for 24hr. pharmacy listings. MC/V.

Hospital: Ospedale Civile Maggiore (☎045 80 71 111), on Borgo Trento in P. Stefani in the north part of town.

Internet Access: Internet Train, V. Roma, 17/A (☎045 80 13 394). From P. Brà, turn right on V. Roma. 2 blocks ahead on left. €2.50 for 30min. 1st-time users get a bonus hr. after paying €5 for 1st hr. Modern, high-speed computers. Open M-F 11am-10pm, Sa-Su 2-8pm. Free for cardholders M-F 9-9:30pm. Card accepted at Bar Roma across the street. MC/V. **Realtà Virtuale,** V. del Pontiere, 3/C (☎045 59 76 57; fax 045 59 31 33). From P. Brà, walk for about 5min. along the wall near the tourist office as it curves and turn right on V. Pontiere. €4 per hr. Open M-F 9am-1pm and 3-7pm, Sa 9am-noon. V.

Post Office: P. Viviani, 7 (☎045 80 59 311). Follow V. Cairoli from P. delle Erbe, the post office appears across a small parking lot on the right. Open M-F 8:30am-6:30pm and Sa 8:30am-1pm. Cash only. **Branch** office, V. C. Cattaneo, 23 (☎045 80 59 911). Open M-Sa 8:30am-6:30pm. **Postal Code:** 37100.

ACCOMMODATIONS

Budget hotels are sparse in Verona, and those that do exist fill quickly. Make reservations ahead of time, especially during the opera season (June-Sept.). Prices are significantly lower in the low season.

Ostello della Gioventù Villa Francescatti (HI), Salita Fontana del Ferro, 15 (☎045 59 03 60; fax 045 80 09 127). Take bus #73 or night bus #90 to P. Isolo. By foot from the Arena, turn on V. Anfiteatro and walk for 10min. until crossing Ponte Nuovo on V. Carducci. Turn left and follow V. Giusti, then turn right on Vco. Borgo Tascherio and follow yellow signs up the hill. Frescoed walls and gorgeous gardens make for a great atmosphere, though the lengthy lockout period is a downside. HI members only. Dinner €8. Laundry €2.50 wash or dry. Internet €5.16 per hr. Check-in 5pm. Lockout 9am-5pm. Curfew 11:30pm, opera-goers allowed back until 1:30am. Lights out at midnight. 5-night max. Reservations accepted for family rooms. Dorms €13.50; family rooms €15 per person. Cash only. ❶

Locanda Catullo, Vco. Catullo, 1 (☎045 800 27 86, fax 59 69 87). At V. Mazzini, 40, turn on V. Catullo, then turn left on Vco. Catullo. Reception on the 2nd fl. Right near the *centro*, an elegant hallway leads to simple, spacious rooms. Advance payment required. Reception 9am-11pm. Advance reservations only for stays of 3 or more nights. Singles €40; doubles €55, with bath €65; triples €80/95. Cash only. ❸

Casa della Giovane (ACISJF), V. Pigna, 7 (☎045 59 68 80; info@casadellagiovane.com). From P. delle Erbe, turn right at Palazzo Maffei on C. S. Anastasia and take 1st left on V. Rosa; V. Pigna is 3rd street on the right. A narrow courtyard spills light into bright rooms. Women only. Showers until 10pm. Laundry €1.55 for wash or dry. Internet €5.16 per hr. Lockout 9am-1pm. Curfew 11pm, except for opera-goers (must present a ticket upon return). Reserve ahead by email. Advance payment required. Dorms €13; singles €18; doubles €28, with bath €34; triples €39/42. Cash only. ❶

Hotel Europa, V. Roma, 8 (☎045 59 47 44; www.veronahoteleuropa.com), minutes from P. Brà. A professional hotel with refreshing colorful decor and within sight of the Piazza Brà. Rooms have bath, A/C, TV, minibar, and phone. Breakfast included. Singles €65, with bath €103; doubles €164; triples €185. Prices fall as much as 25% for winter and extended stays. AmEx/MC/V. ❺

FOOD

Verona is famous for its wines, among them the dry white *Soave* or the red *Valpolicella*, *Bardolino*, *Recioto*, and *Amarone*. For a large selection, try **Enoteca dal Zovo** ❶ (see below), which supplies wine to many local *trattorie*. Local culinary specialties include *gnocchi*, pasta with beans, and asparagus from Rivoli. *Pandoro*, a Christmas cake, is available year-round. **PAM** supermarket, V. dei Mutilati, 3, sells the essentials. From P. Brà, pass through the arch to C. Pta. Nuova and turn right on V. Mutilati. (Open M-Sa 8am-8pm, Su 9am-8pm. AmEx/MC/V.)

Ristorante S. Eufemia, V. Emilei, 21/B (☎045 80 06 865; www.s.eufemia.it). Perfect for a pre-opera romantic meal, this restaurant serves dishes like the homemade *Tagliatelle S. Eufemia* (with mushrooms, asparagus, and tomatoes; €9) in a Roman *palazzo*. *Primi* €6-16, *secondi* €8-16. Cover €2. Open June-Aug. daily noon-2:30pm and 6-10:30pm; Sept.-May M-Sa noon-2:30pm and 7:30-10:30pm. AmEx/MC/V. ❹

Enoteca dal Zovo, Vco. S. Marco in Foro, 7/5 (☎045 80 34 369; www.enotecadalzovo.it), off C. Pta. Borsari. Though the cluttered shelves of bottles make this small winery seem more like an apothecary shop, this *enoteca* occupies a converted chapel with original frescoes still adorning the ceiling. Owners Oreste and Beverly dal Zovo serve impressive wines (from €0.75 a glass), and the potent Elixir of Love (an herbal after-dinner liqueur) while imparting insider knowledge about Verona. Open M-Th 8am-1pm and 2-8:30pm, F-Su 8am-1pm and 2-9pm. Cash only. ❶

Ristorante/Pizzeria Redentore, V. R. Redentore 15, (☎045 80 05 932), right across Ponte Pietra. The food at this neighborhood pizzeria will please your palate, but the view of the city is the real prize. Try dinner at sunset to see the Veronese landscape surrounded by a golden halo. Pizza €4.50-7. *Primi* (with good vegetarian options) €6.50-8.50. Cover €1.30. Open Tu-Su noon-2:30pm and 7-midnight. AmEx/MC/V. ❷

Antica Bottega del Vino, V. Scudo di Francia, 3 (☎045 80 04 535; www.bottegavini.it), off V. Mazzini. Turn left at Banco Nazionale Lavoro; 1st door on the left. Soft light glows through century-old stained glass windows, illuminating specialties like *equine pastissada de caval* (horse meat served with polenta; €16). *Primi* €6.50-12, *secondi* €8-21. Cover €3.70. Open M and W-Su 10:30am-3pm and 6pm-midnight. AmEx/MC/V. ❹

San Matteo, Vco. del Guasto, 4 (☎045 80 04 538; fax 045 59 39 38), from P. Erbe on C. P. Borsari, walk 5min. and turn left. This elegant restaurant is housed in a striking church building right off C. Borsari. Call ahead on Sa night to pre-order *crêpes suzette* prepared by the chef who visits weekly. *Primi* €8.50-11, *secondi* €10-14. Open M-Su noon-2:30pm and 6:30pm-12:30am. AmEx/MC/V. ❹

Caffè Tubino, C. Pta. Borsari, 15/D (☎045 80 31 313), near the intersection of Pta. Borsari and V. Fama. Housed in a 17th-century *palazzo*, this alternative to the average cafe serves up healthy doses of coffee and kitsch with its rich brews and floor-to-ceiling wall of teacups. Seating is scarce, but most come for the popular ground coffee (€15-23 per kg). Espresso €0.85. Cappuccino €1.30. Open daily 7am-9pm. Cash only. ❶

M27 Caffè, V. Mazzini, 27 (☎329 13 41 978; fax 045 80 37 111), just down V. Mazzini from P. Brà. Exhausted power shoppers sip cocktails (€3-5) in this bar with immense white walls and colorful abstract paintings. Stairs lead to a 2nd fl. with Internet access and couches. Open Tu-Su 9am-2am. Cash only. ❶

 SIGHTS

⚡**TIP**

MY VERONA. Looking to save some cash while traveling? The **Verona Card** (day pass €8, 3 days €12) is an excellent money-saving option, covering entry to all museums, churches, and sights, excluding only the Giardino Giusti and the Scavi Scaligeri. Purchase it at any participating museum or church. Churches also offer their own pass, permitting entrance to the basilica, *duomo*, San Fermo, S. Zeno, and S. Lorenzo. (€5, students and seniors €4.)

▨**SHAKESPEAREAN HUBRIS.** Verona's most prized attraction is the **Casa di Giulietta,** where tourists pose on the stone balcony or photographically assault the bronze Juliet below. Lovestruck teens and modern day *amanti* crowd the courtyard, where graffitied professions of undying love cover the walls. The rooms inside the *palazzo* are filled with paintings of the lovers, period dress, and a rather suggestive lone double bed which was used in Franco Zeffirelli's famous 1968 film version of the tragic romance. Contrary to popular belief, the del Cappello (Capulet) family never lived here. *(V. Cappello, 23. ☎045 80 34 303. Open M 1:30-7:30pm, Tu-Su 8:30am-7:30pm. Ticket office closes 6:45pm. €4, students €3. Cash only.)* A canopy shades the walkway into the ▨**Museo Degli Affreschi,** which houses an array of Veronese artwork. In the museum's garden is the **Tomba di Giulietta,** a cave with a single window illuminating the sepulcher. *(V. del Pontiere, 5. ☎045 80 00 361. Open M 1:30-7:30pm, Tu-Su 8:30am-7:30pm. Ticket office closes 6:45pm. €3, students €2.)* The **Casa di Romeo,** reportedly once the home of the *Montecchi*

(Montague) family, sits around the corner from P. dei Signori at V. Arche Scaligeri, 2. The villa is privately owned and closed to the public.

■**PIAZZA DELLA ERBE AND PIAZZA DELLA SIGNORI.** Architecture reminiscent of an earlier era surrounds a market selling fruit and shamelessly self-promotional souvenirs. In the center of the *piazza*, pigeons hop around tiers of the **Madonna Verona's Fountain.** Ironically, fruit vendors' awnings nearly hide the pedestal of the **Berlina**, a platform on which medieval convicts were pelted with produce. The nasty-looking chains still dangle from the platform today. P. delle Erbe lies near **Via Mazzini,** where pink marble leads local *glitterati* to Gucci and Louis Vuitton along the city's pedestrian-friendly fashion row. The **Arco della Costa** (Arch of the Rib) connects P. delle Erbe to **Piazza dei Signori.** A whale rib, prophesied to fall on the first passing person who has never told a lie, still dangles from the arch, and a statue of Dante Alighieri stands in the center of the *piazza*. The della Scala family lived here in the **Palazzo degli Scaligeri.** The 15th-century **Loggia del Consiglio** sits in the *piazza* just behind Dante's back. The view of Verona from the 83m-high ■**Torre dei Lamberti** (1172) is stunning; climb 368 stairs for panoramic views reaching from P. delle Erbe to hillsides miles away, or pay an extra fee to take the elevator and enjoy the same panorama. *(Turn right after Arco della Costa when P. dei Signori begins.* ☎*045 80 32 726. Open M 1:30-7:30pm, Tu-Su 8:30am-7:30pm. Ticket sales end 45min. before closing. Elevator €4, students €3; stairs €3. Cash only.)* Through the arch in P. dei Signori along V. Arche Scaligeri lie the medieval **Tombs of the Scaligeri.**

THE ARENA. A 12th-century earthquake toppled much of the outer wall of this first-century Roman amphitheater, but a lone marble slab still stands tall over 44 remaining seating tiers and interior tunnels. Each summer, the stadium gears up with sets and concession stands to become Verona's **opera house,** where the city stages the famed **Verona Opera Festival.** *(In P. Brà.* ☎*045 80 03 204. Wheelchair accessible. Open M 1:45-6:30pm, Tu-Su 8:30am-6:30pm. Closes 4:30pm on opera nights. Ticket sales end 45min. before closing. €4, students €3, children 7-14 €1 with accompanying adult.)*

BASILICA DI SANT'ANASTASIA. This Gothic church, the largest in Verona, hides artistic treasures behind crumbling brick doors, and side towers capped with weeds. Inside, rose windows illuminate a multicolored marble floor and side altars and chapels. To the left of the main altar, the **Cappella del Rosario** boasts three stories of marble cherubs, Palladian arches, and paintings of Passion scenes by Bernardi and Ridolfi; to the right, the **Cappella Pellegrini** depicts the life of Christ with Michele da Firenze's series of 24 terra-cotta reliefs. *(At the end of C. S. Anastasia. For information, call the Associazione "Chiese Vive" at* ☎*045 59 28 13. Open Mar.-Oct. M-Sa 9am-6pm, Su 1-6pm; Nov.-Feb. Tu-Su 10am-1pm and 1:30-4pm. €2. Cash only.)*

DUOMO AND ENVIRONS. Thermal baths occupied the areas beneath and surrounding the *duomo* during the Roman period; the 12th-century church now rests on the remains of two previous basilicas. The excavated area, called the Church of St. Elena, is accessible through the *duomo*, just left of the apse, and is itself a cooler simpler version of the church above. The *duomo* has been recently restored. Titian's *Assumption of the Virgin* is in the first chapel on the left, which is a less potent version of the his later painting of the same subject that now hangs in Venice. *(At the end of V. Duomo. From the basilica, turn on V. Massalongo, which becomes V. Duomo.* ☎*045 59 28 13. Open Mar.-Oct. M-Sa 10am-5:30pm, Su 1:30-5:30pm; Nov.-Feb. Tu-Sa 10am-1pm and 1:30-4pm, Su 1:30-5pm. €2.50. Cash only.)*

TEATRO ROMANO AND ENVIRONS. A crumbling **Roman theater** comes alive with productions of Shakespeare's works translated into Italian (see **Entertainment,** p. 342). Behind the theater's seats, crumbling Roman stairs weave up a small hillside to the city's **archaeological museum.** Built in 1480, the former Jesuit monastery, the museum was built in 1480 and now displays Roman and Greek artifacts excavated from the area. In the center sits the **Grande Terrazza**, a quiet, leafy garden lined with Roman bas-reliefs and pedestals. *(V. R. Redentore, 2. Cross Ponte Pietra from the city center and turn right.* ☎ *045 80 00 360; fax 045 80 10 587. Open M 1:15-7:30pm, Tu-Su 8:30am-7:30pm. Ticket office closes 6:45pm. €3, students €2. Cash only.)* Behind a brown facade, the gates of the 16th-century **Giardino Giusti** open onto a spacious hillside dotted with gurgling moss-covered fountains and rows of meticulously trimmed hedges—including **Il Labirinto**, a thigh-high hedge maze open to visitors. The cypress-lined avenue gradually winds upwards to a series of picturesque porticoes and curving balconies with breathtaking views of Verona. *(Down V. S. Chiara from Teatro Romano at V. Giusti, 2.* ☎ *045 80 34 029. Open daily 9am-8pm. €4.50, under 18 free. Cash only.)*

CASTELVECCHIO AND ENVIRONS. The castle was built in the 14th century by the della Scala family, whose coat of arms and frescoes still line the interior walls. The Veronese added "Vecchio" (old) to the castle's title to distinguish it from another later built by the Visconti. These days, the castle houses a **museum** of sculptures and paintings, among them Pisanello's celebration of natural paradise in *Madonna della Quaglia*. **Ponte Castelvecchio** to the left of the castle provides a lovely view of Verona along the swirling **Fiume Adige.** *(At the end of V. Roma from P. Brà on C. Castelvecchio, 2.* ☎ *045 80 62 611; www.comune.verona.it/castelvecchio/cvsito. Open M 1:30-7:30pm, Tu-Su 8:30am-7:30pm. Ticket office closes 6:45pm. €4, students €3. Cash only.)* Scipione Maffei's devotion to preserving stone inscriptions lives on in the nearby **Museo Maffeiano,** where much of the sizable array of Greek, Roman, and Etruscan art is over 2000 years old. *(At the corner of V. Roma and C. Pta. Nuova.* ☎ *045 59 00 87. Open M 1:30-7:30pm, Tu-Sa 8:30am-7:30pm, Su 8:30am-1:30pm. €3, students €2. Cash only.)*

SAN ZENO MAGGIORE. Named for Verona's patron saint, who converted the city to Christianity in the 4th century, this massive brick church 25min. outside of the city is one of Verona's finest examples of Italian Romanesque architecture. An urn in the crypt holds Zeno's remains, while the Porphyry Basin, which the saint famously commanded the Devil to move, rests near the base of the nave. *(From Castelvecchio, walk up Rigaste S. Zeno and turn left at the piazza on V. Barbarani, which leads to the church. For information, call the Associazione "Chiese Vive" at* ☎ *045 59 28 13. Open Mar.-Oct. M-Sa 8:30am-6pm, Su 9am-12:30pm and 1:30-6pm; Nov.-Feb. M 8:30am-noon and 3-5pm, Tu-Sa 8:30am-1pm and 1:30-5pm, Su 9am-12:30pm and 1:30-5pm. €2.50. Cash only.)*

OUT, OUT, BRIEF CANDLE

On August 10, 1913, Giuseppe Verdi's *Aida* opened the Verona Opera Festival. Performed before thousands of spectators in the Arena di Verona, it echoed through the theater on a particularly balmy and auspicious evening, Verdi's 100th birthday. Still several years before the installation of electric lights, the theater was dark, the stage dim, and the programs impossible to read. Despite the less-than-ideal conditions, the audience remained eager, as on that night each audience member had brought a candle, the light of which kept the arena glowing throughout the night.

Soon after, the advent of electricity meant that the Arena di Verona traded candlelight for the spotlight and the tradition quickly fell out of favor. But in the mid-1980s, a wealthy patron of the arts decided to revive the sparkling ritual by making candles available to modern opera goers. Now boxes of candles greet spectators as they enter the theater for every summer performance. Just before the first act, as if on silent cue, everyone in the theater lights his candle, setting the entire arena ablaze with twinkling lights. Over the course of the performance, the candles are left to burn out on their own. As the acts unfold, one by one, individual candles wink out, allowing only the actors to shine.

♫ ENTERTAINMENT

The Arena di Verona is the venue for the world-famous ◼**Verona Opera Festival,** which attracts opera buffs in droves every year from June to September. Operas scheduled for 2006 include Bizet's *Carmen*, Puccini's *Tosca* and *Madame Butterfly*, Leoncavallo's *Pagliacci*, and Verdi's *Aida*. (Tickets and information at V. Dietro Anfiteatro 6/B, along the side of the Arena. ☎045 80 05 151; www.arena.it. Open M-F 9am-noon and 3:15-5:45pm, Su 9am-noon. During 2006 opera season (June 24-Aug. 27), open on performance days from 10am-9pm, non-performance days 10am-5:45pm. General admission on the Roman steps M-Th and Su €16.50-24.50, F-Sa €18.50-26.50. General admission ticket-holders should arrive 1hr. before showtime. Reserved seats €73-157. AmEx/MC/V.) Also in summer, the Teatro Romano stages dance performances and Shakespeare plays performed in Italian. June brings the Verona jazz festival. (Info ☎045 80 66 488 or 045 80 66 485; www.estateteatraleveronese.it. Ticket office at Palazzo Barbieri, V. Leoncino, 61. Open M-Sa 10:30am-1pm and 4-7pm. Tickets for both €10.33-20.66.)

TREVISO ☎0422

Treviso, provincial capital of the Veneto, is known by two other names, *Città d'Acqua* (City of Water) and *Città Dipinta* (Painted City). Treviso's predominant feature, however, is its wealth. In the birthplace of Benetton, fashion aficionados peer at the glitzy storefronts of ornate palaces, while budget travelers explore the wide cobblestone lanes and quiet canals that weave through the old city.

⊏ TRANSPORTATION. Treviso is the main stop on the busy Venice-Udine train line. The **train station** is in P. Duca d'Aosta, south of the city center. (☎0422 89 20 21. Ticket counter open daily 6am-8pm. AmEx/MC/V.) Trains depart to: Trieste (2½hr., 15 per day 4:51am-10:25pm, €7.90); Udine (1½hr., 36 per day 12:04am-11:29pm, €5.73); and Venice (30min., 58 per day 5:06am-11:46pm, €2.05). Trains to Milan or Padua connect in Venice. A variety of carriers operate from the **bus station** at Lungosile A. Mattei, 21 (☎0422 57 73 60), off C. del Popolo where it crosses the river. From the train station, turn left on V. Roma. **La Marca** (☎0422 57 73 11; www.lamarcabus.it) services the Veneto region and the **Palladian Villas,** sending buses to Padua (1½hr., 29 per day 6am-7:45pm, €3.70) and Vicenza (1½hr., 11 per day 6:15am-5:10pm, €4.20). The ticket window is open daily (6:25am-7:45pm). **ACTV** (☎041 52 87 886; informazioni@actv.it) runs buses to Venice (1hr., 40 per day 4:10am-8:10pm, €2.40). All buses run reduced service Saturday to Sunday.

◼ ⚐ ORIENTATION AND PRACTICAL INFORMATION. Treviso lies 30km inland from Venice. Surrounded by the Sile, the old city walls encompass Treviso's historical center and most points of interest. From the **train station,** the **ACTT** (intracity) bus hub is across from **Piazza Duca d'Aosta.** Left of the buses, **Via Roma** leads over the river, between the crumbling walls and into the city center; it then becomes **Corso del Popolo,** crosses the river, and enters **Piazza della Borsa.** From there, a walk up **Via XX Settembre** leads to **Piazza dei Signori,** Treviso's main square. Pedestrian-dominated **Via Calmaggiore** leads to the *duomo.*

The **tourist office,** P. Monte di Pietà, 8 (☎0422 54 76 32; www.provincia.treviso.it), on the side of Palazzo dei Trecento from P. dei Signori, has city **maps,** regional accommodations listings, and itineraries for walking tours along the Sile River. (Open M 9am-12:30pm, Tu-F 9am-12:30pm and 2-6pm, Sa-Su 9am-12:30pm and 3-6pm.) **Luggage storage** is available at the train station. (€3 for 1st 12hr., €2 each additional 12hr. Open M-F 7am-8pm and Sa-Su 8:30am-6pm. Cash only.) In case of **emergency,** call ☎113 or an **ambulance** ☎118. The **police** are located at V.

Carlo Alberto, 37 (☎0422 57 71 11). **Ospedale Civile Ca' Foncello** is at P. Ospedale, 1 (☎0422 32 21). Find info on employment opportunities at **Informagiovani**, P. Duomo, 19 (☎0422 65 85 40; www.informagiovani.tv.it. Open Tu-Sa 9am-12:30pm and W-F 3-6pm) and **Internet** at **Western Union**, P. Justinian 4, right behind V. Roma. (☎0422 58 24 47. Open daily 10am-9pm. €2 per hr. Cash only.) The **post office**, P. Vittoria, 1 (☎0422 65 32 11), is at the end of V. Cadorna, off C. del Popolo (open M-Sa 8:30am-6:30pm). **Postal Code:** 31100.

⌂⌂ ACCOMMODATIONS AND FOOD. Albergo Focola ❹, P. Ancilotto, 4, is situated behind Palazzo dei Trecento. One of the better deals in town, it offers rooms with bath, TV, phone, and yellow decor. (☎/fax 0422 56 601. Breakfast €5. Reception 24hr. Reserve ahead. Singles €52; doubles €83. AmEx/MC/V.) To reach **Da Renzo ❹**, V. Terraglio, 108, exit the train station, turn right, mount the stairs to the overpass, and head right down Str. Terraglio for 10min., or take bus #7, 8, or 11 (€0.80). Ask the driver for Da Renzo or the Borgo Savoia stop. The charming rooms of this villa share a tiled breakfast nook. All rooms have bath, nighttime air-conditioning, and phone. (☎0422 40 20 68; www.locandadarenzo.it. Breakfast included. Reception 7am-12:30am. Singles €48; doubles €68; triples €88. AmEx/MC/V.) The **Hotel Carlton ❺**, Largo Porta Altinia, 15, right off of V. Roma, 2min. from the train station, has rooms with air-conditioning, satellite TV, phone, and minibar. Marble pillars and garden terrace are complemented by professional service. (☎0422 41 16 61; www.hotelcarlton.it. Breakfast buffet included. Reception 24hr. Singles €95-118; doubles €120-150; triples €170. AmEx/MC/V.)

Treviso is famous for its cherries, which ripen in June, *radicchio*, which peaks in December, and *tiramisù*, a heavenly combination of espresso-and-rum-soaked cake layered with the delectable, mild *mascarpone* cheese. Its name means, literally, "pick me up," and it's the rumored dessert of choice among those with frustrated libidos. In summer, try a cool scoop of *tiramisù gelato*. To taste these delights, head to the Saturday and Tuesday morning produce **market** at the Stiore stop of the #2 or 11 bus. The fish and vegetable **market** is on tiny Isola dell'Pescheria, surrounded by the canals. (Open Tu-Sa 7:30am-12:30pm.) Head to the **PAM** supermarket, V. Zorzetto, 12, off C. del Popolo, for basics. (☎0422 58 39 13. Open M-Sa 8:30am-7:30pm. AmEx/MC/V.) **La Vera Terra, ❷** V. G. di Treviso, 5, across from Hotel Carlton, offers hearty vegetarian dishes in an elegant setting. Low prices and delicious plates like the *gazpacho adaluse al cumino* (€4.50) and *maccheroni al tofu e fiori di zucca* (€4.50) draw clientele ranging from hip locals to well-dressed businesspeople. Visit the adjoining market for meals to go. (☎0422 41 02 03; laveraterra@libero.it. *Primi* from €4.50, *secondi* from €5. Cover €1. Open M-Sa 10am-2:30pm and 8-11pm. MC/V.) **All'Oca Bianca ❸**, V. della Torre, 7, is on a side street off V. Calmaggiore. This casual trattoria serves excellent fish dishes from a fresh seasonal menu. (☎0422 54 18 50. *Primi* €6-7, *secondi* and fish €7-16. Cover €2, includes mineral water. Open M-Tu and Th-Su 12:15-2:15pm and 7:30-11pm. AmEx/MC/V.)

◙ SIGHTS. From V. XX Settembre, skirt the right side of the busy, cafe-lined *loggias* of **Piazza dei Signori** to find the marble-staircase of the **Palazzo dei Trecento,** a *de facto* memorial to the 1944 Good Friday air raid that devastated the small town. A marble plaque under the stairs commemorates local citizens killed in German concentration camps. (☎0422 65 82 35. Closed to the public. Call to make a reservation or contact the tourist office about group tours.) To see and be seen, strut the busy and boutique-laden Calmaggiore, flowing from beneath the arcades of the P. dei Signori to the white and gray Palladian arch of the seven-domed **Neoclassical duomo.** In the stark moulded white and gray interior, its **Cappella Malchiostro** dates from 1519 and contains works by sworn enemies Titian and Pordenone. (Open M-Sa 7:30am-noon and 3:30-7pm, Su 7:30am-1pm and 3:30-8pm. Free. Cappella illumination €0.30.)

THE DOLOMITES (I DOLOMITI)

Somewhere between Trieste and Innsbruck lies a land of shattered rocky peaks etched smooth with the passage of time. This surreal landscape takes its name from the hard magnesium-laced mineral of which it is largely composed. Its secluded heights have ensured the continued existence of groups such as the Ladins, who speak a 2000-year-old linguistic hybrid of Latin and Celtic. One glance at the lush conifers and snow-covered peaks of this panorama explains why back-packers and skiers still flock to the area Le Corbusier once called "the most beau-tiful natural architecture in the world." The Dolomites stretch from Trentino Alto-Adige, through the Veneto, and into Friuli-Venezia Giulia. Public transportation can be a little spotty, but planning goes a long way in an area used to travelers and their needs. From mountain refuges to luxury hotels, the Dolomites offer custom-ized adventure and beauty for any appreciative wayfarer.

 THE REAL DEAL. The Dolomites are tricky to navigate and if you don't have a car and a burning desire to see the mountains up close, you might be better off skirting around the edges, where transportation is more reliable and speedy. If you do plan on making a foray into the interior, know that you'll be dealing with multiple bus lines as regions change. —*Morgan Kruger*

BELLUNO ☎ 0437

On the southeastern border of the Dolomites, Belluno is the budget traveler's dream. With easy transportation to neighboring towns, but inexpensive dining and lodging just kilometers from gorgeous biking paths, trails of every level of diffi-culty, and beautiful views, visitors could ask for little more.

◗◗ TRANSPORTATION AND PRACTICAL INFORMATION. Belluno runs trains to a number of cities, but plan ahead because some lines run much less fre-quently than others. **Trains** run to Padua (2hr., 14 per day 6am-10:46pm, €6.10) via Conegliano (1hr., 9 per day 6:08am-7:31pm; €3), on the Venice-Udine line. Some scheduled trains run directly to Conegliano, but many require a change in nearby Ponte nelle Alpi. (☎0437 89 20 21. Ticket office open daily 5:50am-7.30pm.) Bel-luno's **bus station,** across P.le della Stazione from the train station, is a regional hub for **Dolomiti Bus,** which serves the pre-Alps to the west and the eastern Dolomites. **Buses** run to: Calalzo (1hr., 12 per day 6:15am-8:05pm, €3); Cortina (2hr., 13 per day 6:25am-6:50pm, €3.70) via Calalzo and Feltre (40min., 16 per day 6:20am-7:10pm, €2.50). For info, call ☎0437 94 11 67 or 0437 94 12 37. (Ticket office open M-F 7am-12:15pm and 3-7:15pm, Sa 7am-12:15pm. When closed, buy ticket from tourist office.) Orange **local buses** (€0.80) stop in Ple. della Stazione.

The city center, **Piazza dei Martiri,** is a 5min. walk from the **train** and **bus stations** in **Piazzale della Stazione.** From the train terminal, cross the parking lot and follow **Via Dante** through **Piazzale Battisti** and across **Via Caffi** to **Via Loreto.** Turn left on **Via Matteotti** so that P. dei Martiri, overlooking several fountains and sculpted gar-dens, is in sight. For **maps,** a list of Internet points, and hiking info, cross through the garden in P. dei Martiri and pass through **Porta Dante** onto **Via XXX Aprile.** The **tourist office** is at P. del Duomo, 2. (☎0437 94 00 83; www.infodolomiti.it. Open daily 9am-12:30pm and 3:30-5:30pm.) To get to **Club Alpino Italiano (CAI),** P. S. Gio-vanni Bosco, 11, from the tourist office, cross the *piazza* and turn right into P. V. Emanuele, then continue straight ahead and down the stairs. Cross the river and take V. S. Antonio. When the road forks, take V. S. Giuseppe to P. S. Giovanni

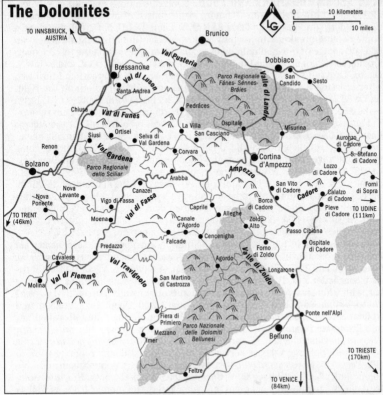

The Dolomites

0 | 10 kilometers
0 | 10 miles

TO INNSBRUCK, AUSTRIA

Brunico

Val Pusteria

Dobbiaco

Bressanone

Val di Luson

Santa Andrea

Parco Regionale Fánes- Sénnes- Bráies

San Candido

Sesto

Valle di Landro

Chiusa

Val di Funes

Pedráces

La Villa

Ospitale

Misurina

Siusi

Ortisei

Selva di Val Gardena

San Casciano

Renon

Val Gardena

Corvara

Cortina d'Ampezzo

Auronzo di Cadore

S. Stefano di Cadore

Bolzano

Parco Regionale dello Sciliar

Arabba

Ampezzo

Lozzo di Cadore

Forni di Sopra

Nova Levante

Canazei

Cadore

Nova Ponente

Vigo di Fassa

Val di Fassa

Caprile

Borca di Cadore

San Vito di Cadore

Calalzo di Cadore

Pieve di Cadore

TO UDINE (111km)

TO TRENT (46km)

Moena

Canale d'Agordo

Alleghe

Zoldo Alto

Predazzo

Falcade

Cencenigha

Passo Cibiana

Cavalese

Val Travignolo

Agordo

Forno di Zoldo

Ospitale di Cadore

Molina

Val di Flemme

San Martino di Castrozza

Valle di Zoldo

Longarone

Fiera di Primiero

Parco Nazionale delle Dolomiti Bellunesi

Ponte nell'Alpi

Mezzano

Imer

Belluno

TO TRIESTE (170km)

Feltre

TO VENICE (84km)

Bosco. The office is ahead, across the *piazza*. Buy membership for a reduced price at mountain *rifugi*. (☎/fax 0437 93 16 55; http://digilander.libero.it/caibelluno. Open Jan.-Apr. Tu 6pm-8pm; May-Oct. F 8:30pm-10:30pm.) **Banks** with similar exchange rates and 24hr. **ATMs** line P. dei Martiri. In case of **emergency,** call ☎113; the **police** (☎0437 94 55 11), on V. Volontari d. Libertà; or an **ambulance** at ☎118. **Pharmacies** post a list of after-hours rotation; **Farmacia Dott. Perale,** P. V. Emanuele, 12, is centrally located and open late. (☎0437 25 271. Open M-F and Su 8:45am-12:30pm and 4-7:30pm, Sa 8:45am-12:30pm. AmEx/MC/V.) The **hospital** is at V. Loreto, 32 (☎0437 16 111). **Ki Point,** V. Feltre, 192 (☎0437 94 05 33; fax 0437 29 87 01.) is a five-minute walk down V. Feltre from the train station. €1.30 per 15min., €3 per hr., with ID. Open M-F 8:30am-12:30pm and 3:30-6:30pm, Sa 8:30am-12:30pm. Closed 1 week in Aug. Cash only.) Belluno's **post office** offers fax and photocopy services just off P. Duomo at P. Castello, 14/A. (☎0437 95 32 11. Open M-Sa 8:30am-6:30pm.) **Postal Code:** 32100.

CULTURE SHOCK. The people of the northern Dolomites have been ethnically and linguistically German and Austrian for centuries. This means that most natives' first language is German, with Italian coming in second, and English a distant third.

ACCOMMODATIONS AND FOOD. Central locations and cliff-side balconies come at low nightly rates. Inquire at the tourist office about accommodations and *affittacamere.* **La Cerva B&B ❷,** V. Paoletti, 7/B, has great views and a home-cooked breakfast in a sunny yellow house. Globetrotting students can take advantage of the mountain bikes available, or hang out on the terrace overlooking the Dolomites. Exit the train station, cross the parking lot, and follow V. Dante. Turn left on Vle. Volantari Libertà, then cross V. Fantuzzi and turn left. After crossing the street near V. Col di Lana, look for V. Paoletti on the right. (☎338 82 53 608; www.lacerva.it. Breakfast €2. Singles €18; doubles €31. Extra bed €8.50. Cash only.) Take Vle. Volontari Libertà from the station. Turn right on V. Fantuzzi, which changes to V. J. Tasso; V. Ricci branches off. At the **Albergo Cappello e Cadore ❹,** V. Ricci, 8, elegance and a friendly staff exist among cheerful carpeted rooms and Klimt-lined hallways. Rooms in the 1843 building come with minifridge, TV, Internet port, and phone; some have a jacuzzi and balcony. (☎0437 94 02 46; www.albergocappello.com. Breakfast included. Singles €40-50; doubles €85-105; triples €110. AmEx/MC/V.) **Casa per Ferie Al Centro ❷,** P. Piloni, 11, has utilitarian rooms off of basic hallways, but its central location, spacious bathrooms, and friendly staff make it a good deal. All rooms have phone and bath. (☎0437 94 44 60; casaferie@diocesi.it. Breakfast €3.50. Reception 6:30am-1am. Singles €25; doubles €40; €10 for each extra person. AmEx/MC/V.)

Dining options in the *centro* are plentiful and inexpensive. **Supermarket per Dolomiti,** P. dei Martiri, 9/10, has a hot deli as well as groceries. (☎0437 94 20 00. Open M-Tu and Th-Su 8am-1pm and 4-7:30pm, W 8am-1pm. V.) **La Trappola Birreria e Spaghetteria ❷,** P. le Cesare Battisti, 6, serves massive portions in a lively bar, with whimsical pictures of boozing monks on the walls. (☎0437 27 417. *Spaghetti primo* €6-8. Flavored regional *grappa* €2.50. Open M-F 11am-3pm and 5:50pm-2am, Sa 5pm-3am. AmEx/MC/V.) Descend through the red-walled bar into **Ristorante Taverna ❸,** V. Cipro, 7, where local specialties like *galletti alla diavola* (devilish chicken; €7) and *lumache alla Bellunese con polenta* (snails served with polenta; €9) are served in the traditional dining room. (☎0437 25 192. *Primi* €5.50-6, *secondi* €7-13. Cover €1. Open M-Sa noon-2:30pm and 7:30-10pm. AmEx/MC/V.) **La Buca ❷,** V. Carrera, 15/C, offers the pizza *Rianata* (lombard cheese, parmesan, anchovies, oregano, garlic, and more; €9.80) as well as an extensive menu of meats and pastas. (☎0437 94 01 91. *Primi* €5-12, *secondi* €6.50-12. Cover €1-1.60. Open daily noon-2:30pm and 6pm-midnight.) **Al Mirapiave ❷,** V. Matteotti, 29, serves 60 types of pizza (with a great seasonal menu) on a cliff-side balcony with a dramatic panorama. (☎0437 94 18 13. Pizza €5.60-7.60. Pasta €4.80-9. Cover €1. Open M and W-Su 11:30am-3:30pm and 6pm-1am. MC/V.) At **Ristorante delle Alpi ❷,** V. J. Tasso, 15, fresh fish is served in a warm pink dining room; ask about the freshest catches. (☎0437 94 03 02. *Primi* €5-9.30, *secondi* €11-15.50. Open M-Sa 12:30-2:30pm and 7:30-10:30pm. MC/V.)

SIGHTS. Changes in the city's government can be traced in the architecture of the **Piazza del Duomo.** On the gate of the **Palazzo Miari,** a residence of the Miari family, a 2nd coat of arms appeared when Belluno switched branches of the family tree from the 16th to 17th century. (Around the right corner of the post office. Privately owned, no entry.) In the mid-17th century, academics gathered in the nearby **Palazzo dei Giuristi,** whose benefactors' busts line the facade. Since 1876, the building has housed the **Museo Civico,** exhibiting pottery, jewelry, and works by Caffi; the 2nd floor's metal flowers and Ridolfi's *Deposizione nel Sepolcro* are highly recommended. (☎0437 94 48 36; www.comune.belluno.it. Open Apr.-Sept. Tu-Su 10am-1pm and 4-7pm; Oct.-Apr. M-Sa 9am-1pm and Th-Su 3-6pm. €2.30; students, over 60, or groups of 10 or more €1.20, under 5 free. Ticket office closes 20min. before museum.) Since 1838, the town government has rested next to the information office in the **Palazzo Rettori,** which now houses the city's **Municipio.** The vast **Parco Nazionale di Dolomiti Bellunesi** (Bellunese Dolomites National Park) starts at the northern edge of city. (☎0439 33 28; www.dolomitipark.it.) For a more high-flying travel package, visit the **Botanical Garden of the Eastern Alps** rests at the top of a chairlift on the western slope of nearby **Monte Faverghera.** Buses from Belluno service the chairlift, which zooms 1500m up the mountain. (☎0437 94 48 30. Tourist office updates bus and chairlift schedules. Open June-Sept. Tu-Su 9:30am-noon and 1-5:30pm. €1.50, 14 and under €0.80.)

 HIKING. Belluno offers excellent, well-marked hiking trails; one of the best is along the *altavia,* stretching north and south from Braies and Belluno, respectively. Hiking the entire *altavia* would take between eight and 15 days, but the hike along the first stretch, from Belluno to **Rifugio #7,** can be done in a day. From Belluno's P. dei Martiri, take V. J. Tasso, which changes to V. Fantuzzi, and then V. Col di Lana. Follow this for about 1km until a sign points right, toward Bolzano; walk uphill about 9km. The paved road is easily cycled or walked in about 3hr., ending at **Casa Bortot** (707m). Stock up on food here—it's the last stop before Rifugio #7. Follow the small gravel path to the left, leading to the Parco Nazionale di Dolomiti Bellunesi, or the start of **Altavia #1.** The route is well-marked and sticks close to the river gorge, with views of waterfalls and deep pools etched out of the dolomite rock. A 3-4hr. hike leads to a small meadow and Rifugio #7 at **Pils Pilon.** (☎0437 94 16 31, in winter 0445 66 11 28. Call ahead to confirm availability. Serves hot meals. Open June-Sept. Rooms €16, CAI members €8. Inquire about the more difficult hikes. Cash only.) For information on the *altevie,* visit www.dolomiti-altevie.it. For more info on hiking, visit the **CAI office** (see **Practical Information**).

> **TIP** **CLUB ALPINO ITALIANO (CAI).** Those intending to do a serious amount of hiking in Italy should consider purchasing a **Club Alpino Italiano membership.** CAI runs many mountain *rifugi,* and members pay half-price for lodgings. *Rifugi,* which generally operate from late June to early October, may also rent out *vie ferrate* hiking equipment essentials. Membership is €36, under 18 €11.50, with a €5.50 supplement for new members and €18 surcharge for non-Italians. It can be purchased at a CAI office; bring a passport photo.

CORTINA D'AMPEZZO ☎0436

As ski season heats up, the winding, brightly lit streets of Cortina d'Ampezzo suddenly fill with multinational *glitterati* (up to 40,000 during holidays) who find themselves drawn to the powdery snow, stylish boutiques, and vast array of adventure sports offered by this mountain paradise. But trust-fund deficient travelers aren't left out in the cold, as hotel and restaurant prices plummet in the low season to spread the area's (natural) wealth.

TRANSPORTATION AND PRACTICAL INFORMATION. Cortina's location high in the Dolomites makes it difficult to reach without a car. The nearest **train station** is in Calalzo, but hourly buses depart for Cortina (1hr., 17 per day 7:33am-9:23pm, €2.50). Trains run to Calalzo from Belluno (1hr.; 9 per day 5:40am-7:29pm, €3), Milan (8hr.), and Venice (3hr.). **Buses** run from Cortina to Belluno (3hr., 9 per day 5:35am-5:55pm, €3.70); Milan (7hr., June-Aug. F-Sa, €40); Venice (5hr.; June 23-Aug. daily, Sept.-June 22 Sa-Su; €10.60). Train information is available from local public phones at ☎ 0436 89 20 21. The orange **urban buses** service Cortina and the Valle d'Ampezzo, and the nine lines are useful for reaching hotels, trails, and cable cars outside town. Buy tickets (€0.80) at newsstands, *tabaccherie*, and bars near bus stops. For longer visits, buy urban bus passes in books of six (€4.20) or 12 (€8), or buy a Guest Card (€10.33) for a week of transportation in the province on urban and Dolomite bus lines. For more info on all buses, call or stop by the **Dolomiti Bus information desk**, in the Cortina bus station. (☎ 0436 86 79 21. Open M-F 8:15am-12:30pm and 2:30-6pm, Sa 8:15am-12:30pm. MC/V.) For **RadioTaxi**, dial ☎ 0436 86 08 88. (24hr.)

Pedestrian thoroughfare **Corso Italia,** lined with boutiques and anchored by the *duomo's* bell tower, runs through the center of town. From the **bus station,** cross **Via Marconi,** head left, and take the long, sloping **Largo Poste** downhill to the *centro*. The **tourist office** is in Piazzetta S. Francesco, 8, off V. Mercato, on the opposite side of the *duomo* from the station and to the left. Buy an extensive regional hiking trail **map** (€2.50), or ask for information on hiking, skiing, and local culture. (☎ 0436 32 31. Open daily M-F 9am-12:30pm and 3:30-6:30pm.) For a less-crowded alternative, try the virtually identical **branch** at P. Roma, 1, just down the street behind the *duomo*. (☎ 0436 27 11; www.infodolomiti.it. Open daily 9am-12:30pm and 3:30-6:30pm.) The **Banca di Trento e Bolzano,** C. Italia, 15, offers **currency exchange,** an **ATM,** and cashes **traveler's checks.** (☎ 0436 86 62 48; fax 0436 86 64 08. Open M-F and Su 8:20am-1:20pm and 2:45-4:15pm.) In case of **emergency,** dial ☎ 113, or call the **police** (☎ 0436 86 62 00), on V. Marconi. **Farmacia Internazionale,** C. Italia, 151, offers long hours and posts a list of after hours rotations. (☎ 0436 22 23. Open M-Sa 9am-12:45pm and 4-7:30pm.) **Ospedale Cortina** (☎ 0436 88 31 11) is on V. Cademai. For those with money to spare, **Internet** is available at **Dolomiti Multimedia,** L. Poste, 59. (☎ 0436 86 80 90; fax 0436 86 67 04. €4.50 per 30min. €9 per hr. Open M-F 9am-12:30pm and 3-6:30pm, Sa 4-7pm. Cash only.) The **post office** and **ATM** are at L. Poste, 18. (☎ 0436 88 24 11; fax 0436 88 24 40. Open M-F 8:30am-6:30pm, Sa 8:30am-1pm.) **Postal Code:** 32043.

> **TIP** **CRACKING THE CODE.** German keyboards are for the most part configured the same as American ones, with one notable difference. The "z" and "y" keys are switched. To avoid wasting time and money, ask the proprietor of whatever Internet cafe you find yourself in to configure it American-style for you.

 ACCOMMODATIONS AND FOOD. Cortina is full of upscale hotels for the wealthy tourists who descend on the town in August and winter, but rates plummet in the low season. **Hotel Oasi ❸,** V. Cantore, 2, offers soft bedding and TVs to hikers with a lust for luxury. Behind the bus station, look left to where Oasi sits on a small hill. (☎ 0436 86 20 19 91; www.hoteloasi.it. Breakfast included. Reception 8am-10pm. Singles €43-85; doubles €66-150. Extra bed €21.50-40. MC/V.) The cheapest in the *centro* is the **Hotel Montana ❸,** C. Italia, 94, right next to the *duomo*. Rooms are clean with phone and wood floors. Breakfast included. (☎ 0436 86 21 26; montana@cortina-hotel.com. Singles €34-60; doubles €62-100. AmEx/MC/V.) **Hotel Fiames ❹,** Località Fiames, 13, books rooms with bath and meals in Fiames, 5km north of town. Take bus #1 (10min., 14 per day 7:30am-7:34pm, €0.80) from the station to the last stop. (☎ 0436 23 66; fax 0436 57 33. Breakfast included. Lunch or dinner €18. Singles €40-65; doubles €80-130.) **International Camping Olimpia ❶,** is in Località Fiames. Bus #1 stops at the access road just before Hotel Fiames; ask the driver for Olimpia. Grounds have a post office, sauna, bar, and restaurant. There is a list of rules to uphold—strict noon check-out, cars are barred from entry, silence is enforced from 1-3pm and 11pm-7am, and visitors are charged the guest fee after 1hr. (☎/fax 0436 50 57. Reception 9am-noon and 3-7pm. Adults €4.50-7.50, children under 10 €2.50-4, dogs €1; RVs and cars with tents or trailers €7-9. Bunks €19-20 per day. Cash only.)

Panificio Pasticceria ❶, V. del Mercato, 10, offers fresh breads, local *strudel* (€2 for a chunk), and pizza by the slice in a little bakery right in the *centro*. (Open M-Tu and Th-Su 6:30am-1pm and 3-7:10pm, W 6:30am-1pm. Cash only.) At **Pizzeria Il Ponte ❶**, V. B. Franchetti, 8, enjoy German influence in the Dolomites with the *Wurstel* (pizza with frankfurt *Wurstel*; €5.50), or sit outside and soak in the view of a romantic arched bridge. From the bus station, turn left on V. Marconi and follow the road as it curves down the hill to reach V. B. Franchetti. (☎/fax 0436 86 76 24; www.ilpontez.supereva.it. Open Tu-Su 10am-3pm and 6:30pm-midnight. MC/V.) Across the street you'll find produce, packaged meats, and a sizable liquor arcade at **Kanguro** supermarket, V. B. Franchetti, 1. (☎ 0436 48 36. Open M-Sa 8:30am-12:30pm and 3:30-7:30pm. MC/V.)

◨ **SIGHTS.** Cortina's tourist office has a wealth of advice on local skiing, hiking, water sports, and nature walks. For those looking for a less strenuous mountain excursion, a flat 7km *passeggiata* (pedestrian and bike path) traverses town from Cortina's famous ski-jump platform to the town of Fiames. V. Marconi (outside the train and bus stations) comprises the middle section of the *passeggiata*, so hikers can join halfway on either end of the street. One major plus is the magnificent view of **Croda del Pomogagnon,** a band of towering rock spires to the east. For more information and trail locations, contact the tourist office.

TRENTINO-ALTO ADIGE

The Mediterranean feel of Italy's southern regions fades under Germanic influences in the peaks of the Dolomites in Trentino-Alto Adige. At the onset of the 19th century, Napoleon conquered this part of the Holy Roman Empire, only to relinquish it to the Austro-Hungarian Empire. Trentino and the Südtirol (South Tyrol) came under Italian control at the end of WWI, a transition that left diverse linguistic patterns and cultural traditions scattered throughout the region. Though Germany thwarted Mussolini's brutal efforts to Italianize the region, Benito did manage to give every German name an Italian equivalent, which explains the dual street and town names used today. Mussolini found spicy *Wurst* carts, Austrian dolls, and shocks of blond hair slightly harder to control, and an aura of Germania bears witness to a deep-rooted Austrian culture that still thrives today.

BOLZANO (BOZEN)   ☎ 0471

Bolzano is most famous for the 5000-year-old Ice Man, a partially decayed body found frozen in 1991. The best sights in the city, however, don't charge admission: snowy peaks beckon hikers in winter, while summer visitors head to the crystal-green Talvera River, catch an afternoon nap at Castel Roncolo, or gaze at the steep hills, resplendent with rows of grape vines. From the *duomo's* boxy Romanesque base and soaring Gothic spires to the two languages—Italian and German—on every street sign, Bolzano weaves competing histories together to create a cultural atmosphere oblivious of national borders.

TRANSPORTATION

Trains: ☎0471 48 89 93, in P. Stazione. Office open M-F 8am-7pm, Sa 8am-5pm, Su 9am-1pm and 2-5pm. **Luggage storage** available. To: **Bologna** (4hr., 21 per day 1:53am-1:07am, €12.34); **Bressanone** (30min., 31 per day 4am-10:31pm, €3.25); **Munich** (4hr., 9 per day 2:25am-6:32pm); **Trent** (45min., 39 per day 1:53am-10:41pm, €2.89); **Venice** (4hr., 2 per day 3:44am-3:30pm, €15.62); **Verona** (1¾hr., 14 per day 8:15am-8:35pm, €6.82).

Buses: SAD, V. Perathoner, 4 (☎0471 45 01 11), between train station and P. Walther. Bus station and tourist office distribute schedules detailing extensive service to the western Dolomites. Reduced service Su and after 6pm. Office open M-Sa 7am-7:25pm, Su 7am-1:15pm. MC/V.

Funicular: 3 cableways, located at the edges of Bolzano, regularly carry visitors to nearby mountain towns. Contact the tourist office for schedules.

Funivia del Colle, V. Campiglio, 7 (☎0471 97 85 45), the world's oldest cableway, leads from V. Campiglio to **Colle** or **Kohlern** (9min.; every 30min. 7am-7pm; round-trip €2.60, bikes €2.10).

Funivia del Renon, V. Renon, 12 (☎0471 97 84 79), a 5min. walk from the train station, heads from V. Renon to **Renon** or **Ritten** atop **Monte Soprabolzano** (12min.; 3 per hr. 7:10am-8:20pm; one-way €2.50, round-trip €3.50, bikes €1, luggage €1-2).

Funivia San Genesio, V. Rafenstein, 15 (☎0471 97 84 36), off V. Sarentino, across the Talvera River near Ponte S. Antonio, connects Bolzano to **Salto's** high plateaus (9min.; 2-3 per hr. daily 10am-12:30pm and 2:30-7pm; round-trip €3.20, bikes €1).

Public Transportation: SASA (☎0471 45 01 11 or 800 84 60 47). All lines stop in P. Walther or the station at V. Perathoner, 4. Buy tickets (€0.90) at *tabaccherie* or from machines near some stops.

Taxi: RadioTaxi, V. Perathoner, 4 (☎0471 98 11 11). 24hr.

Car Rental: Budget-National-Maggiore, V. Garibaldi, 34 (☎0471 97 15 31; fax 0471 30 94 55). From €70 per day. 21+. Open M-F 8am-12:30pm and 3-7pm, Sa 8am-12:30pm. AmEx/MC/V.

Bike Rental: Silver (☎0471 97 55 92) on Vle. Stazione right off P. Walther. Main office at V. Carduci. €1 for 1st 6hr., €2 for 7+ hr. Open daily Apr.-Oct. 7:30am-6:50pm; Nov.-Mar. 7:30am-7:50pm. Cash only.

ORIENTATION AND PRACTICAL INFORMATION

The *centro storico* lies between the **train station** and the **Talvera River** (Talfer Fluss). All major *piazze* are within walking distance. Street and place names appear in Italian and German, and most maps mark both. A walk through the park on **Viale Stazione** (Bahnhofshalle), from the train station, or **Via Alto Adige** (Südtirolerstrasse), from the bus stop, leads to **Piazza Walther** (Waltherplatz) and the *duomo*. Beyond, **Piazza del Grano** leads left to **Via Portici** (Laubenstrasse) and the swankiest district. Here, German and Italian merchants set up shop on opposite sides of the arcade. To reach **Ponte Talvera,** take V. Portici past **Piazza delle Erbe.**

Tourist Office: AST, P. Walther, 8 (☎0471 30 70 00; www.bolzano-bozen.it), has city **maps** and a list of lodgings and daily activities throughout the city. Organizes horseback-riding expeditions, publishes *Bolzano a Passeggio* (a guide to 14 walks in the surrounding hills), and distributes the *funivia* schedule. Open M-F 9am-7pm, Sa 9am-6pm.

Alpine Information: Club Alpino Italiano, P. delle Erbe, 46, 2nd fl. (☎0471 97 81 72; fax 0471 97 99 15). Ring bell. Info on hiking, climbing, and tours. Open M-F 11am-1pm and 5-7pm.

Currency Exchange: Banca Nazionale del Lavoro, next to tourist office at P. Walther, 10. Good rates. Open M-F 8:20am-1:20pm and 2:30-4pm. An **ATM** is around the right corner of the bank and down the stairs, but plenty of others exist throughout the *centro.*

Laundromat: Lava e Asciuga, V. Rosmini, 81, near Ponte Talvera. 35min. wash €3, 20min. dry €3. Plastic bags €0.20. Detergent €1. Open daily 7:30am-10:30pm.

Emergency: ☎113. **Ambulance:** ☎118. **Police:** ☎112.

Pharmacy: Farmacia all'Aquila Nera, V. Portici, 46/B. Open M-F 8:30am-12:30pm and 3-7pm, Sa 8:30am-12:30pm. After-hours rotation posted outside.

Hospital: Ospedale Regionale San Maurizio (☎0471 90 81 11), on V. Lorenz Böhler. Take bus #10 to last stop.

Internet Access: MultiKulti, V. Dott Streiter, 9 (☎0471 05 60 56; www.multi-kulti.com), one street past V. Portici. Offers international calling, fax, and Internet. Internet €1 per 15min., €3 per hr. Open daily 10am-10pm. Cash only. **Caffe Brennpunkt,** V. Brennero, 7 (☎0471 98 29 53) is a slick bar with an even slicker flatscreen computer. First 30min. free, every additional 15min. Open M-W and Su 7:30am-8pm, Th-F 7:30am-8:30pm, Sa 7:30-2am.

Post Office: V. della Posta, 1 (☎0471 32 22 81), by the *duomo.* Open M-F 8am-1:30pm, Sa 8am-12:30pm. **Postal Code:** 39100.

⚑ ACCOMMMODATIONS AND CAMPING

The tourist office lists affordable *agriturismi* options, but most require private transportation—rent a bicycle and enjoy the countryside or reserve ahead for the inexpensive accommodations in the *centro* that fill up quickly in July and August.

Youth Hostel Bolzano, V. Renon, 22 (☎0471 30 08 65; fax 0471 30 08 58). Squeaky clean rooms and cutting-edge decor make this brand-new hostel a great deal. Sheets, breakfast, showers, and lockers (with €1 deposit) included. Internet €2 per hr. Reception daily 8am-9pm with key available for late-arrivals. €19 per person; €2 surcharge for 1-night stay. AmEx/MC/V. ❷

Feichter Hotel, V. Grappoli, 15 (☎0471 97 87 68; fax 0471 97 48 03). From the train station, cross to the park and follow V. Laurin to V. Grappoli; Feichter is on the right. Sunny alpine decor complements view of rooftops and grassy hillsides. TV, phone, bath, and proximity to the *centro* provide plenty to keep guests occupied. Breakfast included. Reserve ahead for mountain view. Singles €55; doubles €80. MC/V. ❹

Garni Thuille, V. Thuille, 5 (☎0471 26 28 77). A 15min. walk from train station. Cross Ponte Talvera, heading away from city center. Turn left on V. S. Quirino, take 1st right onto V. Peter Mayr, then turn left on V. Thuille. Spacious rooms with wooden floors are quiet and well-managed. Breakfast €3. Singles €30-45; doubles €60-80. Cash only. ❷

Schwarze Katz, Stazione Maddalena di Sotto, 2 (☎0471 97 54 17; fax 0471 32 50 28), near V. Brennero, 15min. from the city center. From the train station, turn right at V. Renon; keep left along V. Renon as you pass the cable car station, and look for signs that lead 20m up an alley on the left. A bustling local restaurant gives this hotel a warm, friendly feel. All rooms with sinks, TV; some with bath. Breakfast included. Reception in restaurant in summer M-Sa 7am-2am; in winter M-F 7am-midnight, Sa 7am-9pm. Reserve ahead. Singles €25-30; doubles €45-50. MC/V. ❷

Moosbauer, V. S. Maurizio, 83 (☎0471 91 84 92; www.moosbauer.com). Take SAD bus (15 per day, 7am-10:20pm) toward Merano; ask driver to stop at Moosbauer. Though slightly off the beaten path, beautifully tended campsite has pool, bar, Internet cafe (€0.10 per min.), market, playground, and laundry service (€3 for wash or dry). Shower included. Reception open 8am-noon and 4-9pm. Adults €6-7; children under 12 €4.50-5.50, dogs €3-4, tents €5-5.50, cars €5-5.50. MC/V after 1st night. ❶

■ FOOD

No trip to Bolzano would be complete without a sampling of the city's unique Austrian gastronomic culture. For a full smorgasbord, start with a bowl of *Rindgulasch*, a tasty beef stew; then munch on *Wurst*, thick, spicy sausage, or *Speck*, smoked bacon that tops pizzas and breads across mainland Italy. Hearty *Knödel* (dumplings) come in dozens of rib-sticking varieties. For dessert, try three types of flaky *strudel: Apfel* (apple), *Topfen* (soft cheese), and *Mohn* (poppyseed). Local vineyards bustle during the week-long *Südtiroler Törgelen* tasting spree each fall. An all-day **market** in P. delle Erbe and along V. della Roggia sells fine produce and cold meats (open M-F 7am-7pm, Sa 7am-noon). For a quick regional staple, try the market's **Wurst stand** at the intersection of V. Museo and P. delle Erbe. (*Wurst*, bread, and sauces €2.70. Beer €1.55. Open M-Sa 8am-7pm. Cash only.) A **Despar** supermarket is downstairs in the indoor shopping center at V. della Rena, 40. (☎0471 97 45 37. Open M-F 8:30am-7:30pm, Sa 8:30am-6pm.)

Exil Lounge, P. del Grano, 2 (☎0471 97 18 14). Dishes like "Fit 4 Fun," a bowl of yogurt, granola, and seasonal fruits (€3.70), or the Exil Salad, piled high with *finocchi*, tomatoes, *rucola*, carrots, and Bufala cheese (€5) will delight vegetarians and *Wurst*-intolerant travelers. Open M-W 10am-midnight and Th-Su 10am-1am. Cash only. ❶

Hopfen & Co., P. Erbe, 17 (☎0471 30 07 88). A no-frills pub with just 3 types of beer—dark, light, and double malt—and a sizeable Bavarian menu with a variety of specialties cooked in (what else?) beer. Glasses run at €3.50, while the *gulasch* goes for €12. Open M-Sa 9:30am-1am, Su 10:30am-midnight. MC/V. ❸

Lowengrube, P. Dogana, 3 (☎0471 97 68 48) is close enough to the *centro* to be convenient but far away enough away to be restful. Cheerful Austrian decor and crowds of locals attest to its popularity. *Panini* €3.40, beer €1.60. Open daily 8am-1am. MC/V. ❶

Hostaria Argentieri, V. Argentieri, 14 (☎0471 98 17 18). This upscale Italian restaurant specializes in fish and classy dining. Shrubs around the patio hide a quiet, candlelit interior under soft blue and yellow arches. *Primi* €7.50-15.50, *secondi* €8.50-19.30. Cover €1.50. Open M-Sa noon-2:30pm and 7-10:30pm. AmEx/MC/V. ❹

Blackout, V. Isarco, 11 (☎0471 30 02 56). Lives up to its name with ultra-low lighting and a young clientele that flits like moths around tiki torches outside. More bar than club, but with loud music, cheap drinks (beer or cola €1.80), and a late option for those unwilling to call it a night. Open M-Sa 8pm-1am. Cash only. ❶

■ ■ SIGHTS AND HIKING

The tourist office in Bolzano offers a Museum Card (€2.50) for a free guided city tour, and discounted entry to five city museums as well as the Castel Roncolo. Nearby, the **duomo** is a veritable case study on the transition from Romanesque to Gothic religious architecture—dark, heavy doors are one of the only interruptions in an otherwise square and unadorned base; Gothic influences added the spined hollow spire of the bell tower and the ornate masonry around the eaves. (In P. Walther. Open M-F 9:45am-noon and 2-5pm, Sa 9:45am-noon. Free.) Outside of P. Walther, quiet, cobblestone streets hide gems like the **Chiesa dei Francescani**, V. dei Francesca, 1, identifiable by the mosaic of St. Francis. From the main doors, the crucifix in the expansive apse seems to float in front of three tall stained-glass windows that fill the white-walled church with vibrant color. (Off P. delle Erbe. Open M-Sa 10am-noon and 2:30-6pm. Free.) The **South Tyrol Museum of Archaeology** traces the region's history from the Mesolithic Era to the Copper Age, but most tourists come to file by the giant refrigerator housing **Ötzi**. This famous 5000-year-old Neanderthal was found by hikers in the Alps who mistook him for a modern man, only recently frozen on the mountain. (V. Museo, 43, near Ponte Talvera. ☎0471 32 120; www.iceman.it. Wheelchair accessible. Open Tu-W and F-Su 10am-5pm, Th 10am-7pm. €8, students and seniors €5.50, under 6 free. Audioguides €2. Tour guides €2 for groups of 15+ and must be booked 14 days in advance, call ☎0471 32 021.) Perched on the vine-covered hills above town, **Castel Roncolo** is the most accessible of Bolzano's medieval fortresses. The winding path to the castle offers a spectacular view of the city, and inside lavish frescoes and small nooks provide insight on castle life. (Up V. Weggerstein to V. S. Antonio. Take city bus #12 from P. Walther; every 30min. M-Sa 7:05am-7:15pm. €0.90. ☎0471 32 98 08; www.comune.bolzano.it/roncolo/ie. Open Tu-Su 10am-6pm. Gates for frescoes close 5:30pm. Adults €; groups of 10+, students, and seniors €5.50.)

Bolzano is technically located in the pre-Alps, despite local allegiance to the Dolomites. The hiking here pales in comparison to that in the Alps to the west or the Dolomites proper to the east. The **CAI office** (see **Alpine Information**, p. 350) is likely to be far more helpful than the tourist office for information on outdoor activities. The best hikes can be accessed by the three *funivie* that surround the town, which run straight to vista level. While **Funivia del Renon** and **Funivia del Colle** have limited marked trails, **Funivia San Genesio** services extensive marked trails of moderate difficulty. On Funivia del Renon, the ride itself is an attraction, giving a bird's eye view of curving grape arbors. All three *funivie* offer free **maps** that should suffice for the easier hikes. Drop by the San Genesio **tourist office** (☎0471 35 41 96; www.jenesien.net) before starting out. The gentle walk from the San Genesio Funivia to the Edelweiss rest house, and then to the Tachaufenhaus and back to the *funivia* via the Locher rest house, makes for a pleasant 4½hr. hike. Even on the easiest hikes, take precautions against dehydration and exposure.

BRESSANONE (BRIXEN)　　☎0472

Northwest of the Dolomites and south of Austria, Bressanone's Alpine valley dazzles visitors with unimpeded views of green mountains, crystalline rivers, and rows of pastel houses. Its layout blends patches of urbanity with vast expanses of green space, where winding cobblestone roads coexist with swirling rivers and shady arbors. Modern touches like community theaters and tapas bars rub right against the outer walls of the *centro;* but inside, pedestrians pad through the walkways of the Altstadt, where public gardens and old buildings create a *Brigadoon*-like detachment from the bustle endemic to many other mountain towns.

■■ 🛈 **ORIENTATION AND PRACTICAL INFORMATION.** Bressanone is an easy daytrip by train or bus from Bolzano or Trent. **Trains** run to: Bolzano (30min., every hr. 1:21am-12:24am, €3.25); Brennero (45min., every hr. 4:27am-11:04pm, €4.65); Munich, Germany (5hr., 3-4 per day 8:33am-6:57pm, €50); Trent (1-1½hr., 17 per day 1:21am-12:34am, €4.65); Verona (2hr., 23 per day 4:27-11:04, €8.99). Train info is available at ☎0472 89 20 21 or www.trenitalia.com. **Luggage storage** is available out the main doors and to the right. (€3.87 per day. Open M-

F 6:15am-8pm, Sa 6:35am-8pm.) To reach the *centro* in **Piazza Duomo**, turn left from the bus and train stations onto **Viale Stazione**, walk 500m past the tourist office, on the right, and when Vle. Stazione becomes **Via Bastioni Minore**, turn immediately right through the arch on the right to enter the courtyard of the **Palazzo Vescovile**. P. Duomo is to the left. The **tourist office**, Vle. Stazione, 9, distributes town **maps** and info on suggested hikes; hotel listings outside list up-to-date vacancies throughout town. (☎0472 83 64 01; www.brixen.info. Open M-F 8:30am-12:30pm and 2:30-6pm, Sa 9am-12:30pm.) **ATMs** line V. Bastioni Maggiore, at the end of Viale Stazione. In case of **emergency,** dial ☎113 or call an **ambulance** at ☎118. A sign in the window of **Farmacia di Corte Principevescovile**, V. Portici Minori, 2/A, posts a list of after-hours rotations outside. (Open M-Tu and Th-Su 8am-12:30pm and 3-7pm, W 8am-12:30pm.) The **hospital** (☎0472 81 21 11) is on V. Dante, toward Brenner. **Green and Clean,** V. Dante, 13, offers self-service **laundry.** Enter through parking garage. (Info ☎335 65 19 904. Wash €3 per 8kg; €6/18kg. 20min. dry €3. Open daily 7am-11pm. Cash only.) **Currency exchange** is available at Bressanone's **post office,** behind the tourist office at V. Cassiano 4/B. (☎0472 27 20 01; fax 0472 27 20 40. Open M-Sa 8am-1:30pm.) **Postal Code:** 39042.

⌐⌐ ACCOMMODATIONS AND FOOD. Oddly, many of the more expensive hotels are near the river; the *centro* has three-star rooms in convenient locations for €40-50. Head from P. del Duomo into P. Palazzo, then turn left on V. Bruno to find **Ostello della Gioventù Kassianeum ❷**, V. Bruno, 2. Friendly staff, clean rooms, and buffet breakfast make this hostel worth the extra money. The dazzling view is priceless. (☎0472 27 99 99; jukas@jukas.net. Buffet breakfast and sheets included. Reception M-Sa 8am-8pm, Su 8am-6pm. Dorms €19-27. MC/V.) From the train station, turn left and follow Vle. Stazione until it connects with V. Bastioni in front of **Hotel Goldenes Kreuz (Croce d'Oro) ❹**, V. Bastioni Minori, 8. This well-located hotel has spacious rooms with comfortable furnishings. Pay extra for the sauna, hot tub, tanning bed, or solarium. (☎0472 83 61 55; www.goldeneskreuz.it. Breakfast included. Singles €45-70; doubles €70-120. Cash only.) From P. Stazione, walk down Vle. Mozart for 15min. Turn left on the first street after the river or take a Skibus to the left of the train station and ask to be let off at the three-star **Hotel Senoner ❹**, V. Plose, 22/A. Fall asleep to the sound of the rushing river in this 15th-century hotel with modern furnishings. Enjoy dinner in the restaurant or plasma TV in the breakfast nook. (☎0472 83 25 25; fax 0472 83 24 36. Breakfast €7. Singles €45-54; doubles €76-86. AmEx/MC/V.)

A **Despar** supermarket, V. B. Minori, 4, is near the *centro*. (☎0472 83 70 32. Open M-F 8am-7:30pm, Sa 8am-7pm. MC/V.) **Finsterwirt ❸**, Vco. Duomo, 3, first served wine in the 12th century, but has since given its classic Tyrolean fare an international twist. Grape arbors and stone fountains create a breezy setting for the *osteria* downstairs. Walk directly away from the *duomo* doors; Vco. Duomo is the alley to the left. (☎0472 83 55 43; fax 0472 83 56 24. *Primi* €9.50-11, *secondi* €15.50-19. Open Tu-Sa 12:30-2:30pm and 6:30-10:30pm, Su 12:30-2:30pm. MC/V.) At the 100 year-old **Fink ❷**, Portici Minor, 4, waitresses in traditional garb serve dishes like *rösti*, a pizza-sized mat of fried potatoes and veggies (€7), and Alto Adige wines (€3-5.20), while pastries await those still hungry for dessert. (☎0472 83 48 83; fax 0472 83 52 68. *Primi* €6.70-7.80, *secondi* €11.90-12.50. Open M-Tu and Th-Su 11am-11pm. AmEx/MC/V.) Sit indoors or under the canopy at **Torre Bianca ❶**, V. Torre Bianca, 6, which serves a wide variety of pizzas (€5.20-8.90) and traditional Tyrolean food on a quiet street in the *centro*. Walk past the left side of the cloister's *campanile* and pass through the arch. (☎0472 83 29 72. Cover €1. Open M and W-Su 9am-11:30pm. MC/V.)

◐ ◪ **SIGHTS AND HIKING.** For a break from the boutiques and traffic of central Bressanone, follow Ponte Aquila behind the *duomo* and cross the bridge to the winding footpaths of the **Altstadt** (old town), where shops and pastel houses huddle along quiet streets. For more directed sightseeing, head to **Piazza del Duomo.** A few meters south of the *piazza*, look for a golden lamb-topped monument in P. Palazzo, where the pale yellow **Palazzo Vescovile,** completed in 1595, houses the **Museo Diocesano.** Its predominantly ecclesiastical collection traces the development of Western Christianity. Medieval and Renaissance portraits, including copies of works by Hans Klocker and Albrecht Dürer, round out the exhibits. Explanatory info is in Italian and German only. (☎0472 83 05 05. Open Mar. 15-Oct. 31 Tu-Su 10am-5pm; Dec. 1-Jan. 31 daily 2-5pm. €5.) The candy-colored **duomo** is as colorful inside as out—Baroque and Neo-Classical additions in 1595, 1754, and 1790 covered almost every inch with frescoes. To the right of the *duomo*, the squat gray **cloister** displays traditional Stations of the Cross, but the large gilded organ in the back reveals a touch of stunning ornamentation. The garden contains floral arrangements and a monument to local soldiers killed in both World Wars. (Both open daily 8am-noon and 3-6pm. Guided *duomo* tours meet M-Sa at 10:30am and 3pm just left of the main doors. Free.)

The **Plose Plateau,** towering over Bressanone at heights of over 2000m, is a popular area for skiers, made accessible by the **Sant'Andrea Cable Car** (July 7-Oct. 3. 10min.; 2 per hr. M-F 9am-12pm and 1-6pm, Sa-Su 9am-6pm; round-trip €7, bikes €3), which operates from the nearby hillside town of **Sant'Andrea. SAD bus #126** makes round-trips between the Bressanone train station and S. Andrea (20min., 7 per day 7:54am-7:15pm) and Bressanone (7:15am-7:25pm, round-trip €2). Buy tickets on the bus. From the upper cable-car station, **trail 30** leads along the smooth terrain of the Plose's western slope, and **trail 17** follows the meadows on the Plose's southern slope. For a longer, more strenuous hike, **trail 7** traverses the three summits of the Plose Massif, Monte Telegrafo, Monte Fana, and Monte Forca, reaching altitudes of 2600m. Before tackling this hike, check the weather and plan for possible overnights in *rifugi*. Two *rifugi*, **Plose** and **Rossalm,** also offer hot meals. A tourist office brochure details three easy 3-6hr. hikes on the Plose. Verify bus and lift schedules and be prepared to face rough terrain and high altitudes.

TRENT (TRENTO, TRIENT)   ☎0461

Within the Alpine threshold but connected to the Veneto by a deep valley, Trent was the Roman's strategic gateway to the north. For centuries to follow, the region was the base for fortresses like the Castello del Buonconsiglio. Political ownership of Trent, contested in the 19th-century, was finally settled in Italy's favor at the end of WWI, though Germanic influences are still highly evident. Trent was recently named Alpine City of the Year in 2004 for its local pride and carefully preserved culture, manifested in a year-round rotation of festivals, tours, and exhibits.

▐ **TRANSPORTATION**

Trains: V. Dogana, ☎0461 89 20 21. Ticket office open daily 5:40am-8:30pm. Info office open M-F 8:30am-12:15pm and 1:15-4:30pm. **Luggage storage** is available at the train station. To: **Bologna** (3hr., 9 per day 1:38am-9:41pm, €10.12); **Bolzano** (45min., 35 per day 1:40am-10:51pm, €2.89); **Venice** (3-4hr., 12 per day 4:15am-5:20pm, €7.90); **Verona** (1hr., 2 per hr. 2:26am-9:12pm, €4.65).

Buses: Atesina and **Trentino Transporti** (☎0461 82 10 00; www.ttspa.it), on V. Pozzo next to the train station. Info office in terminal open M-Sa 7am-7:30pm. To: **Riva del Garda** (1¾hr., every hr. 5:57am-7:50pm, €3.20) and **Rovereto** (50min., every hr. 5:57am-7:50pm, €3.60).

Public Transportation: Atesina operates an extensive local bus network. Tickets on sale at dispenser in the bus station or *tabaccherie* for €0.90 (valid for 70min.).

Cableways: Funivia Trento-Sardagna (☎0461 23 21 54), on Lung'Adige Monte Grappa. From bus station, turn right on V. Pozzo; take 1st right on Cavalcavia S. Lorenzo. Cross bridge over train tracks and head across the intersection to the building to the left of the river bridge. To **Sardagna** on Mt. Bondone (4min.; every 15-30min.; €0.90 for 70min. ticket, €1.20 for 120min. ticket. Open daily 7am-10:30pm. Cash only).

Taxi: RadioTaxi: ☎0461 93 00 02. 24hr.

Bike Rental: Public Bike Rental, V. Belenzani, 19 (☎0461 88 44 53) is across the street from the train terminal. €5 key deposit. Office open M-F 9am-6pm and Sa 9am-noon. Bicycles available 6am-8pm daily. Late drop fee €5 plus €2 for each additional day. **Moser Cicli,** V. Calepina, 63 (☎0461 23 03 27), rents mountain bikes. €15 per day. Open M 3-7pm and Tu-Sa 9am-noon and 3-7pm. MC/V.

✦ 🛈 ORIENTATION AND PRACTICAL INFORMATION

The **bus** and **train stations** are on the same street, between the **Adige River** and the gardens and circle-of-hell statue of **Piazza Dante.** The town center lies east of the Adige. From the stations, walk right to the intersection with **Via Torre Vanga.** Continue straight as **Via Pozzo** becomes **Via Orfane** and then the curving **Via Cavour** before reaching **Piazza del Duomo** in the town's center. **ATMs** are nearby. For **Castello del Buonconsiglio,** follow **Via Roma** eastward, away from the river as it becomes **Via Manci,** then **Via San Marco.**

Tourist Office: APT, V. Manci, 2 (☎0461 98 38 80; www.apt.trento.it). Turn right from the train station and left on V. Roma, which becomes V. Manci. Offers information on biking, theater, and frequent festivals. Offers guided tours of the city and the castle; both include wine tasting. Meet at the office, no reservation required; tours limited to groups of 10 or less. City tours July-Aug. Th and Sa 3pm, Sept.-June Sa 3pm; €3. Castle tours July-Aug. Th and Sa 10am; Sept.-June Sa 10am; €3. Open daily 9am-7pm.

Luggage Storage is available at the train station. €2 for 1st 2hr., €1 next 3hr., €2 for 6+ hr., 24hr. max. Open daily 8:30am-12:15pm and 1:30-5:30pm. Cash only.

Bookstore: Libreria Disertori, V. A. Diaz, 11 (☎0461 98 14 55; infolibreriadisertori@virgilo.it), near Ple. C. Battisti. Classic literature and thrillers comprise a slim selection of English books. Local, regional, and international **maps** aplenty. Open M 3-7pm, Tu-Su 9-12am and 3-7pm. AmEx/MC/V.

Emergency: ☎113. **Ambulance:** ☎118. **Police,** P. Mostra, 3 (☎112).

Pharmacy: Farmacia dall'Armi, P. Duomo, 10 (☎0461 23 61 39). Serving the city since 1490. After-hours rotation posted in window. Open July-Aug. M-Sa 8:30am-12:30pm and 3:30-7pm; Sept.-June M-Sa 8:30am-12:30pm and 5-7pm. Cash only.

Hospital: Ospedale Santa Chiara, Largo Medaglie d'Oro, 9 (☎0461 90 31 11), up V. Orsi past the swimming pool.

Internet Access: Call Me, V. Belenzani, 58 (☎0461 98 33 02), off P. del Duomo. Internet (€3 per hr.), fax, **Western Union,** phone booths, and international phone cards available. Open daily 9am-9pm. Laptop users can find affordable wireless access at **Caffè Olimpia,** V. Belenzani, 33/1 (☎0461 98 24 45). €2.50 per hr. Open M-Sa 11am-11:30pm; bar open M and W 6am-9pm, Tu and Th-Sa 6am-midnight. Cash only.

Post Office: V. Calepina, 16 (☎0461 98 47 15), offers fax services just off P. Vittoria. Open M-F 8am-6:30pm, Sa 8am-12:30pm. **Branch:** V. Dogana (☎0461 98 23 01) next to train station. Open M-F 8am-6:30pm, Sa 8am-12:30pm. **Postal Code:** 38100.

ACCOMMODATIONS

▨ **Ostello Giovane Europa (HI),** V. Torre Vanga, 11 (☎0461 26 34 84; fax 0461 22 25 17). Exit train station and turn right; hostel is the white building on the corner, past the bus station. 6-bed dorms are spotless and offer private bathrooms, desk, and phone. Downstairs, guests enjoy the sunny terraces and restaurant. Breakfast, shower, phone, and sheets included. Buffet breakfast €3. 3-course menù (primi, secondi, and dessert) Laundry available €9. (qash €4, dry €2). Internet €5.16. Lockers €3. Reception 7:30am-11pm. Check-out 10am. Curfew 11:30pm (ask for door code to return later). Reserve ahead. 6-bed dorms €13.50; singles €25; doubles €40. AmEx/MC/V. ❶

Hotel Aquila d'Oro, V. Belenzani, 76 (☎0461 98 62 82; www.aquiladoro.it). Just 2 doors down from P. del Duomo, Aquila D'Oro's professional staff and spacious well-decorated rooms set the gold standard. Rooms feature TVs (Italian channels free, additional options €10.50 per day), in-room Internet lines (€5.50 for 1 day), and phone. Breakfast included. Singles €63; doubles €95; triples €120. AmEx/MC/V. ❺

Casa Pompermaier, V. Lavisotto, 69 (☎0461 82 21 90; fax 335 84 89 376). Take bus #8 from the stop across P. Dante from the train station, at the intersection of V. Vannetti and V. Gazzoletti. Get off at the Rotatoria stop on V. Maccani (the 6th stop) and turn right just before the Poli supermarket. Hotel is 100m ahead on the right. A friendly family rents out 4 comfy rooms with spacious bathroom and access to a kitchen. Singles €35; doubles €60. Cash only. ❸

Hotel Venezia, P. Duomo, 45 (☎/fax 0461 23 41 14). Parquet wooden floors and wrought-iron beds give this hotel a dated feel, but big bathrooms and a winning location make for a pleasant stay. Breakfast included. Singles €45; doubles €65. MC/V. ❹

FOOD

Trentino cuisine owes much to the local production of such sterling cheeses as nostrano, tosela, and the highly prized vezzena. Piatti del malgaro (herdsman's plates) include cheeses, polenta, mushrooms, and sausage. Another favorite is the chewy minestrone trippe (tripe soup). A Germanic undercurrent shows itself in the exceptional local version of Apfelstrudel. The **open-air market** around P. del Duomo sells flowers and produce every Thursday. (Open 8am-1pm.) **Supermercati Trentini** lies across P. Pasi from the duomo at P. Lodron, 28. (☎0461 22 01 96. Open M 2:30-7:30pm, Tu-Su 8:30am-7:30pm. MC/V.) The **Poli** supermarket sits where V. Orfane meets V. Roma at V. Orfane, 2. (☎0461 98 50 63. Open M-Tu 8:30am-7:15pm, W 8:30am-1pm, and Th-Sa 8:30am-7:15pm. AmEx/MC/V.)

▨ **Osteria Il Cappello,** P. Lunelli, 5 (☎0451 23 58 50). From the stations, turn right, then left on V. Roma. After 4 blocks, turn right on V. S. Pietro, then take the tunnel by #27. This classy restaurant overlooking a private courtyard serves Trentino cuisine with an international twist. Primi €8-8.50, secondi €12.50-15.50. Cover €2. Open Tu-Sa noon-2pm and 7:30-10pm, Su noon-2pm. AmEx/MC/V. ❸

Ristorante Al Vo, Vco. del Vo, 11 (☎0461 98 53 74; www.ristorantealvo.it). From the stations, turn right and walk to V. Torre Vanga. Turn left; the restaurant is 200m down on the right. A friendly staff has been serving Trentino classics since 1345 in a quiet, airy atrium. Menu changes daily, but lunch with primo, secondo, and side dish costs €13. Open M-W and Sa-Su 11:30am-3pm, Th-F 11:30am-3pm and 7-9pm. AmEx/MC/V. ❺

Graziano's, V. Esterle 9 (☎0461 26 05 44; grazianospizza@hotmail.com) near the *duomo*. Travelers and locals on a budget or on the go fill up on 2 slices of pizza for €1.60-2.00. Open M-F 11am-2:30pm and 5:30-9pm, Sa 5:30-9pm. AmEx/MC/V. ❶

La Cantinota, V. San Marco, 22/24 (☎0461 23 85 27). From the stations, turn right and then left on V. Roma. Take another left on V. San Marco. Cantinota offers everything from champagne in the elegant gold and ivory piano bar upstairs to horse pizza (€10) in the stone and wood *trattoria* on ground level. *Primi* €7.50-9, *secondi* €13-17, single plate meals €10-12. Restaurant open M-W and F-Su noon-2:30pm and 7pm-midnight; piano bar open M-W and F-Su 10pm-2:30am; closed in Aug. MC/V. ❸

Forst Birreria/Ristorante, V. Oss Mazzurana, 38 (☎0461 23 55 90). When heading up V. Roma from the stations, turn right onto V. O. Mazzurana. Light, flaky pizza (from €3.90) and quick service make the patio perfect for a short, affordable meal. A full menu and helpful staff keep the extensive bar and tables in the Austrian-influenced dining room full of faithful patrons. *Primi* €6-10, *secondi* €5.40-11. Cover €1.09. Open Tu-Su noon-3pm and 5:30-11:30. AmEx/MC/V. ❷

La Gelateria, V. Belanzani, 50, near P. del Duomo. This colorful *gelateria* serves up intimidatingly large scoops of rich *gelato*—flavors include violet and 2 different types of pistachio. 3 huge scoops €2. Open daily 10:30am-midnight. Cash only. ❶

⊙ SIGHTS

Trent's **Piazza del Duomo** offers everything from religious history to modern shops and services. The **Fontana del Nettuno** at the center of the *piazza* is anchored by a majestic Neptune waving a trident as mer-people spit incessantly around his feet. Nearby stands the **Cattedrale di San Vigilio,** whose somber interior housed the historical Council of Trent during the sacred public relations blitz of the Counter-Reformation. Dark, rich art adorns the massive incense-filled building, illuminated only by sunlight and clusters of red votive candles. (Open daily 7am-noon and 2:30-6pm. Masses are mornings and evenings, open to tourists 10am-5pm. Free.) Underneath, the **Basilica Sotterranea di S. Vigilio,** entered from the left of the altar, displays altars and statues uncovered in excavations around the *duomo*. (Open M-Sa 10am-noon and 2:30-6pm. €1, ages 12-18 €0.50.) Nearby, the dull white stone castle with the square tower houses the **Museo Diocesano,** officially reopened by Pope John Paul II in 1995 after renovations for elaborate tapestries, paintings, and illuminated manuscripts from various regional churches. (P. del Duomo, 18. ☎0461 23 44 19; www.museodiocesanotridentino.it. Museum open June-Sept. M and W-Su 9:30am-12:30pm and 2:30-6pm, Oct.-May M and W-Su 9:30am-12:30pm and 2:30-5:30pm. Hours extended during exhibitions. Ticket counter close 15min. before museum. €3, ages 12-18 €0.50. Entrance includes access to the archaeological excavations beneath the church. Free audioguides in English with ID deposit.) The **Castello del Buonconsiglio** contains a wealth of history from the medieval period to WWI. In the **loggia** at the end of the castle's rooftop garden, the ceiling features Diana depicted as the moon and Apollo as the sun with scenes from Greek, Roman, and Hebrew history and mythology in the lunettes. Stairs lead down from the *loggia* to the **Fossa dei Martiri,** the castle's old moat and execution site of famed martyrs Cesare Battisti, Damiano Chiesa, and Fabio Filzi in 1916. The castle is most famous, however, for the famed **Ciclo dei Mesi,** a series of International Gothic paintings representing an ideal feudal society. For access, ask about tours of the **Torre dell'Aquila.** Tours depart from the *loggia*. (10 per day from 10:30am-5:15pm. €1. Free audioguides in multiple languages.) Take V. Belenzani and turn right on V. Roma. (☎0461 23 37 70. Castle open Apr.-Sept. Tu-Su 9am-noon and 2-5:30pm; Oct.-Mar. Tu-Su 9am-noon and 2-5pm. €6, students and under 18 or over 60 €3. Torre d'Aquila an additional €1. Ticket price includes admission to museum and Tridentum, an excavation of Roman ruins under P. Battisti.)

ROVERETO ☎0464

Nestled in the Dolomites, the town of Rovereto is far from the attention of camera-toting tourists. Cobblestone alleys weave around frescoed buildings, decorative stone fountains dot the *piazze*, and mountain breezes waft delicately through the streets. The *centro* feels decidedly urban, but the small shops along pedestrian side streets retain a more rural air. The surrounding country offers opportunities for biking, hiking, walking, and horseback-riding, while a museum of Modern art is the star attraction for those more interested in an air-conditioned interior.

📑🖉 **TRANSPORTATION AND PRACTICAL INFORMATION.** The **train station** is at P. Orsi, 11. **Trains** run to: Bologna (3hr., 14 per day 5:25am-9:58pm, €8.99); Bolzano (1hr., 24 per day 2:59am-10:36pm, €4.30); Trent (15min., 32 per day 2:59pm-11:35pm, €2.40); Verona (1hr., 31 per day 2:42am-9:58pm, €3.36). Check schedules at ticket office. (☎0464 89 20 21. Ticket office open M-F 5:50am-7:30pm, Sa 9am-6:30pm. AmEx/MC/V.) The **bus station** is at C. Rosmini, 45. **Buses** run frequently to Riva del Garda (1hr., 24 per day 6:41am-10:30pm, €2.40) and Trent (50min., 24 per day 5:07am-6:56pm, €4.15). Check station for schedules. (Open M-Sa 6:30am-7:15pm. MC/V.) The **tourist office,** C. Rosmini, 6/A, provides a town **map,** lodgings guide, and info on activities in the area. (☎0464 43 03 63; www.apt.rovereto.tn.it. Open M-F 9am-12:15pm and 2:30-6:30pm.) On weekends, visit the **branch** at C. A. Bettini, 43 in the MART. (☎0464 42 52 06. Open Tu-Su 10am-1pm and 2-5:30pm.) There is an **ATM** in the train station; others are located throughout town. **Internet** is available at C. A. Bettini, 58. (€3 per hr. Open Tu-Th 9:30am-noon, 3-7pm, and 9-11:30pm, F-Sa 9:30am-noon and 3-7pm). To reach the **police station,** V. Sighele, 1 (☎046 44 84 611), follow the signs across the street from the train station. A **pharmacy** lies between the bus and train stations at V. Dante, 3. (☎0464 42 10 30. Open M-F and Su 8:30am-12:15pm and 3-7pm, Sa 8:30am-12:15pm.) The **post office,** V. Largo Posta, 7, is up C. Rosmini from the bus station. (☎0464 40 22 18. Open M-F 8am-6:30pm, Sa 8am-12:30pm. MC/V). **Postal Code:** 38068.

🛏🍴 **ACCOMMODATIONS AND FOOD.** Low tourist traffic means that budget hotels are scarce in Rovereto. The tourist office offers a printed list of local lodgings, but affordable living may require a short hike. To reach **Lizzanella ❷,** C. Verona, 115, exit the *centro* along V. Dante, cross the bridge at the end, and turn right on C. Verona at the fork with V. Santa Maria. After about 15min., the hotel appears on the right. The friendly Proserpio family maintains two stories of spacious rooms with shared baths, bright windows, and kitchens in a quiet area down the hill from the Campana della Pace. (☎0464 43 85 93. Breakfast included. Call before arrival. Singles €30; doubles €50. Cash only.)

Celebrate Austrians and Italians at **Vecchia Trattoria Birrara Scala della Torre ❷,** V. Scala della Torre, 7, where Venetian masks look upon Austrian fare. For €11, try the *Gulasch nach trentino con polenta.* From P. delle Erbe, ascend the staircase to the left of the fountain. (☎0464 43 71 00. *Primi* €5.20-6.20, *secondi* from €6.70-13. Bread and cover €1. Open daily noon-2:30pm and 7:30-9:30pm. AmEx/MC/V.) **Trentini** supermarket, at V. Mazzini, 65, stocks basics. (☎0464 42 11 97. Open M 8:30am-1:30pm, Tu-Sa 8:30am-12:30pm and 3:15-7:15pm. V.)

🎭🎶 **SIGHTS AND ENTERTAINMENT.** An unlikely sight in a small town, the gargantuan ▓**Museo d'Arte Moderna e Contemporanea** (commonly known as "Il

Mart"), C. A. Bettini, 43, is the largest modern art museum in Italy. Banners unfurling on every street corner direct visitors to its glass-and-steel cupola. Inside, 5600 sq. m of sleek rooms house over 7000 pieces. Fortunato Depero's massive *Scenario Plastico per le Chant du Rossignol* anchors the Futurist wing, while 20th-century Italian pieces and American works like Warhol's *Four Marilyns*, Lichtenstein's *Hot Dog*, and Rosenquist's *Sliced Bologna* complete the collection. (☎0464 43 88 87; www.mart.trento.it. Open Tu-Th 10am-6pm, F 10am-9pm, Sa-Su 10am-6pm. €8, under 18 €5. Audioguides in Italian or English €3. AmEx/MC/V.) Looming from its perch high above the city, the gray **Castello di Rovereto**, V. Castelbarco, 7, has served mostly military purposes since its construction in the 4th century. From P. Podestà, follow V. Della Terra (near the cannon), turn right on V. Castelbarco, and head up the stairs. The **Museo della Guerra** (Museum of War) now fills the castle with war materials ranging from medieval spears and chain mail to bombshells and newspapers from WWII. The collection also includes a set of samurai armor. Above the museum, an observation deck affords a 360° view of Rovereto. (☎0464 43 81 00; www.museodellaguerra.it. Open Tu-Su 10am-6pm. €5.50, ages 6-18 €2. MC/V.) About an hour walk uphill from the *centro*, the **Campana della Pace** (Bell of Peace) on V. Miravalle commemorates war casualties. The largest ringing bell in the world, the *campana* was cast in 1924 from 226.39 tons of bronze recycled from the cannons of the 19 nations involved in WWI and later blessed by Pope Paul VI. It tolls 100 times for victims of war each night. (☎0464 43 44 12. Open Nov.-Dec. 9am-4:30pm; Mar. and Oct. 9am-6pm; Apr.-Sept. 9am-7pm and public bell-ringing 9-9:30pm. €2, children 6-14 €0.50. Cash only.) The **Civic Museum,** Borgo Santa Caterina, 41, provides tours of the astronomical observatory on Monte Zugna and of the **Dinosaur Tracks** in the southern part of Rovereto. Over 200 million years ago, 250 herbivores and carnivores paced along an ancient landslide. From various places along the mountain trail, their tracks are still visible in the gray hillside (☎0464 43 90 55; fax 0464 43 94 87. Call to arrange a tour.)

Nightlife in Rovereto is fairly tame, but **Bacchus ❶**, V. G. Garibaldi, 29, manages to keep its patrons out late with trademark drinks like the decadent *Shakerato* (€3.50). The warm yellow interior, filled with barrel-shaped tables, is deceptively small, but patrons always manage to find a place at the bar or just outside in the street. (Open M and W-Su 11am-1:30pm and 5pm-close. Cash only.)

RIVA DEL GARDA ☎0464

With lake waters lapping at the foot of the Brenta Dolomites, Riva is a spot for those who love *belle viste* (beautiful views) but who are traveling on *pochi soldi* (a tight budget). Gentle mountain winds make Garda ideal for windsurfing, and Riva's aquatic sports schools are internationally renowned. The area is also a prime location for hiking, canoeing, whitewater rafting, kayaking, bicycling, and swimming—all made accessible and affordable by the attractive youth hostel.

⌐ TRANSPORTATION

Buses: Vle. Trento, 5 (☎0464 55 23 23). Ticket office open M-Sa 6:30am-7:15pm, Su 9:05am-noon and 3:35-7:05pm. Urban tickets available at dispenser in station. To: **Rovereto** (1hr., 18 per day 7:39am-10:04pm, €2.40); **Trent** (1½hr., 20 per day 7:39am-10:04pm, €3.20-3.40); **Verona** (2hr., 14 per day 6:15am-7:10pm, €5.20).

Ferries: Navigazione Lago di Garda (☎030 91 49 511; fax 030 91 49 520), in P. Catena. To **Gardone Riviera** (1½-3hr., 8:40am-5pm, €6.80-9.60) and **Sirmione** (2-4hr., 8:40am-5pm, €8-11.30). Ticket office open 20min before each departure.

Taxi: ☎0464 55 22 00.

Bike Rental: Cicli Pederzolli, Viale dei Tigli, 24 (☎/fax 0464 55 18 30). Mountain and city bikes €8-13 per day. Ask for multiple-day discounts and free guided tours. Open M-Sa 9am-noon and 3-7pm. AmEx/MC/V.

Scooter Rental: Sembenini Dainese Pro Shop, Vle. Dante, 3 (☎0464 55 45 48). €18 per 2hr., €47 per day, €178 per week. Open daily 9:30am-12:30pm and 4-7:30pm. MC/V.

ORIENTATION AND PRACTICAL INFORMATION

To reach the town center from the **train station**, walk straight on **Viale Trento**, then cross the traffic circle and go behind the church taking **Via Roma** to reach **Piazza Cavour.** The **tourist office,** Giardini di Porta Orientale, 8, is near the water's edge on V. della Liberazione. It lists hotel vacancies and offers a variety of cheap regional tours. Ask for a city **map** and hiking routes. (☎0464 55 44 44; www.gardatrentino.it. Free guided tour to the neighboring town of Arco Su 9:30am-noon. Free Riva tour Sa 9:30am-12:30pm. Electronic booking board outside. English spoken. Wheelchair accessible. Open M-Sa 9am-noon and 3-6:30pm, Su 10am-noon and 4-6:30pm.) In case of **emergency,** call ☎113, contact the **carabinieri** at ☎112, or call an **ambulance** at ☎118. There are **pharmacies** at V. Dante Alighieri, 12/B (☎0464 55 25 08; open M-F 8:45am-12:30pm and 3:30-7:30pm), and V. Maffei, 8 (☎0464 55 23 02; open M-Sa 8:45am-12:30pm and 3:30-7:30pm, Su 9am-12:30pm and 3:30-7pm), in P. delle Erbe. For speedy **Internet** access, try **Caffè Italia,** P. Cavour, 8. (☎0464 55 25 00. €1 per 10min., €4 per hr. Open daily 7am-1am. Cash only.) The **post office** and **ATM** are at V. Disciplini, 32. (☎0464 57 87 43. Open M-F 8am-6:30pm, Sa 8am-12:30pm.) **Postal Code:** 38066.

ACCOMMODATIONS AND CAMPING

Ostello Benacus (HI), P. Cavour, 10. (☎0464 55 49 11; www.garda.com/ostelloriva), is a gem for its location alone, right in the center of town. From bus station, walk down V. Trento, cross the traffic circle to V. Roma, turn left under the arch, and cross left through P. Cavour. Breakfast, sheets, and hot shower included. Dinner €9. Laundry €4 per wash. Internet €2 per hr. Reception 7-9am and 3pm-midnight. Silence at 11pm; ask for key to return after midnight. Reserve ahead. Dorms €14. AmEx/MC/V. ❶

Locanda La Montanara, V. Montanara, 20 (☎0464 55 48 57; fax 0464 56 15 52), off V. Florida. 9 bright and comfortable rooms with hardwood floors, some with bath, surround a sunny central staircase. Restaurant downstairs. Breakfast €6. Reserve 1 month ahead in summer. Singles €17; doubles €32, with shower €36; triples €49. MC/V. ❷

Albergo Garni Rita, V. Brione, 19 (☎/fax 0464 55 17 98). Friendly owners run a spacious B&B with large private pool, stone terrace, and rooms with TV and bath in a quiet area 25min. outside of the city center. Breakfast included. Call ahead for reservations. Open Mar. 10-Nov. 3. Singles €38; doubles €53. Cash only. ❸

Albergo Ancora, V. Montanara, 2 (☎0464 52 21 31; hotelancora@rivadelgarda.com). Light-hued furniture and embroidered curtains give the individually furnished rooms an antique vibe, but all have modern amenities, including bath, telephone, and TV. Wheelchair accessible. Discount for extended stay and groups of 10 or more. Singles €58-59; doubles €84-92; triples €120; quads €170. AmEx/MC/V. ❹

Hotel Benini, V. S. Alessandro, 25 (☎0464 55 30 40; www.hotelbenini.com). 1km from the city center. Simple, pleasant hotel offers garden, pool, and bicycle rental. All rooms have bath, A/C, phone, and TV. Wheelchair accessible. Buffet breakfast included. Reception 8am-midnight. Singles €43; doubles €72; triples €108. AmEx/MC/V. 4

Villa Maria, V. dei Tigli, 19 (☎0464 55 22 88; www.garnimaria.com). A 10min. walk from the city center. Though the exterior is rather plain, rooms offer great views of the mountains as well as soft mattresses and homey carpets. All rooms have bath, TV, and Internet jacks. Breakfast included. Reception 8am-10pm. Singles €35; doubles €60. AmEx/MC/V. ❸

Bavaria, V. Rovereto, 100 (☎0464 55 25 24), on road toward Torbole. Pizzeria on premises. Take lessons in windsurfing, sailing, and canoeing right behind the campground at Surfsegnana (see **Sights and Outdoor Activities**). Hot shower €1. Camping reception daily 8am-1pm and 2:30-7pm. Silence 11pm-8am and 3-5pm. No entry by car 11pm-7am. Open Apr.-Oct. €7 per person, children 3-12 €5.80, €9 per site. AmEx/MC/V for €60 or more. ❶

Camping Monte Brione, V. Brione, 32 (☎0464 52 08 85; www.campingbrione.com). Flowering trees shade a pool, bar, laundry services, and minimarket situated 800m from the lake, next to biking trails. Free hot showers. Reception 8am-1pm and 3-7pm. Reserve ahead. €6.50-7.50 per person, €7.50-8.70 per small site without electricity; €9.40-11 per large site at foot of hill with parking and electricity. MC/V. ❶

🍴 FOOD

An **open-air market** sells produce in P. delle Erbe. (Open M-Sa mornings.) A **Despar** supermarket sells standard grocery fare just outside the *centro* at V. Roma, 19. (Open M-Sa 8:30am-1pm and 3:30-7:15pm, Su 9am-12:30pm. Cash only.)

Leon d'Oro, V. Fiume, 28 (☎0464 55 23 41). Wide windows open onto the bustling V. Fiume, but diners in the cool interior are more drawn to the flavorful dishes before them. Try the summer-perfect *risotto mantecato alle code di gambero* (with lemon-marinated prawns; €10). *Primi* from €6.50, fish *secondi* from €8.50. Bread and cover €1.30. Open daily mid to March-mid-Nov. 11:30am-3pm and 5:40-11pm. AmEx/MC/V. ❸

Birreria Spaten, V. Maffei, 7 (☎0464 55 36 70), in P. delle Erbe. Traditional goulash and wurstel are served on the ground floor of the late Baron Menghin's palace, where a rustic homey interior and free-flowing beer belie its noble origins. *Wurstel* €7.50. Goulash from €8.50. Large beer €3.70. Open M-Tu and Th-Su 11am-3pm and 5:30pm-midnight. AmEx/MC/V. ❷

Ristorante-Pizzeria La Leonessa, V. Maffei, 24 (☎0464 55 27 77), just off P. delle Erbe. Bright yellow tablecloths and colorful wall paintings make this a great family restaurant. Try the *sorpresa della casa* (pasta with capers, olives, and tomatoes wrapped inside pizza dough; €6). Pizza €4.50-8. *Primi* €5-10, *secondi* €8-10. Open M-Tu and Th-Su noon-2:30pm and 6-10pm. AmEx/MC/V. ❷

Ristorante Ancora, V. Montanara, 2 (☎0464 52 21 31). Fresh fish perfectly complements the maritime decor in the sunny interior, or sun-kissed rooftop terrace. Try *la trota del lago salmonata alla griglia*, juicy salmon with a crispy, flavorful exterior (€9.50). *Primi* €5-10, *secondi* €9-13. 10% discount for patrons of attached hotel. Open daily noon-2:30pm and 7pm-midnight; June-Sept. closed for lunch. AmEx/MC/V. ❸

👁 🛶 SIGHTS AND OUTDOOR ACTIVITIES

For stunning views, swimming, or pebbly sunbathing, follow the lakeside path behind the tourist office and head away from the mountains. Three kilometers outside Riva, the 20,000-year-old **Cascata Varone** has chiseled a huge gorge in the mountain. Foliage arches over surrounding mountain paths, making them ideal for easy strolls. (Take bus #1 or 2 from V. Martiri. ☎0464 52 14 21. Open daily May-Aug. 9am-7pm; Mar. and Oct. 10am-12:30pm and 2-5pm; Apr. and Sept. 9am-6pm. €4. Cash only.) On the lake itself, find **Noleggio Rudderboat Rental** along Lungalago Marinai d'Italia for hourly paddle boat rentals and low-key fun. (☎335 60 54 454. 2

people €7, 4 people €8, 5 people €9. Open daily 8:30am-7pm. Cash only.) Located behind campground Bavaria Surfsegnana offers windsurfing, sailing, and canoeing lessons. (☎0464 50 59 63; www.surfsegnana.it. Open daily 8am-6pm)

In the cliffs above the lake, historical hotspots draw hikers out of the city *centro*. Follow V. Dante to the mountains as it changes to V. Bastione, then take a left up the ramp and follow the winding cobblestone path for 20min. to the 15th-century **Bastione**, a circular fortress that survived Napoleon's onslaught in 1796 but lost its upper half as a result. Today, hikers can explore the edges of the historical treasure or admire the aerial view of Riva in miniature with tiny boats dotting the vibrant blue of Lake Garda. Farther up, a steep 1hr. hike leads to **Chiesetta Santa Barbara,** a tiny chapel poised over misty mountains and the valley below.

NIGHTLIFE

Lakeside clubs are popular weekend spots, while pubs are an evening or weekday alternative. **Party boats** cruise across the lake to Latin techno beats. Ask at the tourist office for a listing of free musical concerts. (Cover €12.50 includes 1 drink. Reservation required. Cruises late July-Aug.) **Chico's,** Vclo. dei Fabbri, 11, is a typical Italian bar with a spicy Brazilian twist. Flashing lights illuminate hanging flags while merengue and salsa music keep it steamy. From P. Cavour, take V. Disciplini onto V. Diaz. V. dei Fabbri is at the intersection with V. Fiume. (☎033 33 00 81 15. Open daily 8pm-1am. MC/V.) **Pub Barracuda,** P. Catena 7, has plenty of seats looking out on the lake, but interior is decorated by modern paintings from local artists that change monthly. Owner Jimmy offers fresh fruity concoctions (like the *kaipiroska alla fragola*, €5) as well as rums (€3-8 a glass) in a wide selection. (Open daily 8pm-2am. MC/V.) **Pub All'Oca,** V. S. Maria, 9, has three themes: Scotland, sailing and jazz. Old leather booths attract a fashionable crowd to sip fresh *Mojitos* (€5.50) in this ivy-covered classic. (☎0464 55 34 57. Open daily 6pm-2am. Cash only.) **Cafe Latino,** V. Giacomo Cis, 15, is a swanky tri-level *discoteca* overlooking the lake. Pick out the bartenders by their glittery facial tattoos. (☎0464 55 57 85. Cover €8, includes 1 drink. Get a drink card to keep track of drink purchases—lose it and pay €70. Open F-Sa 11pm-4am. AmEx/MC/V.)

FRIULI-VENEZIA GIULIA

Bounded by the Veneto to the west and Slovenia to the east is the kaleidoscope that is Friuli-Venezia Giulia. The region derives its formal name from several distinct provinces unified by the clergy between the 6th and 15th centuries and claimed by the Hapsburgs in the early 1700s as an important economic center for Austria and Hungary. Since then, parts have circulated between countries for decades, resulting in a potpourri of cuisines, styles, and architecture. James Joyce wrote the bulk of *Ulysses* in coffee houses that still dot Trieste; Ernest Hemingway found part of his plot for *A Farewell to Arms* in the region's Carso cliffs; and Franz Liszt, Sigmund Freud, and Rainer Maria Rilke all worked in Friuli, inspired by its natural beauty. While smaller towns retain their idyllic charm, its growing gothams make Friuli-Venezia Giulia one of Italy's most international provinces.

HIGHLIGHTS OF FRIULI-VENEZIA GIULIA

EXPLORE the city of **Trieste,** Italy's gateway to Slovenia (below).

TREAT YOURSELF to the luxuries of **Grado,** the former official treatment resort of the Austro-Hungarian Empire (p. 370).

SOAK UP historical vibes at medieval **Cividale del Friuli** on the banks of the Natisone River (p. 375).

TRIESTE   ☎040

After volleying between Italian, Austrian, and Slavic allegiances for hundreds of years, Trieste (pop. 241,000) has finally settled down, celebrating its 50th anniversary as an Italian city in 2004. Nonetheless, subtle reminders of Trieste's Central European past are manifest in city architecture, the cuisine, and the Hapsburg rulers smirking from the portraits that line the walls of museums. While hip locals strut along bustling quays, the sapphire waters of the Adriatic Sea frame Trieste's constant excitement and drama with breathtaking natural beauty.

◖ TRANSPORTATION

Flights: Aeroporto Friuli-Venezia Giulia/Ronchi dei Legionari, V. Aquileia, 46 (☎0481 77 32 24 or 0481 77 32 25), 20km from the city center. To get to the airport, take bus #51 from the bus station next to the train station (1hr., M-Sa every hr., €3.50). Ticket counter open daily 7am-noon and 1-7pm.

Trains: P. della Libertà, 8 (☎040 89 20 21), down C. Cavour from the quay. Ticket counter open daily 6:05am-8:10pm. Info office open daily 7am-9pm. To: **Budapest, Hungary** (12hr., 2 per day 10:52am-10:32pm, €80-90); **Ljubljana, Slovenia** (3hr., 3 per day 10:52am-10:32pm, €19.60); **Udine** (1½hr., 37 per day 5am-9:19pm, €5.45); **Venice** (2hr., 29 per day 4:30am-9:25pm, €7.90).

Buses: P. della Libertà, 11 (☎040 42 50 20), next to train station. Ticket office open M-Sa 7am-7pm, Su 6:30am-1pm.

Ferries: Depart on a number of lines for **Croatia, Greece, Slovenia,** and **Albania. Agemar Viaggi,** P. Duca degli Abruzzi 1/A (☎040 36 37 37; fax 040 63 81 72), off C. Cavour, has detailed departure schedules and sells tickets for most lines. Open M-F 9am-12:30pm and 3-6pm.

Public Transportation: ACT orange buses travel city and provincial routes to **Carso, Miramare,** and **Opicina.** Tickets (€0.90 for 1hr., €2.95 for 24hr.) for sale at *tabaccherie* and bars. A **funicular** links P. Oberdan with Opicina, a city on the Carso Plateau above Trieste. From P. Oberdan (25min., every 20min. 7:11am-8:11pm, €0.90).

Taxis: RadioTaxi (☎040 30 77 30). Available 24hr.

Car Rental: Maggiore (☎040 42 13 23), in the train station. €70 per day, €303 per week. Open M-F 8:30am-12:30pm and 3-7pm, Sa 8:30am-12:30pm.

✦ 🔁 ORIENTATION AND PRACTICAL INFORMATION

The center of Trieste is a grid, bounded to the east by **Via Carducci,** which stretches south from **Piazza Oberdan** toward the historical **Capitoline Hill.** To the west, **Corso Italia** runs from the spectacular **Piazza dell'Unità d'Italia,** a vast square beside the harbor. The two streets intersect at busy **Piazza Goldoni.** Steps from P. dell'Unità d'Italia along C. Italia lies **Piazza della Borsa,** where *Triestini* come to see and be seen.

Tourist Office: APT, P. dell'Unità d'Italia, 4/B (☎040 34 78 312; fax 040 34 78 320), has great info and lists of *manifestazioni* (artistic events). Open daily 9:30am-7pm.

Consular Services: UK and **US,** V. Roma, 15 (☎040 34 78 303). Open M-F 10am-noon.

Currency Exchange: Deutsche Bank, V. Roma, 7 (☎040 63 19 25). Cash advances on V. Open M-F 8:20am-1:20pm and 2:35-3:35pm.

Emergency: ☎113. **Ambulance:** ☎118. **Police:** ☎112.

Pharmacy: Farmacia alla Borsa, P. della Borsa, 12/A (☎040 36 79 67). Open M-F 8:30am-1pm and 4-7:30pm, Sa 8:30am-1pm. After-hours rotations posted in the window or at the tourist office.

Internet Access: One Net, V. S. Francesco d'Assisi, 28/C (☎040 77 11 90). €5.50 per hr. Open M, W, and Sa 10am-1pm and 4-9pm, Tu and Th 4pm-9pm. **Rosario Service,** V. Milano 22/C (☎040 34 78 246), is off V. Carducci. €2 per hr. Open daily 10am-9pm. Cash only.

Post Office: P. V. Veneto, 1 (☎040 67 64 111), along V. Roma. From the train station, take 3rd right off V. Ghega. Open M-Sa 8:30am-7pm. **Postal Code:** 34100.

Friuli-Venezia Giulia

FRIULI-VENEZIA GIULIA

Trieste

ACCOMMODATIONS
Camping Obelisco, **3**
Hotel Alabarda, **4**
Locanda Valeria, **2**
Nuovo Albergo Centro, **5**
Ostello Tergeste (HI), **1**

FOOD
Al Bragozzo, **14**
Antica Trattoria Suban, **9**
Casa della Musica, **13**
L'Elefante Bianco, **8**
Fratelli la Bufala, **6**
Pizzeria Barattolo, **7**

NIGHTLIFE
Bar Unità, **12**
Via Roma Quattro, **10**

 DOLLAR STORE. NineTNine Cent stores are perfect for travelers on a budget—they're in every major city (and in many small ones, too) and offer a wealth of high-quality products for dirt cheap. While you're not buying Armani, what you can get will do the job and last for as long as you're traveling.

ACCOMMODATIONS AND CAMPING

Ostello Tergeste (HI), V. Miramare, 331 (☎040 22 41 02; ostellotrieste@hotmail.com), 4km from the city center. From train station, take bus #36 (€0.90) from V. Miramare. Ask for the Ostello stop. Seaside villa has breathtaking views and plenty of tree-covered terraces. Rooms are small, but staff is friendly. Breakfast included. Dinner €9. Internet

€2 per hr. Reception 8am-10am and 3:30-midnight. Lockout 10am-3:30pm. Curfew midnight. Reserve ahead online. Dorms €14. Non-HI members add €3. Cash only. ❶

▨ **Hotel Alabarda,** V. Valdirivo, 22, 3rd fl. (☎040 63 02 69; www.hotelalabarda.it). From the train or bus station, head south on C. Cavour and turn left on V. Valdirivo. A cheerful staff and wide hallways complement 18 pleasant rooms with satellite TV. Breakfast included. Internet €5.16 per hr. Wheelchair accessible. Singles €35, with bath €52; doubles €45/68; triples €63/92. 10% discount with *Let's Go.* AmEx/MC/V. ❸

▨ **Nuovo Albergo Centro,** V. Roma, 13 (☎040 34 78 790; www.hotelcentrotrieste.it). Spacious, centrally located rooms have wooden floors, minibar, phone, and satellite TV. Breakfast included. Internet €6 per hr. Singles €35, with bath €48; doubles €50/68; triples €68/92; quads €85/116. 10% discount with *Let's Go.* AmEx/MC/V. ❸

Locanda Valeria, Str. per Vienna, 52 (☎040 21 12 04; info@trattoriavaleria.com), in Opicina, 7km east of Trieste. From P. Oberdan, take either bus #2 or 4. Valeria is 3 blocks away. This newly renovated hotel is far away from the bustle of Trieste. Reservation recommended. Singles €50-60; doubles €90. AmEx/MC/V. ❹

Camping Obelisco, Str. Nuova per Opicina, 37 (☎040 21 16 55; fax 0421 21 27 44), in Opicina. Take tram from P. Oberdan to Obelisco stop and follow the signs. Showers, bar, and tents provided. €4.40 per person, €5.70-7.25 per tent. Cash only. ❶

🚩 FOOD

Trieste's cuisine has distinct Central European overtones, evident in the city's sauerkraut, strudel, and *iota* (sauerkraut, bean, and sausage stew). There's no shortage of quality restaurants along Riva N. Sauro and Riva Gulli that cater to seafood lovers. *Osmizze,* informal seasonal restaurants, sprouted in 1784, when a decree allowed peasants living on the Carso, a plateau outside Trieste, to sell produce for eight days each year. Families in the Carso still celebrate the proclamation by serving regional vegetables and wine (such as *Terrano del Karso,* a dry red) to the public three weeks every year. Ask the tourist office for schedules and locations. The *alimentari* on V. Carducci provide an ideal place to dine without worrying about your wallet. Most cooking needs can be found at the well-stocked **Euro Spesa** supermarket at V. Valdirivo, 13/F, off C. Cavour. (☎040 76 39 38. Open M-Sa 8am-8pm.) At Trieste's **covered market,** V. Carducci, 36/D, dishware booths and magazine vendors surround tables piled high with fruits and cheeses. (On the corner of Vle. della Majolica. Open M and W 8am-2pm, Tu and Th-Su 8am-6:30pm.)

▨ **Antica Trattoria Suban,** V. Comici, 2 (☎040 54 368). Take bus #35 from P. Oberdan. Austrian, Hungarian, and Italian dishes (including veal croquettes with *parmigiano* and egg) so heavenly that even Pope John Paul II was known to indulge. *Primi* €6-8, *secondi* €11-16. Cover €2.50. Open M 7:30-10:15pm, W-Su 12:30-2:30pm and 7:30-10pm. Closed 1st 3 weeks in Aug. Reservation recommended. AmEx/MC/V. ❸

Pizzeria Barattolo, P. S. Antonio, 2 (☎040 63 14 80; www.albarattolo.it). The setting sun warms dozens of happy diners munching on signature pizzas at tables lining the *piazza.* A menu in Italian, English, and German describes favorites like *schiacciata* (€7), a pizza with vegetables, cheese, basil, and garlic. Pizza €4.90-8. *Primi* €5.20-9.50, *secondi* €5.20-11. Service 15%. Open daily 8:30am-midnight. AmEx/MC/V. ❷

Fratelli la Bufala, V. Roma, 12 (☎040 34 81 31 61). Try something a little different here. Both food and decor are inspired by (what else?) buffaloes. Pizza €7-8.50. *Primi* €7-8.50, *secondi* €9-18. Open daily noon-3:30pm and 7-11:30pm. AmEx/MC/V. ❹

L'Elefante Bianco, Riva III Novembre, 3 (☎040 36 26 03; www.elefantebianco-trieste.com). Dine in the candlelit interior or outside on the terrace, but be warned—rooms may be reserved for Italian pop stars or politicos who come for the hand-selected ingredients and international wine list. *Primi* €9-14, *secondi* €14-18. 7-course tasting *menù* €43. Open M 7:15-11:45pm, Tu-Sa 12:30-3pm and 7:15-11:45pm. AmEx. ❺

La Portizza, P. della Borsa, 5 (☎040 36 58 54). Take a break from marathon shopping and let one of the good-looking, pink-shirted staffers serve up one of Portizza's big salads (€4.50-5) or sandwiches (€1.80) right on the *piazza*. Open in summer M-Sa from 6:30am-late; in winter 6:30am-9pm. AmEx/MC/V. ❶

Casa della Musica, V. Capitelli, 3 (☎040 30 73 09) on the ground floor of the Scuola di Musica, 55. Turn right off Largo Riccardo Pitteri onto V. Sebastiano and then onto C. Capitelli. Enjoy a *panini* among hardworking music students at the red backlit bar. Because it's part of the school, only open until 8pm, but ask about concert times, when music calls for extra hours. Wine €1.50-1.80. *Panini* €1.50-2. Open daily 8am-8pm. ❶

Al Bragozzo, Riva Nazario Sauro, 22 (☎040 30 30 01; www.albragozzo.com). Fish are everywhere in this small specialty *trattoria,* from the cart of fresh catches where you select your meal to the delicacies grilled and prepared right at your table. *Primi* €5-9, *secondi* €5-9.50. Open daily noon-3pm and 7-10pm. AmEx/MC/V.

◉ SIGHTS

CITY CENTER

MUSEO REVOLTELLA. The Revoltella, also known as the Galleria d'Arte Moderna, displays temporary modern art exhibits and an extensive permanent collection. Don't miss Magni's *Fontana della Ninfa Aurisiana*, a marble fountain of a woman representing Trieste. *(V. Diaz, 21. ☎040 67 54 250; www.revoltella.it. Open M 9am-1:30pm and 4-7pm, W-Sa 9am-1:30pm and 4pm-midnight, Su 10am-7pm. €5, students €3.)*

 TRIESTE TRIP. A great way to experience Trieste is the T For You Card. Available at the tourist office for €8 (24hr.) or €10 (48hr.), the card grants entrance to all civic museums, travel on local buses, a visit to the Grotta Gigante, a tour, and more. Modest discounts at local hotels and restaurants are another perk.

CITTÀ NUOVA. The oldest areas in the southern half of Trieste sport a tangle of roads in no discernible pattern; in the 1700s, Empress Maria Theresa of Austria commissioned a Città Nuova plan which 19th-century Viennese urban planners implemented between the waterfront and the **Castello di San Giusto.** The resulting grid, lined with Neo-Classical palaces, centers around the Canale Grande. Facing the canal from the south is the Serbian Orthodox ▨**Chiesa di San Spiridione,** a 9th-century church with blue domes and an array of Greek crosses frescoed throughout the interior. *(Open Tu-Sa 9am-noon and 5-8pm, Su 9am-noon. Modest dress required.)* The vast **Piazza dell'Unità d'Italia,** Italy's largest square along the waterfront, provides a full view of the coastline of the Adriatic. On the eastern side of the *piazza,* the **Municipio** (Town Hall) faces the Mazzoleni Fountain of the Four Continents, representing the world as it was known upon the fountain's completion in 1750.

PIAZZA DELLA CATTEDRALE. This hilltop *piazza* on the site of an ancient Roman basilica overlooks the Adriatic and downtown Trieste. The remains of the old Roman city center lie directly below, and the restored **Cattedrale di San Giusto** is across the street. San Giusto assumed a roughly square shape rather than the traditional cross design after a 14th-century renovation combined the original church with the basilica of S. Maria Assunta. The mosaics from both original apses still grace the chambers on either side of the main altar. *(☎040 30 93 62. Open Tu-Sa 8am-noon and 2:30-6:30pm, Su 8am-8pm; closed to tourists Su mornings for mass. Free. Printed guides available for €1 in English, French, German, and Italian.)*

TEATRO ROMANO. In the first century AD, the Emperor Trajan supervised the building of this amphitheater, which staged both gladiatorial games and dramatic performances. Today, the structure is overtaken by weeds and a thriving community of stray cats, though it is still impressive when illuminated after dusk. *(On V. del Teatro Romano, off C. Italia. From Capitoline Hill, descend toward P. Ponterosso. Free.)*

MUSEO DI STORIA E D'ARTE. This museum provides an archaeological history of Trieste and the upper Adriatic. Cases of Greek and Egyptian jewelry, glass, and pottery surround a mummy and sarcophagus. Outside, the **Orto Lapidario** (Rock Garden) arranges pieces of Roman architecture in a garden of history, but heavy weeds and broken benches dampen the experience. *(P. Cattedrale, 1. ☎040 31 05 00 or 040 30 86 86. Open Tu and Th-Su 9am-1pm, W 9am-7pm. Adults €2, with youth discount €1.)*

CITY ENVIRONS

▨CASTELLO MIRAMARE. Archduke Maximilian of Austria commissioned this castle in the mid-19th century. This was, of course, before he was assassinated in Mexico and his wife Carlotta went crazy from grief. Lavishly decorated apartments feature crystal chandeliers, tapestries, and Asian porcelain. Legend holds that visitors can still hear the wailing ghost of Carlotta, whose player piano plucks notes in a particularly eerie upper room. On a promontory over the gulf, Miramare's turrets are easily visible from the Capitoline Hill in Trieste and most points along the **Barcola,** a boardwalk extending 7km between the Castello and Trieste. *(To reach Miramare, take bus #36 (15min., €0.90) to Ostello Tergete (see above), and walk along the water for 15min. ☎040 22 47 013. Open M-Sa 9am-7pm and Su 8:30am-7pm. Ticket office open daily 9am-6:30pm. €4, EU citizens 18-25 €2, EU citizens under 18 or over 65 free. Guided English tours €3.50; audioguides €3.50 or 2 for €5. Gardens open daily 8am-6pm. Free.)*

MARINE PARK. In the gardens of **Castelletto Miramare,** this small World Wildlife Federation aquatic museum offers scuba tours of an underwater landscape just off the Mediterranean shore, as well as an aquarium that simulates ocean life. *(☎040 22 41 47; www.riservamarinamiramare.it. Sea watching M-F. Adults €14, for children under 14 €7 (includes equipment and wet-suit). Scuba diving Sa-Su. €19 for land dive, €27 for night dive or boat dive. Scuba certification and reservation required. Must be in groups of 6-10; ask to be grouped with others if your group is less than 6. Call ahead to inquire about guided tours. Office open daily 9am-7pm. Admission to Castelletto's Marina Museum €4, children under 17 €2.50.)*

NAPOLEONICA AND GROTTA GIGANTE. The tram to Opicina from P. Oberdan is one of the longest running in Europe, and while it's under repairs for the next year, buses #2 and 4 have taken over its route. After a steep climb, they run past vineyards and breathtaking views of the Adriatic coastline. Hop off at the Obelisk stop to meet up with the Napoleonica, a popular trail that cuts along the sides of the Carso cliffs. At the end of the tram route, local bus #42 takes you close to Grotta Gigante, claimed to be the world's largest touristed cave. Staircases wind in and around the 107m interior, which could fit St. Peter's Basilica comfortably inside. *(V. Donota, 2. Bus #42 arrives in the small parking lot across V. Nazionale from the tram stop. Buy tickets in town for return journey. ☎040 32 73 12. Open Apr.-Sept. daily 10am-6pm; Oct.-Mar. closed M. Entrance by guided tour only, every 30min. €7.50, groups of 25 or more €5.50.)*

RISIERA DE SAN SABBA. Italy's only WWII concentration camp occupied this abandoned rice factory outside Trieste. The *risiera* now houses a museum detailing Trieste's role in the Slovenian-born resistance movement fighting Nazi occupation. *(Ratto della Pileria, 43. Bus #8. ☎040 82 62 02. Open daily 9am-7pm. Free.)*

FARO DELLA VITTORIA. Built on the foundations of Fort Kressich, this lighthouse is a tribute to those who gave their lives at sea in WWI. Inaugurated in 1927 in the presence of Vittorio Emanuele III, the 70m tower incorporates the anchor of the first Italian ship to enter the harbor during the 1918 liberation. *(Str. del Friuli, 141. Bus #42. ☎040 41 04 61. Open Apr.-Sept. Tu-Th 3-7pm; Oct.-Mar. M-Sa 10am-3pm. Free.)*

FRIULI-VENEZIA GIULIA

🎵 📷 ENTERTAINMENT AND NIGHTLIFE

The night heats up early at the new ■ **Via Roma Quattro,** whose name is also its address. The animal-print seat cushions are barely visible in the sea of young trendsetters sipping Mandorlino's (€2.50). (☎040 63 46 33. Open daily 7:30am-10:30pm. AmEx/MC/V.) Trieste's glitterati are out in full force along the bars of **Capo di Piazza A. Santin,** part of the pedestrian district that connects P. della Borsa to P. dell'Unità. On summer evenings, the crowd gravitates toward fresh cocktails and Europop at **Bar Unità,** at Capo di P. A. Santin 1/B, on the southwestern corner of P. dell'Unità. (☎040 36 80 33. Open M-Sa 6:30pm-1am.) On the 2nd Sunday in October, Trieste stages the annual **Barcolana,** a regatta that blankets the harbor with thousands of billowing sails. The acclaimed **Teatro Verdi** hosts operas from November to May and a six-week operetta season from July to mid-August. Buy tickets or make reservations at the **box office,** Riva III Novembre, 1. Enter on the other side of the building at P. Giuseppe Verdi. (☎040 67 22 298; www.teatroverdi-trieste.com. Open Tu-Sa 9am-noon and 4-7pm, Su 9am-noon. Tickets €8-40.)

GRADO ☎0431

Visitors come to Grado for spa treatments at the **terme,** a set of spas along the lagoon on Grado's south side. They're willing to pay top dollar for proximity to the solariums and saunas that keep tourists flocking to the tiny island. For those reluctant to splurge on eternal youth, fees for the beach along the *terme* vary based on time of day and season, but tickets are usually available along V. Regina Elena for less than €10. **Santa Eufemia** (☎/fax 0431 80 146), a 7th-century basilica along P. Duca d'Aosta, hosts visitors under its soaring ceiling, and nearby an unearthed mosaic is on display from a raised walkway. The basilica itself had a piece of floor removed to reveal a mosaic from the late 4th century hidden underneath.

Though downtown hotels are pricey, a couple of options are within walking distance of the sea. **Hotel Capri ❸,** Vle. Vespucci, 1, is on the lagoon and offers guests amazing views and a palette of seafoam green. Spacious rooms have balconies, A/C, phone, TV, and bath; some have jacuzzis and lounges. (☎0431 80 091; www.hotelcaprigrado.it. Breakfast €5 extra. Reception open 7am-midnight. Open Easter-Nov. Singles €30-40; doubles €60-80. AmEx/MC/V.) Genial proprietors run **Meublé Al Sole ❷,** Vle. Del Sole, 31, one block from the lagoon with furnished balconies and a sunny breakfast patio. (☎0431 80 370; alsole@aliceposta.it. Breakfast included. Open Easter-Nov. Singles €27-33; doubles €48-60. MC/V.)

COOP supermarket, Vle. Europo, 35/B, has the essentials and more. (☎0431 81 237. Open M-F 8am-1pm and 5-8pm, Sa 8am-8pm, Su 8am-1pm. MC/V.) Combining Austrian and Italian influences, **Ristorante Al Canevon ❹,** Calle Corbatto, 11, offers perfectly grilled fish in a luxurious interior. (☎/fax 0431 81 662. *Primi* €7.50-11.50, *secondi* €11-14. Cover €2.10. Open in summer daily noon-2pm and 7-10pm; in winter M-Tu and Th-Su noon-2pm and 7-10pm. AmEx/MC/V.) If a leisurely meal isn't in the cards, grab some rich, hearty pizza across from the post office on the corner of V. Morosini and V. Caprin at **Pizza Number One ❶,** V. Morosini, 21, a small pizzeria with enormous helpings. The location is perfect to nab a mouthful of the spicy salami pizza (€1.80) or crisp salad (€2) and head to the beach. (☎0431 80 477. Open W-Su 11:15am-3pm and 6pm-1am.) Head south on P. Duca d'Aosta to reach **Agli Artisti ❹,** Campiello Pta. Grande, 2, where traces of Roman walls are still visible in the floor. Seating in the small *campa* offers views of the P. Duca d'Aosta or a maze of medieval streets. (☎/fax 0431 83 081. *Primi* €5-11; *secondi* €5-15. Cover €2.50. Open M and W-Su noon-2:30pm and 6-10pm. AmEx/MC/V.)

This spa resort town is accessible by **bus.** Buses run to: Aquileia (15min., 31 per day 5:35am-11pm, €1.45); Trieste (1½hr., 6 per day 6:20am-7pm, €3.90); Udine (1¼hr., 20 per day 5:35am-11pm, €3.25). Buses arrive from Trieste (1½hr., 4 per day 9:07am-10:07pm) and Udine (1¼hr., 18 per day 8am-10:20pm). **City buses** 37A and 37B (€1) stop at major points across the island and at the wide array of spas and hotels along the south side of the island. From the bus station, take **Via Roma,** continue on **Via Venezia,** then turn left on **Via Dante Alighieri** to reach the **tourist office,** V. D. Alighieri, 72, which provides **maps** of the island and listings of spa treatments and prices. (☎0431 87 71 11; www.gradoturismo.info. Open daily 8am-5pm.) For a **pharmacy,** leave the bus station, walk toward the bay, and bear left on P. S. Marco on V. Orseolo. (☎0431 80 058. Open Tu-Su 8:30am-12:30pm and 4-7pm.) The **police** are directly across the street. Find **Internet** at **Tabacchi Tarallo,** V. A. Manzoni, 25. (☎/fax 0431 87 70 50. €1 per 10min., €6 per hr. Open daily June-Aug. 8am-1pm and 4-10:30pm; Sept.-May 8am-1pm and 4-8pm.) A **hospital** is on V. Amalfi, 1. (☎/fax 0481 53 30 34. Open daily 8am-2pm.) A **post office** at V. Caprin, 34, has an **ATM** as well. (Open M-F 8:30am-2pm, Sa 8:30am-1pm.) **Postal Code:** 34073.

AQUILEIA ☎0431

After passing a series of small towns and hurtling through a handful of gateways, low vegetation is replaced by glimpses of Roman pillars still standing (more or less) along the road, marking the entrance to Aquileia (pop. 3300). This former Roman city and gateway to the Adriatic retains a sense of peaceful detachment from the major thoroughfare that cuts its quiet streets in half. Strolls along back roads reveal small canals and churches that don't appear on any major map.

▐▛ TRANSPORTATION AND PRACTICAL INFORMATION. Aquileia can be reached by **bus** from Udine (1hr., 16 per day 6:10am-9:40pm, €2.75). From Cervignano, a **train station** on the Trieste-Venice line, buses leave to Aquileia *centro* (15min., every 30min. 6am-8:30pm, €1.40). For a list of budget accommodations and nearby camping, including the island of Grado (15km south on V. Beligna, the main thoroughfare), consult the **APT Tourist Office,** P. Capitolo, 4. From the bus stop facing the basilica, head toward the church; the office is on the left. (☎0431 91 087. Open daily Apr.-Oct. 9am-6:30pm; Nov.-Mar. 9am-noon.) In case of **emergency,** dial ☎113, or call the **police** (☎0431 91 034), on V. Semina. The largest local **pharmacy** is on C. Gramsci, 18, two blocks from Albergo Aquila Nera. (☎0431 91 00 01. Open M-F 8:30am-12:30pm and 3:30-7:30pm, Sa 8:30am-12:30pm.) For **currency exchange** and **postal services** July through September, walk two blocks along V. Augusta (toward Cervignano) to the **Poste Italiane** kiosk. (Open M-F 9am-12:30pm and 3:30-5pm.) Otherwise, the central **post office** is in P. Cervi, off C. Gramsci. (☎0431 91 92 72. Open M-F 8:30am-2pm, Sa 8:30am-1pm.) **Postal Code:** 33051.

▐▐ ACCOMMODATIONS AND FOOD. While Aquileia has many hotels around the basilica, the real gems are hidden in quieter areas. **Domus Augusta (HI) ❶,** V. Roma, 25, has clean dorms just minutes from the bus station, but rather small common areas. (☎0431 91 024; www.ostelloaquileia.it. Breakfast and sheets included. Internet €4. Bike rental €2 per hr. Reception 2-11:30pm. Check-out 10am. Lockout 10am-2pm. Curfew 11:30pm. Dorms €15; singles with bath €23. MC/V.) At **Albergo Aquila Nera ❸,** P. Garibaldi, 5, a short walk up V. Roma from V. Augusta, all cavernous rooms feature phone, A/C, TV, safe, and bath. Restaurant and bar downstairs are popular in the neighborhood. (☎/fax 0431 91 045. Breakfast included. Wheelchair accessible. Singles €35; doubles €70; triples €95. AmEx/MC/V.) Sleep near ruins at **Camping Aquileia ❶,** V. Gemina 10, which features a pool and a restaurant seconds from the ruins Porto Fluviale. (May 15-Sept. 15 ☎0431 91 042; Sept. 16-May 14 0431 91 95 83. Reception 8am-11pm. One electrical hookup per campsite. May 15-Sept. 15 €5.25-€6.50 per person; Sept. 16-May 14 €4.40 per person. Tent sites €7.30-9.30, 3-person bungalow €38-47; 4-person bungalow €55-68. MC/V.)

Dimeglio supermarket, P. Garibaldi, 1, sells the basics. (☎0431 90 073. Open M and W 8am-12:30pm, Tu and Th-Sa 8am-12:30pm and 4-7:30pm, Su 8am-noon. Cash only.) Grab a pink table at **La Colombara ❸,** V. S. Zilli, 42, and sample the fresh *sardelle in savor* (sardines in onions; €5.50), or call ahead about "At Table with the Ancient Romans," a theme meal during which the waiters don togas. From the bus stop across from the basilica, turn left, then right on V. Gemina, and follow the road as it curves. (☎0431 91 513; www.lacolombara.it. *Primi* €3.50-9, *secondi* €5.50-13. Open Tu-Su noon-2:30pm and 7-10:30pm. AmEx/MC/V.) From the basilica, exit the *piazza* back to the main road to Cervignano. Turn left on V. G. Augusta and **La Pergola ❷,** V. Beligna, 4, is on the left. Baked shin of pork with potatoes (€11.30), is the house specialty, served outside on picnic tables. 10% discount when staying at Domus Augusta. (☎0431 91 97 40. *Primi* €4.80-6.50, *secondi* €6.20-11.30. Open Mar.-Dec. M and W-Su 10am-3pm and 5-10pm. AmEx/MC/V.) **Ristorante Aquila Nera ❸,** serves fish to a crowd of locals. In case the extensive *menu di pesce* doesn't give away the theme, nets and fish hooks are draped everywhere. (☎0431 91 045. *Primi* €4.80-7.50, *secondi* €6.50-11.)

FERMATA FRENZY. Taking the bus in Italy is easy, affordable, and a great way to get around, but there's one thing you should know. Most bus stops that aren't in major *piazze* are only "fermata prenotata" stops; the bus driver won't stop there unless he sees somebody waiting or somebody already onboard the bus asks him to stop. Unfortunately, bus drivers often miss travelers waiting quietly on the side of the road, so make your presence known. Wave your hands, step out on the curb, make eye contact; you might look stupid but you'll look and feel a lot worse if the bus drives right by and you have to wait an hour.

🖸 **SIGHTS.** Aquileia's ▨basilica still functions as a religious site, but just barely. Plexiglass and steel walkways allow tourists to take flashless pictures of the interior. The church's floor, a remnant of the original building, is a giant mosaic of over 700 sq. m of geometric patterns and images of animals, cherubs, and field workers. Beneath the altar, 12th-century frescoes illustrate the trials of Aquileia's early Christians in addition to scenes from the life of Christ. Damp catwalks guide visitors through the **Cripta degli Scavi** and its half-uncovered mosaics. The first-century Roman house is buried in other artifacts and variated stone. (☎0431 91 067. Basilica open daily 9am-7pm. Free. Crypt entrance €2.60, under 10 free.) The nearby **campanile** (bell tower) was constructed in 1031 using the remains of the Roman amphitheater. Visitors sweat their way up 127 steep, sharply turning steps before enjoying unobstructed views of the countryside. (Open daily 9:30am-1pm and 3-6:30pm. €1.10.) **Porto Fluviale,** the cypress-lined alley behind the basilica that spans the former dockyard of Aquileia's river harbor, is listed as one of UNESCO's most valuable World Heritage Sites and conveniently leads to the Roman ruins at the forum. The **Museo Archeologico,** at the corner of V. Augusta and V. Roma, features the preserved remains of a boat used by Roman citizens. (☎0431 91 016. Open M 8:30am-2pm, Tu-Su 8:30am-7:30pm. €4, between 18 and 25 €2, under 18 or over 65 free.) From there, cross V. Gemina and follow signs to the **Museo Paleocristiano** in P. Pirano to see mosaics that document the region's transition from paganism to Christianity. (☎0431 91 131. Open daily 8:30am-1:45pm. Free.)

UDINE
☎ 0432

Udine's Piazza della Libertà blends arches, platforms, and monuments in a firestorm of regional pride. The "City of Tiepolo" features the Renaissance painter's works in many of its landmarks, from courtrooms to small chapels. Once ruled by the Patriarch of Aquileia, Udine (pop. 95,000) later changed hands among Venetian, French, and Austrian powers, and suffered severe bombing in WWII. Because the city is easily accessible, visitors might want to take advantage of the accommodations available in the neighboring towns of Aquileia, Trieste, and Cividale.

⊟⏻ TRANSPORTATION AND PRACTICAL INFORMATION. Udine is best accessed by **train.** The **train station** is on V. Europa Unità. The ticket counter (☎ 0432 89 20 21) is open 7am-8:30pm. Trains run to: Milan (4½hr., 5:45am and 6:49pm, €25.20); Trieste (1½hr., 36 per day 5:20am-11:43pm, €5.95); Venice (2hr., 33 per day 4:39am-10:32pm, €6.82); and Vienna, Austria (7hr., 5 per day 9:52am-1:45am, €54.87). **Buses** run from V. Europa Unità. Cross the street from the train station and walk one block to the right. **SAF** (☎ 0432 50 40 12) runs buses to: Aquileia (every hr. 6:50am-9:10pm, €2.75); Cividale (every hr. 6:40am-7:15pm, €1.90); and Trieste (2 per hr. 5:05am-10:50pm, €4.65). For a **taxi,** call ☎ 0432 50 58 58.

Udine's **train** and **regional bus stations** are both on **Via Europa Unità,** in the southern part of town. All local bus lines pass the train station, but only buses #1, 3, and 8 (€1.20) run from V. Europa Unità to the center, passing by **Piazza della Libertà** and **Castello Hill.** To walk from the station (15min.), go right to **Piazza D'Annunzio,** then turn left under the arches to **Via Aquileia.** Continue up **Via Veneto** to P. della Libertà. From the southern end of P. della Libertà, turn right on **Via Manin** to reach the **tourist office,** P. 1° Maggio, 7, which distributes **maps** and info for Udine, Trieste, and Aquileia. (☎ 0432 29 59 72; www.udine-turismo.it. Also accessible by bus #2, 7, or 10. Open M-F 9am-1pm and 2-6:30pm, Sa 9am-6:30pm, Su 9:30am-1pm. Closed Su in summer.) **Currency exchange** is available in the streets around P. della Libertà, all with comparable rates. In case of **emergency,** call ☎ 113, an **ambulance** at ☎ 118, or the **carabinieri,** Vle. Trieste, 28 (☎ 112 or 0432 505380). A **pharmacy** is at P. della Libertà, 9. (☎ 0432 50 28 77. Open M-Sa 8:30am-12:30pm and 3:30-11pm. Ring bell 11pm-8am.) Check **Internet** at **InternetPlay,** V. Francesco, 33. (☎ 0432 21 584; www.internetplay.it. €1 per 15min., €4 per hr. Open M-Sa 9am-12:45pm and 3:30-7:45pm.) The **post office,** V. Veneto, 42, has *fermoposta* and fax. (☎ 0432 22 33 54; fax 0432 26 889. Open M-Sa 8:30am-7pm.) **Postal Code:** 33100.

⏺ ACCOMMODATIONS. Most hotels in downtown Udine would send any budget traveler into shock, but moderately priced options do exist outside the city center. While many opt to stay in nearby Aquileia and take the bus to Udine, for those who choose to spend the night here, the best options are in Ple. Cella, a 10min. walk down V. Europa Unità. At **Hotel Quo Vadis ❸,** Ple. Cella, 28, the 38 clean, professional rooms all have bath, TV, and A/C, making it a popular option with university guests and passersby. (☎ 0432 21 091; hotelquovadis@libero.it. Reception 7am-midnight. Reserve ahead. Singles €40; doubles €65; triples €85. AmEx/MC/V.) The owners of the **Albergo Da Brando ❷,** Ple. Cella, 16, offer simple rooms for students that share a hallway bathroom. The restaurant downstairs offers dinner options. The prices are notably low for such close proximity to the *centro.* (☎ 0432 50 28 37. Reception in restaurant downstairs. €20 per person. AmEx/MC/V.) Exiting the train station, cross the street, turn right, and walk 50m to **Hotel Europa ❹,** V. Europa Unità, 47. An elegant red-velvet lobby welcomes visitors to slightly dated rooms, but in close proximity to the train station. All rooms have bath, A/C, TV, and minibar. (☎ 0432 50 87 31 or 0432 29 44 46; fax 0432 51 26 54. Breakfast included. Singles from €50; doubles €75. AmEx/MC/V.)

FOOD. Udinese cuisine blends Italian, Austrian, and Slovenian influences into regional specialties like *brovada e museto*, a stew made with turnips and sausage. Shop for produce on weekday mornings in the **market** in P. Matteotti near P. della Libertà. **Dimeglio** is a well-stocked supermarket on Vle. Cesare Battisti, 9, between P. XX Settembre and P. Garibaldi. (☎0432 50 48 19. Open M-Sa 8:30am-7:30pm.) At ⬛**Al Vecchio Stallo ❷**, V. Viola, 7, local cuisine is served in a playful interior filled with Americana-like farm tools, license plates, and modern paintings. The jovial proprietor rightfully insists that the rich *frico* (potatoes, cheese, and chicken) is a must-have. (☎/fax 0432 21 296. *Primi* €5-6, *secondi* €6-10. Lunch *menù* €10. Cover €1. Open M-Sa 11am-3:30pm and 7pm-midnight. Cash only.) Sidle up to one of the wooden tables at ⬛**Trattoria al Chianti ❷**, V. Marinelli, 4, just off V. Veneto and try *cjalsons* (ravioli sweetened with ricotta) and *frico*. One of over 40 wines will go well with any dish. (☎0432 50 11 05. *Primi* €4.50-5.50, *secondi* €4.50-10. Cover €1. Open M-F 8am-3pm and 6pm-midnight; kitchen closes at 10:30pm. MC/V.) ⬛**Ristorante Vitello d'Oro ❹**, Vle. E. Valvason, 4, has been dishing out Udinese classics in its elegant interior since 1849. Try their *menù tradizione* for €32. (☎0432 50 89 82. *Primi* €8.50-9, *secondi* €14-18. Cover €2.60. Open in summer M 7-11pm, Tu-Sa noon-3pm and 7-11pm; in winter M-Tu and Th-Su noon-3pm and 7-11pm. AmEx/MC/V.) The cafeteria dining room of student favorite **Zenit ❷**, P. XX Settembre, 22, has neon accents and fresh entrees. Lunch of *prìmo*, *secondo*, and dessert under €10. (☎0432 50 29 80. Open M-F 8:30am-3pm, Sa 11:30am-3pm. MC/V.) Grab a *menù* of regional favorites at cozy, family-owned **Ristorante da Brando ❷**, Ple. Cella, 16. (☎0432 50 28 37. *Primi* from €3.65, *secondi* from €4.65. Cover €1.55. Fixed *menù* €10. Open M-Sa 8am-midnight. AmEx/MC/V.)

SIGHTS AND ENTERTAINMENT. The multi-tiered **Piazza della Libertà** has morphed from the political center of old Udine to the city's social center. Along one edge are the Gothic arches of the narrow **Arcado di San Giovanni**, and atop the bell tower, two automated Moorish figures gong out the hours. Across from the arcade, the **Loggia del Lionello**, built in 1488, serves as a public gathering place. In the highest corner of the square, through the **Arco Bollani**, a castle is accessible by road, stone staircase, or arched promenade. Once home to Venetian governors, it now holds the **Civici Musei e Galleria di Storia ed Arte Antica**, which contains paintings like Bellunello's *La Crocifissionè*. (☎0432 27 15 91. Open Tu-Sa 9:30am-12:30pm and 3-6pm, Su 9:30am-12:30pm. €3, ages 6-18 or over 60 €1.50.) Upon exiting the museum, turn left and follow the walkway until you reach **Chiesa di Santa Maria di Castello**, Udine's oldest church. The mossy exterior attests to its almost 500 years atop the hill. Church hours vary, but inside visitors will find a relatively untouristed haven. The **duomo** was consecrated in 1335 as Santa Maria Annunziatta and renovated in 1909. Frescoes by Tiepolo appear on the first and 2nd altars on the right side. The squat brick **campanile** houses the small **Museo del Duomo** with 14th-century frescoes by Vitale da Bologna. (☎0432 50 68 30. Open Tu-Sa 9am-noon and 4-6pm, Su 4-6pm. Free.) Udine has been called the "City of Tiepolo," and some of the Baroque painter's finest works adorn the **Oratorio della Purità**, across from the *duomo*. The *Assumption* (1759) on the ceiling and the *Immaculate Conception* on the altarpiece demonstrate his love of light and air. The **Museo Dicesane e Galleria de Tiepolo** occupies a 16th-century *palazzo* and displays Tiepolo's early frescoes, most notably, the chilling *Solomon's Judgement* in the Patriarch's red courtroom. (P. Patriarcato, 1, at the head of Vle. Ungheria. Entrance beneath the ornate coat of arms. ☎0432 25 003. Open W-Su 10am-noon and 3:30-6:30pm. €5, under 10 €4. Arrange in advance for free guided tours.)

In summer, P. 1° Maggio becomes the fairgrounds for **Estate in Città**, a series of outdoor concerts and guided tours of the city. **Bar Americano**, P. della Libertà, 7, provides an outstanding vantage point from which to people-watch at night. (☎0432 24 80 18. Open daily in summer 6:30am-midnight; in winter 6:30am-9pm.)

Pray at the altar of Guinness at **The Black Stuff,** V. Gorghi, 3/A, where Irish beer is not only inspiration for the drink and decor, but also a way of life. (☎ 0432 29 78 38. Open M and W-Su 6pm-3am. Cash only.)

CIVIDALE DEL FRIULI ☎ 0432

On the banks of the Natisone River, this tiny town (pop. 11,000) is perhaps the most enchanting in Friuli. Founded by Julius Caesar as Forum Iulii, Cividale became the capital of the first Lombard duchy in AD 568 and flourished as a meeting point of artists and nobility in the Middle Ages. Now, mainly pastry shops flourish, though the town has retained its fiercely independent character.

█ ⁊ TRANSPORTATION AND PRACTICAL INFORMATION. Cividale is best reached by **train** (15min., 25 per day 6am-8:05pm, €1.90). Buy tickets in the *tabaccherie* in the Udine train station. **Buses** from Udine (€1.60) are less frequent. The **train station,** Vle. Libertà, 43, is close to the center of town. (☎ 0432 73 10 32. Open M-Sa 5:45am-8pm, Su 7am-8pm.) From the train station, take **Via G. Marconi** and turn left through the stone gate, **Porta Arsenale Veneto,** when the street ends. Cross **Piazza Dante** and turn right on **Via San Pellico,** then left on **Largo Boiani.** The **duomo** is straight ahead. The **tourist office,** P. Diacono, 10, also serves as the **Informagiovani** for Cividale, which helps youths find **work opportunities** in the area, and offers free **Internet.** (☎ 0432 71 04 60; www.cividale.net. Open daily 9:30am-noon and 3:30-6pm.) **Banca Antoniana Popolare Veneto,** Largo Boiani, 20, has an **ATM** (open M-Sa 8:20am-1:20pm and 2:35-3:35pm, Su 8:20am-11:20pm), as does the post office. In case of **emergency,** dial ☎ 113, the **police** at ☎ 0432 70 61 11, on P. A. Diaz, off P. Dante, or contact the reference desk of **Ospedale Cividale** (☎ 0432 70 81), in P. dell'Ospedale. **Farmacia Minisini** is at Largo Boiani, 11. (Open M 3:30-7:30pm, Tu-F and Su 8:30am-12:30pm and 3:30-7:30pm, Sa 8:30am-12:30pm.) The **post office,** Largo Boiani, 37-39, has an ATM and phone booths outside. (☎ 0432 70 57 11; fax 0432 70 57 40. Open M-F 8:30am-2pm, Sa 8:30am-1pm.) **Postal Code:** 33043.

█ █ ACCOMMODATIONS AND FOOD. Quiet Cividale lacks a wide variety of budget accommodations, but lists of *affittacamere* (rooms for rent) are available at the tourist office. Thirty meters down C. P. D'Aquileia from P. del Duomo, turn right on Str. Matteotti to reach **Casa Il Gelsomino ❷,** Str. Matteotti, 11, a small but well-furnished villa with friendly proprietors and views of the town. Two double rooms each have a shower. (☎ 0432 73 19 62. Breakfast included. Reserve ahead. €25 per person, €23 for longer stays. Cash only.) At the centrally located **Al Pomo d'Oro ❹,** P. S. Giovanni, 20, you can expect sunny yellow decor and friendly service, but ask for rooms with private balconies for something a little special. (☎ 0432 73 14 89; www.alpomodoro.com. Breakfast included. Wheelchair accessible. Rooms held until 6pm. Singles €55; doubles €75. AmEx/MC/V.) **Casa Franca ❸,** V. Alto Adige, 15, is a 5min. walk from the train station. Turn left as you exit the station, then left on V. Bottego and follow it until it becomes V. S. Moro. V. Alto Adige is the first street on your right. The large apartment has three spacious rooms with shared bath and homey decor. (☎ 0432 73 40 55. Breakfast included; ask for rooms without for €4 less. Singles €30; doubles €60. Cash only.)

Regional culinary specialties are *frico* (a cheese and potato pancake) and *gubana* (a large fig- and prune-filled pastry laced with *grappa*). Cividale's **open-air market** fills P. Diacono every Saturday from 8am to 1pm. **Coopca,** V. A. Ristori, 17, sells groceries. (☎ 0432 73 11 05. Open M and W 8:30am-12:45pm, Tu and Th-Su 8:30am-12:45pm and 4-7:30pm. Cash only.) Try the flaky *gubana* or sweet fruit tart (both €0.75), some of the best desserts in the region, at █ **Gubane Cividalese ❶,** C. P. D'Aquileia, 10. (☎ 0432 73 21 52. Open daily 7:30am-1:30pm and 3:30-8pm. Cash only.) At **Antica Trattoria Dominissini ❷,** in the courtyard of Casa il Gelsomino on

FRIULI-VENEZIA GIULIA

Str. Matteotti, 11, try the *gnocchi alla carniga* (stuffed with meat; €7) under a canopy of vines. (☎ 0432 73 37 63. *Primi* €5-7, *secondi* €5.20-14. Cover €1. Open Tu-Su 10am-3pm and 6-11pm. AmEx/MC/V.) **Antica Osteria alla Speranza ❸**, Foro Giulio Cesare, 15, across from the post office on Largo Boiani, offers a rotating menu and Friulian wine under frescoed ceilings. (☎ 0432 73 11 31. *Primi* €6.20, *secondi* €9-12. Cover €1.20. Open M and W-Su 9am-2:30pm and 6pm-midnight. MC/V.) **Mandi Mandi ❸**, C. P. D'Aquileia, 8, has great pizza for even better prices. A slice and a pastry from the shop next door make a great meal. (Open Tu-Su 8am-1pm and 4pm-8pm. Cash only.) **Alla Frasca ❸**, V. Stretta de Rubeis, 11, has an entire menu of mushrooms in addition to its regular menu. (☎ 0432 73 12 70. *Primi* €6.20, *secondi* €10-15. Cover €1.80. Open in summer Tu-Su 12:30-2:30pm and 6.30-10pm; in winter Tu-Su 12:30-2:30pm and 7-9:30pm. AmEx/MC/V.)

🔲 **SIGHTS.** In the town center, the 16th-century **duomo's** towering pillars are accented by a variety of wooden confessionals and red marble fonts. The Renaissance sarcophagus of Patriarch Nicolò Donato is left of the entrance. Annexed to the *duomo* is the **Museo Cristiano,** where displays include the octagonal **Battisterio di Callisto,** commissioned by the first Aquileian patriarch in Cividale, and the **Altar of Ratchis,** a Lombard sculpture from AD 740. (☎ 0432 73 11 44. *Duomo* and museum open M-Sa 9:30am-noon and 3-6pm, Su 3-6pm. Free.) Upon exiting the *duomo* itself, circle around the right side to the back of the building and follow Riva Pozzo di Callisto to the bottom of the stairs where signs point to the **Tempietto Longobardo,** an 8th-century sanctuary built on the remains of Roman homes. Inside, a sextet of stucco figures, called *The Procession of Virgins and Martyrs,* stare down at the stalls from their high perch. (☎ 0432 70 08 67. Open Apr.-Sept. M-F 9:30am-12:30pm and 3-6:30pm, Sa-Su 9:30am-1pm; Oct.-Mar. M-F 9:30am-12:30pm and 3-5pm, Sa-Su 9:30am-12:30pm and 2:30-6pm. €2, students €1.)

From the *duomo,* follow C. P. D'Aquileia to **Ponte del Diavolo,** a 15th-century stone bridge set between verdant cliffs 22m above the emerald green **Natisone River.** Cross the bridge, turn right, and descend the stairs to the river to get a clear view of the stone Satan himself, supposedly tossed under the bridge. Head behind the **Chiesa San Martino** to reach another lookout point on the river from private balconies that line the steep banks. Explore the silent, steep stone tunnels of **Ipogeo Celtico,** Monastero Maggiore, 10, an ancient Roman prison with open-jawed skulls engraved in the walls to indicate its former status as a graveyard. (Turn off C. P. D'Aquileia on Vle. Monastero Maggiore right before the bridge. ☎ 0432 70 12 11. Open Tu-Su 7am-10pm. On M, call the tourist office. 10-person maximum. For the key to the door, visit Bar all'Ipogeo at Monastero Maggiore, 2. Free.)

LIVING LA DOLCE VITA

When I accepted a teaching position at an international school in Italy, I imagined it would be a wonderful way to experience life in another country. I would be that "American living abroad" tasting *la dolce vita*. However, I soon understood it was not all glamour and adventure. I had no television, no telephone; I did not have a real bed, and felt disoriented in Trieste, the small, northern Italian city I was to call home. I felt disconnected.

At the international school I was a pre-nursery assistant, working with two-year-olds under the supervision of a permanent teacher. Most of the children were Italian; there were only three foreign students in the classroom. I thought it was slightly ironic that children could be called "foreign students" *(stranieri)* at an international school, but that's the way it was. Not knowing Italian, I only spoke to the children in English, although Italian was spoken in the classroom. Of course, I didn't think that was fair to the non-Italian speakers, but I wasn't in charge. Despite the language barrier, however, I began to adjust to the job. I would play with the children, sing songs with them, do activities like painting, coloring, and reading—basic nursery activities. I grew really close with the kids, and their parents were nice to me even if we couldn't communicate in a common language.

Adjusting to daily life in Trieste itself was harder. Located right on the Adriatic, the city used to be a major Hapsburg port, but its importance has since diminished. There are beautiful hills behind the city, with the sea in front, creating picturesque views from the coast. There are some beautiful buildings: the Castello Miramare, built as Maximillian's summer retreat outside the city, and the Castello San Giusto and the duomo, both of which celebrated their 700th anniversaries in 2003. There is also the Barcola, Trieste's paved beach area, that's great for sunning and swimming in warm weather. At first inspection, it seems like the makings for another lovely Italian city.

Trieste can in fact be lovely, but what you don't realize as a tourist is that bitter winters and the *bora*, a tremendous northern wind, can make it really unpleasant. Furthermore, when you're living there— though you might not notice if you were only visiting for a day—you can sense a sort of stagnation. People and things here are set in their ways, with little progression. Most of the population is elderly, a growing problem throughout Italy as the average age of the population continues to rise due to plummeting birth rates. To find something fun to do on the weekends, young people usually have to drive out of the city. There are some bars and cafes, but if you want to go to a nice club you need a car or a friend who'll give you a ride.

I think that teaching in Italy, rather than just traveling as a tourist through the country, allowed me to see real Italian life, beyond the pasta eating and wine drinking I imagined it to be. It's easy to travel somewhere as a tourist and think how "cute" and "rustic" everything is, then go back to your hotel room and watch MTV like you're not far from home. Having to ride the bus everyday, I saw the fatigue of people who dragged themselves to low-paying jobs every day—I even began to recognize some regulars. I had to learn the unspoken rules of the daily bus commute in Trieste, sometimes the hard way: after being yelled at by three elderly women on a crowded bus for standing too close to the exit too soon before my stop, and at other times for not getting up there soon enough, I began to get the hang of things. From the frequent bus strikes to the lack of orderly lines, things were definitely different in Trieste, but you eventually discover that life goes on and things don't have to be the same as back at home. It was less convenient, but not unmanageable.

Ultimately, teaching in Italy was an experience that has changed the way I approach my life. For me, experiencing life abroad meant working toward assimilation. I wanted to be a part of those living around me. I learned the streets, shops, and restaurants of neighboring Venice and Florence without needing to consult a map. I learned how to enjoy a three hour meal and not ask for the check, and how not to take immediate offense if a salesperson didn't offer the service I'd been used to at home. I learned that florists are closed Monday and Wednesday afternoons for no reason I could discern and that you shouldn't take showers after 11pm, or your elderly neighbors might confront you in the hallway. While I may never feel quite Italian or entirely American again, living and teaching in Italy taught me to carve a new identity that just might belong anywhere.

Abby Garcia, from Goliad, Texas, graduated from Harvard University in 2003 with a degree in Psychology. This former collegiate cheerleader recently returned to her native Texas after 10 months living in Italy and traveling throughout Europe. She hopes to one day return to Europe to live and work for an extended period.

EMILIA-ROMAGNA

Italy's wealthiest wheat- and dairy-producing region, Emilia-Romagna spans the fertile plains of the Po River Valley and fosters some of the finest culinary traditions on the Italian peninsula. Gorge on Parma's famous *parmigiano-reggiano* and *prosciutto*, Bologna's fresh pasta and *mortadella*, and Ferrara's *salama* and *grana* cheese while complementing these dishes with regional wines like the sparkling red *Lambrusco*. Although the Romans originally settled this region, most of the visible ruins are remnants of medieval structures and today travelers find bustling urban scenes that have escaped the heavy tourism of other major Italian cities. Offering authentic cuisine without the omnipresent *menù turistico*, well-preserved sights with low admissions fees, and enough quiet to contemplate both art and natural beauty, Emilia-Romagna is one of Italy's most impressive regions.

HIGHLIGHTS OF EMILIA-ROMAGNA

SAVOR Bologna's delectable regional **cuisine,** some of Italy's finest (below).

ESCAPE Italy proper for majestic views off **San Marino's Rocca Guaita** (p. 414).

BIKE Ferrara's 9km lamp-lined **medieval wall** (p. 385).

PARTY with students and backpackers at **Rimini's superb clubs** (p. 406).

BOLOGNA ☎051

Affectionately referred to as the *grassa* (fat) and *dotta* (learned) city, Bologna (pop. 369,955) has a legacy of excellent food, education, and art. While the Po Valley provides tables with hearty egg pasta and savory local wines, Bologna's museums and churches house priceless artistic treasures. The city also hosts Europe's oldest university, a law school founded in 1088 to settle disputes between the Holy Roman Empire and the Papacy. Academic liberalism drove political activism, and the city's history as a hotbed of the 19th-century socialist movement earned it the nickname "Red Bologna," which its citizens still wear with pride.

▣ TRANSPORTATION

Flights: Aeroporto G. Marconi (☎051 64 79 615; www.bologna-airport.it), at Borgo Panigale, northwest of the city center. The **Aerobus** (☎051 29 02 90) runs to the airport from Track D outside the train station (every 15min. 5:30am-11:10pm, €4.50).

Trains: Info office open daily 7am-9pm. Information through Trenitalia (☎89 20 21). **Disability assistance** (☎199 30 30 60) at the west platform assistance office; open daily 7am-9pm. To: **Florence** (1½hr., 53 per day 5:13am-10:46pm, €4.65); **Milan** (3hr., 63 per day 3:44am-10:15pm, €10.12); **Rome** (4hr., 39 per day 1:34am-9:36pm, €19.37); **Venice** (2hr., 25 per day 4:35am-9:42pm, €7.90).

Buses: Terminal Bus (☎051 24 21 50), next to ATC ticket counter, provides **Eurolines** bus service. Open M-F 9am-6:30pm, Sa 8:30am-6pm, Su 3-6:30pm. Cash only.

Public Transportation: ATC (☎051 29 02 90) runs efficient **buses** that get crowded in the early afternoon and evening. Intra-city tickets (€1) are good 1hr. after validation onboard. Purchase at newsstands, self-service machines, or *tabaccherie*. Buses #25 and 30 run up V. Marconi and across V. Ugo Bassi and V. Rizzoli from the train station.

Car Rental: Hertz, V. Amendola, 16/A (☎051 25 48 30). Turn right from the train station, and left on V. Amendola. Cars start at €55 per day. 25+. Open M-F 8am-8pm, Sa 8am-1pm. AmEx/MC/V.

Taxis: **C.A.T.** ☎051 53 41 41. **RadioTaxi** ☎051 37 27 27. Available 24hr.

✦ ⁊ ORIENTATION AND PRACTICAL INFORMATION

From the **train station**, turn left on **Viale Pietro Pietramellara** and head to **Piazza XX Settembre**. From there, take **Via dell'Indipendenza,** which leads to **Piazza del Nettuno;** behind it is **Piazza Maggiore,** the city center. At P. del Nettuno, V. dell'Indipendenza intersects **Via Ugo Bassi,** which runs west, and **Via Rizzoli,** which runs east to **Piazza Porta Ravegnana. Via Zamboni** and **Strada Maggiore** lead out of this *piazza.*

> ❗ **NO BOLOGNA.** Treat Bologna like a big city—use caution and hold on to your wallet. At night, solo travelers may want to avoid the train station, northern V. dell'Indipendenza, and the areas surrounding the university.

Tourist Office: P. Maggiore, 1 (☎051 24 65 41), in Palazzo del Podestà. Offers **maps** and info on events and lodgings. Open daily 9am-8pm. **Branch** in train station. Open M-Sa 9am-7pm, Su 9am-1pm. **Call Center** (☎051 24 65 41) open M-Sa 9am-7pm.

CST: P. Maggiore (☎800 85 60 65 or 051 64 87 607; www.cst.bo.it) is an accommodations service. Open M-Sa 10am-2pm and 3-7pm, Su and holidays 10am-2pm.

Budget Travel: CTS, Largo Respighi, 2/F (☎051 26 18 02 or 051 23 75 01), across Largo Respighi from the Teatro Communale. Open M-F 9am-12:30pm and 2:30-6pm. Resources include ISICs (€10), train tickets, tour packages, and discounts on air and sea travel. Posters concerning accommodations rentals are outside. MC/V.

Luggage Storage: At the train station. Max. bag weight 20kg. €3.80 for 1st 5hr., €0.60 per hr. for next 6hr., 7hr.+ €0.20 per hr. Open daily 6am-midnight. Cash only.

English-Language Bookstore: Feltrinelli International, V. Zamboni, 7/B (☎051 26 80 70). Wide selection of classics, new novels, and travel guides. Open M-Sa 9am-7:30pm. AmEx/MC/V.

GLBT Resources: ARCI-GAY, V. Don Minzoni, 18 (☎051 64 94 416; www.cassero.it). Sociopolitical organization with a reference and counseling center. Nightclub downstairs (see **Nightlife,** p. 385). Open M-Sa 3-7:30pm.

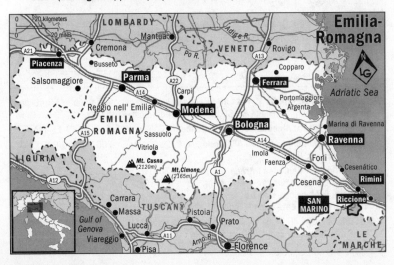

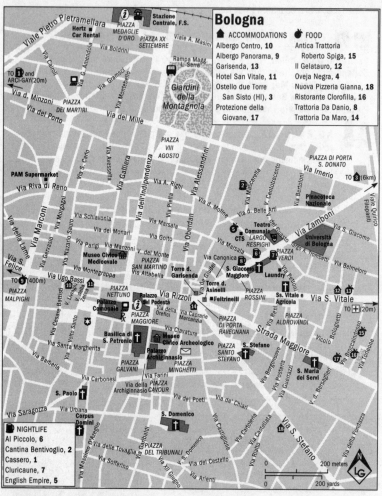

Bologna

🏠 ACCOMMODATIONS
Albergo Centro, **10**
Albergo Panorama, **9**
Garisenda, **13**
Hotel San Vitale, **11**
Ostello due Torre
　San Sisto (HI), **3**
Protezione della
　Giovane, **17**

🍴 FOOD
Antica Trattoria
　Roberto Spiga, **15**
Il Gelatauro, **12**
Oveja Negra, **4**
Nuova Pizzeria Gianna, **18**
Ristorante Clorofilla, **16**
Trattoria Da Danio, **8**
Trattoria Da Maro, **14**

🌙 NIGHTLIFE
Al Piccolo, **6**
Cantina Bentivoglio, **2**
Cassero, **1**
Cluricaune, **7**
English Empire, **5**

Laundromat: Lavarapido, V. Petroni, 38/B, off P. Verdi, near V. Zamboni. €3.40 per 8kg, 25min. wash. Detergent €0.60. Open daily 9am-9pm. Cash only.

Emergency: ☎ 113. **Ambulance:** ☎ 118. **Police:** P. Galileo, 7 (☎ 051 16 40 11 11).

Pharmacy: Farmacia Comunali AFM Bologna, P. Maggiore, 6 (☎ 051 23 85 09). Open 24hr. AmEx/MC/V.

Internet Access: Cambusa Intrage, V. Amendola 2/G (☎ 051 23 96 90; fax 051 26 63 10), has 12 fast computers. €6 per hr. Open M-F 10am-7pm. Cash only. **Sportello Iperbole,** P. Maggiore, 6 (☎ 051 20 31 84). Free Internet provided by the city. Requires ID. Reserve a few days ahead. Limit 1hr. per week. Open M-F 9:30am-6pm.

Post Office: ☎ 051 80 31 60. On P. Minghetti, 4, southeast of P. Maggiore, off V. Farini. Open M-F 8am-6:30pm, Sa 8am-12:30pm. **Currency exchange** available. **Postal Code:** 40100.

ACCOMMODATIONS

Bologna's hotels are rather pricey; reservations are recommended. The most affordable establishments are located around V. Ugo Bassi and V. Marconi.

Albergo Panorama, V. Livraghi, 1, 4th fl. (☎051 22 18 02; www.hotelpanoramabologna.it). Take V. Ugo Bassi from P. del Nettuno, then take the 3rd left. Spacious rooms off a small hallway have charming decorations and good views. All rooms have sink, TV, and shared bath with tubs. Reception 7am-3am. Curfew 3am. Singles €50-60; doubles €60-70; triples €75-85; quads €85-95; quints €100. ❹

Ostello due Torre San Sisto (HI), V. Viadagola, 5 (☎/fax 051 50 18 10), off V. S. Donato, in Località di S. Sisto. Take bus #93 from V. Marconi, 69 (15min., M-Sa every 30min. 6:16am-8:06pm) or 301 from bus station (limited service). Exit at S. Sisto. Social, but out-of-the-way hostel with laundry (€2.60 per wash or dry), basketball court, Internet (€5.16 per hr.), satellite TV, and DVDs. Wheelchair accessible. Reception 7:30-10am and 3:30-11:30pm. Lockout 10am-3:30pm. Curfew 11:30pm. Dorm €15, non-HI members add €3; doubles €33; family rooms €15 per person. AmEx/MC/V. ❶

Garisenda, Galleria Leone, 1, 3rd fl. (☎051 22 43 69; fax 051 22 10 07). Take V. Rizzoli and turn right into the gallery. A hallway lined with antiques leads to 7 spacious rooms with basic modern furnishings. Breakfast included. Singles €45-50; doubles €65-70, with bathroom €95; triples €100/120. MC/V. ❹

Protezione della Giovane, V. S. Stefano, 45 (☎051 22 55 73). Past the church, on the right. Ring buzzer and climb the large staircase at the end of the long hallway. Gorgeous building with frescoed ceilings and French windows overlooks a garden filled with potted trees. Several rooms partitioned into smaller singles. Women only. Breakfast included M-Sa. Curfew 10:30pm. Reserve ahead. Dorm €15. Cash only. ❶

Hotel San Vitale, V. S. Vitale, 94 (☎051 22 59 66; fax 23 93 96). Follow V. Rizzoli past the towers to V. S. Vitale. Ring bell to enter. 17 retro rooms with bath and TV share sunny, interior courtyard. Wheelchair accessible. Reception until 2am. Singles €52-62; doubles €72-86; triples €90-110; quads €110-128. AmEx/MC/V. ❹

Albergo Centro, V. della Zecca, 2, 3rd fl. (☎051 22 51 14; werterg@tin.it). Take V. Ugo Bassi from P. del Nettuno, then 2nd left on V. della Zecca. A snazzy hotel with blue furnishings, professional staff, and bright halls. All rooms with TV and A/C. Singles and triples have bath; some doubles do not. Breakfast €8. Singles €70; doubles €75, with bath €96; triples €120; quads €140. Extra beds €20. AmEx/MC/V. ❺

FOOD

Pasta comes in all shapes and sizes in Bologna. The best of the stuffed variety are *tortellini*, with ground meat, and *tortelloni*, with ricotta and spinach. Bologna is also known for its variety of salamis and hams, including *mortadella*, a sausage-like creation that bears little resemblance to America's processed bologna. Restaurants cluster on side streets near the *centro;* try the areas around V. Augusto Righi, V. Piella, and V. Saragozza. The vast, indoor **Mercato delle Erbe,** V. Ugo Bassi, 27, sells produce, cheese, meat, and bread. (Open in summer M-W 7am-1:15pm and 5-7:30pm, Th and Sa 7am-1:15pm, F 7am-1:15pm and 4:30-7:30pm; in winter M-W and F 4:30-7:30pm. Cash only.) Buy essentials at **PAM** supermarket, V. Marconi, 26. (Open M 8am-7pm, Tu-Su 11am-midnight. AmEx/MC/V.)

Il Gelatauro, V. S. Vitale, 98/B (☎051 23 00 49). With *gelato* widely touted as the best in Italy, this *gelateria* flanks flavors like ginger and *aurora* (pine nut) with classics *strac-*

ciatella and lemon. Kids under 14 can spin the Wheel-of-Gelatauro for a free cone. 2 scoops €1.90. Open daily 11am-11pm. Closed Aug. Cash only. ❶

Nuova Pizzeria Gianna, V. S. Stefano, 76/A (☎051 22 25 16). Locals know this hidden gem as "Mamma's." Owner Gianna crafts fresh pizzas (€2.90-6.80) behind a busy bar. Seating is limited, so devour the special *Gianna* (€6.80) from a stool or get a slice (€1.80) to go. Open M-Sa 8:30am-11:00pm. Closed 2 weeks in Aug. Cash only. ❶

Trattoria Da Maro, V. Broccaindosso, 71/B (☎051 22 73 04; trattoriamaro@libero.it), between Str. Maggiore and V. S. Vitale. This popular neighborhood *trattoria* is colorful not only in its clientele, but also in its neon decor. Try the favorite *pasta con le sarde* (with sardines) amid cluttered bottles, hanging baskets, and old advertisements. *Primi* €9-10, *secondi* €10-13. Cover €1.50 for lunch, €2 for dinner. Open Tu-Sa noon-2:30pm and 8-11pm. AmEx/MC/V. ❸

Oveja Negra, Largo Respighi, 4 (☎051 22 46 79). Country music, funky furniture and modern art come together at this popular cafe adorned with its signature sheep logo. Espresso €0.90. *Panini* from €3. Open M-F 8am-midnight. Cash only. ❶

Antica Trattoria Roberto Spiga, V. Broccaindosso, 21/A (☎051 23 00 63), between Str. Maggiore and V. S. Vitale. Black and white photos of old Bologna line the walls of this traditional, family-run restaurant. Menu changes daily. Bologna specialty €14 (W only). *Primi* €6.50-7, *secondi* €6-9.50. Cover €1.50. Open M 8-11pm, Tu-Sa noon-3:00pm and 8-11pm. Closed Aug. MC/V. ❷

Ristorante Clorofilla, Str. Maggiore, 64/C (☎051 23 53 43). Get your fruits and veggies at this trendy, organic eatery with the motto "eat your way to good health." Serving almost exclusively vegetarian meals, this restaurant prepares a fabulous couscous with tofu, vegetables, beans, and tomato sauce (€6.00) complemented by organic wine (from €2.80 per *caraffe*). Hot entrees from €5.90, salads from €5.80. Cover €1. Open M-Sa 12:15-2:45pm and 7:30-11pm. Closed Aug. AmEx/MC/V. ❷

Trattoria Da Danio, V. S. Felice, 50/A (☎/fax 051 55 52 02). This casual *trattoria*, open since 1937, offers huge portions of Bolognese cuisine. The 3-course meal with drinks (€11.50) and *menù turistico* (€7.50) are a good deal. *Primi* from €5.50, *secondi* from €4.50. Open daily noon-3pm and 7-11pm. AmEx/MC/V. ❷

⚲ SIGHTS

The 40km of porticoed buildings lining Bologna's streets were the city's answer to a 14th-century housing crisis during which a singular array of Gothic, Renaissance, and Baroque styles emerged.

▨ PIAZZA MAGGIORE. Aristotle Fioravanti, designer of Moscow's Kremlin, remodeled the Romanesque **Palazzo del Podestà**, now the boxy brick home of various cafes, shops, and information centers lining its *piazza*-level *loggia*. The 15th-century building is a feat of engineering: the weight of the palace rests on columns, not on the ground itself. Directly across the *piazza* sits the **Basilica di San Petronio,** designed by Antonio da Vincenzo in 1390. The *Bolognesi* originally plotted to make their basilica larger than St. Peter's in Rome, but the jealous Church ordered that the funds be used to build the nearby Palazzo Archiginnasio. The cavernous Gothic interior hosted both the Council of Trent and the 1530 ceremony in which Pope Clement VII gave Italy to German Kaiser Karl V. Golden panels and cherubs fill the **Cappella di S. Petronio** left of the entrance, where opulence contrasts with the bare walls of other chapels in the basilica. From the base of the nave nearby, a marble track dotted with constellation symbols and a single golden line extends across the church's floor to create the largest **zodiac sundial** in the world. The tiny **museum** contains beautiful chalices and illuminated books. (*P. Maggiore, 3. ☎051 22 54 42. Basilica and museum open daily 7:30am-1pm and 2:30-6pm. Free.*)

⬛ PALAZZO ARCHIGINNASIO. This *palazzo*, the first seat of the city's university, features thousands of names and coats of arms of professors and students who worked here—most of them reconstructed after an Allied air raid decimated the structure in 1944. The building now houses the **Biblioteca dell'Archiginnasio**, a city library with over 800,000 texts. Above the 30 arches of the central courtyard sits the **Teatro Anatomico**, a wooden lecture hall. A marble table marks where dissections were performed under the watchful Apollo and other star-adorned ceiling decorations. *(V. Archiginnasio, 1, next to the Museo Archeologico. Follow signs from P. Maggiore. ☎ 051 27 68 11. Palazzo open daily 9am-6:45pm. Closed 1st 2 weeks in Aug. Free.)*

PIAZZA DEL NETTUNO. This *piazza* contains Giambologna's 16th-century stone and bronze fountain *Neptune and Attendants*. Affectionately called "The Giant," a nude Neptune reigns over a collection of water-babies and sirens spraying water from every bodily orifice. Nearby, a wall of portrait tiles commemorates members of the Bolognese resistance to Nazi occupation, while a Plexiglas plaque lists the names and ages of more recent victims of fascist terrorism from the 1974, 1980, and 1984 bombings of the Bologna train station and two individual trains.

PINACOTECA NAZIONALE. The Pinacoteca displays artwork spanning from the Roman era to Mannerism, with pieces by Giotto, Titian, and Giovanni Battista. For impressive works by Bologna's own Guido Reni, try **Gallery 24's** triumphant *Sampson Victorious and the Pietà detta dei Mendicanti*, a floor-to-ceiling canvas. **Gallery 26** displays Francesco Albani's beautiful *Madonna e Bambino* and **Gallery 22** holds several large canvases, including Vasari's *Christ in Casa di Marta*. *(V. delle Belle Arti, 56, off V. Zamboni. ☎ 051 42 09 411; www.pinacotecabologna.it. Open Tu-Su 9am-7pm. Tickets close at 6:30pm. €4, EU students €2, under 18 or over 65 free. Cash only.)*

PALAZZO COMUNALE. Nicolò dell'Arca's terra-cotta *Madonna* and an Alessandro Menganti bronze statue of Pope Gregory XIV adorn the outskirts of this *palazzo*. The top floors house the **Collezioni Comunali d'Arte,** a collection of scantily clad allegorical figures mingling with overdressed, stern-looking *Bolognesi*. *(P. Maggiore, 6. Office ☎ 051 20 36 31; tickets 051 20 35 26. Open Tu-Sa 9am-6:30pm, Su 10am-6:30pm. €4, students €2. Cash only.)* The stark, adjoining **Museo Morandi** displays numerous oil paintings and watercolors and the reconstructed V. Fondazza studio of early 20th-century painter Giorgio Morandi, famous for his muted oil still-lifes of jugs, cups, and bottles. *(P. Maggiore, 6. ☎ 051 20 36 46; www.museomorandi.it. Wheelchair accessible. Open Tu-Su 10am-6pm. €4, students and seniors €2. Cash only.)*

MUSEO CIVICO MEDIOEVALE. Anything remotely associated with Bologna is featured here, including a collection of the patron saints of Bologna, wax seals of local nobility, weaponry, and an impressive collection of sepulcher lids. Watch for a 17th-century dagger that splits apart once inside the body and the 17th-century Roman *Sileno con Otre*, a rare example of an obese marble statue. *(V. Manzoni, 4. Off V. dell'Indipendenza, near P. Maggiore. ☎ 051 20 39 30; www.comune.bologna.it/iperbole/MuseiCivici. Open Tu-Sa 9am-6:30pm, Su 10am-6:30pm. €4, students €2. Cash only.)*

THE TWO TOWERS. After seismic shifts left Bologna's observational defense system with the unexpectedly angular **Torre degli Garisenda,** the determined city strove for height (and architectural accuracy) with 97.2m of brown brick in the soaring **Torre degli Asinelli.** Breathless climbers mount 498 narrow wooden steps past four landings to a breezy perch where a sea of red rooftops, Gothic church spires, bright yellow villages, and miles of uninterrupted horizon sit stories below. *(P. Porta Ravegana, at the end of V. Rizzoli. Open daily 9am-6pm. €3. Cash only.)*

MUSEO CIVICO ARCHEOLOGICO. This museum of artifacts unearthed near Bologna features long glass cases and shelves brimming with Roman inscriptions, red and black Greek pottery, and two dirt-swaddled, half-unearthed Etruscans. An impressive Egyptian collection in the basement displays items from 2640 BC, including stone reliefs from the tomb of one-time Pharaoh Horemheb. *(V. Archiginnasio, 2. Follow signs from P. Maggiore. ☎ 051 27 57 211; www.comune.bologna.it/Musei/Archeologico. Open Tu-Sa 9am-6:30pm, Su 10am-6:30pm. €4, students €2. Cash only.)*

CHURCHES

■**CHIESA SANTO STEFANO.** This cluster of buildings and courtyards assumed its shape from remains of a group of temples used by Egyptian monks—a stone tablet marks it as the former shrine to the goddess Isis. Four of the seven churches of the original **Romanesque basilica** remain. Built to hold the relics of Saints Vitalis and Agricola, the **Cripta** now contains the tomb of Martin the Abbot. In the small **Chiesa di San Sepolcro**, another of Bologna's patron saints, San Petronio, is entombed in the towering **Edicola del Santo Sepolcro,** supposedly modeled from Christ's sepulcher in Jerusalem. In the rear courtyard is the **Cortile di Pilato** (Basin of Pilate), where the governor reportedly absolved himself of responsibility for Christ's death. *(In P. Santo Stefano. Follow V. S. Stefano from V. Rizzoli. ☎ 051 22 32 56. Open M-Sa 9am-noon and 3:30-6pm, Su 9am-12:45pm and 3:30-6:30pm. Modest dress required. Free.)*

CHIESA DI SANTA MARI DEI SERVI. A long walkway with dark, badly marred lunettes and faded patches of fresco hides the bottom half of this soaring *basilica* from street-level view. Inside the well-preserved Gothic structure, octagonal columns support an unusual blend of arches and ribbed vaulting covering shallow altars flanking the nave. Cimabue's *Maestà* hangs in a chapel behind an exquisite altar sculpted by Giovanni Antonio Montorsoli, a pupil of Michelangelo. *(Take Str. Maggiore to P. Aldrovandi. ☎ 051 22 68 07. Open daily 8am-12:30pm and 3:30-7:45pm. Free.)*

CHIESA DI SAN DOMENICO. Tall marble columns line the clean interior of San Domenico, but its signature minimalism stops at the two transept chapels. In the **Cappella di San Domenico,** the body of St. Dominic lies in a marble tomb with religious figures sculpted by Nicolò Pisano and Michelangelo. Across the nave in the **Cappella del Rosario,** 15 small paintings by Fontana, Carracci, and others depict the mysteries of the rosary and frame a statue of the Virgin. The chapel is especially notable here, since St. Dominic is largely credited with the institution of the rosary as a conventional form of Christian prayer. *(From P. Maggiore, follow V. Archiginnasio to V. Farini and turn right on V. Garibaldi. ☎ 051 64 00 411. Open M-Sa 9:30am-12:30pm and 3:30-6:30pm. English tours daily at 3pm; ask for Tarcisio. Free.)*

CHIESA DELLE SANTISSIME VITALE E AGRICOLA. With its polygonal brick spire peering out above the walls of local homes, this small church incorporates shards of capitals and columns from Roman temples into its facade. Underneath the building, an 11th-century crypt holds paintings by Francia and Sano di Pietro. Look for a sculpture of Christ based on the Shroud of Turin's (p. 158) anatomical clues. *(V. S. Vitale, 48. ☎ 051 22 05 70. Open daily 8am-noon and 3:30-7:30pm.)*

CHIESA DI SAN GIACOMO MAGGIORE. The exterior combines Romanesque and Gothic styles. The artwork inside is impressive, even during the current restoration. The aging church is next to the **Oratorio di Santa Cecilia,** which contains a colorful fresco cycle depicting St. Cecilia's marriage and martyrdom. *(Follow V. Zamboni to P. Rossini. ☎ 051 22 59 70. Open daily 7am-noon and 3:30-6pm. Enter Oratorio from V. Zamboni, 15. Open daily in summer 10am-1pm and 3-7pm; in winter 10am-1pm and 2-6pm. Free.)*

🎵 ENTERTAINMENT

Every year from June to September the city sponsors an **entertainment festival** of dance, music, cinema, and art. Many events are free, but some cost €5. Summer visitors should contact the tourist office for a program. The **Teatro Comunale,** Largo

Respighi, 1, hosts world-class operas, symphonies, and ballets. To order tickets ahead, call or sign up outside the ticket office two days before performances. (☎051 52 99 99; www.comunalebologna.it. 10% surcharge for pre-order. Tickets €8-999. Box office open M-F 3:30-7pm, Sa 9:30am-12:30pm and 3:30-7pm. AmEx/MC/V.) See the pride of Bologna play *calcio* (soccer) at the **Stadio Comunale,** V. Andrea Costa, 174. Take bus #21 from the train station or 14 from Pta. Isaia. The season runs from September to June, with matches on Saturday or Sunday afternoons. Tickets for matches against Juventus or AC Milan go fast. The Bologna Football Club (☎390 51 61 11 11; www.bolognafc.it) provides info and tickets.

◧ NIGHTLIFE

Bologna's student population accounts for the city's large number of bars, pubs, and nightclubs. Call ahead for hours and cover, as info changes frequently. In June and July, clubs close and the party scene moves outdoors. The tourist office has a list of outdoor music venues. But don't expect much activity in August—even the outdoor *discoteche* shut down, and locals head to the beach.

Cluricaune, V. Zamboni, 18/B (☎051 26 34 19). This Irish pub draws local students to its low stools and extensive beer selection. Pints €3.10-4.20. Happy hour W 7:30-10:30pm; pints €2.50. Open M-F and Su noon-midnight, Sa 4pm-3am. AmEx/MC/V.

Cassero, V. Don Minzoni, 18 (☎051 64 94 416). Take V. Marconi to P. dei Martiri and turn left on V. Don Minzoni. This popular gay club draws chatty crowds of men and women down a steel catwalk to the basement and breezy wooden terrace of a former 17th-century salt warehouse. Drinks €3-6. ARCI-GAY card required. Open M-F 10pm-2am, Sa-Su 10pm-3am. Cash only.

English Empire, V. Zamboni, 24, near the University. Drawing crowds of loyal patrons from all of Italy, this bar mixes old-world pub with the pumping music and flashing lights of a new-world club. Enjoy wine (from €3.50 per glass), light meals (burger, drink, and coffee for €4.50), and conversation. Open M-F noon-3am, Sa-Su 6pm-3am. Cash only.

Cantina Bentivoglio, V. Mascarella, 4/B (☎051 26 54 16), near Largo Respighi and the Teatro Comunale. Pricey food by day and cheap drinks by night, this bar has live jazz, a relaxed atmosphere, and an umbrella-covered patio. Wine from €4.50 per glass. Open daily 8pm-2am; in summer M-Sa. MC/V.

Al Piccolo, P. Verdi, 1 (☎340 34 93 534), specializes in a unique assortment of Sicilian wines (€4), frozen drinks (€5), and electrofunk music amid black lights and exposed piping. Open M-Sa 10am-2am.

FERRARA   ☎0532

Rome has its mopeds, Venice its boats, and Ferrara its *biciclette.* In a city with a ratio of 160,000 bicycles to 135,000 residents, bikers are a far more common sight than pedestrians. Businessmen with cell phones, elderly ladies, and girls in stilettos dodge the tiny cars that brave the low arches and narrow streets of the area outside the *centro.* On the city's outskirts, biking aficionados can spend a day cycling a gorgeous 9km bike path atop the crumbling medieval walls, while old palaces full of period furniture, art museums, and an ominous *castello* offer eye-candy and adventure to the exertion-phobic crowd.

◧ TRANSPORTATION

Trains from Ferrara run to: Bologna (30min., 52 per day 1:41am-11:47pm, €2.90); Padua (1hr., 39 per day 3:52am-11:48pm, €4.30); Ravenna (1hr., 22 per day 6:33am-8:15pm, €4.20); Rome (3-4hr., 11 per day 4:40am-7:50pm, €30.73); and

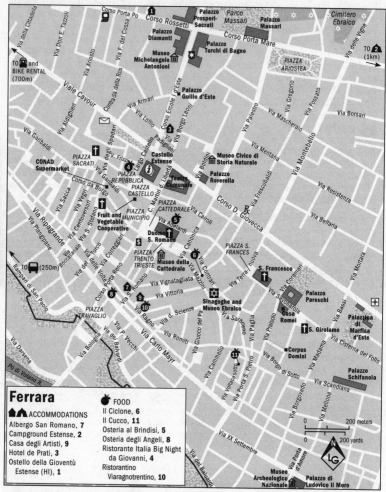

Ferrara

🍎 **ACCOMMODATIONS**
Albergo San Romano, **7**
Campground Estense, **2**
Casa degli Artisti, **9**
Hotel de Prati, **3**
Ostello della Gioventù
   Estense (HI), **1**

🍎 FOOD
Il Ciclone, **6**
Il Cucco, **11**
Osteria al Brindisi, **5**
Osteria degli Angeli, **8**
Ristorante Italia Big Night
   da Giovanni, **4**
Ristorantino
   Viaragnotrentino, **10**

Venice (1½hr., 26 per day 5:02am-10:10pm, €6.10). The ticket office is open daily
6:15am-9:10pm. (Infoline ☎0532 89 20 21. AmEx/MC/V.) **ACFT** (☎0532 59 94 92),
GGFP, and most other **buses** leave from the train station. Buses run to: local
beaches (1½hr., 12 per day 7:30am-6:50pm, €4.23); Bologna (1½hr., 15 per day
5:20am-7:50pm, €3.31); and Modena (2hr., 13 per day 5am-7:32pm, €4.65). From
the bus #2 stop, turn on V. S. Paolo for the ticket office, open daily 6:30am-7:00pm.
(Reduced service Su. Cash only.) **RadioTaxi** (☎0532 90 09 00) is available 24hr.
Head to Pirani e Bagni, P. Stazione, 2, for **bike rental.** (☎0532 77 21 90. €2 per hr.,
€7 per day. Open M-F 5:30am-8pm, Sa 6:30am-noon. Cash only.)

✸ 🛈 ORIENTATION AND PRACTICAL INFORMATION

To get to the *centro storico*, turn left from the **train station** on **Viale Costituzione,**
which becomes **Viale Cavour** and runs to the **Castello Estense.** Alternatively, take

bus #2 to the Castello stop or bus #1 or 9 to the post office (every 15-20min. 5:42am-8:30pm, €0.83). Turn right after the *castello* on **Corso Martiri della Libertà**. The **tourist office** is in Castello Estense, near P. Castello. (☎0532 20 93 70; www.ferrarainfo.com. Open M-Sa 9am-1pm and 2-6pm, Su 9:30am-1pm and 2-5:30pm.) **Currency Exchange** is available at **Banca Nazionale de Lavoro**, C. Pta. Reno, 19. (☎0532 78 16 11. Open M-F 8:20am-1:20pm and 2:35-4:05pm, Su 8:20-11:50am.) **Luggage Storage** is available in the train station. (€2-2.50 per hr. Coin operated. Open 24hr.) In case of **emergency** call ☎113, an **ambulance** ☎118, or the **police**, C. Ercole I d'Este, 26 (☎0532 41 86 00), off Largo Castello. **Fides Pharmacy,** C. Giovecca, 125, is open 24hr. (☎0532 20 25 24. AmEx/MC/V.) **Internet** is available at **Speedy Internet Club,** C. Pta. Po, 37. From the youth hostel, cross the street and turn right. (☎0532 24 80 92. €4 per hr. Also offers printing, photocopy, and fax services. Open M-Sa 9am-9pm. Cash only.) The **post office,** Vle. Cavour, 29, is a block toward the train station from the *castello*. (☎0532 29 72 11. Offers *fermoposta*. Windows #7-11 provide currency exchange. Open M-F 8am-6:30pm, Sa 8am-12:30pm.) **Postal Code:** 44100.

ACCOMMODATIONS AND CAMPING

Minutes from the *centro*, ▨ **Ostello della Gioventù Estense (HI)** ❷, C. B. Rossetti, 24, boasts large, clean rooms with frescoed ceilings and beautiful wooden doors. From the *castello*, walk up C. Ercole I d'Este, then turn left on C. Rossetti. (☎/fax 0532 20 42 27. Breakfast included. Internet €5.16 per hr. Reception 7-10am and 3:30-11:30pm. Lockout 10am-3:30pm. Curfew 11:30pm. Dorms €16; private rooms for 2-5 people €16 per person. AmEx/MC/V.) From C. Martiri d. Libertà, turn left at the cathedral, right on V. S. Romano, left on V. Ragno, and then immediately left to reach ▨**Casa degli Artisti** ❷, V. Vittoria, 66. Spacious rooms have stone floors and ensuite sink. Guests share access to an ivy-covered garden, minibar, and gas burners. (☎0532 76 10 38. Curfew 12:30am. Singles €25; doubles €43, with bath €60. Cash only.) It doesn't get much better than the **Hotel de Prati** ❹, V. Padiglioni, 5, where a central location, friendly staff, and tasteful rooms with TV, refrigerator and A/C make it worth the splurge. (☎0532 24 19 05; www.hoteldeprati.com. Buffet breakfast included. Wheelchair accessible. Singles €47-70; doubles €70-105; suites €110-140. Extra bed €16. AmEx/MC/V.) **Albergo San Romano** ❹, V. San Romano, 120, has large rooms with tile floors and simple decorations. All rooms with TV and phone, some with A/C and view of town. (☎0532 76 94 59; fax 0532 79 82 09. Singles €45, with bath €50; doubles with bath €60; triples €85; quints €105.) Take bus #1 to P. S. Giovanni (€0.83) then V. Gramicia for 15min. through the traffic circle to **Estense** ❶, V. Gramicia, 76, a campsite 1km from the city center. Driving from the *castello*, take C. Ercole I d'Este, turn right on C. Pta. Mare and left on V. Gramicia. Grounds are past V. Pannonio. (☎/fax 0532 75 23 96. Open daily 8am-10pm. Closed mid-Jan. to late Feb. Bike rental €3.50 per half-day, €6 per day. €5 per person, under 8 free. €6.50 per car and tent space; RVs for rent €26 per night. Electricity €2. Free hot showers. MC/V (€50 min.).)

FOOD

Ferrara's specialties include *salama da sugo* (pork, spices, and wine) and *pasticcio alla ferrarese* (sweet bread stuffed with macaroni and meat sauce). Eel, clams, scallops, sea bass, and mullet are integral to the seafood-heavy regional diet. Corpus Domini nuns invented Ferrara's famous *pampepato* (chocolate cake with almonds, candied fruit, and chocolate icing). For wine, try the slightly sparkling *Uva D'Oro* (Golden Grape). A **CONAD** supermarket is at V. Garibaldi, 53. (Open daily 8:30am-8pm. MC/V.) **Ferrara Frutta,** a local produce cooperative, is in P. Castello, 24-26. (☎0532 20 31 36. Open M-W, F, and Su 8am-1pm and 5-7:30pm; Th and Sa 8am-1pm. Cash only.) ▨**Osteria degli Angeli** ❸, V. delle Volte, 4, serves hearty regional fare served inside a 16th-century dining room. From the *basilica*, take C. Pta. Reno and turn left under the arch. (☎0532 76 43 76. *Primi* €7-8, *secondi* €7-16. Open daily 6pm-11pm. MC/V.) The oldest *osteria* in the world, **Osteria al Brindisi ❸**, V.G. degli Adelardi 11, operates in the shadow of the *duomo* among rows of dusty wine bottles. It's been serving luminaries like Titian, Cellini, and Pope John Paul II since 1435. (☎0532 20 91 42; info@albrindisi.com. Cover €2. Open Tu-Su 9am-1am. AmEx/MC/V.) The swanky **Ristorantino Viaragnotrentino ❹**, V. Ragno, 31/A, is the place to go for local seafood specialties like the *spaghetti allo scoglio* (with clams, mussels and squid; €13) and other eclectic dishes. (☎0532 76 90 70. *Primi* €7-16, *secondi* €9-20. Open M and W-Su 12:30-2:30pm and 7:30-10:30pm. AmEx/MC/V.) On a quiet side alley is **Il Ciclone ❷**, V. Vignatagliata, 11, 2nd fl., where the specialty is *Pizza Ciclone* (€7), a whirlwind of pepperoni, ricotta, and mozzarella. (☎0532 21 02 62; fax 21 23 22. *Primi* €6.50-13.50, *secondi* €8-16. Fixed-price *menù* €12. Cover €1.50. Open Tu-Su noon-3pm and 7pm-1am. AmEx/MC/V.) Inspired by the struggling Italian brothers of the film *Big Night*, **Ristorante Italia Big Night da Giovanni ❺**, V. Largo Castello, 38, presents elegant dishes like *taleggio* cheese with pears, nuts, and red turnip sauce. (☎0532 24 23 67. *Primi* €10-20, *secondi* €17-28. Cover €3. Open M-Sa 12:30-2:15pm and 8:15-10:15pm. AmEx/MC/V.) Nestled in a residential neighborhood of the medieval part of town, **Il Cucco ❷**, V. Voltacasotto, 3, has been serving traditional Ferrarese cuisine for more than 30 years. Their *cappellacci di zucca al burro e salvia* (pasta with pumpkin, butter and sage; €7) can be enjoyed at cozy indoor tables or outside on the terrace. (☎0532 76 00 26. *Primi* €5.50-7. *Secondi* €6-11.50. Open daily 12:30-2pm and 7:30-10pm. AmEx/MC/V.)

◎ SIGHTS

Leonello d'Este, ruler and patron of the arts, molded Ferrara into an important artistic center with its own school of painting, the *Officina Ferrarese*. Works by Pisanello, Alberti, Piero della Francesca, and Titian grace the city's palaces and monuments. Those yearning for arboreal beauty can ride or walk down the tree- and lamp-lined 9km concourse that runs along—and atop—the city's medieval wall, stopping only for the panoramic view from one of its stone outcroppings.

▧ CASTELLO ESTENSE. This castle debuted as a small fortress in the 14th century. Today visitors wander through themed rooms like the Chambers of Games, Dawn, and Poisons. The red-tiled **Garden and Loggia of the Oranges,** where Eleonora of Aragon filled her terrace with orange trees, was added later. Less heartwarming are the tunnels of the dank **prigioni** (prisons), where Nicolo III's son, Ugo, and 2nd wife, Parisina, literally lost their heads after the king got wind of their illicit affair. *(☎0532 29 92 33. Open Tu-Su 9:30am-5pm. Admission €6, students and 65 and over €5. Supplement for tower €1. Audioguides €3 for adults, €2.50 for minors. Cash only.)*

▧ DUOMO SAN ROMANO. Dedicated to the city's patron saints, the cathedral is a stunning masterpiece of *loggia*, rose windows, and bas-reliefs. Rosetti designed the arches and terra-cotta apse, and Alberti fashioned the pink *campanile*. A dim interior houses the beautiful Santuario Beata Vergine delle Grazie. Across the street, the **Museo della Cattedrale** displays the church's precious works, including *Jacopo Quercia's* statue, Madonna of the Pomegranate. *(Museum across the street from the duomo, through the courtyard on V. S. Romano. Duomo open M-Sa 7:30am-noon and 3-6:30pm, Su 7:30am-12:30pm and 3:30-7:30pm. Museum ☎0532 76 12 99. Open Tu-Su 9am-1pm and 3-6pm. Ticket office closes 30min. before museum. €5, students €3. AmEx/MC/V.)*

PALAZZO DIAMANTI. Built in 1493 by Biagio Rossetti, the palace is easily recognizable by the innumerable white triangles that cover its facade. Inside is the **Pinacoteca Nazionale,** a collection of art including a series of tablets by El Greco depicting scenes from Christ's life. *(C. Ercole I d'Este, 1. ☎0532 20 58 44. Just before the intersection with C. Rossetti. Open Tu-W and F-Sa 9am-2pm, Th 9am-7pm, Su 9am-1pm. Tickets close 30min. before museum. €4, over 65 and students €2. Cash only.)*

MUSEO MICHELANGELO ANTONIONI. This small museum contains a handful of posters for the *Ferrarese* director's internationally acclaimed films as well as Antonioni's own "Enchanted Mountain" paintings, a craggy, muted series created in the 1970s and 80s. Upstairs find his other notable experiments, including watercolors and oil paintings, some smaller than a thumbnail. *(C. Ercole I d'Este, 17, near Palazzo Diamanti. ☎0532 21 08 30. Open Tu-Su 9am-1pm and 3-6pm. Tickets sales end 30min. before closing. €3, EU students €2, under 18 free. Cash only.)*

PALAZZO MASSARI. Once a 16th-century residence, the *palazzo* now houses three separate museums. The **Padiglione d'Arte Contemporanea** has temporary modern art exhibitions. The **Museo d'Arte Moderna e Contemporanea Filippo de Pisis** displays a large collection by Ferrarese masters. Upstairs, tapestry-covered walls accent Giovanni Boldoni's works in the **Museo Ferrarese dell'Ottocento/Museo Giovanni Boldini.** *(C. Pta. Mare, 9. Turn right off C. Ercole I d'Este. ☎0532 20 99 88. Museums open Tu-Su 9am-1pm and 3-6pm. Ticket office closes 5:30pm. Filippo de Pisis €3, students €2. Ottocento/Boldini €5/3. Combination ticket €8/3. Cash only.)*

SINAGOGHE E MUSEO EBRAICO. The city's Jewish museum is in the heart of the ghetto and contains art and documents the history of the Jews of Ferrara. Inquire here for directions to the **Cimitero Ebraico** (Jewish Cemetery), where most of Ferrara's 19th- and 20th-century Jewish community is buried. The tourist office also provides a map of Jewish itineraries throughout the city. *(V. Mazzini, 95. From the duomo, the museum is on the left side of the street. ☎0532 21 02 28. Guided tours M-Th and Su 10, 11am, and noon. Admission €4, students €1.50. Cemetery: head down C. Giovecca from the castello. Turn left on V. Montebello and continue to end. Open F-Sa.)*

PALAZZO SCHIFANOIA. Delicate ivory sculptures and statues like Fanelli's *San Giorgio che uccide il drago* fill the ground floor. The **Hall of the Months,** a Renaissance fresco series representing each month, its astrological sign, and its corresponding Greek deity, is the *palazzo*'s main attraction. *(V. Scandiana, 23. ☎0532 64 178. Open Tu-Su 9am-6pm. €5, students €3. With Palazzina Marfisa, €8/5. Cash only.)*

CASA ROMEI. After a legal tug-of-war, this 15th-century Renaissance showpiece, halfway house, and one-time candidate for demolition opened as a museum in 1952. Giovanni Romei, an ambitious merchant, constructed the brick *palazzo* to bolster his reputation and it became the prototype of the aristocratic house. Rooms are filled with ceiling frescoes, artwork from destroyed churches, and the remains of one of Ferrara's oldest thermals. *(V. Savonarola, 30. Take V. Adelardi left of the duomo and follow it until it becomes V. Savonarola. ☎0532 24 03 41. Open Tu-Su 8:30am-7:30pm. Ticket sales end 30min. before closing. €2, EU students €1, under 18 free. Cash only.)*

PALAZZINA MARFISA D'ESTE. The furniture in this brick dwelling are positioned as if the *palazzina* were still in use. Note the walnut benches supported by Ionic columns that have been called one of the most perfect creations of Tuscan furniture of the 1500s. *(C. Giovecca, 170. Follow C. Giovecca from Largo Castello, or take bus #9. ☎0532 20 74 50. Open Tu-Su 9am-1pm and 3-6pm. €3, over 65, under 18 €2. Combination with Palazzo Schifanoia and Museo della Cattedrale €6.50, students €4.50. Cash only.)*

MUSEO ARCHEOLOGICO NAZIONALE. Two walls of a neighboring low brick building and two stories of marble *loggia* compose the courtyard of the Palazzo di Ludovico il Moro, built in 1495 for an official of the d'Este court. Glass cases display artifacts from Spina, the Greek-Etruscan city that disappeared in the Adriatic 2000 years ago, and painted maps of Etruscan territories. *(V. XX Settembre, 122. A* *short walk down V. Pta. d'Amore from Palazzo Schifanoia. From P. Trento Trieste, follow V. Mazzini, which becomes V. Saraceno, to the end; turn left on V. Mayr, then right on V. Borgovado.* ☎ 0532 66 299; mnafe@tiscalinet.it. Open Tu-Su 9am-2pm. €4, students €2. Cash only.)

> **TIP** | **BIRD'S EYE VIEW.** For a different perspective, rent a bike and survey Ferrara from atop the Roman Walls that surround the city.

▒ FESTIVALS

On the last Sunday of May, Ferrara revives the ancient **Palio di San Giorgio.** Dating from the 13th century, this event begins with a lively procession of delegates from the city's eight *contrade* (districts), followed by a series of four races held in P. Ariostea: the boys' race, the girls' race, the donkey race, and the great horse race (☎ 0532 75 12 63; www.paliodiferrara.it). During the last full week of August, street performers display their talents at the **Busker's Festival.** (☎ 0532 24 93 37; www.ferrarabuskers.com.) Even the finicky will appreciate the countless methods of eel-preparation at the annual **Eel Festival,** celebrated at the beginning of October in the province of Comacchio (for more information, dial ☎ 0532 33 10 161).

MODENA   ☎ 059

On Sunday evenings, the side streets of Modena (pop. 170,000) are quiet, but Piazza Grande is bustling. At the end of mass, locals gather in front of the *duomo* to chat with the priest and each other. While the rhythm of life here appears to follow a simple beat, don't be fooled: Modena is a small town that packs a big punch, boasting Luciano Pavarotti, the Ferrari and Maserati factories, and internationally renowned balsamic vinegar. While enjoying Modena to the full may require advance planning and reservations for entrance into many of its monuments, its ornate structures, tantalizing flavors, and cultural history make it worth a stop.

◪ TRANSPORATION AND PRACTICAL INFORMATION

The **train station** is in P. Dante Alighieri. (☎ 059 89 20 21. Info office open daily 8am-7pm; ticket office open daily 5:30am-11:10pm.) Trains run to: Bologna (30min., every 30min. 5:09am-12:55pm, €2.50); Milan (2hr., every hr. 4:06am-9:46pm, €8.95); Parma (30min., 2 per hr. 4:06am-1:16am, €3.25); and Verona (4hr., 8 per day 5:58am-11:05pm, €4.65). **ATCM buses** (☎ 199 11 11 01 or 800 11 11 01; www.atcm.mo.it; open M-F 6:30am-7:30pm, Sa 7am-2pm) leave from V. Fabriani, off V. Monte Kosica to the right of the train station, for Maranello (every 1-2hr., €2.42), and also run throughout the city. Call a **taxi** at ☎ 059 37 42 42 (24hr.).

From the **train station,** take bus #7 (dir: Policlinico) or 11 (dir: Zodiaco) to **Piazza Grande** and the town center. On foot, take **Via Galvani** from the station and turn right on **Viale Monte Kosica.** A left on **Via Ganaceto** leads to **Via Emilia,** Modena's main thoroughfare. Continue through **Piazza Matteotti** to **Piazza Torre,** which opens into P. Grande. V. Emilia changes names from **Via Emilia Ovest** on the west side to **Via Emilia Centro** in the center to **Via Emilia Est** in the east. From P. Grande, take V. Castellaro and then the first left to reach the **tourist office,** V. Scudari, 12. (☎ 059 20 66 60. M 3-6pm, Tu-Sa 9:30am-12:30pm and 3-6pm, Su 9:30am-12:30pm.) **Modenatur,** V. Scudari, 10, next to the post office, offers tourist information as well as help arranging themed tours in English, Italian, and German of the city's cars, food, and castle. (☎ 059 22 00 22; www.modenatur.it. Open M-F 9am-1pm and 2:30-6:30pm.) **Informagiovani,** P. Grande, 17, is geared

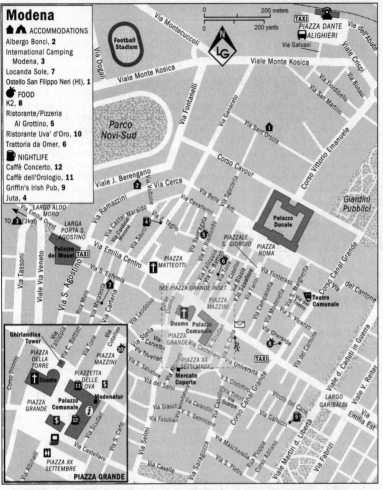

Modena

▲▲ ACCOMMODATIONS
Albergo Bonci, **2**
International Camping
   Modena, **3**
Locanda Sole, **7**
Ostello San Filippo Neri (HI), **1**

🍴 FOOD
K2, **8**
Ristorante/Pizzeria
   Al Grottino, **5**
Ristorante Uva' d'Oro, **10**
Trattoria da Omer, **6**

🍷 NIGHTLIFE
Caffè Concerto, **12**
Caffè dell'Orologio, **11**
Griffin's Irish Pub, **9**
Juta, **4**

EMILIA-ROMAGNA

toward younger travelers and provides travel info, job listings, alternatives to
tourism (see **Beyond Tourism,** p. 90), and **Internet.** (☎ 059 20 65 83. M-Tu and Th-Sa
9am-1pm, W 9am-1pm.) **Currency exchange** is available at **Credito Italiano,** V.
Emilia Centro, 102. (☎ 059 21 80 86. Open M-F 8:20am-1:20pm and 2:45-4:45pm,
Sa 8:20am-12:45pm.) **ATMs** are at **Unicredit Banca,** P. Grande, 40 (Open M-F
8:20am-1:20pm and 3-4pm, Sa 8:20-11:50am.) In case of **emergency,** call ☎ 118, the
police ☎ 113, or an **ambulance** (☎ 059 34 31 56). **Farmacia del Pozzo,** V. Emilia Est,
416 (☎ 058 36 00 91), is open 8am-8pm. Look for the green sign outside any pharmacy to see which has late-night service. **Internet** access is available at **Internet
Point,** P. Grande, 34. (☎/fax 059 21 20 96. €1 for 15min. Open M-Sa 10am-8pm.)
The **post office,** V. Emilia Centro, 86 (☎ 059 20 53 211), is open Monday to Friday
8am-6:30pm and Saturday 8am-12:30pm. **Postal Code:** 41100.

ACCOMMODATIONS AND CAMPING

To reach **Ostello San Filippo Neri (HI) ❶**, V. S. Orsola, 48-52, walk down V. Galvani from the station, turn right along Vle. Monte Kosica, left on V. Ganaceto, and another left on V. S. Orsola. A pleasant staff tends this multi-level hostel with full amenities: clean shared bathrooms, sturdy closets with locks, Internet (€3 per hr), public phone, and TV. Wheelchair accessible. (☎/fax 059 23 45 98. Lockout 10am-2pm. Curfew midnight. Dorms €15. Non-HI members add €3. After 6 nights, receive a complementary 1-year HI membership. HI card available for €18. AmEx/MC/V.) **Albergo Bonci ❸**, V. Ramazzini, 59, has clean, spacious rooms with TV, sink and phone. Shared bath. From the station, turn left down V. Ganaceto, right on V. Cerca, and keep straight. (☎/fax 059 22 36 34. Reception 7am-1am. Reserve in advance. Price higher in fall and winter. Singles €38; doubles €62; triples €78 with *Let's Go* discount. A/C €15 per day. AmEx/MC/V.) From V. Ganaceto, turn right on V. Emilia, then left, to reach **Locanda Sole ❸**, V. Malatesta, 45, with its central but quiet location and rooms with sink, TV, and shared older bathrooms in hall. (☎059 21 42 45. Closed 1st 3 weeks in Aug. Summer singles €30-35; doubles €50-60. Fall-winter singles €45; doubles €65. Price negotiable for longer stays. A/C €15 per night. Cash only.) To reach **International Camping Modena ❶**, V. Cave Ramo, 111, in Località Bruciata, take bus #19 (dir: Rubiera, 6:20am-8:30pm) and ask the driver to stop in front of the Arbe factory. Walk to the right around the factory for 800m. Out of the way location and relatively expensive camping facilities. (☎059 33 22 52. Open Mar.-Oct. €14 for 1 person and tent, €6 for each additional person.)

FOOD

Modena specializes in *prosciutto crudo* and the sparkling *Lambrusco* red wine, but its most prominent product is fragrant balsamic vinegar, poured over salads in liberal quantities. The social ◨**Mercato Coperto di Via Albinelli**, down V. Albinelli from the clothing stalls of P. XX Settembre, was built by the city in 1931 to house a food market that's been around since medieval times. Vendors sell produce, flowers, wines, and even squid. (Open June-Sept. M-Sa 6:30am-2pm; Oct.-May M-F 6:30am-2pm, Sa 6:30am-2pm and 4:30-7pm.) Feast on elaborate salads (€7-8) at outdoor tables or in the elegant interior of **Ristorante Uva' d'Oro ❸**, P. Mazzini, 38, where Modenese specialties are prepared to perfection. (☎059 23 91 71. *Antipasti* €9-12. *Primi* €7-10, *secondi* €7-14. Cover €2. Open M-F noon-2:30pm and 7:30-10:30pm. AmEx/MC/V.) The classic **Ristorante/Pizzeria Al Grottino ❸**, V. del Taglio, 26, has outdoor seating on a wide street. Takeout also available. Follow V. Rismondo one block from V. Emilia. (☎059 22 39 85. Pizza €3.50-8.50. *Primi* €5-7.50, *secondi* €6.50-18. Cover €2. Open M-Tu and Th-F noon-2:30pm and 7:30-10:30pm, Sa-Su 7:30-10:30pm. AmEx/MC/V.) Grandma's kitchen goes gourmet at **Trattoria da Omer ❷**, V. Torre, 33, off V. Emilia, across from P. Torre, where all dishes, including macaroni, *scaloppe*, and *salmone* are €8. (☎059 21 80 50. *Primi* and *secondi* €8. Open M-Sa 1-2pm and 7:30-10pm. Reserve ahead. AmEx/MC/V.) At **K2 ❶**, C. Canal Grande, 67, off V. Emilia, each cone is sculpted into a flower shape. (☎059 21 91 81. Cones from €1.70. Open M-Tu and Th-Su 9am-11pm. Cash only.)

SIGHTS

DUOMO. Modena's Romanesque *duomo* is built over the grave of its patron saint, San Geminiano. The church houses a relic of Geminiano, an encased arm which is paraded around in a religious procession in January. Legend holds that he prevented Attila the Hun from destroying the city by shrouding it in mist. Sculptor Wiligelmo and his students decorated most of the *duomo* with carvings of local,

Roman, biblical, and Celtic themes; scenes from the Old Testament and Gemi-niano's travels frame the door. Visit the three-dimensional clay nativity scene in a cave on the right wall. *(P. Grande.* ☎ *059 21 60 78; www.duomodimodena.it. Open daily 7am-12:30pm and 3:30-7pm. Free.)* The **Museo del Duomo**, V. Lanfranco, 6, allows visitors to see gold chalices, crosses, and embroidered ecclesiastical robes that in centuries past were paraded out only on holy feast days. *(☎059 43 96 969. Open Oct.-Mar. Tu-Su 9:30am-12:30pm and 3:30-6:30pm; Apr.-Sept. Tu-Su 9:30am-12:30pm and 3:30-7pm.)*

PALAZZO DEI MUSEI. Inside the *palazzo*, the **Biblioteca Estense** holds a collec-tion of exquisitely illuminated books, including a 1501 Portuguese world map. The library's **Sala Campori,** available by appointment only, houses the **Biblia di Borso d'Este,** a 1200-page Bible partially illustrated by Emiliano, the painter Taddeo Criv-elli. Above the library, the **Galleria Estense** displays huge canvases like Velázquez's *Portrait of Francesco d'Este* and Bernini's bust of the same subject. In the **Archaeological Ethnological Civic Museum** and the **Civic Art Museum,** large glass cases contain musical instruments, 19th-century scientific instruments, and artifacts from the Americas, Asia, and Africa. *(In Largo S. Agostino at the western side of V. Emilia. Biblioteca* ☎ *059 22 22 48; www.cedoc.mo.it/estense. Exhibits open M-Sa 9am-1pm. Call the library in advance to see the Sala Campori and Biblia di Borso d'Este. €2.60, under 19 or over 65 free. Galleria* ☎ *059 43 95 711; www.galleriaestense.it. Open Tu-Su 8:30am-7:30pm. €4, stu-dents €2. Civic museums* ☎ *059 20 01 00. Open Tu-Sa 9am-noon and 3-6pm, Su 10am-1pm and 3-7pm. €4, students €2. Cumulative ticket to all museums €6, good for 2 days.)*

GHIRLANDINA TOWER. This 95m tower, built in the 13th century, incorporates Gothic and Romanesque elements. Climb to the top for a view of Modena's stucco rooftops. A photo memorial to those who died fighting the Nazis and Fascists dur-ing WWII stands at the base. *(P. Torre off P. Grande. Open Apr.-July and Sept.-Oct. Su and holidays only 9:30am-12:30pm and 3-7pm or with a reservation through the tourist office. €1.)*

FERRARI FACTORY. Modena's flashiest claim to fame is the Ferrari, created in 1940 by Enzo Ferrari. The factory is southwest of Modena in **Maranello,** which can be easily reached by bus. Visitors are allowed to sneak a peek into this complex only if they own a Ferrari, but antique and modern Ferraris, Formula One racers, trophies, and a recreated Grand Prix, complete with pits and track, are on display at **Galleria Ferrari,** the company's museum. *(Galleria at V. Dino Ferrari, 43. From Ferrari fac-tory bus stop, continue along road in same direction as bus for 200m; turn right at Galleria Ferrari sign.* ☎ *0536 94 32 04; galleria@ferrari.it. Open daily Oct.-May 9:30am-6pm; June-Sept. 9:30am-7pm. €12, seniors and students under 18 €7.)* Modenatur also runs tours for car enthusi-asts that include the Galleria Ferrari, the **Maserati Factory,** and a number of other car-related museums in the area. *(☎059 21 82 64; www.motorsite.it. Tours start at €35.)*

ADMINISTRATIVE BUILDINGS. The **Ducal Palace,** built in 1634, was home to the Este court for two centuries and serves today as the **Military Academy.** Guests wish-ing to visit the **Hall of Honor** and **Apartment of the Princes** should make a reservation for a guided tour. *(☎059 22 00 22. At the intersection of C. Cavour and C. V. Emanuele. Guided tours Su at 10am and 11am. €6.)* The **Sale Storiche of the Palazzo Comunale** in P. Grande served as the city's council chambers in the 17th and 18th centuries and still is occasionally used for meetings. Decently preserved frescoes, wooden elders' stalls, and the *Secchia Rapita* (Stolen Bucket) are all on display. *(☎059 20 66 60. Open M-Sa 8am-7pm, Su 3-7pm. €1, free on weekdays. Combined ticket with Ghirlandina Tower €1.50.)*

🎵 🎭 ENTERTAINMENT AND NIGHTLIFE

Most years, near the end of May or beginning of June, Modena's Parco Novi Sud fills with aria enthusiasts for **Pavarotti and Friends,** a benefit concert with the Three Tenors. (For information, contact the Pavarotti International Organization at ☎059 46 06 60 or visit www.lucianopavarotti.com.) In May, Modena demonstrates its love of all things fast with the **Land of Motors** festival, featuring parades of vintage cars, shows, and other spectacles. (☎059 20 66 60.) In June and July, Modena stages the **Serate Estensi,** a week-long festival with jousting, art shows, fireworks, and a Renaissance costume show. (☎059 20 32 707; www.comune.modena.it/seratestensi.) Perhaps the most important event is **Balsamica** (www.comune.modena.it/balsamica), the festival that reflects the dedication of the *Modenesi* to their balsamic vinegar. The event runs for three weeks from mid-May and features exhibitions, tastings, and cooking classes.

For excitement in the evening, try ▉**Griffin's Irish Pub,** Largo Hannover, 65/67. Sit at an outdoor table or enjoy a stiff Guiness at the bar. (At the corner with V. Gallucci. ☎059 22 36 06; www.griffins.it. Happy hour 6-8:45pm. Beers from €3. Open Tu-Th and Su 6pm-1am, F-Sa 6pm-2am. MC/V.) **Caffe Concerto** in P. Grande offers simple fare, drinks, and occasional live music. (☎059 22 22 32; www.caffeconcertomodena.it. Drinks €1-8. *Primi* €8.50-9.50, *secondi* €8.50-12.50. Open M and W-Su 7:30am-1am. MC/V.) **Juta,** V. del Taglio, 91, is a cross between artsy coffee shop and sizzling bar. (☎059 21 94 49. Sa and Su DJ-spun music from 8pm. Open daily 5pm-2am. Cash only.) Cross V. Emilia from P. Mazzini to hit **Caffè dell'Orologio,** Piazzetta delle Ova, 4. Relax with espresso inside or indulge in an evening cocktail at one of the outdoor tables. (☎338 92 56 608. Live music. Cocktails from €6. Open M and W-Su in summer 7am-midnight, in winter 7am-9pm. Cash only.)

PARMA ☎0521

Although a trip to Parma (pop. 172,000), where platters overflow with aged parmesan cheese and rosy-pink *prosciutto*, will certainly never leave the taste buds unsatisfied, Parma's artistic excellence is not confined to the kitchen. In the 16th century, Mannerist painting flourished under native artists Parmigianino and Correggio. The city was also the birthplace of composer Giuseppe Verdi, who resided in Parma while writing some of his greatest works, while pervasive French influences inspired Stendhal to choose the picturesque town as the setting of his 1839 novel *The Charterhouse of Parma.* Parma combines the mannered elegance of its heritage with the youthful energy of the nearby Università degli Studi di Parma.

▐ TRANSPORTATION

Flights depart from **G. Verdi Airport,** V. dell'Aeroporto, 44/A (☎0521 98 26 26; fax 0521 99 20 28) to both national and international destinations. Parma lies northwest of Bologna on the Bologna-Milan line. **Trains** leave the station in P. Carlo Alberto della Chiesa (☎0521 89 20 21 or 0521 77 14 26; ticket office open 5:55am-12:05am) for: Bologna (1hr., every hr. 4:33am-10:38pm, €4.70); Florence (2hr., 2 per day 9:46am and 12:49pm, €14.46); Milan (1½hr., every hr., €11.47); and Turin (3hr., 8 per day 7:15am-7:21pm, €19.88). **Buses** to nearby towns including Bardi, Busseto, and Colorno stop at P. C. A. della Chiesa, 7/B, to the right of the train station. (☎0521 27 32 51. Ticket office open M-Sa 6am-7:45pm, Su 7am-1pm.) **Intra-city buses** run throughout Parma from the front of the train station. Call a **taxi** (☎0521 25 25 62) for 24hr. service. **Car rental** is available at the airport from **Avis** (☎0521 29 12 38.) For **bike rental, Parma PuntoBici,** Vle. P. Toschi, 2, offers city bikes and electric scooters. (☎0521 28 19 79; www.parmapuntobici.it. €.70 per hr. for the first 4 hr., €.40 for each additional hour. Scooters €.90 per hr. Open M-Sa 9:30am-1pm and 3:30-7pm, Su 10am-1pm and 3:30-7:30pm.)

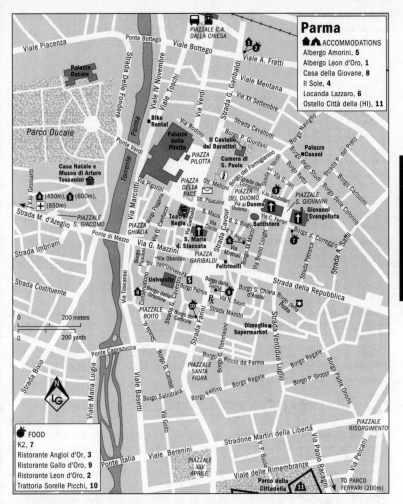

Parma

▲🏠 ACCOMMODATIONS

Albergo Amorini, **5**
Albergo Leon d'Oro, **1**
Casa della Giovane, **8**
Il Sole, **4**
Locanda Lazzaro, **6**
Ostello Città della (HI), **11**

🍴 FOOD
K2, **7**
Ristorante Angiol d'Or, **3**
Ristorante Gallo d'Oro, **9**
Ristorante Leon d'Oro, **2**
Trattoria Sorelle Picchi, **10**

EMILIA-ROMAGNA

✷ 🛈 ORIENTATION AND PRACTICAL INFORMATION

To get to the city, exit the station, keeping the fountain on the right. Turn left on **Viale Bottego,** right on **Strada Garibaldi,** and follow it 1km into town. Turn left on **Strada Mazzini** to reach **Piazza Garibaldi,** the town center. **Strada della Repubblica, Strada Cavour,** and **Strada Farini,** Parma's main streets, all branch out of the *piazza*.

Tourist Office: Str. Melloni, 1/A (☎0521 21 88 89; http://turismo.comune.parma.it/turismo). From train station, walk left on Vle. Bottego, turn right on Str. Garibaldi, then left on Str. Melloni. Open M-Tu and Th-Sa 9am-7pm, W 9am-1pm and 3-7pm, Su and holidays 9am-1pm.

Bank: Banca Antonveneta, Str. dell'Universita, 2, just off P. Garibaldi. Open M-F 8:20am-1:20pm and 3-4pm, Sa 8:20-11:50am. Also has 24hr. **ATM.**

Western Union: Infinitho, Str. M. D'Azeglio, 23/A (☎0521 23 45 55; www.hopera.net), just across the river over Ponte di Mezzo from V. Mazzini. Internet access also available. Open M-Sa 9am-8pm, Su 10am-1pm and 4-8pm.

Beyond Tourism: Informagiovani, Str. Melloni, 1 (☎0521 21 87 49; http://informagiovani.comune.parma.it), next to the tourist office. Posts jobs, volunteer and translation work, and apartment listings. Information on study abroad, cultural events, social activities, professional associations, European and Italian travel and tourism advice also available. English spoken. Free Internet and study room. Open M-Tu and F-Sa 9am-1pm and 3-7pm, W 9am- 1pm, Th 9am-7pm (see **Beyond Tourism,** p. 90).

English-Language Bookstore: Feltrinelli, Str. della Repubblica, 2 (☎0521 23 74 92), on the corner of P. Garibaldi. 2nd floor collection of British and American authors as well as contemporary works. Open M-Sa 9am-8pm, Su 10am-1pm and 4-8pm.

Laundromat: H2O Lavanderie Self-Service, Str. M. D'Azeglio, 108/A (☎338 10 28 597). Wash €3.50 per 7.5kg, €6 per 16kg. Dry €3.50 per 20min. Detergent €1. Open daily 7:30am-10:30pm.

Emergency: ☎113. **Ambulance:** ☎118. **Police:** (☎0521 87 30) on Viale Villetta, 12/A.

Pharmacy: Farmacia Guareschi, Str. Farini, 5/C (☎0521 28 22 40). Open M-F 8:30am-12:30pm and 3:30-7:30pm. After-hours rotation posted outside all pharmacies.

Hospital: Ospedale Maggiore, V. Gramsci, 14 (☎0521 99 11 11 or 0521 25 91 11), over the river past the Parco Ducale.

Internet Access: Web'n'Wine, Str. M. D'Azeglio, 72/D (☎0521 03 08 93; www.webnwine.it), across the river, on the left side of the street. €1 per 10min., €2.50 per 30min., €5 per hr. Wine sold separately. Open M-F 9am-6pm.

Post Office: ☎0521 22 24 13, on Str. Pisacane, 1/A. Turn left on Str. Cavour, heading from P. Garibaldi, then left again on Str. Pisacane. Open M-F 8am-6:30pm, Sa 8am-12:30pm. **Currency exchange** also available. **Postal Code:** 43100.

▛ ACCOMMODATIONS AND CAMPING

Albergo Leon d'Oro, Vle. Fratti, 4 (☎0521 77 31 82). 1 block left from train station, just after intersection with Str. Garibaldi. Required advance payment may seem unorthodox, but guests will find clean rooms with large windows and big beds. Shared bath. Restaurant (see **Food,** p. 397). Closed in Aug.; call for exact weeks. Singles €35, half pension €45; doubles €55/65; triples €75. AmEx/MC/V. ❸

Casa della Giovane, Str. del Conservatorio, 11 (☎0521 28 32 29; www.casadellagiovane.it). From Str. Mazzini, turn left on V. Oberdan; hotel is on the right. Upbeat community atmosphere and pink, semi-private rooms give this place character. Shared bath. Women only. Breakfast (8am) and choice of lunch (12:30-1:45pm) or dinner (7pm, 7:30pm in July and Aug.) included. Laundry and refrigerator available. Curfew Su-Tu and Th-F 10pm, W and Sa 11pm. €26 per person, under 25 €21. 8-month stays available for students (single €550 per month; double €365). Cash only. ❷

Locanda Lazzaro, Borgo XX Marzo, 14 (☎0521 20 89 44; fax 0521 38 56 00), between Str. della Repubblica and P. Duomo. Upstairs from ivy-draped popular restaurant. 8 simple but well-decorated rooms with sink, some with bath. Reception open during restaurant hours; daily 12:30-2:30pm and 7:30-10:30pm, otherwise call ahead before arrival. Reserve ahead. Hotel closed first 2 weeks in Aug. Singles €35, with bath €42; doubles €60/65; triples €75. MC/V. ❸

Albergo Amorini, V. Gramsci, 37 (☎/fax 0521 98 32 39) across the river over Ponte di Mezzo from V. Mazzini. While hotel may be a bit far from the major sights, these rooms with sink, TV, and shared bath are a steal. Reception 4pm-12:30am. Singles €35; doubles €55, with bath €70. AmEx/MC/V. ❸

Il Sole, V. Gramsci, 15/D (☎0521 99 51 07), across the river over Ponte di Mezzo from V. Mazzini, 750m down Str. M. D'Azeglio on the right. This hotel behind a *tavola calda* offers clean rooms with sink and shared bath. Singles €33; doubles €60. MC/V. ❸

Ostello/Camping città della (HI), Parco della cittàdella (☎0521 96 14 34; ostellocittàdella@libero.it). From station, take bus #9 (€0.80); exit when bus turns left on Str. M. della Libertà. Turn right on V. Passo Buole to enter park; hostel and campsite are to the left, housed in the corner of a 15th-century fortress. Hostel: Social atmosphere shared with campsite spices up spacious rooms with 3-4 beds. Communal showers and squat-style toilets also shared with campers. Access to park's recreational facilities includes basketball courts and soccer field. HI members only. 3-night max. Lockout 9:30am-5pm. Curfew 11pm. Call for availability. Open Apr.-Oct. Dorms €10.50. Campsite: Camping in area next to hostel. Open Apr.-Oct. €7 per person plus €11 for camper or tent site. Showers and electricity included. Cash only. ❶

◖ FOOD

Parma's cuisine is rich, delicious, affordable, and renowned throughout Italy. Crumbly parmesan cheese and silky-smooth *prosciutto crudo* fill the windows of the *salumerie* along V. Garibaldi. The local *Malvasia* is the wine of choice. When exported, this sparkling white loses its natural fizz, so carbon dioxide is usually added to compensate—pour a glass to sample the real thing. An **open-air market** comes to P. Ghiaia, off V. Marcotti near the intersection with Str. Mazzini, every Wednesday and Saturday morning. There is a **Dimeglio** supermarket located at Str. Ventidue Luglio, 27/C. (☎0521 28 13 82. Open daily 8:30am-1:30pm and 4:30-8pm.)

▨ **Trattoria Sorelle Picchi,** Str. Farini, 27 (☎0521 23 35 28). From P. Garibaldi, walk down Str. Farini several blocks, restaurant is on your left hidden behind a *salumeria* of the same name. This city secret known only to locals serves traditional dishes including roast pheasant, homemade lasagna, and tantalizing sweet and sour onions. Go early before the crowd of savvy locals comes in. *Primi* €7.50-8, *secondi* €8.50-13. Cover €2. Open for lunch only M-Sa noon-3pm. *Salumeria* open 8:30am-7pm. MC/V. ❸

▨ **K2,** Str. Cairoli, 23 (☎0521 28 55 42), next to the Chiesa di San Giovanni Evangelista. The creamiest of *gelati* deftly sculpted into a flower by workers in pink-and-white uniforms. Try the *amarena* (bitter cherry) or stick with the classic *fiordinutella* (hazelnut). Cones and cups from €1.50. Open M-Tu and Th-Su 11am-midnight. ❶

Ristorante Gallo d'Oro, Borgo della Salina, 3 (☎0521 20 88 46). From P. Garibaldi, take Str. Farini and turn left. Find an impressive list of local wines and traditional foods like pasta with *agnello* (donkey) in a cozy, 14th-century building. Outdoor dining in summer. *Primi* €6.50-8, *secondi* €6.50-9.50. Wines €3 per ¼-bottle, €4 for ½-bottle, €7-11 for full bottle. Open M-Sa noon-2:30pm and 7:30-11pm. AmEx/MC/V. ❷

Ristorante Angiol d'Or, Vco. Scutellari, 1/A (☎0521 28 26 32), off P. del Duomo. Delicacies like quail garnished with grapes, *parmigiano* cheese flan, and pasta in a *foie gras* and champagne cream sauce are tantalizing enough to make the splurge in this candlelit dining room. Menu changes weekly. *Primi* €10-14, *secondi* €15-20. Open M-Sa 12:30-2:30pm and 7:30-10:30pm, Su 12:30-2:30pm. AmEx/MC/V. ❺

Ristorante Leon d'Oro, V. Fratti, 4 (☎0521 77 31 82), off Str. Garibaldi (see **Accommodations,** p. 396). Huge platters of colorful *antipasti* and *dolci* tempt diners in a sunny dining room. *Primi* €5.50-8, *secondi* €10.50-13. Open daily 12:30-3:30pm and 8pm-midnight. Reservation recommended on weekends. AmEx/MC/V. ❸

SIGHTS

PALAZZO DELLA PILOTTA. Built in 1602, the palace's grandeur suggests the ambitions of the Farnese dukes. Today the *palazzo* houses several museums, accessible through the courtyard up the stairs on the left. Though there have been no actual performances in the theater since the curtain last fell in 1732, the elegant, wooden **Teatro Farnese,** completed in 1618, underwent restorations in the 1950s to repair damage inflicted by WWII bombs. Through the theater, the **Galleria Nazionale** contains numerous medieval polyptychs and portraits, including Leonardo Da Vinci's *Testa d'una Fanciulla* (Head of a Young Girl), as well as a gallery devoted to Parmigianino and Correggio. *(From Str. Cavour, turn left on Str. Pisacane and cut across P. della Pace to P. Pilotta. ☎0521 23 33 09 for both theater and gallery. Theater open Tu-Su 8:30am-1:45pm, ticket office closes 1pm. €2, students €1. Gallery open Tu-Su 8:30am-1:45pm. €6, students €4.)* Downstairs, the **Museo Archeologico Nazionale** displays bronzes, and sculptures of ancient origin. *(☎0521 23 37 18. Open Mar.-Sept. Tu-Su 8:30am-6:30pm; Oct.-Feb. 8:30am-1:30pm. €2, students €1.)*

DUOMO, BATTISTERO, AND MUSEO DIOCESANO. Parma's 11th-century Romanesque **duomo** balances vibrant paintings of clouds with more austere masterpieces like the Episcopal throne and Benedetto Antelami's bas-relief *Descent from the Cross* (1178). The stunning dome features Correggio's *Virgin* ascending to heaven. The pink- and white-marble **baptistry** displays early Medieval frescoes of enthroned saints and apostles that rise to the pinnacle of each of the dome's sixteen sides. Diagonally across the *piazza* from the baptistry, the **Museo Diocesano** holds examples of 12th- and 13th-century sculpture while preserving Roman ruins in the basement. *(In P. del Duomo. From P. Garibaldi, follow Str. Cavour and turn right on Str. al Duomo. ☎0521 23 58 86. Duomo open daily 9am-12:30pm and 3-7pm. Free. Baptistry ☎0521 23 58 86. Open daily 9am-12:30pm and 3-6:45pm. €4, students €2. Museo Diocesano ☎0521 20 86 99; www.fabbriceriacattedraleparma.it. Open daily 9am-12:30pm and 3-6:30pm. €3, students €1.50. Cumulative ticket with baptistry €5/3.)*

IL MONASTERIO DI SAN PAOLO. This aged monastery boasts several rooms with detailed ceiling frescoes, but most impressive is the central vault of the **Camera di San Paolo,** depicting the coat of arms of the Abbess, under whose direction the monastery prospered. The complex of St. Paul also houses **Il Castello dei Burattini** (Puppet Castle), a collection of over 1500 puppets. The **Pinacoteca Stuard** holds 270 paintings from the 14th to the 19th century. *(From P. Garibaldi, head up Str. Cavour, turn left on Str. Melloni, and follow the signs. Camera ☎0521 23 33 09. Open Tu-Su 8:30am-1:45pm, ticket office closes at 1pm. €2, ages 18-25 €1, under 18 or over 65 free. Puppet castle ☎0521 23 98 10; fax 0521 22 15 91. Open Tu-Su 9am-5pm, €2.50, students €1.50. Pinacoteca ☎0521 23 12 86. Open M and W-Sa 9am-6:30pm, Su 9am-6pm. €4, students €3.)*

CHIESA MAGISTRALE DI SANTA MARIA DELLA STACCATA. Built in 1521 to house a miraculous picture of the Virgin Mary, the icon is suspended above the altar between red marble columns. This Renaissance church also features impressive frescoes by Parmigianino. Ask the priest to see the **Crypt of the Farnese Dukes,** including the famous Alexander, whose helmet and sword still sit above his tomb, and Antonio Farnese, the last Duke of Parma. The **Sacrestia Nobile,** also accessible by special permission, is a wooden room that was completed by a team of Renaissance artisans in only five years. The column-like carvings, made from a single tree trunk, ascend from floor-level mythical figures into ceiling-height saints. *(Head up V. Garibaldi from P. Garibaldi. ☎0521 23 49 37. Open daily 7:30am-noon and 3-6:30pm. Free.)*

TEATRO REGIO. Commissioned by Marie Louise in 1821, the Teatro Regio is known worldwide. Its Neo-Classical facade is complemented by Borghesi's decorations inside and its four tiers of Baroque balconies feature red velvet seats interrupted only by the large crowned ducal box that faces the stage. *(Str. Garibaldi, 16/ A, next to P. della Pace. ☎0521 03 93 93; www.teatroregioparma.org . Open Tu-Sa 10:30amnoon. €2, students €1. Guided tours in Italian only, offered every 30min.)*

CHIESA DI SAN GIOVANNI EVANGELISTA. This 10th-century church is a longstanding Italian classic. The dome was frescoed by Correggio, while frescoes by Parmigianino run along the left nave and over the first, 2nd, and 4th chapels. The belltower was constructed in 1613. *(In P. S. Giovanni, behind the duomo. ☎0521 23 53 11. Open M-F 8-11:45am and 3-7:45pm, Sa and Su 8am-12:45pm and 3-7:45pm.)*

PARMIGIANO AND PROSCIUTTO FACTORIES. *Parmigiano* cheese fans should contact the **Consorzio del Parmigiano-Reggiano** to arrange a 2hr. tour of factories around Parma. Tours are offered infrequently, but many small factories outside the city are accessible by car anytime. Most give free samples. *(V. Sonnino, 35/A. ☎0521 29 27 00; www.parmigiano-reggiano.it.)* Visits to a *prosciutto* factory are available only during the Proscuitto Festival in the first week of September. *(For more information call the Consorzio del Prosciutto di Parma. ☎0521 24 39 87; fax 0521 24 39 83.)*

FRENCH GARDENS AND COMPOSERS. Although many French palaces were destroyed during WWII, Marie Louise's gardens still thrive by the Baroque **Palazzo Ducale** in **Parco Ducale.** *(West of Palazzo della Pilotta across Ponte Verdi. Park: ☎0521 23 00 23. Open May-Sept. daily 6am-midnight; Oct.-Apr. 7am-8pm. Free. Palazzo: ☎0521 28 28 68. Open M-Sa 9:30am-noon. €3, students €2.)* Music enthusiasts can visit nearby **Casa Natale e Museo di Arturo Toscanini** to see memorabilia. *(Borgo Rodolfo Tanzi, 13. ☎0521 28 54 99; www.museotoscanini.it. Tours in English. Open Tu-Su 9am-1pm and 2-6pm. €2, students €1.)* Across the river, the **Palazzo Cusani,** or **Casa della Musica,** served first as the seat of the University of Parma and later as the Mint of the Duchy of Parma. Today it houses a museum. *(Ple. San Francesco, 1. Follow Borgo del Parmigianino from the tourist office, then turn right on V. Daimazia. ☎0521 03 11 70. Open Jan.-June and Sept.-Dec. Tu-Sa 9am-6pm, Su 9am-1pm; July-Aug. Tu-Sa 9am-1pm and 4-7pm. €2, students €1.)*

SAVE MONEY. The **Museums and Monuments Pass,** good for eight days after purchase from the tourist office, has three distinct itineraries. The **Music Itinerary** (€5) provides entrance to the Teatro Regio, the Casa della Musica, and the Casa Natale e Museo di Arturo Toscanini. The **Imagination and Culture Itinerary** (€5) provides visits to the Galleria Stuard, the Palazzo Ducale, the Puppet Castle in St. Paul, and the Palazzetto Eucherio Sanvitale. The **Music and Art Itinerary** (€8) combines these two options, and allows guests into the Casa della Musica, the Galleria Stuard, the Puppet Castle, the Casa Natale e Museo Arturo Toscanini, and the Palazzo Ducale.

🎵 ENTERTAINMENT

The **Teatro Regio** (Str. Garibaldi, 16/A, next to P. della Pace; ☎0521 03 93 69; www.teatroregioparma.org) is one of Italy's premier opera houses, hosting operatic, cultural, and theatrical extravaganzas throughout the year. The opera season runs from November to April, while the popular **Verdi Festival,** honoring the native composer, takes place each year from April to June at the *teatro.* October and November bring **Parma Danza,** an international festival of ballet and modern dance. **E' grande Estate** brings classical music, opera, jazz, and tango concerts to

Ple. della Pilotta in July. (☎ 0521 21 86 78. Tickets from €10-35.) Information for all events may be obtained at the *teatro's* ticket office. A counterpoint to Parma's classical offerings is the free **Rock Festival** that takes place the first week of July (☎ 349 45 11 826). The **Cinema Astra,** V. Rondizzoni, 1 (☎ 0521 96 05 54; www.cinema-astra.it) also hosts a summer movie festival, **Estive Astra,** in June and July. All movies begin at 9:30pm and cost €5.50, students €4. Last but not least, the annual **Prosciutto Festival** occurs around the first weekend in September; contact the Consorzio del Prosciutto di Parma. (☎ 0521 24 39 87; fax 0521 24 39 83.)

PIACENZA ☎ 0523

One of the first Roman colonies in Northern Italy and the long-time headquarters of Julius Caesar, modern Piacenza (pop. 95,132) draws shoppers seeking the latest fashions to C. V. Emanuele II and V. XX Settembre. Meanwhile, P. dei Cavalli gets packed during concerts underneath the gazes of *Farnese* horsemen and Galleria Ricci Oddi offers an exhibit of modern Italian art. Reluctant to encourage a tourist economy, Piacenza was nevertheless recently voted one of Italy's most hospitable cities. It is an ideal stopover on the way to Parma, Bologna, or Milan.

🖃 🛯 TRANSPORTATION AND PRACTICAL INFORMATION

Trains from P. Marconi to: Bologna (2 hr., every hr. 6:01am-10:00pm, €7.65); Milan (1¼hr., every hr. 4:30am-11:29pm, €4.85); and Turin (2½hr., 9 per day 4:46am-9:28pm, €10.20). The ticket office (☎ 0523 89 20 21) is open 5:25am-11:40pm. **City buses** leave from the front of the station on Vle. S. Ambrogio. For a **taxi,** call ☎ 0523 59 19 19. **Car rental** is available from **Europcar,** close to the station at V. Alberoni, 93. (☎ 0523 33 22 76. Open M-F 8:30am-12:30pm and 3-7pm, Sa 8:30am-12:30pm.)

From the **train station,** walk on **Via dei Mille** and turn right on **Via Giulio Alberoni.** Follow it to **Via Roma,** and then turn left on **Via Daveri,** which leads to **Piazza Duomo.** From there, a right on shop-lined **Via XX Settembre** leads straight to **Piazza dei Cavalli.** The **IAT Tourist Office,** P. dei Cavalli, 7, is on the left side of **Palazzo Gotico** behind the horse statues. (☎ 0523 32 93 24; www.comune.piacenza.it. Open Tu-Su 9am-1pm and 3-6pm.) There is a **Banca Agricola Mantovana,** P. Marconi, 41, at the intersection of P. Marconi with Vle. dei Mille. (Open M-F 8:20am-1:20pm and 3:30-4:30pm, Sa 8:20am-1:20pm.) An **ATM,** P. Marconi, 5, is left of the train station outside McDonald's. For those seeking tourism alternatives, the **Centro Informagiovani,** V. Taverna, 37 (☎ 0523 33 40 13), has information on volunteer work, study abroad, professional associations, and travel. **Public restrooms** are inside the Palazzo Gotico behind the tourist office. **Farmacia Dr. Parmigiani,** P. Duomo, 41, posts after-hours rotations. (Open daily 8:30am-12:30pm and 3:30-7:30pm.) In case of **emergency** call ☎ 113, an **ambulance** ☎ 118, or the **police,** V. Rogerio, 3 (☎ 0523 49 21 08). A **hospital, Ospedale G. da Saliceto,** is on V. Taverna, 49 (☎ 0523 30 11 11). The **post office,** V. Sant'Antonino, 38-40, **exchanges currency.** (☎ 0523 31 64 68. Open M-F 8am-6pm, Sa 8am-12:30pm.) **Postal Code:** 29100.

🛏🍴 ACCOMMODATIONS AND FOOD

From C. V. Emanuele, turn right on V. del Tempio for 🖾**Protezione della Giovane ❸,** V. Tempio, 26. Immaculate rooms are tended by nuns. Lounge area, refrigerator, chapel, and laundry (€1) available for guest use. (☎ 0523 32 38 12. Women only. Reception 6:30am-10:30pm. Curfew M-Th and Su 10:30pm, F-Sa midnight. Singles €28, with breakfast €30. Doubles with bath €56, with breakfast €60. Weekly singles with breakfast €16 per night plus €30 registration fee. Weekly doubles with breakfast €27 per night plus €30 registration fee. Cash only.) To reach **Hotel Astra ❸,** V. Boselli, 19, take Bus #8 from the station (€0.85) to the intersection of V.

Boselli and V. G. M. Damiani. The hotel is on the right. Ten simple rooms, situated above a street cafe, allow guests to relax in the lounge or garden patio. (☎0523 45 70 31. Curfew 11pm. Reserve ahead. Singles €26; doubles €34. Cash only.)

An **open-air market** is held every Wednesday and Saturday morning in P. Duomo and P. dei Cavalli. A small supermarket, **Dimeglio,** is at V. Roma, 98. (☎0523 31 23 82. Open daily 8am-1pm and 4:30-7:30pm. Closed Th afternoon.) Enjoy dinner outdoors or inside the charming dining room at **Osteria del Trentino ❸**, V. del Castello, 71, off P. Borgo past the police station. Options include seasonal meat and fish menus and regional pastas. (☎0523 32 42 60. *Primi* from €7, *secondi* from €10. Open M-Sa noon-3pm and 7:30pm-midnight. AmEx/MC/V.) **Trattoria dell'Orologio/ Pizzeria da Pasquale ❸**, P. Duomo, 38, serves delicious pizza (from €4.50) and traditional cuisine in sight of the *duomo*. Takeout available. (☎0523 32 46 69. *Primi* €6.50-8, *secondi* €10.50-13. Open M-W and F-Su 11am-3pm and 6pm-1am. AmEx/ MC/V.) A popular Spanish restaurant, **Taberna Movida ❷**, V. Daveri, 35, offers tapas and in a modern indoor setting. (☎0523 31 81 31; www.tabernamovida.it. Tapas and entrees €4.50-12.50. Open M-F 12:30-2:30pm and 7:30pm-1am, Sa 7:30pm-2am, Su 5pm-1am.) Find delicious chocolate and apricot jam cake at **Panificio Remondini Alessandro ❶**, V. Calzolai, 52, which also sells cookies and rolls in bulk. (☎0523 32 17 06. Pastries and breads €0.50-5. Open daily 6:45am-1pm and 5-7:30pm.)

👁 🎵 SIGHTS AND ENTERTAINMENT

PIAZZA DEI CAVALLI. The central square is named for the two 17th-century equestrian statues that grace the *piazza* in tribute to Duke Rannucio I and his father, Duke Alessandro Farnese. The true gem is the Gothic **Palazzo del Comune,** or **Il Gotico,** constructed in 1280, when Piacenza led the Lombard League, one of Italy's most powerful trade groups. A monument to war veterans sits under the *palazzo*, with the **Palazzo del Governatore** directly across. Completing the square's trio of impressive buildings is the **Basilica di San Francesco,** adorned inside with 17th-century frescoes. *(Open M-Sa 9am-6pm, Su 7:30am-5:30pm.)*

IL DUOMO. The church, constructed between 1122 and 1233, contains a wealth of sculpture dating to the 12th century. The **crypt,** a maze of thin columns, is pretty spooky. A vigil is kept over the bones of Santa Giustina at its center. *(P. Duomo. Duomo open daily 7:30am-noon and 4-7pm. Modest dress required.)*

MUSEUMS. A great collection of obscure modern Italian art can be found in ▓**Galleria Ricci Oddi,** which displays art from the early 1800s to the present. Works are divided among 19 rooms according to the regions in which the artists originated. The collection includes **Bruzzi's** scenes of the countryside and **Michetti's** episodes of villagers in the landscape. Works to note include Ritratto's 1914 *Toilette*, of a mostly nude woman at her dresser, and Mancini's thickly applied, almost three-dimensional oil paintings, including the stunning *Donna alla Toeletta*, of a woman in a hat looking pensively over her shoulder. *(V. S. Siro, 13. Take C. V. Emanuele from P. dei Cavalli and turn left on V. S. Siro. Continue 2 blocks. ☎0523 32 07 42; www.riccioddi.it. Open Tu-Sa 10am-noon and 3-6pm. €4, students and groups €3.)* The commanding **Palazzo Farnese** houses the **Museo Civico,** the **Pinacoteca,** the **Museo del Risorgimento** and the **Museo delle Carrozze.** The Museo Civico's Etruscan and Roman collection from the 2nd and 3rd century AD is a highlight, while the most notable work in the Pinacoteca is a Botticelli fresco depicting Christ's birth. *(P. Cittàdella, 29, at the end of V. Cavour before it becomes Vle. Risorgimento. Take V. Cavour from P. dei Cavalli and turn left on V. Bacchiochi. ☎0523 32 69 81; fax 0523 32 82 70. Open Tu-Th 8:45am-1pm, F-Sa 8:45am-1pm and 3-6pm, Su 9:30am-1pm and 3-6pm. Museo Civico and Pinacoteca €4.20, students €3.15; Museo delle Carrozze €2.10, students €1.60. Cumulative ticket to all the museums €5.25, students €4.20.)*

RAVENNA ☎ 0544

Liguria has its beaches, Tuscany has its wines, and Ravenna has its mosaics. They appear under your drink at the bar, behind the glass windows of tourist shops, and in almost every major site. The streets paved with colored stones are almost entirely car-free, and travelers walk past monuments like Dante's tomb (to the ire of Florentines, who maintain an empty sepulcher for their exiled son). After the decline of the Roman empire, Ravenna rose from the ashes as a bejeweled pillar of strength. Justinian and Theodora, rulers of the Byzantine Empire, selected the city as the central administrative point for restoring order in the anarchic West and created a thriving artistic culture still visible in its churches and baptisteries.

▌▐ TRANSPORTATION

The **train station** is in P. Farini. **Trains** run to Bologna (1hr., 19 per day 5:07am-8:35pm, €4.60); Ferrara (1hr., 22 per day 6:20am-9:33pm, €4.20), with connections to Florence and Venice; and Rimini (1hr., 30 per day 12:05am-9:35pm, €2.90). (The ticket counter is open daily 6:05am-8:35pm and accepts AmEx/MC/V.) The station is open daily 4:45am-12:30am. Call Trenitalia (☎ 0544 89 20 21). **ATR** (regional) and **ATM** (municipal) **buses** leave outside the train station for Lido Adriano (20min.; every 30min., every 15min. in the summer, 5:40am-8:10pm; €1) and Marina di Ravenna (20-30min., every 30min. 5:40am-7:55pm, €1). Tickets (3-day pass €3) are sold at the booth marked "PUNTO" to the right when you exit the station. Return tickets are hard to get outside Ravenna but can be bought onboard with a surcharge. (☎ 0544 68 99 00. Office open M-Sa 6:30am-8:30pm, Su 7am-8:30pm; during the school year M-Sa 6:30am-7:30pm, Su 7:30am-7:30pm. AmEx/MC/V.) **RadioTaxi** (☎ 0544 33 888), in P. Farini, is available 24hr.

▌▐ ORIENTATION AND PRACTICAL INFORMATION

The **train station** is in **Piazza Farini** at the eastern end of town. **Viale Farini** leads from the station to **Via Diaz,** which runs to **Piazza del Popolo,** the center of town. Ask about city **maps** and accommodations listings at the **tourist office,** V. Salara, 8. Walk to the end of P. del Popolo, turn right on V. Matteotti, and follow the signs. (☎ 0544 35 404; www.turismo.ravenna.it. Open Apr.-Sept. daily 8:30am-7:30pm; Oct.-Mar. M-Sa 8:30am-6pm. **Luggage storage** is available to the left of the train station exit. In case of **emergency,** call ☎ 113, **first aid** ☎ 118, or the **police,** V. Rocca Brancaleone, 1 (☎ 0544 48 29 99). The **hospital, Santa Maria delle Croci,** is at Vle. Randi, 5 (☎ 0544 28 51 11). To get there, take minibus #2 or 444 from the station. **Internet** is available at the **Internet and Phone Center,** V. Rocca Brancaleone 4/6, right off P. Mameli. (☎ 0544 33 744, €1.50. Open daily 9am-11pm.) The **post office,** P. Garibaldi, 1, is off V. Diaz before P. del Popolo. (☎ 0544 24 33 04; fax 0544 38 485. Open M-F 8am-6:30pm, Sa 8am-12:30pm. Cash only.) **Currency exchange** is also available. **Postal Code:** 48100.

▌ ACCOMMODATIONS AND CAMPING

A former orphanage has aged gracefully into the **Residenza Galletti Abbiosi ❹,** V. Roma, 140, now offering A/C, TV, and baths in brightly lit rooms. (☎/fax 0544 31 313; info@galletti.ra.it. Breakfast included. Reception M-F 8am-6:30pm, Sa-Su 8am-6pm. Singles €47; doubles €89; triples €112-129; quads €135-164. AmEx/MC/V.) Take V. Farini and turn right across P. Mameli to reach **Albergo Al Giaciglio ❸,** V. Rocca Brancaleone, 42, just outside the *centro,* where the cheery staff runs simple rooms with TV, fan, and sink. (☎/fax 0544 394 03; mmambo@racine.ra.it.

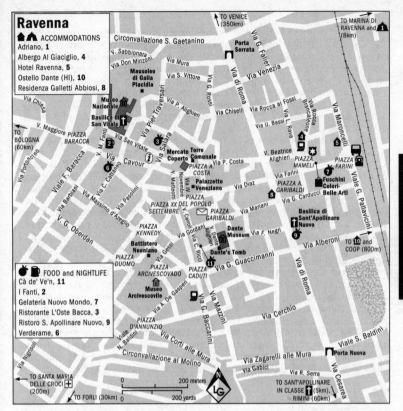

Ravenna

🏠🏠 **ACCOMMODATIONS**
Adriano, **1**
Albergo Al Giaciglio, **4**
Hotel Ravenna, **5**
Ostello Dante (HI), **10**
Residenza Galletti Abbiosi, **8**

🍎 **FOOD and NIGHTLIFE**
Cà de' Ve'n, **11**
I Fanti, **2**
Gelateria Nuovo Mondo, **7**
Ristorante L'Oste Bacca, **3**
Ristoro S. Apollinare Nuovo, **9**
Verderame, **6**

EMILIA-ROMAGNA

Breakfast €5. Restaurant downstairs open M-F. Singles €25-38, with bath €30-43; doubles €42-55/60-65. Extra bed €10. MC/V.) To reach **Ostello Dante (HI) ❶,** V. Nicolodi, 12, take bus #1, 70, or the Linea Rosso from V. Pallavicini, across from the station (every 10-20min. 5:40am-8:10pm, every 30-40min. 8:30-11:30pm). An industrial-style building houses foosball tables, couches, and board games. (☎0544 42 11 64; hostelravenna@hotmail.com. Breakfast included. Safes available. Laundry €2.50 per wash and dry. Wheelchair accessible. Reception 7-10am and 5-11:30pm. Lockout 9:30am-5pm. Curfew 11:30pm. Dorms €13.50; family rooms €14 per person. Non-HI members add €3. MC/V.) At **Hotel Ravenna ❹,** V. Maroncelli, 12, 26 small rooms have tile floors, fans, satellite TV, and a convenient location near the train station (☎0544 21 22 04; fax 0544 21 20 77. Wheelchair accessible. Reception 7am-midnight; notify if leaving after hours. Singles €35-40, with shower €40-48; doubles €40-55/45-70; triples €90-94; quads €110-119. AmEx/MC/V.) Bus #1 departs across from the train station (every 30min. 6:30am-8pm, every hr. 8:30-11:30pm) and stops at camping **Adriano ❶,** V. di Campeggio, 7, in Marina di Ravenna, 8km from the *centro*. Near a public beach, these four-star facilities have a pool, *bocce* courts, and a soccer field. (☎0544 43 72 30; info@campingparkadriano.com. Bungalows require reservation. Reception daily 8:30am-1pm and 3-9pm. Open mid-Apr. to mid-Sept. €4-9.50 per person, €7.50-16.50 per tent. MC/V.)

EMILIA-ROMAGNA

📂 FOOD

The distinctive flavors of Ravennese salt, extra virgin olive oil, and chestnuts characterize Ravenna's cuisine. Accompany a filling meal with a full-bodied *Albana* or *Trebbiano* wine. For dessert, try *zuppa inglese*, a combination of biscuits and custard with a splash of cordial. A spin on the dessert is the creamy *zuppa inglese gelato* at **Gelateria Nuovo Mondo ❶**, V. Farini, 60, where a double cone goes for €2 and low-fat options are also available. (☎0544 355 38. Open daily 10am-midnight. Cash only.) Hostel guests benefit from the convenient **Coop**, across the street at V. Aquileia, 110. (Open M 3-8pm, Tu-Sa 8am-8pm.) Fruit, meat, and cheese stands fill the **covered market** at P. A. Costa, 2, up V. IV Novembre from P. del Popolo. (Open M-Th and Sa 7am-2pm, F 7am-2pm and 4:30-7:30pm. Most stands cash only.) From P. Garibaldi, turn right on V. Gordini, then left on V. Ricci for 🍴**Cà de' Ve'n ❷**, V. Ricci, 24. With vaulted Byzantine ceilings and a distinctive wine-bottle decor, this dark *enoteca* offers an ever-changing selection of fresh meats and pastas. (☎0544 301 63. *Primi* and *secondi* from €6. Open in summer Tu-Su 11am-2:15pm and 6-10:30pm; in winter Tu-Su 11am-2:15pm and 5-10:30pm. AmEx/MC/V.) Grab lunch at the self-service **Ristoro S. Apollinare Nuovo ❷**, V. di Roma, 53, where locals crowd for a simple, cheap, and delicious meal. (☎0544 35 679. Entrees from €3.50. Open daily noon-2:30pm. AmEx/MC/V.) An attentive staff serves hearty regional specialties at **Ristorante L'Oste Bacca ❸**, V. Salara, 20. Try the *tortellaci di ortica* (pasta stuffed with cheese and served with fish and tomatoes), *piadine* (hot, triangular pieces of flatbread) dipped in melted *squaquerone* (a mild local cheese), or the *mortadella*, a round sausage covered with cheese and served on a bed of lettuce. (☎0544 353 63. *Primi* €5.50-7, *secondi* €7-14. Cover €1.60. Open M and W-Su 12:15-2:30pm and 7:15-10:30pm. AmEx/MC/V.) For a blast of local color, try **Verderame ❶**, V. Cavour, 82, where the gold and maroon interior is almost as unique as the famous hot chocolate. (☎/fax 0544 322 48. Open in summer daily 8am-midnight; in winter M-Th and Su 8:30am-8pm, F-Sa 8:30am-midnight. Cash only.)

🔆 SIGHTS

🔳**BASILICA DI SAN VITALE.** Light from thin windows illuminates the octagonal **Basilica di San Vitale**, lending a glow to the interior mosaics. Above the apse, Christ Pantocrator sits on a globe with the *Book of Seven Seals*. On either side, Byzantine mosaics depict Empress Theodora offering a golden chalice, and Emperor Justinian's presentation of a gilded plate. *(V. S. Vitale, 17. From tourist office, turn right on V. Cavour, then again on V. Argentario. ☎0544 21 62 92. Open daily Apr.-Sept. 9am-7pm; Mar. and Oct. 9am-5:30pm; Nov.-Feb. 9am-4:30pm.)* Across the courtyard and behind the church, mosaics cover the interior of the tiny brick **Mausoleo di Galla Placidia**, where a single lamp reveals three stone sarcophagi said to contain the remains of Costanzo III, Empress Galla Placida, and Valentiniano III. Above the door, a pastoral mosaic depicts Christ caring for his flock. *(Behind S. Vitale. Same hours as basilica.)*

BASILICA DI SANT'APOLLINARE IN CLASSE. This spacious, 6th-century brick church is lined with little more than unlabeled marble sepulchers—the real draw is the massive mosaic above the apse, where St. Apollinare and flocks of sheep fill the enormous half-dome. *(In Classe, south of the city. Take bus #4 or 44; both stop across from the train station. ☎0544 344 24. Open M-Sa 8:30am-7:30pm, Su 9am-7pm. Tickets close 30min. before basilica. €2, €1 for EU students 18-25, under 18 or over 65 free. Combo with Museo Nazionale €6.50/3; Su 9am-1pm free. Cash only.)*

RAVENOUS FOR ART. The Ravenna Card provides admission to five museums and monuments: the Museo Arcivescovile, Battistero Neoniano, Basilica di Sant'Apollinare Nuovo, Basilica di San Vitale, and the Mausoleo di Galla Placidia. Individual tickets to the sites are not available. From June 16 through February, the card costs €7.50, students €6.50; March 1 to June 15 €9.50, students €8.50. Purchase it at any participating site. For information on the card or any of the churches, contact the Ufficio Informazioni e Prenotazioni dell'Opera di Religione della Diocesi di Ravenna, V. Canneti, 3 (☎0544 54 16 88; fax 0544 54 16 80), open M-F 9am-12:30pm and 3:30-6pm.

DANTE'S TOMB AND THE DANTE MUSEUM.

Ravenna's most popular monument is the unassuming green-domed tomb of Dante Alighieri, who was exiled from Florence in 1301 and died in Ravenna in 1321. A suspended lamp has burned with Florentine oil since 1908 and illuminates a relief of Dante leafing through his books. The nearby Dante Museum contains Wostry Carlo's illustrations of Dante's works, the fir chest that held the poet's bones, 18,000 scholarly volumes on his works, and the trowel and hammer that laid the cornerstone of Rio de Janeiro's Dante Monument. *(V. D. Alighieri. From P. del Popolo, cut through P. Garibaldi to V. D. Alighieri. Museum ☎0544 336 67. Tomb open daily 9am-7pm. Free. Museum open Apr.-Sept. Tu-Su 9am-noon and 3:30-6pm; Oct.-Mar. 9am-noon. €2, under 18 free. Cash only.)*

MUSEO NAZIONALE. This former Benedictine monastery features Roman, early Christian, Byzantine, and medieval works like the 6th-century bronze cross from the roof of the S. Vitale cupola and the original apse vault of St. Apollinare in Classe. *(On V. Fiandrini. Ticket booth to the right of entrance to Basilica di San Vitale. Museum is through courtyard. Info and tickets ☎0544 34 424. Open Tu-Su 8:30am-7:30pm. Tickets close 30min. before museum. €4, EU students €2, under 18 or over 65 free. Cash only.)*

BASILICA DI SANT'APOLLINARE NUOVO. The 6th-century basilica, which passed into Christian hands a mere 40 years after its construction, features arched windows, white tile floors, and mortar made from crushed seashells. Long mosaics of saints line the central aisle, and frescoes in the central apse recount miracles performed by Jesus.

THE BIG SPLURGE

STONE BY STONE

Numerous art enthusiasts have scoffed at shapeless squiggles on modern canvases, exclaiming, "I could've drawn that myself!" But how many could say the same for a Roman mosaic?

In fact, a unique studio in the colorful city of Ravenna will teach you the necessary skills to rival ancient masters. This school is run by Luciana Notturni, a famous artist, specializing in reproductions of Roman and Byzantine mosaics, as well as "translating" modern art into mosaic form.

Scorning more contemporary, industrial techniques, Luciana and her team of mosaicists honor the ancients by cutting each individual *tesserae* (stone) by hand between a *martellina* (hammer) and a *tagliolo* (chisel). Her students learn this method as well, in intimate, four- to five-person clases. By the end of the five-day workshop, students use over 3000 colors to complete three different mosaics. Throughout the class they remain entirely immersed in local culture; lessons often take place at Luciana's home, where aspiring mosaicists also have the opportunity to mingle with their teacher's family.

Each five-day course costs €660 and includes materials (lime, board, tiles) but not tools (hammer, chisel), food, or lodging which cost another €100. Contact Luciana Notturni at Via F. Negri, 14, 48100 Ravenna, at ☎335 56 18 485, or visit www.mosaicschool.com.

Outside, a tall circular brick *campanile* spirals up six stories over the church's sloping red tile roof. *(On V. di Roma. ☎0544 21 95 18. Open daily Apr.-Sept. 9am-7pm; Mar. and Oct. 9:30am-5:30pm; Nov.-Feb. 9:30am-4:30pm.)*

BATTISTERO NEONIANO. Next door to the *duomo*, the central dome of this pint-sized baptistry features a mosaic of Jesus and John the Baptist in the Jordan River, with a representation of the river as a nude old man. You really have to see it to get it. The mosaic is one of the many that Bishop Neon ordered in AD 452, giving the baptistry its name. The baptismal font is at the center of the room, 3m above the now-covered Roman bath that Bishop Ursus built upon in the early 5th century. *(From P. del Popolo, follow V. Cairoli, turn right on V. Gessi, then head toward P. Arcivescovado. Open daily Apr.-Sept. 9am-7pm; Mar. and Oct. 9:30am-5:30pm; Nov.-Feb. 9:30am-4:30pm. Duomo open daily 7:30am-noon and 3:30-6:30pm.)*

MUSEO ARCIVESCOVILE. This one-room museum displays tattered priestly garments, a flower-shaped marble Easter calendar from AD 532-626, and detailed mosaics of the Virgin Mary and four saints from the now-destroyed Ursian Basilica. The real showpiece is the *See of Maximilian*, an ivory throne trimmed with ornate vines, tiny fowl, and relief panels of the life of Christ, which sits illuminated in the center. *(To the right of the Battistero Neoniano. ☎0544 21 52 01. Open daily Apr.-Sept. 9am-7pm; Mar. and Oct. 9:30am-5:30pm; Nov.-Feb. 9:30am-4:30pm.)*

♫ ▓ ENTERTAINMENT AND FESTIVALS

A host of fairly similar bars and cafes stay open late around P. del Popolo. One notable night spot is **I Fanti**, at V. M. Fanti, 9/A, off V. Cavour. A hip bar in a brick cave hosts partyers, poetry readings, and showings of original art and film throughout the summer. (☎0544 35 135. Open M-Sa 8am-11pm. AmEx/MC/V.) If the mosaics of the basilica left you breathless, channel your slack-jawed awe at **Fuschini Colori-Belle Arti,** P. Mameli, 16, off Vle. Farini, which sells *tesserae* so people can make their own personalized mosaics. (☎0544 37 387. Open M-W, F, and Su 9am-12:30pm and 4:30-7:30pm, Th and Sa 9am-12:30pm. AmEx/MC/V.) Watch for the **Organ Music Festival,** held annually in late July in the basilica. Since 1990, some of the world's most famous performers have come together each June and July for the **Ravenna Festival.** (Info office at V. D. Alighieri, 1. ☎0544 24 92 44; www.ravennafestival.org. Ticket office at V. Mariani, 2. Open M-W and F-Sa 10am-1pm, Th 4-6pm. During festival, open M-Sa 10am-1pm and 4-6pm, Su 10am-1pm. Reserve ahead for popular events. Tickets from €10-15.) In the 2nd week of September, Dante's legacy comes to life with the exhibits and theatricals of the **Dante Festival** (☎0544 30 252).

RIMINI   ☎0541

Given the lack of surprise on doormen's faces when they let in mojito-stained lodgers at 3am, Rimini is clearly a city that's used to playing fast and loose. Inland, the historic center preserves its Roman heritage with an alluring jumble of streets overshadowed by the Malatesta Temple and the Augustan Arch. Buses crammed with sleeveless teens singing drinking songs and colorful explosions of impromptu fireworks are normal sights after midnight. Pastel hotels, beaches, and wide boardwalks filled with small boutiques, fortune tellers, and caricature artists all contribute to a society where it's perfectly acceptable—and admirable—to collapse into bed and wish the rising sun good night.

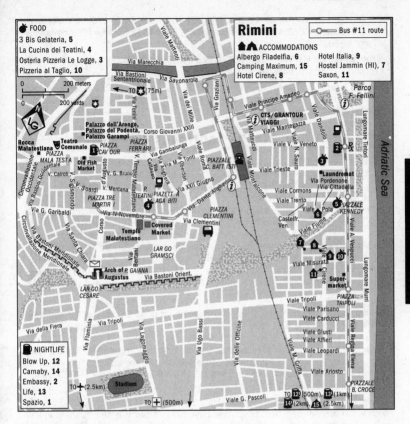

Rimini

◁═⊙═▷ Bus #11 route

🏠🏠▲ ACCOMMODATIONS

Albergo Filadelfia, **6**   Hotel Italia, **9**
Camping Maximum, **15**   Hostel Jammin (HI), **7**
Hotel Cirene, **8**   Saxon, **11**

🍴 FOOD
3 Bis Gelateria, **5**
La Cucina dei Teatini, **4**
Osteria Pizzeria Le Logge, **3**
Pizzeria al Taglio, **10**

🎵 NIGHTLIFE
Blow Up, **12**
Carnaby, **14**
Embassy, **2**
Life, **13**
Spazio, **1**

EMILIA-ROMAGNA

TRANSPORTATION

Flights: Miramare Civil Airport (☎0541 71 57 11), on V. Flaminia. Mostly charter flights. Serves many European cities. Bus #9, across from the train station, goes to the airport (every 20min. 5:37am-10:52pm and 1:02am, €1).

Trains: in P. C. Battisti and V. D. Alighieri (☎0541 89 20 21). Open daily 5am-12:30am. Info office open M, Th, and Sa 8:30am-7:30pm, Tu-W, F, and Su 7:30am-7:40pm. Ticket office open daily 5:15am-10:15pm. To: **Ancona** (1¼hr., 51 per day 12:14am-10:35pm, €4.65); **Bologna** (1½hr., 58 per day 2:28am-11:02pm, €6.45); **Milan** (3hr., 25 per day 2:28am-8:05pm, €15.44); **Ravenna** (1hr., 34 per day 5:20am-10:53pm, €2.80); **Riccione** (10min., 45 per day 4:13am-9:53pm, €1). Cash only.

Buses: TRAM intercity bus station (☎0541 30 05 33; www.tram.rimini.it), at V. Roma in P. Clementini, near the station. From the train station, follow V. D. Alighieri and take 1st left. Urban bus tickets available (valid for 90min.; €1, €1.50 if purchased onboard; 24hr. €3). 24hr. service to many inland towns (€1.03-€3.36). Local bus #11 travels to Riccione. Ticket booth open daily 6:10am-12:20am, to the right of the train station.

Taxis: RadioTaxi (☎0541 50 020). Available 24hr.

Car Rental: Avis, Vle. Trieste, 16/D (☎0541 51 256; fax 0541 56 176) off V. Vespucci. Bus #11: stop 12. 25+. Small cars from €66. Open M-Sa 8:30am-12:30pm and 3-7pm. AmEx/MC/V.

Bike Rental: On Vle. Fiume off Vle. Vespucci (☎0541 39 10 72). Bus #11: stop 12. Open daily Apr.-Oct. 9am-midnight. €3 per hr. Cash only.

Scooter Rental: P. Kennedy, 6 (☎0541 27 016). Rentals start at €13 per hr. Also rents *ciclocarrozzelle* (pedal-powered cars) for €7-12. Open daily Apr.-Oct. 9am-midnight. AmEx/MC/V.

◼ ◼ ORIENTATION AND PRACTICAL INFORMATION

To reach the beach from the **train station** in **Piazzale Cesare Battisti,** turn right from the station, take another right into the tunnel at the yellow arrow indicating *al mare,* and follow **Viale Principe Amedeo.** To the right, **Viale Vespucci,** the hub of Rimini activity, runs one block inland along the beach. Bus #11 runs to the beach from the train station and continues along Vle. Vespucci and V. R. Elena (every 15min. 5:30am-2am). Bus stops are numbered. Buy tickets at the kiosk in front of the station or at *tabaccherie.* To reach the historical center, take **Via Dante Alighieri** from the station and continue to **Piazza Tre Martiri.** The center of Rimini is **Marina Centro. Rimini Sud** (south) branches out from the main city along the coast and comprises the neighborhoods of Bellariva, Marebello, Rivazzurra, and Miramare. **Rimini Nord** (north) goes toward the less-visited Rivabella, Viserba, and Viserbella.

Tourist Offices: IAT, P. Fellini, 3 (☎0541 56 902; fax 0541 56 598), at the beginning of V. Vespucci. Bus #11: stop 10. Open daily in summer 8:30am-7pm; in winter 9:30am-12:30pm and 3:30-6:30pm. **Branch,** P. C. Battisti, 1 (☎0541 51 331; www.riminiturismo.it), left after the train station. Open in summer M-Sa 8:30am-7pm, Su 9:30am-12:30pm; in winter M-Sa 10am-4pm. Hotel reservations office attached. (☎0541 24 760. Open June-Aug. M-Sa 8:15am-8pm; Sept.-June M-Sa 9:30am-12:30pm and 3:30-6:30pm.)

Budget Travel: CTS/Grantour Viaggi, V. Matteucci, 4 (☎0541 51 001 or 0541 55 525), off V. Principe Amedeo. Sells tickets and ISICs (€11). Open M-W and F 9am-noon and 3:30-6:30pm, Th 9am-4pm, Sa 9:30am-noon. Cash only.

Luggage Storage: In train station. €2.10-3.70 for 24hr. Coin-operated.

Laundromat: Lavanderia Trieste Express, Vle. Trieste, 16 (☎0541 26 764). Wash €5, dry €5. No self-service. Open M-F 8:30am-12:30pm and 3-7:30pm, Sa 2-6pm.

Emergency: ☎113. **Ambulance:** ☎118. **Police:** C. d'Augusto, 192 (☎0541 51 000). Dial ☎112 for emergencies.

Pharmacy: Farmacia del Kursaal, V. Vespucci 12/E (☎0541 21 711). Open daily 8:30am-1pm and 4-10pm. Cash only.

Hospital: Ospedale Infermi, V. Settembrini, 2 (☎0541 70 51 11). In case of **emergency,** call ☎0541 70 57 57 or 0541 78 74 61 (specifically for tourist emergencies).

Internet Access: Central Park, Vle. Vespucci, 21 (☎0541 37 44 50). 9 coin-operated computers. €1 for 10min., €2 for 30min., €5 for 80min. Open daily in summer 9am-2am; in winter 10am-2am. Cash only.

Post Office: C. d'Augusto, 8 (☎0541 78 16 73), off P. Tre Martiri, near the Arch of Augustus. Open M-F 8am-6:30pm, Sa 8am-12:30pm. **Currency exchange** available. **Postal Code:** 47900.

▐ ACCOMMODATIONS AND CAMPING

The smaller streets off Vle. Vespucci and Vle. R. Elena between stops 12 and 20 of bus #11 are filled with more hotels than homes. Prices peak in August and reservations are necessary far in advance. If plans fall through, the tourist office provides a complete list of hotels and campgrounds.

Hostel Jammin (HI), Vle. Derna, 22 (☎0541 39 08 00; www.hosteljammin.it). Bus #11: stop 13. Brand new hostel just seconds from the beach boasts enthusiastic owners and amenities that include mosaic bathrooms, free bike rental, Internet (1st 10min. free, €2 per hr.), and lockers (€1 per 24hr.). The owners try to accommodate Rimini's partying lifestyle and though the front door isn't open all night, disco-goers can buzz in at 1:30am and 3:30am. Sheets and breakfast included. Lockout 1:30-5:30pm. Closed Jan. Dorms €16, €18 with bath. Non-HI members add €3. AmEx/MC/V. ❷

Hotel Italia, Vle. Misurata, 13 (☎0541 39 09 94; www.hotelitaliarimini.it). Bus #11: stop 13. Newly refurbished rooms are clean, bright, and maintained by a friendly staff. Buffet breakfast included. Reception 24hr. Half or full pension required during the middle 2 weeks of August (€53/51). Rooms €20-30 per person. Surcharge for single room €8. AmEx/MC/V. ❸

Hotel Cirene, Vle. Cirene, 50 (☎0541 39 09 04; www.hotelcirene.com). Bus #11: stop 13. Lodgers enjoy rich-colored linens, porcelain bathrooms, and stellar service. All rooms have bath, phone, and TV, and some have a balcony. Breakfast included. Half and full pension available. Open May-Sept. Singles €30-35; doubles €46-50; triples €55-60; quads €65-70. AmEx/MC/V. ❸

Albergo Filadelfia, V. Pola, 25 (☎0541 23 679; fax 0541 27 338). Bus #11: stop 12. From V. Trento, turn left on V. Sauro. An affable couple runs this 3-story hotel with rooms of various sizes and shapes. Breakfast buffet €4. Open Apr. 15-late Sept. Prices vary seasonally and according to occupancy. Singles €20-26; doubles €36-48; triples €51-69. AmEx/MC/V. ❸

Saxon, Vle. Cirene, 36 (☎/fax 0541 39 14 00). Bus #11: stop 13. Exit bus to the left, turn right on V. Misurata, then left on V. Cirene. This 30-room hotel in close proximity to the beach has small rooms and even smaller bathrooms with sea-green decor. All rooms have TV, phone, and minibar. Breakfast included. Doubles €60. AmEx/MC/V. ❹

Camping Maximum, Vle. Principe di Piemonte, 57 (☎0541 37 26 02; fax 0541 37 02 71). Bus #11: stop 33. Right across from the beach on the way from Rimini to Riccione, this lively campground is sandwiched between other seaside hotels. Reception daily 7am-9pm. Open June-Sept. €6-8.50 per person, €4-5 per child, €8.50-12 per tent. Bungalows from €60. MC/V. ❶

▐ FOOD

Rimini's **covered market** between V. Castelfidardo and the Tempio provides an array of foods. (Open M, W, and Th-Sa 7:15am-1pm and 5-7:30pm, Tu 7:15am-1pm.) The **STANDA** supermarket, Vle. Vespucci, 133, is between P. Kennedy and P. Tripoli. (Open daily 8am-9pm. AmEx/MC/V.)

Osteria Pizzeria Le Logge, Viale Trieste, 5 (☎0541 55 978). Off the main drag, clusters of grapes and palm awnings surround crowds of happy eaters. Look out for the specialty *Nino*, a huge pizza with mozzarella, gorgonzola, spicy salami, and crisp red onions (€6.80). Pizza €3.60-9.50. Cover €1. Open daily 7pm-midnight. AmEx/MC/V. ❷

La Cucina dei Teatini, P. Teatini, 3 (info ☎0541 28 008, reservations 0541 33 92 38 76 95), just off V. IV Novembre, close to the temple. A young staff serves artistically crafted dishes in an interior filled with modern art or on the shaded deck in the neighboring park, which looks out onto a romantic brick grotto. *Primi* €9-10, *secondi* €10-16. Open M-F 12:30-2:30pm and 7:30-10:30pm, Sa 7:30-10:30pm. AmEx/MC/V. ❹

Pizzeria al Taglio, Vle. Misurata, 5 (☎0541 39 28 78), off Vle. Vespucci, close to P. Kennedy. Thick slices like the *caprese* (cheese, basil, and tomato; €4.80) delight the local teens crowding the interior. Takeout available. Pizza €3-6. Open daily noon-3pm and 5:30pm-2am. Cash only. ❶

3 Bis Gelateria, Vle. Vespucci, 73 (☎328 26 18 979). This hip *gelateria*-creperie, with flat-screen TVs and bustling crowds, has rich gourmet *gelato* heaped high with cookies and fresh berries. Try the *pan di stelle,* a divinely sweet concoction of cookies-and-cream (€1.50 for a scoop) or hot crepes (€2.50-3.50) stuffed with fresh fruit, Nutella, cream, or *gelato.* Open daily Mar.-Sept. noon-1am. Cash only. ❶

👁 🏖 SIGHTS AND BEACHES

Rimini's cultural life once relied largely on Sigismondo Malatesta, a 15th-century lord who refurbished the **Tempio Malatestiano** with funereal chapels for himself and his 4th wife. To the right of the apse, Piero della Francesca's *Sigismondo Pandolfo Malatesta in preghiera davanti a San Sigismondo* shows Malatesta kneeling in front of his castle in Rimini; in the first chapel, a statue of the ruler sits atop two elephants, the family emblem. The apse holds a painted crucifix by Giotto, the only work by the artist in Rimini today. On the exterior, the small brick protrusion was added by Leon Battista Alberti to resemble the Arch of Augustus (see below) as per Malatesta's orders. (On V. IV Novembre. Follow V. D. Alighieri from the train station. ☎054 15 11 30. Open daily 8:30am-1pm and 3:30-7pm. Free.)

Piazza Cavour, Rimini's center, contains an assortment of architecture from the centuries. Shops and bars surround the 18th-century **pescheria** (fish market) under the brick arches in the *piazza.* The four stone fish in the corners of the interior arcade once spouted water for cleaning fish on the market tables. The stone pillars of the Renaissance **Palazzo Garampi**—the first building on the right facing away from the *pescheria*—bear almost no resemblance to the connected brick **Palazzo dell'Arengo** and the smaller **Palazzo del Podestà.** Perpendicular to the municipal building lies the modern **Teatro Comunale,** which lost its auditorium in WWII. In the center of the *piazza,* **Fontana della Pigna** is a four-tiered marble fountain from 1543, adorned with an inscription by Leonardo Da Vinci. In the center of the square a very militant Pope Paul V sits on a throne, his fierce gaze little protection against the cape of pigeons he usually wears. (Check with tourist office about exhibits at the Palazzo del Podestà.) Farther south on the Corso D'Augusto lies **Piazza Tre Martiri,** complete with a large oval foundation and colorful buildings.

Grassy debris is piled at the base of the impressive **Arch of Augustus,** whose construction in 27 BC establishes it as Italy's oldest surviving Roman archway. The arch was designed as a peace offering after decades of Roman civil war. The top of the structure, probably destroyed by an earthquake, is refinished with brick ramparts from the Middle Ages while the arch itself still features original marble pillars in relief, depictions of the gods, and an inscription honoring Augustus. (Follow V. IV Novembre to P. Tre Martiri and turn left on C. d'Augusto.)

Most of the shoreline is privately owned by hotels, which offer guests a strip of beach for a minimum charge of about €3.50 for a lounge chair, use of whirlpools, volleyball courts, lockers, Internet, and other facilities. The fun continues at night with bars and live music. Vendors along the beach offer water sports equipment. A public beach, located at the top of the shore, is slightly less picturesque and offers no storage or lounge amenities; however, the beach is free and the waves are huge.

🔋 🌺 NIGHTLIFE AND FESTIVALS

Rimini is notorious for its non-stop partying, with clubs near the *lungomare* in Rimini Sud. During the high season, 🚌**bus #11** is an institution in and of itself—by 11pm, expect a crowd of strangers singing drinking songs, comparing outfits, and cheering on the rare occasion a group waiting at the stop can successfully fit inside. The route runs from Rimini to the bus station in Riccione, where bus #46 allows easy access to seven more nightclubs grouped together in a valley. Clubs change their hours and prices frequently, and many close in winter.

Many clubs offer free bus services (check at the travel agency in P. Tripoli for schedules; open M-Sa 8:30am-7pm, Su 9am-noon), but there is also a **Blue Line bus** (mid-July to Aug., every 10-20min., €3) for disco-goers. It departs from the station and travels the bus #11 route to the nearby beach towns. Buy tickets onboard. The last bus leaves around 5:30am, after which bus #11 resumes service.

A bustling nightlife scene lights up the historical center by the old fish market. From P. Cavour, follow **Via Pescheria,** where pubs and bars stay open until 3am. 🟦**Embassy,** Vle. Vespucci, 22, a 5min. walk from P. Kennedy, is the only nightclub within walking distance of Rimini *centro*. Past a brightly lit waterfall lies this garden paradise, where drinks flow freely from five bars. A glamorous young crowd socializes on the spacious garden-style patio or heads inside for some steamy dancing. (☎0541 23 934. Drinks €6. Cover €13-25; discount cards often handed out at the door. Open daily midnight-4am.) At **Blow Up,** Vle. Regina Elena, 209, an older crowd grooves to hip hop and techno in this basement complete with retro marble and neon staircase. Take bus #11 to stop 21. (☎0541 38 60 60; www.blow-updisco.it. Drinks €3-7. Cover €10-15. Open daily 10pm-4am. Cash only.) In Bellariva, **Life,** V. R. Margherita, 11, hosts nightly theme parties for two floors of party-goers, from teenagers to a more mixed crowd later in the night. The top level has a laidback bar, while the bottom kicks it up a notch with a fog machine and an elevated stage. Take bus #11 to stop 22; the club also offers a free bus service. (☎0541 37 34 73. Free drink at 2:30am. Cover €9 with discount pass, available near the door. Open daily 10pm-4am. Cash only.) Right on P. Cavour, **Spazio** attracts an older clientele to their strikingly trendy bar and central patio. (☎054 12 34 39. Wine from €3 a glass. Open M-Sa 5pm-7am. AmEx/MC/V.) Past the yellow VW bug wedged above the door at **Carnaby,** V. Brindisi, 20, in Rivazzurra, a teenage crowd packs a 3rd-floor bar, a 2nd-floor disco, and "the Cave," an underground dance floor that reeks of neon and puberty. Take bus #11 to stop 26, turn right, then turn left down V. Brindisi or use the free bus service. (☎0541 37 32 04; www.carnaby.it. Cover €12-25, with discount pass €10. Open daily 10pm-4am. Cash only.)

In September of even-numbered years, Rimini hosts a wild **beach festival.** Classical concerts and parties erupt beneath fireworks displays, lighting up a constant stream of festivities.

🔋 DAYTRIP FROM RIMINI

SAN LEO

San Leo is accessible by buses operated by Ferrovie Emilia-Romagna. Buses depart across from the Rimini train station at 8:40am, 12:10, 1:10, 5:30pm; all but the 12:10pm departure require a brief connection via van at Pietrascuta. Vans leave San Leo at 8am, 1, 6pm. Direct trips €2.53. Connecting trips €1.96 for the 1st leg, €1 for the 2nd. Buy Ferrovie Emilia-Romagna tickets at the kiosk outside the Rimini train station. Buy tickets for the connection on the van. Ask the Rimini tourist office about schedule changes.

Perched atop the Apennines and surrounded by craggy cliffs, San Leo has a fascinating history. Once a Kingdom of Italy under King Berengard II and later the

Papacy's maximum-security prison, San Leo is most famous as the place of detention of Count Cogliostro, a prisoner held here for causing innumerable scandals in the European court. No longer a prison, today the tiny hamlet offers a quiet, untouristed alternative to the swarming streets of nearby San Marino. It takes only 2hr. to explore the entire area, but plan to linger and indulge in San Leo's timeless charm. Across from the tourist office sits **La Pieve**, a tiny church made of sandstone blocks that contains one row of pews and a simple brick apse; in the basement, the 18th-century statue *Madonna del Rosario col Bambino* houses a relic of patron St. Leo. On either side sit 17th-century painted wood depictions of St. Leo and St. Marino. (Open daily 9am-12:45pm and 3-7:00pm. Free.) Just before P. D. Alighieri, signs point up a rocky path that zig-zags steeply to the **fortress.** Inside, glass cases contain fortress relics, but the view of the sweeping hills from the cliffside and the history of the famous prisoners held there is more inspiring. (☎0541 91 63 02. Open daily in summer 9am-7pm; in winter 9:30 am-12:30pm and 2:30-6:00pm. €8, students and over 65 €5, ages 6-14 €3. Cash only.)

Though an ideal daytrip from Rimini, San Leo has a few good lodging options. **Albergo Rocca's ❹** seven simple rooms with bath are charming, but the real draw is the outdoor terrace that looks out on the rooftops of San Leo. (☎0541 91 62 41. Breakfast €5. Reception 8am-10:30pm. Singles €40-47; doubles €50-65; triples €70-91; quads €90-117. AmEx/MC/V.) **Albergo Castello ❹**, in the main *piazza*, has great views of the valley and the *piazza*, and 16 rooms with TV, phone, and bath. (☎0541 91 62 14; albergo-castello@libero.it. Singles €35; doubles €55. AmEx/MC/V.) **Il Bettolino ❸**, V. Montefeltro, 4, serves piles of pasta in the quiet interior or at canopied tables along the street. (☎0541 91 62 65; federico.calcagnini@libero.it. Pizza €2.10-6.70. *Primi* €5.20-7.20, *secondi* €5.70-10.30. Cover €1. Open M-Tu and Th-Su noon-3pm and 7-10pm. AmEx/MC/V.) After exiting the tourist office, turn left for **La Corte ❷**, V. Michele Rosa, 74, which offers traditional dishes (like the meaty *salsiccia di San Leo*, €6.80) on a wooden deck or booths inside. The attached **gelateria** has *gelato* from €1.50 a scoop. For lighter eaters, the *conini* (tiny cones of gelato dipped in chocolate) are just €0.50. (☎0541 91 61 45; osteria-lacorte@libero.it. *Primi* €6.50-7.50, *secondi* €6.50-9.50. Cover €1.50. Open M-F 12:15-2pm and 7:15-9pm, Sa 12:15-2:30pm and 7:15-10pm, Su 12:15-2:30pm and 7:15-9pm. Closed Tu in winter. MC/V.) The **tourist office** at the far end of P. D. Alighieri provides **maps** and brochures. (☎0541 91 63 06 or 800 55 38 00; fax 0541 92 69 73. Open daily Sept.-June 9am-7pm; July-Aug 9:30am-10:30pm.)

RICCIONE ☎0541

In Riccione, a tangible rift exists between the shady lanes where residents make their homes and the steamy streets by the beach, where bewildered vacationers wander through wide boardwalks lined with brightly lit video arcades, risqué sex shops, and a constant stream of busy disco-bars and hotels. The city itself is humming with electricity and neon until early in the morning, but the die-hard divas will swoon over a hillside of world-renowned *discoteche* just a bus ride away.

🖪🖬 TRANSPORTATION AND PRACTICAL INFORMATION. The **train station** (☎0541 89 20 21), between Ple. della Stazione and Ple. Vittorio Veneto, is open 5:40am-8:30pm; binario #1 is open all night (tickets 5:45am-8:17pm). There's no luggage storage, so leave bags behind if clubbing overnight. Trains run to: Bologna (1¾hr., 25 per day 5:55am-10:35pm, €6.45); Pesaro (20min., 52 per day 12:42am-10:05pm, €1.90); and Rimini (10 min., 39 per day 5:08am-11:30pm, €1). **Local bus #11** (€1, €1.50 if purchased onboard) runs along the waterfront from the south of Riccione and travels north to Rimini. The bus stops are numbered.

To get to the beach, exit the train station toward Ple. V. Veneto and walk down **Viale Martinelli** and turn left on **Via Gramsci;** then head right on V. Ceccarini for two blocks to **Piazzale Roma.** The public beach is on the other side of the *piazzale.* The *lungomare* runs along the sea. An **IAT Tourist Office,** Ple. Ceccarini, 10, offers accommodations booking and a free **map.** (☎0541 69 33 02; iat@comune.riccione.rn.it. Open daily June-Aug. 8am-10pm; Sept. 8am-8pm; Oct.-May 8am-7pm.) In case of **emergency,** call ☎113, an **ambulance** at ☎118, or the **police,** V. Cortemaggio, 6/A (☎0541 64 94 44). **Ospedale G. Ceccarini** is at V. Cervi, 48 (☎0541 60 85 11). **Internet** is available at **Phone Center and Internet Point,** V. Amendola 17/C. (☎0541 69 76 66; phoneserv@interfree.it. €1 for 15min., €4 per hr. Open daily 9am-midnight. Cash only.) **Currency exchange** is available at the **post office,** V. Corrodoni, 13. (☎0541 47 39 01. Open M-F 8am-6:30pm, Sa 8am-12:30pm.) **Postal Code:** 47838.

⌂⌂ ACCOMMODATIONS AND FOOD. Hotel reservations are essential for the high season. The rest of the year, bargains abound. The **Hotel Garden ❹** offers free bikes to guests on the go, but rooms with TV, bath, and balcony comfort those who stay. (☎0541 60 15 00; www.hotelgardenonline.com. Reception 24hr. Half and full pension available. €28-45 per person. AmEx/MC/V.) **Hotel La Nidiola ❸,** V. Bixio, 30, is by the beach. Exit the train station and turn right on V. Trento e Trieste. Walk straight 10min.; the hotel is on the left, and offers bright rooms with TV, bath, and balconies. (☎0541 60 15 58; www.lanidiola.com. Reception 24hr. Half pension singles €34-57, full pension singles €37-60; doubles €60-102/66-108. AmEx/MC/V.) The tall **Hotel Nizza ❹,** Lungomare D'Annunzio, 165, features a TV room, rooftop terrace, and large rooms with TV, bath, and balcony. Some are newly refurbished. Walk to the waterfront and take bus #11 to stop 40. (☎0541 64 14 93; www.hotelnizza.it. Reception 24hr. Open May-Sept. €37-58 per person. Prices vary seasonally. AmEx/MC/ V.) Take bus #11 one stop past Hotel Nizza and walk two blocks to reach **Hotel Maris Stella ❸,** Vle. Oriani, 7. Rooms include TV, phone, and fans; half have balcony. (☎0541 64 23 75; www.marisstella.it. Full pension €33-55. Singles supplement €5. Prices vary seasonally. MC/V.)

In a town with so many tourists, conformity reigns in countless cookie-cutter cafes and pizzerias. On the main thoroughfare, **Supermarket Angelini,** Vle. Dante 18, stocks a plentiful selection. (Open M-Sa 7:45am-1:15pm and 4-10:30pm, Su 7:45am-1:15pm. AmEx/MC/V.) A unique place (and a reprieve from the stiflingly humid summer air) is **Campi di Fragole ❶,** V. Dante, 180, a *gelateria* named for the Beatles's "Strawberry Fields Forever." After sampling the freshly made *gelato,* add your tag to the graffiti-covered mirrors with neon gel pens from the counter. (1 scoop €1.50, 2 scoops €2. Open daily Apr.-Sept. 10am-2am. Cash only.) On one of the main pedestrian malls, the self-service **Hot Café ❶,** Vle. Dante, 170/A, offers a well-priced pasta *menù.* (Just off Vle. Dante. ☎0541 64 63 28. Pasta dishes about €4-7. Open daily 6am-3am. AmEx/MC/V.) Grab your meal in **Makkaroni ❸,** a hip bar with wicker chairs and views of a fountain outside. (☎0541 60 38 48. *Primi* €8-10, *secondi* €10-12. Open daily 3pm-7am. AmEx/MC/V.) One of the biggest of the standard pizzerias near the *centro* is **Frankly ❷,** V. Ceccarini, 113, where pizzas like the Frankly (with cheese, cherry tomatoes, prosciutto, and arugula; €8.50) are served in an open-walled interior. (☎/fax 0541 69 33 27. Pizza €4.10-8.50. Pasta and seafood €6.15-19. Open daily noon-3pm and 6pm-2am. AmEx/MC/V.)

▨ NIGHTLIFE. The real action is in the clubs, conveniently nestled together in a valley accessible by bus. From the bus station near the waterfront, take bus #46 to the Discoteche stop—from there, signs point to **Peter Pan** (Viale Abruzzi, 147; ☎0541 64 13 35), **Byblo's** (see below), **Prince** (☎0541 69 48 39), and **Villa delle Rose** (V. Camilluccia, 33; www.villadellerose.net), and down another street to **Cocorico** (see below), **Peschio** (V. Sardegna, 1; ☎0541 60 42 07), and **Acquafan** (V. Pistoia, 13; ☎0541 60 30 50). **Cocorico,** V. Chietti, 44, looks like a suburban house with a white picket fence, but the parties here are far from the Tupperware variety. (☎0541 60

51 83. Cover €28, including 1 drink. Open F-Sa. Call for hours.) In Miramare, **L'Altro Mondo Studio's**, V. Flaminia, 388, is off the beaten path but worth the effort. Lights illuminate a huge floor lined with portals, sliding doors, and steel platforms. A stylish, international crowd of all ages grooves to house and techno, pausing only for the laser show around midnight. (☎0541 37 31 51; www.altromondo.com. Cover about €15, discount for groups. Open daily 11pm-4am, though closing time depends on the crowd. Cash only.) Sophisticated **Byblo's Disco Dinner Club**, V. P. Castello, 24, in Misano, lures chic 20-somethings to its outdoor floor with a siren's song of house and Latin. (☎0541 69 02 52; www.byblosclub.com. Cover about €18. Open W and F-Sa 9:30pm-6am.) For no worries for the rest of your days, try **Hakuna Matata**, Vle. d'Annunzio 138, where the party happens all year long amid bamboo splendor. (☎0541 64 12 03. Drinks €4-7. Open M-Su 8am-5am. AmEx/MC/V.)

 BARS ON A BUDGET. Bars in Riccione have a tendency to be pretty expensive. Plan ahead by hanging on to the **discount passes** that promoters distribute along V. Vespucci and V. R. Elena.

SAN MARINO ☎0549

San Marino is one of three independent states in Italian borders. It was founded in AD 301 by Marinus, a pious stone-cutter who fled to Mt. Titano to escape the caresses of an overly affectionate girl. When the son of the pagan woman who owned Mt. Titano tried to attack Marinus, God paralyzed him. His mother swore to convert to Christianity and to give Marinus and his followers her mountain if God restored her son. God agreed, and Marinus's mountain now hums with life as a heavily touristed independent republic—in proportion to its population of 29,000, the 26 sq. km country is the most visited in the world. Tax-free shopping, friendly locals, and monuments ranging from the seat of the Republic's modern Parliament to three towering castles keep visitors streaming in by the busload.

 STAYING IN TOUCH WITH SAN MARINO. San Marino's country code is ☎378. It is only necessary to dial it when calling from outside Italy. Within Italy and San Marino, just dial the city code, ☎0549.

▢ TRANSPORTATION

The closest train station is in Rimini. **Fratelli Benedettini** (☎0549 90 38 54) and **Bonelli Bus** (☎0541 37 24 32) run from San Marino's center to Rimini's train station (50min., 12 per day 6:30am-7pm, €3.10). Arrive 15min. before departure. In town, a **funivia** (cableway) connects Borgo Maggiore to the *centro storico*. (☎0549 88 35 90. Every 15min. in summer 7:50am-8:30pm; in winter 7:50am-6:30pm; from July 26-Sept. 3, special hours from 7:50am-1am. Round-trip €4.) **Taxis** (☎0549 99 14 41) are in P. Lo Stradone.

▰ ▱ ORIENTATION AND PRACTICAL INFORMATION

To get from one monument to another, follow signs but be aware that the city is difficult to navigate and you'll probably get lost. San Marino's streets wind around **Monte Titano**. From the bus, exit to the left, climb the staircase, and pass through the **Porta San Francesco** to to begin the ascent. **Via Basilicus** leads to **Piazza Titano**. From there, turn right to **Piazza Garibaldi,** then follow **Contrada del Collegio** to **Piazza della Libertà**. The **tourist office**, Contrada del Collegio, 40, stamps passports for

€2.50 and provides a free map. (☎0549 88 29 14; www.visitsanmarino.com. Open M-F 8:30am-6:30pm and Sa-Su 9am-1:30pm and 2-6:30pm. Cash only.) San Marino mints coins interchangeable with the euro, though they're more collector's items than anything else. Pick them up at the **Coin and Stamp Office**, P. Garibaldi, 5. (☎0549 88 23 70. Open M 8:30am-1pm, Tu-Th 8:30am-5:30pm, F 8:30am-2pm, Sa-Su 9am-1pm and 2-6pm. MC/V.) In case of **emergency**, call ☎113, an **ambulance** at ☎118, or the **police** at ☎0549 88 88 88. The **post office** is at Vle. Onofri, 87. (☎0549 88 29 09. Open M-F 8:30am-6pm, Sa 8:30am-noon. Cash only.) **Postal Code:** 47838

THE STRACCIATELLA TEST. A good way to tell if *gelato* is homemade is to look at the *stracciatella* (vanilla with chocolate swirl) flavor. Homemade *stracciatella* will have streaks and strips of chocolate instead of specks, which are produced by machines. "Stracciate" in Italian means "shredded" and refers to the shreds of chocolate mixed into this delectable flavor of *gelato*.

ACCOMMODATIONS AND FOOD

Most of San Marino's affordable hotels are family-run affairs above adjoining restaurants. Other options are mostly four-star hotels. Book ahead to ensure a decently priced room. With frescoed staircases and wrought-iron railings, the **Diamond Hotel ❹**, Contrada del Collegio, 48, across from the Basilica di San Marino, offers five large rooms with bath, high ceiling, and ornate furniture. The attached **restaurant ❸** serves large portions of pizzas and entrees. (☎/fax 0549 99 10 03. Open daily Mar.-Oct. 8:30am-10pm. Pizza €4.50-8. *Primi* €7.50-9, *secondi* €6.20-18. Breakfast included. Doubles €55; triples €78. AmEx/MC/V.) At **Hotel La Rocca ❹**, Salita alla Rocca, 33, down the street from the castle, the TVs are big, the views from the spacious rooms are fantastic, and there's a **restaurant ❸** downstairs. (☎0549 99 11 66; fax 0549 99 24 30. *Primi* €5-8.50, *secondi* €5.50-15. Breakfast included. Singles €32-52; doubles €47-70; triples €60-92; quads €67-116. AmEx/MC/V.) The streets are full of bars and restaurants offering fixed-price *menùs*.

Fresh produce is available at the small **market**, Contra Omereli, 2, just off P. Titano. (☎0549 99 16 13. Open June-Sept. daily 8am-8pm; Oct.-May M-Sa 8am-1pm and 3-7pm, Su 9am-noon. Cash only.) Find supermarket fare at **Alimentari Chiaruzzi**, Contra del Collegio, 13, between P. Titano and P. Garibaldi. (☎0549 99 12 22; daniloc@omniway.sm. Open daily Aug. 7am-midnight; Sept.-July 8am-7:30pm. AmEx/MC/V.) For a sizable sampler of regional pastas right inside the main gate, try **Buca San Francesco ❷**, Francesco Piazzetta Placido Feretrano, 3, past the Pta. S. Francesco where the specialty is *Tris della Buca* (€7), a plate of ravioli, *tagliatelle*, and cheesy lasagna in a light *ragù*. (☎0549 99 14 62. *Primi* €4.50-7, *secondi* €6-7.50. *Piatto unico* with drinks and side dish €10. Bar open daily 9:00am-6:30pm, restaurant open daily noon-3pm. AmEx/MC/V.) To escape the packed streets, slip into the serene **Caffè del Titano ❶**, Piazzetta del Titano, 4. The gooey *brioche cioccolato* (€1.20) and rich cappuccino (€1.70) cannot be surpassed. (☎0549 99 24 73. Open daily 7:30am-10:30pm. Cash only.)

SIGHTS AND ENTERTAINMENT

The late 19th-century **Palazzo Pubblico** is the seat of San Marino's parliament. The marble interior features the **Sala del Consiglio** (Hall of the Council), where the city is still run amid lunettes of Justice (holding a broadsword) and Peace (at a slight disadvantage with an olive branch). The changing of the guard takes place in front of the palace from April to September at half past the hour from 8:30am to 6:30pm. Arrive 10min. early to secure a spot. (P. della Libertà. ☎0549 88 31 52. Open daily

June-Sept. 8am-8pm; Oct.-May. 9am-5:12pm. Tickets sales end 30min. before closing. €3, €4.50 includes Museo San Francesco. Cash only.) Three points along San Marino's defensive network are open to the public, but poking along their in-between paths offers many of the same views without the fee. The first tower is the **Castello della Guaita,** an 11th-century structure carved out of the mountain. Climb to the top of the tower for some great views, but be careful descending the narrow ladder. (Follow signs from P. della Libertà. ☎0549 99 13 69. Open daily Apr.-Sept. 8am-8pm; Oct.-Mar. 9am-5pm. Tickets close 30min. before castle. €3, combined with Castello della Cesta €4.50. MC/V.) Farther along the trail, the **Castello della Cesta** houses the **Museo delle Armi Antiche,** an arms museum with a selection of fierce weapons. Die-hard castle lovers can follow the trail to the 3rd tower, **Torre del Montale,** a squat, mossy turret closed to the public. Nearby, stone outcroppings offer quiet views of the fields. (☎0549 99 12 95. Open daily Apr.-Sept. 8am-8pm; Oct.-Mar. 9am-5pm. Ticket sales end 30min. before closing. €3, combined with Castello della Guaita €4.50. MC/V.) In the **Museo della Tortura,** browse torture toys, from the gruesome *schiacciatesta,* a helmet that shrinks to squeeze out the victim's brain, to the humiliating "Good for Nothing's Necklace," a chain laden with wooden cards and dice, worn by gamblers through the streets. (Near P. S. Francesco, to the right after the main gate. ☎0549 99 12 15; www.museodellatortura.com. Open daily July-Aug. 9am-midnight; Sept.-May 10am-6pm. €6, students €4, groups of 10 or more €3. Family discount available. Cash only.)

In late summer, a **medieval festival** brings parades, food, musicians, and jugglers to San Marino. September 3 is the day of independence for San Marino; the **Palio delle Balestre,** or crossbowman's show, also in early September, commemorates this event; increased bus service makes dropping in for the day easy. (For dates and info, call ☎0549 88 29 98 or the tourist office.)

TUSCANY (TOSCANA)

Recently, popular culture has glorified Tuscany as a sun-soaked sanctuary of art, nature, and culture. For once, popular culture has gotten it right. In Tuscany, every town was home to a Renaissance master, every highway provides vistas of ancient hills, and every year, locals celebrate their illustrious history with costumed parades, festivals, and galas. The region's concentration of art, architecture, and world-renowned wine and cuisine lures millions of visitors each year. Tour groups shuffle from *duomo* to museum, trying to capture "the real Tuscany" through the lenses of their flashing cameras. While it's nearly impossible to get completely off the beaten path, a little effort can yield memorable personal moments. You don't need an art-history degree to stroll through the silent sanctuary of a hidden 15th-century Romanesque church, to admire fields of sunflowers that seem to stretch to infinity, or to bike leisurely atop Lucca's *baluardi* (city walls). So go ahead and pose against the tower in Pisa, gaze open-mouthed at the Botticellis in the Uffizi, and loiter in Siena's Il Campo. Just remember that patience, good timing, and a bit of wanderlust can ensure an even richer experience.

HIGHLIGHTS OF TUSCANY

BASK in the rays of the summer sun on the glamorous beaches of **Elba** (p. 492).

SIP the unique Brunello wine at one of the many local vineyards in **Montalcino** (p. 465).

ROOT for your favorite horse and jockey team during Siena's famed **Palio** (p. 448).

BROWSE the chic boutiques and corner markets of **Florence** (p. 445).

FLORENCE (FIRENZE)   ☎055

Florence is the city of the Renaissance: city of rebirth, city of ingenuity, city of progress. Ravaged by the Black Death, floods, famine, and war, it is surprising that Florence has played a pivotal in the formation of the western world. By the 14th century, Florence had already become one of the most influential cities in Europe. The imposing Palazzo Vecchio, still Florence's town hall, was a municipal powerhouse, and Florentines Boccaccio, and Dante, and Giotto had already created their influential masterpieces. In the 15th century, Florence gained distinction for artistic excellence as the Medici family amassed a peerless collection, supporting masters like Donatello, Botticelli, Brunelleschi, and Michelangelo. When the Arno flooded in 1966, swamping Santa Croce and the Uffizi, Florentines and foreigners braved 6m of water to rescue the paintings, sculptures, and books yielded by this golden age. These days, the tourists who flood streets are captivated by the Florence's distinct character, creative spirit, and timeless beauty.

✈ INTERCITY TRANSPORTATION

Flights: ☎055 30 615; www.aeroporto.firenze.it. In the suburb of Peretola. Mostly domestic and charter flights. The orange **ATAF bus #62** connects the train station to the airport (€1). Buy tickets from *tabaccherie* on the upper level of the airport, departure side. **SITA**, V. S. Caterina da Siena, 157 (☎800 37 37 60 46 or 055 28 46 61), runs buses (€4) between the station and the airport. **Galileo Galilei Airport** (☎050 50 07 07), in **Pisa.** Take airport express from Florence train station (1¼hr., 10 per day,

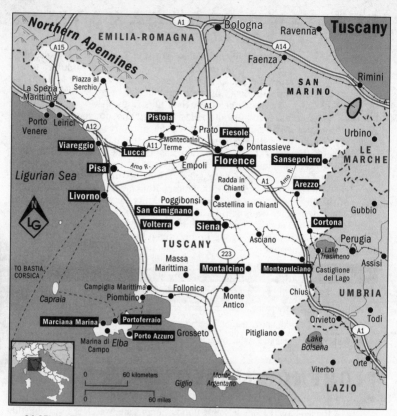

€4.85). In Florence, ask for info at the "air terminal" (☎ 055 21 60 73) halfway down platform **#5** in the train station. Open daily 7:30am-5pm.

Trains: Stazione Santa Maria Novella, just north of S. Maria Novella church. Info office open daily 7am-9pm; after hours call national train info ☎ 848 88 80 88. **Luggage storage** and lost property services available. Trains depart every hr. to: **Bologna** (1hr., 5:48am-1:47am, €7.75); **Milan** (3½hr., 6am-1:47am, €22); **Rome** (3½hr., 5:55am-10:55pm, €15-22); **Siena** (1½hr., 5:31am-11:07pm, €5.93); **Venice** (3hr., 5:18am-1:47am, €15.94). Check out www.trenitalia.it for up-to-date schedules.

Buses: 3 major bus companies serve Tuscany's towns. Offices near P. della Stazione.

SITA, V. S. Caterina da Siena, 15r (☎ 800 37 37 60 46 or 055 28 46 61; www.sita-on-line.it). To: **Arezzo** (2½hr., 3 per day, €6.40); **Poggibonsi** (1hr., 11 per day, €6.10); **San Gimignano** (1½hr., 14 per day, €7.60); **Siena** (1½hr., 2 per day, €5.90); **Volterra** (2hr., 6 per day, €14) via **Colle Val D'Elsa.**

LAZZI, P. Adua, 1-4r (☎ 055 35 10 61; www.lazzi.it). To: **Lucca** (every hr. 7am-8:15pm, €4.70); **Pisa** (every hr.; 6am-8:15pm, €6.10); **Pistoia** (7am-6pm, €2.70); **Prato** (6am-11pm, €2.20).

CAP, Largo Alinari, 9 (☎ 055 21 46 37; www.capautolinee.it). To **Prato** (1hr., 6:40am-8pm, €2.20).

✦ ORIENTATION

From the front steps of **Stazione Santa Maria Novella,** a short walk down **Via Panzani** and a left on **Via dei Cerrentari** leads to the **duomo,** the heart of the city. Most streets

WHAT'S BLACK AND WHITE AND RED ALL OVER? Florence's streets are numbered in red and black sequences. Red numbers indicate commercial establishments and black (or blue) numbers denote residences (including most sights and hotels). Black addresses appear here as a numeral only, while red addresses are indicated by a number followed by an "r." If you reach an address and it's not what you expected, you've probably got the wrong color.

in Florence lead to this instantly recognizable dome, which soars high above every other city structure and makes being lost a little easier to remedy. **Via dei Calzaiuoli,** dominated by throngs of pedestrians, leads south from the *duomo* to the statue-filled **Piazza della Signoria** in front of the **Palazzo Vecchio** and the **Uffizi Gallery.** The other major *piazza* is the **Piazza della Repubblica,** down **Via Roma** from the *duomo.* Major streets run from this *piazza* north back toward the *duomo* and south toward the shop-lined **Ponte Vecchio** (literally, "Old Bridge"). The Ponte Vecchio is one of five bridges that cross from central Florence to the **Oltrarno,** the district south of the **Arno River.** When navigating Florence, note that most streets change names unpredictably, often every few blocks. For guidance, grab a free **map** (one with a street index) from the tourist office across from the train station.

⊟ LOCAL TRANSPORTATION

Public Transportation: Orange **ATAF buses** cover most of the city 6am to 1am. Buy tickets at any newsstand, *tabaccherie,* or coin-operated ticket dispenser. €3.90 for 4 tickets; €1 per 1hr., €1.80 per 3hr., €4.50 per 24hr., €7.20 per 3 days, €16 per week. Validate ticket onboard using orange machine or risk €50 fine. Once validated, ticket allows unlimited bus travel for the allotted time. Tickets sold on buses 9am-6pm (€1.55). From the train station, ATAF info office (☎800 42 45 00; www.ataf.net) is on the left. Open M-F 7:15am-1:15pm and 1:45-7:45pm, Sa 7:15am-1:15pm. Free map. Bus **#7** to **Fiesole, #10** to **Settignano, #17** to **Villa Camerata** (€1).

Taxis: ☎055 43 90 or 055 47 98 or 055 42 42. Outside the train station.

Car Rental: Avis (☎055 31 55 88; www.avis.com), at airport. 25+. Open daily 8am-7pm. **Hertz,** V. Finiguerra, 33 (☎055 23 98 205; www.hertz.com). 25+. Open M-F 8am-8pm, Sa 8am-7pm, Su 8am-1pm. **Maggiore** (☎055 31 12 56; www.maggiore.it), at airport. 19+. Open daily 8:30am-10:30pm. Also at V. Finiguerra, 11r (☎055 29 45 78). Open daily 8:30am-10:30pm. **Branch:** also at Borgo Ognissanti, 128r (☎055 21 36 29). Open M-F 8am-7pm, Sa 8am-1pm.

Bike and Scooter Rental: Alinari Noleggi, V. Guelfa, 85r (☎055 28 05 00; fax 055 27 17 871), rents scooters for €30-60 per day; bikes €15-20 per day. Open M-Sa 9:30am-1pm and 2:45-7:30pm, Su and holidays 10am-1pm and 3-6pm. AmEx/MC/V. **Florence by Bike,** V. S. Zanobi, 120/122r (☎055 48 89 92; www.florencebybike.it), rents bikes (€3.70 per hr., €19-28 per day) and **scooters** (50-650cc; €30-95 per day). Bike rental includes helmet, water, locks, spare tubes, pump, insurance, maps, and suggested itineraries. Reserve ahead. Open daily Mar.-Oct. 9am-7:30pm. AmEx/MC/V.

◪ PRACTICAL INFORMATION

TOURIST AND FINANCIAL SERVICES

Tourist Offices: Informazione Turistica, P. della Stazione, 4 (☎055 21 22 45 or 055 23 81 226; turismo3@comune.fi.it), directly across the *piazza* from station's main exit. Info on cultural events, walking-tour brochures, listings of hours for all sights in the city, and free **maps.** Ask for a map with street index. Open M-Sa 8:30am-7pm, Su and holi-

TUSCANY

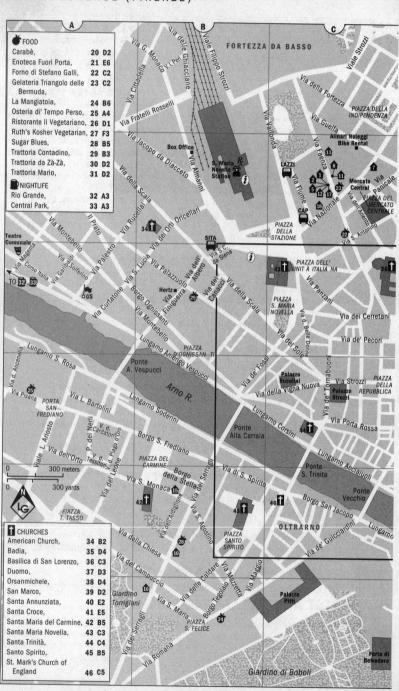

FOOD

Carabè,	**20**	D2
Enoteca Fuori Porta,	**21**	E6
Forno di Stefano Galli,	**22**	C2
Gelateria Triangolo delle Bermuda,	**23**	C2
La Mangiatoia,	**24**	B6
Osteria di' Tempo Perso,	**25**	A4
Ristorante Il Vegetariano,	**26**	D1
Ruth's Kosher Vegetarian,	**27**	F3
Sugar Blues,	**28**	B5
Trattoria Contadino,	**29**	B3
Trattoria da Zà-Zà,	**30**	D2
Trattoria Mario,	**31**	D2

NIGHTLIFE

Rio Grande,	**32**	A3
Central Park,	**33**	A3

CHURCHES

American Church,	**34**	B2
Badia,	**35**	D4
Basilica di San Lorenzo,	**36**	C3
Duomo,	**37**	D3
Orsanmichele,	**38**	D4
San Marco,	**39**	D2
Santa Annunziata,	**40**	E2
Santa Croce,	**41**	E5
Santa Maria del Carmine,	**42**	B5
Santa Maria Novella,	**43**	C3
Santa Trinità,	**44**	C4
Santo Spirito,	**45**	B5
St. Mark's Church of England	**46**	C5

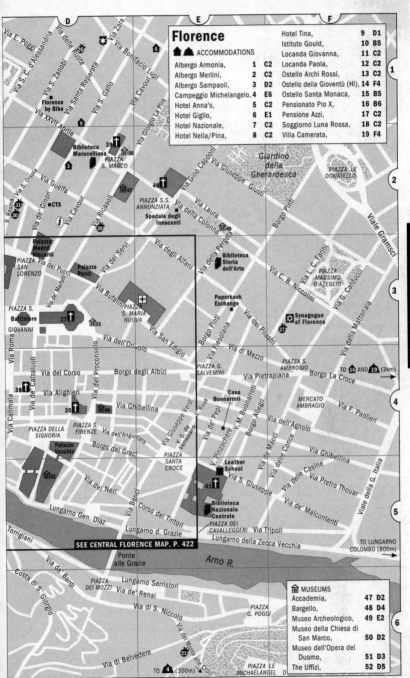

Florence

▲▲ ACCOMMODATIONS

Albergo Armonia,	1	C2
Albergo Merlini,	2	C2
Albergo Sampaoli,	3	D2
Campeggio Michelangelo,	4	E6
Hotel Anna's,	5	C2
Hotel Giglio,	6	E1
Hotel Nazionale,	7	C2
Hotel Nella/Pina,	8	C2
Hotel Tina,	9	D1
Istituto Gould,	10	B5
Locanda Giovanna,	11	C2
Locanda Paola,	12	C2
Ostello Archi Rossi,	13	C2
Ostello della Gioventù (HI),	14	F4
Ostello Santa Monaca,	15	B5
Pensionato Pio X,	16	B6
Pensione Azzi,	17	C2
Soggiorno Luna Rossa,	18	C2
Villa Camerata,	19	F4

TUSCANY

SEE CENTRAL FLORENCE MAP, P. 422

TO LUNGARNO
COLOMBO (800m)

Arno R.

▥ MUSEUMS		
Accademia,	47	D2
Bargello,	48	D4
Museo Archeologico,	49	E2
Museo della Chiesa di San Marco,	50	D2
Museo dell'Opera del Duomo,	51	D3
The Uffizi,	52	D5

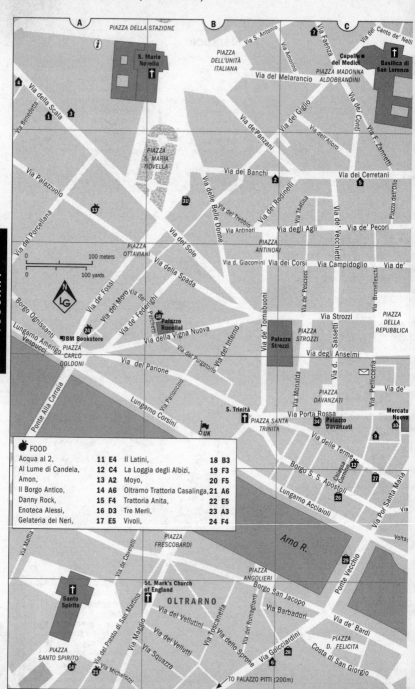

FOOD

Acqua al 2,	11 E4		Il Latini,	18 B3
Al Lume di Candela,	12 C4		La Loggia degli Albizi,	19 F3
Amon,	13 A2		Moyo,	20 F5
Il Borgo Antico,	14 A6		Oltrarno Trattoria Casalinga,	21 A6
Danny Rock,	15 F4		Trattoria Anita,	22 E5
Enoteca Alessi,	16 D3		Tre Merli,	23 A3
Gelateria dei Neri,	17 E5		Vivoli,	24 F4

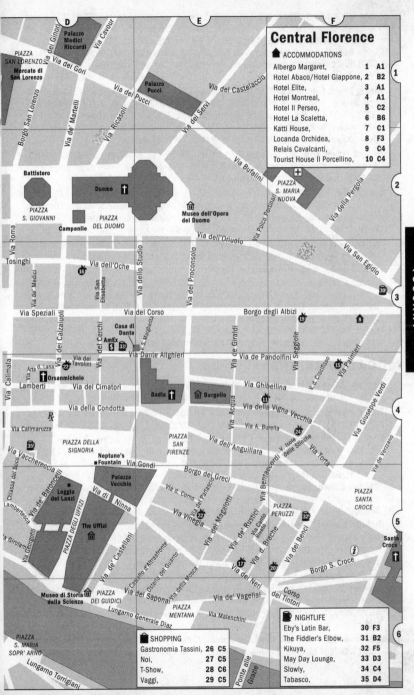

Central Florence

🏠 ACCOMMODATIONS

Albergo Margaret,	1	A1
Hotel Abaco/Hotel Giappone,	2	B2
Hotel Elite,	3	A1
Hotel Montreal,	4	A1
Hotel Il Perseo,	5	C2
Hotel La Scaletta,	6	B6
Katti House,	7	C1
Locanda Orchidea,	8	F3
Relais Cavalcanti,	9	C4
Tourist House Il Porcellino,	10	C4

TUSCANY

🛍 SHOPPING

Gastronomia Tassini,	26	C5
Noi,	27	C5
T-Show,	28	C6
Vaggi,	29	C5

🍸 NIGHTLIFE

Eby's Latin Bar,	30	F3
The Fiddler's Elbow,	31	B2
Kikuya,	32	F5
May Day Lounge,	33	D3
Slowly,	34	C4
Tabasco,	35	D4

days 8:30am-2pm. **Branches:** V. Cavour, 1r (☎055 29 08 32 or 055 29 08 33); Borgo Santa Croce, 29r (☎055 23 40 444); V. Manzoni, 16 (☎055 23 320); airport (☎055 31 58 74). **Consorzio ITA** (☎055 28 28 93 and 055 21 95 37), in train station by track #16 next to pharmacy, offers help finding accommodations. Lines can be long. €3-8.50 commission depending on the star rating of the hotel; not always the best value. **Maps** €0.50-4. Open M-Sa 8:30am-7:30pm; in winter M-Sa 8:30am-6:30pm.

Biking Tours: Florence by Bike, V. S. Zanobi, 120/122r (☎055 48 89 92; www.florencebybike.it), leads tours of historical Florence, the Chianti region, and Florentine hills (€23.24-60.43). Reserve ahead. Open daily 9am-7:30pm. **I Bike Italy** (☎055 23 42 371; www.ibikeitaly.com) offers 1- and 2-day bike tours and hikes of varying difficulty through Fiesole, Chianti, and Tuscan vineyards. Reserve ahead.

Budget Travel: CTS, V. dei Ginori, 25r (☎055 28 95 70), provides Transalpino tickets, discount airfares, car rentals, organized trips, and ISICs. Get there early and take a number. Open M-F 9:30am-1:30pm and 2:30-6pm, Sa 9:30am-12:30pm.

Consulates: UK, Lungarno Corsini, 2 (☎055 28 41 33). Open M-F 9:30am-12:30pm and 2:30-4:30pm. Can be reached by phone M-F 9am-1pm and 2-5pm. **US,** Lungarno Amerigo Vespucci, 38 (☎055 23 98 276), at V. Palestro, near the station. Open M-F 9am-12:30pm. For any consulate not listed, consult www.corpoconsolarefirenze.it.

Currency Exchange: Local banks offer the best exchange rates—beware of independent exchange services with high commissions. Most banks open M-F 8:20am-1:20pm and 2:45-3:45pm. 24hr. **ATMs** all over the city.

American Express, V. Dante Alighieri, 22r (☎055 50 98 220; fes.florence@aexp.com). From *duomo*, walk down V. dei Calzaiuoli, turn left on V. dei Tavolini, and continue to the small *piazza*. Cashes personal checks for cardholders. Mail for cardholders and traveler's check customers at no cost; all others €1.55 per inquiry. €1.55 to leave messages. For lost traveler's checks, call ☎800 87 20 00, lost cards 067 22 80 371. Open M-F 9am-5:30pm. Open for only financial services Sa 9am-12:30pm.

LOCAL SERVICES

Luggage Storage: In train station at track #16. €3.80 for 1st 5hr., €0.60 per hr. 6-12hr., €0.20 per hr. 13hr.+ for up to 5 days. Open daily 6am-midnight.

Lost Property: Ufficio Oggetti Rinvenuti (☎055 23 52 190), next to the baggage deposit in train station. **Lost and Found,** V. Circondaria, 17/B (☎055 32 83 33).

English-Language Bookstores: ▓**Paperback Exchange,** V. Fiesolana, 31r (☎055 24 78 154; www.papex.it). Offers store credit in exchange for used books. Special *Italianistica* section features novels about Brits and Americans in Italy. Open M-F 9am-7:30pm, Sa 10am-1pm and 3:30-7:30pm. Closed 2 weeks in mid-Aug. AmEx/MC/V. **BM Bookstore,** Borgo Ognissanti, 4r (☎055 29 45 75). English-language books on every subject imaginable. Stocks textbooks for American study-abroad programs. Open Mar.-Oct. M-Sa 9:30am-7:30pm, Su afternoons; Nov.-Feb. M-Sa 9:30am-7:30pm.

Bulletin Boards: The American Church lists ads for roommates, English teachers, and baby-sitters, as well as religious and cultural activities in English. Open Tu-F 9am-1pm. Also, bulletin boards with job openings and room rentals are often found at popular casual restaurants, Internet cafes, and bookstores.

Box Office: V. Alamanni, 39r (☎055 21 08 04; www.boxol.it), sells tickets for performances in Florence and Fiesole, including rock concerts. Advance booking service. Online and phone reservations only with credit cards. Open M 3:30-7:30pm, Tu-Sa 10am-7:30pm. Pick up a listing of events in any tourist office or buy the city's entertainment monthly, *Firenze Spettacolo* (€1.85).

Laundromats: Wash and Dry Lavarapido, V. dei Servi, 105r, 2 blocks from *duomo*. Other locations at V. della Scala, 52-54r and V. del Sole, 29r. Self-service wash and dry

€6. Detergent €0.80. Open daily 8am-10pm. **Onda Blu,** V. degli Alfani, 24r. Self-service wash and dry €6. Open daily 8am-10pm.

EMERGENCY AND COMMUNICATIONS

Emergency: ☎113. **Carabinieri:** ☎112. **Ambulance:** ☎118. **Fire:** ☎115.

Police: Central Office (Questura), V. Zara, 2 (☎055 49 771). **Branch:** P. del Duomo, 5. Open M-Th 8:15am-6pm, F-Sa 8:15am-2pm. **Tourist Police: Ufficio Stranieri,** V. Zara, 2 (☎055 49 771), for visa or work-permit problems. Open M-F 8:30am-noon. To report lost or stolen items, go around the corner to **Ufficio Denunce,** V. Duca d'Aosta, 3 (☎055 49 771). Open M-Sa 8am-8pm, Su 8am-2pm. Also, check out the **Lost and Found,** V. Circondaria, 17/B (☎055 32 83 33).

Pharmacies: Farmacia Comunale (☎055 28 94 35), at the train station by track #16. **Molteni,** V. dei Calzaiuoli, 7r (☎055 28 94 90). Both open 24hr.

Tourist Medical Service: V. Lorenzo il Magnifico, 59 (☎055 47 54 11; medserv@tin.it). General practitioners and specialists. English-speaking doctors on-call 24hr. Office visits €45; house calls €65 during day, €80 at night. AmEx/MC/V.

Internet Access: Walk down any busy street and an Internet cafe is sure to pop up. **Internet Train,** Via Guelfa 54/56r, has 15 locations in the city, all listed on www.internettrain.it. Offers telnet, email, and web-cruising. €4 per hr., students €3. Hours vary slightly depending on location. Most open M-F 9am-midnight, Sa 10am-8pm, Su noon-9pm. AmEx/MC/V. **Libreria Edison,** P. della Repubblica, 27r, has a great relaxed atmosphere amid books and coffee upstairs. €3 per hr. Open daily 10am-8pm.

Post Office: ☎055 27 36 480. On V. Pellicceria, off P. della Repubblica. To send packages, go behind the building to V. dei Sassetti, 4. Open M-Sa 8:15am-7pm. Telegram office open 24hr. **Postal Code:** 50100.

ACCOMMODATIONS

Because of the constant stream of tourists, it is best to reserve a room at least 10 days ahead, especially for visits in Easter or during the summer. Most *pensioni* prefer reservations in writing with at least one night's deposit in the form of a money order; others simply ask for a phone confirmation. Florence has such a large number of budget accommodations that it is possible to find a room even without a reservation, but last-minute options are often of significantly lower quality. The **Consorzio ITA** in the train station (see **Tourist and Financial Services,** p. 419) provides info on available rooms and one-star *pensioni* and private *affittacamere*. Hotel owners are often willing to suggest alternatives if their establishments are full, so don't hesitate to ask. Complaints should be lodged with the **Ufficio Controllo Alberghi,** V. Cavour, 37 (☎055 27 601). The municipal government strictly regulates hotel prices, so proprietors must charge within the approved range for their category and must also post these rates in a place visible to guests. Rates uniformly increase around 10% every year, and new rates take effect in March or April. For **long-term housing** in Florence, check **bulletin boards** (p. 424), classified ads in *La Pulce*, published three times weekly (€2), or *Grillo Fiorentino*, a free monthly paper. Reasonable prices range €200-600 per month.

HOSTELS

▩ **Ostello Archi Rossi,** V. Faenza, 94r (☎055 29 08 04; www.hostel archirossi.com), 2 blocks from the train station. Excellent, busy place in easy location. Floor-to-ceiling murals, ceramic tiles, and brick archways. Courtyard patio and dining/TV room. Home-

> **DON'T LET THE BED BUGS BITE.** Each day at Stazione Santa Maria Novella, boosters assail unwitting travelers with offers of rooms at ridiculously cheap prices. These fly-by-night operations are illegal and best avoided. The police routinely evacuate illegal *pensioni* during the night, leaving bleary-eyed backpackers to fend for themselves in the wee hours of the morning. As these establishments are unregulated by the government, they may also be dangerous. To be on the safe side, book your accommodations in advance or use the last-minute booking service at the station. All hotels, hostels, campsites, and *affittacamere* in Tuscany are subject to government inspections and must post their official rating outside their establishment (from 1 to 5 stars).

cooked breakfast included. Dinner €3.60-4.20. Laundry €5.20. Free Internet. Luggage storage. Reserve online a week ahead, especially during summer. Room lockout 11am-2:30pm; no hostel lockout. Curfew 2am. Some wheelchair-accessible rooms. 9-bed dorms €20; 6-bed dorms €24; 4-bed dorms €25. Single-night stay €20. ❷

■ **Istituto Gould,** V. dei Serragli, 49 (☎055 21 25 76; www.istitutogould.it), in Oltrarno. Take bus #36 or 37 from the station to the 2nd stop across the river. The building is not well marked; look for the signs of the larger Istituto Gould complex, then buzz yourself in to the courtyard. 88 beds and a large colonnaded courtyard in a busy residential area. Reception M-F 8:45am-1pm and 3-7:30pm, Sa 9am-1:30pm and 2:30-6pm. 3- or 4-bed dorm €21, with bath €24; singles €36/€41; doubles €50/58. MC/V. ❷

Ostello Santa Monaca, V. S. Monaca, 6 (☎055 26 83 38; www.ostello.it). Follow directions to Istituto Gould, but turn right on V. S. Monaca. 114 beds stacked in high-ceilinged rooms. Friendly management. Kitchen facilities; bring utensils. Breakfast €2.50-3.50. Lunch or dinner €10. Hot water for showers 7-9am and 2-11pm. Sheets included. Laundry €6.50 per 5kg. Internet €5 per hr. June-Sept. arrive before 9am. 7-night max. stay. Reception daily 6am-1pm and 2pm-1am. Lockout 9:30am-2pm. Curfew 1am. Reserve by email or fax 3 days ahead. 10-bed dorms €17. AmEx/MC/V. ❷

Ostello della Gioventù Europa Villa Camerata (HI), V. Augusto Righi, 2-4 (☎055 60 14 51; fax 055 61 03 00). Take bus #17 outside train station (near track #5), or from P. dell'Unità; ask for Salviatino stop. Walk 10min. up driveway, passing a vineyard. Tidy and crowded, in a beautiful but remote villa with 322 beds and a roofed open-air arcade, bar, and TV room with English-language movies every night at 9pm. 4, 6, or 8 beds per room. Breakfast and sheets included. Dinner €8.50. Self-service laundry €5.20. 3-night max. stay. Reception 7am-12:30pm and 1pm-midnight. Lockout 10am-2pm. Strict midnight curfew. Dorms €16.50. Non-HI members add €2.58. ❷

Pensionato Pio X, V. dei Serragli, 106 (☎/fax 055 22 50 44), a few blocks beyond Istituto Gould, in the courtyard on the right. Rooms are nothing fancy, but very clean and quiet. 54 beds with 3-5 beds per room. Dark, co-ed shared bath; bring flip-flops. Check-out 9am. Curfew midnight. Dorms €17, with bath €19. Cash only. ❷

HOTELS

PIAZZA SANTA MARIA NOVELLA AND ENVIRONS

The budget accommodations around this *piazza* in front of the train station offer convenient access to the *duomo* and town center.

■ **Hotel Abaco,** V. dei Banchi, 1 (☎055 23 81 919; www.abaco-hotel.it). 7 beautifully extravagant rooms named after Renaissance greats, with reproduction 17th-century headboards, noise-proof windows, and prints of famous works. All rooms have phone and TV. Breakfast and A/C free when bill is paid in cash, €5 each otherwise. Laundry €7 per load. Free Internet. Parking €24 per day. Doubles €75, with bath €90; triples €110; quads €135. 10% discount with *Let's Go*. Accepts traveler's checks. MC/V. ❺

Soggiorno Luna Rossa, V. Nazionale, 7 (☎055 23 02 185). Airy rooms popular with students have trim furnishings, TV, fan, and colorful stained-glass windows. Small shared baths. Breakfast included. 8-bed dorm €20-22. Singles €25, with bath €30; doubles €60; triples €75, with shower €90; quads with shower €100. Cash only. ❷

Hotel Elite, V. della Scala, 12 (☎055 21 38 32; fax 055 21 53 95). Exit train station right on V. D. Orti Oricellari, which leads to V. della Scala; turn left. Friendly family owners make reservations for guests at Uffizi and other sights. Cozy breakfast and sitting areas enhance these well-maintained rooms, all with TV, phone, and A/C. Quieter rooms in the back with enormous bathrooms. Breakfast €6. Singles €70; doubles with shower €75, with full bath €90; triples €110; quads €120. AmEx/MC/V. ❺

Hotel Giappone, V. dei Banchi, 1 (☎055 21 00 90; www.hotelgiappone.com). Follow directions to Hotel Abaco, Giappone is 1 floor above. Close to the *duomo*. 10 refined rooms sport large beds, phone, TV, A/C, and Internet jacks. Immaculate shared bath. Singles €50, with bath €55; doubles €72/85. Extra bed €26. MC/V. ❹

Albergo Margaret, V. della Scala, 25 (☎055 21 01 38; www.dormireintoscana.it/margaret). An English-speaking staff runs 7 rooms decked in red linens and puffy orange quilts. Rooms have TV and A/C. Curfew midnight. June-Aug. singles €60; doubles with shower €70, with full bath €90. Discounts Sept.-May and for longer stays. Cash only. ❺

Hotel Montreal, V. della Scala, 43 (☎055 23 82 331; www.hotelmontreal.com). Follow directions to Hotel Elite. 22 tasteful, wood-furnished rooms with phone, TV, and A/C. Breakfast €5, free fridge access. Flexible curfew 1:30am. Singles €50-60; doubles €70-90; triples €110-120; quads €120. Cash only. ❸

OLD CITY (NEAR THE DUOMO)

Closest to Florence's most famous monuments, this area is full of high-quality accommodations that are also extremely expensive. Follow V. Panzani from the train station and turn left on V. dei Cerretani to reach the *duomo*.

Hotel Il Perseo, V. dei Cerretani, 1 (☎055 21 25 04; www.hotelperseo.com). Exit the train station and take V. Panzani, which becomes V. dei Cerretani. Aussie-Italian couple and English-speaking staff welcome travelers to 19 bright rooms and large, gleaming baths. All have fans, some have views of the *duomo*. Cozy bar and TV lounge decorated with proprietor's art. Breakfast included. Internet €1.50 for 15min. Parking €15.50 per day. Singles €55; doubles €75, with bath €95; triples €97/120; quads €118/140; quints €133/155. MC/V (3-night min. stay). ❹

Locanda Orchidea, Borgo degli Albizi, 11 (☎055 24 80 346; www.hotelorchideaflorence.com). Turn left off V. Proconsolo from the *duomo*. Dante's wife was born in this 12th-century *palazzo,* built around a still-intact tower. Rooms with marble floors and famous Renaissance prints on the walls; some with garden view. Friendly and helpful native English-speaking management. Book exchange. Clean shared baths, some rooms with shower. Singles €55; doubles €75; triples with shower €100; quads €120. Cash only. ❹

Relais Cavalcanti, V. Pellicceria, 2 (☎055 21 09 62; www.relaiscavalcanti.com), steps from P. della Repubblica. Mother-daughter owners Anna and Francesca welcome guests to gold-trimmed rooms with antique wardrobes. Look for the cookie jar and English-language magazines in the shared kitchen. All rooms have bath, A/C, phone, satellite TV, and fridge. Free luggage storage. Singles €70-85; doubles €90-125; triples €130-160. 10% discount with *Let's Go.* MC/V. ❺

Tourist House Il Porcellino, P. del Mercato Nuovo, 4 (055 21 85 72; www.hotelporcellino.com), on the western side of Mercato Nuovo. In one of oldest buildings in Florence, this recently renovated hotel boasts 2 singles and 6 doubles adorned with paintings of pigs. Rooms with wrought-iron beds, handpainted furniture, bath, TV and phone can be noisy, request one at the back. 3 rooms with A/C. Pay for portion of stay in advance. Singles €70; doubles €100; triples €120. AmEx/MC/V. ❺

TUSCANY

VIA NAZIONALE AND ENVIRONS

From P. della Stazione, V. Nazionale leads to budget hotels that are a short walk from both the *duomo* and the train station. The buildings on V. Nazionale, V. Faenza, V. Fiume, and V. Guelfa are filled with inexpensive establishments, but rooms facing the street may be noisy due to throngs of pedestrians. Women should use caution when walking alone in this area at night.

Katti House, V. Faenza, 21 (☎055 21 34 10; www.kattihouse.com). From the train station, take V. Nazionale for 1 block and turn right on V. Faenza. Well-kept lodgings feature handmade drapes and 400-year-old antiques. Attentive staff. Large rooms have TV, A/C, and bath. Singles €55; doubles €75; triples and quads €105. Prices drop significantly Nov.-Mar. MC/V. ❺

Hotel Nazionale, V. Nazionale, 22 (☎055 23 82 203; www.nazionalehotel.it). From train station, turn left on V. Nazionale. 9 sunny and spacious rooms overlooking a busy street were renovated in 2004. All with comfy bed, bath, and A/C. Breakfast served in room 8-9:30am for €6. Singles €63-95; doubles €70-95; triples €100-125. MC/V. ❺

Via Faenza, 56. These 5 *pensioni*, all with the same amenities, are among the best deals in the area. Turn left on V. Faenza from V. Nazionale.

Pensione Azzi (☎055 21 38 06; www.hotelazzi.com), enter on ground floor next door to main building. Presents itself as a *locanda degli artisti* (an artists' inn) with stylish prints on the walls. But all travelers, not only bohemians, will appreciate the friendly management and relaxing terrace, and 12 large rooms with bath. Splurge on the huge suite with a whirlpool. Breakfast included. Wheelchair accessible. Singles €70; doubles €110. Extra bed €25. AmEx/MC/V. ❺

Hotel Anna's (☎055 23 02 714; www.hotelannas.com), 2nd fl. The only 2-star option in the main building features large, bright rooms with TV, minibar, phone, A/C, and bath. Breakfast €5. Singles €40-60; doubles €80-130. Extra bed €20. AmEx/MC/V. ❹

Locanda Paola (☎055 21 36 82), 3rd fl. 7 bright minimalist rooms with plush armchairs. Curfew 2am. Dorms €25; doubles €65, with bathroom €110. Extra bed €25. Cash only. ❷

Albergo Merlini (☎055 21 28 48; www.hotelmerlini.it), 3rd fl. Murals and geraniums freshen the solarium, and owner creates a jovial atmosphere. Some rooms have views of the *duomo*. Breakfast €5. Flexible 1am curfew. Doubles €75, with bath €90; triples €105; quads €115. MC/V. ❺

Albergo Armonia (☎055 21 11 46), 1st fl. Posters of American films adorn 7 basic rooms with high ceilings and wooden beds. Shared baths. Singles €30-42; doubles €35-60; triples €90; quads €100. Prices drop in winter. ❸

Via Faenza, 69. 2 comfortable, no-frills accommodations under the same roof:

Locanda Giovanna (☎/fax 055 23 81 353). 7 fair-sized, well-kept rooms, some with garden views on the top floor of building. Cheerful staff. Singles €40; doubles €60, with bath €70; triples €75/90. Prices drop about €5 in winter. ❸

Hotel Nella/Pina, (☎055 26 54 346; www.hotelnella.net), 1st and 2nd fl. 14 basic but functional rooms with wood paneling and clean shared bath at good prices. Nella rooms have A/C, phone, and satellite TV. Nella: singles €55, with bath €60; doubles €85. Extra bed €20. Pina: singles €47; doubles €62. 10% discount with *Let's Go.* AmEx/MC/V. ❹

NEAR PIAZZA SAN MARCO AND THE UNIVERSITY

This area is calmer and quieter than its proximity to the center and university would suggest. All accommodations listed are within a few blocks of the delicate beauty of the infrequently touristed Chiesa di San Marco. To reach this neighborhood, exit the train station and turn left on V. Nazionale. Then turn right on V. Guelfa, which intersects V. S. Gallo and V. Cavour.

Albergo Sampaoli, V. S. Gallo, 14 (☎055 28 48 34; www.hotelsampaoli.it). Clean and comfortable rooms with fan and hair dryers; some have balcony. Large common room. Refrigerator available. Free Internet (30min.). Singles €42, with bath €50; doubles €65/85; triples €90/105. Extra bed €25. AmEx/MC/V; cash preferred. ❹

Hotel Tina, V. S. Gallo, 31 (☎055 48 35 19; fax 055 48 35 93). Small *pensione* with blue carpets and bright bedspreads. Cozy sitting room stocks the *Herald Tribune* and other international magazines. Carpeted rooms with A/C and phone. Larger shared baths upstairs. Doubles with shower €75, with bath €85. Extra bed €25. MC/V. ❹

Hotel Giglio, V. Cavour, 85 (☎055 48 66 21; www.hotelgiglio.it). Fantastic staff and veritable overflow of luxuries—hard wood floors, embroidered drapes, ornate furnishings, fluffy towels, and a price tag to match the extra perks. All rooms have bath, A/C, TV, safe, and phone. Breakfast included. Internet €2.50 per 30min. Singles €85-115; doubles €105-155; triples €145-180; quads €170-205. Discount with *Let's Go*. AmEx/MC/V. ❺

IN THE OLTRARNO

Across the Arno and only 10min. from the *duomo*, this area offers a respite from the busy *centro*. From Chiesa di San Spirito to Palazzo Pitti and the Boboli gardens, there are enough sights nearby to make this an attractive location, and a significant population of bohemian students keep the atmosphere lively.

▨ **Hotel La Scaletta,** V. Guicciardini, 13/B (☎055 28 30 28; www.hotellascaletta.it). Cross the Ponte Vecchio and continue on V. Guicciardini. 13 gorgeous rooms filled with antiques and connected by stairways and alcoves. Most rooms have A/C. Rooftop terrace with spectacular view of Boboli Gardens. Breakfast included. Singles €70-100; doubles €85-150; triples €100-170; quads €120-190. 10% *Let's Go* discount with cash payment. MC/V. ❹

CAMPING

Campeggio Michelangelo, V. Michelangelo, 80 (☎055 68 11 977; www.ecvacanze.it), beyond Ple. Michelangelo. Take bus #13 from the station (15min., last bus 11:25pm). Very crowded, but offers a distant vista of the city and a shady olive grove. *Alimentari,* Internet (€7.50 per hr.), laundry (€8), towels (€1), sheets (€3), and bar available for use. Reception daily 7am-11:30pm. Apr.-Nov. tent rental €10.50. €9.50 per person, €6 per tent, €5 per car, €4.40 per motorcycle. MC/V for over €100. ❶

Villa Camerata, V. A. Righi, 2-4 (☎055 60 03 15; fax 055 61 03 00). Take bus #17 outside train station (near track #5), or from P. dell'Unità across from station; ask driver for Salviatino stop. Same reception and same entrance as HI hostel (p. 426), with basic but comfortable shaded sites. Breakfast at hostel €2. Reception daily 7am-12:30pm and 1pm-midnight; 6-night max. stay. Check-out 7-10am. €6 per person, €4.80 with camping card; €5-€10.50 per tent. €10.50 per car. Bungalows €50. ❶

◖ FOOD

Florentine cuisine developed from the peasant fare of the surrounding countryside. Characterized by rustic dishes prepared with fresh ingredients and simple recipes, Tuscan food ranks among Italy's best. White beans and olive oil are two staple ingredients. A famous specialty is *bruschetta*, toasted bread doused with olive oil and garlic, usually topped with tomatoes, basil, and anchovy or liver paste. For *primi*, Florentines favor the Tuscan classics *minestra di fagioli* (a delicious white bean and garlic soup) and *ribollita* (a hearty bean, bread, and black cabbage stew). Florence's classic *secondo* is *bistecca alla Fiorentina* (thick sirloin steak); locals order it *al sangue* (very rare; literally "bloody"), though it's also available *al puntito* (medium) or *ben cotto* (well-done). The best local cheese is pecorino, made from sheep's milk. A liter of house wine usually costs €3.50-6 in a *trattoria;* stores sell bottles for as little as €2.50. Avoid ordering soda at restaurants; it usually costs over €3 per can, though prices are often not marked on menus. The local dessert is *cantuccini di prato* (hard almond cookies with egg yolk) dipped in *vinsanto* (a rich dessert wine from raisins).

MEAT CHEAT SHEET

For centuries, meat has been a hearty staple at Tuscan tables. Use this quick guide to distinguish between the numerous options for carnivores. **Carpaccio,** paper-thin slices of raw beef, is usually seen on *antipasti* menus, served with slices of parmesan cheese and drizzled with olive oil. Look out for signs advertising **porchetta** in markets and local *macellerie* (butcher shops) where thick pieces of pork are carved straight from the roast for the perfect sandwich. For more adventurous eaters, **cinghiale,** the flavorful wild boar that is popular throughout the region is always a hit. Die-hard fans eat it plain, but it's best when accompanied by a thick pasta like *tagliatelle.* On the rare occasion of bad weather, **osso bucco,** a hearty beef stew, is sure to warm your bones. It is best complemented by a glass of red wine and a side of *patate frittate* (fried potatoes similar to French fries). **Coniglio,** or rabbit, is a sophisticated choice often found on five-star menus and in local *osterie.* This tender meat is usually served in an olive sauce. Go for the gold and order **bistecca alla Fiorentina,** traditionally served extremely rare. Don't necessarily expect silverware—it's perfectly acceptable to pick up your steak and attack it with gusto. Tuscany has the best livestock in Italy, and this is by far the best way to enjoy it.

Buy fresh produce or tripe at the **Mercato Centrale,** between V. Nazionale and S. Lorenzo. (Open June-Sept. M-Sa 7:30am-2pm; Oct.-May Sa 7am-2pm and 4-8pm.) For basics, head to the **STANDA,** V. Pietrapiana, 1r. Turn right on V. del Proconsolo and the first left on Borgo degli Albizi. Continue straight through P. G. Salvemini; the supermarket is on the left. (Open M-Sa 8am-9pm, Su 9:30am-1:30pm and 3:30-6:30pm.) From behind the *duomo,* turn right on V. del Proconsolo and left on Borgo degli Albizi. Head two blocks down to find **La Loggia degli Albizi,** Borgo degli Albizi, 39r. A hidden treasure, this bakery offers an escape from the tourist throng. (☎055 24 79 574. Pastries from €0.80. Coffee from €0.80. Open M-Sa 7am-8pm.) Several health-food markets cater to vegetarians. The two best are named after the American book **Sugar Blues.** One is at V. XXVII Aprile, 46r, 5min. from the *duomo.* (☎055 48 36 66. Open M-Sa 9am-1:30pm and 5-7:30pm, Su 9am-1:30pm.) The other is next to the Istituto Gould (see **Accommodations: Hostels,** p. 425), in the Oltrarno at V. dei Serragli, 57r. (☎055 26 83 78. Open M-Sa 9am-2pm and 4:30-8pm, Su 9am-2pm.) Also try **La Raccolta,** V. Leopardi, 2r. (☎055 24 79 068. Open daily 8:30am-7:30pm.) **Ruth's Kosher Vegetarian,** V. Farini, 2, serves kosher fare on the 2nd floor of the building to the right of the synagogue. (☎055 24 80 888; kosherruth@katamail.com. Open M-Th and Su 12:30-2:30pm and 8-10:30pm.)

OLD CITY (NEAR THE DUOMO)

■ **Trattoria Anita,** V. del Parlascio, 2r (☎055 21 86 98), behind the Bargello. Traditionally Tuscan in design and cuisine. Fare includes filling pastas and an array of meat dishes from roast chicken to *bistecca alla Fiorentina.* Outgoing staff engages in friendly banter. Clientele is frequently young and American, so you can puzzle out the menu together. Unbeatable prices. *Primi* €4.70-5.20, *secondi* from €5.20. Fantastic lunch *menù* €5.50. Cover €1. Open M-Sa noon-2:30pm and 7-10pm. AmEx/MC/V. ❷

■ **Al Lume di Candela,** V. delle Terme, 23r (☎055 26 56 561), halfway between P. S. Trinità and P. della Signoria. Candlelit meals showcasing unique interpretations of Tuscan and Venetian favorites, served on golden platters. Try the fabulous *agnello in salsa di melagrana* (lamb in pomegranate sauce; €12.90). Service might be too slow for those on the go, but this is food to be savored. *Primi* €6.80-9.50, *secondi* €8.90-15.90. Open M-Sa noon-2:30pm and 7:30pm-1am. AmEx/MC/V. ❸

Danny Rock, V. dei Pandolfini, 13r (☎055 23 40 307), 3 blocks northwest of the Bargello. Casual pizzeria favored by locals with outdoor patio and large dining room that turns into a hot night spot after hours. Check the specials, as they often feature toppings from different Italian regions. Pizza from €5. Cover €1.50. Open M-Th 12:15-3pm and 7:30pm-1am, F 12:15-3pm and 7:30pm-1:30am, Sa 7:30pm-2am, Su noon-3pm and 7:15pm-1am; closed Su mornings July.-Aug. MC/V. ❷

Moyo, V. dei Benci 23r (☎055 24 79 738), near P. Santa Croce. New and modern, this hip spot is crowded with young Italians lunching on fresh salads and tasty burgers. Try the *insalata Moyo* (lettuce, strawberries, nuts, and feta cheese; €7). Lunch options from €5. Open daily noon-4pm. AmEx/MC/V. ❷

Acqua al 2, V. della Vigna Vecchia, 40r (☎055 28 41 70), behind the Bargello. A snug, air-conditioned restaurant popular with young Italians and foreigners. The *assaggio* (a selection of pastas; €8.01) and *filetto al mirtillo* (steak in a blueberry sauce; €11.03) demand a taste. Salads from €5. *Primi* around €7, *secondi* €7.23-19. Cover €1.03. Service 10%. Reservations strongly recommended. Open daily 7:30pm-1am. AmEx/MC/V. ❸

SANTA MARIA NOVELLA AND ENVIRONS

▨ **Il Latini,** V. dei Palchetti, 6r (☎055 21 09 16; www.illatini.com). You'll see the crowd outside before you see the restaurant. Convivial spirit pervades this old favorite with long wooden tables and solid Tuscan classics. *Bistecca alla Fiorentina* (€16) is a crowd-pleaser. Waiters keep the house wine flowing. *Primi* €6-8, *secondi* €10-18. Open Tu-Su 12:30-2:30pm and 7:30-10:30pm. Reserve ahead. AmEx/MC/V. ❸

▨ **Trattoria Contadino,** V. Palazzuolo, 71r (☎055 23 82 673). Casual, home-style meals. Only offers a fixed *menù* (€9.50), but this is no *menù turistico*—it's the real deal, including *primo, secondo,* bread, and 0.25L of house wine served to an almost exclusively Italian crowd. Airy dining room has black and white decor and a relaxed atmosphere. Open M-Sa 11am-3pm and 7pm-midnight. AmEx/MC/V. ❷

Tre Merli, V. del Moro, 11r (☎055 28 70 62). Another entrance on V. de' Fossi, 12r. In a dining room close to the river with cushioned banquettes, matching ceramic tableware, and soft red light, settle down for a sumptuous meal. Talented chef prepares tender, delicious dishes like *spaghettino all'Imperiale* (with mussels, clams, and shrimp; €13.50). Delightful owner Massimo welcomes *Let's Go* readers with a free glass of wine and 10% discount. *Primi* €7.50-13.50, *secondi* €12-18.50. Lunch *menù* €12. Cover €2. Open daily 11am-11pm. AmEx/MC/V. ❸

Amon, V. Palazzuolo, 28r (☎055 29 31 46), look for the blue-and-white sign. Cheerful owner cooks his own bread and serves scrumptious Middle Eastern food. Try *mousaka* (baked eggplant-filled pita) or *foul* (seasoned beans). Stand-up or takeout. Falafel €2.60-3.20. Shish kebab €3-5. Open Tu-Su noon-3pm and 6-11pm. Cash only. ❶

THE STATION AND UNIVERSITY QUARTER

▨ **Trattoria da Zà-Zà,** P. del Mercato Centrale, 26r (☎055 21 54 11). Wooden ceilings, brick arches, and wine racks greet diners. The outdoor patio is perfect for a summer dinner. Try the *tris* (bean and vegetable soup; €7) or the *tagliata di manzo* (beef; €13-18). Cover €1.55. Open M-Sa noon-3pm and 7-11pm. Reserve ahead. AmEx/MC/V. ❹

▨ **Trattoria Mario,** V. Rosina, 2r (☎055 21 85 50), around the corner from P. del Mercato Centrale. Informal and friendly lunch establishment with incredible pasta, cheap eats, and rabid following of Florentines and foreigners in the know. *Primi* menu offers a variety of traditional Tuscan soups from €3.10-3.40. *Secondi* €3.10-10.50. Cover €0.50. Open M-Sa noon-3:30pm. Closed most of Aug. Cash only. ❷

Ristorante Il Vegetariano, V. delle Ruote, 30r (☎055 47 50 30), off V. S. Gallo. True to its name, this self-service restaurant is popular with students and fills the vegetarian niche, offering fresh dishes like *risotto al pesto* (€5.50) in a peaceful bamboo garden or indoor dining rooms. Salads €4-5. *Primi* from €5, *secondi* from €6. Open Sept.-July Tu-F 12:30-3pm and 7:30pm-midnight, Sa-Su 7pm-midnight. Cash only. ❷

Forno di Stefano Galli, V. Faenza, 39r (☎055 21 53 14). **Branches:** V. delle Panche, 91, and V. Bufalini, 31-35r. Wide variety of fresh breads and scrumptious pastries. Adorable small tarts (€1.50) topped with fruits and custard. Pastries €0.80-2.50. Loaves of bread from €1. Open daily 7:30am-7:30pm. Cash only. ❶

THE OLTRARNO

▨ **Il Borgo Antico,** P. S. Spirito, 6r (☎055 21 04 37). Trendy spot with many student customers. Pastas and fantastic salads (€7) come with shrimp, avocado, or fresh mozzarella. Pizza €7. *Primi* €7, *secondi* €13-18. Cover €2. Reserve ahead. Open daily June-Sept. noon-12:30am; Oct.-May 12:45-2:30pm and 7:45pm-1am. AmEx/MC/V. ❹

▨ **La Mangiatoia,** P. S. Felice, 8r (☎055 22 40 60). Cross Ponte Vecchio, continue on V. Guicciardini, and pass Palazzo Pitti. Grab a table in the back dining room, or sit at the stone counter to watch the cooks baking pizza in a brick oven. Satisfying pasta and quality local fare. Extensive takeout menu. Pizza €4-7.50. *Primi* €3.50-5.50, *secondi* €4-9. Cover €1.50. Open Tu-Su 11am-3pm and 6:30-10pm. AmEx/MC/V. ❷

Osteria di' Tempo Perso, V. Pisana, 16r (☎055 22 31 45). Cross Ponte Alla Carraia; turn right on Borgo S. Frediano and exit through Pta. S. Frediano. Enthusiastic owner of this grapevine-canopied garden knows his seafood. Great deals on rotating daily *menù* for €9.50. *Primi* €6.50-9, *secondi* €7-17. Cover €1.50. AmEx/MC/V. ❸

Oltrarno Trattoria Casalinga, V. Michelozzi, 9r (☎055 21 86 24), near P. S. Spirito. Basic, authentic Tuscan dishes and specialties. Popular with locals. Good quality for the price. Try the *ravioli al sugo a coniglio* (ravioli with ham and sausage; €11.50.) *Primi* €4-4.50, *secondi* €5-10. Cover €2. Open M-Sa noon-2:30pm and 7-10pm. MC/V. ❷

GELATERIE

▨ **Vivoli,** V. Isole delle Stinche, 7 (☎055 29 23 34), behind the Bargello. The household name of Florentine *gelaterie,* Vivoli is a long-standing contender for the best ice cream in Italy. Pint-sized interior and even smaller portions, but flavors like the heavenly chocolate mousse make it worthwhile. Pay first and order with receipt. Cups from €1.50. Open Tu-Sa 7:30am-1am, Su 9:30am-1am. AmEx/MC/V.

▨ **Gelateria dei Neri**, V. dei Neri 20-22r (☎055 21 00 34). Watch through the window as dozens of delicious flavors are mixed right before your eyes. *Crema Giotto,* with coconut, almond, and hazelnut, is incredible. *Gelato* from €1.40, *granita* from €1.50.

Gelateria Triangolo delle Bermuda, V. Nazionale, 61r (☎055 28 74 90). *Gelato* so good, you'll never want to escape. *Crema venusiana,* a blend of hazelnut, caramel, and merengue, is absolute bliss; so are strawberry and rose sorbets. Outdoor seating area on busy V. Nazionale is a great spot for people watching, but there's an extra charge for sitting at the table. Cones from €1.60. Open daily 11am-midnight.

Carabè, V. Ricasoli, 60r (☎055 28 94 76; www.gelatocarabe.com). Enjoy pistachio, *nocciola,* and the unusual *susine* (plum). Owners Antonio and Loredana get the lemons for their lemon *gelato* from Sicily every week. The *granita* (from €2.20) is outstanding, particularly *mandorle* (almond) and *more* (blackberry). Cups from €1.70. Open daily May-Sept. 10am-midnight; Oct. and Mar.-Apr. noon-midnight.

ENOTECHE (WINE BARS)

Check out an *enoteca* to sample some of Italy's finest wines. A meal can often be made out of free side-dishes (cheeses, olives, toast and spreads, and salami).

THE REAL DEAL. *Gelato* is said to have been invented in Florence centuries ago by the Buontalenti family; you'll want to make sure you get the most authentic kind. Before shelling out €1.50 for a *piccolo cono*, assess the quality of an establishment by looking at the banana flavor: if it's bright yellow, it's from a mix—keep walking. If it's slightly gray, real bananas were used. Metal bins also signify homemade *gelato*, whereas plastic tubs indicate mass-production. Most *gelaterie* also serve *granite*, flavored ices that are easier on the waistline. *—Jen Rugani*

Enoteca Alessi, V. dell' Oche, 27/29r (☎055 21 49 66; fax 055 23 96 987), 1 block from the *duomo*. Among Florence's finest, stocking over 1000 wines in the cavernous interior. Doubling as a chocolate and candy store, it offers nibbles between sips. Cool, spacious, and high-ceilinged. Open M-F 9am-1pm and 4-8pm. AmEx/MC/V. ❷

Enoteca Fuori Porta, V. Monte alle Croce, 10r (☎055 23 42 483; www.fuoriporta.it), in the shadows of S. Miniato. This more casual *enoteca* is free of tourists but crowded with young Italians. Reasonable meals of traditional Tuscan pasta, with an extensive *bruschetta* and *crostino* menu. On the way down from Piazzale Michelangelo, it's a great alternative to the expensive hilltop cafes. Open M-Sa 10am-2pm and 5-10pm. ❷

SIGHTS

With the views from Brunelleschi's dome, the perfection of San Spirito's nave and the overwhelming array of art in the Uffizi Galleries, it's hard to take a wrong turn in Florence. For comprehensive listings on museum openings, check out www.firenzeturismo.it. To make phone reservations, call **Firenze Musei.** (☎055 29 48 83; www.firenzemusei.it. Open M-F 8:30am-6:30pm, Sa 8:30am-12:30pm.)

VENI, VIDI, MEDICI. Sadly, capital letters at most museums in Florence remind visitors that there are NO STUDENT DISCOUNTS. The price of a ticket should not, however, keep any visitor from seeing the best collections of Renaissance art in the world. Choose carefully and plan to spend a few hours at each landmark. Also consider investing in cheap audio tours, as their descriptions provide a valuable context for understanding the works and most labels are written solely in Italian. Additionally, many of Florence's churches are free treasuretroves of great art. In the summer, inquire at the tourist office about Sere al Museo, evenings when certain museums are free 8:30-11pm.

PIAZZA DEL DUOMO AND ENVIRONS

■**THE DUOMO (CATTEDRALE DI SANTA MARIA DEL FIORE).** In 1296 the city fathers commissioned Arnolfo di Cambio to erect a cathedral so magnificent that it would be "impossible to make it either better or more beautiful with the industry and power of man." Arnolfo succeeded, completing the massive but domeless nave by 1418. Finally, Filippo Brunelleschi, after studying Classical methods of sculpture, devised the ingenious techniques needed to construct a dome large enough for the nave. For the *duomo's* sublime crown, now known simply as **Brunelleschi's Dome,** the architect designed a revolutionary doubleshelled structure that incorporated self-supporting, interlocking bricks. During construction, Brunelleschi, an obsessive task-master, built kitchens, sleeping rooms, and lavatories between the two walls of the cupola so the masons would never have to descend. The **Museo dell'Opera del Duomo** (p. 435) chronicles Brunelleschi's engineering feats in an in-depth exhibit. A 16th-century Medici rebuilding campaign removed the *duomo's* incomplete Gothic-Renaissance facade. The walls remained naked until 1871, when Florentine architect Emilio de Fabris won the commission to create a facade in neo-Gothic style. Especially when viewed from the southern side, his beautiful green, white, and red marble walls are impressively grand.

Today, the *duomo* claims the world's 3rd-longest nave after St. Peter's in Rome and St. Paul's in London. It rises 100m into the air, making it as high as the hills surrounding Florence and visible from nearly every corner of the city. Though ornately decorated on the outside, the church's interior is rather chilly and stark, with unadorned dark stone left mostly bare, and aimed at encouraging devotion through modesty. One notable exception to this sober style is the extravagant frescoes on the ceiling of the dome, where visions of the apocalypse glare down at visitors in a stunning display of color and light. Notice, too, Paolo Uccello's celebrated *trompe l'oeil* monument to the mercenary captain Sir John Hawkwood on the cathedral's left wall, and his *orologio* (clock) on the back wall. The clock doesn't give the time of day, however; this 24hr. timepiece runs backward, starting its cycle at sunset, when the *Ave Maria* is traditionally sung. *(Duomo open M-Sa 10am-4:45pm, Su 1:30-4:45pm; 1st Sa of the month 10am-3:30pm. Shortest wait at 10am and just before closing. Mass daily 7am, 12:30pm, and 5-7pm. Ask inside the entrance, to the left, about free guided tours in English.)* Climb the 463 steps inside the dome to Michelangelo's lantern for an expansive view of the city from the external gallery. Halfway up, visitors can enjoy a great view of the dome's frescoed interior just inches from their faces. *(Entrance on southern side of the duomo. ☎ 055 230 28 85. Open M-F 8:30am-7pm, Sa 8:30am-5:40pm. €6.)*

▧ ORSANMICHELE. Built in 1337 as a granary, the Orsanmichele was converted into a church after a great fire convinced city officials to move grain operations outside the city walls. The *loggia* structure and ancient grain chutes are still visible from the outside. Secular and spiritual concerns mingle in the statues along the facade. Within the numerous small niches, the patient searcher will find Ghiberti's *St. John the Baptist* and *St. Stephen*, Donatello's *St. Peter* and *St. Mark*, and Giambologna's *St. Luke*. Inside, a Gothic tabernacle designed by Andrea Orcagna encases Bernardo Daddi's miraculous *Virgin*, an intricately wrought, expressive marble statue of Mary at her most beatific. The top floor occasionally hosts special exhibits. Across the street, the **Museo di Orsanmichele** exhibits numerous paintings and sculptures from the original church. *(V. Arte della Lana, between the duomo and P. della Signoria. ☎ 055 28 49 44 for church and museum. Church open daily 9am-noon and 4-6pm. Museum open daily 9am-noon. Both closed 1st and last M of the month. Free.)*

BATTISTERO. Though built between the 5th and 9th centuries, in Dante's time the octagonal baptistry was believed to have originally been a Roman temple. The building's exterior has the same green- and white-marble patterning as the *duomo*, and the interior contains magnificent 13th-century Byzantine-style mosaics. Dante was christened here and later drew upon the murals of damnation as inspiration for *Inferno*. Florentine artists competed fiercely for the commission to execute the famous **bronze doors,** which depict scenes from the Bible in exquisite detail. In 1330 Andrea Pisano left Pisa to cast the first set of doors, which now guard the southern entrance (toward the river). In 1401 the cloth guild announced a competition to choose an artist for the remaining two sets. Two young artists, Brunelleschi (then 23 years old) and Ghiberti (then 20), were asked to work in partnership to enter the competition, but the uncompromising Brunelleschi left in an arrogant huff, allowing Ghiberti to complete the project alone. Their separate entries into the competition are displayed side by side in the Bargello. Ghiberti's project, completed in 1425, was so admired that he immediately received the commission to forge the final set of doors. The ⬛**Gates of Paradise,** as Michelangelo reportedly called them, are nothing like Pisano's earlier portals. Originally intended for the northern side, they so impressed the Florentines that they were placed in their current position facing the cathedral. Best admired in the morning or late evening after the tourist crowds have thinned, the doors are truly a masterpiece, and each individual panel is a work of art in itself. *(Opposite the duomo. Open M-Sa noon-7pm, Su 8:30am-2pm. Mass M-F 10:30am and 11:30am. €3. Audioguide €2.)*

CAMPANILE. Also called "Giotto's Tower," the 82m bell tower next to the *duomo* has a marble exterior that matches its neighboring monuments. Three great Renaissance minds contributed to its construction: Giotto drew the design and laid the foundation in 1334, but died soon after. Andrea Pisano added two stories to the tower, and Francesco Talenti completed the construction in 1359. The original exterior decoration is now in the Museo dell'Opera del Duomo. The 414 steps to the top, somewhat steeper reveal successive views of the *duomo*, the baptistry, and the rest of the city. The best time to make the trek up the stairs is in the early morning, when there is no smog to obscure the view. *(Open daily 8:30am-6:30. €6.)*

MUSEO DELL'OPERA DEL DUOMO. Most of the *duomo's* art resides in this modern-looking and slightly less-crowded museum, including a late *Pietà* by Michelangelo, up the first flight of stairs. He started working on it in his early 70s, and the soft curves and flowing lines of the marble and limpness of Christ's body are said to reflect the artist's conception of his own mortality. Allegedly, Michelangelo severed Christ's left arm with a hammer in a fit of frustration. An over-eager apprentice touched up the work soon after, leaving visible scars on Mary Magdalene's head. Also in the collection are Donatello's wooden *St. Mary Magdalene* (1455), Donatello and Luca della Robbia's *cantorie* (choir balconies with bas-reliefs of cavorting children), and four frames from the baptistry's Gates of Paradise. A huge wall displays all of the paintings submitted by architects in the 1870 competition for the *duomo's* facade. *(P. del Duomo, 9, behind the duomo. ☎055 23 02 885. Open M-Sa 9am-6:50pm, Su 9am-1pm. €6. Audioguide €4.)*

PIAZZA DELLA SIGNORIA AND ENVIRONS

From P. del Duomo, V. dei Calzaiuoli, one of the city's oldest streets, leads to P. della Signoria. Built by the Romans, V. dei Calzaiuoli now bustles with crowds, chic shops, street vendors, and *gelaterie*.

⬛**THE UFFIZI.** Giorgio Vasari designed this palace in 1554 for Duke Cosimo and called it the Uffizi because it housed the offices (*uffizi*) of the Medici administration. An impressive walkway between the two main branches of the building, full of human statues, street performers, and vendors hawking trinkets and prints, leads from P. della Signoria to the Arno River and is surrounded every morning by a line of art-hungry tourists waiting to enter the museum. Beautiful statues overlook the walkway from niches in the columns; play spot-the-Renaissance-man and try to find Leonardo, Vespucci, Machiavelli, and Petrarch. To avoid disappointment inside the museum, keep in mind that a few rooms are usually closed each day and famous pieces often go on temporary loan, so not all works are always available for viewing. A sign outside the ticket office lists the rooms that are closed for the day; ask if they will reopen the next day.

Before visiting the main gallery on the 2nd floor, stop to see the exhibits of the **Cabinet of Drawings and Prints** on the first floor to the left. These include rare sketches by Botticelli, Leonardo, Raphael, del Sarto, and Michelangelo. Upstairs, in a U-shaped corridor, is a collection of Hellenistic and Roman marble statues. Arranged chronologically in rooms off the corridor, the collection promises a thorough education on the Florentine Renaissance, as well as a choice sampling of German and Venetian art. Framing the entrance to **Room 2** are three gold Madonnas by the great Renaissance forefathers Cimabue, Duccio di Buoninsegna, and Giotto. **Room 3** features art from 14th-century Siena, including works by the Lorenzetti brothers and Simone Martini's Annunciation. **Rooms 5** and **6** hold examples of International Gothic art, popular in European royal courts. Check out the rounded war-horses in the The Battle of San Romano, Paolo Uccello's noble but not quite successful effort to conquer the problem of perspective.

Room 7 houses two paintings by Fra Angelico (also called Beato Angelico) and a *Madonna and Child* by Masaccio. Domenico Veneziano's *Sacra Conversazione (Madonna with Child and Saints)* is one of the first paintings of Mary surrounded by the saints. Piero della Francesca's double portrait of Duke Federico and his wife Battista Sforza stands out for its translucent color and honest detail. (A jousting accident gave the Duke's nose its unusual hooked shape.) **Room 8** has Filippo Lippi's touching *Madonna and Child with Two Angels*. Works by the Pollaiolo brothers and Botticelli's *Return of Judith* occupy **Room 9.**

Rooms 10-14 are a shrine to Botticelli—the resplendent *Primavera, Birth of Venus, Madonna della Melagrana,* and *Pallas and the Centaur* glow from recent restorations. **Room 15** moves into the High Renaissance with Leonardo Da Vinci's *Annunciation* and the remarkable, unfinished *Adoration of the Magi.* **Room 18,** the tribune designed by Buontalenti to hold the Medici treasures, has a mother-of-pearl dome and a collection of portraits, most notably Bronzino's *Bia de' Medici,* Vasari's *Lorenzo il Magnifico,* and del Sarto's *Woman with the Petrarchino.* Also note Rosso Fiorentino's oft-duplicated *Musician Angel.* **Room 19** features Piero della Francesca's students Perugino and Signorelli. **Rooms 20** and **22** detour into Northern European art. Note the contrast between Albrecht Dürer's life-like *Adam and Eve* and Lucas Cranach's haunting, more surreal treatment of the same subject Bellini's *Sacred Allegory* and Mantegna's *Adoration of the Magi* highlight **Room 23.**

Room 25 showcases Florentine works, including Michelangelo's only oil painting in Florence, *Doni Tondo.* Raphael's *Madonna of the Goldfinch* and Andrea del Sarto's *Madonna of the Harpies* rest in **Room 26. Room 28** displays Titian's erotic and inviting *Venus of Urbino.* Parmigianino's eerily lovely and regal *Madonna of the Long Neck,* now in **Room 29,** was discovered unfinished in the artist's studio following his death. Works by Paolo Veronese and Tintoretto dominate **Rooms 31** and **32. Room 33,** in fact a corridor, holds Vasari's *Vulcan's Forge* and an El Greco. The staircase vestibule **(Rooms 36-40)** contains a Roman marble boar, inspiration for the brass Porcellino in Florence's New Market. **Rooms 41** and **43-45** house many works by Rembrandt, Goya, Rubens, and Caravaggio, currently on display after lengthy restorations. Vasari's designs included a secret corridor running between the Palazzo Vecchio and the Medici's Palazzo Pitti. The corridor runs through the Uffizi and over the Ponte Vecchio, housing more art, including a special collection of artists' self-portraits. The corridor is opened sporadically and requires both separate entrance fee and advance booking. *(From P. B. S. Giovanni, go down V. Roma past P. della Repubblica, where the street turns into V. Calimala. Continue until V. Vacchereccia and turn left. The Uffizi is straight ahead. ☎055 23 88 651. Open Tu-Su 8:15am-6:35pm. €8.50. Save hours of waiting by reserving tickets in advance for €3 extra. Pick up reserved tickets at Door 1 before entering at Door 3 on the other side of the walkway. Audioguide €4.65.)*

▧ **PALAZZO VECCHIO.** Arnolfo del Cambio designed this fortress-like *palazzo,* built between 1299 and 1304 as the seat of the *comune's* government. The massive brown stone facade has a thin square tower rising from its center and turrets along the top. Its apartments once served as living quarters for members of the *signoria* (city council) during their two-month terms, when they prayed, ate, and lived together in complete isolation from the outside world. The building later became the Medici family home, and in 1470, Michelozzo decorated the **courtyard**, now open to the public at no cost. He filled it with religious frescoes and placed ornate stone pediments over every door and window. The courtyard also has stone lions and a copy of Verrocchio's 15th-century *Putto* fountain. Once inside the palace, visitors can take advantage of numerous tour opportunities. The worthwhile Activities Tour ticket includes both the "Secret Routes" and "Invitation to Court" tours. "Secret Routes" fulfills Clue®-fans' fantasies of hidden passages with visits to stairwells tucked in walls behind beautiful oil paintings, an area between the ornate ceiling and the roof of the Salone, and the private chambers of Duke Cosimo I de' Medici. "Invitation to Court" includes reenactments of Medici court life, complete with a tour guide playing Cosimo's wife, Eleonora di Toledo, decked out in Renaissance finery. "The Encounter with Giorgio Vasari" tours through the **Monumental Apartments** with a guide playing the part of Vasari, Duke Cosimo I de' Medici's court painter and architect and a biographer of Renaissance artists. The Monumental Apartments, which house the *palazzo's* extensive art collections, are accessible both by tour and as a museum. The rooms contain 12 interactive terminals with virtual tours of the building's history and detailed computer animations. (☎055 27 68 224 or 055 27 68 558; www.museoragazzi.it. Office open daily 9am-7pm. Tours daily in English and French. 20-person group max. Reservation recommended. "Monumental Apartments" tour €6, ages 18-25 €4.50; Activities Tour €8/5.50.)

The city commissioned Michelangelo and Leonardo Da Vinci to paint opposite walls of the **Salone del Cinquecento,** the meeting room of the Grand Council of the Republic. Although they never completed the frescoes, their preliminary sketches for the *Battle of Cascina* and the *Battle of Anghiari*, both powerful depictions of humans and horses in strenuous motion, were studied by Florentine artists for years. The Salone's ceiling is so elaborately decorated with mouldings and frescoes that the walls can hardly support its weight; an intricate network of beams between the ceiling and roof suspend each wall painting. The tiny **Studio di Francesco I,** built by Vasari, is a treasure trove of Mannerist art, with paintings by Bronzino and Vasari as well as bronze statuettes by Giambologna and Ammannati. The Mezzanino houses some of the *palazzo's* best art, including Bronzino's portrait of the poet Laura Battiferi and Giambologna's *Hercules and the Hydra*. (☎055 27 68 465. Open M-W and F-Sa 9am-7pm, Su 9am-1pm. Palazzo vecchio €6, ages 18-25 €4.50; courtyard free. Cumulative ticket with Cappella Brancacci and Palazzo Vecchio €8/6.)

PIAZZA DELLA SIGNORIA. With the turreted Palazzo Vecchio to the west and a corner of the Uffizi Gallery to the south, this 13th-century *piazza* is now one of the most touristed areas in the city. The space fills daily with photo-snapping onlookers who return after the sun goes down for drinks and dessert at one of the many upscale cafes that line the sides of the square. The *piazza* indirectly came into existence because of the struggle between Guelph and Ghibelline factions, when the Guelphs destroyed many Ghibelline homes in the 13th century and created a gaping open space in the middle of the city. With the construction of the Palazzo Vecchio, the square blossomed into Florence's civic and political center. In 1497, religious zealot Girolamo Savonarola convinced Florentines to light the Bonfire of the Vanities in the *piazza*, barbecueing some of Florence's best art, including, legend has it, all of Botticelli's secular works held in public collections. A year later, disillusioned citizens sent Savonarola up in smoke on the same spot, marked today by a comparatively discreet commemorative disc near the fountain of Neptune. Monumental sculptures cluster around the Palazzo Vecchio, including Donatello's *Judith and Holofernes*, a copy of Michelangelo's *David*, Giambologna's equestrian *Cosimo I*, and Bandinelli's *Hercules*. The awkward *Neptune*, to the left of the Palazzo Vecchio, so revolted Michelangelo that he decried the artist: "Oh, Ammannato, Ammannato, what lovely marble you have ruined!" Apparently, most *Fiorentini* share his opinion. Called *Il Biancone* (The Big White One) in derision, *Neptune* is regularly subject to attacks of vandalism by angry aesthetes. The 14th-century stone Loggia dei Lanzi, adjacent to the Palazzo, originally built as a stage for civic orators, is now one of the best places in Florence to see world-class sculpture for free. Indeed, as a sign near the entrance proclaims, the towering works of marble are "on par with the gallery in the Uffizi."

THE PONTE VECCHIO. Built in 1345, this is indeed the oldest bridge in Florence. In the 1500s, butchers and tanners lined the bridge and dumped pig's blood and intestines in the river, creating an odor that, not surprisingly, offended the powerful bankers as they crossed the Arno on their way to their offices. In an effort to improve the area, the Medici clan kicked out the lower-class shopkeepers, and the more decorous goldsmiths and diamond-carvers moved in. Today, their descendants line the street in medieval-looking boutiques, and the bridge glitters with rows of the most chic Florentine necklaces, brooches, and charms. While technically open to vehicles, it is chiefly tourists and street musicians who swamp the roadway. The Ponte Vecchio was the only Florentine bridge to escape German bombs during WWII. A German commander who led his retreating army across the river in 1944 couldn't bear to destroy it, choosing instead to make it impassable by toppling nearby buildings. From the neighboring **Ponte alle Grazie,** the heart-melting sunset ▨view of the Ponte Vecchio, with its glowing buildings and the shimmering Arno running beneath, is more beautiful than even the finest piece of the gold that has made the bridge so famous. *(Toward P. Santa Croce. From the Uffizi, turn left on V. Georgofili and right at the river.)*

THE BARGELLO AND ENVIRONS

▨**BARGELLO.** In the heart of medieval Florence, this dour 13th-century brick fortress was once the residence of Florence's chief magistrate. Later it became a brutal prison with public executions held in its courtyard. In the 19th century, the Bargello's one-time elegance was restored, and it now gracefully hosts the spectacular yet largely untouristed **Museo Nazionale,** an underappreciated treasury of Florentine sculpture. From the outside, the Bargello looks like a three-story fortress, but the arched windows of the inner courtyard offer glimpses of refined, sculpture-lined colonnades. On the 2nd floor and to the right is the spacious, high-ceilinged **Salone di Donatello,** which contains Donatello's bronze *David*, the first free-standing nude since antiquity. David's playful expression and youthful posture provide quite the contrast to Michelangelo's determined figure of chiseled perfection in the Accademia. (Donatello's earlier marble *David*, fully clothed and somewhat generic, stands near the left wall.) On the right are two beautiful bronze panels of the *Sacrifice of Isaac* submitted by Ghiberti and Brunelleschi to the baptistry door competition (p. 434). The next floor contains some dramatic works by Andrea del Verrochio, teacher of Leonardo Da Vinci, as well as a vast collection of small bronzes and coins. Dominating the ground floor are some of Michelangelo's early works, including a debauched *Bacchus*, an intense bust of *Brutus*, and an unfinished *Apollo*. Baccio Bandinelli's *Adam and Eve*, in the same room, seem to have been captured by a snapshot in a moment of relaxed conversation. The spacious courtyard is filled with plaques of dozens of noble Florentine families' coats of arms. *(V. del Proconsolo, 4, between the duomo and P. della Signoria.* ☎ *055 23 88 606. Open daily 8:15am-1:50pm; closed 2nd and 4th M of the month. Hours and closing days vary by month. €4. Audioguide €3.80.)*

BADIA. This was the site of medieval Florence's richest monastery. Buried in the interior of a residential block, a quiet respite from the busy streets, the church's simple facade belies the treasures within. Filippino Lippi's stunning *Apparition* *of the Virgin to St. Bernard*, one of the most appreciated paintings of the late-15th century, hangs in eerie gloom to the left of the church. Note the beautiful frescoes and Corinthian pilasters, and be sure to glance up at the intricately carved dark wood ceiling. Visitors are asked to walk silently among the prostrate, white-robed worshippers. *(Entrance on V. Dante Alighieri, off V. Proconsolo. ☎055 26 44 02. Officially open to tourists M 3-6pm, but respectful visitors can walk through the church at any time.)*

MUSEO DI STORIA DELLA SCIENZA. This impressive and unique collection is well worth a visit between jolts of Botticelli. It boasts scientific instruments from the Renaissance, including telescopes, astrological models, clock workings, and wax models of anatomy and childbirth. The stellar **Room 4** displays a number of Galileo's tools, including his embalmed middle finger and the objective lens through which he first observed the satellites of Jupiter in 1610. Detailed English guides are available at the ticket office. *(P. dei Giudici, 1, behind Palazzo Vecchio and the Uffizi. ☎055 26 53 11. Open M and W-F 9:30am-5pm, Tu and Sa 9:30am-1pm; Oct.-May also open 2nd Su of each month 10am-1pm. €6.50, under 18 €4.)*

CASA DI DANTE. This residence is reputedly identical to the house Dante inhabited. Anyone who can read Italian and has an abiding fascination with Dante will enjoy the displays, which trace the poet's life from youth to exile and pays homage to the artistic creation that immortalized him. Check out Giotto's early but representative portrait of Dante on the 3rd floor. Nearby is a facsimile of the abandoned and melancholy little church where Beatrice, Dante's unrequited love and spiritual guide in *Paradiso*, attended mass. *(Corner of V. Dante Alighieri and V. S. Margherita within 1 block of the Bargello. ☎055 21 94 16. Ring bell to enter. All captions in Italian. Open M and W-Sa 10am-5pm, Su 10am-2pm. €3, groups over 15 €2 per person.)*

PIAZZA DELLA REPUBBLICA AND FARTHER WEST

After hours of contemplating great Florentine art, visit the area that financed it all. In the early 1420s, 72 banks operated in Florence, most in the area around the Mercato Nuovo and V. Tornabuoni. With a lower concentration of famous sights, this area is more residential and commercial, though still crowded with visitors. Surrounding cafes and stores are often overpriced.

■**CHIESA DI SANTA MARIA NOVELLA.** The wealthiest merchants built their chapels in this church. Constructed between 1279 and 1360, the Dominican *chiesa* boasts a Romanesque-Gothic facade considered one of the greatest masterpieces of early Renaissance architecture. The facade, made of Florentine marble, is geometrically pure and balanced, a precursor to the Classical revival of the high Renaissance. The church was originally a home to Dominican friars, or *Domini canes* (Hounds of the Lord), who took a bite out of sin and corruption. Thirteenth-century frescoes covered the interior until the Medici family commissioned Vasari to paint new ones. Fortunately, Vasari spared Masaccio's powerful ■**Trinity,** the first painting to use geometric perspective. This fresco, on the left side of the nave, creates the illusion of a three-dimensional tabernacle. The **Cappella di Filippo Strozzi,** to the right of the high altar, contains cartoon-like frescoes by Filippo Lippi, including a green Adam, a woolly Abraham, and an excruciating *Torture of St. John the Evangelist.* Brunelleschi's *Crucifix* stands in the **Gondi Chapel** as a response to Donatello's *Crucifix* in Santa Croce, which Brunelleschi found to be too full of "vigorous naturalism." Supposedly, Donatello had just finished grocery shopping when Brunelleschi unveiled his work; upon the unveiling, Donatello, in admiration and awe, dropped his bag of eggs on Brunelleschi's kitchen floor. A cycle of Ghirlandaio frescoes covers the **Tournabuoni Chapel** behind the main altar. *(☎055 21 59 18. Open M-Th and Sa 9am-5pm, F and Su 1-5pm. €2.50, ages 13-18 €1.50.)*

PIAZZA DELLA REPUBBLICA. The largest open space in Florence, this *piazza* teems with crowds and street performers in the evenings. An enormous arch filling in the gap over V. Strozzi marks the western edge of the square. The rest of the *piazza* is lined with overpriced cafes, restaurants, and *gelaterie*. In 1890 the *piazza* replaced the Mercato Vecchio as the site of the city market, but has since traded market stalls for the more fashionable Guess and Pucci. The inscription *"Antico centro della città, da secolare squalore, a vita nuova restituito"*—the "ancient center of the city, squalid for centuries, restored to new life"— makes a derogatory reference to the fact that the *piazza* is the site of the old Jewish ghetto. When the "liberation of the Jews" of Italy in the 1860s allowed Jews to live elsewhere, the ghetto slowly diminished. An ill-advised plan to demolish the city center's historical buildings and remodel Florence caused the destruction of the Old Market, but an international campaign successfully thwarted the razing, leaving the present-day gathering space as a vibrant center for city life.

CHIESA DI SANTA TRINITÀ. Hoping to spend eternity as they had lived—in elite company—the most fashionable *palazzo* owners commissioned family chapels in this church. The facade, designed by Bernardo Buontalenti in the 16th century, is almost Baroque in its elaborate ornamentation, and is an exquisite example of late-Renaissance architecture. Scenes from Ghirlandaio's *Life of St. Francis* decorate the **Sassetti chapel** in the right arm of the transept. The famous altarpiece, Ghirlandaio's *Adoration of the Shepherds*, is in the Uffizi. The one here is a convincing copy. *(In P. S. Trinità. ☎055 21 69 12. Open M-Sa 8am-noon and 4-6pm, Su 4-6pm.)*

MERCATO NUOVO. Under their Corinthian-columned splendor, the *loggie* of the New Market have housed gold and silk traders since 1547. Today, the occasional piece of gold makes an appearance among the more prominent vendors selling imitation designer purses, belts, and clothes. Pietro Tacca's pleasantly plump statue, *Il Porcellino* (The Little Pig; actually a wild boar) appeared some 50 years after the market opened. Rubbing its snout is reputed to bring good luck, but it won't turn the purse you buy into real leather. *(Off V. Calimala, between P. della Repubblica and the Ponte Vecchio. Vendors hawk wares from dawn-dusk.)*

PALAZZO DAVANZATI. As Florence's 15th-century economy expanded, its bankers and merchants flaunted their new wealth by erecting grand edifices. The great *quattrocento* boom began with construction of the Palazzo Davanzati. Today, the cavern-like *palazzo* finds life as the Museo della Casa Fiorentina Antica. Though the interior of the building has been closed since 1995, the courtyard is adorned with antique furniture, restored frescoes, and wooden doors and ornaments, giving visitors a small glimpse of the 15th-century merchants' luxury. *(V. Porta Rossa, 13. ☎055 23 88 610. Open daily 8:30am-1:50pm. Closed 1st, 3rd, and 5th M and 2nd and 4th Su of the month. Video screenings about the Palazzo 10, 11am, and noon, on 4th fl. Free.)*

SAN LORENZO AND FARTHER NORTH

ACCADEMIA. It doesn't matter how many pictures you've seen of him—when you come around the corner and see Michelangelo's triumphant ■**David,** towering in self-assured perfection under the rotunda designed just for him, you will be blown away. From 5 ft. away, Michelangelo's painstaking attention to details, like the veins in David's hands and at the back of his knees, bring the statue to life, and the sheer size of the work gives new appreciation to the genius of Michelangelo's skill with stone. In a series of unfortunate events, the statue's base was struck by lightning in 1512, damaged by anti-Medici riots in 1527, and was finally moved here from P. della Signoria in 1873 after a stone hurled during a riot broke David's left wrist in two places. If this real *David* seems a bit different from the copy in front of the Palazzo Vecchio, there's a reason: Michelangelo exaggerated his head and torso to correct for distortion from viewing far below; the statue here stands on a higher pedestal and appears a bit less top-heavy. In the hallway leading up to the *David* are Michelangelo's four ▒**Slaves** and a *Pietà*. The master left these statues intentionally unfinished—chipping away only enough to show the figures emerging from the marble, he remained true to his theories about "releasing" his figures from the living stone. Also worth a look are Botticelli's Madonna paintings as well as works by Uccello. Two panel paintings, Lippi's *Deposition* and Perugino's *Assumption*, sit in the room just before the rotunda. The Serviti, who commissioned the two-sided panel, disliked Perugino's depiction so much that they only displayed Lippi's portion in their church. An impressive collection of Gothic triptychs lurks on the second floor in **Room 2**. *(V. Ricasoli, 60, between the churches of San Marco and S. S. Annunziata. Line for entrance without a reservation begins at V. Ricasoli, 58. ☎055 29 48 83. Most areas wheelchair accessible. Open Tu-Su 8:15am-6:50pm. €8.)*

BASILICA DI SAN LORENZO. In 1419 Brunelleschi designed this spacious basilica, another Florentine example of early-Renaissance simple lines and proportion. Because the Medicis lent the funds to build the church, they retained artistic control over its construction. Their coat of arms, featuring five red balls, appears all over the nave, and their tombs occupy the two sacristies and the Cappella dei Principi (see below) behind the altar. The family cunningly placed Cosimo dei Medici's grave in front of the high altar, making the entire church his personal mausoleum. Donatello created two **pulpits**, one for each aisle; his *Martelli Sarcophagus* (in the left transept) takes the form of a wicker basket woven in marble. Michelangelo designed the church's exterior, but disgusted by the murkiness of Florentine politics, he abandoned the project to study architecture in Rome, which accounts for the basilica's still unadorned brown stone facade. *(Open M-Sa 10am-5pm. €2.50.)*

The **Cappelle dei Medici** (Medici Chapels) consist of dual design contributions by Matteo Nigetti and Michelangelo. Intended as a grand mausoleum, Nigetti's **Cappella dei Principi** (Princes' Chapel) emulates the baptistry in P. del Duomo. Except for the gilded portraits of the Medici dukes, the decor is a rare glimpse of the Baroque in Florence. Michelangelo created and sculpted the entire **New Sacristy**—architecture, tombs, and statues—in a mature, considered style that reflects his study of Brunelleschi. Designed to house the bodies of four of the Medici family, the room contains two impressive tombs for Medici dukes Lorenzo and Giuliano. Lounging on the tomb of the military-minded Lorenzo are the smooth, minutely rendered female *Night* and the muscle-bound male *Day*, both left provocatively "unfinished." Michelangelo rendered the hazier *Dawn* and *Dusk* with more androgynous figures for the milder-mannered Giuliano's tomb, which is closer to the entrance. Some of the artist's sketches are in the basement. *(Walk around to the back entrance in P. Madonna degli Aldobrandini. ☎055 23 88 602. Open daily 8:15am-5pm; closed 1st, 3rd, and 5th M of the month and 2nd and 4th Su. €6.)* The adjacent **Laurentian Library** houses one of the world's most valuable manuscript collections. Michelangelo's famous entrance portico confirms his virtuosity; the *pietra serena* sandstone staircase is one of his most innovative architectural designs. *(☎055 21 07 60. Open daily 8:30am-1:30pm. Free with entrance to San Lorenzo.)*

MUSEO DELLA CHIESA DI SAN MARCO. Remarkable works by Fra Angelico adorn the Museo della Chiesa di San Marco, one of the most peaceful and spiritual places in Florence. A large room to the right of the courtyard contains some of the painter's major works. The 2nd floor houses Angelico's most famous *Annunciation*, across from the top of the stairwell, as well as the monks' quarters. Every cell in the convent contains its own Fra Angelico fresco, each painted in flat colors and with sparse detail to facilitate the monks' somber meditation. To the right of the stairwell Michelozzo's library, based on Michelangelo's work in S. Lorenzo, is a simple space for reflection. In Cells 17 and 22, underground artwork peeks through a glass floor, excavated from the medieval period. Look also for Savonarola's cell, which displays some of his relics. On the way out, the **Museo di Firenze Antica** of Florence's ancient roots is worth a quick visit. These two rooms showcase numerous archaeological fragments, mostly pieces of stone work from Etruscan and Roman buildings in the area. Be sure to peek in to the church itself, next door to the museum, to admire the elaborate altar and vaulted ceiling. *(Enter at P. di San Marco, 3.* ☎ *055 23 88 608 or 055 23 88 704. Open M-F 8:15am-1:50pm, Sa 8:15am-6:50pm, Su 8:15am-7pm. Closed 2nd and 4th M and 1st, 3rd, and 5th Su of the month. €4, EU citizens 18-25 €2, over 65 or under 18 free. English guides available near the entrance.)*

PALAZZO MEDICI RICCARDI. The palace's facade is the work of Michelozzo. This stands as the archetype for all Renaissance palaces. The private chapel inside features Benozzo Gozzoli's beautiful, wrap-around fresco of the **Three Magi** and several Medici family portraits. The *palazzo* hosts rotating exhibits ranging from Renaissance architectural sketches to Fellini memorabilia. *(V. Cavour, 3.* ☎ *055 27 60 340. Open M-Tu and Th-Su 9am-7pm. €4, children €2.50.)*

MUSEO ARCHEOLOGICO. Unassuming behind its bland plaster facade, the archaeological museum has a surprisingly diverse collection. Its rooms teem with collections of statues and other monuments of the ancient Greeks, Etruscans, and Egyptians. A long, two-story gallery devoted to Etruscan jewelry runs the length of the plant-filled courtyard. In almost any other city in the world, this museum would be a major cultural highlight, but in Florence, it's possible to enjoy it without large crowds. Don't miss the *Chimera d'Arezzo* in **Room 14.** *(V. della Colonna, 38.* ☎ *055 23 575. Open M 2-7pm, Tu and Th 8:30am-7pm, W and F-Su 8:30am-2pm. €4.)*

PIAZZA SANTA CROCE AND ENVIRONS

▓**CHIESA DI SANTA CROCE.** The Franciscans built this church as far as possible from their Dominican rivals at S. Maria Novella. Started in 1210 as a small oratory, the ascetic Franciscans ironically produced what is arguably the most splendid church in the city, with a unique Egyptian cross layout. Breathtaking marble sculptures adorn the grand tombs of the luminaries of Florence past on both sides of the main aisle, frozen in expressions of grief and mourning. The Renaissance greats buried here include Michelangelo, who rests near the beginning of the right aisle (his tomb is by Vasari, but his body is actually buried in the floor slightly to the left); Galileo, directly opposite in the left aisle; and Machiavelli, farther down and on the right. Donatello's *Crucifix*, which so agitated Brunelleschi, is in the Vernio Chapel of the left transept under heavy scaffolding; the artist's gilded *Annunciation* is to the right of humanist Leonardo Bruni's tomb. The Florentines, who banished Dante, eventually prepared a tomb for him here. Dante died in Ravenna, however, and the literary necrophiles there never sent him back. To the right of the altar, the frescoes of the **Cappella Peruzzi** vie with those of the **Cappella Bardi.** Giotto and his school painted both, but unfortunately, the works are badly faded. While wandering through the church, note the water mark about 8ft. up on the walls and pillars, an enduring reminder of the 1966 flood. *(*☎ *055 24 46 19. Open Mar. 15-Nov. 15 M-Sa 9:30am-5:30pm, Su and holidays 1-5:30pm; Nov. 16-Mar. 14 M-Sa 9am-5:30pm, Su and holidays 3-5:30pm. €4, under 18 €2.)*

The **Museo dell'Opera di Santa Croce,** which forms three sides of a peaceful courtyard, is accessible through a door from the right aisle of the church. At the end of the cloister next to the church is Brunelleschi's ▓**Cappella Pazzi,** a humble marvel of perfect proportions. Its decorations include Luca della Robbia's *tondi* of the apostles and Brunelleschi's moldings of the evangelists. Across the courtyard down a gravel path, a former dining hall contains Taddeo Gaddi's fresco *The Tree of the Cross* and his *Last Supper*. Also in the room is Cimabue's *Crucifixion*, left in a tragic state by the 1966 flood. *(Enter through the loggia in front of Cappella Pazzi. Hours same as church. Free with entrance to church.)*

SYNAGOGUE OF FLORENCE. This synagogue, also known as the **Museo del Tempio Israelitico,** sits behind a hefty iron gate and is resplendent with Sephardic domes and horseshoe arches. David Levi, a wealthy Florentine Jewish businessman, donated his fortune in 1870 for the construction of "a monumental temple worthy of Florence," in recognition of the fact that Jews were newly allowed to live and worship outside the old Jewish ghetto. Architects Micheli, Falchi, and Treves created one of Europe's most beautiful synagogues. (*V. Farini, 4, at V. Pilastri.* ☎ *055 24 52 52 or 055 24 52 53. Open M-Th and Su 10am-6pm, F 10am-2pm. €4, students €3. The museum includes free, informative tours every hr.; book in advance.*)

CASA BUONARROTI. This little museum houses Michelangelo memorabilia and two of his most important early works, *The Madonna of the Steps* and *The Battle of the Centaurs.* Both pieces on the 2nd-floor. He completed these panels, which illustrate his growth from bas-relief to sculpture, when he was 16. Some of his rare sketches are on rotating display. (*V. Ghibellina, 70.* ☎ *055 25 17 52. From P. S. Croce, follow V. dei Pepi and turn right on V. Ghibellina. Open daily 9:30am-4pm. €6.50, students €4.*)

IN THE OLTRARNO

The far side of the Arno is a lively, unpretentious quarter filled with students and young people that grants a small reprieve from the tourist throngs. Though you'll likely cross over the Ponte Vecchio on the way to the Oltrarno, consider coming back along V. Maggio, a street lined with Renaissance palaces, many of which have markers with historical descriptions. Head over the Ponte S. Trinità, which affords excellent views of the Ponte Vecchio, or dally a bit in P. San Spirito, which thrives with markets in the day and street artists at night.

▓ **PALAZZO PITTI.** Luca Pitti, a 15th-century banker, built his *palazzo* east of S. Spirito against the Boboli hill. The Medici family acquired the *palazzo* and the hill in 1550 and enlarged everything they could. During Italy's brief experiment with monarchy, the structure served as a royal residence. Today, the **Palazzo Pitti** is fronted with a vast uninhabited *piazza* and houses a gallery and four museums, providing enough diversions for a lengthy and unhurried visit. (*Ticket office is on the right before the Palazzo.* ☎ *055 29 48 83. Cumulative 3-day ticket €12.50.*) The ▓**Galleria Palatina** was one of only a few public galleries when it opened in 1833. Today, it houses Florence's second-most important collection (after the Uffizi). Its artistic smorgasbord includes works by Botticelli, Tintoretto, Veronese, Velasquez, Titian, Perugino, del Sarto, Raphael, Vasari, Canova, Caravaggio, and Rubens.

The **Appartamenti Reali** (Royal Apartments), at the end of the galleria house, are lavish reminders of the time when the *palazzo* served as the royal House of Savoy's living quarters and hold a few Renaissance and Baroque greats. (*Open Tu-Su 8:15am-6pm. Cumulative ticket for Palatine Gallery and Royal Apartments €8.50, EU students €4.25.*) In the **Galleria d'Arte Moderna** lies one of Italian art history's big surprises, the early 19th-century proto-Impressionist works of the Macchiaioli group. The collection also includes Neo-Classical and Romantic pieces, like Giovanni Dupré's sculptural group *Cain and Abel.* Find out if the clothes make the Medici in the **Galleria del Costume,** a decadent display of the family's finery. (*Open daily 8:15am-1:50pm; closed 1st, 3rd, 5th M and 2nd and 4th Su of the month. Modern Art Gallery and Costume Gallery €5, EU students €2.50.*) The **Museo degli Argenti** on the ground floor exhibits the Medici family treasures, including cases of precious gems, ivories, silver pieces, and Lorenzo the Magnificent's famous collection of vases. The Salone depicts a floor-to-ceiling fresco of a blind Homer and the nine muses leaving Mount Parnassus, alluding to scholars who fled to Tuscany from Greece after the Turkish invasion of 1453.

An elaborately landscaped park, the ▓**Boboli Gardens** are an exquisite example of stylized Renaissance gardens and provide seemingly endless pathways that meander past beautifully groomed lawns. A large oval lawn sits just up the hill from the back of the palace, marked by an Egyptian obelisk and lined with a hedge dotted by marble statues. Labyrinthine avenues of cypress trees lead eager wanderers to bubbling fountains with graceful nudes. Be sure to see the fountain of a portly Bacchus, sitting astride a very strained turtle. While the gardens seem like the perfect picnic spot, visitors are unfortunately prohibited from bringing in outside food. The **Museo della Porcellana**, hidden in back of the gardens, exhibits fine ceramics from the Medici collection. *(Gardens open June-Aug. 8:15am-7:30pm; Apr.-May and Sept.-Oct. 8:15am-6:30pm; Nov.-Feb. 8:15am-4:30pm and Mar. 8:15am-5:30pm. Porcellana Museum and Silver Museum open daily 8:15am-7:30pm. Closed 2nd and 4th M and 1st, 3rd, and 5th Su of the month. Cumulative ticket for all 3 sights €6, EU students €3.)*

CHIESA DI SANTA MARIA DEL CARMINE. Inside this church, the ▨**Brancacci Chapel** holds Masaccio's stunning 15th-century frescoes, declared masterpieces in their own time. Fifty years later, a respectful Filippino Lippi completed the cycle. Masolino's *Adam and Eve* and Masaccio's pain-filled *Expulsion from Eden* stand face to face, demonstrating the latter's innovative depiction of human forms. With such monumental works as the *Tribute Money*, this chapel became a school for many later Renaissance artists, including Michelangelo himself. *(P. del Carmine, 14. Church open daily 9am-noon. Free. Chapel open M and W-Sa 10am-5pm, Su 1-5pm. €4, ages 18-25 €3, under 18 €1.50, included in cumulative Palazzo Vecchio ticket €8/6/3.)*

SAN MINIATO AL MONTE AND ENVIRONS

▧**PIAZZALE MICHELANGELO.** This is a must. With its copy of Michelangelo's *David*, Piazzale Michelangelo is the best place in all of Florence for a romantic moment. At sunset, waning light casts a warm glow over the city; views from here are even better (and certainly cheaper) than those from the top of the *duomo*. Make the challenging uphill trek at around 8:30 during the summer to arrive at the *piazza* in time for sunset. The large *piazza* doubles as a parking lot, home to hordes of tour buses on summer days, and occasionally hosts concerts as well. *(Cross Ponte Vecchio and turn left, walk through the piazza, and turn right on V. de' Bardi. Follow it uphill as it becomes V. del Monte alle Croci, where a staircase to the left heads to the piazzale.)*

▨**SAN MINIATO AL MONTE.** One of Florence's oldest churches, San Miniato gloriously surveys all of Florence. Its inlaid marble facade and 13th-century mosaics provide a prelude to the incredible floor inside, patterned with lions, doves, and astrological signs. Inside, the **Chapel of the Cardinal of Portugal** holds a collection of superlative della Robbia terra cottas. The cemetery is an overwhelming profusion of tombs and mausoleums. For a special treat, visit at 5:40pm, when monks perform chants inside the church. *(Take bus #13 from the station or climb stairs from Ple. Michelangelo.* ☎ *055 23 42 731. Open daily 8am-7:30pm. Free.)*

⏏ ▧ ENTERTAINMENT AND FESTIVALS

Florence disagrees with England over who invented modern soccer, but every June, the various *quartieri* turn out in costume to play their own medieval version of the sport, known as **calcio storico.** Two teams chase a wooden ball in *piazze* around the city; unsurprisingly, matches often blur the boundary between athletic contest and riot. A makeshift stadium in P. Santa Croce hosts three nights of matches in June. Check newspapers or the tourist office for the exact dates and locations of historical or modern *calcio*, and always book tickets ahead. The **stadio,** north of the center, hosts modern soccer matches. Tickets (from €10 in the bleachers to €40 in the smaller, less crowded stands along the sidelines) are sold at the **Box Office** and at **Marisa,** the bar across the street from the stadium. Take the #25 bus from the station to the **Giardini del Drago** for a pick-up game of soccer.

The most important of Florence's traditional festivals celebrates the patron saint, **San Giovanni Battista** on June 24. A tremendous fireworks display in Ple. Michelangelo starts around 10pm—grab a spot anywhere along the Arno and watch for the specially coordinated combinations of red, purple, and white fireworks in honor of Florence's newly Series-A soccer team. The summer also swings with music festivals, starting in late April with the classical **Maggio Musicale.** Take in an evening of opera or ballet with locals in the **Teatro Comunale;** ticket prices range €15-150. To avoid an obstructed view, always ask to see a seating chart before springing for the cheapest seats. The **Estate Fiesolana** (June-Aug.) fills the Roman theater in Fiesole with concerts, opera, theater, and film.

In summer, the **Europa dei Sensi** program hosts **Rime Rampanti,** nightly cultural shows with music, poetry, and food from a chosen European country. Call the information office (☎348 58 04 812; www.rimerampanti.it) for reservations. The same company also hosts **Le Pavoniere,** with live music, pool, bar, and pizzeria, in the Ippodromo delle Cascine (along the river and past the train station). Call the office (☎055 32 17 541) for info and reservations. The **Festa del Grillo** (Festival of the Cricket) is held the first Sunday after Ascension Day, which is 40 days after Easter. Crickets in wooden cages are sold in the Cascine Park to be released into the grass—Florentines believe that a cricket's song brings good luck.

▢ SHOPPING

Florentines design their window displays (and their wares) with flair. For both the budget shopper seeking a special gift and the big spender who's looking to make the splurge of a lifetime, Florence offers ample options and many temptations to drop some cash. Watch for store windows to flood with "Saldi" signs in January and July, which mark the end-of-season sales. In July and August, Florentine families rush to the beach for the weekend and nearly all stores close early on Saturday. Some close for the entire month of August.

V. Tornabuoni's swanky boutiques and well-stocked goldsmiths on the Ponte Vecchio serve a sophisticated clientele. To join this crowd, try **Vaggi,** Ponte Vecchio 2/6r and 20r. Charms start at €25, and 18k gold earrings cost €40 or more. (☎055 21 55 02. Open M-Sa 9am-7:30pm.) Florence makes its contribution to *alta moda* with a number of fashion shows, including the biannual **Pitti Uomo,** Europe's most important exhibition of menswear in January and June.

The city's artisan traditions thrive at the open markets. **San Lorenzo,** the largest, cheapest, and most touristed, sprawls for several blocks around P. S. Lorenzo. In front of the leather-shops, stands stock all kinds of goods—bags, clothes, food, toys, and flags. High prices are rare, but so are quality and honesty. (Open daily 9am-twilight.) Stands throughout the city stock the same small selection of generic t-shirts; skip these and try **T-Show,** V. Guicciardini, 15r, with two stories' worth of *Italia-* and *Firenze*-printed merchandise. Most t-shirts cost €8-15; bags are €10. (☎055 28 47 38. Open M-Sa 9:30am-7:30pm, Su 10am-7pm. MC/V.) For everything from pot-holders to parakeets, shop at the market in **Parco delle Cascine** on Tuesday morning, which begins four bridges west of the Ponte Vecchio at P. V. Veneto and stretches along the Arno River. For a flea market specializing in old furniture and postcards, visit **Piazza Ciompi,** off V. Pietrapiana from Borgo degli Albizi. (Open Tu-Sa.) Even when prices are marked, don't hesitate to bargain. As a general guideline, start with half of the price offered or at least show disinterest to get the price lowered; but never ask for a price you're not willing to pay. Brush up on your Italian shopping phrases, as vendors are more likely to lower the price for shoppers who can talk the talk. Don't bargain if paying by credit card.

Books, paper goods, and **art reproductions** make great souvenirs. **Alinari,** L. Alinari, 15, stocks the world's largest selection of art prints and high-quality photographs from €25, as well as a selection of journals and *carta fiorentina*, paper covered in intricate floral designs. (☎055 23 951. Open M-F 9am-1pm and 2:30-6:30pm, Sa 9am-1pm. AmEx/MC/V.) Epicures shouldn't miss a visit to **Gastronomia Tassini,** V. Apostoli, 24r, which offers authentic and affordable tastes of Italy. Jars of hit pasta sauces—pesto, olive, *cinghiale* (boar), and *tartufo* (truffle)—start at €2. *Let's Go* readers get a discount, as well as cooking tips and recipes from the friendly owner Giorgio and staff. All products are bubble-wrapped and vacuum-packed to travel. (☎055 28 26 96. Open M-Sa 8:30am-2pm and 4:30-7:30pm. MC/V.)

Florentine **leatherwork** is affordable and known worldwide for its high quality. Some of the best leather artisans in the city work around P. S. Croce and V. Porta S. Maria. The **Santa Croce Leather School,** in Chiesa di Santa Croce, offers first-rate products at reasonable prices, as well as the chance to observe the craftsmen making fine leather bags and jackets. (On Su, enter through V. S. Giuseppe, 5r. ☎055 24 45 33 and 055 24 79 913; www.leatherschool.it. Open Mar. 15-Nov. 15 M-Sa 9am-6:30pm, Su 10:30am-12:30pm and 3-6pm; Nov. 16-Mar. 14 M-Sa 9am-12:30pm and 3-6pm.) **NOI,** at V. delle Terme, 8, produces leather apparel of superb quality for hotshot clientele but also carries more affordable goods. (Wallets from €25; bags €60-200; jackets from €250. 10% discount with *Let's Go*.)

◧ NIGHTLIFE

For reliable info, consult the city's entertainment monthly, *Firenze Spettacolo* (€2), or the entertainment website, www.informacittafirenze.it. **Piazza Santo Spirito** in Oltrarno has live music in the summer. For clubs or bars that run late and are far from the *centro*, keep in mind that the last bus may leave before the fun winds down, and taxis are rare in the area of the most popular discos, so plan ahead and make sure you have the number of a taxi company.

BARS

May Day Lounge, V. Dante Alighieri, 16r (www.maydayclub.it). This eclectic lounge is lit by all manner of lamps and light installations and filled with quirky Italians. Play pong on the 80s gaming system or sip mixed drinks (€4.50-6.50) to a funk beat. Try the "banana cow" shot (rum, creme of banana, panna, granatina; €3). Draft beer €4.50. Happy hour 8-10pm. Th is watermelon night. Open daily 8pm-2am. AmEx/MC/V.

The Fiddler's Elbow, P. S. Maria Novella, 7r (☎055 21 50 56). Ex-pat bartenders serve cider and beer (€4.50 per pint) to crowds of convivial foreigners. Don't be surprised if impromptu rounds of karaoke arise in the wee hours. Patio overlooks P. Santa Maria Novella. Open daily M-Th and Su 3pm-1am, F-Sa 2pm-2am. AmEx/MC/V.

Eby's Latin Bar, V. dell' Oriuolo, 5r (☎338 65 08 959). Shake it to the Latin music on the palm-covered patio while waiting in line for fresh-fruit cocktails blended with seasonal ingredients. Fantastic nachos and burritos. Beer €3.50, cocktails €5.50-7. Happy-hour M-Tu 6pm-midnight, W-Sa 6-9pm. Open M-Sa noon-3pm and 6pm-3am.

Kikuya, V. Benci, 43r (☎055 23 44 879). An international blender—a Japanese name for a neighborhood Irish pub cherished by local Florentines and foreigners of all ages. Dimly lit bar room and comfortable red-cushioned benches make for lively conversations over a pint (€4.50) and a burger (€5). Open daily 7:30pm-2am. MC/V.

Slowly, V. Porta Rossa, 63r (☎055 264 53 54). Sleek room with jazzy pop sets a suave tone. The place for trendy Italian 20-somethings to see and be seen. Cocktails and long drinks worthy of applause; don't miss the popular mojito (€8). Cocktails €7-10. *Primi* €10-12. Open M-Sa 10am-2:30am. MC/V.

DISCOS

Central Park, in Parco delle Cascinè. Open-air dance floors pulse with hip-hop, reggae, and Italian "dance rock." Favored by Florentine and foreign teens and college students. Mixed drinks €8. No cover for foreign students before 12:30am, after that, the regular €11 cover is charged. Open M-Tu and Th-Sa 11pm-late, W 9pm-late. AmEx/MC/V.

Rio Grande, V. degli Olmi, 1 (☎055 33 13 71; www.rio-grande.it), near Parco delle Cascinè. This and Central Park are the most popular of Florence's discos, with Rio Grande catering to a slightly older crowd. Open-air dance floors make for wild summer nights. Special nights include soul, hip-hop, house, and reggae. Call for schedule. €16 cover includes 1 drink; each subsequent drink €7. Open Tu-Sa 11pm-4am. AmEx/MC/V.

Tabasco Gay Club, P.S. Cecilia, 3r (☎055 21 30 00), in tiny alley across P. della Signoria from Palazzo Vecchio. This dark basement club features smoke machines, strobe lights, and low-vaulted ceilings. Caters to gay men. 18+. Cover €10 before 1am, €13 after 1am, includes 1st drink. Open Tu-Su 10pm-4am. AmEx/MC/V.

◢ DAYTRIP FROM FLORENCE

FIESOLE

A 30min. bus ride from Florence. Catch the ATAF city bus #7 (€1) from the train station and exit near track #16 or P. S. Marco; it stops at P. Mino da Fiesole in the town center. The tourist office, V. Portigiani, 3 (☎055 59 87 20; www.comune.fiesole.fi.it), is next to the Teatro Romano, half a block off P. Mino da Fiesole, directly across the piazza from the bus stop. Office provides a free map with museum and sights listings. Open Mar.-Oct. M-Sa 9am-6pm, Su 10am-1pm and 2-6pm; Nov.-Feb. M-Sa 9am-5pm, Su 10am-4pm.

Fiesole is the site of the Etruscan settlement which later extended down the hill to become Florence. Fiesole has long been a welcome escape from the sweltering summer heat of the Arno Valley and a source of inspiration for famous figures: Alexander Dumas, Anatole France, Paul Klee, Marcel Proust, Gertrude Stein, and Frank Lloyd Wright all had productive sojourns here. Leonardo Da Vinci even used the town as a testing ground for his famed flying machine.

Facing away from the bus stop, walk across P. Mino da Fiesole and down V. Dupre half a block to the entrance of the **Museo Civico,** V. Portigiani, 1 (☎055 59 477). One ticket provides admission to three constituent museums. The **Teatro Romano** includes the perfectly rectangular foundations of Etruscan thermal baths and the toppled columns and sturdy archways of temple ruins. The well-preserved structure of the amphitheater is gussied up in modern sound equipment and spotlights for summer concerts. The amphitheater grounds leads into the **Museo Civico Archeologico,** housing an extensive collection of Etruscan artifacts, well-preserved Grecian urns, a reconstructed tomb with skeleton, and vases from *Magna Graecia* (present-day Southern Italy under the Greek Empire). Hop across the street to breeze through the **Museo Bandini,** V. Dupre, 1, which holds a collection of 15th-century Italian paintings. (☎055 59 477. Ruins and museums open Apr.-Oct. daily 9:30am-7:30pm; Nov.-Mar. closed Tu. €6.50, students and over 65 €4.50.) Additionally, a walk uphill from the bus stop and to the left leads to the **Convento Francesco** and **public gardens.** The climb is steep but short, and the panorama of the valley below is perhaps the only spot from which Brunelleschi's massive *duomo* appears small. The monastery contains a frescoed chapel and a tiny museum of precious Chinese pottery, jade figurines, and Egyptian artifacts including a mummy brought back by Franciscan missionaries. (☎055 59 175. Open June-Sept. Tu-F 10am-noon and 3-6pm, Sa-Su 3-6pm; Oct.-May Tu-F 10am-noon and 3-5pm, Sa-Su 3-5pm.)

Accommodations in Fiesole are expensive, but the town is a great place for lunch. Grab a bite at **Pizzeria Etrusca ❸**, in P. Mina da Fiesole, next to the bus stop. (☎055 59 94 84. Pizza €5-10. *Primi* from €5.50, *secondi* from €9. Cover €1.30. Open M-W and F-Su noon-3:30pm and 6pm-1am. AmEx/MC/V.) Take in the fantastic view of the Arno Valley over coffee (from €0..) or *gelato* (from €1.60) at **Blu Bar ❷**, P. Mino, 10. The table charge can be expensive, so enjoy your snack at the bar. (Crepes €6. Pizza €5-6. Cocktails €10. Open Apr.-Oct. daily 8am-1am; Nov.-Mar. M and W-Su 8-1am.)

SIENA ☎0577

Siena's vibrant character and local energy make it a distinctly Tuscan city. Locals are fiercely proud of their town's history, which dates back to the 13th century when the first *Sienese* crafted a sophisticated metropolis rich in wealth and culture. The city's vehement (and still palpable) rivalry with Florence resulted in grandiose Gothic architecture and soaring towers, though the arrival of the Black Death stunted much of Siena's potential for innovation. These days, the *Sienese* celebrate their heritage with festivals like the semi-annual Palio, an intoxicating display of pageantry in which jockeys race bareback horses around the central square. Situated in the heart of Tuscan wine country, Siena (pop. 50,000) also makes an ideal base for exploring the surrounding countryside. No matter which country you call home, while you're in Siena, you're Italian.

▌ TRANSPORTATION

Trains: In P. Rosselli, 15min. by bus from city center. Ticket office open daily 5:50am-12:30pm and 1-7:30pm. From points south of the city, change in Chiusi; from points north of the city, change in Florence. Trains to **Florence** (1¾hr., 19 per day 5am-9:22pm, €5.50) and **Rome** (3hr., 12 per day 5:57am-8:18pm, €16.30) via **Chiusi.**

Buses: TRA-IN/SITA (☎0577 20 42 46). Ticket offices are in the underground terminal in P. Gramsci and at the train station. Open daily 5:45am-8:15pm. Some intercity buses leave from P. Gramsci and others from the train station. To: **Arezzo** (8 per day, €4.60); **Florence** (every hr., €6.50); **Montalcino** (8 per day, €3); **Montepulciano** via **Buonconvento** or **Torrenieri** (20 per day, €4.30); **San Gimignano** via **Poggibonsi** (31 per day, €5.20); **Volterra** (M-F 4 per day, €2.50; get off at Colle Val d'Elsa and buy tickets at newsstand for a **CPT** bus to Volterra). TRA-IN also runs buses within Siena. Buy tickets (valid for 1hr., €0.90) at the office in P. Gramsci or from any vendor that displays a TRA-IN sign. All buses have reduced service Su.

Taxis: RadioTaxi (☎0577 49 222) is open daily 7am-9pm.

Car, Bike, and Scooter Rental: Perozzi Noleggi, V. dei Gazzani, 16-18 (☎0577 23 73 85). Cars €72 per day; vans €115 per day; bikes €10 per day; scooters €26-€52 per day. Insurance included. Open M-Sa 9am-7pm, Su 9am-1pm. AmEx/MC/V.

▐ ORIENTATION AND PRACTICAL INFORMATION

From the **train station,** cross the street and take bus #3, 4, 7, 8, 9, 10, 14, 17, or 77 to the town center. These buses stop in **Piazza del Sale** or **Piazza Gramsci.** Some buses stop just before P. Gramsci, making it difficult to know when to get off; ask the bus driver. From either *piazza,* follow the signs to **Piazza del Campo,** Siena's historical center. Buy local bus tickets from vending machines by the station entrance or at the *biglietteria* (€0.90). From the **bus station** in **Piazza San Domenico,** follow the signs to P. del Campo. **Piazza del Duomo** lies 100m west of **Il Campo.**

Tourist Office: APT, P. del Campo, 56 (☎0577 28 05 51; infoaptsiena@terresiena.it). Knowledgeable staff provides snappy brochures on sights in and around Siena but are

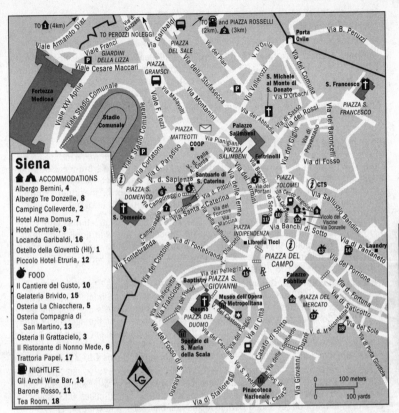

Siena

♠ ♠ ACCOMMODATIONS
Albergo Bernini, **4**
Albergo Tre Donzelle, **8**
Camping Colleverde, **2**
Hotel Alma Domus, **7**
Hotel Centrale, **9**
Locanda Garibaldi, **16**
Ostello della Gioventù (HI), **1**
Piccolo Hotel Etruria, **12**

🍴 FOOD
Il Cantiere del Gusto, **10**
Gelateria Brivido, **15**
Osteria La Chiacchera, **5**
Osteria Compagnia di
San Martino, **13**
Osteria Il Grattacielo, **3**
Il Ristorante di Nonno Mede, **6**
Trattoria Papei, **17**

NIGHTLIFE
Gli Archi Wine Bar, **14**
Barone Rosso, **11**
Tea Room, **18**

generally swamped with inquiries and unable to grant much personal attention. Open Mar. 16-Nov. 14 daily 9:30am-1pm and 2:30-6pm; Nov. 15-Mar. 15 M-Sa 8:30am-1pm and 3-7pm, Su 9am-1pm. **Prenotazioni Alberghi e Ristoranti** (☎0577 94 08 09; fax 0577 28 02 90), in P. S. Domenico, finds lodgings for a €2 commission. Also books reservations for walking tours of Siena (2hr. tour M-F 4:30pm; book by 1pm; €20) and San Gimignano. Open Apr.-Oct. M-Sa 9am-8pm; Nov.-Mar. M-Sa 9am-7pm.

Budget Travel: CTS, V. Sallustio Bandini, 21 (☎0577 28 58 08). Student travel services. Open M-F and Su 9am-12:30pm and 3:30-7pm.

Laundromat: Lavorapido, V. di Pantaneto, 38. Wash €3 per 8kg. Dry €3. Open daily 8am-10pm. **Onda Blu,** Casato di Sotto, 17 (☎0800 86 13 46). Wash €3 per 7kg. Dry €3. Open daily 8am-10pm.

English-Language Bookstore: Libreria Ticci, V. delle Terme, 5/7 (☎0577 28 00 10). Extensive selection. Open M-Sa 9am-7:30pm. **Feltrinelli,** V. Banchi di Sopra, 64 (☎0577 27 11 04; www.lafeltrinelli.it). Classic and popular fiction; English-language magazines. Open M-Sa 9am-7:30pm, Su 11am-1:30pm and 3:30-7:30pm. MC/V.

Luggage Storage: At TRA-IN ticket office beneath P. Gramsci. €2 per half day (7am-1pm or 1-7:45pm), €3.50 per full day. No overnight storage. Open daily 7am-7:45pm.

Emergency: ☎113. **Police:** (☎112), on V. del Castoro near the *duomo.* **First Aid:** ☎118. **Ambulance:** V. del Porrione, 49 (☎0577 431 11).

Pharmacy: Farmacia del Campo, P. del Campo, 26. Open in summer daily 9am-noon and 4-8pm; in winter 9am-noon and 3:30-7:30pm. Posts list of after-hours rotations.

Hospital: V. Le Scotte, 14 (☎0577 58 51 11). Take bus #3 or 77 from P. Gramsci.

Internet Access: Cafe Internet/International Call Center, Galleria Cecco Angiolieri, 16. €0.99 for 1st 20min. €0.03 per each additional min. Open daily 9am-11pm. **Internet Train,** V. di Città, 121 (☎0577 22 63 66). Wireless connections available for laptops. €5.16 per hr. Open M-F 10am-8pm, Sa-Su noon-8pm.

Post Office: P. Matteotti, 36, offers **currency exchange.** €2.58 fee for amounts over €5.16. Open M-Sa 8:15am-7pm. **Postal Code:** 53100.

ACCOMMODATIONS

Finding a room in Siena can be difficult and expensive in the summer. Book far ahead for the Palio (see **Entertainment,** below). For visits over a week, *affitta-camere* are an attractive option. The APT and Prenotazioni Alberghiere tourist offices can provide a list of these private rooms and help with booking.

Piccolo Hotel Etruria, V. Donzelle, 3 (☎0577 28 80 88; www.hoteletruria.com). Family-run establishment maintains immaculate, modern rooms with floral bedspread, phone, TV, and hair dryer at some of the best prices in Siena, and only a stone's throw from Il Campo. Breakfast €5. Curfew 1am. Singles €45, with bath €50; doubles €80; triples €105. Extra bed €25. AmEx/MC/V. ❹

Ostello della Gioventù "Guidoriccio" (HI), V. Fiorentina, 89 (☎0577 52 212), in Località Lo Stellino, a 20min. bus ride from town. Take bus #10 or 15 from P. Gramsci. Bus #15 stops at front door. For bus #10, continue from stop in bus's direction and take 1st right. Continue past McDonald's and gas station, hostel is on the right about 50m down. With mostly 2- to 3-person rooms, the hostel is an excellent value and has a young, friendly atmosphere. Breakfast €1.55. Dinner €9.75. Key deposit €1. Lockout 9:30am-3pm. Curfew midnight. Reservation recommended. Dorms €13.75. ❶

Albergo Tre Donzelle, V. Donzelle, 5 (☎0577 28 03 58; fax 0577 22 39 33). Basic rooms have tasteful wood furnishings and lots of space. Close to Il Campo, but often noisy as a result. Friendly English-speaking staff. Curfew 1am. Singles €33; doubles €46, with bath €60. Extra bed €18, in rooms with bath €19. AmEx/MC/V. ❸

Albergo Bernini, V. della Sapienza, 15 (☎0577 28 90 47; www.albergobernini.com). Antique-laden rooms have picture-perfect views of the *duomo* and San Domenico soaring above red rooftops. Outdoor patio is lined with plants, which makes for the perfect setting for a serenade by the welcoming, accordion-playing owner. Breakfast €7. Curfew midnight. July-Sept. singles with bath €78; doubles €62, with bath €82. Extra bed €25. Sept.-July prices drop 20%. Cash only. ❺

Locanda Garibaldi, V. Giovanni Dupré, 18 (☎0577 28 42 04). Wood-trussed ceilings and low-vaulted sitting area with sleek and classy decor. Most rooms with bath. Reception in restaurant downstairs. Curfew midnight. Reservation recommended, very popular in summer. Doubles €75, with bath €82; triples €90; quads €115. ❸

Hotel Alma Domus, V. Camporeggio, 37 (☎0577 44 177; fax 0577 47 601), next to Santuario di S.Caterina in a quieter part of town. The rooms are comfortable and have bath, handsome, polished stone floors, and refreshing A/C. Breakfast €6. Curfew 11:30pm. Singles €42; doubles €60; triples €75; quads €90. Cash only. ❹

Hotel Centrale, V. C. Angiolieri, 26 (☎0577 28 03 79; hotelcentrale.siena@libero.it). Don't be deceived by the dark staircase—this hotel is well-kept and comfortable. Rooms with beamed ceilings, hair dryer, fridge, phone, satellite TV, fan and views of La Torre and the *duomo.* Breakfast €5. Singles €50-55; doubles €70-80. AmEx/MC/V. ❹

Camping Colleverde, Strada di Scacciapensieri, 47 (☎0577 28 00 44; www.terresiena.it). Take bus #3 from train station or bus #8 from P. del Sale. Confirm destination with driver.

Buses run every 30min. Campsite is well-maintained, with grocery store, restaurant, and access to nearby bar. Open late Mar. to mid-Nov. Reception 7:20am-11pm. Pool €1.55, children €1.03. €7.75 per person, €3.50 per tent, ages 3-11 €4.13. MC/V. ❶

▣ FOOD

Siena specializes in rich pastries. The most famous is *panforte*, a concoction of honey, almonds, and citron, first baked as trail mix for the Crusaders. For a lighter snack, try *ricciarelli*, soft almond cookies with powdered vanilla on top. Sample either (€2.10 per 100g) at the **Bar/Pasticceria Nannini,** the oldest *pasticceria* in Siena, with branches at V. Banchi di Sopra, 22-24, and throughout town. **Enoteca Italiana,** in the Fortezza Medicea near the entrance off V. Cesare Maccari, sells fine wines (from €1.60 per glass), including *Vernaccia*. (☎0577 28 84 97. Open M noon-8pm, Tu-Sa noon-1am. MC/V.) Siena's **open-air market** fills P. La Lizza each Wednesday (8am-1pm). For groceries, head to **CONAD,** in P. Matteoti (Open M-Sa 8:30am-8:30pm, Su 9am-1pm and 4-8pm), or the **COOP** a few blocks from the train station. Turn left from the station, then left again one block down at the overpass; it's in the shopping complex immediately to the right. (Open M-Sa 8am-7:30pm.)

▧ **Il Cantiere del Gusto,** V. Calzoleria, 12 (☎0577 28 90 10; www.cantieredelgusto.com), behind the curve of P. del Campo off V. Banchi di Sotto. Delicious aromas waft up from the intimate and elegant dining area downstairs. Friendly waitstaff serves hearty Tuscan classics like *tagliatelle al ragù di coniglio* (with rabbit sauce; €6.50). *Primi* €6-7, *secondi* €7-13. Cover €1. Service 10%. Open daily 12:30-2:30pm and 7-10pm. MC/V. ❸

▧ **Osteria La Chiacchera,** Costa di S. Antonio, 4 (☎0577 28 06 31), next to Santuario di S. Caterina. Frequented by young Italians, the restaurant offers delicious food at extremely low prices in a casual and lively atmosphere. *Primi* €4.50-5, *secondi* €5-5.50. Open M and W-Su noon-3:30pm and 7pm-midnight. AmEx/MC/V. ❷

▧ **Trattoria Papei,** P. del Mercato, 6 (☎0577 28 08 94), on the far side of Palazzo Pubblico from Il Campo. Shady outdoor tables and a large stone-arched dining room can get crowded and noisy. Vast range of homemade pasta dishes, including scrumptious *tagliolini al sugo d'anatra* (with duck sauce; €6.50), and traditional *secondi* like savory *coniglio all'arrabbiata* (rabbit with sage and rosemary; €8). Wines are served by the bottle (1L €7), but you're charged only for what you drink. Cover €2. Open Tu-Su noon-3pm and 7-10:30pm. AmEx/MC/V. ❸

Il Ristorante di Nonno Mede, V. Camporeggio, 21 (☎0577 24 79 66), down the hill to the left of San Domenico. Although indoor seating is cramped, choose from an extensive menu of white pizzas and enjoy in the expansive outdoor seating area that has great views of the *duomo*. Delicious *antipasto* buffet €7.80. Pizza €5-6.50. Open M and W-Su 12:30-3pm and 7pm-midnight. MC/V. ❷

Osteria Il Grattacielo, V. dei Pontani, 8 (☎0577 28 93 26), on a tiny street between V. dei Termini and V. Banchi di Sopra. Culinary delights abound here, including baby artichokes, sun-dried tomatoes in oil, olives, and hunks of salami and pecorino. Half the fun here is ordering—just point at the jars and create your dream lunch. A full meal with wine runs less than €10. Open M-F 10am-3pm and 5:30-7pm, Su 6-8pm. Cash only. ❷

Osteria Compagnia di San Martino, V. del Porrione, 25 (☎0577 49 306), off P. del Campo. Tuscan food, like *tagliatelle al cinghiale* (flat noodles with wild boar; €6), served in no-frills outdoor area or dining room with A/C. *Primi* €5-6, *secondi* €6-15. Open M-Sa noon-3pm and 7-10:30pm. AmEx/MC/V. ❸

Gelateria Brivido, V. d. Pellegrini, 1-3 (☎0577 28 00 58). *Gelato* in flavors like kiwi and watermelon served in a standing-room only store. Don't miss the sinfully good *biscotto* packed with crumbs of chocolate cookie. Cones from €1.50. Open daily 10am-9pm. ❶

SIGHTS

> **TIP**
> **BANG FOR YOUR BUCK.** Siena offers two *biglietti cumulativi* (cumulative tickets). The first allows two days of entry to the Museo Civico, the Spedale di S. Maria della Scala, and the Palazzo Papesse (€10). The second covers those three plus the Museo dell'Opera Metropolitana, the baptistry, and the Oratorio di San Bernardino, and is valid for seven days (€16). Both tickets can be bought at any of the included sights.

■ **IL CAMPO.** Siena radiates from the **Piazza del Campo,** the shell-shaped brick square designed for civic events and affectionately referred to as "Il Campo." The *piazza's* brick paving is divided in nine sections, representing the city's medieval Council of Nine. Il Campo is the center of Sienese lifestyle and tradition. Dante referred to the square in his account of the real-life drama of Provenzan Salvani, the heroic Sienese merchant who panhandled in Il Campo to pay for a friend's ransom. Later Sienese mystics like San Bernadino used the *piazza* as a public auditorium. For €1-2, claim a table and an espresso at one of the many cafes lining the curved walkway, or better yet, grab a bottle of wine and stake out a seat on the cobblestone *piazza* itself. Twice each summer, the **Palio** morphs the mellow Campo into a chaotic arena as horses race around its edge (see **Entertainment**). At the top of the slope is the **Fonte Gaia,** a rectangular marble fountain nestled into the slanted *piazza*. The water here emerges from the same 25km aqueduct that has refreshed Siena since the 14th century. Standing at the bottom of the *piazza* is the imposing **Palazzo Pubblico,** with its looming bell tower, the **Torre del Mangia.** In front of the *palazzo* is the **Cappella di Piazza,** which was started in 1348 but took 100 years to complete due to the untimely arrival of the Black Death.

■ **PALAZZO PUBBLICO.** This impressive medieval building was home to Siena's Council of Nine in the Middle Ages. It still houses city government offices, but the main tourist draw is the **Museo Civico.** Although the Sienese art pieces here range from medieval triptychs to 18th-century landscapes, the greatest treasure is the collection of late medieval to early Renaissance painting in the distinctive Sienese style. The large and airy **Sala del Mappamondo,** named for a lost series of astronomical frescoes, displays Simone Martini's *Maestà*, which combines religious overtones with civic and literary awareness: the Christ Child holds a parchment inscribed with the city motto of upholding justice, *Expertus fidelem,* and the steps of the canopied throne are engraved with two stanzas from Dante's *Divine Comedy.* In the next room, the **Sala dei Nove** exhibits Pietro and Ambrogio Lorenzetti's famous frescoes, the *Allegories of Good and Bad Government and their Effects on Town and Country,* with opposing visions of utopia and damnation on the right and left walls. *(Open daily Nov.-Feb. 10am-5:30pm; Mar.-Oct. 10am-7pm. €7, students €4.50, under 11 free.)* The Palazzo Pubblico's other star attraction is the **Torre del Mangia,** named for gluttonous bell-ringer Giovanni di Duccio, or "Mangiaguadagni" (Eat the profits). At 102m, the tower is Italy's tallest secular medieval monument. Persistence pays off when over 500 dizzying and narrow stairs (claustrophobes beware) conclude just underneath the highest bell of the tower. Siena's tile rooftops, farmlands, and vineyard hills form an enchanting mosaic. It gets crowded in the afternoon, so arrive early. *(Open daily Nov.-Mar. 15 10am-4pm; Mar. 16-Oct. 10am-7pm. €6, or €10 combined ticket with Museo Civico.)*

■ **DUOMO.** Atop one of the city's seven hills, the *duomo* is one of few full Gothic cathedrals south of the Alps. To prevent the massive apse from hanging over the side of the hill, the **baptistry** was built below. A huge arch, part of a striped wall facing the front of the cathedral, is the sole remnant of Siena's 1339 plan to construct a new nave, which would have made this *duomo* the largest church in all Christendom. The grandiose effort ended when the Black Plague decimated the working populace. One of the *duomo's* side aisles has been enclosed and turned into the **Museo dell'Opera Metropolitana** (p. 453). Statues of philosophers, sibyls, and prophets, all by Giovanni Pisano, hold sway beneath impressive spires.

The bronze sun symbol on the facade of the *duomo* was the creation of St. Bernadino of Siena, who wanted the feuding Sienese to relinquish their loyalty to emblems of nobility and unite under this symbol of the risen Christ. Alas, his efforts were in vain—the Sienese continue to identify with the animal symbols of their *contrade* (districts). The marble floor, like the rest of the *duomo*, is richly ornate, depicting such widely varying and often violent themes as alchemy and the Slaughter of the Innocents. A series on the left showing multi-ethnic sibyls represents the spread of Christianity. Most of the pieces are covered for preservation purposes, except in September when visitors can look for the works by Machese d'Adamo, perhaps the most spectacular in the entire building. Halfway up the left aisle is the **Piccolomini altar,** designed by Andrea Bregno in 1503. The altar contains niches that house four small life-like statues; St. Paul, on the lower right with the most elaborate drapery, was sculpted by Michelangelo early in his career. In the neighboring chapel is Donatello's bronze statue of St. John the Baptist, graceful even in his emaciation. The statue was honorably built to host a very special holy relic—St. John's right arm. The lavish **Libreria Piccolomini,** commissioned by Pope Pius III, houses the elaborately illustrated books of his uncle Pius II. *(Duomo open Mar. 15-Oct. M-Sa 7:30am-7:30pm; Nov.-Mar. 14 M-Sa 7:30am-5pm; Su 2-5pm. €3, €4-5.50 when floor is uncovered in Sept. Library open Mar. 15-Oct. 9am-7:30pm; Nov.-Mar. 14 M-Sa 10am-1pm and 2-5pm, Su 2-4:45pm. €1.50. Cumulative ticket for duomo, baptistry, crypt, Museo dell'Opera Metropolitana, and Oratorio San Bernardino €16. Modest dress required.)*

MUSEO DELL'OPERA METROPOLITANA. The cathedral museum holds all the art that won't fit in the church. The first floor contains some of the foremost Gothic statuary in Italy, all by Giovanni Pisano. Upstairs the 700-year-old *Maestà*, by Duccio di Buoninsegna, originally served as a screen of the cathedral's altar. Other noteworthy works are the Byzantine *Madonna degli Occhi Coressi*, paintings by Lorenzetti, and two altarpieces by Matteo di Giovanni. Climb the **Scala del Facciatore,** in **Room 4** on the upper floor, to a balcony over the nave. A very narrow spiral staircase leads to a tiny tower for an unadvertised but beautiful view of the entire city. *(Museum entrance outside of duomo, exit portals and turn left. Open daily Mar. 15-Sept. 9am-7:30pm; Oct. 9am-6pm; Nov.-Mar. 14 9am-1:30pm. €6.)*

SPEDALE DI S. MARIA DELLA SCALA. Built as a hospital in the 13th century, the Spedale is now a museum, displaying its original frescoes, chapels, and vaults, as well as beautiful paintings and statues. The Sala del Pellegrinaio, or the Pilgrims' Hall, used as a ward until the late 20th century, contains an expressive fresco cycle by Vecchietta which tells the narrative history of the hospital building. The Sagrestia Vecchia, or Cappello del Sacro Chiodo, houses masterful 15th-century Sienese frescoes. On the way downstairs, duck into the dim underground chapels and vaults, sites of rituals and "acts of piety for the dead" performed by various *contrada* fraternities. One level down is the entrance to the **Museo Archeologico,** included in admission to the Spedale. Established in 1933 to collect and preserve Etruscan artifacts from the Siena area, the museum is now almost entirely in the eerie medieval underground water works of the city. Signs point the way through dank, labyrinthine passageways before emerging into rooms containing well-lit glass cases of Etruscan pottery and coins. *(Opposite the duomo. Open daily Mar.-Nov. 10:30am-6:30pm; Dec.-Feb. 10:30am-4:30pm. Ticket office closes 30min. before museum. €6 without advanced booking, €5.50 with booking, students €3.50/3.)*

HORSE POWER

The Palio is only about 90 seconds long. The rope suddenly drops, the horses lunge onto the track, and then, in a minute-and-a-half blur of trampling hooves and brightly colored jerseys, it's over as quickly as it began, and a new *contrada* can call itself the Palio victor. At least until August.

Though the semi-annual bareback horse race around Siena's Il Campo is very brief, ceremonies leading up to the event begin several days in advance, as 10 *contrade*, or districts, of Siena prepare their horses and jockeys for victory with trial runs around the converted *piazza*. The night before the race, Siena's streets are full of music and revelry as locals toast victories past, sing rewritten (and often obscene) lyrics to popular children's songs, and rekindle old *contrada* rivalries.

Spectators begin to pack Il Campo early on the morning of the race, with prime free spots near the rails going to die-hard Palio fans. Those lucky (or wealthy) enough to secure bleacher seats file in at around 3:00pm, after the horses have been led into their *contrada* churches and blessed. A 2hr. parade of heralds, flag-throwers, and city dignitaries follows, prefacing the anarchy to come with traditional regal pomp. The final piece is the victory prize, the Palio itself, a banner depicting the Madonna and Child alongside a

PINACOTECA NAZIONALE. Siena's superb art gallery displays works by every major artist of the highly stylized Sienese school. The masters represented include the seven followers of Onccio—Simone Martini, the Lorenzetti brothers, Bartolo di Fredi, Da Domenico, Sano di Pietro, and Il Sodoma—as well as many others. The museum is refreshingly free of the tourist hordes that can make it difficult to appreciate many of Siena's prime collections. (*V. S. Pietro, 29, in the Palazzo Buonsignori down V. del Capitano from the duomo. Open M 8:30am-1:30pm, Tu-Sa 8:15am-7:15pm, Su 8:15am-1:15pm. €4, EU citizens and students 18-26 €2, EU citizens under 18 or over 65 free.*)

SANTUARIO DI SANTA CATERINA. This sanctuary honors the Sienese Caterina, who had a miraculous vision in which Christ came to her with a ring and proposed marriage. Known for her outspoken manner, her eloquence persuaded Pope Gregory XI to return to Rome from Avignon; in 1939 she was proclaimed the patron saint of Italy. The complex of brick buildings and airy courtyards, converted into a Renaissance *loggia*, branches into many Baroque chapels. The **Chiesa del Crocefisso** on the right is impressive, but don't overlook the beautiful, smaller **Oratorio della Cucina** on the left. (*Entrance at the intersection of Costa di S. Antonio and V. dei Pittori, down from P. S. Domenico on V. Sappienza. Open daily 9am-12:30pm and 3-6pm. Free.*)

BAPTISTRY. Lavish and intricate frescoes depicting the lives of Christ and St. Anthony decorate the baptistry. On the left is Vasari's *Morte del Generale Collignon.* The centerpiece, however, is the hexagonal Renaissance **baptismal font** (1417-30). Panels include Ghiberti's *Baptism of Christ* and *John in Prison*, as well as Donatello's *Herod's Feast.* (*Behind the duomo. Open daily Mar. 15-Sept. 9:30am-8pm; Oct. 9am-6pm; Nov.-Mar. 14 10am-1pm and 2:30-5pm. €3.*)

OTHER SIGHTS. As in many Italian towns, Siena's Franciscan and Dominican basilicas rival each other from opposite ends of town. The **Chiesa di San Domenico** contains Andrea Vanni's portrait of S. Caterina and several other dramatic frescoes illustrating her miraculous acts. The exquisite *cappella* inside, dedicated to S. Caterina, was built in 1460 to store her preserved head and half of one of her fingers, still on display today for the curious and not squeamish. (*In P. S. Domenico. Open daily Nov.-Apr. 9am-1pm and 3-5:30pm; May-Oct. 7am-1pm and 3-7pm. Free. Modest dress required.*) Those interested in the Palio may enjoy one of Siena's 17 **contrada museums.** Each neighborhood organization maintains its own collection of costumes, banners, and icons. *(Most require an appointment—ask at the tourist office. Schedule visits at least 1 week in advance.)* Take time out from sightseeing for a stroll within the brick walls of the **Fortezza Medicea,** filled with fountains and towers. *(Free.)*

ENTERTAINMENT AND NIGHTLIFE

Siena's ▧**Palio,** hands-down the highlight of the town's entertainment, overtakes the city twice each year, on July 2 and August 16, transforming it into an exciting frenzy as people pack P. del Campo to watch the bare-backed horse race. Even when it doesn't involve barbaric bareback horse races, Siena's nightlife is kept booming by the large local and foreign student population. At new and popular **Gli Archi Wine Bar,** V. Pantaneto, 22, try an assortment of vintages paired with deliciously cheap *antipasti* trays. (☎0577 24 75 79; www.gliarchi.it. *Antipasti* €6-8, €3.50 for one portion. Pasta dishes €4.50-6. M-F noon-3pm and 7-11pm, Sa 12-3.) The study-abroad crowd gets down at **Barone Rosso,** V. dei Termini, 9, where themed parties, music, and alcohol are all in abundance. (☎0577 28 66 86; www.baronerosso.com. Open daily 9pm-3am.) For a slightly calmer evening out, head to **Tea Room,** V. di Porta Giustizia, 9, down a small staircase to the left behind P. Mercato, where a friendly crowd sips drinks and student performers display their talents. (☎0577 22 27 53; www.tearoomportagiustizia.com. Tea and other drinks from €2. Open daily 9pm-3am.)

▣ DAYTRIPS FROM SIENA

> ⚡TIP⚡ **BABY YOU CAN DRIVE MY CAR.** Bus service in and out of Siena is less than reliable. Enjoy daytrips from Siena by renting a car, which will spare you the agony of waiting for, flagging down, and chasing after buses.

THE CHIANTI REGION

Buses connect Siena to Radda in Chianti (1hr., 4 per day, €5.20 round-trip), a major base for exploring vineyards. Buses also connect Radda to Florence (1½hr.; 3 per day; last bus to Florence 6:10pm, last bus to Siena 6:40pm). In the morning, buses arrive at and depart from the same spot on V. XX Settembre. In the afternoon, return buses to Florence and Siena leave from a stop across the street about 100m down. This stop is not well marked, so flag down the bus as it approaches.

rearing horse, drawn in a cart by four white oxen.

By 7:30pm, the starting time of the race, the energy and volume of the crowd has reached a fever pitch. But suddenly, absolute silence engulfs the *piazza* as the crowd waits with bated breath to hear the line-up order of the horses, randomly decided in secret just before the race. Riders battle for spots behind the starting line until the announcer decides that all is in order and signals for the rope to drop without warning. During the three laps around the *piazza,* traditional medieval rules apply, and jockeys have free rein to whip, jostle, or push their opponents as they like. This becomes especially precarious around the first curve, notoriously the most difficult, where it is not uncommon for riders to be thrown, trampled, or even killed. The frenzied crowd, however, is focused only on the horse at the head of the pack, and as the cannon shot announces the winner of the race the *piazza* erupts into outbursts of joy, despair, mania, and disbelief. Only 90 seconds, true. But what a 90 seconds it is.

Celebration by the winning *contrada* continues until the fall, when the official victory dinner is held in the *piazza.* And occupying the seat of honor? Why, the winning horse, of course.

(The Palio is run every year on July 2 and August 16. Contact Siena's APT tourist office for more info and a copy of the program.)

Siena lies within easy reach of the Chianti region, a harmonious landscape of green hills, ancient castles, tiny villages, and of course, uninterrupted expanses of vineyard. In the Middle Ages, the small countryside towns of Castellina, Radda, and Gaiole formed a military alliance against invading French and Spanish invaders, adopting the black rooster as their symbol. Today the rooster adorns the bottles of Chianti wines, which are famous throughout the world.

Peaceful **Radda in Chianti** is just 9km from Siena on bus #125 and makes a great base for exploring the surrounding countryside. Radda's **tourist office,** in P. del Castello, has a multilingual staff willing to help find accommodations. Ask here about the few wineries within walking distance of the town center. To reach the tourist office, walk from the bus stop down V. XX Settembre with the city walls on the left. Turn left at the public gardens on V. Roma, the main street in town, and right on Sdrucciolo del Castello. (☎0577 73 84 94; proradda@chiantinet.it. Open Mar.-Oct. M-Sa 10am-1pm and 3-7pm, Su 10:30am-12:30pm.)

Radda has very few budget accommodations, so it's hard to beat **Le Camere di Giovannino ❹**, V. Roma, 6-8, where the rooms and the amiable owners are full of country character. Rooms have wood-trussed ceilings and vases of dried flowers on every bureau. All come with kitchen access, bath, and TV. (☎/fax 0577 73 56 01. Rooms €52, with breakfast €62.) Like all towns in the Chianti region, Radda is home to numerous *enoteche*. Inside the vault of the reputable **Porciatti Alimentari ❷**, P. IV Novembre, 1-3, master butchers sell aged, handmade salami, pork sausages, and cheese that are also available for tasting. Wine bottles start at €7. (☎0577 73 80 55; www.casaporciatti.it. Open May-Oct. M-Sa 7:45am-1pm and 5-8pm, Su 7:45am-1pm; Nov.-Apr. M-Sa 8am-1pm and 4:30-7:30pm. MC/V.) The cheapest place to pick up wine is the **COOP** supermarket, V. Roma, 26, which stocks bottles from €3.10. (Open M-Tu and Th-Sa 8am-1pm and 4:30-8pm, W 8am-1pm.) The casual **Pizzeria da Michele ❸**, P. IV Novembre, down a flight of stairs from the main bus stop, has valley views and interesting dishes on a menu that changes daily. (☎0577 73 84 91. Pizza served only at dinner. *Primi* €6.50-7.50, *secondi* €11-14. Cover €2. Open Tu-Su noon-2:30pm and 7pm-midnight.) Another option is the delicious **Enoteca Dante Alighieri ❶**, P. Dante Alighieri, 1, across from the bus stop. It specializes in *bruschette* and *crostini* (from €2.25) and has an extensive wine list (from €2 a glass). Takeout is also available. (☎0577 73 88 15. Open M-F and Su 7am-10pm.) After a rigorous day of wine tasting, relax in the shaded **public gardens** outside the city walls.

For more information on touring the nearby wineries, vacation rentals, and excursions to the countryside, inquire at **A Bit of Tuscany,** V. Roma, 39. (☎0577 73 86 37; www.divinetours.com. Open M-F 10am-1pm and 3-6pm.) Most wineries in the area give free tastings, but cellar tours often require reservations—the tourist offices provide booking services. **Internet** is available at **Snappy Bar,** V. XI Febbraio, 2. (☎0577 73 87 11. €5 for 1st hr. €4 per additional 1st hr. Wireless connection for laptops €4 for the first hr., €2 per additional hr. Open Tu-Su 7am-10:30pm.)

MONTEPULCIANO

A TRA-IN bus connects Siena to Montepulciano (1½hr., M-Sa 5 per day, €4.50), some via Buonconverto. A bus also runs to Florence (2hr., €7.70).

Stretched along the crest of a narrow limestone ridge, this small medieval hamlet (pop. 14,000) is Tuscany's highest hill town. Sixteenth-century palaces, squares, and churches grace Montepulciano's narrow streets and arched walkways. Though neglected for centuries after the Renaissance, today the walled town is wealthy and heavily touristed, largely as a result of its famous red wine industry.

The **Chiesa di San Biagio,** built on a wide, grass-covered plateau, is a stunning example of high-Renaissance symmetry. The cavernous interior was redone in the

17th century in overwrought Baroque, but the simplicity of the original still shines through. The surrounding area has great vistas of the countryside, and in the summer, blooming lilacs. (From P. Grande, follow V. Ricci to V. della Mercezia. Turn left down staircase before Piazzetta di S. Francesco. Follow signs, through the city walls, and along V. di San Biagio. Open daily 9am-1pm and 3:30-7pm.) Montepulciano's main square, **Piazza Grande,** is surrounded by an unfinished *duomo* to the south, the 14th-century Palazzo Comunale to the west, the Palazzo Tarugi to the north and the Palazzo Contucci to the east. The interior of the *duomo* is somber, its simplicity marked by several great oil paintings on the bare walls. Note the Sienese master Taddeo di Bartolo's poignant *Assumption of the Virgin* above the altar. (In P. Grande, at the top of the hill. Open daily 9am-12:30pm and 3:15-7pm.)

Tourists to Montepulciano keep themselves plenty busy browsing the wine stores and tasting free samples. Enjoy a few sips at the shop at Porta di Bacco, on the left immediately inside the city gates. (Open daily 9am-8pm.) For a delicious selection of typical Tuscan food, visit ◼**Osteria dell'Acquacheta ❷**, V. del Teatro, 22, off the Corso, where you savor a platter of *pecorino di pienza al tartufo* (aged cheese with truffles; €5.20) while chatting with the dynamic and amiable staff. (*Primi* €5.20-7; *secondi* by weight, €2.10-2.80 per 100g. Open M and W-Su 12:30-3pm and 7:30-10:30pm. MC/V.) Try the *pollo e coniglio all'Etrusca* (Etruscan-style chicken and rabbit; €10.40) at **Il Cantuccio ❸**, V. delle Cantine, 1/2, where tuxedo-clad waiters and dim lighting create a romantic atmosphere. (☎0578 75 78 70. *Primi* €7.30-9.40, *secondi* €8.60-15.50. Service 12%. Open Tu-Su 12:30-2:30pm and 7:30-11pm. MC/V.) Since most lodgings in Montepulciano are three- or four-star hotels, *affittacamere* (rooms for rent) are the best option. Should you plan to stay the night, **Ristorante Cit-**

Montepulciano

🏠 ACCOMMODATIONS   🍴 FOOD

Ristorante Cittino, **2**   Il Cantuccio, **1**
Osteria dell'Acquacheta, **3**

tino ❸, V. della Nuova, 2, off V. di Voltaia del Corso, has three family-run rooms that are spacious and comfortable, while delicious smells drift up from the restaurant below. (☎0578 75 73 35. Reserve ahead. Open M-Tu and Th-Su 9am-11pm. Singles €28-35; doubles €55.)

The **tourist office**, P. Grande, 7, provides **maps** and bus schedules, makes free arrangements for hotels and *affittacamere* in the town and countryside, and sells tickets for wine and oil tours. **Farmacia Sorbini** (☎0578 75 73 52), on V. Calamandrei, fills urgent prescriptions. The **post office**, V. delle Erbe, 12, uphill from P. delle Erbe and the Corso, offers currency exchange for a €0.50 commission. (Open M-F 8:15am-7pm, Sa 8:15am-12:30pm.) **Postal Code:** 53045.

AREZZO
☎0575

Arezzo (pop. 90,000) and its neighboring valleys were once home to Renaissance titans Piero della Francesca and Michelangelo, the poet Petrarch, the humanist Bruni, and the artist and historian Giorgio Vasari. It's also the hometown of Roberto Benigni, director and star of the Oscar-winning *La Vita è Bella* (*Life is Beautiful*), who shot many of the film's key scenes in the surrounding countryside. Though largely urban and commercial, the more subdued historical district preserves many vestiges of past genius, from Vasari's stunning architecture in P. Grande to Francesco's unparalleled *Legend of the True Cross* in the Basilica di San Francesco. Escape the busy city center with a stroll outside the eastern portion of the medieval city walls, which yields striking views of the countryside, and glimpses into backyards full of olive trees, flowerbeds, and vegetable gardens.

■ TRANSPORTATION

Arezzo lies on the Florence-Rome train line. From P. della Repubblica, **trains** run to Florence (1½hr., 2 per hr. 4:30am-9:50pm, €5.10-8) and Rome (2hr., every 1-2hr. 6:30am-10:11pm, €11.50-18). The ticket booth is open M-Sa 5:50am-8:50pm. To the left of the train station, **TRA-IN**, **SITA**, and **LFI buses** run to: Cortona (1hr., every hr., €2.60); Sansepolcro (1hr., every hr., €3.10); and Siena (1½hr., 7 per day, €4.60). Call ☎0575 38 26 51 for more info. Buy tickets at ATAM ticket office, in front and to the left of train station exit. (☎800 38 17 30. Open daily 6:20am-7:40pm.) For **taxis**, contact **RadioTaxi**. (☎0575 38 26 26; open 24hr.) **Car rental** is available at **Autonoleggi Ermini**, V. Perrenio, 21. (☎0575 35 35 70. €55-105 per day. 21+. Open M-F 8:30am-12:30pm and 3:30-7:30pm, Sa 8:30am-12:30pm.)

■ ORIENTATION AND PRACTICAL INFORMATION

Via Guido Monaco, which begins directly across from the **train station** at **Piazza della Repubblica**, parallels **Corso Italia**; together they form the backbone of the commercial district. To get to the historical center, follow V. Guido Monaco from the station to the traffic circle at **Piazza Guido Monaco**. Turn right on **Via Roma** and then left on the pedestrian walkway, C. Italia, which leads to the old city. **Piazza Grande** lies to the right, 250m up C. Italia. **Via Veneto** begins a block to the right of the train station, going under the train tracks and continuing to the back of the station.

Tourist Office: APT, P. della Repubblica, 28 (☎0575 20 839; www.apt.arezzo.it). Turn right after exiting station. English spoken. Free **maps** and brochures on nearby valleys. Open Apr.-Sept. M-Sa 9am-1pm and 3-7pm, Su 9am-1pm; Oct.-Mar. M-Sa 9am-1pm and 3-6:30pm.

Budget Travel: CTS, V. Veneto, 25 (☎0575 90 78 09 or 0575 90 78 08), sells Eurail passes and plane tickets. Open M-F 9am-1pm and 3-7:30pm, Sa 9am-1pm.

Currency Exchange: Banks line V. G. Monaco between the train station and P. G. Monaco. **Banca Nazionale del Lavoro,** V. G. Monaco, 74, has a 24hr. **ATM.** Open M-F 8:20am-1:35pm and 2:50-4:05pm, Sa 8:20-11:50am.

Emergency: ☎113. **Carabinieri:** ☎112. **Ambulance:** ☎118.

Police: V. Dardano, 9 (☎113 or 0575 90 66 67), off V. Fra Guittone by the train station.

Pharmacy: Farmacia Comunale, Campo di Marte, 1 (☎0575 90 24 66), next to CONAD supermarket on V. Veneto. Open 24hr.

Hospital: Ospedale Civivo, V. Fonte Veneziana (☎0575 25 51). **Misericordia** (☎0575 24 242).

Internet Access: InformaGiovani, P. G. Monaco, 2 (☎0575 37 78; informagiovani@comune.arezzo.it). Free access with a 30min. limit. Open M-Sa 9:30am-7:30pm.

Post Office: V. G. Monaco, 34 (☎0575 33 24 11). **Currency exchange** (€0.50 commission) at booth #9 (same hours). Open M-Sa 8:15am-7pm. **Postal Code:** 52100.

⌂ ACCOMMODATIONS

Hotels fill to capacity during the **Fiera Antiquaria** (Antique Fair) the first weekend of every month. Otherwise, finding a cheap room should be a cinch. **Ostello Villa Severi ❶,** V. Redi, 13, is a bit of a hike from town. Take bus #4 (€0.90) from P. G. Monaco to two stops (7min.) after Ospedale Vecchio. Disembark when the town park is on the left; the hostel is inside the park. The yellow villa is a decent budget option with small showers, high ceilings, and wood-beam detail. (☎0575 29 90 47; www.peterpan.it/ostello.htm. Breakfast €3. Lunch or dinner, including several courses and wine, €11. Reserve ahead for meals. Reception daily 9am-1pm and 6-11:30pm. Lockout 1-6pm. Dorms €15.) To get to **Albergo Cecco ❸,** C. Italia, 215, follow V. G. Monaco from the train station, turn right on V. Roma and another right on C. Italia. Do not follow signs for Hotel Cecco; they are misleading. The rooms are basic but spacious and clean, and all come with TV, phone, and large windows. (☎0575 20 986; fax 0575 35 67 30. Breakfast €3. Singles €30, with bath €40; doubles €45/60; triples €60/78; quads with bath €92. AmEx/MC/V.)

◖ FOOD

A well-stocked **CONAD** supermarket is on the corner of V. Veneto and V. L. B. Alberti, behind the train station. (Open M-Tu and Th-Sa 8am-8:30pm, W 8am-1:30pm.) An **open-air market** takes place in P. Sant'Agostino on weekdays until 1pm. Head to **La Mozzarella,** V. Spinello, 25, across from the train station, for a great variety of cheeses. (Open M-Sa 8am-1pm and 4-8pm.)

Trattoria Il Saraceno, V. Mazzini, 6 (☎0575 27 644), off C. Italia. This local spot boasts *Arezzese* specialties like duck and pecorino cheese in honey. Sardine-like seating. Pizza €6-8. *Primi* €6.50-7.50, *secondi* €6.50-10.50. Cover €2. Open M-Tu and Th-Su noon-3:30pm and 7:30-11pm. AmEx/MC/V. ❸

Ristorante Chicco di Riso, P. San Gemignano, 1 (☎0575 30 24 20). From C. Italia, turn right on V. Garibaldi, then left uphill to the *piazza.* Fish dishes and lots of veggies and all-organic meals like brown rice *risotto.* Student special includes soup and entree sampler (€4.50). Open M-Sa 12:30-2:30pm and 7:30-9:30pm. ❷

Paradiso di Stelle, V. G. Monaco, 58 (☎0575 27 448). First-rate homemade *gelato,* especially the *nocciola* and *tiramisù* (from €1.50). Try a toasty Nutella-filled crepe (€2.30). Open Mar.-Sept. Tu-Su 10:30am-midnight; Oct.-Feb. 10:30am-9pm. ❶

👁 SIGHTS

BASILICA DI SAN FRANCESCO. This extraordinary 11th-century basilica houses gorgeous frescoes, among them Piero della Francesca's ▣**Leggenda della Vera Croce** (Legend of the True Cross), in the chapel behind the main altar, which portrays the story of the crucifix and its role in early Christianity. The narrative begins with the death of Adam and proceeds to major events such as the conversion of Emperor Constantine. St. Francis is the figure kneeling at the foot of the cross. *(Up V. G. Monaco from train station, right into P. San Francesco. Basilica open daily 8:30am-noon and 2-7pm. Free. Chapel containing della Francesca's frescoes open M-F 9am-7pm, Sa 9am-6pm, Su 1-6pm. Visitors admitted in groups of 25 every 30min.; last visit begins 30min. before closing. Reservation required. Call ☎ 0575 20 630 or visit the office to the right of the church. €6, EU students 18-25 €4, art students or EU citizens under 18 €2. Upper portion of the fresco cycle free.)*

PIAZZA GRANDE. This square contains the **Chiesa di Santa Maria della Pieve**, a spectacular Romanesque church that dates from the 12th century and is one of Arezzo's most impressive monuments. Elegant columns and rounded arches frame Benedetto da Maiano's 15th-century portico. On the elevated presbytery sits Pietro Lorenzetti's brilliantly restored polyptych, depicting the *Annunciation* and *Madonna and Child.* Below lies the 9th-century church upon which the Pieve was built. The adjoining pock-marked tower is known appropriately as the "Tower of a Hundred Holes." *(Open M-Sa 8am-noon and 3-7pm, Su 8:30am-noon and 4-7pm.)* Surrounding the church is Arezzo's best architecture: the 14th-century Romanesque **Palazzo della Fraternità dei Laici** and the hulking 16th-century Baroque **Loggiato dei Vasari.** The *piazza* also hosts the monthly **antique fair** and the semi-annual **Giostra del Saraceno** (see **Festivals**) each summer.

DUOMO. The massive 13th-century cathedral, built in Tuscan Gothic, houses Arezzo native Piero della Francesca's *Maddalena* and Bishop Guido Tarlati's tomb, on the left side of the nave near the altar. Carved reliefs relate stories about the iconoclastic bishop's unconventional life. The six circular teal- and purple-stained-glass windows were designed by Guglielmo de Marcillat. The *Capella della Madonna del Conforto*, off the severe nave, holds a terra-cotta *Crucifixion* by Andrea della Robbia. *(Up V. Andrea Cesalpino from P. S. Francesco. ☎ 0575 23 991. Open daily 7am-12:30pm and 3-6:30pm. Modest dress required.)*

CHIESA DI SAN DOMENICO. As was often the case, the Dominicans built their church on the end of town opposite the Franciscan establishment. The church contains a superb Cimabue crucifix (1265), Spinello Aretino's *Annunciation*, and a Marcillat rose window depicting St. Augustine. *(Take V. Andrea Celaspino from P. S. Francesco, turn left at P. Libertà on V. Ricasorli, then right on V. di Sassoverde, leading to the church. Open daily 8:30am-1pm and 3:30-7pm. Hours may vary. Closed during mass.)* Near the church lies the **Casa Vasari,** which the historian and artist built for himself and decorated with impressive portrait-frescoes of Michelangelo and del Sarto. In the adjacent room, Vasari's depictions of the muses crown the ceiling; one is in the likeness of his fiancee, Niccolosa. He even painted himself contemplating the lovely view from one of the windows. *(V. XX Settembre, 55. Just off V. San Domenico. ☎ 0575 22 906. Open M and W-Sa 8am-7:30pm, Su 8am-1pm. Ticket sales end 30min. before closing. €2, EU students €1. Ring bell to enter.)*

🎊 FESTIVALS

Arezzo's **antique fairs** take place in and around Piazza Grande on the first weekend of every month. Beautiful antique furniture and religious paraphernalia would be tough to lug home through customs, though sundry bric-a-brac can make nice souvenirs. The **Giostra del Saracino,** a medieval joust, happens on the 3rd Sunday of June and the first Sunday of September, though celebrations engulf the town for the entire week before the event. In a ritual recalling the Crusades and fostering intercultural tolerance, "knights" representing the four quarters of the town charge a wooden effigy of a Turk with lances drawn. For more information, call ☎0575 36 64 60 or contact giostradelsaracino@comune.arezzo.it. Every July, crowds of dreadlocked and tattooed teens descend upon Arezzo for the **ArezzoWave Love Festival.** Stop at the outdoor stages to hear local and international alternative bands, watch a poetry reading, or dance to the spins of a local techno DJ.

◤ DAYTRIP FROM AREZZO

SANSEPOLCRO

Sansepolcro is most easily accessible by the hourly SITA bus from Arezzo (1hr., 15 per day, €3.10). Some routes require a change in Le Villel; ask the driver. The bus arrives just outside the walls of the old city. From the bus stop, enter the old city on V. N. Aggiunti. Follow the street 5 blocks, until passing the Museo Civico on the right. Turn right under an arch on V. G. Matteotti, and turn immediately left into P. Garibaldi. Sansepolcro's tourist office, P. Garibaldi, 2, is 1 block ahead on the left. (☎/fax 0575 74 05 36. Open daily 9:30am-1pm and 3:30-6:30pm.)

Nestled in the valley of the Tiber at the foot of the Apennines, Sansepolcro's claim to fame is native Piero della Francesca. The **Museo Civico,** V. Aggiunti, 65, displays some of della Francesca's finest works. *The Resurrection* features a triumphant Jesus towering above sleeping guards, resting one foot on his coffin and staring intently out at the viewer. Look closely at the guard in the red on the lower right—it's actually a self-portrait of della Francesca himself. (☎0575 73 22 18. Open daily June-Sept. 9am-1:30pm and 2:30-7:30pm; Oct.-May 9:30am-1pm and 2:30-6pm. €6, over 65 €4.50, ages 10-16 €3. Groups €4.50 per person. Audioguides €2.) The left chapel of the Romanesque **duomo,** begun in 1002, shelters the town's other cherished sight, the mysterious **Volto Santo** (Holy Face), a large wooden crucifix depicting a blue-robed Jesus. Believed by some to be much older than its 12th-century attribution, the Holy Face's Assyrian features suggest Oriental origins. Scholars speculate that the same artist produced the much-celebrated *Volto Santo* in Lucca. (V. Matteotti, just off P. Torre di Berta. Open 8am-noon and 3-6pm.)

CORTONA   ☎0575

The ancient town of Cortona surveys Tuscany and Umbria from its vine-ringed mountain peak. Though currently peaceful, the city once rivaled Perugia, Arezzo, and even Florence in power and belligerence. In 1411 Cortona lost autonomy and was appropriated by the king of Naples, who soon sold it to the rival Florentines. For all its grumbling, Cortona enjoyed peace and prosperity under Florentine rule; impressive art collections and architecture from this period of grandeur linger within the small city's walls, including two altarpieces by Fra Angelico and the paintings of Luca Signorelli, the great precursor to Michelangelo. Today, Cortona has become a tourist hot spot known best for its role in *Under the Tuscan Sun.* Indeed, the view from P. Garibaldi as the sun sets over the valley below and lights glow in a dusky haze would make anyone want to look up real estate listings.

▐ TRANSPORTATION

Trains depart **Camucia-Cortona station** to Florence (every hr., €6.40) and Rome (every 1-2hr., €9.10). **LFI buses** (☎0575 30 07 48) run to Cortona's P. Garibaldi from this station (15min., €1) and from **Terontola train station** (30min., every hr., €1.60; buy ticket from *bar* in train station). Buses also arrive in P. Garibaldi from Arezzo (1hr., 12 per day, €2.50). Buy LFI bus tickets from the tourist office, or any *bar* or *tabaccheria*. For **taxis**, call ☎335 81 96 313.

▟ ▞ ORIENTATION AND PRACTICAL INFORMATION

Buses from neighboring cities stop at **Piazza Garibaldi** just outside the city wall. Enter the city by following **Via Nazionale**, which leads to **Piazza della Repubblica**, the center of town. Diagonally across the *piazza* is **Piazza Signorelli**, Cortona's main square. The **tourist office**, V. Nazionale, 42, provides **maps**, bus schedules, and tickets for buses, trains, and tours. (☎0575 63 03 52; www.apt.arezzo.it. Open June-Sept. M-Sa 9am-1pm and 3-7pm, Su 9am-1pm; Oct.-May M-Tu and Th-F 9am-1pm and 3-6pm, W and Sa 9am-1pm. Train tickets not sold Sa-Su.) **Currency exchange** and a 24 hr. **ATM** are available at **Banca Etruria**, V. S. Margherita, 5. (Open M-F 8:20am-1:20pm and 2:35-3:35pm, Sa 8:20-11:50am.) In case of **emergency**, dial ☎113, call an **ambulance** at ☎118, or reach the **police** at V. Dardano, 9 (☎0575 60 30 06). **Farmacia Centrale** is at V. Nazionale, 38. (☎0575 60 32 06. Open M-Sa 9am-1pm and 4:30-8pm.) The **hospital** is on V. Maffei (☎0575 63 91). Use the **Internet** at the novelty shop at V. Guelfa, 36. At the end of V. Nazionale, turn left on V. Guelfa and walk halfway down the hill. (☎0575 60 52 35. €5 per hr., ISIC cardholders €4. Open M-F 9am-1pm and 4-8pm, Sa 9am-1pm.) **Telenet**, V. Roma, 20, also offers **Internet**, a phone center, **Western Union**, cell phone rental and shipping services; English spoken. (☎0575 63 17 35. €5 per hr. Open M-Sa 9:30am-1pm and 4-8pm, Su 4-8pm.) The **post office** is uphill from P. della Repubblica at V. Santucci, 1. (☎0575 60 30 21. Open M-F 8:15am-1:30pm, Sa 8:15am-12:30pm.) **Postal Code:** 52044.

▐ ACCOMMODATIONS

🛏 **Ostello San Marco (HI)**, V. Maffei, 57 (☎0575 60 17 65; www.cortonahostel.com). From bus stop, walk 5min. uphill on V. S. Margherita and follow signs curving left to the hostel. Clean and bright rooms with comfortable beds and linens make for an enjoyable stay. Breakfast included. Dinner €9. Reception 7-9am and 5pm-midnight. Open to individuals mid-Mar.-Nov., year-round for groups. Dorms €12. Cash only. ❶

Casa Betania, V. G. Severini, 50 (☎0575 62 829; fax 0575 60 42 99), downhill on V. Severini from P. Garibaldi. Cross the street and take an immediate right through the gates. Simply furnished rooms have small sinks and large, sunny windows looking out over the chapel next door. Singles €26, with bath €31; doubles €37/42. MC/V. ❸

Istituto Santa Margherita, V. Cesare Battisti, 15 (☎0575 63 03 36; fax 0575 63 05 49). Downhill on V. Severini from P. Garibaldi. The Istituto is on the corner of V. Battisti, on the left. Get thee to this nunnery (actually a former college). Rooms with large baths. Breakfast €3. Flexible midnight curfew. Singles €32; doubles (no unmarried couples) €46; triples €56; quads €66. Cash only. ❸

Hotel San Luca, P. Garibaldi, 1 (☎0575 63 04 60; www.sanlucacortona.com). Wide hallways lead to refined rooms, some with balcony and sweeping vistas of the Val di Chiena valley and Lake Trasimeno. Comfortable common areas. All rooms have bath, satellite TV, A/C, phone, and minibar. Breakfast included. Singles €70; doubles €100; triples €136; quads €173. AmEx/MC/V. ❺

🗎 FOOD

Cortona's restaurants serve home-style Tuscan dishes at reasonable prices. The best beef in Tuscany is raised in the surrounding valleys, so consider making the modest splurge on *bistecca alla Fiorentina*, a massive hunk of red meat served *al sangue* (very rare). Steak is so popular that restaurants sell it per 100g. Complement dinner with the fine local wine, *Bianco Vergine di Valdichiana*. Pennypinchers can pick up a €2.50 bottle at **Despar,** P. della Repubblica, 23, which also stocks picnic supplies and makes *panini* with fresh ingredients for €3. (☎0575 63 06 66. Open Apr.-Oct. M-Sa 7am-1:30pm and 4-8pm, Su 7:30am-1:30pm; Nov.-Mar. M-Tu and Th-Sa 7am-1:30pm and 4:30-7:30pm, W 7am-1:30pm. AmEx/MC/V.) On Saturday P. Signorelli hosts an **open-air market.** (Open 8am-1pm).

🍴 **Trattoria La Grotta,** P. Baldelli, 3 (☎0575 67 80 67), turn left into courtyard at the P. della Repubblica end of V. Nazionale. The *gnocchi di ricotta e spinaci* (€7.50) draw tears of gastronomic joy. Follow up with the *carpaccio con rucola e parmiggiano* (€8.50). Seating in converted wine cellar or outside in a secluded courtyard. *Primi* €6.50-9, *secondi* €8-16. Open M and W-Su 12-2:20pm and 7:30-11pm. MC/V. ❸

Pizzeria Fufluns, V. Ghibellina, 3 (☎0575 76 41 40; www.fufluns.net), off P. della Repubblica. A wide variety of pizzas and pasta have won this tiny, stone-walled restaurant many fans. The ivy-covered patio and indoor tavern fill during lunch and dinner hours with adoring *Cortonesi* and happy tourists. Pizza €4-6. *Primi* €5-7.50, *secondi* €7-15. Open M and W-Su 12:30-2:30pm and 7:30pm-12:30am. MC/V. ❸

Trattoria Dardano, V. Dardano, 24 (☎0575 60 19 44). Filled with tourists in the know and families offer simple, filling dishes, with notably ample *secondi* portions. Succulent meat dishes, including a very affordable steak (€2.50 per 100g). *Primi* €5-7, *secondi* €5-8. Cover €1. Open M-Tu and Th-Su noon-4pm and 7pm-midnight. Cash only. ❷

Ristorante Preludio, V. Guelfa, 11 (☎0575 63 01 04). Dress up for Tuscan meals with a twist, like *gnochhi di prugne* (plum pasta dumplings; €9). Stone portals, high ceilings, and flowers on tables add a classy touch. Roasted meats €4-5 per 100g. *Primi* €7-10, *secondi* €7-18. Cover €2. Open daily 12:30-3pm and 7:30-10:30pm. MC/V. ❹

IN RECENT NEWS

IT'S A GIRL THING

While traveling alone is undoubtedly an exhilarating experience, it can also be an intimidating one—especially for female travelers. Recognizing this fact, a collection of accommodations, tourist offices, and businesses in Tuscany have formed a coalition called **Tuscany Welcomes Women** to ensure that the experience of independent female trekkers is a happy and secure one.

Tuscany Welcomes Women offers tourist services and programs designed to meet the needs of women who travel to Tuscany each year. For example, accommodations in the program provide offers for mothers with children, discounts on laundry and beauty services, special dietary menus, luggage transport, and a "room welcoming" pack with much appreciated amenities like conditioner and a hair dryer.

If the program becomes successful within the region, Tuscany Welcomes Women hopes to expand their scope to perhaps one day becoming Italy Welcomes Women. Until then, female visitors to popular Tuscan destination like Florence and Siena can rest assured that a network of tourist services is ready and eager to answer their questions, make their stay safer and more comfortable, and, of course, point to the nearest salon.

(For more information, visit http://www.rete.toscana.it/sett/turismo/benvenute_guida.pdf)

Gelateria Snoopy, P. Signorelli, 29. Charlie Brown and his cartoon beagle adorn the walls as patrons young and old line up at the counter for homemade waffle cones filled with ■ **5 scoops** for €2 and other delicious treats. Open daily 10am-9pm. Cash only.

👁 SIGHTS

■ **MUSEO DELL'ACCADEMIA ETRUSCA.** Perfectly preserved Egyptian sarcophagi and mummies, Roman coins, and golden altarpieces mingle to fantastic effect in this extravagant collection. Also check out oil paintings by old masters and native sons Luca Signorelli and Pietro Berrettini (called Pietro da Cortona), as well as by the Futurist Gino Severini. In the main hall on the first floor is an unusual 5th-century BC Etruscan chandelier, decorated with intricate allegorical carvings. In the Medici Room, lined with coats of arms, are two 1714 globes by Silvestro Moroncelli; one depicts the "Isola di California" floating in the Pacific, the other sports vivid illustrations of all the constellations. *(P. Signorelli, inside the courtyard of Palazzo Casli, to the right of P. della Repubblica. ☎057 63 72 35; www.accademia-etrusca.org. Open Apr.-Oct. daily 10am-7pm; Nov.-Mar. Tu-Su 10am-5pm. Guided visits daily at 10:30am, 6 person max. €4.20, with guide €7, groups of 15+ €2.50 per person.)*

THE REAL DEAL. With the recent popularity of *Under the Tuscan Sun,* visitors to Cortona may find themselves approached by taxi drivers offering cheap rides out to the farmhouse featured in the book and film. Before embarking on this mini-pilgrimage, remember that it's a residence, not a tourist attraction, and ask yourself if it's really worth the money—or the potential of being ripped off by a less-than-honest driver. —*Jen Rugani*

■ **MUSEO DIOCESANO.** The upstairs gallery of this small Renaissance art museum houses the stunning *Annunciation* (c. 1432-4) by Fra Angelico in **Room 3** as well as Luca Signorelli's masterpiece, *The Deposition* (1502), a vivid portrayal of the removal of Christ's dead body from the cross that combines Classical Roman and medieval detailing. Christ's agonized face looks down from Pietro Lorenzetti's fresco of *The Way to Calvary,* and Severini's modern interpretations of traditional biblical scenes line the stairwell. *(From P. della Repubblica, pass through P. Signorelli and follow the signs. ☎0575 62 830. Open daily Apr.-Oct. 10am-7pm; Nov.-Mar. 10am-5pm. €5, 14 and under €3. Audioguides available for €3.)*

FORTEZZA MEDICEA. Views of the Val di Chiana and Lake Trasimeno beyond are better at this fortress than from P. Garibaldi. The courtyards and turrets contain temporary art installations, and shrines decorated with mosaics based on Severini's series in the Museo Diocesano, line the uphill path. On the way, the white marble facade of the **Basilica di Santa Margherita** belies bold combinations of primary colors within—blue ceilings are fancifully dotted with gold stars. The body of Santa Margherita rests eternally in a glass coffin at the center of the altarpiece. *(A thigh-burning 15min. walk up V. S. Margherita from P. Garibaldi. To reach the fortress, take a right out of the church and climb the small uphill road. ☎0575 60 37 93. Fortress open daily July-Aug. 10am-7pm; Mar-June and Sept.-Oct. 10am-6pm. Closed during bad weather. €3, under 12 €1.50. Basilica free. Modest dress required.)*

PALAZZI AND PIAZZE. In P. della Repubblica, the 13th-century **Palazzo Comunale** overlooks the surrounding shops and cafes. At night, people gather on the steps to enjoy their *gelato* and people-watch. **Palazzo Casali,** to the right and behind the Palazzo Comune, dominates P. Signorelli. Only the courtyard walls lined with coats of arms remain from the original structure; the facade and interlocking staircase are 17th-century additions. **Piazza del Duomo** lies to the right and downhill from the Palazzo Casali. Inside the simple **Cattedrale di Santa Maria** are paintings by Signorelli and del Sarto, as well as an impressive Baroque-canopied high altar and rich dark wood pulpit built in 1524. *(Duomo open 7:30am-12:30pm and 3-6:30pm.)*

❄ FESTIVALS

When August 14-15 rolls around, Italian cows start trembling. Yes, it's time for the **Sagra della Bistecca** (Steakfest), the most important town festival, when the populace converges upon piles of superb steak in the public gardens behind the church of S. Domenico. The next culinary extravaganza follows in the 3rd weekend in August with the **Festa dei Porcini,** which fills the gardens with mushroom-lovers. Tickets are sold at the garden entrance. In early June, neighborhoods commemorate a nobleman's 1397 marriage with religious ceremonies, period dress, and the **Giostra Dell'Archidado,** a crossbow challenge in which participants compete for the *verretta d'oro* (golden dart). Musical and theatrical events come in July, when Cortona absorbs the spillover from the Umbria Jazz Festival (p. 498). Relax in the gardens or join in the *passeggiata* in the park, which screens movies in the original language (usually English) weekly from mid-June through early September. (Visit www.teatrosignorelli.com for lists of films and info. Films start 9:45pm. In bad weather screenings in Teatro Signorelli. Tickets €5.)

MONTALCINO ☎ 0577

Perched atop a hill overlooking vineyards and stately clusters of cyprus, Montalcino (pop. 5000) is yet another Tuscan wine town with a view. But unlike some of its neighbors, Montalcino boasts a relatively low influx of tourists, allowing visitors to stroll leisurely along narrow alleys and steep stairways that have changed little since medieval times. A former Sienese stronghold, its heavy walls are enduring evidence of prior belligerence, but the tiny town has long since traded warmongering for wine making. Its foremost industry today is the production of the heavenly albeit pricey *Brunello di Montalcino*, a wine acknowledged as Italy's finest red. Sample the *Brunello* in the numerous wine shops or leave the city walls for a winery tour and a free taste.

▐█ TRANSPORTATION AND PRACTICAL INFORMATION. To reach Montalcino, take one of the daily **TRA-IN buses** from Siena (1¼hr., 7 per day, €3). The last bus to Montalcino departs at 10:20pm, and the last bus back to Siena departs at 8:30pm from Montalcino's P. Cavour. In Siena, the buses leave from the **train station,** not P. Gramsci, but both TRA-IN ticket windows sells tickets (see **Siena: Transportation,** p. 448). Coming from Montepulciano (1¼hr., €3.50), change buses at Torrenieri. There is no actual bus stop, so flag the bus down as it approaches. Contact the **Pro-Loco tourist office,** Costa del Municipio, 8, for information about tours of the local vineyards, free **maps,** hotel booking, and **currency exchange.** From P. Cavour, where the bus stops, walk up V. Mazzini to P. del Popolo. The tourist office is under the clock tower on the right. (☎0577 84 93 31; www.prolocomontalcino.it. Open Apr.-Oct. daily 10am-1pm and 2-5:50pm; Nov.-Mar. Tu-Su 10am-1pm and 2-5:40pm.) Rent a **mountain bike** (€13 per day) or **scooter** (from €26 per day) at **Minocci Lorenzo Noleggio,** V. P. Strozzi, 31, in the gas station. (☎0577 84 82 82; montalcinolmnoleggio@libero.it. Open by appointment only from 9am, so call first.)

▐▌ ACCOMMODATIONS AND FOOD. Hotel rooms are expensive and scarce in Montalcino; *affittacamere* are generally well-kept and run €42-52 for a double with bath. The tourist office provides a list of all hotels and *affittacamere* in the area. ▨**Anna Affittacamera ❹,** V. S. Saloni, provides luxury for a low price. Rooms have ceiling frescoes, comfortable beds, TV, and bath. (☎0577 84 86 66; fax 0577 84 81 67. Singles €42; doubles €64. Apartment with kitchen and terrace €60-80.) Closest to the bus stop is **Albergo Il Giardino ❸**, P. Cavour, 4, where the friendly owner is more than willing to share his extensive knowledge and collection of local wines. The large, tasteful rooms all have spacious baths. (☎0577 84 82 57. Singles €35-38; doubles €53; triples €72.) **Il Barlanzone Affittacamere ❹**, V. Ricasoli, 33, rents four color-coordinated rooms and an apartment with TVs, large baths, and an unobstructed view of the fortress. (☎0577 84 61 20. Singles €45; doubles €55; apartment €75. Weekly rentals receive 10% discount. MC/V.)

Montalcino's wine menus are generally twice as thick as the food menus. The best deals on *Brunello* (€16-27) are at the **COOP**, on the corner of V. Sant'Agostino and V. della Libertà. (Open M-Tu and Th-Sa 8am-1pm and 4-8pm, W 8am-1pm.) *Enoteche* line V. Mazzini, the town's main street, all offering huge selections of *Brunello* and tasty snacks like *bruschette* and cheese and meat plates (€3-7). In the rustic and brightly painted **Taverna Il Grappolo Blu ❸**, Scale di V. Moglio, 1, down a small staircase off of V. Mazzini, a memorable ravioli with pecorino cheese and *ragù* (€8) is just one of many superior options. (☎0577 84 71 50. Cover €1.50. Open M-Th and Sa-Su noon-3pm and 7-10pm. AmEx/MC/V.) Complement a meal at Maria Pia's **Re di Macchia ❹**, V. S. Saloni, 21, with *Il Consiglio di Antonio* (€14), four of Montalcino's premier wines. (☎0577 84 61 16. *Primi* €8, *secondi* €10-12. Cover €2.50. Open M-W and F-Su noon-2pm and 7-9pm. AmEx/MC/V.)

🄶 **SIGHTS.** The ▓**Abbazia di Sant'Antimo,** is in Castelnuovo, a town 10km from Montalcino on the same La Peschiera route as the Fattoria dei Barbi; return times at 7:45am, 2:25, and 4:55pm (€1.10 one-way). The walk from Castelnuovo to the abbey takes about 8min. and passes the sloping hills and cypress trees characteristic of the Tuscan countryside. Lore holds that Charlemagne founded the abbey in AD 780 as thanksgiving for the miraculous curing of the plague that was scourging his army. The actual structure standing was built in the early 12th century, with a rounded apse and carved alabaster capitals, and is one of Tuscany's most beautiful Romanesque structures. Inside, monks perform mass in **Gregorian chant** seven times per day (during which time the church is closed to the public). Chants float through speakers throughout the rest of the day. (☎0577 83 56 69; www.antimo.it. Open M-Sa 10:30am-12:30pm and 3-6:30pm, Su 9-10:30am and 3-6pm.)

Back in town stands Montalcino's 14th-century **fortezza,** which sheltered a band of republicans escaping the Florentine siege of Siena in 1555. The fortress is almost perfectly preserved, with five towers and part of the town walls incorporated into the structure. Two interior courtyards, one shaded by foliage, the other sunny and cheered by geraniums, make nice picnic spots. Many visitors bypass the fortress itself in favor of the sophisticated **Enoteca La Fortezza,** which offers free tastings, cheese plates (€8) and local wines (€3-9 per glass; *Brunello* €6.50-15). A climb up the stairs, through the turret, and onto the panoramic walls is €3.50, but you can enjoy great views from the ground for free. (Fort and *enoteca* open Apr.-Oct. daily 9am-8pm; Nov.-Mar. Tu-Su 9am-6pm.)

To appreciate the area vineyards, use the local shuttle service, **La Peschiera,** (☎0564 95 31 34) to visit **Fattoria dei Barbi.** Shuttles depart daily from P. Cavour at 7:10am, 1:45, 2:45, and 7pm; return 7:45am, 2:25, and 4:55pm. Ask the driver to stop at the Fattoria. Shuttle stops at the bottom of an 800m driveway; walk up to the entrance. Tours of the extensive cellars are followed by a tasting of three different kinds of *Brunello*. Tastings are available any time during open hours; ring the bell for service. The winery also includes a restaurant, which is open for lunch and dinner. (☎0577 84 11 11; www.fattoriadeibarbi.it. Open M-F 10am-1pm and 2:30-7pm, Sa-Su 2:30-7pm. Free 30min. tours given M-F every hr. 11am-noon and 3-5pm.)

VOLTERRA ☎0588

Atop a huge bluff known as *Le Balze*, Volterra stands alone in a surrounding checkerboard of green and yellow farmland. Once an important Etruscan settlement, the town shrunk to its current size during the Middle Ages, when outlying parts fell from the eroding hillside. With its Roman amphitheater and Etruscan-era alabaster statues standing among medieval palaces and modern *enoteche*, Volterra blends centuries of Tuscan tradition with a friendly and much-touristed atmosphere. If you've ever wondered why the Tuscan countryside is so popular with visitors, take a short walk to the city's perimeter and admire the sprawling fields and distant mountains—you'll understand what all the fuss is about.

⌐ TRANSPORTATION

The **train station** that services Volterra is in the nearby town of Cecina. To get there, take the **CPT bus** to Saline (6 per day, Su and Aug. 2 per day; €1.50). From Saline, transfer to another CPT bus to Cecina for trains to Pisa (€6.50) and the coast. Service to Cecina via Saline runs five times per day during the week (last bus at 6:20pm), and only two times on Sunday. For other schedules and information, consult the tourist office or call ☎0588 86 150. **Buses** (☎0588 86 150) are in P. Martiri della Libertà, with daily departures to Florence (1½hr., €6.56). **TRA-IN** connects to San Gimignano (1½hr., €4.25), Siena (1½hr., €4.40), and other points in Tuscany. Most destinations require a change at Colle Val d'Elsa; be sure to anticipate plenty of time for connections, and pick up a schedule from the tourist office. **CPT** runs buses between Volterra and Colle Val d'Elsa, and also runs to Pisa (2hr., 10 per day, €4.91) via Pontedera. Buy tickets at **Associazione Pro Volterra**, at *tabaccherie*, or at vending machines near the bus stop. **TRA-SITA** runs buses from Colle Val D'Elsa to other points in Tuscany. Buy tickets at travel agencies or ticket offices in towns. For **taxis,** call ☎0588 87 257.

✳ ⁊ ORIENTATION AND PRACTICAL INFORMATION

To get from the bus stop in **Piazza Martiri della Libertà** to the town center in **Piazza dei Priori,** turn right from the bus stop, walk into town and turn left on **Via Ricciarelli.** Most of Volterra's main streets radiate from P. dei Priori

Tourist Office: Consorzio Turistico, P. dei Priori, 19 (☎0588 86 099; www.volterra-tur.it). Provides **maps,** brochures, and audio walking tours (€7 per person, €10 for 2). Also makes hotel and taxi reservations for free. Open daily 10am-1pm and 2-6pm.
Associazione Pro Volterra, V. Turazza (☎0588 86 150; www.provolterra.it), just off P. dei Priori, sells CPT bus tickets and provides schedule and fare information on trains to Pisa and buses to Florence, Pisa, Saline di Volterra, San Gimignano, and Siena.

Currency Exchange: Cassa di Risparmio di Volterra, V. Matteotti, 1, has a 24hr. exchange machine and an **ATM** outside. Also in P. Martiri della Libertà. Open M-F 8:20am-1:20pm and 2:35-3:35pm, Sa 8:20-11:20am.

Emergency: ☎113. **Ambulance:** ☎118.

Pharmacy: Farmacia Amidei, V. Ricciarelli, 2 (☎0588 86 060). Open M-Sa 9am-1pm and 4-8pm; open Su for emergencies, call number posted in window.

Hospital: ☎0588 91 911. On Borgo S. Lazzaro.

Internet Access: ▧**Web and Wine,** V. Porte all'Arco, 11/13 (☎0588 81 531; www.webandwine.com). After surfing the web, kick back with a glass of Chianti or one of 37 different kinds of hot chocolate and cast an eye over Etruscan ruins visible through the glass floor. €5 per hr. Open Tu-Su 7am-1am. **SESHA,** P. XX Settembre, 10. €6 per hr. Open daily 9am-1pm and 3:30-8pm. MC/V.

Post Office: P. dei Priori, 14 (☎0588 86 969). Open M-F 8:15am-7pm, Sa 8:15am-12:30pm. **Postal Code:** 56048.

☗ ACCOMMODATIONS AND CAMPING

Hotels can get expensive, so ask the tourist office for a list of *affittacamere*. Singles start at €30, doubles at €40.

▧ **La Torre,** V. Guarnacci, 47 (☎0588 80 036 or 348 72 47 693). From bus stop, turn right into town, then left and immediately right on V. Matteoti, which becomes V. Guarnacci right after it crosses V. Gramsci. Great *affittacamere* in the historical center. Rooms sport matching wood furniture, comfy beds, large bath, and TV. Owner supplies city maps and generously stocks free drinks. Call ahead or book through tourist office. Singles €33; doubles €42. Cash only. ❸

▧ **Seminario Vescovile,** V. V. Veneto, 2 (☎0588 86 028; fax 0588 90 791), in P. S. Andrea, next to the church. Follow directions to La Torre, but turn right on V. Gramsci, walk through P. XX Settembre, then turn left. Exit city through Pta. Marcoli and follow the road, turn left on V. V. Veneto and continue until Sant'Andrea is visible. High, arched ceilings, frescoed doorways, and views of the walled city and Tuscan countryside. 2- to 4-person rooms, no unmarried couples. Breakfast €3. Reception 8am-midnight. Curfew midnight. Reservation required. Rooms €14, with bath €18. AmEx/MC/V. ❷

Albergo Etruria, V. Matteotti, 32 (☎0588 87 377). Walk into town, turn left, then make the 1st right on V. Matteotti; the Etruria is a few blocks down. Carefully decorated cream-colored rooms with TV and phone, private garden, and a classy lounge make this a congenial place. Breakfast €6. Singles €60; doubles €80. Extra bed €30. MC/V. ❹

Hotel La Locanda, V. Guarnacci 24/28 (☎0588 81 547; www.hotel-lalocanda.com). A former convent turned 4-star hotel. Rooms adorned with matching bedspreads, curtains, and upholstered furniture are hung with artwork from a local gallery. All have bath, satellite TV, fridge, Internet port, and safe. Buffet breakfast included. Doubles €85-120, double room for one person is 20% off double-price; wheelchair-accessible double €80-105; suite with massaging shower and sauna €250. AmEx/MC/V. ❺

Le Balze, V. Mandringa, 15 (☎0588 87 880). Exit through Pta. S. Francesco and bear right on Strada Provincial Pisana. Turn left on V. Mandringa after 20min. Campground has pool and bar. Store sells tickets for bus into town (every hr. 8:18am-9:21pm). Showers included. Reception 8-10am and 3:30-10pm. Cars must be parked by 11pm. Open Apr.-Oct. €6 per person, €4 per tent, €7 per camper. AmEx/MC/V. ❶

☐ FOOD

Excellent local cheeses and game dishes are available at any of the *alimentari* along V. Guarnacci and V. Gramsci. Sample *salsiccia di cinghiale* (wild boar sausage) and pecorino (sheep's milk cheese). For a sweet snack, try *ossi di morto* (bones of the dead man), a rock-hard local confection made of egg whites, sugar, hazelnuts, and a hint of lemon, or *pane di pescatore* (fisherman's bread), a dense and delicious sweet bread full of nuts and raisins. Pick up groceries at **Despar,** V. Gramsci, 12. (Open M-F 7:30am-1pm and 5-8pm, Sa 7:30am-1pm.)

▩ **L'Ombra della Sera,** V. Gramsci, 70 (☎0588 86 663), off P. XX Settembre. A local favorite whose candlelit outdoor patio on busy V. Gramsci makes for great people watching during a summer evening. Rich Volterran classics, like *tagliolini al tartufo* (€9) are stellar choices. *Primi* €6-9, *secondi* €9-13.90. Cover €1.30. Service 10%. Open Tu-Su noon-3pm and 7-10pm. AmEx/MC/V. ❸

Trattoria Il Poggio, V. Porte all'Arco, 9 (☎0588 85 257). Pasta dishes with meat sauces and a "medieval" *menù* (€13) featuring local cheeses are the highlights at this casual restaurant, accompanied by interesting medieval paraphernalia, like giant crossed axes hanging from the walls. Pizza €4.50-6.50. *Primi* €5-8, *secondi* €6-13. MC/V. ❸

Pizzeria/Birreria Ombra della Sera, V. Guarnacci, 16 (☎0588 85 274). Frantic cooks toss pizzas with crispy crusts, while diners relax under sleek cross-vaulted ceilings and the warm glow of red lanterns. Takeout available. Pizza €4.20-7.20; salad €6; pasta €5.50-7. Cover €0.90. Service 10%. Open Tu-Su noon-3pm and 7-10pm. MC/V. ❶

Ristorante Etruria, P. dei Priori, 6/8 (☎0588 86 066). Volterran dinner spot has shaded outdoor seating amid towers and palaces on the main *piazza*. Rich soups and local game featured in varying preparations (€13.50-22.50). *Primi* €4-10, *secondi* €4.50-16. Service 10%. Open M-Tu and Th-Su noon-3pm and 7-10pm. AmEx/MC/V. ❸

⊙ SIGHTS

PINACOTECA COMUNALE. This graceful building contains Volterra's best art, held in dimly lit rooms with few labels. The first floor showcases two dramatic works: Rosso Fiorentino's spectacular *Deposizione della Croce*, in which Christ's body has a greenish tinge (most likely from aging and poor restoration); and Luca Signorelli's far richer *Annunciazione*, filled with finely-realized details of architecture and cloth. Fiorentino's painting spills from the canvas onto the frame, creating the mesmerizing illusion that his subjects are not confined to the flat surface. *(V. dei Sarti, 1. Up V. Buonparenti from P. dei Priori. ☎0588 87 580. Open daily 9am-7pm. €8, students €5, children under 10 free. Combination ticket including Pinacoteca, Museo Etrusco, and Museo dell' Opera del Duomo di Arte Sacra is sold at any sight.)*

PIAZZA DEI PRIORI AND FORTEZZA MEDICEA. Life in Volterra revolves around P. dei Priori, which is surrounded by sober, dignified palaces. The **Palazzo dei Priori,** the oldest governmental palace in Tuscany (1208-1254), presides over the square. Regal coats of arms line the walls of the first floor. Inside, the council hall and antechamber are open to the public. Jacopo di Cione Orcagna's damaged *Annunciation with Four Saints* occupies the right wall. The *sinopia*, the fresco's preliminary drawing, is in the adjoining antechamber. *(Open daily 10am-1pm and 2-6pm. €1.)* Across the *piazza*, **Palazzo Pretorio's** 13th-century buildings and towers house municipal offices.

CATTEDRALE DI SANTA MARIA ASSUNTA. Construction began on Volterra's pre-Romanesque cathedral in the 12th century and continued for three centuries. By the time the choir at the end of the nave was completed, architects had already switched to a Gothic design, indicated by the transition from rounded arches to pointed ones. The chapel off the left transept holds frescoes by Rosselli, including the luminous *Missione per Damasco.* On the right, a chapel holds the remains of Volterran Saints Ugo and Ottaviano—their skulls are still visible in the glass chambers. *(Down V. Turazza from P. dei Priori to P. S. Giovanni. Open daily 8am-12:30pm and 3-7pm.)*

MUSEO ETRUSCO GUARNACCI. The Etruscan museum displays over 600 finely carved funeral urns from the 4th to the first centuries BC. The pieces are not well displayed and lack explanatory signs, but an audio tour (€4.50) covers a few rooms. The first floor (Room XIV) holds the museum's most famous piece, the elongated bronze figure dubbed *l'Ombra della Sera* (Shadow of the Evening). The farmer who unearthed it used it for years as a fireplace poker until a visitor recognized it as an Etruscan votive figure. In Room XIX, the famous urn *Urna degli Sposi* depicts an obviously embittered married couple. *(V. Minzoni, 15. From P. dei Priori, head down to V. Matteotti, turn right on V. Gramsci, and follow it to V. Minzoni. ☎0588 86 347. Gallery and museum open daily mid-Mar. to Oct. 9am-7pm; Nov. to mid-Mar. 9am-2pm.)*

ROMAN AMPHITHEATER. These impressive ruins include partly grass-covered stone seating and Corinthian columns salvaged from the stage. The admission fee allows you to walk the edge of the ruins behind metal rails, but the vantage point from V. Lungo le Mura is free and just as gratifying. *(Just outside the city walls next to Pta. Fiorentina. From P. dei Priori, follow V. delle Prigioni, turn right at the T-junction and left on V. Guarnacci. Proceed out the porta and through the parking lot to the left. Open daily Mar. 16-Nov. 1 10:30am-5:30pm; Nov. 2-Mar. 15 Sa-Su 10am-4pm. €2.)*

PALAZZO VITI. This private residence is still home to descendants of the wealthy Viti family, but 12 rooms are open to the public. The furnishings and alabaster collections date from the 15th century to the present, and the beautiful interior was used as a film set by Italian director Luchino Visconti. *(Via dei Sarti, 41, down the street from the Pinacoteca. Open daily 10am-1pm and 2:30-6:30pm. €4, students €2.50.)*

SAN GIMIGNANO ☎0577

The hilltop village of San Gimignano looks like an illustration from a medieval manuscript. Prototypical towers, churches, and palaces loom above the city's walls as if from a fairy tale. San Gimignano's 14 famous towers, all that remain of the original 72, date from a period when prosperous families battled, using their towers to store grain for sieges. They were also conveniently used for dumping boiling oil on attacking enemies. After WWII, the skyline began to lure tourists, whose tastes and wallets resuscitated production of the golden *Vernaccia* wine. With hordes of daytrippers, an infestation of souvenir shops, and innumerable eateries, San Gimignano now has something of the feel of a medieval Disneyland. But the fortress-top sunsets, nighttime *gelato* strolls, and ample spots for lounging on *piazza* steps make an overnight stay worthwhile.

⌐ TRANSPORTATION

The nearest **train station** is in Poggibonsi; buses from the station to town (20min; M-F every 30min. 6:05am-8:35pm, Sa-Su every hr. 7:35am-8:20pm; €1.35). **TRA-IN buses** (☎0577 20 41 11 or 0577 93 72 07) leave from P. Montemaggio, outside Pta. S. Giovanni. Schedules and tickets are at Caffè Combattente, V. S. Giovanni, 124, on the left after entering the city gates. Tickets are also available at *tabaccherie* or the tourist office. Change at Poggibonsi for Florence (1½hr., every hr., €6). Buses also run to Siena (1½hr., every 1-2hr., €5.20). For **bike** and **car rental** try **Bruno Bellini**, V. Roma, 41, 200m down the hill from Pta. S. Giovanni. (☎0577 94 02 01; www.bellinibruno.com. Bikes €7-11 per hr., €15-21 per day. Scooters from €31 per day. Cars from €67 per day. Open daily 9am-1pm and 3-8pm. AmEx/MC/V.)

✈ ? ORIENTATION AND PRACTICAL INFORMATION

Buses to San Gimignano stop in **Piazzale Martini Montemaggio,** just outside the city walls. To reach the center, pass through **Porta San Matteo** and climb the hill, following **Via San Giovanni** to **Piazza della Cisterna,** which merges with **Piazza del Duomo** on the left. The other main street in town, **Via San Matteo,** extends down from the opposite side of P. del Duomo. Addresses in San Gimignano are marked in both faded black stencil and etched clay tiles; since most establishments go by the black, these are listed.

Tourist Office: Pro Loco, P. del Duomo, 1 (☎0577 94 00 08; prolocsg@tin.it), has lists of hotels and rooms for rent, as well as bus and train schedules and bus tickets. Self-guided audio tours of the town available (€5). Excellent free **maps.** Offers 2hr. tours of wineries Tu 11am and Th 5pm. Includes multiple tastings (all with food) and transportation by bus for €26 (€18 with own transportation). Reserve by noon the day before. Also makes private room reservations in person. Open daily Mar.-Oct. 9am-1pm and 3-7pm; Nov.-Feb. 9am-1pm and 2-6pm.

Accommodations Services: Siena Hotels Promotion, V. S. Giovanni, 125 (☎0577 94 08 09; fax 0577 94 01 13), on the right entering the city gates; look for *"Cooperativa Alberghi e Ristoranti"* sign. Reserves hotel rooms in San Gimignano and Siena for 5% commission. Open M-Sa 9:30am-7pm. **Associazione Strutture Extralberghiere,** P. della Cisterna, 6 (☎/fax 0577 94 31 90). Patient staff makes free reservations for *affitta-camere,* or private rooms. Doubles with bath €50-60. Call a week ahead to stay in the countryside; the city center is easier to book. Open Mar.-Nov. daily 9:30am-7:30pm.

Currency Exchange: Pro Loco tourist office and post office offer best rates. Rip-offs elsewhere. **ATMs** scattered along V. S. Giovanni, V. degli Innocenti, and P. della Cisterna.

Police: ☎112. **Ambulance:** ☎118. **Carabinieri:** (☎0577 94 03 13), on P. Martiri.

Pharmacy: P. della Cisterna, 8 (☎0577 94 03 69). Fills urgent prescriptions all night; call ☎0368 71 36 675. Open M-Sa 9am-1pm and 4:30-8pm.

Internet Access: Edicola La Tuscia, outside the gates at the beginning of V. S. Matteoti. €4.50 per hr. Open M-Tu and Th-Sa 7am-1pm and 2:30-8pm, W and Su 7am-6pm.

Post Office: P. delle Erbe, 8, behind the *duomo.* Open M-F 8:15am-4pm, Sa 8:15am-12:30pm. **Currency exchange** available. **Postal Code:** 53037.

▐ ACCOMMODATIONS AND CAMPING

San Gimignano caters to wealthy tourists, and most accommodations are well beyond budget range. *Affittacamere* provide an alternative to overpriced hotels, with most doubles with bath from €50-60. Look for the signs for "Camere/Rooms/Zimmer" that hang in souvenir shops, restaurants, and other storefront windows along main streets. The tourist office and the **Associazione Strutture Extralberghiere** (see **Practical Information,** above) has lists of budget rooms.

Camere Cennini Gianni, V. S. Giovanni, 21 (☎347 07 48 188; www.sangiapartments.com). Enter through Pta. S. Giovanni. Reception is at the *pasticceria* at V. S. Giovanni, 88. Each room is homey and luxurious, with large bath, heated towel-rack, and lovely views of the surrounding vineyards. Use of kitchens for groups of 4, €15 extra. Reserve ahead. Singles €47; doubles €55; triples €65; quads €75. Cash only. ❹

Albergo Il Pino, V. Cellolese, 6 (☎/fax 0577 94 04 15), just off V. S. Matteo before exiting Pta. S. Matteo. Rustic and spacious rooms owned by the restaurant downstairs have quilted comforters and dark wood furnishings, comfy sofa chairs, and TV. Dogs allowed. Reservation recommended. Singles €45; doubles €55. AmEx/MC/V. ❹

Hotel La Cisterna, P. della Cisterna, 24 (☎0577 94 03 28; www.hotelcisterna.it). Large rosemary-scented rooms with flowing, floral curtains complement the pastoral panorama. All rooms have bath, A/C, safe, and satellite TV. Buffet breakfast included. Singles €70; doubles €90, with view €105-116. Extra bed €30. AmEx/MC/V. ❺

Il Boschetto di Piemma (☎0577 94 03 52; www.boschettodipiemma.it), at Santa Lucia, 2.5km downhill from Pta. S. Giovanni. Buses (€0.50) run from P. dei Martiri. Confirm destination with driver before boarding. Small, wooded sites close together, but near community pool. Bungalows available for €20. Bar and market on premises. Reception daily 8am-1pm and 3-10pm. Open year-round. €7.20 per person, €4.50 per child, €6.50 per small tent, €3 per car. Hot showers free. ❶

🎨 FOOD

If the sad glass eyes of stuffed tuskers around town aren't enough of a hint, San Gimignano specializes in boar and other wild game. It also caters to less daring palates with mainstream Tuscan dishes at higher prices. A weekly **open-air market** is in P. del Duomo and P. della Cisterna. (Open Th 8am-1pm.) Purchase the famous *Vernaccia di San Gimignano*, a light, sweet white wine, from **La Buca**, V. S. Giovanni, 16, for around €4.50. This cooperative also offers tastes of terrific sausages and meats produced on its own farm. The boar sausage *al pignoli* (with pine nuts; €2.07 per 100g) and the oddly satisfying *salame con mirto* (with blueberry) are delicious. (☎0577 94 04 07. Open daily Apr.-Oct. 9am-8pm; Nov.-Mar. 9am-7pm. AmEx/MC/V.)

■ **Trattoria Chiribiri**, P. della Madonna, 1 (☎0577 94 19 48). From the bus stop, take the 1st left off V. S. Giovanni and climb a short staircase. Tiny restaurant serves amazing local fare at unusually affordable prices. The dining room can get overheated, but the attentive servers are ready and waiting with cooling fans. *Primi* €5-7, *secondi* €6.80-11. Open Mar.-Oct. M-Tu and Th-Su 11am-11pm; Nov.-Feb. M-Tu and Th-Su noon-2pm and 7-10pm. Cash only. ❷

■ **Pluripremiata Gelateria**, P. della Cisterna, 4 (☎0577 94 22 44). 3 counters hold *gelato* flavors never seen before. Try the *champelmo*, a mix of champagne and grapefruit, or the creative *Vernaccia*, a *gelato* version of the region's famous wine. Cups start at €1.50. 3 flavors in a chocolate-lined cone €2.20. Open daily 11:30am-9pm. ❶

La Stella, V. S. Matteo, 77 (☎0577 94 04 44). Food made with produce from the restaurant's own farm and served in the long narrow dining room with an alleyway of tables. Sample homemade pasta with wild boar sauce (€7.80) or try an assorted *primi* platter (€8.75). Extensive wine list includes the crisp *Vernaccia*. *Primi* €4.65-8.75, *secondi* €7.50-12.45. *Menù turistico* €15. Cover €1.85. Open Apr.-Oct M-Tu and Th-Su noon-2:30pm and 7-9:30pm; Nov.-Mar. noon-2pm and 7-9pm. AmEx/MC/V. ❸

Ristorante Perucà, V. Capassi, 16 (☎0577 94 31 36). Behind V. S. Matteo. Charming benches and lanterns welcome diners to a quieter spot hidden away from the tourist bustle. Experimental types will love the *semifreddo ai zafferano*, an ice cream dessert made with saffron (€5). *Primi* €5-9, *secondi* €9-16. Cover €2. Open M-W and F-Su noon-2:30pm and 7-10:30pm. AmEx/MC/V. ❸

👁 SIGHTS

Famous as the *Città delle Belle Torri* (City of the Beautiful Towers), San Gimignano has always appealed to artists. During the Renaissance, they came in droves, and the collection of their works complement San Gimignano's cityscape. Now the narrow, car-less streets cater to throngs of sightseers and souvenir-hunters.

■ **PIAZZA DELLA CISTERNA AND PIAZZA DEL DUOMO.** As in any other proper hill town, the central P. della Cisterna (1237) is surrounded by towers and palaces and is the bustling center of life in San Gimignano. It adjoins P. del Duomo, site of the impressive tower of the **Palazzo del Podestà**. To its left, tunnels and intricate *loggie* riddle the Palazzo del Popolo. To the right of the *palazzo* rises its **Torre Grossa**, the town's highest tower and the only one people can climb. Also in the *piazza* stand the twin towers of the Ardinghelli, truncated due to a medieval zoning ordinance that regulated tower envy by prohibiting structures higher than the Torre Grossa. A perch on one of the steps in either *piazza* offers ample opportunity for watching scenery and people.

MUSEO DELLA TORTURA. This disturbing museum (a sign near the entrance to the first room actually forbids the entrance of "sensitive people") displays over 50 torture devices put to use from the Middle Ages to the present. The nine rooms are filled with axes, swords, chastity belts, spiked collars, guillotines, the rack, an Iron Maiden, and even a primitive electric chair. Morbidly fascinating captions in multiple languages explain the history and mechanics of the devices. If that wasn't enough, diagrams accompany each display, depicting the torture device in use—particularly instructive in the case of the rectal pear. *(V. del Castello, 1, off P. della Cisterna. Open daily Apr.-Oct. 10am-8pm; Nov.-Mar. 10am-6pm. €8, students under 18 €5.)*

PALAZZO COMUNALE. A frescoed medieval courtyard leads to the entrance to the **Museo Civico** on the 2nd floor. The first room of the museum is the **Sala di Dante,** where the bard spoke on May 8, 1300 in an attempt to convince San Gimignano to side with the Florentines in their ongoing wars with Siena. On the walls, Lippo Memmi's sparkling *Maestà* overwhelms the accompanying 14th-century scenes of hunting and tournament pageantry. Up the stairs, Taddeo di Bartolo's altarpiece, *The Story of San Gimignano,* tells the tale of the city's namesake saint, originally a bishop of Modena. Within the museum lies the entrance to the 218-step climb up **Torre Grossa.** While the final steps are precarious (watch your head on the low ceiling at the top), they are well worth it, as the tower offers views of a half dozen of San Gimignano's towers, the ancient fortress, several *piazze* and the Tuscan landscape stretching to the horizon in all directions. The tower's bell rings daily at noon. *(Palazzo del Popolo, Museo Civico, and Tower open daily Mar.-Oct. 9:30am-7pm; Nov.-Feb. 10am-5:30pm €5, students €4.)*

BASILICA DI SANTA MARIA ASSUNTA. The bare facade of this 12th-century church seems unfit to shelter such an exceptionally frescoed interior. Off the right aisle, the **Cappella di Santa Fina** is covered in Ghirlandaio's frescoes of the life of Santa Fina, the town's ascetic local saint who was stricken with a fatal disease at the age of 10. In the main church, Bartolo di Fredi painted beautiful frescoes of Old Testament scenes along the north aisle, while Barna da Siena provided the extremely impressive New Testament counterparts along the south aisle. *(In P. del Duomo. Church and chapel open M-Sa 9:30am-3pm and 5:15-7:30pm, Su 12:30-5pm. Closed Feb. €3.50, students under 18 €1.50.)*

FORTEZZA. Follow the signs past the Basilica di Collegiata from P. del Duomo to this tiny, crumbling fortress. The courtyard is often full of street artists and musicians, and the turret offers a beautiful view of the countryside. Park benches protected by trees make for a great picnic or lounge spot when visitors clear out in the evening. There are weekly screenings of movies in the courtyard at night from June to August. *(Schedule and info at the tourist office. Movies €6, children €4.)*

TUSCANY

PISTOIA   ☎ 0573

Many travelers regard Pistoia (pop. 84,000) only as a stop on the train between Florence and Lucca. It's a small but surprisingly urban Tuscan city that is worth a day's visit. In the perfectly flat P. del Duomo, the black- and-white-checkered cathedral, baptistry, and *campanile* dominate the scenery. Pistoia's history is as checkered as its buildings. In 1177 the town joined several other Italian city-states in declaring its independence, but was soon surpassed by its neighbors in military, political, and economic strength. Thereafter, Pistoia became a murderous backwater, whose inhabitants Michelangelo maligned as "enemies of heaven." Lending its name to the pistol and *pistole* dagger, the town's bloody reputation spawned a debauched and enduring mythology. Today, the more peaceful residents prefer to pick their battles, haggling over produce prices in the open-air markets of P. della Sala or rooting for the closest soccer team.

▐ TRANSPORTATION

Pistoia is accessible by train or bus. The **train station** is in P. Dante Alighieri. **Trains** run to: Florence (40min., every hr. 4:40am-11pm, €2.60); Pisa (1hr., every 2hr. 6:50am-11:30pm, €4); Rome (4hr., every hr., €25-32) via Florence; and Viareggio (1 hr., every 2hr. 6:15am-10:30pm, €4). **COPIT buses** run from the train station to Empoli (1¼hr., 6:20am-8pm, €3.10) and Florence (1hr., 5am-10:20pm, €3.10). Buy tickets at COPIT vendors or across from the train station at V. XX Settembre, 71. **Cooperative Pistoia Taxi** (☎ 0573 21 237 or 0573 24 291) is in P. Garibaldi, P. San Francesco, and at the train station. Night service is available until 1am. **Cicli Bencini**, C. Gramsci, 98, rents mountain **bikes** for €15 per day. (☎ 0573 25 144. Open M-Sa 8:30am-1pm and 2:30-7:30pm. AmEx/MC/V.)

✦ ▐ ORIENTATION AND PRACTICAL INFORMATION

To reach the *centro* from the **train station**, walk up **Via XX Settembre** and continue straight as it changes names to **Via Vanucci** and then to **Via Cino**. Turn right on **Via Cavour**, then left on **Via Roma**, which leads to **Piazza del Duomo**, the heart of the town. Local buses #1 and 3 (€0.60) stop at **Piazza Gavinana**. From there, turn right on Via Cavour and left on Via Roma to P. del Duomo. An **APT Tourist Office**, P. del Duomo, 4, is in Palazzo dei Vescovi. The English-speaking staff distributes free **maps** and brochures and helps find accommodations. (☎ 0573 21 622; fax 0573 34 327. Open daily 9am-1pm and 3-6pm.) **Currency exchange** (traveler's checks and cash) is available at **Cassa di Risparmio di Pistoia e Pescia**, V. S. Matteo, 3. (☎ 0573 36 91. Open M-F 8:20am-1:20pm and 2:50-3:50pm.) In case of **emergency**, call the **police** at ☎ 112 or an **ambulance** at ☎ 118. A **pharmacy** is at V. Cino, 33. (☎ 0573 36 81 80. Open daily 8:30am-1pm and 3:30-8pm.) For the **hospital**, call ☎ 0573 35 21. **Internet** is available at the tourist office (€5 per hr.) and at **Telnet Internet Point**, V. G. Carducci, 7. (☎ 0573 99 35 71. €3 per hr. Open M-F 9:30am-1pm and 3:30pm-midnight, Sa 9:30am-1pm and 3:30-8pm, 2nd and 4th Su of the month 3:30-8pm.) The **post office**, V. Roma, 5 (☎ 0573 99 53 03), near the bank, exchanges currency and American Express Traveler's Cheques. (Open M-Sa 8:15am-7pm.) **Postal Code:** 51100.

▐ ▐ ACCOMMODATIONS AND FOOD

Most rooms are centrally located and somewhat expensive. *Affittacamere* listings are available from the tourist office, but most of the cheaper rooms are in localities far from town. As one happy guest wrote in their guest book, staying at **Bed & Breakfast Canto alla Porta Vecchia ❸**, V. Curtatone e Montanara, 2, is living like a real Pistoian. Take V. XX Settembre from the train station; the road changes names several times before becoming V. Curtatone e Montanara. There is no sign, so watch for the address in front. In front of the large wooden doors, walk up the steps to buzz in. Carved dark wooden beds, red satin couches, antique furniture, and original sketches furnish the four frescoed rooms. Friendly owners Anna and Giovanni serve complimentary drinks and guests gather on the terrace to chat. (☎/ fax 0573 27 692. Singles €30; doubles €60, with bath €70. Cash only.) Up the street to the left, **Albergo Firenze ❸**, V. Curtatone e Montanara, 42, offers basic rooms and relative value. All rooms have A/C, satellite TV, minibar, high ceilings, and lace curtains. (☎0573 23 141; www.hotel-firenze.it. Breakfast and Internet included. Singles €45, with bath €62; doubles €65-84. Extra bed €25. AmEx/MC/V.)

Grocery stores and specialty shops line the side streets. Bargain hunters browse the **open-air market** in and around P. del Duomo for deals on items from shower curtains to silver jewelry. (Open W and Sa 7:30am-2pm.) P. della Sala has hosted a fruit and vegetable **market** since medieval times. (Open daily 8am-7pm.) A **Dimeglio** supermarket is on V. Veneto, across from the train station and to the right. (Open M-Tu and Th-Su 8am-10pm, W 8am-1:30pm.) **Trattoria dell'Abbondanza ❸**, V. dell'Abbondanza, 10, serves an excellent *panzanella di Farro* (€6), a summer salad of oil-soaked bread, basil, tomatoes, parsley, and garlic. (☎0573 36 80 37. *Primi* €6-8, *secondi* €7-12. Open M,W, and F-Su 12:15-2:15pm and 7-10:30pm, Tu and Th 7-10:30pm. MC/V.) Sample from the lengthy wine list at **La Botte Gaia ❸**, V. Lastrone, 17/19, or try gourmet cheeses, salads, and other delectable *antipasti* at outdoor tables with stylish residents of Pistoia. The *bruschette* (€3.50) with sun-dried tomato and pecorino (sheep's milk cheese) are small but heavenly. (☎0573 36 56 02. *Antipasti* from €3. *Primi* and *secondi* €6-12. Cover €1.50. Open Tu-Sa 10:30am-3pm and 6:30pm-1am, Su 6:30pm-1am. Reserve ahead. AmEx/MC/V.) Menus in multiple languages present the ample choices at **Ristorante San Jacopo ❸**, V. Crispi, 15. The emphasis is on meaty Tuscan dishes and the dining room is airy, with cream table cloths and vaulted walls. (☎0573 23 141. *Primi* €6-9, *secondi* €7.50-12. Open Tu-Sa 12:15-2:30pm and 7-10pm, Su 12:15-2:30pm. AmEx/MC/V.)

👁 SIGHTS

CATTEDRALE DI SAN ZENO. Activity in Pistoia converges on the flat cobble-stones of P. del Duomo. The green- and-white marble **Cattedrale di San Zeno** houses a store of early Renaissance art tucked into pocket-sized niches on multiple floors, as well as San Zeno's greatest treasure, the ◪**Dossale di San Jacopo.** Between 1287 and 1456, nearly every significant Tuscan silversmith (including the young Brunelleschi) lent a hand to this altarpiece, a tremendously ornate affair with relief work detailing biblical scenes and a procession of saints in a plain chapel off the right aisle. Visitors can enter the chapel for a small fee (€2), or observe the work from afar for free. (☎0573 25 095. Open daily 7am-12:30pm and 3-7pm. Altar open 11:20am-noon and 4-5:30pm. Modest dress required.) Across from the *duomo* is the octagonal **baptistry,** designed by Andrea Pisano in the 14th century. Nino and Tom-maso Pisano's sculpture *Virgin and Child* brightens a modest interior. (Open in summer daily 8am-6pm; in winter M and Su 9:30am-6pm, Tu-Sa 9:30am-12:30pm and 3-6pm.) The **campanile,** adjacent to the *duomo*, has sounded the hour since the 12th cen-tury. With its pyramid-shaped spire rising 66m, on clear days vistas from the small arched windows span to Florence. (☎0573 21 622. Open M and F-Su 9am-1pm and 3-6pm. Visits must be booked beforehand at the tourist office. €5.)

PALAZZO COMUNALE. A 13th-century structure next to the *duomo* facing the *piazza.* Left of the central balcony on the dark brick facade, about halfway up, an arm reaches out of the wall, brandishing a club above the black marble head below—a tribute to the 1115 Pistoian victory over the Moorish King Musetto. Inside, the **Museo Civico** houses artwork dating to the 13th century. With its Gothic windows and archways, the courtyard is also well worth a peek. (☎0573 37 12 96. *Open Tu-Sa 10am-6pm, Su 9:30am-12:30pm. Museum €3.50, under 18 or ISIC cardholders free. Cumulative ticket for museum, the Centro Marini, and other museums €6.50, students €5.20.)*

CENTRO MARINO MARINI. Escape an overdose of Renaissance paintings with a visit to this modern collection celebrating one of Italy's most renowned 20th-century artists, native Marino Marini. The collection's pieces are connected by a maze of stairs and include sculptures (many of the sensuous Pomono, ancient Roman fertility goddess), studies, and paintings. *(C. Silvano Fedi, 30, in the Palazzo del Tau. ☎0573 30 285; www.museomarinomarini.it. Open May-Sept. M-Sa 10am-6pm; Oct.-Apr. M-Sa 10am-5pm. €3.50.)*

CHIESA DI GIOVANNI FUORCIVITAS. The single-naved interior of the 12th-century construction is a vast space with vibrant stained-glass windows punctuating stark stone walls. The church contains Luca della Robbia's terra-cotta *Visitation* (1445) on the left and a Romanesque relief of *The Last Supper* on the lintel. Giovanni Pisano's font and Guglielmo de Pisa's pulpit are both among the finest of 13th-century carving. *(At the intersection of V. Cavour and V. Crispi. Open daily 7:30am-6pm.)*

CHIESA DI SANT'ANDREA. This typically Pisan-Romanesque church was founded in the 8th century. In 1298 Giovanni Pisano carved the pulpit, now considered his masterpiece. Supported by seven red marble columns, the pulpit's five white marble panels have delicately carved figures illustrating the *Nativity, Adoration of the Magi, Massacre of the Innocents, Crucifixion,* and *Last Judgment. (Exit P. del Duomo by V. del Duca, from the corner opposite the duomo, and continue as it changes to V. dei Rossi and then V. Sant'Andrea. ☎0573 96 41 30. Open daily 7:30am-6pm.)*

NIGHTLIFE AND FESTIVALS

With Staropramen, Hopf Weizen, and Bass on tap (€4 per pint), **Vecchia Praga,** P. della Sala, 6, at the end of V. del Lastrone, is a beer-lover's haven. Cocktails, liquor, wine, and light food are also available to the mostly Italian crowd. (☎0573 31 155. Open Jan.-July and Sept.-Dec. M-Sa 10am-1am, Su 6pm-1am; Aug. daily 6pm-1am. MC/V.) Europe's remaining flower children converge each July in P. del Duomo for the **Pistoia Blues** concert series. The past two summers featured Santana, Jethro Tull, and Ike Turner. (☎0573 35 86; www.pistoiablues.com.) During the festival, the city allows free camping in designated sites near the stadium. On July 25, Pistoia holds the **Giostra dell'Orso** (Joust of the Bear). In accordance with 13th-century custom, 12 contemporary knights from four competing districts joust a defenseless bear-shaped target, earning points for the accuracy of their lunges. Pistoians and visitors fill the stands in the P. del Duomo, cheering on their favorite knight and recording wins and losses on the free scorecards given out by the city.

DAYTRIP FROM PISTOIA

MONTECATINI TERME

Montecatini Terme's 2 train stations are 2min. apart. Most trains stop at both. Get off at the 2nd Montecatini stop, Stazione Centro. From Stazione Centro, walk straight ahead up V. Manzoni and through P. XX Settembre until arriving at P. del Popolo. Walk across the piazza to Vle. Verdi. Use free Internet and pick up a map and a list of spa locations at the tourist office, Vle. Verdi, 66-68. (☎0572 77 22 44; apt@montecatini.turismo.toscana.it). Open M-Sa 9am-12:30pm and 3-6pm, Su 9am-noon.

Just a 10min. train ride from Pistoia, Montecatini Terme offers a taste of the affluent life without draining the wallet. Famous for its thermal baths, Montecatini is a classic spa town: upper-crust Italians and European tourists lazily pass their days shopping at glamorous boutiques and relaxing under palm trees. Time moves slowly in Montecatini, and so do its mostly older residents, seen strolling down the well-manicured streets. The town's most famous bath is the impressive Neo-Classical ■Tettuccio, sitting in prominence at the end of Vle. Verdi and filled with rotundas, gardens, and bubbling fountains. The spa is famous for the healing waters that spring from the fountains, allegedly soothing for liver and digestive problems. Visitors can pay €0.50 for a plastic cup or bring an empty bottle to drink and see for themselves. (☎0572 77 85 01. Open May-Oct. 7:30am-noon and 5-7pm. €12.50, 11am-noon and 5-7pm €5.) For winter visitors, the **Excelsior** offers spa services year-round. (☎0572 77 85 11. Bath open M-F 7:30am-noon and 4-7pm, Sa 7:30am-noon. Beauty treatments available M-F 8:30am-8pm, Su 9am-2pm. Thermal wellness available M-F 7:30am-noon and 4-6:30pm, Su 7:30am-noon.)

Montecatini has several fine hotels and restaurants. **Hotel Corona D'Italia ❸**, V. Verdi, 5, is open year-round. All rooms have antique furnishings, marble floors, TV, phone, and bath. Reserve ahead for a double with balcony at no extra cost. (☎0572 79 217; hcorona@italway.it. Breakfast €6. Singles €36; doubles €50. Extra bed €10. AmEx/MC/V.) For a lavish dining experience at a reasonable price, eat at the expansive patio restaurant of ■**Grand Hotel Tettuccio ❺**, V. Verdi, 74. Servers decked in black ties and vests weave elegantly between tables to serve guests on satin-cushioned chairs. Try the fabulous *maccheroni all'Astice* (€12), flat noodles topped with half a lobster. (☎0572 78 051. *Primi* €10-12, *secondi* €14-20. Cover €4. Open daily noon-2pm and 7-10pm. AmEx/MC/V.) Near the station, family-run **Corsaro Verde ❸**, P. XX Settembre, 11, serves a large selection, including *giganti alle erbe* (€6), ravioli stuffed with curd cheese and spinach. (☎0572 91 16 50. *Primi* €5-7, *secondi* €7-15. Open Tu-Su noon-3pm and 7-11pm. AmEx/MC/V.)

LUCCA ☎0583

Comfortably settled behind a ring of Renaissance walls, the handsome provincial capital of Lucca has the unusual ability to host a multitude of visitors without ever feeling crowded. The town began as a Roman colony and during the Middle Ages rivaled Florence and Siena in military and political might. The scenic, tree-lined promenade running atop the impressive 4km stone walls draws cycling *Lucchese* daily and provides the perfect vantage point for viewing the red-roofed historical center and the surrounding Tuscan countryside. With booming textiles and olive industries, and calm but steady flow of tourists, Lucca quietly maintains a tradition of eminence and commercial prosperity. It offers many fine Romanesque churches, medieval storefronts, and for opera enthusiasts, the childhood home of Giacomo Puccini.

■ TRANSPORTATION

Trains: (☎0583 47 013), in P. Ricasoli, just outside the city walls. Trains provide the most convenient transport to Lucca. Info booth open daily 8am-noon and 3-8:30pm. To: **Florence** (1½hr., every hr. 5:10am-10:19pm, €4.75); **Pisa** (30min., every hr. 6:40-12:17am, €2.95); **Viareggio** (20min., every hr. 6:22am-11:11pm, €2.95).

Buses: Lazzi (☎0583 58 40 76), in Ple. Verdi, next to tourist office. To: **Florence** (1½hr., every hr. 6:25am-7:45pm, €5) and **Pisa** (50min., every hr. 5:55am-8pm, €3).

Taxis: (☎0583 58 13 05), in Ple. Verdi; (☎0583 49 49 89), in P. Stazione; (☎0583 49 26 91), in P. Napoleone; (☎0583 49 41 90), in P. S. Maria.

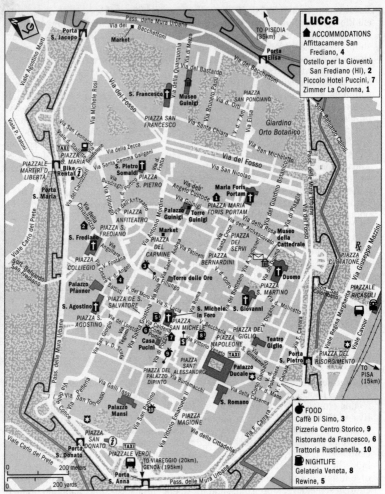

Lucca

▲ ACCOMMODATIONS
Affittacamere San
  Frediano, **4**
Ostello per la Gioventù
  San Frediano (HI), **2**
Piccolo Hotel Puccini, **7**
Zimmer La Colonna, **1**

🍎 FOOD
Caffè Di Simo, **3**
Pizzeria Centro Storico, **9**
Ristorante da Francesco, **6**
Trattoria Rusticanella, **10**

🍸 NIGHTLIFE
Gelateria Veneta, **8**
Rewine, **5**

Bike Rental: Cicli Bizzari, P. S. Maria, 31 (☎348 38 00 126), 2 doors down from the regional tourist office, offers a large selection of bikes and multi-day rentals. Basic bikes €2.10 per hr., €9.30 per day; mountain and racing bikes €3.15/19.90; tandem bikes €5.15 per hr. Open daily 9am-8pm. **Antonio Poli**, P. S. Maria, 42 (☎0583 49 37 87; www.biciclettepoli.com), on the other side of the regional tourist office, offers virtually identical services and prices. Open daily 8:30am-8pm.

✳🕐 ORIENTATION AND PRACTICAL INFORMATION

To reach the city's historical center from the **train station,** cross the road and turn left. Enter the city with the traffic at **Porta San Pietro** to the right, then head left on **Corso Garibaldi.** Turn right on **Via Vittorio Veneto** and follow it one block to **Piazza Napoleone** (P. Grande), the hub of the city. If arriving by bus, walk to the right through **Piazzale Verdi** and follow **Via San Paolino** toward the center of town and turn on V. V. Veneto to reach P. Napoleone.

Tourist Office: Centro Accoglienza Turistica (☎0583 44 29 44), in Ple. Verdi. English-speaking staff provides free **maps**, as well as train and bus info. Books guided tours (www.turislucca.com; tours run Tu, Th, and Sa 3pm; €10). Self-guided audio tours (€9 for 1 unit, €6 each additional unit) and bike rental (€2.50 per hr.). Free room reservation service, but not for the cheaper hotels. Open daily 9am-7pm. **Agenzia per il Turismo**, P. S. Maria, 35 (☎0583 91 99 21). Office is between the bike shops. Detailed brochures and free hotel and *affittacamere* reservation service. Open daily 9am-8pm.

Currency Exchange: UniCredit Banca, P. S. Michele, 47 (☎0583 47 546) Open M-F 8:20am-1:20pm and 2:35-4:05pm, Sa 8:20am-12:45pm. 24hr. **ATM.**

Luggage Storage: At tourist office in Ple. Verdi. €2 per hr.

Laundry: Lavanderia Niagara, V. Michele Rosi (☎335 62 92 055). Open daily 8am-10pm.

Emergency: ☎113. **Carabinieri:** ☎112. **First Aid:** ☎118.

Pharmacy: Farmacia Comunale, in P. Curtatone, heading right from the exit of the train station. Open 24hr.

Hospital: Campo di Marte (☎0583 97 01).

Internet Access: Mondo Chiocciola Internet Point, V. Gonfalone, 12 (☎0583 44 05 10). €5 per hr. Open M-Sa 9am-1pm and 3:30-8pm.

Post Office: ☎0583 43 351. On V. Vallisneri, off P. del Duomo. Open M-Sa 8:15am-7pm. **Postal Code:** 55100.

ACCOMMODATIONS

Ostello per la Gioventù San Frediano (HI), V. della Cavallerizza, 12 (☎0583 46 99 57; www.ostellolucca.it). 15min. from P. Napoleone. Walk 2 blocks on V. Beccheria, then turn right on V. Roma and left on V. Fillungo. After 6 blocks, turn left into P. S. Frediano and right on V. della Cavallerizza. Signs point the way. The hostel is on the left. Good-sized rooms and immaculate bathrooms. Breakfast €1.60; dinner €8. Towels €1.50. Sheets included. Laundry facilities available. Reception daily 7:30am-10am and 3:30-midnight. Check-out 9:30am. Lockout 10am-3:30pm. Curfew 1am. Dorms €16.50; family rooms (2-6 people) with bath €23 per person. Non-HI members add €3. ❷

Affittacamere San Frediano, V. degli Angeli, 19 (☎0583 46 96 30; www.sanfrediano.com). Follow directions to hostel, but turn left on V. degli Angeli 2 blocks before P. S. Frediano. Thank-you cards to the English-speaking staff line the stairway leading to rooms with TV, big windows, and antique furniture. Matching color schemes and fluffy quilts make these rooms a delight. Large, clean shared baths have tubs. Breakfast included. Singles €45, with bath €55; doubles €55/70. AmEx/MC/V. ❹

Zimmer La Colonna, V. dell'Angelo Custode, 16 (☎/fax 0583 44 01 70 or 339 46 07 152), off P. Maria Foris Portam. Hallways lined with columns lead to spacious rooms with TV and quaint antique decor; windows open onto a courtyard. Clean shared baths. Doubles €50, with bath €65. Extra bed €16. ❹

Piccolo Hotel Puccini, V. di Poggio, 9 (☎0583 55 421; www.hotelpuccini.com), around the corner from Puccini's birthplace. Each room is decorated with framed playbills from his operas. Attentive staff speaks English, Spanish, and French. 14 cozy, comfortable rooms have bath, TV, phone, and safe. Singles €60; doubles €85. AmEx/MC/V. ❹

FOOD

The central **market** occupies the large building on the east side of P. del Carmine. (Open M-Sa 7am-1pm and 4-7:30pm.) An **open-air market** overruns V. dei Bacchettoni. (Open W and Sa 8am-1pm.) The closest supermarket is **Pam**, V. Diaz, 124. Turn right from Pta. Elisa, and turn left on V. Diaz. It's at the end of the block. (☎0583 49 05 96. Open M-Tu and Th-Su 8am-8pm, W 8am-1:30pm.)

FAMILY MATTERS

■ **Trattoria Rusticanella,** V. S. Paolino, 32 (☎0583 55 383). Tavern setting caters to regulars returning home from work as well as foreigners returning from a day on the road. Jovial atmosphere, warm peppered bread, and delicious food. 3-course lunch *menù* €7.50. Pizza from €5. *Primi* €4-5, *secondi* €7-13. Cover €1. Open M-Sa 11am-3pm and 6-10:30pm. MC/V. ❷

■ **Ristorante da Francesco,** Corte Portici, 13 (☎0583 41 80 49), off V. Calderia between P. S. Salvatore and P. S. Michele. Ample patio seating and well-prepared dishes in sometimes skimpy *secondi* portions. The delicious *raviole lucchese* (meat ravioli with ragù; €5.70) could be a meal on its own. *Primi* €4.70-5.70, *secondi* €8-12. Wine €7.20 per L. Cover €1.50. Open Tu-Su noon-2:30pm and 8-10:30pm. Cash only.❷

Pizzeria Centro Storico, V. S. Paolino (☎0583 53 409), at the intersection with V. Galli Tassi. English- and German-speaking owner Michele has many fans. Pizza €1.60-3. *Primi* €5-8, *secondi* €5-9.50. Takeout available and is cheaper than sitting at the outdoor tables. Open daily 9am-midnight. AmEx/MC/V. ❶

Caffè Di Simo, V. Fillungo, 58 (☎0583 49 37 40) gleams with chandeliers and a zinc bar. Bow-tied waiters serve delicious coffee and bite-size cakes (€1.50) while mellow jazz plays in the background. Coffee €0.90, at table €2.10. Open Tu-Sa 8am-10pm. ❶

🕓 SIGHTS

■ **BALUARDI.** No tour of Lucca is complete without seeing the perfectly intact city walls, or *baluardi* (battlements). The shaded 4km path along the walls, closed to cars, passes grassy parks and cool fountains. An excellent way to appreciate the layout of the city and the beautiful countryside high above the moat, the path is perfect for a breezy afternoon picnic or a sunset bike ride.

■ **DUOMO DI SAN MARTINO.** Architects designed the multi-layered, arched facade of this ornate, asymmetrical *duomo* around its bell tower, constructed two centuries earlier. The 13th-century reliefs that decorate the exterior include Nicola Pisano's *Journey of the Magi* and *Deposition*. Matteo Civitali, Lucca's famous sculptor, designed the floor and contributed the statue of St. Martin to the right of the door. His prized *Tempietto*, halfway up the left aisle, houses the 11th-century **Volto Santo** (Holy Face). Reputedly carved by Nicodemus at Calvary, this wooden crucifix is said to depict the true image of Christ. Other highlights include Tintoretto's *Last Supper* (1593), in the 3rd chapel on the right, and

Madonna and Saints by Ghirlandaio, in the sacristy off the ~~~ **della Cattedrale,** left of the *duomo,* holds religious objects from ~~~ enlightening guided audio tour costs €1. *(P. S. Martino, between bell ~~~ office. From P. Napoleone, take V. del Duomo. Duomo open M-F 9:30am-5:45pm, ~~~ 6:45pm, Su between masses 9-9:50am, 11:30-11:50am, and 1-5:45pm. Free. Sacristy op~~ F 9:30am-5:45pm, Sa 9:30am-6:45pm, Su 9-9:50am, 11:30-11:50am, and 1-5:45pm. €~~ Museo della Cattedrale open Apr.-Oct. daily 10am-6pm; Nov.-Mar. M-F 10am-2pm, Sa-Su 10am-5pm. €4. Combination ticket for Sacristy, Museo della Cattedrale, and Chiesa di S. Giovanni €6.)*

CHIESA DI SAN MICHELE IN FORO. Looking at its current setting in a busy central *piazza,* it's hard to tell that construction on this church actually began in the 8th century on the site of a Roman forum. The church's large interior holds beautiful and dramatic oil paintings. Lippi's bold *Saints Helen, Roch, Sebastian, Jerome* hangs toward the end of the right aisle; Robbia's *Madonna and Child* is near the front. Original religious statues were replaced in the 19th century with likenesses of Cavour, Garibaldi, and Napoleon III. *(Open daily 9am-noon and 3-6pm. Free.)*

CHIESA DI SAN GIOVANNI. This unassuming church hides an archaeological treasure trove. The simple plaster dome off the left transept crowns the entrance to a recently excavated 2nd-century AD Roman complex, which includes the mosaic pavement and ruins of a private house and bath (the church's foundations), a Longobard burial site, and a Paleochristian chapel, as well as 12th-century crypt. *(Walk past San Giovanni from P. S. Martino and around the corner to the right. Open Apr.-Oct. daily 10am-6pm; Nov.-Mar. M-F 10am-2pm, Sa-Su 10am-5pm. €2.50.)*

TORRE GUINIGI AND TORRE DELLE ORE. These towers are two of the 15 towers remaining of medieval Lucca's original 250. The narrow **Torre Guinigi** rises above Lucca from the mute stone mass of Palazzo Guinigi, which is not open to the public. At the top of 230 stairs, a grove provides a shaded view of the city and the hills beyond. *(V. S. Andrea, 41. From P. S. Michele, follow V. Roma for 1 block, turn left on V. Fillungo and right on V. S. Andrea. ☎0583 31 68 46. Open daily June-Sept. 9am-11pm; Oct.-Jan. 9am-4pm; Feb.-May 9am-6pm.)* For more exercise, climb the 207 steps of the **Torre delle Ore** (Clock Towers), where you can stop to watch the inner workings of the city's tallest timepiece. *(V. Fillungo, 22. Open daily in summer 10am-7pm; in winter 10am-5:30pm. €3.50, students €2. Combination ticket for both towers €5.50/4.)*

CASA PUCCINI. Music lovers shouldn't miss the birthplace and childhood home of Giacomo Puccini (1858-1924), composer of *La Bohème* and *Madama Butterfly.* The 4th-floor apartment displays original compositions and scribbled revisions, letters, and assorted playbills. The final room holds the Steinway piano on which Puccini had been composing *Turandot* before he succumbed to throat cancer. *(V. di Poggio, 30. Near P. San Michele. ☎0583 58 40 28. Open June-Sept. daily 10am-6pm, Mar.-May and Oct.-Dec. Tu-Su 10am-1pm and 3-6pm. €3.)*

PIAZZA NAPOLEONE. Also called "Piazza Grande" by locals, this central *piazza* is the town's administrative center. The 16th-century **Palazzo Ducale** now houses government offices. In the evening, prime *passeggiata* time, *Luccese* young and old pack the *piazza.* **Piazza Anfiteatro** is also quite popular with locals and tourists, its closely packed buildings creating a nearly seamless oval wall.

🎵 🎭 ENTERTAINMENT AND NIGHTLIFE

For evidence that Lucca is a sleepy Tuscan town at heart, look no farther than **Gelateria Veneta,** V. Vittorio Veneto, 74, the epicenter of activity for the throngs on V. Vittorio Veneto. The place to see and be seen late on Saturday nights, Veneta

wank seating. (☎0583 46 70 37. Cones €1.80-3.50,
...1-F and Su 10am-1am, Sa 10am-2am.) For liquid
...ewine, V. Calderia, 6, has an expansive selection of
...e) on display in the trendy, loud interior. Head to the
...etting. (*Anitpasti* and *primi* €7.50. Open at 8am for
..., and 6-10pm for drinks.)

...es with artistic and musical performances, especially in
...mer Festival (☎0584 46 477; www.summer-festival.com)
...ut July and has featured performances by pop stars like
...on, James Taylor, Dido, and Oasis. Sample **Teatro Comunale**
...eason, starting at the end of September, or their ballet sea-
...uary. The king of Lucca's festivals is the **Settembre Lucchese**
(Se... ...ively jumble of artistic, athletic, and folkloric presentations.
Lucca a... ...s annual **Palio della Balestra,** a crossbow competition dating
from 1443 and revived for tourists in the early 1970s. Participants don traditional costume on July 12 and September 14 for the competition.

PISA ☎050

Each year millions of tourists arrive in Pisa to marvel at the famous Leaning
Tower, forming a *gelato*-slurping, photo-snapping mire. But a journey through the
rest of the city and surrounding countryside reveals that Pisa is far more than a
torre pendente. Fortunately, the marvel of the precariously leaning tower
attracted enough tourist interest to revive the other historical landmarks of the P.
del Duomo and, indeed, the entire city. Commanding a beautiful stretch of the
Arno River and sheltering enough monumental architecture to trump any souvenir stand, Pisa also has a surprisingly diverse array of cultural and artistic diversions for those who are willing to look for them. In the Middle Ages, the city
earned its living as a port and had a trade empire extending to Corsica, Sardinia,
and the Balearics; with time though, silt began to fill the Arno, stopping its flow
and drying up Pisa's fortunes. Home to one of Italy's most prestigious universities, Pisa has also thrived as a haven for opinionated and exuberant students. So
after that hackneyed Kodak moment, take some time to wander the sprawling
university neighborhood though *piazza* Cavalieri and Dante Alighieri, along
alleys lined with elegant buildings and impassioned political graffiti.

▐ TRANSPORTATION

Flights: Galileo Galilei Airport (☎050 50 07 07; www.pisa-airport.com). Trains that
make the 5min. trip (€1) between train station and airport coincide with flight departures and arrivals. Bus #3 runs between the airport, train station, and other points in
Pisa and environs (every 20min., €0.85). Charter, domestic, and international flights.
To: **Barcelona** (3½hr., 2 per day); **London** (2¼hr., 11 per day); **Paris** (2hr., 3 per day).

Trains: ☎147 80 888. In P. della Stazione, at southern end of town. Info office open
daily 7am-9pm. Ticket booth open 6am-9:30pm; self-service ticket machines available
24hr. To: **Florence** (1hr., every hr. 4:12am-12:49am, €5.05); **Genoa** (2½hr., 6am-
10:40pm, €8.10); **Livorno** (20min., every hr., €1.50); **Rome** (3hr., 12 per day €15.40-
23.50). Regional trains to **Lucca** (20min., every 30min. 6:24am-9:40pm, €2.10) also
stop at Pisa's **San Rossore,** closer to the *duomo* and the youth hostel. If leaving Pisa
from S. Rossore, buy tickets at *tabaccherie,* as there is no ticket office in the station.

Buses: Lazzi (☎050 46 288; www.lazzi.it) and **CPT** (☎800 01 27 73; www.cpt.pisa.it)
in P.S. Antonio, are located near train station. To: **Florence** (change in Lucca; 2½hr.,
every hr., €7.40); **La Spezia** (3hr., 4 per day, €7.40); **Lucca** (40min., every hr.,

LUCCA ■ 481

right aisle. The Museo ...
...of the duomo. An ...
...ower and post ...
...9:30am-M...

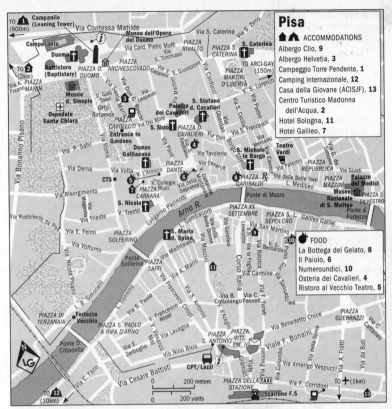

Pisa

🏛🏠 ACCOMMODATIONS
Albergo Clio, **9**
Albergo Helvetia, **3**
Campeggio Torre Pendente, **1**
Camping Internazionale, **12**
Casa della Giovane (ACISJF), **13**
Centro Turistico Madonna
    dell'Acqua, **2**
Hotel Bologna, **11**
Hotel Galileo, **7**

🍴 FOOD
La Bottega del Gelato, **8**
Il Paiolo, **6**
Numeroundici, **10**
Osteria dei Cavalieri, **4**
Ristoro al Vecchio Teatro, **5**

€2.20). To: **Livorno** (45min., 5am-7:30pm, €2.37) and **Volterra** (1½hr., 7 per day, €5.11) via **Pontederra.**

Taxis: RadioTaxi (☎050 54 16 00 or 050 41 252), in P. della Stazione; (☎050 56 18 78), in P. del Duomo; (☎050 28 542), at the airport.

Car Rental: Avis (☎050 42 028; 25+), **Hertz** (☎050 43 220; 23+), and **Maggiore** (☎050 42 574; 21+) have offices at the airport. From €61 per day.

🔷📍 ORIENTATION AND PRACTICAL INFORMATION

Pisa lies near the mouth of the **Arno River,** which splits the town. Most sights lie to the north of the Arno; the main **train station** is to the south. To reach the **Campo dei Miracoli (Piazza del Duomo)** from the station, take bus #3 (€0.85). Alternatively, walk straight up **Viale Gramsci,** through **Piazza Vittorio Emanuele,** and stroll along the busy **Corso Italia.** Cross **Ponte di Mezzo** and follow the river left, turn right on **Via Santa Maria** which hits the *duomo* and Leaning Tower after 30min.

Tourist Office: (☎050 42 291; www.turismo.toscana.it.) In P.V. Emanuele II. Walk straight from station exit and take left at large *piazza*. English-speaking, knowledgeable staff provides detailed **maps.** Detailed list of local hotels and campsites, including prices and locations, is available. Open M-F 9am-7pm, Sa 9am-1:30pm; another **branch** (☎050 56 04 64) is behind the Leaning Tower. Open M-Sa 9am-6:30pm.

Budget Travel: CTS, V. S. Maria, 12 (☎050 48 300 or 050 29 221; fax 050 45 431), by the Hotel Galileo. International tickets and boats to nearby islands. English spoken. ISIC discounts available. Open M-F 9am-1pm and 3:30-7pm, Sa 9am-1pm.

Luggage Storage: At the airport. Drop-off available 10am-6pm, pick-up 8am-8pm. €6 per bag per day.

English-Language Bookstore: The Bookshop, V. Rigattieri, 33/39 (☎050 57 34 34). Best selection in town. Classics, guide books, and some contemporary titles. Open Aug.-June M-F and Su 9am-8pm; July 9am-1pm and 4-8pm.

GLBT Resources: ARCI-GAY Pride! V. S. Lorenzo, 38 (☎050 55 56 18; www.gay.it/pride). Ring bell to enter. Open M-F 1:30-7:30pm.

Laundromat: Bucato Point, V. Corridoni, 50m from train station (☎800 08 04 03). Wash €3. Dry €3 for 7kg. Soap €0.70. Open daily 8am-10pm.

Emergency: ☎113. **Ambulance:** ☎118. **Police:** ☎050 58 35 11.

Pharmacy: Farmacia, V. Lugarno Mediceo, 51 (☎050 54 40 02). Open 24hr.

Hospital: Santa Chiara (☎050 99 21 11), on V. Bonanno near P. del Duomo.

Internet Access: Internet Point 77, V. F. Corridoni, 77, 2 blocks from the train station. €3 per hr. Open M-Sa 11am-10pm. **Internet Planet,** P. Cavolloti, 3/4 (☎050 83 07 02; info@internetplanet.it). From P. del Duomo, follow V. S. Maria and take 2nd left. €2.10 per 30min., €3.10 per hr. Open M-Sa 10am-midnight, Su 3pm-midnight.

Post Office: P. V. Emanuele, 8 (☎050 18 69), near the station, left of the large traffic circle. Open M-Sa 8:30am-7pm. **Postal Code:** 56100.

■ ACCOMMODATIONS AND CAMPING

Albergo Helvetia, V. Don G. Boschi, 31 (☎050 55 30 84), off P. Arcivescovado, near *duomo*. Bright, well-kept rooms—fluffy quilts, TV, ceiling fan, and phone. Small shared baths. Welcoming bar downstairs. Staff speaks English, French, and Spanish. Breakfast €5 (order night before). Reception 8am-midnight. Singles €35, with bath €45; doubles €50, with bath €62. Extra bed €15. ❸

Hotel Galileo, V. S. Maria, 12, 1st floor (☎050 40 621; hotelgalileo@pisaonline.it). A solar system of stellar rooms in the university district, all with frescoed ceilings, TVs, and antique tiling and furniture. Narrow baths. Singles €45, with bath €60; doubles €48, with bath €66. Extra bed €15. ❹

Centro Turistico Madonna dell'Acqua, V. Pietrasantina, 15 (☎050 89 06 22), behind old Catholic sanctuary 2km from the Tower. Bus #3 from station (4 per hr., last 9:45pm); ask to stop at *ostello*. Board bus across the street from 1st departure point in *piazza*, outside Hotel Cavalieri. Located by a creek, which attracts mosquitoes and chirping crickets. Kitchen available. Sheets €1. Reception daily 6pm-midnight. Check-out 9am. Dorms €15; doubles €42; triples €54; quads €64. MC/V. ❶

Casa della Giovane (ACISJF), V. F. Corridoni, 29 (☎050 43 061), 10min. right of station, in a commercial neighborhood removed from the town's main attractions. Large abode with basic furnishings, large baths, and free breakfast. Sheets provided, but no towels or daily cleaning service. Women only. Reception daily 7am-11pm. Check-out 9am. Curfew 11pm. Singles €30; doubles €40. Cash only. ❸

Albergo Clio, V. S. Lorenzino, 3 (☎050 28 446), off C. Italia, 1 block from the Ponte Mezzo. Vintage Hollywood lobby: pink chairs, black-and white-tiled floor, and mirrored moldings. Tiled hallways lead to bare rooms and small bathrooms. Singles €30; doubles €45, with bath €55; triples with bath €65. Cash only. ❸

Hotel Bologna, V. Mazzini, 57 (☎050 50 21 20; www.albergobologna.com). Great management, elevators, and wood floors. Rooms have bath, TV, minibar, A/C, and cherubic paintings. Breakfast included. Internet €2 per hr. Check-out 11am. Singles €90-120; doubles €110-140; triples €130-160; quads €150-180. AmEx/MC/V. ❺

Campeggio Torre Pendente, V. delle Cascine, 86 (☎050 56 17 04; www.camping-toscana.it/torrependente), 1km from tower. Bus #3 to P. Manin. With city wall on right, walk 2 blocks and turn left on V. delle Cascine, following camping signs. Walk above long and dark concrete underpass, then past industrial-looking buildings; campground is on the right, in a convenient location. Swimming pool, market, planned excursions, and decent bathrooms; some sites not shaded. Reception 8:30am-11pm. Open Mar.-Oct. €8 per person, €4.50 per child; €6.50 per tent. Bungalows €45-100. AmEx/MC/V only for purchases of more than €100. ❶

Camping Internazionale (☎050 35 211; www.pisacamping.com), 10km away on V. Litoranea in Marina di Pisa, across from its private beach. Take CPT bus (intercity bus) from P. S. Antonio to Marina di Pisa (buy ticket in CPT office entering P. S. Antonio from P. V. Emanuele; €1.50). Sites are small but partially shaded, with clean shared bathrooms. Bar and market on premises. Open May-Sept. €8 per person, €7 per child; tents €6-15. July-Aug. prices increase by €1-2. AmEx/MC/V. ❶

▣ FOOD

Steer clear of the countless touristy pizzerias near the tower and head for the river; the restaurants here offer a more authentic ambience and consistently high quality. Cheap meals are plentiful in the university area. In P. Vettovaglie, an **open-air market** spills into nearby streets. Bakeries and *salumerie* fill Pisa's residential quarter. For a wide selection of groceries, try **Pam**, V. Pascoli, 8, just off C. Italia. (Open M-Sa 8am-8pm.)

▣ **Il Paiolo,** V. Curtatone e Montanara, 9 (☎050 42 528), near the university. Lively pub atmosphere with bench seating and great music. Order the hearty *bistecca* for €2.70 per 100g (make sure to get a weight or price quote), or try some heavenly *risotto* with mussels, tiny calamari, and chunks of salmon (€5.50) with the light, sweet house white wine (0.25L for €2.10). *Primi* and *secondi* €4.70-7.25. Cover €1. Open M-F 12:30-3pm and 7:30pm-2am, Sa-Su 7:30pm-2am. Cash only. ❷

▣ **Numeroundici,** V. S. Martino, 47. Munch on generously sized sandwiches (€2.50) and superb vegetable torte (€2.30) on wooden benches in this casual and popular establishment. High-ceilinged dining room filled with Tibetan lanterns. Self-service. *Primi* €4, *secondi* €6. Open M-F noon-10pm, in summer open until 11:30pm. MC/V ❶

La Bottega del Gelato, P. Garibaldi, 11, right off the Ponte di Mezzo. Wide range of flavors, plus specials of the day. Nutella, yogurt, limoncello... Decide before reaching the counter, or end up swallowed in the crowd. Busiest after sundown. 2 generous scoops in a small cup or cone €1.30. Open M-Tu and Th-Su 11am-1am. ❶

Ristoro al Vecchio Teatro, P. Dante, 2 (☎050 20 210). Delicious, traditional Pisan cuisine built around fresh vegetables and seafood. Try the *risotto mare* (with seafood; €7) or the buttery *sfogliata di zucchine* (zucchini torte; €7). *Primi* and *secondi* €6-7. Dessert €3. Cover €1.50. Open M-Sa noon-3pm and 8-10pm. Closed Aug. AmEx/MC/V. ❷

Osteria dei Cavalieri, V. San Frediano, 16 (☎050 58 08 58). Wine-laden dining room with slick jazz posters hops with tourists and locals. Classy place to sample some traditional *trippa, coniglio,* or *cinghiale* after a busy day of sightseeing. *Primi* €7-9, *secondi* €10-15. Open M-F 12:30-2pm and 7:45-10pm, Sa 7:45-10pm. MC/V. ❸

👁 SIGHTS

🏛 LEANING TOWER. *Campo dei Miracoli* (Field of Miracles) is an appropriate nickname for the *piazza* that houses the Leaning Tower, *duomo*, baptistry, and *Camposanto*. But look closely—*all* of the buildings are leaning at different angles, thanks to the mischievous, shifty soil. Of course, none lean quite so dramatically as the famous *campanile* of the *duomo*, which tilts 5.5° to the south. Bonanno Pisano began building it in 1173, and construction on the tower was repeatedly delayed as the soil shifted and the building began to lean. The tilt intensified after WWII, and thanks to those tourists who climb its 294 steps, it continues to slip 1-2mm every year. In June of 2001, the steel safety cables and iron girdles that had imprisoned the Tower during a several-year stabilization effort were finally removed. One year later, the Tower reopened, albeit on a tightly regulated schedule: once every 30min., guided groups of 30 visitors are permitted to ascend. *(Make reservations at the ticket offices in the Museo del Duomo or next to the tourist information office. Tours depart daily June-Aug. 8:30am-11pm; Sept.-May 8:30am-7:30pm. Assemble next to information office 10min. before scheduled time. Childen under 8 not permitted, under 18 must be accompanied by an adult. €15. Cash only. Free baggage storage.)*

LUNAR LEANER. The wait to climb the Leaning Tower can sometimes take hours out of your day. Save the ascent until after sundown—the tower is open during the summer until 11pm—to escape the crowds. You'll get a unique view of the city illuminated by moonlight.

🏛 BATTISTERO. The baptistry, an enormous barrel of a building, was begun in 1152 by a man known as Diotisalvi ("God save you"). It measures 107m in girth and is 55m tall. Blending architectural styles, it incorporates Tuscan-Romanesque stripes with a multi-tiered Gothic ensemble of gables, pinnacles, and statues. Guido Bigarelli's fountain (1246) dominates the center of the ground floor. Nicola Pisano's pulpit (1260) recaptures the dignity of classical antiquity and is one of the harbingers of Renaissance art in Italy. The dome's acoustics are astounding: a choir singing in the baptistry can be heard 2km away. A staircase embedded in the wall leads to a balcony level just below the dome; farther up, a space between the interior and exterior of the dome yields teasing views of the surrounding *piazza*. *(Open daily late Apr.-Sept. 8am-7:30pm; Oct. and Mar. 9am-5:30pm; Nov.-Feb. 9am-4:30pm. €6, includes entrance to 1 other museum or monument on the combination ticket list.)*

CAMPOSANTO. This cloistered courtyard cemetery, covered with earth that Crusaders brought back from Golgotha, was once considered one of the architectural wonders of the world. Fragments of enormous frescoes shattered by Allied bombs during WWII line the galleries which hold the Roman *sarcophogi* whose reliefs inspired Nicola Pisano's pulpit in the baptistry. The **Cappella Ammannati** contains haunting frescoes of Florence succumbing to the plague; its unidentified 14th-century creator is known as the "Master of the Triumph of Death." *(Next to the duomo. Open daily late Apr.-late Sept. 8am-7:30pm; Mar. and Oct. 9am-5:30pm; Nov.-Feb. 9am-4:30pm. €6, includes entrance to 1 other museum or monument on the combination ticket list.)*

DUOMO. The dark green and white facade of the *duomo* is the archetype of the Pisan-Romanesque style; indeed, this is one of the most important Romanesque cathedrals in the world. Begun in 1063 by Boschetto (who is now entombed in the wall), the cathedral is the Campo's oldest structure. Enter the five-aisled nave through Bonanno Pisano's richly decorated bronze doors (1180). Although a 1595 fire destroyed most of the interior, the cathedral was masterfully restored, and original paintings by Ghirlandaio still hang along the right wall, Cimabue's spectacular gilded mosaic *Christ Pantocrator* graces the apse, and bits of the intricately patterned marble Cosmati pavement remain. The cathedral's elaborate chandelier is falsely rumored to have inspired Galileo's theories of gravity. Giovanni Pisano's last and greatest pulpit, designed to outdo his father's in the baptistry, sits majestically in the center, with ornately sculpted reliefs and supports that demonstrate the artist's undeniable skill. *(Open Apr.-Sept. M-Sa 10am-7:45pm, Su 1-7:45pm; Mar. and Oct. M-F 10am-5:30pm, Su 1-5:45pm; Nov.-Feb. M-F 10am-12:30pm and 3-4:30pm, Su 3-4:30pm. €2. Free during Su mass, but the roped-off area at the end of the nave provides only a partial view.)*

 TOWER POWER. The city offers a joint ticket to the **duomo, baptistry, Camposanto, Museo delle Sinopie,** and **Museo del Duomo** (€10.50), to one of the above monuments (€5), two of the above monuments (€6), and to everything but the *duomo* (€8.50). Tickets for just the *duomo* are €2. Tickets for the Leaning Tower are sold separately (€15). Combination tickets can be bought at the two *biglietteria* on the *Campo dei Miracoli* (at the *Museo del Duomo* and next to the tourist office behind the tower).

MUSEO NAZIONALE DI SAN MATTEO. Thirty rooms showcase panels by Masaccio, Fra Angelico, and Simone Martini. Sculptures by the Pisano clan and a bust by Donatello also grace this converted convent. *(Off P. Mazzini on Lugamo Mediceo. Open Tu-Sa 8:30am-7:30pm, Su 8:30am-1:30pm. €4, ages 18-26 €2, under 18 or over 65 free.)*

MUSEO DELL'OPERA DEL DUOMO AND MUSEO DELLE SINOPIE. The Museo dell'Opera del Duomo displays artwork from the three buildings of P. del Duomo, and gives excellent historical information about the art and construction of the famous buildings. Work by the Pisano clan abounds, including the sensitive sculpture *Madonna del Colloquio* (Madonna of the Conversation) by Giovanni Pisano, which was named for the expressive gazes exchanged between mother and child. The display also includes a collection of Egyptian art, works by Tino Camaino and Nino Pisano, and an assortment of Roman and Etruscan pieces tucked into the church in the Middle Ages. *(Behind the Leaning Tower. Open daily Apr.-Sept. 8am-7:20pm; Mar. and Oct. 9am-5:20pm; Nov.-Feb. 9am-4:20pm. €6, includes entrance to 1 other museum or monument on the combination ticket list.)* Across the square near the Battistero, the **Museo delle Sinopie** displays fresco sketches by Traini, Veneziano, and Gaddi, as well as other sketches uncovered during the post-WWII restoration of the Camposanto. *(Same hours and admission cost and conditions as Museo dell'Opera del Duomo.)*

PIAZZA DEI CAVALIERI. Designed by Vasari and built on the site of the Roman forum, this *piazza* once held the town hall. Now it is the seat of the **Scuola Normale Superiore,** one of Italy's premier universities. Though not open to the public, a walk around the exterior is worth it. The wrought-iron baskets on either end of the **Palazzo dell'Orologio** (Palace of the Clock) were once receptacles for the heads of delinquent Pisans. In the *palazzo*'s **tower,** Ugolino della Gherardesca was starved to death in 1208 along with his sons and grandsons, as punishment for treachery. This murky episode in Tuscan politics is commemorated in Shelley's *Tower of Famine*, as well as in Dante's *Inferno* with gruesome cannibalistic innuendos.

OTHER SIGHTS. Of Pisa's many churches, one merits special attention. The **Chiesa di Santa Maria della Spina** (Church of Saint Mary of the Thorn), which faces Gambacorti near the river, is quintessentially Gothic. It was built to house a thorn taken from Christ's Crown of Thorns. Visitors can view the interior only during Italy's annual Culture Week. *(From the* Campo, *walk down V. S. Maria and over the bridge. Ask the tourist office for info.)* For an afternoon trip away from the busy downtown, take the CPT bus from P. S. Antonio to the hillside suburb of Calci, where the **Certosa Monumentale di Calci** awaits amidst shady groves of olive trees. The monk's cloister has beautiful grounds and an adjoining museum, available for viewing only with a guide. *(Open Tu-Sa 8:30am-6:30pm, Su 8:30am-12:30pm. Guided tours every hour. €4, students €2.)*

 THE REAL DEAL. Though the dozens of souvenir shops lining the P. del Duomo are easy to dismiss as a rip-off, smart and patient shoppers can find some great bargains amidst the deluge of Leaning Tower shot glasses. Stick to the carts on the outside of the city wall and be ready to bargain. —Jen Rugani

♫ ▓ ENTERTAINMENT AND NIGHTLIFE

Occasional concerts take place in the *duomo*. Call **Opera della Primaziale** (☎050 56 05 47). The annual **Gioco del Ponte** revives the city's tradition of medieval pageantry. Pisans divide into multiple teams, pledging their allegiance to their own city neighborhood. Pairs of teams converge on the *Ponte di Mezzo* and joust to see which side's cart can claim the largest portion of the bridge. (☎050 92 91 11; last Su in June.) The night before the holiday of the patron saint Nicholas in mid-June, the **Luminara di San Ranieri** brings the illumination of Pisa (including the tower) with 70,000 lights. The main street of the University District, which runs up from P. Garibaldi on the river, changing names from Borgo Stretto to V. Oberdan to V. Carducci, is lined with places to drink beer, sip coffee, or enjoy *gelato*—as is C. Italia, toward the station. Young students also converge for drinks and heated debate in the bar-lined P. Dante.

VIAREGGIO ☎0584

The resort town of Viareggio sits at the foot of the Riviera, tucked between the colorful beach umbrellas of the Versilian coast and the olive and chestnut groves cloaking the foothills of the Apuan Mountains. Young Italians arrive each morning to slather on oil and soak up the sun, but usually return to the inland cities by evening to avoid the often costly accommodations. At night, European tourists stroll along the shore's promenade, taking in grandiose 1920s architecture and glitzy boutiques.

▐ TRANSPORTATION. Viareggio lies on the Rome-Genoa and Viareggio-Florence train lines. **Trains** service Florence (2hr., 5:45am-10pm, €5.90); Genoa (2½hr., 3:02am-12:30am, €11.50); La Spezia (1hr., 5:52am-3:02am, €5.30); Livorno (30min., 5:39am-2:32am, €4.85) via Pisa; Rome (3hr., every hr., 5:39am-2:32am, €26). **Lazzi buses** (☎0584 46 233) connect Viareggio to: Florence (2¼hr., every hr., €5.70); La Spezia (2hr., 4 per day, €3.50); Lucca (45min., every hr., €2.50); Pisa (20min., 20 per day, €2.50). All buses stop in P. Mazzini, the town's main square near the waterfront. **Taxis** (☎0584 45 454) are available at the train station. Rental cars are available at **EuropCar,** right at the train station. (☎0584 43 05 06. Open M-F 9am-12:30pm and 3:30-6:30pm, Sa 9am-12:30pm.)

⚠️ 🔢 ORIENTATION AND PRACTICAL INFORMATION. A **tourist office** at the train station has good **maps,** local bus schedules, and information on hotels. (Open Tu 9:30am-1pm, W-Sa 9:30am-1pm and 4-6pm.) To reach the main **tourist office,** V. Carducci, 10, from the main exit of the train station walk directly across the *piazza,* then head right. Take the first left and down V. XX Settembre to P. Mazzini. At the other end of the *piazza,* turn right on V. Carducci and walk two and a half blocks. Office is on the right in between two banks. The personable staff supplies decent maps, brochures, and information on hikes and car tours. Train schedules are posted outside. (☎0584 96 22 33; www.versilia.turismo.toscana.it. Open M-Sa 9am-2pm and 3-7pm, Su 9am-1pm.) Adjacent to the tourist office, the **booking office** has hotel information and can reserve rooms for a 5% commission. (☎0584 31 781. Open May-Sept. W-Sa 9:30am-12:30pm and 3-5:30pm, Su 9:30am-noon; reduced hours Oct.-Apr.) **Luggage storage** is available at the train station, left before the exit and after the bar. (€3 for 12hr. Open daily 8am-8pm.) **Currency exchange** is available at the post office or at any of the banks along V. Garibaldi. In case of **emergency,** dial ☎113; for **first aid,** call ☎118. An all-night **pharmacy** is at V. Mazzini, 14. The **post office** is at the corner of V. Garibaldi and V. Puccini. (☎0584 30 345. Open M-F 8:15am-7pm, Sa 8:15am-12:30pm.) **Postal Code:** 55049.

🏠 🍴 ACCOMMODATIONS AND FOOD. Amid splendor and pretense a few budget accommodations. Many, however, turn into *pensioni* in the summer, catering to Italians on extended holidays and making it difficult to find short-term accommodations in July and August. Call several weeks ahead. Close to the beach, **Hotel Albachiara ❹,** V. Zanardelli, 81, offers modest rooms with bath. From V. XX Settembre, turn left on V. IV Novembre and walk to V. Zanardelli. (☎0584 44 541. Breakfast included. Sept.-June doubles €65; full pension €52. July-Aug. doubles €70; full pension €54-58. AmEx/MC/V.) **Hotel Rex ❹,** V. S. Martino, 48, has small and refined rooms with bath, TV, phone, and A/C. English-speaking staff. (☎0584 96 11 40; hotelrex.vg@libero.it. Breakfast included. Late June-Aug. singles €65; doubles €80-110; triples €120. Low-season prices drop considerably. AmEx/MC/V.)

Accustomed to catering to a wealthy clientele, Viareggio's restaurants are none too cheap. To avoid high cover charges, head away from the waterfront to **Ristorante da Giorgio ❺,** V. Zanardelli, 71, to savor fresh seafood in a dining room filled with photos of the port. (*Primi* €9, *secondi* €25. ☎0584 44 493. Open Tu-Su noon-2:30pm and 7:30-10pm. AmEx/MC/V.) For an affordable splurge and terrific people watching, drop €4.50 on coffee and dessert at the ritzy terrace of the **Gran Cafe Margherita ❷,** overlooking the sea. From P. Mazzini facing the sea, turn left on the main drag; the restaurant is ahead on the right.

🎭 🏖️ ENTERTAINMENT AND BEACHES. Most of the shoreline has been roped off by the owners of Viareggio's private beaches. This doesn't mean visitors can't walk through these areas to the water; they just can't park beach towels there. Walking to the left facing the water across the canal along Vle. Europa, 30min. from P. Mazzini, leads to the **free beach,** at the southern edge of town. Or, take city bus #9 (tickets €0.80, €1.50 if bought onboard) from the train station and save some precious tanning time. Bus #10 returns from the beach to the station. The crowd here is younger, hipper, and noticeably less pretentious than the private beach set. Every year, revelers from all over Italy flock to Viareggio to celebrate **Carnevale.** The town is famous for its colorful parades, hilarious performances, and riotous parties as the streets fill with food and music for the nationwide holiday.

LIVORNO
☎ **0586**

Dwarfed by monstrous ocean liners awaiting departure for destinations like Sardinia, Corsica, Greece, and Spain, Livorno is a rough-and-ready port town with a convenient ferry system. Henry James's assertion that Livorno "may claim the distinction, unique in Italy, of being the city of no pictures" is true enough; nevertheless, visitors usually find the town perfectly serviceable for an evening stay and early morning departure. Those awaiting ferries will find fresh and affordable seafood, views of the surrounding countryside, and inexpensive accommodations.

▣ TRANSPORTATION

Trains: Frequent service connects Livorno to: **Florence** (1½hr., €5.95); **Piombino** (1½hr., €5); **Pisa** (15min., €1.60); **Rome** (3½hr., €14.80).

Buses: ATL (☎0586 88 42 62; www.atl.livorno.it) sends buses from P. Grande to **Piombino** (8 per day, €6.46) and **Pisa** (16 per day, €2.17).

Ferries: At Stazione Marittima. From the train station, take bus #1 to P. Grande (buy ticket from *tabaccheria;* €1). Ticket offices open before and after arrivals and departures. From P. Grande, take PB 1, 2, or 3 bus, or take V. Cogorano, cross P. Municipio, and turn left on V. S. Giovanni, following it to the water. Turn right and cross the overpass, leading to the port and Stazione Marittima (10min.). Stazione Marittima has **currency exchange** and **luggage storage.** Schedules and docks vary by season. Prices increase in summer and on weekends. Port taxes (€3-8) may apply. **Corsica Marittima** (☎0586 21 05 07; www.forti.it/sncm/Inglese/homeing.html) runs quick service to **Bastia, Corsica** (2hr., Apr.-Sept. 2-4 per day, €16-30) and **Porto Vecchio, Corsica** (10hr., June-Sept. 1-2 per week). **Moby Lines** (☎0586 82 68 25; www.moby.it) runs to **Bastia** (3hr., June-Sept. daily, €15-28) and **Olbia, Sardinia** (8-10hr., daily Mar.-Sept., €20-46). **Corsica** and **Sardinia Ferries** (☎0586 88 13 80; www.corsicaferries.com) runs to **Bastia** (4hr., daily May-Sept., €16-28) and **Golfo Aranci, Sardinia** (6-8hr.; June-Aug. Tu-Su 2 per day, greatly reduced service in low season; €21-47).

Taxi: Radio Taxi ☎0586 88 20 20.

✦ ⓘ ORIENTATION AND PRACTICAL INFORMATION

From the **train station,** take bus #1 to reach **Piazza Grande,** the town center. Buses #2 and 8 also stop at P. Grande, but only after trips to the suburbs. Buy tickets (€1) at the booth outside the station, at *tabaccherie,* or at one of the orange vending machines. The **tourist office** is at P. Cavour, 6, 3rd fl., up V. Cairoli from P. Grande. (☎0586 89 81 11; www.costadeglietruschi.it. Open M-F 9am-1pm and 3-5pm, Sa 9am-1pm; reduced hours Sept.-May.) Near P. Grande, a right on V. Corogano leads to a tourist kiosk in P. Municipio that supplies well-detailed street **maps.** (☎0586 82 01 11. Open daily 9:30am-7pm.) There is also a **branch** office in Stazione Marittima. (☎0586 89 53 20. Open June-Sept. M 8am-1pm and 4-8pm, Tu and Th-Su 8am-1pm and 2-8pm, W 8:30am-2pm and 3-8pm.) **Currency exchange** is available at the train station (open daily 8-11:45am and 3-5:45pm), Stazione Marittima, the post office, and the banks on V. Cairoli. Self-service **luggage storage** lockers are in the train station. (€2-4 per 24hr. No large bags.) In case of **emergency,** dial ☎113, call an **ambulance** ☎118, or contact the **hospital** at ☎0586 22 31 11. **Farmacia Comunale,** P. Grande, 8 (☎0586 89 44 90), is open 24hr. The **post office** is at V. Cairoli, 12/16. (☎0586 27 641. Open M-F 8:30am-7pm, Sa 8:30am-12:30pm.) **Postal Code:** 57100.

ACCOMMODATIONS

Hotel Cavour, V. Adua, 10 (☎/fax 0586 89 96 04). From the main tourist office, cross P. Cavour and follow V. Michon to V. Adua. Simple but spacious rooms with big bright windows and clean baths. Satellite TV in the lounge. Singles €26, with bath €40; doubles €48, with bath €55; triples €60; quads with bath €85. Cash only. ❸

Hotel Marina, C. Mazzini, 24 (☎0586 83 42 78). From main tourist office, continue through P. Cavour, follow V. Ricasoli 1 block, and turn right on C. Mazzini. Handsome stone tiles, soft beds, and immaculate baths in huge rooms with TV. Common room has TV, pool table, and board games. Singles €47; doubles €62; triples €72. MC/V. ❹

Ostello/Albergo Villa Morazzana, V. Collinet, 40 (☎0586 50 00 76), just within city limits. Bus #1 to P. Grande (€1) and transfer to bus #3. (20min., M-F every hr.) #3 buses run different routes, so ask at info booth in P. Grande which goes to hostel, or call hostel for exact directions. Some of the clean, simple rooms in this 17th-century villa have views of the countryside and sea. Minutes from a quiet beach. Breakfast included. Wheelchair accessible. Lockout 9:30am-5pm. Curfew 11:30pm. Dorms €18; singles €50; doubles with bath €75. AmEx/MC/V. ❷

FOOD

Livorno owes its culinary specialties to the sea. The city has its own variation of bouillabaise: a fiery, tomato-based seafood stew they call *cacciucco*. Fill up at the **Central Market** in P. Cavallotti (open M-F 5am-3pm, Sa 5am-8pm), or **STANDA,** V. Grande, 174, off P. Grande. (Open Mar.-Oct. M-Sa 8:30am-12:30pm and 4-8pm, Su 9am-1pm and 4-8pm; Nov.-Feb. M-Sa 8:30am-12:30pm and 3:30-7pm.) Head to **Osteria del Mare** ❸, Borgo dei Cappuccini, 5, for elegant and affordable meals. The *risotto mare* (€6.20) is a specialty. From P. Mazzini, near Hotel Boston, take V. Navi to Borgo dei Cappuccini. (☎0586 88 10 27. *Primi* €6.20-6.70, *secondi* €8-13 or €3.62-4.91 per 100g. Cover €1.55. Open M-W and F-Su noon-3pm and 7:30-10:30pm. AmEx/MC/V.) **Ristorante Vecchia Livorno** ❸, Scali delle Cantine, 32, across from Fortezza Nuova, is in a quieter spot away from the city center classic Livornese fare. (☎0586 88 40 48. *Primi* €5.50-8, *secondi* €8.20-12.95 or €5-6 per 100g. Cover €1.50. Open M and W-Su noon-2:30pm and 7-10pm. Cash only.) Two blocks from Hotel Marina is **Luna Rossa** ❷, C. Mazzini, 222, which serves cheaper food in a relaxed interior. The takeout pizza *menù* (€13-22) is extensive and popular. (☎0586 88 14 42. *Primi* €4-6.50, *secondi* €5-11. Cover €1.50. Service 10%. Open Tu-Su noon-3pm and 7:30-10pm. MC/V.)

SIGHTS AND ENTERTAINMENT

Livorno is more of a transportation hub than a tourist spot, so sights are extremely limited. The **Fortezza Nuova,** circled by a large moat, is in the heart of **Piccola Venezia,** where canals course through the city. In mid-July, rowers in the **Palio Marinaro** race boats toward the old port. At the end of the month, **Effeto Venezia** transforms Livorno's Piccola Venezia into a theater with 10 days of concerts and exhibitions.

ELBA
☎ 0565

According to legend, the enchanting island of Elba grew from a precious stone that slipped from Venus's neck into the Tyrrhenian Sea. Since then, Elba has seen its share of notable visitors, its 150km of coastline drawing the likes of Jason and the Argonauts and eminent Roman patricians. Elba, nicknamed Aethalia, or "Sparks," by the Greeks and renowned since Hellenic times for its mineral wealth, also derived considerable fame from its association with Napoleon. The Little Emperor was sent into his first exile here in 1814, creating both a temporarily war-free Europe and the famous palindrome: "Able was I ere I saw Elba." All vanquished conquerors of Europe should be so lucky. Elba's turquoise waters, dramatic peaks, velvety beaches, and diverse attractions can accommodate almost any interest. A popular spot for foreign tourists as well as Italian daytrippers in search of a brief tropical sojourn, each zone of the island attracts a distinct variety of visitor—families lounge in Marina di Campo and Marciana Marina, beach bums and club kids waste away in Capoliveri, yacht-clubbers gallivant in Porto Azzurro, and nature lovers gravitate to the island's mountainous northeastern tip.

 TRANSPORTATION TO ELBA. Elba's **airport** (☎0565 97 60 11; fax 0565 97 60 08) in Marina di Campo, sends flights to Milan, Munich, Parma, Rome, Vienna, and Zurich. The best way to reach Elba is to take a **ferry** from Piombino Marittima (or Piombino Porto), on the mainland, to Portoferraio, Elba's largest city. Ferries also dock at Porto Azzuro, on the opposite side of the island. **Trains** on the Genoa-Rome line travel straight to Piombino Marittima but usually stop at Campiglia Marittima (from Florence, change at Pisa). From Campiglia Marittima, a connecting **intercity bus** (30min., €1.20), timed to meet incoming trains, connects to Piombino Marittima. Tickets to Piombino purchased at a **train station** include the bus ticket. Meet the bus when exiting the station. Both **Toremar** (ferry 1hr., €5.70-7.51; hydrofoil in summer 30min., €6.74-9.84) and **Moby Lines** (1hr., 6:40am-10:30pm, €6.50-9.50) run about 20 trips to Elba per day. The ticket offices of Toremar (☎0565 311 00; www.toremar.it) and Moby Lines (☎0565 22 52 11; www.moby.it) are in the **Stazione Marittima** at the ferry docks in Piombino; buy tickets for the next departing ferry at these offices or at the FS booth in the Campiglia Marittima train station. Remember to allow 10min. to descend from the ticket office to the dock.

PORTOFERRAIO
☎ 0565

Portoferraio (pop. 10,000) has split personalities: to the west of the Medici Fortress is a modern, rather unattractive port, while to the east lies a picturesque Tuscan beach town. However, the western side is also home to many of the town's budget accommodations, snack bars, and *gelaterie*. As the island's main port, it is probably Elba's liveliest city and contains most of its essential services. Though frequent boats make Portoferraio the easiest area to access from the mainland, the imposing sealiners keep at a comfortable distance from centuries-old sights and gorgeous stretches of white, pebbly beaches.

▐ TRANSPORTATION

Ferry service is at **Toremar,** Calata Italia, 22 (☎0565 91 80 80), and **Moby Lines,** V. Elba, 4 (☎0565 91 41 33; fax 0565 91 67 58). Portoferraio can be accessed by

Elba

Ligurian Sea

0 ___ 4 kilometers
0 ___ 4 miles

Tyrrhenian Sea

Isole del Topi
Cavo
Mt. Grosso (347m)
Mt. Strega (428m)
Portoferraio
Cala d'Enfola
Marciana Marina
Golfo della Biodola
Golfo di Procchio
La Biodola
Carpani
Bagnaia
Rio nell'Elba
Rio Marina
TO PIOMBINO
TO PIOMBINO
Marciana
Procchio
Villa Napoleonica di S. Martino
S. Martino
Mt. Castello (390m)
Poggio
M. Perone
Mt. Capanne (1019m)
S. Ilario in Campo
La Pila
Mt. Orello (377m)
Sp. di Barbarossa
Porto Azzurro
Pomonte
Cavoli
Marina di Campo
Lacona
Golfo di Campo
Golfo di Lacona
Golfo Stella
Capoliveri
Isola di Corbella
Pareti
Mt. Calamita (412m)
Isole Gemini
Palazzo

bus from Elba's other towns. **ATL,** V. Elba, 20, across from the Toremar landing, runs hourly **buses** to Capoliveri, Cavo, Lacona Marciana, Marciana Marina, Marina di Campo, Pomonte, Porto Azzuro, and Rio Elba. (☎0565 91 43 92. Open daily June-Sept. 8am-8pm; Oct.-May M-Sa 8am-1:20pm and 4-6:30pm, Su 9am-12:30pm and 2-6:30pm. Tickets €1.20-3.10. Day pass €6.50, 6-day pass €18.) For **taxis,** call ☎0565 91 51 22. **Rent Chaippi,** Calata Italia, 38, rents **cars** (€45-65 per day), **mopeds** (€35-40), and **mountain bikes** (€10) for exploring the island. (☎0565 91 66 87; www.rentchiappi.it. Open M-Sa 8am-8pm and Su 9:30am-12:30pm and 3:30-6:30pm.)

⚹ 🛈 ORIENTATION AND PRACTICAL INFORMATION

Though it's Elba's largest city, Portoferraio has a tiny *centro*. From the center of the harbor (in front of the Toremar docks), a left leads to **Calata Italia** and a right to **Via Emanuele II; Via Manzoni** cuts between them. From Calata Italia, a right turn on **Via Elba** goes farther inland toward services like banks and grocery stores. V. Emanuele II turns into **Calata Mazzini,** which curves with the borders of the harbor; follow street signs and turn left through a brick arch, **Porta Medicea,** to **Piazza Cavour.** Cut through the *piazza* to reach **Piazza della Repubblica,** the center of town.

Tourist Offices: APT, Calata Italia, 44 (☎0565 91 46 71; www.aptelba.it). From the Toremar docks facing away from the water, proceed left. Walk past a series of private tourist companies and cafes and cross V. Elba. Office is ahead on the right. Accommodations info for all of Elba, bus schedules, and restaurant listings. Open in summer daily 8am-8pm; in winter 8am-1pm and 4-8pm.

Boat Excursions: Linee di Navigazione Archipelago Toscano (☎0565 91 47 97; www.elbacrociere.com) offers tours of Elba's coast as well as excursions to nearby islands (€25.80-36.20). Information and booking in tourist office. Less expensive but more crowded, **Visione Sottomarina** (☎328 70 95 470) runs trips along the coast (€15) in glass-bottomed boats for prime underwater views. Arrive 20min. early for decent seats. Tickets sold onboard. Also departs from Marciana Marina.

UMBRIA AND LE MARCHE

HIGHLIGHTS OF UMBRIA AND LE MARCHE

JOURNEY to one of Italy's most revered pilgrimage sites, the **Basilica di San Francesco** in Assisi, an elaborate monument to the ascetic St. Francis (p. 513).

SAMPLE world-famous Perugina chocolate in **Perugia** (p. 498).

RELAX AND REFLECT like St. Francis did at the **Eremo delle Carceri** (p. 515).

UMBRIA

 Umbria is known as the "green heart of Italy." This landlocked region is rich in wild woods and fertile plains, craggy gorges and gentle hills, tiny cobblestoned villages and lively international universities. Three thousand years ago, Etruscans settled this regional crossroads between the Adriatic and Tyrrhenian coasts. Another conqueror, Christianity, transformed Umbria's architecture and regional identity. St. Francis shamed the extravagant church with his legacy of humility, pacifism, and charity that persists in Assisi to this day. The region holds Giotto's greatest masterpieces and produced medieval masters Perugino and Pinturicchio, and Umbria's artistic spirit gives life today to the internationally acclaimed Spoleto Festival and Umbria Jazz Festival.

PERUGIA   ☎ 075

The citizens of Perugia (pop. 160,000) rose to political prominence after chasing the *Umbri* tribe into surrounding valleys. Obscure wars with neighboring cities dominate the Perugia's history, but periods of prosperity during peacetime gave rise to the stunning artistic and architectural achievements for which the city is known today. Pietro Vannucci, mentor to Raphael, is known as "Perugino" because of his long association with the town, which proudly displays many of his frescoes. Perugia is very walkable; visitors quickly become familiar with the layout of the winding streets and hilltop monuments. With a renowned jazz festival, decadent chocolate, and two universities, Perugia is a city of variety and character.

▐ TRANSPORTATION

Trains: Stazione Fontiveggio, in P. V. Veneto. Lies on the Foligno-Terontola line. Info office open M-Sa 8:10am-7:45pm. Ticket window open daily 6am-8:40pm. To: **Arezzo** (1½hr., 1 per hr., €3.82); **Assisi** (25min., every hr., €1.60); **Florence** (2½hr., 18 per day, from €7.90); **Foligno** (40min., every hr., €2.20); **Orvieto** (1½hr. 5 per day, €9) via **Terontola** (40min., 5 per day, €9); **Passignano sul Trasimeno** (30min., every hr., €2); **Rome** (2½hr., 6 per day 4:55am-6:10pm, €10.12) via **Terontola** (1 per day) or **Foligno** (1 per day); **Spoleto** (1½hr., every hr., €3.50) via **Foligno** (3 per day). A secondary station is **Perugia Sant'Anna,** in P.le Bellucci. The commuter rail runs to **Sansepolcro** (1½hr., 14 per day 6:18am-8:31pm, €3.90) and **Terni** (1½hr., 19 per day 7:31am-12:30am, €4.30) via **Todi** (1hr., 5 per day 6:53am-8:39pm, €2.70).

Buses: City buses in P. dei Partigiani, down the escalator from P. Italia. Bus #6 (€0.90) runs to the train station. **APM** (☎075 57 31 707), in P. dei Partigiani. To: **Assisi** (1hr., 8 per day 6:25am-8:05pm, €2.80); **Chiusi** (1½hr., 7 per day 6:20am-6:35pm, €4.80); **Gubbio** (1¼hr., 11 per day 6:40am-8pm, €4); **Todi** (1½hr., 8 per day 6:30am-7:30pm, €4.80). Reduced service Su. Additional buses leave from the train station. Tickets at RadioTaxi Perugia, to the right of the train station. To: **Siena** (every 2hr., €9).

Taxis: In P. Italia (☎075 57 36 092), and on C. Vannucci (☎075 57 21 979).

Car Rental: Hertz, P.V. Veneto, 2 (☎337 65 08 37), near the train station. Cars from €85 per day. Open M-F 8:30am-12:30pm and 3-7pm, Sa 8:30am-1pm.

✦ ❷ ORIENTATION AND PRACTICAL INFORMATION

From Fontiveggio train station, buses #6, 7, 9, 13d, and 15 run to **Piazza Italia** (€0.90). Otherwise, it's a 2km trek uphill to the city center. To get to P. Italia from the **bus station** in **Piazza dei Partigiani** or from the nearby **Perugia Sant'Anna train station** at **Piazzale Belucci,** follow the signs to the **escalator** that runs beneath the old city (open 6:15am-1:45am; free). From P. Italia, **Corso Vannucci,** the main shopping thoroughfare, leads to **Piazza IV Novembre** and the *duomo*. Behind the *duomo*, is **Piazza Braccio Fortebraccio** and the university district. One block off C. Vannucci is **Via Baglioni,** which leads to **Piazza Matteotti,** the municipal center.

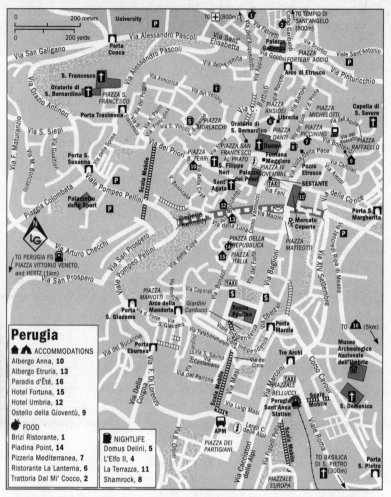

Perugia

⌂ ▲ ACCOMMODATIONS

Albergo Anna, **10**
Albergo Etruria, **13**
Paradis d'Été, **16**
Hotel Fortuna, **15**
Hotel Umbria, **12**
Ostello della Gioventù, **9**

● FOOD

Brizi Ristorante, **1**
Piadina Point, **14**
Pizzeria Mediterranea, **7**
Ristorante La Lanterna, **6**
Trattoria Dal Mi' Cocco, **2**

■ NIGHTLIFE

Domus Delirii, **5**
L'Elfo II, **4**
La Terrazza, **11**
Shamrock, **8**

Tourist Office: P. IV Novembre, 3 (☎075 57 23 327 or 075 57 36 458; fax 075 57 39 386). The knowledgeable staff provides **maps** and info on accommodations, restaurants, and cultural events. Ask for a free ■**Perugia Little Blue** guide in English, which is especially helpful for long-term stays in Perugia. Open M-Sa 8:30am-1:30pm and 3:30-6:30pm, Su 9am-1pm. **Info Umbria,** L. Cacciatori delle Alpi, 3/B (☎075 57 32 933; www.guideinumbria.com), next to the bus station. Private office provides maps, sells tickets to concerts, shows, and sporting events, and provides free booking for many hotels. Internet €3 per hr. Luggage storage €1.30 for 1st hr., €0.80 each additional hr. Open M-F 9am-1pm and 2:30-6:30pm, Sa 9am-1pm.

Budget Travel: CTS, V. del Roscetto, 21 (☎075 57 20 284), off V. Pinturicchio toward the bottom of the street, offers vacation deals to ISIC holders. Open M-F 10am-1pm and 3-6pm. **SESTANTE Travel,** C. Vannucci, 2 (☎075 57 26 061), books flights, sells train tickets, and rents cars. Open M-F and Su 9am-1pm and 3-7pm.

Currency Exchange: Banks have the best rates; those in P. Italia have 24hr. **ATMs.** The Perugia FS train station charges no commission for exchanges of less than €40.

Luggage Storage: In the **FS train station.** €3.87 per 24hr. Open daily 6am-9pm. Also available at **Info Umbria** (see above).

English-Language Bookstore: Libreria, V. Rocchi, 3 (☎075 75 36 104). Small selection of classics, a few recent best sellers, and travel guides. Open M-Sa 10am-1pm and 3:30-8pm, Su 10:30am-1pm.

Laundromat: 67 Laundry, V. Fabretti, 7/A. Wash €3 per 7kg, dry €6. Open daily 8am-9pm. **Bolle Blu,** C. Garibaldi, 43. Wash €3 per 8kg, dry €3. Open daily 8am-10pm.

Emergency: 113. **Ambulance:** ☎118. **Police:** V. Cortonese, (☎112 or 075 50 621).

Pharmacy: Farmacia S. Martino, P. Matteotti, 26 (☎075 57 22 335). Open 24hr.

Hospital: Central line (☎075 57 81). **Ospedale Silvestrini** (☎075 57 82 296).

Internet Access: Perugia has many cheap and reliable Internet cafes. Don't pay more than €1.50 per hr. **InformaGiovani,** V. Idalia, offers free Internet, but is often crowded. Go early. Open M and W 10am-1:30pm and 3:30-5pm, Tu and Th-F 10am-1:30pm.

Post Office: In P. Matteotti. Open M-Sa 8am-6:30pm. Offers **currency exchange** M-F 8am-6:30pm, Sa 8am-1pm. **Postal Code:** 06100.

⚡TIP CLIFF'S NOTES. While the tourist office in town is a valuable resource, student travelers should also stop by the Palazzo Galenga in P. Fortebraccio, home of the Università per Stranieri (University for Foreigners). The helpful, English-speaking staff at the information desk on the ground floor is specifically suited to help young people, and can provide student-friendly tips about the town.

🏠 ACCOMMODATIONS AND CAMPING

Reserve ahead in July, when the Umbria Jazz Festival draws crowds to Perugia.

 Ostello della Gioventù/Centro Internazionale di Accoglienza per la Gioventù, V. Bontempi, 13 (☎075 57 22 880; www.ostello.perugia.it). Good cheer and terrace with great views of the city. Check out the 300-year-old frescoed ceilings. Kitchen, lockers, spacious showers, lobby phone, Internet, and TV room. Sheets €1.50. Lockout 9:30am-4pm. Curfew midnight, 1am in summer. 2-week max. stay. Open Jan. 16-Dec. 14. Groups can request 8-person room with bath. Dorms €13. AmEx/MC/V. ❶

Albergo Anna, V. dei Priori, 48 (☎/fax 075 57 36 304), on the corner of Piazza B. Ferri off C. Vannucci. Climb 3 floors to chandeliered hallways and cozy 17th-century rooms, some with ceramic fireplaces and great views of the city rooftops. Singles €30, with bath €37-40; doubles €48/54, with veranda €62. AmEx/MC/V. ❸

Albergo Etruria, V. della Luna, 21 (☎075 57 23 730), down a staircase off C. Vannucci. Well-located rooms have antique furnishings and bath. Immense 13th-century sitting room with English magazines and a low, arched roof. Buzzing in can be a hassle. Curfew 12:30am. Singles €27; doubles €54; triples €75. Cash only. ❸

Hotel Umbria, V. Boncambi, 37 (☎075 57 21 203; www.hotel-umbria.com), off P. della Repubblica. Narrow rooms with TV and spacious, clean baths. Singles €38-48; doubles €55-70. Prices vary depending on length of stay and payment method. AmEx/MC/V. ❹

Hotel Fortuna, V. L. Bonazzi, 19 (☎075 57 22 845; www.umbriahotels.com). This converted 13th-century *palazzo* has fluffy towels, a rooftop terrace, and free Internet 8pm-8am. All rooms have bath, A/C, phone, TV, minibar, and hair dryer. Breakfast included. Singles €67-86; doubles €97, with bath €124. AmEx/MC/V. ❺

Paradis d'Eté, V. del Mercato, 29/A (☎/fax 075 51 73 121), 8km from town, in Colle della Trinità. Take a city bus from P. Italia (dir: Colle della Trinità; every 1-2hr.) and ask the driver to stop at the campgrounds. Attractive camping with free hot showers and pool access. €6.20 per person, €4.80 per tent, €3 per car. AmEx/MC/V. ●

📷 FOOD

Although you'd be insane to bypass the world-famous Perugian chocolate at **Perugina,** C. Vannucci, 101 (open M 2:30-7:45pm, Tu-Sa 9:30am-1:30pm and 2:30-7:45pm, Su 10:30am-1:30pm and 3:30-7:45pm), make sure to try the city's other specialties, too. Both *torta di formaggio* (cheese bread) and the *mele al cartoccio* (apple pie) are available at **Ceccarani,** P. Matteotti, 16. (☎075 57 21 960. Open M-Sa 7:30am-8pm, Su 9am-1:30pm.) For other confections, like *torciglione* (sweet almond bread) and *baci* (chocolate-hazelnut kisses), follow aromas to **Pasticceria Sandri,** C. Vannucci, 32. (Open Tu-Su 8am-10pm.) Check out the **covered marked** in P. Matteotti; on summer nights, it becomes an outdoor cafe. (Entrance is below street level. Open M-F 7am-1:30pm and 4:30-7:30pm.) The **COOP,** P. Matteotti, 15, stocks essentials. (Open M-Sa 9am-8pm.) Complement meals with one of the region's native wines: try *Sagrantino Secco,* a dry red, or *Grechetto,* a light white.

🍴 **Trattoria Dal Mi' Cocco,** C. Garibaldi, 12 (☎075 57 32 511). This unpretentious local favorite leaves diners stuffed and giddy. Overwhelming €13 *menù* includes your choice of *antipasti,* side dish, *primi* and *secondi* of the day, dessert, and a glass of liqueur. Open Tu-Su 1-3pm and 8:30pm-midnight. Reservations recommended. MC/V. ❸

Pizzeria Mediterranea, P. Piccinino, 11/12 (☎075 57 21 322). From P. IV Novembre, walk to the right of the *duomo* and turn right. A college crowd descends by night for upscale pizza at downscale prices (€3.70-5). Take food to the *piazza* for a more lively atmosphere. Cover €1.10. Open daily 12:30-2:30pm and 7:30-11pm. AmEx/MC/V. ●

Brizi Ristorante, V. Fabretti, 75/79 (☎075 57 21 386). From P. IV Novembre, walk right of the *duomo,* go left through P. Danti, and right down V. Rocchi to P. Fortebraccio. On far side of *piazza,* turn left on V. Fabretti. If you've had your fill of pizza and pasta, try the mixed grill with lamb, sausage, and chicken (€6.20). *Primi* €5, *secondi* from €5. *Menù* €10.50. Cover €1.30. Open M and W-Su noon-2:30pm and 7-10:30pm. MC/V. ❷

Ristorante La Lanterna, V. Rocchi, 6, near the *duomo.* Walk past an extensive collection of Victorian dolls in the entryway to enjoy *gnocchi lanterna* (ricotta and spinach dumplings with mushrooms and cheese; €7.50) in brick-vaulted rooms. Waiters in formal dress hover attentively. *Primi* €7.50-10, *secondi* €10-14.50. Cover €2. Open daily May-Aug. noon-3:30pm and 7:30-10:30pm, Sept.-Apr. closed Th. AmEx/MC/V. ❹

Piadina Point, V. Bonazzi, 7 (☎0267 35 20 546). Regional specialty *piadine* (crunchy flat breads) are made with your choice of cheeses, meats, and veggies (€3). Open daily 11am-3pm and 5-9pm. Cash only. ●

👁 SIGHTS

PIAZZA IV NOVEMBRE AND ENVIRONS

🏛 **PIAZZA IV NOVEMBRE.** The social center of Perugian life, P. IV Novembre presents a pageant of young, lively locals and internationals against a backdrop of beautiful monuments. Perugia's most visited sights frame P. IV Novembre on the northern end of the city, and most other monuments lie no more than a 15min. walk away. The Fontana Maggiore, designed by Fra' Bevignate and decorated by Nicola and Giovanni Pisano, sits in the center of the *piazza.* Bas-reliefs depicting both religious and Roman history cover the double-basin fountain. Students congregate at all hours on the steps bordering the *piazza* to people-watch and chat over pizza and wine. Bottles aren't allowed on the steps after 8pm, but never fear—neighboring cafes happily dole out drinks in plastic cups.

 PERUGIA PASS. The Perugia Citta Museo card grants admission to up to 12 of the city's fine artistic and historical sites, including the Galleria Nazionale dell'Umbria, the Pozzo Etrusco, and the Museo Archeologico. A one-day pass for four attractions is €7, a three-day pass for all 12 sights is €12.

PALAZZO DEI PRIORI AND GALLERIA NAZIONALE DELL'UMBRIA. The 13th-century windows and turrets of this *palazzo*, on the left when looking at the Fontana Maggiore, are remnants of an embattled era. This building, one of the finest examples of Gothic communal architecture, shelters the impressive **Galleria Nazionale dell'Umbria.** The collection contains magnificent 13th- and 14th-century religious works by Duccio, Fra Angelico, Taddeo di Bartolo, Guido da Siena, and Piero della Francesca. Among these early masterpieces, Duccio's skillful rendering of the transparent garments in his *Virgin and Child and Six Angels* in **Room 2** is worth a closer look. Another highlight is della Francesca's detailed *Polyptych of Saint Anthony* in **Room 11.** Native sons Pinturicchio and Perugino share **Room 15.** The former's *Miracles of San Bernardino of Siena* uses colors and rich tones that contrast with Perugino's characteristic soft pastels. Upstairs, three rooms display Baroque and Neo-Classical works as well as a collection of jewelry and textiles. *(In P. IV Novembre at C. Vannucci, 19. ☎075 57 21 009; www.gallerianazionaledellumbria.it. Open daily 8:30am-7:30pm, ticket office closes at 6:30pm. Closed Jan. 1, May 1, Dec. 25, and 1st M of the month. €8.50, EU citizens 18-25 €4.25, EU citizens under 18 or over 65 free.)* To the right of the Galleria sits the **Sala dei Notari,** once the citizens' assembly chamber. Thirteenth-century frescoes adorning the eight Romanesque arches that support the vault portray scenes from the Bible and Aesop's fables. *(Up the steps across from the fountain and across from the duomo. Open daily June-Sept. 9am-1pm and 3-7pm; closed M Oct.-May. Free admission. Sometimes closed for public performances.)*

DUOMO (CATTEDRALE DI SAN LORENZO). Perugia's imposing Gothic *duomo* was begun in the 14th century, but builders never completed the facade. Though not as ornate as other cathedrals in Tuscany and Umbria, its 15th- to 18th-century embellishments contribute to the elegance of the church, enhanced occasionally by organ music at night. The church holds the Virgin Mary's wedding ring, snagged from Chiusi in the Middle Ages, though it is kept out of public view and under lock and key. *(P. IV Novembre. Open M-Sa 9am-12:45pm and 4-5:15pm, Su 4-5:45pm.)*

COLLEGIO DELLA MERCANZIA AND COLLEGIO DEL CAMBIO. The walls of these audience chambers, on either side of Palazzo dei Priori, are covered in magnificent wood panelling and elaborate frescoes. The elegant carved bench in the **Collegio della Mercanzia** (Merchants' Guild) stands near illuminated lists of members of the merchants' guild. In the **Collegio del Cambio** (Exchange Guild), the **Sala dell'Udienza** (audience chamber) holds Perugino's frescoes, which portray heroes, prophets, and even the artist himself. The 88 members of Perugia's merchant guild have met in this richly paneled structure to debate tax laws and local commerce since 1390. *(Collegio della Mercanzia: C. Vannucci, 15, next door to Galleria Nazionale dell'Umbria. ☎075 57 30 366. Open Mar.-Oct. and Dec. 20-Jan. 6 M-Sa 9am-12:30pm and 2:30-5:30pm, Su and holidays 9am-1pm; Nov.-Dec. 19 and Jan. 7-Feb. Tu and Th-F 8am-2pm, W and Sa 8am-4:30pm, Su 9am-1pm. Collegio del Cambio: at C. Vannucci, 25. ☎075 57 28 599. Open Mar.-Oct. and Dec. 20-Jan. 6 M-Sa 9am-1pm and 2:30-6:30pm, Su and holidays 9am-1pm; Nov.-Dec. 19 and Jan. 7-Feb. Tu-Su 9am-1pm. €2.60, combination ticket including Collegio della Mercanzia €3.10, groups or over 65 €2.60.)*

VIA DEI PRIORI. Don't be fooled by the street's present-day calm and *pietra serena* (stone-like serenity). V. dei Priori, which begins under the arch at Palazzo dei Priori, was one of the goriest streets of medieval Perugia: the spikes on the lower walls of the street were once used to impale the rotting heads of executed criminals. The Baroque **Chiesa di San Filippo Neri** resides solemnly in P. Ferri; Santa Maria di Vallicella's heart is kept here, along with many large, bright paintings. *(2 blocks farther from Chiesa di San Filippo Neri. Open daily in summer 7am-noon and 4:30-7:30pm; in winter 8am-noon and 4-6pm.)* **Piazza San Francesco al Prato** is a grassy square that invites leisurely lounging and strolling. At its edge is the colorful **Oratorio di San Bernardino.** Carved reliefs and sculptures embellish its Renaissance facade, built between 1457 and 1461. *(Near San Filippo Neri, down V. San Francesco. Open daily 8am-12:30pm and 3:30-6pm.)*

THE NORTHEAST

VIA ROCCHI. From behind the *duomo*, medieval V. Rocchi, the city's oldest street, winds through the northern city and straight underneath the **Arco di Etrusco,** a perfectly preserved Roman arch built on Etruscan pedestals. Walk straight through P. Braccio Fortebraccio, where V. Rocchi turns to C. Guiseppe Garibaldi, and follow it for 10min. toward the jewel-like **Tempio di Sant'Angelo** (also known as Chiesa di San Michele Arcangelo), a 5th-century circular church constructed with stone and wood taken from ancient pagan buildings. The **Porta Sant'Angelo,** an arch and tower that welcomes visitors to the city, stands next door. *(Past Palazzo Gallenga, to the right near the end of C. Garibaldi. ☎ 075 57 22 624. Open Tu-Su 10am-noon and 4-6pm.)*

CAPPELLA DI SAN SEVERO. This chapel is home to *The Holy Trinity and Saints,* one of many collaborations by Perugia's favorite mentor-student tag-team, Perugino and Raphael, who painted the lower and upper sections respectively. Raphael's natural talent was apparent even in his first fresco. Check out the *piazza* wall opposite the chapel where a plaque engraved with a quote from Dante's *Paradise* praises the city. *(In P. Rafaello. ☎ 075 57 33 864. Open daily Apr.-Oct. 10am-1:30pm and 2:30-6:30pm; Nov.-Mar. 10:30am-1:30pm and 2:30-5pm. €2.50, including Pozzo Etrusco and Casero di Porta Sant'Angelo.)*

POZZO ETRUSCO. With a depth of 36m, the Pozzo Etrusco (Etruscan Well) dates to the 3rd century BC and was once Perugia's main water source. Perugians were forced to use the well again during World War II, when bombs destroyed the water lines to the city. Descend stairs to the footbridge spanning the well just meters above the water. *(P. Danti, 18, across from the duomo. Look for the "Pozzo Etrusco" sign above a small alleyway. ☎ 075 57 33 669. Open M and W-Su 10:30am-1:30pm and 2:30-5pm.)*

THE EAST SIDE

BASILICA DI SAN PIETRO. This 10th-century church consists of a double arcade of closely spaced columns that lead to a choir. Its art-filled interior contains solemn, majestic paintings and frescoes depicting saints and soldiers, all in brilliant color on a dramatic scale. Look for Perugino's *Pietà* along the northern aisle. At the far end is a garden; its lower section offers a must-see view of the surrounding countryside. Downstairs, an ancient Etruscan crypt is on display. *(At the end of town on V. Borgo XX Giugno, past Pta. S. Pietro. Entrance to church is on the far left side of the court-yard, garden is through the courtyard on the right. Open daily 8am-noon and 3-6:30pm.)*

CHIESA DI SAN DOMENICO. This cathedral is the largest church in Umbria. The Gothic rose window brightens the otherwise simple white interior, rebuilt in 1632. The magnificently carved **Tomb of Pope Benedict XI** (1325), by Lorenzo Maitani, rests in the Capella del Santissimo Sacramento to the right of the high altar. *(In P. Giordano Bruno, on C. Cavour. Open daily 8am-noon and 4pm-sunset.)*

GIARDINI CARDUCCI. These well-maintained public gardens are named after the 19th-century poet Giosuè Carducci. From the garden wall, enjoy the splendid panorama of the Umbrian countryside; a castle or an ancient church crowns every hill. *(Behind P. Italia at the far end of C. Vannucci, the main street leading from P. IV Novembre.)*

ROCCA PAOLINA. The *rocca* is the underground remains of a grandiose fortress built by the architect Antonio Sangallo il Giovane on the order of Pope Paolo III Farnese. An escalator goes through it and connects the upper and lower parts of the city—peek into old passageways as you ride up to P. Italia. *(Beneath P. Italia. Entrances there and across from bus station in P. Partigiani. Open daily 6:15am-2am. Free.)*

NIGHTLIFE AND FESTIVALS

Perugia has more nightlife options than any other city in Umbria, and its large student population keeps clubs packed nearly every night of the week from September to May. During the academic year, join the nightly bandwagon at **Piazza Fortebraccio,** where free buses depart for several nearby clubs (starting at 11pm). Once there, cover charges of €13-26 put patrons in the thick of deafening electronic music and scantily clad clubbers. In the city, one of Perugia's hottest discos is **Domus Delirii,** V. del Naspo, 3, just off P. Morlacchi. **Shamrock,** P. Danti, 18, is down a small side street on the way to the Pozzo Etrusco. Each pint of Guinness (€4.50) comes with a free shot of whiskey. (☎075 57 36 625. Happy hour 6-9pm. Open daily 6pm-2am.) Head to the student hangout **La Terrazza,** in P. Matteotti, on the rooftop terrace behind the covered market. It often hosts concerts, movies, and book readings. (Open daily 6pm-3am, weather depending.) **L'Elfo II,** V. del Verzaro, 39, off P. Morlacchi near the university, hosts a crowd of international students. (Beer €3.50-3.80. Cocktails €5.50. Open daily 9pm-2am.) Late-night cafes along V. Mazzini and P. Matteotti are a popular alternative to bar-hopping.

Every July, the 10-day ■Umbria Jazz Festival draws world-class performers like B.B. King and Alicia Keys. Grab a *panini* and a bottle of wine and head to one of the free outdoor concerts, or dance all night by the stage in P. IV Novembre. (For info call ☎800 46 23 11, visit www.umbriajazz.com, or go to the ticket office, V. Mazzini, 9, off C. Vannucci. Open M-Sa 10am-1pm and 3:30-7:30pm. Tickets €12-50, some events free.) In September, the **Sagra Musicale Umbra** occurs in many Umbrian cities and fills Perugia's churches with religious and classical music. Check Palazzo Gallenga or www.sagramusicaleumbra.com for event listings. Contact the tourist office or www.eurochocolate.perugia.it about the week-long **Eurochocolate Festival** at the end of October, when chocolate becomes the focus of fanciful creations and throngs of chocolate devotees wait for their free samples.

▶ DAYTRIP FROM PERUGIA: LAKE TRASIMENO

Thirty kilometers west of Perugia, Lake Trasimeno is a refreshing oasis. After advancing down the Alps in 217 BC during the Second Punic War, Hannibal's elephant-riding army routed the Romans just north of the lake, killing 16,000 soldiers. Thankfully, neither elephants nor bloodshed can be found any longer in Castiglion del Lago, the main town. A system of ferries connects Castiglion del Lago with Passignano sul Trasimeno, Tuero, San Feliciano, and Lake Trasimeno's two largest islands—Isola Maggiore and Isola Polvese.

CASTIGLION DEL LAGO

The easiest way to Castiglion del Lago from Perugia is by bus (1hr., 6 per day, €4.20) from P. Partigiani. Buses stop in P. G. Marconi. From there, walk up the stairs into P. Dante Alighieri, which leads up to the city entrance. The tourist office, P. Mazzini, 10, in

LOVE THE LAKE? If you plan to spend a long time exploring Lake Trasimeno, consider participating in the **Museo Aperto** museum tour, sponsored by the region's tourist offices. One ticket costs €6.20 and includes admission to attractions in Castiglion del Lago, Citta della Pieve, and Panicale. A €1.60 supplement includes a tour on Isola Maggiore with tastings of local products. Inquire at the tourist office in any of the four towns to buy tickets or book tours.

the main square, provides boat schedules, exchanges money, and helps find rooms in hotels or private residences. ☎075 96 52 484. Open M-F 8:30am-1pm and 3:30-7pm, Sa 9am-1pm and 3:30-7pm, Su and holidays 9am-1pm and 4-7pm.

Castiglion del Lago is now a much quieter town than in past centuries, when it was conquered by Byzantium, Arezzo, Cortona, and finally Perugia in 1184. Clinging to a limestone promontory covered in olive groves, its medieval walls enclose two main streets and a single square. At the end of V. V. Emanuele, next to the hospital, stand the **Palazzo della Corgna** and the medieval **Rocca del Leone.** The 16th-century *palazzo* is notable for its frescoes by Niccolò Circignan. The courtyard of the crumbling Rocca is free and open to the public, and its grass lawn sometimes serves as a venue for open-air concerts. (☎075 96 58 210. Open daily Mar 21.-Apr. 9:30am-1pm and 3:30-7pm; May-June 10am-1:30pm and 4-7:30pm; July-Aug. 10am-1:30pm and 4:30-8pm; Sept.-Oct. 10am-1:30pm and 3:30-7pm; Nov.-Mar. 20 9:30am-4:30pm. Combination ticket €3.) Visitors can also catch a ferry to the nearby **Isola Maggiore**, one of Lake Trasimeno's only inhabited island*s*.

Budget lodgings are scarce in the immediate vicinity of Castiglion del Lago, but **Il Torrione ❹**, V. delle Mura, 2/4, right on V. Battisti just inside the gates, is a worthy option. The peaceful garden leads to suites that have bath and picturesque views of the lake. (☎075 95 32 36; www.trasinet.com/iltorrione. Singles €55; doubles €65.) **La Torre ❹**, V. V. Emanuele, 50, offers rooms with bath, TV, air-conditioning, and refrigerators in the heart of the old town. (☎075 95 16 66; www.trasinet.com/latorre. Breakfast €5. Singles €50; doubles €65-75; triples €85. AmEx/MC/V.)

Gourmet food shops line the busier streets, while cheap pizzerias, where prices average €4-6 per person, crowd V. V. Emanuele. For a fancier dining experience, try **La Cantina ❸**, V. V. Emanuele, 93, a certified Umbrian cuisine restaurant with beautiful views and an attentive waitstaff. (*Primi* €5-7.50, *secondi* €8.20-19. Cover €1.80. Open June-Sept. M and W-Su 12:30-3pm and 7pm-1am; Oct.-May W-Su 12:30-3pm and 7-10:30pm. AmEx/MC/V.) **Ristorante L'Acquario ❸**, V. V. Emanuele, 69, offers a variety of lunch *menù* options (€13-17). (*Primi* €6-8.50, *secondi* €8-30. Cover €1.80. Open Mar.-Oct. M-Tu and Th-Su noon-2:30pm and 7-10:30pm; Nov.-Feb. Tu and Th-Su noon-2:30pm and 7-10:30pm. AmEx/MC/V.)

TODI   ☎075

APM (☎075 89 42 939 or 800 51 21 41) runs buses to and from Perugia (1¼hr.; M-Sa 8 per day; last bus from Todi 5pm, last bus from Perugia 7:30pm; €4.80). The bus station is in P. Consolazione, a short ride on city bus A or a 1km walk uphill from the centro. Todi is also accessible by train on the Perugia-Terni line from Ponte Rio (45min., 13 per day 6:30am-1pm and 3:30-8pm, €2.70). The last train leaves from Terni at 8:10pm and from Perugia at 8:50pm; city bus C runs to the station at P. Jacopone until 7:45pm. The IAT Tourist Office, P. del Popolo, has free maps, schedules, and info on restaurants and lodgings. (☎075 89 42 526. Open M-F 9:30am-1pm and 3:30-7pm, Sa-Su 10am-1pm and 3:30pm-7pm.) Farmacia Pirrami (☎075 89 42 320) is at P. del Popolo, 46. (Open daily 9am-1pm and 4:30-8pm.) Postal Code: 06059.

According to legend, the founders of Todi built their city on the spot where an eagle landed after stealing a tablecloth from their dinner feast. At the foot of Todi's hills lies the Renaissance **Tempio di Santa Maria della Consolazione,** whose elegant green domes and detailed reliefs are thought to have been based on architectural genius Bramante's early draft for St. Peter's in Rome. Equally impressive are the magnificent altarpiece and 12 enormous statues of the region's saints. (Open daily 9am-12:30pm and 2:30-6:30pm.) Follow a sinuous dirt path (Vle. della Serpentina) from P. della Consolazione or the less curvy V. della Consolazione to reach **La Rocca,** a ruined 14th-century castle that fronts a quaint public park. From the park follow V. della Rocca to the towering **Tempio di San Fortunato.** Built by the Franciscans between the 13th and 15th centuries, the church features a high vaulted ceiling with decorative medallions, intricate sculptures and reliefs, and aged frescoes like *The Madonna and Jesus With Angels* by Masolino da Panciale. (Open M 3-7pm, Tu-Su 9am-1pm and 3-7pm.) From San Fortunato, head through P. Jacopone to the **Piazza del Popolo,** encircled by three palaces-turned-municipal-centers, half a dozen souvenir shops, two *gelaterie*, and a 900-year-old church. The 12th-century **duomo** is at the far end of P. del Popolo atop a flight of broad stone steps. The rose window cuts through a huge 🔳**fresco** of the Last Judgement for a breathtaking effect. (Open daily 8:30am-12:30pm and 2:30-6:30pm.)

High-priced luxury hotels are located inside the city walls while less expensive options are about a 20min. walk downhill from the center. The best budget option, however, is **Crispolti Holiday House ❸,** near P. del Popolo. Walking down V. del Duomo, turn right on V. di S. Prassede and wind to the right until V. Cesia, 96.This hostel-style accommodation is in an old church building and has a bar, an inexpensive restaurant, a meeting room, a beautiful terrace, a TV room, and an Internet point. (Breakfast included. Dorms €30; doubles €80; quads €152. Group discounts available.) **Antica Hosteria de la Valle ❷,** V. Ciuffelli, 19, serves pleasant meals (*primi* €7-12, *secondi* €7-9, full course dinner €18-25) in a stately room of brick and wood. (☎075 894 48 48. Open Tu-Su noon-2:30pm and 7-10pm. MC/V.) Just down the street is a sitting area with park benches.

GUBBIO ☎075

With picturesque streets and a rugged mountainside setting, Gubbio (pop. 30,000) is a town that preserves its past. The town's famous Eugubine Tablets—one of the only existing records of the ancient Umbrian language—offer a glimpse into Umbria's history and provide important evidence of an Umbrian and Roman alliance against the invading Etruscans. Gubbio also boasts its own school of painting, a thriving ceramics trade, and its favorite son Bosone Novello Raffaelli, Italy's first novelist. A convenient daytrip from Perugia but certainly worthy of a night's stay, Gubbio is filled with comfortable accommodations and friendly residents who punctuate their seasons with unique traditions and celebrations.

🔳🔢 TRANSPORTATION AND PRACTICAL INFORMATION

The nearest **train station** is in **Fossato di Vico,** 19km away on the Rome-Ancona line. Trains run to: Ancona (1½hr., 15 per day, from €4.23); Rome (2½hr., 10 per day, €10.12); Spoleto (1¼hr., 10 per day, €3.36). **APM buses** (☎075 50 67 81) run to and from Perugia (1hr.; M-F 11 per day, Sa-Su 4 per day; €4) and are much more convenient than the train, though the twisting, hilly road can be slightly stomach-churning. The **bus** is the easiest way to reach Gubbio from Fossato (M-Sa 12 per day, Su 6 per day; €2). Tickets sold at the newsstand in P. Quaranta Martiri, at the

Perugia bus stop, and at the newsstand in Fossato's train station. If stranded in Fossato without bus service, call a **taxi** at ☎075 91 92 02 or 033 53 37 48 71. In Gubbio, taxis (☎075 92 73 800) are available in P. Quaranta Martiri.

Gubbio is a tangle of twisting streets that open into squares. Buses stop in **Piazza Quaranta Martiri.** A short uphill walk on **Via della Repubblica** from the bus station leads to **Corso Garibaldi.** Signs point uphill to **Piazza Grande,** the civic headquarters on the hilltop. Some of the best ceramics are sold on **Via dei Consoli** and in P. Grande. The **IAT Tourist Office,** P. Oderisi, 6, off C. Garibaldi, offers bus schedules and **maps.** (☎075 92 20 693; www.umbria2000.it. Open daily Mar.-Oct. M-F 8:30am-1:45pm and 3:30-6:30pm, Sa 9am-1pm and 3:30-6:30pm, Su 9:30am-12:30pm and 3:30-6:30pm; Nov.-Feb. 8:30am-1:45pm 3-6pm. A 24hr. **ATM** is at P. Quaranta Martiri, 48. In case of **emergency,** dial ☎113, call an **ambulance** at ☎118, the **hospital** is at ☎075 23 94 67, or contact the **police** (☎075 22 15 42), on V. Leonardo Da Vinci. **Farmacia Luconi** is at C. Garibaldi, 12. (☎075 92 73 783. Open Apr.-Sept. M-Sa 9am-1pm and 4:30-8pm; Oct.-Mar. 9am-1pm and 4-7:30pm.) The **post office** is at V. Cairoli, 11. (☎075 92 73 925. Open M-F 8am-1:30pm, Sa 8am-12:30pm.) **Postal Code: 06024.**

🏠🍴 ACCOMMODATIONS AND FOOD

A private garden and enthusiastic staff make 🔲**Residenza di Via Piccardi ❸,** V. Piccardi, 12, an ideal place to relax. Six large and bright rooms all have bath and TV. (☎075 92 76 108; e.biagiotti@tiscali.it. Breakfast included. Check-in before 8pm. Singles €35; doubles €50; triples €60. Extra bed €10. Cash only.) **Residenza Le Logge ❹,** V. Piccardi, 7/9, is to the right off P. Quaranta Martiri. Big, clean rooms are the standard in this *pensione* run by a friendly owner. For a splurge, ask for the massive double suite with a whirlpool tub. (☎075 92 77 574; www.paginegialle.it/residenzalelogge. Breakfast included. Singles €52-60; doubles €62-80; suite €80.) Walk up from P. Quaranta Martiri on V. Della Repubblica, and turn right on V. Gioia to reach **Hotel Grotta dell'Angelo ❸,** V. Gioia, 47. Spacious rooms all have bright linens, TV, phone, and bath. (☎075 92 71 747; www.grottadellangelo.it. Breakfast €4. Singles €35-38; doubles €50-55; triples €65. AmEx/MC/V.)

Every Tuesday brings a bustling **market** under P. Quaranta Martiri's *loggie.* Sample local delicacies at **Prodotti Tipici e Tartufati Eugubini ❶,** V. Piccardi, 17, including *salumi di cinghiale o cervo* (boar or deer sausage) and the region's white-truffle oil. (Open daily 10am-1pm and 2:30-8pm.) **Taverna del Buchetto ❷,** V. Dante, 30, inside a converted granary near Pta. Romana off C. Garibaldi, prepares hearty meals. (☎075 92 77 034. Pizza €3.62-7. *Primi* €4.13-7.75, *secondi* €7-11. Cover €1.29. Open Tu-Su noon-3pm and 7-11pm. AmEx/MC/V.) Mushrooms and truffles are the specialties at **La Cantina Ristorante/Pizzeria ❸,** V. Francesco Piccotti, 3, off V. della Repubblica. (☎075 92 20 583. Pizza €4.50-7. *Primi* €6.50-10.50, *secondi* €6.50-13. Cover €1. Open Tu-Su noon-2:30pm and 7-10pm; open for pizza noon-3pm. MC/V.) The stone dining room of **San Francesco e il Lupo ❹,** at V. Cairoli and C. Garibaldi, pumps out pizzas to hungry crowds. (☎075 92 72 344. Pizza €4-7.50. *Primi* €5-10, *secondi* €6-25. Cover €2. Open M and W-Su noon-2pm and 7-10pm. MC/V.) The elegant dining rooms of **Ristorante La Lanterna ❸,** V. Gioia, 23, caters to all with staples of Eugubine fare. (☎075 92 76 694. *Primi* €5.80-9, *secondi* €7.50-11. Open M-W and F-Su noon-3pm and 7:30-10:30pm. MC/V.)

👁 SIGHTS

PIAZZA QUARANTA MARTIRI. In the middle of the *piazza* stretches the **Giardino dei Quaranta Martiri** (Garden of the 40 Martyrs), a memorial to those slain by the Nazis in reprisal for the assassination of two German officials. The understated **Chiesa di San Francesco,** one of multiple places claiming to be the site where St.

Francis experienced his conversion, stands on one side of the square. The central apse holds the *Vita della Madonna*, a partially destroyed 15th-century fresco series by Ottaviano Nelli, Gubbio's most famous painter. V. Matteotti runs from P. Quaranta Martiri outside the city walls to the **Teatro Romano**, which still stages productions. The nearby **Antiquarium**, built on an archaeological excavation, displays impressive mosaics found in the city. *(Church open daily 7:15am-noon and 3:30-7:30pm.)*

PALAZZO DEI CONSOLI. This white stone palace was built in 1332 for the high magistrate of Gubbio. Inside, the **Museo Civico** displays a collection of Eugubine and Roman artifacts. In a room upstairs are the **◼Tavole Eugubine** (Eugubine Tablets), comparable to the Rosetta Stone for their linguistic significance. Five of these seven bronze tablets, dating from 300 to 100 BC, form one of the few remaining documents of the ancient Umbrian language. The last two tablets are in Latin. An illiterate farmer discovered them in 1444 in an underground chamber of the Roman theater just outside the city walls; he was subsequently tricked into swapping them for a worthless piece of land. The texts spell out the social, religious, and political organization of early Umbria and describe how to read religious omens from animal livers. *(In P. Grande. ☎ 075 92 74 298. Open daily Apr.-Oct. 10am-1pm and 3-6pm; Nov.-mid-Mar. 10am-1pm and 2-5pm. €5, ages 7-25 €2.50, under 7 free.)*

DUOMO. The unassuming pink Gothic *duomo* sits tucked away up a hill from P. Grande, displaying 12th-century stained-glass windows, art by Perugino's student Dono Doni, and Pinturicchio's *Adoration of the Shepherds*. *(Follow the signs from P. Grande. Open daily Apr.-Sept. 9am-7pm; Oct.-Mar. 10am-5pm.)*

MONTE INGINO. Hop into the rather shaky cages of the **◼funivia** (6min.) which climbs to the peak of Monte Ingino, a place with splendid views and picnic spots. Work up an appetite by climbing the hill up to the **Basilica and Monastery of Sant'Ubaldo**, which houses the saint's pickled body in a glass case above the altar. The stained glass at the entrance tells the story of his life, and the three *ceri*, large wooden candles carried in the **Corsa dei Ceri** procession each May, are also on display. Each December, lights transform the entire hill until it looks like the world's earthiest Christmas tree. Follow the dirt trail behind the basilica up to the scaffolding where the star is placed atop the "tree" and then continue up to an ancient but well-preserved tower for spectacular 360° panoramas of the mountains and valleys of Umbria. *(To reach the funivia, turn left out of Pta. Romana. From the uphill entrance to the basilica, bear left and continue upward on a dirt path to the top of the mountain. Chairlift open June M-Sa 9:30am-1:15pm and 2:30-7pm, Su 9am-7:30pm; July-Aug. M-Sa 8:30am-7:30pm, Su 8:30am-8pm; Sept. M-Sa 9:30am-1:15pm and 2:30-7pm, Su 9:30am-1:15pm and 2:30-7:30pm; Mar. M-Sa 10am-1:15pm and 2:30-5:30pm, Su 9:30am-1:15pm and 2:30-6pm; Apr.-May M-Sa 10am-1:15pm and 2:30-6:30pm, Su 9:30am-1:15pm and 2:30-7pm; Oct. daily 10am-1:15pm and 2:30-6pm; Nov.-Feb. daily 10am-1:15pm and 2:30-5pm. €4, round-trip €5.)*

🐝 FESTIVALS

The annual **Corsa dei Ceri**, 900 years old and still going strong, takes place every May 15, the day of patron saint Ubaldo's death. Intended to represent candles, three *ceri* (wooden boxes) are carved like hourglasses and topped with little statues of saints. Each one corresponds to a distinct section of the populace: the masons (S. Ubaldo), the farmers (S. Antonio Abate), and the artisans (S. Giorgio). After 12 hours of furious preparation and frenetic flag-twirling, squads of *ceraioli* (runners) clad in Renaissance-style tights heave the heavy objects onto their shoulders and run a wild relay race up Monte Ingino. This raucous festival turns Gubbio's quiet streets to a chaotic stomping ground bristling with intense ritual fervor. Visitors will be entranced; locals will almost certainly be drunk. During the **Palio della Balestra,** held in P. Grande on the last Sunday in May, archers from Gubbio and nearby Sansepolcro have gathered for a fierce crossbow contest since 1461. The contest provides an excellent excuse for Gubbio to throw a huge party every year and maintain an industry in medieval-weaponry toys.

ASSISI
☎ 075

Assisi's serene atmosphere and renowned spirituality stem from the legacy of St. Francis, patron saint of Italy and the town's favorite son. The 12th-century monk founded the Franciscan order and sparked a revolution within the Catholic Church through his audacious asceticism. Franciscan monks and nuns dressed in brown *cappucci* robes still inhabit Assisi, resembling the tiny votive statues that overflow souvenir stands. Fervent religiosity, however, is hardly a prerequisite for a visit to Assisi. Many people come simply for the intricate architecture of the city; the Basilica di San Francesco is perhaps the most frequented sight in Umbria, housing the saint's relics and Giotto's renowned fresco series of St. Francis's life. Local ruins attest to Assisi's Etruscan and Roman roots, while grand palaces and majestic *rocce* (castles) from a later era tower above tile roofs. Though renovations have repaired most of the damage caused by devastating earthquakes in 1997, unsightly construction cranes still mar the beautiful views today.

▐ TRANSPORTATION

Trains: Station near Basilica di Santa Maria degli Angeli. Assisi is on the F. S. Foligno-Terontola line. Office open 6am-8pm (☎075 80 40 272). **Luggage storage** available (see **Practical Information,** p. 512). Trains to **Florence** (2-3hr., 13 per day 5:54am-7:30pm, €8.99); **Perugia** (30min., 1-2 per hr. 5:54am-10:45pm, €1.65); and **Rome** (2½hr., 14 per day 5:15am-8:38pm, €8.99).

Buses: Buses leave from P. Unità d'Italia. Buy **SULGA** (☎075 50 09 641; www.sulga.it) tickets onboard. To: **Florence** (2½hr., 7am, €6.40) and **Rome** (3¼hr.; 1:45, 4:30pm; €8.26). Buy **APM** (☎800 51 21 41) tickets at newsstands. To: **Foligno** (1hr., M-Sa 10 per day 6:55am-7:10pm, €3.36) via **Spello** and **Perugia** (1½hr., 12 per day 6:30am-6:25pm, €2.70). Buy **SENA** (☎0577 28 32 03) tickets onboard. Bus to **Siena** (2hr., 2 per day, €9) leaves from S. Maria degli Angeli. Schedules at tourist office.

Public Transportation: Local buses (2 per hr., €0.80) run along **Linea A** from the train station to bus stops at P. Unità d'Italia, Largo Properzio, and P. Matteotti. Buy tickets onboard or at *tabaccherie* in the train station. Minibuses (€0.80) run around the inner city to select points on the outside along 2 lines, A and B.

Taxis: In P. del Comune (☎075 81 31 93), P. San Chiara (☎075 81 26 00), P. S. Pietro (☎075 81 23 78), and at the train station (☎075 80 40 275). **RadioTaxi** can be reached at ☎075 81 31 00.

▐ ▞ ORIENTATION AND PRACTICAL INFORMATION

Towering above the city to the north, the **Rocca Maggiore** can help orient those lost among Assisi's winding streets. The bus from the train station stops first at **Piazza Unità d'Italia;** get off here for direct access to the Basilica di San Francesco. Stay on the bus until **Piazza Matteotti** to access the *centro* from above. To reach **Piazza del Comune,** from P. Matteotti take **Via del Torrione** to **Piazza San Rufino,** take the downhill left in the *piazza,* and then walk down **Via San Rufino. Via Portica** becomes V. Fortini, V. di Seminario, and, finally, V. San Francesco and connects P. del Comune to the Basilica di San Francesco. Heading in the opposite direction from P. del Comune, **Corso Mazzini** leads to the Chiesa di Santa Chiara.

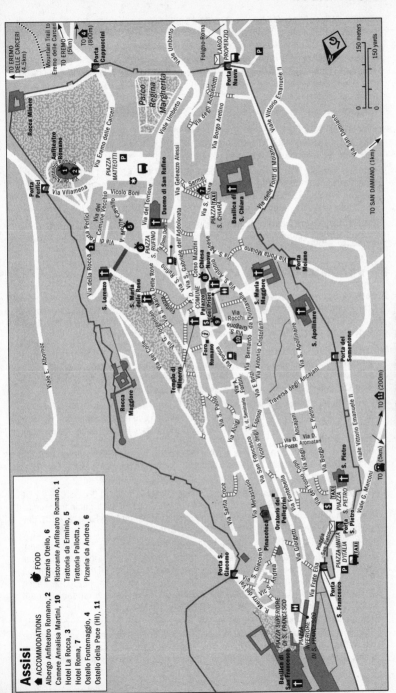

Assisi

▲ ACCOMMODATIONS
Albergo Anfiteatro Romano, **2**
Camere Annalisa Martini, **1**
Hotel La Rocca, **3**
Hotel Roma, **7**
Ostello Fontemaggio, **4**
Ostello della Pace (HI), **11**

♣ FOOD
Pizzeria Otello, **6**
Ristorante Anfiteatro Romano, **1**
Trattoria da Erminio, **5**
Trattoria Pallotta, **9**
Pizzeria da Andrea, **6**

UMBRIA AND
LE MARCHE

Tourist Office: P. del Comune (☎075 81 25 34; www.assisi.umbria2000.it). Walking into P. del Comune on V. S. Rufino, office is at far end of the *piazza*. Provides brochures, bus info, train timetable, and a decent **map**. Open M-Sa 8am-2pm and 3-6pm, Su and holidays 9am-1pm.

Currency Exchange: To exchange traveler's checks, try **Banca Toscana,** in P. S. Pietro, or **Banca dell'Umbria,** in P. del Comune. Banks open M-F 8:20am-1:20pm and 2:35-3:35pm. **ATMs** outside.

Luggage Storage: In train station. €2.60 per 12hr. Open daily 6:30am-7:30pm.

Emergency: ☎ 113. **Ambulance:** ☎ 118. **Carabinieri:** P. Matteotti, 3 (☎075 81 22 39).

Hospital: Ospedale d'Assisi (☎075 81 391), on the outskirts of town. Take the *Linea A* bus from P. del Comune and get off at stop 7.

Internet Access: Bar, V. Portica, 29B (☎075 81 62 46). €2 per 1st 15 min., €1 per each additional 15min. Open daily 9am-11pm. **Caffeteria Pasticceria,** V. S. Gabriele dell'Addolorata, 25 (☎075 81 68 93). DSL line €2 per 30min., €3.50 per hr. Open M-Sa 11am-1pm, Su 4-9pm.

Post Office: Largo Properzio, 4, up the stairs to the left just outside Pta. Nuova. Open M-Sa 8:35am-1:25pm. **Branch** at P. S. Pietro, 41. Open M-F 8:10am-7pm, Sa 8:10am-1:25pm. **Postal Code:** 06081.

ACCOMMODATIONS AND CAMPING

Reservations are crucial around Easter and Christmas and strongly recommended for the **Festa di Calendimaggio** in early May. If you don't mind turning in around 11pm, ask the tourist office for a list of **religious institutions**. The tourist office also provides a list of *affittacamere*, rooms for rent in private residences.

▨ **Camere Annalisa Martini,** V. S. Gregorio, 6 (☎/fax 075 81 35 36; cameremartini@libero.it). Bright rooms, some with balconies, surround a charming courtyard. Central location, soft beds, and truly friendly atmosphere. Laundry €5. Singles €24, with bath €26; doubles €38; triples €52; quads €62. Cash only. ❷

Ostello/Hotel/Camping Fontemaggio, V. per l'Eremo delle Carceri, 7 (☎075 81 36 36; fax 075 81 37 49). V. Eremo begins in P. Matteotti and leads through Pta. Cappuccini; follow 1km up the road and then bear right at the sign. Hotel, hostel, campground, and bungalows available for those who don't mind the trek. Onsite restaurant. Checkout 10am. Curfew 11pm. Dorms €20; singles €35; doubles €52; triples €72.50; quads €96; 4- to 8-person bungalows €50-140. Camping €5.50 per person, €4.50 per tent, €2.50 per car. Cash only. Hostel ❷/ Hotel ❸/Campground ❶

Albergo Anfiteatro Romano, V. Anfiteatro Romano, 4 (☎075 81 30 25; fax 075 81 51 10), off P. Matteotti. Modest rooms with views of the *Rocca* are built within the foundation of an old amphitheater. Hotel check-in is at the restaurant (see **Food,** p. 513). Singles €22; doubles €36, with bath €46. AmEx/MC/V. ❷

Ostello della Pace (HI), V. di Valecchi, 177 (☎075 81 67 67; www.assisihostel.com). From the train station, take the bus to P. Unità d'Italia. From P. Unità d'Italia, walk downhill on V. Marconi, then turn left at sign and walk for 500m. Bright rooms with 2-3 bunk beds and shared baths. Breakfast included. Dinner €8. Laundry €3.50. Reception 7-10am and 3:30-11:30pm. Lockout 9:30am-3:30pm. Reserve ahead. HI card required; on sale at hostel. Dorms €15, with bath €16. MC/V. ❶

Hotel La Rocca, V. di Pta. Perlici, 27 (☎075 81 22 84). From P. del Comune, follow V. S. Rufino uphill and cross the *piazza*, heading up V. di Pta. Perlici until you reach the old arches. All rooms have bath; many have great views of the *Rocca*. Restaurant downstairs. Open Feb. 5-Jan. 15. Singles €39; doubles €46; triples €63. AmEx/MC/V. ❸

Hotel Roma, P. S. Chiara, 13 (☎075 81 23 90; fax 075 81 67 43). Rooms have pleasant decor and many offer spectacular views of the *piazza* and surrounding countryside. Request rooms without breakfast for a lower price. All rooms have bath, TV, and phone. Singles €40, with breakfast €45; doubles €65. MC/V. ❹

🍴 FOOD

Assisi's alluring sweets and nut breads includes the mouth-watering *torrone* (a sweet nougat of almonds and egg whites; €2.90 per 100g) and the divine *brustengolo* (packed with raisins, apples, and pinenuts; €2.10 per 100g). **Pasticceria Santa Monica,** V. Portica, 4, right off P. del Comune, sells these and other treats. (Open daily 10am-9pm.)For fresh produce on weekdays, head to V. S. Gabriele.

Pizzeria Otello, V. S. Antonio, 1 (☎075 81 24 15). On the far left of the Palazzo dei Priori. Roast in the cool shadow of the Chiesa Nuova. Pizza at excellent value and in many varieties, sized for 1 (€5-7). Or try the deliciously creamy *strangozzi al tartufo* (pasta with truffles; €6.80). Open daily noon-4pm and 7-10:30pm. AmEx/MC/V. ❷

Trattoria da Erminio, V. Monte Cavallo, 19 (☎075 81 25 06). Real men don't eat *tartufi*—this *trattoria* is *the* place for carnivores. The savory aroma of crackling, roasting meat wafts down the street. *Primi* €5-9.50, *secondi* €4.70-11. Cover €1.50. Open M-W and F-Su noon-2:30pm and 7-9pm. AmEx/MC/V. ❷

Pizzeria da Andrea, P. S. Rufino, 26 (☎075 81 53 25). From the P. del Comune walk up V. S. Rufino. Look for the *pizza al taglio* sign on the right side of the piazza. Pleasant seats on the fountain outside make this a great rest from sightseeing. Pizza (€0.90-3.20). Panini (€3). Open daily 8:30am-8:30pm. Cash only. ❶

Ristorante Anfiteatro Romano, V. Anfiteatro Romano, 4 (☎075 81 30 25), off P. Matteotti. Downstairs from the hotel. Hearty portions of Umbrian fare served on the refreshing vine-rimmed patio or in the dining room adorned by a Roman fresco. *Primi* €4-8, *secondi* €5-9. Cover €1.60. Open daily noon-2:30pm and 7-9pm. AmEx/MC/V. ❷

Trattoria Pallotta, Vco. della Volta Pinta, 13 (☎075 81 26 49), off P. del Comune, tucked under the arch opposite Tempio di Minerva. Succulent Umbrian classics served beneath stone arcades. Excellent veggie options. *Primi* €5-9, *secondi* €7-9. Cover €2.50. Open M and W-Su noon-2:30pm and 7:15-9:30pm. AmEx/MC/V. ❸

🔆 SIGHTS

At age 19, St. Francis (1182-1226) abandoned his military and social ambitions, rejected his father's wealth, and embraced asceticism. His love of nature, devoted humility, and rejection of the Church's worldliness earned him a huge European following and posed an unprecedented threat to the decadent papacy and corrupt monastic orders. St. Francis continued to preach chastity and poverty until his death, when the order he founded was gradually subsumed into the hierarchy that it had criticized. Ironically, the Church has glorified the modest saint in countless cathedrals, many of which can be found in Assisi.

BASILICA DI SAN FRANCESCO. A major pilgrimage site, **Basilica di San Francesco** is one of the greatest spiritual and artistic attractions in Italy. When its construction began in the mid-13th century, the Franciscan order protested, complaining that the elaborate church was an impious monument to the conspicuous consumption that St. Francis had scorned. Brother Elia, the vicar of the order, insisted that a double church be erected, the lower level built around the saint's crypt, the upper level used for services. The walls of the upper church are covered with Giotto's renowned *Life of St. Francis* fresco cycle, while Cimabue's magnificent *Madonna and Child, Angels,* and *St. Francis* grace the

UMBRIA AND LE MARCHE

ON A WING AND A PRAYER

Father Pasquale Magro is a monk of the Franciscan order who has lived in the Convent of the Basilica di San Francesco for 13 years. He is also in charge of the historical research library Biblioteca del Sacroconvento in Assisi.

On his youth: My mother was a housewife and my father was a government worker. I was an altar boy from very young age. I wanted to become a pilot, an air pilot, but this was only a child's dream.

On becoming a monk: My brother had to become a priest but I had no intention. I don't know how or when I entered the convent. It was quite smooth, no shock, nothing. It was not possible to become a pilot in Malta.

On the monastic lifestyle: One has to control and guide his instincts, otherwise life becomes instinctive. Life is hard for everybody. You have to live courageously as a friar or nun. Life is not advantages. Life is advantages and disadvantages.

On the basilica: This is one of the greatest places of Christendom. It's the explosion of human spirit. There is one exhibition happening here of religious Christian images made of bombs from WWI. There is a dove made out of a hand bomb, which splinters into wings.

On St. Francis: St. Francis's mission was to bring together, not to divide. He was an authority against division because the world is all too full of conflict.

right transept. Some of Cimabue's frescoes in the transepts and apse have so deteriorated that they now look like photographic negatives. Pietro Lorenzetti decorated the left transept with his outstanding *Crucifixion, Last Supper,* and *Madonna and Saints.* Also stunning are Simone Martini's frescoes in the first chapel on the left, depicting the life of St. Martin. **St. Francis's tomb,** the inspiration for the entire edifice, lies below the lower church. The coffin itself was hidden in the 15th century for fear of the war-mongering *Perugini,* and it wasn't rediscovered until 1818. The stone coffin sits above the altar in the crypt, surrounded by the sarcophagi of four of the saint's dearest friends. (☎075 81 90 084. *Info window open daily 9am-noon and 2-5pm. Lower basilica and tomb open daily 9am-6:45pm. Upper basilica open daily 8:30am-6:45pm. Modest dress required. Unguided visits to the basilica free. Tours (€1) given by monks begin outside lower basilica daily 9am-noon and 2-5:30pm. Arrange in advance; call or visit info window across from entrance to lower basilica. Modest dress required.)*

ROCCA MAGGIORE. The Rocca Maggiore looms uphill from the *duomo.* Check out the view of the town and the Basilica di San Francesco from the gravel lot outside the fortress, or pay a nominal fee to enter the fortress and eerie 50m tunnel to Torre Poligonale. The ◪**view** is breathtaking— miles of countryside stretch in all directions—but the trip through the tunnel is not recommended for claustrophobes. *(From P. del Comune, follow V. S. Rufino to P. S. Rufino. Continue up V. Pta. Perlici and take 1st left up a narrow staircase. Open daily 10am-sunset. Closed in bad weather. €2, students €1.50. All-inclusive ticket for Pinacoteca, Foro Romano, and Rocca €5.20, students €4.)*

BASILICA DI SANTA CHIARA. The Basilica di Santa Chiara stands out with its buttresses, but it is the surrounding ◪**courtyard** with fountains and views that make it dazzling. Standing on the site where St. Francis attended school, the church shelters the tomb and relics of St. Claire, as well as the crucifix that supposedly spoke to St. Francis, instigating his conversion. The nuns in the convent are sworn to seclusion. (☎075 81 22 82. *Open daily 6:30am-noon and 2-7pm. Free.)*

DUOMO (CHIESA) DI SAN RUFINO. V. S. Rufino climbs steeply from P. del Comune between closely packed houses, opening onto P. S. Rufino to reveal the squat *duomo* and its massive bell tower. Peer through glass tiles on the floor into the Roman ruins below. (☎075 81 27 12. *Open daily 7am-1pm and 3-6:30pm. Church free. Museum and crypt €3, students €2.50; tickets on sale in the museum).*

OTHER SIGHTS. From Basilica di San Francesco, V. S. Francesco snakes between medieval buildings and their 16th-century additions. Not far along, the pink facade of the **Palazzo Vallemani** shelters the **Pinacoteca,** a museum containing works by important Umbrian artists like Dono Doni and a collection of Renaissance frescoes lifted from city gates and various shrines. Up the street, the colorfully frescoed **Oratorio dei Pellegrini** (Pilgrim's Oratory) is worth a brief peek. Built in 1457, this oratory was used to care for the health of poor pilgrims who came to visit the tomb of St. Francis. At the end of the street, P. del Comune sits on the **Foro Romano.** Enter from the crypt of St. Nicholas on V. Portica and walk among the columns and statues of the old Roman forum, which stretches the length of P. del Comune. *(Forum ☎ 075 81 30 53, Pinacoteca 075 81 20 33. Both open daily Mar. 16-Oct. 15 10am-1pm and 2-6pm; Oct. 16-Mar. 15 10am-1pm and 2:30-7pm. Admission to each €3.50, students €3.)* Above ground sits the **Tempio di Minerva,** a majestic Roman temple turned into a Christian church. Guarded by six crumbling Corinthian columns, the temple sits snug between the bell tower of the city and a cafe. *(Open daily 7am-7pm.)* Finally, just off the square, the beautiful and silent **Chiesa Nuova** stands on the site of St. Francis's boyhood house, and features high domes, a rounded central apse, and a heavily frescoed interior. *(☎ 075 81 23 39. Open daily 6:30am-noon and 2:30-5pm.)*

> **TIP**
>
> **THREE BIRDS WITH ONE STONE.** Consider investing in a combined ticket (adults €4.50, students €3.50) which grants visitors entrance to the Foro Romano, Pinacoteca, and Rocca Maggiore.

🎵 ENTERTAINMENT

All of Assisi's religious festivals involve feasts and processions. An especially long, dramatic performance marks **Easter Week.** A play reenacts the Deposition from the Cross on Holy Thursday, and traditional processions trail through town on Good Friday and Easter Sunday. Assisi welcomes spring with the **Festa di Calendimaggio** (first Th, F, and Sa of May). A queen is chosen and dubbed *Primavera* (Spring), while the upper and lower quarters of the city compete in a musical tournament. Ladies and knights overtake the streets in celebration of the young St. Francis, who wandered the streets of Assisi singing serenades at night. According to legend it was on one such night that he encountered a vision of the *Madonna della Povertà* (Lady of Poverty). Classical music concerts and organ recitals occur once or twice each week from April to October in the various churches. October 4 marks the **Festa di San Francesco,** which kicks off in **Chiesa di Santa Maria degli Angeli,** the site of St. Francis's death. Aside from various religious ceremonies, the highlight of this celebration is the offering of oil for the cathedral's votive lamp. Each year a different region of Italy offers the oil, as well as traditional dances and songs.

▶ DAYTRIPS FROM ASSISI

EREMO DELLE CARCERI AND MONTE SUBASIO

From P. Matteotti, exit Assisi through Pta. Cappuccini and immediately turn left up the dirt road, parallel to the city wall. At the Rocca Minore, follow the trail uphill to the right. Follow the paved road to the right, instead of crossing and taking the trail uphill. Loose rocks can make the descent difficult. For an easier walk (or drive) from Pta. Cappuccini, follow the dirt trail next to the paved road uphill and take shortcuts via dirt roads on the right to bypass long, winding turns for cars. Eremo is about 4km away. ☎ 075 81 23 01. Open 6:30am-7pm, 6:30am-5pm in winter. Taxis make the climb for €8-12 from the centro.

An intense but gorgeous 1hr. hike up Monte Subasio reveals the inspiring sanctuary ▒**Eremo delle Carceri,** where St. Francis often retired in prayer. Though cars crowd the front gates, once inside visitors can relax among shady trees. The central courtyard gives access to the **Grotta di San Francesco,** a series of tiny cells and chapels where St. Francis slept and prayed. (Modest dress is required, so bring a scarf or other appropriate attire in addition to hiking clothes.) The trails that run through the natural beauty of St. Francis's preferred retreat, Monte Subasio, can be easily navigated with a Kompass map (€6.95) or the less-detailed Club Alpino Italiano map (€8), available from any bookshop or newsstand in Assisi.

OTHER RELIGIOUS SITES AROUND ASSISI. Several churches associated with St. Francis and St. Claire stand in the immediate vicinity of Assisi. A 15min. stroll down the steep road outside Pta. Nuova leads to the **Convent of San Damiano,** where St. Francis heard his calling and later wrote the *Canticle of the Creatures.* Be sure to visit the convent, the entrance to which is inside the church by the altar. (☎075 81 22 73. Open daily 6:30am-noon and 2-7pm.) The train to Assisi passes **Basilica di Santa Maria degli Angeli.** From Assisi, take the frequent bus marked "S. M. degli Angeli" and get off one stop after the train station. Take the first left, over the tracks, on Vle. Patrono d'Italia. The Renaissance facade of the basilica will emerge on the left. St. Francis built the small **Porziuncola** and died in the small cell in the right transept called the **Cappella del Transito.** In order to overcome temptation, St. Francis supposedly flung himself on the thorny rosebushes in the garden outside, staining the leaves eternally red. Through the rose garden lies the **Museo di Santa Maria degli Angeli,** which houses relics from the Porziuncola chapel. (☎075 80 51 432. Basilica open daily Oct.-June 6:15am-7:45pm; July-Sept. 6:15am-9pm. Museum open daily 9am-12:30pm and 3-6:30pm. Free.)

SPOLETO ☎0743

A magnificent gorge and thick walls surround Spoleto, sheltering the town full of fine medieval and Roman monuments. Travelers have always admired Spoleto's dramatic gorge, spanned by the 14th century Ponte dell Torri, but it wasn't until 1958 that tourism took off. In that year, the composer Giancarlo Menotti selected Spoleto as the trial site for a summer arts festival, and his *Festival dei Due Mondi* (Festival of Two Worlds) hasn't left since.

▣▟ TRANSPORTATION AND PRACTICAL INFORMATION

The **train station** (☎0743 48 516) is in P. Polvani. Ticket window is open daily 6am-8pm. Trains run to: Ancona (2hr., 12 per day, €7.90); Assisi (40min., 20 per day, €3); Orte (1hr., 22 per day, €2.89); Perugia (1½hr., 17 per day, €3.50); Rome (1½hr., every 1-2hr., €6.82). Trains to Assisi and Perugia sometimes run via Foligno. **SSIT buses** (☎0743 21 22 09; www.spoletina.com) depart from P. della Vittoria for Foligno (45min., M-F 6 per day, €2.60) and Perugia (2hr., 2 per day, €5.40). Schedule and tickets are available at **Tabaccheria Scocchetti,** P. della Vittoria 24. (Open daily 7:30am-2pm and 3-8:30pm.) **Taxis** are in P. della Libertà (☎0743 44 548), in P. Garibaldi (☎0743 49 990), and at the train station (☎0743 22 04 89).

Have patience with Spoleto's narrow streets; a map, available from the tourist office in **Piazza della Libertà,** makes them more navigable. To get there from the train station, take an orange ATAF bus (direct to *centro,* €0.80). Buy tickets in the station at the newsstand, marked with a yellow Lotto sign. From **Corso Mazzini,** turn left up **Via del Mercato** to **Piazza del Mercato,** the bustling center from which **Via del Municipio** runs to **Piazza del Municipio** and **Piazza Campello** and **Via Saffi** leads to **Piazza del Duomo.** Most of the city's sights are in these three squares.

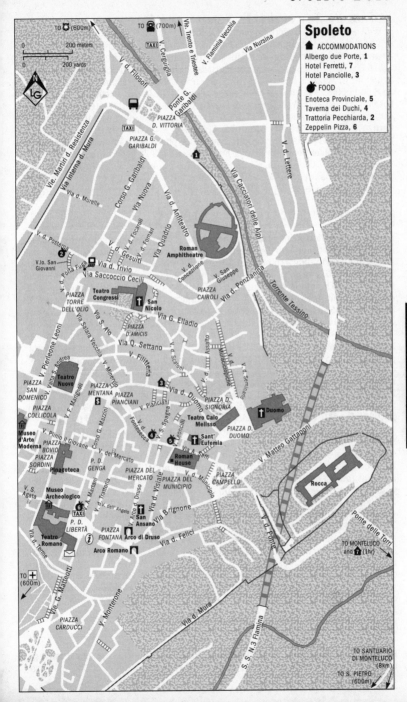

The **tourist office**, P. della Libertà, 7, offers detailed info about tours and lodgings as well as English and German maps of the city and nearby trails. (☎0743 23 89 20 or 23 89 21; info@iat.spoleto.pg.it. Open Apr.-Oct. M-F 9am-1pm and 4-7pm, Sa-Su 10am-1pm and 4-7pm; Nov.-Mar. M-F 9am-1pm and 3:30-6:30pm, Sa 10am-1pm and 3:30-6:30pm, Su 10am-1pm.) The **bank**, Cassa di Risparmio di Spoleto, P. Mentana, 3, just off C. Mazzini, has a 24hr. **ATM**. (Open M-F 8:20am-1:20pm and 2:50-3:50pm, Sa 8:20-11:50am.) In case of **emergency**, call ☎113, or for an **ambulance** at ☎118. A **hospital** is located on V. Madonna di Loreto, outside the southwestern walls of the center. The **police** station (☎0743 22 38 87) is located at V. dei Filosofi, 57. **Farmacia Betti**, Vle. Trento e Trieste, 63 (☎0743 22 31 74), is on the way to town from the train station and posts information about other pharmacies in the area. **Internet** is available at **Spider Service**, V. Porta Fuga, 11. (☎0743 22 5165. Open M-F 9:30am-10:00pm, Sa-Su 10am-10pm. €1.25 per hr. Also phone center and **Western Union** point.) There is a **post office** at V. L. G. Matteotti, 2. (☎0743 40 373. Open M-F 8:10am-6pm, Sa 8am-12:30pm.) **Postal Code:** 06049.

ACCOMMODATIONS AND FOOD

Finding accommodations is almost impossible during the summer music festival (the last week of June and the first week of July). Contact **Conspoleto**, P. della Libertà, 7, for help finding a room. (☎0743 22 07 73; www.conspoleto.com. Open M-Sa 9am-1pm and 3-7pm). Prices are higher during the festival. Central ⬛**Hotel Panciolle ❸**, V. del Duomo, 3, has rustic rooms that overlook the countryside. Follow V. del Duomo out of P. del Duomo to reach the hotel. (☎0743 456 77. Breakfast €5. Singles €40; doubles €55; triples €65. Cash only.) **Albergo Due Porte ❸**, P. della Vittoria, 5, is a 10min. walk from the train station. Go straight down Viale Trento e Trieste and bear right into P. della Vittoria. Friendly, English-speaking management, a garden, and large rooms with bath, TV, and phone make this a pleasant stop. (☎0743 22 36 66. Breakfast included. Wheelchair accessible. Singles €35; doubles €57; triples €75; quads €100. Cash only.) High above Spoleto, **Hotel Ferretti ❸**, Loc. Monteluco, 20, is 5min. from the bus stop or a 30min. walk on trail #1. It's more likely to have openings than places downtown. There's a piano in the common room and rooms have bathroom, TV, and phone. (☎0743 498 49; fax 0743 22 23 44. Breakfast included. Singles €38; doubles €59. Required half pension.)

A small **open-air market** sells fresh produce in P. del Mercato. (Open M-Sa 8:30am-1pm.) At the stylish **Enoteca Provinciale ❸**, V. Saffi, 7, torch lamps burn outside as diners enjoy food on sturdy wooden benches. (☎0743 22 04 84. *Primi* €5-10, *secondi* €6-11. Open M and W-Su 11am-3pm and 7-11pm. AmEx/MC/V.) The pleasant **Taverna dei Duchi ❷**, V. Saffi, 1, cooks all manner of Umbrian specialities with truffles and goat cheese. Don't fill up completely on the superior bread basket, and try the simple *spaghetti alla bolognese* for €5.50. (☎0743 44 088. *Primi* €4.50-10.50. Tender grilled meats €5-11.50. Pizza from €6, evening only. Open M-Th and Su 12:15-2pm and 7-10pm, F noon-2pm, Sa 7-10pm. MC/V.) For a good deal on thin-crust pizza (from €1) and *panini* (€2-4), locals frequent **Zeppelin Pizza ❶**, in P. della Libertà. (Open daily 10:30am-3:30pm and 5-9:30pm. Cash only.) At **Trattoria Pecchiarda ❸**, Vco. San Giovanni, 1, guests can dine on regional cuisine on an outdoor patio. From P. Garibaldi, follow C. Garibaldi, turn right on V. della Posterna, and turn left up the stairs. (☎0743 22 10 09. *Primi* and wood-grilled *secondi* €7-13. Open daily 1-3:30pm and 8pm-midnight. AmEx/MC/V.)

SIGHTS

ROCCA ALBORNOZIANA AND PONTE DELLE TORRI. The Rocca, a **papal fortress** up V. Saffi from P. del Duomo, served as a high-security prison until 1982 and was used during WWII. In 1943, the prisoners staged a dramatic escape to join the partisans in the Umbrian hills. The complex's only drama now exists in the restored frescoes from the 15th century in the **Camera Pinta.** On the far side of the Rocca is the massive ■**Ponte delle Torri,** a stunning achievement of 14th-century engineering built on an ancient Roman aqueduct. Ten 80m arches support the bridge, and the view across the Tessino Gorge is riveting. *(☎0743 43 707. Open daily June 11-Sept. 12 10am-8pm; Sept. 13-Oct. 31 M-F 10am-1pm and 3-6pm, Sa-Su 10am-7pm; Nov. 1-Mar. 14 M-F 2:30-5pm, Sa-Su 10am-5pm; Mar. 27-June 10 M-F 10am-1pm and 3-7pm, Sa-Su 10am-7pm. Entrance only with the hourly guided tours. €4.65, ages 7-14 and over 60 €3.62.)*

MONTELUCO. The 800m trail along Spoleto's steep "mountain of the sacred grove" crosses over Ponte delle Torri and through a canopied forest. The zig-zagging footpath then passes abandoned mountain shrines and a few spots with downhill views. At the crest of the mountain are hotel-restaurants, a flat grass clearing perfect for picnics, and the tiny 13th-century sanctuary, **Santuario di Monteluco,** once the refuge of St. Francis of Assisi and St. Bernadino of Siena. *(Open 9am-noon and 3-6pm.)* The path back to Spoleto passes the churches of **San Giuliano** and **San Pietro.** Rain turns the path into a rocky stream, so it's best to travel on a sunny day or when buses are running. *(Buses leave P. della Libertà for Monteluco every 1½hr. from mid-June to early Sept. Cross the Ponte delle Torri and follow the stairs up to trail #1 (marked by red dots or red and white stripes), which leads to the sanctuary. Wear proper footwear, as the trail is challenging, and be certain to ask at the tourist office for a trail map.)*

 Rain makes the trail to Monteluco impassible, even the day after a storm. Always wear proper footwear, as the trail is rocky and difficult at times.

DUOMO. Spoleto's Romanesque cathedral was built in the 12th century and was later expanded by a portico (1491) and 17th-century interior redecoration. Eight rose windows, the largest one bearing the symbols of the four evangelists, animate the elegant facade. Inside, brilliantly colored scenes by Fra Filippo Lippi fill the domed apse. ■**The Coronation** in the dome of the main apse features Lippi at his most colorful. Check out the 15th-century Cappella dell'Assunta covered in eroding frescoes and the more lavish 17th-century Cappella della' Santa Icone. Lorenzo de' Medici commissioned Lippi's tomb, which was decorated by the artist's son, Filippino, and is now in the right transept. The soaring bell tower is a mixture of styles and materials: stone blocks, fragments of inscriptions, friezes, and other remnants of the Roman era combine to form this structure. *(Down shallow flight of steps from Casa Romana. Open daily 8:30am-12:30pm and 3:30-7pm.)*

CHIESA DI SAN ANSANO AND CRIPTA DI SAN ISAACO. Heading away from P. Mercato on V. dell'Arco di Druso, the Chiesa di San Ansano is at the corner on the left. Built on the ruins of a Roman temple dating to the first century BC, San Ansano now stands with a Renaissance facade and interior. The stairs to the left of the main altar lead down to the foundations of the 11th-century church. Haunting, well-preserved frescoes detail scenes from the life of St. Isaac, who lies in a sarcophagus dating from AD 550 at the center of the room. *(☎0743 40 305. Open daily Apr.-Oct. 7:30am-noon and 3-7pm; Nov.-Mar. 7:30am-noon and 3-6:30pm.)*

THE MUSEUM OF MODERN ART. A refreshing alternative to ancient ruins and holy frescoes, this impressive permanent collection of art critic Giovanni Carandente includes early works by Moore, Consagra, Pomodoro, Leoncillo, and Calder. *(Follow V. Mercato as it turns into V. Giovane and go down a flight of stairs. The museum lies straight ahead. ☎0743 464 34. Open daily Mar. 16-Oct. 14 10:30am-1pm and 4:30-7pm; Oct. 15-Mar. 15 10:30am-1pm and 3-5:30pm. €4, ages 15-25 or over 65 €3, ages 7-14 €1.50. Ticket including Pinacoteca and Casa Romana €6/4/ 1.50.)*

ROMAN RUINS. Spoleto's ruins, a testament to the city's prominence in Roman times, are found mainly in P. della Libertà. The **amphitheater** stands just beyond the Roman walls. Take V. S. Agata from the *piazza* to reach the entrance of the **Museo Archeologico,** which houses ceramic artifacts found in the area. *(☎0743 22 32 77. Open daily 8:30am-7:30pm. €2.50, EU citizens ages 18-25 €1, EU citizens under 18 or over 65 free.)* The **Arco Romano,** at the top of V. Monterone, once marked the town's entrance. Off P. Fontana, the **Arco di Druso** commemorates Emperor Drusus's military triumphs at what was once the entrance to the forum (now P. del Mercato).

CASA ROMANA. Duck into the first-century "Roman house," ancient home of Vespasia Polla, Emperor Vespasian's mother, which features well-preserved tiled floors and household artifacts. *(Beneath city hall, entrance at V. di Visiale, 9. From P. del Duomo, take stairs opposite* duomo *entrance, then 1st left. ☎0743 22 46 56. Open daily Mar.16-Oct.14 10am-8pm; Oct.15-Mar.15 8am-6pm. €2.50, ages 15-25 or over 65 €2, ages 7-14 €1. Ticket including Museum of Modern Art and Pinacoteca €6/4/1.50 available.)*

PINACOTECA. A small museum with six rooms that house works by Umbrian artists from the Middle Ages and on. The museum has made a permanent move to Palazzo Spada in P. Sordini. *(☎0743 46 434. Open by appointment only. Call at least 3 days in advance. Ticket including Museum of Modern Art and Casa Romana available; see above.)*

🎵 🎇 ENTERTAINMENT AND FESTIVALS

The renowned **Stagione del Teatro Lirico Sperimentale di Spoleto,** an experimental opera season, runs from late August to September. The Istituzione Teatro Lirico Sperimentale di Spoleto, P. G. Bovio, 1, provides info (☎0743 22 16 45). The ▓**Spoleto Festival** (known as the **Festival dei Due Mondi**) has become one of the world's most prestigious international arts events. Each June and July it features concerts, operas, and ballets, and also brings films, modern art shows, and craft displays to town. Purchase tickets beginning in late April from the ticket office at P. della Libertà, 12. (☎800 56 56 00; www.spoletofestival.it. Open daily 9am-1pm and 3-7pm.) During the festival, box offices at **Piazza del Duomo, Teatro Nuovo,** and **Rocca Albornoziana** open 1hr. before the start of most performances in addition to regular hours (Tu-Su 10:30am-1pm and 4-7pm). For those under 26 a €12 weekly pass is available. You can also get a discount of 15% if you buy tickets to more than 3 events on the same day. Book ahead. For more details write to the Associazione Festival dei Due Mondi, Biglietteria Festival dei Due Mondi, 06049 Spoleto, Italia.

▶ DAYTRIP FROM SPOLETO

TREVI

Take an SSIT bus from Foligno, the transfer point for the Rome-Florence line (20 min; every hr. 7am-10pm; €1.82.) Walk straight from train station to reach the bus station. Take the orange municipal bus to Trevi (30min.; M-Sa 8 per day; last bus to Trevi 7pm, last bus to Foligno 6:30pm; €0.85). Foligno train schedule is posted outside the Trevi tourist office and at the tabaccheria next to P. Garibaldi in Trevi.

Removed and unhurried in comparison to other more trafficked Umbrian hill towns, Trevi lies along near-vertical slopes striped with olive groves. The **Pinacoteca Rascolta d'Arte di San Francesco** houses a collection of religious Renaissance art, including some dramatic large-scale works. The unique **Museo della Città Dell'Ulivo** offers a history of the city's staple industry as well as free olive oil samples and Italian recipes. Follow V. S. Francesco from P. Mazzini to reach the museums. (☎0742 38 16 28; www.sistemamuseo.it. Open June-July Tu-Su 10:30am-1pm and 3-7pm, Aug. daily 10:30am-1pm and 3-7:30pm, Oct.-Mar. F-Su 10:30am-1pm and 2:30-5pm, Apr.-May and Sept. Tu-Su 10:30am-1pm and 2:30-6pm. €3, students

€2.) The **Flash Art Museum,** V. P. Riccardi, 4, showcases avant-garde art in a 15th-century *palazzo*. The small museum is associated with the trendy contemporary Italian art magazine *Flash* and hosts rotating exhibits of modern art. (☎0742 38 10 21; www.treviflashartmuseum.org. Open Tu-Su 3-7pm.) The **Illumination Procession,** one of Umbria's oldest religious festivals, takes place January 28.

The **Pro Loco Tourist Office,** P. del Comune, 5, offers great free **maps** and assistance in renting one of the abundant *affittacamere*, as hotels in Trevi are expensive. (☎0742 78 11 50; www.protrevi.it. Open daily 9am-1pm and 4-8pm.) From P. Garibaldi, take V. Roma to P. Mazzini. The quaint **Ristorante Maggionlini ❷,** V. San Francesco, 20, has a bar for sampling Trevi's olive oil. (*Primi* €6.40-8.30, *secondi* €5.90-11.40. Open M and W-Su noon-3pm and 7-10pm. MC/V.)

ORVIETO
☎ 0763

A city upon a city, Orvieto (pop. 20,000) was built in layers. Medieval structures stand over ancient subterranean remains: in the 7th century BC, Etruscans burrowed for *tufo* (a volcanic stone out of which most of the medieval quarter is built), creating a companion city beneath Orvieto's ground surface which has provided archeologists and tourists alike with plentiful opportunities for exploring the Etruscan heritage of the area. Five centuries later, Romans sacked and reoccupied the plateau, calling their "new" city, strangely enough, *urbus ventus* (old city), from which the name Orvieto is derived. Here fervent Christians planned their crusades and Thomas Aquinas lectured in local academies. Today, the town is a tourist destination made popular by its spectacular *duomo*, brooding underground chambers, and delightful *Orvieto Classico* wine; on any given day Americans may outnumber Italians. To escape the crowds, skip the ceramic shops on C. Cavour and head to the side streets, full of artisans' shops and panoramas.

▌⊏ TRANSPORTATION

Orvieto is about half way between Rome and Florence train line. **Trains** run to: Arezzo (1hr., every hr. 7:30am-11:57pm., €5.80); Florence (2½hr., every hr. 7:30am-8:44pm, €9.90) via Cortona (45min.); and Rome (1½hr., every hr. 4:27am-11:28pm,

UMBRIA AND
LE MARCHE

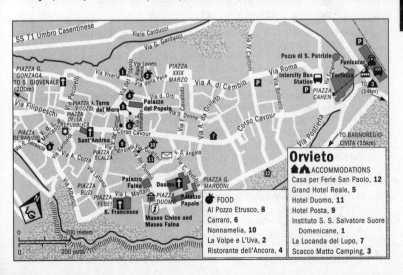

Orvieto

▲▲ ACCOMMODATIONS
Casa per Ferie San Paolo, 12
Grand Hotel Reale, 5
Hotel Duomo, 11
Hotel Posta, 9
Instituto S. S. Salvatore Suore
    Domenicane, 1
La Locanda del Lupo, 7
Scacco Matto Camping, 3

● FOOD
Al Pozzo Etrusco, 8
Carraro, 6
Nonnamelia, 10
La Volpe e L'Uva, 2
Ristorante dell'Ancora, 4

€6.82). **Buses** leave from P. Cahen and the train station. **COTRAL** (☎0763 73 48 14) runs buses to Viterbo (8 per day 6:20am-5:45pm, €2.80). Purchase tickets at *tabaccherie*. **ATC** buses (☎0763 30 12 24) stop in P. Cahen and go to Perugia (1½hr., 5:55am, €6) and Todi (1hr., 1:45pm, €4.80). Purchase tickets at the funicular ticket office, at *tabaccherie* on C. Cavour, or on the bus with a surcharge. The ◪**funicular** ascends Orvieto's hill, connecting the train station with the city's historical center at P. Cahen (every 10min.; €.80, with shuttle to P. del Duomo €0.90). The tickets for the funicular are valid for 1hr., which allows for multiple journeys between the hilltop and the *centro storico*. For a **taxi,** call (☎0763 30 19 03).

⊹ 🛈 ORIENTATION AND PRACTICAL INFORMATION

Across from the **train station,** the **funicular** travels up the hill to **Piazza Cahen**. There begins **Corso Cavour,** which runs slightly uphill from P. Cahen to **Piazza della Repubblica**. About 10min. from P. Cahen, C. Cavour crosses **Via del Duomo**. At this intersection, turn left down V. Duomo to reach—surprise—the *duomo*. Two blocks down, a right turn on **Via della Piazza del Popolo** will deliver you to—surprise again—**Piazza del Popolo**. Most of the city's restaurants, hotels, and shops are found between V. del Duomo and the P. della Repubblica along C. Cavour. The **tourist office,** P. del Duomo, 24, supplies great free **maps** and info on hotels, restaurants, and sights. The office also offers deals on underground tours of Orvieto and sells the **Orvieto Unica card** (€12.50, students €10.50), which includes an underground tour, round-trip ticket for funicular-minibus or 5hr. of parking, and entrance to Museo Faina, the Torre del Moro, and the Cappella della Madonna di San Brizio, as well as discounts at participating businesses. (☎0763 34 17 72; fax 0763 34 44 33. Open M-F 8:15am-1:50pm and 4-7pm, Sa-Su and holidays 10am-1pm and 3-6pm.) **Luggage storage** is available at the train station. In an **emergency,** call an ambulance ☎113, or the **police** ☎112 or 0763 34 00 88, in P. della Repubblica. The **hospital** (☎0763 30 71) is across the tracks from the train station in Loc. Ciconia. A **post office** (☎0763 34 09 14) is on V. Ravelli, off C. Cavour. (Open M-Sa 8:10am-4:45pm, last day of the month 8:10am-noon.) **Postal Code:** 05018.

🏠 ACCOMMODATIONS AND CAMPING

▧ **Grand Hotel Reale,** P. del Popolo 25 (☎0763 34 19 09), offers an unparalleled deal in a 13th-century *palazzo* which once housed King Umberto. This luxurious hotel features stunning views of the Palazzo del Popolo and a friendly and helpful staff. All rooms have bath, TV, and phone; the more expensive rooms are adorned with magnificent frescoes and Murano glass light fixtures. Breakfast in opulent dining room €8. Singles €35, with bath €66; doubles €55/68, with frescoes €88; triples €114; quad €140. ❸

▧ **La Locanda del Lupo,** C. Cavour, 231 (☎0763 34 13 88; www.lalocandadellupo.it), about halfway between P. Cahen and the intersection with V. del Duomo. 3 spacious and comfortable rooms above a traditional restaurant, serving enormous cracker-crust pizzas and exquisite pork with rosemary and fennel. Rooms €23-35 per person. ❸

Hotel Posta, V. Luca Signorelli, 18 (☎0763 34 19 09). Housed in an old *palazzo*, this quirky hotel is undergoing renovations. New mattresses are very comfortable and staff is friendly. Murano glass light fixtures and lush outdoor patio. Breakfast €6. Reserve 3weeks ahead in summer. Singles €26-37; doubles €43-56. Cash only. ❸

Instituto S. S. Salvatore Suore Domenicane, V. del Popolo, 1 (☎0763 34 29 10). Behind thick doors and run by kindly nuns. Rooms fill up quickly during high season and religious holidays; reserve ahead. Breakfast €3. 2-night min. stay. Curfew in summer 10:30pm; in winter 9:30pm. Closed July. Singles €45-50; doubles €52. Cash only. ❹

Casa per Ferie San Paolo, V. Postierla, 20 (☎0763 34 05 79 or 349 69 32 121; cscor-vieto@tiscalinet.it). Face the *duomo* and follow street which runs to the right of Palazzo Papale for 10min. Enter gate on right; reception in building on the left. A trek from P. del Duomo, but these quality rooms are close to the train station. Curfew 1am. Reserve 4-5 days ahead. Singles €26; doubles €47. Cash only. ❸

Hotel Duomo, Vicolo Maurizio, 7 (☎0763 34 18 87; www.orvietohotelduomo.com), facing the *duomo*. Go down the left wall and down the stairs on Vlo. Maurizio, at the yellow sign. Rooms feature artwork by a prominent Orvietan artist and a view of the *duomo*. A/C, satellite TV, hair dryer, and minibar. Breakfast included. Free Internet in lobby. Singles €60-70; doubles €90-105; triples €120-130; quad €150. AmEx/MC/V. ❺

Scacco Matto Camping (☎0744 95 01 63; fax 0744 95 03 73), on Lago Corbara, 14km from town. From station take infrequent Orvieto-Baschi bus. Beach and free hot showers. €5.50 per person, €5.50 per tent, €3 per car. Cash only. ❶

◨ FOOD

In antiquity, Orvieto was known as *Oinarea*, or the "city where wine flows." The stream is still steady, with bottles as cheap as €2.50. Pair a light bottle of *Classico* with local treats like baked *lumachelle* (snail-shaped buns with ham and cheese), *tortucce* (fried bread dough), or *mazzafegate* (sweet or salty sausages). Most restaurants serve game meat. Also prevalent are *tartufi* (truffles) served frequently and cheaply in many dishes—sometimes even grated at your table. The sociable **Panini Imbottiti,** V. del Duomo, 36, sells bottles of *Classico* from €3.30. (Open M-Tu and Th-Sa 7:30am-noon and 5:15-9pm, W 7:45am-2pm.) To sample before investing in a whole bottle, stop by **Cantina Freddano,** C. Cavour, 5, which offers free wine-tasting. Bottles start at €4. (☎0763 30 82 48. Open daily 9:30am-7:30pm.)

▨ **Carraro,** C.Cavour, 101 (☎0763 34 28 70), before the intersection with V. del Duomo as you walk toward Torre del Moro. Marked by a giant stuffed boar, Carraro is a 57-year-old family tradition. This shop sells homemade truffle spread (€15 for a small jar) as well as a variety of fresh, local cured meats, cheeses, and baked goods. Indulge in wild boar and truffle sausage (€24 per kg) and award winning *cennerino* cheese (€22 per kg). Picnic lunch for under €5. Open daily 7:15am-1:30pm and 4:30-8:30pm. ❶

▨ **Nonnamelia,** V. del Duomo, 25 (☎0763 34 24 02), to the right of the *duomo*. With 2 shaggy white stuffed animals greeting you at the door, Nonnamelia never fails to please, from its creative, fresh recipes to the detailed carved-wood decorations. The generous portion of *penne* with saffron, zucchini, and *scamorza* (€7) and the lamb chops with fried artichokes (€8.50) provide a unique alternative to Umbria's ubiquitous wild boar. Pizza €3.50-7.50. Open daily noon-3pm and 7-11pm. Cash only. ❸

Al Pozzo Etrusco d'Aronne, P. de' Ranieri, 1/A (☎0763 34 44 56). Basic, hearty food beloved by locals served in an intimate dining space, complete with an actual Etruscan well and outdoor *piazza* seating. Very traditional dishes including *scamorza* and pecorino mousse (€6) as well as a vegetarian menu (€15). *Primi* €5-8, *secondi* €7-12. Open M and W-Su noon-3pm and 7-10pm. AmEx/MC/V for over €26. ❸

La Volpe e L'Uva, V. Ripa Corsica, 2/A (☎347 79 99 876), behind Palazzo del Popolo. Snug interior and friendly staff serve excellent vegetarian fare as well as a variety of simple, local-style meat dishes (€6-10). Open W-Su 1-3:30pm and 8-11pm. MC/V. ❸

Ristorante dell'Ancora, V. della Piazza del Popolo 7/11 (☎0763 34 27 66; www.argoweb.it/ristorante_ancora), offers a peaceful retreat from the busy streets. Eat in indoors or opt to sit in the large, sheltered garden at this somewhat upscale restaurant. *Primi* €8-10, *secondi* €8-13. Open daily noon-4pm and 7-10pm. AmEx/MC/V. ❸

UMBRIA AND LE MARCHE

👁 SIGHTS

■**DUOMO.** Orvieto's architectural claim to fame, the *duomo* is nothing short of dazzling. Designed in the late 13th century by Sienese architect Lorenzo Maitani, the facade of Orvieto's pride and joy is an example of the transitional Romanesque-Gothic style. With carved marble pillars, spires, sculptures, and mosaics, the *duomo* awes admirers with scrupulous details and brilliant use of color. The bottom level features carved bas-reliefs of the Genesis and Old Testament prophecies as well as the final panel of Maitani's *Last Judgment*. Surrounding the rose window by Andrea Orcagna (1325-1364), bronze and marble sculptures emphasize the Christian canon. Thirty-three architects, 90 mosaic artisans, 152 sculptors, and 68 painters worked for over 600 years to improve the *duomo*, and the work continues—the bronze doors were installed in 1970. *(☎0763 34 11 67. Duomo open M-Sa 7:30am-12:45pm and 2:30-7pm, Su and holidays 2:30-6:45pm; closes 1-2hr. earlier in winter. Crypt open M-F 10am-noon. Free. Modest dress required.)*

Cappella della Madonna di San Brizio, also called the Cappella Nuova, off the right transept, includes Luca Signorelli's floor-to-ceiling frescoes of the Apocalypse. His vigorous craftsmanship, mastery of human anatomy, and dramatic compositions inspired Michelangelo in his work on the Sistine Chapel. Also note da Fabriano's *Madonna and Child* and the marble *Pietà* by di Scalza. Opposite the San Brizio chapel is the ■**Cappella Corporale,** which features stunning frescoes by Ugolino di Prete Ilario and holds the gold-encrusted **Reliquario del Corporale** (chalice-cloth) from the miracle of Bolsena in 1263, said to have been soaked with the blood of Christ. *(Tickets and information at tourist office. €3, children under 10 free.)*

PALAZZO PAPALE. From this austere, 13th-century "Palace of the Popes," Pope Clement VII rejected King Henry VIII's petition to annul his marriage with Catherine of Aragon, thereby excommunicating Catherine and condemning English Catholicism. Set back in the *palazzo* is the **Museo Archeologico Nazionale,** where visitors can examine Etruscan art from the area and walk into a restored tomb decorated with faded 4th-century frescoes. *(To the right facing the duomo. Open daily 8:30am-7:30pm. €3, with entrance to Etruscan Necropolis €5, students 18-25 €1.50; EU citizens under 18 or over 60 free.)* Above the archaeological museum is the **Museo dell'Opera del Duomo,** which displays art and cultural artifacts from the 13th through 17th centuries. Featured pieces include Simone Martini's *Politico di S. Domenico,* Andrea Pisano's *Madonna and Child,* and Francesco Mochi's marble *Annunciation. (Accessible only in guided tours.☎0763 34 35 92; www.opsm.it. Currently under renovation. Guided visits Tu, Th, Sa, Su and holidays for up to 10 people €5. Call ahead or check at the tourist office.)*

UNDERGROUND CITY. Underground City Excursions runs the most complete and accessible tours of the dark, twisted bowels of the city. The ancient Etruscan town Velzna occupied the soft *tufa* of the cliff below modern Orvieto. Although Velzna was sacked by the Romans, its cisterns, mills, pottery workshops, quarries, wine cellars, and burial sites lie preserved beneath the earth. *(☎0763 34 48 91; speleotecnica@libero.it. 1hr. tours leave from the tourist office daily 11am, 12:15, 4, and 5:15pm. €5.50, students €3.50, children under 5 free.)*

CHIESA DI SAN GIOVENALE. Built in AD 1000, the city's oldest church was dedicated to the city's first bishop, who is represented in a fresco near the entry. Directly next to the doors on the left is a 14th-century "Tree of Life"—a family tree of the church's founders. The courtyard outside the church offers ■**views** of the countryside below. Graves of victims of the Black Death of 1348 fill the slope below P. San Giovanni. *(From P. della Repubblica, walk downhill along V. Filippeschi, which turns into V. Malabranca. The church is at the end of the street on the right.)*

MUSEO CIVICO AND MUSEO FAINA. Ensconced in the Palazzo Faina directly opposite the *duomo*, the museums hold an extensive collection of Etruscan artifacts. Exhibits include collections of over 3000 coins, bronze urns, Roman ornaments, and red and black figure vases attributed to Athenian artists from the 6th century BC—all collected by Claudio Faina during hazardous excavations of local *necropoli*. *(Piazza del Duomo, 29. ☎ 0763 34 15 11. Open daily Apr.-Sept. 9:30am-6pm; Oct.-Mar. Tu-Su 10am-5pm. €4.50, students and seniors €3.)*

▓ FESTIVALS

Though nightclubs are virtually non-existent in Orvieto, the city has no shortage of festivals. No matter when you come, locals are always celebrating: look for craft fairs, food and wine tasting events, and theater and music festivals. Spring brings the **Palio dell'Oca,** which has tested dexterity on horseback since medieval times. On Pentecost, 50 days after Easter, Orvieto celebrates the **Festa della Palombella.** At the stroke of noon, Campo della Fiera lights up with fireworks when a white dove descends across a wire to ignite the explosives. In June, the **Procession of Corpus Domini** celebrates the Miracle of Bolsena when a communion wafer is transformed to flesh and blood. A week of medieval banquets and dancing precedes the procession. Also in June is the **Festa della Repubblica,** during which entertainers blast trumpets and make balloon animals for throngs of kids and tourists. From December 29 to January 5, **Umbria Jazz Winter** swings in theaters, churches, and palaces, with the grand finale in the *duomo*. For details contact **Servizio Turistico Territoriale IAT dell'Orvietano,** P. Duomo, 24 (☎ 0763 34 19 11 or 0763 34 36 58), or **Informazioni Turistiche** (☎ 0763 34 17 72; fax 0763 34 44 33), at the same address.

LE MARCHE

Green foothills separate the umbrella-laden beaches along the Adriatic Sea from the craggy Apennines. Remains of the Gauls, Picenes, and Romans fill the rural towns in these hills. The legacy of Raphael and Donato Bramante in Urbino, the palm-lined boardwalk of San Benedetto del Tronto, the windy streets of Ascoli Piceno, and the hidden beauty of Ancona all form the highlights of Le Marche.

PESARO ☎ 0721

Pesaro strikes a balance between hip Rimini and laidback Fano, offering a blend of culture, *couture*, and seaside serenity. The historical center is appealing, the beaches relatively uncrowded, and though overpriced boutiques dominate the larger *piazze*, Pesaro also has many back-alley bookshops and street concerts.

> **⬥TIP** **PROPER PESARO.** The pronunciation of this town's name is not intuitive. Unlike most Italian words, in which emphasis falls on the penultimate syllable, "Pesaro" is pronounced with stress on the first syllable, making it "PEZ-are-oh."

TRANSPORTATION

The **train station** is at the end of V. Risorgimento and Vle. della Liberazione. (Ticket counter is open daily 6:10am-8:30pm. AmEx/MC/V.) **Luggage storage** is available (see **Practical Information,** below). **Trains** depart to: Ancona (1hr., 55 per day

(sidebar) UMBRIA AND LE MARCHE

12:35am-11:51pm, €2.94); Bologna (2hr., 29 per day 5:35am-10:13pm, €7.40); Fano (15min., 44 per day 4:55am-10:56pm, €1.24); and Rimini (30min., 43 per day 4:48am-11:11pm, €2.40). The **bus depot** (☎0721 32 401; cash only) is 50 ft. to the right of the train station when facing the town. Buses #10, 11, 14, 20, 30, 40, 50, 60, 70, 130, and C/S also stop at P. Matteotti, and run to Fano (15min., every 30min. 6:30am-9pm, €1) and Gradara (20min., every hr. 6:08am-7:08pm, €1.25). **SOGET** (☎0721 54 96 20) runs buses to Urbino from the train station (55min.; M-Sa 11 per day 6:50am-8:05pm, Su 6 per day 8:30am and 2:20-8:20pm; €2.05). **Bucci** runs a bus to Tiburtina station in Rome from Ple. Matteotti (4½hr., 6am and 2pm, €20.75). Buy tickets on the bus. **Taxis** are available at the train station (☎0721 31 111; available 24hr.), P. del Popolo (☎0721 31 430), and P. Matteotti (☎0721 34 053). **Bicycle rental** (☎347 75 29 634) is available in Ple. d'Annunzio, at the intersection of Vle. Trieste and V. Verdi. (€2 per hr. Open late Apr.-Sept. 9am-midnight. Cash only.)

✈ 🛈 ORIENTATION AND PRACTICAL INFORMATION

From the **train station**, take **Via Risorgimento** and walk straight to reach **Piazza del Popolo**, the old city center. **Corso XI Settembre** runs west toward Chiesa di Sant'Agostino, while **Via San Francesco** runs east to **Piazzale Matteotti** and the bus station. **Via Rossini** runs straight toward **Largo Aldo Moro**, which leads to **Viale della Repubblica**, **Piazzale Libertà**, and the sea. **Viale Trieste** runs along the beach. The **IAT Tourist Office** in P. Libertà, to the right of the giant bronze globe, organizes guided tours of town sights. (☎0721 69 341; iat.pesaro@regione.marche.it. Open daily in summer 8:30am-1:30pm and 3-7pm, in winter M-Sa 9am-1pm and 3:00-6:00pm.) For more guided tours, call ☎0721 38 77 14. The **Provincial Tourist Office**, V. Rossini, 41, is past P. del Popolo on the left, off Largo Aldo Moro. It has info on the region, including tours and recommended sights. (☎800 56 38 00; www.turismo.pesarourbino.it. Open M-Sa 9:30am-1pm and 4-7pm, Su and holidays 9:30am-12:30pm.) **Luggage storage** is near the "Taxis" sign outside the train station. (€3 for 1st 12hr., €2 for each additional 12hr. Open daily 6am-11pm. Cash only.) In case of **emergency**, call ☎113 or 0721 21 344, an **ambulance** at ☎118, or the **police** at ☎0721 42 551. Speedy **Internet** is available at **Max3D**, V. Passeri, 177. (☎0721 351 22. €5 per hr., €3 when you buy a renewable membership card for €10. Open M-Sa 9:30am-1pm and 3:30-9pm. Cash only.) The **post office** is at P. del Popolo, 28. (☎0721 43 22 85. Open M-F 8am-6:30pm, Sa 8am-12:30pm.) **Postal Code:** 61100.

🏠 🍴 ACCOMMODATIONS AND FOOD

Though the availability of reasonably priced lodgings makes Pesaro a real low-season deal, bargains are harder to find in the summer. ⬛**Hotel Athena ❸**, Vle. Pola, 18, is a 20min. walk from the train station. Follow Viale della Liberazione to Viale Mameli, then turn right; after the street changes to V. Fiume, turn left on V. Tripoli and walk one block. Simple rooms with bath, phone, and TV are complemented by a sunny lobby, gracious staff-members, and a 5min. walk to the

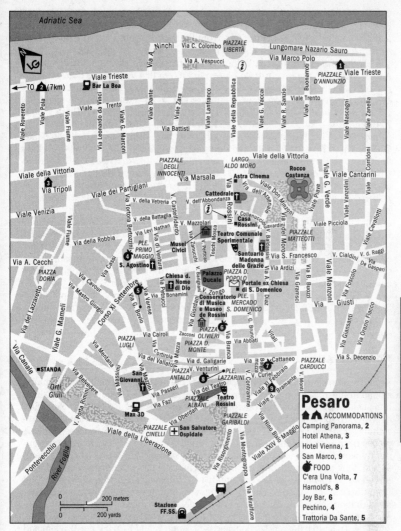

Pesaro

▲ ACCOMMODATIONS
Camping Panorama, 2
Hotel Athena, 3
Hotel Vienna, 1
San Marco, 9
🍴 FOOD
C'era Una Volta, 7
Harnold's, 8
Joy Bar, 6
Pechino, 4
Trattoria Da Sante, 5

beach. (☎0721 30 114; fax 0721 33 878. Breakfast included. Singles €35; doubles €50; triples €60. AmEx/MC/V.) Only seconds from the beach are the simple rooms of **Hotel Vienna ❸**, Ple. D'Annunzio, 5, with TV, telephone, and bath. (☎0721 31 256; fax 0721 31 114. Breakfast included. Singles €32-37; doubles €42-50; triples €58-64. AmEx/MC/V.) To get to **San Marco ❹**, Viale XI Febbraio, 32, follow V. Risorgimento from the train station and bear right into Ple. Garibaldi, then turn right on the busy Viale XI Febbraio. A friendly staff runs 40 spacious rooms with bath, phone, and TV in a busy, industrial neighborhood near the train station. (☎0721 31 396; sanmarco@abanet.it. Breakfast included. Wheelchair accessible. Reception 24hr. Singles €40; doubles €65; triples €80. AmEx/MC/V.)

UMBRIA AND LE MARCHE

Camping Panorama ❶ has free hot showers, electricity, and a pool. (7km north of Pesaro on Str. Panoramica toward Gabicce Mare. ☎0721 20 81 45; www.panoramavillage.it. Take bus #14, 4 per day, from Piazzale Matteotti and stop at Fiorenzuola. Open May-Sept. €5.50-8 per person, €7-10 per tent. AmEx/MC/V.)

A **STANDA** supermarket is at V. Canale, 41. (Open M-Sa 8am-8pm, Su 7am-2pm. AmEx/MC/V.) At the tavern-style *trattoria* ◧**C'era Una Volta ❸**, V. Cattaneo, 26, just off Piazzale Lazzarini, the main attraction is the pizza, massive in both diameter and variety—there are over 75 options. For an adventure, try their specialty *Cartoceto* (€6.70)—for a challenge, try to finish it. (☎0721 30 911. Pizza €2.50-7.50. *Primi* €4.70-7.50, *secondi* €5-24. Open Tu-Su noon-2:30pm and 7pm-1am. AmEx/MC/V.) Celebrate Pesaro's proximity to the Adriatic at **Trattoria da Sante ❸**, V. Bovio, 27, with delicious seafood pasta. (☎072 13 36 76. Follow C. XI Settembre north from P. del Popolo and turn left on V. Bovio. *Primi* €6-8, *secondi* €8-10. Daily special €8. Cover €1. Reserve for weekend dinner. Open daily noon-2:30pm and 7-10:30pm. Cash only.) If you've had your fill of pasta and *panini*, try **Pechino ❶**, V. Tortora, 7, an Italian-style Chinese restaurant where *maiale in salsa agrodolci* (sweet and sour pork; €4.10) will leave both travelers and their wallets full. (☎0721 35 316. *Antipasti* €1.40; main courses from €3.80. Open daily 11am-4pm and 6pm-midnight.) Three doors down from Teatro Rossini, **Harnold's ❶**, P. Lazzarini, 34, offers affordable fare served by talkative owner Patrick. You may have to wait for service at the busy outdoor tables, but the food, ranging from fresh *panini* and salads to the "Big Ben" double-decker cheeseburger (€4.20), is well worth it. (☎0721 65 155. From P. del Popolo, follow V. Branca away from the sea. *Panini* €2-4.20. Open daily 8am-3am. Closed Su in winter. AmEx/MC/V.) Satisfy your sweet tooth at **Joy Bar ❶**, where sugary cappuccinos (€1), creamy *gelato* (€1.50), and mounds of caramels and sweets abound in a quirky atmosphere. (☎0721 33 895. Open daily 7am-8pm. Cash only.)

◉ SIGHTS

Pesaro's main square, **Piazza del Popolo,** holds the massive **Palazzo Ducale,** commissioned in the 15th century by Alessandro Sforza. (Open to visitors only for exhibitions held in the interior. Ask the tourist office about scheduled events.) Rich clay deposits from the nearby river Folgia have made the crafting of ceramics a long-standing tradition in Pesaro. The **Musei Civici** showcase several centuries worth of pieces from regional kilns, ranging from prehistoric artifacts to colorful contemporary works. Nearby, a gallery holds the fiery *Fall of the Giants* by Guido Reni, four still-life paintings by Benedetto Sartori, and Bellini's remarkable *Incoronazione della Vergine,* an image surrounded by 15 panels depicting scenes ranging from Christ's Nativity to St. George (somewhat unimpressively) slaying an iguana-sized dragon. (V. Toschi Mosca, 29. From P. del Popolo, head down C. XI Settembre and turn right on V. Toschi Mosca. ☎0721 38 75 41; www.museicivicipesaro.it. Open July-Aug. Tu and Th 9:30am-12:30pm and 4-10:30pm, W and F-Su 9:30am-12:30pm and 4-7pm; Sept.-June Tu-W 9:30am-12:30pm, Th-Su 9:30am-12:30pm and 4-7pm. €4, under 26 or over 65 €2, under 15 free. Cash only.) Opera enthusiasts can spend hours in the **Casa Rossini** where the 1792 birthplace of Gioachino Rossini now houses a museum displaying photographs, theatrical memorabilia, signed opera scores, and even Rossini's piano. Extend a visit with opera screenings in the brick cellar. (V. Rossini, 34. ☎0721 38 73 57. Open July-Aug. Tu and Th 9:30am-12:30pm and 4-10:30pm, W and F-Su 9:30am-12:30pm and 4-7pm; Sept.-June Tu-W 9:30am-12:30pm, Th-Su 9:30am-12:30pm and 4-7pm. €4, under 26 or over 65 €2, under 15 free. Cash only.)

♫ ENTERTAINMENT

Pesaro hosts the **Mostra Internazionale del Nuovo Cinema** (The International Festival of New Films) during early June and late July (☎0721 38 75 110). Live theater and movie screenings are held in buildings along V. Rossini and at the **Teatro Comunale Sperimentale** (☎0721 38 75 48), an experimental theater on V. Rossini, just off P. del Popolo. Native composer Rossini founded the **Conservatorio di Musica G. Rossini**, P. Olivieri, 5, which sponsors events year-round. Contact **Teatro Rossini**, P. Lazzarini, 29 (☎0721 38 76 26), off V. Branca, for show times and prices. The annual **Rossini Opera Festival** begins in early August, with performances continuing through September. Reserve tickets at the box office of Teatro Rossini starting April 21. (☎0721 38 00 294; www.rossinioperafestival.it. Info line open M-F 10am-1pm and 3-6pm. Teatro Rossini box office open Aug. daily 10am-noon and 4-6:30pm and at the theater 1hr. before the performance.) **Astra Cinema**, V. Rossini, 82, shows international blockbusters in Italian soon after their initial release. (☎0721 341 39. Screenings nightly at 8:30 and 10:30pm. Tickets €7, reduced prices W. Cash only.)

♫ DAYTRIP FROM PESARO

FANO

Fano is accessible from Pesaro by train (10min., 33 per day 4:30am-11:02pm, €1.30) and from Bucci by bus (€2). For the beach, exit the train station right on V. Cavallotti and turn right on V. C. Battisti. To reach P. XX Settembre, the town center, turn left on V. Garibaldi from V. Cavallotti and then right on C. Giacomo Matteotti.

Fano is a sleepy town stretching 12km along the coast from Pesaro to some of the quietest seaside retreats. Even in summer, vacationers are scarce on the beaches to the north; further inland, a quiet *centro* offers relatively untouristed churches and many restaurants serving regional seafood specialties. Best viewed from its Western side, the town's oldest highlight, the **Arco d'Augusto**, is a tall Roman arch dating from AD 2 and squeezed between two buildings. Though hotels reserve most of the shoreline for their guests, the first entrance to the public **beach** sits across from Viale Adriatico, 150. Though this beach is convenient, the large rocks require substantial padding for sunbathing. (Open daily 5am-11pm. Free.) The **tourist office**, Viale Battisti, 10, provides a city **map** and a list of local events. (☎0721 80 35 34; www.turismofano.com. Open M-F 9am-1pm and 3:30-6:30pm, Sa and holidays 9am-1pm.) Although Fano makes a nice daytrip, overnighters can contact **Associazione Albergatori**, Viale Adriatico, 132, an organization that offers travelers free help with finding lodgings. (☎0721 82 73 76; fax 0721 82 57 10. Open Oct.-May M-F 9am-12:30pm and 4-7pm; June-Sept. M-Sa 9am-12:30pm and 4-7pm, Su 9:30am-12:30pm.) A **PuntoSMA** supermarket is at V. Garibaldi, 53. (Open M-W and F-Su 8am-12:45pm and 5-8pm, Th 8am-12:45pm. MC/V.) Inland, **La Vecchia Fano ❸**, V. Vecchia, 8, serves meat-heavy authentic *Fanese* plates like *tagliolini al farro* (€6.50) in a cool traditional atmosphere. Turn right off V. Cavour away from P. XX Settembre. (☎/fax 0721 80 34 93. *Primi* €6.50-7.50, *secondi* €6.50-18. Open Tu-Su noon-2:30pm and 7:30-10:30pm. AmEx/MC/V.) Bluefish is everywhere on the menu at **La Pesce Azzuro ❷**, V. d'Adriatico 48, where a brightly painted ship's hull welcomes visitors to this funky self-service restaurant north of town. (☎0721 80 31 65. Lunch and dinner *menù* €9.50. Open daily Apr.-Oct. noon-2pm and 7:30-10pm.)

URBINO
☎**0722**

With picturesque stone dwellings scattered along steep city streets and a turreted palace ornamenting its skyline, Urbino encompasses all that is classic Italy. The fairy-tale city is home to many artistic treasures and Renaissance monuments, including Piero della Francesca's *Ideal City* and Raphael's childhood home. The cultural beauty within the city walls is rivaled only by the magnificence of the region's surrounding mountains and valleys. Urbino's youthful vitality endures owing to its university population and stream of international visitors.

⌸ TRANSPORTATION

Buses stop in Borgo Mercatale. Bus timetables are posted at the beginning of C. Garibaldi, in P. della Repubblica, under the portico at the corner bar. Blue **SOGET** (☎0722 22 333) buses run to P. Matteotti and the depot outside the train station in Pesaro (55min.; M-Sa 11 per day 6:40am-6:45pm, Su 6 per day 7:30am-8:05pm; €2.05). Buy a ticket onboard. **Bucci** (☎0721 32 401) runs buses to Rome (5hr., 4pm, €22). **Luggage storage** is available (see below). **Taxis** are in P. della Repubblica (☎0722 25 50) and near the bus stop (☎0722 32 79 49).

✦🛈 ORIENTATION AND PRACTICAL INFORMATION

A short walk up **Via Mazzini** from **Borgo Mercatale** leads to **Piazza della Repubblica,** the city's hub, from which **Via Raffaello, Via Cesare Battisti, Via Vittorio Veneto,** and **Corso Garibaldi** radiate. Another short walk uphill on V. V. Veneto leads to **Piazza Rinascimento** and the **Palazzo Ducale.**

Tourist Office: V. Puccinotti, 35 (☎0722 26 13; iat.urbino@regione.marche.it), across from Palazzo Ducale. Open M and Sa 9am-1pm, Tu-F 9am-1pm and 3-6pm. **Info booth** (☎0722 26 31) in Borgo Mercatale. Open M-Sa 9am-6pm, Su 9am-1pm.

Budget Travel: CTS, V. Mazzini, 60 (☎0722 32 92 84), sells train or plane tickets and offers student tour info. Open M-F and Su 9am-1pm and 3:30-7:30pm, Sa 9am-1pm.

Luggage Storage: At the car-parking office in Borgo Mercatale. 24hr. per bag €1. Open daily 8am-8pm. Cash only.

Laundromat: Powders, V. Battisti, 35 (☎0722 21 96). Wash €3.75 per kg. Dry €2. Open M-Sa 9am-10pm. Cash only.

Emergency: ☎113. **Ambulance:** ☎118. **Police:** ☎112 or ☎0722 30 93 00.

Hospital: (☎0722 30 11), on V. B. da Montefeltro, off V. Comandino. Bus #1 and 3 from Borgo Mercatale stop.

Internet Access: Tourist office allows free 10min. **The Netgate,** V. Mazzini, 17 (☎/fax 0722 24 62), has over 20 computers. €4 per hr., students €3.20. Open M-F 10am-11pm, Sa noon-11pm, Su noon-10pm. Cash only.

Post Office: V. Bramante, 28 (☎0722 37 791), off V. Raffaello. **Currency exchange** and **ATM** available. Open M-F 8am-6:30pm, Sa 8am-12:30pm. **Postal Code:** 61029.

🏠 ACCOMMODATIONS AND CAMPING

Cheap lodgings are relatively rare in Urbino, and reservations are a good idea. One alternative is to stay in Pesaro and make Urbino a daytrip.

Pensione Fosca, V. Raffaello, 67 (☎0722 32 96 22 or 0722 32 25 42), on the top floor. A central location and pleasant waitstaff make up for the utilitarian rooms and the hike up an unpleasant staircase. Shared bath. Call ahead and arrange a check-in time. Singles €21; doubles €35; triples €45. Cash only. ❷

Hotel San Giovanni, V. Barocci, 13 (☎0722 28 27 or 0722 32 90 55). From P. della Repubblica, head toward V. Mazzini and turn right, following the signs. Modern hotel has big, simple rooms with phone and tiny bathrooms. Restaurant downstairs. Closed last 3 weeks of July. Singles €25, with bath €35; doubles €38/55. Cash only. ❸

Piero della Francesca, V. Comandino, 53 (☎0722 32 84 28; fax 0722 32 84 27), in front of hospital. Bus #1 from Borgo Mercatale or a 15min. walk from P. della Repubblica. Modern rooms have bath, TV, phone, and balconies with views of the misty hills. Reception 24hr. Singles €31; doubles €52; triples €68. AmEx/MC/V. ❸

Hotel Italia, C. Garibaldi, 32 (☎0722 27 01; www.albergo-italia-urbino.it), just off P. della Repubblica. Just across the street from the towering Palazzo Ducale, chic rooms have all the amenities as well as handsome blonde wood fixtures. Breakfast €8. Reception 24hr. Singles €45-65; doubles €65-115; triples €115-140. AmEx/MC/V. ❹

Camping Pineta (☎0722 47 10), on Loc. Monti delle Cesane, 2km from Urbino. Take bus #7 from Borgo Mercatale; ask to be let off at camping. Secluded sites have view of the city. Open 1 week before Easter-Sept. Office open daily 9am-10pm. €6 per person, €13 per car. Free showers and electricity. July-Aug. prices rise 10%. Cash only. ❶

◨ FOOD

Urbino's *caciotta* is a delicate cheese that pairs well with a glass of *Bianchello del Metauro*. **Supermarket Margherita,** at V. Raffaello, 37, has meats, cheeses, and packaged food but no fruits or veggies. (☎0722 32 97 71. Open M-Sa 7:30am-1:55pm and 4:30-8pm. Cash only.) For something a little greener, try **Frutta e Verdura,** 18/A V. Bramante. (Open daily 7am-1pm and 5-8pm. Cash only.) The university **Mensa** on V. Budassi, offers a huge dinner for around €4 with student ID. (Closed June-Aug.) At **Bar del Teatro ❶,** C. Garibaldi, 88, enjoy the best view in town: a theater next door, the Palazzo Ducale on one side and the valley on the other. (☎0722 29 11. Espresso €0.80; cappuccino €1.10. Open M-Sa 7am-midnight. Cash only.)

▨ **Pizzeria Le Tre Piante,** V. Voltaccia della Vecchia, 1 (☎0722 48 63). From P. della Repubblica, take V. Veneto, turn left on V. Nazario Sauro, right on V. Budassi, and left and down the stairs on V. Foro Posterula. Packed with locals, this gem serves sizeable pizzas (€2.50-6). Watch the sun set over the Apennines from the terrace. *Primi* €5.50-6, *secondi* €8-13. Open Tu-Su noon-3pm and 7-11pm. Cash only. ❸

La Trattoria del Leone, V. Battisti, 5 (☎0722 32 98 94). Fine dining at affordable prices, just off the *centro*. Try regional specialties like the *galletto al coccio* (a whole rooster served in a crockpot; €7.50). *Primi* €6-7.50, *secondi* €5-12. Cover €1.70. Open daily 12:30-2:30pm and 7:30-10:30pm. AmEx/MC/V. ❷

Ristorante Ragno d'Oro, Viale Don Minzoni, 2/4 (☎0722 32 77 05). Follow V. Rafaello to the statue at the top of the hill. Turn right on Vle. Don Minzoni. At noon, a stream of students make the hike to this *trattoria*. Try the signature pizza, the *Ragno d'Oro*, topped with mozzarella, spinach, ricotta, and speck (€5.70) with some of the German beer kept on tap. Pizza €2.50-7.50. *Primi* €5-7.50, *secondi* €6-14.50. Cover €1.50. Open daily noon-2:30pm and 7-11:30pm. AmEx/MC/V. ❸

Un Punto Macrobiotico, V. Pozzo Nuovo, 4 (☎0722 32 97 90). From P. della Repubblica, take C. Battisti and 1st right. Eager waitstaff and long benches promote a community feel in this cafeteria-type eatery. Organic menus are more balanced than meat-heavy ones elsewhere. Prices of individual meals change, though most are around €6 (students eat for half price). Open M-Sa 12:30-2:30pm and 7:30-9pm. Cash only. ❸

Caffè del Sole, V. Mazzini, 34 (☎0722 26 19). Popular student hangout with sunny decor serves *panini*, drinks, and hearty helpings of local personality. Look out for the giant mouth mural taking over the back wall. Jazz concerts Sept.-May W-Th nights. Open M 7am-1am, Tu-Sa 7am-2am. AmEx/MC/V. ❶

⊙ SIGHTS

The turreted silhouette of the Renaissance ⬛**Palazzo Ducale** dominates the Urbino skyline. A stairway inside leads to the **Galleria Nazionale delle Marche,** in the former residence of Duke Frederico da Montefeltro. The gallery contains the most important art collection in Urbino, including works like the *Ideal City* by Piero della Francesca. In the last rooms, Berruguete's *Portrait of Duke Federico with a Young Guidubaldo,* Raphael's *Portrait of a Lady,* and Paolo Uccello's narrative panel *The Profanation of the Host* are also on display. Ambrogio Barocchi designed the *palazzo's* facade. The building also contains the **Museo Archeologico's** varied collection of Roman art and artifacts. The subterranean servants quarters have cavernous tunnels and are also worth visiting. Free art exhibits are on display in the **Sale del Castellare;** the entrance is next to the *duomo.* (In P. Rinascimento. ☎0722 32 26 25. Open M 8:30am-2pm, Tu-Su 8:30am-7:15pm. Ticket sales end 1hr. before closing. €4, students 18-25 €2.)

The site of Raphael's birth in 1483, **Casa Natale di Raffaello,** V. Raffaello, 57, is now filled with period furnishings and paintings. The only decoration in the museum attributed to the artist himself is a fresco of the Virgin and Child, in the room to the left when facing the *Annunciation,* a work by Raphael's father Giovanni Santi. (☎0722 32 01 05. Open Mar.-Oct. M-Sa 9am-1pm and 3-7pm, Su 10am-1pm; Nov.-Feb. M-Sa 9am-2pm, Su 10am-1pm. Ticket office closes 20min. before museum. €3. Cash only.)

Next to Palazzo Ducale sits the stark facade of the **duomo.** Inside hang notable paintings like Veronese's fantastic *Traslazione della Santa Casa e Sant'Andrea.* (Open daily 7:30am-1pm and 2-7pm. Free.) The Gothic frescoes by L. J. Salimbeni (1416) decorating the 14th-century **Oratorio di San Giovanni Battista** represent events from the life of St. John; its painters are said to have drawn their sketches with lamb's blood. (At the end of V. Barocci. From P. della Repubblica, take V. Mazzini and turn right up the small path on the right, following the sign. ☎347 67 11 181. Open M-Sa 10am-12:30pm and 3-5:30pm, Su 10am-12:30pm. €2. Cash only.)

▣ ▧ NIGHTLIFE AND FESTIVALS

The main *piazze* stay lit well into the night, when people head to cafes for one last shot of espresso (and/or tequila, as the case may be). There isn't much excitement before 11pm, but this student town keeps things going until well after 3am. Bars are well stocked with German beers, hard liquor, and even the occasional bottle of absinthe. Check out **The Bosom Pub,** V. Budassi, 24, with its dark wood paneling and beer paraphernalia. Happy hours yield some great deals, with the beer of the week going two for one, and two bottles of wine for €10. (☎0722 47 83. Bottled beer €3-4; cocktails €4. Open daily Aug.-May 6pm-3am; June-July 9pm-3am. Cash only.) A black lit entrance welcomes visitors to the **Art Cafe,** V. Valerio, 28, a chic bar with leather couches. (☎338 91 71 336. Cocktails €4-5; shots €2-3. Open daily 11pm-2am.) In July the town resounds with Renaissance music during the **Antique Music Festival.** Saturdays are amateur nights—those with 3rd-century lutes, feel free to rock and roll. The 3rd Sunday in August brings the **Ceremony of the Revocation** of the Duke's Court, and the night before the festival, jousting matches erupt. The **Festa dell'Aquilone,** held on the first Sunday in September, is a fierce kite-flying competition between different cities. (The rain date is the 2nd Su of Sept.)

ANCONA   ☎071

Midway down the boot, Ancona is Northern Italy's major transportation hub for boats to Croatia, Slovenia, and Greece. As a result, most travelers only pass through Ancona on their way to more exotic locales. Those who choose to linger in Ancona will enjoy the centuries-old *duomo* and the sparkling Passetto beach.

▐ TRANSPORTATION

Trains: In P. Rosselli. Ticket office open daily 5:55am-8:45pm. To: **Bologna** (2½hr., 43 per day 1:25am-9:31pm, €10.12); **Milan** (5hr., 24 per day 1:32am-7:13pm, €19.37); **Pesaro** (45min., 41 per day 4:40am-10:22pm, €3.10); **Rimini** (1½hr., 50 per day 1:32am-10:22pm, €4.65); **Rome** (3-4hr., 10 per day 3:37am-7:07pm, €13.22); **Venice** (5hr., 4 per day 2:25am-6:14pm, €22.20). AmEx/MC/V.

Ferries: Ancona offers ferry service to **Croatia, Greece,** and **Northern Italy.** Schedules available at **Stazione Marittima** (☎071 20 78 91) on the waterfront. Call the day before departure to confirm, as cancellations can occur. Reserve July-Aug. **Luggage storage** available (see below).

Adriatica (☎071 50 21 16 21; www.adriatica.it). To: **Durazzo, Albania** (15hr.; €64, July-Aug. €85); and **Spalato, Croatia** (8hr., €40.80). AmEx/MC/V.

ANEK (☎071 20 72 346; www.anekitalia.com). Offers 20% discount for those under 26 and 10% discount for families and those over 65. To **Igoumenitsa, Greece** (15hr.) and **Patras, Greece** (20hr.; €54, July-Aug. €73). Round-trips discounted 30%. AmEx/MC/V.

Jadrolinija (☎071 20 43 05; www.jadrolinija.tel.hr/jadrolinija) runs to **Split, Croatia** (9hr.; €36.50, late June-Aug. €47; 20% discount on round-trip). AmEx/MC/V.

SEM Maritime Co (SMC; ☎071 20 40 41; www.marittimamauro.it). To: **Split, Croatia** (9hr.; €37, round-trip €68; prices increase 20% late July-late Aug.) and **Hvar Island.** AmEx/MC/V.

▐ ❼ ORIENTATION AND PRACTICAL INFORMATION

The **train station** is a 25min. walk from **Stazione Marittima.** Buses #1, 1/3, and 1/4 head along the port toward Stazione Marittima and up **Corso Stamira** to **Piazza Cavour,** the city center. Buy tickets (€0.90) at *tabaccherie.* For Stazione Marittima, disembark at **Piazza Repubblica,** walk back toward the water and turn right on the waterfront. The **tourist office,** located across the street in the Largo Dogane, offers a good **map** of the town. (☎071 20 79 029. Open in summer M 9am-7pm, Tu 11am-7pm, W-Su 10am-7pm.) There's a **branch** in Stazione Marittima that has ferry info. (☎071 20 11 83. Open daily July-Aug. 9am-7pm.) Info on long-term housing, employment, and cultural opportunities is at **InformaGiovani,** V. Palestro, 6/A, which also offers 30min. free Internet. (☎071 54 958, ext. 8; www.anconagiovane.it. Open M and Sa 10am-1pm, Tu and Th 10am-1pm and 4:30-7pm, F 4:30-7pm. No Internet within 30min of closing.) **Luggage storage** is available in Stazione Marittima. (Open daily 8am-8:30pm. €1 per bag per day for 1st 2 days, €2 per bag per day thereafter. Cash only.) In case of **emergency,** call ☎112 or 113, the **police** (☎071 22 881), an **ambulance** (☎118), or **first aid** (☎071 59 64 012). The hospital, **Ospedale Regionale Umberto I** (☎071 59 61) is on V. Conca-Torrette. **Internet** is available at New International Service, Cso. Stamira. 81. Facing the port, go to the far left of P. Cavour and turn the corner. (☎071 20 76 981. Open daily 9am-midnight. €1 per 15min., €1.50 per 30min.) The **post office** is at P. XXIV Maggio, 2, off P. Cavour (☎071 50 12 280. Open M-F 8am-6:30pm and Sa 8am-12:30pm.) **Postal Code:** 60100.

> **▐TIP◀** **CASH MONEY.** Though many hotels advertise that they accept credit cards, be sure to carry cash in case the credit card machine is broken.

▐ ACCOMMODATIONS

Ostello della Gioventù (HI) ❶, V. Lamaticci, 7, houses clean rooms with dark wood bunkbeds and spotless bathrooms. From the train station, cross the *piazza* and turn left. Take the first right and make a sharp right behind the newsstand. This is a good place to stay if you're coming and going by train. (☎/fax 071 42 257. Reception 6:30-11am and 4:30pm-midnight. Check-out 9:30am. Lockout 11am-4:30pm. Curfew midnight. Dorms €14. HI members only. AmEx/MC/V.) Sparsely furnished rooms offer little more than an inexpensive place to sleep at **Pensione Euro ❷**, C. Mazzini, 142, 2nd fl., off P. Cavour. Bring earplugs, as foot traffic on C. Mazzini is audible well past midnight. (☎071 20 34 22. Singles €25; doubles €40; triples €50. Cash only.) The clean rooms at **Hotel City ❹**, V. Matteotti, 112/114, all have bath, A/C, TV, and minibar. From P. Cavour, facing away from the port, turn left on the street just before Largo XXIV Maggio, and turn left at the end on V. Matteotti. (☎071 20 709 49; www.hotelcityancona.it. Buffet breakfast included. M-Th singles €60; doubles €96; triples €103. F-Su singles €56; doubles €92; triples €98. AmEx/MC/V.) Facing away from the port, walk to the far end of P. Cavour, turn right on V. Vecchini, walk straight and go up the staircase to **Pensione Milano ❷**, V. Montebello 1/A. Fourteen clean, non-descript rooms off a simple hallway come with basic furnishings and shared baths. (☎071 20 11 47. Reception 7am-11:30pm. Singles €21; doubles €31. Cash only.)

🔳 FOOD

The best **grocery** deals are at **Di per Di**, V. Matteotti, 115. (Open M-W and F 8:15am-1:30pm and 5-7:35pm, Sa 8:15am-1pm and 5-7:40pm. Cash only.) From P. Roma, head toward the horse fountain and turn right on V. Mazzini. Then, turn left into P. delle Erbe for **Mercato Pubblico,** P. delle Erbe, 130. Pack a meal for the ferry ride at this old-fashioned indoor market. (Open in summer M-Sa 7:30am-12:45pm and 5-8pm; in winter M-Sa 7:30am-12:45pm and 4:30-7:30pm. Most vendors cash only.) At **La Cantineta ❷**, V. Gramsci, 1, find a *trattoria* teeming with locals at tightly packed tables. Don't be deceived by the cracked tile floor—a genial, welcoming staff offers huge bread baskets, heavy portions of regional cuisine like *stoccafisso* (€13.50), and reasonable prices. At least locally, this secret is out—come early or be prepared to wait. (☎071 20 11 07. Open Tu-Su noon-2:45pm and 7:30-10:45pm. *Primi* €2.60-7.50, *secondi* €4.20-13.50. Cover €1.60. AmEx/MC/V.) From P. Roma, head toward the horse fountain and turn left to find **Bontà delle Marche ❸**, C. Mazzini, 96, an indoor specialty deli and lunch restaurant. Trays of gourmet meats and cheeses from Le Marche tempt from the display cases, while crisp white tables dot the pedestrian thoroughfare outside. (☎071 53 985; www.bonta-dellemarche.it. Market open M-Sa 8am-8pm. Restaurant open M-Sa 12:30-3:30pm. AmEx/MC/V.) For low-key dining, head to **Osteria Brillo ❷**, C. Mazzini, 109. This small, pub-style eatery right off the *centro* serves hearty Italian fare at reasonable prices. *Primi* specials change daily. From P. Roma, head toward the horse fountain and turn right on C. Mazzini. (☎071 20 72 629. Pizza €5.50-7.50. *Secondi* €5.50-15.50. Open M-Sa 12:30-3pm and 7:30-11pm. AmEx/MC/V.)

⬡ SIGHTS

Far from the port's industrial clutter, **Pasetto Beach**—though not the sandiest—offers a taste of natural beauty. Families flock here for the sapphire-blue waves, and sunbathers spread out on the wide railing. Above the beach, marble vistas and hundreds of stairs lead to the snow-white **Monumento ai Caduti,** a tribute to the soldiers in WWII. (In P. IV Novembre. Take bus #1/4 from the station or from P. Cavour along Vle. della Vittoria to the shoreline. Free.) In the **old city,** in the **Piazzale del Duomo** stands the **Cattedrale di San Ciriaco,** a Romanesque church built above the remains of an early Christian basilica and an even earlier Roman temple to Venus. Look in the basement on the left for the tomb of St. Ciriaco and a rather gruesome view of the body. From P. Cavour, follow C. Mazzini to the port and turn right on V. Gramsci at P. Repubblica. Continue to P. Del Senato and climb 247 steps to the duomo. (☎071 52 688. Open in summer M-Sa 8am-noon and 3-7pm; in winter M-Sa 8am-noon and 3-6pm. Free.) Ancona's painting gallery, the **Pinacoteca Comunale Francesco Podesti,** in the **Palazzo Bosdari,** V. Pizzecolli, 17, features works by the Camerte school including Carlo Crivelli's *Madonna con Bambino* and Titian's *Apparition of the Virgin.* From P. Roma, head down C. Garibaldi toward the port. Turn right at P. Repubblica on V. Gramsci and go straight. (☎071 22 25 045. Open M 9am-1pm, Tu-F 9am-7pm, Sa 8:30am-6:30pm, Su 3-7pm. €4.30, ages 16-25 €3.25. Cash only.) The enormous 16th-century **Palazzo Ferretti** houses Le Marche's foremost archaeological museum, the **Museo Archeologico Nazionale delle Marche,** an impressive collection including the Ionian Dinos of Amandola, Greek pottery, and jewelry unearthed by regional excavations in the 1900s. (V. Ferretti, 6. From Palazzo Bosdari, continue toward the *duomo.* ☎071 20 26 02; museo.ancona@archeomarche.it. Open Tu-Su 8:30am-7:30pm. €4. Cash only.)

ASCOLI PICENO   ☎0736

According to legend, Ascoli was founded by Sabines guided westward out of central Italy by a *picchio* (woodpecker). The bird not only gave the city its name, but also gave Le Marche a feathered mascot. By other accounts, Ascoli was the metropolis of the Piceno, a Latin tribe that controlled much of the coastal marches and had the woodpecker as its totem. Whatever the origins of its name, the city is one of Le Marche's most interesting, offering travelers a variety of sights, spirited local festivals, and a *centro storico* composed of ancient towers and elegant *loggie* made from bright travertine, a mineral consistently included in local architectural projects for the past 2000 years.

▛ TRANSPORTATION

The **train station** is in Piazzale della Stazione, at the end of V. Marconi. (Ticket counter open M-Sa 8am-noon and 3-6pm.) **Trains** depart to San Benedetto (30min., M-Sa 16 per day 6:24am-9:05pm, €2.40), but require a transfer at the P. d'Ascoli station from July to early September. **Buses** to San Benedetto are more crowded than trains and take twice as long, but run much more consistently. Buses leave from Vle. Gasperi, behind the *duomo.* **Start** sells bus tickets from **Agenzia Cameli,** V. Dino Angelini, 129 (☎800 44 30 40; www.startspa.it), off P. Roma, and runs buses to San Benedetto (1hr.; M-Sa 34 per day 5:10am-11:30pm, Su 15 per day 7am-10:40pm; €1.70) and Acquasanta Terme (1¼hr., 13 per day 5am-7:15pm, €3.45). Buses to Rome (3hr.; M-Sa 4 per day 3:20am-4:30pm, Su 4 per day 3:20am-5:30pm; €11.90) depart from P. Orlini. (☎0736 25 90 91. Ticket agency open M-Sa 9am-12:45pm and 4-7pm, Su 9-9:30am and 4-4:30pm.)

▟ ▞ ORIENTATION AND PRACTICAL INFORMATION

From the **train station,** walk one block to **Viale Indipendenza,** turn right, and continue straight to **Piazza Matteotti.** Turn right on **Corso Mazzini;** follow it into **Piazza del Popolo** (10min.). The main bus stop is on **Viale Gasperi,** behind the *duomo.* Walk around the *duomo* to **Piazza Arringo,** then to **Via XX Settembre** and **Piazza Roma.** From there, **Via del Trivio** leads to C. Mazzini and P. del Popolo. Two tourist offices serve Ascoli: **Centro Visitatori,** P. Arringo, 7 (☎0736 29 82 04 or 0736 29 82 12; www.comune.ascolipiceno.it; open daily 9:30am-12:30pm and 4-7pm), and **Ufficio Informazioni,** P. del Popolo, 17 (☎0736 25 30 45; open M-F 8:30am-1:30pm and 3-6pm, Sa 9am-1pm). Head to **Banca Nazionale del Lavoro,** C. Mazzini, 160, for **currency exchange.** (☎0736 29 61. Open M-F 8:20am-1:20pm and 3-4:30pm, Sa 8:20am-11:50pm.) In case of **emergency,** dial ☎113, call the **police** ☎112, or an **ambulance** ☎118. There is a **pharmacy** at P. Roma, 1. (☎0736 25 91 83. Open daily 9am-1pm and

Ascoli Piceno

🏠 **ACCOMMODATIONS**
Cantina dell'Arte, 2
Ostello dei Longobardi, 1

🍴 **FOOD**
Caffè Meletti, 5
Cantina dell'Arte, 3
Ristorante dal Vagabondo, 4

4:30-8pm.) **Libreria Cattolica**, P. Arringo, 21, has one computer with **Internet**. (☎0736 24 72 95. €5 per hr. Open M 4-8pm, Tu-Su 8:30am-1pm and 4-8pm. Cash only.) Ascoli's **post office**, on V. Crispi, provides **currency exchange**. (☎0736 24 22 83. Open M 4-8pm, Tu-Sa 8:45am-12:45pm and 4-8pm.) **Postal Code:** 63100.

🏠 🍴 ACCOMMODATIONS AND FOOD

Accommodations in Ascoli Piceno are cheap and rustic, but not run-down. The best deal in town is the pleasant **🛏Ostello dei Longobardi ❶**, R. dei Longobardi, 12. An 11th-century building with 20th-century plumbing, this quiet hostel offers 16 beds separated into single-sex dorms. From P. del Popolo, take C. Mazzini to P. S. Agostino and turn right on V. delle Torri, then left on V. Soderini. (☎0736 26 18 62; www.hostels-aig.org. Reception open daily 7-9am and 6pm-midnight. Dorms €14. Cash only.) In the heart of town, **Cantina dell'Arte ❸**, V. della Lupa, 8, is a quaint hotel decorated with family photos. Rooms have marble floors, bath, TV, and phone. Follow C. Trento e Trieste to P. S. Maria Inter Vineas and turn right on V. delle Canterine, then right on V. della Lupa. (☎0736 25 57 44. Reserve ahead. Singles €30; doubles €40; quads €65; quint with kitchen €100. AmEx/MC/V.)

Ascoli's cuisine relies on local produce, including wild mushrooms, onions, capers, garlic, fennel, and anise. Fried sweet-cream ravioli and savory anise-flavored cakes topped with powdered sugar are holiday favorites. The region's wines include *Rosso Piceno* and *Falerio dei Colli Ascolani*. An **open-air market** is in P. S. Francesco, behind P. del Popolo. (Open M-Sa 8am-1pm.) **Tigre** supermarket is at P. S. Maria Inter Vineas, 1, at the end of C. Trento e Trieste. (Open M-W and F-Sa 8:30am-7:30pm, Th 8:30am-1pm. MC/V.) Take C. Mazzini from P. del Popolo and turn left, following signs for **🍴Ristorante dal Vagabondo ❸**, V. D'Argillano, 29. Admire tasteful modern art on the walls while Gennaro serves up heaping plates of tasty Ascoli-Picenian fare to Italian tourists and local residents. (☎0736 26 21 68. *Primi* €5-7, *secondi* €10. Lunch *menù* €10. Open daily noon-3pm and 7-11pm. AmEx/MC/V.) There's no better place to try local *Anisetta Meletti* (€5 per glass, €12.40 per bottle) than **🍴Caffè Meletti ❶**, P. del Popolo, 20, the spacious, 100-year-old cafe where Silvio Meletti first pushed his now-famous liqueur. (☎0736 25 96 26. Open in summer daily 7am-midnight, in winter Tu-Su 7am-midnight. AmEx/MC/V.)

Quell a ravenous appetite at **Cantina dell'Arte ❷**, V. della Lupa, 5, across from the hotel of the same name (see above). The medieval stone interior renders the generously portioned *menù* (€10) even more delectable. (☎0736 25 56 90. *Primi* €4-5, *secondi* €5-6. Open M-Sa noon-3pm and 7-10:30pm, Su noon-3pm. MC/V.)

👁 SIGHTS

PIAZZA DEL POPOLO. This vast *piazza* was once the Roman forum, and it still buzzes with political and consumer activity along *loggie* filled with cafes, boutiques, and city offices. The gleaming pavement is made of travertine, an off-white mineral that's been used to construct the city's major buildings and squares for over two millennia. **Palazzo dei Capitani**, the city's former town hall, welcomes visitors to its paved open-air courtyard. During a Christmas Day squabble in 1535, an angered papal commissioner ordered that the building be burned after a group of rebels barricaded themselves inside; a decade later, the contrite arsonist dedicated the refurbished palace to Pope John III and erected a statue in his honor. The *palazzo* stood without controversy until 1938, when it served as a seat of the Fascist Party. (☎0736 24 49 75. Open daily 9am-1pm and 3-7pm. Free.) The eastern end of the Romanesque-Gothic **Chiesa di San Francesco** contains a wood crucifix, the only art saved from the 1535 fire. The church's "singing columns," two sets of low columns flanking the outer door on the V. del Trivio side, sound a dull pop if you draw your hand quickly across them. (Open daily 8am-noon and 3:30-7:30pm. Free.)

PIAZZA ARRINGO. The Oration Square which derives its name from its role as a local podium. On one end, the travertine **duomo** combines Classical, Romanesque, and Baroque styles and holds work from the 5th through 18th centuries. A Roman basilica serves as the transept, topped by an 8th-century octagonal dome. Inside, freshly restored frescoes decorate the ceiling, while stairs on the right lead down into the dim **Cripta di San Emidio,** where shimmering mosaics and sculptures adorn the tomb of Ascoli's first bishop and patron saint. According to legend, the tomb only holds the body of San Emidio—the head of the decapitated martyr is housed in Chiesa di San Emidio alle Grotte (see below). Next to the cathedral stands the squat 12th-century **baptistry.** (Duomo open daily 7am-12:30pm and 5:30-7:45pm. Free.)

PINACOTECA CIVICA. Medieval and Renaissance works by Crivelli, Titian, van Dyck, and Reni line the walls of the art museum, housed amid period furniture and frescoed ceilings in the massive Palazzo Arringo. Check out the sunny courtyard garden and the life-like sculptures scattered throughout the building—Ascoli native Romolo del Gobbo's ▧**Paolo e Francesca** is especially striking. (To the left after exiting the duomo in P. Arringo. Enter the garden courtyard, turn immediately left, then another left up the staircase. ☎0736 29 82 13. Open daily 9:30am-12:30pm and 4-7pm. €5. Cash only.)

MUSEO ARCHEOLOGICO STATALE. Inside the **Palazzo Panichi** is a three-floor museum with a collection of Greek and Roman artifacts, some excavated from nearby San Benedetto. The most impressive piece is a mosaic floor that depicts the face of a boy in the center; when viewed from the opposite side, it becomes the face of an old man. (P. Arringo, 28. Open Tu-Su 8:30am-7:30pm. €2, students €1.)

OTHER SIGHTS. From the Piazza del Popolo, turn left on C. Mazzini and right on V. del Trivio. Bear left on V. Cairoli, which becomes V. delle Donne, then pass the church on the left and follow tiny V. di Solestà as it curves to the right. V. di Solestà leads to the single-arched **Ponte di Solestà**, one of Europe's tallest Roman bridges. From the bridge, take V. Rigante, turn right on Viale M. Federici, turn left on V. Carso, and follow it under the roadway to reach **Chiesa di Sant'Emidio alle Grotte**, whose Baroque facade is crafted from the natural rock wall. Inside, **catacombs** contain the remains of the first Ascoli Christians and the head of San Emidio.

FESTIVALS

Ascoli's **Carnevale** is one of Italy's liveliest; insanity reigns on the days preceding Ash Wednesday. On the first Sunday in August, the colorful medieval pageant of **Tournament of Quintana** honors the city's patron Saint Emidio, with 1500 enthusiasts in medieval garb, man-on-dummy jousting and a torch-lit procession, ultimately culminating in a fierce competition where all six neighborhoods of the town bandy for the coveted winner's banner, the *Palio*. On the third Sunday of each month except July, an **Antique Market** unfolds in the *centro*.

SAN BENEDETTO DEL TRONTO ☎0735

With over 7000 palm trees and nearly as many children playing under their waving fronds, San Benedetto draws summering Italian families and a smattering of foreign tourists. Don't come expecting to split beach time with cultural enrichment—the height of the local art scene are the sand castles along the miles of beach.

 TRANSPORTATION. The **train station** is at Via Gramsci, 20/A. The ticket counter is open daily 6:40am-8:35pm (AmEx/MC/V). **Trains** run to: Ancona (1hr., 28 per hr. 12:28am-9:13pm, €4.30); Bologna (3hr., 12 per day 12:28am-8:31pm, €24); and Milan (5-6hr., 6 per day 12:38am-4:14pm, €35). **Start** runs **buses** from the train station to Ascoli Piceno (1hr.; M-Sa 34 per day 6am-12:10am, Su 15 per day 7am-midnight; €1.70). Buy tickets at the train station or at Caffè Blue Express (open 3am-8pm) across from the station. **Local buses** stop in front of the train station. Bus #2 departs across the street from the station (every 10-20min. 5:57am-12:45am, €0.75). **Taxis** (☎0735 58 41 27) run from F. S. Stazione.

 ORIENTATION AND PRACTICAL INFORMATION. From the **train station,** cross the street and take bus #2 to the **seaside,** or turn left on **Via Gramsci** and left again on **Via Monfalcone** toward the beach. **Viale Trieste,** the *lungomare,* intersects V. Monfalcone and runs along the shore, changing from **Viale Marconi** to **Viale Europa/Scipioni,** and then to **Viale Rinascimento. Via Trento,** which becomes **Via Volta,** runs parallel to the *lungomare.* To reach the **tourist office,** Viale delle Tamerici, 5, turn left from the train station on V. Gramsci, then left on V. Fiscaletti; follow it to the sea and turn right on Vle. dei Tigli. The office is housed in a brown building, facing the main shore. (☎0735 59 50 88; www.rivieradellepalme.it. Open June-Sept. M-Sa 9am-1pm and 4-7pm, Su 9am-1pm.) In case of **emergency,** call ☎113, an **ambulance** at ☎118, or the **police** at ☎112. The **Ospedale Civile** (☎0735 79 31) is on V. Silvio Pellico. From the train station, turn left on V. Gramsci and right on V. Montello, then left on V. Silvio Pellico. **Farmacia Mercuri,** Viale de Gasperi, 61/63 (☎0735 78 01 51), posts a 24hr. rotation outside. (Open M-Sa 9am-1pm and 4-7pm.) Across from the train station, **Easy Connect,** V. Roma, offers cheap **Internet.** (Open daily 10am-11pm. €1 per hour.) **Currency exchange** is available at the **post office,** V. Roma, 125, which is located in the parking lot outside the train station. (Open M-F 8am-1:30pm and Sa 8am-12:30pm.) **Postal Code:** 63039.

 BEACH FOR FREE. The free beaches in San Benedetto are superb, don't waste money paying for the private ones. The best free beach (with the fewest people) is all the way at the end of the promenade.

 ACCOMMODATIONS. Most hotels include private beach access in their fee, and public beaches are marked *"spiaggia libera."* Numerous shacks rent storage cabins (€5.20 and up) and umbrellas (€6.20 and up). To get to **La Playa ❷,** V. Cola di Rienzo, 25/A, take bus #2 to the rotunda stop at V. del Mare. Continue straight on V. dei Laureati and turn right on V. F. Ferrucci. Walk one block and turn left on V. Cola di Rienzo. The staff and oversized rooms with polished tile floors, bath, TV, minibar, and balcony make this budget locale feel like a splurge. (☎/fax 0735 65 99 57. Open June-Oct. No singles in Aug. Singles €26-32; doubles €36-60. Prices rise in July and Aug. Cash only.) The **Albergo Patrizia** ❹, V. Volta, 170, has a private beach and offers guests a free chair, umbrella, and bicycles. All 33 rooms have bath, TV, and phone; some have balcony. From the station, take bus #2. (☎0735 817 62; www.albergopatrizia.it. Breakfast included. Open June-Sept. Doubles €55-65; triples €70. Full pension €36-67 per person. Prices peak in Aug. MC/V.) Campers appreciate **Seaside** ❷, V. dei Mille, 125, for its pool, market, restaurant, electricity, and hot showers, in a spacious grove walled off from the *centro* traffic outside. Take bus #2, or on foot from Vle. Rinascimento, turn right on V. A. Negri and bear left on V. dei Mille. (☎0735 65 95 05; seaside@libero.it. Open June-Sept. €7-10 per adult, €3-5 per child ages 3-7, €7 per half-site, €12-18 per site, €2.50-5 per car.)

❏ FOOD. On Tuesday and Friday morning, head to the **open-air market,** on V. Montebello. The **Tigre** supermarket is at V. Abruzzi, 28. (Open in summer M-Sa 8:30am-1pm and 5-8pm, Su 9am-1pm. AmEx/MC/V.) Dine by candlelight at the chic **▨Bagni Andrea** ❸, Vle. Trieste, on the left heading away from the train station between beaches #8 and 9. The elegant beach-side restaurant specializes in fish. Reserve ahead for dinner on the weekends. (☎0735 83 834. *Primi* €8; *secondi* €10-18. F-Sa piano bar 10pm. Open daily 1-3pm and 8:30-11pm, but late-night Latin/swing disco closes at 3am. AmEx/MC/V.) Dim globe lights illuminate the comfortable, pub-like interior of **Bar San Michele** ❷, V. Piemonte, 111. From the train station, turn left on Vle. Gramsci, which becomes V. Ugo Bassi then V. Piemonte. (☎0735 82 429. Pizza €2.10-6.50. *Panini* €4-6. *Primi* €4-6, *secondi* €4-8. Cover €1.50. Open M-Sa noon-3pm and 7:15pm-2:30am. AmEx/MC/V.)

ABRUZZO AND MOLISE

The foothills of the Apennine mountains are home to medieval castles, Roman ruins, and a sprawling, varied wilderness. The people of this region have been shepherds since the Bronze Age, and only in the last half century has their way of life changed. One can still follow millennia-old shepherds' paths through the countryside. About 2hr. from Rome and not yet discovered by tourists, these highlands offer natural beauty and a unique retreat. Youths nod to their CD players, shirtless men lead donkeys, and women tote copper water jugs. A single region until 1963, Abruzzo and Molise lie at the juncture of Northern and Southern Italy. Abruzzo, the wealthier of the two, offers resorts, lakes, lush pines, and stunning wildlife in Abruzzo National Park. The smaller Molise, dubbed a religious center by the Samnite order, is home to phenomenal ruins, medieval festivals, and flavorful food.

HIGHLIGHTS OF ABRUZZO AND MOLISE

GLIMPSE herds of wild horses on the **Gran Sasso d'Italia** (p. 543)

FIND OUT why **L'Aquila** is 99 times better than any other town in the region (below).

HUDDLE in your tent in **Abruzzo National Park,** where the village of **Opi** beckons the adventurous (p. 549).

SPEND time, not money, exploring each of **Tremiti's verdant isles** (p. 553).

L'AQUILA
☎ 0862

In 1254, 99 lords from 99 castles banded together to build L'Aquila (The Eagle), Abruzzo's majestic capital. The lords honored the founding of the city by constructing a 99-spout fountain—a stately structure that flows today just as steadily as it did some 700 years ago. Local legend claims that the town has 99 medieval streets, 99 *piazze*, and 99 churches, one of which tolls its bells 99 times at 9:09 every evening. Local legend also claims that the "fresh mountain air" renders hotel air-conditioning unnecessary—a myth that remains unsubstantiated.

 TRANSPORTATION

> **TRANSPORTATION TROUBLES.** Traveling by car in Abruzzo and Molise is advisable, since bus service can be inconvenient and inconsistent. Before setting out, always double check at the APT office, the bus station, and with the driver before boarding a bus. Be sure also to confirm the return routes. Thanks to technology, schedules and information are available by phone or Internet.

The **train station** (☎0862 41 92 90) is on the outskirts of town. Take **bus #M11, 5,** or **8** to V. XX Settembre to reach the center, taking a left on C. Federico II. On foot, follow signs to the Fontana delle 99 Cannelle and hike 2km uphill. **Trains** go to Sulmona (1hr., 8 per day 6:27am-8:25pm, €4.62) and Terni (2hr., 10 per day 6:27am-7:57pm, €5.89). L'Aquila has two **bus** systems: ARPA regional buses (☎0862 41 28 08) and municipal buses. Monday through Saturday, blue **ARPA buses** go to: Avezzano (50min., 26 per day 5:55am-8:30pm, €4.50); Pescara (1½hr., 7 per day 6am-9:10pm, €7); Rome (1¾hr., 17 per day 4:40am-8pm, €8.50); and Sulmona (40min, 7 per day 6:20am-7:20pm, €4.50). The **station ticket office** (☎0862 41 28 08) is open Monday through Saturday 5:30am-8:30pm, Sunday 7:30am-1:15pm and 2:30-8pm.

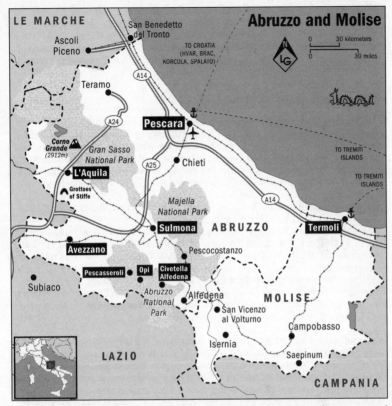

The yellow **municipal buses** stop at **AMA** markers and serve surrounding towns and sights (☎0862 31 98 57; www.amaaq.191.it. One-way €0.85, 1½hr. €1, 1 day €1.90). Tickets are available at *tabaccherie*, newsstands, bars, and at the **City Bus Station**, past P. del Collemaggio on V. G. Caldora. A subterranean tramway connects the station with P. del Duomo. **Taxis** (☎0862 22 115) are available at the bus station.

🔲🔢 ORIENTATION AND PRACTICAL INFORMATION

Corso Vittorio Emanuele II, the main street, stretches between the **Castello Cinque-centesco** in the north and **Piazza del Duomo,** the heart of L'Aquila's historical district, in the south. Beyond P. del Duomo, the street continues as **Corso Federico II** until reaching the gardens of the **Villa Comunale** and **Via XX Settembre.** Pick up a map at the tourist office; L'Aquila's often unlabeled streets are difficult to navigate.

The **APT branch office,** P. Maria Paganica, 5, has info on hotels, sites, and transport. Visitors planning to explore the park should pick up an information booklet. Turn left off C. V. Emanuele II on V. Leosini. (☎0862 41 08 08 or 41 03 40. Open M-Sa 9am-1pm and 3-6pm, Su 9:30am-1pm.) The main **APT Tourist Office,** V. XX Settembre, 8, stocks an indispensable free **map.** (☎0862 223 06. Open M-Sa 9am-1pm and 3-6pm, Su 9am-1pm.) **Club Alpino Italiano,** V. Sassa, 34, offers hiking information, including maps and guide references. (☎0862 243 42. Open M-Sa 7-8:15pm.) The **Centro Turistico Gran Sasso,** C. V. Emanuele II, 49, has bus and train schedules and info on the Gran Sasso park. (☎0862 221 46. Open M-F 9am-1pm and 4-7pm, Sa 9am-1pm.) The **police** (☎112 or 113) are at V. del Beato Cesidio. **Internet** is at C. P. Umberto, 20. (☎0862 273 64. €5 per hr. Open M-Sa daily 9am-11pm, Su 4-11pm.) Take C. V. Emanuele II from the *duomo*, turn left on C. P. Umberto. It's at the end of the colonnade on the left. The **post office**, in P. del Duomo, **exchanges currency**. (☎0862 63 71. Open M-Sa 8am-6:30pm.) **Postal Code:** 67100.

🏠🍴 ACCOMMODATIONS AND FOOD

There are no true budget accommodations in L'Aquila, only three- and four-star hotels. The two hotels listed here are among the most reasonably priced and offer some of the best values for your money. **Hotel San Michele ❺**, V. dei Giardini, 6, is luxurious. All rooms are equipped with Internet, satellite TV, air-conditioning, minifridge, and fluffy towels. On the 3rd and 4th floors, windows look out on the mountains south of town. Follow C. Federico II from P. del Duomo and turn right on V. dei Giardini to reach the hotel. (☎0862 42 02 60; www.stmichelehotel.it. Impressive buffet breakfast included. Parking €8 per night. Singles €65; doubles €80-90. MC/V.) The rooms in the centrally located **Hotel Duomo ❹**, V. Dragonetti, 6. are small, but many have splendid *duomo* views, and all have a bath, TV, and phone. V. Dragonetti is across from the *duomo* and to the left. (☎0862 41 07 69; www.hotel-duomo.it. Breakfast €5. Singles €55-60; doubles €75-80. AmEx/MC/V.)

Torrone, a honey and almond nougat, is L'Aquila's specialty. Some of the more popular kinds are available at **Caffè Europa ❶**, C. V. Emanuele II, 38, for €8 per box. Though on the touristy side, Europa still attracts locals who linger at the counter over *caffè macchiati*. (Open daily 7am-7:50pm.) **Le Mangiatoie ❸**, V. Dragonetti, 22/24, next to Hotel Duomo, is known for its fresh cuisine. While the menu is short, each Abruzzese specialty is excellently prepared. Their *gnocchi al ragù* (€5) is light and simple, and their *macedonia* (fruit salad; €2.50) is hard to top. (☎0862 24 639. *Primi* €5-6, *secondi* €6-11. Open M and W-Su 1-3pm and 8:30pm-12am. MC/V.) New in L'Aquila is the *enoteca/gastronomia* **Il Girone dei Golosi ❷**, V. Santa Giusta, 9-13. Sample small plates of regional meats and cheeses, and quench thirst with well-priced bottles of wine in the most romantic courtyard in town. From P. del Duomo, follow V. Dragonetti and turn right onto V. Santa Giusta. (☎0862 41 30 46. *Gastronomia* €3-9, bottles of wine €5-18. Open M-Sa 6pm-midnight. MC/V.) Find everything from fresh fruit and cured meats to clothes at the busy **market** in P. del Duomo. (Open M-Sa 8am-noon.) A small **STANDA** supermarket, C. Federico II, is two blocks from V. XX Settembre. Enter on the corner of V. Monteguelfi and V. S. Agostino. (☎0862 264 82. Open M-Sa 8am-8pm. AmEx/MC/V.)

👁 SIGHTS

Chiesa di San Bernardino, built in the 15th century and restored after an earthquake in 1703, peers over the mountains south of L'Aquila. Though bereft of its original rose windows, the towering church remains a stunning sight. The interior boasts the tomb of San Bernardino and somewhat disturbing X-rays of his tomb taken in 1931. Each year on May 22 schoolchildren from Siena make a pilgrimage to L'Aquila to bring oil that will light the lamp in front of the church's mausoleum for the rest of the year. Across from the church, a stairway frames a breathtaking mountain view; to reach it, walk down V. S. Bernardino from C. V. Emanuele II. (Open daily 7:30-10am and 6-8pm. Modest dress required.)

Commissioned in 1272, the **Fontana delle 99 Cannelle** (Fountain of 99 Spouts) is L'Aquila's oldest monument. Take V. Sallustio from C. V. Emanuele and bear left onto V. XX Settembre. Follow the small roads down the hill, staying to the left.

Within the walls of the fort, the **Museo Nazionale di Abruzzo** showcases local art and artifacts: sacred paintings, Roman sarcophagi, Renaissance tapestries, a ▓**million-year-old mammoth skeleton,** and some local modern art. (☎0862 63 31. Open Tu-Su 8:30am-7:30pm. €4; ages 18-25 €2; university students, children under 18, and adults over 65 free.) To find the ▓**Basilica di Santa Maria di Collemaggio,** take C. Federico I past V. XX Settembre, or the tramway to the bus station from P. del Duomo, and turn left on V. di Collemaggio after Villa Comunale. At the request of Pietro da Marrone (later Pope Celestine V), L'Aquila's citizens began this church in 1287. The pink- and white-checkered facade belies an austere interior, as Baroque embellishments were stripped away in 1972 to restore the striking medieval design. In the evening, take a stroll through the grounds with locals.(Open in summer daily 9am-1pm and 3-8pm; winter hours vary. Modest dress required.) L'Aquila's **Castello Cinquecentesco** dominates the park at the end of C. V. Emanuele. The Spanish viceroy Don Pedro da Toledo built this fort in the 16th century to defend himself against the rebelling *Aquilesi.* Naturally, they were forced to pay for its construction. The moat's outer wall drops 12m to the courtyard below.

Outside L'Aquila are the well-preserved ruins at historian Sallust's birthplace, **Amiternum,** an ancient Sabine town conquered by the Romans in 293 BC. The remains of a theater, amphitheater, and aqueduct survive from the Roman era, and may be explored daily between 9:30am and 1pm (free). **ARPA buses** service this sight from both L'Aquila and Sulmona (1-2hr., 2-3 per day, €1-2). In L'Aquila, take **bus #15** from the rotary in front of the Castello to San Vittorino.

DAYTRIPS FROM L'AQUILA

GROTTOES OF STIFFE

Take the white Paoli bus (☎0862 810 825) from the lower level of the bus station (25min., 1 per day, €2.65). Bus schedules are subject to change so check with the APT office in L'Aquila for more info.

⭐**TIP** **DRESS FOR THE WEATHER.** Be sure to wear proper clothing and footwear—the temperature inside the grottoes is around 10°C (50°F) all year round, and the pathways through the caves are slippery and uneven.

The Grottoes of Stiffe at San Demetrio ne' Vestini, 21km southeast of L'Aquila, were formed in prehistoric times when an underground river carved the caverns and rock formations that now form waterfalls and small lakes. The beautiful caves are famous for both the visual and sound effects created by the water. During the Christmas season, nativity scenes are set up throughout the caves. (☎0862 86 142; www.grottestiffe.it. Open year-round. Tours 10am, 1pm, 3pm, and 6pm. Ticket window open daily 10am-1pm and 3-6pm. €8, students €6.50, ages 6-10 €6.) The bus drops off passengers near the ticket booth, on V. del Mulino. Reaching the actual grottoes requires a 2km hike uphill or a short drive. While tours are given only in Italian, the ticket booth has explanatory brochures in English

OTHER DAYTRIPS

GRAN SASSO D'ITALIA (GREAT ROCK OF ITALY). The snow-capped Gran Sasso d'Italia, the highest mountain ridge within Italy's borders, looms 12km north of L'Aquila. Midway up the Sasso (and above the tree line), a flat plain called **Campo Imperatore** is home to herds of wild horses, shepherds, and never-ending landscapes. On a clear day, you can see both of Italy's coasts from the **Corno Grande,** the range's highest peak (2912m). The trail map (€8), available at the Club Alpino

ABRUZZO AND MOLISE

Italiano in town or at the base of the mountain, is useful for planning hikes. *Sentieri* (paths) are marked by difficulty. Only the more taxing routes reach the top. The peaks are snowed in from September to July and only experienced mountaineers should venture out during this period. In the summer a **funicular** (☎0862 60 61 43; every hr. when functioning 8:30am-5pm; round-trip €13) ascends the 1008m to Campo Imperatore, making the Sasso an easy afternoon excursion from L'Aquila.

In winter Gran Sasso teems with **skiers.** The trails around the funicular are among the most difficult, offering one 4000m and several 1000m drops. Ten trails descend from the funicular and the two lifts. Purchase a weekly pass at the *biglietteria* at the base of the funicular. **Campo Felice** (☎0862 91 78 03), at nearby Monte Rotondo, has 16 lifts, numerous trails of varying difficulty, and a ski school. From **L'Aquila,** take yellow **bus #76** or blue shuttle **M6** (30min., 12 per day, €1) from the bus station. Buy tickets at newsstands, *tabaccherie,* or the station. The funicular is closed in parts of June and October. Trails start at the upper funicular station. Call **Club Alpino Italiano** (☎0862 243 42; www.cai.it) for current conditions. For info on mountain guides, inquire at the tourist office or Club Alpino Italiano, or write to Collegio Regionale Guide Alpine, V. Serafino, 2, 66100 Chieti (☎0871 693 38).

The map and the info booklet from L'Aquila's APT office list overnight *rifugi* (hiker's huts), which run €8-14. Another option is the hostel **Campo Imperatore ❶,** which offers bunkbeds and shared bathrooms. Call from the lower ropeway station to be picked up. (☎0862 40 00 11. Dorms €15 per person.) **Camping Funivia del Gran Sasso ❶** is located on a secluded field downhill from the lower ropeway where people pitch tents. (☎0862 60 61 63; campingfuniviagransasso@virgilio.it. Hot showers available. €4-6.50 per person, €6-7 per large tent, €1 per car.) Call these lodgings before setting out, and bring food and warm clothing as it's windy and cool at Campo Imperatore year round.

SULMONA   ☎0864

Hidden deep in Abruzzo's Pelignia Valley, Sulmona is enveloped by the hulking Apennines. Small and often overlooked by tourists, the town has pleasant public gardens, a signature candy (*confetti*), and great pride in its famous son, Roman poet Ovid. The letters "SMPE," adorning Sulmona's streets and inscribed on buildings, are shorthand for the poet's famous proclamation, *"Sulmo mihi patria est"* ("Sulmona is my homeland"). The mountains around Sulmona tempt many travelers with leisurely walks and hikes, although a day spent simply meandering the friendly city streets can be equally enjoyable.

◪ **TRANSPORTATION.** Two kilometers outside the city, the **train station** (☎0864 21 10 41) joins the Rome-Pescara and Carpione-L'Aquila-Terni lines. The way into town is long and hilly, so it's best to take **bus A** (5:30am-8pm, €0.70) from the train station to the *centro;* ask to stop at P. XX Settembre. Catch the bus back to the train station from the stop next to the public gardens. **Trains** run to: Avezzano (1½hr., 11 per day 4:47am-7:49pm, €3.50); L'Aquila (1hr., 9 per day 6:34am-8:30pm, €3.36); Naples (4hr., 4 per day 6:29am-3:26pm, €12.34); Pescara (1-1¼hr., 21 per day 5:10am-9:18pm, €3.36); and Rome (1½-2½hr., 5 per day 5:47am-5:23pm, €7-12). **ARPA** (☎0864 20 91 33) runs a **bus** to Castle di Sangro in Abruzzo National Park (1hr., 3 per day 8:10am-6:10pm, €6.55; reduced service Su). For a **taxi,** call ☎0864 317 47 in the center, or ☎0864 314 46 at the train station.

◪◪ **ORIENTATION AND PRACTICAL INFORMATION. Viale Stazione** runs from the train station to Sulmona. It town, it becomes **Viale Roosevelt** and continues past the public gardens where it becomes **Corso Ovidio,** the main street. C. Ovidio runs past **Piazza XX Settembre** and **Piazza Garibaldi,** then exits the *centro* *storico* through **Porta Napoli.** The regional tourist office, **IAT,** C. Ovidio, 208, provides free city **maps,** as well as hotel and restaurant listings. It also offers guided tours of the countryside, and sells **Club Italiano Alpino** maps for €5-7. (☎/fax 0864 532 76. Open M and W 9am-1pm and 4-8pm, Tu and F 9am-1pm.) A cheery crew mans the **UST Tourist Office,** across the street in Palazzo dell'Annunziata, providing detailed hiking information, train and bus schedules, Club Alpino Italiano maps, free city maps, and references for local mountain guides. (☎0864 21 02 16; www.comune.sulmona.aq.it. Open daily 9am-1:30pm and 4-8pm.) In case of an **emergency,** reach the **police** at ☎113. For an **ambulance,** call ☎118. Access the **Internet** at **Totoricevitora,** V. Marselli, 8, at the far side of P. Garibaldi. **Western Union** service is also available. (☎0864 21 27 14. Open M-Sa 9am-1pm and 3:30-8:30pm. €6 per hr., students €5.) The **post office** is in P. Brigata Maiella, behind P. del Carmine. (☎0864 452 637. Open M-F 8am-6:30pm, Sa 9:15am-1pm.) **Postal Code:** 67039.

█▐ ACCOMMODATIONS AND FOOD. Make reservations in summer, since this region is popular with mountain bikers and hikers. A former *palazzo*, the vine-covered **Hotel Italia ❷,** P. S. Tommasi, 3, to the right off P. XX Settembre, has rustic rooms with high ceilings, some with balconies and views of mountains as well as the dome of S. Annunziata—a good deal for the location. (☎0864 523 08. Singles €25, with bath €35; doubles €42/55. Cash only.) The recently renovated **Albergo Stella ❹,** V. Panfilo Mazara, 18/20, off C. Ovidio, features spacious, beautifully decorated rooms. All rooms have bath, phone, TV, hair dryers, and card entry. The management speaks no English but strives to accommodate all needs. Guests also have access to the new *enoteca* that connects to the hotel's restaurant. (☎0864 52 653; www.hasr.it. Breakfast included. Singles €50; doubles €70. MC/V.) Close to P. Plebiscito and the tomb of Ovid, **Bed and Breakfast "Il Giullare" ❷,** V. Spezzato, 12, offers intimate rooms at a reasonable price. (☎347 79 16 188. Breakfast included. €25 per person. Cash only.) The UST tourist office rents three **apartments ❶** in the center of town, two of which hold up to four people (€39 per night) and one that holds up to seven (€52-72 per night). Rooms include beds, microwave, sink, stove, fridge, TV, and bath. Call for info and booking. (☎0864 21 02 16.)

❚Da Gino ❸, P. Plebiscito, 12, beloved by locals, opens only for lunch. Dynamic waiters juggle the crowd gracefully, serving up simple dishes made with off-the-farm fresh ingredients. Their *risotto* dishes (€7), made with delectable pecorino cheese, are excellent (☎0864 52 289. *Primi* €7, *secondi* €8-12. Open M-Sa 12:15-2:45pm. Cash only). **Cesidio ❷,** V. Solimo, 25, has been preparing local fare at reasonable prices for 50 years. The house specialty, spicy *spaghetti al Cesidio* (€5), is pasta perfection. (☎0864 527 24. *Menù* €13. Open Tu-Su noon-3:30pm and 7-10:30pm. AmEx/MC/V.) The chic and colorful **Osteria Del Tempo Perso ❷,** Vco. del Vecchio, 7, serves splendid pizzas (€4-7) to a packed house; an impressive selection of vegetarian toppings is available. Heaping plates of *antipasti* (from €6.50) are accompanied by fresh *focaccia*. (☎0864 525 45. Open M and W-Su 12:30-3pm and 7:30pm-2am. AmEx/MC/V.) A **market** occurs every Wednesday and Saturday morning in P. Garibaldi, and a supermarket CRAI is on V. Stazione Introdaqua, just outside of town on the way to the Pelino factory. (Open daily 8am-8pm.)

SULMONA FOR POCKET CHANGE. Start the day off right, with candy for breakfast at the **Pelino factory** (free). On the way back to the center of town, buy a picnic lunch at **supermarket CRAI,** and head for the hills. Wander aimlessly, use the **bus** (€0.75) to set out for the **sanctuary of Hercules** (free). In the late afternoon, visit **Museo Nazionale, churches,** and enjoy the **sunset** over P. Garibaldi (all free).

A B R U Z Z O A N D M O L I S E

JOUST A LITTLE BIT

There's nothing like a little jousting to celebrate the heritage of a city. A few years ago, Sulmona resurrected its valiant tradition of chivalrous games, originally held in the 15th century to display the city's wealth and power.

These were not your average Hollywood style jousts, however. Instead of two knights with lances seated on charging horses, in Sulmona, the focus was on one knight at a time, and one very unlucky target chosen from the audience. Each mounted knight had three runs to hit the seated, immobile target, who was graciously allowed to wear armor, though it did little when the winning strokes were the ones to the middle of the forehead. In fact, the winning knight was the one who made the target bleed the most.

Luckily for modern-day spectators, the focus now is less on blood and more on history, culture, and skill. Knights representing the seven medieval districts now use their lances only to pierce rings. And the citizens of Sulmona have even invited their international brethren to participate: in addition to Sulmonese lords and ladies, visitors today will be able to observe Spanish horsemen, Excalibur knights, French *culverins*, and Alemanian mortar-men.

(For more info, visit the website of Sulmona's Tourist Office:
www.comune.sulmona.aq.it.)

☉ ♫ **SIGHTS AND ENTERTAINMENT.** Sulmona is overflowing with interesting museums, panoramas, hikes, and medieval churches. The Romanesque-Gothic **Cattedrale di San Panfilo** is at the end C. Ovidio, near the public gardens. Its center was built 1000 years ago on the ruins of a temple to Apollo and Vesta. From the gardens near P. XX Settembre, follow C. Ovidio to the **Chiesa di Santissima Annunziata,** with carved cherubs in high relief staring down from the facade. The 15th-century Gothic *palazzo* adjacent to the church has a very small **museum** presenting rare Sulmonese Renaissance goldwork. There is also a collection of wooden statues from local churches. (☎0864 21 02 16. Open Tu-F 9am-1pm, Sa-Su 10am-1pm and 4-7pm. €1.) In same building, the **Museo Nazionale** features intact ruins of an ancient Roman house. (Open Tu-Su 9am-1pm, 3-7pm. Free.) The colossal **Piazza Garibaldi** surrounds the Renaissance **Fontana del Vecchio,** which flows with mountain water channeled from the nearby **medieval aqueduct.** With its backdrop of towering Apennines, P. Garibaldi is a lovely sight, particularly in the early evening.

Sulmona's *confetti* candy is made at the **Pelino factory,** V. Stazione Introdaqua, 55. Turn right after the arch at the end of C. Ovidio on V. Trieste, continue 1km down the hill as it becomes V. Stazione Introdaqua, and enter the Pelino building. The Pelino family has been making *confetti* since 1783 with traditional machinery, some of which is displayed in the free **museum.** Check out the somewhat sacrilegious pictures of prior popes and Padre Pio munching on candied religious instruments. (☎0864 21 00 47. Open M-Sa 9am-12:30pm and 4-7pm.)

The last weekend of July heralds the **Giostra Cavalleresca di Sulmona,** a festival in which beacon-bearing knights ride figure-eights around P. Garibaldi. Each knight's crest represents one of the seven *borghi* (neighborhoods) of medieval Sulmona. Purchase a seated ticket from the UST, or stand on tiptoe in the crowd to watch for free. In preparation for the big event, the *borghi* host public festivals on June weekends and hang crest-flags from windows. The first weekend of July brings another joust, the **Giostra Cavalleresca di Europa,** this time featuring international knights. In October, Sulmona hosts international film and opera festivals.

🅝 **HIKING.** The mountains of **Majella National Park** (also spelled "Maiella") tower over Sulmona. The park's headquarters are in Guardiagrele (☎0871 800 713). Several trails are easily accessible by foot or **ARPA bus** from the town center; the UST tourist office has information on the capricious bus schedule. High up on the cliffs, one can visit the cave retreat of the saintly hermit who became Pope Celestine V, the only pope to renounce his post. It's a fairly easy hike (1½hr. round-trip) from the town of **Badia,** which is accessible by bus (20min., 11 per day 7:35am-7:40pm, €1; reduced service Sa-Su) from Sulmona's public gardens; purchase tickets from *tabaccherie.* Several longer routes can be reached from **Campo di Giove,** accessible by bus (25min., 4 per day 6:30am-6pm, €2.20, reduced service Sa-Su) from Sulmona. For information on hiking, consult the UST tourist office and the helpful **Club Alpino Italiano** (☎084 210 635) maps (€5-7), available from the tourist offices. Each hike is designated by a series of colored blazes placed along the trails at regular intervals. The difficulty levels in the Club Alpino Italiano guide refer to mountaineering experience, not hiking experience—so hikes of "moderate difficulty" may be challenging for those not used to mountain climbing. The beginning sections of almost all trails are manageable. **Hike 7a** is 45min. from the village of Fonte D'Amore to the ruins of a **sanctuary** dedicated to Hercules, the guardian of shepherds (or, according to old Sulmonese lore, a villa belonging to Ovid). Take the 5km hike through forested hills to Morrone to find the sacred site. The sanctuary can also be reached from Badia. These trailheads, 4km from Sulmona, are served by local buses. Schedules are available from the tourist office; when planning a hike, keep mid-afternoon service gaps in mind.

ABRUZZO NATIONAL PARK

As you arrive in Parco Nazionale d'Abruzzo (Abruzzo National Park), it is nearly impossible to tear your eyes away from the beautiful landscape. The highest peaks in the Apennines provide spectacular views of lush woodlands and crystal-clear lakes as frigid as they are pristine. Within the park, 44,000 hectares of wilderness bristle with wildlife. Grazing wild horses, white *Abruzzese* sheep-dog packs, herds of chamois, and aloof Marsicano brown bears are the current proprietors of abandoned castles and pre-Roman ruins. Avezzano is the gateway to the park, while Pescasseroli, the park's administrative center, provides the best base for exploration. And while the wild creatures and landscapes are diverse, the human inhabitants of the park are unified in their unfailing warmth and generosity.

 BABY, YOU CAN DRIVE MY CAR. Because the ARPA bus falls short of many of Abruzzo National Park's marvelous sights and quaint villages, renting a car is certainly worth it. Those with cars can request the free Guide to Abruzzo's Hidden Wonders at the park's tourist office.

■‖ ‖ TRANSPORTATION AND PRACTICAL INFORMATION

Trains run from Avezzano to Pescara (2-3hr., 7 per day 6:13am-8:10pm, €7); Rome (2hr., 13 per day 4am-8:50pm, €6); and Sulmona (1 hr., 10 per day 6:13am-8:10pm, €3.60). An **ARPA bus** (☎0863 26 561 or 0863 22 921) runs from Avezzano through the park to Castel di Sangro (2¾hr., M-Sa 5 per day 6:40am- 4:15pm, €5.20), making five stops en route: Pescasseroli (1½hr., €3.90); Opi (1¾hr., €4.20); Villetta Barrea (2hr., €4.20); Civitella Alfadena (2hr., €4.20); and Barrea (2¼hr., €4.40). Buses run to Pescasseroli from Rome (3hr., 7:45am, one-way €14).

In Avezzano, a **post office** is directly to the right of the train station exit. (Open M-F 8am-1:30pm, Sa 8:30am-12:30pm.) **Rt.com Services,** V. Montello, 1, offers **Internet** at €3 per hr. and serves as a **Western Union** point. (Open daily 10am-11pm.) In Pescasseroli, check out the **Centro Accoglienza Turistici,** Vico Consultore, 1, the national park's tourist office, and pick up the essential park **map** (€6). From the

ABRUZZO
AND MOLISE

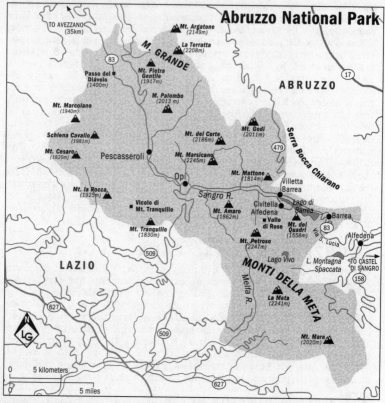

bus stop in P. Antonio, take the first left on V. della Piazza toward the center of town. (☎0863 91 13 242; www.parcoabruzzo.it. Open daily 10am-1pm, 2-6pm.) The **IAT Information Office,** V. Piave, 2, off P. Antonio, provides info on lodgings and restaurants. (☎0863 91 04 61; www.pescasseroli.net. Open daily 9am-1pm and 4-7pm.) For **police,** call ☎0863 91 07 16. For the **guardia medica,** call ☎0863 91 06 75. The **Farmacia del Parco,** P. V. Emanuele, 12, stocks everything from aloe to moleskin. (☎0863 91 07 53. Open M-F 9am-1pm and 5-8pm, Sa-Su 4-8pm.) **Punto Internet** is located on I Traversa di Fiume Sangro, off V. Principe di Napoli. (☎338 33 69 547. Open 9:30am-1pm and 2-8pm. €2.50 per 30min.) The **post office** is at V. Piave, 1/A. (☎0863 91 07 31. Open M-F 8am-1:30pm, Sa 8am-noon.) **Postal Code:** 67032.

🏠🍴 ACCOMMODATIONS AND FOOD

AVEZZANO. If there is one thing to be said about Avezzano, it's that it was beautiful once upon a time. In 1915, however, an earthquake shook the town to pieces, and today its primary aesthetic features are the *telespazio* (a satellite transmission system) and several ghastly fountains (the most offensive is in front of the train station). Beauty aside, the town is unquestionably the most convenient gateway to Abruzzo National Park. Buses to the park depart from the **bus station,** directly behind the **train station;** a *sottopassaggio* (underground passageway) connects the two. Most of Avezzano's accommodations are on the expensive side, but

Hotel Creati ❷, V. XX Settembre, 297, stands out as a budget option; the 10min. walk from the train station is worth it. Comfortable rooms all have a TV and most have a shared bath. Follow the stonewall left of the train station, turn right on V. Collelungo, then left on V. XX Settembre. (☎0863 41 33 47. Singles €18-20; doubles €32-36; triples €40-48. Cash only.) **COAL** supermarket, 304 V. XX Settembre, stocks the basics. (☎0863 41 09 09. Open M-Sa 8am-1pm and 4-8pm. AmEx/MC/V.)

PESCASSEROLI. In the middle of the park, this town is a popular place to stay. Solo travelers may have a hard time finding a single room, since most establishments offer only doubles. Inquire at the IAT office about *affittacamere* (rooms for rent). Close to the IAT office is ■ **Pensione Clemente ❷**, V. Isonzo, 1, run by the welcoming Elena. Rooms are furnished with hand-stitched quilts, each with bath and TV. From the bus stop, follow V. Piave, turn right on V. Principe di Napoli, and left on V. Isonzo. (☎0863 91 05 06. €20 per person. Cash only.) **Hotel Raffaello ❸**, V. Carmelo Sipari, 3, offers guests unparalleled comfort and elegance. Housed in a 15th-century *palazzo* once owned by the founder of the park, the rooms all have bath, TV, and minibar. (☎0863 91 28 57; www.pescasseroli.net/raffaello. Breakfast included. Singles €40; doubles €60. MC/V.) **Pensione al Castello ❹**, V. Gabriele d'Annunzio, 1, has seven pleasant rooms, all with bath and TV. (☎0863 91 07 57. Breakfast €3. Doubles €42; triples €53; quads €64. MC/V.) The best camping option is **Campeggio dell'Orso ❶**. One kilometer from Pescasseroli on the road to Opi, these quiet grounds are a choice spot. Call ahead to reserve. (☎0863 91 95 or 339 76 43 656. €9 per adult, ages 5-10 €5.)

For picnic supplies, look to the many *alimentari* and produce shops in the town center. The **alimentari** on V. Principe di Napoli makes fresh *panini* for €2.50 and under. (Open M-Sa 8am-1pm and 3pm-8pm.) **Pasticceria Alpina ❶**, Traversa Sangro, 6, serves an array of award-winning sweets. (☎0863 91 05 61. Open Tu-Su 7am-10pm. Cash only.) Pescasseroli's restaurants close early, so expect to eat early. For traditional fare, head to **Ristorante Vecchie Arcate ❸**, at V. della Chiesa, 57. Chefs prepare delicious *carrati* (€6.50), the Abruzzese take on *gnocchi*, with vegetables and cheese. (☎0863 91 06 18. *Primi* €5-7, *secondi* €7-10. Cover €2. Open June-Sept. and Dec.-Apr. Tu-Su noon-3pm and 7:30-10pm. AmEx/MC/V.) For a delicious slice of pizza (from €0.80), a filling *panini* (from €2), or an Italian hamburger (€2.50), **Pizzeria Saltarelli ❶**, with the green- and white-striped awning on V. Principe di Napoli, is the place to go. (Open daily 11am-10pm. Cash only.)

■**OPI.** ARPA buses follow the park road to the village of Opi, named for the pagan goddess of abundance whose temple rested here in ancient times. A drive through Opi gives travelers glimpses of wild horses and access to some of the main hiking trails. To find more information about the lodgings listed here as well as others in Opi, consult www.opionline.it. Both accommodations listed here can be reached at info@opionline.it. **La Sosta ❷**, V. Nazionale, 17, is a spotless and comfortable six-room B&B .5km past Opi on the park's bus route. Owners Incoronata and Elio welcome guests with homemade breakfast. A fantastic backyard terrace provides peace and quiet, while balconies in every room offer mountain views. All rooms have bath, and some have TVs. (☎0863 91 60 57; www.opionline.it. Breakfast included. €20-25 per person. Cash only.) **Vecchio Mulino ❶**, occupies a peaceful spot 2km past the village on the bus route. This campground, owned by friendly Bostonian Paolo, has a restaurant, bar, and access to trails. (☎0863 91 22 32; ilvecchiomulino@tiscalinet.it. €5.50-6 per person, €5.50 per tent. AmEx/MC/V.)

CIVITELLA ALFEDENA. This tiny medieval village overlooks the icy Lago di Barrea from the top of a small mountain. Approaching the town, the ARPA bus passes the entrance to **Camping Wolf ❶**, with partially wooded and terraced sites. (☎0864 89 03 60. €4.39 per person, €4.65 per large tent. Cash only.) In the historical center, **Alberghetto La Torre ❹** and **Albergo Antico Borgo ❹**, V. Castello, 3, both owned by friendly and English-speaking Antonio, offer rooms with bath, TV, phone, and beautiful views of the Sentiere delle Valdirose mountains. Parking lot and garden are across the street. (☎0864 89 01 21; www.albergolatorre.com. Breakfast included. Singles €30-45; doubles €40-55; half pension €35-45 per person, includes dinner. Cash only.) The **Museo del Lupo**, on the left when entering town, documents the history of the Apennine wolf and lynx. Though not as thrilling as an actual wildlife encounter, it's likely your only opportunity to see the creatures. (☎0864 89 01 41. Open daily 10am-1pm and 2-6pm; closed M in winter. €3.)

 NOT TO BE CONFUSED WITH . . . Keep in mind that Civitella Alfedena and Alfedena are two different locations separated by 10km. Before setting out from Pescasseroli, verify with the bus driver the correct stop for your intended destination.

HIKING

The ascent from Avezzano to Pescasseroli is breathtaking; this trail, which marks the beginning of the park, passes by fields of poppies, dazzling valleys, and rocky outcrops. The indispensable trail map (€6) from the **Pescasseroli Centro Accoglienza Turistici**, indicates prime viewing spots for brown bears, deer, wolves, and eagles. If the park's creatures prove elusive, there's always Pescasseroli's **Centro di Visita**, Viale Colle dell'Orso, 2, off V. S. Lucia heading toward Opi, which has a museum and a small zoo. (☎0863 91 131. Open daily 10am-1pm and 3-7pm. €5.) The trails are arranged such that all paths beginning with the same letter start from the same point. For a short hike, take trail **B1** to the castle ruins at Monte Ceraso (50min. round-trip). Easier options are **F2** and **G5**. F2 begins in Grotta Fondillo, accessible from the highway between Opi and Villetta Barrea, and ends at **Il Passagio dell'Orso** (Passage of the Bear). G5 begins just to the east of Villetta Barrea from the main highway, and ends at Cascate, an optimal place for viewing the chaimois (hooved, goat-like animals with horns). To really stretch those legs, tackle the beautiful 5hr. round-trip hike on trail **C3** to **Vicolo di Monte Tranquillo** (Tranquil Mountain Pass, 1673m). The trail starts at the southern end of town and leads up through the green Valle Mancina, past the Rifugio Della Difesa station. The climb to the pass is lined by forests of graceful birch trees and boasts mighty views of the mountain peaks to the north. Trail **C5**, which intersects trail C3, weaves along the ridges. True adventurers can take on one of the park's highest peaks, **Monte Marsicano** (2245m), with the steep and arduous trail **E6** from Opi (7-8hr. round-trip). Clever coordination of hikes with the ARPA bus schedule can enable travelers to venture farther afield. From Civitella Alfedena, take trail **I1** to **K6** through the beautiful **Valle di Rose** to see the park's largest herd of chamois. K6 is one of the more difficult trails. From mid-July to early September, this area can only be explored with a guide (€7 per person). Go to an *ufficio di zona* the day before a planned excursion for more information about the trails or to obtain a permit and reserve a guide. From Barrea, 20km from Pescasseroli, trail **K5** runs to the **Lago Vivo** (5hr. round-trip), which dries up between June and October.

Ecotur, V. Piave, 7, 2nd fl., in Pescasseroli, offers organized excursions. They also rent **mountain bikes**. (☎0863 91 27 60; www.ecotur.org. Open daily 9am-1pm and 3:30-7pm.) Several paths, including trail C3, are great for biking. During winter, this area offers excellent skiing, with challenging slopes and heavy snowfall. Package deals called *settimane bianche* (white weeks) provide accommodations, lift tickets, and half pension. For ticket info, call **Gestione Impianti Sportivi Pescasseroli**, ☎0863 91 11 18. For the snow bulletin, call ☎0862 66 510. Pescasseroli's website, www.pescasseroli.net, also has information on winter sports.

PESCARA   ☎ 085

The central transportation hub for Abruzzo and Molise, Pescara holds little in the way of aesthetic appeal but offers exciting nightlife in the summer and great shopping year-round. Italian vacationers swarm on its 20km shoreline in July and August and leave its lackluster buildings deserted during the rest of the year. Even so, travelers waiting for a train or boat to Croatia can manage to find something worthwhile besides the beach. In the old city, several museums and traditional restaurants deftly showcase the best of local culture. Mid-July brings the city's celebrated jazz festival, which attracts internationally known musicians—recent years have brought the likes of Chic Corea, Tony Bennett, and Bobby McFerrin.

🖪🖊 TRANSPORTATION AND PRACTICAL INFORMATION. Domestic and international **flights** leave from **Aeroporto d'Abruzzo** (☎ 085 43 24 21). Bus #38 (€0.70) runs between the train station and the airport. **Trains** run from Stazione Centrale on C. V. Emanuele to: Bari (3½-4hr., 17 per day 1am-8:08pm, €13-28); Lecce (6hr., 12 per day 3am-8:08pm, €19-34); Milan (6½hr., 11 per day 12:44am-11:59pm, €37-42.25); Naples (5-7hr., 11 per day 3:32am-8:08pm, €14.31-34.54); Rome (4hr., 11 per day 6:15am-10:12pm, €11.21); Sulmona (1hr., 18 per day 5:13am-10:12pm, €3.60); and Termoli (1½hr., 23 per day 3am-9pm, €6.15). **ARPA buses** run from the train station. Buses to L'Aquila, Avezzano, Rome, and Sulmona run on varying schedules. Consult the info booth in front of the train station for departure times. **Ferries** depart from beyond the harbor in the old city. **SNAV** (☎ 071 20 76 116; www.snavoli.it) runs ferries June to September to the Croatian islands of Hvar, Brac, Korcula, and Spalato. Call for times (one-way €64-84). **Jetline** (☎ 085 45 16 241) runs ferries to the Tremiti Islands (2½hr., 8am, €20.50).

Buses and trains stop at **Stazione Centrale** in the center of the new city, on the main street, **Corso Vittorio Emanuele.** To the right, C. V. Emanuele extends toward the **River Pescara.** Across the bridge to the right is the old city, and a short walk to the left leads to the **tourist harbor.** Straight across the bridge is the extensive public park. The main stretch of beach runs parallel to C. V. Emanuele, a few blocks straight out of the train station. To reach the **APT Tourist Office,** turn right in front of the train station on C. V. Emanuele; it will be the first establishment on the right. (☎ 085 42 90 01; www.abruzzoturismo.it. Open M-F 10am-1pm.) The English-speaking staff provides a good **map** and advice on accommodations, museums, hiking, and restaurants. For **police,** dial ☎ 113; the station is at P. Duca d'Aosta. Inquire for locations of **Internet** points. The **post office** is on C. V. Emanuele between the station and the river. (☎ 085 47 07 101. Open M-Sa 8am-6:30pm.) **Postal Code:** 65100.

🖬🖪 ACCOMMODATIONS AND FOOD. The best budget lodgings are off C. V. Emanuele, across from the train station. Beachfront hotels aren't worth the prices—the only views are of Pescara's beach-umbrella forest, and the train station isn't that far from the beach. At ☒ **Hotel Marisa ❸,** V. R. Margherita, 39, closest to the public beach, Silvio and his family welcome guests with social breakfasts. Rooms are spacious, some with couches, all with TV, phone, and bath. Follow C. Umberto from the station and turn left on V. Fabrizi, which becomes V. R. Margherita. (☎ 085 27 345; hotelmarisa@virgilio.it. Singles €35; doubles €60. Cash only.) **Hotel Adria ❸,** V. Firenze, 141, is a pleasant option; turn right on the street parallel to C. V. Emanuele, one block toward the waterfront. Thirty modestly sized rooms come with fridge, bath, and TV. (☎ 085 42 24 246; fax 085 42 22 427. Singles €40; doubles €70. MC/V.) **Hotel Alba ❹,** V. M. Forti, 14, has more spacious rooms, some with A/C, TV, phone, and bath. (☎ 085 38 91 45; www.hotelalba.pescara.it. Breakfast and parking included. Singles €50-65; doubles €60-100. AmEx/MC/V.)

Food of choice in Pescara falls into two categories: seafood and traditional Abruzzese cuisine. The local wines, including the white *Trebbiano* and red *Montepulciano*, satisfy broad tastes. The best seafood options are along the water. On summer weekends, reservations are essential. Excellent seafood can also be found at ▧ **Wine and Wine ❷**, V. Chieti, 14, right off C. V. Emanuele toward the river, a relaxed family-run establishment that also specializes in wine. There is never a menu, only what is freshest from the market. (☎085 42 23 180; winewine_ilgabbiano@hotmail.com. Open daily 1-3pm and 8-10pm.) **Jambo ❸**, Vle. Rivera, 38, features elegant patio dining, a colorful bar, and an excellent waitstaff. The *gnocchi agli scampi* (€9) has seafood fans rejoicing. (☎085 42 12 79 49. Open daily 8am-3am. AmEx/MC/V.) The popular **La Cantina di Jozz ❷**, V. delle Caserme, 63, offers outdoor seating across from the museum in the old city, one of the most happening nightlife areas. Patrons linger over plates of *pesce fritto* (€4.50) late in the evening. (☎085 4 51 88 00. Open Tu-Sa noon-3pm and 8pm-midnight, Su noon-3pm. AmEx/MC/V.) For picnic supplies, head to **Le Tigre** supermarket at V. N. Fabrizi, 59, where a range of foodstuffs are available for cheap. Follow directions for Hotel Marisa. (☎085 42 16 896. Open M-Sa 8:15am-7:45pm.)

◨ ▣ SIGHTS AND ENTERTAINMENT. All the attractions of a seaside resort and shoreline town crowd Pescara's vibrant **beach:** basketball, soccer, volleyball, music, windsurfing, and miles of sunbathing. Almost all of the shoreline is private; admission costs €5-7 depending on location. A paltry public stretch is 5min. left of P. I. Maggio when facing the sea. Pescara's cultural area is on the other side of the river, with a couple of decent museums and a pleasant harbor. Cross the bridge and take the first right to reach the **Museo delle Genti d'Abruzzo**, V. delle Caserme, 24, which celebrates 4000 years of Abruzzo's history. Chronological galleries show the development of local crafts from Paleolithic times to the present. (☎085 45 10 026. Open Sept.-June M-Sa 9am-1pm, and Tu, Th, Su 4-7pm; July-Aug. M-F 9am-1pm, and Tu-Su 7-11pm. €5, EU students and citizens under 18 or over 65 €2.) Straight across the bridge, the **Museo Civico**, V. Marconi, 45, celebrates the remarkable artwork of six members of the influential Cascella family. (☎085 428 35 15. Open Tu and Th-Su 9am-1pm, and Tu and Th and 4-6pm. €2.50, EU citizens 18-24 €1.50, EU citizens under 18 or over 65 free.) For nightlife, pick up the monthly brochure *Giorno e Notte*, available at restaurants and stores around the city. Pescaresi prefer a stroll down the streets around V. Caserme or along the beach.

Pescara hosts a world-renown annual **jazz festival** in mid-July, attracting Italian and international acts. (☎085 29 220; www.pescarajazz.com. Tickets €10-25.) The popular annual **film festival,** also in July, screens both Italian and international films in several of Pescara's cinemas. Contact the APT tourist office for more information. (☎085 42 90 01; www.abruzzoturismo.it. Tickets €10 and up.)

TERMOLI   ☎0875

Despite its pristine coastline and quaint streets, Termoli is less visited than other coastal towns. Most travelers come through on the way to the Tremiti Islands. The **FS train station** lies at the western end of town. Trains run to Bari (14 per day 4:01am-9:04pm, €13-21); Milan (11 per day 2:27am-12:06am, €40); Naples (1 per day 11:24am, €12.34); Pescara (22 per day 12:06am-11:55pm, €4.40-9.15); and Rome (2 per day 6:52am-5:46pm, €17.45-34.23). Across the street, **Corso M. Milano** extends to **Lungomare Colombo,** a waterfront strip lined with hotels. Restaurants and shops line **Corso Umberto** from the station to the old town. To get to the **port,** walk down C. Milano and turn right on Lungomare Colombo. The ferry docks and ticket offices are on the breakwater past the fishing boats. The **tourist office, Azienda Autonoma di Soggiorno e Turismo,** is at the back of P. Bega. The friendly staff offers **maps**, directories, and brochures on Termoli's lesser known attractions.

From the station, turn right on C. Umberto I. At the galleria, walk through the underpass and to the right to the back of the building. Buzz the office to take *Scala A* (stairway A) to the 2nd floor. Ring again to enter the office. (☎0875 70 39 13; aasttermoli@virgilio.it. Open M and W 8am-2pm and 3-6:30pm, Tu, Th, and F 8am-2pm and 4:50-6:30pm, Sa 8am-1:10pm.) For **Internet,** try **Digipl@net,** C. M. Milano, 24.(☎0875 71 44 36. Open M-F and Su 4:30-9pm. €3 per hr.)

Travelers have several options for accommodations and food. The best is **Pensione Villa Ida ❸,** C. M. Milano, 27, between the station and the beach. Its 23 generously sized rooms have A/C, bath, TV, and phone. (☎0875 70 66 66; www.pensionevillaida.it. Breakfast included. Singles from €44; doubles €65. AmEx/MC/V.) **Hotel Rosary ❹,** Lungomare Colombo, 24, at the intersection with C. M. Milano, is a short walk from the station and the beach. All rooms have bath and TV. (☎0875 84 944. Open Apr.-Oct. Doubles €57; triples €75; quads €95. AmEx/MC/V.) For groceries, go to **Sisa Supermercato,** V. Adriatica, 5, right off C. M. Milano. (☎0875 70 72 53. Open M-Sa 7:30am-12:45pm, 5-9pm. MC/V.) From the train station, follow C. Umberto I, turn left on C. Nazionale, right on V. Alfano, then left on V. Ruffino for **La Sacrestia ❶,** V. Ruffini, 48. Divine pizzas (€3-6) served steaming from the oven. (☎0875 70 56 03. Open daily noon-2pm and 7:30-11pm. MC/V.) **Lineapane ❶,** C. M. Milano, 18, is the perfect place to pick up quality baked goods. The locally famous *cancellate* (€0.50), flat iron-cooked cookies, are a sure bet. (Open M-Sa 7am-1:15pm and 4:30-9pm, July-Aug. Su 7am-1pm. Cash only.)

TREMITI ISLANDS ☎0882

Covered with lush vegetation and rich in natural resources, the Tremiti Islands are a relatively well-kept secret. San Domino, the largest in the archipelago, is dubbed the "Green Pearl of the Adriatic" because of its complex flora. Its neighbor, San Nicola, the only island populated year-round, was most famously home to Emperor Augustus's daughter Julia, exiled there for her naughty behavior. When summer hits, the four islands swell with Italian daytrippers, but after the evening ferries depart they become peaceful and relaxing retreats. Just 35km from the Gargano Peninsula on the mainland, *Isole Tremiti* make a fun daytrip—each can be crossed on foot in less than 2hr.—or a base for more prolonged exploration.

⌐ TRANSPORTATION. Ferry service from Termoli operates June-Sept. **Hydrofoils** make the trip in 1hr., ferries in 1½hr. Several companies serve the islands: the popular **M/N Venere** (☎0875 70 51 98; www.adriaticshippinglines.it; 1 per day 8:40am, return 6:40pm; €7.50-8.50); **Navigazione Libera** (☎0875 70 48 59; www.navlib.it; daily June 10-Sept. 9 8:40, 9:15, 10:55am, 5:20pm; return 9:45am, 4:10, 5:30, 6:40pm); and **Adriatica** ferries (☎0875 70 235; M-Th 8:40am, return 4pm; F-Su 9:35am, return 4, 7pm). Ferries dock on San Nicola, forcing passengers to take small motorboats to the dock (€1.50). Only the hydrofoils dock directly at San Domino.

⚡🔟 ORIENTATION AND PRACTICAL INFORMATION. There are four Tremiti islands: **San Domino, San Nicola, Capraia,** and **Pianosa.** San Domino is the largest, with the archipelago's only hotels, while San Nicola is home to an 11th-century abbey. The last two are small and desolate, hospitable to seagulls but not much else. **Motorboats** (€1.50) run throughout the day between San Nicola and San Domino. For **carabinieri** on both islands, call ☎112. A 24hr. **first aid station** (☎0882 46 32 34) is at the port in San Domino, the 2nd building on the left when heading uphill on the main road. A **pharmacy** is in the village on San Domino (☎0882 46 33 27. Open daily June-Sept. 9am-1pm and 5-9pm; Oct.-May 9:30am-12:30pm and 5-7:30pm.) **Post offices** are on San Domino (☎0882 46 32 59) and San Nicola (☎0882 46 30 21). Postal service is spotty at best.

ACCOMMODATIONS AND FOOD. San Domino hosts the islands' only hotels, most of which offer doubles, require half or full pension, and raise prices in July and August. True budget accommodations are nonexistent. Reservations are a good idea in summer, as the few rooms fill up quickly. **Albergo Rossana ❸**, just up the hill from the port on San Domino, has six simple but spacious rooms, all with double bed, bath, and A/C. (☎0882 46 32 98. Breakfast included. €25-34 per person. Prices peak at €57 in Aug. MC/V.) At the top of the hill on San Domino, **Pensione Carluccetta ❹**, V. Aldo Moro, offers five rooms, all with A/C and TV. Half pension required. (☎0882 46 32 64. €50 per person; July-Aug. €62-65 per person. Cash only.) Popular **Villagio International ❸**, up the hill and to the right from the port, on Punta del Diamante, is in a quiet area near the shore. There are two housing options: bungalows and pre-fabricated hut/tent hybrids. (☎0882 46 34 05. www.puntadeldiamante.it. Pre-fab units €30-36 per person, required half pension in Aug. €58. Bungalows €46-54 per person, required half pension in Aug. €78. MC/V.) **Ristorante Al Faro ❸**, V. Aldo Moro, in the village on San Domino, serves a short but excellent menu of local seafood dishes. (☎0882 46 34 24. Open daily noon-3pm and 8-10pm. *Primi* €6-8; *secondi* €10-14.) At **Ristorante Bel Mare ❷**, San Domino Marina, 1, the only restaurant on the beach of San Domino, customers choose their favorite seafood dishes from a large self-service table. (☎339 68 74 457. *Primi* €6, *secondi* €8. Open daily in summer 9am-6pm.)

OUTDOOR ACTIVITIES AND SIGHTS. Paths snake through the thick **pine forest** on San Domino. Many lead down to the small rocky coves along the coast, where vacationers swim in sapphire waters in secluded spots, *sans* suits. Some Italians take to the seas with **spear guns** for fishing adventures, while others are content to contemplate marine life more peacefully while **snorkeling**. The **Marlin Club**, up the hill and to the left (☎0882 46 37 65; www.marlintremiti.it), affiliated with Hotel Eden, offers **scuba diving instruction** at many experience levels, for €70 with equipment and guide. **M.G.M.**, in the colorful kiosk farthest left on the port, offers two tours of the archipelago's natural caves, both in a glass-bottomed boat; the long tour (€13) includes all of the islands while the shorter tour (€9) covers only San Nicola and San Domino (☎368 70 00 341 or 333 58 32 718.) The fortified **Abbazia e Chiesa di Santa Maria** (Abbey of Santa Maria) has crowned the cliffs of neighboring island San Nicola since the 11th century. The dreary structure might be more interesting for its historical value than its architecture. Emperor Augustus's adulterous daughter Julia was banished here in the 1st century and in the early 20th century so were victims of the Fascist regime's purges. The monastery is accessible by a short path from the harbor or by an elevator (€1). **Alidaunia's** 15min. helicopter tours are a quick way to see the islands, though they miss much of the beautiful scenery found in local caves. (☎088 16 17 961 or 16 10 267. Depart from Termoli 8:45am and 4pm. €22.) One of the islands' only clubs, **Discoteca Diomede**, P. Sandro Pertini, 1, San Domino, has a huge dance floor and attractive green and white decor. Though entrance is free, there is an obligatory drink; try Cuba Libera for €4.50. (☎0882 46 34 03. Open daily 8am-3am.)

GOT ACQUA? Buying water in Abbazia di Santa Maria is expensive; plan ahead and buy water from the *alimentari* in the village on San Domino.

CAMPANIA

Sprung from the shadow of Mt. Vesuvius, Campania thrives in defiance of natural disasters. The submerged city at Baia, ash-smothered Pompeii, and ruins of Cumae attest to a land resigned to harsh natural outbursts. While the thriving city of Naples and the beaches of the Amalfi Coast continue to reel in tourists, Campania remains one of Italy's poorest regions and is often looked down on by the prosperous North. But despite catastrophes, centuries of foreign invasion, and blistering summers heat, the people of Campania have cultivated a unique attitude towards life, which, in the end, is the region's true treasure.

HIGHLIGHTS OF CAMPANIA

DESCEND underneath the city of **Naples** to tour **catacombs** and **aqueducts** (p. 569).

PEER into the crater **Mt. Vesuvius,** mainland Europe's only active volcano (p. 578).

RECOVER from all your ailments at **Ischia's** therapeutic **hot springs** (p. 590).

SIP a *granita* or *limoncello* in the shade of **Amalfi's lemon groves** (p. 597).

NAPLES (NAPOLI)   ☎081

Italy's 3rd-largest city is Southern Italy at its best. From zipping Vespas to bustling throngs, Naples moves a million miles per minute. Neapolitans spend every waking moment out on the town, eating, drinking, shouting, laughing, and enjoying themselves. Surrounded by the ancient ruins of Pompeii and the gorgeous Amalfi Coast, Naples is the anchor of Campania, full of excitement and energy. Despite its reputation as a city of crime and grime, Naples is one of Europe's greatest cities: recently, UNESCO declared Naples's historical center the most architecturally varied in the world, an honor the city's world-renowned treasure trove of *piazze*, palaces, and exquisite churches well deserves. The birthplace of pizza and the modern-day home of tantalizing seafood and pasta, Naples will please even the pickiest of gourmands. Once you get used to the heartbeat of Naples, everywhere else seems just a bit boring in comparison.

✈ INTERCITY TRANSPORTATION

Flights: Aeroporto Capodichino, V. Umberto Maddalena (☎848 88 87 77 or info line 081 78 96 259; www.gesac.it), northeast of the city. The convenient **Alibus** travels between the port near P. Municipio, P. Garibaldi near the McDonald's (Stazione Centrale), and the airport (15-20min., 6am-11:30pm, €3). The **3S** city bus also runs from P. Municipio and P. Garibaldi (Stazione Centrale) to the airport (€1). Buy ticket at any *tabbacheria*. Although cheaper than the Alibus, the city bus makes many more stops and is a target for pickpockets. A **taxi** from P. Municipio costs €19. Taxis to and from the airport have set prices, depending on your desired location. The taxi driver should not turn on the meter, and there should be no supplementary fees or charges. **Alitalia,** (☎081 75 11 494), **British Airways** (☎199 71 22 66), **Lufthansa** (☎199 40 00 44), **Easy Jet** (☎848 88 77 66) all fly from Naples.

Trains: Naples is served by 3 train companies from **Stazione Centrale** in P. Garibaldi. (www.napolipiazzagaribaldi.it).

   FS: ☎081 56 72 430. Ticket offices open daily 6:10am-9:40pm. To: **Brindisi** (5hr., 5 per day 6am-6pm, €17); **Milan** (9hr., 13 per day 4:30am-10:30pm, €50); **Rome** (2hr., 40 per day 4:30am-

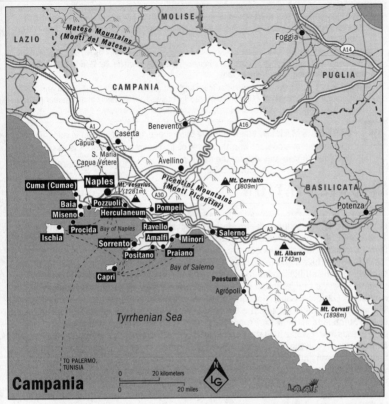

Campania

10pm, €10); **Salerno** (45min., 37per day 4:50am-10:30pm, €3); **Siracusa** (10hr., 6 per day 8am-10pm, €40).

Circumvesuviana: ☎081 77 22 11 11; www.vesuviana.it. To: **Herculaneum** (€1.70); **Pompeii** (€2.30); **Sorrento** (€3.10). Trains depart every 30min. 5:09am-10:42pm.

Ferrovia Cumana and **Ferrovia Circumflegrea:** ☎800 00 16 16; www.sepsa.it. Luggage storage available (see **Practical Information,** p. 562). Trains from Montesanto station to **Cumae** and **Puzzuoli.** Trains depart every 20min. Info booth in Stazione Centrale open daily 7am-9pm.

Ferries: The daily newspaper *Il Mattino* (€0.80) carries up-to-date ferry schedules. Port taxes may apply. Hydrofoils depart from **Mergellina, Molo Beverello, Pozzuoli,** and and ferries from **Stazione Marittima** (on **Molo Angioino**) and **Molo Beverello.** Molo Angioino is for longer trips to **Sicily** and **Sardinia.** Molo Beverello is at the base of P. Municipio. Take the R2, the 152, the 3S or the Alibus from P. Garibaldi to P. Municipio.

Alilauro: ☎081 55 13 352 or 081 55 22 838. Ticket office at Molo Angioino. Depart from Molo Beverello. Open daily 9am-7pm. Ferries to **Ischia** (8 per day 7:35am-8pm, €10-20).

Caremar: ☎081 55 13 882. Ticket office on Molo Beverello. Open daily 6am-10pm. Ferries and hydrofoils to: **Capri** (ferry: 1½hr., 3 per day 7:35am-6:40pm, €4.80; hydrofoil: 1hr., 4 per day 5:40am-9:10pm, €9.60); **Ischia** (ferry: 1½hr., 8 per day 6:25am-9:55pm, €4.80; hydrofoil: 1hr., 5 per day 7:50am-6:55pm, €9.60); **Procida** (ferry: 1hr., 5 per day 6:25am-7:20pm, €4.80; hydrofoil: 40min., 5 per day 7:40am-5:55pm, €7.90).

Metro del Mare: ☎199 60 07 00; www.metrodelmare.com. Ticket office at Molo Beverello and Mergellina. Recently created addition to Naples' public transportation system. Up to 6 lines connect Naples to Sorrento, Capri, Monte di Procida and the areas between.

SNAV: ☎081 42 85 555. Open daily 9am-7pm. Hydrofoils Apr.-Oct. to: **Capri** (1hr., 6 per day 7:10am-6:10pm, €10); **Ischia-Casamicciola Terme** (1hr., 4 per day 8:20am-6:45pm, €10); **Procida** (40min., 4 per day 8:20am-6:40pm, €10); and ferries to **Palermo** (10hr., 8pm, €27) from Stazione Marittima.

Siremar: ☎081 58 00 340. Ticket office at Molo Angioino. Open daily 9am-7pm. Depart from Stazione Marittima. 2 ferries per week in summer; 3 per week in winter. To: **Lipari** (12hr.); **Stromboli** (8hr.); **Vulcano** (13hr.). Prices vary.

Tirrenia: ☎199 12 31 99. Ticket office at Molo Angioino. Open daily 8:30am-1:15pm and 2:30-5:30pm. Ferries to **Cagliari** (16hr., depart weekly, bi-weekly in summer) and **Palermo** (11hr., depart daily). Required supplemental port tax. Schedules and prices vary.

 STREET SMARTS. When crossing busy streets in Naples, keep in mind that if you make eye contact with the driver of an oncoming vehicle, it is assumed that you will stop and wait for the car to pass.

ORIENTATION

Think of central Naples as divided into four areas: **Stazione Centrale, waterfront** (from P. del Mercato to Mergellina), **centro storico (Spaccanapoli)**, and **Plebiscito** (including V. Toldeo and the Spanish Quarter). Stazione Centrale sits prominently at the head of **Piazza Garibaldi**, directly opposite the statue of Garibaldi. Although sometimes a gridlocked mess of buses and *motorini*, the Stazione Centrale district is worth exploring to check out the ethnic food markets and to hone your bargaining skills with the street vendors. Several budget lodgings lie nearby, but the area is fairly seedy, so exercise caution. P. Garibaldi is also the central hub for the many bus lines that service Naples. The waterfront district spans the entire length of Naples from P. del Mercato in the east to Mergellina in the west. From P. Garibaldi, take a left on **Corso Garibaldi** and walk until it ends at the water in **Piazza Guglielmo Pepe**. With the water on your left, **Via Nuova Marina** stretches all the way to **Piazza Plebiscito**, passing through **Piazza del Mercato**, and near **Piazza Bovio** and **Piazza Municipio** (the end of the R2 bus line) along the way. The waterfront district is full of little restaurants and shops tucked away on tiny side streets. Mergellina is accessible by Metro line #2. **Via Toledo**, a chic pedestrian shopping street, links the waterfront to the Plebiscito district and the **Spanish Quarter**. The well-to-do hang around P. Plebiscito and shop at the **Galleria Umberto,** and the narrow streets of the Spanish Quarter are a prime place to watch loud neighbors shout to each other from their balconies. **Piazza Dante** and **Piazza Carità**, along V. Toledo, lie on the western extreme of the *centro storico* (Spaccanapoli). Walking away from the waterfront, a right at any of these will lead to the winding roads of the beautiful historical district. A right off V. Toledo on **Via Maddaloni** leads through the central *piazze* of the historical district, **Piazza Gesù Nuovo** and **Piazza San Domenico Maggiore;** shortly after, the street intersects **Via Duomo**, after which a right and then a left leads to P. Garibaldi.

 Although violent crime is rare in Naples, theft is common. For the love of San Gennaro, be smart. Don't carry money in wallets or purses. Don't wear flashy jewelry or flaunt a camera. Women should travel in groups when possible and avoid eye contact with strangers. When choosing accommodations, always ask to see a room before committing, and never stay anywhere that feels unsafe. The city has many excellent hostels and hotels, but many awful ones, too.

LOCAL TRANSPORTATION

One "UnicoNapoli" (☎081 55 13 109; www.napolipass.it) ticket is valid for all modes of transportation in Naples: **bus, Metro, train,** and **funicular.** Tickets are available at *tabaccherie* in three types: 1½hr. (€1), full-day (€3), and weekend

CAMPANIA

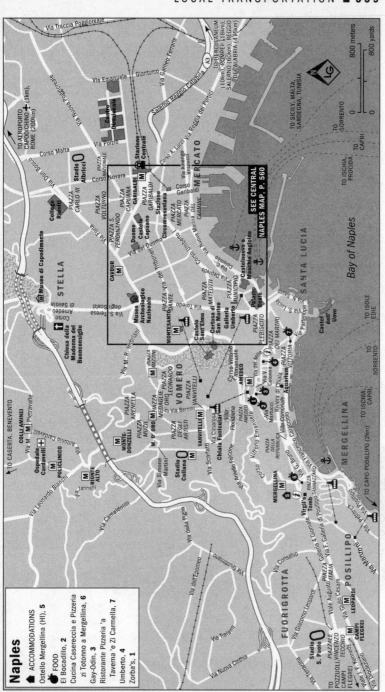

Naples

ACCOMMODATIONS
Ostello Mergellina (HI), **5**

FOOD
El Bocadillo, **2**
Cucina Casereccia e Pizzeria
zi Totonno a Mergellina, **6**
Gay-Odin, **3**
Ristorante Pizzeria 'a
Taverna 'e Zi Carmella, **7**
Umberto's, **4**
Zorba's, **1**

SEE CENTRAL
NAPLES MAP, P. 560

CAMPANIA

TO MUSEO CAPODIMONTE (1km)

Via Santa Teresa degli Scalzi

PIAZZA CAVOUR

CAVOUR

Via Luigi

Via Matteo Imbriani

Via Salvator Rosa

Museo Archeologico Nazionale

Via Forìa

Via d. Anticagi

Vico Gigante

Via Francesco Saverio Correra

Via S. Tomassi

PIAZZA MUSEO NAZIONALE

Via Santa Maria Costantinopoli

Viale C. de Crecchio

Via Pisanelli

S. PAOLO Maggiore

Salita Pontecorvo

Via d. Sapienza

Via Atri

Via Paolo

5

Napoli PIAZZA
Sotterranea SAN GAETANO

6

Via E. Pessina

Via Bellini

PIAZZA BELLINI

PIAZZA MIRAGLIA

SPACCANAPOLI

Salita Tarsia

7

Via S. Pietro a Maiella

9

Cappella San Severo

Via Ventaglieri

PIAZZA DANTE

S. Domenico Maggiore

Via S. D. Maggiore P. NILO

Via San Biagio de

MONTESANTO

Via Montesanto

Supero

Via S. Sebastiano

14 13

16

PIAZZA S. ANGELO

PIAZZA SAN DOMENICO MAGGIORE

MONTESANTO

V. Porta Medina

Stazione Cumana

PIAZZA PIGNASECCA

S. Spirito

Via Toledo

Via Capitelli

Chiesa di Gesù Nuovo

Via Benedetto Croce

Mouse Club

Universal Books

Via Mezzocannone

University

Via A. Tar

PIAZZA GESÙ NUOVO

17

S. Chiara

Via Santa Chiara

Via Pignatelli

TO VOMERO (500m)

Via P. Scura

V. S. Liborio

V. Monteoliveto
V. Oliveto

18

19

PIAZZA MONTEOLIVETO

Chiesa di Monteoliveto Sant'Anna dei Lombardi

P. S. Maria La Nova

Via Sedile di Portome

V. Porta di Mass

Via Francesco Girardi

PIAZZA CARITÀ

Via C. Battisti

Via G. Oberdan

PIAZZA MATTEOTTI

PIAZZA BOVIO

Via G. Sanfelice

TO CERTOSA DI SAN MARTINO and CASTEL SANT'ELMO (200m)

PIAZZA SAN SEPOLCRO

Corso Vittorio Emanuele

Vco. Giardinetto

Via Toledo

20

Via A. Diaz

Rua Catalana

Via Campodisola

Via Cristoforo Colombo

Vco. San Sepulcro
Via Portacarrese

Feltrinelli

Via San Tommaso d'Aquino

Via P. di Tappia

Via Cervantes

Via Medina

Via S. Bartolomeo

Via A. de Gasperi

SPANISH QUARTER

22

Via De Pretis

Via Merisago

23

24

TO VOMERO (500m)

Palazzo Municipio

Via P. E. Imbriani

PIAZZA MUNICIPIO

25

Via San Mattia

Salita S. A. di Palazzo

Via Santa Brigida

Via G. Verdi

Via Vittorio Emanuele III

Castelnuovo o Maschio Angioino

Molo Beverello

Via Santa Caterina Da Sien

Via Giovanni Nicotera

Funicular to Vomero

Galleria Umberto

26

Via San Carlo

S. Fernando

27

Teatro San Carlo

Via San Carlo

PIAZZA TRIESTE E TRENTO

Via Ferdinando Acton

Molo Beverello

Via Chiaia

Entrance
Palazzo Reale

Via Parco D. Castello

TO MERGELLINA, VILLA COMUNALE (350m), U.S. CONSULATE (1km)

Via Eglìaca a Forcella

PIAZZA PLEBISCITO

S. Francesco di Paola

CAMPANIA

N

LG

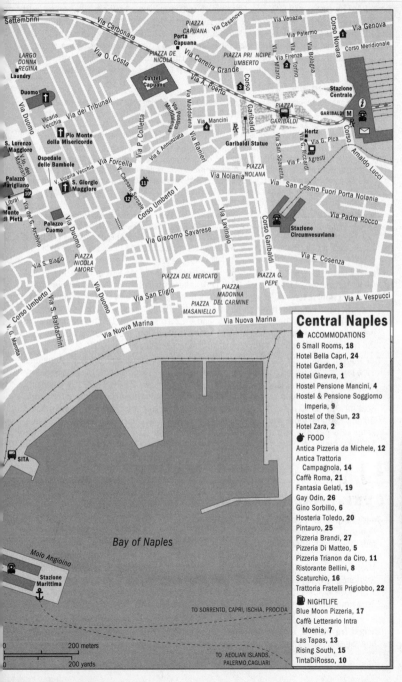

Central Naples

ACCOMMODATIONS
6 Small Rooms, **18**
Hotel Bella Capri, **24**
Hotel Garden, **3**
Hotel Ginevra, **1**
Hostel Pensione Mancini, **4**
Hostel & Pensione Soggiorno
  Imperia, **9**
Hostel of the Sun, **23**
Hotel Zara, **2**

FOOD
Antica Pizzeria da Michele, **12**
Antica Trattoria
  Campagnola, **14**
Caffè Roma, **21**
Fantasia Gelati, **19**
Gay Odin, **26**
Gino Sorbillo, **6**
Hosteria Toledo, **20**
Pintauro, **25**
Pizzeria Brandi, **27**
Pizzeria Di Matteo, **5**
Pizzeria Trianon da Ciro, **11**
Ristorante Bellini, **8**
Scaturchio, **16**
Trattoria Fratelli Prigiobbo, **22**

NIGHTLIFE
Blue Moon Pizzeria, **17**
Caffè Letterario Intra
  Moenia, **7**
Las Tapas, **13**
Rising South, **15**
TintaDiRosso, **10**

CAMPANIA

(good for Sa or Su, €2.50). Weekly tickets (€9) are also available. The buses and Metro stop running around midnight, and the *notturno* (nighttime) buses are unreliable and unsafe. Transportation around the environs of Naples includes the **Metro del Mare** (see **Intercity Transportation,** p. 556), the **Circumvesuviana** train to Pompeii and the **Metro** to Pozzuoli. All transportation in Campania is on one ticketing system; ticket costs depend upon the *fascia* (zone) of your destination.

Public Transportation:

Buses: Look for the orange buses. All stops have signs indicating their routes and destinations. **R1** travels from P. Bovio to Vomero (P. M. Oro) and **R2** runs from P. Garibaldi to P. Municipio. **3S** connects the 3 stations: the airport, the Stazione Centrale in P. Garibaldi, and Molo Beverello, where boats leave for the islands in the Bay of Naples and more distant destinations.

Subway: Info: ☎800 56 88 66; www.metro.na.it. To cover long distances (e.g., from the train station to P. Cavour, Montesanto, P. Amedeo, or Mergellina), use the efficient Metro that runs west to Pozzuoli from P. Garibaldi. Go to platform #4, 1 floor underground at Stazione Centrale. Line #1 stops at **Piazza Cavour** (Museo Nazionale), **Montesanto** (Cumana, Circumflegrea, funicular to Vomero), **Piazza Amedeo** (funicular to Vomero), **Mergellina,** and **Pozzuoli.** Transfer at P. Cavour for line #2. For Procida or Ischia, take the Metro to Pozzuoli.

Funiculars: Info: ☎800 56 88 66; www.metro.na.it. 3 connect the lower city to Vomero: **Centrale,** most frequently used, runs from V. Toledo to P. Fuga; **Montesanto** from P. Montesanto to V. Morghen; **Chiaia** from V. del Parco Margherita to C. Cimarosa. Centrale and Chiaia make intermittent stops at C. V. Emanuele. A 4th, **Mergellina,** connects Posillipo to Mergellina. Open M-Sa 4 per hr. 7am-10pm, Su reduced service 8am-7pm.

Taxis: Consortaxi: ☎081 55 25 252. **Free:** ☎081 55 15 151. **Napoli:** ☎081 55 64 444. **Partenope:** ☎081 55 60 202. Only take taxis with meters, and inquire about prices up front; even well-known companies have been known to charge dubiously high rates. For all taxis, the meter starts at €2.60; and an additional €0.05 is charged for every 70m. Expect to pay a min. €4.15, and a €2.10 surcharge 10pm-7am. From Molo Beverello to Stazione Centrale, €9.50. Service to and from the airport is at a set rate. *Qui Napoli* lists the prices for airport service, or inquire at the tourist office.

Car Rental: Avis in the airport (☎081 78 05 790; www.avisautonoleggio.it). Additional 12% tax on cars rented at the airport. Open M-F 8am-7:30pm, Sa 8:30am-1pm and 4-6pm, Su 9am-1pm. AmEx/MC/V. **Hertz,** V. Ricciardi, 5 (☎081 20 62 28; www.hertz.it). For prices, call the info center (☎199 91 12 211). Another office by the airport at V. Scarfoglio, 1 (☎081 78 02 971). Additional 12% tax applies. Open M-F 8am-1pm and 2-7pm, Sa 8am-noon. AmEx/MC/V. **Maggiore** (☎081 28 78 58), in Stazione Centrale. From €86 per day, €430 per week. Open M-F 8am-1pm and 3-7pm, Sa 8:30am-1:30pm. AmEx/MC/V.

🛂 PRACTICAL INFORMATION

TOURIST AND FINANCIAL SERVICES

Tourist Office: EPT (☎081 26 87 79; www.enteturismo.info), at Stazione Centrale. Calls hotels and ferry companies. Grab a free **map** and the indispensable 📖 **Qui Napoli,** a monthly tourist publication full of schedules, events, and listings (newest editions found at the airport). English spoken. Open M-Sa 9am-7pm, Su 9am-1pm. **Main office,** P. dei Martiri, 58 (☎081 41 07 211; enturna@virgilio.it). Open M-F 9am-2pm. **Branch** at Stazione Mergellina (☎081 76 12 102). Open M-Sa 9am-7pm. **AASCT** (☎081 25 25 711; www.inaples.it), at Palazzo Reale in P. Plebiscito, offers friendly information on accommodations and sights. Open M-F 9am-3pm. **Branch** at P. Gesù Nuovo (☎081 551 27 01). Open M-Sa 9am-1:30pm and 2:30-7pm.

Budget Travel: CTS, V. Mezzocannone, 25 (☎081 55 27 960), off C. Umberto on the R2 line. Student travel info, ISIC and FIYTO cards, and booking services. Open M-F 9:30am-

6:30pm, Sa 10am-1pm. **Branch:** V. Cinthia, 36 (☎081 76 77 877. Open M-F 9:30am-1pm and 4-7pm, Sa 9:30am-1pm). **CIT**, P. Municipio, 70 (☎081 55 25 426), is a general travel agency. Open M-F 9am-1pm and 3-6pm. **Italian Youth Hostel Organization** (☎081 76 12 346), at the Ostello Mergellina (see **Accommodations**, p. 564), supplies HI cards (€15). Open M-F 9am-1pm and 3-6pm.

Consulates: Canada, V. Carducci, 29 (☎081 40 13 38). **UK**, V. dei Mille, 40 (☎081 42 38 911). Open in summer M-F 8:30am-1:30pm. **US**, P. della Repubblica at the western end of Villa Comunale. (☎081 58 38 111, 24hr. emergency 033 79 45 083. Open M-F 8am-1pm and 2-5pm.)

Currency Exchange: Several banks operate in P. Municipio and P. Garibaldi. **Thomas Cook** at airport has decent rates. Open M-F 9:30am-1pm and 3-7pm. **Branches:** P. Municipio, 70 (☎081 55 18 399). **Stazione Centrale** has expensive 24hr. currency exchange. Smaller offices along C. Umberto I charge more reasonable fees.

American Express: Every Tour, P. Municipio, 5 (☎081 55 18 564). Open 9:30am-1pm and 3-7pm. Offers currency exchange. **Branch** in Stazione Centrale. AmEx/MC/V.

LOCAL SERVICES

Luggage Storage: In Stazione Centrale on the ground floor near the info desk. €3.80 for first 5hr., €0.60 per hr. 6-12hr., €0.20 per hr. 13hr.+.

English-Language Bookstores: The area near the university teems with bookstores. Near the Spanish Quarter, **Feltrinelli**, V. S. T. d'Aquino, 70/76 (☎081 55 21 436), just north of the Municipio. Extensive selection awaits upstairs. Open M-F 9am-8pm, Sa 9am-2pm and 4-8:30pm. AmEx/MC/V. **Libreria Universal Books**, C. Umberto, 22 (☎081 25 20 069; unibooks@tin.it), in a *palazzo* off C. Umberto by P. Bovio. Open daily 8:30am-1pm and 4-7pm. MC/V.

Laundromats: Self Service Lavenderia, Largo Donnaregina, 5 (☎328 61 96 341). From C. Umberto, take a right on V. Duomo. 1 block past the *duomo* on the right. Wash and dry €7-11. Free detergent. Open M-Sa 8:45am-7:30pm. Cash only.

EMERGENCY AND COMMUNICATION

Emergency: ☎113. **Police:** ☎081 794 11 11. **Carabinieri:** ☎112. **Ambulance:** ☎081 75 28 282 or 081 75 20 696.

Tourist Police: Ufficio Stranieri, at the **Questura**, V. Medina, 75 (☎081 79 41 111), near P. Municipio on the R2 bus line. Assists with passport problems and helps travelers who have been victims of crime.

Pharmacy: ☎081 26 88 81, at Stazione Centrale by FS ticket windows. Open 24hr., with a few exceptions on Su and holidays. When closed, the **Farmacia Helvethia**, P. Garibaldi, 111 (☎081 55 43 164; fax 081 554 19 20), across from station, is open daily 4pm-1pm. *Il Mattino* lists the schedule.

Hospital: Cardarelli (☎081 74 72 859 or 081 74 72 848), north of town on R4 or OF bus line.

Internet Access: Mouseclub, V. Pignatelli, 45 (☎081 55 13 683; www.mouseclub.it). Take V. Toldeo from P. Municipio. Turn right at V. Capitelli. V. Pignatelli is the 2nd right after P. Gesù Nuovo. Bar, lounge, and Internet cafe. €1.50 per hr. Open daily 9am-9pm. **Phone Center Sama**, V. Ricciardi 9 (☎/fax 081 28 51 48), a 2min. walk from train station, to the left off P. Garibaldi. €1.50 per hr. Open daily 9am-9pm.

Post Office: ☎081 552 42 33. In P. Matteotti, at V. Diaz. Take the R2 line, a view into true Neapolitan life like nothing else. Also in Galleria Umberto I (☎081 55 23 467) and outside Stazione Centrale. Notoriously unreliable *fermoposta*. Open M-F 8:15am-6pm, Sa 8:15am-noon. **Postal Code:** 80100.

BATHROOM BASICS. It's always a good idea to carry a package of tissues when traveling through Southern Italy, since it's a common to find no toilet paper available in public bathrooms.

▲ ACCOMMODATIONS

Hotels litter the hectic and seedy-by-night area around **Stazione Centrale.** Don't trust anyone who approaches you in the station—people working on commission are happy to lead naïve foreigners to unlicensed, overpriced hotels. Stazione Centrale has several comfortable and inexpensive options that are quiet despite their bustling surroundings. The **waterfront** and **centro storico** areas are more expensive. **Vomero,** albeit a 15min. commute to the sights, provides views and tranquility. Be cautious when selecting a place to stay. Don't surrender documents or passports before seeing a room, always agree on the price in writing *before* unpacking, and look for an intercom system or night attendants. For camping, check out **Pozzuoli** (p. 576) and other small towns on the Bay of Naples.

STAZIONE CENTRALE

▩ **Hostel Pensione Mancini,** V. Mancini, 33 (☎081 55 36 731; www.hostelpensioneman-cini.com), off far end of P. Garibaldi from station. Friendly owners often share their extensive knowledge of Naples. Roomy, renovated, and with expected additions of a common room and kitchen. Breakfast included. Check-in and check-out noon. Reservations suggested 1 week in advance. Dorms €20; singles €35, with bath €45; doubles €50/60; triples €75/80; quads €90/100. 10% discount with *Let's Go.* Cash only. ❷

Hotel Zara, V. Firenze, 81 (☎081 28 71 25; www.hotelzara.it). Quiet, spacious, renovated rooms, all with TV, A/C, and bath; some with LAN hookup and radio. Breakfast €4. Internet €4 for 1hr. Reservations recommended. Singles €35; doubles €45, with bath €65; triples €80; quads €95. 5% discount with *Let's Go.* AmEx/MC/V. ❸

Hotel Ginevra, V. Genova, 116, 2nd fl. (☎/fax 081 28 32 10; www.hotelginevra.it). Exit P. Garibaldi on C. Novara, turn right on V. Genova. A short walk from the train station, good for late-night arrivals. Clean, comfortable, and family-run. English and French spoken. Internet €2.50 per hr. Reserve 1 week ahead. Singles €35, with bath €55; doubles €55/65; double "Superior" rooms (include minibar, safe, bath, and A/C) €80. 10% discount with *Let's Go* in hand and cash payment. AmEx/MC/V. ❸

Hotel Garden, C. Garibaldi, 92 (☎081 28 43 31; www.hotelgardenapoli.it). Lovely rooftop terrace. Spacious rooms all have TV, phone, balcony, A/C, and bath with hair dryer. Breakfast included. Some rooms have wireless Internet. Reservations recommended May-Sept. With *Let's Go,* singles €62-73; doubles €73-93. AmEx/MC/V. ❺

WATERFRONT

▩ **Hostel of the Sun,** V. Melisurgo, 15 (☎081 42 06 393; www.hostelnapoli.com). Take R2 bus from station, exit at V. De Pretis. Buzz #51. €0.05 for elevator during business hours. First-rate hostel with good-spirited and helpful staff and dynamic owners. Dorms and private rooms are large, clean, and have free lockers. Common room with satellite TV, DVDs, and small library. Kitchen and refrigerator available. Breakfast included. Fast Internet €3 per hr. Laundry €3. Dorms €20; singles €45, with bath €50; doubles €55/70; triples €80/90; quads €90/100. 10% discount with *Let's Go.* Cash Only. ❷

Ostello Mergellina (HI), V. Salita della Grotta, 23 (☎081 76 12 346, fax 081 76 12 391). M: Mergellina. From Metro, make 2 sharp rights. Driveway after overpass. 200 well-maintained beds. Breakfast, shower, and sheets included. Internet and free storage. Towels €3. Laundry €5.20. Lockout 9am-3pm. Strict curfew 12:30am. Reservations recommended July-Aug. Dorms €14; double as a single €21; doubles €34; family rooms €16 per person, €13 with more than 2 beds squeezed in. Cash only. ❶

Hotel Bella Capri, V. Melisurgo, 4 (☎081 55 29 494; www.bellacapri.it). Across the street from Hostel of the Sun. Perfect spot for repose before ferry departures. Rooms all with bath, A/C, TV, and phone, some with balconies. Breakfast included. Internet €3 per hr. Dorms €22; singles €45-50, with bath €57-69; doubles €50-60/66-80; triples €66-84/80-100; quad €80-96/97-110. 10% discount with *Let's Go*. AmEx/MC/V. ❷

CENTRO STORICO (SPACCANAPOLI)

6 Small Rooms, V. Diodato Lioy, 18 (☎081 79 01 378; www.6smallrooms.com). Take the Metro to P. Dante; change line at P. Cavour. From P. Dante, turn left on V. Toledo, left on V. Senise, and right on V. Lioy. Look for the name on the call button. Small, cozy, with a great vibe. Big rooms. Kitchen and English video collection available. Key (€5 deposit) available for after midnight curfew. Call for dorm beds after 10pm the night before arrival. Dorms €20; doubles €55, with private bath €65. Cash only. ❷

Hostel and Pensione Soggiorno Imperia, P. Miraglia, 386, 6th fl. (☎081 45 93 47; www.eds.it/soggiornoimperia). Take R2, exit at the University, take V. Mezzocannone through P. S. D. Maggiore. Buzz 1st green doors to left on P. Miraglia. Climb 6 flights to reach this 16th-century *palazzo* and its 9 big, bright rooms. Reserve ahead. Singles €30, with bath €50; doubles €50/65; triples €75/90; quad €90/100. Cash only. ❸

VOMERO

Pensione Margherita, V. Cimarosa, 29, 5th fl. (☎081 57 82 852; pensione.margherita@tiscali.it). Take the funicular from near P. Plebiscito, exit at the station. Go around the corner to the right. Buzz to enter (in the same building as the Centrale funicular station). 19 cavernous rooms share 6 spotless baths. A little out of the way, but leaving the bustle of Naples behind as you head to the quiet hills of Vomero is worth the trek. Check-out 11am. Curfew 1am. Singles €40; doubles €70; triples €95. Closed Aug. 1-15. Cash only. ❹

▣ FOOD

PIZZERIAS

If you ever doubted that Neapolitans invented pizza, Naples's pizzerias will take that doubt, beat it into a ball, throw it in the air, spin it on their collective finger, punch it down, cover it with sauce and mozzarella, and serve it *alla margherita*.

▨ **Gino Sorbillo**, V. dei Tribunali, 32 (☎081 44 66 43; www.accademiadellapizza.it), in the historical center near Vco. S. Paolo. 21 children of this generation man the kitchen. Peer inside to watch the frenzied action and original, flame-spewing oven. No reservations, so expect long waits. Favorites include *marinara* (tomato, garlic, oregano, oil; €2.10), and *margherita* (tomato, mozzarella cheese, basil; €3). Service 10%. Open daily noon-3:30pm and 7-11:30pm. MC/V. ❶

▨ **Pizzeria Di Matteo**, V. dei Tribunali, 94 (☎081 45 52 62), near V. Duomo. A brick oven churns out the best *marinara* around (€2). Extremely popular with Neapolitans. Pizzas burst with flavor and the building bursts with aficionados—sign up on the list, and try some of the fried zucchini while you wait. Open M-Sa 9am-midnight. Cash only. ❶

Antica Pizzeria da Michele, V. Caesare Sersale, 1/3 (☎081 55 39 204; www.damichele.net), at the corner of V. Colletta. From P. Garibaldi, take C. Umberto I and turn right. Huge line outside says "Quality!" more loudly than a legion of reviews. Serves only *marinara* and *margherita* pizzas. Watch sweltering chefs toss pies from pizza-board to flame-licked oven, plates—all with superhuman grace and dexterity. Pizza €3.50-4.50. Drinks from €1.20. Open M-Sa 10am-11pm. Cash only. ❶

Pizzeria Brandi, Salita S. Anna di Palazzo, 1 (☎081 41 69 28; www.brandi.it), off V. Chiaia. In 1889, Raffaele Esposito invented the *margherita* in Brandi's ancient oven to symbolize Italy's flag with the green of basil, red of tomato sauce, and white of mozzarella. Famous customers include Luciano Pavarotti, Isabella Rossellini, and Gérard Depardieu. *Margherita* €4.20. Cover €1.50. Service 12%. Open Tu-Su 12:30-3:30pm and 7:30pm-midnight. Weekend reservations recommended. AmEx/MC/V. ❷

Pizzeria Trianon da Ciro, V. Pietro Colletta, 42/44/46 (☎081 55 39 426; www.pizzeria-trianon.com), 1 block off C. Umberto I. Spacious interior boasts elusive A/C and amicable service. House speciality is the enormous *gran trianon* pizza (€6.50), with 8 distinct sections of top-notch toppings. Pizza €2.80-7. Beer €1-3. Service 15%. Open M-Sa 10am-3:30pm and 7-11pm. Cash only. ❷

RESTAURANTS AND TRATTORIE

Local fish and shellfish enjoy an exalted place on the city's tables. Devour plentiful *cozze* (mussels) with lemon or as a soup. Savor *vongole* (clams) in all their glory, and don't miss their more expensive cousin, the *ostrica* (oyster). Try not to gawk as true Neapolitans suck the elusive juices from the heads of *aragosta* (lobster) or devour *polipo* (octopus). For fresh fruits and seafood, the bustling **market** on V. Soprammuro, off P. Garibaldi, is the place to go. (Open M-Sa 8am-1:30pm.) Fruit stands, groceries, and pastry shops line V. Tribunali in Spaccanapoli. Fruit stands are often closed on Monday afternoons, fishmongers on Thursday afternoons. A large supermarket, **Supero,** is one block across the street from P. Dante, at Vico San Domenico Soriano, 20. (Open M-Sa 8:30am-8pm, Su 8:30-1:30pm. MC/V.) The **waterfront** offers a combination of traditional Neapolitan fare and a change of culinary pace. Take the Metro or C25 bus to P. Amedeo, on the waterfront in Mergellina, for informal, hearty seafood. In the *centro storico* (Spaccanapoli), small shops cling to side streets, away from the more expensive *trattorie.* Some of the cheapest, most authentic options lie along V. dei Tribunali in Spaccanapoli.

CENTRO STORICO (SPACCANAPOLI)

🏷 **Hosteria Toledo,** Vco. Giardinetto, 78/A (☎081 42 12 57), in the Spanish Quarter. Prepare yourself for a long meal full of Neapolitan comfort food. The *gnocchi* (€6) is hearty enough to be its own meal. Ask the staff for their recommendations—you won't be disappointed. If you are feeling adventurous, try the chef's surprise. *Primi* and *secondi* €5-12. Cover €1. Service 10%. Open daily 8pm-midnight. AmEx/MC/V. ❸

🏷 **Trattoria Fratelli Prigiobbo,** V. Portacarrese a Montecalvario, 96 (☎081 40 76 92). From V. Toledo walking from waterfront, turn left on V. Portacarrese. Intimate and friendly; great for a quiet lunch away from the V. Toledo mob or a leisurely dinner with friends. Accommodating owners cater to all culinary desires, especially those of gluttony. Filling *primi* including *gnocchi alla mozzarella* (€3) and seafood including roasted calamari (€4), though servings are small. Pizza from €2.50. House wine €2.50 per bottle. Open M-Sa 8am-midnight. Cash only. ❷

Ristorante Bellini, V. Santa Maria di Constantinopoli, 79-80 (☎/fax 081 45 97 74), just off P. Bellini. Come for obliging service and an evening *al fresco,* surrounded by screens and fragrant flowers. Try the *linguine al cartoccio* (€11) or anything from the *pesce* menu. *Primi* €6.50-9, *secondi* €8.50 and up. Open daily 9am-4pm and 7pm-12am. Closed Su in summer. MC/V. ❸

Antica Trattoria Campagnola, Piazzetta Nilo, 22 (☎081 55 14 930). Heaping portions of regional cuisine at this outstanding *trattoria,* including excellent *fritto di aliei.* Simple outdoor seating offers a calm alternative to the bustling pizzerias nearby. Fast service and wide selection of wines. *Menù* €12. Open daily 10am-midnight. AmEx/MC/V. ❷

WATERFRONT

Zorba's, V. Martucci, 5 (☎081 66 75 72). M: Mergellina. 2 blocks off P. Amedeo, to the right exiting the station; turn left at the sign, it's 3 doors down. This delightful change from the relentless pasta parade serves Greek cuisine. *Satanas* (devilishly spicy mini-sausages; €7) are sure to spark strong reactions. Fresh baklava €3. Open Tu-F and Su 8:30pm-1am, Sa 8:30pm-3am. Cash only. ❷

Ristorante Pizzeria 'a Taverna 'e zi Carmela, V. Nicolo' Tommaseo 11-12 (☎081 76 43 35 81), on the corner of V. Partenope. Dining on a breezy side street overlooking the ocean is a great way to escape the midday heat. Known by locals for the excellent seafood, especially *polpo* (octopus). Ask waiters for their suggestions on seafood to get the best dishes of the day. *Primi* €3.50-12, *secondi* €5-12. Open in summer daily 11:15am-1:30pm and 7:30pm-1am. Cash only. ❸

Cucina Casereccia e Pizzeria Zi Totonno a Mergellina, P. Sannazzaro, 69 (☎081 66 65 64). At this seafood restaurant all imaginable sea creatures are fried, sautéed, and stewed to perfection by a welcoming staff. A *zuppa di cozze* (€7) comes heaping with succulent mussels and pieces of octopus, though good luck with finishing the *zuppa di cozze super* (€9.50). Open M-Sa noon-6am. MC/V. ❸

Umberto, V. Alabardieri, 30/31 (☎081 41 85 55; www.umberto.it). M: Mergellina. V. Alabardieri leads out of P. dei Martiri; restaurant on the left. Accented with tea lights and bamboo, this swanky but affordable locale serves local fare with flair. House specials is *tubettoni d' 'o treddeta* (tube pasta stuffed with seafood; €9.50). *Primi* €4.50-9.50, *secondi* €5-9. Cover €1.85. Service 12%. Open Tu-Su 12:30-3:30pm and 7pm-1am. Closed 2 weeks in Aug. Reservations recommended. AmEx/MC/V. ❸

El Bocadillo, V. Martucci, 50 (☎081 66 90 30). M: Mergellina. Real, honest Brazilian-style barbecue, i.e., juicy slabs of name-your-animal. The campy decor may not be inspiring, but the delicious cuisine is. Entrees €3.60-10. *Paella* €8.50. 1L sangria from €5. Open daily 7pm-3am. MC/V. ❷

GELATERIE AND PASTICCERIE

Naples's most beloved pastry is *sfogliatella*, filled with sweetened ricotta cheese, orange rind, and candied fruit. It comes in two forms: the popular *riccia*, a flaky-crust variety, and a softer, crumblier *frolla*. Many vendors sell atrocious concoctions laden with unnatural dyes and carrying a mass produced label. Avoid these and look for creamy textures and muted colors instead.

▦ **Fantasia Gelati**, V. Toledo, 381 (☎081 55 11 212), comes close to *gelato* perfection. The shop's fruit flavors, including heavenly *arancia* (orange) and tangy papaya, are made with real juices, yielding tart, refreshing results. Very generous scoops. Cones €1.30-2. Open daily 7am-11pm. Cash only. ❶

▦ **Gay-Odin**, V. V. Colonna, 15/B (☎081 41 82 82; www.gay-odin.it), off P. Amedeo. Also at V. Toledo, 214 (☎081 40 00 63). No Norse gods, just delicious chocolate treats. Try the *foresta*, a sweet and crumbly chocolate stalk (from €2.20 for a small twig to €8.40 for a branch best shared with friends). Open M-Sa 9:30am-1:30pm and 4:30-8pm, Su 10am-2pm. AmEx/MC/V. ❶

Scaturchio, P. S. Domenico Maggiore, 19 (☎081 55 16 944; www.scaturchio.it). With divine desserts and a quiet spot in the *piazza*, it's the perfect place to pass the afternoon watching Neapolitans go by. A contender for the best *sfogliatelle* (€1.30) in the city. Specialty is *ministeriale*, a chocolate and rum pastry (€2.50), and excellent *gelato* (cones from €1.30). Open M and W-Su 7:20am-8:40pm. AmEx/V. ❶

Pintauro, V. Toledo, 275 (☎081 41 73 39). This tiny bakery invented *sfogliatella* in 1785. Try it piping hot from €1.30. *Meringues* €1.30. Open in summer M-Sa 8:30am-8pm; daily in winter with same times. Cash only. ❶

Caffè Roma, V. Toledo, 325 (☎081 40 68 32). Huge variety of *panini* and pastries (try the *profiterolles;* €1.50). For a quick snack, go for *focaccia* (from €0.80) or a *granita* (€1.80) instead. Open M-Sa 9am-9pm. Cash only. ❶

👁 SIGHTS

The exquisite architecture that forms a backdrop to daily life in Naples is a narrative of successive conquests, featuring Greek, Roman, and Spanish styles. Excavations *in sito* can be found at the Museo Archeologico Nazionale or Museo and Gallerie di Capodimonte. The Palazzo Reale's apartments and the city's castles give a taste of 18th-century royal Neapolitan life. Reduced price tickets are given to EU citizens 18 to 24 years unless otherwise noted. The **Campania Artecard** is a worthwhile investment for those taking a few days to tour regional sights, granting free admission to two of 48 museums and sites in and around the city (including Pompeii), and half-price admission to the rest. Free public transportation, special transportation on weekends, and discounts on audioguides is also included. They are available at the airport, train stations, travel agencies, and all the museums and sites included on the card throughout the region. (☎800 60 06 01; www.campaniartecard.it. Last entrance to museums 1hr. before closing. All religious sites require modest dress. Sites and transportation in Naples and Campi Flegrei €13, ages 18-25 €8. Sites and transportation in all of Campania €25, ages 18-25 €18.)

> **TOURING CAMPANIA.** The three-day Campania Artecard (€25) may be an especially worthwhile investment for those traveling to Pompeii, Herculaneum, and Vesuvius. With access to the entire transportation network, as well as free admission to two sights and half-price admission to the rest, cardholders can save up to €10 on transportation and entrance fees.

CENTRO STORICO (SPACCANAPOLI)

Naples's most renowned neighborhood is replete with brilliant architecture. The main sights get lost among ornate banks, *pensioni*, and *pasticcerie*, so watch for the shoebox-sized signs on buildings. To get to the historical center from P. Dante, walk through Pta. Alba and past P. Bellini before turning down V. dei Tribunali, the former route of a Roman road that now contains some of Naples's best pizzerias.

MUSEO ARCHEOLOGICO NAZIONALE. Situated in a 16th-century *palazzo* and former barracks, the world's oldest archaeological museum houses treasures from Pompeii and Herculaneum. Unreliable labeling makes the guidebooks or a tour a worthy investment. The ground floor's Farnese Collection displays sculptures snatched from Pompeii and Herculaneum, as well as imperial portraits and colossal statues from Rome's Baths of Caracalla. The massive Farnese Hercules depicts the hero after his last labor, though which labor remains unclear; a diverging mythical account extends the traditional 12 labors to include a 13th: bedding 100 women in one night. Check out the Farnese Bull, the largest extant ancient statue. Sculpted from a single slab of marble, the bull was further freed from the stone by a benevolent Michelangelo. The mezzanine contains a room filled with exquisite mosaics from Pompeii, most noticeably some delicious-looking fruits and the Alexander Mosaic, which shows a young and fearless Alexander the Great routing a Persian army. Though most people have heard of the lovely Aphrodite, the *Gabinetto Segreto*, or Secret Cabinet, will introduce the curious to her lesser-known counterpart, Hermaphrodite, who was blessed with a curvy feminine form and handy masculine member. The collection, specializing in erotic paintings and objects from Pompeii, includes everything from images of (intimate) godly love to phallic good luck charms replete with hanging bells. Check in at the ticket desk to gain entrance. *(M: P. Cavour. Turn right from the station and walk 2 blocks. ☎ 081 44 01 66. Open M and W-Su 9am-7:30pm. Admission €6.50, EU students €3.25, under 18 or over 65 free. Included under Campania Artecard. Audioguides in English, French, Italian; €4.)*

CATACOMBS AND THE UNDERGROUND OF NAPLES. The catacombs of San Gennaro, San Gaudioso, and San Severo all date back to the early centuries AD, and provide a glimpse of ancient Neapolis. Tours of the city's subterranean alleys are fascinating, but not for the claustrophobic: guides set people crawling through narrow underground passageways, grottoes, and catacombs, spotting Mussolini-era graffiti, exploring Roman aqueducts, and entering Neapolitan homes to point out how ancient Roman theaters have been incorporated into architecture over the ages. **Napoli Sotterranea** drags the intrepid underneath the historical center. *(P. S. Gaetano, 68. Take V. Tribunali and turn left right before San Paolo Maggiore. ☎ 081 29 69 44; www.napolisotterranea.org. Tours every 2hr. M-F noon-4pm; Sa-Su, and holidays 10am-6pm. €5.)*

DUOMO. Naples's *duomo* lies on V. Duomo, its modest 19th-century facade belying an ornate interior. Inaugurated in 1315 by Robert of Anjou, the *duomo* has been subject to many additions and renovations. Inside on the right, the main attraction is the **Cappella del Tesoro di San Gennaro,** decorated with Baroque paintings. A beautiful 17th-century bronze grille protects the high altar, which possesses a reliquary containing the saint's head and two vials of his coagulated blood. According to legend, disaster will strike the city if the blood does not liquefy on the day of the **Festa di San Gennaro** (see **Entertainment and Festivals,** p. 572). Behind the main altar of the church lies the saint's **crypt,** decorated with Renaissance carvings in white marble. Visitors can also view the newly opened underground **excavation site,** an intimate tangle of Greek and Roman roads constructed over several centuries. The entrance is halfway up the right side of the church. *(Walk 3 blocks up V. Duomo from C. Umberto I or take the #42 bus from P. Garibaldi. ☎ 081 44 90 97. Open M-Sa 9am-noon and 4:30-7pm, Su 9am-noon. Free, excavation site €3.)*

CAPPELLA SAN SEVERO. The chapel, founded in 1590, is now a private museum. Several remarkable 18th-century statues inhabit its lovely corridors, including the *Veiled Christ* by Giuseppe Sanmartino. Laced throughout the Christian artwork are allusions to Masonry, as the founder of the chapel, Prince Raimondo of the S. Severi, reached Grand Master status. In masonry symbology, the swastika labyrinth design on the marble flooring represents

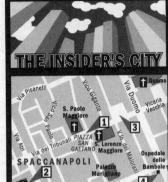

the exploration of the mysteries of the universe. Three major symbols of Masonry can be found at the Veiled Christ's feet: a hammer, a compass, and pliers. Legend claims that the chapel's builder, alchemist Prince Raimondo of the S. Severi, murdered his wife and her lover by injecting them with a poison that preserved their veins, arteries, and vital organs. *(V. De Sanctis, 19. Near P. S. Domenico Maggiore. ☎081 55 18 470; www.museosansevero.it. Open M and W-Sa 10am-5:40pm, holidays 10am-1:30pm. 20% discount with Campania Artecard. Admission €5, students under 26 €2.50, high school students €2, 9 and under free.)*

CHIESA DI SANTA CHIARA. Santa Chiara was built in the 1300s by the rulers of the house of Anjou. Since then, it has been renovated several times, most recently after a WWII bombing. Stained-glass windows stretch up the walls, casting a golden glow over the interior. The church is littered with sarcophagi and tombs from the Middle Ages, including the 14th-century tomb of Robert of Anjou. The first chapel to the left is dedicated to Neapolitan-born Salvo D'Acquisto. During WWII, while working for the *carabinieri* in Rome, he sacrificed his life to appease German calls for retribution after one of their officers was killed. As they were rounding up 26 innocent women and children, Salvo made a hero's sacrifice. Check out the garden, archaeological site, and monastery, adorned with Gothic frescoes and *majolica* tiles. *(From P. Dante, take V. Toledo and turn left on V. B. Croce. The church is in P. Gesù Nuovo. ☎081 552 15 97; www.santachiara.info. Open M-F 9:30am-6:30pm, Su 9:30am-2:30pm. €4, EU students €2.50. 10% discount with Artecard.)*

CHIESA DI GESÙ NUOVO. Originally built for the Prince of Salerno, the church's 15th-century Jesuit facade suggests simplicity, but from inlaid marble floors to colorful ceiling frescoes, the interior is awash in opulent Baroque decor. The magnificent main altar, featuring a triumvirate of marble statues and a towering gold sun, is overwhelming. Outside the church is a spectacular spire glorifying the lives of Jesuit saints. *(Across from the Chiesa di Santa Chiara, in P. Gesù Nuovo. ☎081 55 18 613. Open daily 7am-12:30pm and 4-7:30pm. Modest dress required.)*

PIO MONTE DELLA MISERICORDIA. This chapel was built by a group of nobles dedicated to helping the needy and sick, housing pilgrims, and ransoming Christian slaves held by infidels. The church has seven arches, each with an altar and painting, and the main archway holds Caravaggio's *Our Lady of Mercy.* In the *piazza* outside, a spire is dedicated to S. Gennaro for having saved the city from the 1656 plague. *(V. Tribunali, 253, 1 block after V. Duomo, in a small piazza. ☎081 44 69 44; www.piomontedellamisericordia.it. Call to book a tour (Tu, Th, and Sa, 9:30am-1:30pm.) Tickets €5, EU students, over 65, and under 14 €3, with Artecard €4.)*

PIAZZA PLEBISCITO

■ **PALAZZO REALE AND BIBLIOTECA NAZIONALE.** Statues of the various rulers of Naples decorate the *palazzo* in P. Plebiscito. Vomero, towering majestically in the distance, provides a picturesque backdrop for the square's superb architecture. Inside the 17th-century *palazzo* is the **Museo di Palazzo Reale,** comprised of opulent royal apartments with original Bourbon furnishings, paintings, statues, and porcelains. Immense chambers reveal lavish royal life, including the king's throne and walls lined with mirrors and paintings. *(Take the R2 bus from P. Garibaldi to P. Trieste e Trento and walk around the palazzo to the entrance on P. Plebiscito; or, make the short walk from anywhere in the historical center. ☎84 88 00 288. Open M-Tu and Th-Su 9am-7:30pm. Included with Artecard. Entrance €7.50, reduced €3.75. Ages under 18 and above 65 free.)* The *palazzo* is an intellectual mecca, housing the 1,500,000-volume **Biblioteca Nazionale.** The library contains carbonized scrolls from the Villa dei Papiri in Herculaneum. *(☎081 78 19 231. Visits are possible with a reservation M-F 10am-1pm.)* Also in the *palazzo* is the famous **Teatro San Carlo,** built in 1737 and reputed to have better acoustics than La Scala in Milan (p. 249). For information on performances, see **Entertainment and Festivals,** p. 572. *(Theater entrance on P. Trieste e Trento. ☎081 66 45 45; www.itineranapoli.com. Open daily 9am-6:30pm. Tours held daily, meeting in foyer.)*

CASTELNUOVO O MASCHIO ANGIONO. It's impossible to miss this five-turreted landmark towering over the Bay of Naples. Built in 1286 by Charles II of Anjou as his residence in Naples, the fortress's most stunning feature is the triumphal entrance, with reliefs commemorating the arrival of Alphonse I of Aragon in 1443. The castle also holds the magnificent Hall of the Barons, where King Ferdinand once trapped rebellious barons and where Naples's city council still holds spirited meeting. The splendid Cappella Palatina, also called the Chapel of St. Barbara, is a cool retreat from the castle's open churchyard. *(P. Municipio. Take the R2 bus from P. Garibaldi or walk from the historical center. ☎081 795 58 77. Open M-Sa 9am-7pm. €5.)*

GALLERIA UMBERTO I. Although now a shopping mall complete with street vendors selling designer knock-offs, the building itself is one of the most beautiful in Naples. In the shape of a cross, the atrium has a high, arched ceiling covered in glass panes. It seems a bit out of place in Naples, and is more architecturally akin to buildings in Milan, but it is a unique treat to shop in this 17th-century wonder. *(P. Trieste e Trento. Stores open daily 10am-1pm and 4-8pm. Building is open all day.)*

CHIESA DI SAN DOMENICO MAGGIORE. This 13th-century church, founded when Naples was a center of learning in Europe, has been restructured several times over the years, finally ending in a 19th-century, spiked Gothic interior. To the right of the altar in the Chapel of the Crucifix hangs the 13th-century painting that allegedly spoke to St. Thomas Aquinas, when he lived in the adjoining monastery. Fine Renaissance sculptures decorate the side chapels, but many have been moved to the Capodimonte museum. *(P. S. Domenico Maggiore. ☎081 45 91 88. Open daily 8:30am-noon and 4:30-7pm.)*

CAPODIMONTE

◾**MUSEO DI CAPODIMONTE.** Housed in a royal *palazzo*, the museum sits inside a pastoral park where youngsters play soccer and lovers, well, play. In addition to its plush royal apartments, the palace houses the Italian National Picture Gallery. The **Farnese Collection** on the first floor is full of masterpieces, many of them removed from Neapolitan churches for safety's sake. Among these incomparable works are Bellini's *Transfiguration*, Masaccio's *Crucifixion*, and Titian's *Danae*. The 2nd floor traces the development of the Neapolitan realist style, from Caravaggio's visit to Naples (his *Flagellation* is on display) to Ribera and Luca Giordano's adaptations. *(Take bus #24, 110, M4, or M5 from the Archaeological Museum and exit at the gate to the park, on the right. The park has 2 entrances, Pta. Piccola and Pta. Grande. ☎081 74 99 111; www.capodimonte.selfin.it. Open M-Tu and Th-Su 8:30am-7:30pm. €7.50, reduced tickets and entrance after 2pm €3.75.)*

VOMERO

MUSEO NAZIONALE DI SAN MARTINO. Once the monastery of St. Martin, the cloisters are now home to an excellent museum of Neapolitan history and culture. In addition to extensive galleries, the monastery sports a lavish chapel, festooned with Baroque marbles and statuary. Collection highlights include Riberia's *Deposition of Christ*, held to be one of his finest works, and a *Nativity* by Guido Renis. Numerous balconies and a multi-level garden allow views of the city below, but beware of amorous couples, who monopolize most available benches. *(From V. Toledo, take the funicular to Vomero and turn right on V. Cimarosa. Continue straight up 2 flights of stairs, along V. Scarlatti, and then veer left, walking for about 10min., keeping left; Castel*

Sant'Elmo and Piazzale S. Martino emerge on the right. ☎ 081 55 85 942; www.pierreci.it. Open Tu-Sa 8:30am-7:30pm. €6, EU students €3. Included under Campania Artecard.) The massive **Castel Sant'Elmo** next door was built to deter rebellion and hold political prisoners. Nowadays, however, it's more concerned with tourism and glamor. There are grand views from the battlements. *(☎ 848 80 02 88; www.civita.it. Open M-Tu and Th-Su 10am-7pm, reduced €1.50. Special exhibits around €6. Included with Artecard.)*

MUSEO DUCA DI MARTINA. Ceramics fans should visit this crafts gallery inside the lush gardens of the **Villa Floridiana** for 18th-century Italian and Asian porcelain. Though on the smaller side, this collection is thoughtfully presented and full of treasures. *(V. Cimarosa, 77. To get to the entrance, take the funicular to Vomero from V. Toledo, turn right out of the station, then turn left on V. Cimarosa. Enter the gardens and keep walking downhill. ☎ 081 57 88 418; www.pierreci.it. Open M and Th-Su 8:30am-2pm. €2.50, EU students €1.25, EU citizens under 18 or over 65 free. 20% discount with Artecard.)*

WATERFRONT

■ **VIRGIL'S TOMB.** *Mirabile dictu!* Anyone who studied Latin in high school may have at least a passing interest in seeing the poet's resting place at Salita della Frotta. Below the tomb is the entrance to the closed **Crypta Neapolitana,** a tunnel built during the reign of Augustus; the Metro line of antiquity, it connected ancient Neapolis to Pozzuoli and Baia. Nearby lies the tomb of Leopardi, moved from the church of S. Vitale in Fuorigrotta in 1939. Call ahead and arrange a translator to describe and explain the inscriptions, or just come for the amazing view. *(M: Mergellina, take 2 quick rights. Entrance between overpass and tunnel. Guided tours upon request. ☎ 081 66 93 90. Open daily 9am-1hr. before sunset. Free.)*

CASTEL DELL'UOVO (EGG CASTLE). This massive Norman castle of yellow brick and odd angles was built on a large chunk of tufa rock. Once a monastery, by the end of the 5th century the structure was used as fortress defense against invaders. It offers beautiful views of the water and Naples, especially during sunset. *(Take bus #1 from P. Garibaldi or P. Municipio to S. Lucia and walk across the jetty. ☎ 081 24 00 055. Only open for special events; call ahead.)*

AQUARIUM. On the waterfront, in Villa Comunale, this world-class aquarium is a proud reminder of Naples's attachment to the sea. Founded in the late 19th century, it's Europe's oldest, displaying 30 tanks with 200 local species. *(Easily accessible by bus #1 from P. Garibaldi or P. Municipio. ☎ 081 58 33 111. Open Tu-Sa 9am-5pm, Su 9:30am-2pm. €1.50, children €1.)*

♪ ※ ENTERTAINMENT AND FESTIVALS

Once famous occasions for revelry, Naples's religious festivals are now excuses for sales and shopping sprees. On September 19 and the first Saturday in May, the city celebrates the **Festa di San Gennaro.** Join the crowd to watch the procession by the *duomo* in May and see the patron saint's blood miraculously liquefy in a vial. The **Festa di Madonna del Carmine** (July 16) features a mock burning of Fra' Nuvolo's *campanile* and culminates in fireworks. In July, P. S. Domenico Maggiore holds concerts, while summers are full of neighborhood celebrations, sporting events, music, and shows. The **Neapolis Festival** in July hosts pop concerts at Arena Flegrea in Campi Flegrei. **Teatro S. Carlo** (☎ 081 79 72 111) at Palazzo Reale hosts opera performances (Oct.-June) and the symphony (Oct.-May). Gallery tickets start at €12 and should be purchased in advance. Consult the ticket office and *Il Mattino* for schedules. Catch a soccer match at **Stadio S. Paolo** (☎ 081 23 95 623), in Fuorigrotta, for a truly accurate portrait of Neapolitan life. Take the Metro to

Campi Flegrei. **Napoli**, in Serie C, the 3rd division, is still a powerhouse, attracting spectators for matches from August through June. Tickets start at €20.

Two weekends of every month (1 per month in June and July) **Fiera Antiquaria Napoletana** hosts flea markets filled with ancient and expensive artifacts. Though such items come with hefty price tags, hundreds wander through the stands along V. F. Caracciolo on the waterfront to browse stamps, books, coins, and art. (☎081 62 19 51. Open 8am-2pm.) From early December to early January, Neapolitan artisans gather along the Spaccanapoli and surrounding streets to hand-work fine porcelain Nativity scenes renowned throughout Europe for their delicate beauty. This spectacle draws a huge international crowd.

⬛ SHOPPING

A thriving black market and low prices make Naples an enticing place for shopping. Just keep this in mind: street vendors are craftier than you are. If a transaction seems too good to be true, it is. Clothing is usually a good deal, though that new shirt may come apart in the washing machine or turn everything a ghastly shade of purple. **Never buy electronic products from street vendors!** Even brandname boxes have been known to be filled with newspaper or rocks. Cases of music and computer CDs and DVDs often contain old copies of Microsoft DOS or simply are blank, so try them out if possible. And do *not* fall for those Mickey Mouse dolls that "dance" to a boombox—they're ingenious deceptions.

That said, designer knock-off belts, purses, and sunglasses are plentiful, and none of your friends will know the difference. A word about bargaining: do it. In the dog-eat-dog world of unregulated transactions, bargaining is the law. The most aloof is the king. The moment a vendor notices a happy person carrying a backpack and admiring the goods with reverent awe, he doubles the prices and lays on the compliments. So offer less than half, and be damned if you're going to budge.

Via Santa Maria di Constantinopoli, south of the Archaeological Museum, has old books and antique shops. **Spaccanapoli** and its side streets near the Conservatorio house small music shops with inexpensive manuscripts. **Via Toledo, Corso Umberto I,** and **Via Duomo** provide high-class shopping for a lower budget, and the streets south of **San Lorenzo Maggiore** house Neapolitan craftsmen. For formal shopping, **Piazza Martiri** houses a roll call of major Italian designers. **Galleria Umberto** has plenty of higher-end stores. The most expensive shopping district is in the hills of **Vomero** along the perpendicular **Via Scarlatti** and **Via Luca Giordano.** Many artisans' workshops inhabit the streets nearby, hawking everything from wrought iron to delicate cameos. For jeans, head to the market off **Porta Capuana.** (Most markets open M-Sa 9am-5pm, but many close at 2pm.)

◪ NIGHTLIFE

Content to groove at the small clubs and discos during winter, Neapolitans return to the streets and *piazze* in warmer weather. Each *piazza* hosts a slightly different nighttime crowd. In winter, clubs and pubs open at around 11pm and remain open until everyone goes home at around 4 or 5am. In summer, the Sunday evening *passeggiata* fills the Villa Comunale along the bay (bus #1), and young couples flood picturesque V. Petrarca and V. Posillipo. As night goes on, *piazze* fill with laughing Neapolitans, beer and wine in hand, who just hang out and disturb the neighbors. *Il Mattino* and *Qui Napoli* print decent club listing's. **ARCI-GAY/Lesbica,** Vico San Geronimo alle Monache, 17-20 (☎081 55 28 815; open for males M, W, and F and females Tu, Th, and Sa 5-8pm) across from Mondadori Books on V. Benedetto Croce, has information on gay and lesbian nights at different clubs.

TAKE TO THE STREETS

Travelers hoping to dance the night away may be surprised by the lack of discos in Naples. But the city has a unique nightlife of its own—come summer Neopolitans pack *piazze* by the hundreds, *Peronis* and pizza slices in hand. To maximize your enjoyment of the city's bustling nocturnal scene, here is a crash course in *piazza* personalities:

Piazza Gesù Nuovo: At night, university students break from their relentless bongo-playing but not from their firm convictions in the "healing powers" of certain botanicals. Plentiful fast food satisfies hunger cravings.

Piazza Santa Maria La Nova: Always stuffed to bursting, and frequented by sociable Neopolitans of all ages. Vendors sell hot dogs late at night, and liquor flows freely from local bars.

Piazza Bellini: Quieter, and replete with outdoor seating and hanging plants. The bars here, hosting a mix of locals and tourists, are on the expensive side. But the low-key ambience might well provide the respite you crave after a hard day of sightseeing.

Piazza Vanvitelli: Chic, young, happening, and just a short funicular ride up V. Toledo. Don't bother showing up unless you pass for under 28 and don't mind weaving through amorous couples. (Beware: buses and funiculars may not run past 11pm.)

CAFES, BARS, AND PUBS

Caffè Letterario Intra Moenia, P. Bellini, 70 (☎081 29 07 20; www.intramoenia.it). Appeals to the intellectual crowd by keeping books out for skimming. Top off the sumptuous setting with a cocktail (€6-7), beer (€3.50-6), or the delightful *dolce, delizia caprese* (€8). Open daily 10am-2am. Cash only.

Blue Moon Pizzeria, V. T. de Amicis 4, right in P. Gesu Nuovo. Supplier of €1 large bottles of Peroni beer to the masses, as well as all the food needed for a night of socializing in the *piazza*. Open daily 7pm-late. Cash only.

Las Tapas, V. Paladino, 56 (☎081 55 22 168). A low-key favorite of university students, close to the bustling nightlife of P. San Domenico Maggiore. Outdoor seating in an alcove just down V. Nilo from V. dei Tribunali. Enjoy sangria (glass, €1.60; 1L, €9). Service 10%. Open daily 7pm-2am.

NIGHTCLUBS

Rising South, V. S. Sebastiano, 19 (☎333 653 42 73; www.risingsouth.it), nearby P. Gesu Nuovo. *Enoteca*, bar, cultural association, cinema—this club does it all. Plush oriental carpets, vintage chandeliers, and a sound-proof main hall carved from tufa set the scene as one of the university students' favorite spots. Drinks around €4. Open daily as a bar Oct.-May, with special events scheduled in the summer.

TintaDiRosso, V. S. Biagio dei librai, 39 (☎081 79 01 27; www.tintadirosso.it), formerly jazz club Riot. A cultural hot spot in Naples for local musicians and contemporary theater. The complex includes a bar and is surrounded by a dense garden. Check website for weekly events. Cocktails from €4. Open Th-Su 10:30pm-3am. Cash only.

◪ DAYTRIPS FROM NAPLES

▧ HERCULANEUM (ERCOLANO)

To reach Herculaneum, take a Circumvesuviana train from Naples's Stazione Centrale to the "Ercolano Scavi" stop (dir: Sorrento; 20 minutes). Walk 500m downhill to the ticket office. The Municipal Tourist Office, V. IV Novembre, 84, is on the way (☎081 78 81 243; open M-Sa 9am-2pm). The archaeological site is open Apr.-Oct. daily 8:30am-6pm, exit at 7:30pm; Nov.-Mar. 8:30am-3:30pm, with exit at 5pm. €10, EU students €5, EU citizens under 18 or over 65 free. The guided tours are especially enlightening; inquire at the tourist office. Grab an illustrated guidebook (€4-6) at the shops that flank the entrance, or pick up the free Brief Guide to Herculaneum *and map at the entrance.*

Neatly excavated and intact, the remains of the prosperous Roman town of Herculaneum hardly deserve the term "ruins." Indeed, exploring the 2000-year-old houses, complete with frescoes, furniture, mosaics, small sculptures, and wooden doors, can make even the most respectful visitor feel like a *voyeur*. Herculaneum is much more intact and better preserved than Pompeii and displays artifacts in context, which lends to a very rewarding and informative experience.

Though archaeologists long held the opinion that most of Herculaneum's residents escaped the eruption that destroyed Pompeii, recent discoveries of tangled remains suggest that much of the fleeing population was buried in avalanches of volcanic mud. Only the southeastern quarter, about 45% of the city, has been excavated; between 15 and 20 of these excavated houses are open to the public. One of the more alluring is the **House of Deer,** named for the grisly statues of deer being mauled by packs of ghoulish creatures. Here, archaeologists also found the statues *Satyr with a Wineskin* and *Drunken Hercules*, a majestic marble representation of the hero struggling to relieve himself. The **palestra,** a gym and exercise complex, still holds shelves once laden with massage oils and the *strigiles* used to scrape the skin clean after a rubdown. The large vaulted swimming pool, *caldarium* (warm bath), and *frigidarium* (cold bath) in the **baths** are still largely intact. Towering columns in the atrium and bits of delicate stone carving attest to ancient opulence. The **House of the Mosaic of Neptune and Anfitrite** is famous for the breathtaking **mosaic** that gives the structure its name. Two textured, shimmering figures stand beneath a vivid fan of blues and greens, and to the left, bizarre masks cast indelible expressions overhanging flower garlands. In front of the house is a remarkably well-preserved **wine shop.** A mock stucco colonnade distinguishes the **Samnise House.** Down the street, the **House of the Wooden Partition** still has a door in its elegant courtyard, and a clothes press around the corner. Outside the site, 250m to the left on the main road, lies the theater, perfectly preserved, though buried underground. (☎ 081 73 90 963. Occasionally open for visits; call to check.) The **Villa dei Papiri,** 500m west of Herculaneum, was recently the site of quite a stir when a trove of ancient scrolls from the library appeared to include works by Cicero, Virgil, and Horace. (Rarely open to the public; Campania Artecard holders can view the site by special arrangement. Contact the municipal tourist office at ☎ 081 78 81 243.)

CAMPI FLEGREI

SEPSA buses run from P. Municipio to the towns of Campi Flegrei (www.infocampi-flegrei.it). The blue SEPSA bus is in the direction of Monte di Procida/Torregaveta, while the yellow SEPSA bus is labeled #152. To Baia, take the blue or yellow SEPSA bus from M: Pozzuoli (30min.). Don't be confused by the outdated signs on the Ferrovia Cumana; this rail line no longer goes through Baia. In Baia, buy an Unico Fascia 1 ticket (€1.70) and ride all modes of transportation all day. To Cumae, take the SEPSA bus marked Miseno-Cuma from the train station at Baia to the last stop in Cumae (15min., €0.60), and walk to the end of the V. Cumae. The "Cuma" stop on the Ferrovia Circumflegrea is in the modern town, several kilometers from the archaeological sites. Reach Miseno using the Miseno-Cuma SEPSA bus from either Baia or Cumae, and Pozzuoli using the Ferrovia Cumana, Ferrovia Circumflegria, or Naples Metro.

 COOL BUS. When planning your trip to Baia, keep in mind that the blue SEPSA bus is air-conditioned, while the yellow SEPSA bus is not.

The Campi Flegrei (Phlegraean Fields) are a group of tiny coastal towns west of Naples nestled among a chain of lakes and inactive volcanoes. Ancient Greeks colonized this area and associated the thermal nature of the land with Hades, god of the Underworld. The Greek legacy lives on in the ruins at **Cumae,** also immortalized in Virgil's *Aeneid* as Aeneas's landing point in Italy. Later, the Roman elite used the region's hot springs for the intricate bath houses that still stand on the hill over **Baia**, and built an impressive amphitheater near their believed gate to hell in **Pozzuoli**. Today, Italians cover the scorching yet breezy coast of **Miseno** with their fishing boats, relaxing beaches, pizzerias, and restaurants. The sights are too far apart to walk from one to another, so use the omnipresent yellow and blue SEPSA buses. Frequent bus stops are on the side of the road; the front of the bus will list the towns that its route stretches between, and you can always tell your driver your intended destination and ask him to tell you when to get off.

Perched on a hill overlooking the bustling port center of **Baia**, where SEPSA buses drop passengers off, is Baia's central attraction: the luxurious **Roman Baths.** Climb up the stairs and stroll through the well-preserved ruins, remarkable for their multiple stories, beautiful mosaics, and detailed ceilings. At the base of the hill sits the gem of the bath houses, known misleadingly as the ◪**Tempio di Mercurio,** or the Temple of Echoes. Light shines through the oldest domed ceiling in the world, bounces off the water, and reflects on the wall. Faint of heart be warned: lizards and snakes abound in the ancient stone walls. (☎081 86 87 592; www.ulixes.it or www.pierreci.it. Open Tu-Su 9am-7pm. Two-day **archaeological pass** grants admission to the Baths, the Archaeological Museum in Baia, the *scavi* in Cumae, and the Amphitheater in Pozzuoli. €4, with student pass €2. Sold at all participating sites. Included with Artecard.) A short bus ride from the center of Baia accesses the **Castello Aragonese** and the **Museo Archeologico dei Campi Flegrei** with a small collection of ancient artifacts and a beautiful view of Baia's harbor. (☎081 52 33 797, www.pierreci.it. Open Tu-Sa 9am-1hr. before sunset, Su 9am-7pm. Entrance with archaeological pass. Included with Artecard.) For a less conventional view of ruins, try the glass-bottomed boat *Cymba* out of Baia's port to see the **Submerged Roman City.** The boat runs from March 15th to November 2 and can hold 48 people. (☎081 52 65 780; www.associazionealiseo.it. Launches Sa noon, 4pm; Su 10:30am, noon, and 4pm. €7.75, children 6-12 €6.20, under 5 free.)

Cumae (Cuma), founded in the 8th century BC, was the earliest Greek colony on the Italian mainland. Legend claims it was the place where Aeneas, father of Rome, washed up after being shipwrecked in Virgil's *Aeneid.* The highlight of Cumae's *scavi* (excavations) (☎081 85 43 060; www.pierreci.it; included with Artecard) is the ◪**Antro della Sibilla,** a cave gallery that was used as a pizza oven until 1932, when archaeologists realized what it actually was. Stroll through the cave and see where the mythical Sibyl, the most famous oracle this side of Delphi, gave her prophecies. Then gape at the **Augustan Tunnel,** a shaft used for transportation inland from the coast. Remnants of Cumae's Greek past are found in the **Tempio di Apollo,** one flight of stairs above Sibyl's cave, and the **Tempio di Jupiter,** a short hike up the hill from the Temple of Apollo. According to legend, the Tempio di Apollo was constructed by Daedalus, who landed in Cumae after escaping captivity in Crete with his hand-crafted wings. Little remains of the original temples, but the spectacular view of Ischia and the coastline make the hike worthwhile.

Pozzuoli, the Campi Flegri town most accessible from Naples, is a busy port. Be sure not to miss the famous volcanic crater **Solfatara,** accessed either by hiking from the center of Pozzuoli (follow the frequent signs) or by riding bus #152. Solfatara was believed by the ancients to be a portal to Hades—not an unwarranted superstition, considering its eerie glowing yellow rocks, jets of sulfuric gas, rank odor, and unnatural warmth. (☎081 15 26 23 41; www.solfatara.it. Open daily Apr.-Sept. 8:30am-7pm; Oct.-Mar. 8:30am-1hr. before sunset. €5.50, children 5-10 €3. 20% discount with Artecard.) Beneath the crater, a short walk from both the waterfront and the train station, is the ◪**Flavian Amphitheater,** built in the first century AD, the 3rd largest in Italy. The remarkably well-preserved subterranean structures below the floor of the stadium have given engineers an idea of how the

Romans were able to raise caged beast up to the floor of the stadium. (☎081 52 66 007; www.pierreci.it. Open in summer M and W-Su 9am-8pm; in winter 9am-7pm. Entrance with the archaeological pass. Included with Artecard)

Although Baia and Cumae are ideal daytrips from Naples, the pleasant beachfront hotels in **Miseno** make for a fine overnight stay. Take the SEPSA bus from Baia or Cumae to Miseno. The **Hotel Villa del Mare ❸**, V. Misena, 30, is at the last Miseno bus stop. This modern and comfortable choice is steps from the beach. (☎081 523 14 96; www.hotelvilladelmare.it. 15 rooms all with bath, TV, A/C and telephone. Breakfast included. Singles €40; doubles €60. AmEx/MC/V. Call from bus stop for directions.) On the other side of the Miseno Port, there is the **Hotel Miseno ❹**, V. della Shoah, 145, with breezy, small rooms overlooking fishing boats. (☎081 52 35 000; www.hotelmiseno.it. 17 rooms with bath. Breakfast included. Singles €50; doubles €80. AmEx/MC/V.) Close to both Naples and the sites of the Campi Flegrei, **Hotel Gauro ❹**, V. Campi Flegrei, 30, in Pozzuoli, offers guests rooms with balconies, views of the port, A/C, TV, telephone, and minibar. There is also breakfast included, wireless Internet access on the first floor, and parking available. SEPSA buses pass right by it. (☎081 85 30 730; www.gauro.com. With *Let's Go*, singles €55; doubles €73; triples €80; quads €95. Weekends from June 24 to Sept. F-Su nights, singles €45; doubles €55. Deals for extended stays. MC/V.)

MOUNT VESUVIUS

Trasporti Vesuviani buses (☎081 96 34 420) run from Herculaneum and Pompeii to the crater of Vesuvius (From Herculaneum, round-trip €7.60, 2 per day 8:25am and 12:45pm. From Pompei, 10 per day between 8:05am-3:35pm, €8.60. Buy tickets on the bus; schedule at the tourist office or on the bus). Buses leave from the Ercolano Circumvesuviana station. Vesuvius stop is part way up the crater; it's a 20-30min. walk to the top. Admission €6.50. Open in summer 8am-6pm; in winter 8am-3pm.

Climb to the top of the only active volcano on mainland Europe, and watch steam ominously rise from its crater. In the good old days (around 1700) visitors could clamber about in the crater to their hearts' content. Now they have to settle for a front row seat on Vesuvius's steep lip. Every eruption (a total of 28 since AD 79) has helped widen and deepen the aperture, each fiery belch expanding the cavern. Vesuvius hasn't blown its top since March 31, 1944—the longest it has lain dormant in several centuries. A geological station closely monitors tectonic rumblings, and local governments are always ready with a comprehensive evacuation plan. In the summer of 2003, a geological station near the site detected significant subterranean activity, prompting much speculation and concern. Experts agree that the next eruption will likely be the most violent since the blast of 1631, which boasted almost as much force as the AD 79 blast that buried Pompeii.

CASERTA   ☎0823

Caserta is easily accessible by train. Trains to and from Naples (40min., 35 per day 4:50am-9:20pm, €2.80). The Caserta train station is a major stop for local buses (€0.77-0.88). The Reggia is directly opposite the train station. EPT tourist offices operate inside the Reggia and at C. Trieste, 43, at the corner of P. Dante. (☎0823 32 11 37. Both offices open M-F 9am-1-40pm.) For Capua, take the train to "Santa Maria Capua Vètere" (€1.25), walk straight 1 block, and make the 1st left. Take the next left on V. Achille, walk 150m, and turn right on V. E. Ricciardi, which becomes V. Amfiteatro. Or take the blue bus from the Caserta train station (€0.88) to P. Adriano near the ruins. Buses leave for Naples from the intersection 1 block north of the Capua train station.

Few palaces, no matter how opulent, can hold a candle to Caserta's glorious ■**Reggia**, often referred to as "The Versailles of Naples." A world apart from the brutality of Pompeii and more vivacious than Naples's quiet churches, the palace and grounds resonate with a love of art and a passion for beauty. When Bourbon King

Charles III commissioned the palace in 1751, he intended it to rival that of Louis XIV, outshining the Sun King's spectacular abode. The vision endures; the grounds are lovely, and the palace's interior leaves most tripping over their own jaws. Completed in 1775, the expansive lawns, fountains, sculptures, and carefully pruned trees culminate in a 75m man-made waterfall—setting for the final scene of *Star Wars* (1977). On the 3km walk through the park, visitors can peer into the rippling pools, where fish dart among a trove of aquatic plants. At the base of the waterfall are many exquisite sculptures, notably a grouping showing Diana transforming the hunter Octane into a deer. To the right are the **English Gardens**, complete with fake ruins inspired by Pompeii and Paestum (inquire at the Reggia ticket desk for info on guided tours). Instead of making the walk to the waterfall, another option is to take a horse-and-buggy ride from the entrance to the gardens (or a less-romantic trip on one of the park's rattling orange mini-buses). The **palazzo** itself boasts 1200 rooms, 1742 windows, 34 staircases, and a preposterously ornate bassinet: it's overseen by an angel, suspended over a bed of bronze fruit, and held aloft by a cherub. Clocks and an intriguing collection of 18th-century children's toys also inhabit the halls. The main stairway, guarded by a pair of sculpted lions, is a highlight of the palace's architecture. Frescoes and intricate marble floors adorn the royal apartments, some boasting beds guarded by sculptures of fearsome mythical beasts. (☎0823 32 14 00. Open Tu-Su 9am-7:30pm; park open 9am-6:30pm. €6.50 for entrance to *palazzo* and gardens. Gardens only, €2. Included with Artecard.) One train stop from Caserta lies **Capua** and an impressive **Roman amphitheater**, much smaller but as intact as the Colosseum in Rome. The *hypogeum*, an elaborate basement with tunnels, brought gladiators and beasts into the arena. It was the site of many bloody *munera* (gladiatorial contests) and *venationes* (spectacularly staged beast hunts) in antiquity. (☎0823 79 88 64. Open Tu-Su 9am-6:30pm. €2.50, students €1.25. Included with Campania Artecard.)

POMPEII (POMPEI)   ☎081

On the morning of August 24, AD 79, a deadly cloud of volcanic ash from the eruption of nearby Mt. Vesuvius overtook Pompeii, engulfing the city in black clouds and catching the prosperous residents by surprise. Mere hours after the eruption, stately buildings, works of art, and human bodies were sealed in casts of ash—natural tombs that would remain undisturbed for centuries. Today visitors to the site bear witness to an intimate record of the town's demise. Since excavation efforts began in 1748, archaeologists have continually turned up new discoveries in their ongoing mission to understand life in the Roman era. Most of the interesting artifacts from Pompeii are in the Museo Archeologico Nazionale in Naples; what remains at the site are homes, streets, and public buildings. If you are looking to learn about how people lived around AD 79 when Vesuvius erupted, start your day at the museum at Naples looking at the extensive Pompeii collection.

HEAT EXHAUSTION. The sites at Pompeii afford visitors few water fountains and little shade. Bring lots of water and keep cool to avoid heat stroke. Around 15 people per year die from heat-related illnesses at Pompeii. If you need medical attention, flag down a guide or call ☎113.

◪▨ TRANSPORTATION AND PRACTICAL INFORMATION

The quickest route to Pompeii (25km south of Naples) is the **Circumvesuviana train** (☎081 77 22 444). Board at Naples's Stazione Centrale (dir: Sorrento; 40min., 2 per hr. 5:40am-10:40pm, €2.30), or from Sorrento's station. Get off at the "Pompei Scavi" stop. Eurail passes are not valid. The Porta Marina entrance to the ruins is

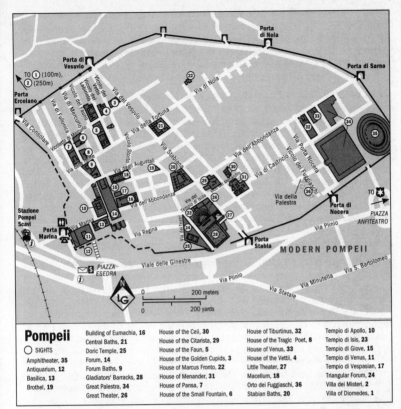

Pompeii

○ SIGHTS

Amphitheater, **35**
Antiquarium, **12**
Basilica, **13**
Brothel, **19**

Building of Eumachia, **16**
Central Baths, **21**
Doric Temple, **25**
Forum, **14**
Forum Baths, **9**
Gladiators' Barracks, **28**
Great Palestra, **34**
Great Theater, **26**

House of the Ceii, **30**
House of the Citarista, **29**
House of the Faun, **5**
House of the Golden Cupids, **3**
House of Marcus Fronto, **22**
House of Menander, **31**
House of Pansa, **7**
House of the Small Fountain, **6**

House of Tiburtinus, **32**
House of the Tragic Poet, **8**
House of Venus, **33**
House of the Vettii, **4**
Little Theater, **27**
Macellum, **18**
Orto dei Fuggiaschi, **36**
Stabian Baths, **20**

Tempio di Apollo, **10**
Tempio di Isis, **23**
Tempio di Giove, **15**
Tempio di Venus, **11**
Tempio di Vespasian, **17**
Triangular Forum, **24**
Villa dei Misteri, **2**
Villa of Diomedes, **1**

downhill to the left. Less frequent FS trains also leave from the Naples station, stopping at modern Pompeii en route to Salerno (30min., every hr., €2.20). The FS train station is a 10min. walk from the excavation's eastern entrance; to reach this entrance, walk to the end of V. Sacra and turn left on V. Roma.

The excavations stretch along an east-west axis, with the modern town (with hotels and restaurants) at the eastern end. Stop by the **tourist office,** V. Sacra, 1 (☎081 85 07 255; www.pompeiisites.org), or the info booth at the site, for a free **map.** From the Pompei Scavi stop, take a right; follow the road down the hill to the **branch office** at P. Porta Marina Inferiore, 12. (☎800 01 33 50. Both offices open M-F 8am-3:30pm, Sa 8am-2pm.) Free **luggage storage** is available at the entrance to the ruins. There is a **police station** and **post office** at the site entrance, at P. Schettini, 1 (☎081 85 06 164), and another police station at P. B. Longo, where V. Roma ends.

👁 SIGHTS

Pompeii entrances are open April-October daily 8:30am to 7:30pm, with last entrance at 6pm, and November-March 8:30am-5pm, last entrance at 3:30pm. A comprehensive exploration takes all day. (Tickets €10, EU students €5, EU citizens under 18 or over 65 free.) The budget-conscious in search of an engaging tour should consider the excellent **audioguides,** available at the site's entrance. Consult the free **map** and punch in the site's audio code to hear an informative description

(€6.50, 2 guides for €10, children's guide €4.50). Call **GATA Tours** (☎ 081 861 56 61) for information on **guided tours,** which are more expensive than the audioguides and usually available only to groups. However, guides also gather solo travelers by the ticket office to form tour groups. A tour is a worthwhile investment; otherwise, endure hefty admission fees and a poor labeling system to get a peek at the ruins, many of which are under restoration and covered by scaffolding.

NEAR FORUM. The **basilica** walls, to the right upon entering the ruins, are decorated with faux-marble stucco. Before the eruption, lawyers and prominent citizens fought legal battles on this floor. Walk farther down V. D. Marina to reach the **forum,** ringed by a marble colonnade. Once dotted with statues of emperors and gods, this site was the commercial, civic, and religious heart of the city. Glass display cases house gruesome body casts of Vesuvius's victims, contorted in surprise and agony. The wasted **Tempio di Giove**—largely destroyed by an earthquake that struck 17 years before the eruption—stands at the upper end of the forum. To the left, the **Tempio di Apollo** contains statues of Apollo and Diana (originals displayed in the **Museo Archeologico Nazionale,** p. 568) and a column topped by a sundial. On the opposite side of the forum, the **Tempio di Vespasian** retains a delicate frieze depicting the elaborate preparation for a sacrifice. To the right, the **Building of Eumachia** has a door frame carved with animals and insects in acanthus scrolls.

NEAR HOUSE OF THE FAUN. At the **Forum Baths,** archaeologists have chipped away parts of body casts to reveal teeth and bones beneath. Over the course of the excavations, the **House of the Faun** has yielded stunning treasures, among them a dancing bronze faun and the spectacular Alexander Mosaic (originals now in the **Museo Archeologico Nazionale,** p. 568). The building's opulence leads archaeologists to believe that it was the dwelling of one of the richest men in town. The **House of the Vettii** was the home of two brothers whose rivalry is apparent on every wall. A famous painting of the fertility god Priapus, flaunting his very ample endowment, is in the vestibule. Phalli were believed to scare off evil spirits in ancient times. *(Exit Forum through the upper end by the cafeteria; Forum Baths are on the left. A right on V. della Fortuna leads to the House of the Faun. Continuing on V. della Fortuna, turn left on V. dei Vettii to reach the House of the Vettii on the left.)*

NEAR BROTHEL. A quick right off V. degli Augustali, a well-worn road frozen in a perpetual state of reconstruction, leads to the small brothel, the **Lupanare** (literally, dwelling of she-wolves). Above each bedstall, a pornographic painting advertises the specialty of its occupant with unabashed precision. Even 2000 years later, this is still the most popular spot in town—expect a wait. The street continues down to the main avenue, V. dell' Abbondanza. The **Stabian Baths,** to the left, were privately owned and therefore fancier than the Forum Baths. More body casts—some of the site's most affectingly macabre—rest in dusty glass cases. The separate men's and women's sides both include a dressing room, cold baths (*frigidarie*), warm baths (*tepidarie*), and hot steam baths (*caldarie*); on the women's side there is an impressive marine-creature mosaic. Look down to see the remnants of the *hypocaust,* an intricate system used to channel hot steam underneath the floor. *(From V. dei Vettii, cross V. della Fortuna over to V. Storto, and turn left on V. degli Augustali.)*

NEAR GREAT THEATER. The **Great Theater** was built during the 2nd century BC. Many stone-walled cells, once home to gladiators during their training, line the edges of the field in front. Music and dance concerts were held in the **Little Theater,** built slightly later. North of the theaters stands the **Tempio di Isis,** Pompeii's monument to the Egyptian fertility goddess. Through the exit on the right, the road passes the fine **House of the Ceii** and the **House of Menander.** At the end of the street, take a left to re-connect to the main road. The altar here was built to ward off evil spirits, which Romans believed gathered at crossroads. *(Across the street, V. dei Teatri leads to the Great Theater and the Little Theater.)*

NEAR AMPHITHEATER. Red graffiti crowds the walls along V. dell'Abbondanza, expressing everything from political slogans to insults to declarations of love. Popular favorites include "Albanus is a bugger," "Restitutus has deceived many girls many times," and the lyrical "Lovers, like bees, lead a honey-sweet life." At the end of the street await the **House of Tiburtinus** and **House of Venus**, where gardens have been replanted according to modern knowledge of ancient horticulture. Nearby is the oldest standing **amphitheater** in the world (80 BC), which once held crowds of 12,000. The spectators determined whether a gladiator would live or die during battle with a casual thumbs down or thumbs up. In the **Orto dei Fuggiaschi**, the body casts of victims fleeing the city are displayed in a glass case. The ash formed such a perfect casing that it is still possible to see the expressions and individual facial features of some. Director of the excavations from 1860 to 1875, Giuseppe Fiorelli created the method of filling the cavities in the ash left by bodies with plaster to form the casts that can be seen today.

VILLA DEI MISTERI. The **Villa dei Misteri** is the best-preserved Pompeiian villa. The **Dionysiac Frieze** depicts a bride's initiation into the cult of Dionysus. Nearby, the famed **Cave Canem mosaic** still guards the entry to its master's villa, though now it only aims to protect the home from the myriad flashbulbs of tourists. Head through the *porta* for a great view of the entire city. *(For the Villa dei Misteri go to the far western end of V. della Fortuna, turn right on V. Consolare, and walk all the way up Pta. Ercolano.)*

BAY OF NAPLES

The Bay of Naples is nestled in the horseshoe between Naples and Sorrento, both convenient departure points to explore the pleasure islands of Capri, Ischia, and Procida. Each island offers unique amenities to the weary traveler. On Capri expensive shops and pristine waters are the playground of the rich and the envy of everyone else. Ischia's hot springs and therapeutic waters beckon those seeking health of mind and body. Procida, the quietest island, retains winding streets and empty shores that call to the independent voyager. July and August are busy, but a low-season jaunt ensures a break from crowds and intense sunshine. Veer fearlessly from main avenues and take narrow side streets to glimpse town life. Merge with crowds at the famous villas and grottoes, but come back later to take a private dip. Above all, just take it easy.

SORRENTO ☎081

Built on the cliffs above the glittering Bay of Naples, the magic of Sorrento (pop. 16,000) lies in its tiny alleys and quiet side streets. Its *piazze* and roads are overrun with tourists and the 13,000 hotel beds are often full during summer. However, Sorrento's old city and Marina Grande offer areas to window shop or stroll. More significantly, Sorrento is a convenient stopover, thanks to cheap accommodations, swift transportation connections, and proximity to the Amalfi Coast.

▐ TRANSPORTATION

Circumvesuviana railway (☎081 77 22 444), just off P. Lauro, runs 39 **trains** per day (6:17am-11:55pm) to: Herculaneum (45min., €1.80); Naples (1hr., €3.20); and Pompeii (30min., €1.80). Ferries and hydrofoils depart for the Bay of Naples islands. The port is accessible from P. Tasso by bus (€1). **Linee Marittime Partenopee** (☎081 80 71 812) runs **ferries** (40min., 5 per day 8:35am-4:55pm, €7.50) and **hydrofoils** (20min., 19 per day 7:20am-6:20pm, €10.50) to Capri. It also runs ferries to Positano (20min., 3 per day 8:50am-3:30pm, €6) and hydrofoils to Naples (35min., 8 per day 7:20am-8:25pm, €7.50). **Caremar** (☎081 80 73 077; www.caremar.it) runs ferries to Capri (50min., 4 per day 7:45am-7pm, €5). **Metrò del Mare** (☎199 60 07 00) goes to Amalfi (30min., 4 per day 8:30am-6pm, €6). Ticket offices open just before boats depart. **SITA buses** leave from Circumvesuviana station for the Amalfi Coast and are the best way to connect to south of the city. Twenty-one buses per day 6:30am-9:30pm head to Amalfi (1¼hr., €2.40) and Positano (40min., €1.30). The city runs orange **internal buses** (€1) every 20min. Buy tickets for SITA and local lines at a bar, *tabaccherie*, or at the hotel in P. Lauro. The Sorrento tourist office has ferry, bus, and train schedules. **Cars** and **scooters** are available for rent at **Rent A Car,** C. Italia, 253. Scooters start at €33 per day. (☎081 87 82 801. Insurance included. Driver's license and credit card required. Cars with chauffeurs available. 18+. Open daily 8am-1pm and 4-8:30pm. AmEx/MC/V.)

✦ 🛈 ORIENTATION AND PRACTICAL INFORMATION

Most of Sorrento rests atop a flat shelf that descends steeply to the Bay of Naples. Festooned with flags from the home countries of its visitors, **Piazza Tasso** is at the town's center. Steep stairways and roads connect it to **Marina Piccola. Corso Italia** runs through P. Tasso; facing the sea, the **train** and **bus stations** are in **Piazza Lauro** to the right, and the old city is to the left. **Corso S. Caesaro** runs parallel to C. Italia on the old city side of P. Tasso.

Tourist Office: Lungomare de Maio, 35 (☎081 80 74 033; www.sorrentotourism.com). From P. Tasso, take Lungomare de Maio to the far end of P. S. Antonio and continue toward the port. Office is to the right in the Circolo dei Forestieri compound. Free **maps.** Open M-Sa Apr.-Sept. 8:30am-6:30pm; Oct.-Mar. 8:30am-2pm and 4-6:15pm.

Currency Exchange: No-commission currency exchange is everywhere and easy to find. **Western Union** kiosk at V. S. Cesareo, 26 (☎081 87 73 552). Open in summer daily 10am-2pm and 4-10pm; closed in winter.

English-Language Bookstore: Libreria Tasso, V. S. Cesareo, 96 (☎081 80 71 639; www.libreriatasso.com), stocks thrillers, including the incomparable 🔳**Let's Go.** Classics and new fiction also available. Open M-Sa 9:30am-1:15pm and 5-10:45pm, Su 11am-1:30pm and 6:30-11pm. MC/V.

Laundromat: Wash and Dry, V. Fuoro, 3, just off C. Italia. 6 washers and 6 dryers. €8 per load. Open daily 8am-8pm.

Emergency: ☎113. **Police:** ☎(081 807 30 88), on Vco. 3° Rota. From the station, go right on C. Italia and turn left after V. Nizza.

Hospital: Ospedale Civile di Sorrento, C. Italia, 129 (☎081 53 31 111).

Internet Access: Matilda, P. Tasso, 1 (☎081 87 73 236; www.matildaclub.net). Down the staircase behind the flags in P. Tasso. 8 computers with ADSL connections. €3 per 30min., €5 per hr. Check email while singing karaoke (daily 9pm) and dancing like a fiend. You're bound to find something fun in this 6-floor complex that spans from P. Tasso to the road for the marina. Open daily 4pm-4am.

Post Office: C. Italia, 210 (☎081 80 72 828), near P. Lauro. Open M-F 8am-6:30pm, Sa 8am-12:30pm. **Postal Code:** 80067.

🏠 ACCOMMODATIONS AND CAMPING

Reasonably priced accommodations and a well-run transportation network make Sorrento a convenient gateway to the Amalfi Coast or more southern destinations.

Many visitors head to nearby beaches and towns during the day and return to Sorrento's hotels at night, a great way to avoid inflated prices for lodging and food on the Amalfi Coast. Reserve ahead in summer. To avoid being overcharged, ask hotel managers to see an official price list. Prices below are for high season.

■ **Residenza Maresca**, C. Italia, 5, (☎ 081 87 84 616). The proprietors of Ristorante Giardinello rent out immaculate apartments and rooms around Sorrento. All have TV, refrigerator, bath. Most have A/C, a cooking area, and great views of the city and surrounding hills. On top of that, guests have the option of in-room massage therapy at a large discount (€10 per 30min., €20 per hr.). Breakfast at restaurant included. Reservations recommended at least 15 days in advance. With *Let's Go*, doubles €60. ❹

Ostello Le Sirene, V. degli Aranci, 160 (☎081 80 72 925; www.hostel.it.). From the station, turn left and follow the signs. A good base for daytrips, this busy, conveniently located hostel is next door to a popular bar. Dorms, though slightly cramped, each have their own bathroom. They also offer cheaper dorms in nearby town of Sant'Angelo (€14 per night). Breakfast and sheets included. Four-bed dorms €20; 6-bed dorms €18; 8-bed dorms €16; doubles €60. ❷

Hotel Elios, V. Capo, 33 (☎081 87 81 812), halfway to the Punta del Capo. Take bus A from in front of the flags of P. Tasso. The 14 rooms are not impressive, but 2 large terraces and a hilltop location make for great views. A hike from Sorrento's bus and train stations, but quiet as a result. Open Apr.-Oct. Singles €35-40; doubles €60-65; triples €80; quad €100. Cash only. ❸

■ **Nube d'Argento**, V. del Capo, 21 (☎081 87 81 344; www.nubedargento.com). Bus A from P. Tasso. Manicured grounds and helpful staff make Nube d'Argento a comfortable option. Seaside camping complex with pool, hot showers, market, and restaurant. Laundry €7. Reservations required for bungalows; reserve 2 months ahead for Aug. €7-9 per person, €8-9.50 per large tent. 2-person bungalows €50-60; 4-person bungalows €65-100; 6-person bungalows €80-100. 10% discount with *Magic Europe* camping brochure (available at any campsite) or International Camping Card. AmEx/MC/V. ❶

🍴 FOOD

Forgo the crowded tourist haunts, skip the unappetizing British cuisine, and seek out Sorrento's *trattorie* and restaurants for decent Italian fare. Many places offer good prices and substantial portions. Local favorites include *gnocchi alla Sorrentina* (potato dumplings in tomato sauce, mozzarella, and basil) and *cannelloni* (pasta stuffed with meat or cheese). **Fabbrica Liquori**, V. S. Cesareo, 51, provides free samples of *nocillo*, a mysterious dark walnut liqueur, and *limoncello*, its lemon cousin. Follow V. S. Cesareo from P. Tasso for a **market** where sweet, ripe fruit awaits. There's a giant **STANDA** supermarket on C. Italia, 225. (Open M-Sa 8:30am-1:20pm and 5-8:55pm, Su 9:30am-1pm and 5-8:30pm. AmEx/MC/V.)

■ **Ristorante e Pizzeria Giardiniello**, V. dell'Accademia, 7 (☎081 87 84 616; ristorante-giardiniello@libero.it). Take 2nd left off V. Giuliani, which runs off C. Italia at the cathedral. Mamma Luisa does the cooking in this family-run nook. Try her delightful *gnocchi* (€5) or *linguini al cartoccio* (with mixed seafood; €7). Finish a meal with arguably the best fruit *gelato* in Italy. Secluded seating in a bamboo enclosure. Cover €1.50. Open June-Sept. daily 11am-2am; Oct.-May M-W and F-Su 11am-2am. AmEx/MC/V. ❷

■ **Davide**, V. Giuliani, 39 (☎081 87 81 337), right off C. Italia, 2 blocks from P. Tasso. Enjoy excellent *gelato* from a seat on the bar's garishly postmodern furniture. It's nearly impossible to choose from over 50 flavors including "Peach Delicate," "Fig Heavenly," and the mysterious "Perfume of Sorrento." Cones from €2. Open daily 9am-midnight. Closed Nov.-Mar. Cash only. ❶

Bollicine Wine Bar, V. dell'Accademia, 9/11 (☎081 87 84 616; www.vineriabolli-cine.com). The perfect place to grab a light lunch. All produce is fresh and local, the wine list is long, and the classy dark wood interior provides an escape from the typical tourist fare. *Bruschette* from €4.50, *panini* €3.50-5, wine from €2. Open Tu-Su 11:30am-3pm and 6pm-2am. MC/V. ❶

La Pasteria Di Corso, V. Pietà, 3/5 (☎081 87 73 432), in the alley behind the Tasso statue in P. Tasso. Dine by candlelight on old-style *cucina Sorrentina.* Close to the main *piazza* but quietly secluded around a corner. Enjoy *antipasti* with fresh cucumber and eggplant (€10-13) and a delectable fruit brandy after dinner. *Primi* €7-9, *secondi* €9-12. Cover €2. Open W-Su 7pm-midnight. AmEx/MC/V. ❸

The Red Lion, V. Marziale, 25 (☎081 80 73 089; www.theredlion.it), a right off C. Italia on the way to the train station from P. Tasso (follow the signs). Popular among tourists for its low prices and roaring atmosphere (especially during soccer games) it's packed every night—expect lines in summer. Full meal €12. AmEx/MC/V. ❷

🅖 🎵 SIGHTS AND ENTERTAINMENT

Sorrento's popularity among tourists, compared to the more beautiful and serene towns nearby on the Amalfi Coast, is remarkable. If you're willing to conquer the stairs, the **Marina Grande,** far from the crowds swarming around P. Tasso, provides a pleasant setting for relaxing on a bench after a long day of walking, beaching, or daytripping. A walk to **Punta del Capo** is another fine option, as the ruins of **Villa di Pollio Felice** are clustered around a beautiful cove. Take bus A from P. Tasso to the end of the route, then take the footpath to the right of the stop. Bring a suit and a towel for a memorable swim among the ruins.

The **old city** and the area around **Piazza Tasso** heat up after dark. Hands-down the most stylish bar in Sorrento, **Photo Bar,** formerly Gatto Nero, V. Correale, 19, has a garden and creative interior with giant color photos. (☎081 87 73 686. Open Tu-Su noon-3pm and 7pm-late.) At the rooftop lemon grove of **The English Inn,** C. Italia, 56, a fun-loving crowd gathers after 10:30pm on summer nights to dance to blasting music. They return the next morning for a hearty, foreign breakfast (€5-7) of eggs, sausages, and bacon. (☎081 80 74 357. Open daily 9am-1am, later on weekends.).

ISLAND HOPPING. Ferries (*traghetti*) or faster, more expensive **hydrofoils** (*aliscafi*) depart from Naples and Sorrento, and connect a few islands to each other. For trips to Ischia and Procida from the mainland, traveling via Pozzuoli (easily reached on the Naples Metro, line #1) is shortest and cheapest; for Capri, Sorrento makes an efficient base. The most frequented routes to Capri and Ischia are through Naples's Mergellina and Molo Beverello ports. To reach Molo Beverello from Stazione Centrale, take bus R2 from P. Garibaldi to P. Municipio on the waterfront. For Mergellina, take the Naples Metro, line #1 to the "Mergellina" stop (accessible from Stazione Centrale in P. Garibaldi). Ferries and hydrofoils also run between the islands, but with less frequency than between the major ports.

PROCIDA   ☎081

Calmly rippling waters and netted fishing boats bobbing in the port create a scene so exquisite that Procida (pop. 11,000) has been used as a setting for numerous films, including as *Il Postino* and *The Talented Mr. Ripley*. Sun-baked buildings quietly crowd a port awash in cheery pastels. From the fresh seafood to the citrusy sweetness of the many lemon groves, Procida awakens your senses as you stumble upon the most authentic, untouristed island in the Bay of Naples; cross your fingers and hope that others don't do the same.

▐ TRANSPORTATION

Ferries and hydrofoils: To **Naples, Pozzuoli,** and **Ischia.** All boats dock at Marina Grande, near the ticket offices.

Caremar (☎081 89 67 280) runs to: **Ischia** (ferries: 35min., 10 per day 7:30am-11pm, around €2.30; hydrofoils: 20min., 3 per day 10:35am-3:45pm, €3.10); **Naples** (ferries: 1hr., 5 per day 7:15am-8pm, €4.50; hydrofoils: 40min., 6 per day 6:50am-6:50pm, €7.90); **Pozzuoli** (ferries: 50min., 3 per day 8:55-6:05pm, €2.60; hydrofoils: 30min., 8:25am, €3.10).

Procida Lines (☎081 89 60 328). Hydrofoils to **Pozzuoli** (30min., 8 per day 4am-7:15pm, €6).

SNAV (☎081 89 69 975; www.snav.it) runs hydrofoils to **Naples** (40min., 4 per day 7:35am-5:40pm, €9) and **Ischia** (40 min., 8 per day 7:50am-9:10pm, €3.56). Confirm times and prices at port ticket offices.

Buses: SEPSA buses (€0.80 at *tabaccherie*, €1.10 onboard) depart from the port and serve entire island. Frequency and times vary seasonally; see schedules available at the tourist office or posted at many *tabaccherie* and hotels.

L1 covers the middle section of the island, running past most of the hotels and campgrounds before stopping at the port of **Chiaiolella,** the site of the liveliest restaurants and beaches. (Every 20min. 6:10am-11pm.)

C1 follows much the same route, but also covers the less populated northwestern part of the island. (Every 40min. 6:50am-8:25pm.)

C2 runs to the northeastern part of the island. (Every 40min., 6:55am-8:25pm.)

L2 serves the southeastern part. (Every hr., 6:25am-8:25pm.) Bus drivers rarely call out stops; tell your driver where you want to get off and ask him to remind you when the stop approaches.

Taxis and **microtaxis:** ☎081 896 87 85. Taxi stand near the docks. However, walking around Procida can be an adventure, as cars, trucks, and *motorini* don't like to share the narrow streets with pedestrians. Flatten up against the nearest wall when they come speeding by. Street names and numbers are more like suggestions than cold, hard facts, so be prepared to get lost, which is half the fun of Procida.

▐ PRACTICAL INFORMATION

The **AAST Tourist Office,** V. Roma, 92, is to the right from the dock on the main port, in the same building as the ferry ticket offices. Free **maps** are available with street names and site locations. (☎081 81 01 968; www.procida.net. Open daily 9am-1pm and 3-6pm.) There is an **ATM** by the port, at V. Roma, 103. **Western Union** is available at **Navigator,** V. P. Umberto, 33, on the way to Terra Murata (Open daily 10am-1pm 5-8pm.) In case of **emergency,** call an **ambulance** at ☎118 or the **carabinieri,** V. G. da Procida, 22 (☎112 or 081 89 67 160). A 24hr. **emergency clinic,** V. V. Emanuele, 191 (☎081 89 69 058), is accessible by bus L1, L2, or C1. **Internet** access is available at **Bar Capriccio,** V. Roma, 99, to the left of the ferry ticket office when facing away from the water. (☎081 89 69 506. Open daily 7am-2am. €3 per 30min., €5 per hr.) The **post office,** at the corner of V. V. Emanuele and V. Liberta, also has an ATM. (☎081 89 60 740. Open M-F 8am-1:30pm, Sa 8am-12:30pm.) **Postal Code:** 80070.

⌂ ACCOMMODATIONS

Spending an inexpensive night on Procida is difficult, so budget travelers may want to make the island a daytrip from Naples. For those able or willing, however, Procida offers gorgeous options.

La Rosa dei Venti, V. Vincenzo Rinaldi, 32 (☎081 89 68 385; www.vacanzeaprocida.it). Take a taxi from the port to this ideal space for secluded relaxation. Located on the northwestern part of the island, it is difficult to reach on foot. Like living in the Garden of Eden, 20 *cassette* ("boxes" with kitchenette and dining area) are surrounded by lush flowers and offer a break from the outside world. Private beach access. Breakfast included. Internet €2.50 per hr. 2-6 person *cassetta* €25-37 per person, per night. Mandatory €100 refundable security deposit. AmEx/MC/V. ❷

Pensione Savoia, V. Lavadera, 32 (☎081 89 67 616; hotelsavoiaprocida@virgilio.it). Take bus L2. Recently renovated accommodations sport *majolica* tiles, cheery yellow rooms, high ceilings, and great views. Hotel has friendly management and a pleasant atmosphere. Breakfast €4. Rooms €40-75 per person. Cash only. ❸

Rooms by Prochyta Bar, Marina Chiaiolella (☎081 89 60 061; www.procida.it/prochyta). To the right just before V. Giovanni da Procida opens up to Marina Chiaiolella. Decently priced rustic rooms are a stone's throw from the port. Jovial management and kitchen access. Breakfast included. All rooms with bath. Doubles €50-85. ❺

Hotel Celeste, V. Rivoli, 6 (☎081 89 67 488; www.hotelceleste.it). From Marina Chiaiolella, walk 1 block up V. Giovanni da Procida, taking the first right on V. Rivoli. 35 spacious rooms share interior courtyard and have bath, TV, phone, and A/C. Terraces have views of the vineyard. Attentive staff. Easy access to beaches. Reserve ahead in summer. Mandatory half pension in Aug. Singles €50-60, half pension €90; doubles €60-92/€140. AmEx/MC/V. ❹

Hotel Riviera, V. Giovanni da Procida, 36 (☎/fax 081 89 67 197; www.hotelrivieraprocida.it). Take bus L1 or L2, then ascend the winding drive. 25 comfortable rooms have bath, A/C, TV, and phone. Convenient access to beaches at Ciraccio and Ciracciello. Breakfast included. Reserve ahead. Open Apr.-Sept. Singles €42-60; doubles €60-90. 10% discount with *Let's Go,* excluding July-Aug. AmEx/MC/V. ❹

Campeggio Caravella (☎081 810 18 38), on V. IV Novembre. Take bus L1 or C1. Clean, pleasant grounds with snack bar and flowers. 15min. from beach at Ciraccio. Reserve in June for Aug. Open June 15-Sept. 15. €6 per person, €6 per tent. Cash only. ❶

▯ FOOD

Like accommodations, Procida's dining options are not designed for the budget-minded. For snacks on the go, try the **Supermerc SISA,** V. Libertà, 72 (☎081 89 68 246), across the street from the **post office.** For those willing to pay, many excellent restaurants are located in both the **Porto** and **Chiaiolella** parts of town. Family-run **Il Galleone ❸,** V. Marina Chiaiolella, 35, distinguishes itself from the more touristy restaurants along the marina with open-air seating and very attentive service. Settle down for great seafood *antipasti* (€5-8) and watch the boats come and go. (☎081 89 69 622. *Primi* €7-8, *secondi* €8-13. Daily *menù* €16. Cover €1.50. Open daily noon-4pm and 7:30-11pm. AmEx/MC/V.) Come to **Da Michele ❸,** V. Marina Chiaiolella, 29, for Procidan fare just above the harbor. Try the succulent rabbit (€7), a highlight of island cuisine. (☎081 89 67 422. Pizza €2.50-6.50. *Primi* €4-9, *secondi* around €10. Cash only.) One of the many Porto restaurants is **Ristorante Lo Sfizio ❷,** V. Roma, 81 Enjoy the fresh seafood, just pulled from the harbor, as you watch people stroll down V. Roma. (☎081 89 69 931; www.ristorantesfizio.it. Pizza €3.10-6.50. *Primi* €7-10, *secondi* €6-10. Daily *menù* €15. Open M-Tu and Th-Su noon-3pm and 7:50pm-12am. AmEx/MC/V.) After dinner, ask at any bar for the syrupy *limoncello,* made from Procidan lemons.

👁 SIGHTS

Take bus C2 to the **Abbazia San Michele Arcangelo** (Abbey of St. Michael the Archangel), or make the steep uphill trek to Procida's easternmost and highest hilltop. From the left side of the port (facing away from the water), walk up V. V. Emanuele, taking the first left on V. P. Umberto. A plain yellow facade guards splendid 15th-century gold frescoes and eerie bleeding Christ figures within. The abbey's opulent scroll work and stately archways prove a jarring contrast to the quaint, unornamented island outdoors. Take a moment to admire the deeds of St. Michael emblazoned on the domes. (☎081 89 67 612. Open daily 9:45am-12:45pm and 3pm-5:30pm. Free.) En route to the abbey, the medieval walls of **Terra Murata** are downhill from the monastery, on V. S. Michele. Procida's oldest settlement, this area has winding streets, squat stone buildings, and islanders roaring around on *motorini*. The **lookout point** before the old city walls opens onto the idyllic marina of **Corricella;** pack a picnic and enjoy the breeze. The night view is especially nice.

Procida has several **beaches,** most of which remain pleasantly uncrowded. The dark sand and calm water of **Ciraccio** stretch across the western shore and are sprinkled with snack bars and drink stands. Its western end, near Chiaiolella, is at the end of the L1 line. Another popular beach is **Chiaia,** on the southeastern cove, accessible by L1, L2, and C1. Perhaps the prettiest of them all, **Pozzo Vecchia** (a.k.a. Il Postino Beach, after the movie was filmed here) rests amid striking layered cliffs. Don't forget to pay homage to Sophia Loren, whose pictures adorn the entrance. **Procida Diving Center** runs scuba diving tours that introduce participants to a host of interesting sites and sea life. One dive and full equipment rental for €28. Kids, beginners, and advanced divers are all welcome. The offices are at Marina di Chiaiolella. (☎339 43 58 493; www.procidadiving.it. Open M-Sa 9am-1pm and 3:30pm-7pm.) Lemons are ubiquitous in Procida and honored for their place in Procidan culture in the **Festa del Limone.** Besides food tastings featuring lemons, highlights include a fashion show and a debate on—what else—the lemon.

ISCHIA ☎081

Ischia's combination of sea, sand, and sky presents a rich, earthy beauty so perfect, it's almost eerie. The island (pop. 55,000) was once an active volcano, and hot springs, ruins, and lemon groves create an atmosphere that is downright Edenic. Travelers have sought out Ischia since ancient times (gaining it mention in the *Iliad* and *Aeneid*), and the appeal has scarcely abated. The island is popular with German tourists, so prepare to step off the ferry in summer to German signs, newspapers, and voices. The Italians keep to the therapeutic hot springs and thermal spas that, according to locals, bring relief from any ailment. Bargains and breathing room are hard to find, but *la dolce vita* is ever-present.

◪ TRANSPORTATION

Ferries: From Ischia, ferries and hydrofoils run to **Pozzuoli, Naples, Procida, Capri,** and **Sorrento.** Most ferries arrive and leave from **Ischia Porto,** where the main ticket offices are located. Some ferries arrive and depart from **Casamicciola,** on the northern side of the island. Take the #1, 2, or CS bus from Ischia Porto. Schedules and prices are subject to change. Call individual ferry lines for details.

Caremar (☎081 98 48 18; www.caremar.it) runs to: **Naples** (ferries: 1½hr., 8 per day 6:45am-8:10pm; hydrofoils: 1hr., 6 per day 6:50am-7:10pm, €10.50, €6); and **Pozzuoli** (ferries: 1hr., 3 per day 8:25am-6:55pm, €3.60); **Procida** (ferries: 35min., 8 per day 6:45am-7:30pm; hydrofoils: 20min., 3 per day noon-4:15pm, €3.10, €4). Most Caremar ferries leave from Ischia Porto. Ticket offices open approximately 30min. before departure of 1st boat.

Traghetti Pozzuoli (☎081 99 28 03; www.traghettipozzuoli.it) runs to **Naples** (1½hr., 7 per day 6:40am-6:50pm, €8) and **Pozzuoli** (1hr., 6 per day 2:30am-7pm, €8). Ticket offices open approximately 30min. before departure of 1st boat.

Alilauro (☎081 99 18 88; www.alilauro.it) runs hydrofoils to: **Capri** from Ischia Porto (40min., 10:40am, €12.20); **Naples**, Mergellina (45min.; from Ischia Porto 11 per day 8am-7pm, €11.50; from Forio M and F-Su 4 per day 1-8:30pm, Tu-Th 1 per day 3:40pm, €13); **Naples**, Molo Beverello (45 min.; from Ischia Porto 11 per day 6:35am-7pm, €12; from Forio 3 per day 12:50-6pm, €13); **Sorrento** from Ischia Porto (daily, 5:20pm, €14.50).

Buses: Orange **SEPSA buses** depart from the intersection on V. Iasolino and V. B. Cossa. Take a right from Molo 1 or a left from Molo 2 and walk along the port, following the road as it curves away from the port. The main lines are **CS, CD,** and **#1. CS** circles the island counter-clockwise, hitting Ischia Porto, Casamicciola Terme, Lacco Ameno, Forio, Panza Cava Grado (Sant'Angelo), Serrara, Fontana, Buonopane, and Barano. **CD** follows the same route in a clockwise direction (both every 15-30min., 4:20am-1am). **Bus #1** follows the CS route as far as Cava Grado (Sant'Angelo) and then comes back (every 15-30min., 5:05am-4:15pm). Other routes are shorter, run less frequently, and stop earlier; use these for reaching specific sites or more remote locations (€0.95 for 60min., €1.20 for 90min., 1-day pass €4, 2-day pass €6). Don't expect breathing space; island buses are packed with passengers until the bitter, early-morning end.

Taxis: The pricey **Microtaxi** fleet (☎081 99 25 50) and **taxis** (☎081 33 31 093) wait at a taxi stand in front of the ticket offices on V. Iasolino. They take on many customers who would rather not go for a crowded bus ride inside someone else's armpit.

 TICKET TIP. When purchasing bus tickets on Ischia, ask specifically for the €0.95 tickets (valid for 60min.), since some vendors may attempt to pass off the €1.20 tickets (valid for 90min.) as the cheapest ones available.

⚡🛈 ORIENTATION AND PRACTICAL INFORMATION

Ischia's towns and points of interest lie largely on the coast; the main road (S.S. 270) wraps around the island and connects most of these places. In **Ischia Porto,** the main harbor town, **Corso V. Colonna** runs parallel to **Via de Luca** from the port, one block from the waterfront. Counterclockwise, **Casamicciola, Lacco Ameno,** and **Forio** continue along the coast. And in the south, **Fontana,** reached by the CS and CD lines, is a good departure point for **Monte Epomeo.** An **AACST Tourist Office** is on V. Iasolino. Turn right off the boat and follow the port to the information sign. The staff provides local tour listings, a free **map,** a much better map for €2.60, and accommodations info. Baggage storage is €3 for 2hr. (☎081 50 74 231; www.ischiaonline.it. Open M-Sa 9am-2pm and 3-8pm, Su 9am-2pm.) **Internet** is available at the **Pointel Store,** P. Trieste e Trento, 9, right off of the main bus stop near the port. Open M 4:30-8:30pm, Tu-Sa 9:30am-1pm, 4:30-8:30pm. €3.60 per 30min., €6 per hr. The **police** are at V. delle Terme, 78, two blocks from V. de Luca in Ischia Porto. They offer help with passport problems. (☎081 99 13 36. Open M, W, and F 9am-noon, Tu and Th 9am-11am.) In case of **emergency** dial ☎112 or call an **ambulance** ☎118. **Ospedale Anna Rizzoli,** V. Fundera in Lacco Ameno (☎081 50 79 111), is accessible by bus #1, CS, or CD.

🏠 ACCOMMODATIONS

Despite the island's immense popularity, Ischia has several budget options, located in Forio. Hotels in Ischia Porto, Casamicciola Terme, and Lacco Ameno tend to be very expensive, since many hotels have pools fed (allegedly) by hot springs. Ischia's many tourists ensure the presence of hotels everywhere, and among these, some are truly appealing to the budget-minded traveler.

CAMPANIA

FORIO

Apartments in Ischia, V. Catello, 4 (☎081 98 25 94 or 347 05 64 203; EDP1@inter-free.it). Call English-speaking management for directions. 6 well-maintained apartments with terrace and easy beach access in 300-year-old family home full of antiques. Call or email for reservations and directions. Apartments hold up to 6 people. With *Let's Go*, prices start at €25 per person. Stays of 2 nights or more are preferred. Cash only. ❷

Ostello Il Gabbiano (HI), Str. Statale Forio-Panza, 162 (☎081 90 94 22), on the road between Forio and Panza. CS, CD, and #1 bus stop outside. Though a bit out of the way, this hostel provides a pool and easy beach access. 100 beds. 4-, 6-, and 8-bed rooms. Breakfast, shower, and sheets included. Lockout 10am-2pm. Curfew 2am. Open Apr.-Sept. All beds €16 per person. Cash only. ❷

Pensione di Lustro, V. Filippo di Lustro, 9 (☎/fax 081 99 71 63; pensionedilustro@virgilio.it). Take the CS, CD, or #1 bus to Forio, exit at the seaside stop on V. Colombo, and make a slight left. Truman Capote slept here in 1968. This hotel has 10 comfortable rooms with bath, A/C, and TV. Domed ceilings and painted tiles provide beautiful accents. Breakfast included. In summer €40 per person; in winter €30. €5 discount in winter with *Let's Go*. Half pension €45-60 per person. AmEx/MC/V. ❸

Hotel Villa Verde, V. Matteo Verde, 34 (☎/fax 081 98 72 81; www.villaverdehotel.it). Follow directions to Pensione di Lustro, continuing on V. Filippo di Lustro and then taking left on V. Matteo Verde. Quiet, family run hotel in the center of Forio. Rooftop patio with garden and sweeping views of port and Monte Epomeo. All rooms with A/C and TV. Breakfast included. €25-45 per person. ❸

Hotel Villa Franca and **Baia Verde,** S.S. 270, #183 (☎081 98 74 20; fax 081 98 70 81). From Ischia Porto, take bus CS, CD, or #1. Exit at the stop after S. Francesco stop (ask bus driver) between Forio and Lacco Ameno. Continue walking in the same direction; the hotel will be on the left. 2 hotels near the beach share 35 rooms and same management. Relax in beautiful garden or heat things up in the solarium. 3 pools (2 cold mineral baths and 1 thermal bath). Breakfast included. Half pension required in July and Aug. €39-62 per person, supplement for single room €5. AmEx/MC/V. ❹

ISCHIA PORTO

Albergo Macri, V. Iasolino, 96 (☎081 99 26 03), along the docks, near where buses board. A quiet, family-run hotel away from the noise and bustle of V. Porto; follow signs. Though somewhat plain, the 22 rooms have comfortable beds and spotless bath. With *Let's Go*, singles €22-27; doubles €51-64; triples €70-83. AmEx/MC/V. ❷

Pensione Crostolo, V. Cossa, 48 (☎081 99 10 94. www.crostolohotel.com or www.valeryhotel.com). From Ischia Porto bus station, ascend the main street and turn right. Expected name change to Valery Hotel summer 2006. Offers lovely terraces overlooking the sea. 15 basic rooms have bath, TV, fridge, and safe. With *Let's Go*, singles €30; doubles €50; triples €75; quads €100. Cash only. ❸

Hotel Villa Ciccio, V. Quercia, 26 (☎081 99 32 30; www.villaciccio.it). From Porto Ischia bus station, a short walk uphill to the right on V. Quercia. Small hotel offering greater luxury near the port. Quiet, garden-surrounded thermal swimming pool and patio. All rooms with terrace or balcony, A/C, minibar, safe, and telephone. Per person €45-65, supplement for single room €5. MC/V. ❹

◧ FOOD

While *cucina Ischitana* is a treat, it is difficult to find an eatery that is not tourist-oriented. Explore side streets to escape the omnipresent €4 *margherita*. Seafood and fruit are excellent, but the local delicacy is *coniglio* (rabbit).

Emiddio, V. Porto, 30 (☎081 99 24 32), at the docks in Porto. This family-run restaurant bustles with locals and tourists. Enjoy large portions and excellent desserts. Choose your fish from the many varieties just pulled from the water. *Primi* €5-8, *secondi* €10-16. Cover €1. Open daily noon-3pm and 7pm-midnight. AmEx/MC/V. ❸

Nuova Pizza Village, V. Iasolino, 48 (☎081 98 24 61), across from the port and close to Matsu Peppe. Big slices of pizza heaping with vegetables and more outlandish toppings, like french fries. Slices start at €1.50. Open daily 10:30am-12am. Cash only. ❶

La Tinaia, V. Matteo Verde, 39 (☎081 99 84 48), in Forio, is a standout for its creamy, tasty *gelato*. Try the espresso in a chocolate dipped cone (€4), or simply sip it as you watch the people go by. Cones from €1.20. Open daily 8:30am-midnight. Cash only. ❶

Mastu Peppe, V. Iasolino, 10 (☎081 98 19 12), on the water near the ferry docks of Porto. With your back to the bustle of V. Porto, enjoy the pleasant seaside seating and lively waitstaff. Fare is hearty and simple, and a good meal runs cheap. *Antipasti* €4-8. *Primi* €4-10, *secondi* from €6. Cover €1.50. Open daily noon-3:30pm. Cash only. ❷

👁 🏔 SIGHTS AND OUTDOOR ACTIVITIES

🏞**MORTELLA GARDENS.** Lady Suzanna Walton, wife of British composer Sir William Walton (1902-1983), planned and cultivated the exotic gardens, with over 800 rare and exotic plants. Named "Best Garden in Italy" in 2004, the park houses stately buildings, including a monolithic, modern sun temple and an incongruous Thai shrine nestled among vines, vivid blooms, and lily-covered pools. Allow at least an hour to fully absorb the site's beauty; the map given at the entrance can help. Victoria's House has tropical plants and a gigantic Amazonian waterlily, one of the rarest flowers in the world. A fantastic panorama of Ischia's coast crowns the landscape just above the garden tea house. (*Take the CD or CS bus to the stop before S. Franceso; ask driver for V. Calise. Walk downhill, following signs for "spiaggia" (beach). Garden entrance is on the right, V. Calise, 39.* ☎ *081 98 62 20; www.ischia.it/mortella. Open Tu, Th and Sa-Su 9am-7pm. €10. Concerts in the summer €15, call for schedule and information.*)

CASTELLO ARAGONESE. Perched atop its own tiny island called Ischia Ponte, the Castello broods in lofty isolation. Connected to the rest of civilization by a 15th-century footbridge, this former stronghold hosts both the holy and the macabre. The castle cathedral, largely destroyed by WWII bombing, revels in a heady mix of Roman and Baroque styles. Below, the crypt houses colorful 14th-century frescoes by craftsmen from the school of Giotto. The nuns' cemetery has a ghastly history: whenever a nun died, the order would prop her decomposing body up on a stone chair as a fragrant reminder to the other nuns of their own mortality. For more family fun, visit the castle's Museum of Arms and Instruments of Torture, 200m past the main ticket booth. Here misbehaving visitors can be introduced to some tools that make even the strongest stomachs turn. (*Bus #7 runs to Ischia Ponte from Ischia Porto.* ☎ *081 99 28 34. Open daily 9am-7:30pm. €10.*)

BEACHES AND HOT SPRINGS. Nestled on an inlet and surrounded on three sides by tall rock, the stunning Citara beach boasts coarse white sands and azure waters. Leave your frisbee at home; there won't be room for it on the crowded shore. (*Take bus #2 from Ischia Porto.*) Martoni, on the island's south side, has calm water and a great view. (*Take bus #5 from Ischia Porto*). For a steamier experience, the hot springs at Sorgeto on the far side of the island range from tepid to boiling. The beach is the perfect spot to lounge and soak aching feet. Locals say that the lather formed by rubbing the light-green porous rocks together is fantastic for the skin. The springs are occasionally closed due to falling rocks, so ask the tourist office before setting out. (*Reach the beach from Panza by a 20min. hike. Lacco Ameno and Casamicciola Terme are densely packed with the thermal*

To Do:
Buy Let's Go Europe
Buy Eurail Pass
Check euro conversion rate
Ask about Roman hostels
Visit letsgo.com

Photo credits, clockwise from top left: Jeremy Todd, Samuel Perwin, Kristin Lee, Yaa Bruce, Nick Elprin, Dham Choi

LETSGO.COM
Here today, wherever you're headed tomorrow.

Whether you're planning your next adventure or are already far afield, LETSGO.COM will help you satisfy your wanderlust. Peruse our feature articles and destination write-ups as you select the spots you're off to next. Consult fellow travelers on our discussion and photo forums or search for anecdotal advice in our researchers' blogs. From embassy locations to passport laws, we keep track of all the facts, so discover what you need to know, book that high-season hostel bed, and hit the road. *READY. SET. LETSGO.COM.*

baths that originally attracted visitors to Ischia. Hikers should take the CS or CD bus to Fontana, a good departure point for a trek to the 788m peak of Monte Epomeo. On clear days, the summit overlooks Capri and Terracina.)

NIGHTLIFE

Ischia's liveliest nocturnal scene is in Ischia Porto, along V. Porto and C. V. Colonna. The best of the bunch is the *discoteca* **New Valentino,** C. V. Colonna, 97, where young Italians grab each others' sweat-soaked bodies to blaring music. (☎081 99 26 53. Open F-Su 11pm-6am.) **Blue Jane,** on V. Iasolino, at Pagoda Beach near the port, features a packed disco and a smooth, floor-side hangout. Energetic bum-shakers vie for the coveted central spot on the dance floor. (☎081 99 32 96. Cover €10-20. Open July-Aug. daily 11:30pm-4am; June and Sept. F-Su 11:30pm-4am.) For something more low-key, try a leisurely *passegiata* along the ocean front streets of Forio.

CAPRI AND ANACAPRI

Gem-like in size and sparkle, Capri has been a destination of the rich and famous for thousands of years. Augustus fell in love with Capri in 29 BC but traded its rocky cliffs for the fertile, volcanic Ischia. His successor Tiberius passed his last decade here, leaving scattered villas and a legacy of idyllic retirement homes. In the late 19th century, writer Axel Munthe was bewitched by Anacapri, building his final abode amid sunlit walkways and flowering vines. Today, the truly glamorous flit like hummingbirds between ritzy boutiques and top notch restaurants. Perched on the hills above Capri (pop. 7000), the quaint Anacapri (pop. 5000) is a relative oasis of budget hotels, lovely villas, and deserted mountain paths. Both share access to the island's beautiful attractions, including the aqua waters of the Blue Grotto and the majestic views of the Faraglioni peaks. A languid stroll along Capri's cobblestone paths, admiring the many beautiful sun-bathing faces, reveals that any season here is splendid.

TRANSPORTATION

Ferries and Hydrofoils: Capri's main port is **Marina Grande.** Naples and Sorrento are the main gateways to Capri; several different companies service these cities. Check ticket offices at Marina Grande for details.

Caremar (☎081 83 70 700) runs to **Naples** (ferries: 1¼hr., 3 per day 5:45am-2:50pm, €5.60; hydrofoils: 40-50min., 4 per day 10:25am-10:20pm, €10.50) and **Sorrento** (hydrofoils: 25min., 4 per day 7am-6:15pm, €5.80).

THE HIDDEN DEAL

A DAY AT THE BATHS

Though it was the Greeks who believed that Ischia's thermal springs had supernatural powers, it was the Romans who developed a penchant for their luxury—and their profit. Historically used as a cure for weak spirits, a pre-antibiotic remedy for war wounds, and plumbing for Roman public baths, the thermal springs in Ischia have erupted into a major destination for the rich, famous, and ailing.

While their growing popularity has made the number of affordable spas scarce, there's still hope for those without VIP credentials. **'O Vagnitiello,** a hotel and spa, is one of the world's finest destinations for mud wallowing, seaweed wrapping, and Jacuzzi soaking, accessible even to budget travelers. The least expensive on the island, it offers six different pools of thermal water, saunas, and a beach swimming area filled with inner tubes. Along the beach, umbrellas line the gardened terraces overlooking the sea, while dense forests shade the grounds. Unlike any other spa on Ischia, a whole day of "therapy" costs only €10 and for those who wish to extend their stay, one night, including breafast and access to the baths, costs only €50.

To reach the spa, take the CD, CS or #1 bus from the port toward Casamicciola. Ask driver for O Vagnitiello stop, and follow the narrow path uphill. (☎081 99 39 75; www.vagnitiello.it.)

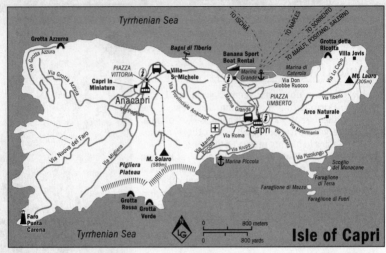

Isle of Capri

SNAV (☎081 83 77 577) runs hydrofoils to **Naples** (40-50min., 6 per day 9:10am-8:10pm, €10.30). Ticket office opens around time of first departure.

Linea Jet (☎081 83 70 819) runs hydrofoils to **Naples** (40-50min., 11 per day 8:30am-6:25pm, €12) and **Sorrento** (25min., 15 per day, 7:20am-6:20pm, €9.50). Ticket office opens around time of first departure.

Public Transportation: SIPPIC buses (☎081 83 70 420) depart from V. Roma in Capri for Anacapri (every 15min., 6am-1:40am), Marina Piccola, and points in between. In Anacapri, buses depart from P. Barile, off V. Orlandi, for the Grotta Azzurra (Blue Grotto), the *faro* (lighthouse), and more. Direct line between Marina Grande and P. Vittoria in Anacapri (every hr. 5:45am-10:10pm; €1.30, day pass €7). Visitors rarely use the all-day pass enough to make it worthwhile, so buy individual tickets as needed. A **funicular** runs from Marina Grande to Capri (every 10min. 6:30am-1:30am, €1.30).

Taxis: Ride in style in a convertible cab. Available at main bus stop in Marina Grande (☎081 83 70 543), at bus stop in Capri (☎081 83 70 543), or in P. Vittoria, in Anacapri (☎081 83 71 175). To avoid being overcharged, tell the driver to start the meter.

✦🛈 ORIENTATION AND PRACTICAL INFORMATION

There are two towns on the isle of Capri: **Capri** proper, near the ports, and **Anacapri,** higher up the mountain. Ferries dock at **Marina Grande,** below the town of Capri. The alternative to taking the funicular from the marina to Capri town is a steep and winding 1hr. hike past people's yards and up a stairway. Expensive boutiques and bakeries line the streets that radiate from **Piazza Umberto. Via Roma,** to the right exiting the funicular, leads to Anacapri. The bus to Anacapri ends at **Piazza Vittoria;** Villa San Michele and the Monte Solaro chairlift are nearby. **Via Giuseppe Orlandi,** running from P. Vittoria, leads past several restaurants on the way.

Tourist Office: AAST (☎081 83 70 634; www.capritourism.com) in Capri, at the end of the dock at Marina Grande. **Branches:** Capri in P. Umberto (☎081 83 70 686). Under the clock. Open daily 9am-1pm and 3:30-6:45pm. Anacapri at V. Orlandi, 59 (☎081 83 71 524), right from bus stop. Open M-Sa 9am-1pm and 2:30-7:40pm. All provide detailed **maps** (€2), ferry and bus info, and the magazine *Capri è...*, with detailed information about the island's accommodations and restaurants. Reduced hours Oct.-May.

Currency Exchange: V. Roma, 31 (☎081 83 74 768), across from the main bus stop, and in P. Umberto. Another agency in the center of Anacapri at P. Vittoria, 2 (☎081 83 73 146). No commission. Open in summer daily 8am-6pm, winter hours vary.

Luggage Storage: Outside Capri's funicular. €2.85 per bag per 2 hr. Open daily in summer 8am-8pm; in winter 8:15am-6pm.

English-Language Bookstore: Librerie Studio La Conchiglia, Vle Botteghe, 12 (☎081 83 76 577), in Capri, off P. Umberto. Open daily in summer 9am-1:30pm and 3-10:30pm; in winter 9am-1:30pm and 3-9pm. Classics, new fiction, and beach trash. Smaller location in Anacapri, V. G. Orlandi, 205 (☎081 83 72 646). Open daily in summer 9:15am-1:15pm and 4:30-9pm; in winter 9am-1pm and 4-8pm.

Emergency: ☎113 or 081 838 12 05. **Police,** V. Roma, 70 (☎081 83 74 211). **Ambulance:** ☎081 83 81 205.

Hospital: Ospedale Capilupi, V. Provinciale Anacapri, 5 (☎081 83 81 111), a few blocks down V. Roma from P. Umberto.

Tourist Medical Clinic: V. Caprile, 30 (☎081 83 81 240), in Anacapri.

Internet Access: Capri Internet Point (☎081 83 73 283), P. Vittoria, 13, in Anacapri, has 4 fast computers. €4 per hr. Open daily 8am-9pm.

Post Office: Anacapri, V. de Tommaso, 8 (☎081 83 71 015). Open M-F 8:30am-1:30pm, Sa 8:30am-noon. **Capri,** V. Roma, 50 (☎081 97 85 211). Open M-F 8:30am-7pm, Sa 8:30am-1pm. **Postal Codes:** Anacapri 80071; Capri 80073.

▌ ACCOMMODATIONS

Lodgings in Capri proper are pricey year-round and become even more expensive in the summer. Anacapri offers serenity and economy, as well as proximity to Capri. The lower prices listed usually apply from October to May. Call ahead to confirm reservations and prices. **Makeshift camping is illegal and heavily fined.**

ANACAPRI

▓ **Bussola di Hermes,** V. Traversa La Vigna, 14 (☎081 83 82 010; www.bussolahermes.com). Call from P. Vittoria in Anacapri for pick-up rather than navigate Anacapri's tangled streets. By far the best budget lodgings on the island. It's difficult to find more welcoming owners than Rita and Ciro, who know everything about Capri and love hosting young travelers. Recently renovated rooms filled with accents like *majolica* tiling and a complimentary bottle of *limoncello*. Breakfast included. Reserve early. Dorms €27-30; singles €25-35; doubles €70-110; triples €85-130; quads €90-140. 8% discount with *Let's Go*. AmEx/MC/V. ❸

Villa Mimosa Bed and Breakfast, V. Nuova del Faro, 48/A (☎081 83 71 752; ferdyok@libero.it). 100m on the right past the last stop of the Marina Grande-Anacapri bus. Relax in rooms that would make Martha Stewart proud, or lay out on a terrace enveloped by flowering plants. Every detail is attended to by helpful staff. All rooms with satellite TV, A/C, and bath. Breakfast included. Doubles €80-100. Cash only. ❺

Cala di Limmo, V. Nuova del Faro, 122 (☎/fax 081 83 72 488). Accessible by bus to Punta del Faro. 3 rustic rooms, each with bath and fan, in the shadow of the volcanic cliff Migliera. Access to trails for the Grotta Azzurra, and a private path to the best swimming on Capri, at Faro beach. Breakfast included. Doubles €70. Cash only. ❺

CAPRI

Vuotto Antonio, V. Campo di Teste, 2 (☎081 83 70 230). Take V. V. Emanuele out of P. Umberto, a left on V. Camerelle, a right on V. Cerio, and left. Housed in "Villa Margherita." Rooms decorated in antiques and *majolica* tiles. The hotel is devoid of modern distractions, leaving guests to happily contemplate the perfect views of the Faraglioni and southern coast from their private terraces. Doubles €60-90. Cash only. ❺

Pensione 4 Stagioni, V. Marina Piccola, 1 (☎081 83 70 041; www.hotel4stagionicapri.com). From P. Umberto, walk 5min. down V. Roma. Turn left at the 3-pronged fork in the road and look for green gate on the left. Rooms are small and plain but pristine. Pricier doubles enjoy garden access and sea views. Breakfast included. Open Apr.-Nov. Singles €40-70; doubles, depending on view, €70-120. Extra bed €20. AmEx/MC/V. ❺

Bed and Breakfast Parco Augusto, Viale Matteoti, 8/A (☎081 83 70 868). From P. Umberto, follow V. V. Emanuele to V. Sirena, turn right on V. Matteoti, and follow staircase up hill on the right. Great views of the Gardens of Augustus and the dramatic southern coast. Breakfast served on patio secluded by woods. Doubles €60-115. ❺

◨ FOOD

Capri's food is glorious. Savor creamy white local mozzarella served with sweet red tomatoes, glistening yellow olive oil, and deep green basil in an *insalata caprese*—many consider it the *sine qua non* (must-have; literally "without which not") of summer dining. *Ravioli alla caprese* are hand-stuffed with a blend of local cheeses. Conclude with the indulgent *torta di mandorle* (chocolate almond cake), also known as *torta caprese*. Local wines bear *Tiberio* or *Caprese* labels. A step up (particularly price-wise) is the *Capri Blù*. Restaurants often serve *Capri DOC*, a light white. But beware: it's easy to pay a lot and receive very little. Be discerning around P. Umberto, where restaurants can serve €3 sodas and equally overpriced stale pastries. Fruit stands around the island sell delectable cherries and ripe tomatoes at low prices. In Anacapri, try the well-stocked **supermarket,** V. G. Orlandi, 299. (☎081 83 71 119. Open M-Sa 8:30am-1:30pm and 5-8:30pm, Su 8:30am-noon.)

ANACAPRI

🅖**Ristorante Il Cucciolo,** V. La Fabbrica, 52 (☎081 83 71 917). Follow the signs for Villa Damecuta from bus stop or call for free ride from P. Vittoria. Fresh food at low prices, served on a seaside terrace. *Bruschette pomodori antipasto* (€3.50) is unsurpassed. *Ravioli caprese* €5. Considerable *Let's Go* discount: *primi* and *secondi* €6-9. Cover €1.50. Service 12%. Open Mar.-Oct. M and W-Su noon-2:30pm and 7:30-11pm. Reservations recommended F-Su. AmEx/MC/V. ❷

Ristorante Materita Bar-Pizzeria V. Orlandi, 140 (☎081 83 73 375; fax 081 83 73 881). Endure cramped outdoor seating to enjoy delicious pizza (from €4.50). In addition to *primi* and *secondi* (from €7.50), enjoy a complimentary aperitif or *limoncello* with *Let's Go* in hand. Cover €1.50. Service 12%. Open daily 11:45am-3:30pm and 6:45pm-midnight; Nov.-Mar. closed Tu. AmEx/MC/V. ❸

La Rondinello, V. Orlandi, 295 (☎081 83 71 223), near P. Vittoria, on the left. Enjoy a romantic, candlelit feast under a canopy of thick bougainvillea with fresh *antipasti* and extensive seafood offerings. The *gamberoni* (shrimp; from €15) are particularly succulent. *Primi* €8-12, *secondi* €8-15. Cover €2. Service 11%. Open daily noon-3pm and 7-11:30pm. AmEx/MC/V. ❸

Trattoria Il Solitario, V. Orlandi, 96 (☎081 83 71 382; maxichef@yahoo.com). A vine-covered path leads to a serene outdoor dining area. Treat taste buds to a *pizza rossa* (€4-6) or delightful *pizza bianca* (€5-8). Fixed *menù* €9, with *primo*, side, and dessert. Cover €1.50. Open M and W-Su noon-3pm and 7:30-11pm. AmEx/MC/V. ❷

CAPRI

■ **Villa Verde,** Vico Sella Orta, 6/A (☎081 83 77 024; www.villaverde-capri.com). Follow the signs from V. V. Emanuele, off P. Umberto. Reserve ahead to eat as few have eaten before. Large portions of fresh fish, lobster, and vegetables. Prices are VIP, as are the walls (plastered with pictures of celebrity visitors), but top-notch quality and quantity are worth the extra dough. House specialties are *linguini fra diavolo* (with lobster; €30) and rich desserts (€5-7). Daily specials €10-20. Pizza €5.50-12. *Primi* €5.50-30, *secondi* €12-25. Service 12%. Open daily noon-4pm and 7pm-1am. AmEx/MC/V. ❺

■ **Longano da Tarantino,** V. Longano, 9 (☎081 83 70 187), just off P. Umberto. Possibly the best deal in town, featuring a sea view and a €15 *menù* (with *primo, secondo,* coffee, dessert, and a shot of *limoncello* to finish it off). Seating is cramped, but service is friendly and efficient. Excellent grilled seafood (€12). Pizza from €4. Cover €0.80. Open Mar.-Nov. M-Tu and Th-Su noon-3:30pm and 7pm-midnight. Reservations recommended. AmEx/MC/V. ❷

Aurora Pizzeria, V. Fuorlovado, 20 (☎081 83 70 181). Just off P. Umberto. Celebrity pictures cover a wall of this cozy establishment, which serves some of the best pizza on the island. The *pizza aurora* (with eggplant) is tasty and has the perfect crust. Pizza €8-9. €2 cover. Service 15%. AmEx/MC/V. ❷

Buca di Bacco, V. Longano, 35 (☎081 83 70 723), off P. Umberto. A less exclusive spot to savor superior cuisine. While enjoying the view, try pizza (€4-8; served for dinner only) or one of many pasta options (€6-12). Open Sept.-July M-Tu and Th-Su noon-3pm and 7pm-midnight; Aug. daily noon-2:30pm and 7pm-midnight. AmEx/MC/V. ❷

Salumeria Simeoli, V. Botteghe, 12/A (☎081 83 75 543), off P. Umberto. Tiny deli boasts fine *panini* (from €1.50), fresh *prosciutto* and *mortadella,* and a wide selection of cheeses, including creamy mozzarella. Cold beverages and *limoncello* (€10 and up) available at what might be the least exorbitant prices in town. Grab cold cuts to go for a tasty picnic lunch. Open daily 8am-2pm and 5-9pm. AmEx/MC/V. ❶

👁🄰 SIGHTS AND OUTDOOR ACTIVITIES

COAST. Daily **boat tours** (€11.50) reveal the ins and outs of the gorgeous coast, including the **Blue Grotto** (though it costs extra to enter; see below). Departures from Marina Grande are at 9:30, 10:30, and 11:30am. *(Tickets and info at Grotta Azzurra Travel Office, V. Roma, 53, across from the bus stop. ☎081 83 70 466; g.azzurra@capri.it. Open M-Sa 9am-1pm and 3:30-7pm, Su 9am-12:30pm.)* Cavort in the clear water amid immense lava rocks, or rent a **motor boat** (€80 for 2hr.) from **Banana Sport,** in Marina Grande. *(☎081 83 75 188 or 330 22 70 64. Open daily 9:30am-6pm.)* Many pebbly **beaches** surround the island. Take a boat (€5) from the port or descend between vineyards to **Bagni di Tiberio,** a bathing area set within ruins of an imperial villa. *(Take an internal bus. On foot, take V. Roma from P. Umberto to the 3-pronged fork in the road; take the fork farthest to the left and head down the path to the left. A gorgeous stretch of Marina Piccola awaits at the bottom.)*

VILLA SAN MICHELE. Henry James once declared this Anacapri enclave a clustering of "the most fantastic beauty, poetry, and inutility." Built in the early 20th century by Swedish author-physician Axel Munthe, this magnificent building displays 17th-century furniture and Roman sculpture on the site of a former Tiberian villa. Glorious gardens, complete with flowering arbors, miniature streams, and a panoramic view of the Capri coast, host Friday night concerts from June to August. *(Upstairs from P. Vittoria and to the left, past Capri's Beauty Farm. ☎081 83 71 401. Open daily 9am-6pm. €5. Concert information available at ticket desk and Capri tourist offices.)*

SOLE OF CAPRI

Everyday, shoemaker Antonio Viva sits on a stool outside his shop in Anacapri. His hands are always moving as he makes shoes and talks to passersby. There are many shoemakers on Capri, but Signor Viva is the only one with a personality big enough to make him, and not just his shoes, a tourist attraction. With his two sons, Giancarlo and Antonio, Signor Viva does the same thing day after day as the world around him changes.

On Capri: My family has been on Capri for generations, and I've been making shoes here for 50 years. There are so many people here now, I don't know what will happen to Capri. It's hard in Italy now. Not many jobs. People are working very hard.

On himself: People come here for me. The shoes are good, but they come to talk to me. It's like a museum when I'm here. People come and look. I am here, there, everywhere. Posters, billboards, TV. People take pictures with me. Viva is like Julia Roberts.

On selling shoes: If a poor man comes to me, I try to give him shoes cheaper. I can see he is not rich. I can see he is not a bad man. I work for everyone. Workers, presidents, everyone in the middle. Everyone needs shoes. I want people to be happy. If you are nice and sit and talk, I'll help you and make a deal.

To visit Signor Viva, go to L'Arte del Sandalo Caprese, V. Orlandi, 75, (☎081 837 35 83), in Anacapri.

THE BLUE GROTTO. The walls of La Grotta Azzurra, a water-filled cave carved into the cliffside, shimmer vivid blue when sunlight radiates from beneath the water's surface. Some who visit find the water amazing; others think it's pretty, but not pretty enough to justify €8 for a 6min. boat ride. Despite the narrowness of the cave opening and the sign warning that swimming is "strictly forbidden," many choose to take dips in the grotto during the organized tour or after boats stop at 5pm. Check with the tourist office to make sure that the grotto is not closed due to choppy water. *(Take the bus marked Grotta Azzurra from the intersection of V. De Tomaso and V. Catena. The grotto opening is accessible with the island boat tour as well.)*

CLIFFS. An exploration of the island's natural beauty can be a much-needed break from crowded *piazze* and commercial streets. For those who prefer land to sea, trails lead to stunning panoramas. At the island's eastern edge, a 1hr. walk connects the **Arco Naturale**, a majestic stone arch, and the **Faraglioni,** the three massive rocks featured on countless postcards. Parts of the path are unpaved dirt, so wear proper footwear. *(V. Tragara goes from Capri Centro to the Faraglioni, while the path to the Arco Naturale connects to the route to Villa Jovis through V. Matermania.)* Hike a steep uphill path 1½hr. to check out the ruins of Emperor Tiberius's magnificent **Villa Jovis.** Tiberius lived here during his more eccentric final years, in the largest of his 12 Capri villas. Always the gracious host, the emperor was prone to tossing those who displeased him over the precipice; he also kept a school of young boys (whom he referred to as "minnows") on hand for purposes unprintable. The view from the **Cappella di Santa Maria del Soccorso,** built onto the villa, is unrivaled. *(V. Longano from P. Umberto. Don't miss the left on V. Tiberio. Open daily 9am-6pm. Free.)*

OTHER SIGHTS. Capri's location makes it ideal for surveying Italy's topography. Viewed from the peak of ◨**Monte Solaro,** the Apennines loom ahead to the east; the mountains of Calabria are to the south on the right. A 12min. chairlift from P. Vittoria to the summit dangles from precipitous heights. *(☎081 83 71 428; montesolaro@tiscali.it. Chairlift open Mar.-Oct. daily 9:30am-4:45pm. €6 round-trip.)* A difficult hike also leads up the mountain, starting from the base near the Villa San Michele. A bus from P. Vittoria leads to the **Punta Carena Faro,** Italy's 2nd-tallest lighthouse. The pedestrian stretch of V. G. Orlandi, off P. Vittoria in Anacapri, leads to the least expensive (yet still pricey) **tourist shopping** on Capri.

🎵 🎭 ENTERTAINMENT AND NIGHTLIFE

Nocturnal action carries a hefty price tag, though Anacapri's prices are slightly lower. In typical Italian fashion, no one bothers heading out until around midnight. Underground, V. Orlandi, 259, is one of the town's most popular night spots, although the atmosphere is less than chic. No cover and €5 cocktails make it popular among squealing study-abroad students and Italian locals. For a more low-key evening, Zeus, V. Orlandi, 103, a few blocks from P. Vittoria, is a cinema popular with locals that also serves great *gelato*. (☎081 83 79 16.) The Capri scene is classier and much more expensive. Covers are high and gatherings exclusive at the lounges and clubs near P. Umberto. Squeeze into the sweaty, frenzied Number Two, V. Camerelle, 1 (☎081 83 77 078), the hotspot for an older and wealthier crowd, including celebrities. Also in Capri is Bara Onda, V. Roma, 8 (☎081 83 77 147), which enjoys theme nights on many weekends. Both clubs are open all night. Those sufficiently self-assured to hang with dressed-to-kill Italians should recall that buses stop running at 1:40am.

AMALFI COAST

It happens almost imperceptibly: after the exhausting tumult of Naples and the compact grit of Sorrento, the highway narrows to a two-lane road that zigzags down the coastline. The hazy horizon becomes illuminated with lemon orchards and bright village pastels, and suddenly the Amalfi Coast hits the bloodstream and the euphoria kicks in. Positano, Amalfi, and Praiano combine simplicity and sophistication, earning the favor of Emperor Augustus, Ernest Hemingway, and Jacqueline Kennedy Onassis, though the region's ultimate appeal rests in the tenuous balance it strikes between man and nature. Whitewashed homes cling defiantly to rock, and scooters brazenly hug cliff-side bends. For all human enterprise, no attraction outdoes the coast's unassuming grandeur.

POSITANO   ☎089

When John Steinbeck visited Positano (pop. 4000) in the 1950s, the town was a posh haven for artists and literati. Jack Kerouac and Tennessee Williams sought solitude in this Bohemian retreat, where the fashion avant-garde invented the bikini and creativity ran as wild as the bougainvillea. This classy reputation soon drew ordinary millionaires in addition to the writers, painters, actors, and filmmakers who made it famous and today its beachfront teems with vacationers from all walks of life and from all over the world. Steinbeck had estimated that Positano's cliffs could stack no more than 500 visitors at a time. He clearly underestimated local ingenuity: the *Positanesi* have managed to squeeze in over 2000 hotel beds, and crowds now overrun the tiny footpaths and narrow stairways. Though the nature of tourism here has changed considerably since Steinbeck's time, Positano remains the most fashionable of Amalfi's coastal towns.

🚌 TRANSPORTATION

Overland, Positano is best reached by **bus.** Blue **SITA** buses run to Amalfi and Sorrento (7am-9pm, 25 per day, €1.30). There are two stops in Positano along the main coastal road, Via Marconi (see **Orientation**). Walk downhill from either stop to reach the *centro.* Tickets are sold at the friendly Bar Internazionale, by the Chiesa Nuova stop on V. Marconi, or at *tabaccherie.* **Ferries** and **hydrofoils** run between the coast and islands. **Linee Marittime Salernitane** (☎089

CAMPANIA

81 11 64; www.amalficoastlines.com) runs ferries (50min., 8:45 and 10am, €11) and hydrofoils (30min.; 11am, 2:10, and 5:10pm; €13.50) to Capri. **Travelmar** (☎089 87 29 50) runs ferries to Amalfi (25min., 6 per day 10am-6:30pm, €5); Minori (30min., 4 per day noon-5:20pm, €5.50); and Salerno (1¼hr., 6 per day 10am-6:30pm, €6). Call ahead to confirm times and prices.

✈ 🛈 ORIENTATION AND PRACTICAL INFORMATION

Positano clings to two huge cliffs overlooking the Tyrrhenian Sea. Coming from Sorrento, **Chiesa Nuova** is the first SITA stop in town on **Via Marconi**, in front of Bar Internazionale. From here, if you don't mind the steep downhill walk, take **Viale Pasitea,** or wait for one of Positano's frequent **internal buses** marked "Positano Interno" (every 15-30min. 7:15am-midnight, €1); the bus route ends downtown in **Piazza dei Mulini.** The 2nd SITA stop is at the intersection of V. Marconi and **Via Cristoforo Colombo;** internal buses don't run here, so walk 10min. downhill on V. C. Colombo to reach P. dei Mulini, where V. C. Colombo becomes Vle. Pasitea. Also from P. dei Mulini, **Via dei Mulini** winds through town, past the church of Santa Maria, and to **Spiaggia Grande,** the main beach. Take the footpath from Spiaggia Grande to get to the cozier **Fornillo** beach.

Tourist Office: V. del Saraceno, 4 (☎089 87 50 67; www.aziendaturismopositano.it), in a red building near the church, provides a **map,** hotel listings, and ferry and bus schedules. Open in summer M-Sa 8am-2pm and 3-8pm; in winter M-Sa 9am-3pm, Su 8:30am-noon.

Currency Exchange: P. dei Mulini, 6 (☎089 87 58 64), on the V. Mulini side of the *piazza.* Open in summer 9:30am-1:30pm and 4-9:30pm; in winter 9:30am-1pm and 3:30-7:50pm. Decent rates, but commission on traveler's checks. (€1 per check, €3 per min.)

English Language Bookstore: La Libreria, V. C. Colombo, 165 (☎089 81 10 77). Selection of classics, new fiction, and Italian cookbooks in a basement with A/C. Open daily 10am-1:30pm and 5-8:30pm. Reduced hours in winter. MC/V.

Emergency: ☎113. **Carabinieri:** (☎112 or 089 87 50 11), near the top of the cliffs down the steps opposite Chiesa Nuova. The nearest **hospital** is in Sorrento; a **tourist medical clinic** is in Amalfi.

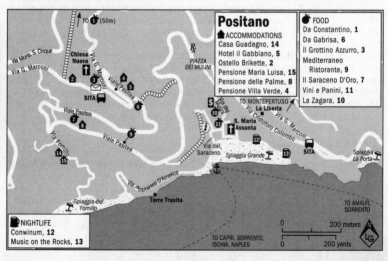

Positano

▲ ACCOMMODATIONS
Casa Guadagno, **14**
Hotel il Gabbiano, **5**
Ostello Brikette, **2**
Pensione Maria Luisa, **15**
Pensione delle Palme, **8**
Pensione Villa Verde, **4**

🍴 FOOD
Da Constantino, **1**
Da Gabrisa, **6**
Il Grottino Azzurro, **3**
Mediterraneo Ristorante, **9**
Il Saraceno D'Oro, **7**
Vini e Panini, **11**
La Zagara, **10**

🎵 NIGHTLIFE
Conwinum, **12**
Music on the Rocks, **13**

CAMPANIA

Pharmacy: Viale Pasitea, 22 (☎089 87 52 26). Open in summer M-Sa 9am-1pm and 5-9pm, Su 9am-1pm; in winter M-W and F-Sa 9am-1pm and 4-8pm, Su 9am-1pm.

Internet Access: Conwinum, V. Rampa Teglia, 12 (☎089 81 16 87; www.positano.conwinum.it), below Buca di Bacco, provides fast Internet with printing. €6 per hr. Drinks available while you surf. Open daily 9am-late.

ACCOMMODATIONS

Staying in Positano can be rough on the wallet, so budget travelers might consider making Positano a daytrip from Sorrento or Salerno. For those looking to stay in the village, however, there are a few very good budget options. Contact the tourist office for help in arranging *affittacamere* for longer stays.

Ostello Brikette, V. Marconi, 358 (☎089 87 58 57; www.brikette.com). Accessible by orange Interno bus or SITA bus; exit both at "Chiesa Nuova" stop and walk 100m to the left of Bar Internazionale; hostel is on the right. On foot, take Vle. Pasitea and turn left on V. Marconi. Clean rooms and sublime views from large terraces. Helpful staff gives guests advice on sights and restaurants. Breakfast and sheets included. Internet €4 per hr. Lockout 10am-2:30pm. Lights-out curfew varies from midnight to 2am depending on nightlife. Reserve early. Open late Mar.-Nov. Dorms €24; doubles €70. MC/V. ❷

Pensione Villa Verde, Vle. Pasitea, 338 (☎089 87 55 06; www.pensionevillaverde.it). Take Interno bus to "Casale." Simple rooms cling to the side of a valley overlooking Positano. All rooms with terrace and bath. TV and A/C available on request. Breakfast included. €30-40 per person. Cash only. ❸

Pensione Maria Luisa, V. Fornillo, 42 (☎ 089 87 50 23; www.pensionemarialuisa.com). Take the Interno bus down Vle. Pasitea to V. Fornillo. Kind owner Carlo welcomes guests to 14 bright rooms with private baths and views from seaside terraces. Simple and quiet, this *pensione* promises comfort. Guests have refrigerator access. Singles €50; doubles €70. Cash only. ❹

Casa Guadagno, V. Fornillo, 36 (☎089 87 50 42; fax 089 81 14 07). Take the Interno bus down Vle. Pasitea to V. Fornillo. Tiled floors, incredible views of the coast, and winter heating. Friendly husband and wife management team. Enjoy breakfast (included) on the hotel's idyllic covered terrace. All rooms have bath, minifridge, and private terrace overlooking the sea. Reserve ahead. With *Let's Go,* doubles €85. Cash only. ❺

Pensione delle Palme, Vle. Pasitea, 252 (☎089 87 51 62; www.positanovilladellepalme.com). In the same building as Saraceno D'Oro restaurant. With 4 generations watching over this hotel, guests are welcomed into the family. Rooms full of quirky antiques. All with bath and terrace. Breakfast around €5. Singles €55-60; doubles €70-80; triples €100-110. Cash only. ❸

Hotel Il Gabbiano, Vle. Pasitea, 310 (☎089 87 53 06; www.ilgabbianopositano.com). All rooms have harbor views, bath, and TV. Antiques provide tasteful accents. Breakfast included. Doubles €110-130; triples €145; quads €180. MC/V. ❹

FOOD

The *granita al limone* is a slushy *Amalfitan* specialty. The best kind boasts pieces of frozen lemon rind. Don't bother with the commercial machines that pompously whirl their contents: they simply can't compare to the homemade, sun-ripened variety. Look no further than the ■**granita stand** in P. dei Mulini, near the Interno bus stop, and wait in what may be a long line for lemony ice piled over the brim of a cup. (*Granita* €1.50. Open in summer daily 8am-10pm.) As for the rest of food in Positano, generally speaking, high prices reflect high quality.

Da Gabrisa, Vle. Pasitea, 219 (☎089 81 11 70; fax 089 81 16 07). Bright, cheery atmosphere and great service. Savor the tender pumpkin in the grilled vegetable *anti-pasto* (€5). The simple *pasta alla norma* (pasta in tomato sauce with eggplant; €8) is a treat. *Primi* €6-10, *secondi* €8-15. Open daily 7-11pm. AmEx/MC/V. ❸

Da Constantino, V. Corvo, 95 (☎089 87 57 38). From V. Marconi, with your back to Vle. Pasitea, walk left until the stairs just past Ostello Brikette; walk up the stairs and turn right when you hit the real road. The elevated sea view overshadows even the most succulent meal. Sea breezes and inviting atmosphere make this the spot to cap off a long day. Try the specialty *crespolini al formaggio* (crepes filled with cheese; €5.50). Pizza from €4. *Primi* €5-10, *secondi* €8-13. Open in summer daily noon-3:30pm and 7pm-midnight; in winter Tu-Th noon-3:30pm and 7pm-midnight. AmEx/MC/V. ❸

Mediterraneo Ristorante, Vle. Pasitea, 236-238 (☎089 81 22 828; www.ristorante-mediterraneo.com). Variety of offerings, outdoor seating, attentive service. Try fried zucchini flowers or *calamarato con polipetti e pomodorini* (squid-shaped pasta with octopus and tomato; €12). Live folk music M, W, and F evenings. *Primi* €6-17.50, *secondi* €6-20. Cover €2. Open daily 12:20-3:30pm and 7pm-midnight. MC/V. ❹

Vini e Panini, V. del Saraceno, 29-31 (☎089 87 51 75), near the tourist office. Well-stocked shop sells fresh sandwiches, cheese, and excellent produce. Wander the aisles for all manner of scrumptious Italian foodstuffs. *Panino* with mozzarella and tomato €3. Bottle of *limoncello* €10. Open Mar.-Dec. M-Sa 8am-2pm and 4:30-9pm. Cash only. ❶

Il Grottino Azzurro, V. G. Marconi, 158 (☎089 87 54 66), next to Bar Internazionale. Excellent fish priced right. Guests linger for hours in simple but inviting interior. Home-made pasta dishes €6-10, fresh seafood from €8. Cover €2. Open M-Tu and Th-Su 12:30-2:30pm and 7:30-11pm. Closed Dec. to mid-Feb. Cash only. ❸

Il Saraceno D'Oro, Vle. Pasitea, 254 (☎089 81 20 50). If you are looking to avoid a traditionally lengthy Italian dinner, enjoy delicious pizza to go (dinner only) from €4.50. The incredible *gnocchi alla sorrentina* (€7) comes covered in perfectly baked mozzarella. Cover €1.50. Open in summer daily noon-3pm and 7-11:30pm; in winter M-Tu and Th-Su 1-3pm and 7-11pm. Cash only. ❷

La Zagara, V. dei Mulini, 8/10 (☎089 87 59 64; www.lazagara.com). For a snack after a day of trekking or just for an after-dinner dessert, join the crowds and try the invitingly named *torta afrodisia* (€3). Prices are higher on the patio, which becomes a piano bar in the evening. Open daily 8am-1:30am. Cash only. ❶

👁 📷 SIGHTS AND BEACHES

People looking to lighten their pocketbooks find ample opportunities in Positano. The tragically chic spend entire days, or at least unbearably hot afternoons, in exorbitant boutiques. Others take boat excursions along the coast and to neighboring islands. Frequent cruises embark to the **Emerald** (p. 602) and **Blue Grottoes** (p. 595), beautiful water-filled caves nearby. As numerous boating companies compete for these excursions, prices can sometimes be reasonable for shorter trips; check the tourist office and booths lining the port.

For most, Positano's beaches are its main attraction. The biggest, busiest, and priciest is **Spiaggia Grande,** in the main stretch by the docks. At the less crowded, private **Lido L'incanto** (☎089 81 11 77), guests revel in the fact that they are surrounded only by other people who shelled out €10 for a *lettino* (beach chair), umbrella, shower, and changing room. Outside the entrance, **Blue Star** (☎089 81 18 88; www.bluestarpositano.it) rents motorboats and rowboats, and provides boat tours of the Blue Grotto and Emerald Grotto; call for prices and information. The serene and secluded **Fornillo Beach** is hidden from the docks and downtown blitz by a shady, rocky walkway. Take **Via Positanese d'America,** a footpath that starts from the left side of the port facing away from the water and winds past **Torre Trasita.** Three private beaches on this end offer amenities for a small fee. **Marinella** (€7) features a little sand underneath a time-worn boardwalk. Sit among chattering teenagers while flipping through this summer's beach-book or trashy magazine of choice. **Fratelli Grassi** (€12) and the slightly crowded **Puppetto** (€7) offer boat excursions to those with cash to burn.

The three **Isole dei Galli,** peeking out of the waters off Positano's coast, were allegedly home to Homer's mythical Sirens, who lured unsuspecting victims with their spellbinding songs. In 1925 the quartet of Stravinsky, Picasso, Hindemith, and Massine bought one of the *isole*, perhaps in honor of this legend. While swimming around these beautiful islands is permitted, setting foot on them is not.

Positano offers tremendous **hikes** for people with quads of steel. **Montepertuso,** a high mountain pierced by a large *pertusione* (hole), is one of three perforated mountains in the world (the other two are in India). Hike the 45min. trail up the hillside or take the bus, which leaves from P. dei Mulini near the port.

♫ ♟ ENTERTAINMENT AND NIGHTLIFE

The swank piano bar and disco **Music on the Rocks,** on the far left side of the beach facing the water, packs well-dressed 30-somethings into a large cave with one side open to the water. Celebrities including Sharon Stone and Luciano Pavarotti have been known to drop in, and classy threads are a prerequesite. (☎089 87 58 74. Cover varies, but can reach €20.) For less exclusive revelry, head to **Conwinum** to meet young locals. No cover and €5 cocktails make this spot equally popular with the backpacking crowd; the low lighting and red interior set the right mood. (☎089 81 20 76. Open daily from 9am as an Internet cafe.) People looking to quench their thirst begin to arrive around 10pm.

PRAIANO ☎089

Praiano's vast coastline is just as beautiful as Positano's, but far less crowded. Towers that once kept watch over the sea are now crumbling, picturesque ruins punctuating landscape. Whether you choose the 25min. bus ride (€1.30) or the 1hr. walk from Positano, the quiet of Praiano (pop. 2000) is a welcome change from the hordes of tourists on the rest of the Amalfi Coast.

♠ ♘ ACCOMMODATIONS AND FOOD. Close to the beach but far from the rush of the modern world, **Le Sirene ❹,** V. S. Nicola, 10, caters to those looking for peace, quiet, and natural beauty. Follow the signs from Praiano's *duomo*, near Trattoria di San Gennaro. All rooms have A/C, telephone, and terraces overlooking the coast. (☎089 87 40 13; www.lesirene.com. Buffet breakfast included. Double as a single €60; doubles €80-100; triples €110-120.) Enjoy the panorama from the campground **Residence La Tranquillità ❶** and the **Hotel Continental ❹,** V. Roma, 21, housed in the same complex on the road leading to Amalfi (ask the driver to stop at Ristorante Continental). Don't miss the domed, decorated ceilings inside. Plush apartments, with TV, telephone, and kitchen are available for week-long stays. A long stairway descends to a stone dock extending out onto shimmering waters. (☎089 87 40 84; www.continental.praiano.it. Breakfast and shower included. Parking available. Camping €10 per person, €15 per tent. Doubles and 2-person bungalows €68-88. Simpler accommodations €45 per person. Apartments for 3-6 people

from €500 per wk. Discounts with cash payment. MC/V.) **La Perla ❹**, V. Miglina, 2, 100m toward Amalfi from La Tranquillità on the main road, offers large rooms with bath and a rooftop terrace overlooking the sea. All rooms have satellite TV, minifridge, A/C, and swipe-card access. (☎089 87 40 52; www.perlahotel.it. Breakfast included. Internet €6 per hr. Singles €40-60; doubles €80-90. Sea view €20 per day. 10% discount with *Let's Go* in hand. AmEx/MC/V.) Walk toward Positano from Trattoria San Gennaro to find decent budget accommodations at **Casa di San Gennaro ❹**, on V. Capo Vettica. Ten spotless rooms have TV, A/C, minifridge, and bath. Breakfast included. (☎089 87 42 93; www.ilsangennaro.it. Scooter rental from €25 per day. Doubles €35-50, with sea view €50-80. AmEx/MC/V.)

On the road from Positano, next to the Chiesa di San Gennaro (with blue and gold domes), is **Ristorante Continental ❸**, below Villagio La Tranquillità, which specializes in seafood. Enjoy local wine (from €5) and sea views in the bright white interior. (☎089 87 42 93. Daily changing menu, around €15. Cover €1.70. Open Easter-Nov. daily noon-3pm and 8pm-midnight. MC/V.)

🖂 🎭 SIGHTS AND ENTERTAINMENT. Praiano's openness and natural beauty make it the coast's best spot for a scenic **scooter** ride, though the abundance of winding roads often makes rental companies hesitant to rent out scooters to first-time drivers. Casa di San Gennaro (see above) rents scooters at dirt-cheap rates. From **Torre a Mare**, a well-preserved tower that serves as an art gallery for the works of sculptor and painter Paolo Sandulli, and around the bend from Praiano toward Amalfi, a ramp leads down **Via Terramare** to **Marina di Praia.**

A bit farther down V. Terramare toward Amalfi, the **Grotta Smeraldo** (Emerald Grotto) lures tourists with the promise of luminous green water. This 22m cavern is perfect for people who missed Capri's Blue Grotto or haven't had their fill of watery caves. The green water gives off a slight glow, and the cave's walls drip with stalactites. SITA buses stop at the grotto's above-ground elevator, which leads to the cave. Boats also depart from Amalfi's Molo Pennello daily from 9:30am-4pm and approach the grotto by sea. Multilingual guides reveal an underwater nativity scene, as well as a rock formation that is said to resemble Garibaldi. No swimming is allowed in the grotto. (Tour €7. Open daily 9am-4pm.)

AMALFI ☎089

It is almost impossible to decide on Amalfi's greatest attraction. It may be its location between the jagged rocks of the Sorrentine peninsula and the azure waters of the Tyrrhenian, or the lemon groves that bask under the sun, or even the plump lemons themselves, which seem to give everything from icy *granita* to the afternoon breeze an unparalleled citrus zing. Monuments like the fanciful Arab-Norman *duomo* and medieval paper mills also add to the city's character. Amalfi (pop. 5500) was furthermore the seat of Italy's first sea republic and the preeminent maritime powerhouse of the southern Mediterranean, thanks in part to the compass, invented here by Flavio Gioia. Sadly, Amlafi's universal appeal is also responsible for the throngs of tourists and exorbitant prices that characterize the town today.

🚍 TRANSPORTATION

The **bus terminal** is in P. F. Gioia, on the waterfront. **SITA buses** (☎089 26 66 04; www.sita-on-line.it) go to: Positano (40min., 25 per day 6:30am-11pm, €1.30); Salerno (1¼hr., 20 per day 6am-10pm, €1.80); and Sorrento (1¼hr., 29 per day 5:15am-11pm, €2). Buy tickets from *tabaccherie*. **Ferry** and **hydrofoil** tickets and departures are at the dock off P. F. Gioia. **Travelmar** (☎089 87 31 90; www.coop-santandrea.it) runs hydrofoils to: Minori (5min., 4 per day 12:45-6:20pm, €1.50); Positano (25min., 7 per day 9:20am-6pm, €5); and Salerno (35min., 6 per day 10:40am-7:10pm, €4). **Metro del Mare** (☎199 60 07 00; www.metrodelmare.com) runs to Sorrento (30min., 4 per day, 7:30am-3:25pm, €6). Rent **scooters** at **Financial Tour Travel** (see **Practical Information**). Call **taxis** at ☎089 87 22 39.

ORIENTATION AND PRACTICAL INFORMATION

Think of Amalfi as if it were in the shape of a T, with the top running along the shore and the stem, **Via Lorenzo di Amalfi**, running from the shore to the town's main square, **Piazza Duomo.** To reach P. Duomo, take V. L. di Amalfi from **Piazza Flavio Gioia** away from the sea and through the white arch. **Piazza Municipio** is a 100m walk along the coast in the direction of Atrani, up **Corso Repubblica Marinara** (on the left when facing the sea). Ferries and buses stop in P. F. Gioia, the intersection of the two roads. Facing the water, Atrani lies to the east and and the left, and Praiano is west to the right. Go through the tunnel on C. Repubblica Marinara to reach Atrani, 750m down the coast, or follow the public path through the restaurant just next to the tunnel, on the side facing the sea. The walk takes 10min.

The **AAST Tourist Office,** C. Repubblica Marinara, 27, is through a gate on the left on the road toward Atrani. Grab a free **map,** along with hotel and restaurant listings. Ferry and bus timetables are also available. (☎089 87 11 07; www.amalfitouristoffice.it. Open May-Oct. M-Sa 8:30am-1:30pm and 3:30-6:30pm, Su only the kiosk near the marina is open; Nov.-Apr. M-Sa 8am-2pm.) The **police,** V. Casamare, 19, are on the left, up V. di Amalfi (☎089 87 10 22). For **medical assistance** dial ☎118 or contact **American Diagnostics Pharmaceutics** (☎089 32 98 24 or 089 32 94 22 90 33), with doctors fluent in English, French, German, and Medicinal Japanese on-call 24hr. The facilities are clean and modern, and doctors perform blood tests and lab procedures. For **Internet,** head to **Financial Tour Travel,** V. di Amalfi, 29, which has three computers. It also offers **Western Union** services and rents **scooters** from €32 per day. (☎089 87 10 46. Internet €4 per hr. Open daily 9am-2pm and 4-8pm.) The **post office,** C. Repubblica Marinara, 35, next to the tourist office, offers **currency exchange** with good rates. (☎089 87 29 96. Commission €0.52, €2.58 on checks over €51.65. Open M-F 8am-6:30pm, Su 8am-12:30pm). **Postal Code:** 84011.

ACCOMMODATIONS

Lodgings fill up in August, so reserve far ahead. Those on a budget should consider Salerno or Sorrento for excellent lodging at lower prices.

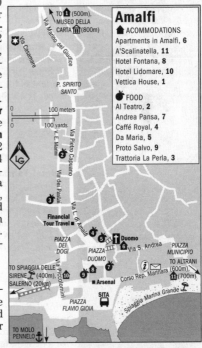

Amalfi

🏠 ACCOMMODATIONS
Apartments in Amalfi, 6
A'Scalinatella, 11
Hotel Fontana, 8
Hotel Lidomare, 10
Vettica House, 1

🍴 FOOD
Al Teatro, 2
Andrea Pansa, 7
Caffé Royal, 4
Da Maria, 5
Proto Salvo, 9
Trattoria La Perla, 3

Hotel Lidomare, V. Piccolomini, 9 (☎089 87 13 32; www.lidomare.it), through the alley across from the *duomo,* left up the stairs, then across the *piazzetta.* 15 cavernous rooms have terrace, TV, phone, fridge, A/C, and fantastic bath (most with jacuzzi). Locally made antiques adorn the halls. Small library available for perusal. Breakfast included. Singles €50-55; doubles €99-120. AmEx/MC/V. ❹

A'Scalinatella, P. Umberto, 6 (☎089 87 19 30 or 089 87 14 92; www.hostelscalinatella.com), 10min. from Amalfi in Atrani. Take C. Repubblica Marinara through the tunnel, then the stairs immediately on your right. Follow the road to P. Umberto. A 100m walk from Atrani's beach and a perfect starting point for hikes. Welcoming owners also rent rooms in Atrani, plus campsites and scenic rooms above Amalfi. Laundry €5.50. Dorms €10-21; doubles €30-60, with bath €50-83. Cash only. ❷

Vettica House, V. Maestra dei Villaggi, 96 (☎089 87 18 14; www.hostelscalinatella.com), shares management with A'Scalinatella. Call Gabriele for directions. A haven of tranquility amid natural beauty, 10 bright rooms with bath sit above lemon groves. Quick access to great hiking trails (not including the 270 stairs up from the road). Kitchen available. Dorms from €12.50 with *Let's Go;* doubles €52; quads €60. Call ahead to confirm prices. Cash only. ❶

Apartments in Amalfi, V. S. Andrea (☎089 87 28 04; www.amalfiapartments.com), next to the *duomo* at Suportico S. Andrea, rents 2 small apartments with views of the sea and the *piazza.* The double apartment can fit 4 while the studio apartment is perfect for a couple; they share a fantastic terrace. Friendly proprietors serve home-brewed *limoncello.* Reserve 1 month ahead and call for directions through the winding maze of stairs. €65 for 2 people; €90-110 for 4 people. Cash only. ❸

Hotel Fontana (☎089 87 15 30; www.hotel-fontana.it), in P. Duomo, 7, has comfortable rooms in an optimal location. High ceilings and gigantic mirrors. All rooms with bath, satellite TV, A/C, and minifridge. Breakfast included. Singles €50-75; doubles €80-100. €30-40 per additional bed. Suites also available. AmEx/MC/V. ❹

🏠 FOOD

Food in Amalfi is good but expensive. Indulge in fish, *scialatelli* (a coarsely cut local pasta), and the omnipresent pungent liqueur *limoncello,* made from local lemons. The town's many *paninoteche* are perfect for a tight budget.

▓ **Da Maria** (☎089 87 18 80), in P. Duomo. The 1st stop in a quest for quality. Friendly owners serve daily seafood specials, as well as traditional favorites like *scialatelli* and delectable seafood *risotto* (€13). Fast service despite the crowds. Pizza from €4.50. *Primi* from €10, *secondi* from €12. Fixed menu €20. Cover €3, for pizza €1.50. Open Tu-Su noon-3:30pm and 6:30-11:30pm. Reservations recommended. AmEx/MC/V. ❹

▓ **Trattoria La Perla,** V. dei Pastai, 5 (☎089 87 14 40), around corner from Hotel Amalfi. Excellent local cuisine in a quiet *piazza* served by knowledgeable owner Emilio. Try the *baccala fritto* (fried fish; €13), and for dessert, don't miss the decadent *melanzane fritta alla ciocolatta* (fried eggplant in chocolate; €4). *Menù* with dessert €16.50. Cover €2. Open Mar.-Nov. and Aug.-Sept. daily noon-3pm and 7pm-midnight; Apr.-Oct. M and W-Su noon-3pm and 7-11:30pm. AmEx/MC/V. ❸

▓ **Caffé Royal,** V. Lorenzo di Amalfi, 10 (☎089 87 19 82), near the *duomo*. The fantastic *gelato* made here (a labor of love) is the best on the Amalfi Coast. The biggest cones and 30+ flavors at great prices (€2-3). Profiteroles covered in lemon cream (€3) are a specialty. Open daily 7am-2am; Jan.-Feb. closed F. AmEx/MC/V. ❶

Proto Salvo (☎338 18 81 800), in P. Duomo. This is *the* place for great takeout snacks of pizza and sandwiches (€3). Thick *focaccia* with toppings from €1. Lunch and early evening bring large crowds, so plan to wait. Mixed salads and vegetarian *panini* available. Open daily 8:30am-midnight. Cash only. ❶

Al Teatro, V. E. Marini, 19 (☎089 87 24 73). From V. L. di Amalfi, turn left up Salita degli Orafi immediately after a shoe store, then follow the signs. Decent food at reasonable prices. Try the *scialatelli al Teatro* (with tomato and eggplant; €7). *Primi* and *secondi* from €4.50. *Menù* €14.50. Cover €1.50. Open M-Tu and Th-Su 11:30am-3:15pm and 7-11pm. Closed early Jan. to mid-Feb. AmEx/MC/V. ❷

Andrea Pansa, P. Duomo, 40 (☎089 87 10 65; www.pasticceriapansa.it). Opened in 1830, Amalfi's oldest pastry shop bears a bounty of outstanding confections, some made seasonally. In winter try the *sprocollati* (fig with ground almond); year-round, the *baba au limon* (€2) and *baba con crema* (€1.50) are delicious. Open daily 7am-midnight. AmEx/MC/V. ❶

◢ SIGHTS

The 9th-century **Duomo di Sant'Andrea** is the dominant feature of P. Duomo, and perhaps the most dominant feature of Amalfi. Its facade has intricate geometric designs of vividly contrasting colors, typical of the Arab-Norman style. The **bronze doors,** crafted in Constantinople in 1066, are so handsomely wrought that they started a bronze door craze throughout Italy. (☎089 87 13 24. Open daily 9am-9pm. Modest dress required.) To its left, the **Chiostro del Paradiso** (Cloister of Paradise), a 13th-century cemetery for Amalfitan nobles, has 120 striking marble columns and an intricate fresco of the crucifixion. The elegant interlaced arches of both the cloister and the church, like the bell tower in the square, show a Moorish influence. The church **museum** houses mosaics, sculptures, and the church's treasury. Underneath, the crypt contains the body of the church's namesake, St. Andrew the Apostle, whose remains were brought to Amalfi during the Crusades. (Open daily in summer daily 9am-9pm; in winter 10am-5pm. Free multilingual guides available. Cloister, museum, and crypt €2.50.) In the center of the *piazza*, the **Fontana di Sant'Andrea** does its best to counteract the church's stately influence, featuring a marble female nude with water trickling from her nipples. Those who can put their Freudian complexes aside might venture a drink from the fountain, which was rebuilt in the 19th century according to an original medieval plan.

The 9th-century waterfront **arsenal** majestically guards the entrance to the city center and contains relics of Amalfi's former maritime glory, including examples of Amalfitan currency (the *Tari*), and early compasses by Flavio Gioia. To inject an ailing diet with a fiber-packed kick, head to the **Museo della Carta** (Paper Museum). From the arsenal, take V. di Amalfi; the road changes to **Via delle Cartiere.** The museum, in a 13th-century paper mill, exhibits the history of paper production, including paper samples made from pressed flowers and the water-powered machines that made Amalfi a paper-producing powerhouse. (☎328 31 88 626; www.museodellacarta.it. Open daily 10am-6:30pm. €2.) Shops in town sell hand-bound reproductions of traditional Amalfitan books made from local paper.

🎵 ENTERTAINMENT

There are two small **beaches** in Amalfi; one is sandy, the other is rocky. The sandy beach, though not stunning, is a stretch near the marina. Better (and free) options are at nearby **Atrani**, a 15-20min. walk away. After the tunnel from Amalfi, descend a winding staircase to the beach and P. Umberto. Past P. Umberto, a stairway leads to **Chiesa di San Salvatore de Bireto,** with beautiful 11th-century **bronze doors** from Constantinople. The church's name refers to the hat placed on the Republic's *doge*, or ruler, when he was inaugurated. Atrani used to be home to the Amalfi Republic's leaders; with about 1000 inhabitants today, it's a quiet place to escape Amalfi's crowds by day and enjoy lively bars and music at night. Try **La Risacca**, P. Umberto, 1, with friendly bartenders and a fun-filled atmosphere. (☎089 87 28 66. Open daily 8-2am. MC/V.) To watch a soccer match head to **Bar Directo**, P. Umberto, 2 (☎328 53 49 153; open daily 7-3am; cash only), with plentiful outdoor seating.

Hikers often tackle paths from Amalfi and Atrani to the imposing **Monti Lattari**, winding through lemon groves and mountain streams. From Amalfi, the **Antiche Scale** lead to the charming village of **Pogerola**. Trek through the ◪**Valley of the Dragons,** named for the torrent of water and mist which plumes like smoke from a dragon and explodes out to sea every winter. Another favorite is the 4hr. **Path of the Gods,** leading from Bomerano to **Positano**, with great views along the way. The beautiful hike from Atrani to **Ravello** (1½-2hr.) runs through gently bending lemon groves, up secluded stairways, and down into green cliff valleys. From Ravello, it's only about 1hr. downhill to **Minori's** beautiful beaches, past quaint village churches and bountiful grapevines. SITA runs frequent bus service from both Minori and Ravello to Amalfi. Hike past the old paper mills in **Valle delle Ferriere**, which begins at the paper museum (see **Sights**). Naturally, the hikes can get steep, and a good map is essential (available at the tourist office in Amalfi). For a shorter walk, head from Amalfi's center to its terraced cliffs to reach the cliff where famous rebel Masaneillo hid from Spanish police. Although the cave is sporadically closed, the astounding views are a nice payoff along the way.

🔁 DAYTRIP FROM AMALFI

MINORI

SITA buses from Amalfi stop on V. G. Capone, which becomes V. G. Amendola as it heads 1km northwest to Amalfi.

With a decidedly low-key character and many pleasant seafront cafes, Minori is serene and inviting. Smaller and less touristed than Amalfi or Positano, the town is home to large stretches of beautiful **free beaches.** Sunbathers seeking the perfect day at the beach and hikers in search of the optimal trail-end spot can find peace and relaxation here. The difficult 1hr. hike from Atrani (via Ravello) is enjoyable for its cliff vistas and shady lemon groves. For a lunchtime *panino* (€3-6) or tasty *gelato* (€2), try **Suzy Beach ❶**. With plenty of breezy outdoor seating, this is the perfect place to reward tired feet after a long day's hike—or to further cultivate sloth-like tendencies after a long day of sunning.

RAVELLO ☎089

Far from the beach on its cliff-top perch, Ravello (pop. 2500) presides over a patchwork of villages and ravines that tumble into the sea. Romans founded the town in AD 500, and Barbarians and Saracens later invaded, but artists and intellectuals have ultimately claimed the natural beauty and romantic decay of this once-formidable settlement. The gardens of Villa Rufolo inspired part of Boccaccio's *Decameron* and Wagner's opera *Parsifal* and to this day, Ravello is known as *La Città della Musica*, because of the performances it hosts all year.

⌗❼ TRANSPORTATION AND PRACTICAL INFORMATION. Take the blue **SITA bus** from Amalfi (20min., 30 per day 6:30am-midnight €1.30) marked "Ravello-Scala." For a gorgeous walk, hike along hills and lemon groves from Minori (1hr.), Atrani (2hr., via Scala), or Amalfi (2½hr., via Pontone). Ask at the tourist office in Amalfi for details. For a **taxi**, call ☎089 85 80 00. The **AAST Tourist Office** is at V. Roma, 18, off P. Duomo. (☎089 85 70 96; www.ravellotime.it. Open daily 9am-7pm.) The English-speaking staff provides brochures, event and hotel listings, and a **map**. The **carabinieri** (☎089 85 71 50) are on V. Roma, near P. Duomo. A **pharmacy**, P. Duomo, 14, is on the left side of the *piazza* facing the *duomo*. (☎089 85 71 89. Open daily in summer 9am-1pm and 5-8:30pm; in winter 9am-1pm and 4:30-8pm. Closed Dec.) Clean **public toilets** are located next to Cafe Calce (see **Accommodations and Food**, below). Across the street is an **ATM**; another is at P. Duomo, 5. Look for a faded bronze sign to the left of the kiosk. The **post office** is at P. Duomo, 15. (Open M-F 8am-1:30pm, Sa 8am-12:30pm.) **Postal Code:** 84010.

⌗❸ ACCOMMODATIONS AND FOOD. Ravello offers mainly opulent options. To get to **Hotel Villa Amore ❹**, V. dei Fusco, 4, follow V. San Francesco out of P. Duomo toward Villa Cimbrone, and take a left on V. dei Fusco. Twelve clean, white-washed rooms share a garden overlooking cliffs and the sea. As its welcome sign says, "A stay at Villa Amore gives peace to the soul and joy to the heart." All rooms have terrace and view; some have bath. (☎/fax 089 85 71 35. Breakfast included. Reserve 1 month ahead. Singles €48-56; doubles €80-90. MC/V.) **Albergo Garden ❺**, V. G. Boccaccio, 4, before the tunnel to Ravello, by the SITA bus stop, lacks intimacy but compensates with great views. All 10 rooms have bath and balconies. (☎089 85 72 26; www.hotelgardenravello.it. Breakfast included. Reserve 1 month ahead for Aug. Closed Nov. 15-Feb. 15. Doubles €110. Extra bed €20.)

Wines with Ravello labels are revered around the globe, and as you stroll down V. Roma, step into one of the many wine shops and have a taste or even buy a bottle. **Cumpà Cosimo ❸**, at V. Roma, 44, has a large menu and a staff willing to chat about Ravello. The restaurant's atmosphere is informal and laid-back, perfect for casual meals. The *mista di pasta fatta in casa* (€14) mixes five delectable homemade pastas. (☎089 85 71 56. Cover €2. Open daily noon-4pm and 7pm-midnight. AmEx/MC/V.) **Cafe Calce ❶**, V. Roma, 2, serves excellent pastries, coffee, and *gelato*. *Limoncello* costs €11 per bottle. (☎089 85 71 52. Cappuccino €2. *Gelato* €2. Open M-Tu and Th-Su 8am-1am. MC/V.)

CAMPANIA

⬚ ⬚ SIGHTS AND ENTERTAINMENT. The beautiful churches, ivy-covered walls, and meandering paths of the 13th-century **Villa Rufolo** inspired Wagner's magic garden, seen in the 2nd act of his opera *Parsifal*. In summer, the villa puts on a concert series with performances in some of its most picturesque spaces (for details, see below). A medieval tower with Norman-Saracen vaulting and statues representing the four seasons serves as the entry to the famous **Moorish cloister.** Enter through the arch off P. Duomo near the tunnel. The main hall frequently hosts exhibits by big-name artists. (☎089 85 76 57. Open daily 9am-8pm. €5, under 12 or over 65 €2.50.) The Amalfi Coast's 3rd set of famous **bronze doors,** cast by Barisano of Trani in 1179, is in the portal of Ravello's **duomo.** The doors have 54 panels depicting detailed scenes from the Passion of Christ. Inside, antique columns set off two pulpits with elaborate mosaics. An image of the town's patron saint stands in the **Cappella di S. Pantaleone.** Behind the painting, his blood is preserved in a cracked vessel. St. Pantaleone was beheaded on July 27, AD 290, at Nicomedia. Every year on this day the city holds a **religious festival,** during which the saint's blood is mysteriously liquefied. The **museum** within depicts the *duomo's* history through pagan and Christian eras with beautiful ancient mosaics and sculptures. Follow V. San Francesco out of P. Duomo to **Villa Cimbrone.** Renovated by Lord Greenthorpe in the 19th century, the villa sports floral walkways and majestic gardens, including the panoramic **Terrace of the Infinite.** The **Temple of Bacco** and the **Grotto of Eva** lie along the twisting paths, as well as some of the most magnificent views on the Amalfi Coast. A procession of notables has made the villa a famous retreat; visitors include Greta Garbo, Leopold Stokowski, and Jacqueline Kennedy, a resident in 1962.

During the year, internationally renowned musicians perform at **classical music festivals,** held around New Year's, Easter, and all summer. In warm weather, concerts can be heard in the gardens of Villa Rufolo; in winter they move inside the villa or *duomo.* Each season's festival is unified by a Wagnerian *leitmotif,* and includes screenings of films and panel discussions on a range of topics. Tickets, usually €10-20, are sold at the Ravello Festival Box Office, V. Roma 10-12. (☎089 85 84 22; www.ravellofestival.com. Open daily 9am-2pm and 3-8pm.)

SALERNO ☎089

As the capital of the Norman Empire from 1077 to 1127 and home to Europe's first medical school, Salerno (pop. 144,000) once played host to a proud, powerful culture. During WWII, however, the city was blasted by Allied bombs and much of its medieval past was turned to rubble. Unlike the dreamy villages of the Amalfi Coast, Salerno is an urban reality, with an industrial core, a university, and one of the liveliest nightlife scenes on the peninsula. The cosmopolitan city gives travelers a wonderful taste of modern Italy, and though it serves well as a cheap base for visiting the Amalfi Coast and the ruins at Paestum, Salerno itself is a worthwhile destination. The snaking alleyways of the old city are charming, and those who take time to look can find a treasure trove of excellent restaurants and cafes.

⬚ TRANSPORTATION

Trains: (☎089 25 50 05) In P. Veneto. To: **Naples** (45min., 40 per day 3:41am-10:32pm, €5-10); **Paestum** (40min., 16 per day 5:52am-9:52pm, €3); **Reggio Calabria** (3½-5hr., 16 per day, €17-35); **Rome** (2½-3hr., 22 per day, €21-33); **Venice** (9hr., 11 per day 2:54am-8:50pm, €36-43).

Buses: SITA buses leave from the train station for **Amalfi** (1¼hr., 24 per day 5:15am-10pm, €3) and **Naples** (1hr., 38 per day 5:05am-10:10pm, €3). Buy tickets from a bar or *tabaccherie* and ask where your bus leaves (either P. Veneto or P. della Concordia). **CSTP** runs buses from P. della Concordia to **Paestum** (1½hr., 12 per day 6:30am-7:30pm, €2.50) and from P. Veneto to **Pompeii** (1hr., 14 per day 6:10am-9pm, €3).

Ferries and Hydrofoils: Most ferries leave from P. della Concordia, 2 blocks from the train station. Others leave from Molo Manfredi, up the waterfront. **Linee Marittime Salernitane** (☎089 23 48 92; www.amalficoastlines.com) runs hydrofoils from Molo Manfredi to **Capri** (2½ hr.; 3 per day after July 1 8:15am, 11:05am, and 5pm; €12). **Travelmar** (☎089 87 29 50) runs to many destinations on the Amalfi Coast: **Amalfi** (35min., 6 per day 8:40am-3:30pm, €4); **Minori** (30min., 4 per day 7:50am-2:10pm, €4); and **Positano** (1¼hr., 6 per day 8:40am-3:30pm, €6).

Public Transportation: Orange and blue **CSTP buses** connect the train station to the rest of the city. For routes and schedules, check the ticket booth in P. Veneto. 1hr. tickets €0.80; full-day pass €1.40.

Taxis: ☎089 75 75 75 or 089 71 26 96.

Car Rental: Travel Car, P. Veneto, 33 (☎089 22 77 22). Cars from €45 per day. Open daily 8am-1pm and 3-7:30pm. AmEx/MC/V. **Avis** and **Hertz** also have offices to the right as you exit the train station.

◼ 🔁 ORIENTATION AND PRACTICAL INFORMATION

Salerno's **train station** is in **Piazza Vittorio Veneto.** The pedestrian **Corso Vittorio Emanuele** veers right out of the *piazza*, becoming **Via dei Mercanti** upon reaching the old quarter, the liveliest and most historically interesting area of Salerno. **Via Roma,** home to many of the city's best restaurants, runs parallel to C. V. Emanuele, one block toward the waterfront. Along the waterfront in front of the train station is **Piazza della Concordia,** from which many intercity buses depart, and **Lungomare Trieste,** which runs to Salerno's port, **Molo Manfredi.**

Tourist Office: EPT (☎089 23 14 32), in P. V. Veneto, to the right when leaving the train station. Friendly staff provides free **maps** and brochures on hotels and restaurants, as well as comprehensive bus and train info. Open M-Sa 9:15am-2pm and 3:15-8pm.

Work Opportunity: Ask the P. V. Veneto tourist office about short-term work options (see **Short-Term Work,** p. 90).

English-Language Bookstore: Libreria Mondadori, C. V. Emanuele. Decent selection of classics and new fiction. Open M-Sa 9am-1:30pm and 5-9pm. MC/V.

Emergency: ☎113. **Carabinieri:** ☎112. **Ambulance:** ☎118.

Hospital: S. Leonardo (☎089 30 12 03).

Internet Access: Attendere Prego, V. Roma, 26, has 6 fast computers and printers. €3.50 per hr. Open daily 9am-9pm.

Post Office: C. Garibaldi, 203 (☎089 25 72 11). Open M-Sa 8:15am-6:15pm. **Branch** (☎089 22 99 98) at P. V. Veneto. Open M-Sa 8:15am-1:30pm. **Currency exchange** at main office only. **Postal Code:** 84100.

🏠 ACCOMMODATIONS

▨ **Ostello Ave Gratia Plena,** V. Canali (☎089 23 47 76; www.ostellionline.org). Take C. V. Emanuele into the old district, where it becomes V. dei Mercanti, then turn right on V.

Canali. A 15min. walk with a backpack. The hostel is past the church, on the right. Good location, with proximity to restaurants and nightlife. Clean, comfortable rooms and a great indoor courtyard. Sheets and hot shower included. Towels €2.50. Internet €3.50 per hr. Lockout 10:30am-3pm. Curfew 12:30am. Single-sex and co-ed dorms available. Dorms €14; singles €23; doubles €34; triples €46.50. MC/V. ❶

Hotel Salerno, V. Vicinanza, 42, 5th fl. (☎089 22 42 11; www.albergosalerno.com), 1st left off C. V. Emanuele. Bright and clean with a comfortable TV lounge. Remarkably quiet considering its location by the train tracks. Some rooms have phone and TV, all have a fan. A/C €8. Singles €35, with bath €45-50; doubles €42/65. AmEx/MC/V. ❸

Hotel Montestella, C. V. Emanuele, 156 (☎089 22 51 22; fax 089 22 91 67) is a 10min. walk from the train station, on the right. Though the lounge is eclectic and minimalist, the rooms are elegant and generously sized. Preparing for renovations in fall 2005. All rooms have TV, phone, and A/C; some with balcony. Breakfast included. Singles €60; doubles €94; triples €104; quads €114. AmEx/MC/V. ❹

Albergo Santa Rosa, C. V. Emanuele, 14, 2nd fl. (☎089 22 53 46; alb.srosa@tiscali.net), 1 block from the train station on the right. 12 clean, comfortable rooms. Somewhat removed from most of Salerno's restaurants and bars, but within walking distance and still an excellent value. Internet point in building. Singles €28, with bath €38; doubles €38-60. ❸

◨ FOOD

▨**Hosteria Il Brigante,** V. F. Linguiti, 4 (☎089 22 65 92). From P. Duomo, head up the stairs and look for the sign on the left. As authentic as it gets: 1 menu, hand-written on brown laminated paper, and just 1 waiter/manager visible. Try the *pasta alla sangiovannara* (€3), a hodge-podge of pasta, tomato, cheese, and sausage. Open Tu-Su 1:30-2:30pm and 9-11:30pm. Cash only. ❷

▨**Il Caminetto,** V. Roma, 232 (☎089 22 96 14). Enjoy delicious seafood for the lowest prices in town at an outdoor seating area protected from the noise and fumes of the busy V. Roma. Try the heaping dish of *zuppa di cozze* (mussels in marinara sauce; €4) or the slightly tangy *pasta fagioli* (€4). Cover €1.50. *Primi* €4-8, *secondi* €4-10. Open daily 12:30-3:30pm and 7:30pm-1am. Closed W lunch. MC/V. ❷

▨**Gerry,** V. G. Da Procida, 33 (☎089 23 78 21). Packs of locals vie nightly to be next in line for Salerno's best *gelato*. Homemade and creamy, this treat is worth the wait. Traditional (*fragola*) and more ambitious (*golosone*) flavors. Cones from €1.50 (generous) to €2 (semi-insurmountable). Open daily 10am-1pm and 5pm-1am. Cash only. ❶

Panineria Sant Andrea, P. Sedile del Campo, 13 (☎089 75 04 18). Every kind of sandwich you could imagine from *polipo* (octopus; €6.50), to the simple mozzarella with various meats (from €2). Takeout window and popular outdoor seating in summer. Open Tu-Su noon-3pm and 9pm-1am. Cash only. ❶

◉ ♫ SIGHTS AND ENTERTAINMENT

To take in the evening air, stroll down C. V. Emanuele or sit in the lush gardens of the **Villa Comunale.** For a bit of historical flavor, the old city is a pleasing tangle of alleys and little shops. A particularly nice walk starts at C. V. Emanuele, turns right off V. Mercanti or V. Roma on V. Duomo, then runs uphill to **Duomo San Matteo.** First constructed in AD 845, the *duomo* was destroyed and rebuilt 200 years later by the Norman leader Robert Guiscard. When Pope Gregory VII fled to Salerno in 1084, he consecrated the *duomo*. Its cosmopolitan design stands out among the city's other buildings, and the arches of the portico, the floor of the apse, and the two pulpits in the nave bear beautiful geometric mosaics. The *duomo* also harbors a tooth from Evangelist Matthew, a hair from the Virgin Mary, and a splinter from the True Cross. (☎089 23 13 87. Open M-F 9am-6pm, Sa-Su 1-6pm.) To soak up some rays, take the bus along Lungomare Trieste and head to the sandy **beach** beyond the sailboat harbor. Nearby **Vietri sul Mare** is home to hundreds of artisans and a pleasant beach. Buses #4 and 9 run from the station (10min., €0.80).

Through July, the **Salerno Summerfestival,** at the Arena del Mare, near the Molo Manfredi, includes a concert series with jazz and blues. (☎089 66 51 76. Concerts usually start 10pm. Prices vary. Contact tourist office for info.) At night, younger crowds gather near the fountain at **Bar/Gelateria Nettuno,** V. Lungomare Trieste, 136-138. (☎089 22 83 75. Open daily 9am-2am.) The many bars along V. Roma are perfect spots to hang with locals or watch a soccer match.

⚡ DAYTRIP FROM SALERNO

PAESTUM

The simplest way to get to Paestum is to take the train from Salerno (30min., 19 per day, €2.90). Exiting the Paestum station, walk straight for 7min. until you see the museum and entrance to temples on the right. There are also CSTP buses from Salerno, P. della Concordia (1½hr., 12 per day 6:30am-7:30pm, €3.20), which stop at V. Magna Graecia, the main modern road. Buy tickets from tabaccherie. While consistently air-conditioned, buses are often caught in traffic on the way to Paestum, and the trains run much more frequently. The tourist office in Salerno provides a list of return buses and trains from Paestum. The AAST Tourist Office, V. Magna Graecia, 887, is next to the museum. (☎0828 81 10 16. Open June-Sept. 15 M-Sa 9am-7pm, Su 9am-1pm; Sept. 16-June M-Sa 9am-1pm and 2-5pm.) Restoration work occasionally leaves temples fenced off or obscured. (Temples open in summer daily 9am-7:30pm; in winter 9am-4pm. Museum open daily 9am-6:30pm. Ticket sales end 1hr. before closing. Museum and temples closed 1st and 3rd M of the month for restoration. Museum admission €4, EU students €2, EU citizens under 18 or over 60 free. Ruins and museum €6.50, EU students €3.25, EU citizens under 18 or over 60 free. Included with Artecard.)

Not far from the Roman ruins of Pompeii and Herculaneum, Paestum's three ▓**Doric temples** rank among the best-preserved and most complete in the world, rivaling those of Sicily and Athens. Amazingly, these masterfully constructed structures were built without any mortar or cement, yet remained standing after the great earthquake of AD 69 reduced Pompeii's Temple of Jupiter to a pile of rubble. The town began as a Greek colony dedicated to sea god Poseidon, and then was conquered by the Romans, who expanded the settlement. It may seem like you missed your bus stop. Fear not the dearth of urban squalor, gentle traveler: *ruins* are the destination. The ancient Greeks built Paestum on a north-south axis, marked by the **Via Sacra;** in some places tracks are still visible, worn in the stone. Farther south on V. Sacra is the **Roman forum,** larger than the one at Pompeii though more dilapidated. The Romans leveled most of the structures in the city's center to build this proto-*piazza*, the commercial and political arena of Paestum. To the left, a shallow pit marks an ancient **gymnasium.** East of the gymnasium lies the Roman **amphitheater,** built during the reign of Julius Caesar.

When excavators first uncovered the three temples in the 18th century, they misnamed them. Although recent scholarship has provided new info about the temples's dedications, the old names have stuck. There are three entrances.

CAMPANIA

The northernmost (closest to the bus stop) leads to the **Templo di Cere.** Built around 500 BC, this temple was used as a church in the early Middle Ages. South of the forum lies the 5th-century BC **Templo di Poseidon** (actually dedicated to Apollo). More sophisticated and complete than the temple of Ceres, this temple incorporates many of the refinements found in Athens's Parthenon. Small lions' heads (now on display in the museum) served as gargoyles on the temple roof. The southernmost temple, known as the **basilica,** is also the oldest, dating from the 6th century BC. Its unusual plan, with a main interior section split by a row of columns down the middle, has inspired the theory that the temple was dedicated to two gods, Zeus and Hera, rather than one. A ■**museum,** on the other side of V. Magna Graecia, houses extraordinary pottery, paintings, and artifacts taken primarily from Paestum's tombs. The presentation is outstanding, with descriptive essays in several languages. Look up at the dramatic friezes that encircle the first floor, which depict Hercules struggling against his foes. The museum also holds samples of 2500-year-old honey and paintings from the famous **Tomb of the Diver,** dating from 475 BC. The 2nd floor of the museum houses an exhibit of the artist Bartolomeo Gatto.

PUGLIA, BASILICATA, AND CALABRIA

HIGHLIGHTS OF PUGLIA, BASILICATA, AND CALABRIA

JOURNEY to the end of the **Appian Way,** the oldest and most famous Roman road, marked by one remaining column in Brindisi (p. 627).

REPOSE in the shelter of cliff-side **Tropea** as azure waves lap sandy shores (p. 645).

DISCOVER buried treasures at **Reggio di Calabria's Museo Nazionale** (p. 638).

PUGLIA

The ports of Brindisi, Bari, and Otranto are as bustling and international today as they were hundreds of years ago when the Greeks and Romans coveted them as trade routes to the East. Yet tourism has only recently begun to materialize in this rustic, sun-baked region, and Puglia remains a refreshing pause from Italy's more frequented destinations. The area, located in the middle of the Mediterranean, also maintains great cultural wealth, laying claim to remote medieval villages, cone-roofed *trulli* houses, and ports with a distinct Middle Eastern flavor. Its arresting castles and cathedrals eloquently recall the Middle Ages, when an onslaught of invaders shaped local culture. Travelers to Puglia will welcome its passionate and unique cultural heritage and distinctly Southern zest for life.

BARI   ☎080

Exquisite Puglian cuisine and nightlife fueled by the city's university population add to the complexity of this busy port (pop. 300,000), the main Italian transportation hub for those traveling to Greece. Clothing shops and *gelaterie* tempt on every street, and the sea is never more than a few blocks away. Amid the constant commotion, reckless drivers zoom about and pick-pockets dart down alleys. Although Bari does not figure prominently on most itineraries, its bustling lifestyle is sure to excite, if only for a few days.

▶ TRANSPORTATION

Flights: Palese Airport (☎080 58 35 200; www.seap-puglia.it), 8km west of the city. **Alitalia, Air France, British Airways,** and **Lufthansa** fly to major European cities. Shuttle bus #16 leaves from P. Aldo Moro (12 per day 5:15am-6:30pm, €0.77).

Trains: Bari is connected to 4 railways, all of which leave **Bari Centrale** (☎080 52 40 148) in P. Aldo Moro: **Ferrovie Dello Stato** (FS), **Ferrovie Sud Est** (FSE) (behind the FS tracks), **Ferrotramviaria Nord** (you must exit and re-enter the station), and **Ferrovie Appulo Lucana** (FAL). All regional (non-FS) trains have reduced service on Su.

FS, which serves large cities, runs trains to: **Brindisi** (1½-1¾hr., 22 per day 4:50am-11:11pm, €5.73-10.33); **Foggia** (1½-2hr., 39 per day 12:03am-11:55pm, €6.70-13.94); **Lecce** (2hr., 21 per day 4:50am-9:21pm, €7.50-12.19); **Milan** (9½-10hr., 13 per day 12:03am-10:56pm, €37.70-61.93); **Naples** (4½hr., 7 per day 12:13am-6:42pm, €19.17-27.47); **Reggio di Calabria** (7½-8hr., 6 per day 12:14am-10:44pm, €27.13-36); **Rome** (5-7hr., 7 per day 12:13am-6:42pm, €26.12-36); **Termoli** (2-3hr., 15 per day 12:03am-9:39pm, €10.12-21.28).

Puglia, Basilicata, and Calabria

FSE (☎080 54 62 444; www.fseonline.it) runs trains from track 11 to **Alberobello** (1½hr., 13 per day 6:28am-8:25pm, €4).

Ferrotramviaria Nord (☎080 52 13 577; www.ferrovienordbarese.it), to the left of Centrale. Departs for: **Ruvo** (45min., €2.30). On Su the Ruvo route is served by bus from P. Aldo Moro.

FAL (☎080 52 44 881; www.fal-srl.it), next door to the Nord station in P. Aldo Moro. Trains depart for **Matera** (1½hr., 8 per day 6:25am-7:05pm, €4) via **Altamura.**

Buses: SITA (☎080 55 62 446; www.sita-on-line.it) buses leave from V. Capruzzi, 226, behind the train station.

Ferries: Some companies are listed below, but call ahead: schedules and prices vary, especially on weekends. Obtain tickets and info at the Stazione Marittima or at the offices. **Check-in at least 2hr. before departure.** Try to avoid walking through the desolate area surrounding the Stazione Marittima and port. Visit www.greekferries.gr for more info on ferries to Greece.

Marlines (☎080 52 31 824 or 080 52 75 409, reservations 080 52 10 206; www.marlines.com). To **Durres, Albania** (schedules vary weekly July-Sept.; €62-130 in the high season, €45-105 in low season).

Superfast Ferries (☎080 52 82 828; www.superfast.com) sails overnight to **Greece**. To **Corfu** (8 hr.; all odd dates of July, even dates of August, and odd dates in Sept. until Sept. 9.), **Igoumenitsa** (8½hr., M-Sa 1 per day 10pm) and **Patrasso** (14½hr., M-Th and Sa 10pm), the line to **Corfu** is operated by partner company **Blue Star Ferries**. High season €95-430, low season €83-393 depending on the preferred type of seating.

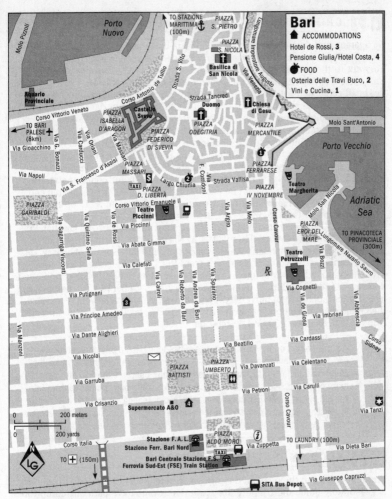

Bari

🏠 ACCOMMODATIONS
Hotel de Rossi, 3
Pensione Giulia/Hotel Costa, 4

🍅 FOOD
Osteria delle Travi Buco, 2
Vini e Cucina, 1

Ventouris Ferries, V. Piccinni, 133, c/o P. Lorusso & Co. (☎080 52 17 699; www.ventouris.gr). Windows #18-20 in Stazione Marittima. To **Corfu-Igoumenitsa** (10hr.; 2 per week Feb. 2-Apr. 29, 5 per week May 2-Dec. 29) and **Durres, Albania** (13hr.). Call for prices.

Public Transportation: Local buses leave from P. Aldo Moro, in front of the train station. Tickets sold at *tabaccherie* (€0.80) or on the bus (€1). **Bus #20** makes hourly trips between Stazione Marittima and the train stations.

Taxis: ☎080 55 43 333 (for **RadioTaxi**) and 080 52 10 600 (for the taxi station). For RadioTaxi, you must leave message after beep with departure and destination.

↳ **ARRIVEDERCI, ITALIA.** Bari is an important port for ferries to **Greece, Turkey, Albania, Israel, Bosnia-Herzegovina,** and **Serbia and Montenegro.** Many lines offer special student rates and discounts on round-trip tickets. Don't forget your passport!

PUGLIA, BASILICATA, AND CALABRIA

ORIENTATION AND PRACTICAL INFORMATION

Via Sparano runs from the train station to **Piazza Umberto I,** Bari's main square. The end of V. Sparano intersects **Corso Vittorio Emanuele II** and the edge of the old city. To walk to the **port,** skirt the old city's winding streets by turning left on C. V. Emanuele II and right at **Piazza della Libertà** on **Via Giuseppe Massari.** Circle the castle, head right, and follow the coast. Otherwise, take bus #20 from the station (every hr.). For a calmer route to the sea (not the port), turn right off V. Sparano on C. V. Emanuele II, continuing past **Corso Cavour** to **Piazza Eroi del Mare.**

Head right from the train station to reach the **APT Tourist Office,** P. Aldo Moro, 33/A, 2nd fl. The office supplies free **maps** of Puglia and Bari. (☎080 52 42 361; www.pugliaturismo.it. Open M-F 9am-noon.) There is also a small kiosk across from the station that gives out information about Bari. There is a **laundromat** at V. Toma, 35. Take the pass over the train tracks to C. Cavour and continue straight. V. Toma is on the left. (☎080 55 67 056. Wash €3, dry €2. Open M-Sa 9am-1pm and 4-6pm.) In case of **emergency,** dial ☎113; reach the **carabinieri** at ☎112 or at the station located on V. Tanzi, 5. Walk east on V. Carulli and turn left 2 blocks after the highway on V. Abbrescia to find the station straight ahead. The local **hospital,** Policlinino is at P. Giulio Cesare, 11 (☎080 54 21 854). From FSE exit of Bari Centrale, follow V. Capruzzi west, taking Viale Salandra left into P. Cesare. A **pharmacy, Lojacono di Berrino,** C. Cavour, 47, is across from the Teatro Petruzzelli. (☎080 52 12 615. Open M-F 8:30am-1pm and 5-8:30pm.) Check **Internet** in the air-conditioned **Netcafe,** V. Andrea da Bari, 11. (Open M-Sa 9am-10pm. €4 per hr.) The **post office** is in P. Battisti, behind the university. From P. Umberto, turn left on V. Crisanzio, then immediately right on V. Cairoli. (☎080 57 57 187; fax 080 57 57 053. Open M-F 8am-6:30pm, Sa 8am-12:30pm.) **Postal Code:** 70100.

> **!** A strategic port on the Italian coast, Bari has long been a prime target for invaders. To keep them at bay, citizens built the old city as a labyrinth in which they could hide or take attackers by surprise. Today thieves often benefit from the maze of streets, and careless tourists are their favorite prey. **Do not venture into the old city at night.** Use maps discreetly, avoid wearing jewelry, and hold tightly to purses, bags, and cameras. At the same time, don't skip the sights solely for fear of petty crime; the old city is historically interesting and well worth exploring.

ACCOMMODATIONS AND FOOD

Though located in the heart of downtown, ▓**Hotel de Rossi ❸,** V. de Rossi, 186, is reasonably quiet and friendly. Its attractive rooms have bath, air-conditioning, and TV. (☎080 52 45 355; fax 080 52 45 502. Breakfast included. Singles €35; doubles €60. AmEx/MC/V.) Three hotels occupy the same building at V. Crisanzio, 12, across the street from the university library. **Pensione Giulia ❹** has country-style rooms with air-conditioning. (☎080 52 16 630; www.hotelpensionegiulia.it. Breakfast included. Internet €1 per 10min. Singles €42, with bath €52; doubles €52/65; triples €75; quads €90. AmEx/MC/V.) Another alternative is the **Hotel Costa ❺,** which has modern rooms, with phone, TV, and either air-conditioning or fan. (☎080 52 19 015; www.hotelcostabari.com. Singles €62; doubles €88. AmEx/MC/V.)

Outside the old city walls, stock up for the ferry ride at **Supermercato A&O,** which has an ATM inside. (Open M-Tu and Th-Su 8am-2pm and 4:30-8:15pm, W 8am-2pm.) Eating in the old city can feel like a time warp; often, restaurants provide neither menus nor itemized checks. Just off of Piazzale 4 Novembre, ▓ **Vini e Cucina ❷,** V. Vallisa, 23, is such a place. Sit at the nearest free seat, let the waiters tell you what you're ordering, and enjoy the most authentic food Bari has to offer. (☎330 43 30 15. *Antipasti* €2. *Primi* €3.50, *secondi* €4. Cover €0.50. Open M-Sa noon-3pm and daily 7pm-midnight. Cash only.) ◗**Osteria delle Travi Buco ❸**, Largo Chiurlia, 12, at the end of V. Sparano in the old city, serves fresh food in large portions. Try the *orecchiette con cavallo* (with horse meat) or the pasta with arugula. (☎339 15 78 848. *Primi* €5, *secondi* €5. *Menù* with drink €16-19. Open Tu-Su 1:30-4pm and 7:30-11:30pm. MC/V.)

👁 SIGHTS

Looks like mom and dad were wrong—there really is a Santa Claus, and the ▨**Basilica di San Nicola** proves it. In 1087 60 *Baresi* sailors stole St. Nicholas's remains from Turkey; the sailors initially refused to cede the body to local clergy, but ultimately gave it up when the Church built this spartan basilica as Santa's final resting place. Inside, 17th-century paintings enliven the gaudy ceiling. St. Nick himself occupies the crypt in the chapel, ready to receive homage and Christmas wish lists. On the back wall, several paintings commemorate the jolly saint's good deeds, including his resurrection of three children who were sliced to bits and plunged into a brine barrel by a nasty butcher. (Open daily 7am-noon and 4-7:30pm, except during mass.) Just outside the old city, off C. V. Veneto near the water, is the colossal **Castello Svevo,** built in the 13th century by Frederick II on Norman and Byzantine foundations. Isabel of Aragon and Sona Sforza added bulwarks in the 16th century. Visitors can't climb the ramparts, but the medieval cellar displays art from the region's cathedrals and castles. (☎080 52 86 111, for tickets 080 62 25. Open daily except major holidays 9am-7pm. €2, ages 18-25 €1.) Down Lungomare N. Sauro past P. A. Diaz is the **Pinacoteca Provinciale,** on the 4th floor. The gallery displays landscapes and works by Veronese, Tintoretto, Bellini, De Nittis, and Francesco Netti, acclaimed hometown artist, as well as a vast collection of Greek art from the 1800s. (☎080 54 12 422. Open daily 9am-1pm and 4-7pm, Su 9am-1pm; Aug. open only in the morning. €2.58, students €0.52.)

🎵 🎭 ENTERTAINMENT AND NIGHTLIFE

Bari is the cultural nucleus of Puglia. On C. V. Emanuele, **Teatro Piccinni** offers a spring concert season and opera year-round. Purchase tickets at the theater. (☎080 52 10 878. Open M-F 10:30am-12:30pm and 5-8pm, Sa-Su 10:30am-12:30pm.) Consult the ticket office or the *Sera* section of *La Gazzetta del Mezzogiorno* (the local newspaper) for the latest information. From September through June, sports fans can catch **soccer matches** on any Sunday. (Tickets start at €15 and are available at the stadium or in bars.) On May 7-9, *Baresi* celebrate their stolen saint in the **Festival of San Nicola,** featuring a parade of children and traditional foods.

Most of Bari's clubs are open nightly from 8pm until 1 or 2am (3am on Sa), but they generally close in August, when the town university is on holiday. V. Sparano and P. Umberto are packed by night, and on weekends, students cram into P. Ferrarese and other *piazze* along the breezy waterfront east of the old city.

🏞 DAYTRIPS FROM BARI

CASTELLANA GROTTE

FSE trains depart from Bari for "Grotte di Castellana Grotte" (2hr.; 8:22, 9:52, 11:50am, and 4:20pm; €3). Caves are across the parking lot and to the left. 50min tours every hr. daily in summer 8:30am-7pm; in winter 8:30am-1pm; €8. 2hr. tours every hr. in summer daily 9am-6pm except 1 and 2pm; in winter 10am-noon; €13. English 50min. tour 1 and 6:30pm; 2hr. tour 11am and 4pm.

> **‡TIP‡ WHAT'S IN A NAME.** Not all trains heading for Castellana Grotte actually stop at the grottoes. The stop "Castellana Grotte" is for the city, 2km away. The next, unmarked stop is for the grottoes. Confirm with the conductor when boarding that the train actually stops there.

Superstitious locals once feared that these breathtaking natural caverns were an entrance to hell. The Castellana Grotte, discovered in 1938, are famed for their impressive size and eerie beauty. Over time, stalactites and stalagmites have developed into all sorts of whimsical shapes, including a Virgin Mary, a camel, a wolf, an owl, and an ice-cream cone. Even if the resemblances don't seem obvious, the various formations invite the imagination to run wild. Those with time to kill can even watch them grow—at the rate of 3cm per century. Visitors must take one of two **guided tours:** a short 1km jaunt and a longer 3km trek both start at La Grave, the enormous pit that was considered the opening to hell. The longer tour culminates in the stunning **Grotta Bianca** (White Cave), a giant cavern filled with white stalactites. (☎080 02 13 976 or 080 49 98 211; www.grottedicastellana.it.)

ALBEROBELLO   ☎0804

The mere sight of the *trulli*-covered hills is well worth the trek out to Alberobello (pop. 10,000). The structures are associated in Italian lore with magic and mystery—one glance at the fantastical landscape, populated by gnarled olive trees, rust-colored earth, and the white, conically domed *trulli*, and it's easy to understand why. Unfortunately, the origin of *trulli* in Alberobello proper is far less glamorous. In the 17th century, they were constructed at the behest of a count so that he could populate the area with dwellings that appeared impermanent in order to fool imperial inspectors and avoid paying taxes. The typical *trullo* contains a central shared space with several offshooting bedrooms, each with its own conical roof. Inhabitants inscribed symbols into the roofs, reputedly to ward off evil spirits. While some remain occupied, more than 1000 *trulli* of Alberobello are a UNESCO World Heritage site and primarily a tourist attraction.

⌐✸ TRANSPORTATION AND PRACTICAL INFORMATION. Alberobello is just south of Bari. Take the **FSE train** from Bari (1½hr., 14 per day M-Sa 5:30am-7:15pm, €4). To reach the *trulli* from the train station, bear left and take **Via Mazzini,** which becomes **Via Garibaldi,** to **Piazza del Popolo.** The **Pro Loco Tourist Office,** at V. Monte Nero, 1, in the *trulli* district, is helpful and can provide information on sights, directions, lodgings and guided tours. (☎0804 32 28 22. Open in summer daily 9am-9pm; in winter M-Sa 9am-1pm and 4-8:30pm.) Visit www.alberobellonline.it for more info on the city. For **police,** P. del Popolo, 32, call ☎0804 32 52 40. In case of **emergency,** call the **carabinieri** at ☎112 or an **ambulance** at ☎348 86 14 543.

⌐✸ ACCOMMODATIONS AND FOOD. Because visiting Alberobello can be expensive, budget travelers may opt for a daytrip to this town. But if you decide to stay, ▓**Trullidea ❺,** V. Monte Nero, 18, rents *trulli* for the night. Facing the *trulli*, V. Monte Nero goes uphill. Suites come with furnishings, kitchen, bath, and breakfast at a nearby restaurant. Hot summers are not a problem as *trulli* remain cool. (☎/fax 0804 32 38 60; www.trullidea.it. Singles €68; doubles €86; triples €102. AmEx/MC/V.) To reach **Didi Hotel ❸,** V. Piave, 30, take C. V. Emanuele from P. del Popolo, turn left on C. Trieste and left again on V. Piave. The hotel is notable for its great value: the 30 rooms each have air-conditioning, TV, phone, bath, and fridge; many sport a balcony with great views. (☎0804 32 34 32; www.dorosrl.it. Singles €35-40; doubles €45-50.) For camping info call **Camping dei Trulli** (☎0804 32 36 99).

L'Olmo Bello ❷, V. Indipendenza, 33, to the left before entering the *trulli* district, serves specialties in a century-old *trullo*. Try the *orecchiette alla buongustaio*, ear-shaped pasta in a tomato-basil sauce. (☎0804 32 36 07; www.ristoranteolmobello.it. Cover €1.60. Open M and W-Su noon-2:30pm and 8-11pm. MC/V.) **Ristorante Terminal ❸**, V. Indipendenza, 4, provides an escape from the scorching sun and makes for a low-key lunch break. Partake in meals with bread and Puglian olive oil. (☎0804 32 41 03; fax 0804 32 75 18. *Primi* and *secondi* €6.50-12. Cover €1.50. Service 15%. Open Tu-Su noon-3pm and 6:40pm-midnight. AmEx/MC/V.)

◖ **SIGHTS.** Any trip to Alberobello should begin with a tour of the ▨ **Museo del Territorio.** From P. del Popolo, turn left at Eritrea store to P. XXVII Maggio. (Open M-F 10:30am-7:30pm, Sa-Su 10:30am-10pm. Free. Tour €2.) **Sylva Tour** operates out of the museum, offering excursions into the countryside and guided walks around town. (☎0804 32 18 38; www.sylvanet.it. 1½hr. museum and town tour €9.) To reach the **Trullo Sovrano,** take C. V. Emanuele from P. del Popolo and continue past the church at the end. Built as a seminary in the 16th century, this two-story structure is decorated to show how *trulli* were originally used. (Open daily 10am-7:30pm. €1.50.) For a nominal fee, taste several local olive oils on rustic bread at the **Oil Museum.** (Open Tu-Su 9:15am-12:45pm and 3-7pm. Call ahead. €0.25.)

SALENTO PENINSULA

Foreign tourists often overlook Italy's sun-baked heel, home to hidden grottoes, medieval fortresses, and the beaches of two seas. With cultural roots stretching back to Ancient Greek times, the Salento modestly bears the laurels of centuries. Its art and architecture are some of the best preserved in Italy and its vistas pristine and unrivaled. Transportation within the peninsula can sometimes be complicated, but with some planning a sojourn along the varied coastline or inland in olive and wine country is both possible and worth the effort.

BRINDISI   ☎0831

As Italy's gateway to the East, Brindisi has always been more of a departure point than a destination. Pompey made his escape from Julius Caesar's army here in the 1st century BC, and Crusaders used the port to sail for the Holy Land. The city's streets are crowded with travelers who stay only long enough to pick up their ferry tickets. But Brindisi is worth more than just a cursory stop. As the one-time terminus of the Appian Way and a present-day port of industry and travel, Brindisi has a striking mix of historical sights and modern Italian flavor. And as neighboring Lecce and Ostuni attest, this region amply repays travelers who stop to explore.

◰ **TRANSPORTATION**

Trains: In P. Crispi. Ticket office open daily 8am-8pm. **Luggage storage** available. **FS** to: **Bari** (1¼-1¾hr., 26 per day 4am-10:44pm, €6-13); **Lecce** (20-35min., 27 per day 6:01am-10:47pm, €2.32); **Milan** (9-12hr., 10 per day 7:48am-11:24pm, €54-85); **Rome** (6-9hr., 9 per day 6:23am-10:45pm, €27-45); **Taranto** (1¼hr., 20 per day 4:45am-10:44pm, €3.62).

Buses: FSE, at the train station, handles buses throughout Puglia. **Marozzi** buses travelers to **Rome** (7½-8½hr., 3 per day 11am-10pm, €35.65). **Miccolis** runs to **Naples** (5hr., 3 per day 6:35am-6:35pm, €23.60). Be sure to ask where you should catch the bus, since neither Marozzi nor Miccolis buses leave from the town center. Buy tickets for

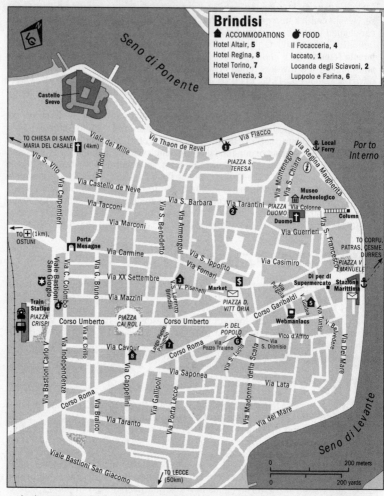

Brindisi

■ ACCOMMODATIONS

Hotel Altair, **5**
Hotel Regina, **8**
Hotel Torino, **7**
Hotel Venezia, **3**

🍴 FOOD

Il Focacceria, **4**
Iaccato, **1**
Locanda degli Sciavoni, **2**
Luppolo e Farina, **6**

both companies at the helpful and efficient **Grecian Travel,** C. Garibaldi, 79 (☎0831 56 83 33; fax 0831 56 39 67). Open M-F 9am-1pm and 4:30-8pm, Sa 9am-1pm. It's also a **CTS** budget-travel information point.

Ferries: Ferries leave from Costa Morena for **Corfu** (8hr.); **Igoumenitsa** (10hr.); **Kephalonia** (16½hr.); **Patras** (17hr.); **Paxi** (13hr.). Catamarans operated by **Italian Ferries** (C. Garibaldi, 96/98; ☎0831 59 08 40), sail to **Corfu** (4hr.) and are only slightly pricier than ferries. The catamarans leave from Stazione Marittima. Prices for each ferry line are fixed by the transport authority, and all agencies charge the same amount for tickets. Unfortunately, some agencies are more than happy to book passage for a full or nonexistent ferry, so exercise caution—use a reputable agency and always ask for other options to avoid scams. Well-established ferry lines include **Med Link Lines,** C. Garibaldi, 49 (☎0831 52 76 67), and **Fragline,** V. Spalato, 31 (☎0831 54 85 34). Port tax (€6) and the deck reservation fee (€3) are not included in ticket price. Most

PUGLIA, BASILICATA, AND CALABRIA

ARRIVEDERCI, ITALIA. Brindisi is a central port for passenger boats to **Greece.** To get to Athens, take the ferry from Brindisi to Patras (see **Transportation,** below) and then a train or bus from Patras to Athens (2½hr.); you can buy these tickets at Brindisi's Stazione Marittima. Ferries also run from Brindisi to Çesme, **Turkey** (30hr.) and Durres, **Albania** (9hr.). Brindisi is the only Adriatic-side port that accepts Eurail and Interrail passes, and only **Hellenic Mediterranean Lines** and **Italian Ferries** (see **Ferries**) do so officially; however, almost all companies provide unofficial discounts. No Eurail and Interrail passes are accepted on ferries to Çesme, Turkey or Durres, Albania.

lines provide a **free shuttle** that runs 1km from Stazione Marittima to Costa Morena, where ferries depart. **Check-in 2hr. before departure.** Bring your own food to avoid the overpriced seagull fodder found in the snack bars onboard.

Public Transportation: City buses (☎0831 54 92 45) run between the train station and port and to destinations around the city. **Local ferries** depart from the tourist office on V. Margherita every 10min., crossing the Seno di Ponente and landing near the Chiesa Maria del Casale. Purchase bus and ferry tickets at bars and *tabaccherie* for €0.70.

Taxis: ☎0831 59 79 01. Make sure to take a licensed taxi, as unofficial taxi services tend to overcharge. Always agree on a price before taking off. Taxis from Stazione Marittima to Costa Morena cost €17.

ORIENTATION AND PRACTICAL INFORMATION

Corso Umberto runs from the train station to **Piazza Cairoli** and through **Piazza del Popolo** and **Piazza della Vittoria.** At P. della Vittoria, it becomes **Corso Garibaldi,** which ends at the port. The **Stazione Marittima** is on **Via Regina Margherita,** to the right. Taking a left at the end of C. Garibaldi, V. Regina Margherita curves around by the column that marked the end of the Appian Way, becoming **Via Flacco** and then **Via Thaon de Revel;** this area is full of bars and restaurants.

The **APT Information Office,** V. Regina Margherita, 5, provides a free **map** and advice about local services, and sights. From C. Garibaldi, turn left on V. Margherita. (☎0831 52 30 72; aptbrindisi@pugliaturismo.it. Open daily 8am-2pm and 3-8pm.) **Luggage storage** is available at the train station. (€5-10 per 24hr., depending on bag size. Open daily 6:30am-10:30pm.) In case of **emergency,** call ☎113, the **police** at ☎0831 22 95 22, or the **carabinieri** at ☎112 or 0831 15 29 11. **Ospedale Di Summa** (☎0831 53 71 11) offers emergency care. **Internet** is available at **Webmaniacs,** Vico Sacramento, off of C. Garibaldi. (☎0831 52 15 32. €3 per hr. Open M-Sa 9am-8:30pm.) The **post office** is at P. Vittoria, 10. (☎0831 47 11 11. Open M-F 8am-6:30pm, Sa 8am-12:30pm.) **Branch** in the Stazione Marittima. **Postal Code:** 72100.

ACCOMMODATIONS

■ **Hotel Altair,** V. Giudea, 4 (☎/fax 0831 56 22 89; www.hotelaltair.191.it), is close to the port and town center. From Stazione Marittima, walk up C. Garibaldi and take the 3rd left. Rooms have TV and fridge at this family-run hotel. A/C only in rooms with bath, €10 extra. Reserve 1 week ahead. Singles €20, with bath €35; doubles €35-€50; triples with shower €60. AmEx/MC/V. ❷

Hotel Venezia, V. Pisanelli, 4 (☎0831 52 75 11), is equidistant from the train station and Stazione Marittima. From the train station, pass the fountain and take the 2nd left off C. Umberto on V. S. Lorenzo da Brindisi, following the signs pointing right on V. Pisanelli. 12 comfortable rooms have high ceilings and shared baths. Reserve 4 days ahead. Singles €15; doubles €25, with bath €35; quads €13 per person. Cash only. ❶

Hotel Torino, Largo Pietro Palumbo, 6 (☎0831 59 75 87; www.brindisiweb.com/ torino). 14 spacious and inviting rooms with bath, A/C, and satellite TV. Garage parking available. Singles €40-50; doubles €60-70; triples €75-80. AmEx/MC/V. ❹

Hotel Regina, V. Cavour, 5 (☎0831 56 20 01; www.hotelreginaweb.com), off P. Cairoli. This American-style hotel offers a modern alternative to the smaller accommodations in town. All 43 rooms have A/C, fridge, and TV. Buffet breakfast included. Laundry service and Internet available. Singles €44-70; doubles €55-90. AmEx/MC/V. ❺

🔲 FOOD

Avoid the restaurants and cafes on C. Garibaldi near the port, where the ubiquitous *menù turistico* yields small portions, steep drink prices, and insipid dishes. Better options lie on nearby side streets. An **open-air market**, off P. della Vittoria on V. Fornari, sells fresh fruit. (Open M-Sa 7am-1pm.) Pick up supplies for your ferry ride at **Di per Di,** C. Garibaldi, 106, one block from the port. (☎0831 56 25 66. Open M-Sa 8am-1:30pm and 4:30-8:30pm, Su 9am-1pm.)

Iaccato, V. Flacco (☎0831 56 70 45), directly on the water. Since 1950 this little fishermen's shack has been serving some of the town's top seafood. Watch the staff expertly fillet the salmon right in front of you (with green peppers; €6.70). *Primi* €5.16-15.49, *secondi* €6.20-31. Cover €1.53. Open daily noon-3pm and 7-11pm. MC/V. ❺

Il Focacceria, V. Cristoforo Colombo, 5 (☎0831 56 09 30), offers more than its name implies. A favorite of sailors on leave in the port, this simple restaurant dishes out excellent lasagna (€3) and takeout pizza (€3-5.50). Open daily 8am-11pm. Cash only. ❶

Luppolo e Farina, V. Pozzo Traiano (☎0831 59 04 96), just off C. Garibaldi near P. del Popolo. Wood-fueled oven masters have pizza tossing down to a science. The house pizza, with mozzarella and sun-dried tomatoes (€5.30), is especially good. Pizza €4-9. *Primi* €4-8, *secondi* €4-10. Cover €1. Open daily 7pm-midnight. AmEx/MC/V. ❷

Locanda degli Sciavoni, V. Tarantini, 43 (☎0831 52 20 50), a short walk from the front of the *duomo*. Favored by locals and tourists, the simple decor and lively atmosphere are fine accents to the traditional cuisine. The *spaghetti alle scampi* is a winning ticket. *Primi* €3-8, *secondi* €5-8. Cover €1.50. Open M-Sa 7pm-midnight. MC/V. ❸

👁 🎵 SIGHTS AND ENTERTAINMENT

Turning left at the seaside end of C. Garibaldi, V. Regina Margherita passes a set of marble steps. The huge ■**column** here, recently restored, once marked the end of the **Appian Way.** Figures of Jove, Neptune, Mars, and tritons grace the marble capital. The column's twin, which stood on the adjacent base, now resides in Lecce. The **Monumento al Marinaio d'Italia** across the bay watches over Brindisi's seamen with solemn beatitude. V. Colonne runs from behind the column to P. Duomo. In the 11th-century **duomo** (rebuilt in the 18th century), Emperor Frederick II married Jerusalem's Yolande. (Open daily 7am-noon and 4:30-7:30pm.) Nearby in P. Duomo, the **Museo Archeologico** traces Brindisi's history with pottery and other artifacts. (☎0831 56 55 01. Open M, W, and F 9:30am-1pm and 3:30-7pm, Tu, Th, and Sa 9:30am-1pm. Free.) Follow the signs from the train station to the outskirts of town to see the **Chiesa di Santa Maria del Casale** and its 13th-century frescoes, including one of Mary blessing the Crusaders. (Open daily 7am-noon and 4-7pm.)

🔁 DAYTRIP FROM BRINDISI

■OSTUNI

Ostuni is on the train line between Brindisi (30min., 16 per day 4am-10:44pm, €2.32) and Bari (1-1¼hr., 15 per day 6am-10:55pm, €4.10). From train station (☎0831 30 12

68), take the orange city bus to P. della Libertà at the center of town (15min.; M-Sa every 30min., Su every hr. 7am-9:30pm; €0.70). Buy tickets at the train station bar (€0.70) or on board (€1.50). Buses are not numbered, so tell the driver your intended destination before boarding. The AAST Tourist Office, C. Mazzini, 6, just off P. della Libertà, provides assistance with lodging, maps of the centro storico, and a booklet of the town's historical information. (☎0831 30 12 68. Open M-F June-Aug. 8:30am-1:30pm and 3:30-6:30pm, Sept.-May 8:30am-noon and 4-7pm.) In case of emergency, call the carabinieri at ☎112.

Rising from a landscape of sea, dark-red earth, and olive trees, Ostuni's *città bianca* (white city) appears ethereal. The *centro storico's* walls protect the city from the elements and lend a fairy-tale touch to the serpentine streets. The terrace at the top of C. V. Emanuele boasts a view of the old city. Just off P. della Libertà, the small church of **Santo Spirito** features a doorway with reliefs from the late medieval period. From the *piazza*, V. Cattedrale runs through the old town center, leading to the **Convento delle Monacelle** (Convent of Little Nuns), V. Cattedrale, 15, an architecture student's dream, with a Baroque facade and a white-tiled dome. Inside, a 24,500-year-old human skeleton resides at the **archaeological museum.** Crowning Ostuni's hill, the **duomo** was the last Byzantine building to be erected in southern Italy. The facade in the Spanish-Gothic style, with its intricate rosette, contrasts sharply with the Norman styles more common in Puglia. (Open daily 7:30am-12:30pm and 4-7pm.) On August 26, Ostuni celebrates Sant'Oronzo with the **Cavalcata,** a parade of costumed horses and riders. Many praise Ostuni's **beaches,** accessible from P. della Libertà by the STP bus. (☎800 23 20 42; www.stp-brindisi.it. Dir: "Torre Canne." 6 buses per day 5:50am-2:25pm, €.90. *Tabaccherie* in the square post schedules. Ask bus driver to tell you when you have reached your destination.) The closest beach is at **Villanova;** the most popular **Costa Merlata.** Buses pick up travelers near the statue at the center of P. della Libertà.

Unfortunately, there are few affordable options for those planning to stay the night; accommodations in Ostuni tend to be overpriced and poorly located. However, the oldest hotel in Ostuni is now a budget traveler's delight. At **Hotel Orchidea Nera ❸,** a 5min. walk from P. della Libertà at C. Mazzini, 188, the owner, Carmen, lets big, airy rooms, all with bath. (☎0831 30 13 66. Singles €36; doubles €62; triples €67. Cash only.) Consult the tourist office for *agriturismi* options.

For lunch or dinner, try one of the small taverns and *osterie* that abound in the old city. The streets can be tricky to navigate, but signs everywhere point to restaurants. Head to **Locanda dei Sette Peccati ❶** for pizza in casual alleyway seating or for a picnic lunch to go, taking a right off V. Cattedrale on V. Franc Ant Arc. Zaccania, then left on V. Francesco Campani. (☎0831 33 95 95. *Panini,* pizza, and pasta dishes, from €3.50. Cover €1. Open daily noon-3:30pm and 7pm-2am. AmEx/MC/V.) **Porta Nova ❹,** V. Gaspare Petrolo, 38, is a little pricey but has fresh seafood and a pastoral view. (☎0831 33 89 83; www.ristoranteportanova.it. *Primi* €8-10, *secondi* from €10. Cover €2. Open in summer daily noon-3pm and 7pm-midnight; closed in winter. AmEx/MC/V.) Near P. della Libertà on Largo Lanza, **Ristorante Vecchia Ostuni ❸** has quiet outdoor seating and a menu specializing in all types of meat and fish (from €6.50). Call 30min. ahead to have special fish prepared. (☎0831 30 33 08. Open M and W-Su noon-3:30pm and 7pm-midnight. AmEx/MC/V.) On V. Cattedrale, the highly air-conditioned, highly stylish **Madrif Caffe ❶** serves caffeinated beverages with music videos blaring from flat screen TVs on the walls. (Open M-Sa 9:30am-late. Cash only.)

LECCE ☎0832

One of Italy's hidden pearls, Lecce (pop. 90,000) is where Italians go when foreign tourists invade their country. Although a succession of conquerors—Cretans, Romans, Saracens, Swabians, and more—passed through here, the Spanish Hapsburgs wielded enduring influence in the 16th and 17th centuries, resulting in the beautiful buildings seen today. Most of the city's churches and palaces are sculpted from *tufigna*, the soft, locally quarried "Lecce stone" that hardens when exposed to air. At night, the lighted buildings make for a memorable *passeggiata* for posh and pampered vacationers. Lecce, the "Florence of the South," is a great starting point for a tour of the Salento Peninsula, in the heel of Italy's boot.

■ TRANSPORTATION

Trains: Lecce is the southeastern terminus of the state railway. The **FS Station** is in P. Massari, a short walk down V. Oronzo Quarta from the town center. Buses #24 and 28 (€0.62) run from in front of the station on V. Oronzo Quarta to the center of town. **FS** runs trains (☎0832 30 10 16) to: **Bari** (1½-2hr., 21 per day 5am-10:14pm, €6-13); **Brindisi** (20-40min., 23 per day 5:00am-10:14pm, €2.32-8.26); **Rome** (6-9½hr., 7

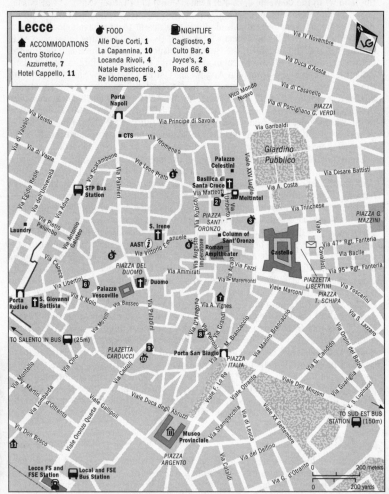

Lecce

ACCOMMODATIONS
Centro Storico/
Azzurrette, **7**
Hotel Cappello, **11**

🍴 FOOD
Alle Due Corti, **1**
La Capannina, **10**
Locanda Rivoli, **4**
Natale Pasticceria, **3**
Re Idomeneo, **5**

🍷 NIGHTLIFE
Cagliostro, **9**
Culto Bar, **6**
Joyce's, **2**
Road 66, **8**

per day 6am-11pm, €30-44). **FSE** trains (☎0832 66 81 11; www.fseonline.it) criss-cross the Salento Peninsula. Trains run M-Sa to **Gallipoli** (1hr., 11 per day 6:56am-8:50pm, €4.20) and **Otranto** (1¼hr., 7 per day 6:56am-5:43pm, €2.80) via **Maglie.**

Buses: The **FSE Station** (☎0832 34 76 34; www.fseonline.it), on V. Boito, is easily acces-sible by bus #4 (€0.70) from the train station. FSE buses depart from the **FSE Garage,** across from the train station on the left, and stop at the FSE station on their way out of town. Tickets are available in the train station *bar.* To **Gallipoli** (1hr., 5 per day, €2.84); **Taranto** (2hr., 5 per day 7am-4pm, €4.58). **STP** (☎0832 30 28 73), on V. Adua, heads to smaller towns of the Salento Peninsula. Pick up a schedule at the tourist office. In July and Aug., **Salento in Bus** (☎0832 35 03 76; www.salentoinbus.it) is the most convenient way of traversing the peninsula, with buses running to **Gallipoli** (1¼-1¾hr., 7 per day 7:05am-9:53pm, €3.50) and **Otranto** (1hr., 9 per day 7:13am-12:23am, €3.50), as well as to other towns on the peninsula. Buses stop on V. Pitagora, close to the FS station.

Taxis: (☎0832 24 79 78), at the train station. (☎0832 30 60 45), in P. S. Oronzo.

✦ 🛈 ORIENTATION AND PRACTICAL INFORMATION

Lecce lies 35km south and inland from Brindisi. From the **train station,** take **Viale Oronzo Quarta** straight to **Via Cairoli** to get to the streets of the old city. Turn left on **Via Paladini** and wind around the **duomo,** stopping at **Via Vittorio Emanuele.** To the left, **Via Libertini** passes **Piazza Duomo** and **Chiesa di San Giovanni Battista** and exits the old city walls through **Porta Rudiae.** To the right lies **Piazza Sant'Oronzo,** Lecce's main square, with the Roman amphitheater to the left and the *castello* beyond.

Tourist Office: APT Lecce, V. V. Emanuele, 24, near P. Duomo (☎0832 24 80 92; www.pugliaturismo.it). Has good **maps** and a comprehensive booklet on the numer-ous B&Bs of Lecce.

Budget Travel: CTS, V. Palmieri, 89 (☎0832 30 18 62). From P. S. Oronzo, take V. Emanuele and turn right on V. Palmieri. Provides flight and train info and sells tickets. Open M-F 9am-1pm and 4:30-8pm.

Laundromat: Lavanderia Self-Service, V. dell'Università, 47 (☎339 68 36 396), half-way between Pta. Rudiae and Pta. Napoli. Wash €3-€6.50. Dry €1.50 per 20min. Open M-F 9:30am-2pm and 4-8pm

Public Bathrooms: In P. S. Oronzo, at the corner with V. Imperatore Augusto.

Emergency: 113. **Carabinieri:** V. Calabria (☎112 or 0832 27 98 64), north of the city walls.

Hospital: Ospedale Vito Fazzi (☎0832 66 11 11), on V. S. Cesario. In case of emer-gency, call ☎0832 66 14 03.

Internet Access: Meltintel Phone Center, V. Matteoti 23/B (☎0832 30 71 67) has 6 fast computers. Close to P. S. Oronzo. €0.50 for 1st 10min, €3.60 per hr. Also has money transfer services. Open M-Sa 9:30am-1:30pm and 4-10pm, Su 4-10pm.

Post Office: ☎0832 27 40 64. In P. Libertini, across from the *castello.* Open M-F 8am-6:30pm, Sa 8:30am-noon. **Postal Code:** 73100.

🏠 ACCOMMODATIONS

Lecce lacks ultra-cheap accommodations. B&Bs are an alternative to impersonal hotels, and the tourist office lists affordable *affittacamere* (rooms for rent).

Centro Storico, V. A. Vignes, 2/B (☎0832 24 27 27; www.bedandbreakfast.lecce.it). Centrally located. From P. S. Oronzo, take V. Augusto Imperatore until it becomes V. Federico D'Aragona. V. Vignes is on the left. 5 large rooms in well-tended B&B have A/C, TV, cooking facilities, and terrace with views of the city. Reserve 2 weeks ahead. Sin-gles €31-35; doubles €52-57, with bath 70-80. Extra bed €20. Cash only. ❸

Azzurrette, V. A. Vignes, 3/B, shares management and building with Centro Storico. The 4 suites are spacious and have big, sunny, windows. All have A/C, TV, kitchen, and balcony. Reserve 1-2 weeks ahead. Singles €40; doubles €60. Cash only. ❸

Hotel Cappello, V. Montegrappa, 4 (☎0832 30 88 81; www.hotelcappello.it). From the station, take the 1st left off V. Quarta on V. Don Bosco and follow the signs. This modern hotel has a friendly staff and 35 rooms, all with A/C, TV, and fridge. Bar in the lobby. A great value. Singles €35; doubles €48-50. AmEx/MC/V. ❸

🗂 FOOD

Leccese food is a delight. Regional specialties range from the hearty *cicerietria* (chickpeas and pasta) and *pucce* (sandwiches made with olive-bread rolls) to *confettoni* (traditional chocolate candies). The venerable **Salumeria Loiacono,** V. Fazzi, 11, in P. S. Oronzo, has been providing picnic supplies for over a century. (Open daily 7am-2pm and 4:30-8:30pm.)

🍽 Alle Due Corti, Corte dei Giugni, 1 (☎0832 24 22 23; www.alleduecorti.com), at the corner of V. Prato. Dedicated to the preservation of Leccese culture through cuisine—it's so authentic, even the menu is written in dialect. *Lu ranu te la Spagna,* a hearty dish of wheat seeds, chicken, pork, mussels, cuttlefish, peppers, peas and tomatoes (€7) is a touted specialty. *Primi* €5-8, *secondi* €6-10. Cover €1.50. Open M-Sa 12:30-2pm and 8-11:30pm. Reservations recommended in evenings. AmEx/MC/V. ❷

Re Idomeneo, V. Libertini, 44 (☎0832 38 18 93), a few blocks from the *duomo.* A reasonably priced spot that crowds up in the evening. Endearing staff, generous portions, and a fun atmosphere. Traditional *cicerietria* (€6) makes great comfort food in the winter. *Primi* €5-7, *secondi* €6 and up. Open daily noon-3pm and 7-11pm. Cash only. ❷

La Capannina, V. Cairoli, 13 (☎0832 30 41 59), between the train station and P. Duomo. Attentive service and pleasant outdoor seating in stately, nearly private *piazza.* Pasta specialty is *orecchiette a casareccia* (with meat, tomato, and cheese sauce; €6). Pizza for dinner only (€3.50-6). *Primi* €4-8, *secondi* €5-10. Cover €1.30. Open Tu-Su 9am-2pm and 7pm-midnight. Reservations recommended in evenings. AmEx/MC/V. ❷

Locanda Rivoli, V. Augusto Imperatore, 19 (☎0832 33 16 78). Hearty food comes in generous portions at this older establishment, which dates back to the early 1900s. The *risotto allo champagne* (€12) is a chic treat. The rustic, laidback indoor and outdoor seating buzzes with activity after 10pm. *Primi* €5-8, *secondi* €12-25. *Menù* €12.50. Open in summer M and W-Su 7pm-midnight. Hours vary in winter. AmEx/MC/V. ❸

Natale Pasticceria, V. Trinchese, 7 (☎0832 25 60 60), near McDonald's in P. Oronzo. This copper-ensconced pastry shop is full of so many locals, pastries, candies, and flavors of *gelato* that your head will spin. Almond is their specialty. Cones €2-4. Local cream-filled delights from €0.70. Open daily 8am-midnight. MC/V. ❶

👁 SIGHTS

Get an education in Baroque architecture by touring the churches and palaces of downtown Lecce, all about a 10min. walk apart.

BASILICA DI SANTA CROCE. Constructed between 1549 and 1695, the most outstanding of Lecce's churches is a masterwork of Leccese Baroque. Most of the area's architects contributed their skills to its facade at some point. Look closely to see the profile of Gabriele Riccardi, the basilica's original designer, hidden between the upper window and the column to its left. Two rows of massive Corinthian columns tower inside, their acanthus leaves dancing majestically. F. A. Zantimbalo's 1614 altar adorns the chapel to the left of the apse. *(From P. S. Oronzo, head down V. Templari. Open daily 8am-1pm and 4:30-8:30pm. Modest dress required.)*

PALAZZO CELESTINI. The lower half of this *palazzo's* facade was designed by Giuseppe Zimbalo, nicknamed "Lo Zingarello" (The Gypsy) for his tendency to wander from one project to another. The upper half is by Giuseppe Cino, Zimbalo's pupil, to whom he characteristically passed his unfinished projects. Though now an office space, visitors can view its inner courtyard, which hosts rock and classical music concerts in the summer. Keep an eye out for posters or ask at the AAST office for more information. *(Next to Basilica d. S. Croce.)*

DUOMO. Constructed in 1114, the *duomo* was "Zingarelloed" between 1659 and 1670. Except for two Leccese altars, the interior dates from the 18th century. At night, misty streams of light pour out of the **campanile** that rises from the left side of the cathedral. Opposite, the **Palazzo Vescovile** (Bishop's Palace) has been remodeled several times since its construction in 1632. On the right, with a Baroque well in its center, stands the **seminary,** designed by Giuseppe Cino in 1709. *(From P. S. Oronzo, take V. Emanuele. Duomo open daily 6:30am-noon and 5-7:30pm.)*

ANCIENT RUINS. The **Column of Sant'Oronzo,** one of two that marked the termination of the Appian Way in Brindisi (p. 622), towers melodramatically over P. S. Oronzo. A flowing-robed statue of the saint now tops the column. Nearby, the ruins of a 2nd-century amphitheater recede into the ground. In its prime, it held 20,000 spectators; these days, at least that many young people seem to gather there to flirt on summer nights. Near the station, the **Museo Provinciale** contains Apulian ceramics from the 5th century BC. *(V. Gallipoli, 28. ☎0832 24 70 25. Open M-Sa 9am-1pm and 2:30-7:30pm, Su 9am-1pm. Wheelchair accessible. Free.)*

OTHER SIGHTS. The wildly intricate **Chiesa di San Giovanni Battista** was Lo Zingarello's last work. The artist who used Baroque norms as a basis for innovation decorated the columns with unfettered glee. Fifteen altars within, surrounding a Roman Cross design, testify to his disdain for moderation. *(From P. del Duomo, take V. Libertini.)* The ornate **Porta Napoli** once stood on the road from Naples. The arch was erected in 1548 in honor of Holy Roman Emperor Charles V, whose coat of arms adorns the front. *(From P. del Duomo, take V. Palmieri.)*

🎵 🍸 ENTERTAINMENT AND NIGHTLIFE

Cagliostro, V. Cairoli, 11, near the *duomo*, is a favorite among university students. (☎0832 30 18 81. Draft beer and cocktails from €3. Open daily 8pm-3am. Cash only.) **Joyce's,** V. Matteo da Lecce, 5, is another hot spot, with walls covered in creeping vines, U2 album covers, and glass cases containing texts of *Ulysses.* (Walk out of P. S. Oronzo toward the basilica and turn left on V. Matteo da Lecce. ☎0832 27 94 43. Open daily 8pm-2am.) The raucous **Road 66,** at V. dei Perroni, 8 (☎0832 24 65 68), near Pta. San Biagio, and the trendy **Culto Bar,** V. Libertini, 17, are also good bets for nocturnal action. Most nightclubs, especially during the summer, are on the coast and only accessible by car. For up-to-date information on the hottest nightlife options, chat with locals in the bustling *piazze* or consult the monthly publication *Salento in Tasca*, available at local bars. The yearly **MedFest** brings classical music concerts to the Castello Carlo V throughout the summer. Call ☎082 24 23 68 for info.

Lecce's soccer team has bounced between Serie A and Serie B in recent years, and its fans have rallied behind it 100% at every step of the way. Those who visit the city during a match are likely to get caught up in the infectious cheering and flag-waving in the *piazza*. (Matches held Sept.-June. Buy tickets at *tabaccherie* and lottery agencies, or contact the stadium at ☎0832 39 61 40. Tickets from €15.) The AAST office distributes the *Calendario Manifestazioni*, which describes Lecce's annual summer festivals and lists seasonal events in the province.

OTRANTO
☎ 0836

Although throngs of Italian tourists descend upon Otranto (pop. 5000) in July and August, its winding streets, crystal-clear waters, and medieval sights make it worth visiting year-round. Earlier visitors included Turkish pirates who converted to Christianity after conquering the city. Unable to force Otranto's devoted Christian inhabitants to renounce their god by threatening them with gruesome deaths, the Turkish invaders instead gave up Islam—so convinced were they by the piety of these people. The bones of the Martiri d'Otranto (Martyrs of Otranto) attract some visitors but most are content to just wade in Otranto's clear, warm waters.

TRANSPORTATION AND PRACTICAL INFORMATION. Otranto is 40km southeast of Lecce, and it can be downright hard to reach by public transportation. Rustic **FSE trains** run from Lecce (1¼hr., 9 per day 6:45am-7:30pm, €2.58) to Maglie. Get off in Maglie and take the awaiting bus to Otranto. The FSE ticket to Lecce covers both. In July and August, **Salento in Bus** (☎0832 35 03 76; www.salentoinbus.it) runs straight to Otranto's castle (2 hr., €3.50). Pick it up in Lecce on V. Gallipoli, in front of the Bar Rossa Nera. The town's main beach is along the **Lungomare d'Otranto,** ending at the **public gardens.** On the left after the gardens, V. V. Emanuele leads to **Piazza de Donno** and the entrance to the *centro storico*. Enter through the city gate and turn right on **Via Basilica** to reach the **duomo;** to the left is a narrow passage leading to the *piazza*; here, the **APT Tourist Office** offers advice on lodgings and transportation to towns on the peninsula. (☎0836 80 14 36. Open daily 9am-2pm and 3-9pm.) For the **carabinieri,** call ☎0836 80 10 10. **Farmacia Ricciardi** is at V. Lungomare, 101. (☎0836 80 10 36. Open daily 8:30am-1pm and 4:30-8pm.) Down the road toward the *centro storico* stop by **Giardini Caffe** for **Internet.** (☎338 648 81 00. €5 per hr. Open M-Sa 7am-2am.) The **post office** is by the stoplight on V. Pantaleone. (☎0836 80 10 02. Open M-Sa 8:15am-6pm.) **Postal Code:** 73028.

ACCOMMODATIONS AND FOOD. Lodgings in Otranto are very expensive from mid-July to August, when most hotels require half pension and all require reservations. The tourist office can help find *affittacamere*. ■**Hotel Miramare ❺,** V. Lungomare, 55, is right on the beach, with nicely furnished rooms, all with balcony, fridge, and TV. Call in March to reserve a room for July or August. (☎0836 80 10 23; www.miramareotranto.com. Buffet breakfast included. Internet available. Singles €65-80; doubles €100-130. AmEx/MC/V.) The **Bellavista Hotel ❺,** V. V. Emanuele, 19, directly across from the public gardens and beach, has rooms with bath, TV, and air-conditioning. (☎0836 80 10 58; www.hotelbellavista.assovia.com. Singles €48-97; doubles €70-124. AmEx/MC/V.) A 10min. walk from the beach and near the FSE train station, the more rustic **B&B Hotel Pietra Verde ❺,** V. P. Presbitero, has rooms with phone, TV, air-conditioning, bath, and balcony. (☎0836 80 19 01; www.hotelpietraverde.com. Singles €40-80; doubles €60-110. AmEx/MC/V.)

For seaside essentials, visit the **market** by P. de Donno which sells fruit, meat, and fish. (Open daily 8am-1pm.) Across from the public gardens, **Boomerang Self-Service ❶,** V. V. Emanuele, 14, serves tasty dishes cafeteria-style. (☎/fax 0836 80 26 19. Pizza €3.10-5.50. *Primi* €4.50, *secondi* €4.50-7. Open Mar.-Sept. daily noon-12:30am.) The friendly **Acmet Pascià ❹,** at the end of V. V. Emanuele, provides outdoor dining with a gorgeous view. (☎0836 80 12 82. *Primi* €6-18, fish *secondi* €11-18. Cover €2. Open Tu-Su 10am-3:30pm and 7pm-1:30am. AmEx/MC/V.)

SIGHTS. The *centro storico*, ensconced in stout ramparts, guards many of Otranto's proudest historical sites. Dante stayed here while writing parts of the *Divine Comedy*. The majestic ■**duomo** is paved with a phenomenal 11th-century floor mosaic of the Tree of Life. The mosaic extends the length of the nave and depicts religious and historical figures from Adam and Alexander the Great to King Arthur—and that's just the A's. Another section depicts the 12 zodiac signs and seasonal agriculture work. Equally impressive is the ceiling, a colored and gilded affair well worth the pain in the neck. In the **Cappella dei Martiri,** a small chapel in the *duomo's* crypt, lie the skulls and bones of all 800 *Otrantini* who died for their faith. (*Duomo* open daily 8am-noon and 3-6:30pm, excluding mass. Modest dress required.) Frescoes of the Garden of Eden brighten the musty interior of the Byzantine **Chiesa di San Pietro.** Take C. Garibaldi to P. del Popolo and follow the signs up the stairs on the left. (Open daily on request 9:30am-1pm and 3:30-7:30pm.) The **Aragonese castle,** with its imposing walls and moat, still looks ready for a siege. A gate in the ramparts leads to the refuge of Otranto's picturesque sailboat harbor. (Open daily 10:30am-12:30pm and 6-11:30pm.) Every Wednesday a **market** surrounds the castle. (Open 9am-1pm.)

⚶⚶ ENTERTAINMENT AND BEACHES. In August, Otranto's **beaches** show less shore than skin as Italian vacationers stake claims to every patch of land. For those seeking fewer crowds, the fine sand and azure waters are just as enjoyable in early summer. The free public strips along the *lungomare* and farther along on V. degli Haethey are the most accessible. For €5, the beach closest to V. Pantaleone provides bathrooms and changing facilities, but umbrellas and chairs cost another €10. The beach one block down the road heading away from V. Presbitero is free, although the proximity of old freighters, which belch smoke as they dock, can make for a less than idyllic setting. In the evening, vendors arrive to feed the crowds—try the delicious *noccioline zuccherate* (candy-coated peanuts; €1). If exploring the depths of the salty brine sounds more appealing than sunning on the sand, **scuba diving** is available by appointment at V. S. Francesco di Paola, 43. (☎/fax 0836 80 27 40; www.scubadiving.it.) For a relaxing stroll, grab a friend and head to the beautiful **Chiesa S. M. dei Martiri,** walking straight out of the old city on V. Ottocento Martiri. This complex, with stone steps and a beautiful view, provides a respite from the beach buzz.

After dark, Otranto's *lungomare* fills with people walking along the waterfront and hitting up the pubs, while those with cars head to the discos 5-6km away. The public gardens sport numerous food-stands with nuts and snacks (from €1.50) and, in summer, carnival-style rides for children. On August 13-15, Otranto welcomes tourists to the **Festa dei Martiri d'Otranto,** a festival in honor of the martyrs. On the first Sunday in September, the town celebrates the **Festa della Madonna dell'Altomare** (Festival of the Virgin of the High Seas).

TARANTO
☎ 0994

Mythology claims that Taranto (pop. 200,000) was founded over 2500 years ago when Poseidon saved the Taras from an Ionian shipwreck. Dolphins, summoned from the depths by the temperamental sea god, escorted Taras through the sea to the shores, where he established the colony that became known as Taranto. Today the image of the dolphin is omnipresent in the city, a reminder of ancient prosperity as Taranto attempts to refashion itself after a blighted period. Unemployment, government corruption, welfare dependency, and Mafia control have cast a shadow over the city, obscuring its seaside charm. However, young professionals are working to spark urban renewal and attract visitors with the city's reasonably priced accommodations, inexpensive seafood, and sailboat-packed beaches.

⬛ TRANSPORTATION. The **train station** (☎ 147 88 80 88) is in P. Libertà, across from the old city over Ponte Pta. Napoli. **FS** runs **trains** to: Bari (1¾hr., 16 per day 4:40am-10:22pm, €8); Brindisi (1¼hr., 10 per day 5:08am-10:21pm, €3.62);

Naples (4hr., 8 per day 5:13am-11:30pm, €14-18); and Rome (6-7hr., 12 per day 5:35am-11:30pm, €23.50-37). A number of companies run **buses** from P. Castello. **Marozzi,** C. Umberto I, 67 (☎0994 59 40 89), a block from P. Garibaldi, has information on many of them. Daily services run to Bari (1¾hr.) and Lecce (1¾hr.). **SITA buses** (www.sita-on-line.it) run to Matera (1¾hr., 4 per day 6:20am-7:20pm, €4.81). Local **AMAT buses** sell tickets (€0.70, 90min. ticket €0.95, 1-day ticket €1.65). Buy tickets at any *tabaccherie* or bar.

⑦ PRACTICAL INFORMATION. The buildings of Taranto's **old city** crowd atop a small island between two promontories. Bridges join the old city to the new **port** area and the **train station.** From the station, buses to the new city stop near **Piazza Garibaldi,** the main square. On foot, take **Via Duca d'Aosta** over **Ponte Porta Napoli** and bear left to reach **Piazza Fontana** in the old city. Walk for 20min. along the shore to **Piazza Castello** and cross the swinging bridge to the new city. P. Garibaldi is one block ahead. The **APT Tourist Office,** C. Umberto I, 113, offers free **maps.** Walk out of P. Garibaldi, heading away from the old city. (☎0994 53 23 92; apttaranto@pugliaturismo.com. Open M-F 9am-1pm and 4:30-6:30pm, Sa 9am-noon.) A **booth** in P. Garibaldi also provides **maps.** (Open M-F 8:30am-1:40pm.) To reach the **public restrooms**, facing away from the old city, take V. Cavour out of P. Garibaldi and turn right on V. Pitagora; restrooms are on the right. In case of **emergency,** call ☎113 or the **police** at ☎112. The **hospital** is located on V. Bruno, a left onto V. Crispi off Viale Virgilio walking away from the old city. **Internet** access is available at **Chiocciolin@it,** C. Umberto I, 85, next to P. Garibaldi. (☎/fax 0994 53 80 51. €4 per hr. Open M 4:30-8:30pm, Tu-Su 9am-1pm and 4:30-8:30pm.) The **post office** is the massive, orange-stone building on Lungomare V. Emanuele. (☎0994 35 951. Open M-F 8am-6:30pm, Sa 8am-12:30pm.) **Postal Code:** 74100.

> **!** Be wary of pick-pockets in the old city, especially during *siesta* hours in summer, when streets are empty. At night avoid the area entirely.

⬛⬛ ACCOMMODATIONS AND FOOD. Albergo Pisani ❷, V. Cavour, 43, off P. Garibaldi, is conveniently located, reasonably priced, and comfortable. (☎0994 53 40 87; fax 0994 52 54 41. Breakfast included. Singles with bath €25; doubles €44, with bath €46. Cash only.) Continue down P. Cavour and turn left on the *lungomare;* 500m down find the **New Astor Hotel ❸,** Viale Virgilio, 4, with rooms dressed in plush upholstery. In the lounge, leather chairs overlook the glimmering Ionian sea. All rooms have TV, air-conditioning, and bath. (☎/fax 0994 59 59 10. Singles €35; doubles €45. Cash only.) **Hotel Plaza ❹,** in P. Garibaldi at V. d'Aquino, 46, spices up bland rooms with full amenities—bath, A/C, and TV. (☎0994 59 07 75. Breakfast included. Singles €60; doubles €80. AmEx/MC/V.)

Taranto's fishing industry fuels a seafood-heavy local cuisine; fish dishes here are plentiful and inexpensive. Try *cozze* (mussels) in basil and olive oil or spaghetti with *vongole* (clams). ◪**Ristorante Basile-Luzzi ❷,** V. Pitagora, 76, offers delectable seafood, impeccable service, and outdoor seating across the street from a park. Their specialty, *risotto alla pescatore* (€6), is excellent. (☎0994 52 62 40. Pizza €3-4.50. *Primi* €2-6, *secondi* €4-7.) At **Nautilus ❹,** V. Virgilio, 2, find a feast for the senses: savor subtly flavored seafood dishes inside a gleaming dining room with seaside views. (☎0994 53 55 38. *Primi* €8-10.50, *secondi* €9.50-13. Cover €1.50. Open noon-2:30pm and 8pm-1am. AmEx/MC/V.) **Panificio due Mari ❶,** between P. Garibaldi and the bridge at V. Matteotti, 16, is the place to chow on sandwiches, pizza, and fresh bread. (Open M-Sa 7:30am-midnight.) Another option for quick eats is the **market** in P. Castello. (Open daily 7am-1:30pm.)

⊙⊡ SIGHTS AND ENTERTAINMENT. The **Museo Nazionale Archeologico,** currently at Palazzo Pantaleo, Lungomare V. Emanuele II, houses one of the world's largest terra-cotta figurine collections, in addition to ancient pots, sculptures, mosaics, jewelry, and coins, although unfortunately all labels are in Italian. (☎0994 71 84 92. Permanent address C. Umberto I, 41, in P. Garibaldi. Open daily 8:30am-7:15pm. €2, under 18 or over 65 free.) From P. Garibaldi, a **swinging bridge,** built in 1887, hangs over the shipping canal. The first of its kind, it opens sideways to let ships through. The bridge still swings, and it's fun to watch— check the daily schedule of opening times posted on either side.

Via d'Aquino pulses every night between 6pm and midnight; from throngs of kids to bands of promenading grandmothers, people of all types stroll its walkways. A quieter atmosphere can be found on the **Lungomare Vittorio,** where people gather on benches to chat or munch cones of *gelato.* In P. Garibaldi, the Italian Navy Band in peak form accompanies the lowering of the flag at sundown. Taranto's **Holy Week Festival,** beginning the Sunday before Easter, has a ceremony steeped in medieval Spanish ritual; sheet-covered men parade papier-mâché statues around the town.

BASILICATA

Mountainous and largely land-locked, Basilicata never attained the strategic importance of neighboring coastal regions, nor the economic prominence characteristically associated with booming port cities; as such, Basilicata is a land where foreigners rarely venture. Fortunately for those who do make the trip, its fascinating prehistoric caves, breathtaking vistas, colorful local culture, and smooth beaches retain a raw, untapped beauty. Basilicata is truly the hidden gem of Italy, its value known only to its inhabitants and astute Italian vacationers.

MATERA   ☎0835

Matera's claim to fame are the *sassi*, ancient homes carved directly in the rocky terrain. Until 1952, when the government declared the 7000-year-old homes unsafe and unsanitary, locals still inhabited these residences without the benefits of electricity or running water. Today, 50 years after the cliffs' inhabitants were moved to government-built suburban housing, trendsetters and professional firms have started occupying *sassi*, sparking a wave of renovations. As restaurants, hotels, and office buildings creep into the cliffs, the once dismal dwellings have become quite swank. Life has come anew to Matera (pop. 56,000), so beautiful and oddly captivating that the city's evocative landscape has even earned it a special place in movie-making history as a stand-in for ancient Jerusalem, most recently with biblical epics *The Passion of the Christ* and *King David.* Riding this wave of enthusiasm and possibility, Matera has become the 2nd-largest city in Basilicata. Despite the relative isolation of the city and the fact that it is the only provincial capital in Italy not connected by FS trains, Matera's extraordinary sights, inexpensive accommodations, and engaging local culture make a visit worth the effort.

▄ TRANSPORTATION

The train station, **Matera Centrale,** is in P. Matteotti. **FAL trains** (☎0835 33 28 61; www.fal-srl.it) run to Altamura (30min., M-Sa 13 per day 5:10am-8:47pm, €2.20) and Bari (1½hr., M-Sa 13 per day 5:10am-8:47pm, €4). **FAL buses** leave from P. Matteotti for Bari on Sunday (1¾hr., 6 per day 6:15am-2:05pm, €4), when train service is suspended. Buy tickets at the station. **SITA buses** (☎0835 38 50 70; www.sita-online.it) leave from P. Matteotti and run to: Altamura (30min., 3 per day 1:10-6:30pm,

€1.29); Metaponto (1hr., 5 per day 8:15am-5:30pm, €2.63); and Taranto (1½hr., 6 per day M-Sa 6am-5pm, €5.16). There is reduced service on Sunday. Buy bus tickets at the ticket office across the street. For a **taxi**, call ☎0835 33 43 48.

✳ 🛈 ORIENTATION AND PRACTICAL INFORMATION

Matera's grottoes split into two small valleys that overlook a deep canyon in the **Parco della Murgia Materana**. From the **train** and **bus stations** at **Piazza Matteotti**, head down **Via Roma** or **Via Minzoni** to **Piazza Veneto**, the heart of the city and the entrance to the *sassi*. **Sasso Barisano**, the modern area located in the first valley, is straight ahead, through the stairway across from the Banco di Napoli. To reach the cavernous **Sasso Caveoso**, continue to the right on **Via del Corso**, which bears right on **Via Ridola**, then descend left at **Piazza Pascoli**. The more important *chiese rupestri* (rock churches) are on the other side of the ridge opposite the Sasso Caveoso. The tourist office and most hotels offer a detailed map of the *sassi*.

The **APT Tourist Office** is at V. de Viti de Marco, 9. From the station, walk down V. Roma and take the 2nd left. (☎0835 33 19 83; www.comune.matera.it. Open in summer daily 9am-1pm and 4-6:30pm; in winter M-F 9am-1pm, Tu and Th 4-6:30pm.) The city also has an **information office**, on V. Madonna della Virtù, the road along the ridge in the *sassi* district. (Open daily Apr.-Sept. 9:30am-12:30pm and 3:30-6:30pm.) A helpful website about the town is www.sassiweb.it. In case of **emergency**, call ☎113 or an **ambulance** at ☎0835 24 32 70. The **police** (☎112) are on V. Minzoni. **Ospedale Madonna Delle Grazie** (☎0835 24 31) is on Cda. Cattedra Ambulante. For **Internet**, head to **Qui PC Net**, on V. Margherita, to the left of the Banco di Napoli. (☎0835 34 61 12. €1.40 per 15min., €4 per hr. Open daily 8am-1pm and 5-8:30pm.) The **post office** is on V. del Corso, off P. Veneto. (☎0835 33 25 91. Open M-F 8am-6:30pm, Sa 8am-noon.) **Postal Code:** 75100.

🏠 ACCOMMODATIONS

Excellent budget accommodations abound in Matera, making it a great base for exploring other areas of Basilicata and Puglia.

▨ **Le Monacelle**, V. Riscatto, 9/10 (☎0835 34 40 97; www.lemonacelle.it). Facing the *duomo*, V. Riscatto skirts the left side. Hostel, hotel, conference center, and host to world-class concert series, there's not much that this complex doesn't do. Though housed in cloisters built in the 1500s, modern amenities abound, including Internet access for guests and a movie screening room. Breakfast included. All rooms with A/C, bath, TV. Dorms €16; singles €55, doubles €86. AmEx/MC/V. Hostel ❷/Hotel ❹

Sassi Hostel (HI), V. S. Giovanni Vecchio, 89 (☎0835 33 10 09; hotelsassi@virgilio.it). From the station, take V. Minzoni to P. Veneto and V. S. Biagio to the church, where signs leading to the hostel appear on the right. Anything but primitive, the rooms in this hostel are renovated *sassi*. Guests are invited to cavort inside prehistoric caves and fulfill their troglodyte fantasies. English, French, and Spanish spoken. All rooms have bath. Sheets and towels included. Curfew midnight. Dorms €16. AmEx/MC/V. ❷

Bed and Breakfast Capriotti, P. Duomo (☎0835 33 39 97 or 329 61 93 757; www.capriotti-bed-breakfast.it). Facing the *duomo*, Capriotti is on the left. *Sassi* caves with sleeping, cooking, and living nooks also have views of Sasso Barisano. Both are equipped with bath, A/C, and refrigerator. €30-40 per person. Cash only. ❸

Locanda di San Martino, V. Fiorentini, 71 (☎0835 25 66 00; www.locandadisanmartino.it), offers the inimitable experience of sleeping inside what was once a Neolithic temple. Located in the *sassi*, these luxurious rooms have TV, phone, A/C, and stylish bath. Doubles and suites €86-120. AmEx/MC/V. ❺

Albergo Roma, V. Roma, 62 (☎0835 33 39 12), by tourist office. Newly renovated rooms are basic but comfortable, clean and close to transportation. All rooms with bath, TV, and A/C. Singles €35; doubles €50. Cash only. ❸

🔦 FOOD

Though small, Matera has managed to concoct several local specialties worth sampling, including *favetta con cicore* (soup of beans, celery, chicory, and croutons, mixed in olive oil) and *frittata di spaghetti* (pasta with anchovies, eggs, bread crumbs, garlic, and oil). Experience true Materan grit with *pane di grano duro*, made with extra-hard, local wheat. Fruit can be found at the **open-air market** off V. Minzoni near P. Veneto. (Open daily 9am-1pm.)

▧ **Cantina U'Ciddar,** V. Purgatorio Vecchio, 25, in Sasso Caveoso. Near Santa Lucia alle Malve, look for the signs. Like being invited to lunch at an old friend's *sassi* house. The intersection of Materan cuisine, culture, and colorful local characters make this hidden spot an experience not easily duplicated anywhere else. No set menu, full meals for less than €10. Open daily for lunch. Cash only. ❷

▧ **L'Osteria,** V. Fiorentini, 58 (☎0835 33 33 95). From P. Veneto entrance to *sassi*, V. Fiorentini is the main street. Simple, Materan *cucina tipica* at low prices and big servings. The *capunti con cicerchie e funghi* (local pasta with beans and mushrooms; €5.50) is light and full of flavor. *Primi* €4-5.50, *secondi* €5-8. Cover €1. Open M-Tu and Th-Su noon-3pm and 7:30-11pm. AmEx/MC/V. ❷

Trattoria del Corso, V. La Vista, 12 (☎0835 33 28 92), off P. Veneto near V. Manzoni. This local favorite serves fantastic Basilicatan specialties and authentic charm you won't find at its pricier counterparts. *Primi* €4.50-6, *secondi* €6-9. Cover €1.50. Open M-Th and Sa-Su noon-3pm and 7-11:30pm. Call ahead in Aug. AmEx/MC/V. ❸

Trattoria Lucana, V. Lucana, 48 (☎0835 33 61 17), off V. Roma. Try the *orecchiette alla materana* (ear-shaped pasta with tomatoes and vegetables; €5.86) or the house specialty, *bocconcini alla lucana* (veal with mushrooms; €6.70). Cover €1. Service 10%. Open M-Sa 12:30-3pm and 8-10:30pm. Closed early Sept. AmEx/MC/V. ❸

Ristorante Osteria Arti e Mestieri La Stalla, V. Rosario, 73 (☎0835 24 04 55). From P. Veneto, take V. S. Biagio until the archway on the right; walk through, down the stairs, and follow signs to the restaurant. The perfect lunch break after trekking up those *sassi* stairs. Cool, rustic dining room. *Primi* €3-6, *secondi* €6-9. Open daily 12:30am-4pm and 7pm-12:30am. AmEx/MC/V. ❷

Caffè Terrazza dell'Annunziata, P. Veneto (☎0835 33 65 25; www.terrazzadellannunziata.com), on the top floor of the *palazzo* holding the public library, across from the *sassi* entrance. Stylish decor and unique *granita* flavors enhance the views of *sassi* from the roof top terrace. *Granita* and *gelato* €2. Open M-Sa 9am-late. Cash only. ❶

Gran Caffè, P. Veneto, 6 (☎0835 23 23 02). Behind an unassuming storefront lies a huge selection of pastries and fresh bread. No seating. Grab a sandwich, soda, and *cannoli* for less than €5 and enjoy them on the *piazza's* benches. *Gelato* €1. Open M and W-Su 6am-midnight. Cash only. ❶

👁 SIGHTS

ON THE WAY TO THE SASSI. The 7000-year-old homes lie in a maze of pathways, and a detailed map is necessary to negotiate them properly. To enter the heart of *sassi* zone, start from P. Veneto and head onto V. del Corso; immediately past the Chiesa di S. Francesco d'Assisi, turn left into P. Sedile. From there, V. Duomo leads to the **Puglian-Romanesque duomo.** Its towering spire and carved outer portals are certainly worth pausing to admire. Inside, the 15th-century carved choir stalls are just as intricate. *(Open daily 8am-1pm and 3:30-6pm.)* Retracing the path back to the Chiesa di S. Francesco d'Assisi, V. Ridola leads past the skeleton-and-skull-covered facade of the **Chiesa del Purgatorio.** The **Museo Ridola** looms on the right and is home to some of the region's finest archaeological treasures. Don't miss the exhibit on 20th-century excavation techniques or the collection of prehistoric and Classical art housed in a monastery. *(V. Ridola, 24. ☎0835 31 12 39. Open M 9am-12pm, Tu-Su 9am-noon and 3-8pm. €2.50, students 18-24 €1.25, under 18 or over 65 free.)*

THE SASSI. Little is known about the people who first built and inhabited the *sassi*. The dwellings themselves are carved in several styles from limestone calcarenite. The oldest, inhabited around 7000 years ago, are the crumbling structures that line **Sasso Barisano** (along V. Addozio). The valley east of the *duomo* around **Sasso Caveoso** contains the second type of *sassi*, the carved nooks dating from around 2000 BC. The most elaborate *sassi*, and, at a little more than 1000 years old, some of the most recent constructions, are clustered near V. Bruno Buozzi (off V. Madonna delle Virtù near the *duomo*). Most of the 6th-century *chiese rupestri* (rock churches) remain unmodified, with remnants of some 12th-century frescoes. Until 1952, groups of up to 12 people still lived in these windowless caves, often sharing dwellings with the family livestock. Local children roam the *sassi* offering tours of the caves to visitors; the organized ones are more enlightening. Try **Sassi Tourism,** V. B. Buozzi, 141/143 (☎0835 31 94 58; www.sassitourism.it). For a self-guided tour, buy a book at any magazine stand. In the *sassi*, the **Cooperative Amici Del Turistica** offers information and tours in English, French, German, and Italian. The **Sassi by Night** tour is a good one. *(V. Fiorentini, 30. ☎0835 33 03 01; www.amicidelturista.it. Open in spring and summer daily 8am-1pm and 4-9pm; in fall and winter 9am-noon and 4-7pm. €10 per person for groups of 4 or more.)* A public bathroom (€0.50) is near the bottom of the *sassi* area. *(Open daily 9am-6pm.)*

CHURCHES. Rock-hewn churches periodically punctuate the *sassi* along V. Bruno Buozzi. From P. V. Veneto, walk past the Museo Ridola on V. Ridola and bear left until reaching the end of the P. Pascoli; descend the stairs and head straight until hitting V. Bruno Buozzi on the left. It's also possible to follow signs reading "Turistico Itinerario" and "Convicino di S. Antonio" from the bottom of V. Bruno Buozzi. Follow the path along the cliffs to reach the churches of **San Pietro Caveoso, Santa Maria d'Idris,** and **Santa Lucia alle Malve,** which preserve beautiful 11th-century Byzantine frescoes in their caves. *(Open daily 9am-1pm and 3-7pm. 1 church €2.50, 4 churches €5, all 7 churches €6.)* A nearby *sasso* is furnished as it was when 10 people and two horses shared its two small rooms. Tours of the cave are available in English. *(☎/fax 0835 31 01 18. Open daily 9am-9:30pm. €2.)* Farther along lies the multi-level complex of **Madonna delle Virtù** and **S. Nicola dei Greci,** which contains frescoes, houses, and the modern sculpture of artist Leoncillo. Informational tours are offered in English. *(Open daily 9am-9pm. €2.50, students €1.25.)*

PARCO DELLA MURGIA METERANA. The park straddles the ridge across the canyon from the *sassi* and offers some of the area's best **hiking.** The park entrance is off Str. Statale, down V. Annunziatella and then V. Marconi. The terrain, lush in some patches and bare in others, is odd and intriguing; over 150 rock churches dot the landscape in addition to the strange *jazzi*, caves built by shepherds to shelter their flocks. The park was recently expanded to create even more hiking options. The tourist office has information on private tour guides.

FESTIVALS

At the end of June and beginning of July, Matera celebrates the ■**Festa di Santa Maria della Bruna,** which features numerous musical and cultural events, nightly fireworks displays, and open-air markets selling everything from power tools to psychic readings by exceedingly gifted parakeets. The revelry culminates with the **Assalto al Carro** on July 2. The *sassi* house an **International Sculpture Exhibition** from June to October in the churches of Madonna delle Virtù and San Nicola dei Greci.

DAYTRIPS FROM MATERA

ALTAMURA

Altamura is on the FAL line between Bari (1hr., 15 per day 5:50am-9:57pm, €3) and Matera (40min., 15 per day 5:08am-10:27pm, €2.20). Vle. Regina Margherita runs from the station to the old city, where it becomes V. Federico di Svevia. Just after the old city, V. Federico di Svevia splits into V. Pietro Colletta and V. Matera. The hospital (☎0803 10 811) is on Vle. Regina Margherita; for the medical clinic, call ☎0803 10 82 01. The carabinieri (☎0830 14 10 14) are in P. S. Teresa, down V. N. Melodia from P. Duomo.

The urban center of Puglia's farm country, Altamura boasts a **Romanesque cathedral** and some rather unusual archaeological finds. The cathedral, located in P. Duomo in the old city, is captivating with its rose window and intricately decorated church portals. Scenes from the life of Christ surround the picturesque yet lugubrious *Cenacolo. (Open daily 7am-noon and 4-8pm.)* The Altamura **Archaeological Museum** displays a collection of relics from Greek and prehistoric tombs. At the entrance to the old city, turn left and continue until signs for the museum appear. (☎080 31 46 409. Open M-Sa 9am-7:30pm, Su 8:30am-1:30pm. €2.20.)

GRAVINA

Gravina is best reached from Altamura by FAL train (10min., 18 per day 7:08am-10:59pm, €1.20), while FS trains run to rural spots in the area. Museo Ettore Pomarici Santomasi is on V. Museo, 20. (☎080 32 51 021; www.fondazionesantomasi.it.) Open M-F 9am-1pm and 4-7pm, Sa 9:30am-12:30pm and 4:30-7:30pm, Su 9:30am-12:30pm. For the carabinieri, call ☎0803 26 42 72. The Ospedale Civile is on V. San Domenico (☎112). A helpful website about Gravina is www.gravinainpuglia.it.

Gravina takes its name from the steep gorge over which it perches. This stunning ravine is one of the town's main highlights, as are the many historical and architecturally diverse buildings. Both train stations are at the end of the **Corso Aldo Moro** (on the other side of the tracks from the FAL station), which runs to the old city. The *corso* becomes **Via V. Veneto,** which turns into the tangled roads that comprise most of the old city. Head downhill to reach P. Notar Domenico and the **Chiesa del Purgatorio,** decorated with statues of skeletons that recline with an eerie cheerfulness. The bears supporting the columns of the church represent the ancient dominance of the Roman Orsini family, once feudal lords of Gravina. Next to the church in a large *palazzo,* the archaeological museum **Ettore Pomarici Santomasi** huddles unobtrusively. Free admission includes tours of the collection of Lucanian grave relics, including some Greek *amphorae.* Next to the stations, the facade of **Chiesa di Madonna delle Grazie** bears a relief of an eagle. On C. Aldo Moro, heading away from the stations, turn left down V. Fontana La Stella to the stone bridge leading across the ravine for a spectacular view of the cliffs and the town.

METAPONTO ☎0835

Most people go to Metaponto for the **beach,** and for good reason: the sand is soft and the waters of the Ionian sea refreshing. Plan carefully, as Metaponto can feel abandoned and run-down during much of the year, though from mid-July through August, campsites swell with city-dwellers escaping to the sea. If the crowds become unbearable, catch bus #1 to the *borgo* and see the area where the Greek mathematician **Pythagoras,** inventor of the Pythagorean theorem, taught until his death in 479 BC, and where Spartacus staged his famous slave revolt. Or stop by the **Museo Archeologico,** V. Aristea, 21, which displays jewelry, vases, and figurines—most from nearby ruins. Past the post office and down a lonely country road lie the ruins of the **Doric Templo di Apollo Licius** and a **Greek theater** from the 6th century BC. It's another 5km to the **Tavole Palatine,** the ruins of a Greek temple of Hera and the best-preserved temple in Metaponto. (☎0835 74 53 27. Open M 2-8pm, Tu-Su 9am-8pm. €2.50, ages 18-26 €1.25, under 18 or over 60 free.)

Most of Metaponto's accommodations line the beach and fall into two categories: costly or camping. **Kammel Camping ❶,** V. Lido, 1, is at the end of V. Magna Grecia. The lively rhythms of the campground's *discoteca* invade the silence of the adjacent national forest. The site also provides tennis courts, game rooms, bars, a swimming pool, and a beach shuttle. (☎0835 74 19 26; www.kammel.it. Open July 21-Aug. 25. €13 per person, €8.50 per tent, €3.50 per car. Electricity €3.50. AmEx/MC/V.) A good value is **Hotel Residence Kennedy ❹,** Viale Jonio, 1, just off P. Nord. Call from train station for pick-up. Good-sized rooms have bath, air-conditioning, TV, and fridge; some have kitchen facilities or a balcony. (☎/fax 0835 74 19 60; www.hrkennedy.it. Breakfast included. Singles €50-61; doubles €70-85. AmEx/MC/V.) **L'Oasi Ristorante Pizzeria ❸,** V. Lido, 47, is a good choice for a beachside lunch break, with tasty, cheap seafood and pizza. (☎0835 74 18 83. *Primi* €4-5, *secondi* €5-6. 4-course *menù* €17. Open daily noon-3pm and 7pm-midnight. AmEx/MC/V.) **Alimentari di Maria,** a mini-market off P. Nord on V. Magna Grecia, makes tasty *panini* for under €2. (Open daily 7am-6pm.) The scent of fresh bread entices sunbathers to stop by **Macelleria 2000** (not to be confused with Mercato 2000), a butcher shop near the beach entrance at the end of P. Nord. Its tasty sandwiches or roast chicken (€5.50) can satisfy any hunger pang. (Cash only.)

Metaponto is best reached by train. **Trains** run to: Bari (2hr., 11 per day 4:50am-9:34pm, €13.63); Reggio di Calabria (5hr., 11 per day 1:29am-7:07pm, €25.20); Rome (6hr., 8 per day 7:45am-11:45pm, €32.28); Salerno (4hr., 7 per day 6:35am-5:35pm, €10.10); and Taranto (40min., 23 per day 4:50am-11:45pm, €3.60). Many longer routes from Metaponto require bus transfers, usually in Battipaglia. Blue **SITA buses** run from the train station and V. Magna Grecia near the rotary to Matera (1hr., 5 per day 7:05am-4:30pm, €2.63). Local Chiruzzi buses (☎0835 54 33 50) serve the immediate area. Bus #1 runs between the train station, the museum, and the *lido* (13 per day 5:05am-7:55pm, €0.70). A good place to get on is in front of Camping Internazionale on V. Magna Grecia. **Bike rental** is available at the beach. The town has four sections: **scalo** (train station), **borgo** (museum), **lido** (beach and hotels), and the Greek **ruins.** While *scalo, borgo,* and the ruins are all 1-2km apart, the *lido* is farther away. Both the beach and the ruins can be reached by a short bus ride from the station. **V. Magna Grecia** runs parallel to the shore, one block inland from the road closest to the shore, **Via delle Sirene.** In case of **emergency,** call ☎0835 74 19 97. The **post office** is near the Museo Archeologico, a 10min. walk straight ahead from the train station. (Open M-Sa 8am-1:15pm.) **Postal Code:** 75010.

CALABRIA

Sometimes called the last great oasis of the Mediterranean, Calabria is an undiscovered land of inspiring history and unspoiled natural beauty. Though one of Italy's most under-developed regions, it is also the most under-appreciated. Two and a half millennia ago, when the northern cities that sniff at her today were small backwaters, Calabria was of worldwide importance, home to leading philosophers, artists, and athletes. Fortunately for local pride, traces of this illustrious past remain in abundance, from the Greek ruins at Locri to the Norman Castle at Cosenza. Many of the region's excavation sites remain untouched since antiquity, providing a view of the way the ancients lived—and a marked contrast to the more developed regions that have paved over their Greek and Roman heritage.

REGGIO DI CALABRIA ☎0965

Though many regard the area as merely a departure point for Sicily, Reggio and its environs actually comprise some of the finest landscapes in Italy. The provincial capital of Reggio di Calabria was one of the earliest and proudest Greek settlements on the Italian mainland, but it slid into neglect and disarray following centuries of raids and natural disasters. After a devastating 1908 earthquake, a new city arose from the rubble, crowded with designer stores and turn-of-the-century palaces but somewhat devoid of historical interest or charm. More inspired settings are very close at hand on the Tyrrhenian Coast to the north and the Ionian Sea to the east. The nearby towns of Scilla and Locri offer one of Italy's most attractive beaches and some fine archaeological treasures, respectively.

▛ TRANSPORTATION

Aeroporto dello Stretto (☎0965 64 05 17) is 5km south of town. Orange buses #113, 114, 115, 125, or 131 from P. Garibaldi outside Stazione Centrale to the airport (€0.90). Flights service Bologna, Florence, Milan, Rome, and Turin. Reggio's main **train station** is **Stazione Centrale** (☎0965 27 427), on P. Garibaldi at south end of town. The information office is open M-Sa 7am-9pm. Trains run to: Cosenza (2½hr., 5 per day 5:20am-5:45pm, €11-21); Naples (4½hr., 10 per day 5:55am-8:40pm, €21.59); Rome (8hr., 11 per day 12:15am-10:21pm, €29.59); Scilla (30min., 20 per day 5:20am-8:40pm, €1.76); Trope (2hr., 4 per day 6:16am-8:40pm, €5). **Lirosi** runs **buses** from P. Garibaldi to: Florence (11hr., 6:45pm, €47) and Rome (8hr.; 7am, 11:45am, 10pm; €35). **Costaviola** (☎0965 75 15 86) runs buses from P. Garibaldi to Scilla (45min., 12 per day 7:20am-8:10pm, €1.70). Buy tickets onboard. **Ferries** depart from the port, at the northern end of the city. Boats and hydrofoils serve Messina and the Aeolian Islands. **FS** (☎0965 81 76 75), all the way to the left when facing the port, shares hydrofoil service with **Ustica** (☎090 66 25 06 or 090 36 40 44), to the right of FS. FS office open daily 6:30am-8:15pm; Ustica's hours vary. **NGI** is across from Onda Marina to the right of the port entrance. ([335 84 27 784. Open M-F 12:20am-10:20pm, Sa 12:20am-8:20pm. **Meridiano** (☎0965 81 04 14) is on the corner nearest the port entrance. Ferries run from Monday to Saturday from 2:10am-11:50pm with reduced service on Sundays.

▛▟ ORIENTATION AND PRACTICAL INFORMATION

Reggio's main thoroughfare is **Corso Garibaldi,** which runs parallel to the sea and to all the major sights. Facing away from **Stazione Centrale,** walk straight through **Piazza Garibaldi** to C. Garibaldi; a left turn leads to the heart of town. At the end of C. Garibaldi and down V. L. G. Zerbi is Reggio's **port,** from which hydrofoils and boats run to Messina and the Aeolian Islands. One block to the left of the station, the twin roads **Corso Vittorio Emanuele III** and **Viale Matteotti** trace the *lungomare.* City buses run continuously up and down C. Garibaldi and northward along the two roads. At its center, C. Garibaldi becomes a pedestrian route, perfect for an evening *passeggiata* past the many bars and designer outlets that line the street.

The APT **tourist office,** which provides free **maps** and information, is located at the central train station. (☎0965 27 120. Open M-Sa 8am-2pm and 2:30-7:30pm. Branch at airport ☎0965 64 32 91.) For **currency exchange,** head to Banca Nazionale del Lavoro, C. Garibaldi, 431. (☎0965 85 11. Open M-F 8:20am-1:20pm and 2:35-4:05pm.) **ATMs** line C. Garibaldi. In an emergency, call ☎113, the **carabinieri** ☎112, or the **police** ({0965 53 991), near Stazione Centrale. **Farmacia Centrale** is at C. Garibaldi, 543. (☎0965 33 23 32. Open M-F 8:30am-1pm and 5-8:30pm.) There is a **hospital,** Ospedale Riuniti, on V. Melacrino (☎0965 39 111). Turn left from P. Italia on C. Garibaldi to reach the **post office,** V. Miraglia, 14. (☎0965 31 52 68. Open M-F 8:30am-6:30pm, Sa 8:30am-12:30pm.) **Postal Code:** 89100

ACCOMMODATIONS

High-quality, cheap accommodations are nearly impossible to find in Reggio, so you might as well splurge on **Hotel Palace Masoanris ❺**, V. V. Veneto, 95. This three-star hotel next to Museo Archeologico offers rooms with bath, air-conditioning, phone, minibar, and balconies; ask for a room on the street side for no extra charge. (☎0965 26 433; www.montesanohotels.it. Breakfast included. Singles €90; doubles €120; triples €162. AmEx/MC/V.) If you're not a big spender, try **Hotel Diana ❸**, V. Diego Vitrioli, 12, off C. Garibaldi. While some of the rooms have TV, phone, and air-conditioning, others are less appealing. Make sure to see a room before deciding to spend the night. (☎0965 89 15 22. Reserve 1 month ahead in Aug. Singles €27.50; doubles €55, with A/C €65; triples €74. Cash only.) If you're planning to stay for awhile, save money by staying outside the city at **B&B Villa Maria ❺**, V. Marina Arenile, 3, in Gallico Marina. Take bus #110 from P. Garibaldi, walk to the waterfront (10min.) and turn right. Villa Maria is on V. Marina Arenile behind the "Ottica" shop. Villa Maria offers rooms near the coast with terrace. (☎0965 37 26 33 or 333 74 48 064. Breakfast included. Terrace suite €50, €25 for each additional person. Other rooms €40, plus €20 per person. Cash only.)

FOOD

Chefs in Reggio serve *spaghetti alla calbrese* (with pepper sauce), *capocollo* (a ham spiced with local hot peppers), and *pesce spada* (local harpoon-hunted swordfish). Stock up at **Dì per Dì**, a supermarket opposite the train station. (Open daily 8:30am-1:30pm and 5-8:30pm.) *Bars* along C. Garibaldi often offer baked goods, so sweeten the day with a few of the region's beloved *biscotti*. For a good cheap meal, try **Cordon Bleu ❶**, C. Garibaldi, 230. Despite chandelier lighting and a haughty French *nom*, this versatile joint serves cheap *tavola calda* goodies from €1. (☎965 33 24 47. Open daily 6:30am-11pm; food served 11am-9pm. MC/V.) **Le Palme ❸**, C. V. Emanuele III, serves up seafood pizzas on palm-lined patio. (☎0965 81 00 86. Pizza €4-7. *Primi* €9, *secondi* €10. Open daily noon-3:30pm and 7:30pm-2am. MC/V. For cheaper pizza, head to **Pizzeria Rusty ❶**, V. D. Romeo, next to the museum. Double-folded Neapolitan slices the size of tables, priced by weight (€7.75 per kg) and *tavola calda* favorites like *arancini* (€1.30) distinguish this tiny *rosticceria* from nearby ice cream-vending bars. (0965 20 012. Open M-Tu and Th-Su 9am-1:30pm and 6pm-midnight. Cash only.)

SIGHTS

The preeminence Reggio di Calabria enjoyed in antiquity as a great Greek *polis* may have passed, but the ▧**Museo Nazionale** preserves the city's historical claim to fame with one of the world's finest collections of art and artifacts from Magna Graecia (Greater Greece). In the first-floor galleries, a wealth of *amphorae* and *pinakes* (wine jars and votive tablets) show scenes from mythology and daily life. The floor above the gallery has a large coin collection and a 2300-year-old novelty sarcophagus shaped like a huge, sandaled foot. Downstairs, treasures formerly submerged in the Ionian Sea, such as pottery and broken statues, comprise the **Sezione Subacquea.** If the Subacquea is the centerpiece, **I Bronzi di Riace** are the crowning jewels. Rescued from the sea in 1972, the Riace Bronzes are among the best (and arguably the most valuable) ancient Greek sculptures in the world; dating from the 5th century BC, they represent nude male warriors in stunning detail. Muscular and assured, the bronzes share gallery space with the estimable **Head of the Philosopher,** which some point to as the Greek tradition's first life-like portrait. A display before entering the gallery documents the bronzes' restoration process. (P. de Nava, on C. Garibaldi toward the Stazione Lido. ☎0965 81 22 55. Open Tu-Su 9am-7:30pm. €6, ages 18-25 €3, under 18 or over 65 free. Cash only.)

🄫🎵 BEACHES AND ENTERTAINMENT

As the day cools, *Reggiani* mingle on the **lungomare,** a long, narrow botanical garden stretching along the seaside that Italian author d'Annunzio immortalized as the "most beautiful kilometer in all of Italy." When they want to take a dip, travelers sprawl on the beach near **Lido Comunale.** Playgrounds, an elevated boardwalk, and monuments to the city's more famous citizens dot the *lungomare*, while the quiet beauty of a sunset behind the misty blue mountains of nearby Sicily provides a final natural touch to a pleasant afternoon swim. Calabrians finish the summer with the **Festival of the Madonna della Consolazione.** The four-day festival, celebrated in mid-September, concludes with an elaborate fireworks display.

🄫 DAYTRIPS FROM REGGIO DI CALABRIA

SCILLA

Scilla is accessible from Reggio by train (30min., 20 per day, €2.10) or by bus (20min., 12 per day, €1.29). Scilla's train station does not sell tickets, so purchase a round-trip ticket from Reggio or ask at nearby bars for regional train tickets.

Walk along the beach and listen for mermaids singing; local legend has it that merfolk still dwell off the Scillan coast. Homer immortalized the town's great cliffs in *The Odyssey* as the home of the menacing Scylla, a terrible monster with six heads, 12 feet, and a fierce temper. The mythical creature devoured many a ship that steered away from Charybdis, a hazardous whirlpool in the straits where Sicily and Italy meet. Travelers today can expect a more hospitable welcome. Only 23km from Reggio, this fishing-village-turned-resort's languorous pace and distinctive geography (it is built directly into cliffs enclosing a sandy beach) can make the real world seem far away. Except, that is, for when the meteorological oddity *Fata Morgana* creates a natural magnifying glass out of the light over the sea, making the Sicilian city of Messina appear to be floating just over the water.

THE IONIAN COAST

Trains along the Ionian Coast often have erratic schedules and multiple connections, so allow ample travel time when planning an itinerary.

From Reggio to Riace, the Ionian Coast offers miles of marvelous beaches. White sands, rocks, and dunes cater to every taste and provide a contrast to the mountains visible in the distance. Though the ancient Greeks once made these shores as crowded as modern Tropea, now it is primarily locals who frequent these waters and relish their unexploited beauty. Even the more established sites at the villages of **Bovalino Marina, Bianco,** and **Soverato** are relatively unknown.

COSENZA ☎ 0984

One of the most important cultural and industrial centers of Calabria, Cosenza is full of intrigue. From the plundered riches that King Alaric I supposedly buried in the city's Busento River in AD 410 to its Norman castle and 12th-century *duomo*, Cosenza's treasures mirror its unusual history. Though usually ignored by tourists due to its inland location far from the beaches, Cosenza has plenty to offer visitors, from its charming *centro storico* to its thriving nightlife. Beautifully situated in the mountains, Cosenza is a city that lives for itself and not for tourists.

🖵 TRANSPORTATION

Trains depart from **Stazione Cosenza** (☎ 0984 39 47 46), on V. Popilia, 4km north of the city center. The ticket office is open daily 6:10am-12:42pm and 1:50-8:22pm. Trains go to: Naples (4½hr., 8 per day 8:17am-6:48pm, €20.86); Reggio)2½hr., 12 per day 6:40am-7:30pm, €11.46); Rome (6½hr., 8 per day 8:17am-6:45pm, €31.35). **Ferrovie della Calabria** sends trains to Camigliatello (1½hr., M-Sa 9:18am, €1.91). It also sends regional blue **buses** to Camigliatello (8 per day 6:50am-7:05pm, €1.91) and San Giovanni (2hr., 10 per day, €3) from the station on V. Autostazione and the train station. The ticket office is opposite the train ticket window and is open daily 6am-2:20pm and 4-7:30pm. All orange **city buses** stop at P. Matteotti. Tickets (€0.77) are sold at magazine kiosks (main kiosk at V. Trieste with C. Mazzini, near P. dei Bruzi) and at most *tabaccherie*. Buses **#4T, 22,** and **23** serve the *centro storico*, departing from P. Bruzi and stopping in P. Prefeturra (every 30min. 5:30am-11pm). Buses **#15, 16,** and **27** run between P. Matteotti and the train station (every 7min. 5am-midnight; reduced service Su). Routes posted on yellow hanging street signs in P. Matteotti and at all bus stops. Call ☎ 800 24 24 00 for info.

> ❗ Since none of the bus stops are marked, the yellow schedules at bus stops and in P. Matteotti are the only way to distinguish stops. Ask the driver where you should get off.

ORIENTATION AND PRACTICAL INFORMATION

The **Busento River** divides the city in two: the traffic-heavy new city, north of the Busento, and the relaxed old city, south of the river. **Corso Mazzini**, the main thoroughfare and shopping center, begins near the river at **Piazza dei Bruzi**, continues through the **Piazza Kennedy**, and ends in **Piazza Fera**. To get to C. Mazzini, hop on any bus to **Piazza Matteotti** and, facing away from the bus stop, walk a block up **Corso Umberto** to P. dei Bruzi. The bus station is on **Via Autostazione**, to the right off P. Fera at the end of C. Mazzini, where the *corso* splits seven ways. Cosenza's *centro storico* lies across the **Ponte Mario Martiri**, three blocks to the right from P. Matteotti when facing away from P. dei Bruzi. A labyrinth of medieval stone buildings, the old city has winding "roads" and cobblestone staircases. The only discernible street, the narrow **Corso Telesio**, begins in **Piazza Valdesi**, near the Busento, and climbs to the statue of Telesio in the **Piazza Prefettura (Piazza XV Marzo)**.

Go up to the lot in C. Mazzini, turn right and look for the sign for the **APT Tourist Office**, C. Mazzini, 92, which has a wealth of information and a helpful staff. In case of **emergency**, call ☎ 113, the **carabinieri** ☎ 112, or the **police** ☎ 0984 25 422, in P. dei Bruzi, behind the town hall. For an **ambulance**, dial ☎ 0984 68 13 21, or call the **Red Cross**, V. Popilia, 35 (☎ 0984 40 81 16). **Farmacia Berardelli** is at C. Mazzini, 40. (☎ 0984 26 452. Open M-F 8:30am-1pm and 4:30-8pm. Posts after-hours rotation.) The hospital, **Ospedale Civile dell'Annunziata** (☎ 0984 68 11), is on V. Felice Migliori.

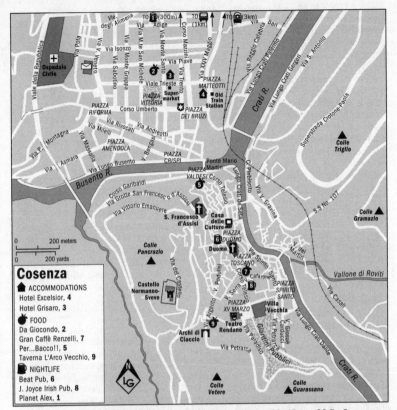

Cosenza

ACCOMMODATIONS
Hotel Excelsior, 4
Hotel Grisaro, 3

FOOD
Da Giocondo, 2
Gran Caffè Renzelli, 7
Per...Bacco!!, 5
Taverna L'Arco Vecchio, 9

NIGHTLIFE
Beat Pub, 6
J. Joyce Irish Pub, 8
Planet Alex, 1

For free **Internet,** head to **Casa delle Culture,** C. Telesio, 98. (Open M-Sa 8am-noon and 4-7pm.) The **post office,** V. Veneto, 41 (☎0984 22 162), is at the end of V. Piave, off C. Mazzini. (Open M-F 8am-6:30pm, Sa 8am-12:30pm.) **Postal Code:** 87100.

ACCOMMODATIONS

Hotel Excelsior ❹, P. Matteoti, 14, offers antique, high-ceilinged rooms with air-conditioning, TV, phone and 24hr. reception. (☎0984 74 383; fax 0984 74 384. Breakfast included. Singles €40; doubles €60. AmEx/MC/V. To reach **Hotel Grisaro ❸,** V. Monte Santo, 6, walk one block up C. Mazzini from P. dei Bruzi, then turn left on V. Trieste. V. Monte Santo is one block up on the right, marked by a bright sign. Rooms are spacious and comfortable, with balcony, TV, and fluffy bed. (☎0984 27 952, fax 0984 27 838. Wheelchair accessible. Curfew 1am. Reserve ahead. Singles €28.50, with bath €36; doubles €52; triples €67; quads €78. MC/V.)

FOOD

Cosenza is a well-fed city. Its restaurants draw on rich mushrooms and fresh *prosciutto* of the Sila forests, plentiful fish from the Tyrrhenian Sea, and the fruit of the region's orchards. For fresh, juicy produce, stop at **Cooper Frutta,** Vle. Trieste,

25/29, a block from C. Mazzini, and pick up everything else from **Cooperatore Alimentare,** next door at Vle. Trieste, 35. (Open M-Sa 7am-2:15pm and 4-8:30pm.) Take a picnic to nearby P. Vittoria and enjoy a peach, a loaf, and the old men playing *gioca tresete,* a local card game. Take bus 4t to the hillside village, or follow signs along V. Petrarca to reach **Taverna L'Arco Vecchio ❸,** at P. Archi di Ciaccio, 21. Done up in elegant wood, this restaurant offers guests a range of salads (€6-8) and entrees in a garden dining area. Enjoy the marvelous location by the city's old arch and the large wine selection. (☎0984 72 564. *Primi* €5-8, *secondi* €5-11. Cover €1.50. Open M-Sa 1-3pm and 8-11pm. AmEx/MC/V.) Owned and operated by the same family since 1803, **Gran Caffé Renzelli ❶,** C. Telesio, 46, specializes in home-made sweets; their *varchiglia alla mocale* is a chocolate-covered almond treat made from a recipe from the 1300s. The "Gran Caffe" is as pretty as it is powerful, with steamed milk, coca, and *vov,* an egg liqueur. (☎0984 26 814; www. grancaffer-enzelli.it. Mini pizza *rustica* €1.03. *Gelato* €2.60. Cover €0.52. Open M-F and Su 8am-midnight, Sa noon-midnight. Closed W in winter. Cash only.) On a warm summer night, head to **Per...Bacco!! ❸,** P. dei Valdesi, 3. This outdoor wine bar/restaurant dishes up specialties in a tree-lined *piazza.* (☎0984 79 55 69; www.perbaccowine bar.it. *Primi* €5, *secondi* €7-11. Live music Tu-F in summer. Open M-Sa 1-3pm and 8pm-midnight.) To reach **Da Giocondo ❷,** V. Piave, 53, turn left off of C. Mazzini on V. Piave and walk two blocks. This three-room restaurant beams with local charm. Bow-tied waiters serve fresh fish, regional specialties, and tasty fruit desserts to complement a long wine list. (☎0984 29 810. *Primi* from €4, *secondi* from €5. Cover €2. Open M-Sa noon-3pm and 7-10pm. AmEx/MC/V.)

👁 SIGHTS

CHIESA DI SAN FRANCESCO D'ASSISI. This small church's plain exterior, rebuilt after an earthquake in 1854, hides a lavish but somewhat worn Baroque interior. In the far right aisle, a portal leads to the main attraction, the ornate **Cappella di Santa Caterina,** which is graced by the paintings of Flemish artist William Borremons. Behind the altar, a wooden tomb puts the angelic but shriveled body of a 500-year-old Franciscan monk on full display. The chambers above, accessible by a stairway from the adjoining sacristy, reveal views of the city. They aren't generally open to the public, so ask church officials nicely. (☎*0984 75 522. Cross Ponte Mario Martiri, turn left up narrow C. Telesio to the duomo. Continue on C. Telesio just past the cathedral's facade, then turn right on V. del Seggio. Turn right at the top; the church is around the corner. Open Tu-Su 10am-7:30pm. Free.)*

DUOMO. The *duomo* was erected in the middle of the 12th century with a Romanesque design, only to be almost entirely rebuilt in 1184 after another earthquake struck. When the *duomo* was reconsecrated in 1222 after an earthquake, Frederick II gave the city a gilt **Byzantine crucifix** containing a splinter said to be from the True Cross. Now the cross is in the Galleria Nazionale at the Palazzo Arnone. Call ahead to see it. Inside the *duomo* is Cosenza's most prized work of art after the famed cross: *La Madonna del Pilerio,* a 12th-century painting in the Byzantine style with influences from Sicily and Campania. It is in a Baroque chapel, the first on the left side of the church entrance. The next chapel belongs to the *Arciconfraternità della Morte* (Archbrotherhood of Death). This religious order was charged by ancient privilege to aid those condemned to death. Many *Cosentini* executed for their part in the Risorgimento are buried in this humble chapel near Isabella of Aragon, on the right side of the cathedral. *(Cross Ponte Mario Martiri into the old city, and head left up C. Telesio. Or take bus #22 or 23 to P. Prefettura, and facing away from P. del Governo, turn right down C. Telesio. Open mornings and late afternoons. For the cross, go to the Palazzo Arnone on V. Gravina, but call ☎0984 79 56 39 ahead.)*

CASTELLO NORMANNO-SVEVO (NORMAN CASTLE). This fairy-tale structure on a hill high above the city predates most of the *centro storico* and, in its ruined state, provides a meditative testament to the city's tumultuous past. Originally built by the Saracens but refurbished by Frederick II after the *Cosentini* tried to overthrow him, the castle offers views of the city. Now serene and barely visited, the castle has functioned as a barracks, a prison, and a seminary. Earthquakes have destroyed many of the ornaments, but its columns and long, high-ceilinged halls remain. *(Take bus #22 or 23 to P. Prefettura, and facing Teatro Rendano, walk up the stairs to the left of the theater about 200m, going left at the P. Archi di Ciaccio and continuing up the stairs opposite Taverna L'Arco Vecchio. Or take bus 4T to the elevated village and follow signs 10-15min. uphill. The climb is steep; bring water on hot days. Open daily 8am-8pm. Free.)*

TEATRO RENDANO. Calabria's most prestigious performance venue, this theater was constructed in 1895 and destroyed by WWII bombing. It has since been restored to its former glory and its plush interior has even showcased the likes of José Carreras. Reservations for non-*Calabresi* or unconnected foreigners are extremely difficult to get during the opera season (Oct.-Dec.); seats for the theater season (Jan.-May) may be somewhat easier to come by. The Rendano also hosts regional performance groups during the summer, with readily available tickets. *(Behind the statue of Telesio in P. Prefettura. ☎0984 81 32 20. For plays, tickets may be available 10am-1pm and 5-8pm on day of performance, but availability can't be checked by phone. From €18. Student discounts.)*

◪ NIGHTLIFE

Cosenza is the center of action for smaller towns. ◪**Beat Pub,** P. Duomo, 4/6, right next to the *duomo*, is huge, with more than 50 Belgian beers to choose from (€4). There is also live music on Thursdays and Fridays in the winter. (☎0984 22 799.

Open daily 7:30pm-3am. AmEx/MC/V.) **Planet Alex,** P. XI Settembre, 12, off C. Mazzini, is a disco-pub in the new city that blasts DJ music until late. (☎0984 79 53 37. DJs F-Su. Open M-F, Su 1-3pm and daily 6:30pm-3am.) Get a taste of the Emerald Isle at the **J. Joyce Irish Pub,** V. Cafarone, 19, a lively bar that's packed on the weekends. (☎0984 22 799. Open daily from 8pm. AmEx/MC/V.)

CAMIGLIATELLO AND SILA MASSIF ☎0984

"Its nature will amaze you," a billboard near Sila's train station proudly states. Indeed, the Sila wilderness is an untainted landscape of fertile green, with lakes, mountains, and woods that burst with wildflowers in the spring. Covering the widest part of the Calabrian peninsula, the Sila was once a huge forest, exploited from its earliest days to provide fuel and material for the buildings and fleets of Rome. Today, the cutting of trees is rigidly controlled, and the area offers some of Italy's most spectacular natural settings and a wealth of activities to satisfy intrepid explorers. Camigliatello, a resort town with many bus connections and access to hikes and ski slopes, is the best base in the Sila.

◧⃰ TRANSPORTATION AND PRACTICAL INFORMATION. FS trains run from Cosenza (1½hr., 9:18am, €1.91), but their schedules are fairly erratic, so **buses** from Cosenza **Autostazione** are usually the most reliable form of transport (40min., 9 per day 6:30am-7pm, €1.91). Find bus hours at the tourist office and buy tickets at Bar Pedace, the bar closest to the bus stop. **Maps** and information on Sila and surrounding attractions, events, and trails can be found at the **Pro Loco Tourist Office,** V. Roma, 5, uphill from the train station and bus stop. (☎0984 57 81 59. Open daily 9am-1pm and 3:30-7pm.) **Banca Carime** is at V. del Turismo, 73. (☎0984 57 80 27. Open M-F 8:30am-1:20pm and 2:35-3:35pm.) For **medical emergencies,** call ☎0984 57 83 28. Camigliatello's **post office,** on V. Tasso, is at the intersection of V. del Turismo and V. Roma, next to Hotel Tasso. (☎0984 57 80 76. Open M-Sa 8am-1pm.)

▞◩ ACCOMMODATIONS AND FOOD. Hotel Meranda ❸, V. del Turismo, 29, offers modern rooms in a secluded area off the main road. Facilities include an elegant restaurant/bar and *discoteca*. (☎0984 57 80 22, fax 0984 57 92 93. Singles €28-40; doubles with half pension €34-60, with full pension €39-60. Extra bed €35-52.) **B&B Villa Guido ❸,** V. Napoli, 19, in Moccone, is 1.5km up the road from V. Roma. At the intersection with Moccone, turn right and follow the signs—call ahead for pick-up from Camigliatello. Four doubles and a four-bed suite for families, all with bath and TV, share a balcony and living room. (☎0984 57 80 66; www.villaguido.it. Breakfast included. Closed Nov. Singles €40; doubles €60. Cashes only.) Buses run from Camigliatello to **La Fattoria ❶** campsite, 5km from Camigliatello, near a vineyard. (☎0984 57 83 64. Tent provided. €5.60 per person. Cash only.)

Le **Tre Lanterne ❸,** V. Roma, 142, is a popular spot that specializes in *funghi porcini* (€9). (☎0984 57 82 03. Pizza from €3.50. *Primi* from €5, *secondi* from €8. Cover €1.50. Open Tu-Su 10:30am-3:30pm and 7-11:30pm. AmEx/MC/V.) For mushrooms, mushrooms, and more mushrooms, visit **La Casa del Fungo ❷,** on P. Misasil, at the op of V. Roma. They also serve meat, cheese, and a few dishes that do not include mushrooms. (☎0984 57 80 00. Open M and W-Su 9am-8:30pm.) Dine by lantern light at **Ristorante Hotel Lo Sciatore ❷,** V. Roma, 128, an upscale restaurant with a ski-lodge feel which serves creamy mushroom *risotto*. (☎0984 57 81 05. Wood-stove pizza from €2.60. *Primi* from €4.50, *secondi* from €4. Cover €1.60. Open daily 12:30-3pm and 7:30-10pm. AmEx/MC/V.) There are also a number of *salumerie* that overflow with cheeses, cured meats, and marinated mushrooms. Picnic grounds lie 10min. from the *centro*, up V. Tasso past the post office.

⚠️🎿 OUTDOORS AND SKIING. Want snow? There's plenty of it at the **Tasso Monte Curcio Ski Trail**, 2km from town up V. Roma and left at Hotel Tasso. Go right at the fork in the road. In winter, minibuses leave for the trailhead from Camigliatello's bus stop. Buy tickets onboard. Though Tasso offers 35km of cross-country skiing, it has only two downhill trails that are 2km each. (☎0984 57 81 36 or 0984 57 94 00. When snow is on the ground, lifts are open daily 8am-5pm. Round-trip lift ticket €4, weekends €5; full-day pass €15/20.) Getting to the **Parco Nazionale di Calabria** (☎0984 57 97 57), 10km northwest, is more tricky; just two buses head into the park daily, in the morning and afternoon, at varying times. **Altipiani**, V. Corado, 20 (☎0984 57 81 54; www.inaltipiani.it), offers guided tours of the park in Italian to large groups, as well as moonlit bikes trips. Arrange times and prices through reservation. Altipiani also rents bikes (€5 per hr., €18 per day; discount for multi-day rental) and snowshoes (€5 per hr., €12 per day; discount for multi-day rental).

TROPEA   ☎0963

Resounding with the crash of waves against imposing rock faces, the ancient buildings and rock-hewn grandeur of Tropea are the stuff of dreams. Poised at the edge of a severe precipice, the town's winding streets create a maze of hidden *piazze* and dignified churches. Though empty during the day when the beach's white sands beckon, these streets flood after sundown with a carnival-like procession of bronzed vacationers in skimpy designer wear, cradling creamy *gelato* cups that somehow never settle on their thighs. Tropea's traditional (if anomalous) dual claims to fame were its nobility and its red onions; the nobility has long since withered, but the onions remain as potent as the summer sun.

📇📞 TRANSPORTATION AND PRACTICAL INFORMATION. Trains run from the Reggio train station (2hr., 10 per day, €5). There are three direct returns to Reggio; all others change at **Rosarno**. As the station has no ticket office, buy tickets at **Valentour**, P. V. Veneto, 17. (☎0963 62 516. Open M-Sa 9am-1pm and 4-10pm, Su 6-10pm). **AutolineeSav** (☎0963 61 129) operates convenient *pullmini* (little blue buses) that pick up passengers on V. Stazione every 30min. The vans (€0.83-€1) travel 27 routes, going as far as 24km afield; they are often the easiest way to access some of the more remote attractions around Tropea. For exact stops, ask the English-speaking staff at the **Pro Loco Tourist Office,** down V. Stazione at P. Ercole. (☎0963 61 475. Open June-Oct. daily 9am-1pm and 4:30-8:30pm; Nov.-May. M-Sa 10am-noon and 4-7:30pm.) **Banca Carime,** on V. Stazione, has an **ATM** and **currency-exchange** machine. (Open M-F 8:20am-1:20pm and 2:35-3:35pm.) In case of **emergency,** call the **police** (☎113 or 0963 60 42 11) or the **carabinieri** (☎112 or 0963 61 018). For an **ambulance,** call ☎0963 61 366. From the Pro Loco, walk up C. V. Emanuele through P. Ercole, **Internet,** at **Quelila,** is on the left. If you've walked off the cliff and plummeted into the ocean, you've gone too far. (Open M-Sa 10am-1pm and 5pm-midnight, Su 5pm-midnight.) The **post office** is on C. Rigna. (☎0963 60 44 49. Open M-F 8am-1:30pm, Sa 8am-12:30pm.) **Postal Code:** 89861.

🏠🍴 ACCOMMODATIONS AND FOOD. To reach 📷**Da Litto di Anne Lise Moisan ❷,** V. Carmine, 25, walk 10min. uphill along hairpin-curves or call in advance to be picked up. Each bungalow in the garden has a patio, kitchen, and TV. (☎0963 60 33 42. Reserve in advance. Sept.-June €18 per person. July and late-Aug. €34. Early Aug. €47.) For camping by the sea, try the shaded **Campeggio Marina dell'Isola ❶,** on V. Marina dell'Isola, at the bottom of the stairs leading to the beach. (☎0963 61 970, in winter 0963 60 31 28; www.maregrande.it. €6 per person. Electricity €7. Prices vary seasonally. Free hot showers. AmEx/MC/V.)

Tropea's red onions and pepper-hot cheeses spice up local dishes, along with the famous *Vecchio Amaro del Capo*. **La Boheme ❸,** V. Roma, 21, has seating beneath the *duomo*. (☎0963 60 30 53. *Primi* €6-8, *secondi* €7-12. Cover €1.50. Open daily noon-3pm and 7pm-midnight. AmEx/MC/V.) Head to the elegant **Pimm's Restaurant ❹,** Largo Migliarese, next to the lookout at the end of C. V. Emanuele, to dine to the sound of waves crashing over the shoreline. (☎0963 66 61 05. *Primi* from €8, *secondi* €10-18. Cover €2.50. Open in summer daily 12:30-2:30pm and 7:30-11pm; in winter Tu-Su 12:30-2:30pm and 7:30-11pm. MC/V.) **Ristorante Porta Vaticana ❸,** through the gate on V. Regina Margherita, serves enticing *risotto afrodite* (€7.50). (☎0963 60 33 87. Cover €1.50. *Primi* from €5.70, *secondi* from €6.50. Open daily Feb.-Oct. noon-3pm and 7:30pm-midnight. MC/V.) **Night and Day ❷,** V. Umberto I, serves a variety of *panini*, crepes (€4-7), and alcohol right in the middle of tourist mayhem. (Wine by the glass €2.50. Beer from €3. Cocktails €4-5. Meal-size salads €8.50. Open June-Sept. daily 10am-6pm.) En route to the beach, grab a sandwich and a cool drink at the **Alimentari Pandullo Marco ❶,** Largo S. Michele, 20, on V. Stazione across from V. Umberto I.

◧◪ SIGHTS AND BEACHES. The gleaming **Santuario di Santa Maria dell'Isola** presides over the white cliffs at the edge of town. Featured on postcards sold from Reggio to Cosenza, the church's sequestered beauty and historical significance warrant the fierce local pride. To honor the Madonna, townsmen take the church's *Holy Family* statues out to sea every August 15 in a procession of hundreds of small boats. The naval parade tours nearby towns and ends with a display of fireworks in the evening. (Sanctuary open daily 9:30am-noon and 2:30-8:30pm. No swimwear allowed. Church €1, museum and terrace €0.50.) Up the cliff is Tropea's graceful **Norman cathedral.** Besides some elegant polychrome marble work and several sword-bearing dead *Tropeani*, the interior houses two bombs that miraculously failed to destroy Tropea when an American warplane dropped them in 1943. To reach the **beach,** take a winding set of stairs down the cliffs at the end of V. Umberto (turn off C. V. Emanuele to the left).

SICILY (SICILIA)

An island of contradictions, Sicily's complex culture is the result of a millennia of diverse influences. Sicily has either owned or been owned by every great Mediterranean empire since the arrival of the Phoenicians in 900 BC. Greek dominance followed, and Sicily soon sported more Greeks and Greek temples than Greece itself. Roman theaters, Arab mosques, and Norman cathedrals round out the physical remnants of the island's ancient diversity. The island's separation from the mainland is a literal reinforcement of its residents' determined independence, assimilating foreign influences into a unique cultural pastiche. Ancient Greeks lauded the golden island as the second home of the gods, but it is better known to many of today's tourists as the home of *The Godfather*. While the Mafia remains an unspoken presence in Sicilian society, its power has weakened in recent years, and represents only one minor element in the island's complex cultural tapestry. Under the ominous shadow of Mt. Etna, chic resorts, archaeological treasures, and fast-paced urban cities welcome adventurous travelers to this enigmatic island.

HIGHLIGHTS OF SICILY

BASK in the glow of Byzantine gold at Monreale Cathedral near **Palermo** (p. 654).

FLIT between visions of paradise as you choose a favorite **Aeolian isle** (p. 663).

SCALE famed **Mt. Etna** (p. 689) in the morning and party all night in **Catania** (p. 689).

COMMUNE with the sultry spendors of **Pantelleria's azure-lapped shores** (p. 719).

PALERMO
☎ 091

Simultaneously turbulent, exquisite, and intense, Italy's 5th largest city is a strangely alluring mix of beauty and decay. A gritty metropolis with over one million inhabitants, Palermo's pace of life dispels any myth of a sleepy Sicily, with its racing stream of cars, buses, and scooters setting the city's breakneck pace. Those who do opt to slow down will be amply rewarded with its impressive sights, living relics of past *Palermitano* grandeur. While poverty, bombings, and centuries of neglect have taken their toll on much of Palermo, the city is currently experiencing a revival. The 1993 election of an anti-Mafia mayor brought an end to the mob's knee-bashing control, and with political cleanup underway, Palermo is now at work restoring its architectural treasures.

✈ INTERCITY TRANSPORTATION

Flights: Falcone Borsellino Airport at Punta Raisi (☎848 86 56 43), 30min. from central Palermo. Prestia & Comande (☎091 58 04 57) runs buses every 30min. from P. Castelnuovo (45min.) and Stazione Centrale (1hr., €4.65). Taxis (☎091 59 16 62) charge at least €30-50 and are parked outside the airport. Look for the "shuttle to trains" sign. Free shuttles run every 10-20min. to and from the nearby train station at Punto Raisi. At the station, head left and down the escalator. Trains to Stazione Centrale run every 30min. from 4am-10pm (€4.85).

Trains: Stazione Centrale, in P. Giulio Cesare. At the foot of V. Roma and V. Maqueda. Ticket office (☎091 60 31 111) open 6:45am-8:40pm. **Luggage storage** available (see **Practical Information**, p. 651. To: **Agrigento** (2hr., 14 per day 7:35am-8:20pm, €6.60); **Catania** (3½hr., 9 per day 5:55am-8:45pm, €11); **Messina** (3½hr., 14 per day 4am-

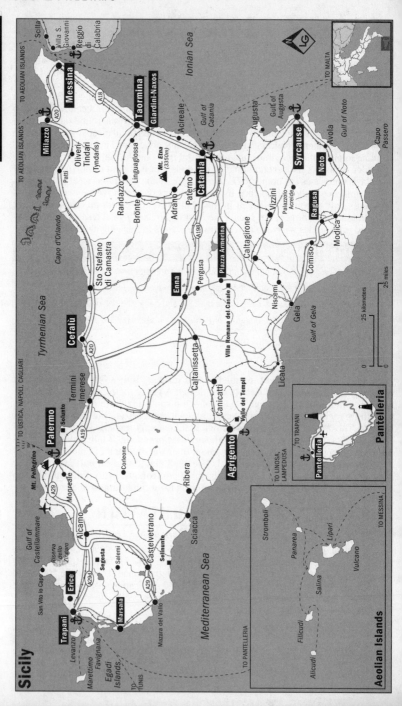

SICILY

Sicily

Tyrrhenian Sea

Gulf of Castellammare

San Vito lo Capo

Riserva dello Zingaro

✈ Trapani ⚓
Levanzo
Favignana
Egadi Islands
Maretimo
TO TUNIS

Erice
✈
Marsala
Mazara del Vallo

Segesta
Salemi
Selinunte
Castelvetrano

Alcamo
Monreale
A29
A29

Corleone

Ribera

Sciacca

Mediterranean Sea

Mt. Pellegrino ▲
✈ ⚓ Palermo
A19
Solunto ▪
Termini Imerese
A20

Cefalù
A20

Sto Stefano di Camastra
Patti
Capo d'Orlando

Oliveri Tindari (Tyndaris)
Milazzo ⚓
TO AEOLIAN ISLANDS
TO AEOLIAN ISLANDS
Messina ⚓
Villa S. Giovanni ⚓
Scilla
Reggio di Calabria

A18
Taormina
Giardini-Naxos
Acireale

Randazzo
Linguaglossa
▲ Mt. Etna (3350m)
Bronte
Adrano
Palermo
Catania ⚓ ✈

Gulf of Catania

Ionian Sea

A198

Enna
Pergusa
Piazza Armerina
Villa Romana del Casale ▪

Caltanissetta
Canicatti
Valle dei Templi ▪
Agrigento ⚓
TO LINOSA, LAMPEDUSA

Licata
Gela
Gulf of Gela

Nisċemi
Caltagirone
Comiso
Modica
Ragusa
Vizzini
Palazzolo Acreide

Noto
Avola
Capo Passero

Syrcause ⚓
Augusta
Gulf of Augusta
Gulf of Noto

TO USTICA, NAPOLI, CAGLIARI

TO MALTA

N
LG

25 miles
25 kilometers
0
0

Pantelleria

TO TRAPANI
⚓ Pantelleria

TO PANTELLERIA

Aeolian Islands

Stromboli
Panarea
Lipari
Salina
Filicudi
Alicudi
Vulcano
TO MESSINA

Palermo

ACCOMMODATIONS
Campeggio
 dell'Ulivo, 18
Hotel Ariston, 5
Hotel Confort, 15
Hotel del Centro, 17
Hotel Moderno, 11
Hotel Regina, 12
Hotel Sicilia, 16

FOOD
Antica Focacceria
 San Francesco, 13
Hostaria al Duar, 2
Il Mirto e la Rosa, 3
Lo Sparviero, 6
Margo' Ristorante/
 Pizzeria, 10
Pizzeria Bellini, 14
Renna Self Service, 4
Sesto Canto, 7

NIGHTLIFE
I Candelai, 9
Via di Mezzo Librothèca, 8
Volo, 1

SICILY

SPARE SOME CHANGE. When purchasing train tickets at the Stazione Centrale, avoid using large bills if possible, as the machine gives change back up to only €4.50. If your change exceeds €4.50, you will receive a ticket which is credited to that amount and can be used in the machine at a later date.

8:45pm, €10.20); **Milazzo** (3hr., 15 per day 4am-8:45pm, €9.20); **Falcone Borsellino Airport** (40min., 23 per day 4:45am-10:10pm, €4.50); **Rome** (11hr., 9 per day 4am-8:45pm, €45); **Trapani** (2½hr., 10 per day 6:40am-8:40pm, €6.85).

Buses: All 4 lines run along V. P. Balsamo, by the train station. Facing away from the tracks, turn right; exit with McDonald's on the left and newsstands on the right; V. P. Balsamo is straight ahead, hidden by an army of buses. When purchasing tickets, ask exactly where your bus will be arriving and find out its logo.

Cuffaro, V. Balsamo, 13 (☎091 61 61 510). To **Agrigento** (2½hr.; M-Sa 7 per day 5:45am-8pm, Su 8am, noon, and 3:30pm; €7:20).

SAIS, V. Balsamo, 16 (☎091 61 66 028). To: **Catania** (3hr.) and **Catania Airport** (2½hr.; M-Th 14 per day, F 16 per day, Sa 13 per day 5am-8pm, Su 9 per day 8am-8pm; €12.50); **Messina** (3hr.; M-F 9 per day 5am-8pm, Sa 5 per day 9am-8pm, Su 4 per day 9am-8pm; €13.30); **Piazza Armerina** (2½hr.; M-F 8 per day, Sa 4 per day 6:15am-8pm, Su 4 per day 9am-8pm; €7).

Segesta, V. Balsamo, 14 (☎091 61 69 039). Buses marked "Sicilbus," "EtnaTransport," or "Interbus." To: **Alcamo** (1hr.; M-F 10 per day 6:30am-8pm, Sa 8 per day 6:30am-8pm, Su 11:30am and 8pm; €5.20, round-trip €7.90); **Rome** (12hr.; Th and Su from Politeama 6:30pm, from Stazione Centrale 6:40pm, Sa 7:45am from Politeama, 8am from Stazione Centrale; €45, round-trip €76.50); **Terrasini** (1hr.; M-Sa 6 per day 6:30am-8pm, Su 11:30am and 8pm; €2.60, round-trip €4.20); **Trapani** (2hr.; M-F 27 per day 6:00am-9pm, Sa every hr., Su 5pm and 9pm; €7.80).

Ferries and Hydrofoils:

Grimaldi Group (☎091 58 74 04; www.gnv.it), on the waterfront on V. del Mare, off V. Francesco Crispi. These luxury ships have gyms and discos. Ticket office open M-F 8:45am-1pm, 2:15pm departure; Sa 9am-noon, 4:30pm departure; Su 4:30pm departure. Ferries to **Civitavecchia** (12hr.; Tu 10pm, Th 11pm, Su 6:30pm; €43-65) and **Genoa** (20hr., summer daily 8:30pm, €63-100). Check ahead, as schedules are likely to change.

Siremar, V. Francesco Crispi, 118 (☎091 58 24 03), on the last street before the waterfront, between V. A. Gravina and V. E. Amari, runs ferries to (2½hr.; M-Sa 9am, Su 8:15am; €10.60, July-Aug. €11.60). Also runs hydrofoils June-Sept. (1¼hr., M-Th and Sa 8:15am and 5:15pm, F and Su 8:15am, 3:30 and 7pm, €16.80). Ticket office open daily 8:30am-1pm and 4-6:30pm. €1.50 surcharge per ticket for reservations. Leaves from Stazione Marittima.

Tirrenia (☎091 60 21 111), 100m south of Grimaldi, next to the parking lot. Open M-F 8:30am-12:30pm and 3:30-8:45pm, Sa 3:30-8:45pm, Su 5-8:45pm. Ferries to **Naples** (10hr.; Oct.-May 8:15pm, June 8:45pm; €35-80) and **Cagliari, Sardinia** (14hr.; Oct.-July 15 Sa 7pm, July 15-Aug. Sa 5pm; €30-60).

Ustica (☎091 33 33 33) runs hydrofoils twice a day to the **Aeolian Islands.** Ticket office at end of Stazione Marittima. Open daily 9am-1pm and 5-7pm. All hydrofoils stop in: **Alicudi** (2½hr.; €19.60, in winter €17.60); **Filicudi** (3hr., €25.10/22.60); **Lipari** (4hr., €31.30/28.20); **Salina** (3½hr., €30.40/27.40); and **Vulcano** (4½hr.; summer daily 7am and 4:45pm, winter M, W, and F 7am; €31.30/28.20).

✚ ORIENTATION

Palermo's newer half follows a grid pattern, but older sections to the south, near the **train station,** form a tangled knot. The train station dominates **Piazza Giulio Cesare,** from which two primary streets define Palermo's central axis. **Via Roma** begins directly across the *piazza* from the front of the station and runs the length of the old city, ending at V. E. Amari, just to the right of the **Politeama.** On the left side of P. Giulio Cesare, facing out from the front of the station, and running parallel to V. Roma, **Via Maqueda** meets **Via Vittorio Emanuele** at the **Quattro Canti,** and this intersection forms the center of the old city. Continuing up V. Maqueda will take you to **Piazza Verdi** and **Teatro Massimo.** Turning right at P. Verdi on **Via Cavour** will take you past V. Roma and out to the port. At P. Verdi, V. Maqueda becomes **Via Ruggero Settimo,** which leads to **Piazza Castelnuovo** and the Politeama. From there V. Ruggero becomes **Via della Libertà** and leads to the **Giardino Inglese.**

🄴 LOCAL TRANSPORTATION

Public Transportation: Orange **AMAT city buses.** Main terminal in front of Stazione Centrale, under dark green overhang. Tickets €1 per 2hr., €3.35 per day. Buy tickets from *tabaccherie* or ticket booths. Pick up a free **transit map** from the tourist office or any AMAT info booth. Most bus stops are labeled and have route maps posted. Palermo also has the **Metropolitana** subway system, but it's usually faster to take a bus or even walk.

Taxis: Station office ☎091 61 62 001. **Autoradio** ☎091 51 27 27. **RadioTaxi** ☎091 22 54 55, in front of Stazione Centrale, next to the bus stop.

PRACTICAL INFORMATION

TOURIST AND FINANCIAL SERVICES

Tourist Office: P. Castelnuovo, 34, in the Banco di Sicilia building (☎091 60 58 111; www.palermotourism.com). **Maps,** brochures, and *Agenda,* a seasonal information packet. Open year-round M-F 8:30am-2pm and 2:30-6pm. Branches at the train station (☎091 61 65 914) and the airport (☎091 59 16 98; open daily 8:30am-8pm).

Consular Services: UK, V. C. Cavour, 117 (☎091 32 64 12). Open daily 10am-noon. **US,** V. G. B. Vaccarini, 1 (☎091 30 58 57). Emergencies only. Open M-F 9am-12:30pm.

Currency Exchange: *Cambio* at the central post office and train station. **Banca Nazionale del Lavoro,** V. Roma, 201, and **Banco di Sicilia,** on V. R. Settimo, both open M-F 8:20am-1:20pm. **ATMs** can be found on V. Roma and V. Maqueda; the Bancomat 3-plus ATMs are newer and sometimes more reliable.

American Express: G. Ruggieri and Figli Travel, V. E. Amari, 40 (☎091 58 71 44). From P. Castelnuovo (Politeama), follow V. E. Amari toward the water. Cashes **Traveler's Cheques** for cardholders only. Ask for the red city map *Palermo in Your Pocket.* Open M-F 9am-1pm and 4-7pm, Sa 9am-1pm.

LOCAL SERVICES

Luggage Storage: In the train station at track #8. €3.80 per bag for the first 5hr., €0.60 each additional hr. up to 12hr., €0.20 each additional hr. Open daily 6am-midnight.

English-Language Bookstore: Libreria Feltrinelli, V. Maqueda, 395 (☎091 58 77 85), a few blocks before Teatro Massimo from the train station. An impressive selection of classics and bestsellers. Open Sept.-June M-Sa 9am-8pm, Su 10am-1:30pm and 5-8pm; July-Aug. M-Sa 9am-1pm and 4-8pm.

EMERGENCY AND COMMUNICATIONS

Emergency: ☎113. **Carabinieri:** ☎112. **Ambulance:** ☎118.

Police, V. Dogali, 29 (☎113 or 091 69 54 111).

Pharmacy: Lo Cascio, V. Roma, 1 (☎091 61 62 117). Look for green cross near the train station. Open 24hr. except 1-4:30pm. **Di Naro,** V. Roma, 207 (☎091 58 58 69), on the right after C. V. Emanuele. Open M-F 8:30am-1pm and 4-8pm.

Hospital: Policlinico Universitario, V. del Vespro, 127 (☎091 65 51 111), or **Ospedale Civico,** V. C. Lazzaro (☎091 66 61 111; in case of emergency 091 60 62 243), near the station.

Internet Access: Aboriginal Internet C@fé, V. Spinuzza, 51 (☎091 66 22 229, www.aboriginalcafe.com), across P. Verdi from the Teatro Massimo, look for the "Internet Point" sign. Photos of the Outback and shark jaws adorn this Internet hangout. (20min. minimum €1, €3.50 per hr. Student discounts before 8pm. Open daily 10am-3am.) Among a multitude of no-frills internet points scattered around the city, the best is **Centro Internet Point,** V. V. Emanuele, 304 (☎091 61 14 559), with 7 new and fast computers. (15min. minimum €0.50, €2 per hr.)

Post Office: V. Roma, 322 (☎091 160 or 091 75 31 111). Massive white-columned building 5 blocks up V. Roma past V. V. Emanuele. Open M-Sa 8am-6:30pm. Branch: Stazione Centrale (☎091 61 75 357), to the right of the station, beside the tracks. Open M-F 8am-6:30pm, Sa 8am-12:30pm. **Postal Code:** 90100.

⌐ ACCOMMODATIONS AND CAMPING

When it comes to finding a place to stay, Palermo is pricey. For the sake of comfort and, more importantly, safety, plan on spending a little more in Palermo and budget your trip accordingly.

Hotel Sicilia, V. Divisi, 39, 1st. fl. (☎091 61 68 460). From P. Giulio Cesare, 5 blocks up V. Maqueda on the right. Marble staircases lead you to Palermo's best deal: all rooms have bathroom, A/C, TV, balcony, high arched ceilings and breakfast included. €40 per person. Internet available for €8 per hr. Curfew 2am. Apr.-Oct. singles €45; doubles €72; triples €84. Nov.-Mar. singles €39/62/70. ❹

Hotel del Centro, V. Roma, 72, 2nd fl. (☎091 61 70 376; www.hoteldelcentro.it), 5 blocks up V. Roma from the station. Rooms have towering ceilings, classy curtains, and cream-colored details. Bath, A/C, and free Internet and wi-fi. Breakfast included. Singles €48-62; doubles €72-85. Extra bed 35% more per person. Cash only. ❺

Hotel Regina, C. V. Emanuele, 316 (☎091 61 14 216; www.hotelreginapalermo.it), at the intersection of V. Maqueda and C. V. Emanuele, across from the larger Hotel Centrale. Near the old city. Carved bureaus and glass globe lighting fixtures adorn pastel rooms, 3 of which have balconies. Be sure to double-check your reservation before arriving. TV in lobby. Beach passes available. Singles €23, with bath €37; doubles €42/50, triples with bath €72. Credit card required for reservation. AmEx/MC/V. ❷

Hotel Ariston, V. M. Stabile, 139, 6th fl. (☎091 33 24 34). Take V. Roma 4 blocks past V. Cavour, or bus #122 from the station and get off before V. Amari. Between Teatro Massimo and the Politeama. 7 bright, modern rooms in minimalist style have bath, A/C, and TV. 1st night must be paid with reservation. Singles €40; doubles €60. AmEx/MC/V. ❸

Hotel Moderno, V. Roma, 276 (☎091 58 86 83 or 091 58 82 60; fax 091 58 86 83), at V. Napoli. Quiet rooms with somewhat plain decor. All but 3 have windows that open to silent inner courtyard. Bath, A/C, and TV. Bar and communal TV room. Breakfast included. Singles €55; doubles €75; triples €95; quads €105. AmEx/MC/V. ❹

Hotel Confort, V. Roma, 188 (☎091 32 43 62; fax 091 33 17 41). From the station, on the left side of V. Roma just past V. Divisi. Simply furnished rooms with dark wood-paneling, shared bath, and a location so central you'll want earplugs to block the noise. TV lounge by front desk. 1am curfew. Singles €25; doubles €39-45. Cash only. ❷

Campeggio dell'Ulivo, V. Pegaso, 25 (☎/fax 091 53 30 21), 35min. outside Palermo. Take bus #101 from Palermo's central station to P. de Gasperi; then take bus #628 to V. Sferracavallo. Walk downhill a block and turn right on V. dei Manderini just after the post office. Campground is on the right. Free hot showers. €7 per person. Tent rental €5 per day. Double bungalows €25, quads €40. Cash only. ❶

◖ FOOD

The best restaurants in town are between Teatro Massimo and the Politeama. Palermo's bustling markets provide fresher and more interesting selections than most supermarkets. **Ballarò** sprawls through the streets behind V. Maqueda and C. V. Emanuele, while **Capo** covers the streets behind Teatro Massimo. **Vucciria** completes the trio in the area between C. V. Emanuele and P. S. Domenico. All three are open Monday through Saturday during daylight hours. Saturday morning is most chaotic. Try *Palermitano* specialty *cassata*, a sweet ricotta pastry. If you don't feel like haggling, however, head to **Supermercato GS**, Salita Partanna, 1. In P. Marina with Villa Garibaldi on your left, walk straight toward Chiesa di. S. Maria dei Miracoli; turn right when you get there. (Open M-Sa 8:30am-8pm.)

Sesto Canto, V. S. Oliva, 26 (☎091 33 68 36), from V. Ruggero facing P. Castelnuovo, turn left and walk into P. S. Oliva, continue toward the Villa Fillipina; Sesto Canto will be around the corner on the left. Taking their restaurant's name from Dante's *Divine Comedy*, the Serafino sisters serve heavenly gluten-free cuisine. From the sesame salmon to the steak filet smothered in melted *formaggio*, the menu usually satisfies even the pickiest gourmands. *Antipasti* €4-8, *primi* €7-11, *secondi* €12-15. Cover €1.50. Open Tu-Sa 10am-2:30pm and 7pm-midnight, Su 10am-2:30pm. AmEx/MC/V. ❹

Pizzeria Bellini, P. Bellini, 6 (☎091 61 65 691), to the left of P. Pretoria. Outdoor seating among the ancient beauties of Palermo makes this restaurant an ideal spot for a romantic meal. Try their superb *granita (*€3). Pizza €4-7.50. *Primi* €6-8, *secondi* €7-13. Cover €1.50. Open daily noon-midnight. ❸

Lo Sparviero, V. Sperlinga, 23/25 (☎/fax 091 33 11 63), 1 block toward P. Politeama from Teatro Massimo, on the left. Shrouded in antique decor, this local secret serves classic Sicilian cuisine beneath a mounted ram's head. Varied salad options in large portions make interesting vegetarian choices (€4.50). Pizza from €4. *Primi* €5.50-8, *secondi* €6.50-13. Cover €1. Open daily 11am-midnight. AmEx/MC/V. ❸

Il Mirto e la Rosa, V. Principe di Granatelli, 30 (☎091 32 43 53; info@ilmirtoelarosa.com). Traditional fare (including many vegetarian options) amid elegant arches. Try *fettuccine al profumo d'estate* (sauce of tomatoes, pine nuts, peppers, garlic, and basil; €7). *Primi* from €7, vegetarian *secondi* from €5, fish and meat *secondi* from €10. *Menù* €13-21. Open M-Sa 12:30-3pm and 7:30-11pm. AmEx/MC/V. ❸

Margo' Ristorante/Pizzeria, P. Sant'Onofrio, 3 (☎091 61 18 230). Follow Vco. dei Giovenchi off V. Maqueda, opposite intersection of V. Maqueda and V. Bari. Professional staff and upscale environment of rough-cut rock walls and tranquil music. Try specialty *ravioli di cernia, spada, e crema di asparagi* (€8.50). Pizza €4-8. *Primi* €5.50-8.50, *secondi* from €8. Cover €2. Open Tu-Su 8pm-1am. AmEx/MC/V. ❸

Antica Focacceria San Francesco, V. A. Paternostro, 58 (☎091 32 02 64), from V. Roma, take V. V. Emanuele toward the port and turn right on V. Alessandro Paternostro. This expansive *focacceria* has served delighted patrons in a secluded *piazza* since 1834. Behind the counter sits an infamous vat of *milza* (spleen). The brave can try it in a *panino* or with *maritata* cheese (€1.60), while the rest may choose from the extensive menu, featuring both standard Italian fare and options from around the world. 19 salads from €3.60. Self-service menu from €1.50. *Primi* from €4, *secondi* €8-19. Cover €2. Open daily 12:30-3:15pm and 7:45-11:15pm. AmEx/MC/V. ❸

Hostaria al Duar, V. Ammiraglio Gravina, 31 (☎0347 47 35 744 or 0347 70 17 848), off V. Roma, 3 blocks toward the port. Mix of Sicilian and Arabic flavors served on bright picnic tables. *Primi* from €3.50, *secondi* from €6.50. Tunisian *secondi* €2-6.20. Cover €1. Service 10%. Open daily 10am-3:30pm and 7pm-midnight. AmEx/MC/V. ❷

Renna Self-Service, V. Principe di Granatelli, 29 A/B/C (☎091 58 06 61; rennass@tin.it). Fast-food joint as crowded as a high school cafeteria, but Renna doesn't sacrifice the taste or portion size. *Primi* from €2, *secondi* from €3.40. Open M-Th and Sa noon-3:30pm and 7-10pm, F and Su noon-3:30pm. AmEx/MC/V. ❶

👁 SIGHTS

Ancient glory, centuries of neglect, and heavy bombing during WWII have made Palermo a city of splendor and degradation, where ancient and modern ruins stand side-by-side. For much of the 20th century, corrupt politicians and Mafia activity diverted funds and attention from dilapidated landmarks, but the political changes of recent years have made promising strides at cleaning and rebuilding.

SICILIAN STREET SMARTS. Be careful in Palermo. The city can feel deserted at any time of the day, and some of the streets, particularly in the helter-skelter old city south of Teatro Massimo, can be hard to navigate even in daylight. Have a clear idea of where you are headed at all times. Instead of navigating the streets with a map, break your journey into smaller, more digestible bits, setting landmarks as you go. When possible, stay on main streets: **Via Roma, Via Maqueda, Via Ruggero Settimo, Via della Libertà,** and **Via V. Emanuele.** These straight thoroughfares will keep you on track, and the stream of traffic, which continues well into the night, is reassuring.

MONREALE. Palermo's greatest treasure isn't in Palermo, but in little Monreale, just 8km outside the city. The extraordinary Cattedrale di Monreale is an example of Sicilian Norman architecture, mixing Arabic and local styles on the northern template. The interior, however, is a masterpiece of Byzantine design. Its walls glisten with 6340 sq. m of gold mosaics, the largest display of Byzantine religious art outside the Hagia Sofia. The series of panels over the main altar depicts the massive Christ Pantocrator, the mystical flavor of the locale emphasized by the minimal light from the cathedral's windows. Every few minutes someone pays €1 to activate electric lighting in a portion of the church, and the sudden illumination is startling. From the side entrance, Genesis appears at the upper left of the central aisle. The Old Testament narrative continues clockwise with images of Adam and Eve. The quiet **cloister** offers a contrast to the solemn shadows of the cathedral. Though seemingly empty, this courtyard contains one of the most unusual collections of Sicilian sculpture. Two hundred twenty-eight paired columns ring the interior columns alternating with ones decorated by Arabic tiles. Each capital is constructed in Greco-Roman, Islamic, Norman, Romanesque, and Gothic styles. A balcony along the cathedral's apse looks over the cloisters to all of Palermo. Two doors down from the cloister is the entrance to tranquil **gardens.** *(Bus #389 leaves from Palermo's P. Indipendenza for Monreale's P. V. Emanuele. 30min., 3 per hr., €1. To get to P. Indipendenza, take bus #109 or 318 from Palermo's Stazione Centrale. Tourist info to the left of the church ☎ 091 64 04 413. Cathedral open daily 8am-6:30pm. Free. Terrace open daily 8am-6:30pm. €1.50. Modest dress required. Cloister open M-Sa 9am-7pm. €6.)*

CAPPELLA PALATINA. This chapel, in the monstrous conglomerate **Palazzo dei Normanni,** houses a smaller version of the mosaics at Monreale. While one corner to the far left of the altar was designed by local artisans, Norman kings imported artists from Constantinople to cover every inch of the remaining interior with gold and azure. Locally crafted Arabic wall mosaics and ceiling designs complete the effect. Those who prefer this Christ Pantocrator over that of Monreale claim it is the softer and more compassionate of the two. Upstairs, guides lead tours of the **Sala di Ruggero,** every 20min. *(Take V. V. Emanuele past the cathedral on your right and through the Porta Nuova; take a left just before you get to P. Indipendenza. ☎ 091 70 54 879. Chapel open M-Sa 8:30am-noon and 2-5pm, Su 8:30am-12:30pm. Closed Easter M. M and F-Su entire palace €6, chapel €4, under 18 or over 65 €3, teachers and art/architecture students from most countries, but not the US, €3. Tu-Th entire palace €4, chapel €2.)*

TEATRO MASSIMO. Constructed between 1875 and 1897 in a Neo-Classical style, the **Teatro Massimo** is the second-largest indoor stage in Europe. After 30 years of renovation, the theater reopened for its 100th birthday in 1997 with typical Sicilian style: they shot a guy. No, just kidding, there were trumpets and confetti. (Incidentally, it was here that Francis Ford Coppola shot the climactic scene in *The Godfather: Part III.*) Guided tours allow visitors to repose in the VIP guest box and view the beautiful Morano flower light fixtures. Operas, plays, and ballets are performed here all year, while the **Festival della Verdura** brings famous performers in late summer. In this period, shows move from the Massimo to nearby Villa Castelnuovo. *(On P. Verdi. From Quattro Canti walk up V. Maqueda. ☎800 65 58 58 or 091 60 90 831, box office 091 60 53 555. Open Tu-Su 10am-4pm for 20min. tours in English, French, and German. Last tour 3:30pm. €3, under 18 or over 65 €2, under 6 free. No entry during rehearsals.)*

MUSEO ARCHEOLOGICO ANTONINO SALINAS.
Housed in a quiet *palazzo* in the town center, this museum features an impressive collection of Sicilian archaeological treasures. Most impressive are several fine Greek and Roman works, including a large section of the **Punic Temple of Himera,** and the 3rd-century-BC Greek **Ram of Syracuse.** Also not to be missed is the recently restored **Mosaico delle Quattro Stagioni,** depicting the four seasons in a haunting mosaic. Other temple remnants include fantastic renditions of Perseus beheading Medusa and Zeus courting Hera. *(From Teatro Massimo, cross V. Maqueda and head down V. Bara all'Olivella. P. Olivella, 24. ☎091 61 16 805 or 091 61 10 740. Open M and Su 8:30am-1:45pm, Tu-Sa 8:30am-6:45pm. €4.50, EU students €2, EU residents under 18 or over 65 free.)*

CATACOMBE CAPPUCCINI.
Over the course of 350 years, the Cappuchin friars preserved remains of over 8000 men, women, and children. Hanging from niches by wires and nails and lying in glass-sided caskets, many are dressed in their finest and are at various stages of decay. Various notables are buried here, including several bishops and the painter Velàzquez, but the most arresting remains are those of Rosalia, a three-year-old girl who lies in her own tiny glass box. *(Take bus #109 or 318 from Stazione Centrale to P. Indipendenza. From there, hop on #327. Or, from C. V. Emanuele, pass P. Indipendenza and turn right on V. Cappuccini, then right again on V. Il Pindemonte. P. Cappuccini, 1. ☎091 21 21 17. From P. Indipendenza, about a 20min. walk. Open summer daily 9am-noon and 3-5:30pm; in winter daily 9am-noon and 3-5pm. €1.50.)*

PALERMO'S CATHEDRAL.
As a part of their ongoing rivalry, the leaders of Palermo and Monreale competed to construct the most beautiful church. Although many consider the mosaics in Monreale to be superior, Palermo's cathedral is still breathtaking. Renovated from the 13th to the 18th centuries, this structure's exterior shows various styles butting heads. Arabic columns, Norman turrets, and an 18th-century dome crowd the facade and walls. Note the

FROM THE ROAD

EVERYBODY NEEDS A FRIEND

When I began researching the Mafia in Sicily, I quickly realized that a lot about Sicily hasn't been written down in books yet. Then I met an English-speaking expatriate who settled in Sicily 20 years ago. This man enjoys his unique position as a local—a man who knows the way things really work in Sicily—but who can still see things from the perspective of an outsider. I met him in a bar. We didn't talk about the Mafia, we talked about doors.

"In Sicily, you've got to find the side door. You go through the front door, it take you 3 months to buy toothpaste. But to find the side door, you need a friend. And once you've found a friend, and he's done you the favor of showing you the side door, you owe him a favor. And that's the way Sicily works. The whole system runs on favors. And one you have friends and favors, well, now you have a side door, even if you don't want one. It's not enough to go to work and work hard and take care of the things that are yours, it's not enough to open and close your front door responsibly."

People talk about the Mafia, like it's this big dark separate world, but in a way, everybody is a little bit a part of it. You've got to watch your side door, because everybody's got favors, because everybody's got a friend.

—Chris Starr

inscription from the Qur'an on the first left column before the entrance; in 1185 the Palermitano archbishop chose to plunk his cathedral down on top of a mosque, and this column was part of its stonework. The interior is dominated by saint-lined arches and carved rock walls. Flying buttresses connect it to the former **archbishop's palace**, completed in 1460 and even larger and more opulent than the church itself. The palace now serves as the Diocesan Museum of Palermo, and both can be visited with one ticket. *(On C. V. Emanuele. ☎ 091 33 43 76. Cathedral open daily 9:30am-5:30pm. Closed Su morning and during mass. Treasury and crypt open M-Sa 9:30am-5:30pm. Museum open Tu-F 9:30am-1:30pm, Sa 10am-6pm, and Su 9:30am-1:30pm. Closed Monday. €4.50.)*

QUATTRO CANTI AND LA FONTANA PRETORIA. The intersection of V. Maqueda and C. V. Emanuele forms the old city at the **Quattro Canti** (Four Screens). Dividing the old city into four districts, each sculpted corner of this 17th-century *piazza* has three levels. The lowest level has statues of the four seasons, on the middle level are the Spanish viceroys who commanded Sicily and Southern Italy, and on the top level are the city's patron saints. Covered in smog, the sculptural works have recently benefitted from Palermo's city-wide restoration. P. Pretoria, down V. Maqueda, houses the **Fontana della Vergogna** (Fountain of Shame) under Teatro Bellini. The fountain got its name from irate churchgoers who didn't like staring at monsters and nude figures as they left **Chiesa di San Giuseppe dei Teatini** across the street. An even more shameful story explains its shameless size. In the early 16th century, a rich Florentine commissioned the fountain for his villa, sending his son to the marble quarries to ensure its safe delivery. In need of cash, the son sold the fountain to the senate of Palermo and shipped it to Sicily, bringing Albert Mobilio's words to mind: "Sicily is a world where deception is only frowned upon to the degree it lacks artfulness." *(630m down V. Maqueda from the train station.)*

PALAZZO ABATELLIS. Signs in P. Marina point toward this late 15th-century *palazzo*, which houses one of Sicily's best art museums, the **Galleria Regionale Siciliana.** Dozens of religious panel paintings and sculptures from the Middle Ages through the Baroque period culminate with Antonello da Messina's unusual *Annunciation.* The massive and morbid fresco *The Triumph of Death* claims a room of its own on the lower level. *(V. Alloro, 4. From P. G. Cesare in front of train station, take V. Abramo Lincoln, then go left for 2 blocks on V. N. Cervello. ☎ 091 62 30 011. Open daily 9am-1pm, Tu-F also open 2:30-7pm. Ticket counter closes 30min. before museum. €4.50, EU students 18-25 €2, EU residents under 18 or over 65 free.)*

CHIESA DEL GESÙ (CASA PROFESSA). Nicknamed "Il Gesù," this green-domed church has a dazzling marble interior and Surrealist ceiling paintings of the Last Judgment, depicting figures with swords beating the unworthy into Hell and a black-clad man waving a pastel flag with "Jesus" written across it. WWII bombing damaged its courtyard and the **Quartiere dell'Albergheria**, filled with scarred buildings and bomb-blackened facades. *(In P. Casa Professa, on V. Ponticello, across V. Maqueda. Open daily 7-11:30am and 5-6:30pm. No visits during mass.)*

OTHER CHURCHES. The famous **Santa Maria dell'Ammiraglio,** ("La Martorana") was built for an admiral of Norman King Roger II. The Byzantine mosaics inside are the 12th-century equivalent of celebrity photos: Roger I stands with Jesus, and Admiral George admires the Mother of God. *(P. Bellini, a few steps from P. Pretoria. ☎ 091 61 61 692. Open M-Sa 8am-1pm and 3:30-5:30pm, Su 8:30am-1pm.)* Next door lies the smaller **Chiesa di San Cataldo**, dating from 1154, whose domes and arches liken it to a mosque. *(Open M-F 9am-3:30pm, Sa 9am-12:30pm, Su 9am-1pm.)* Perhaps the most romantic spot in Palermo, the garden and cloister of the **Chiesa di San Giovanni degli Eremiti,** come with bulbous pink domes designed by Arab architects, gazebos and little fountains. *(V. dei Benedettini, 3. Walk west from the train station on C. Tukory to Pta. Montalto and turn right. Open M-Sa 9am-7pm, Su 9am-1pm. €4.)*

PUPPETS. There are no small parts, only small wooden actors. For 300 years, Sicilian-made puppets have taken the stage at the **Museo Internazionale delle Marionette,** offering a playful glimpse at Sicilian stage culture. Galleries also display puppets from across the globe; it's a small world, after all. *(P. Niscemi, 5. Follow signs from P. Marina. ☎091 32 80 60; fax 091 32 82 76. Open M-F 9am-1pm and 4-7pm. Closed 1 week around Aug. 15 for celebration of Ferragosto. €3, under 18 or over 65 €1.50. Demonstrations on request.)* Catch a puppet show at Vincenzo Argenti's **Opera dei Pupi.** Tall, armored puppets reenact the chivalric *Orlando e Ronaldo per la Bella Angelica. (V. P. Novelli, 1. ☎091 32 91 94. Shows daily 6pm. €8.)*

GARDENS. The city's fresh gardens and parks provide relief from Palermo's urban jungle. The large **Giardino Inglese,** off V. della Libertà, resembles a paradise more than Hyde Park, harboring many a picnicker under its palms and marble busts. In summer, the park hosts concerts and carnival rides for children. Down C. V. Emanuele toward the port, the **Giardino Garibaldi** in P. Marina features enormous banyan trees. The large Parisian-style **Villa Giulia,** at the end of V. Lincoln, has sand pathways, flower beds, and fountains. *(Open daily 8am-8pm.)*

MONTE PELLEGRINO. Monte Pellegrino, an isolated mass of limestone rising from the sea, is Palermo's principal natural landmark, separating the city from the beach at Mondello. Near its peak, the **Santuario di Santa Rosalia** marks the site where the young Palermitano *ragazza,* Rosalia, sought escape from her marriage and wandered into ascetic seclusion. After dying there, she appeared as an apparition to a woodsman, and told him to carry her bones through the city in a procession. The procession is believed to have ended the plague that was destroying Palermo. The bones of Rosalina, who is now the patron saint of the city, can be found in Palermo's cathedral, and are still paraded around every year on July 15. *(☎091 54 03 26. Open daily 7am-7pm. Take bus #812 from P. Castelnuovo. Buses every 1½hr.)*

▐ NIGHTLIFE

Nightlife is as varied as one would expect for a city of Palermo's size. For information on cultural events, pick up *Un Mese a Palermo,* a monthly brochure available at any APT office, or the *News-News.* **Piazza Olivella,** in front of the Archaeological Museum, and **Via Candelai,** to the left off of V. Maqueda two streets past the Quattro Canti toward Teatro Massimo, and **Via Spinnuza,** across from Teatro Massimo and one street up from V. Bara all'Olivella, are popular nightlife hubs where mobs of the young *Palermitani* flood the dance floors every night.

▨ **Via di Mezzo Librothéca,** V. S. Oliva 20/22 (☎091 60 90 090; viadmezzo@virgilio.it), just up the street from Sesto Canto. The name stands for book+tea+coffee and that describes the vibe at this bistro where the conversation is as vibrant as the music is low-key. Enjoy outdoor seating on a quiet side street, or move indoors to select a book off the shelves or admire the paintings of artist-in-residence/waitress Nicoletta Signorelli. Coffees and tea (€1.40-2.50), beer (€3.50-4), wine (€3), and mixed drinks (€3.50-6).

I Candelai, V. Candelai, 65 (☎091 32 71 51; www.candelai.it.), picks up around midnight with one of central Palermo's few dance floors. Open daily in summer Th-Su 11pm-3am, in winter nightly 11pm-3am.

Volo, V. della Libertà, 12 (091 61 21 284, www.volofood.it). 2 blocks up from P. Castelnuovo, just after V. G. Carducci on the left. Dress to impress and head to Volo, where the Euro-sleek interior and elegant garden exterior are equally perfect settings. DJ on F and Sa nights. Daily happy hour 4-7pm with free hors d'oeuvres. All cocktails €5. Open June-Oct. M-Th 11:30am-1:30am, F and Su 11:30am-2:30am, Sa 9:30am-2:30am; Nov.-May M-Th 11:30am-12:45am, F and Su 11:30am-1:45am, Sa 9:30am-1:45am.

◠ BEACHES

Mondello Lido is a free beach for tourists by day and a playground of clubs and bars by night. All registered hotels provide tickets that must be shown at the entrance. Otherwise, beach-goers pay €8 to set up camp in the area near the Charleston—or sit for free directly on the shoreline. Take bus #101 or 102 from the station to reach the Politeama and V. della Libertà, and then bus #806 in the same direction to reach Mondello; the beach is beyond a tree-filled area known as *la Favorita*. Watch for the frequent vendors that wander around the sand with all types of goodies. *Ciambelle* (donuts caked in sugar; €1) are an essential beach treat.

USTICA   ☎091

The crystal waters of Ustica (pop. 1300) have turned Sicily's first natural marine reserve into a bustling tourist port with abundant outdoor and underwater activities to satisfy the adventurous. Hiking trails wind around the island's 9km scenic coastline, while guided tours explore such archaeological treasures as a prehistoric village and a necropolis. Perhaps the most spectacular attractions are the ancient artifacts buried just below the water's surface, catalogued and labeled for divers to explore. Despite its distance from Palermo, the self-proclaimed "diving capital of the world" is a worthwhile and memorable destination.

▣ TRANSPORTATION

Ustica is accessible by ferry or hydrofoil from Palermo. **Siremar,** V. Capitano Vincenzo di Bartolo, 15, right next to the church, is open daily 9am-1pm and 3:30-7pm (☎091 84 49 002; fax 091 84 49 457). It runs **hydrofoils** (1¼hr.; Sept.-May M-Th and Sa 6:45am and 3pm, F and Su 6:45am, 1 and 5:15pm; July-Aug. daily 6:45am, 1pm and 5:15pm; €16.80) and **ferries** (2½hr.; daily 5pm; €10.60, Aug. €11.60) to Palermo. For public transportation on the island, orange **minibuses** run the entire perimeter of the island, a 30min. round trip. (P. Vito Longo, every 30min., €0.80.) Hotel Clelia and Trattoria da Umberto both rent **scooters** for €20 per day, helmet and gas included. (see **Accommodations**).

◪▟ ORIENTATION AND PRACTICAL INFORMATION

The tiny town center of Ustica consists of two main *piazze* with streets branching out. To get to town from the hydrofoil port, turn right from the port and head up the road until you get to the staircase with an arrow marked "Centro" and follow that to Piazza Umberto I. With your back to the stairs, Piazza Capitano Vito Longo will be up and to your right. To reach the town from **Cala Cimitero,** the ferry port, take the road uphill and turn left at the fork. A 24hr. **ATM** is at **Banco Monte dei Paschi di Siena,** on P. Capitano Vito Longo right next to the church. In case of **emergency,** call the **carabinieri** (☎091 84 49 049), the **hospital** (☎091 84 49 248), or contact **tourist medical assistance** (☎091 84 49 392). A **pharmacy** is in P. Umberto I. (☎091 84 49 382. Open M-F 8:30am-1pm and 5-8:30pm, Su 10:30am-1pm.) The **post office,** Largo Armeria, 13, is off P. Umberto I. (☎091 84 49 394. Open M-F 8am-1:30pm, Sa 8am-12:30pm.) **Postal Code:** 90010.

▛▟ ACCOMMODATIONS AND FOOD

Though reasonable in the low season, accommodations in Ustica can be incredibly pricey in July and August, making the island most suitable for a summer daytrip. If you would like to spend a little more time in Ustica, your best bet is probably renting a vacation home. **Immobiliare Tranchina,** P. della Vittoria, 7, rents furnished **apartments ❸** for two-eight people that include kitchen, bath, double bedrooms, electricity, water, and gas. (☎091 84 49 542 or 091 84 49 225; www.usticatour.it. 3-night min. Extra bed for an additional cost. Additional cost for maid service during stay. A/C available. €20-35 per person per night, depending on the season and number of people.) For the best deal, consider the **Settimana Blu** package: €300 per person provides a week's lodging and 6 days of guided dives, all equipment included. **Hotel Clelia ❺**, V. Sindaco, 29, offers some of the nicest rooms around; all sport cheery yellow walls, TV, air-conditioning, minibar, phone, and hair dryer. (☎091 84 49 039. Breakfast included. Scooter rental available for €20 per day. Internet €4.80 per hr. Shower facilities available to guests after check-out. Singles €32-83; doubles €56-146; triples €81-201; quads €100-260. Ages 5-11 50% discount. AmEx/MC/V.) **Albergo Giulia ❺**, V. San Francesco, 16, has 11 rooms equipped with TV, air-conditioning, phone, minibar, hair dryer, and brightly tiled bathroom. (☎091 84 49 007. Singles €32-70; doubles €50-110. Cash only.)

Ristorante Al Clelia ❸, at Hotel Clelia, provides views of the sea, the perfect setting to enjoy *gamberetto con fiori di zucca* (shrimp tucked into pumpkin flowers; €12), one of Chef Marino's many masterpieces. (*Antipasti* €4-8, *primi* €6-10, *secondi* €10-12. Open daily Apr.-Sept. 8pm-midnight.) At **Trattoria da Umberto ❸**, P. della Vittoria, 7, a wooden overhang and looming trees provide abundant shade for enjoying the *pennette piccanti con capperi e olive* (pasta with capers and olives; €7). (☎091 84 49 542. *Primi* €5-9, *secondi* €9-15.) Directly behind the Municipio, lively **Vai Mo' ❹**, V. Petriera, specializes in local seafood and hosts a piano bar. Indoor and outdoor seating available. (☎091 84 481 20; www.vaimo.it. *Primi* €7-14, *secondi* €10-14. Open daily May-Sept. 12:30-3pm and 8:20-11pm. AmEx/MC/V.) **Mini Market Caminita,** P. Umberto I, 3, sells essentials. (☎091 84 49 474. Open M-Sa 8am-1pm and 4-8pm, Su 8am-1pm.)

👁 SIGHTS AND ENTERTAINMENT

The natural splendor of Ustica's marine reserve is easily accessible both by land and by sea. Whether traversing the island's hiking trails on foot or circumnavigating the island aboard a boat, the views are spectacular. **Boat tours** are a great way to explore the fascinating grottoes dispersed around the coastline, among them the neon blue waters of 🏊**Grotta delle Barche** and **Grotta Azzurra,** a nautical graveyard filled with ancient vessels. Small boat owners advertise cheap rides that circle the island; find them at P. Umberto I or at the port. Set a price before embarking; women traveling alone should attempt to join a larger group before taking a tour. The island's most popular activity, **scuba diving** off rocky coasts, is quite affordable, with opportunities for daytrips and long excursions. **Alta Marea,** on V. Cristoforo Colombo, runs dives from May to October. (☎347 17 57 255; www.altamareaustica.it. Boats leave port daily at 9:15am and 3:15pm. Single immersion €35, with full equipment €55; 6 dives €190; 10 dives €280. Diving class €330.) Once submerged, see the 🏊**underwater archaeological remains** of Roman lead anchors and *amphorae,* part of Ustica's underwater archaeology experiment.

RENAISSANCE MAN. To get around Ustica, you need to know only one man: **Gigi Tranchina.** A lifelong resident of Ustica, Gigi is a one-man tourism bureau who knows everything about the island and will gladly coordinate bike tours, hikes, scooter rentals and diving trips. Head to **Trattoria da Umberto** to find Gigi himself, or check out one of his two websites: www.usticatour.it and www.isoladiustica.it.

After a long day outdoors, you can relax at **Carpe Diem,** Largo Padiglione, 1, which serves beer (€3.50), wine (€2.50), and mixed drinks. Visit their daily happy hour from 4:30-7:30pm, with beer for €2.50 at the bar. (Open Tu-Su.)

CEFALÙ   ☎0921

The Sicilian proverb "good wine comes in small bottles" captures the timeless nature of Cefalù (pop. 14,000), whose heavenly qualities were featured in the Academy Award-winning film *Cinema Paradiso*. Dominated by *La Rocca*, the imposing fortification rising 278m above the old town, Cefalù is a labyrinth of cobblestone streets. The city's aging terra-cotta and stone buildings cling to the water's edge, just as crowds cling to the social *lungomare*. Be aware, though, that Cefalù's charms do not come cheaply: the city's reputation as a beach resort and its proximity to Palermo allow *pensioni* to charge whatever they please.

▐ TRANSPORTATION

Cefalù is best accessed by train. From P. Garibaldi, take V. Matteotti until it hits V. Mazzini and becomes V. A. Moro. Take V. A. Moro to the station. The **train station** (☎0921 89 20 21), in P. Stazione, is three blocks ahead on the left and open daily 4:30am-11:30pm. Tickets can be purchased at the station's bar. Trains to: Messina (3hr., 12 per day 4:45am-9:47pm, €8.50); Milazzo (2hr., 15 per day, €7.95); Palermo (1hr., 34 per day 5:13am-10:20pm, €4.95); and Sant'Agata di Militello (50min., 12 per day 7:02am-9:16pm, €4.45). **Sommatinese,** V. Cavour, 2 (☎0921 42 43 01; segreteria@gvv.it) runs **buses** from the train station and the waterfront along P. Colombo to 26 towns (€1). The station bar's window and tourist office post schedules. **Taxis** are available from **Kefautoservizi,** in P. Stazione (☎0921 42 25 54), in P. Garibaldi (☎0921 42 21 58), or in P. del Duomo (☎0921 42 11 78).

◪ ▐ ORIENTATION AND PRACTICAL INFORMATION

From the **train station,** head right on **Via Aldo Moro,** which curves up to the city's biggest intersection. To the left, **Via Roma** cuts through the center of the new city. Straight and to the left, **Via Matteotti** leads into the old city, changing at **Piazza Garibaldi** into the boutique-lined **Corso Ruggero. Via Cavour,** across the intersection from V. A. Moro, becomes the *lungomare.*

Tourist Office: C. Ruggero, 77 (☎0921 42 10 50; fax 0921 42 23 86), in the old city. English-speaking staff has a vast supply of brochures, **maps,** hotel listings, and schedules. Open M-Sa 8am-8pm, Su 9am-1pm.

Currency Exchange: Banca S. Angelo (☎0921 42 39 22), near train station, at the corner of V. Giglio and V. Roma. Open M-F 8:30am-1:30pm and 2:45-3:45pm. A 24hr. **ATM** is at the **Banca di Sicilia** (☎0921 42 11 03 or 0921 42 28 90), in P. Garibaldi.

Emergency: ☎113. **Carabinieri:** ☎112. **Police:** ☎113 or 0921 92 60 11.

First Aid: ☎0921 92 60 11. **Guardia Medica:** V. Roma, 15 (☎0921 42 36 23), in a modern yellow building in the new city, behind an iron fence. Open daily 8am-8pm.

Pharmacies: Dr. V. Battaglia, V. Roma, 13 (☎0921 42 17 89), in the new city. Open M-Sa 9am-1pm and 4:30-8:30pm. MC/V. **Hospital:** (☎0921 92 01 11) on Cda. Pietra Pollastra, outside the city limits.

Internet Access: Capriccio Siciliano, V. Umberto I, 1 (☎0921 42 05 50; capriccios@libero.it). Mimma and Giuseppe sell a variety of Sicilian specialty products and have decently fast Internet in the back. €3 for 30 min., €5 per hr. Open daily 9am-9pm. **Kefaonline,** P. S. Francesco, 1 (☎0921 92 30 91), where V. Umberto meets V. Mazzini. €5 per hr. Open M-Sa 9:30am-1:30pm and 3:30-7:30pm.

Post Office: V. Vazzana, 2 (☎0921 42 15 28). In a modern concrete building on the right off the *lungomare,* 2 long blocks from P. Colombo. Open M-F 8am-7:30pm, Sa 8am-12:30pm. **Postal Code:** 90015.

ACCOMMODATIONS AND CAMPING

Locanda Cangelosi, V. Umberto I, 26 (☎0921 42 15 91), off P. Garibaldi. This centrally located *affittacamere* is the best deal in the city. Private residence has large rooms, each with a balcony. 2 shared baths. Laundry available €5 per load. Reserve ahead. Sept.-June singles €25; doubles €35; triples €50. July-Aug. €30/40/50. The owner also has 10 fully furnished apartments for €40-50 per night. ❸

Hotel Mediterraneo, V. A. Gramsci, 2 (☎/fax 0921 92 26 06 or 0921 92 25 73), 1 block left from the station. 16 well-furnished rooms boast cloud-like beds, A/C, TV, sparkling bath, hair dryer, and safe for valuables. Buffet breakfast included. Singles €45-80; doubles €60-125; triples €80-145; quads €95-165. ❺

Camping Costa Ponente (☎0921 42 00 85; fax 0921 42 44 92), west of Cefalù on Cda. Ogliastrillo. A 45min. walk or short ride on the Cefalù-Lascari bus (€1) from P. Colombo. Pool, tennis court, and free hot showers. July-Aug. €6 per person, €5 per tent, €4 per car; Sept.-June €5.50/4.50/3.50. ❶

FOOD

Seafood is undoubtedly the specialty in Cefalù, but delicious formerly land-dwelling cuisine is also easily found. Just off the *lungomare*, next door to the post office on V. Vazzana, an **IperSidis** supermarket sells basics, including bathing suits. (☎0921 42 45 00. Open daily 8:30am-1pm and 4:30-8:30pm.)

La Vecchia Marina, V. V. Emanuele, 73/75 (☎0921 42 03 88). Seafood is the specialty at this excellent restaurant, full of model ships and paintings of fishermen. Make a reservation in advance to get a table on the terrace overlooking the harbor. *Primi* and *secondi* €5.50-10. Must order both a *primo* and a *secondo*. Cover €1.60. Open M and W-Su noon-3pm and 7-11:30pm. AmEx/MC/V. ❸

Osteria la Botte, V. Veterani, 6 (☎0921 42 43 15), off C. Ruggero, 2 blocks past P. Duomo. An affordable gem among Cefalù's upscale restaurants. *Primi* and *secondi* from €6.50. Cover €1.50. Open Tu-Su 12:30-3pm and 7:30-11:30pm. July-Aug. open 7pm-midnight only. AmEx/MC/V. ❸

Gelateria di Noto, V. Bagno Cicerone (☎0921 42 26 54), where the *lungomare* meets the old town. More than 40 flavors of some of Sicily's best *gelato*—a great location just off the beach. So good you'll probably come back for seconds. Open daily 7am-3am. ❶

Il Caffè Duomo, Piazza Duomo, 19 (☎393 29 28 642; ristorante@seriocefalu.it). Located in the Palazzo Maria—home at one point to everything from a royal palace to Fascist party headquarters—Caffè Duomo is perfect for an afternoon coffee (€1-2) or glass of wine (from €2). Full dinner menu, and extremely fresh seafood display. *Primi* €9-12, *secondi* €7-15. Open daily June-Oct. 10am-2am. Closed Tu Nov.-May. ❹

L'Arca di Noé, V. Vazzana, 7/8 (☎0921 92 18 73), across from the post office. An astounding variety of foods and decorations crowd wooden booths docked among nautical maps, anchors, and ropes. A ship-shaped *bar* and *gelateria* serve those on the run. Internet available. Pizza from €3.50. Open M-Sa 24hr. AmEx/MC/V. ❶

Ristorante-Pizzeria Trappitu, V. di Bordonaro, 96 (☎0921 92 19 72; www.paginegialle-trappitu.it). Urns and a grinding mill wheel are conversation starters, but filling food (including the house specialty, homemade *tiramisù*) keeps mouths otherwise occupied. Impressive wine list enhances the traditional menu. Pizza €4-8. *Primi* from €6.50, *secondi* €7-18.50. Open M-W and F-Su noon-3pm and 7pm-midnight. AmEx/MC/V. ❸

Al Gabbiano, V. Lungomare G. Giardina, 17 (☎0921 42 14 95). Breezy eatery above the water is ideal for dining at the beach. Pizza €4-8. *Primi* from €4, *secondi* from €8. Open in summer daily noon-3pm and 7pm-1am; closed W in winter. AmEx/MC/V. ❷

👁 SIGHTS

🏛**La Rocca** stands above Cefalù at the center of the city's history. Medieval fortifications lace the edges, while crumbling cisterns and ovens line forgotten avenues. The **Tempio di Diana** first served as a place of sea worship and later as a defensive outpost. At the top of La Rocca is **Il Castello,** a military fort used even by the Byzantines. Most remains date from the 12th and 13th centuries AD, and offer a great place for panoramic views of the landscape. (Take Salità Saraceni to Tempio di Diana, a 20min. uphill hike. From Diana, continue up for another (steeper) 20min. hike. to Il Castello. From P. Garibaldi, follow the signs for "Pedonale Rocca" up V. G. Fiore to Vco. Macell from between the fountain and Banco di Sicilia. Use caution, as the path is slippery when wet. Gates close 1hr. before sunset.)

Tucked away in Cefalù's narrow streets is the city's **duomo.** It was constructed in AD 1131 after King Ruggero II promised to build a monument to the Savior if he lived through a terrible shipwreck. The dramatic, off-white structure combines Arabic, Norman, and Byzantine styles, reflecting the craftsmen hired for its construction. Once a potential fortress with crenellated towers and firing outposts, it now protects only the king's body and stunning Byzantine mosaics. An enormous **Christ Pantocrator** mosaic surveys all who enter with glistening calm. (Open daily 8am-noon and 3:30-7:30pm. Modest dress required.) Stuffed alligator cases and ancient urns get equal footing in the **Museo Mandralisca.** Local baron Mandralisca bequeathed his collection to the city. The 19th-century art connoisseur amassed an array of medieval and early Renaissance Sicilian paintings by anonymous artists, including the centerpiece, the **Ritratto di Ignoto,** by 15th-century Sicilian master Antonello da Messina. The image is inescapable in Cefalù, smirking at tourists from every postcard rack, but the real thing is surprisingly lively. Unfortunately, for every good painting, there are hundreds of seashells and old books, and a half-dozen lamps of questionable taste. (V. Mandralisca, 13, opposite the *duomo.* ☎0921 42 15 47. Open daily 9am-7pm. €4.15, €2.60 per person for groups of 10 or more.)

🎵 ENTERTAINMENT

Cefalù's most attractive **beaches, Mazzaforno** and **Settefrati,** lie west of town on the Cefalù-Lascari bus line. The popular **Attrezzata** is just off the *lungomare.* Crowded for good reason, the beach has white sand, turquoise shallows, and free showers—the area closest to the old city is completely free. The seven stones jutting out from the waves are said to have been placed in memory of seven brothers who died here while trying to rescue their sister from pirates.

Though nightlife is limited, there are a few spots worth checking out. Local favorite **Mas Que Nada Pub,** V. Discesa Paramura, 5/7, serves a variety of drinks (€2.40-5) and coffee (€1-2.50) on a palm-tree covered terrace. (☎338 90 30 367. Just off P. Garibaldi and down the stairs. Open 11:30am-3pm and 6pm-2am.) Head to the open-air garden at **Bar BeBop,** V. Nicola Botta, 4, and share a few laidback beverages (€2-5) beneath the oleander trees. There is a piano bar Thursday and Sunday. (☎0921 92 39 72. Open 7:30pm-2am. From P. Duomo, head down C. Ruggiero toward P. Garibaldi. V. Botta is 2 streets down on the right.) With a great seaside location, **Murphy's Pub,** Lungomare G. Giardina, 5, offers a selection of draft beers (€2-4), a big-screen TV, and the ambience of an Irish pub. (☎0921 42 25 88. *Panini* €2.50-4. Pizza €3.50-8. Open Oct.-May Tu-Su 5:30pm-3am.)

MILAZZO ☎090

Visitors to Milazzo are all thinking the same thing: what time does my boat leave? Once upon a time, only one or two boats a day sailed from Milazzo's port. Now ferries and hydrofoils zip to the Aeolian Islands and to the Italian mainland every hour. Originally a great capital, Milazzo was ransacked by the ancient Romans, though now her safe harbors host hydrofoils full of anxious tourists instead of warships. Welcome to Milazzo: get in, get your boat, and get out.

🖳🚹 TRANSPORTATION AND PRACTICAL INFORMATION. Trains run to Messina (40min., 19 per day, €2.85) and Palermo (2½hr., 12 per day, €9.20). **Giuntabus** (☎090 67 37 82 or 090 67 57 49) runs **buses** to Messina (45min., every hr. 14 per day, €3.40). Both city buses and Giuntabuses arrive in **Piazza della Repubblica** across from the Agip gas station. The port and center are a 10min. orange bus ride from the **train station. Lungomare Garibaldi** runs the length of the port. Turn left down **Via Crispi** and right into **Piazza Caio Duilio;** follow the signs to the **tourist office**, P. C. Duilio, 20. (☎090 92 22 865; www.aastmilazzo.it. Open M-F 9am-1pm and 3-6pm, Sa 9am-1pm.) A **medical clinic** (☎090 92 21 695) is on V. F. Crispi.

🛏🍴 ACCOMMODATIONS AND FOOD. Budget accommodations are limited in Milazzo, and are usually budget for a reason. For those who can afford it, the eco-friendly (and just plain friendly) **Petit Hotel ❺**, Villa dei Mille, 37, is worth a few extra euros. Located right on the port, this hotel provides warmly decorated, naturally cooled rooms tricked out with ionic filters and a bunch of other environmentally friendly extras. An organic **restaurant ❸** downstairs serves delicious food (all either homemade or Fair-Trade approved) and is open to guests around the clock. On the side, owner Antonio serves as a *de facto* tourist information office and general font of goodwill. (☎090 92 86 784; www.petithotel.it. Singles €70-125; doubles €100-195; triples €130-245; quads €160-320. *Primi* €6-8, *secondi* 10-14.) Campgrounds at **Riva Smeralda ❶**, on Str. Panoramica, are 6km from town on Capo Milazzo and can be reached by bus from P. della Repubblica. (☎090 92 87 791. Free showers. €6-8.50 per person, €2.90-4.40 per tent, €2.60-3.90 per car.)

Milazzo gears itself toward travelers on the go, but food doesn't have to be rushed. Bars line the *lungomare*, and fruit vendors are along V. Regis in P. Natasi and at the intersection with V. del Sole. A large **Girasole** supermarket, V. del Sole, 34, provides necessities. (Open M-Sa 10am-8pm. MC/V.) **Blue Pub ❶**, V. A. Manzoni, 4, carries pizza in air-conditioned Tex-Mex splendor. (☎090 92 83 839. Pizza from €3.60. Cover €1. Open daily 7pm-late). For a relaxed meal, **Ristorante Al Gambero ❸**, V. Luigi Rizzo, 5/7 (☎090 92 23 337), has a large, covered patio overlooking the port. (Pizza from €4.50. *Primi* €6.50-7.50, *secondi* €8.50-13. Cover €1.50. Open daily 11am-4pm and 7pm-midnight; closed M in winter. AmEx/MC/V.)

◪ SIGHTS. Milazzo's fantastic **Arab-Norman Castello**, in the historical center, boasts foundations constructed over Greek, Roman, and Byzantine remains and the architectural input of numerous other civilizations, including an Aragonese wall. (Guided tours offered 6 per day; closed M. €3.10, under 18 or over 65 €1.60.)

AEOLIAN ISLANDS (ISOLE EOLIE)

Homer believed this unspoiled archipelago to be a home of the gods; residents deem them *Les Perle del Mare* (Pearls of the Sea). Every summer, boatloads of visitors experience the magic of the rugged shores and pristine landscapes of the Aeolians. Lipari, the central and largest island, has ancient ruins and one of the finest archaeological museums in Italy. Visit nearby Stromboli for its restless volcano, Panarea for inlets and elitism, Salina for sheer cliffs over cerulean waters, and Vulcano for radioactive mud baths and the Great Crater, the long-extinguished home of Vulcan, god of fire. Far more affordable in the low season, the islands see a price increase in July and August. Reservations for this period should be made sooner rather than later, especially for the smaller islands and more elite resorts.

✖ TRANSPORTATION

The islands lie off Sicily, north of Milazzo, the principal and least expensive departure point. **Trains** run to Milazzo from Messina (45min., 19 per day, €2.65) and Palermo (3hr., 12 per day, €9.20). **Giuntabus** (☎090 67 37 82 or 67 57 49) arrives in Milazzo's port from Messina (45min.; M-Sa 14 per day, Su daily; €3.40) and from the **Catania airport** (Apr.-Sept. daily 4pm, €10.33). From Milazzo's train station, the orange **AST bus** runs to the **seaport** (10min., every 30 min., €0.90). **Hydrofoils** and **ferries** run regularly mid-June through September to Lipari from Cefalù (3hr., €21.69); Messina (2½hr., 5 per day 7:10am-6:20pm, €16.50); Naples (5½hr., 8am, €74.90); Palermo (4hr.; 6:55am, 2pm; €31.30); and Reggio Calabria (2-3hr., €17.50). Ferries leave less frequently from Molo Beverello in Naples.

Hydrofoils run twice as fast and often as ferries, but for twice the price. Three hydrofoil and ferry companies serve the islands, all with ticket offices in Milazzo on V. dei Mille, directly across from the docks in the port. High season is July and August. **Siremar,** V. dei Mille, 18, in Milazzo sends ferries and hydrofoils to the islands. (☎090 92 83 242; fax 090 92 83 243. Open daily 5:45am-6:30pm.) It also has offices in Lipari (☎090 98 12 193) and Naples (☎081 25 14 740). **Ustica,** V. dei Mille, 23 (☎090 92 87 821), in Milazzo, sends hydrofoils to the islands. It also has an office in Lipari (☎090 98 12 448). Ustica recently bought SNAV Lines, and some Ustica booths still say SNAV. **Navigazione Generale Italiana (NGI),** V. dei Mille, 26 (☎090 92 84 091; fax 090 92 83 415), in Milazzo; V. Ten. Mariano Amendola, 14 (☎090 98 11 955), at Porto Sottomonastero in **Lipari.** The following table lists ferry and hydrofoil info for both Ustica and Siremar. There is a €1.50 fee to reserve in advance that is not included in the fees listed here. Schedules are subject to change, so call for definitive info. Both offices have convenient portable timetable booklets—just ask for an *orario*.

TO	FERRY FROM MILAZZO		HYDROFOIL FROM MILAZZO	
	TIME	HIGH SEASON	TIME	HIGH SEASON
Vulcano	1½hr.	3 per day; 7, 9am, 6:30pm; €6.30	40min.	16 per day, 6:20am-6:20pm, €10.50
Lipari	2hr.	6 per day, 7am-6:30pm, €6.20	55min.	17 per day, 6:15am-6:10pm, €11.30
Salina	3hr.	2 per day; 7, 9am; €8.40	1½hr.	7 per day, 6:15am-6:10pm, €12.80
Panarea	4hr.	M and W-Su 2:30pm, Tu and Sa at 7am; €7.50	2hr.	5 per day, 6:15am-4:20pm, €13.30

LIPARI
☎090

Centuries ago, pirates ravaged Lipari's shores. Today, boats and hydrofoils let loose packs of equally ravenous buccaneers looking for other kinds of treasures. They descend in swarms upon its beaches and wallow in its waves like listless merpeople; those who prefer the colors of the surrounding sea and mountains to neon umbrellas and skimpy beachwear hike to nearby private beaches. Inexpensive hotels, divine sunbathing, and excellent archaeological museums make this island of 10,000 people an ideal launching pad for exploring the archipelago.

▣ TRANSPORTATION

Autobus Urso Guglielmo, V. Cappuccini, 9 (☎090 98 11 262 or 090 98 11 026), operates **buses** on most of the island. (Ticket office open daily 9am-7:30pm; tickets also available onboard.) Island tours (€3.62) depart daily 9:30, 11:30am, and 5pm. Reservation is required. **De. Sco., V.** Stradale Pianoconte, 5, at the end of C. V. Emanuele, rents shiny scooters, lined up showroom-style. (☎090 98 13 288 or 368 75 35 590. Rental includes gas. €18-24 per day; Aug. €30-36. Open daily 8:30am-8pm. MC/V.) **Ditta Carbonaro Paola,** on C. V. Emanuele, 21, also rents scooters just steps away from De. Sco. (☎090 98 11 994. €15 per day; Aug. €25 per day.) For **taxis,** call ☎090 98 86 077 or 090 98 12 216.

⚒ 🛈 ORIENTATION AND PRACTICAL INFORMATION

The **hydrofoil** and **ferry port** are on the end of the promontory supporting the *castello* and museum. Restaurants and hotels cluster around **Corso Vittorio Emanuele,** the main thoroughfare, and **Via Garibaldi,** which runs mostly parallel to C. V. Emanuele around the base of the *castello* and is accessible by large stone stairs; C. V. Emanuele ends at the docks. Purchase a map at a *tabaccherie* or bike rental.

Tourist Office: AAST, C. V. Emanuele, 202 (☎090 98 80 095; www.aasteolie.info). From the dock, walk down C. V. Emanuele; office is on your left. Info hub for all 7 islands. Ask for *Ospitalità in blu,* which contains helpful visitor information. Open July-Aug. M-F 8am-2pm and 4:30-10pm, Sa 8am-2pm; Sept.-June M-F 8am-2pm and 4:30-7:30pm.

Currency Exchange: C. V. Emanuele is lined with banks and **ATMs.** Exchange money at **Banco Antonveneta** (☎090 98 12 117; open M-F 8:20am-1:20pm and 2:35-3:35pm), **Banco di Roma** (☎090 98 13 275; open M-F 8:30am-1:35pm and 2:50-4:10pm), or at the **post office** (cash only). Some of the smaller Aeolian Islands have few or no ATMs, so get cash on Lipari before visiting them.

Luggage Storage: At Ustica hydrofoil office. €3 per 12hr. €2 overnight surcharge. Open 6:45am-8pm.

English-Language Bookstore: Libreria Mimo Belletti, C. V. Emanuele, 203 (☎090 98 11 282; mimmobelletti@tiscali.it). Small rack of varied English titles.

Laundry: Lavanderia Caprara Andrea, Vico Storione, 5 (☎090 98 13 177), off C. V. Emanuele. Wash and dry €4 per kg (5kg min.). Open M-Sa 9am-1pm and 4:30-8:30pm.

Emergency: ☎113. **Carabinieri:** ☎112 or 090 98 11 333. **Police:** ☎090 98 12 757. Call ☎090 98 80 030 for non-emergencies. **Ambulance:** ☎090 98 95 267. **First Aid:** ☎090 98 85 267 or 090 98 11 010.

Pharmacies: Farmacia Internazionale, C. V. Emanuele, 128 (☎090 98 11 583). Open in summer M-F 9am-1pm and 5-9pm; in winter 9am-1pm and 4-8pm. AmEx/MC/V. **Farmacia Cincotta,** V. Garibaldi, 60 (☎090 98 11 472). Open in summer M-F 9am-1pm and 5-9pm; in winter 9am-1pm, and 4-8pm. After-hours rotation posted outside.

Hospital: Ospedale Civile di Lipari (☎090 98 851), on V. Santana. At southern end of C. V. Emanuele, descend the side street between scooter rental places and turn right on V. Roma. V. Santana is the 2nd left. Open daily 8am-8pm. **Medical Clinic:** ☎090 988 52 26. Office 50m up V. Garibaldi from the waterfront, on the left under the Italian flag. Open M, W, F 8:30am-1pm and Tu, Th 3:30-5:30pm.

Internet Access: Internet Point, C. V. Emanuele, 185. 7 fast computers. €2 per 15min., €3 per 30min., €5 per hr. Open M-Sa in summer 9am-1pm and 5:30pm-1am, Su 5:30pm-midnight; in winter 9:30am-1:30pm and 4:40-9pm. **Net C@fe,** V. Garibaldi, 61 (☎090 98 13 527). 3 computers. €3 per 30min., €5 per hr. Open daily 8am-3am; closed F in winter.

Post Office: Main branch for Aeolians (☎090 98 10 051), on C. V. Emanuele. Open M-F 8am-6:30pm, Sa 8am-12:30pm. **Postal Codes:** Canneto-Lipari 98052; Lipari 98055; all other islands 98050.

SICILY

ACCOMMODATIONS AND CAMPING

As soon as you step off of the hydrofoil exit ramp, you will be bombarded with offers for *affittacamere*. These are often the most affordable way to enjoy the islands, and some of the best deals are listed below. As always, ask to see the room before accepting and **always obtain a price quote in writing.** Also, prices are often fairly negotiable outside of August, so try to bargain your way to a better rate.

Pensione Enzo il Negro, V. Garibaldi, 29, 3rd fl. (☎090 98 13 163, 090 98 12 473, or 368 66 52 83), 20m up V. Garibaldi from hydrofoil dock to the left, under a small doorway. Classy hotel has elegant archways, painted tiles, and a book exchange. 8 rooms have balcony, fridge, A/C, and bath. Singles €30-47; doubles €50-75. AmEx/MC/V. ❸

Casa Vacanze Marturano, V. Mavrolico, 35 (☎333 41 46 212; www.eoliearcipelago.it), off C. V. Emanuele. Residences scattered on all 7 islands. Spacious rooms, most with shared kitchen and bath. Breakfast included in Panarea. Lipari and Salina €20-30. Vulcano, Panarea, Filicudi, Alicudi, and Stromboli €25-45. AmEx/MC/V. ❸

Hotel Rocce Azzurre, V. Maddalena, 69 (☎090 98 13 248; fax 090 98 13 247), on Porto delle Genti. Nestled in a quiet bay, this charming hotel has 33 rooms, all with bath and many with balcony. Breakfast included. €68-74 per person. In Aug. half pension €78-110; full pension €94-120. AmEx/MC/V. ❺

Casa Vittorio di Cassara, Vico Sparviero, 15 (☎/fax 090 98 11 523; casavittorio@net-net.it), off V. Garibaldi, 78, at end of short stairway. Take V. Garibaldi from hydrofoil dock and U-turn at 1st possible left. From small alley, take 1st right. Yellow building with blue window frames. If it's locked, continue to the end of the street and turn right. At red iron gate, ring top left button. Ideal location near port and *centro*. Rooms with bath vary from singles to 5-person apartments. Some include kitchen and sea view terrace. Rooms €15-40. Prices vary seasonally. Cash only. ❸

Baia Unci, V. Marina Garibaldi, 2 (☎090 98 11 909; www.campeggitalia.it/sicilia/baiaunci). Campground near Canneto, 2km from Lipari. 10min. from beach. Self-service restaurant on grounds. Open Mar. 15-Oct. 15. €8-14 per person with tent. Cash only. ❶

FOOD

Legions of lovers have sprinkled sauces, garnished salads, and spiced meats with the island's *capperi* (capers), renowned for their aphrodisiacal powers. After following suit, complete a meal in style with local *Malvasia* dessert wine. Lipari's lip-smacking cuisine can get expensive, so head to **UPIM** supermarket, C. V. Emanuele, 212, for a budget meal. (☎090 98 11 587. Open M-Sa 8am-10pm. AmEx/MC/V.) *Alimentari* along C. V. Emanuele sell cheap fruit every day.

▨ **Da Gilberto e Vera,** V. Garibaldi, 22-24 (☎090 98 12 756; www.gilbertoevera.it), is famous for some of Italy's best *panini* with ingredients like *prosciutto*, capers, tomatoes, olives, mint, etc. Also carries tons of picnic supplies. *Panini* €4. Open daily Mar.-Oct. 7am-4am; Aug. 7am-6am; Nov.-Feb. 7pm-2am. AmEx/MC/V. ❶

La Cambusa, V. Garibaldi, 72 (☎349 47 66 061). Husband and wife team makes this *trattoria* feel like home. Cluster around outdoor tables with *Liparesi* or retreat indoors to enjoy authentic flavors of Sicily. Regulars rave about the pasta (from €5). Cover €1. Open daily noon-3pm and 7-11pm. Reservation recommended. Cash only. ❷

La Piazzetta (☎090 98 12 522; fax 090 98 13 761), off C. V. Emanuele, next to Subba (see below). Walls and menus boast signatures of its many famous satisfied customers, including Audrey Hepburn. The patio extending into a small *piazza* is almost as elegant as the lady herself. Pizza from €7.50. *Primi* from €7, *secondi* from €9.50. Service 10%. Open July-Aug. daily noon-2pm and 7:30-11pm; Sept.-June Tu-Th 7:30-11pm. MC/V. ❹

Ristorante Sottomonastero, C. V. Emanuele, 232 (☎090 98 80 720; fax 090 98 11 084). Tables are always filled at this versatile *ristorante*, which specializes in Aeolian sweets. Pizza from €3.50. *Primi* from €5, *secondi* from €7. Cover €1.30. Open daily 7am-midnight; late July-Aug. 24hr. Kitchen open noon-2pm and 8:30-10pm. AmEx/MC/V. ❷

Pasticceria Subba, C. V. Emanuele, 92 (☎090 98 11 352). Pay by weight, in more ways than one, at the archipelago's oldest *pasticceria*. The *pasta paradiso*, an almond paste dumpling, is a heavenly sweet. Large pastries from €1.55. Open daily May-Oct. 7am-1am; Nov.-Apr. 7am-midnight. Cash only. ❶

👁 SIGHTS

Lipari's best sights—aside from its beaches—are all in the *castello* on the hill, where a **fortress** with ancient Greek foundations dwarfs the surrounding town. In the vicinity is the ▧**Museo Archeological Eoliano,** whose collection, explained in English and Italian, includes Liparite urns, galleries full of Greek and Sicilian figureware pottery from the 4th and 5th centuries BC, and treasures of underwater exploration that range from Greco-Italic amphorae to the a 17th-century Spanish warship wreck. The geological and volcanic section is devoted to the island's natural history. Walk up the stone steps to the right off V. Garibaldi; turn left at San Bartolomeo. (☎090 98 80 174. Museum open daily June-Aug. 9am-1:30pm and 4-7pm; Nov.-Apr. 9am-1:30pm and 3-6pm. Ticket office closes 1hr. before closing. €4.50, EU residents 18-25 €2, EU residents under 18 or over 65 free.) The **Chiesa di San Bartolomeo** is on the same hill. Built in the 12th century, it was sacked by Barbarossa the Turk in 1544. A new Baroque version, dedicated to St. Bartholomew, is done up in blue hues and topped by a painted ceiling. Stratified Greek, Roman, and Stone Age ruins encircle the building. The park's centerpiece is a contemporary Ancient Greek-style **theater.** Ask at the tourist office for programs and ticket prices. (Both sites are across from the museum. Open daily 9am-1pm. Free.)

🎵 ENTERTAINMENT

From July to September, island bus tours (€3.25) run at 2pm from **Autobus Urso Guglielmo** (☎090 98 11 262 or 090 98 11 026) on V. Cappuccini. A better way to see the coastline is from the water, aboard a rented boat from the hydrofoil port. For still better views, take the Lipari-Cavedi bus to the beaches of nearby **Canneto.** The pebbles are prickly and the sun scorching, so bring sunscreen and flip-flops. Rent a raft, kayak, or canoe along the beach at V. Marina Garibaldi (€3-5 per hr., €13-24 per day) to explore the coves flanking **Spiaggia Bianca.** A few kilometers north at **Pomiciazzo,** pumice mines line the road. Farther north at **Porticello,** people bathe at the foot of mines where flecks of stone float on the water's surface. A beach closer to the port is **Porto della Gente.** From the docks at the end of V. Garibaldi, turn left on the *lungomare* and walk up the hill. Turn right up the stairs and take the first left away from the hotel. Turn right on the next road and follow it to the shore. These beaches provide views of Salina, Panarea, and Stromboli. For the best vista, take the Lipari-Quattropani bus to **Pianoconte** and head to **Monte S. Angelo.** The mountain path is narrow and overgrown, so ask for help instead of getting lost.

Summer fever reaches its breaking point (and surpasses the island's capacity) on August 24 with the **Festa di San Bartolomeo.** Processions, parties, and pyrotechnics take over in celebration. The quieter **Wine and Bread Festival** in mid-November features more delectable activities in the Pianoconte district.

For a relaxed evening head to **Bar Luna Quinta,** V. Francesco Crispi, 44. With your back to the dock, V. F. Crispi runs along the water to your right. This self-proclaimed "slow-bar" is an eccentric dive known as a safe haven for visiting mariners and local artists alike. (☎090 38 80 088. Open daily 7:30pm-late.)

VULCANO ☎090

Visitors can usually smell Vulcano long before they see it. The pungent island was once thought to be the home of the Greek god Vulcan, god of smiths, and of Aeolus, keeper of the winds—as well as the gate to Hell—though it is now best known for its volcanic craters and savage landscapes. The largest volcano is the active and heavily touristed Fossa di Vulcano. The great furnace currently lies benign, but geologists forecast an eruption within the next 20 years. Black beaches, bubbling seas, and natural sulfuric mud spas may make Vulcano seem unfriendly, but these untamed natural phenomena usually end up winning over visitors.

▤ TRANSPORTATION

The island is accessible by **hydrofoil** and **ferry. Siremar** (☎090 98 52 149), atop a stone walkway at the Porto Levante intersection, runs hydrofoils to Lipari (10min., 9 per day 7am-7:35pm, €2.50) and Milazzo (40min., 9 per day 7:20am-7:50pm, €10.40). **Ustica** (☎090 98 52 230), directly off the port next to Cantine Stevenson, runs hydrofoils to: Lipari (10min., 11 per day 8am-7:50pm, €2.50); Milazzo (40min., 8 per day, €10.50); Palermo (4hr., 2 per day 7:15am-4:05pm, €31.30). **N.G.I. Biglietteria** (☎090 98 52 401) sells ferry tickets under a blue awning on V. Provinciale, just off P. Levante. Open daily 8:15am-noon, 5:15-6:30pm and 10:30-11:30pm. **Scaffidi Tindaro** (☎090 98 53 047) runs **internal buses** off the port on V. Provinciale, in front of Ritrovo Remigio. Rare buses (€1.95) run to Vulcano Piano. **Bikes** and **scooters** are available for rent at the two **Sprint da Luigi** shops, a block apart on V. Provinciale with almost identical prices. Multilingual owners provide maps and other tourist information. (☎090 98 52 208 or 347 76 00 275. Scooters in May €12.50-15 per day; June €15.50-18 per day; July-Aug. €15-25 per day; Sept. €15.50 per day. Bikes €3-5. €3 each additional day. Tandem bike €8 per hr., €20 per day; minicar €15 per hr., €45 per day. 18+ for anything with a motor.) Find **boat rental** at **Blob Oasi,** Baia di Ponente (☎338 89 69 690) on the Sabbie Nere. Rent rubber-like boats ranging from 2-person (€50) to 20-person (€1000). The store is open daily June-October 9am-6pm. **Centro Nautico,** Baia di Levante, is on the beach behind Ritrovo Remigio, near the hydrofoil dock. (☎339 87 97 238 or 337 27 95. 4-person motorboat €90-150 per day. Gas extra. Open daily 8am-10pm.) For a **taxi** from the port call ☎339 57 91 576 or 347 81 30 631.

▦ ▐ ORIENTATION AND PRACTICAL INFORMATION

Vulcano's casual atmosphere is manifested in the lack of posted street names and address numbers. Frequent directional signs and arrows, however, make this pedestrian island easily navigable. Ferries and hydrofoils dock at **Porto di Levante,** on the eastern side of **Vulcanello,** the youngest of the island's three volcanoes. Facing away from the hydrofoil dock at the far left of the port, **Via Provinciale** heads left toward the Fossa di Vulcane and its **Gran Cratere** (Great Crater). Straight ahead is **Via Porto Levante,** a semicircular road that loops through town and reconnects to the ferry docks. From the hydrofoil docks, V. Porto Levante splits in three directions at the small statue of Aeolus. The pharmacy is straight ahead, while the **acquacalda** and **Laghetto di Fanghi** are on the right. Continue along to the left of the pharmacy, passing green pastures on the way to the black shoreline of **Sabbie Nere.**

Tourist Office: V. Provinciale, 41 (☎090 98 52 028 or 090 98 52 142), has info on *affittacamere*. Open Aug. daily 8am-1:30pm and 3-5pm. All other info at AAST in Lipari.

Bank: Banco Sicilia (☎090 98 52 335), 100m down from the port on V. Provinciale, has an **ATM**. Open M-F 8:30am-1:30pm and 2:45-3:45pm.

Currency Exchange: Ustica Office (☎090 98 52 230), at Porto di Levante.

Emergency: ☎113. **Carabinieri:** ☎090 98 52 110. **Police:** ☎090 98 52 577. **First Aid:** ☎090 985 22 20.

Pharmacy: Farmacia Bonarrigo, V. Favaloro, 1 (☎090 98 52 244; in case of emergency 98 53 113), straight ahead of the port, at the far end of the small *piazza* where V. Provinciale breaks off. Open M-Sa 9am-1pm and 5-8pm, Su 9am-1pm. AmEx/MC/V. Posts list of after-hours rotations.

Internet Access: 2 computers at **DeSpar market** on V. Lentia across from the thermal baths. €4 per hr. Open M-Sa 8am-9:30pm.

Post Office: At Vulcano Piano, down V. Provinciale. Open M-F 8am-1:20pm, Sa 8am-12:20pm. **Postal Code:** 98050.

ACCOMMODATIONS AND CAMPING

Hotel Torre, V. Favaloro, 1 (☎/fax 090 98 52 342), down V. Porto Levante from hydrofoil docks, near pharmacy. Rooms come with bath, A/C, and kitchen; many offer great views. Good location near *acquacalda*. Doubles Oct.-May €40; June-Sept. €50; Aug. €80. Extra person 35%. Solo travelers may receive low-season discount. Cash only. ❹

Residence Lanterna Bleu di Francesco Corrieri, V. Lentia, 58 (☎/fax 090 98 52 178). V. Lentia breaks from V. Provinciale before the pharmacy. 1- or 2-room apartments are tranquil. All come with bath, A/C, kitchenette, and terrace. 400m from thermal and mudbaths. Breakfast €4. May-Sept. singles €42-68; doubles €83-136. Oct.-Apr. singles €31; doubles €62. Extra bed €13-19. AmEx/MC/V. ❹

Campeggio Togo Togo (☎090 98 52 303), at Porto Ponente, on opposite side of Vulcano's isthmus neck, 1.5km from hydrofoil dock and adjacent to Sabbie Nere. Showers, tent, and hot water €0.50. Pizzeria on premises in summer. Open Apr.-Sept. Reserve ahead for Aug. €11 includes tent and light. Larger bungalow with TV and kitchenette July-Aug. up to 4 people €85; Apr.-June and Sept. 1-7 €21 per person. ❶

FOOD

Granita and *gelato* are in abundance at the port, but venture off the main roads for a good meal. The aromatic *Malvasia* wine is a delight. **Tridial Market,** on V. Porto Levante in the *piazza* before the pharmacy, has essentials, plus a sandwich counter. (Open daily 8am-8:30pm.) An **alimentari** on V. Provinciale, toward the crater from the port, sells produce. (Open daily 8am-1pm and 5-8pm.) A small **CONAD** market is right below Hotel Torre. (Open M-Sa 8am-9:30pm.)

Remigio, V. Porto Levante, 1 (☎090 98 52 085), at end of the hydrofoil docks. Popular with tourists and locals, this large bar sells hot and cold sandwiches made to order (€2). Delicious *gelato* and many, many desserts. Free baggage storage for patrons. Horseshoe *ciappe* €1.30. *Cassata* €2.20. Open daily 6am-2am. Cash only. ❶

Cafe Piazzetta (☎090 98 53 267), in Piazzetta Faraglione, down V. Provinciale from hydrofoil docks. Serves *gelato* and cocktails (€5.50), as well as the more substantial pizza (from €5-6.80) or *basiluzzo panino,* with tomato, cheese, lettuce, olive oil, salt, and oregano (€2.80). Live music June-Sept. on the bamboo patio 10pm-1:30am. Free baggage storage for patrons. Open Apr.-Sept. daily 7am-2am. AmEx/MC/V. ❶

Cantine Stevenson (☎090 98 53 247), on V. Porto Levante. Nightlife dive where locals listen to classical music in a pub-like setting. Check out the 60-page wine list. Live music M-W 10:30pm-1:30am. Cocktails €5.50. Pizza €6.50. *Primi* from €6.50, *secondi* from €8. Dessert €4.50. Open daily 1pm-3am. MC/V. ❷

Ristorante-Bar Vincenzino, V. Porto Levante, 25 (☎090 98 52 016; fax 090 98 53 370), down hydrofoil docks, up V. Provinciale. Large, low-key restaurant/bar serves Aeolian specialties. *Gamberoni alla griglia* (grilled prawns; €18) are an expensive treat. *Primi* €7-9, *secondi* €7-20. Cover €1.50. Open daily 8am-10:30pm. AmEx/MC/V. ❹

👁 SIGHTS

Anyone visiting Vulcano for more than a day should tackle the 1hr. hike to the **Gran Cratere** at the summit of Fossa di Vulcano. The crater rewards trekkers with views of the island, sea, and volcanic landscape. The hike winds through yellow *fumaroli*, emissions of noxious smoke, and orange rock formations powdered with dust. Between 11am and 3pm, the sun transforms the volcano face into a furnace. Head out in the early morning or late afternoon, and bring a hat, sunscreen, sturdy climbing shoes, and plenty of water. Segments of the trail are quite strenuous and should be approached with caution. Obey the signs, and don't sit or lie down, as poisonous gases tend to accumulate close to the ground. Some travelers shave a good 30min. off their descent time by sprinting straight down the mountainside; this is an undeniable thrill, but the risk is a nasty spill. (Facing away from the water at the port, turn left on V. Provinciale and follow it until reaching a path with *"Cratere"* signs. The notices point to a turn-off 300m on the left.)

If everyone jumped into a radioactive mudpit, would you? The murky graybrown of the **Laghetto di Fanghi's** water blends right in with the surrounding volcanic rock formations, but the putrid smell makes this natural spa impossible to miss. Undeterred, droves of visitors spread sludge over their bodies for its allegedly curative effects (especially for arthritis). Therapeutic or not, the mud is radioactive and high in corrosive sulfuric acid, which can cause severe burning or blistering. Remove all silver and leather accessories, and keep the actual mud away from the eyes. (Up V. Porto Levante and to the right from the port. €2.) Directly behind the mud pits at the **acquacalda,** Vulcano's shoreline bubbles like a jacuzzi, courtesy of volcanic *fumaroli* beneath the surface. The sulfuric nature of the water has quite an effect on the human blood circulation, creating a heavenly sensation upon emerging—although the mercilessly corrosive acid tends to destroy bathing suits. This is not the place to display the latest in swimwear fashion. Disposable suits are available nearby for €10.

If sulfur burns and radioactive mud don't sound appealing, join carefree sunbathers on Vulcano's best beach, **Sabbie Nere.** Black sands curl up against whitecrested waves, and colorful umbrellas form a rainbow of relaxation. Follow V. Provinciale from the port, then take the road that veers to the left of the pharmacy. Continue along the pastures and past the Hotel Eolie until reaching the shore.

PANAREA ☎090

As is apparent from the constant stream of white linen and Louis Vuitton luggage on the hydrofoil docks, petite Panarea is the island for chic repose. With simple white buildings and a beguiling elegance, Panarea attracts an older, upscale crowd seeking an understated place to relax. In August, however, rambunctious youth overtake the *discoteche*, forcing its once-dignified waterside bars to pump up the volume and party well into the morning.

SICILY

TRANSPORTATION AND PRACTICAL INFORMATION. Panarea is accessible by **ferry** and **hydrofoil** (see **Aeolian Islands: Transportation,** p. 664). The **Siremar** office is at the port. (☎090 98 30 07. Open M, Th, Sa 7am-11:30am; Tu-W, F, Su 2-7:45pm and 2-6:30pm.) Panarea is a purely pedestrian island. Its only vehicles are bikes, scooters, and golf carts that serve as taxis. All directional signs list distances by feet rather than kilometers, and street signs and numbers are very rare. The main road, **Via San Pietro,** runs past Chiesa San Pietro along an undulating stone path to **Punta Milazzese. Banca Antonveneta** has an **ATM** on V. S. Pietro, on the left from the port, and **Banca di Sicilia** has one on the patio of the Hotel Cincotta. Have a back-up plan in case ATMs don't work. The **post office** on V. S. Pietro **exchanges currency** and traveler's checks. (☎090 98 30 28. Open M-F 8am-1:30pm, Sa 8am-12:30pm.) In case of **emergency,** call the **carabinieri** (July-Aug. ☎090 98 31 81; Sept.-June 981 13 33, in Lipari) or the **medical clinic** (☎090 98 30 40). A 24hr. **golf cart taxi** service is run by **Paola+Angelo** (☎333 31 38 610), on V. S. Pietro. Passage to the beach costs around €8. A **pharmacy** is at V. Iditella, 8. (☎090 98 31 48. Open in summer M-Sa 9am-1pm and 5-9pm; in winter M-Tu and Th-Su 9am-12:30pm.)

ACCOMMODATIONS. Hotels are small but costly, and prices peak in July and August. From the docks, turn left, follow the road past the ATM to the steps, and look for the manta ray symbol to spot ◙**Hotel RAYA ❺,** on V. S. Pietro. From striking architecture to amazing views, all aspects of this hotel breathe island elegance. Its *discoteca* is famous on the island (see **Entertainment and Beaches,** p. 672), and service is coolly obliging. (☎090 98 30 13; www.hotelraya.it. Breakfast included. Economy singles €92-142; singles €186-278; doubles €236-440. AmEx/MC/V.) ◙**Quartara ❺,** V. S. Pietro, 15, has the prettiest rooms on the island, evident in the unique decor, with cream-colored canopy, balcony, air-conditioning, TV, bath, hair dryer, and minibar. (☎090 98 30 27. Breakfast included. Singles €70-220; doubles €130-300; with view €150-340. Singles supplement €36-100. Extra bed 20% more. Substantial discounts during low-season.) Turn right from the docks and climb stairs to the white- and blue-houses of **Da Francesco/Pasqualina ❹,** on V. del Porto. All rooms have bath, fan, and sea view. A *trattoria* extends from the deck. (☎090 98 30 23. Breakfast included. Rooms €30-70 per person; half pension €65-100. MC/V.) **Hotel Tesoriero ❺,** on V. S. Pietro, has the basics and more: bath, air-conditioning, TV, and hair dryer, plus a terrace with sea view. (☎090 98 30 98 or 98 31 44; info@hoteltesoriero.it. Breakfast included. Doubles €80-150. Half pension €60-100. Singles supplement €11-52. Extra bed 30% more. AmEx/MC/V.) Indulge in Mediterranean bliss with seaside pool and hydromassage at **Hotel Cincotta ❺,** on V. S. Pietro next to Hotel Raya. Its airy rooms are stocked with bath, TV, minibar, and terrace with view. (☎090 98 30 14; fax 090 98 32 11. Breakfast included. Doubles €130-300; half pension €30 extra per person. Extra bed 20% more. AmEx/MC/V.)

FOOD. Da Bruno minimart is on V. S. Pietro by the post office. (☎090 98 30 02. Open daily July-Aug. 7:45am-9pm; Sept.-June 8am-1pm and 4-9pm.) Locals line up at the **panificio** next door for *focaccia* and pizza slices. (☎090 98 32 84. Open daily Sept.-July 6:30am-1:30pm and 5-8pm; Aug. 6:30am-9pm.) Near the port, at **Ristorante Da Pina ❹,** V. S. Pietro, 14, swaths of gauze create an ethereal mood among the pillowed outdoor benches—guests don't sit, they lounge. *Gnocchi di melanzane* (with eggplants; €14) and *couscous di pesce e aragosta* (with fish and lobster; €10) are the house specials. (☎090 98 30 32 or 090 98 33 24; fax 090 98 31 47. Lobster €150 per kg. *Primi* €10, *secondi* €15. AmEx/MC/V.) Whenever a craving flares, find *gelato* (€2.50), *panini* (€3.50), or a Sicilian sweet at **Ritrovo Naif ❶,** V. S. Pietro, open all night. (☎090 98 31 88; www.barnaif.com. Open in summer 24hr.; winter hours vary.)

♫⛱ ENTERTAINMENT AND BEACHES. The few who seek out Panarea's beaches do so precisely because most others do not. Tiny and unencumbered by umbrellas, these are some of the more natural and intimate coves of the archipelago. From Punta Milazzese, three small beaches extend along the coastline; gradually changing from rocks to sand, the trio gives a wide spectrum of Aeolian shores. Two rights from the center of town lead to **Calcara** (also known as "Spiaggia Fumarole"), near the thermal springs at **Acquacalda**. Reach another beach by following V. S. Pietro's signs for **Spiagetta Zimmari**. In a 30min. stroll along a scenic road alive with darting lizards and flowering cacti, rock gives way to sand. Arrive early to find an empty patch of sand, and stop by the supermarket before heading out, as Spiagetta Zimmari's only bar is pricey. For views of coves and cliffs, embark on a boat tour with **Eolie Mare,** on V. Umberto I. The company also rents boats for private exploration. (☎090 98 33 28. Tour €50 for 2 people. Open daily 24hr.) For scuba diving, **Amphibia** has an office on the *lungomare,* up the stairs next to the hotel Da Francesco. (☎335 61 38 529. Office open daily May-Sept. 9am-1pm and 3-7pm. Single immersion €39, 3 dives €111, 6 dives €215. Wetsuit rental €20.)

Panarea comes alive in summer with disco fever. The spot to be is **Hotel RAYA,** V. S. Pietro, which pumps with energy and exclusivity until the first morning rays. Cover: €30-50. Three cocktails: €30. A party outfit that will get you past the door: €100. Chatting up Italian soccer players, Milanese banking heirs, and actresses from all over? Priceless. (☎090 98 30 13. Open July 23-Aug. 31. Hotel guests free.)

SALINA ☎090

Though close to Lipari in both size and distance, Salina is far removed from its more developed neighbor. Untouched landscapes and the most dramatic beaches on the archipelago make it a tranquil paradise. The island's most astounding rock formations are at Semaforo di Pollara, chosen as the setting of Massimo Troisi's film *Il Postino.* Some of Sicily's best restaurants hide away on Salina's slopes, though the island's limited tourism has led to a dearth of budget accommodations. Ultimately, its tranquil simplicity is a blessing after the bombast of Stromboli, the tourist throngs of Lipari, or the my-yacht-is-better-than-yours elitism of Panarea.

⛴ TRANSPORTATION. Porto Santa Marina is the main port of Salina, accessible by **hydrofoil** (30min., 10 per day, €5.30) and **ferry** (50min., 3 per day, €3.20) from Lipari. The smaller port of **Rinella** on the opposite side of the island receives hydrofoils (45min., €6) and ferries (1½hr., €3.80). **Ustica** (☎090 984 30 03) and **Siremar** (☎090 98 43 004) have offices on either side of the church of Santa Marina, in front of the port in P. S. Marina. Blue **CITIS buses,** V. Nazionale, 10 (☎090 98 44 150), in Malfa, stop at the church. Monthly schedules are posted at the Ustica office. **Buses** run to Pollara (40min., 7 per day 6:05am-5:15pm, €1.80) and Leni, Valdichiesa, Malfa, Gramignazzi, Rinella, and Lingua (12 per day 6:05am-8pm). **Rent scooters** from **Motonoleggio Bongiorno Antonio,** V. Risorgimento, 240, in Santa Marina. Facing away from the hydrofoil docks, turn left up the road that curves uphill. Turn right up the first side street just before a row of parked scooters to reach the office. Caution: Salina's roads are extremely narrow and curvy, and locals drive with a notorious and reckless abandon, so leave driving to the experts. If you do drive, then absolutely wear a helmet. (☎090 98 43 409 or 090 98 43 264. Scooters €8-8.50 per hr., €26-31 per day. Gas extra. Mountain bikes €2.50-3.50 per hr., €8-10.50 per day. Open daily in summer 8:30am-8pm; in winter 8:30am-1:30pm. AmEx/MC/V.)

⛅🛈 ORIENTATION AND PRACTICAL INFORMATION. The main road, **Via Risorgimento,** runs parallel to the *lungomare.* **Banco di Sicilia,** V. Risorgimento,

158-160, cashes **traveler's checks, exchanges money,** and has an **ATM.** (☎090 98 43 365. Open M-F 8:30am-1:30pm.) In case of **emergency,** call the **carabinieri** (☎090 98 43 019), **police** (☎090 98 43 021), or **first aid** (☎090 98 44 005). A **pharmacy,** V. Risorgimento, 211, is at the end of the street. (☎090 984 30 98. Open M 5:30-8:30pm, Tu-F 9am-1pm and 5:30-8:30pm, Sa 9am-1pm.) **Salina Computer,** on V. Risorgimento, 110, has **Internet** and is open daily 8:30am-1pm and 3-8:30pm. (☎090 98 43 444. €6 per hr.) The **post office,** at V. Risorgimento, 130, exchanges **traveler's checks.** (☎090 984 30 28. Open M-F 8am-1:30pm, Sa 8am-12:30pm.) **Postal Code:** 98050.

🏠🍴 ACCOMMODATIONS AND FOOD. Restaurants crowd Santa Marina, the dockside town, but most accommodations are farther away. By the port, consider **Pensione Mamma Santina ❺,** V. Sanità, 40, which offers rooms painted in melon hues. Guests mingle on the terrace, and the owner/chef (recently featured in *Cucina Italiana*) has been known to give cooking lessons to inquisitive onlookers. (☎090 98 43 054; www.mammasantina.it. Breakfast included. Doubles €90-200. Half pension €25 extra per person. €30 surcharge for use of a double as a single. AmEx/MC/V.) Salina's only true budget accommodation, **Campeggio Tre Pini ❶,** V. Rotabile, 1, maintains campsites with a market, bar, and restaurant. (☎090 98 09 155, in winter 090 98 09 041. Take the bus or hydrofoil to Rinella, and confirm destination with driver. Reserve July-Aug. €6-8 per person, €8-11 per tent.)

As always, the cheapest way to eat is a cold lunch: assemble a beach picnic at any **alimentari** on V. Risorgimento. But given Salina's cuisine, it is almost inexcusable not to indulge in a meal. The finest is at 🍴**Ristorante Mamma Santina ❶,** where chef Mario welcomes you to the terrace dining room and treats you to homemade specialties. *Spaghetti alla mamma santina* (€10), a family secret made with 14 fresh herbs and spices, is unbelievable. (*Primi* €5.50-10; *secondi di carne* €8, *di pesce* €12. Open daily noon-3pm and 8pm-midnight. AmEx/MC/V.) An exerting but rewarding 15min. uphill walk leads to 🍴**Ristorante da Franco ❹,** V. Belvedere, 8. Follow the signs starting from the *lungomare* right before the *carabinieri* station. Promising "courtesy, hospitality, and quality" from "the best of nature," the restaurant offers supremely fresh local specialties, not to mention the best views in Salina. (☎090 98 43 287. *Primi* from €9.30, *secondi* from €13. Homemade wine €9.30. Open daily 7:30pm-midnight. Closed Dec. 1-20. AmEx/MC/V.) At night, **Nmi Lausta ❹,** V. Risorgimento, 188, packs gabby patrons into the bar downstairs. Evening diners go upstairs for *pasta modo mio,* or "pasta my way," an oft-changing pasta dish, in the relaxed terrace garden. (☎090 98 43 486. Lunch *menù* €20, dinner *menù* €35. Open daily 1-3pm and 6pm-midnight. Bar closes at 3am. MC/V.)

📷🎉 SIGHTS AND FESTIVALS. Seeing Salina's finest sight involves a 1hr. bus ride from Santa Marina to the striking 📷**Pollara,** a beach 100m straight down from the town's cliffs in the middle of a half-submerged volcanic crater. The trip, though fast-paced, is worth every twist and turn. Black sand, crumbling boulders, and sandstone walls create the crescent of land that hugs the blue water. To the far right, a natural rock archway bursts from the water and suns itself against a cliff. On the other side of the island, **Valdichiesa** rests at the base of **Monte Fossa delle Felci,** the highest point of the Aeolians. Trails lead from the town 962m up the mountain. For less aerobic activity, relax at **Malfa's** beach, which offers equally tantalizing views—of the huge sulfur bubbles known as *sconcassi.* The first Sunday in June, the population of Salina heads to Pollara for the **Sacra del Cappero,** often numbering 1000 celebrators. Each restaurant and volunteering family brings its own special dish in which the *cappero* (caper) is key. Visitors are invited to contribute their own treats, which is an easy way to make friends and get in with the locals.

STROMBOLI
☎ **090**

In Italian geology, "strombolic activity" refers to the most violent type of volcanic eruption. In keeping with its title, the aptly named island of Stromboli harbors the Aeolians' only currently erupting volcano—a fact that keeps residents few (around 370) and visitors many. Though the great Stromboli is always gurgling, the island itself keeps quiet until summer. Sporadic volcanic activity scares away all but the most determined visitors, cleaning out hotel rooms and turning the town into a deserted haven, if a dimly ominous one. The adventurous are drawn to nightly guided hikes up the mountain, but if the volcano's threat seems more intimidating than intriguing, renting a boat is also a great way to visit.

◪ **TRANSPORTATION.** Along the shorefront *lungomare*, **Siremar** (☎090 98 60 16; open daily 9am-1pm, 3-8pm, and 8:30-10pm for service to Naples), **Ustica** (☎090 98 60 03; open daily 8am-1pm and 3-8pm), and **N.G.I.** (☎090 98 30 03) run **ferries** and **hydrofoils** to the islands. **Boat rentals** are available from a number of companies at the port, including the **Società Navigazione Pippo.** (☎090 98 61 35 or 338 98 57 883. Boats from €60 per day; larger boats run up to €200. Gas extra. 3hr. boat tours daily 10:30am and 3:10pm; €20. Open daily 9am-noon, 2-8pm, and 9-10:30pm.)

◪◪ **ORIENTATION AND PRACTICAL INFORMATION.** On the calmer slopes of smoking Stromboli, the three villages of **Scari, Ficogrande,** and **Piscita** have melded into one stretch known as the town of Stromboli. From the ferry docks, the wide *lungomare* is on the right, continuing to the beach and two large hotels, while the narrow **Via Roma** heads from the ticket offices up to the town center. Pick up an excellent **map** at Totem Trekking for €2.50. Twisting uphill to the left, V. Roma passes the **carabinieri** station (☎090 98 60 21), the island's only **ATM** next to the Alimentari da Maria, the **post office** (☎090 98 60 27; open M-F 8am-1:30pm, Sa 8am-12:30pm), and finally the **pharmacy** (☎090 98 67 13; open M-Sa 8:30am-1pm and 4-8:30pm; Sept.-May M-Sa 8:30am-1pm and 4-7:30pm), just before reaching **Piazza San Vincenzo.** V. Roma then dips downhill, becoming **Via Vittorio Emanuele,** which runs past the **medical clinic** (☎090 98 60 97) and leads to the trail up the mountain. **Postal Code:** 98050.

◪◪ **ACCOMMODATIONS AND FOOD.** Unlike the more populated islands, the tourist deluge in Stromboli happens in August. In the low season, many *pensioni* close down and owners are reluctant to rent rooms for fewer than three nights. When hotels are solidly booked, *affittacamere* may be the best bet. Expect to pay between €20 and €30. Ask to see the room before paying, and don't be afraid to check for hot water and comfortable beds. From the main road, follow the small side street across from St. Bartholomew's church at the end of town to reach **Casa del Sole ❷,** on V. Cincotta. Big dormitory rooms face a terrace and shared kitchen, while the upstairs holds doubles painted in sea hues. Four bathrooms are downstairs. (☎/fax 090 98 60 17. Open Mar.-Oct. Dorm beds €13-24 per person; doubles €30-50. Prices vary seasonally.) **Pensione Brasile ❹,** up the street from Casa del Sole, offers simple rooms and home-cooked meals. (☎090 98 60 08; www.netnet-eolie.it/pensionebrasile.it. Breakfast included. Apr.-June 15 and Sept.-Oct. €28 per person; June 16-Sept. 7 half pension doubles €42-70 per person; full pension €60-73 per person. MC/V.) **Pensione Villa Petrusa ❺,** V. Voldato Pannettieri, 4, off V. V. Emanuele, 10min. from the sea, has gardens, a TV room and bar, and 26 comfortable rooms with bath. (☎090 98 60 45. Breakfast included. Singles €40-62; doubles €70-130. Cash only.) **La Lampara B&B ❸,** V. V. Emanuele, 27, has five rooms decorated island-style, with brightly tiled floors, TV, and large bath. (☎090 98 64 09. Breakfast included. Rooms €20 per person; July €35; Aug. €45. AmEx/MC/V.)

Stuff a pre-hike knapsack snack at **Alimentari da Maria,** V. Roma, 191, just before the church. (☎090 98 61 49. Open daily 8:30am-1pm and 4:30-8:30pm, Su 8:30am-1pm. MC/V.) In order to admire the volcano's explosive activity from solid ground, head to ■**L'Osservatorio ❹,** in Punta Labronzo, the last establishment along V. V. Emanuele. The food is slightly overpriced, but the spectacular view of nighttime eruptions makes it well worth it. The restaurant is a serious trek away; bring a flashlight at night and wear sneakers. Taxis also depart for the restaurant from S. Bartolo every hour 5-11pm. (☎090 98 63 60 or 337 29 39 42; fax 090 98 63 60. Pizza from €6.20. *Primi* from €7, *secondi* from €14. Cover €1.50. Open daily 9:30am-midnight. Cash only.) Locals say the best pizza on the island is **La Lampara ❸,** V. V. Emanuele, 27, on the left just after P. San Vincenzo. It shares management with La Lampara B&B. The freshly squeezed lemon *granite* (€2) are amazing, and the owner serves fish he caught himself. The *frittura di pesce misto* (mixed fried fish; €11) offers a nice sampling. (☎090 98 64 09; fax 090 98 67 21. Pizza from €5.50. *Primi* €6-10, *secondi* €10-14. Open Mar.-Nov. daily 6pm-midnight. AmEx/MC/V.) At the *rosticceria* **La Trottola ❷,** V. Roma, 34, delve into the *pizza Stromboli,* a cone-shaped creation bursting with mozzarella, tomatoes, and olives. (☎090 98 60 46. Pizza from €4. Open daily 8am-2pm and 4pm-midnight. MC/V.)

◙ SIGHTS. Strombolicchio, a gigantic rock with a small lighthouse, rises 2km in the distance from the beach at **Ficogrande.** The ravages of the sea have eroded the rock from 56m to a mere 42m in the past century. Beachgoers should check out the cove at the end of V. Giuseppe Cincotta, off V. V. Emanuele near Casa del Sole, where rocks encircle the stretch of black sand.

At the ■**volcano,** rivers of orange lava and molten rock spill over the slope, lighting the **Sciara del Fuoco** (Trail of Fire) at roughly 10min. intervals. The **Società Navigazione Pippo** (☎090 98 61 35), at the port, runs a boat trip for those wishing to view the volcano from the sea (1hr., 10pm, €15), although many visitors prefer to get a bit closer. An ordinance passed in 1990 made hiking the volcano without a guide illegal, and for good reason: a photographer was burned to death after getting too close to the volcanic opening, and in 1998, a Czech diplomat, lost in the fog, walked off the cliff's edge. So if such an end is not in your stars, look into an escorted trip with ■**Magmatrek,** on V. V. Emanuele (☎/fax 090 98 65 768; office open 10am-1pm and 4:30-6:30pm). After being banned for three years, guided tours to the craters are once again allowed. The charismatic **Mario Zaia** (☎368 67 55 73), known as Zaza, is regarded as one of the most reliable volcano guides working today. (Helmets required and provided. All tours offered in English. Departures daily Mar.-June 3:30pm; July-Aug. 6pm; Sept.-Oct. 3:30pm; €22.) **Totem Trekking,** at P. S. Vincenzo, 4, rents equipment and supplies, as well as Internet access for €2.50 per hr. (☎090 986 57 52. Open daily in summer 10am-1pm and 4:30pm-midnight; Dec. 15-Jan. 8 10am-1pm and 4-7pm. Call year-round to arrange rentals. AmEx/MC/V.)

STOP IN THE NAME OF LAVA. Let's Go does not recommend, advocate, or take responsibility for anyone hiking Stromboli's volcano, with or without a guide. A red triangle with a black vertical bar means "danger."

◪ ENTERTAINMENT. The plateau of **Piazza San Vincenzo** is Stromboli's geographic center and its most exciting 46 sq. m (besides the crater itself). Each night around 10pm, islanders flock to **Ritrovo Ingrid** for *gelato* (€1.55) and drinks. (☎090 98 63 85. Open daily July-Aug. 8am-3am; Aug.-July 8am-1am.) Its neighbor, **Ris-**

MESSINA IN STRAITS

Sicily has long prided itself on its physical and cultural separation from the rest of Italy. The isolated island, however, may soon face a significant sort of integration into the mainland: Prime Minister Silvio Berlusconi has set construction of the world's largest suspension bridge, connecting Sicily to the southern tip of Italy, to commence in 2005. The bridge is expected to promote development and employment in two of the poorest regions in Italy.

But many Italians don't see it that way. Controversy concerning the bridge has spawned an anti-bridge campaign spearheaded by a number of political and environmental groups. Campaign supporters, fearful of potential Mafia influence in its construction, are also worried that such a bridge would destroy the area's delicate ecosystem and natural beauty. Ironically, this could help to destroy the very tourism that bridge proponents hope to increase. Furthermore, protesters argue that a bridge would triple crossing costs for locals and leave a projected 3000 ferry and hydrofoil operators out of work.

Even logistics of the bridge itself are under debate: many claim that the bridge is not only impractical but impossible, citing the seismic activity constantly causing Sicily to inch towards the mainland. Despite these objections, however, construction is due to conclude in 2012.

torante-Pizzeria II Conte Ugolino, has a seating area where people gather for conversation. The moon rising directly over the *piazza* with the volcano in the background is a magical sight. (☎090 98 65 765. Cover €3. Service 15%.)

EASTERN SICILY

MESSINA   ☎090

Messina (240,000) is a transportation hub if ever there was one; better air-conditioning and a duty-free shop would turn this fast-paced town into an airport. While its role as a major port and the main commercial connection between Sicily and the mainland has brought prosperity, Messina has also weathered nonstop invasions, plagues, and earthquakes. Despite all obstacles, the town maintains its dignity in points of historical interest and beauty like the *duomo*, the allegorical clock tower next door, and the church of Santa Maria Annunziàta dei Catalani.

▐▀ TRANSPORTATION

Trains: Stazione Centrale FS (☎090 67 97 95 or info 147 88 80 88), in P. della Repubblica. Call ahead; schedules change frequently. To: **Naples** (7hr., 11 per day, €21.59); **Palermo** (3½hr., 14 per day, €10.55); **Rome** (9hr., 17 per day, €41.37); **Syracuse** (3½hr., 9 per day, €8.19); **Taormina** (40min., 21 per day, €2.05). Trains to the west stop in **Milazzo** (45min., €2.35), the main port of the Aeolian Islands.

Buses: Messina has 4 bus carriers, many of which serve the same routes.

AST (☎090 66 22 44, ask for "*informazioni*"). Ticket office in an orange minibus in P. Duomo across from the cathedral. Serves small and less touristed areas all over Sicily and southern Italy.

SAIS, P. della Repubblica, 6 (☎090 77 19 14). Ticket office is behind the trees, across from far left tip of the FS station. To: **Catania airport** (1-2hr., 6 per day, €7.25); **Catania** (1½hr., 9 per day, €6.50); **Florence** (12½hr.; 1 per week, Su; €50); **Naples** (22hr., 3 per week., €25); **Palermo** (1½hr., 8 per day, €13.30).

Interbus, P. della Repubblica, 6 (☎090 66 17 54), has blue offices left of the train station, beyond the line of buses. To: **Giardini-Naxos** (1½hr., 9 per day, €2.50); **Naples** (1 per week, Su; €22); **Rome** (2 per day, €30); **Taormina** (1½hr., 12 per day, €2.50).

Giuntabus, V. Terranova, 8 (☎090 67 37 82 or 090 67 57 49), 3 blocks up V. I Settembre, left on V. Bruno, right on

V. Terranova. To: **Catania Airport** (Apr.-Sept. daily 4pm, €10.60) and **Milazzo** from Terranova (45min.; M-Sa 14 per day 6am-6pm, Su 1 per day; €3.40).

Ferries: Meridiano (☎347 91 00 119 or 347 64 13 234), on the waterfront 300m from the FS station. To **Reggio** (40min.; M-Sa 12 per day, Su 1 per day; €1.50).

Speedboats and Hydrofoils: From Messina, **BluVia**, the waterfront wing of Stazione Centrale, **FS** sends hydrofoils to **Reggio** (25min.; M-F 14 per day 6:10am-7:40pm, Sa and Su 6 per day 7:30am-7:40pm; €2.80) and **Villa San Giovanni** (30min., 2 per hr., €1). From the station facing the *piazza*, turn right and walk toward the waterfront, then look for BluVia signs. Ticket office on the docks. **Ustica** (☎0903 64 044), has offices in a blue building on the waterfront side of C. V. Emanuele, 2km north of the train station off C. Garibaldi. Hydrofoils to: **Aeolian Islands** (2-2½hr., June-Sept. 3-6 per day for each destination); **Lipari** (5 per day, 7:10am-8:20pm, €16.50); **Panarea** (1¾hr., 4 per day 7:10am-2:55pm, €19.10); **Salina** (1¼hr., 5 per day 7:10am-6:20pm, €19.10).

Public Transportation: Orange **ATM buses** leave either from P. della Repubblica or from the bus station, 2 blocks up V. I Settembre from the station, on the right. Buy tickets (€0.90 for 1½hr.) at a *tabaccheria* or newsstand. Bus info on yellow-bordered signs outside the bus station. **Bus #79** stops at the *duomo*, museum, and aquarium, and only runs from P. della Repubblica. **Trams** run from the station to the museum (10min., every 10min. 5am-10pm, €0.90 for 3hr.; buy tickets at *tabaccherie* or newsstand).

Taxis: Radiotaxi Jolly (☎090 65 05), to the right of the *duomo*.

ORIENTATION AND PRACTICAL INFORMATION

Messina's transportation center is **Piazza della Repubblica**, in front of the **train station**, home to two tourist offices and headquarters for several bus lines. The tram leaves from the *piazza*, and ferry and speedboats run from the port right next to the station. **Via G. la Farina** runs in front of the train station. Beyond the highrises to the left, **Via Tommaso Cannizzaro** leads to the center of town, meeting palm-lined **Viale San Martino** at **Piazza Cairoli**. Enter P. della Repubblica from the train station. At the far right end begins **Via I Settembre**, which intersects **Corso Garibaldi**. C. Garibaldi runs along the harbor to both the hydrofoil dock and **Corso Cavour**.

> **Tourist Office: AAPIT**, V. Calabria, 301 (☎090 67 42 71; aptmeinfoturismo@virgilio.it), on the right corner facing P. della Repubblica from train station. Well staffed and very helpful, with a deluge of **maps** and info on Messina, the Aeolian Islands, and Reggio Calabria. Open M-Sa 9am-6:30pm.

> ❗ **MIDNIGHT MESSINA.** Women should not walk alone in Messina at night, and no one should roam the streets near the train station or the harbor after 10pm. Stay near the more populated streets around the *duomo* and the university. Be wary of pick-pockets and purse-snatchers, and keep money in a secure place.

> **Currency Exchange: F. lli. Grosso**, V. Garibaldi, 58 (☎090 77 40 83). Open M-F 8:30am-1pm, Sa 8:30am-12:30pm.

> **ATMs:** Outside the train station and to the right. Also at V. T. Cannizzaro, 24, and **Banco di Napoli** on V. Emanuele facing the port.

> **English-Language Bookstore: Libreria Nunnari e Sfameri**, V. Cannizzaro, 116 (☎090 71 04 69). University bookstore stacks 4 shelves with classics—brush up on Shakespeare and Faulkner. Open M-F 8:30am-1pm and 4-8pm, Sa 8:30am-1pm. MC/V.

> **Emergency:** ☎113. **Carabinieri:** ☎112. **Ambulance:** ☎118.

> **Medical Clinic:** V. Garibaldi, 242 (☎090 34 54 22).

Pharmacy: Farmacia Abate, Vle. S. Martino, 39 (☎090 63 733, for info on all pharmacies in town 090 71 75 89). From the train station take V. del Vespro 4 blocks and turn left. All pharmacies open M-F 8:30am-1pm and 4:30-8pm. After-hours rotation posted outside.

Hospital: Ospedale Piemonte (☎090 22 24 347), on Vle. Europa.

Internet Access: Centro Internet, V. Ghibellina, 87, on the small street across V. Cannizzaro from Libreria Nunnari e Sfameri. Walk down it for a short block and Centro Internet will be at the corner on your left. 4 fast computers. €0.05 per min. Open daily 9:30am-1pm and 4-8pm.

Post Office: ☎0906 68 64 15. In P. Antonello, off C. Cavour and across from Galleria. Open M-Sa 8:30am-6:30pm. **Postal Code:** 98100.

ACCOMMODATIONS

Messina is definitely more fly-by than stop-over, and its handful of hotels caters not to cost-conscious travelers but to deep-pocketed businessmen. Cheaper hotels are found in the shady neighborhood by the station; be careful at night. If you can afford it, make your stay in Messina short and spring for a more expensive option.

Hotel Cairoli, Vle. S. Martino, 63 (☎090 67 37 55). From train station, walk 4 blocks up V. del Vespro and left 1 block. Just off P. Cairoli. A white- and blue-sign is prominent over the doorway. Rooms come with A/C, TV, and phone. Ask at front desk for a free breakfast coupon. Singles €34-40, with bath €46; doubles €50/80. AmEx/MC/V. ❸

The Royal Palace Hotel, V. T. Cannizzaro, 224 (☎090 65 03; reservation.rph@framon-hotels.it). Across the street from the J.G. Cafe, this hotel's rooms have bath, TV, and A/C for a professional clientele. Fancy **restaurant** ❺ on 1st floor. Breakfast €11. Lunch or dinner €30. Singles €86-114; doubles €127-158. AmEx/MC/V. ❺

FOOD

Restaurants and *trattorie* cluster in the area around V. Risorgimento, reached by following V. Cannizzaro two blocks past P. Cairoli. Messina is hooked on sword-fish—baked, fried, or stewed (*pesce stocco*). Another specialty is *caponata*, a dish of fried eggplant, onion, capers, and olives in a red sauce. For dessert, *cannoli* and sugary *pignolata* are both decadent. Art-deco splendor garnishes **Osteria Etnea** ❷, V. T. Cannizzaro, 155-57, near the university. Signature pasta and fish dishes (from €3.10) like *spaghetti etnea* (€4.65) have a flare of their own. (☎090 71 80 40. Cover €2. Open M 8-11:30pm, Tu-Sa 12:30-4pm and 8-11:30pm, Su 12:30-4pm. AmEx/MC/V.) At **Osteria del Campanile** ❸, V. Loggia dei Mercanti, 9-13, behind the *duomo*, locals flood sidewalk tables and the subdued dining room for *fettuccine salmonate* (€6.20) and other staples. (☎/fax 090 71 14 18. *Primi* from €5.20, *secondi* from €6.20. Open M-Sa noon-3pm and 5-11:30pm. AmEx/MC/V.) Follow V. I Settembre away from the *duomo* one block and turn right to **Pizza e Coca** ❶, V. C. Battisti, 47, your red-checkered, cheap-as-anything Little Italy-style pizzeria—in the real Italy. (☎090 67 36 79. *Bruschetta* €3. Pizza from €4, family size from €12. Takeout and delivery available. Open M-Sa noon-2am, Su 5pm-midnight.)

SIGHTS

Though Messina has lost many of its monuments to both natural and man-induced calamities, the town still features a number of great sights. Churches on the out-skirts of town, Montalto, offer sweeping vistas of the city and port.

PIAZZA DEL DUOMO. Flagstones and shady trees provide a relaxing respite from the city that surrounds this central *piazza*. The great **duomo**, built in Norman times and dedicated in 1197 to the Virgin Mary, dominates the square with an enormous facade that can be blinding in the afternoon sun. The long nave rolls past 14 niche sculptures of saints and sweeping tile floors to arrive at a massive altar dedicated to Madonna della Lettera, the city's patron saint. A statue of Archbishop Angelo Paino to the left of the altar commemorates the tireless efforts of the man who rebuilt the *duomo* twice, first after the earthquake of 1908 and again after WWII bombing destroyed half of the church. **Il Tesoro** (The Treasury), a modern two-story museum, houses the church's most valuable possessions, including gold reliquaries and candlesticks. The highlight is the ornate *Manta d'Oro* (Golden Mantle), a special cover decorated with precious stones and jewels used to drape the picture of the Madonna and Child in the church's altar. It is on display after being locked away for three centuries and emerges from the church each year for an annual festival. Plans for the **campanile** began in the early 16th century, and at 90m, it was intended to be the highest in Sicily. After being struck by lightning in 1588, restorations continued until 1933, when the tower acquired its clock. The structure displays man's progression from base being to noble creature. At noon, a creaky recording of the *Ave Maria* booms and a lion lets out a mechanized roar. Below the clock tower, ancient myth and local lore meet in stone at the **Fontana di Orione,** designed in 1547 by Angelo Montorsoli, a pupil of Michelangelo. The intricate fountain glorifies Orion, the mythical founder of Messina. *(Duomo open daily 7am-7:30pm. Guided tours of treasury in English, French, and German. Treasury open Apr.-Oct. M-Sa 9am-1pm and 3:30-7:30pm; Nov.-Mar. M-Sa 9-1pm, Su 4-6:30pm. €2.58, under 18 or over 65 €1.55.)*

MUSEO REGIONALE. A converted spinning mill houses all that was salvaged from the monastery of St. Gregory and churches throughout the city after the devastating earthquakes of 1894 and 1908. Galleries around a quiet courtyard display the development of Messina's rich artistic tradition. Among more notable pieces are *The Polyptych of the Rosary* (1473) by local master Antonello da Messina; Andrea della Robbia's terra-cotta *Virgin and Child;* and Caravaggio's life-sized *Adoration of the Shepherds* (1608) and *Resurrection of Lazarus* (1609). Just past the entrance, door panels tell the story of the Madonna della Lettera. *(Take bus #8 or 79 from the station or P. Duomo to P. Museo. ☎090 36 12 92. Museum open June-Sept. M and F 9am-1:30pm, Tu, Th, Sa 9am-1:30pm and 4-6:30pm; Oct.-May Tu-Sa 9am-2pm, Su 9am-1pm. Ticket sales end 30min. before closing. €2.50; EU residents 18-25 €2; EU residents under 18 or over 65 and students of literature, philosophy, or art free.)*

PORT. The port is more than a place to catch a hydrofoil: Messina's history and character largely center on its former naval prowess. The enormous **La Madonnina,** a 6m golden statue, surveys the city from a 60m column across the water in the port's center. On the city side, the gleaming **Fontana di Nettuno** by Montorsoli graces the intersection of V. Garibaldi and V. della Libertà. The muscular marble god stands triumphant over the chained muscle-bound she-beasts Scylla and Charybdis, extending one arm to calm the seas. The port is dangerous after dark, so make this a daytime excursion.

CHIESA DELLA SANTISSIMA ANNUNZIÀTA DEI CATALANI. Known as "Catalani" because it was given to the guild of Catalan merchants in the 16th century, this church was built between 1150 and 1200 over the remains of a pagan temple and then rebuilt after its front section collapsed in a flood in the Middle Ages. Islamic and Byzantine influences are apparent in the archways and layout. *(On V. Garibaldi.)*

✿ FESTIVALS

The **Festa di Madonna della Lettera** on June 3 celebrates Messina's guardian. Parades throughout the city culminate at the *duomo*, where the *Manta d'Oro* is restored to the altar for one day every year. Messina overflows with approximately 150,000 white-robed pilgrims during the nationally celebrated **Ferragosto Messinese** festival August 13-15. During the first two days of Ferragosto, two huge human effigies called Mata and Grifone zoom around city in the *Processione dei Gianti.*

TAORMINA
☎ 0942

Legend has it that Neptune wrecked a Greek boat off the eastern coast of Sicily in the 8th century BC and that the sole survivor, inspired by the spectacular scenery, founded Taormina (pop. 10,000). Historians tell a different tale: the Carthaginians founded Tauromenium at the turn of the 4th century BC, only to have it wrested away by the Greek tyrant Dionysius. Disputed origins aside, Taormina's beauty is uncontested, with pines and mansions crowning a cliff above the sea. Disoriented, fanny-packed foreigners, hearty backpackers, and elite VIPs all come for a glimpse of what millions of photographic flashes and hyperbolic statements can't seem to dull: a vista that sweeps dizzily from boiling Etna to the straits of Messina.

▛ TRANSPORTATION

Taormina is accessible by bus from Messina or Catania. Although trains from Catania and Messina are more frequent than buses, the train station lies 5km below Taormina, next to neighboring Giardini-Naxos. Buses run from the train station to Taormina (every 30min. 7:35am-11pm, more frequently in the summer) and Giardini-Naxos (7:50am-11:20pm, more frequently in the summer).

Trains: ☎ 0942 89 22 021. To: **Catania** (50min., 25 per day 1:20am-8:16pm, €3.05); **Messina** (40min., 22 per day 4:02am-11:40pm, €3.05); **Palermo** (4hr., 5 per day 7am-6:40pm, €12.70); **Syracuse** (2hr., 11 per day 4:30am-8:09pm, €9.70).

Buses: Interbus (☎ 0942 62 53 01). Ticket office off C. Umberto, at the end of V. Pirandello (open daily 6:20am-11:45pm). To: **Catania** (M-Sa 16 per day 6:30am-8:45pm, Su 12 per day 8:45am-6pm; €4.20, round-trip €6.60) and **Messina** (M-Sa 5 per day 6:20am-5:40pm; Su 8:50am, 4:40, 6pm; €3, round-trip €4.10). Same bus runs to **Giardini-Naxos** and **train station** (dir.: Recanti or Catania; M-F every 30min. 6:50am-midnight; €1.20, round-trip €2), **Gole Alcantara** (M-Sa 4 per day 9:15am-4:45pm, Su 9:15am; round-trip €4.60), and **Isola Bella, Mazzaro,** and **Spisone** (M-Sa 14 per day 6:30am-7:40pm, Su 4 per day 8:40am-5:40pm; €1.50, round-trip €2.20). Pick up a helpful paper schedule at the Taormina bus terminal. **SAT**, C. Umberto, 73 (☎ 0942 24 653; www.sat-group.it), operates day-long tours to Mt. Etna.

Taxis (☎ 0942 23 000 or 0942 23 800) run from the train station to downtown Taormina for €11. Within the city don't pay more than €7. €3 surcharge 10pm-6am.

Car and Scooter Rental: Cundari Rent, Vle. Apollo Arcageta, 12 (☎ 0942 24 700), around corner from post office at the end of C. Umberto. Scooters €25-40 per day, €149 per week. 14+. Cars €55-85 per day, and €265-340 per week. 21+. Gas extra. Open daily 8:30am-1pm and 4-8pm. 10% *Let's Go* discount.

◼✴ ▞ ORIENTATION AND PRACTICAL INFORMATION

To reach the city from the **train station,** hop on the blue **Interbus** that makes the trip uphill (10min., every 30min. 5am-11pm, €1.30). Cars are not allowed on Taormina's steep and narrow streets; automobiles can park in a small lot at the base of **Via Pirandello.** From the bus depot, a short walk left up V. Pirandello leads to the town's main street, **Corso Umberto.** Beginning under a stone archway, the boutique-lined road runs left through four principal *piazze*. Small stairways and side streets wind downhill to a variety of more affordable restaurants, shops, and bars. Accurate and detailed maps are also posted on high brown signs throughout the city, but can be difficult to read.

Tourist Office: AAST (☎0942 23 243; www.gate2taormina.com), in the courtyard of Palazzo Corvaja, off C. Umberto across from P. V. Emanuele. Friendly staff provides several pamphlets and a basic **map;** the turquoise fold-out "SAT Sicilian Airbus Travel" map is more helpful, as is the CST map, both available at the tourist office. Open M-Sa 9am-2pm and 4-7pm.

Tours: CST (☎0942 23 301) offers *Etna Tramonto,* a sunset trip up the volcano (July-Aug. M and W 3:45pm; Sept. M and W 3:15pm; Oct. M and W 2:15pm; €55).

Currency Exchange: Dozens of banks and **ATMs** line C. Umberto and V. Pirandello, as do many currency exchange offices, including **Rocco Frisono,** C. Umberto, 224 (☎0942 24 806), between P. Sant'Antonio and P. Duomo. Open M-Sa 9am-1pm and 4-8pm.

American Express: La Duca Viaggi, V. Don Bosco, 39, 2nd fl. (☎0942 62 52 55), in P. IX Aprile. Mail held. Open M-F Apr.-Oct. 9am-1pm and 4-7:30pm; Nov.-Mar. 9am-1pm and 2-6pm.

International Newsstand: Mr. Frank, C. Umberto, 9 (☎0942 62 61 82). *International Herald Tribune, Wall Street Journal, Sunday Express,* and *Daily Mail,* as well as a small rack of English-language paperbacks (€6.60). Open daily 8am-1pm and 4-9pm.

Emergency: ☎113 or 0942 61 11 11. **Police:** ☎112 or 0942 232 32.

First aid: ☎0942 62 54 19 or 0942 57 92 97.

Pharmacy: Farmacia Ragusa, P. Duomo, 9 (☎0942 24 104). Posts after-hours rotations. Open M-Tu and Th-Su 8:30am-1pm and 5-8:30pm.

Hospital: Ospedale San Vincenzo (☎0942 57 92 97), in P. S. Vincenzo.

Internet Access: Internet Cafe, C. Umberto, 214 (☎0942 62 88 39). 7 fast computers, €2 per 20min., €5 per hr. **Western Union** services. Open July-Aug. daily 9am-9pm; Sept.-June 9am-1:30pm and 4-7:30pm.

Post Office: ☎0942 73 230. In P. Sant'Antonio at the very top of C. Umberto near the hospital. Cashes traveler's checks. Open M-Sa 8am-6:30pm. **Postal Code:** 98039.

⌐ ACCOMMODATIONS

Taormina's popularity as a resort town makes cheap accommodations difficult to find. Those on a tight budget should consider staying in a hostel, or in nearby Mazzarò, Spisone, or Giardini-Naxos (p. 683). Hike down steep trails to Mazzarò and Spisone or take the bus or cable cars; service stops around 1:30am.

▧ **La Campanella,** V. Circonvallazione, 3 (☎0942 23 381; fax 0942 62 52 48). Facing the archway at the intersection of C. Umberto and V. Pirandello, turn left up V. Circonvallazione and look for the "La Campanella" sign. 3 flights of stairs to the entrance make for a great view of Taormina and the Calabrian shore from the top. Bright sitting area and comfortable rooms. Breakfast included. Singles €65; doubles €80. Cash only. ❺

▧ **Taormina's Odyssey Youth Hostel,** Traversa A di V. G. Martino, 2 (☎0942 24 533). A 15min. walk from the intersection of C. Umberto and V. Pirandello. Take V. C. Patrizio to V. Cappuccini. When it forks, turn right onto V. Fontana Vecchia. Follow signs with a picture of a Greek ship. Renowned among backpackers; friendly English-speaking employees, clean rooms, lockers and a great price. 28 dorm-style beds. Breakfast included. Kitchen open 10am-9pm. Towel rental, bag storage, water €1 each. Reserve ahead in summer. €15-18 per person. €45-50 for the 1 double. Cash only. ❷

Hotel Villa Nettuno, V. Pirandello, 33 (☎0942 23 797; villanettuno@tao.it). Walk up stone steps toward the hotel's sign. Charming inn, complete with parlor and beautiful garden. All rooms with bathrooms and fans. Rooms with views at no extra charge. Reserve ahead in summer. Singles €40; doubles €74. Extra bed €16. AmEx/MC/V. ❸

Pensione Svizzera, V. L. Pirandello, 26 (☎0942 23 790; www.pensionesvizzera.com), 3min. from the bus station. Pricey, but worth every euro. Glorious views, palm-laden patio, and terrace. A/C, bath, and TV. Breakfast buffet included. Reservation recommended May-Sept. Closed Jan. 10-Feb. 20. Singles €60-95; doubles €80-120; triples €110-130; quads €125-140. AmEx/MC/V. ❺

Inn Piero, V. Pirandello, 20 (☎0942 23 139). Near base of C. Umberto after gas station in 2 buildings overlooking the sea. Less expensive than most of its neighbors, Piero offers affordable rooms in a great location, all with bath and fan. Breakfast included. 15% discount in downstairs restaurant. Reserve ahead in summer. Singles €35-50; doubles €70-80. Student discount 10%, except in Aug. AmEx/MC/V. ❹

🍴 FOOD

Taormina's restaurants are of consistently high quality; prices tend to vary, though, so shop around for the best deals. An **SMA** supermarket, V. Apollo Arcageta, 21, is at the end of C. Umberto, near the post office. (Open July-Aug. M-Sa 8am-9:30pm, Su 8:30-1pm; Sept.-June M-Sa 8:30am-1pm and 4:30-8:30pm.)

🍴 **Pigghia e Potta,** V. di Giovanni, 23 (☎0942 62 62 86) off P. V. Emanuele. This brightly decorated and friendly hole-in-the-wall restaurant serves very tasty and very cheap food on the go. Pizza (€2), *arancine* (€2), and pasta (€5). Water or soda €1, beer €2-3. Open daily 11am-midnight. ❶

La Cisterna del Moro, V. Bonifacio, 1 (☎0942 23 001), off C. Umberto. Incredible food served on a terrace—this pub is a compromise between pizza joint and formal restaurant. The pizza (€5-8) will leave you full while the view will keep you long after dessert. Try the *lo stuzzichino casereccio* (€10), an *antipasti* plate of vegetables, meats, and cheese. Open noon-3pm and 7pm-midnight (later in summer). AmEx/MC/V. ❷

Bella Blu, V. Pirandello, 28 (☎0942 24 239; www.paginegialle.it/bellablu). One of the most unique views in the city: cable cars glide down the mountain between clusters of cypress trees. Pizza and drink €7.50. *Primi* from €4.50, *secondi* from €6.50. Cover €1.50. Open daily 11am-5pm and 6pm-11pm. AmEx/MC/V. ❷

👁 SIGHTS

The well-preserved **Greek theater** is Taormina's best treasure. Although originally constructed by the Greeks in the 3rd century BC, it was enlarged and largely rebuilt by Romans in the 2nd century. It offers an unsurpassed view of Etna, whose sultry smoke and occasional eruptions rival even the greatest Sophoclean tragedies. In ancient times, the cliff-side arena seated 5000 spectators; that same number packs in for the summer-long festival Taormina Arte (see **Entertainment and Beaches,** p. 683) every year. (☎0942 23 123. From P. V. Emanuele, walk up V. Teatro Greco. Open in summer daily 9am-1hr. before sunset; Apr. and Sept. 9am-6:30; Oct. and Mar. 9am-5pm; Nov.-Feb. 9am-4pm. €4.15, EU residents €2, EU residents under 18 or over 65 free.) From P. V. Emanuele, take C. Umberto to reach the **duomo.** This 13th-century structure, rebuilt during the Renaissance, takes center stage in Taormina today. The Gothic interior shelters paintings by Messinese artists and a statue of the Virgin Mary displayed over marble floors. A two-legged female centaur, Taormina's mascot, crowns the fountain out front. (Opening hours vary; inquire at Museo Sacra, next door.) Behind the tourist office, the **Chiesa di Santa Caterina** protects a small theater, the Roman **Odeon.** The short walk down V. di Giovanni leads to Taormina's public gardens, the **Villa Comunale.** Filled with people relaxing under palms during summer's greatest heat, the gardens look out over Giardini-Naxos below and Etna in the distance. A trek to the **Piccolo Castello** offers an escape from the crowds. V. Circonvallazione, which runs parallel to and above C. Umberto, leads to a small stairway that snakes up the mountainside to the castle. The **Galleria Gagliardi** debuts the latest in art at C. Umberto, 187a. Exhibits change every 15 days. (☎0942 62 89 02. Open daily 10am-1pm and 5-10pm.)

🎵 🏖 ENTERTAINMENT AND BEACHES

While action-packed Giardini-Naxos plays host to the area's wildest nights, in summer Taormina also stays up late. A large variety of chic bars line C. Umberto and its side streets. Don't miss █**Cafe Marrakech**, P. Garibaldi, 2. This exotic bar's cocktails (from €6) and Turkish coffee (€5-6) seduce party-goers both indoors and out. (☎0942 62 56 92. Open Tu-Su 5pm-3am.) **Re di Bastoni,** C. Umberto, 120, has a classy laidback vibe that goes well with the Friday- and Saturday-night live jazz. There's also live music on occasional Thursday and Sundays. (☎0942 23 037; www.redibastoni.it. Open July-Aug. daily 8am-2am; Sept.-June closed M.) The **Casanova Pub,** V. Paladini, 2, coming from C. Umberto on your right before Cafe Marrakech, serves pizza (from €6.50), beer (from €5), and cocktails (from €6). (☎0942 23 945. Open daily 10am-7am. AmEx/MC/V.) **Tutti Ccà,** V. F. Ingegneri, 12, is right off the main tourist drag of C. Umberto, but feels miles away. Relax on the stairs outside or head into the bar for an extensive list of alcohol and a kitchen serving local cuisine. (☎0942 62 54 88. Open M and W-Su noon-3am. Open M in Aug.) Every summer brings **Taormina Arte,** a theater, ballet, music, and film extravaganza. Past performances have featured Jose Carreras, Bob Dylan, and Ray Charles. (☎0942 21 142; www.taormina-arte.com. Box office at C. Umberto, 19.)

Cable cars zip along the *funivia* from V. Pirandello to the beach in a breezy ride (☎0942 23 605. In summer every 15min. M 9am-1am, Tu-Su 8am-1am; €1.70, €3 round-trip.) At the popular **Lido Mazzarò**, lounge-chair rentals (€7.50) from Lido La Pigna include shower, parasol, and changing area—or just enjoy the view while drinking a coffee on the terrace upstairs. A 15min. walk to the right, sparkling waters flow around the tiny █**Isola Bella**, a nature preserve 100m offshore. The strong-stomached can travel the narrow, winding route by bus to Castelmola, the highest point in Taormina, complete with a medieval castle and regal panoramas.

GIARDINI-NAXOS ☎0942

Now the eastern coast's ultimate beach town and a watering hole for throngs of tourists, Giardini-Naxos was the first Greek colony in Sicily in 734 BC. Excavations in the 1960s unearthed traces of a **Greek city** built of lava blocks, founded in the shadow of the volcano. Visit the traces of the fortress ruins, now overgrown with wildflowers, to escape the city bustle. The nearby **Museo Archeologico** records the ancient city's earliest days and includes an inscribed ceramic cup, the colony's earliest surviving writing. (☎0942 51 001. Open 9am-1hr. before sunset. €2.07, EU citizens 18-25 €1, EU citizens under 18 or over 65 free.)

As in Taormina, hotels fill up in July and August, though prices are better; reserve far ahead in summer. Beachfront hotels crowd V. Tysandros, varying considerably in quality and price—better deals can be found on nearby V. Naxos. Just one block from the beach, **Hotel Villa Mora ❹**, V. Naxos, 47, offers well-decorated rooms, some with balcony. All rooms have bath, phone, and TV; some have air-conditioning. (☎0942 51 839; www.hotelvillamora.com. Breakfast included. Open Mar.-Dec. Singles €40-50; doubles €70-96; triples €98-135; quads €120-155. MC/V.) **Hotel Costa Azzura ❸**, V. Naxos, 35, offers bright rooms at an unbeatable price. Doubles have air-conditioning and TV. (☎0942 51 458. Singles €30-40; doubles €50-70; triples €65-80. AmEx/MC/V.) Buy necessities at **Sigma** supermarket, V. Casarsa, s/n. Look for the sign on V. Dalmazia, just of V. Naxos. (Open M-Sa 8:30am-1:30pm and 4:30-9pm, Su 8:30am-1pm.) Located at the tip of the port,

Angelina ❷, V. Calcide Eubea, 2, serves its seafood seaside. Lively regulars enjoy the extensive menu and equally impressive wine shelf. (☎/fax 0942 51 477. *Primi* €5-10, *secondi* €8-15. Open daily noon-4pm and 6:30pm-midnight. AmEx/MC/V.)

Only 5km away from Taormina, Giardini-Naxos shares a train station with its neighbor. **Interbus** runs from Giardini to the **train station** and Taormina's **bus station** (☎0942 62 53 01; in summer 40 per day 7:35am-11:35pm; €1.30). Signs throughout town point the way to the helpful **AAST Tourist Office,** V. Tysandros, 54, along the *lungomare.* (☎0942 51 010. Open M-F 8:30am-2pm and 4-7pm, Sa 8:30am-2pm.) In case of **emergency,** call the **carabinieri** (☎112) or **first aid** (☎0942 539 32). **Post offices** are at V. Erice, 1 (☎0942 51 090), and Lungomare Naxos, 151 (☎0942 57 11 90).

CATANIA ☎095

Catania (pop. 400,000) earns its status as a Sicilian treasure. From the stately grace of its *piazze* to the ancient history of Greek and Roman remains, the city merges tradition with youthful revelry, as university students funnel into its numerous cafes and bars. Leveled repeatedly, sometimes by invaders but most often by nearby Mt. Etna, Catania has been rebuilt several times since its founding in 729 BC. After the monstrous 1693 earthquake, G. B. Vaccarini recreated the city with his Baroque *piazze* and *duomo.* This architectural beauty was later complemented by the musical virtuosity of the operas of favorite son Vincenzo Bellini.

▐ TRANSPORTATION

Flights: Fontanarossa (☎095 34 05 05). Take the alibus from train station or pay about €20 for the 15min. cab ride. 1 flight daily to Malta with **Air Malta,** C. Sicilia, 71 (☎095 34 53 11).

Trains: ☎095 53 27 19. In P. P. Giovanni XXIII. To: **Agrigento** (4hr., 7 per day 5:15am-7:20pm, €8.99); **Enna** (1½hr., 7 per day 5:15am-7:20pm, €4.23); **Florence** (12hr.; 17 per day 3:15am-10:07pm, 2 direct 10:20am and 9:30pm; €43.02); **Messina** (2hr., 17 per day 5:30am-9:20pm, €4.65); **Palermo** (3½hr., 6 per day 5:45am-7:20pm, €11.21); **Rome** (10hr.; 14 per day 3:15am-10:07pm, 3 direct 9:16am, 12:08pm and 7:50pm; €38.37); **Syracuse** (1½hr.; 10 per day 6:10am-8:54pm; €4.23, round-trip €6.04); **Taormina/Giardini-Naxos** (1hr., 23 per day 3:15am-9:30pm, €2.69).

Buses: All companies are on V. D'Amico, across the city-bus-filled *piazza* in front of the train station. Service is significantly reduced on Su, so weekend travelers may wish to take a train instead. Information office inside the train station. **SAIS Trasporti** (☎095 53 62 01) serves **Agrigento** (3hr., 22 per day 6:30am-9pm, €10) and **Rome** (14hr.; 7:50, 9pm; €40, under 26 or over 60 €35). **SAIS Autoline** (☎095 53 61 68) to: **Enna** (1½hr.; M-Sa 8 per day 6:40am-8pm, Su 3 per day 9am-8pm; €6); **Messina** (1½hr.; M-Sa 25 per day 5:15am-8:30pm, Su 6 per day 7am-8:30pm; €7); **Palermo** (3hr., 16 per day 5am-8pm, €12). **Interbus** and **Etna** (☎095 53 27 16) both run to: **Brindisi** (8hr.; 10:30am, 10pm; €36.40); **Noto** (2½hr.; 2, 5:45pm, 7:15pm; €5.60); **Ragusa** (2hr., 10 per day 6am-8pm, €6.20); **Taormina/Giardini-Naxos** (1hr., 12 per day 7:15am-10pm, €4).

Ferries: La Duca Viaggi, P. Europa, 1 (☎095 72 22 295). Walk up V. Africa from train station. Ferry tickets to **Malta** (high season €85.22).

Public Transportation: AMT buses leave from train station in P. P. Giovanni XXIII. **Alibus** goes to the airport and **#27** to the beach. Tickets (€0.77) valid for 1½hr. are sold at *tabaccherie* and newsstands.

Scooter Rental: Hollywood Rent by Motoservice, P. Cavour, 12 (☎095 44 27 20).

▐◀ 🔢 ORIENTATION AND PRACTICAL INFORMATION

Via Etnea, running from the *duomo* to the **Giardini Bellini,** is Catania's chic main street. Several main thoroughfares run perpendicular to V. Etnea from the water-

SICILY

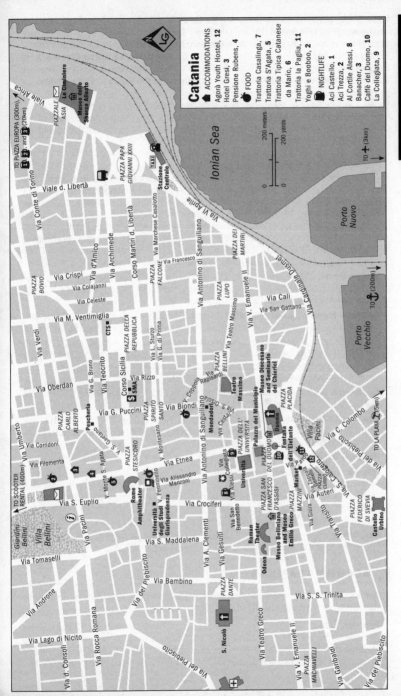

Catania

▲ ACCOMMODATIONS
Agorà Youth Hostel, 12
Hotel Gresi, 3
Pensione Rubens, 4

● FOOD
Trattoria Casalinga, 7
Trattoria S'Agata, 5
Trattoria Tipica Catanese
da Mario, 6
Trattoria la Paglia, 11
Yoghi e Booboo, 2

■ NIGHTLIFE
Aci Castello, 1
Aci Trezza, 2
Al Cortile Alessi, 8
Banacher, 3
Caffè del Duomo, 10
La Collegiata, 9

SICILY

front. From north to south, these are **Via Umberto,** which runs from **Piazza Galatea** on the water to **Villa Bellini** (Bellini Gardens); **Corso Martiri della Libertà,** which runs from the bus and train stations at **P. Giovanni XXIII** before becoming **Corso Sicilia** at **Piazza della Repubblica** and bisecting V. Etnea at **Piazza Stesicoro; Via A. di Sangiuliano,** which runs past **Piazza Bellini** and the **Teatro Massimo** (Teatro Bellini); and **Via Vittorio Emanuele II** which leads straight from the water to **Piazza Duomo.**

As with any city, travelers should be careful of petty thievery. Know where your things are at all times, don't walk around with a map glued to your face, and be wary of manufactured distractions. At night, stick to the populated and well-lit areas along V. Etnea and other main avenues.

Tourist Offices: Municipal Tourist Office, V. Vittorio Emanuele, 172 (☎095 74 25 57 34 or 095 74 25 515; www.catania.it). English-speaking staff provides **maps,** self-guided tours in English, theater schedules, and other useful information. Open M, W, F 8:15am-1:30pm, Tu and Th 8:15am-7:45pm, Sa 8:15am-1:45pm. **AAPIT,** V. Cimarosa, 10 (☎095 73 06 279 or 095 73 06 222), near the Giardini Bellini. From V. Etnea, turn on V. Pacini before the post office and follow signs. English-speaking staff offers brochures on city, region, and Etna. Open M-F 8am-8pm, Sa-Su 8am-2pm. **Branches** at station (☎095 73 06 255); V. Etnea, 63 (☎095 31 17 78); and airport (☎095 73 06 266 or 095 73 06 277). Same hours as downtown office.

Budget Travel: CTS, V. Ventimiglia, 153 (☎095 53 02 23; fax 095 53 62 46), off P. della Repubblica. Useful info on travel in Sicily, Italy, and beyond. Open M-F 9:30am-1pm and 4:30-7:30pm, Sa 9:30am-12:30pm.

American Express: La Duca Viaggi, P. Europa, 1 (☎095 72 22 295), up V. Africa from train station. Mail held for 1 month. Open M-F 9am-1pm and 4-7:30pm, Sa 9am-noon.

English-Language Bookstore: Librerìa Mondadori, V. A di Sangiuliano, 223/225 (☎095 31 51 60). Just down from the Teatro Bellini. Brand-new branch of this national chain offers a decent selection of English titles as well as a reading room and in-store cafe. Open daily 9am-2am.

Emergency: ☎113. **Ambulance:** ☎118 or 095 37 71 22. **Medical Clinic,** C. Italia, 234 (☎095 37 71 22). **Carabinieri:** ☎112. **Police:** ☎095 53 13 33.

Pharmacy: Crocerossa, V. Etnea, 274 (☎095 31 70 53). Open daily 8:30am-1pm and 4:30-8pm. AmEx/MC/V. **Croceverde,** V. G. D'Annunzio, 43 (☎095 44 16 62), at the intersection of C. Italia and C. della Provincia.

Hospital: Ospedale Garibaldi (☎095 75 91 111), in P. Santa Maria del Gesù.

Internet Access: Internetteria, V. Penninello, 44 (☎095 31 01 39), hip young staff serve cappuccino, sandwiches, couscous, and other homemade items in a funky interior with cool music and 12 decently fast computers. Also offers Wi-Fi connection, at same rate as desktop computers. Food €2-6. €1 per 30min., €2 per hr. Open M-F 10am-9pm, Sa 10am-1:30pm and 5-10pm.

Post Office: V. Etnea, 215 (☎095 71 55 111), in the big building next to Giardini Bellini. Open M-F 8am-6:30pm, Sa 8am-12:30pm. **Postal Code:** 95125.

■ ACCOMMODATIONS

A plethora of posh stores lining the streets suggests high hotel prices, but many *pensione* near V. Etnea are affordable. Reserve early for summer.

Pensione Rubens, V. Etnea, 196, 3rd fl. (☎095 31 70 73; fax 095 71 51 713), above the Thai consulate. Amicable owners and attractive, well-kept rooms make this a comforting home away from home. All rooms have bath, A/C, TV, and phone. Reserve ahead in summer. Singles €45-55; doubles €75; triples €95; quads €115. AmEx/MC/V. ❸

Agorà Youth Hostel, P. Curro, 6 (☎095 72 33 010; http://agorahostel.hypermart.net). Standing at the elephant in P. Duomo with your back to V. Etnea, look for the fountain in the corner of the *piazza*. Walk behind the fountain, turn right, and follow the diagonal street for 3 short blocks before turning left. Though loud music from the in-house bar, trains passing on the tracks directly below, and stuffy dorms make this place a bad choice for light sleepers, social types will enjoy the laidback encounters with fellow guests. On-site grotto restaurant and wine bar, complete with underground stream, serve food (*primo, secondo, contorno* or *dolce,* and drink; €8) and drinks (2-for-1 happy hour on cocktails and beer from 7-10pm). Kitchen and refrigerator available 24hr. Breakfast included. Towels €2. 2 computers with Internet (€4 per hr.). Dorms Sept.-June €17; July €18; Aug. €20. ❷

Hotel Gresi, V. Pacini, 28 (☎095 32 27 09; www.gresihotel.com), off V. Etnea before Villa Bellini and post office. Decorated hallways lead to an inviting salon, breakfast room, and spacious social bar. Clean rooms with gorgeously painted ceilings all have bath, A/C, TV, and phone. Breakfast €5. Singles €48; doubles €75. AmEx/MC/V. ❹

⌂ FOOD

When *Catanesi* gather at the table, chances are they'll be dining on local favorites like eggplant- and ricotta-topped *spaghetti alla norma,* named for Bellini's famous opera. Another hit is the fresh *masculini,* or anchovies, rumored to have aphrodisiacal powers. The **marketplace** off P. del Duomo and V. Garibaldi features vendors with fish, fruit, and sweets. The action runs in the morning and early afternoon (M-Sa). An **SMA** supermarket is at C. Sicilia, 50. (☎095 32 60 699. Open M-Sa 8:30am-8:30pm.) **Bar Savia,** V. Etnea, 304, across from Bellini Gardens, serves the best *granite di gelsi* (mulberry iced drinks; €1.60) in town. (Open M-Sa 8am-9:30pm.) Perhaps the best deal, however, is the *arancino*—a filling meat-stuffed fried rice ball available for €1.30 at any bar with a sign reading *"tavola calda."*

▨ Yoghi e Booboo, V. Santa Filomena, 48 (☎095 32 14 30; www.yoghiebooboo.it) The undisputed (if largely unchallenged) champion of Tex-Mex cuisine in Catania, Yoghi e Booboo serves up large portions of southwestern favorites that wouldn't be out of place on either side of the Rio Grande. If you're feeling more East than West, go for the sushi (€12), which the chef learned how to make while working in America. Serves a wide variety of pizzas (€6-8.50), typical Sicilian fare, and meal-size salads (€8-9). *Primi* €4-10, *secondi* €7-16. Open daily 8pm-1am. ❸

Trattoria S'Agata, V. Monte S. Agata, 11-13 (☎095 31 54 53), off V. Etnea. Go left after Stefanel store in P. Stesicoro. Catanese charm accompanies *risotti* and other specialties listed on multi-language menus. *Primi* and *secondi* (from €7). Cover €2. Open daily in summer noon-midnight; in winter noon-4pm and 6pm-midnight. AmEx/MC/V. ❸

Trattoria Casalinga, V. Biondi, 19 (☎095 31 13 19). Popular with the locals, this little restaurant offers *primi* for €5-6 and *secondi* €7. Fixed *menù* (€20) is perfect for larger groups. Cover €1. Open M-Sa noon-4pm and 8pm-midnight. MC/V. ❸

Trattoria la Paglia, V. Pardo, 23 (☎095 34 68 38), brings the bustle of the marketplace indoors, near P. del Duomo. This popular stop makes every effort to pack its customers in, so don't be surprised if you're sharing a table with strangers. Those tired of tomatoes can trade red sauce for black with *spaghetti al nero di seppia* (with squid ink; €4.65). Make sure to come in daytime, as the market shoppers make this place lively. *Primi* €4-8, *secondi* €5.50-11. Open M-Sa noon-4pm and 7pm-midnight. AmEx/MC/V. ❷

Trattoria Tipica Catanese da Mario, V. Penninello, 34 (☎095 32 24 61; www.cataniacity.com/trattoriamario), off V. Etnea near the amphitheater. Fish is the specialty at this family-run restaurant. *Al fresco* dining in summer. *Primi* €4-9, *secondi* €6-9. Cover €1.50. Open M-Sa 12:30-3pm and 6:30pm-midnight. MC/V. ❷

SICILY

SIGHTS

In **Piazza del Duomo,** Giovan Battista Vaccarini's little lava **Fontana dell'Elefante** (1736) commands the city's attention. Vaccarini carved his elephant (the symbol of the city) without visible testicles. When the statue was unveiled, horrified *Cata nesi* men, who construed from this omission an attack on their virility, demanded corrective measures. Vaccarini's acquiescence was, well, monumen-

> **⚡TIP** **WORD TO THE WISE.** While you're staring at the elephant's testicles, make sure nobody steals your purse. This tip is written with Catania's Fontana dell'Elefante in the P. Duomo in mind, but it is also good advice in general.

tal. Residents claim that visitors may attain citizenship by smooching the elephant's nether regions, but the height of the pachyderm's backside precludes the fulfillment of such aspirations. The other buildings on the *piazza*, including the 18th-century **Palazzo del Municipio** on the left and the former **Seminario dei Chierici** on the right, are striped black and white to mirror the *duomo's* side. Visit the **Museo Diocesano,** V. Etnea, 8, next to the *duomo*, to see priestly vestments several centuries old. (☎ 095 28 16 35. Open Tu-Su 9am-12:30pm and 4-7:30pm.)

The 1950 restoration of the **duomo** revealed its interior predating the Baroque makeover. Restorators discovered stumps of columns and pointed arches of the original apses. In the Norman **Cappella della Madonna,** on the right, the walls surround a Roman sarcophagus and a 15th-century Virgin Mary statue. The body of Catania's beloved priest, the Beato Cardinal Dusmet, lies nearby, his head and bony fingers protruding from his vestments. To the right of the main door is **Bellini's tomb,** guarded by a marble angel. The words and music from his *Sonnambula* are inscribed above the tomb and translate as "Ah, I didn't think I'd see you wilt so soon, flower." (Hours vary; closed to visitors during mass. Modest dress required.)

The centerpiece of Catania's restoration efforts rests just up V. Etnea. Marked by an fountain and crooked cyprus trees, the **Giardini Bellini** sprawl over small hills and around tiny ponds. Sunday afternoons find half the city strolling here, *gelato* in hand. Below a Victorian bandstand, a plot displays the day's date in perfect grass figures, replanted daily. A few blocks away in P. Stesicoro, modern streets cradle a sunken pit holding ruins of a 2nd-century **Roman amphitheater,** with visible tunnels that gladiators used to enter the arena. Uphill from P. del Duomo, at V. V. Emanuele, 260, lies the entrance to the **Roman Theater,** built in the 2nd century on the grounds of an earlier Greek theater. Its passageways, lined with the remains of marble columns, spill out into the similar but smaller **Odeon,** with another entrance around the back. Mt. Etna's 1669 eruption coated the marble of both theaters with lava. (☎ 095 71 50 508. Open daily 9am-1:30pm and 3-7pm. €2, EU residents €1.)

Near the train station on V. Africa, a rescued factory complex has been restored as **Le Ciminiere,** a cultural center with free art exhibits, concerts, and a cinema museum. In addition, the ▧**Museo Storico dello Sbarco Alleato in Sicilia-Estate 1943** (Historical Museum of the Allied Landing in Sicily—Summer 1943), skillfully showcases an often ignored aspect of WWII. Exhibits highlight the Allied bombing and subsequent invasion of Sicily by American, British, Canadian, and Australian troops, an event which immediately preceded the defeat of Mussolini and the end of the war with Italy. The museum presents the war in Sicily from the perspective of the average Sicilian, depicting a typical Sicilian city square before and after bombing, as well as Axis and Allied propaganda. Also included are creepy Italian postcards of angelic children dressed up as soldiers and various saints blessing the fascist troops marching under the fascist banner. (☎095 53 35 40; www.provincia.ct.it. Open Tu 3-5pm, Th-Su 9:30am-12:30pm and 3-5pm. Free).

🎵🎭 ENTERTAINMENT AND NIGHTLIFE

Teatro Massimo (Bellini), V. A. di Sanguiliano, 233, mesmerizes audiences in a sumptuous setting. Sink into plush red seats for a symphony or wait for the thrill of opera (Jan.-June). Student discounts are available for all tickets; contact the tourist office. Tours in Italian available upon request. (☎095 71 50 921. Box office open M 9:30am-12:30pm, Tu-F 5-7pm. Information office open M-F 8am-2pm.) The AAPIT's free monthly bulletin *Lapis*, available at bars and the tourist office, details Catania's hot nightlife, movies, concerts, and festivals.

During the cooler months, *Catanesi* love their nightly *passeggiata*, circulating the P. del Duomo and swarming near Teatro Bellini. Cafes pulsate with life on weekends, drawing a sometimes raucous crowd. Local university students and urban 30-somethings frequent neighborhood watering holes. In the late evening, university students swarm the streets near P. Università. ▧**La Collegiata** is a student favorite, with live music and large crowds (open 7pm-4am).

Try **Al Cortile Alessi,** V. Alessi, 30, for courtyard dining under swaying nespola trees. (Open Tu-Su 8pm-late. AmEx/MC/V.) **Caffè del Duomo,** across from the elephant fountain, offers *gelato* and coffee for a nice low-key night in Catania's main *piazza*. (☎095 71 50 556. Open daily 5:30am-3am.) In the summer months, most *Catanesi* leave town. From the *centro*, locals drive to the dance floor of **Banacher,** V. XXI Aprile S.S., 114, a 15min. taxi ride from Catania's center. Lights keep the dancing crowds captive until 5am at what is reputed to be Europe's largest outdoor disco. (☎095 27 12 57. Cover €10. Open Tu-Su 10pm-3am.) Summer crowds also scooter 20min. away to **Aci Castello** and nearby **Aci Trezza,** nearly identical nightlife hubs with a variety of expensive bars and pretty seaside views.

This side of Catania's coast is far from the city chaos but still subject to Etna's fury; huge, black boulders line the jagged shore, hurled there by eruptions of yore. Previous tectonic activity created a series of nearby islands that are now marine reserves, including the **Island of the Cyclops** of Odyssian fame. Catania's biggest feast day honors the city's patron, **Sant'Agata.** Fireworks and non-stop partying in the first five days of February salvage the city from winter gloom. The crowded beach **La Playa** offers a charming view of a nearby power plant. (Take bus #427, which runs June-Sept.) Farther from the port is the more rugged **La Scogliera,** with fiery cliffs and a bathing area. (Take bus #334 from P. del Duomo; 30min.)

🏞 DAYTRIP FROM CATANIA

MOUNT ETNA

An AST bus leaves from Catania's central train station at 8:15am for a 2hr. ride to Rifugio Sapienza. The bus leaves Etna at 4:30pm (times subject to change; round-trip €4.80). In case of emergency, call ☎0942 53 17 77.

The lava-seared wilderness of Mt. Etna is one of Italy's most compelling natural settings. Etna's history of volcanic activity is the longest documented of any volcano—the first recorded eruption was in 1500 BC, though it was probably active long before that. Europe's largest active volcano (at 3350m), it has long held sway over the residents of eastern Sicily: the Greek poet Hesiod envisioned Etna as the home of Typhon, the last monster conceived by Earth to fight the gods before the dawn of the human race. The ancients also claimed its fires were the home of Vulcan, the gods' blacksmith. Apparently Typhon's aggressions aren't over yet: a 1985 eruption

THE LOCAL STORY

ALWAYS TIME TO LEAVE

Volcanoes have fascinated Dominique di Salvo since she was a girl. Twenty-nine years ago, she traded her native Paris for the simmering setting of Sicily's Mt. Etna. When the volcano erupted in summer 2002, destroying her restaurant, di Salvo wasn't ready to give in.

LG: How many people live on Mt. Etna?

A: Three. There are three of us who live here at 2000m: my husband, my son, and me. Other people come only to work.

LG: And you're not afraid?

A: Not at all. This is not like Pompeii that has explosions. No, Etna is not like Pompeii or Vesuvius. Here, lava takes a long time to come down the mountain.

LG: Your restaurant was destroyed by an eruption recently, is that correct?

A: Yes, I said it was safe for people, but not for buildings. I am working in this restaurant while I rebuild mine, and when other restaurants in the area have been destroyed, the owners come to work in mine. We help each other out when an eruption occurs.

LG: What if Etna erupts again?

A: There is always time to leave. Most people who die [here] do so from heart problems or asthma. This happens to people who don't know that at 2000m, or 3000m, people don't feel that well. This is a problem of mountains, not Etna.

destroyed much of the summit tourist station, and eruptions in 2001 and 2002 sent lava rolling down slopes at 100m per hour. The most recent major eruptions occurred in the fall and winter of 2002-2003 and formed two new craters near the volcano's peak. The volcano continues to emit ash and smoke plumes, causing discomfort for area residents.

From Rifugio Sapienza (1900m), where the AST bus stops, a 3hr. hike to the aptly named **Torre del Filosofo** (Philosopher's Tower; 2920m) gives a broad and contemplative view of the looming peaks and Etna's steaming craters. Anyone with sturdy shoes can take a 30min. jaunt to explore the crater in front of the parking area. From the Philosopher's Tower, a 2hr. hike leads to the **craters** themselves. **Valle del Bove,** Etna's first volcanic crater, is on the way down. While the view of the hardened lava, huge boulders, and unearthly craters is incredible, the trail is so difficult and the volcanic activity so unpredictable that sightseers are only allowed access by guided tour. On a certified tour, hikers can hold molten rocks heated by subterranean activity or watch guides burn newspapers on exposed rifts in the rock. Those who brave the trip should take precautions: carry water and bring warm clothing, as winds are ferocious and pockets of snow linger even in mid-July. Windbreakers and hiking boots can be rented at the top of the cablecar for €1.50. Travelers not wishing to hike can take an off-road shuttle up to Philosopher's Tower for €42.50 (includes a guided tour of the nearby craters).

CST, C. Umberto, 99-101, runs tours to 3000m (☎0942 62 60 88; csttao@tiscalinet.it. June-Aug. M and W 3:45pm; Sept. 3:15pm; Oct. 2:15pm; €55) and to 2000m (year-round Tu and Th 8am; €25). Also try **Gruppo Guide Alpine,** V. Etna, 49 (☎095 79 14 755) which runs tours to 3000m for €55.

After an intense hike, campers can curl up at **Camping La Timpa,** V. Santa Maria la Scala, 25, in the countryside of Acireale. They offer **bungalows ❹** with kitchen and bath and **camping ❶.** (☎095 76 48 155; www.campinglatimpa.it. €4.65-8 per person, €7 per 2-person tent, €8 per 4-person tent, €3 per car. Free hot showers. Doubles €100; triples €110; quads €120. Prices rise during high season.)

CENTRAL SICILY

ENNA ☎0935

Dubbed *l'ombelico della Sicilia* (the navel of Sicily), Enna (pop. 30,000) is an isolated city of ancient charms, worn stone streets, churches in a multitude of architectural styles, and some of the most beautiful, far-reaching views in Sicily. At night, the intimate *piazze* spring to life with revelers whose strolls inevitably lead them to railings overlooking dramatic mountainsides. For the best view in town, walk the short distance to the towers of the Castello di Lombardia. On clear days, the imposing silhouette of Etna shimmers in the distance.

▐ TRANSPORTATION

Enna is accessible by both bus and train, but taking the bus sidesteps the 8km uphill hike into town from the train station.

Trains: ☎0935 50 09 10. Buses connect the train station to the town center (see below). To: Agrigento (2hr., 7 per day 7:16am-8:40pm, €6.35); Catania (1¼hr., 7 per day 6:20am-8:15pm, €6.40); Palermo (3hr., 6 per day 7:16am-8:40pm, €7.50).

Buses: All buses depart from the bus station on V. Diaz, a short walk uphill from P. Matteotti. **Interbus** (☎0935 50 23 90) and **SAIS** (☎0935 50 09 02) are under the same roof, with an additional Interbus office (☎0935 50 31 41) on V. Roma by the tourist office. Regional buses also make various stops throughout the city. To: **Catania** (2hr.; M-Sa 6 per day 6:20am-6:15pm, Su 7:15am, 5:15, and 6:15pm; €6.40) continuing to **Noto, Ragusa,** and **Syracuse; Palermo** from Enna and Enna Bassa (2hr., 9 per day, €8.30); **Piazza Armerina** (35min., 11 per day 7am-9:45pm, €2.70).

Public Transportation: City Buses run from the train station to Enna and Calabiscetta from the station (M-Sa 7:20, 8:15, 10:20am, 12:20, 12:50, 2, 2:20, 5:20, 8:05pm, Su 8:15am, 1:20pm.) €1.35 ticket on bus. Make sure you don't get off in Enna Bassa. Ask for Enna Centro.

Taxis: In P. Scelfo (☎0935 50 09 05) and in P. V. Emanuele (☎0935 50 09 06). Be advised that taxis don't always answer the phone, and stop running at about 8:30pm.

◆ ❷ ORIENTATION AND PRACTICAL INFORMATION

The **bus station** lies just outside Enna's central historical district. **Via Vittorio Emanuele** runs from the station to **Piazza Matteotti,** where **Via Roma** branches in two directions. V. Roma passes by **Piazza Vittorio Emanuele** and the *duomo,* toward the Castello di Lombardia. The right fork of V. Roma cuts an arc through residential areas to the **Torre di Federico II.** Beware of V. Roma's disordered addresses; every location often has two sets of street numbers, and very often neither is correct. Ask for directions to prevent confusion.

Tourist Offices: AAPIT, V. Roma, 411-413 (☎0935 52 82 28). Info on Enna province. Open M-Sa 8:30am-1:30pm and 3-7pm. For info on the city, transportation, and lodgings, head to **AAST,** P. Cloajanni, 6 (☎0935 50 08 75; fax 0935 26 119), beside Hotel Sicilia. English and French spoken. Open M-Tu and Th-Sa 8am-2:15pm, W 8am-2:15pm and 2:45-6:15pm, but hours may vary.

Currency Exchange: Banks line V. Roma between P. V. Emanuele and P. Umberto I. Currency exchange also available at the post office.

ATM: In P. Umberto I, on V. Roma.

Emergency: ☎113. **Ambulance:** ☎118. **Police:** ☎0935 52 21 11. **Carabinieri** (☎112 or 0935 50 12 67) in P. Europa.

First Aid: ☎0935 45 245. **Medical Clinic:** ☎0935 50 08 96. Open daily 8pm-8am.

Pharmacy: Farmacia del Centro, V. Roma, 315 (☎0935 50 06 50), posts after-hours rotations, as does **Farmacia Librizzi,** P. V. Emanuele, 21 (☎0935 50 09 08). Open 9am-1pm and 4-8pm.

Hospital: Ospedale Umberto I, Contrada Ferrante (☎0935 45 111), off of V. Boris Giuliano in Enna Bassa.

Internet Access: Ciemme, V. Lombardia, 31 (☎0935 50 47 12; fax 0935 50 67 35), next to the castle, has speedy computers. €3 per hr. Open M-Sa 9am-8pm, closed Su.

Post Office: V. Volta, 1 (☎ 0935 56 23 12). Take a left off V. Roma just before the AAPIT office and walk to the right of the Provincia building. Open M-F 8am-7pm, Sa 8am-12:30pm. **Postal Code:** 94100.

ACCOMMODATIONS

Enna is short on accommodations, though a B&B lies nearby in Calascibetta, accessible by bus. **Affittacamere da Pietro ❸**, Cda. Longobardo da Pietro, is 4km from Enna. To get there, follow the B&B signs from V. Roma or take the bus for Calascibetta and ask to be dropped off at the Affittacamere da Pietro. All rooms have bath and TV. At night, buses and taxis stop running, so if you are staying at da Pietro, plan alternate transportation back. (☎ 0935 33 647 or 340 27 65 76 36. Singles €30; doubles €45. Cash only.) Right in the heart of town, just up V. Roma from the AAPIT office, **Hotel Sicilia ❺**, P. Colajanni, 7, has luxurious decorated rooms complete with bath, TV, hair dryer, antiques, and Botticelli reproductions. Buffet breakfast included, served on a terrace. (☎ 0935 50 08 50; www.hotelsicili-aenna.it. Singles €62-€72; doubles €91; triples €110. AmEx/MC/V.)

FOOD

Enna's relaxed character extends to its dining, making eating out an enjoyable and lengthy affair. Restaurants cluster along Vle. Marconi behind V. Roma and P. Crispi. Find basic supplies at the **Sigma** supermarket right before the castle at V. Lombardia, 21. (Open M-Sa 9am-2pm and 5-9pm.) Picnickers can also investigate V. Mercato Sant'Antonio, lined with *alimentari*, fruit stands, and bakeries. The terrace of ▧**Ristorante La Fontana ❷**, V. Vulturo, 6, in the intimate P. Belvedere, overlooks the valley and offers a lovely meal setting. Try the *spaghetti alla donna concetta* (€6.20), a house specialty. (☎ 0935 25 465. *Primi* from €4.65, *secondi* from €7.80. Cover €1.08. Open daily noon-3:30pm and 7pm-midnight. AmEx/MC/V.) Watch the action outside the *duomo* from the tiny **Bar del Duomo ❶**, in P. Mazzini, while munching selections from rows of perfect cookies. (☎ 0935 24 205. Open M and W-Su 6am-midnight.) Feast on fantastic food in the elegant stone and wood dining room of **San Gennaro da Gino ❷**, Viale Marconi, 6. Start with the extensive *antipasto* buffet (€7) and finish off with delicious *panna cotta* (€3). Piano bar nights are Tuesday and Friday. (☎ 0935 24 067; fax 0935 50 61 91. Pizza from €3.10. *Primi* €6-7, *secondi* €6-10. Cover €1.50. Open M-Tu and Th-Su 12:30-3pm and 8pm-12:30am. AmEx/MC/V.) Head to the mirror-lined walls and refined decor of **Ristorante Pizzeria Ariston ❷**, V. Roma, 353, for a proper indoor meal. (☎ 0935 26 038. Additional entrance on V. Vulturo. Pizza from €4. *Primi* €6-7, *secondi* €6-12. Cover €1.50. Open M-Sa 12:30-2:30pm and 7:30-10:30pm. AmEx/MC/V.)

INSIDER'S INSALATA. We may translate *insalata* as "salad" but that doesn't make them exactly the same thing. Often on Italian menus, *insalate* is used more or less as a synonym for *contorni*, the general term for any vegetable-based side-dish. Thus *insalata al pomodoro* doesn't mean a tomato-based salad, but only tomatoes, lightly sprinkled with salt, pepper, and olive oil and served on a bed of basil. If you want a green-based salad with a variety of vegetables, order an *insalata mista* or the simpler *insalata verde*.

SIGHTS

Although grass and vines have overrun its courtyards, the walls and towers of the **Castello di Lombardia** attest to a time when residents of Enna were more engaged in defending their environment than enjoying it. These days, however, visitors can savor a view of the entire province and, on clear days, Mt. Etna, from ▧**La Pisana,** the tallest of the castle towers. The Swabians constructed the castle, named for a Lombardian siege, in the Norman period. (From the *duomo*, V. Roma curves uphill and becomes V. Lombardia before ending at the Castello. ☎0935 50 09 62. Open daily Apr.-Oct. 8am-8pm; Nov.-Mar. 8am-5pm. Gates often stay open later.) One of the city's other architectural marvels is the **Torre di Federico II,** which concealed Sicilian defenders during WWII. A tunnel runs from the *torre* to the castle at the other end of town. The entrance is visible from within the tower. Adjacent to the castle, a natural **fortress** also offers excellent views of the city. The weeping Demeter supposedly mourned the loss of her daughter Persephone to Hades at the **Rocca di Cerere,** on the path leading to the left of the castle. Turn left on V. IV Novembre for the **public gardens.** (Open daily 9am-8pm. Free.)

Though more than a dozen religious fraternities throughout the city have their own churches, all participated in creating the curious ▓**duomo,** which combines as many architectural styles as there are brotherhoods. Construction began in the early 14th century, but the cathedral was remodeled throughout the 15th and 16th centuries, resulting in a stylistic potpourri. The eclecticism extends to the church's interior, which juxtaposes Gothic doors, medieval walls, Renaissance paintings, and gilded Baroque flourishes. The sacrilegious stretch out on wooden pews to appreciate the marvelous wood-paneled ceiling. (Open daily 9am-1pm and 4-7pm.) The **Museo Alessi,** in the rectory immediately behind the cathedral on V. Roma, matches the schizophrenic spirit of the *duomo* with its own varied collection. Ancient coins and pottery share space with oil paintings and the church's treasures, which include a fine collection of silver pieces. On the ground floor is a stunning gold crown that depicts the story of Christ's ascension, which adorns the head of the Madonna during the annual Festa della Madonna (see **Entertainment,** below). (☎0935 50 31 65. Open daily 8am-8pm. €2.60, students or over 60 €1.50.)

🎵 ENTERTAINMENT

With the opening of ▓**Azimut** in 2005, nightlife has arrived in style in Enna. Located between the Castello and the Rocca di Cerere with superb views of the valley below, Azimut offers an elegant interior befitting its official status as a wine bar, At night things loosen up with a variety of live music shows. On Tuesday for singer-songwriters, Thursday and Friday for rock and blues, and Saturday for turntable nights featuring a rotating cast of regional DJs. (☎333 98 76 159. Wine from €2.50 per glass, €10-28 per bottle. Draft beer €3.50. Cocktails €4-5. Open Tu-Su 11am-3am.) On July 2, Enna celebrates the **Festa della Madonna** with the procession of three enormous votive statues through the streets of the city, followed by fireworks, music, and traditional *mastazzoli* (apple cookies). The party continues through the summer with the feasts of **Sant'Anna** and **Madonna di Valverde** on the last Sundays of July and August respectively. Every Easter, the brothers of each religious fraternity don hoods and capes and parade through the streets. Processions of a speedier sort take place at the **Autodromo di Pergusa** (☎0935 256 60; fax 0935 25 825), which hosts **Grand Prix** auto races from March through October. The most important race is the Formula 3 in May. Otherwise, the Autodromo acts as an all-purpose arena, hosting everything from motorcycle races to dog shows.

PIAZZA ARMERINA   ☎0935

Perched in the Erei Mountains, the medieval city of Piazza Armerina (pop. 21,000) shows few signs of time's passing. Traditional Sicilian music still echoes off the green-domed *duomo* and the rhymes of the singing fruit-truck driver resonate through town at midday. Many streets are little more than twisting stone staircases, but the foothills below contain the city's real attraction: the famed Villa Romana and its remarkably intact ancient mosaics, which are among the largest and most beautiful in the world.

TRANSPORTATION AND PRACTICAL INFORMATION. Buses run to Piazza Armerina from Caltanissetta (1hr., 4 per day 7:40am-6pm, €4.65); Catania (1-2hr., 12 per day 6:05am-5pm, €7); Enna (35min., 8 per day 5:45am-5:10pm, €3.25); Gela (1hr., 5 per day 7am-7:05pm, €3.40); and Syracuse (3-4hr., M-Sa 1pm, €7.75). Buses arrive at the city's northern end in **Piazza Senatore Marescalchi.** Facing away from the **Interbus** office, walk two short blocks before turning left on **Via D'Annunzio,** which quickly becomes **Via Chiaranda,** then **Via Mazzini,** and finally arrives at **Piazza Garibaldi,** the historical center. The **tourist office,** V. Cavour, 1, is in the courtyard of a *palazzo* just off P. Garibaldi. (☎0935 68 30 49. Open M-F 9am-1pm.) In P. Garibaldi, **Farmacia Quattrino** posts after-hours rotations. (☎0935 68 00 44. Open M-F 9am-1pm and 4:30-8pm.) In case of **emergency,** call the **carabinieri** at ☎0935 68 20 14 or 112. For **Internet,** visit **International Point di Perla Enza,** P. Gen. Cascino, 30. (☎0935 68 65 87 or 0935 68 80 08. €3 per hr. Open daily 9am-9pm.)

TIP

BUS BUNGLE. Before buying a round-trip bus ticket, check for a time limit on the return leg. Some tickets expire 90min. after purchase or first use.

ACCOMMODATIONS AND FOOD. Follow the signs to ▣**Ostello del Borgo ❶,** Largo S. Giovanni, 6, a renovated 14th-century monastery on V. Umberto. This gem offers rooms with dignified furniture and a friendly staff. All private rooms include bath and toiletries; dorms have cramped but clean showers and toilets down the hall. Internet access is available on one fast computer for €2 per hr. (☎0935 68 70 19; www.ostellodelborgo.it. Wheelchair accessible. Buffet breakfast included. Dorms €15; singles €43; doubles €57; triples €75; quads €91. AmEx/MC/V.) **Hotel Villa Romana ❹,** V. De Gasperi, 18, offers posh rooms with full amenities, including bath, TV, air-conditioning, and phone. Three restaurants and two bars round out this splurge. (☎0935 68 29 11; www.piazza-armerina.it/hotelvillaromana. Breakfast included. Mar.-Sept. singles €60; doubles €85; triples €115. Oct.-Feb. singles €50; doubles €75; triples €105. AmEx/MC/V.)

A handful of restaurants sprinkle the streets of Piazza Armerina's historical district, though more options are available in other areas. **Ristorante Pizzeria Pepito ❸,** V. Roma, 140, serves Italian comfort food with a distinctly Spanish flair. Enjoy *agnello al forno* (baked lamb; €10) in the formal upstairs dining room with impressive views of the gardens across the street. (☎0935 68 57 37. *Primi* €6-7, *secondi* from €7. Cover €1. Open M and W-Su noon-3pm and 7pm-midnight. AmEx/MC/V.) For great food at a good price, head to **Café des Amis ❶,** V. Marconi, 22. This tiny cafe has outdoor seating and the best *arancini* and pizza in town (both €1.50). It is also open in the afternoon and evenings, when other restaurants are closed. (☎0935 68 06 61; www.cafedesamis.net. Open M-W and F-Su 6am-11pm.) Savvy locals head to **Ristorante Pizzeria da Totó ❷,** V. Mazzini, 29, near P. Garibaldi, for pizza and *insalata capricciosa* (a salad of mixed Sicilian ingredients; €3.60) served in a comfortable ambience. (☎/fax 0935 68 01 53. Pizza €4-5. Cover €1.05. Open Tu-Su noon-3:30pm and 6pm-midnight. AmEx/MC/V.)

SIGHTS. A fertile valley 5km southwest of town shelters the ▣**Villa Romana del Casale.** This remarkable site, known locally as I Mosaici, is thought to have been constructed at the turn of the 4th century, but a 12th-century landslide kept it mostly hidden for another 800 years. In 1916, famed archaeologists Paolo Orsi and Giuseppe Culterra unearthed 40 rooms of stone mosaics, but there are rooms that have yet to be excavated. Glass walls and ceilings shade the mosaics for protection but still allow for a sense of what the villa would have looked like at the height of its glory. Guidebooks from nearby vendors explain the finer points of the villa's construction and history. Enter first through the **baths,** then pass into a large **hall** on the left to find a mosaic depicting a chariot race; the flying legs are all that remain of the driver, believed to have been Maximenius Herculeus. Max's great wealth, fondness for the hunt, and side business as an importer of animals are part of the tiles' tale. One of the largest rooms shows the capture of bulls, tigers, and lions, while the floor of the **Triclinium** depicts the Battle of the Giants and the Feats of Hercules. The **Salle delle Dieci Ragazze** (Room of Ten Girls) showcases ten bikini-clad beauties in the most famous of the villa's mosaics. While the **Cubicolo Scena Erotica** is not quite as scandalous as its title suggests, the bare tush and intimate kiss depicted still make it the raciest mosaic at the villa. A room off the great hall illustrates the battle between Odysseus and Polyphemus, though the artist fudged the finer narrative details, generously allowing the Cyclops three eyes instead of one. *(Buses leave from P. Marescalchi or Hotel Villa Romana. Bus info: V. Umberto, 6.* ☎ *0935 85 605. The 5km walk is well marked with signs pointing to I Mosaici. Bring lots of water— the sun can be brutal. City buses (€0.60) run every hr. 9am-noon and 3-6pm. Return buses run every hr. from 9:30am-12:30pm and 3:30-6:30pm. Villa* ☎ *0935 68 00 36 and ticket office open daily 8am-6:30pm. €4.50, ages 18-25 €2, under 18 or over 65 free. Tour office* ☎ *0935 68 70 27, www.guardalasicilia.it. Guided tours available for groups. Audio tours €5.)*

🎭 🎵 **ENTERTAINMENT AND NIGHTLIFE.** Every year on August 13 and 14, Piazza Armerina relives the glory days of the Middle Ages during its **Palio dei Normanni**, a remembrance of the Norman Count Roger's defeat of the Saracens in 1160. The festival starts with a knightly parade on horseback through the town streets to P. Duomo, where Count Roger (or at least his modern-day stand-in) is given the keys to the city. The following day the crowds head to the football grounds where competitors trade shinguards for saddles and battle it out old-school tournament style. The winner receives the icon of the Holy Mary of Victories, a golden medal first given to Count Roger by Pope Alexander II in 1160.

For an elegant-but-relaxed night on the town, head to 🍷**Pan e Vinu** wine bar, P. Garibaldi, where the friendly staff and laidback atmosphere provide a nice complement to the dignified burgundy and dark-wood interior. (☎347 74 38 344. Open M-Tu and W-Su 11:30am-3pm and 7pm-1am. Wine from €3 per glass and €10 per bottle. Free appetizers with wine; more elaborate fare €3-10.)

SOUTHERN SICILY

SYRACUSE (SIRACUSA) ☎0931

Mixing Baroque beauty with archaeological jewels, Syracuse (pop. 121,000) combines the relics of an ancient Mediterranean powerhouse with the beauty of a seaside town. At its peak in the ancient world, Syracuse cultivated a selection of great contributors to Western culture, including Theocritus, Archimedes, and the Greek lyric poet Pindar. After many conquests, the city's fortunes waned and it receded from the spotlight. Yet Syracuse has elegantly stepped into the 21st century to become the flower of modern Sicily, as the stunning ruins of the Temple of Apollo and the *duomo* sit comfortably beside more contemporary structures.

▟ TRANSPORTATION

Trains: ☎0931 67 964. On V. Francesco Crispi, between Ortigia and the Archaeological Park. To: **Catania** (1½hr., 12 per day 5am-9:35pm, €4.23); **Florence** (14hr.; 10 per day 5am-9:35pm; €44.31, €27 extra for bed); **Messina** (3hr., 9 per day 5am-9:35pm, €8.99); **Milan** (18hr.; 11 per day 5am-9:35pm, 3 direct lines per day 5am, 5:27, 7:50pm; €48.00); **Noto** (30min., 12 per day 5:20am-8:30pm, €2.27); **Ragusa** (2-3hr.; 3 per day 5:20am-5:35pm, some via **Modica**; €6.60); **Roma** (10-13hr., 8 direct per day 5am-9:35pm, €37.70); **Taormina** (2hr., 12 per day 5am-9:35pm, €6.82); **Turin** (18-20hr.; 8 per day 5am-9:35pm, 2 direct per day 1:20, 2:45pm; €49.63).

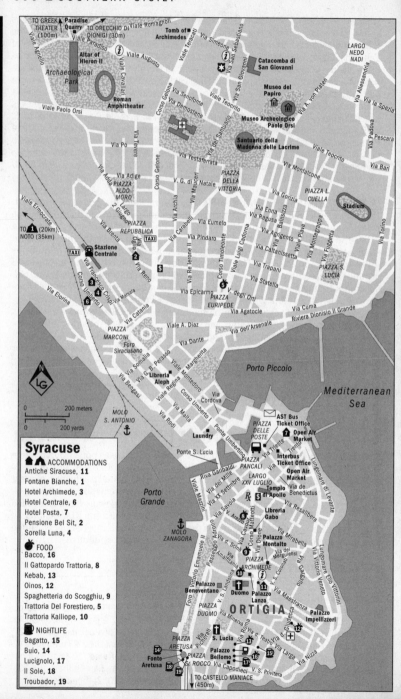

TO GREEK THEATER (100m)
Paradise Quarry
TO ORECCHIO DI DIONIGI (30m)
Viale Romagnoli
Tomb of Archimedes
Viale Paradiso
Viale Agnello
Viale Cavallari
Altar of Hieron II
Archaeological Park
Roman Amphitheater
Viale Paolo Orsi
Via Po
Via Adda
Via Adige
PIAZZA ALDO MORO
Largo 2 Giugno
PIAZZA REPUBBLICA
Via Brenta
Viale Ermocrate
TO (20km); NOTO (35km)
Stazione Centrale
Via Francesco Crispi
Corso Umberto I
Via Elorina
Via Catania
Via Marsala
Via Reno
Via Agnello
Via Augusto
Corso Gelone
Corso Gelone
Via Senofonte
Via Teocrito
Via Demostene
Via San Sebastiano
Via San Giovanni
Via Simeone
Via Teracati
Catacomba di San Giovanni
Museo del Papiro
Museo Archeologico Paolo Orsi
Santuario della Madonna delle Lacrime
Via del Santuario
Via Testaferrata
V. G. di Natale
Via Mauceri
Via Archia
Via Eumelo
Via Carabelli
Via Pindaro
Via Ierone II
Corso Timoleonte
Via Epicarmo
V. degli Orti
PIAZZA DELLA VITTORIA
PIAZZA EURIPIDE
Viale Luigi Cadorna
Via Enna
Via Ragusa
Via Agrigento
Via Caltanissetta
Via Trapani
Via Statella
Via Gorizia
Via Plave
Via Montegrappa
Via Fubagetta
PIAZZA L. CUELLA
PIAZZA S. LUCIA
Stadium
Via Teocrito
Via Montalcone
Viale Teocrito
Via Torino
Via Bari
Via la Spezia
Via Padova
Via Pescara
Via Alessandria
Via A. von Platen
LARGO NEDO NADI
Via Agatocle
Via Cuma
Riviera Dionisio II Grande
PIAZZA MARCONI
Foro Siracusano
Viale A. Diaz
Via Dante
Via dell'Arsenale
Via Sonalia
Via G. B. Perasso
Viale Montedoro
Corso Umberto I
Viale Regina Margherita
Libreria Aleph
Via Cordova
Via Bengasi
Via Malta
Via Rodi
Porto Piccolo
Mediterranean Sea
MOLO S. ANTONIO
Ponte Umbertino
Ponte S. Lucia
PIAZZA DELLE POSTE
AST Bus Ticket Office
Open Air Market
Interbus Ticket Office
Open Air Market
PIAZZA PANCALI
Via Trieste
Via Trentino
Lungomare di Levante
Via de Benedictus
Via Resalibera
Templo d'Apollo
LARGO XXV LUGLIO
Libreria Gabo
Via Mirabella
Laundry
Riva Garibaldi
Viale Mazzini
Riva del Mille
Via XX Settembre
Via V. Arezzo
Via Savoia
Corso Matteotti
Via Dione
Palazzo Montalto
Via del Merguensi
PIAZZA ARCHIMEDE
Palazzo Beneventano
Duomo
Palazzo Lanzo
PIAZZA DUOMO
S. Lucia
PIAZZA ARETUSA
Fonte Aretusa
Palazzo Bellomo
PIAZZA S. ROCCO
Via Capodieci
Via Minerva
Via Roma
Via S. Teatro
Via Pichorali
Via Landolina
Via Maestranza
Via Larga
Via Nizza
ORTIGIA
Porto Grande
MOLO ZANAGORA
Foro Vittorio Emanuele II
Passeggio Adorno
Via Amalfitana
Via S. Landolina
Via V. Mirelli
Via Maestranza
Via Giudecca
Via S. Coronale
Via del Mergulensi
Via Vittorio Veneto
Via Elio Vittorini
Palazzo Impellizzeri
TO CASTELLO MANIACE (450m)
TO ORTIGIA

Syracuse

■▲ ACCOMMODATIONS
Antiche Siracuse, **11**
Fontane Bianche, **1**
Hotel Archimede, **3**
Hotel Centrale, **6**
Hotel Posta, **7**
Pensione Bel Sit, **2**
Sorella Luna, **4**

🍴 FOOD
Bacco, **16**
Il Gattopardo Trattoria, **8**
Kebab, **13**
Oinos, **12**
Spaghetteria do Scogghiu, **9**
Trattoria Del Forestiero, **5**
Trattoria Kalliope, **10**

🍸 NIGHTLIFE
Bagatto, **15**
Buio, **14**
Lucignolo, **17**
Il Sole, **18**
Troubador, **19**

OLD TIME TOURS. Ask at the station about the Val di Noto train tour, a pilot program begun in 2005 which may or may not be around in 2006, consisting of an all-day, €25 tour of southeastern Sicily with guided stops in either Noto and Modica or Ragusa and Scicli to admire the history, regional cuisine, and Baroque architecture, all from a historical steam locomotive.

Buses: AST (☎0931 46 27 11 or 0931 44 92 15), next to the post office on Ortigia, left after the stone bridge. Reduced weekend service. To: **Gela** (4hr., 7am and 1pm, €7.23); **Piazza Amerina** (3hr., 7am, €7.23); **Ragusa** (3hr.; 10 per day 7am-7:30pm, Su 2:20pm only). **Interbus,** V. Trieste, 40 (☎0931 66 710), 1 block from P. delle Poste toward center of Ortigia, 2nd street to left after stone bridge. To: **Catania** (M-F 16 per day 5:45am-7pm; Sa 6:20, 8am, 1, 5pm; Su 9am, 1, 5, 6pm); **Noto** (1hr.; 12 per day 7am-8:30pm, Su 8:50am, 2:20, 8:10pm; €2.75).

Public Transportation: Orange **AST buses** depart from P. delle Poste. Buses #21 and 22 (27 and 28 in summer) run past Fontane Bianche every 2-3hr.; buses #23 and 24 do as well but much less frequently. Tickets (€0.80) sold in *tabaccherie.*

Taxis: ☎0931 69 722 or 0931 60 980. From the train station to Ortigia costs about €8.

ORIENTATION AND PRACTICAL INFORMATION

Ponte Umbertino connects the island of Ortigia to mainland Syracuse. **Ponte Nuovo** (**Ponte Santa Lucia**), just to the left of Ponte Umbertino facing the mainland, is open even when Umbertino is closed to car traffic. On the mainland, **Corso Umberto I** links the bridge to the **train station** and passes through **Piazza Marconi,** from which **Corso Gelone** passes through town to the **Archaeological Park.** C. Umberto continues past **Foro Siracusano** to the train station.

Tourist Office: APT, V.S. Sebastiano, 45 (☎0931 48 12 00 or 0931 67 710). From the station, take V. F. Crispi to V. Catania, which becomes C. Gelone after the tracks. Turn right on Vle. Teocrito after 10min., then left on V. S. Sebastiano; the office is 150m down on the left, across from the catacombs. Useful tourist **map** includes a mini-guide. English spoken. Open M-F 8:30am-1:30pm and 3-6:30pm, Sa-Su 9am-1pm; July-Aug. also open Sa 3:30-6:30pm. **AAT Office: Ortigia,** V. Maestranza, 33 (☎0931 46 42 55). After crossing Ponte Umbertino, turn right through P. Pancali to uphill C. Matteoti. Turn left on V. Maestranza at the fountain in P. Archimede; office is in courtyard of the *palazzo* across from the pharmacy, next to the beauty and wellness store. Open M-F 8am-2pm and 2:45-5:30pm, Sa 8am-2pm.

Luggage Store: In train station. Open daily 7am-1pm and 3-7pm for deposit and pick up; €4 per hr.

English-Language Bookstore: Libreria Aleph, C. Umberto I, 106 (☎0931 48 30 85). A good selection of English-language titles and friendly staff. Also have 2 computers for Internet. €1 per 15min. Open M-Sa 9am-8pm.

Libreria Gabo, C. Matteotti, 38. (☎0931 66 255). Decent selection of English titles. Also offers Internet access on 3 computers, €1.50 per 15min. Open M-Sa 9am-1pm and 4:30-8:30pm, Su 6-8:30pm.

Laundry: Lavenderia ad Acqua, C. Umberto, 13, near the bridge to Ortigia. €3-5 per load, depending on size. Open M-Sa 8:30am-8:30pm, Su 4-8pm.

Emergency: ☎113. **Carabinieri:** ☎112 or 0931 44 13 44. **Police:** ☎0931 49 51 11.

First Aid: Guardia Medica, V. Giudecca (☎0931 48 46 39). Open daily 8am-8pm.

Pharmacy: Mangiafico Farmacia, C. Matteotti, 53 (☎0931 65 643). Open M-Sa 8:30am-1pm and 4:30-8pm. MC/V.

Hospital: Ospedale Generale Provinciale (☎0931 72 41 11), a beige brick monstrosity on V. Testaferrata, off the end of C. Gelone.

Internet Access: Internet Train, V. Roma, 122. 10 fast computers in Ortigia. Min. €1 for 10min. €4.30 per hr., students under 26 €3.20 per hr. Open M-F 10am-1pm and 4pm-8pm, Sa 10am-1pm.

Post Office: P. delle Poste, 15, on Ortigia. Turn left crossing the bridge. Offers **currency exchange.** Open M-F 8:15am-6:30pm, Sa 8am-12:30pm. **Postal Code:** 96100

ACCOMMODATIONS AND CAMPING

Many budget accommodations have staked out the area between the station and the bridge to Ortigia. While prices are good, the quality is very uneven. Don't be fooled by big signs and a lot of flyers. This area is pretty run-down, and at night, visitors should stick to the main, well-lit thoroughfares. Ortigia's options are more expensive, but generally of higher quality.

Sorella Luna, V. Francesco Crispi, 23 (☎0931 21 178; www.sorellalunasrl.it). This B&B retains the beautiful wooden beam ceilings of the convent here before, but everything else is brand-new. All rooms have phone, A/C, bath, wet bar/minifridge, and TV with some English channels. Breakfast included and served on rooftop. May-Sept. singles €50; doubles €80; triples €100; extra bed €20. Oct.-Apr. singles €45/70/85/15. ❹

Hotel Centrale, C. Umberto I, 141 (☎0931 60 528; hotelcentralesr@virgilio.it), near the train station, is a great value. Friendly staff. Clean rooms, some with views, have sink and A/C. Singles €17, with view €18; doubles €28-30, with bath and TV €35-50; triples with bath and TV €65. Cash only. ❷

Antiche Siracuse, V. Roma, 9 (☎0931 46 13 65). 3 beautiful rooms with bath, A/C, TV, phone, and one with kitchen, all located off P. Archimede. Singles €45-50; doubles €65-85; triples €90-100. Breakfast included in the cafe downstairs. AmEx/MC/V. ❹

Hotel Archimede, V. F. Crispi, 67 (☎0931 46 24 58; fax ☎0931 46 20 40). Comfortable rooms and professional staff. Rooms with bath, A/C, and TV. Breakfast included. Singles €35-55; doubles €50-85; triples €70-100; quads €90-128. AmEx/MC/V. ❷

Pensione Bel Sit, V. Oglio, 5, 5th fl. (☎0931 60 245; fax 0931 46 28 82). Follow signs from C. Gelone, close to the train station. Large, simply furnished rooms with colorful bedspreads have fan and airy windows; some with bath. Upstairs rooms also have A/C and TV. Reserve 1 week ahead for July-Aug. Singles €20; doubles €34. Cash only. ❷

Hotel Posta, V. Trieste, 33 (☎0931 21 819; bookinghotelposta@hotmail.com). A classy joint near the waterfront with excellent service and large, comfortable rooms with bath, A/C, wet bar, and TV. Singles €70-75, in winter €50; doubles €95/75. AmEx/MC/V. ❺

Fontane Bianche, V. dei Lidi, 476 (☎0931 79 03 33; fax 0931 79 11 50), 20km from town. Take bus #21 or 22 (€0.77) from P. delle Poste in Ortigia. Showers included. Open May-Sept. €6 per person in high season, €4.50 in low season; €5 per tent. ❶

FOOD

While hotel prices can run fairly high, restaurants are affordable. On the mainland, the area around the station and the Archaeological Park offers some of the best deals. Ortigia has an **open-air market** on V. Trento, off P. Pancali, as well as several budget options on V. Savoia and V. Cavour.

Oinos, V. d. Giudecca, 69/75 (☎0931 46 49 00). The elegance of this restaurant and *enoteca* is matched only by the eccentricity its owner, Milan expat Ivo Vatti, and the sheer virtuosity of resident chef-prodigy, 20-year-old Valentina Galli. Glass cut-outs in the stone floor reveal more than 270 varieties of wine for sale—sample a glass before finishing off one of many homemade desserts. Wine from €3 per glass and €12 per bottle. *Primi* €7-10, *secondi* €13-17. Desserts €4. Cover €2. Internet €3 per hr.; free for patrons. Open Tu-Su 12:30-2:30pm and 7pm-midnight. ❹

Kebab, V. Roma, 104 (☎347 01 88 287 or 347 88 64 076). Santino serves up quick cuisine at this tiny hole-in-the-wall that is both cheap and delicious. Try the kebab (€4) with a little *hasalla* for some extra kick. Also serves a variety of *panini* (€2-3.50), including cheeseburgers, and one with *cavallo* (horse). *Couscous di pesce* €6, *couscous di carne* €5. Open daily 11am-3pm and 7pm-1am. ❶

Trattoria Kalliope, V. d. Consiglio Regionale, 26 (☎0931 46 00 08). In a small *piazza* filled with statues and jazz music, Kalliope serves appetizing pasta and seafood dishes in a casual, outdoor environment. *Primi* from €5, *secondi* from €7. Cover €1. Open M and W-Su noon-3pm and 7pm-midnight. ❷

Trattoria Del Forestiero, C. Timoleonte, 2 (☎0931 46 12 45 or 335 84 30 736), on the mainland. From the start of C. Gelone, take V. Agatocle to P. Euripede; restaurant is on the far side at start of C. Timoleonte. Walk 10min. out of touristy Ortigia and you'll find good, cheap food at this lively local favorite. Try their speciality, a *pizza forestiero*. Pizza from €2.50; takeout available. *Primi* from €3.10, *secondi* from €4.20. Cover €1.10. Open M and Th-Su noon-3:30pm and 7-11:30pm. ❶

Il Gattopardo Trattoria, V. Cavour, 67 (☎0931 21 910), draws a hip, college-aged crowd. Leopard-lined walls pay homage to the *trattoria's* namesake. Kitchen specializes in traditional Sicilian fare, especially *pizza alla norma*. *Primi* and *secondi* €5. Open M-Sa 10am-1pm and 8-11pm. Cash only. ❷

Bacco, V. Roma, 120. A lively dining room and terrace both host above-par Sicilian cuisine. *Primi* €5-10, *secondi* €7-12. Meat *menù* €12, fish *menù* €16; drink not included. Open daily 10:30am-3:30pm and 4:30pm-12:30am. Oct.-May closed Tu. ❸

Spaghetti do Scogghiu, V. D. Scinà, 11, a tiny street off P. Archimede, in Ortigia. An impressive selection of spaghetti—over 20 varieties—in a busy, hole-in-the-wall restaurant in the center of Ortigia. *Primi* and *secondi* from €5.50. Cover €1.50. Open Tu-Su noon-3pm and 6:30pm-midnight. ❷

👁 SIGHTS

MAINLAND SYRACUSE

■ **ARCHAEOLOGICAL PARK.** Syracuse's three centuries as a strategic city on the Mediterranean left behind a collection of immense monuments. The Greek ruins are the most impressive, but Roman remains also attest to a rich heritage. Two theaters, an ancient quarry, and the world's largest altar (see below) share a fenced compound, visited with a single ticket. Walk through the gauntlet of souvenir stands to reach the ticket office. *(Take C. Gelone to V. Teocrito; park entrance down V. Augusto to the left; follow the frequent signs. Information ☎0931 66 206. Park open daily in summer 9am-2hr. before sunset; in winter 9am-3pm. Ticket office open daily in summer 9am-6pm; in winter 9am-2pm. €6, EU residents 18-25 €3, EU residents under 18 or over 65 free.)*

■ **CATACOMBA DI SAN GIOVANNI.** Dating from AD 415-460, this subterranean maze has over 20,000 tombs carved into the walls of what used to be a Greek aqueduct. No corpses linger—only ghostly frescoes, an occasional sarcophagus, and a few wall-carvings. The 4th-century **Cripta di San Marziano,** the crypt of the first bishop of Syracuse, lies below the **Chiesa di San Giovanni** next door. *(Across from tourist office on V. S. Giovanni, off Vle. Teocrito from C. Gelone. ☎0931 64 694; fax 0931 66 751. Open Tu-Su 9am-12:30pm and 2:30-5:30pm. Mandatory guided tours every 15-20min., €3.50, under 15 or over 65 €2.50, school groups €1.50 per person. MC/V.)*

GREEK THEATER. Seated in a theater row that was carved into the hillside in 475 BC, it's easy to understand why Syracuse became such a successful Greek colony. If the 15,000 spectators watching Aeschylus's original production of *The Persians* got bored, they could lift their eyes over the now-ruined scenic building to scan fields, colorful flowers, the sparkling sea—and oncoming attackers, as Syracuse's location was spectacularly strategic. Original Greek inscriptions line the walls along the mid-level aisles, and the track for the *deus ex machina*, a large crane that made the gods "fly," is still in place around the orchestra. *(Closes early during the-ater season (May-June). Included in ticket for the archaeological park and quarry; see above.)*

PARADISE QUARRY. The floral valley next to the theater derives its name from the gardens that line the base of the large, chalky cliffs. These quarries provided most of the characteristic gray stone that built old Syracuse. Two large artificial caves were cut in the walls, the **Orecchio di Dionigi** (Ear of Dionysius) and the **Grotta dei Cordari** (Ropemakers' Cave). The latter is closed to the public for safety reasons, but visitors can still experience the Orecchio di Dionigi, which is famous for the echoes that ricochet off its walls. Legend claims the tyrant Dionysius put his prisoners here so he could eavesdrop on their conversations. Though the acoustics are still impressive, the subversive plots have been replaced by boisterous explanations of tour guides. *(Open daily from 9am-2hr. before sunset.)* Outside this area lies **Ara di Ierone II** (the altar of Hieron II, 241-215 BC), once used for public sacrifices. At 198m by 23m, it is the world's largest altar. Up the hill and through the other gate is a 2nd-century Roman **amphitheater.** Visitors can see the tunnels through which gladiators and their prey entered the arena floor.

MUSEO ARCHEOLOGICO PAOLO ORSI. Named for the most famous archaeologist in Sicily, this museum has a collection of over 18,000 objects from prehistory through ancient Greece and early Christianity (40,000 BC-AD 600). From the introductory room at the museum's core, hallways branch into chronologically arranged galleries that wind through time and space. Exquisite *kouroi* torsos, grimacing Gorgons, elegant vases, and Pygmy elephant skeletons rest in dimly-lit galleries. Otherworldly inhabitants populate gigantic urns and rough tombs in the museum's large garden. *(Vle. Teocrito, 66. ☎0931 46 40 22. Open Tu-Sa 9am-2pm and 3-6pm, Su 9am-2pm. Ticket office open Tu-Sa 9am-2pm and 3-5pm, Su 9am-1pm. €4.50, EU residents 18-25 €2, EU residents under 18 or over 65 free.)*

SANTUARIO DELLA MADONNA DELLE LACRIME. For three days in 1953, a mass-produced statuette of the Madonna reputedly began to weep in the home of the Iannuso family. Since then the number of pilgrims has grown so large that the commanding spire of the **Basilica Madonna delle Lacrime** was built in 1994 on the plans of Frenchmen Michel Arnault and Pierre Parat. Pilgrim or not, a stop at the sanctuary to admire the impressive architecture will be worth it. The **Museum of Lacrymation** and the **Museum of Liturgy** complement the basilica; timetables placed outside of the sanctuary tell the statue's tale. *(☎0931 21 446; www.madonnadellelac-rime.it. Both museums open daily 9am-12:30pm and 4-6pm. Sanctuary open 8am-noon and 4-7pm. Museum of Lacrymation €1.55, Museum of Liturgy €1, both museums €2. Sanctuary free.)*

MUSEO DEL PAPIRO. Long before the printing press and tell-all autobiographies, papyrus scrolls promised the quickest path to earning a place in eternity. This museum, created to promote research on antique and contemporary uses of papyrus, displays pages from the ancient Egyptian *Book of the Dead*, with spells to facilitate entry into the afterlife. Special attractions include invocations (translated into Italian) to the Eater of Souls and the Snake that Rises. There's also an entrancing video on papyrus's history and a collection of texts and woven objects. *(V. Teocrito, 66, near Orsi museum. ☎0931 61 616. Open Tu-Su 9am-1:30pm. Free.)*

ORTIGIA. Across Ponte Umbertino, Ortigia offers more selective restaurants and nightlife than the mainland. Before rescuing Sicily from barbary, the Greeks landed in Ortigia, using the island as a point of embarkment for their attack on the mainland. At the end of the bridge, the fenced-in ruins of the **Tempio di Apollo** gleam white in the setting sun. Dating from 575 BC, it is the oldest peripteral (with columns on all sides) Doric temple in Sicily. The island flourished in the Baroque period, leaving today's smattering of elegant churches and the **Palazzo Impellizzeri,** V. Maestranza, 22. *Siracusani* glide with an air of casual entitlement in the island's streets and *piazze* during the long summer evening's *passeggiate.*

DUOMO. The 18th-century exterior of the cathedral looks like the standard Baroque compilation of architectural fancies. The interior is anything but. A 5th-century BC Temple of Athena first stood on the site, and rather than demolishing the pagan structure, architects incorporated it into their construction. Fluted columns line the interior, recalling the structure's Classical origins. Large, shiny letters proclaim this the first Christian church in the West. Legend has it that the temple became a church with the arrival of St. Paul. The first chapel on the right is dedicated to St. Lucia, the light-bearer and Syracuse's patron saint. Catch a glimpse of her left arm in the elaborate glass reliquary. Hidden from view above the reliquary is a masterpiece of Sicilian silver work, a life-sized statue of Lucia that parades through the streets on her feast day (see **Entertainment,** below). Lest people forget how she died, silversmiths thoughtfully included a dagger protruding from her throat, the punishment dealt the saint by the pagan government of AD 304. *(From P. Archimede, take V. Roma and turn right on V. Minerva. Open daily 8am-noon and 4-7pm. Modest dress required.)*

FONTE ARETUSA. This ancient pond fed by a "miraculous" fresh-water spring near the sea overlooks Pta. Grande. *Siracusani* believe that the nymph Arethusa escaped the enamored river god Alpheus by diving into the sea and that the goddess Diana rescued her by transforming her into this fountain. The river surfaces here at the Fonte Aretusa. *(P. Aretusa. From P. Duomo, walk down V. Picherale.)*

🎵 🎭 ENTERTAINMENT AND NIGHTLIFE

Siracusani, like all Italians, fall prey in summer to ancestral instincts that force them from the cities to the beaches. **Fontane Bianche** is one such beach, well populated and with many discos. The campground there ensures a place to sleep when buses stop. Take bus #21 or 22 (30min., every 2-3 hr., €0.77). In Ortigia, nightlife consists of a tour of the island, stopping at several bars along the way.

Don't miss **🎭Lucignolo,** V. Roma, 154, on your night on the town. Slang for "wicked," Lucignolo lets you play the devil in the red-lit interior. Also organizes boat parties; ask at the bar. (Open Tu-Su 6pm-2am.) **Bagatto,** in the small P. San Giuseppe, often features free live music 10:30pm-midnight, and **Il Sole,** hidden away in the courtyard of an old building, off V. Amalfitania. Piazzetta San Rocco is a nightlife hot spot; the two best bars there are the eclectic **Buio** ("darkness") and the energetic **Troubador,** off P. S. Rocco.

In May and June, the city stages **classical Greek drama** in ancient amphitheaters. The APT office has details. Tickets for **Istituto Nazionale del Dramma Antico** are available at the theater box office, in the Archaeological Park. (☎0931 46 58 31; www.indafondazione.org. Open M-F 10am-6:30pm.) At the **Festa di Santa Lucia,** December 13, men shoulder the silver statue of the city's patron saint in a 6hr. procession from the *duomo* to S. Lucia al Sepolcro on the mainland. After a week, the statue returns to the *duomo* December 20.

▶ DAYTRIPS FROM SYRACUSE

NOTO

Accessible by Interbus from Syracuse (1hr.; 8 per day 7:05am-6pm, return 7 per day 6:55am-4:55pm; €2.50). Ticket office opposite bus stop in Bar Efirmedio. Noto can also be reached by train (30min., 12 per day 5:20am-8:30pm, €2.27). The station is a 15min. walk from town.

A haven of Baroque unity, Noto is a pleasure to the eyes. After a 1693 earthquake shook Sicily's shore, the noble Landolina and Nicolaci families made Noto their favorite renovation project, restoring its elegance with monumental staircases, *putti* moldings, and pot-bellied balconies. Noto has a slower pace than coastal towns, making it a calm retreat from frenzied tourist destinations. Toward the city center from C. V. Emanuele and up four flights of giant steps stands the immense **Chiesa di San Francesco all'Immacolata,** built in 1704 and currently closed for renovation, which houses one of the bloodiest crucifixes in Sicily. On C. V. Emanuele, stop at the **Teatro Comunale Vittorio Emanuele** to gaze up at its painted balconies and bright red drapes. (Play season Nov.-May. Open Tu-Su 9am-1pm and 4-8pm. €1.50, show tickets €10-€25.) From C. V. Emanuele, turn right on V. Niccolaci for a view of the balconies of the **Palazzo Niccolaci,** supported by cherubs, griffins, and sirens. **La panoramica dal Campanile** affords a matchless view of the city from the top of the **Chiesa di San Carlo** (€1.50, under 18 €1). Decent **beaches** are 7km away at **Noto Marina.** Buses depart from the Giardini Pubblici. (July-Aug. M-Sa 8:30am, 12:45pm; €1.20.) The **Hall of Mirrors** at Palazzo Ducezio in P. Municipio on C. V. Emanuele is worth a look if you're into Baroque. Dating from 1760, the frescoes of local history are interspersed with mirrors from which the hall takes its name. (Open June-Sept. Tu-Su 9am-1pm and 4-8pm; Oct.-May 9am-1pm and 3-7pm.)

There are very few budget accommodations in Noto, but reasonably priced bed and breakfasts abound. The rose among the thorns is **⬛B&B Teatro ❸**, P. XVI Maggio, 10, next to the Teatro and across from the tourist office. Three operatically named rooms (*La Tosca, La Norma,* and *La Rigoletta*) are tastefully furnished. All rooms have air-conditioning, full bath, and hair dryer and share a fully stocked kitchen and common room with multilingual magazines and TV. (☎0931 83 85 03; www.bbnoto.com. Breakfast and Internet included. Reservations recommended, especially in summer. Doubles €70-90; triples €80-100; quads €90-110. AmEx/MC/V.) Call to reserve one of two rooms with air-conditioning at ◨**Centro Storico ❸**, C. V. Emanuele, 64. This eclectic hotel is run by a welcoming family. (☎0931 57 39 67; www.centro-storico.com. €25-32 per person, no singles. Reserve ahead.)

A number of reasonably priced *trattorie* line C. V. Emanuele, the best of which is **Trattoria al Buca ❷** which tempts with homemade pasta and fish. Try the ravioli in meat sauce (€6) which showcases their speciality, ricotta cheese. (☎0931 89 47 78. Cover €0.70. *Primi* from €4, *secondi* from €5.50. Open M-Th and Sa-Su noon-3:30pm and 7pm-midnight.) At the **Pasticceria La Vecchia Fonata ❶**, C. V. Emanuele, 150, try the specialty "porchetta"—*panedi spagna* (sponge cake) filled with sweet ricotta (€2.50). *Gelato* €1.30-2.50. *Panini* €2. (☎0931 83 94 12. Open Tu-Su 7am-1am.) Just down the road, at C. V. Emanuele, 125, is **Caffè Sicilia ❶**, one of Noto's classic bars and hangout for ice cream aficionados and wine connoisseurs. Especially popular are the gourmet *granite*, with a variety of hard-to-find flavors like *cappucino ghiacciato* (iced cappucino).

To reach the **APT Tourist Office** from the bus stop at the **Giardini Pubblici** (Public Gardens), cross the paved way with the fountain on the right. Turn left through the tunnel trees and pass under the **Porta Nazionale** (built in 1838) to **Corso Vittorio Emanuele.** The tourist office is six blocks up C. V. Emanuele on the right in the garden of the Villetto Ercole, behind the fountain. Look for the wooden sign. Once there, grab a free **map.** (☎0931 57 37 79; noto.apt@tin.it. Open Mar.-Oct. M-Sa 8:30am-1:30pm and 3:30-6:15pm; Nov.-Feb. M-F 8am-2pm and 3:50-6:30pm, Sa 8am-2pm.) To reach the town center from the **train station,** follow the road leading uphill and to the right until it ends, then walk through the park for a block. A left turn here and 5min. walk will put you at the far end of the town's main street, C. V. Emanuele. From there, follow the directions given above. The **post office,** across from Al Buco, is open Monday to Friday 8am-6:30pm and Saturday 8am-12:30pm.

THE LEG BONE'S CONNECTED TO THE KNEE BONE. Travelers to Sicily will undoubtedly come across the omnipresent **Trinacria.** An unusual combination of mythological references, the island's ancient symbol consists of three legs bent at the knee, radiating equidistantly from Medusa's snake-haired head, adorned with wheat. Famous for turning men into stone with her fearsome gaze, Medusa was in charge of protecting the ends of the earth, which in the days of ancient Greece meant Sicily. The boughs of wheat represent cultivation of Sicily's fertile soil, and the three legs stand for the three corners of the trian-gular island: Capo Pallor at Messina, Capo Passer at Syracuse, and Capo Lille west of Marsala. The leg bent at the knee was a Spartan symbol of power. The Trinacria is most often represented in burnished gold, the color of the sun, which has always—for obvious reasons—been associated with the island of Sicily.

RAGUSA
☎ 0932

The first thing you notice about the little town of Ragusa (pop. 68,000) is that it is actually two even smaller towns: Ragusa Ibla, the old town, and higher up, Ragusa Superiore, the (relatively) new town, built entirely after the earthquake of 1693. Ragusa Ibla and Superiore are divided by a breathtaking valley, full of dense foli-age and waterfalls, which creates a scenic—albeit steep—hike between the two. Visitors will probably want to spend most of their time in Ragusa Ibla, where the combination of antique buildings and sweeping vistas makes for beautiful tours through the twisting streets and open *piazze.*

TRANSPORTATION

The **train station** is at P. Stazione, above P. del Popolo and V. Dante in Ragusa Supe-riore, behind the bus stop. **Trains** run to: Caltanissetta (5hr., 5 per day 4:08am-8:20pm, €9.25); Gela (1¼hr., 6 per day 4:08am-8:20pm, €4.25); Palermo (7hr., 6 per day 4:08pm-8:20pm, €17.80); and Syracuse (2hr.; 6 per day 6:05am-6:30pm, €6.60). **Etna Buses,** in P. del Popolo in Ragusa Superiore run to Catania (2hr.; M-F 10 per day 5:45am-7pm, Sa 6 per day 5:45am-5pm, Su 5 per day 8am-7pm; €6.60). Buy tickets at **Caffè del Viale;** from P. del Popolo with your back to the train station, turn left on Vle. Tenente Lena toward P. Libertà. **AST,** just off P. del Popolo (0932 68 18 18) runs buses from P. del Popolo to Chiaramonte (40min., 8 per day 7:10am-7:30pm, €1.95); Gela (1½hr.; M-Sa 9:45am and 3:15pm, €4.20); Noto (1½hr.; 10 per day 6am-7pm, €4.20); Palermo (4hr.; M-Sa 4 per day 5:25am-5:25pm, Su 3:10pm and 5:25pm; €11.35); and Syracuse (2hr., 10 per day 6am-7pm, €5.80). Connec-tions to Agrigento and Enna run via Gela. Ticket office at P. Libertà.

ORIENTATION AND PRACTICAL INFORMATION

The train station is in **Piazza Stazione** just above **Piazza del Popolo,** the buses stop in P. del Popolo and in nearby **Piazza Gramsci** (P. Pullman). To reach the town center of **Ragusa Superiore,** turn left on **Viale Tenente Lena,** walk through **Piazza Libertà** and across **Ponte Senatore F. Pennavaria,** the first of three bridges spanning the **Vallata Santa,** at which point Vle. Ten. Lena becomes **Via Roma. Corso Italia,** off V. Roma, goes downhill for several blocks, passing the post office in **Piazza Matteotti** before becoming **Via XXIV Maggio.** It ends at Chiesa di Santa Maria della Scala. Here, stairs and roads wind down to **Ragusa Ibla,** the older section of town. City buses run a circuit of Ragusa Ibla and Ragusa Superiore (M-Sa 2 per hr. and Su 1 per hr.).

The **Pro Loco Tourist Office,** V. Largo Camerina, 5, is in Ragusa Ibla. Helpful staff has **maps** and brochures. Look for the signs from P. Duomo. (Open Tu-Sa 9am-noon and 4-6pm, Su 9am-noon. Hours provisional.) The **AAPIT Tourist Office,** V. Cap-

SICILY

itano Bocchieri, 33, is in Ragusa Ibla, beyond the *duomo* and behind a small entry-way with flags above the door. (☎621 42 12 21 525 or 0932 22 15 29. Open M and W-F 9am-1:30pm, Tu 9am-1:30pm and 6-8pm, Sa-Su 9:30am-1pm. Call ahead for exact hours.) In case of **emergency**, call ☎113, the **police** at ☎112 or 0932 62 10 10, an **ambulance** at ☎118, **first aid** (☎0932 62 14 10), or the **medical clinic** (☎0932 62 39 46) in P. Igea. The **Ospedale Civile** (☎0932 24 51 84) is on V. di Vittorio in a peach build-ing. **Ibl@cafe**, P. della Repubblica, 10-11, in Ragusa Ibla, has four fast computers for **Internet** (€3 per hr.), as well as hip owners who serve great *panini* (€2.50-3) on the side. (☎0932 68 31 08; iblacafe@hotmail.com. Open daily 9am-11pm. Closed Su in summer and Tu in winter.) A **post office** (☎0932 23 21 11) is in P. Matteotti, two blocks down C. Italia from V. Roma. (Open M-Sa 8am-6:30pm. Closes at noon last day of the month.) *Fermoposta* services are at V. Ercolano. **Postal Code:** 97100.

⌂ ACCOMMODATIONS

From the train station, cross P. del Popolo to V. Sicilia. Turn right and pass the gas station to find **Hotel Jonio ❷**, V. Risorgimento, 49. The best deal in town, these plain rooms all have TV and bath. (☎0932 62 43 22; fax 0932 22 91 44. Breakfast included. Singles €30, with half pension €41; doubles €50/72; triples €66/99. AmEx/MC/V.) A fancier option, **Mediterraneo Palace ❺**, is across the bridge from the train station, at V. Roma, 189. Despite the odd fisherman's tarp that shields the hotel's entrance from the sun, this palace exemplifies comfort and modernity. Spacious, air-condi-tioned rooms all have pay TV, minibar, and bath, some with bath massage. (☎0932 62 19 44. Wheelchair accessible. Singles €68-92; doubles €90-118. AmEx/MC/V.) Rooms in Ragusa Ibla are pricey, but if you're up for the splurge, **Locanda Don Serafino ❺**, V. XI Febbraio, 15, has elegant rooms with slate floors and stone arch-ways. Rooms have air-conditioning, TV and bath (with hair dryer and toiletries), some with spa baths and/or balcony. (☎0932 22 00 65; www.locandadonserafino.it. Breakfast included. Doubles €110-170. AmEx/MC/V.) Escape the city and head to campsite **Baia del Sole ❶**, on Lungomare Andrea Doria, in Marina. Tumino buses run from P. Gramsci in Ragusa to P. Duca degli Abruzzi in Marina (25min.; 13 per day 6am-8:30pm; €2.20, round-trip €3.60). Keeping the water on the right, walk 1km from the main *piazza* on the *lungomare*. Hot showers are available 7-9am and 5-7pm. (☎0932 23 98 44. €3 per person, €8 per tent; Aug. €6/13 per tent.)

◖ FOOD

Visitors to Ragusa should try the specialty *panatigghie*, thin but savory pastries filled with the unlikely trio of cocoa, cinnamon, and ground meat. Purchase gro-cery essentials at **SMA**, a short walk from the station on Vle. Sicilia. (☎0932 62 43 42. Open M-Sa 8:30am-8pm.) In Ragusa Ibla, a series of cafes and bars line C. XXV Aprile below P. Pola, offering *panini* and other cheap eats to students from the university. From P. Duomo, walk away from the *duomo* and down C. XXV Aprile.

⌘ Gelati Divini, P. Duomo, 20 (0932 22 89 89; www.gelatidivini.it) Gelati Divini offers you the best of both worlds with their *moscato* and *brachetto* flavors, respectively white-and red-wine flavored ice-cream. For the truly adventurous, try the *cioccolato al peper-oncino*, spicy peppered chocolate ice cream. Also sells local cheeses (€2.50) and chocolate (€2.50-5). Bottled wine from €6.50. *Gelato* €2-4. Open daily 10am-1am. Closed Tu in winter; Jan. 15-Feb. 15 open Sa-Su only. ❶

La Valle, V. Risorgimento, 70 (☎0932 22 93 41; www.lavalle.it). Tasty food can be boxed up for takeout, eaten in the quirky mint-green dining room, or enjoyed on the streetside patio. Offers a margherita pizza *menù* with drink and cover included (€7) or a *menù* with *primo, secondo, contorno*, fruit, and water (€13). Pizza €3.50-8. *Primi* €5-9, *secondi* €5-12. Cover €1.50. Open M and W-Su noon-3pm and 7pm-midnight. AmEx/MC/V. ❷

Ristorante Orfeo, V. S. Anna, 117 (☎0932 62 10 35), off V. Roma in the *centro*, serves Sicilian specialties in a classy atmosphere. The aesthetically conscious dining room sports unique table decorations. Fresh fish from €11. *Primi* from €7, *secondi* from €8. Cover €2.60. Service 10%. Open M-Sa noon-3pm and 7-10pm. AmEx/MC/V. ❸

Pizzeria La Grotta, on V. G. Cartia, 8 (☎0932 22 73 70), 2nd right off V. Roma walking away from the bridge. Original variations on standard *tavola calda* fare, including 31 *panini* choices. Wacky creations like pizza topped with french fries or Nutella are wildly popular. Pizza slices €1.40. Open M-Sa 5:30pm-12:30am. ❶

👁 🎵 SIGHTS AND ENTERTAINMENT

The hilltops of Ragusa Superiore and Ragusa Ibla offer fantastic views of the countryside. Ragusa Ibla, the ancient section, is accessible by a steep but lovely 10min. hike down from the church at the bottom of C. Italia (V. XXIV Maggio) or by catching bus #1 or 3 (€0.77) from P. del Popolo. The buses return to the Ragusa Superiore from Largo Camerina, one block from the cathedral in Ibla. The stairs at S. Maria offer a stellar view, crowned by a monastery and the 18th-century dome of **San Giorgio**, which glows turquoise at night. (Modest dress required.) The road to the left after the set of tricky steps to P. Repubblica circumvents the town, passing monasteries and farmland. P. del Duomo di San Giorgio sits at the top of the city. C. XXV Aprile runs downhill from the *piazza*, passes two churches, and ends at the **Giardini Iblei**, pleasant public gardens with views of the valley below, as well as a convent which organizes free art exhibits. (Park open daily 9am-midnight; art exhibits 10:30am-1pm.) Ragusa Superiore's **Museo Archeologico**, below Ponte S. Pennavaria, displays pottery from the Syracusan colony of Camarina. (☎0932 62 29 63. Open daily 9am-1:30pm and 4-7:30pm. €2, ages 18-25 €1, under 18 or over 65 free.)

During the summer, Italians pack their swimsuits, rev up their Vespas, and spend the weekend baking their bodies and splashing in the crystal blue waters at ▓**Marina di Ragusa. Autolinee Tumino** (☎0932 62 31 84) runs buses to Marina from P. Gramsci (25min.; 15 per day, last bus returns at 10pm; €2.20, round-trip €3.60). Ask the bus driver for a schedule with return times and clarification on where the bus returns for pick up.

Since 1990 Ragusa Ibla has played host to the annual **Ibla Grand Prize**, an international piano, voice, and composition competition that runs from late June to early July. Performances are held in the theater of the **Palazzo Comunale**.

AGRIGENTO ☎0922

For a city that incorporates majestic Greek monuments and medieval churches with equal aplomb, Agrigento (pop. 52,000) remains surprisingly under-appreciated. Visitors are treated to some of the Mediterranean's most impressive Greek ruins: a series of intact, ancient Doric temples. The fantastic juxtaposition of this relic-filled valley and the town's complex of urban high-rises creates a surreal scene straight out of a play by local celebrity Luigi Pirandello. Although Agrigento today takes great pride in its modernity, traces of its past still linger in the winding cobblestone streets.

◧ TRANSPORTATION

Trains: The **train station** is in P. Marconi, below P. Aldo Moro. Ticket office open M-Sa 6:30am-8pm. To: **Catania** (3¼hr.; 12:20, 7:45pm; €9.20) via **Enna** (2hr., €5.73) and **Palermo** (2hr., 10 per day 4:50am-8:05pm, €6.70).

Buses: From P. V. Emanuele, buses are to the left in P. Roselli. **Cuffaro** (www.cuffaro.info) runs buses to **Palermo** (M-Sa 4 per day 5:45am-2:30pm, Su 8:15am, 4:30, 6:30pm;

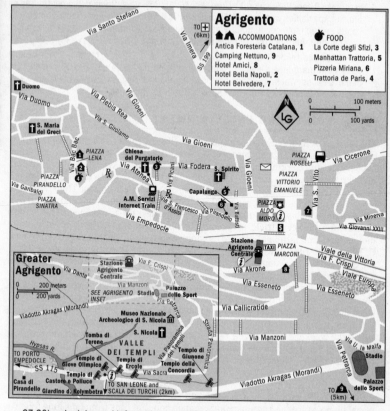

Agrigento

🏠🏠 ACCOMMODATIONS
Antica Foresteria Catalana, **1**
Camping Nettuno, **9**
Hotel Amici, **8**
Hotel Bella Napoli, **2**
Hotel Belvedere, **7**

🍎 FOOD
La Corte degli Sfizi, **3**
Manhattan Trattoria, **5**
Pizzeria Miriana, **6**
Trattoria de Paris, **4**

€7.20); schedules and information available at the bar down from the SAIS offices in P. Roselli. **SAIS Trasporti**, V. Ragazzi del 99 (☎0922 59 59 33), behind the ticket office, runs buses to: **Caltanissetta** (1hr., M-Sa 14 per day 4:30am-7:15pm, €4.13); **Catania** (2¾hr., 11 per day, €11); **Trapani** (M-Sa 6:30, 8:30am, 1:55pm; €10) and the **airport**. Reduced service Su.

Public Transportation: Orange **TUA buses** depart from the train station. Tickets €0.80 valid 1½hr. available at *tabaccherie* (there's one in the train station). Buses #2 and 2/ run to the beach at San Leone; #1/, 2, 2/, 3, and 3/ run to the Valle dei Templi; #1/ runs to Pirandello's house.

Taxis: At train station, in P. Marconi (☎0922 26 670), and in P. Aldo Moro (☎0922 21 899). A trip to the temples should run about €15 on the meter–just make sure it's running.

✦ 🔢 ORIENTATION AND PRACTICAL INFORMATION

Agrigento's **train station** is in **Piazza Marconi**, the main stop for all city buses. Walk up the stairs to find the town's lively park-like central square, **Piazza Aldo Moro**. From P. Aldo Moro, the posh **Via Atenea** leads to the *centro storico*. At the far side of P. Aldo Moro is **Piazza Vittorio Emanuele**, just beyond which is the **bus station.** The temples are a bus ride (#1, 1/, 2, 2/, 3, or 3/) or a long walk away, below the town. (On foot, head out of the station on **Viale delle Vittoria** and follow the signs.)

Tourist Office: AAPIT kiosk in the train station and **AAST,** in P. Aldo Moro, in the center of the square. English-speaking staff, **maps,** and brochures. AAST open daily 9am-1pm, plus W 3-7pm. Train station kiosk open in summer daily 9am-1pm and 3:30-7pm; in winter 9am-1pm. Another summer office is in **Valle dei Templi,** adjacent to parking and bar. English spoken. Open daily 8:30am-1pm and 3pm-sunset.

English-Language Bookstore: ■**Capalunga,** V. Atenea, 123 (☎0922 22 338; www.capalunga.com). Thoughtfully chosen selection English books, art shows, hip decor–curl up in an egg-shaped window seat overlooking the sea–and free high-speed Internet for customers. Open daily 9:30am-1pm and 5:30-9pm; July-Aug. closed Su.

Emergency: ☎113. **Carabinieri:** P. Aldo Moro, 2 (☎0922 59 63 22). **First Aid:** ☎0922 40 13 44.

Pharmacy: Farmacia Averna Antonio, V. Atenea, 325 (☎0922 26 093). Open M-F 9am-1:30pm and 5-8:30pm. **Farmacia Dr Patti,** V. Atenea, 129 (☎0922 20 591). Open M-F 9am-1:30pm and 5-8:30pm. Both post late-night and weekend rotations.

Hospital: Ospedale Civile (☎0922 49 21 11), 6km from town center toward Palermo on Contrada Consolida, off V. San Michele. Take bus #4 from P. Rosselli.

Internet Access: A.M. Servizi Internet Train, Cortile Contarini, 7 (☎0922 40 27 83; www.internettrain.it). 1 block before Chiesa del Purgatorio, make a right off V. Atenea from P. Aldo Moro (look for the orange "Internet Train" sign on V. Atenea). 6 high-speed computers. €3.20 per hr., printing (black-and-white) €0.15 per page. CD burning €4, disc included. Open daily 9am-8:30pm.

Post Office: P. V. Emanuele (☎0922 59 51 50; fax 0922 22 926). Call in the morning for inquiries. Open M-Sa 8am-6:30pm. **Postal Code:** 92100.

▐ ACCOMMODATIONS AND CAMPING

■**Hotel Bella Napoli,** P. Lena, 6 (☎/fax 0922 20 435), off V. Bac Bac. Take V. Atenea 500m uphill and turn right at the sign for Trattoria de Paris. Cheerful yellow hallways lead to bright rooms with bath, A/C, and TV, some with balcony. Rooftop terrace overlooks the valley. Breakfast €3. Singles €35; doubles €65; triples €80. MC/V. ❸

Antica Foresteria Catalana, P. Lena, 5 (☎/fax 0922 20 435). Next door to Hotel Bella Napoli and under the same management, Catalana offers larger rooms with high slanting ceilings and more luxurious decor. All rooms with bath, A/C, phone, and TV, some with balcony. Breakfast €3. Singles €45; doubles €75; triples €95. MC/V. ❹

Hotel Amici, V. Akrone, 5 (☎0922 59 62 88; www.hotelamici.com). Down the stairs and next to the bingo parlor in P. Marconi. Offers 20 quiet rooms with bath, TV, A/C, and some with balcony and sea views. Free parking and breakfast included. Singles €38, July-Aug. €44; doubles €68/73; triples €84/90; quads €96/110. MC/V. ❸

Hotel Belvedere, V. S. Vito, 20 (☎/fax 0922 20 051). Follow clearly marked signs from train station. Friendly staff hosts guests in colorful rooms with fan and telephone. Some rooms overlook a small garden. Breakfast €3. Singles €35, with bath €49; doubles €43/64; triples €76/96. 5% discount with *Let's Go.* Cash only. ❸

Camping Nettuno, (☎0922 41 62 68), on the beach at V. l'Acquameno by the bus stop. Take bus #2 or 2/ from the train station. Market, restaurant, bar, and pizzeria on premises. Showers €0.50. €5 per person, €5 per tent, €2.50 per car. ❶

◖ FOOD

Plenty of *alimentari* line V. Pirandello, and the small stairways tucked off V. Atenea lead to authentic, inexpensive *trattorie.* Indulge a sweet tooth at the candy stalls along V. della Vittoria. The town specialty is *torrone,* a nut-filled, cream-colored nougat. The *Sette Soli,* a smooth local wine, nicely complements most meals.

■ **Trattoria de Paris**, P. Lena, 7 (☎0922 25 413), beside Hotel Bella Napoli. The Paris supplies locals with fresh pasta at a deliciously low price. Try the *cavatell al cartoccio—* homemade pasta with eggplant, basil, and ricotta cheese, and tomato sauce, prepared and served in foil to seal the flavor (€4.50). *Primi* €4.50, *secondi* €5.60. Service 10%. Open M-Sa noon-3pm and 7:30-10:30pm, Su noon-3pm. AmEx/MC/V. ❷

■ **Manhattan Trattoria/Pizzeria**, Salita M. degli Angeli, 9 (☎0922 20 911), up steps off V. Atenea. Don't fold your slice in half New York style—the food here is typically Sicilian. Sit inside or outside on terraced steps. The chef's specialty *ravioli* and *tortellini* options are excellent (€6-7). Try the *involtini di carne all contadina* (breaded rolls stuffed with meat and cheese; €6). *Antipasti* buffet €5. Pizza from €3.50. *Primi* €5-7, meat entrees €5-7, fish entrees €6-12. Cover €1.50. Open noon-3pm and 7-11pm. AmEx/MC/V. ❷

Pizzeria Miriana, V. Pirandello, 6 (☎0922 22 828), at the start of V. Pirandello off P. Aldo Moro. Great food at local joint for an unbeatable price. Pasta €2.50. Friendly cooks serve pizza by the slice (€1) and *panini* from €1.55. Open M-Sa 8am-10pm. ❶

La Corte degli Sfizi, Cortile Contarini, 4 (☎0922 20 052), off V. Atenea. Classic Sicilian dishes served in a peaceful bamboo-enclosed garden. Dinner *menù* €14-16. Pizza €3.50-7. *Primi* €4.50-7, *secondi* €5.50-7. Cover €1.55. Service 20%. Open M and W-Su 11am-3pm and 7pm-midnight. AmEx/MC/V. ❸

👁 SIGHTS

■**VALLE DEI TEMPLI.** Planted on a ridge below Agrigento's hilltop perch, the five temples are a tribute to the indominability of paganism. Having survived the ravages of time, earthquakes, vicious Punic Wars, and the rise of Christianity, the temples are official World Heritage Landmarks. As sunlight transitions to moonlight, the temples cast eerie silhouettes across the countryside; once it's dark, they're illuminated by concealed lighting. From the entrance, a wide avenue heads uphill along the ridge, first passing the **Tempio di Ercole.** One row of solid, squat columns is all that remains of the earliest of the temples. Farther along, the perfectly intact pediment and columns of the **Tempio della Concordia** is the Valle's star attraction. This temple's walls and columns are some of the best preserved remains. Erected in the mid-5th century BC from limestone, it owes its survival to its early use by the archbishop of Agrigento who, after kicking out the demons Eber and Ray, rededicated the temple to Saints Peter and Paul and transformed it into a Christian church. The road through the valley ends at the 5th-century BC **Tempio di Giunone,** with its columns and partially extant pediment. To the left during the ascent, holes in the ground mark an early Christian burial site. Across the street lies the entrance to the eternally unfinished **Tempio di Giove Olimpico.** Had Carthaginian troops not interrupted its construction in 406 BC, it would have been one of the largest Greek temples ever built. The toppled partitioned columns and walls have challenged archaeologists for years, but the temple's most interesting sight are the gigantic *telamones*, 8m sculpted male figures intended to have encircled the temple. One of these massive men has been reconstructed at the site. At the end of the path, past the Tempio di Giove, stand four columns of the long since destroyed **Tempio di Castore e Polluce**, also known as the Tempio dei Dioscuri.

 THE REAL DEAL. At the Valle dei Templi, don't waste money on a tourist map at the ticket office—there are free maps across the street in the parking lot. *—Chris Starr*

The **Museo Nazionale Archeologico di San Nicola**, 1km uphill from the parking lot, has a fabulous collection of red- and black-figureware vases, terra-cotta votive figures, and funerary vessels from the area's necropolis. Escape from the sun and go indoors to see an upright *telamon*, as well as model projections of how a completed Tempio di Giove Olimpico might have looked. The **Chiesa di San Nicola** near the museum displays the sarcophagus of Phaedra, one of the most impressive 3rd-century works of art. *(Valle dei Templi is a 30min. walk from the train station. Starting on V. F. Crispi, follow signs downhill and left at the lower intersection. Buses #1/, 2, 2/, 3, or 3/ run from train station and stop in a dirt carpark with a snack bar. Make sure to bring lots of water, sunscreen, light clothes, and good walking shoes, as there is no break from the relentless Agrigento sun. Visiting when the park first opens or right before it closes is a good way to avoid both heat and crowds. Lower temples open in summer 8:30am-7pm; in winter 8:30am-5pm. Upper temples open in summer M-Sa 8:30am-10pm, Su and holidays 8:30am-midnight; in winter 8:30am-7:30pm. Entrance to temples €6, museum €6, combined ticket €10, EU citizens 18 to 25 combined ticket €5, under 18 or over 65 free. Parking €2.60, €1.50 motorcycle.)*

■ GIARDINO DELLA KOLYMBETRA. Originally used as a garden and irrigation basin by the Greeks in 500 BC, the Gardens at Kolymbetra, translated roughly from the Greek as "the place of giving waters," were used continually as an orchard until the 20th century. Given over to the FAI (Italian Environmental Agency) in the 1990s, the garden is now restored to its formal quiet splendor. Take a break from temple-gazing and enjoy a quiet walk through the shade. *(In the lower portion of the Valle dei Templi, follow the signs to the garden. ☎ 335 12 29 042; www.fondoambiente.it. Open July-Sept. 10am-7pm; Apr.-June 10am-6pm; Oct.-May 10am-5pm. Closed Jan. €2.)*

CHIESA DI SANTA MARIA DEI GRECI. First constructed by the Normans in the 1100s and remodeled by the Byzantines in the 1300s, Santa Maria dei Greci's real attraction is not what's in the church, but what's beneath it. Through its glass floors, visitors can see an ancient Greek temple dedicated to Athena in the 5th-century BC and recently excavated ruins of the first Christian church in Agrigento (built on this site in the 5th century AD). The original Athenian sacrificial altar stands behind the Christian altar in the present church. Down below, pay special attention to the upper-left corner of the church, where the entrance to a tunnel once led all the way to the Valle dei Templi far below. *(Follow the signs up the hill from V. Bac Bac off V. Atenea. ☎ 333 87 02 111. Open M-Sa 9:30am-12:30pm and 3:30-6:30pm, Su upon request. The church has been under restoration for several years, but is expected to re-open in 2005 with a plexiglass floor to showcase the excavated Greek temple beneath the church.)*

CHIESA DEL PURGATORIO (S. LORENZO). The legendary craftsman Serpotta employed all of his wizardry to make this church's stucco sculptures look like marble. The statues of the Virtues were intended to help parishioners stay out of purgatory by reminding them of its unpleasantries. Church elders did a thorough job—it's pretty hard to ignore all the reminders of eternal damnation, including the unusual skull and crossbones on the confessional and countless depictions of roasted sinners. To the left of the church, underneath a sleeping lion, lies the 5th-century-BC entrance to a network of Greek underground aqueduct channels which run the length of the city but are not open to the public. *(In P. Purgatorio off V. Atenea in the centro storico. Open M-Sa 10:30am-1pm and 4-8pm; hours vary. €1.50.)*

TEATRO PIRANDELLO. Dedicated to Queen Margherita on its opening in 1880, the theater was renamed in honor of Agrigento's favorite son, playwright Luigi Pirandello, on the 10th anniversary of his death, December 10, 1946. After brief stints as a movie theater and playhouse, the building was closed for renovation until April 29, 1995. Today it hosts a variety of plays in the winter months, including many works by Pirandello. There are no plays in the summer, but the 19th-century building (designed by another local boy, architect Dioniso Sciascia) is worth a peek. Look out for the four names on the dome ceiling of ancient *Agrigentini* famous for the arts. *(☎ 0922 50 02 73. Open M-F 8am-1pm. Play season from Nov.-May. Schedule posted at the theater or ask at the tourist office. Admission €2.50 with tour in English.)*

CASA NATALE DI LUIGI PIRANDELLO. Aficionados of Pirandello will enjoy a visit to his birthplace a few kilometers outside of the city. Treasures include a series of photographs, playbills, drafts of scripts, and various letters to and from the master. A huge stone marks his gravesite. This site is best-suited for people with a strong interest in the life and work of Pirandello. *(Take the TUA bus #1 to P. Kaos.* ☎ *0922 51 11 02. Open daily 9am-7pm. €2, under 18 or over 65 free.)*

♪ ☀ ENTERTAINMENT AND FESTIVALS

The hills surrounding the Valle dei Templi come alive with the sound of music every year on the first Sunday in February, when Agrigento hosts the **Almond Blossom Festival,** an international folk-dancing fest. The **Settimana Pirandelliana,** a week-long outdoor festival of plays, operas, and ballets in P. Kaos, pays homage to the town's beloved son in late July and early August. (Info ☎ 0922 23 561.) During summer months, *Agrigentini* primarily abandon the town in search of the beach and nightlife at **San Leone,** 4km from Agrigento by bus #2. Just be careful not to tumble down the **Scala dei Turchi,** the beautiful natural steps that descend to **Lido Rossello,** another popular beach, after a night of carousing.

WESTERN SICILY

TRAPANI   ☎ 0923

Unlike any other seaside town, Trapani has an allure all its own. From the ancient rooftops spanning the length of Trapani's old city to the colorful fishing boats and massive ferries plowing the waves just below the horizon, Trapani harbors both packs of roaming wild dogs and throngs of eager tourists. Nevertheless, despite the town's quiet charms, most travelers only pass through. Reliable transportation and extensive lodgings make Trapani a good base for adventures to Segesta's temple, the Egadi Islands, Erice's medieval streets, San Vito's beaches, and the natural splendor of the Lo Zingaro reservation.

▐ TRANSPORTATION

Flights: Vincenzo Florio Airport (☎ 0923 84 25 02), in Birgi en route to Marsala, 16km outside of Trapani. Buses from P. Malta are timed to coincide with flights. Daily flights to Rome and Pantelleria. Not a heavily used airport.

Trains: ☎ 0923 89 20 21. In P. Umberto I. Ticket office open daily 6am-7:50pm. To: **Castelvetrano** (1½hr., 15 per day 4:35am-8:30pm, €4.40); **Marsala** (30min., 14 per day 4:35am-8:30pm, €2.65); **Palermo** (2hr., 11 per day 6:30am-9:30pm, €6.45).

Buses: AST (☎ 0923 21 021). Main station in P. Malta. From the front of the train station, turn left on V. Mazzini, then left again on V. Marinella. P. Malta will be to the left. To: **Erice** (45min.; M-Sa 9 per day 7:30am-8:30pm, Su 4 per day 5:30pm; €2.10, round-trip €3.20); **Marsala** (M-Sa 6:50am, 12:50, 2:10pm; €2.60); **San Vito Lo Capo** (1½hr.; M-Sa 11 per day 7am-8:30pm, Su 4 per day 8am-7:15pm; €3.20). **Segesta** (☎ 0923 21 754) runs buses to local towns and to **Rome** (15hr., 5:30pm, €38).

Ferries: *Traghetti* (ferries) and *aliscafi* (hydrofoils) leave for the **Egadi Islands** (Levanzo, Favignana, and Marettimo), **Ustica, Pantelleria,** and **Tunisia.** Ferries leave from Stazione Marittima across from P. Garibaldi; hydrofoils depart from a dock farther along V. A. Staiti, about 150m toward the train station. Tickets for sale from the travel agents along V. A. Staiti, from ticket booths on the docks, and at Stazione Marittima. Chart below shows high-season (June-Aug.)

times and rates; less frequent and less expensive in low-season. Schedules change with weather. Schedules are available at all ticket offices and at tourist office.

Ustica (☎0923 22 200; www.usticalines.it), in a yellow booth at the hydrofoil dock. AmEx/MC/V.

Siremar (☎0923 54 54 55; www.siremar.it), with ticket offices at a blue- and white-striped water-front booth at the hydrofoil dock and in Stazione Marittima. Open M-F 6:15am-noon, 3-7pm, and 9pm-midnight; Su 3-3:30pm, 5:15-6:45pm, and 9pm-midnight. AmEx/MC/V.

Tirrenia (☎0923 54 54 55; www.tirrenia.it), in Stazione Marittima. Open M 6:30am-1pm and 3-6pm, Tu 9am-1pm and 4-9pm, W-F 9am-1pm and 3-6pm, Sa 9am-noon. AmEx/MC/V.

Public Transportation: Orange **SAU buses** have main terminal at P. V. Veneto, down V. Osorio from the station and right on V. XXX Gennaio, and straight to the water. Office on left when facing water. Posts schedules of all routes. Complete schedules also available at the tourist office. Tickets (€0.80) sold at *tabaccherie*.

Taxis: (☎0923 22 808) in P. Umberto, outside the train station; (☎0923 23 233) in V. A. Staiti, near the port.

DESTINATION	COMPANY	DURATION	FREQUENCY	PRICE
Favignana (Egadi Islands)	Siremar (ferry)	1hr.	3 per day	€3.20
Favignana (E.I.)	Ustica (hydrofoil)	20min.	10 per day	€5.30
Favignana (E.I.)	Siremar (hydrofoil)	25min.	10 per day	€5.30
Levanzo (E.I.)	Siremar (ferry)	1hr.	3 per day	€3.20
Levanzo (E.I.)	Siremar (hydrofoil)	20min.	10 per day	€5.30
Levanzo (E.I.)	Ustica (hydrofoil)	20min.	10 per day	€5.30
Marettimo (E.I.)	Siremar (ferry)	3hr.	1 per day	€6.60
Marettimo (E.I.)	Siremar (hydrofoil)	1hr.	4 per day	€11.60
Marettimo (E.I.)	Ustica (hydrofoil)	1hr.	2 per day	€10.50
Pantelleria	Siremar (ferry)	5½hr.	midnight daily	€20.60
Pantelleria	Ustica (hydrofoil)	2½hr.	6pm daily	€34
Ustica via Favignana	Ustica (hydrofoil)	2½hr.	3 per week	€19
Cagliari (Sardinia)	Tirrenia (ferry)	11½hr.	Tu 9pm	€38.21
Tunis, Tunisia	Tirrenia (ferry)	8½hr.	M 10am	€51.38

⚡🐦 ORIENTATION AND PRACTICAL INFORMATION

Trapani sits on a peninsula 2hr. west of Palermo by bus or train. The old city began at the outer tip of the hook, growing backward from the peninsula until it tripped and spilled new streets and high-rises onto the mainland. The **train station** is in **Piazza Umberto I,** with the **bus station** just to the left and behind the train station in **Piazza Malta. Via Scontrino** runs past the train station; a right from the station leads to an intersection with **Via Garibaldi** at **Piazza Emanuele,** where all the local buses stop. V. Garibaldi becomes **Via Libertà** and moves into the old city. The first left off V. Libertà is **Via Torrearsa,** home to the informational **tourist office.** The next left off V. Libertà, **Via Roma,** leads down to the port. V. Libertà merges with **Corso Vittirio Emanuele,** which runs all the way to the **Torre di Ligny** at the end of the peninsula.

Tourist Offices:

AAPIT (☎0923 29 000; www.apt.trapani.it), in P. Alessandro Scarlatti. Staff provides **maps,** help with lodgings, and info on attractions in and around town. Pick up a *Trapani Hotels* guide. Open M-Sa 8am-8pm, Su 9am-noon.

The Provincial Tourism Office (☎0923 54 55 11; www.apt.trapani.it), off Via Verdi at Via San Francesco d'Assisi, 27. Marked "APT" on maps. Serves the entire province of Trapani. Open M-Tu and Th-Sa 8am-2pm, W 8am-2pm and 2:30-6pm.

Currency Exchange: Banks line many of the city's streets, including C. Italia. They generally have better rates than the train station. The post office also changes money and traveler's checks. **ATMs** are at Stazione Marittima in the old city and along V. Scontrino in front of the train station.

Emergency: Police, P. V. Veneto (☎113 or 0923 59 02 98). **Carabinieri,** V. Orlandini, 19 (☎0923 271 22). **First Aid,** P. Generale Scio, 1 (☎0923 29 629). **Ambulance:** ☎0923 80 94 50.

Pharmacy: Viale Margherita, 9, next to P. V. Veneto. All pharmacies open M-F 9am-1:30pm and 4:30-8pm. After hours rotation posted outside. Look for bright green cross.

Hospital: Ospedale Sant'Antonio Abate (☎0923 80 91 11), on V. Cosenza, far northeast of the city center.

Internet Access: Kei Internet Point, V. XXX Gennaio, 9 (☎0923 59 36 41). From P. V. Veneto on V. Garibaldi, turn left down V. XXX Gennaio. The entrance is 2 streets down and around the corner on the left on V. Bastioni. 10 fast computers. €2 for 30min., €3 per hr. Open M-Sa 10am-2pm and 4:30-9:30pm.

Post Office: P. V. Veneto, 3 (☎0923 43 44 04). Huge building in P. V. Veneto on V. Garibaldi marked "Poste" on one tower and "Telegraph" on the other. **Currency exchange,** booth #18. Open M-Sa 8am-6:30pm. **Postal Code:** 91100.

ACCOMMODATIONS AND CAMPING

Albergo Moderno, V. Genovese, 20 (☎0923 21 247; fax 0923 23 348). From P. S. Agostino on C. V. Emanuele, turn right on V. Roma and left on V. Genovese. The Albergo has a friendly staff and clean, well-kept rooms, all with TV and bath. Reception 24hr. Singles €25; doubles €35; triples €45. AmEx/MC/V. ❷

Pensione Messina, C. V. Emanuele, 71, 4th fl. (☎/fax 0923 211 98). An aged courtyard leads to an eclectic mix of mirrors and statues in this tiny, 9-room hotel. High-ceilinged rooms have antique atmosphere, but location and price couldn't get any better. All rooms have balcony, sink, fridge, and ceiling fan. Shared bath. Breakfast €4. Singles €20; doubles €30-35. Extra bed 35% of cost of room. AmEx/MC/V. ❷

Hotel Vittoria, V. F. Crispi, 4 (☎0923 87 30 44; fax 0923 29 870), off P. V. Emanuele, near train station. 65 large, luxurious rooms offer modern atmosphere, some with view of the rocky coast. Inviting communal area has a bar and TV. Breakfast €5. Singles €53; doubles €79; triples €106. AmEx/MC/V. ❹

Nuovo Albergo Russo, V. Tintori, 4 (☎0923 221 66; fax 0923 26 623), off C. V. Emanuele. Rooms are comfortable and centrally located. All with bath, A/C, and TV. Breakfast €3. Sept.-June singles €40; doubles €70; triples €95. July-Aug. and Easter week singles €42; doubles €85; triples 25% more than doubles. AmEx/MC/V. ❹

Campeggio Lido Valderice (☎0923 57 34 77), on V. del Detince, 15, in seaside town of the same name. Take bus for Bonegia or San Vito Lo Capo (€3.20). Follow flower-lined road opposite bus stop and perpendicular to the highway, and turn right at its end. Well-shaded campground near beaches. €5 per person, €4.50 per tent, €2 per car, €7-10 per camper. Hot showers €0.60. AmEx/MC/V. ❶

FOOD

Trapani's cuisine is heavily influenced by North African and Italian flavors. Couscous prepared with fish is one of the area's specialties as well as the *biscotti con fichi*, the Italian Fig Newton. If you're cooking your own meals, the old city has many *alimentari*, as well as a daily fish and fruit **market** along the northern *lungomare* at the intersection of V. Maggio and V. Garibaldi. In addition, **Supermercato Di per Di,** Via San Pietro, 30, is two streets up from the port between Chiesa di Santa Maria del Jesu and Chiesa di San Pietro (☎/fax 0923 24 620. Open June-Aug. M-Sa 8:30am-1pm and 5-7pm; Aug.-May M-Sa 8:30am-1pm and 4:30-7pm).

■ **Pizzeria Calvino**, V. N. Nasi, 71 (☎0923 21 464), 100m from the *duomo*. With a line out the door every night, this pizzeria is widely considered the best in town. 30 delicious varieties. Order to go or reserve 1-2hr. ahead for a table. Delivery available. Pizza from €3.50. Open M and W-Su 7pm-12:30am. MC/V. ❶

■ **Trattoria da Salvatore**, V. N. Nasi, 19 (☎0923 54 65 30), 1 street toward the port from C. V. Emanuele. Family-style restaurant serves regional pastas like *busiata con sarde* (€4.15) and spicy house couscous (€7.50). *Primi* €4-5, *secondi* €7-8. Cover €1.80. Open M-Sa noon-3pm and 6pm-midnight. AmEx. ❷

■ **Poldo**, P. Lucatelli, 8 (☎347 03 23 231), off V. Turretta near the ferry station. Simple name, elaborate food. Poldo serves delicious *panini* (€1.50-4) at scandalously low prices, including a cheeseburger (€3) that puts most American burger joints to shame. *Primi* from €6, *secondi* from €7. Open daily 9am-5am. ❷

Ristorante Medina, Viale Regina Margherita, 19 (☎0923 29 028). Just across the street from the main gate to the Villa Margherita Gardens. Middle Eastern cuisine and pizza in large portions at great prices. Kebabs (€3.50). Pizza from €1.50 per slice, *panini* €3.50. Open daily noon-4pm and 7-11pm. ❶

Cantina Siciliana, V. Giudecca, 2 (☎0923 28 673; www.cantinasiciliana.it). From the port, walk up V. XXX Gennaio. V. Giudecca is the 1st left past Corso Italia. Look for the sign. Where the locals come to eat couscous (€8). Specializes in Trapanese and Sicilian cuisine. *Primi* €6-12, *secondi* €8.50-12. Open daily 12:30-5pm and 7:30-11pm. MC/V. ❸

Taverno Paradiso, Lungomare Dante Alighieri, 22 (☎/fax 0923 22 303). This classy, blues-playing tavern serves seafood and drinks in a romantic villa-like interior, complete with vine-covered stone walls and cherub sculptures. *Primi* from €9, *secondi* €9-13. Cover €3. Open M-Sa 12:30-3:30pm and 7:30-10:30pm. AmEx/MC/V. ❹

 COFFEE, CASANOVA STYLE. Drink your coffee like a local by downing your espresso in one gulp. Just be sure to let the scalding drink cool before pouring it down your throat.

👁 SIGHTS

Delicate stone statues blend into the gray exterior of the 17th-century Baroque **Chiesa del Purgatorio**. Inside, 20 nearly life-sized wooden sculptures, known as *I Misteri*, depict the passion and crucifixion of Christ. Every year on Good Friday, the sculptures, each requiring the strength of 14-30 men, are dressed up and paraded around the city. The sculptures' 18th-century artists constructed the Roman soldiers to resemble Spanish conquistadors, reflecting Spanish dominance in Sicily at the time. Several statues were damaged in WWII, but have since been reconstructed. (1 block up V. D. G. Giglio from P. Garibaldi, across from Stazione Marittima; follow signs from the port. Open daily 4-6:30pm.)

The main attraction in the modern part of town is the enormous and lavishly decorated **Sanctuario dell'Annunziata**. This church houses a 14th-century statue of the Madonna of Trapani. Legend has it that a boat carrying the statue got caught in a storm; the captain promised God that if he survived, he would leave it as a gift to the first port at which he arrived. In the same complex is the **Museo Nazionale Pepoli**, which features a collection of local sculpture and painting, coral carvings, and folk-art figurines, including a frightening portrayal of Herod's baby hunt. (Take SAU buses #24, 25, or 30 from P. V. Emanuele, 2 blocks to the right of the train station. *Sanctuario* ☎0923 53 91 84; museum 0923 55 32 69 or 0923 53 12 42. *Sanctuario* open M-Sa 8am-noon and 4-7pm, Su 8am-1pm and 4-7pm; museum open Tu-Sa 9am-1:30pm, Su 9am-12:30pm. Call to confirm hours. €2.50, 18-25 €1, under 18 or over 65 free.)

The picturesque **Torre di Ligny,** at the end of a wide jetty off a promontory, is visible from both of Trapani's ports. By day, the rock walls of the tower seem like outcroppings of the rocky shore, as the identically colored brick fortress rises over boulders. By night, the northern coastline appears as a vision of bright lights reflecting off the water. The tower houses the **Museo di Preistoria/Museo del Mare,** with shells, artifacts, and underwater excavation pieces. (☎0923 22 300. Open M-Sa 9:30am-noon, Su 10:30am-12:30pm. €1.55.) At the cusp of the old and new cities, the **Villa Margherita's** gardens offer a change of pace from cobblestone and cement. Banyan trees, palms, and fountains surround avenues. In addition, playgrounds and statuary complete the picture. Each July, the gardens host the **Luglio Musicale Trapanese,** a festival of opera, ballet, and cabaret that draws stars to the temporary stage amid shady trees. Other concerts happen virtually every other month as well. (☎0923 21 454. Shows 9pm. Info booth inside park gates.)

▨ DAYTRIPS FROM TRAPANI

MARSALA

Trains service Marsala from Trapani (30min., 14 per day, €2.65). AST buses (☎0923 23 222) also run from Trapani (40min.; M-Sa 6:50am, 12:50, 2:10pm; €2.75, round-trip €4.60) and back (M-Sa 7am, 1:05, and 2:05pm). From the train station, a right facing V.A. Fazio and then a slight left on V. Roma leads to the centro storico. V. Roma turns into V. XI Maggio and then V. Veneto. The Pro Loco Tourist Office is at V. XI Maggio, 100, before Palazzo Comunale and the duomo. (☎0923 71 40 97; www.prolocomarsala.org. Open M-Sa 8am-8pm, Su 9am-noon.)

An area of both ancient and modern historical interest, Marsala's (pop. 77,000) streets are worthy of a short visit. The city's lack of budget accommodations make it best suited for a daytrip from nearby Trapani. The **Museo Archeologico Regionale Baglio Anselmi** guards the famed **Carthiginian warship.** This now skeletal vessel sank in the final battle of the First Punic War (241 BC), in which Rome defeated Carthage and established its naval supremacy. In addition to the ship, other galleries display objects from Lilybaeum and the Isle of Mozia, including pottery and two life-size sculptures. (☎0923 95 25 35. Open M-Tu, Th, and Sa-Su 9am-1:30pm; W and F 9am-1:30pm and 4-6:30pm. €2, under 18 €1, EU residents over 65 free.) It was at Marsala that Garibaldi and his red-shirted revolutionaries landed in 1860 to launch the Risorgimento. Marsala celebrates this event with its **Porta Garibaldi,** an 18th-century gate erected where Garibaldi first entered the city. Additionally, the **Museo Civico** features a variety of Garibaldi-related artifacts, including thousands of red shirts and Garibaldi's own ostentatious uniform. (In the San Pietro complex on V. XI Maggio. Open Tu-Sa 9am-1:30pm, W and F 9am-1:30pm and 4-6:30pm. €2, under 18 €1, EU residents over 65 free.) Besides battles and revolutionaries, Marsala is famous for its sweet **Marsala wine.** Samples are available at a wide variety of *enoteche* scattered throughout the old city.

For something to soak up all that wine, head to **Trattoria Garibaldi ❷,** P. Addolorata, 5, across from the Sanctuary of Maria S.S. Addolorata. The *trattoria* serves vegetarian omelettes (€4) and a wide variety of Italian cuisine. (*Primi* from €4.50, *secondi* from €6. Cover €1. Open M-F noon-3pm and 7:30-10:30pm, Sa 7-10pm, Su noon-3pm. AmEx/MC/V.) If you decide to spend the night, your best bet is **Hotel Acos ❹,** V. Mazara, 14, with 37 rooms, as well as a bar, restaurant, and swimming pool. All rooms with TV, bath, phone, and air-conditioning. (☎0923 99 91 66; www. acoshotel.com. Breakfast €5. Singles €40-52; doubles €57-130.)

RISERVA DELLO ZINGARO

Bus tickets available in San Vito at Mare Monti, V. Amadeo, 15 (☎0923 97 22 31; info@sanvitomaremonti.com). Buses depart P. Marinella (M, W, F 8am; return M, W, F

7pm; €8, reservation required). Bluvacanze, V. Savoia, 13 (☎ 0923 62 10 85), runs excursions (M, W, F 9am; return 4pm; €15).

For shade and seclusion, escape 10km from San Vito to the Riserva dello Zingaro, Italy's first nature reserve, where rare Bonelli's eagles, mountain trails, and prehistoric caves abound. An unfinished four-lane highway came perilously close to marring the isolation of the pristine reserve, but a 1981 environmental rally halted the highway in its tracks. Once in the reserve, follow the yellow brick road to successive secluded pebble beaches that stretch along the coastline. Due to entrances on both sides of the reserve, the middle two beaches offer the most privacy. Though camping is illegal and motor vehicles are prohibited, the hiking is superb.

SEGESTA

Tarantola buses (☎ 0924 31 020) leave P. Malta in Trapani for Segesta (4 per day 8am-5pm, return 4 per day 7:10am-6:35pm; €3.10, round-trip €4.75). Temple open 9am-7pm; ticket office 9am-6pm. €4.50, EU residents 18-25 €2, EU residents under 18 or over 65 free.

The extraordinary ◪**Doric temple** is one of the best-preserved relics of ancient Greek architecture. Isolated and untouched, it dominates a landscape of sudden valleys and lush vineyards of this former Trojan colony. Roam among the 5th-century BC columns or take a Lilliputian seat on a pedestal to contemplate their dignified tranquility. A wealth of ruins, including a Greek theater, a castle, and a mosque, cluster nearby around Monte Barbaro. It's worth taking the bus (every 30min., €1.20) to avoid the steep uphill trek in the midday sun, but the 25min. walk to the top is quite pleasant on cooler days. The **Greek theater** carved into the top of the hill has a 4000-person capacity and holds performances from mid-July to August. Ask at the Trapani tourist office for details.

ERICE ☎ 0923

Getting to tiny Erice is an adventure in its own right—the road up from Valderice provides breathtaking vistas and hairpin turns in equal measure. Once in Erice, visitors will be charmed by its quiet streets and awed by the panoramic views offered from terraces and parks all over town. A center of worship since the fertility cults of the Phoenician goddess Tanit-Asarte, Erice is home today to a beautiful *duomo*—La Chiesa Madrice (the Mother Church). An interesting history, the grand Castello Normanno, and a landscape that stretches from Pantelleria to Mt. Etna, make Erice well worth weathering the swarms of tourists who flock here annually. Once atop the *campanile* of the *duomo* or the peak of a Castello Normanno tower, it's easy to forget the bustling crowds below and understand why the people of Erice call their home "Il Monte del Dio"—the Mountain of God.

◪◪ **TRANSPORTATION AND PRACTICAL INFORMATION.** The **bus** from Trapani to Erice departs either from P. Malta or neighboring stops listed there (40min.; M-Sa 9 per day 6:40am-8:30pm, last return to Trapani 7:30pm; Su 4 per day 9am-5:30pm, last return to Trapani 6:30pm; €3.05 round trip). Buses stop on **Via Conte Pepoli**, at the base of town. From the **Porta Trapani** (Trapani Gate), a left turn leads to the **duomo** and its hard-to-miss **campanile**. Straight through the Porta Trapani is **Via Vittorio Emanuele** and Erice's central *piazza*, **Piazza Umberto I**. Back at the bus stop, following V. Conte Populi to its end leads to the **Giardino del Balio** (Balio Gardens) and the **Castello Normanno** (Norman Castle), also known as the **Castello de Venere** (Castle of Venus). The **AAST Tourist Office**, on Via Guarrasi, 1 (the street opposite V. V. Emanuele at P. Umberto I), provides colorful town **maps** and brochures (☎ 0923 86 93 88. Open M-F 8am-2:30pm). **ATMs** can be found all over Erice, including one on V. V. Emanuele near P. Umberto I.

SICILY

ᑫᑲ ACCOMMODATIONS AND FOOD. Finding reasonably priced accommodations in Erice might require extra investigation, but the search pays off. **█Ulisse Camere ❸**, V. Santa Lucia, 2, offers clean rooms at half the price of many of its competitors. From the bus stop, walk five blocks down V. Conte Pepoli and watch for the "Ulisse Camere" sign on the left. When reserving ahead, ask for a room with a view (no extra charge), or one that shares the quiet private courtyard. The best is Room 11, which includes a patio, entryway, and gorgeous view, in addition to the full bathroom, TV, and minifridge that are standard. (☎0923 86 01 55; www.sitodiulisse.it. Single with breakfast €32; double with breakfast €62, without €55; triples €79/70. AmEx/MC/V.) Renovated in 2001, **Villa San Giovanni ❸**, V. N. Nasi, 12, has big rooms with balconies and panoramic views. All rooms come with bath, TV, telephone, and minibar. (☎0923 86 91 71; villas.giovanni@libero.it. Breakfast included. Oct.-May singles €36-40; doubles €66-70; half pension €40-43 per person; full pension €50-53. June-Sept., Holy Week, and New Year's singles €38-42/68-72/43-46/53-56. Triples available at half and full pension prices.)

Erice's restaurants are charming, but the prices steep. At **La Vetta ❸**, V. G. Fontana, 5, off P. Umberto I, savor Chef Mario's take on regional favorite couscous and *busiati* (both €7), Sicilian pasta hand-rolled into a narrow tube. (☎0923 86 94 04. Pizza from €4.50. *Primi* €7, *secondi* from €6. Cover for restaurant €2, for pizzeria €1.50. Open M-W and F-Su noon-3:30pm and 7:30pm-midnight. Closed Oct.-Nov. AmEx/MC/V.) If you're looking for fancy, look no farther than **Ristorante Monte San Giuliano ❸**, V. S. Rocco, 7. Tucked neatly under stone archways, San Giuliano offers a variety of regional cuisine on a terrace overlooking the sea. (☎0923 86 95 95; www.montesangiuliano.it. *Primi* €8-9, *secondi* €7-15. Cover €2. Open July-Aug. 7:30am-midnight; Oct.-May 7:30am-10pm. Closed Nov. 2-17 and Jan. 7-27. AmEx/MC/V.) The Giardini del Balio, up Viale Conte Pepoli from the bus stop, have stone benches overlooking the valley, ideal for an enchanting picnic. Stock up on supplies at **Salumeria Bazar del Miele**, V. Cordici, 16, which sells Sicilian specialties. Grab a bottle of the *Marsala* (€8) to accompany your meal. (☎0923 86 91 81. Open daily 9:30am-8pm. AmEx/MC/V.) In addition to fancy pastries like *morbido a coco* (almond-coconut candy specific to Erice; €20 per kg), **Pasticceria Tulipano ❶**, V. V. Emanuele 10-12, serves cheap, quick meals, including *tavola calda* (€2-5), pizza, and pasta. Eat at one of the shaded outdoor tables. (☎0923 86 96 72. Open daily 7:30am-midnight. AmEx/MC/V.) For dessert, snack on sweets at the **Antica Pasticceria del Convento ❷**, V. F. Guarnotti, 1. From P. Umberto I, take V. Cordici. It will be on the first corner on the right in P. S. Domenico. The fresh cookies come in all shapes and colors (€12 per kg). Try the famous *belli e brutti* (pretty and ugly), an almond treat so-named because of its beautiful taste and rather rough appearance. (☎0923 86 93 90. Open daily 9am-1pm and 3:30pm-3am.)

◘ SIGHTS. Erice fits an impressive number of sights inside its 8th-century BC **Elymian walls.** The **Castello Normanno (Castello di Venere)** was built on the site of ancient temples to fertility goddesses. It served as a prison until 1940, but the hollow tub against the wall farthest from the entrance, likely used for human sacrifice, indicates a more ominous legacy. Inquire at the tourist office about guided tours and winter hours. (Open daily 8am-7pm. Donations requested). Next to the castle is a Spanish-style **Torre Medievale,** and at the castle's base, the **█Giardini del Balio** spread green boughs over stone benches. The views from the gardens and castle are incomparable; most of the countryside—the Egadi Islands, Pantelleria, and occasionally Etna and Tunisia—peeking over the horizon. Throughout Erice, 61 churches await exploration, all accessible by joint €0.50 ticket. The 14th-century **Gothic duomo** features ornate ceilings in the Arabian-influenced Neo-Gothic interior. The **bell tower** offers broad views. (Open daily 10am-6:30pm. Open until midnight in Aug. Bell tower only €1; bell tower and *duomo* €2.) In P. Umberto, the

Museo Comunale di Erice, inside the library, houses a small but varied collection primarily relating to the city's fertility goddesses. (Open M-Sa 8:30am-7:30pm. Free.)

EGADI ISLANDS (ISOLE EGADI)

Inhabited since prehistoric times, the Egadi Islands offer some of the best outdoor adventures in Sicily. Lying just off of Trapani, the archipelago of Favignana, Levanzo, and Marettimo is easily accessible by ferry or hydrofoil. Favignana is the largest and most modern of the trio, with plenty of beaches—and enough tourists to pack them. In the port towns of Levanzo and Marettimo, mules and sheep share plains with cacti, while rugged cliffs climb line the coast. To really get to know the islands, dedicate at least an entire day to each, as the best beaches and intriguing discoveries lie far from the ports.

 GOT CASH. Stop by the ATM in Trapani or Favignana before leaving because there aren't any ATMs on Levanzo or Marretimo.

FAVIGNANA ☎0923

Favignana's ample and appealing beaches make it a summer playground for Italians enamored with island living. They build summer homes on the shoreline, while short-term vacationers arrive eager for a tan and expecting the modern conveniences the town's sisters lack.

▐ TRANSPORTATION. Siremar (☎0923 92 13 68) and Ustica (☎0923 92 12 77) both run **hydrofoils** to the islands from Trapani (25-45min. to Favignana and Levanzo, 45min.-1hr. to Marettimo; 11 per day 6:30am-8:20pm; €5.30 to Favignana, €11.80 to Marettimo). Ustica runs hydrofoils between the three islands (Favignana-Levanzo 8 per day 6:55am-9:30pm, €2.50; Favignana-Marettimo 3 per day 10am-4:50pm, €6.90). Siremar runs **ferries** from Trapani to Favignana (1hr., 3 per day 7am-5:15pm, €3.20). **Buses** are necessary to reach the more remote beaches. Tarantola buses (☎0923 92 19 44 or 0923 31 020) run from Porto Florio: **Line 1** (8 per day 8am-4:50pm) to Calamone (5min.), Lido Burrone (8min.), Cala Azzurra (15min.); **Line 2** (8 per day 7:45am-7pm) to Calamone and Cala Rotonda (13min.); **Line 3** (6 per day 8:30am-5:40pm) to Cala Rossa (7min.), Lido Burrone, and Calamone. Buy tickets (€0.60) at *tabaccherie.* **Francesca e Rocco,** Traversa Calamoni, 7, runs minibus excursions around the island. (☎348 58 60 676. Available 24hr. €8 per person, 5-person min.) **Noleggio Isidoro,** V. Mazzini, 40, rents **bikes** and **scooters.** (☎347 32 33 058. Bikes €3 per day, scooters €15 per day. Open daily 7am-8pm.)

▐▐ ORIENTATION AND PRACTICAL INFORMATION. Hydrofoils and ferries drop passengers off at **Porto Florio.** A right out of the port leads to **Piazza Europa** and **Via Vittorio Emanuele,** which connects P. Europa to the main plaza, **Piazza Madrice,** where the **tourist office** is located. Running parallel to V. V. Emanuele between the two plazas is **Via Mazzini.** At P. Madrice, V. V. Emanuele becomes **Via Roma. Via Nicotera** also runs through P. Madrice. Off V. V. Emanuele, Via Garibaldi runs away from the plazas and eventually becomes **Via Libertà** as it heads into the countryside. The most beautiful beaches are about 1km away. A **Pro Loco Tourist Office,** P. Madrice, 8, provides brochures, schedules, and **maps** (€1) of Favignana and other islands. (☎0923 92 16 47. Open in summer M-Sa 9am-1pm and 4-8pm, Su 9am-1pm; in winter daily 10am-noon.) **Banco di Sicilia,** P. Madrice, 12, next to Pro Loco, has an **ATM** and **currency exchange.** (☎0923 92 13 47. Open M-F 8:20am-1:20pm and 2:50-3:50pm.) In case of **emergency,** the **carabinieri** (☎0923 92 12 02) are on V. S. Corleo, near P. Castello, and **first aid** (☎0923 92 12 83) is on Contrada delle Fosse off V.

Calamoni. **Farmacia Barone** is at P. Madrice, 64. (☎347 11 07 716. Open daily 8:30am-12:30pm and 5-8pm.) **Farmacia Dottore Abramo** is at P. Europa, 41. (☎0923 92 16 66. Open M-W and F-Su 8:30am-12:30pm and 5-8:30pm.) Both post after hours rotations outside. The **post office** is at V. G. Marconi, 3, off P. Madrice. (☎0923 92 12 09. Open M-F 8am-1:30pm, Sa 8am-12:30pm.) **Postal Code:** 91023.

⌐⌐ ACCOMMODATIONS AND FOOD. Rustic and rural, Favignana has better camping than hotels. However, the **Casa Vacanze Mio Sogno ❷**, V. Calamoni, 2, is a real steal. Take V. Libertà and turn left on V. Dante. Couched in a castle-like structure, rooms come with bath, kitchenette, TV, and patio, and are arranged around a small garden. (☎0923 92 16 76. Reserve ahead in summer. €20-40 per person.) **Camping Egàd ❶**, Contrada Arena, is a comfortable choice for camping. Tents, bungalows with kitchenettes and bathrooms, and caravans with shared bathrooms are available. A scooter and bike rental shop, diving center, restaurant, market, and disco are all on-site. (☎0923 92 15 55 or 0923 92 15 67; www.campingegad.it. Look for the Camping Egàd shuttle at the port, or call to be picked up. July-Aug. €6.20 per person, €6 per tent; Sept.-June €4.80/4.90 per tent. 2-person bungalows €30-48; 2-person caravans €19-28. Showers €0.30.) **▧Alternative Pub ❷**, P. Europa, 4, serves a variety of salads made-to-order amid a nautical decor. If you're thirsty, you can brave the Lanterna (€7), a very large, very colorful, very potent beverage made according to the owner's secret recipe and served in absurdly large beer steins. (Salads and *panini* from €3; a salad, wine or beer, and coffee €10. Open daily 8:30am-3am.) **▧La Bettola ❸**, V. Nicotera, 45, serves fish fresh out of the water. From P. Madrice, walk down V. Nicotera; it will be toward the end of the street on your left. (☎/fax 0923 92 19 88. *Primi* €5-13.50, *secondi* €4.50-14.50. Cover €1.80. Open daily 1-2:30pm and 8-11pm. Closed Th in winter. AmEx/MC/V.) **Ristorante Aegusa ❸**, V. Garibaldi, 17, down the road from the hotel of the same name, offers three specialty meals per day on a sea of blue and yellow tables. Try the *tonni antichi sapori* (€11.50); this tuna dish made with tomatoes and capers is the chef's personal favorite. (☎0923 92 24 30. *Primi* €6.50-9, *secondi* €8.50-16. Cover €2.50. Open daily 1-2:30pm and 8-10:30pm. AmEx/MC/V.) Tuna is a big part of Favignana's culinary tradition. A variety of tuna products are on sale at the **Antica Tonnara di Favignana ❶**, V. Nicotera, 6. (☎/fax 0923 92 16 10 or 333 45 59 472. Open daily June-Sept. 9am-midnight; Oct.-May 9am-1pm and 5-8pm. AmEx/MC/V). Stock up for a languorous day at the beach at **San Paolo Alimentari**, V. Mazzini, 24. (☎0923 92 16 80. Open M-Tu and Th-Sa 8am-1pm and 5-8:30pm, W 8am-1pm.)

◪⌐ SIGHTS AND BEACHES. The island's most popular beaches are the **Lido Burrone**, and the rockier **Calamone, Cala Rossa**, and **Cala Azzurra. Lido Burrone** is best equipped, including places to change and shower. Both **Cala Azzurra** and the rocky **Cala Rossa** are touted as the most beautiful. All beach areas can be reached by the public **Tarantola buses** (€0.60; see **Transportation**, p. 717). The tip of the island around **Cala Rotonda** and **Galera** makes a gorgeous boat trip but is difficult to access from land. To hire a boat, inquire at the tourist office. With stints as a prison, an Arab lookout tower, and a Norman fortress, the **Castello di Santa Caterina** is a formidable sight on a hill overlooking the city. Funky cafe by day and lively bar by night, **▧Camarillo Brillo**, V. V. Emanuele, 18, is a favorite haunt of youth marooned on the island, offering a happy hour (daily 6-10pm; €5 for a drink and hors d'oeuvres) and nightly live music. Come for the tunes and stay for the Sicilian wine bar. (Wine €3.50 per glass, €10 per bottle. Breakfast buffet daily 8:30-10:30am €5. Open daily Easter-Sept. 8am-3am.)

LEVANZO ☎0923

Levanzo is the smallest of the three Egadi Islands with a town center that is equally diminutive. Little more than a row of white-washed, blue-shuttered buildings, the center is host to two bars above the docks which serve as the island's social center. The one on the right (looking from the port), **Bar delle Zia Sarina,** has homemade almond and cassata *gelati* (€2). The **Ustica hydrofoil office** is on the dock, while the **Siremar office** is up an alley off the *lungomare.* They also have a booth on the dock next to the Ustica office. Right from the harbor is **⊠Albergo Paradiso ❹**, which keeps the island's best rooms, each with bath and air-conditioning, many with sea view. The hotel's cozy restaurant serves traditional and regional specialties. (☎ / fax 0923 92 40 80. Reserve for Aug. by mid-Mar. Half pension €60; full pension €80. Open Mar.-Nov. AmEx/MC/V.) Head down the *lungomare* to visit the island's primary attraction, the **Grotta del Genovese,** a cave containing 14,000-year-old Paleolithic incisions and slightly younger ochre-grease paintings of tuna fish rituals and dancing men (€5, ages 5-11 €3). The tour guide **Natale Castiglione,** in the ceramics shop Grotta del Genovese, offers information on the site. (☎ 0923 92 40 32; nacasti@tin.it. Tour reservation required at least one day in advance. Boat or jeep excursions €13. Shop open 9am-4pm, last tour leaves at 3pm.) A few kilometers along the coastal road, grottoes and beaches await. **Cala Tranate** and **Capo Grosso** (the end of the island where there is a lighthouse) are both about a 1½hr. walk. Be careful—the clear water between the rounded rock beach and the neighboring island has a ripping current when the winds pick up.

MARETTIMO ☎0923

The most physically remote of the Egadi Islands, Marettimo is equally distant in spirit. Because there are few roads, a boat is the best way to see Marettimo's caves. They are available for rent, with a captain, from the port. Beyond the village, the only intrusion into the island's rugged environment is an outstanding set of hiking trails crossing the island. The 2½hr. hike to **⊠Pizzo Falcone** (686m), the highest point on the Egadi Islands, starts at the sea road, past the Siremar office. Along the way, snuggled between cliffs and greenery, stand the **Case Romane,** ruins date back to Roman domination. To the right of the little village and past a beach at **Punta Troia,** a **Spanish castle** tops the cliff. According to legend, when a prince married one of two sisters over the other, the rejected one threw her sister off the cliff. The heartbroken prince then tossed the offending sister down the same route, then followed himself. Locals say that at sunset, the ghosts of the two lovers find each other again at the castle.

A few *piazze* connect the town's maze-like streets. A **cultural center** on V. Scalo Vecchio, along the fishing boat docks, has information on all three islands, as well as a local museum. (Open 8am-noon and 3-8pm.) **Il Corallo ❷**, V. Chiusa, 11, rents furnished apartments with bath, patio, and kitchenette. (☎0923 92 32 26. Apr. and Sept. €15 per person; June-July 15 €20 per person; July 15-Aug. €25-30 per person.) **Al Carrubo ❸**, Contrada Palosa, barbecues fish and serves up pizzas on their large patio. From the old port (Scalo Vecchio) walk into the town on V. G. Pepo and continue until it ends at C. Palosa. (☎0923 92 31 32. Pizza €4.50-6.50. *Primi* €6-12, *secondi* €7.50-10.50. Open daily June-Sept. 7:30pm-3am.) For a peaceful afternoon, head to **Caffé Tramontana ❶**, V. Campi, 11, where the outdoor tables above the old port offer great views of the island and sea. (Coffee €1-2.50. Open daily June-Sept. 8am-3am.) To stock up on supplies for your hike, you can head to **Alimentare Anastasi Clemente,** V. Mazzini, 13. (Open M-Sa 8am-1:30pm and 4-9pm.)

PANTELLERIA ☎0923

Known as *"La perla nera dell'Europa"* ("the black pearl of Europe"), Pantelleria is as African and Middle Eastern as she is European. At once both a world of stark contrasts and seamless integration, its main attractions are its natural beauty and tranquil isolation. Visitors coming for thermal springs, Arab *dammusi*, and sweet, plump capers are quickly seduced by the island's subtle magic and breathtaking beauty. Pantelleria's history has been one of travelers passing through and deciding to stay—after only a few moments on the island, it's easy to see why.

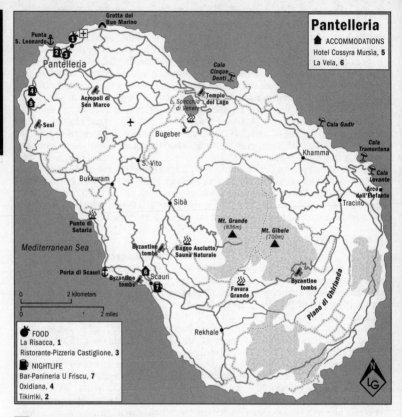

Pantelleria

🏠 ACCOMMODATIONS
Hotel Cossyra Mursia, **5**
La Vela, **6**

🍅 FOOD
La Risacca, **1**
Ristorante-Pizzeria Castiglione, **3**

🍸 NIGHTLIFE
Bar-Panineria U Friscu, **7**
Oxidiana, **4**
Tikirriki, **2**

▄ TRANSPORTATION

Pantelleria is surprisingly expansive. Almost all tourists rent a car or scooter, and consequently public travel resources like buses are few and far between. The midnight ferry from Trapani may save money on a night's hotel, but if spending the night struggling to curl up in a straight-backed ferry chair doesn't sound appealing, opt for the hydrofoil and relax on the noon return ferry instead.

Airport: ☎0923 91 11 72. Flights from the largest Italian cities service the airport, including Rome, Venice, Milan, Palermo, and Catania (14 departures per day 9:45am–6:45pm). **Air Sicily** ☎0923 91 22 13.

Ferries: Ustica hydrofoil tickets for sale at **Agenzia Minardi,** V. Borgo Italia, 15 (☎0923 91 15 02), on the *lungomare,* and in summer at a booth on the port. Open daily 7:30am–1pm and 6–10:30pm. To **Trapani:** (2½hr., 8:30am, €34); also available at **La Cossira** (☎0923 91 10 78), left of Hotel Khamma, where V. Catania meets the *lungomare.* Open daily 9am–1pm and 5:30–7:30pm. **Siremar,** V. Borgo Italia, 65 (☎0923 91 11 04), on the waterfront, runs ferries to **Trapani** (5hr., €20.60–23). Open M-F 6:30am–1pm, 5–6:30pm; Sa-Su 6:30am–1pm.

Island Buses: Infrequent buses run M-Sa from P. Cavour to the airport and the 5 island towns of Khamma-Tracino, Scauri-Rekale, Bukkuram, Sibà, and Bugeber (€1). Check schedule posted outside the tourist office; times are subject to change.

Scooter and Car Rental:

Autonoleggio Princioto Claudio, V. Ponte, 8, Rekhale. (☎0923 91 61 22 or 347 19 71 565). Reserve ahead for a driver to meet you at the port, or just call when you get there. Cars only: June €25, July €35, Aug. €45, Oct.-May €10. Reserve ahead in Aug. Open daily 8am-10pm.

Autonoleggio Policardo, V. Messina, 31 (☎0923 91 28 44; noleggiopolicar@tiscalinet.it), off the port, up the street to the right after the fenced-in scooter lot. Scooters €15-21 per day; in Aug. €40 per day. Cars 21+. €26 per day, €126 per week; €55 per day in Aug. Open daily 8am-8pm.

ORIENTATION AND PRACTICAL INFORMATION

Ferries and **hydrofoils** arrive at the northwest tip of the teardrop-shaped island. The town of Pantelleria borders the curved **port.** The main street, **Via Borgo Italia,** changes to **Lungomare Paolo Borsellino** and stretches from the docks to the private sailboat moorings. At the end of Lungomare P. Borsellino beneath the **Castello, Piazza Almanza** becomes **Piazza Cavour.** Most services are here. Roads at either end of the *lungomare* lead along the coast to other towns. Facing away from the water, the to the left are **Bue Marino, Gadir, Lago Specchio di Venere,** and **Arco dell'Elefante.** The right road leads to the **airport,** the **Sesi, Scauri town,** and **Rekhale.** An inland road above and to the right of the sea highway, past the Agip gas station, leads to **Sibà** and **Montagna Grande.**

Tourist Office: Pro Loco (☎0923 91 18 38), in P. Cavour in the corner of municipal building closest to Banco di Sicilia. Look for the language flags. Lots of brochures, **maps** (€0.77), bus schedules, and help finding lodgings. Open Apr.-Oct. M-F 9am-1pm, Sa-Su 9-11am.

Currency Exchange: Banca Nuova (☎0923 91 27 32), up V. Catania from the *lungomare*. Open M-Sa 8:20am-1:20pm and 2:40-3:40pm, Su 8:20-11:50am. 24hr. **ATMs** located at Banca Nuova, across the street at **Monte dei Paschi di Siena** and **Banco di Sicilia,** in P. Cavour across from the municipal building.

Carabinieri: V. Trieste, 13 (☎0923 91 11 09).

First Aid: P. Cavour, 21 (☎0923 91 02 55), on the far right side of the Municipal building (opposite Banco di Sicilia). Open M-F and Su 8am-8pm, Sa 10am-8pm.

Pharmacy: Farmacia Greco, P. Cavour, 26 (☎0923 91 13 10). Open M-Sa 8:30am-1pm and 4:30-8pm.

Hospital: ☎0923 91 11 10.

Internet Access: Internet Point Da Pietro, V. Dante, 7 (☎0923 91 13 67). Open daily 9:30am-2pm and 4:30-9pm. €0.50 for 5min., €6 per hr., €10 per 2hr. Fax and copy available. Printing €0.15 per page.

Post Office: V. Verdi, 2 (☎0923 69 52 11), behind the municipal building and across from Banco di Sicilia, off P. Cavour. **Exchanges currency** and **traveler's checks.** Open M-F 8am-1:30pm and Sa 8am-12:30pm. **Postal Code:** 91017.

 STREETSMARTS. Use extreme caution when traveling by car or by scooter in Pantelleria. Many roads are steep, narrow, and curvy, and those off the main highway are often unpaved and rocky. When in doubt, park and walk, but be careful on roads without sidewalks or lighting. Whether driving or walking, always hug the shoulder and, most importantly, pay attention.

ACCOMMODATIONS

Most visitors stay in *dammusi*, square-shaped, domed dwellings unique to the island. White roofs and thick lava-stone walls keep the interior cool, while cisterns catch rainwater that runs from the roof. Classic *dammusi* are whitewashed, simply furnished, and include a sleeping alcove There are over 3000 *dammusi* on Pantelleria, and nearly every resident rents one out or knows someone who does. The town of Pantelleria also has reasonable *affittacamere*. Quality varies considerably, and finding a place often requires perseverance. For both *dammusi* and rooms, inquire at the bars lining the beach or the tourist office and look for flyers. Some *dammusi* require a minimum stay and most cost from €20-35. Be ready to haggle. Follow the sea road 10km west from Pantelleria town to Scauri's port, where 15 *dammusi* are for rent from ▧**La Vela ❷**, on Scauri Scalo. All have kitchen, bath, and patio. A beach, bamboo-shaded porches, and a restaurant with sea view should seal the deal. (☎0923 91 18 00 or 349 35 37 154. Reserve 4 months ahead for July and Aug. €25-35 per person. Cash only.) You won't forego modern luxuries at **Hotel Cossyra Mursìa ❺**, along the road from Pantelleria town to Scauri, before the *sesi*. This resort-style hotel overlooking the sea has rooms resembling *dammusi*. Amenities include a deck, three swimming pools, TV lounges, a piano bar, tennis courts, archery ranges, scuba diving, and an acclaimed restaurant. (☎0923 91 12 17; www.mursiahotel.it. Open Mar.-Oct. Rooms are divided into 3 classes: classic, comfort, and superior. Double €110-170/120-180/140-200. Half pension double €90-170/100-180/120-200; single room add €8-30. AmEx/MC/V.)

🍴 FOOD

Arab domination in the 8th century turned Pantelleria away from fishing to the cultivation of its rich volcanic soil. A local specialty, *pesto pantesco*, is a sauce of tomato, capers, basil, garlic, and almonds, eaten with pasta or on *bruschetta*. The local *zibbibo* grape yields grape jelly and the amber *passito* and *moscato* dessert wines. A **SISA** supermarket sits above the *lungomare* at V. Napoli, 17. Hike up the stairs at the 90° bend of the *lungomare*, passing the Banco Nuova sign on the right. (Open M-Tu and Th-Su 8:30am-1pm and 5:30-8:30pm, W 8:30am-1pm. MC/V.) **La Risacca ❷** is at V. Milano, 65. From the port, head toward Sibá. La Risacca is above the port next to the hospital. Pizzas (€4-8), specialties like *spaghetti con gambero* (with shrimp; €8) and *ravioli panteschi* (ravioli stuffed with ricotta and mint, covered in a tomato or butter-herb sauce; €8) are served in a dining room or on a terrace. (Open daily 12:30-2:30pm and 8-11pm. Closed M Oct.-May.) **Ristorante-Pizzeria Castiglione ❸,** V. Borgo Italia, 24, along the *lungomare*, serves 39 kinds of pizza (takeout €4-6 available) in a chic, modern dining room. Fish *secondi* are a particularly good deal. (☎0923 91 14 48. *Primi* €6-8, *secondi* €8. Cover €1. Open daily noon-2pm and 7:30pm-midnight. Closed W Oct.-May. AmEx/MC/V.)

👁 SIGHTS

Pantelleria's natural beauty is unsurpassable, and there are many specific sights worth checking out. Don't plan to hit more than two destinations in a day. Pantelleria's bus system is notoriously unreliable, not infrequently leaving travelers waiting in the sun for half a day, and many inland and coastal sights are a good hour's walk from the scattered bus stops. Relief comes in the form of motorized transportation, an absolute necessity for most destinations inland and to the south.

🏞**BAGNO ASCIUTTO (LA GROTTA DI BENIKULÀ) AND MONTAGNA GRANDE.**
Near the town of Sibà is a rock sauna and the summit of Pantelleria's highest mountain. Signs guide through and beyond Sibà to the sauna; the last 10min. or so must be traveled on foot. Inside, visitors lie face down in a deep, low cave. Bring water and a towel and be prepared to leave and reenter several times. Farther along the sauna path, at the foot of Monte Gibele, the **Favara Grande** is a

fumarole (crater) that emits clouds of hot smoke. Most of the trails that leave from the asphalt road are short, and a shady picnic area in a pine grove near the summit is the perfect place to relax after a dry bath or sauna. If the midday heat is already enough, head to Montagna Grande for the view. The road past Sibà leads almost to the top, with views stretching for miles. Watch for the lush Ghirlanda Plain. *(Take the Sibà bus from P. Cavour (M-F 4 per day 6:40am-7:40pm). Both the Bagno and the mountain are clearly marked. By car or scooter, follow signs from Pantelleria for Sibà. Note that on some maps and signs, the Bagno Asciutto is labeled as "Grotta di Benikulà.")*

THE PUNTO DI SATARIA. At the **Punto di Sataria,** stairs lead down to a cave once thought to be the home of the nymph Calypso, with whom Ulysses resided for seven years of his odyssey. The 40°C (104°F) water in the thermal pools, only a jump away from the much cooler sea, is believed to cure aching joints. Be careful of the surf in the open water. *(Portions of this site may be blocked off due to falling rocks. Buses depart Pantelleria M-F 5 times per day 6:40am-2pm. Be sure to inquire about return times. By car or scooter, follow the road from Pantelleria to Scauri.)*

LO SPECCHIO DI VENERE (THE MIRROR OF VENICE0. Legend has it that Venus used this lake as a mirror before her dates with Bacchus, a fan of Pantelleria for its strong *zibbibo* wine. Mere mortals may also be lured by a glimpse down into this startlingly aquamarine pool, fringed with firm white mud and sunken into a bowl of green hillside. Sulfur springs warm the water and enrich the mud. Local practice recommends letting the sun dry the therapeutic mud to a white cake on the skin and then taking a long swim through the warm waters to wash it off. *(From P. Cavour take the bus to Bugeber; ask driver where to exit and ask about return times. Buses depart Pantelleria M-F 7:50am and 2pm. By car or scooter, head to Bugeber and follow signs for the turn-off.)*

THE SESI. The Bronze Age people who inhabited Pantelleria 5000 years ago left behind the *sesi*, dome-shaped funerary monuments built around 1800 BC. Tunnels in the *sesi* gave access to chambers that stored kneeling corpses. Many have been torn down for building material, but the largest remaining congregation of *sesi* forms a cemetery with 70 tombs. *(On the road from Pantelleria to Scauri. Buses depart Pantelleria M-F 5 times per day 6:40am-2pm. Be sure to inquire about return times. Look for a sign indicating the "zona archeologica" to the left, past the Hotel Cossyra Mursìa.)*

THE NORTHEASTERN COAST AND THE ARCO DELL'ELEFANTE. In the shadow of the black rock structures lining the coast, visitors crowd the best swimming holes off Pantelleria, located in three small inlets along the northeastern coast. The first, Gadir, is one of the more popular *acquacalda* spots on the island. Cement encloses the natural pool next to the sea. Even better swimming is down the coast at **Cala di Tramontana** and **Cala di Levante.** Perfect for sunbathing, these twin coves are actually one, split by a rocky outcropping. Cala di Levante offers a view of the ▧**Arco dell'Elefante,** off to the right. The unofficial symbol of the island, the unusual rock formation looks like a large elephant guzzling up the surf. *(All 3 inlets are on the Khamma-Tracino bus line. Buses leave P. Cavour M-F 6 per day 6:40am-5:20pm. Check return times. By car or scooter, follow signs for Khamma and Tracino, then signs for coastal roads.)*

IL PIANO DI GHIRLANDA (THE GARLAND PLAIN). Surrounded by its own crumbled lip, this fertile crater makes a beautiful 2hr. hike from Tracino. On the way, scope out the terraces where peasants, working out of small, utilitarian *dammusi,* tend fruit orchards and caper fields. Follow signs to the **Byzantine tombs** at Gabbiana; surrounded by a vineyard, these tombs mark the resting place of a family of four from the early Middle Ages. *(By car, take road leading out of Tracino's P. Perugio. Or take Tracino bus to the Byzantine tombs, then follow signs to trails.)*

SICILY

☕ NIGHTLIFE

Pantelleria's most vibrant nightlife is at the port. **Tikirriki,** V. Borgo Italia, 5/7 (☎0923 91 10 79) and **Il Goloso,** V. Borgo Italia, 35 (☎0923 91 18 14), both serve until about 2am and have tables outside by the water. Twelve kilometers away in the town of Scauri is the lively **◪Bar-Panineria U Friscu,** C. da Scauri, 54, which serves as the perfect pre-disco party stop. Try the local white wine. (☎0923 91 83 40. Wine €3 per glass, €15 per bottle.) The only disco open during the summer is **Oxidiana,** on the western seaside road heading out of Pantelleria, on the left just before Hotel Cossyra Mursìa; look for a huge electronic scrolling banner that reads "Tutte le Sere." (☎0923 91 23 19. Open July-Sept. 15.)

◪ ☾ BEACHES AND BOAT TOURS

Pantelleria's beaches aren't really beaches. The closest things to a beach are the pebble-filled coves. Swimming areas around the coast are rated on maps by a three-point scale based on difficulty of access. Rocky coves and swimming grottoes abound but require a trek. Closest to Pantelleria is **Grotta del Bue Marino,** 2km to the east, along the *lungomare* to the right of town when facing the water. Snorkelers hug its coast and sunbathers drape over volcanic rock. **Use extreme caution:** the water is shallow in places, and the bottom is lined with jagged rocks.

A **◪boat tour** is the fastest and most relaxing way to see Pantelleria. Glass-bottomed boats provide a glimpse of hidden caves and colorful marine life. Boats also offer a view of some of Pantelleria's greatest, and otherwise inaccessible, rock formations, including Cinderella's Slippers, *L'Arco dell'Elefante,* and *I Cinque Denti* (The Five Teeth). The boats lining the ports offer diverse advantages: smaller ones can nudge into crevices between rocks, but their larger cousins provide shade, napping cushions, and space to move more freely. **Adriano Minardi,** V. Borgo Italia, 15 (☎/fax 0923 91 15 02), runs tours of the island. Expect to pay about €40 for any service at sea.)

SARDINIA (SARDEGNA)

An old legend says that when God finished making the world, He had a handful of dirt left over, which He threw into the Mediterranean, stepped on, and—behold—created the island of Sardinia. Another myth claims that Sardinia was the land of Atlantis, covered by a tidal wave in the 2nd millennium BC. However it came to be, Sardinia has been bobbled back and forth from country to country for centuries. Shuffled between the Phoenicians and the Carthaginians, Sardinia got a break when the Romans made it an agricultural colony. But by the 13th century, it was again a theater for conflict between the Pisans, the Aragonese, the newly united Spanish, and the *Piemontesi*. Until just decades ago, *padroni* (landlords) controlled the land, and farmers toiled under a system akin to serfdom. The architecture, language, and cuisine of traditional Sardinian life render it a cultural anomaly, a composite society of African, Spanish, Italian, and influences. The latent independence movement, reflected in grafitti and Sardinian flags, speaks to the island's location on the border between many different peoples and cultures.

HIGHLIGHTS OF SARDINIA

CIRCLE Cagliari's medieval town atop the ramparts of **Bastione di San Remy** (p. 731).

SOAK IN the sun on the luxurious beaches of **La Maddalena Archipelago** (p. 744).

SAIL from Alghero's busy waterfront to the luminescent **Grotte di Nettuno** (p. 740).

MARVEL at the colorful streets of **Orgosolo**, where artists have been addressing social issues through large-scale murals since 1975 (p. 757).

▐ TRANSPORTATION

FLIGHTS. Alitalia flights link Alghero, Cagliari, and Olbia to major Italian cities. Though flights are faster than water travel, exorbitant fares discourage most air travelers. Recently, Ryanair and EasyJet have begun to serve Sardinia's airports. EasyJet (www.easyjet.com) flies from Olbia to Berlin and London, and from Cagliari to Luton. Ryanair (www.ryanair.com) sends flies from Alghero to Barcelona, Frankfurt, London, and Rome.

FERRIES. The cheapest way to Sardinia is by ferry from Civitavecchia, Genoa, or Livorno to Olbia; expect to pay €20-75 each way, depending on the company, season, boat speed, and departure time (night trips, fast ferries, and summer ferries cost more). The cheapest fares are for daytime *posta ponte* (deck class) slots on slow-moving boats, but most ferry companies require that *poltrone* (reserved armchairs) be sold to capacity before they open *posta ponte*. In the price ranges below, the low number is the low-season *posta ponte* fare, and the high number is the high-season *poltrone* fare. Expect to pay €10-20 more for a *cabina* with a bed, plus €5-15 depending on the season, duration, and taxes. Travelers with vehicles, animals, or children should arrive 1½hr. before departure; everyone else should arrive 45min. early. Vehicles can cost €50-120, depending on the length of the voyage and the season. The ferry schedule chart below is for summer service. All winter ferries sell at lower prices and run overnight.

> **Tirrenia** (☎199 12 31 99 or 081 31 72 999 for reservations; www.tirrenia.it) has offices in city harbors, including: **Cagliari** (☎070 66 60 65), **Civitavecchia** (☎076 65 81 925 or 076 65 81 926), **Genoa** (☎010 26 981), and **Olbia** (0789 20 71 00). Also Tirrenia offices in **Livorno** (☎0586 42 47 30), on Calata Addis Abeba–Varco Galvani; main

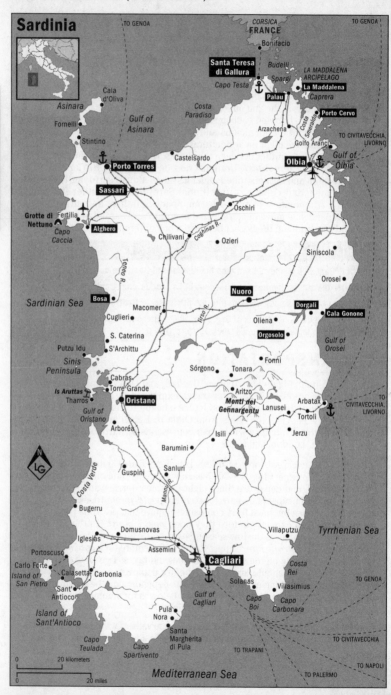

office in **Naples,** Rione Sirignano, 2 (☎081 25 14 721). **Palermo** (☎091 602 11 11), on Calata Marinai d'Italia; **Porto Torres,** V. Mare, 38 (☎079 518 10 11).

Sardinia Ferries (☎019 21 55 11; www.sardiniaferries.com). Offices include **Livorno,** at the Stazione Marittima (☎0586 88 13 80), in **Civitavecchia** (☎0766 50 07 14), at Calata Laurenti, and **Golfo Aranci** (☎0789 46 780), at the Stazione Marittima.

Moby Lines (www.mobylines.it) has offices in **Olbia** (☎0789 27 927 or 0565 27 60 77) and in **Livorno** (☎0586 89 99 50), on V. Veneto, 24 (☎0586 82 68 23), and in **Genoa** (☎010 25 41 513).

Linea dei Golfi (☎0565 22 23 00; www.lineadeigolfi.it) **Olbia** (☎0789 246 56). Ferries from Piombino and Livorno to **Olbia** and **Piombino** (☎0565 22 23 00).

Enermar (www.enermar.it) has offices at **Genoa's** port (☎199 76 00 03) and **Palau** (☎199 76 00 01).

ROUTE	COMPANY	DURATION	FREQUENCY	PRICE
Civitavecchia-Olbia	Tirrenia (unità veloce)	4hr.	1-2 per day, 8:30am	€27.63-45.54
Civitavecchia-Olbia	Tirrenia (traditional)	8hr.	1 per day, 11pm	€19.92-44.91
Civitavecchia-Cagliari	Tirrenia (traditional)	14½hr.	1 per day, 6:30pm	€26.56-54.71
Genoa-Olbia	Tirrenia (traditional)	13¼ hr.	1 per day, 6pm	€21-83.99
Genoa-Porto Torres	Tirrenia (traditional)	10hr.	1-2 per day, 9pm	€27.78-84.34
Naples-Cagliari	Tirrenia (traditional)	16hr.	1-2 per week, 7:15pm	€26.56-60.39
Palermo-Cagliari	Tirrenia (traditional)	13½hr.	1 per week, 7pm	€25.01-55.75
Trapani-Cagliari	Tirrenia (traditional)	10hr.	1 per week, Su midnight	€25.01-55.21
Civitavecchia-G. Aranci (Olbia)	Sardinia Ferries	7-10hr.	3 per day in summer	€17-38
Livorno-Golfo Aranci	Sardinia Ferries	5-8hr.	3 per day in summer	€20-48
Olbia-Livorno	Moby Lines	10hr.	2-3 per day	€20-46
Bonifacio-S. Teresa Bonifacio-S. Teresa	Moby Lines Saremar	1hr.	10 per day in summer	€8-12
Genoa-Palau	Enermar	12hr.	1 most days	€35-59
Genoa-Olbia	Grand Navi Veloci	8-10hr.	1 per day	€42-77
Genoa-Porto Torres	Grand Navi Veloci	11hr.	1-3 per day	€31-74
Piombino-Olbia	Linea dei Golfi	6½hr.	July-Aug. 6-14 per week	€16.50-35

CAGLIARI ☎070

Since the Phoenicians founded the ancient port town of Korales over two millennia ago, several great civilizations have competed for domination of Cagliari (pop. 160,000), Sardinia's capital and largest city. In the 11th century, after defeating the Genoese, the Pisans built the fortified town of Castrum Kolaris, which became one of the most important artistic and cultural centers on the Mediterranean. Cagliari maintains the energy of a modern city, with chic boutiques, a large university, and cafes serving espresso-sipping students. Put on your walking shoes and wander around the ramparts of the Bastione San Remy, the winding cobblestone streets, the broad waterfront, and the still-functioning amphitheater. And when the pulse of city life becomes too strong, a 20min. bus ride will bring you to the sparkling green water and bright sands of Il Poetto, one of the best beaches in all Sardinia.

▔ TRANSPORTATION

Flights: ☎070 21 051. In the village of Elmas. ARST buses run the 8km from the airport to the city terminal at P. Matteotti (30min., 21 per day 5:40am-8:45pm, €0.67).

Trains: FS (☎08 92 021), in P. Matteotti. Stations open daily 6:10am-8:45pm. Ticket office 6:45am-1:30pm and 1:50-8:45pm; 24hr. ticket machines. **Luggage Storage**

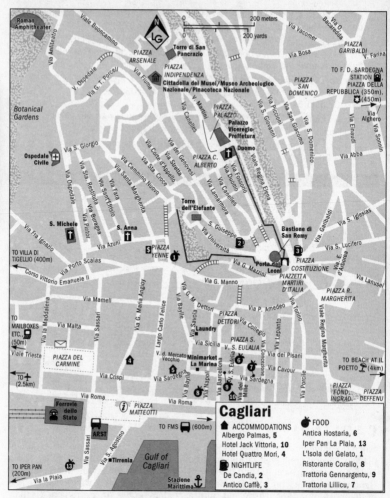

Cagliari

🏠 ACCOMMODATIONS
Albergo Palmas, 5
Hotel Jack Vittoria, 10
Hotel Quattro Mori, 4

🌙 NIGHTLIFE
De Candia, 2
Antico Caffè, 3

🍴 FOOD
Antica Hostaria, 6
Iper Pan La Plaia, 13
L'Isola del Gelato, 1
Ristorante Corallo, 8
Trattoria Gennargentu, 9
Trattoria Lillicu, 7

€2.51 per half-day. To: **Olbia** (4hr., 6:32pm, €12.95) via **Oristano** or **Macomer**; **Oristano** (1½hr., 16 per day 5:30am-10:02pm, €4.55); **Porto Torres** (4hr.; 12:03, 2:50, 4:27pm; €12.95); **Sassari** (4hr.; 6:38am, 12:03, 2:50, 4:27pm; €12.10). Other destinations include S.Gavino, Iglesias, Decimomannu, and Carbonia.

EXTRA! EXTRA! Sardinia's daily newspaper, *L'Unione Sarda*, publishes a page called "Per Chi Viaggia" ("For Travelers") which lists departure times and contact information for all bus, airplane, train and ferry routes serving Cagliari, Alghero, Oristano, Olbia, Arbatax, Porto Torres, Palaue, Nuoro, Lanusei, Sassari, and their small town destinations.

Buses: There are 3 major bus companies that serve Cagliari.

ARST, P. Matteotti, 6 (☎070 40 98 324). Office open M-Sa 8-8:30am, 9am-2:15pm, and 5:30-7pm, Su 1:30-2:15pm and 5:30-7pm. Information in the front entrance area, ticket booth through the McDonald's. When office is closed, buy tickets on bus. Serves local towns, including **Villasimius** (15 per day 5am-8:10pm, €2.89) and **Arbatax** (10:25am-3pm, €7.64). Also runs to **airport** (10min., 24 per day 6:10am-8:45pm, €0.67).

PANI (☎070 65 23 26; www.orginazzazionepani.it) ticket booth in ARST station. Office open M-Sa 8am-2:15pm and 5:30-7pm, Su 1:30-2:15pm and 5:30-7pm. Buses leave from ARST station to: **Nuoro** (3½hr., 4 per day 5:30am-6:15pm, €11.31); **Oristano** (1½hr., 4 per day 5:30am-6:15pm, €5.84); **Sassari** (3hr., 7 per day 5:30am-7pm, €12.60-13.43).

FMS (☎800 04 45 53), on Vle. Colombo, runs to smaller towns. To: **Buggerruruns** (10:07am, 12:20, 5:50pm); **Calasetta, Sant'Antioco-San,** and **Giovanni Suergiu** (6 per day, 10:07am-7:12pm); **Giba** and **Nuxis Santadi** (1:05, 4:25, 6:20pm); **Iglesias** (10 per day, 6:10am-8:21pm), **Portoscuso** (6:10am, 12:20, 1:55, 5:50pm). Buy tickets M-Sa at newsstand across from Farmacia Spanno on V. Roma.

Ferries: Tirrenia (☎199 12 31 99), buy tickets from red building 1 block behind the ARST station. Ferries leave from **Stazione Marrittima;** only ticketholders are allowed in the station. **Luggage storage** available (see **Practical Information,** below). Open M, W, and F 8:30am-7pm, Tu and Th 8:30am-6:50pm, Sa 8:30am-6pm, Su 4-8pm.

Local Buses: ☎070 20 911 or 070 20 91 210. Orange **CTM buses** run from P. Matteotti. Tickets sold in park across from ARST station. €0.77 per 1½hr., €1.29 per 2hr., €2.17 per day. **Buses P, PQ,** and **PF** go to Il Poetto 5:20am-10:50pm, last return 11:25pm; in the summer, lines **3/P, 9/P, Yellow,** and **Arancio** run to Il Poetto.

Taxis: Radiotaxi Quattro Mori (☎070 40 01 01), in front of the train station.

Car Rental: Auto assistance (☎070 68 48 874; www.autoassistance.it), in Stazione Marittima, rents cars (from €70), motor scooters (from €45), and a few mountain bikes (€10 per day). Insurance included. 21+. Open M-F 9am-1pm and 3-7pm. AmEx/MC/V.

◄▶ ORIENTATION AND PRACTICAL INFORMATION

Via Roma greets new arrivals to Cagliari, with the **harbor** and **Stazione Marittima** on one side and outdoor cafes on the other. **Piazza Matteotti,** between V. Roma, **Via Sassari,** and **Largo Carlo Felice,** contains the **train station,** the **ARST station,** and the **tourist office.** Across from P. Matteotti, Largo Carlo Felice climbs the steep hill leading to **Piazza Yenne,** then heads up to the **Castello district,** the *centro storico.* Merchants converge on the terraces of the Bastione di S. Remy for a **flea market** on Sunday morning and a smaller daily ▧**flea market** in P. del Carmine, where visitors hone their bargaining skills and find antiques for low prices.

Tourist Office: ☎070 66 92 55. P. Matteotti, in park across from the train and bus stations. English-speaking staff has substantial info on local sights and posts contact information for lodgings. Open M-Sa 8:30am-1:30pm. Hours vary in winter.

Currency Exchange: Banca di Roma, P. Yenne, 5, at the corner of C. V. Emanuele II. **ATM** outside. Open M-F 8:25am-1:35pm and 2:50-4:10pm, Sa 8:25-11:55am.

Luggage Storage: At Stazione Marittima. Free. Open Sa-Su 7am-7pm. At train station, €2.51 per half-day.

English-Language Bookstore: Le Librerie della Costa, V. Roma, 65 (☎070 65 02 56). Classics, contemporary works, and childrens' books. Internet upstairs; €3 per 30min., €5 per hr. Open M-Sa 9am-8:30pm, Su 10am-1:30pm and 5-9pm. AmEx/MC/V.

Laundry: Ghibli Lavanderia Self-Service, V. Sicilia, 20 (☎070 56 55 21 or 349 43 129), off V. Bayle. Wash €4 per 6 kg, €7 per 16 kg. Dry €3.50. Detergent €1. Open daily 8am-10pm; last wash 9pm.

Emergency: ☎112. **Police:** ☎070 40 40 40. **Ambulance:** ☎118. **First Aid:** Weekends and nights ☎070 50 29 31.

Pharmacy: Farmacia Dr. Spano, V. Roma, 99 (☎070 65 56 83). Open in summer M-F 9am-1pm and 4:50-8:10pm, Sa 9am-1pm; in winter M-F 9am-1pm and 4:30-7:50pm, Sa 9am-1pm. AmEx/MC/V.

SARDINIA

Hospital: V. Ospedale, 54 (☎070 609 33 20), about a 5min. walk from Chiesa di S. Michele. Open daily 8:30am-12:30pm.

Internet: Mail Boxes Etc., V. Trieste, 65/B (☎070 67 37 04), past the post office. 2 computers with fast connection and ports for laptops. €1.50 per 15min., €5 per hr. **Fax** and **UPS service** available. Open M-F 9am-1pm and 4-7:30pm. MC/V.

Post Office: V. Carmine, 27 (☎070 60 311). Take V. Sassari from P. Matteotti. *Fermoposta*, phone cards, and **currency exchange.** Open M-F 8:10am-6:50pm, Sa 8am-1:15pm. **Postal Code:** 09100.

ACCOMMODATIONS

Budget accommodations dot the area just off V. Roma, between Largo Carlo Felice and Vle. Regina Margherita. The best bet in town is **Albergo Palmas ❷**, V. Sardegna, 14. Cross V. Roma and turn right. Take the first left on Largo Carlo Felice and a right on V. Sardegna. Helpful staff runs 14 centrally located simple rooms with high ceilings, tasteful decor, and balcony. (☎070 65 16 79. Shared bath. Reception up flight of stairs. Reserve ahead. Singles €25; doubles €35-40. AmEx/MC/V.) To reach **Hotel Jack Vittoria ❹**, V. Roma, 75, cross V. Roma from the train station or ARST station and turn right. Don't be fooled by the unkempt staircase and unassuming facade—founded in 1938 this is still one of Cagliari's loveliest hotels, holding 20 rooms with Venetian chandeliers, Victorian molding, bath, phone, and air-conditioning. Check-in on 3rd floor. (☎/fax 070 66 79 70. Breakfast €6. Reserve ahead. Singles €50; doubles €82. Extra beds €28. Cash only.) Set back from the port, the **Hotel Quattro Mori ❹**, V. G. M. Angioy, 27, offers 42 rooms with marble floors and dark wood furnishings. Rooms have bath, air-conditioning, TV, DVD player, and refrigerator. (☎070 66 85 35; www.hotel4mori.it. Breakfast included. Reserve ahead. Singles €55; doubles €75; triples €95; quads €120. AmEx/MC/V.)

FOOD

Many small shops sell fruit, cheese, and bread, along V. Sardegna. Try **Mini Market La Marina,** V. Sardegna, 43, which also has a great bakery. (Open M-Sa 7am-2pm and 4:30-8:30pm. MC/V.) The **Iper Pan La Plaia,** in a large shopping complex on V. la Plaia, 15, is the mother of all grocery stores. (Open M-W and Sa 9am-9pm, Th-F 9am-9:30pm, Su 9am-2pm and 5-9pm.) On Sunday mornings, there's a **market** on the far side of the stadium in Borgo S. Elia for fresh fruit and seafood.

▨ **Trattoria Lillicu,** V. Sardegna, 78 (☎070 65 29 70). Run by the same family for 80 years. Small but impeccable selection of Sardinian dishes like *lacetti di agnelle* (lamb; €6.50) and seafood. Dining room, with family-style seating, is loud and packed late; if you're lucky you will be serenaded by the guitar-playing owner. *Primi* €5-7, *secondi* €6-13. Cover €1.55. Open M-Sa 1-3pm and 8-midnight. AmEx/MC/V. Reserve ahead. ❸

▨ **Antica Hostaria,** V. Cavour, 60 (☎070 66 58 70, fax 070 66 58 78). This beautiful restaurant sports Art Nouveau decor and tuxedo-clad waiters, and starts meals off with a sparkling *aperitif*. Try house favorite *fregola con arselle* (tiny semolina pasta in clam broth; €8) or veal in *vernaccia* sauce (€8). *Primi* €7-9, *secondi* €8-13. Cover €2. Open M-Sa 12:45-3pm and 8-11pm. AmEx/MC/V. ❸

▨ **L'Isola del Gelato,** P. Yenne, 4 (☎070 65 98 24). A waterfall in the wall feeds a river running beneath the transparent floor. Fun staff, over 120 *gelato* flavors, a fresh yogurt-and-topping station, and 16 creamy mousses make this a wildly popular *gelateria*. Cups from €1, giant 5-scoop cup €3. Open Mar.-Nov. daily 9am-2am. Cash only. ❶

Ristorante Corallo, V. Napoli, 4 (☎070 66 80 27), off V. Roma. At tables set with complimentary fresh vegetables (radishes, celery, lettuce), enjoy *gnochetti* in a variety of sauces. Suckling pig and roast lamb are the Su specialty. *Primi* €4-7, *secondi* €6.50-9.50. Open M-Sa noon-3pm and 7:30-11pm. AmEx/MC/V. ❸

Trattoria Gennargentu, V. Sardegna, 60/c (☎070 65 82 47). Join locals in this casual *salumeria*-restaurant for spaghetti with sea urchin and smoked fish roe (€7.50) and zesty *salsiccia arrosta* (roasted sausage; €8). *Primi* €5.50-7.50, *secondi* €5-13.50. Cover €1.55. Open M-Sa 12:30-3pm and 7:30-11pm. AmEx/MC/V. ❷

🔘 SIGHTS

▨ BASTIONE DI SAN REMY. Approaching **Piazza Costituzione,** sightseers are dwarfed by an enormous arch and a staircase that seems to be carved into the hillside. Climb up the graceful though graffiti-covered double stairway to the terraces of the 19th-century *bastione* for a spectacular view of Cagliari below. Take particular note of the **Golfo degli Angeli,** the pink flamingos, and the **Sella del Diavolo** (Devil's Saddle), a massive rock formation. The *bastione* divides the modern city and the medieval Castello district. For a stroll through medieval Cagliari, start at the top of the *bastione* and follow the narrow streets past Aragonese churches and Piemontese palaces, then stop at the Pisan wall that runs along the hill.

▨ PALAZZO VICEREGIO. Constructed by the Aragonese in 1216 and later used as a seat for Spanish and Savoyard viceroys, this beautiful palace maintains its original Pisan marble floor and 18th-century furnishings. Portraits inside are by Sardinian masters like Giovanni Marghinotti. The palace serves as Cagliari's provincial seat. *(Next to the duomo in P. Palazzo. Open daily 10am-2pm and 3-7pm; entrance only with tour guide. Tour in English or Italian. Free.)*

MUSEUMS. Although the menacing spear above the entrance recalls the building's original purpose, today the **Cittadella dei Musei** at P. Arsenale houses a modern complex of research museums that includes the **Museo Archeologico Nazionale.** The extensive collection of Sardinian artifacts from the Nuraghic eras to Byzantine includes Mycenean pottery from 1600 BC, Barumini, the largest of Sardinia's *nuraghi,* jewelry and coins from the Punic Phoenician Age, Roman glass works and mosaics, and a 1000-year-old army of tiny bronze figurines. Comprehensive expla-

I'M SO HUNGRY I COULD EAT A CAVALLO

Sardininians are born with a taste for delicacies that are unique to their island. Whether a first-time visitor to Sardinia or a seasoned regular, use this primer as a guide to items you might encounter on the menu.

Cavallo: Horsemeat. Popular throughout the island, it's a specialty in the Sassari area, where it is sautéed with garlic, salt, and olive oil to complement its natural sweetness.

Found at most specialty Sardinian markets, **bottarga** (fish eggs) are ground into a topping for pasta or pizza. Once known as the poor man's caviar, they are the roe of either *tonno* (tuna) or *mugine* (gray mullet).

Arselle, tiny, flavorful clams with speckled grey and black shells, can be found only in Sardinia.

Filled with potato, cheese, and mint, **culurgiones,** small pasta dumplings, are usually served in a light tomato sauce. They are most commonly served as a leaf-shaped ravioli. While they can be bought frozen in the supermarket to cook at home, they are best when made fresh at an authentic restaurant.

Seadas (or Sebadas) are flat dumplings that resemble large raviolis. Available uncooked at most markets, they are filled with cheese and then fried and smothered with either honey or sugar.

nations, with major wall-text displays in English and Italian, use the artifacts to narrate the history of Sardinian occupation. The entire 2nd floor of the museum is devoted to the archaeological history of Cagliari from the Nuraghic to Roman ages. *(Take V. Buoncammino to P. Arsenale and pass under the Torre di S. Pancrazio to the Arsenale. ☎ 070 65 59 11. Open Tu-Su 9am-7:15pm. Wheelchair accessible. €4, students 18-25 €2, under 18 or over 65 free.)* The **Pinacoteca Nazionale**, in the complex with the archaeological museum, displays medieval and Baroque religious paintings and altarpieces. The labyrinthine museum is built around the remains of a 16th-century fortification, visible on the ground floor and discovered during reconstruction of the Citadel in 1966. Be sure to visit the ■**Madonna con Bambino** on the lower floor. *(☎ 070 66 24 96 or 070 67 40 54. Open Tu-Su 9am-8pm. Wheelchair accessible. €2, students 18-25 €1, under 18 or over 65 free. Both museums €5, students €2.50.)*

DUOMO (CATTEDRALE DI SANTA MARIA). The Pisans constructed this massive **Gothic cathedral** during the 2nd half of the 13th century, dedicating it to the Virgin Mary and St. Cecilia. The *duomo* is modeled after the one in Pisa (p. 486) and filled with art by Pisan masters. The pulpits on either side of the main door, carved in 1162, are by Gugliemo, and the four lions at the base of the altarpiece are by Pisano. The ornate wood balcony to the left, in front of the altar, was constructed for the Piemontese king, who refused to sit among the people for fear of regicide. Colorful marble inlays conceal 179 niches housing the remains of about 200 martyred saints from Cagliari. *(P. Palazzo, 4. ☎ 070 16 63 837. Open M-F 8am-12:30pm and 4:30-8pm, Su 8am-1pm and 4-8pm. Free. Modest dress required.)*

ROMAN AMPHITHEATER. Constructed after the Carthaginians succumbed to the Roman juggernaut in 238 BC, this amphitheater conforms to the natural slope of the rocky landscape. It lost its downhill side to the Pisans, who used the wall as a quarry to build their monuments in the 13th century. Underground cages held ferocious animals in the days when the arena hosted gladiatorial combats. Today, summer performances in the theater (see **Entertainment,** below) are just a little more civilized. *(V. Fra Ignazio. ☎ 070 65 25 96; www.anfiteatroromano.it. 30min. guided tours Apr.-Oct. 1 Tu-Su 10am-1pm and 3-6pm; last tour 5:30pm. €3.30, students €2.20, groups €1.65, over 65 free.)*

🎵 🎭 ENTERTAINMENT AND NIGHTLIFE

The **Roman Amphitheater** continues to dazzle spectators with theater, dance performances, opera, and concerts in July and August. Most shows start at 9:30pm and cost €8-50. Buy tickets at the amphitheater from 7pm on performance nights or at the box office, Vle. Regina Margherita, 43. (☎ 070 65 74 28. Open M-F 10am-1pm and 5-10pm, Sa 10am-1pm, Su when there's a show.) **Outdoor movies,** mostly dubbed American films, are screened in July and August around 9pm at the Marina Piccola off Spiaggia del Poetto. Buy tickets (€4) at the Marina.

Most bars and clubs in the city are open from 9pm to 5am, but shut down in the summer when students hit the beaches and the dancing moves outdoors. The crowd at ■**De Candia,** V. De Candia, 1, sways under DJ music and colorful cocktails, including *assenzio* (absinthe) lightened with burnt sugar. The bar is one of several positioned on a terrace on top of the Bastione de San Remy; they all feature lounging couches or hammocks. (☎ 070 65 58 84. Cocktails €5.50-8. Open daily 7am-4am.) Join the famous faces plastered to the walls at the **Antico Caffè,** P. Costituzione, 10/11, who have come for delicious desserts like crepes (€3.50-6) and sinful ice-cream sundaes (€4-7) for over 150 years. Call to reserve a table outside. (☎ 070 65 82 06. Service 20%. Open daily 7am-2am. AmEx/MC/V.) To dance the night away, either find a ride or rent one—most *discoteche* are 15-20km outside of Cagliari, on the beaches. The best night to go out is Friday. On the first of May, Sardinians flock to Cagliari for the **Festival of Sant'Efisio,** honoring a deserter from Diocletian's army who saved the island from the plague but couldn't save himself from a beheading. A costumed procession escorts his effigy from the capital down the coast to the small church that bears his name.

BEACHES

Il Poetto, Cagliari's most popular stretch of beach, spans 10km from the Devil's Saddle to the Margine Rosso (Red Bluff). The beach was famous for its pure white sands until the government dumped several tons of coarse brown sand on top to prevent erosion. Locals claim it's ugly, but only because their gorgeous **Villasimus** and **Chia** allow them to have high standards. And despite the brown sand, the crystal waters are still beautiful. Behind Il Poetto, the salt-water **Stagno di Molentargius** (Pond of Molentargius) provides a habitat for flamingos. (City buses P, PQ, and PF, as well as the 3/P, 9/P, Yellow, and Arancio run frequently to the beaches. 20min., €0.77.) To avoid crowded areas, hold off for a few stops after hitting the beach area. For more private sunning and swimming, head to **Cala Mosca,** smaller and surrounded by dirt paths. A 4.3km circular trail leaves from the road to the left of Il Poetto, dropping first into the isolated **Cala Fighera,** then continuing uphill past the ruins of towers and a cistern from the Punic-Roman age. Alternatively, take city bus #5 to Stadio Amsicora, then bus #11 to the beach.

SASSARI   ☎079

Founded as the first free town of Sardinia in 1294, Sassari (pop. 113,000) held onto its medieval walls until the late 1800s despite being encroached upon Pisans, Genoese, Aragonese, and Austrians. It has since become the island's 2nd largest city and the home to its first university, popularly called "Culleziu," built by the Jesuits from 1559 to 1605. The university's presence has bolstered Sassari's cultural life, crowding its streets with bookstores, museums, tiny restaurants and shops, and plenty of students. With broad *piazze*, winding medieval center, public gardens, and university population, Sassari feels more like a modern Italian city than most other Sardinian destinations—it is quite worth the detour from coastlines and quaint villages to experience this contemporary side of Sardinia.

> **IL TRENINO.** Most Sardinian towns have a small *trenino*, or tourist train, that runs through the town and to some important sights that are hard to reach on foot. Inquire at the tourist office about departure times and destinations.

▐ TRANSPORTATION

Trains: In P. Stazione ☎079 26 03 62, 1 block from P. Sant'Antonio. Take bus #8 from P. d'Italia. Tickets (€0.57) available at bars around town. **Luggage storage** available (see **Practical Information,** below). To: **Alghero** (35min., 11 per day 6:09am-8:55pm, €1.81); **Cagliari** (3½hr., 7 per day 7:06am-6:50pm, €12.10); **Olbia** (2hr., 6 per day 7:06am-8:35pm, €5.60); **Porto Torres** (20min., 9 per day 5:58am-6:45pm, €1.25).

Buses:

ARST (info ☎079 263 92 06 or 236 92 03). Buses depart from V. Italia in the public gardens, and the bus station on V. XXV Aprile, just in front of the train station. To: **Castelsardo** (1hr., 11 per day 7:20am-7:45pm, €2.01); **Nuoro** (1¾hr., 2 per day 9:35am and 2:50pm, €6.30-7.64); **Porto Torres** (35min., 1-2 per hr. 5:20am-10pm, €1.19). Buses run to **Fertilia Airport** (40min., 5 per day 7:25am-7:30pm, €1.76, departures only from the bus station). Tickets sold at Tonni's Bar, C. M. Savoia, 11, and at the ticket office at the bus station.

FDS (☎079 24 13 01). Buses leave from V. XXV Aprile. Tickets are sold on C. Vico, at the bus stop. To: **Alghero** (50min., 13 per day 5:50am-8:15pm, €1.50) and **Castelsardo** (1hr., daily 11:35am, €1.10).

PANI (☎079 23 69 83; fax 267 7560). Buses leave from V. XXV Aprile. Office open M-F 5:30-6:35am, 8:30am-2:15pm, and 5-7:15pm, Sa-Su 5:30-6:35am, 9-9:30am, noon-2:15pm, and 5-7:15pm, or around the time of bus departures. To: **Cagliari** (3-4hr., 7 per day 6am-7:15pm, €13.43); **Oristano** (2¼hr., 4 per day 6:36am-7:15pm, €7.18); **Nuoro** (2½hr., 6 per day 6:36am-7:15pm, €6.77); **Torralba** (1hr., 6 per day 6:36am-7:15pm, €2.32).

Taxis: RadioTaxi (☎079 26 00 60). 24hr.

Car Rental: Avis, V. Mazzini, 2 A/B (☎079 23 55 47). 21+. Open M-Sa 8:30am-12:30pm and 4-7pm. AmEx/MC/V. **Eurorent,** V. Roma, 56 (☎079 23 23 35). Fiats or other small "Class B" vehicles from €60 per day. 21+. Credit card required. Open M-F 8:30am-1pm and 4:30-7pm, Sa 8:30am-noon. MC/V.

✦ 🛈 ORIENTATION AND PRACTICAL INFORMATION

Many buses stop in the **giardini pubblici** before heading to the **bus station.** Since these gardens are close to Sassari's attractions, get off at **Via Italia** in the park. **Emiciclo Garibaldi** lies ahead, a small semi-circular *piazza*, past **Via Margherita di Savoia.** To reach the town center, head straight through Emiciclo Garibaldi to **Via Carlo Alberto,** which spills into **Piazza Italia.** To the right, **Via Roma** runs to the tourist office and the Museo Sanna. To the left lies **Piazza Castello,** packed with people and restaurants, 200m from **Corso Vittorio Emanuele,** a major thoroughfare cutting through the historical town center.

Tourist Office: V. Roma, 62 (☎079 23 17 77; aastss@tiscali.it), a few blocks to the right of P. d'Italia when facing the provincial administration building. Go through the gate and the doorway on the right. English-speaking staff provides **maps** and bus and train schedules. Open M-Th 9am-1pm and 4-6pm, F 9am-1:30pm.

Currency Exchange: Banca Commerciale D'Italia, P. Italia, 22-23, has an **ATM** outside. Open M-F 8:20am-1:20pm and 2:35-4:05pm, Sa 8:20am-11:50pm.

Luggage Storage: ☎079 26 03 62. In the train station. €4 per 12hr. Open daily 6:50am-8:50pm.

English-Language Bookstore: Giunta al Punto, V. Cavour, 16 (☎079 20 13 118). Small selection on 1st floor of mostly British classics. Open daily 9am-8pm. MC/V.

Emergency: ☎113. **Ambulance:** ☎118. **Police:** (☎079 28 35 500), V. Coppino, 1.

Pharmacy: Simon, V. Brigata Sassari, 2 (☎079 23 11 44). Posts after-hours rotations.

Hospital: Ospedale Civile, V. Montegrappa, 82/83 (☎079 20 61 000).

Internet Access: Dream Bar, V. Cavour, 15 (☎079 23 96 26). 4 computers. €3.50 for 30min., €5.20 per hr. Open M-Sa 9am-9:30pm. Cash only.

Post Office: V. Brigata Sassari, 13 (☎079 28 21 267), off P. Castello. Open M-F 8:15am-6pm, Sa 8:15am-1pm. **Currency exchange,** phone cards, and *fermoposta.* **Postal Code:** 07100.

🛏 ACCOMMODATIONS

Sassari has several favorable options both and outside the city limits. ▨**Il Gatto e la Volpe ❷,** Caniga Località Monti di Tesgia, 23, is a funky oasis in the countryside, 5km from the city. Its five rooms have unique color schemes, and some have terrace, kitchenette, and bath. Dynamic young owner Marcello is friendly and accommodating in every way, making guests feel truly at home. Groups of over five people can also book beach and archaeological excursions, sailing trips, and mountain bike rentals (€11 per day). Call for free pick up from the center of town. (☎079 31 80 012 or 328 69 23 248. Breakfast included. Internet and shared kitchen. Reserve ahead. Rooms €22 per person; singles and quads available. Apartments with kitchen €25 for 2, €30 for 1. Extra beds available. Cash only.) **Hotel Leonardo da Vinci ❾**, V. Roma, 79, is worth the splurge. Replete with oriental rugs, imported granite floors, and hallways lined with chandeliers, this hotel also has helpful staff, Internet, and luggage storage in the lobby. The enormous rooms have bath, air-conditioning, phone, minibar, TV, and hair dryer. (☎079 28 07 44; www.leonardodavincihotel.it. Buffet breakfast included. Parking €8 per day. Singles €54-68; doubles €74-92; triples €123. AmEx/MC/V.)

🌀 FOOD

A covered **market** occupies P. Mercato, down V. Rosello from V. V. Emanuele. (Open M-F 8am-noon, Sa 8am-1pm.) A **supermarket** is on the corner of V. Cavour and V. Manno. (☎079 23 72 78. Open M-Sa 8am-9pm.)

Trattoria La Vela Latina, Largo Sisini, 3 (☎ 079 23 37 37), in a *piazza* off V. Arborea. Owner Francesco loves his guests as much as they love his food. Flavorful horse or donkey meat (€10) could win over the most timid of eaters. For something less adventurous, try the *brodo di pesce fresco* (stew of fish, grains, and spices; €8) or *riso alla pescatora (€8)*. Complement your meal with the very popular house red wine. *Primi* €6-10, *secondi* €7-13. Open M-Sa 1-2:30pm and 8-10:30pm. AmEx/MC/V. ❸

Ristorante Trattoria L'Assassino, V. Ospizio Cappucini, 1 (☎079 23 50 41). From V. Battistini, walk through P. Tolla and go down V. Pettinadu, then take a right onto V. Ospizio Cappucini. Comfortable local favorite serves Sardi specialties. Fill up on tender tripe, horse, or roast suckling pig. *Primi* €3.50-8, *secondi* €5-13. 3-course *menù* from land or sea €20. Open M-Sa noon-3pm and 8pm-midnight. Cash only. ❸

Trattoria Da Antonio, V. Arborea, 2/B (☎079 23 42 97), behind the post office. This wood-paneled find is a meat lover's heaven, with a few items available for vegetarians. Ask the waitstaff to recommend horse, donkey, and tentacled creatures. *Primi* €4.50, meat dishes €6-8. Cover €1. Open daily 1-2:30pm and 8:30-10:30pm. MC/V. ❷

Il Senato, V. Alghero, 36 (☎079 27 77 88). Splurge-worthy restaurant, reputedly among Sardinia's best, uses first-rate, seasonally chosen fresh ingredients. Don't miss the *dolce della suocera* (€4), the "mother-in-law cake," with ricotta, almond, and caramelized sugar crust. *Primi* €10, fish €8 per 100g, meat €10-15 per 100g. Open M-Sa 1-3pm and 8-11pm. AmEx/MC/V. ❹

👁 🎵 SIGHTS AND ENTERTAINMENT

Museo Giovanni Antonio Sanna, V. Roma, 64, is an informative and well-presented archaeological museum that gives multilingual guidebooks to visitors. Artifacts dating from the Neolithic Period to the Middle Ages, including arrowheads, tools, ceramics, bronze statuettes, and Romanesque sculptures, chronologically detail the island's history. (☎079 27 22 03. Open Tu-Su 9am-8pm. €2, ages 18-25 €1, EU citizens under 18 or over 65 free.) From the center of town, walk down C. V. Emanuele from P. Castello and turn left on V. al Duomo to P. Duomo to reach Sassari's *duomo*, **Cattedrale di San Nicolò.** Reconstructed in Gothic Catalán style in 1480, only the bell tower remains from the original 13th-century structure. The impressive facade, covered with statues and engravings, conceals an unremarkable interior, though some recently uncovered early frescoes fill the side chapels. (Open daily 8:30am-noon and 4-7:30pm. Free. Modest dress required.)

In the 3rd week in May, the lavish **Sardinian Cavalcade** is Sardinia's largest folk festival. The party includes a parade of costumed emissaries from local villages, a horse exhibition, singing, and dancing. On August 14th, **I Candelieri** brings worker's guilds carrying enormous candles through the streets. The medieval festival is one of the most colorful on the island. Each guild has its own costume, and the candles are decked with flowers and streamers. If it weren't for the **University Pub,** V. Amendola, 49/A, Sassari would be devoid of a hip youth scene. A favorite among locals, the subdued pub offers cheap drinks (beer from €1.60) and overflows with students when school's in session. Request the mysterious Sardinia Island mixed drink (€5.70), with a secret but strong contents. (☎079 20 04 23. Open Sept.-July M and W-Su 8:30pm-1am.)

ALGHERO
☎**079**

Vineyards and ruins are but a short trip away from Alghero's charming palm-lined parks and cobblestone streets. Also known as Barcelonetta, the city has changed hands between everyone from native Sardinians to Spanish *Aragonese* and Ligurian *Genovese*. A distinctly Spanish flair still makes itself felt—in addition to Italian, a dialect of Catalán chimes in the streets. Today, Alghero is known for its proximity to the coastline, dynamic nightlife, and its accessibility for tourists—the recent advent of Ryanair fights to Alghero-Fertilia airport has made Alghero a happening vacation spot.

■ TRANSPORTATION

Flights: ☎079 93 50 39 or 93 52 82. Airport near Fertilia, 6km north of the city. Access via hourly buses from town center and Fertilia. Domestic flights year-round, flights also to Rome, Frankfurt, London, and Barcelona (www.ryanair.com).

Trains: FDS (☎079 95 07 85) on V. Don Minzoni, in the northern part of the city. Take **AP** or **AF bus** from in front of Casa del Caffè in the park (3 per hr.) or walk 1km along port. Taxis €7 from center. Open daily 5:45am-9pm. Buy tickets at **FS stand** in the park and ride the bus to the station for free, or buy from *biglietteria* in station. **Luggage storage** available (see **Practical Information**). To **Sassari** (40min.; 11 per day 6:01am-8:47pm; €1.81, round-trip €3.10). Reduced service Su.

Buses:

ARST (☎800 86 50 42) and **FDS** (☎078 95 04 58). Tickets at stand in the public gardens (☎079 95 01 79). Blue buses depart V. Catalogna, next to park. To: **Bosa** (1½hr., 2 per day 6:35am and 7:30pm, €2.89-3.72); **Porto Torres** (1hr., up to 7 per day 4:45am-8:45pm, €2.32); **Sassari** (1hr., 1-2 per hr. 5:35am-7pm, €2.58).

FDS also runs orange **city buses** (☎079 95 04 58). Buy tickets (€0.57) at *tabaccherie.* Buses run from V. Cagliari (in front of Casa del Caffè) to the airport (20min., 6 per day 5:45am-8:30pm). **Line AF** runs between Fertilia and V. Cagliari, stopping at the port (40min.; every 40min.; from Alghero 7:10am-9:30pm, from Fertilia 7:50am-9:50pm). **AP** (from Vle. della Resistenza) buses run to train station (every 40min. 6:20am-9pm). **AO** (from V. Cagliari) heads to the *lido* (beach) and the hospital (2 per hr. 7:15am-8:45pm). **AC** (from V. Liguria) runs to **Carmine** (2 per hr. 7:15am-8:45pm). Tourist offices provides a complete schedule.

Taxis: On V. Emanuele (☎079 97 53 96) across from the BNL bank, or at the airport (☎079 93 50 35). Both stand and number are quite unreliable late at night—plan ahead if you are going on a crazy night out.

Car Rental: Avis, P. Sulis, 9 (☎079 97 95 77; www.avisautonoleggio.it), or Fertilia airport (☎079 93 50 64). Cars from €60 per day with unlimited mileage. 25+. Credit card required. Open M-F 8:30am-1pm and 4-7pm, Sa 8:30am-1pm. AmEx/MC/V. **Europcar** (☎079 93 50 32; www.europcar.it), at the airport. From €70 per day, including insurance. 150km max. per day. Open daily 8am-11pm. AmEx/MC/V.

Bike and Scooter Rental: Cycloexpress di Tomaso Tilocca (☎079 98 69 50; www.cicloexpress.com), at the harbor near the intersection of V. Garibaldi and V. Spano. Bikes €7-13 per day, tandems €15 per day, electric scooters €15 per day, motor scooters €23-50 per day. Open M-Sa 9am-1pm and 4-8:30pm, Su 9am-1pm. AmEx/MC/V.

🧭 ORIENTATION AND PRACTICAL INFORMATION

ARST buses stop at the corner of **Via Catalogna** and **Via Cagliari,** on the waterfront one block from the **port.** The tourist office, in **Piazza Porta Terra,** lies diagonally across the small park, on the right beyond the easily visible towers of the *centro storico.* The **train station** is a hike from the town center but accessible by local orange buses (lines AF and AP). To walk from the station, follow **Via Don Minzoni** until it becomes **Via Garibaldi** along the waterfront.

Tourist Office: P. Porta Terra, 9 (☎079 97 90 54; www.infoalghero.it), on the right from the bus stop, toward the old city. Multilingual staff offers an indexed street **map,** tours of the city, and daytrips to local villages. Open M-Sa 8am-8pm.

Currency Exchange: Banca Nazionale del Lavoro, V. Emanuele, 5 (☎079 98 01 22), across from the tourist office, has a 24hr. **ATM.** Open M-F 8:20am-1:20pm and 3-4:30pm, Sa 8:20-11:50am. Currency exchange also at the **post office.**

Luggage Storage: In train station. €1 per day.

Emergency: ☎113. **Carabinieri:** ☎112. **Police:** P. della Mercede, 7 (☎113 or 97 20 01). **Ambulance:** ☎118. **First Aid:** ☎079 99 62 33.

Pharmacy: Farmacia Puliga di Mugoni, V. Sassari, 8 (☎079 97 90 26). Posts after-hours rotations. Open May-Oct. M-Sa 9am-1pm and 5-9pm AmEx/MC/V.

Hospital: Ospedale Civile (☎079 99 62 00), on V. Don Minzoni in Regione la Pietraia.

Internet Access: Bar Miramar, V. Gramisci, 2. 3 computers; expect a wait. €1.60 for 15min., €5 per hr. Open daily 8:30am-1pm and 2:30pm-12:30am. Cash only.

Post Office: V. Carducci 33/35 (☎079 972 02 31), has *fermoposta* and **currency exchange.** Open M-F 8:15am-6:15pm, Sa 8am-1:15pm. **Postal Code:** 07041.

🏠 ACCOMMODATIONS AND CAMPING

🏨 **Hostal del'Alguer (HI),** V. Parenzo, 79 (☎/fax 079 93 20 39 or 079 93 04 78), in Fertilia. From the port, take bus AF to Fertilia; turn right and walk down the street. Hostel, an outdoor complex of several buildings, is on the right, with reception in building farthest from street. Fun-loving staff offers 100 beds, bike rental, bar, pool table, and info on attractions. Internet, bus ticket purchase, and phone in lobby. HI members only. Breakfast included. Large lunch or dinner €10. Reception 7am-noon and 3:30pm-midnight. 4- to 6-bed dorms €16; family rooms with 2 beds €18-25. ❶

🏨 **Hotel San Francesco,** V. Machin, 2 (☎ 079 98 03 30; www.sanfrancescohotel.com), in the heart of the *centro storico.* 20 simple, clean rooms in this 4th-century church cloister have bath, A/C, TV, phone, and beautiful stone walls. Enjoy breakfast on a terrace encircling the church courtyard, which hosts a popular classical music festival in the summer. Breakfast included. Reservation required June-Aug. Singles €40-55; doubles €73-90; triple €95-120. MC/V. ❹

Hotel La Margherita, V. Sassari, 70 (☎079 97 90 06; fax 079 97 64 17), near P. Mercedes. 53 spacious rooms with A/C, phone, and TV in a central location. Rooftop terrace has a view of the waterfront and is good for socializing and sunbathing. Free umbrellas and lounge chairs at a local beach. Breakfast included. Singles €55-75; doubles €80-110. Extra bed €10-40. AmEx/MC/V. ❺

CHEWING THE FAT

I have been chatting with Efisio at a cafe. We're talking about Sardinia and how tourism is affecting the lives of country folks such as himself. After finishing off his espresso, he grabs his cellular phone, has an abrupt conversation in Sard, and begins to get up.

"We go hunt pig," he says decidedly.

After having been told, not asked, what I was doing that afternoon, I wonder how one hunts pigs. Pigs live in pigpens, and root around in the mud. They don't seem difficult to hunt. They just sort of stand there. It dawns on me, as Efisio and I enter his rust-covered truck, that my friend's weak command of English has misled me. Surely we're going to his farm to *slaughter* pigs.

My stomach turns. I've never seen an animal slaughtered, and I'm not interested in having this be the first time. But it is too late. We're already speeding down dirt roads through the dry, rocky countryside of Sardinia.

Off we go with Efisio's pals, through stunning country seemingly untouched by human hands. We abruptly pull off the dirt road. They lift the flatbed tarp. Bows, arrows, and spears. Ah, I get it. We're not hunting pigs. We're hunting boars.

I get a 2min. explanation. Shoot arrows at a boar to make him angry and get him to charge. When he charges, grab the spear and make a circle, and stick him when he gets close enough. I

Bed and Breakfast MamaJuana, Vco. Adami, 12 (☎339 13 69 791; www.mamajuana.it), on a side street in the heart of the old town, parallel to V. Roma. 4 eclectic medieval rooms are spruced up with antique furniture and lovely paintings, plus bath and TV. Housekeeping for extra fee. Breakfast included at a nearby cafe. Arrival 9am-9pm, call in advance. Singles €40-60; doubles €60-80. Cash only. ❹

La Mariposa, V. Lido, 22 (☎079 95 03 60; www.lamariposa.it). Campground near the beach, 1.5km from Alghero toward Fertilia, offers restaurant, bar, market, bike rental, diving, and beach access. Laundry €5 per load. Reserve ahead in summer. Open Mar.-Oct. €7-10.50 per person, ages 3-12 €4.80-5, €3-8 per tent, €2-4 per car. Apr.-June tents and cars free. 4-person bungalows €44-75. Hot showers €0.50. AmEx/MC/V. ❶

🍴 FOOD

On Wednesday, there is an **open-air market** on V. Garibaldi and P.le della Pace. Walk about 15min. from the city center to **Antiche Cantine del Vino Sfuso,** C. V. Emanuele, 80, where you can sample and purchase local wholesale red, white, and rose wines for a mere €1.27 per L—bring your own plastic bottle. (Open M-Sa 8:30am-1pm and 4:30-8pm. MC/V.) A **SISA** supermarket is at V. Sassari, 49. (Open M-Sa 8am-9pm, Su 8am-1:30pm and 5-8:30pm.)

▧ Encontre del'Ateneu, Bastioni Marco Polo, 41. Located right along the waterfront, with a funky Mediterranean lounge feeling, Encontre del'Ateneu serves up refreshingly creative dishes like pasta with shrimp, green beans, lime, and mint. In the evening, the adjoining bar fills up with romantics listening to lounge music. *Primi* €8; *secondi* €15, including a *contorno* (vegetable or starch). Open daily 12:30-3pm and 7:30-11pm. ❸

Osteria Taverna Paradiso, V. Umberto, 29 (☎079 97 80 01). Stone-vaulted ceilings and good meat and fish make for charming dining in the *centro storico*. Try the platter of local cheeses (€7.25-8.30) for dessert. *Primi* €6.20-12, *secondi* €7.20-13. 3-course *menù* €13.50-22.50. Open daily noon-2:30pm and 7:30pm-midnight. MC/V. ❸

Trattoria Maristella, V. Kennedy, 9 (☎079 97 81 72). Slightly removed from the historical center, this local haunt serves some of the best fish in town. Come for laidback meals at exceptional value. Try the *fregola con cozze e vongole* (semolina pasta cooked with mussels and clams; €8). *Primi* €7.50-8, *secondi* €7-12.50. AmEx/MC/V. ❸

Ristorante da Ninetto, V. Gioberti, 4 (☎079 97 80 62). From P. Porta Terra, take V. Simon and turn right on V.

Gioberti. Snug restaurant housed in an 8th-century *frantoio* (olive press) with arched stone ceilings. Savory fare includes a fresh fish selection and homemade *seadas* (€4). *Primi* € 8-20, *secondi* €10-20. Open daily 12:15-3pm and 7:15pm-midnight. AmEx/MC/V. ❺

Al Tuguri, V. Maiorca, 113 (☎/fax 079 97 67 72; www.altuguri.it). Delicious variations on traditional cuisine give Tuguri its stellar reputation. Try the exceptional 5-course *menù* with meat, fish, or vegetarian dishes (€34). *Primi* €8.50-9.50, *secondi* €8.50-16. Open M-Sa 12:30-2pm and 8-10:30pm. Reserve ahead. MC/V. ❺

👁 SIGHTS

A leisurely walk through the *centro storico* reveals tiny alleys, half-hidden churches, and ancient town walls. The old city is hard to navigate without a map, so stop by the tourist office before heading inside. The **Torre di Porta Terra** dominates the entrance to the town near the public gardens. It was financed by the Jewish community in the 15th-century and consequently is known as the **Torre degli Ebrei** (Tower of the Jews). Heading down V. Roma, Alghero's **duomo, La Cattedrale di S. Maria,** is at the intersection with V. P. Umberto. Begun in 1552, it took 178 years to construct, resulting in a stunning, motley Gothic-Catalán-Renaissance facade. Rebuilt in the 19th-century, the cathedral has Gothic choirs, a mosaic of John the Baptist, and the original Porta Petita (small door) from the Catalán structure. About a block from the *duomo*, down V. Principe Umberto are the **Teatro Civico,** built in the 19th century, and the **Palazzo Machin,** a classic example of Gothic-Catalán architecture. A right turn from V. Roma on V. Carlo Alberto reveals the **Chiesa di San Francesco.** The heavy Neo-Classical facade conceals a graceful Gothic internal structure and a beautiful marble altar. (Open M-F 9:30am-noon and 5-6:20pm, Su 5-7:30pm. Free. Modest dress required.) Heading away from the harbor, V. Carlo Alberto arrives at the beautiful **Chiesa di San Michele** at P. Ginnasio, built between 1661 and 1675 and dedicated to the patron saint of Alghero. V. Carlo Alberto ends at P. Sulis and the **Torre dello Sperone,** where French soldiers were imprisoned in 1412 after failing to capture the Catalán fortress. In the 19th century, Sardinian patriot Vincenzo Sulis was a prisoner here; on the side of the tower rest two old canons, used now by youngsters as a playground.

The countryside around Alghero is filled with spectacular nature reserves, inland mountains, and cliffs plunging into the sea, making it a popular destination for trekking and bicycling. Inquire at the have no idea how I got myself into this, but I nod and follow along.

We walk into the woods. Efisio stops, grabs my arm, and points. He's excited, and wants me to shoot an arrow. I have no idea what I'm shooting at, but release my arrow. It rips through the woods and lodges in a tree trunk. I'm proud that I shot an arrow without injuring myself, but while I'm admiring my work, Efisio has sent a few arrows toward the boar and everyone is grabbing their spears. I do the same.

As the beast comes charging from the woods, I instinctively run backward. All I know is that some ugly thing with horns is not happy, and is going to try his best not to end up wrapped up in cellophane at the supermarket. I would do the same in his position.

The men begin to close around each other, and as it approaches, they use all their force and shove their spears deep into the boar's back and chest. It squeals and twitches and flails for what seems like 10min. Then all of a sudden, quiet.

Efisio waves me over. I look around and realize that I am a good 200 feet from the rest of them, holding my spear upside-down, ready to do harm to nothing in particular. I walk over. Efisio's buddies are gutting the animal, and on the ground next to it is its tongue that has already been cut out. We sit around, have a few drinks, a few laughs, and a few bites of tongue. All in a day's work, at least in Sardinia.

—Yaran Noti

tourist office for a comprehensive list of itineraries. One of the most popular parks, the **Le Prigionette Nature Reserve,** lies at **Porto Conte,** off the Fertlia-Porto Conte highway on the road to Capo Caccia. Buses heading toward the Grotte di Nettuno pass by the reserve three times daily. Bike and hiking paths wind through mountains past slopping valleys filled with grazing wild horses. The forestry house at the park entrance supplies good **maps** and advice. (☎079 94 90 60. Open daily 8am-4pm.) **FDS buses** also lead directly to Porto Conte (30min.; every hr. 7:10am-11:30pm, last return midnight; €0.88), where a dirt road leads to **Punta Giglio Reserve.** The rough road is a difficult but popular route for bikers, ending after 3km at a limestone peak on Punta Giglio. This point has the most impressive views in the region, as well as several WWII barracks. The seaside highways heading away from Alghero around the Porto Conte and Capo Caccia area are also popular for biking and quite safe thanks to low traffic levels.

🎵 🎭 ENTERTAINMENT AND NIGHTLIFE

Alghero comes alive at night, with people streaming through the cramped streets of the *centro storico* and pouring onto the promenade through the early morning hours. (Hostelers beware: the last bus to Fertilia is at 11:30pm, and taxis are few and far between.) In the summer months, locals in search of warm evening breezes and decent bands head to the open-air bars along **Lungomare Dante,** and along the waterfront all the way to Fertilia. Both locals and tourists also find amusements aplenty at **Poco Loco,** V. Gramsci, 8, heading inland from Lungomare Dante past P. Sulis. Famed for its pizza-by-the-meter (€17-27; 0.5m also available), Poco has many attractions—six bowling lanes, Internet (€5.20 per hr.), and great live music on summer weekends. (☎079 97 31 034. Live music F-Sa 11pm. Beer from €2; cocktails €5.50. Open in summer daily 8pm-3am or later. MC/V.)

🎭 DAYTRIP FROM ALGHERO

GROTTE DI NETTUNO

FDS buses (☎079 95 01 79) run to Capo Caccia (50min.; 3 per day 9:15am-5:10pm, last return 6:05pm; €1.76). Or take the pleasant Navisarda Grotte di Nettuno ferry boat tour. Boats (☎079 97 62 02, 079 95 06 03, or 079 97 89 61) leave Alghero's Bastione della Maddalena (2½hr. round-trip, including tour of caves; June-Sept. 8 per day 9am-5pm; Apr.-May and Oct. 9, 10am, and 3pm; round-trip €12, under 13 €6). Entrance to caves €10.

The Duke of Buckingham dubbed the ◼**Grotte di Nettuno** "the miracle of the gods." These majestic caves, first discovered by fishermen, have been around for 60 to 70 million years and today are one of Sardinia's most frequented tourist destinations. Thanks to modern lighting, the caves today are glorious, with colored lights casting blue, green, and yellow shades on different parts of the grotto—the effect is magical. Well-run 30min. tours are conducted in English, French, German, and Italian. The caves are in **Capo Caccia,** a steep promontory that juts out from **Porto Conte.** Built in 1954, the steep **Escala del Cabirol** provides access to the grotto by land for those brave enough to walk down the 632 steps that plunge to the sea between massive white cliffs. (☎079 94 65 40. Open daily Apr.-Sept. 9am-7pm; Oct. 10am-4pm; Nov.-Mar. 9am-1pm. Groups admitted every hr. €10.) ARST buses to Capo Caccia stop at the **Nuraghi di Palmavera** (☎079 95 32 00; fax 079 98 87 65), 3km past Fertilia, where a central tower surrounded by 50 huts forms a limestone complex dating from 1500 BC. (Open Apr.-Oct. 9am-7pm; Nov.-Mar. 9:30am-4pm.) The **S.I.L.T. cooperative** at V. E. Mattei, 14 (☎079 98 00 40; www.coopsilt.it) offers tours in English, French, German, and Spanish on request only. (Every hr. 9:15am-12:15pm and 4-6pm, €3-5.)

PORTO TORRES   ☎ 079

Founded in 27 BC, the village of Turris Libissonis served as one of the Roman
Empire's principal ports along trade routes between Sicily and Africa. Today, the
Roman ruins and Romanesque 12th-century church are worth a glimpse, but dominated by industry and port bustle, Porto Torres is otherwise quite forgettable and
best visited during an afternoon while you wait for a train to your next destination.

TRANSPORTATION. Trains (☎079 51 46 36), on V. Fontana Vecchia near the
port, are synchronized with ferries, running to Sassari (20min., 1-2 per hr. 5:40am-
9:50pm, €1.25) and continuing to Olbia, and also going to Cagliari via Oristano.
ARST buses (☎079 263 92 00 or 800 86 50 42) run from the port and along C. V.
Emanuele. The bus stop system can be confusing; talk to the driver before getting
on for more specific information. Tickets are available in **Bar Acciaro,** C. V. Emanuele, 38, and the bar **Green Point,** on the port. Buses run to: Alghero (1hr., 7 per
day 6:05am-10:05pm, €2.32); Fertilia Airport (40min., 8:15am and 2pm, €1.55);
and Sassari (35min., 1-4 per hr. 6:05am-10pm, €1.19). **APT** runs local buses
throughout the city. **Taxis** (☎079 51 40 52) are on C. V. Emanuele.

ORIENTATION AND PRACTICAL INFORMATION. Porto Torres has one
major thoroughfare, **Corso Vittorio Emanuele,** which leaves from **Piazza Colombo**
where the buses stop and runs to the sea from the port. From the train station,
take a right on **Via Fontana Vecchia** and then a quick left on **Via Eleanora d'Arborea,**
which ends at C. V. Emanuele. The **Pro Loco Tourist Office,** V. Roma, 3, is in **Piazza
Garibaldi,** the first left off C. V. Emanuele when coming from P. Colombo. The
staff provides **maps,** bus schedules, and info on local sights, beaches, and excursions. (☎079 504 19 97. Open July-Sept. daily 9am-8pm; call for reduced winter
hours.) Farther up the street, the **BNL** bank, C. V. Emanuele, 18/20, has an **ATM**
outside. (Open M-F 8:30am-1:30pm and 2:45-4:15pm, Sa 8:30am-noon.) In case of
emergency, call the **carabinieri** (☎079 50 24 32) or an **ambulance** (☎079 50 80 70).
Farmacia Rubatiu, C. V. Emanuele, 73, is down the block from the bank. (☎079 51
40 88. Open M-Sa 9:15am-1pm and 5-8:30pm.) The **post office** is at V. Ponte
Romano, 83. (Open M-Sa 8:15am-1:15pm.) **Postal Code:** 07046.

ACCOMMODATIONS AND FOOD. Centrally located on the water just off
of P. Colombo, **Hotel Elisa ❹** offers guests spacious rooms with nice wooden furniture, a popular restaurant, and four generations of family experience. All 26 rooms
have bath, TV, phone, hair dryer, and fridge, and most have balcony or windows
with sea views. (☎079 51 32 60; fax 079 51 37 86. Buffet breakfast included. Singles
€45-50; doubles €68-73; triples €86-93; quads €94-113. AmEx/MC/V.) To reach
Albergo Royal ❸, V. S. Satta, 8, from the port or bus stop, walk up C. V. Emanuele
away from the water until you see the yellow sign for the hotel. Turn left and walk
300m along V. Petronia and then left on V. Satta. The rooms have simple but comfortable decor. All come with bath, TV, and A/C, and some with balcony. (☎079 50
22 78. Singles €30-35; doubles €50-65; triples €60-70. Cash only.)

In the morning, an **outdoor market** is at the intersection of V. Delle Vigne and V.
Sacchi. A **SISA** supermarket is on V. Mare, 24. (☎079 50 10 24. Open daily 8am-
8:30pm. AmEx/MC/V.) Locals and visitors flock to **Piazza Garibaldi ❷,** P. Garibaldi,
13, a bright two-floor restaurant with outdoor seating, tasty pizza (€3-8.50), and
late-night drinks. (☎079 50 15 70; www.piazzagaribaldi.net. *Bruschetta* €3.50-4.
Risotto €6.50-7.50. *Primi* €6-7.50. Beer from €1. Open daily 12:15-3:30pm and
7pm-1am. AmEx/MC/V.) Head to **Trattoria La Tana ❷,** V. Cavour, 25, for traditional
gnochetti alla sarda (€4) or a nice fillet of horse (€9) in the comfortable dining
room. (☎079 50 22 46. Pizza €3-6. *Primi* €3-4.50, *secondi* €5.50-10.50. Open in
summer daily noon-4pm and 7pm-midnight; closed Tu in winter.) A fun lunch spot

is **Fuori Orario ❸**, P. XX Settembre, 7, with outdoor or indoor seating and a standard Sardinian menu, including inexpensive *panini*. (☎079 51 32 54. *Panini* €3.50-€4.50. *Primi* €7-13, *secondi* €10-12. Open daily 12:30-4:30pm and 7pm-midnight.)

🄶🄲 **SIGHTS AND BEACHES.** The ruins of the **Roman Thermal Baths** attest to the wealth and success of Turris Libissonis as a Roman grain port. Popularly referred to as **Palazzo Re Barbaro,** the ruins were believed to be the ancient seat of Sardinian Governor Barbaro (slayer of local saints Gavino, Proto, and Gianuario) until excavations turned up the three traditional bath chambers. The baths are accessible from the museum **Antiquarium Turritano**, V. Ponte Romane, 99, which houses ancient Roman artifacts, including mosaics, jewelry, and pottery, with descriptions in Italian. (☎333 25 43 14. Open 9am-8pm. €2.50, students €1.50. Guided visits in English available M-Sa 9:30am-1:30pm and 3:30-7pm.) The town also boasts the 12th-century **Basilica di San Gavino,** the largest and oldest Romanesque-Pisan church in Sardinia; entrances are in the long side-walls, not in the front or back. Soak up some rays at the two **beaches** along Porto Torres's shore. Though framed by the port in the background, **Spiaggia Lungo Scoglio,** 250m from the port, is family-friendly, complete with a metal dolphin diving over a rock that juts out of the water. **Spaggia di Balai,** about 10min. down Lungomare Balai, is larger and more secluded, separated from the road by a small, grassy park.

PALAU   ☎0789

Situated on the luminous waters of Sardinia's northern coast, Palau is both a gorgeous destination and a convenient base for exploring La Maddalena. Palau's most famous sight is the Roccia dell'Orso, an enormous rock that the mistral winds have carved into the shape of a bear. It was an object of intrigue even in Homer's day, and is immortalized in his *Odyssey* with a warning of the ferocious *Lestrigoni* people that lived around it. Palau is now a heavily touristed town composed of modern buildings in Sardinian pastel shades. Though the town does have some nice restaurants and a spectacular pair of camping facilities, the real attraction is the incomparable coastline nearby.

🄴🄻 **TRANSPORTATION AND PRACTICAL INFORMATION.** The port end of **Via Nazionale,** Palau's single major thoroughfare, contains a white building that houses a bar, ferry ticket offices, and a newsstand that sells ARST bus tickets (buses stop outside). **ARST buses** run to Olbia (14 per day; €2.32 to the *centro*, €2.58 to the port) and Santa Teresa di Gallura (7 per day 7:55am-9:25pm, €1.72). **EneRmaR** (☎199 76 00 02) and **Saremar Ferries** (☎0789 70 92 70) serve the island of La Maddalena (15min.; 3 per hr. 7:15am-2am; round-trip €5.80, under 12 €2.20, cars €8.40-16.80, bicycles free).

Palau's ⬛**tourist office,** V. Nazionale, 109, slightly uphill from the center of town on the left as you head away from the port, offers info on beaches, outdoor activities, and tours of neighboring islands, as well as a wealth of publications about Sardinia and the Palau region. (☎/fax 0789 70 95 70. Open M-Sa 8:30am-1pm and 5-8pm, Su 9am-12:30pm and 5-8pm. **Banca di Sassari,** V. Roma, 9, has **currency exchange** and **ATMs** in front. (Open M-F 8:20am-1:20pm and 2:30-3:30pm, Sa 8:20am-12:30pm.) In case of **emergency,** dial ☎113, contact the **carabinieri** at ☎112, or call the **medical clinic** at ☎0789 70 93 96. **Farmacia Nicolai** is at V. delle Ginestre, 19. (☎0789 70 95 16, for urgent needs 0789 70 83 53. Open M-Sa 9am-12:30pm and 5-8pm. AmEx/MC/V.) The **Guardia Medica Turistica,** located on V. degli Achei on the way toward Baia Saraceno from the port, offers quick, friendly checkups and prescriptions for travelers' ailments. Open 9:30am-1:30pm and 4:30-7:30pm, with a doctor always on-call. The **post office** is on the bottom floor of a building complex at the intersection of V. Garibaldi and V. La Maddalena—follow the signs. (☎0789 70 85 27. Open M-F 8:15am-1:15pm, Sa 8:15am-12:45pm.)

ACCOMMODATIONS AND FOOD. Accommodations in Palau are often prohibitively expensive; if you are desperate for air-conditioning and a break from the beach, paying high prices at hotels instead of the campgrounds will be necessary; otherwise, the campgrounds provide a stellar budget option. **Hotel La Roccia ❺**, V. dei Mille, 15, has a lobby built around an enormous boulder, and themed rooms, like "Il Faro" (the lighthouse). All 22 rooms have balcony, air-conditioning, phone, TV, bath, and share a lovely small outdoor garden. (☎0789 70 95 28; www.hotellaroccia.com. Breakfast included. Reserve ahead. Singles €45-85; doubles €75-125. Extra bed additional 35%. AmEx/MC/V.) The fading **Hotel del Molo ❺**, on V. dei Ciclopi, 25, has a pleasant staff and 14 quiet rooms, all with air-conditioning, TV, phone, bath, and fridge, some with balcony and charming sea view. (☎0789 70 80 42. At mid-season, singles €70; doubles €80; triples €120. AmEx/MC/V.) Among the attractive camping options, **Acapulco ❶**, Loc. Punta Palau, has a private beach, a bar with nightly piano music, a pizzeria, and a restaurant. It also arranges underwater spear-fishing and excursions to La Maddalena Archipelago. (☎0789 70 94 97; www.campingacapulco.com. Open Mar.1-Oct. 15. Reserve ahead in summer. Adults €8-16.50, children ages 4-12 €5.50-11, tent and hot shower included. Bungalows with mandatory half pension €38-54. 4-person caravans €52-89. Set of 2 towels €6. Electricity €2.50. AmEx/MC/V.) Another camping option, though less desirable than Acapulco, is **Baia Saraceno ❶**, Loc. Puna Nera, 1. Follow the *lungomare* away from the port and then follow the signs to Baia Saraceno. Located across the docks from the port and behind a man-made forest, Baia Saraceno also offers camping facilities with picturesque beaches 500m outside Palau. There are no singles, and the white stucco bungalows are very expensive for minimal amenities. Restaurant, pizzeria, and a bar are interspersed among trees along the coastline. The facility arranges water sports and trips to nearby islands. (☎078 97 09 403; www.baiasaraceno.com. Adults €8-17, children 4-12 years €5.50-11. Bungalows and *tukuls* with half pension €35-52; bungalows with kitchen €62-115; 4-person caravan €52-89. Electricity €2.50. AmEx/MC/V for over €100.)

Numerous bakeries and stores line V. Nazionale, and a **market** every Friday (8am-1pm) crowds the harbor with fresh cheeses, meats, clothing, and crafts. The friendly waitstaff of **L'Uva Fragola ❶**, P. V. Emanuele, 2, serve a variety of crisp, refreshing salads (€5.50-10.50), spaghetti (€4.50-7), and 39 types of creative pizzas (€3.56-8.00) with toppings like octopus and egg. Savor a homemade dessert at the bright green tables. (☎0789 70 87 65. Cover €1. Open daily noon-3pm and 7-11pm. MC/V.) **Ristorante da Robertino ❸**, V. Nazionale, 20, is a pleasant restaurant with flavorful pastas (spaghetti with shellfish; €11) and delicious fresh fish. (☎0789 70 96 10. *Primi* €5.50-12, *secondi* €8-18. Cover €1.55. Open Tu-Su 1-2:30pm and 8-10pm. Reserve 2 days in advance. MC/V.) **Ristorante Il Covo ❸**, V. Sportiva, 12, serves seafood and traditional, meat-heavy Sardinian cuisine at reasonable prices. The *pasta dello chef* (pasta with fresh vegetables, anchovies, and olives; €8) and the lamb with balsamic vinegar dressing are original options. (☎0789 70 96 08. Pizza €5.80-8. *Primi* €6.80-10, *secondi* €5-14.50. 4-course dinner €30. Cover €1.90. Open daily noon-2:30pm and 7-11:30pm. AmEx/MC/V.)

SIGHTS. The little **Spiaggia Palau Vecchia** is the beach to the left of the port when facing the water. Its shores are shaded most of the day, and therefore not the best for those set on a tan. Check out the **Roccia dell'Orso,** Palau's trademark curiosity, from where you can enjoy stunning views of the countryside and port. **Cara-**

melli buses run to the rock at **Capo d'Orso** (15min.; 5 per day 7:30am-6pm, last return 6:20pm; €0.62) from the port, 3km from town along V. Capo d'Orso. Be sure to bring strong shoes for the long stair climb. If you want to see the Roccia without the exercise, look back toward Palau as you take the ferry to La Maddalena—it can sometimes be seen at the right side of the hill to the left of Palau. Caramelli also runs to **Porto Pollo** (30min.; 5 per day 8:15am-7:20pm, last return 7:55pm; €1.19), a beach where Mediterranean scrub and seaweed sway under the water. Several private boat companies run full-day tours of the archipelago.

LA MADDALENA ARCIPELAGO ☎0789

Corsica and Sardinia were once joined by a massive land bridge; La Maddalena, Caprera, and the 50-plus smaller islands that surround them are its fragmented remains. Though visitors crowd the streets and relax on calm, white-sand beaches, tourism has not spoiled the islands; the entire archipelago is a national park, and commercial development is strictly regulated. In addition, Italian patriots mob La Maddalena for their own reasons: their national hero, the unifier Giuseppe Garibaldi, made the nearby island of Caprera his home while he was in exile. The other main residents of La Maddalena are the members and families of a US Naval Station, located along V. Principe Amedeo, which explains why so many people speak English on the small Sardinian islands.

▐▌ TRANSPORTATION AND PRACTICAL INFORMATION

EneRmaR (☎199 76 00 02) and **Saremar** (☎0789 70 92 70) run **ferries** between Palau and La Maddalena (15min.; 3 per hr. 7:15am-2am; €2.90 per person, €8.40-16.80 per car, bicycles free). For **taxi service,** call ☎0789 73 65 00 or 0789 72 20 80. Rent **bikes** and **motor scooters** at **Nicola,** V. Amendola, 18. (☎0789 73 54 00. Bikes €10 per day. Motor scooters €20-50 per day. Open daily 8am-8pm.)

A **tourist office** is in P. des Geneys, on the waterfront. (☎0789 73 63 21. Open May-Oct. M-Sa 9am-1pm and 5-7pm.) A **Banco di Sardegna,** on V. Amendola off P. XXIV Febbraio, has **currency exchange** and a 24hr. **ATM.** (Open M-F 8:20am-1:20pm and 2:35-4:05pm.) A self-service **laundromat, Azzura Lavanderia,** is at V. Dei Mille, 3. (☎389 97 24 027. Wash €4 per 6kg, dry €5. Open M-Sa 9am-1pm and 4:30-8pm. Cash only.) In case of **emergency,** call the **carabinieri** at ☎0789 73 70 04 or 0789 73 69 43, an **ambulance** at ☎118, or the **hospital** at ☎0789 79 12 00. There is a **pharmacy** at the corner of P. S. Maria Maddalena and V. Marsala which is open 9am-1pm and 5-8:30pm and is able to fill prescriptions. **Patsi Net Internet Point,** V. Montanara, 4, has fast connections. (☎0789 73 10 55; fax 0789 72 19 19. €6 per hr. Open daily 9am-1pm and 5-9:30pm; July-Aug. closed Su. AmEx/MC/V.) A **post office** is in P. Umberto, 1, across the street from the main part of the *piazza.* (☎0789 79 09 00. Open M-F 8:15am-6:15pm, Sa 8:15am-noon.) **Postal Code:** 07024.

▐▌ ACCOMMODATIONS AND FOOD

Hotel Arcipelago ❹, V. Indipendenza, 2, is a good deal, though it's a 20min. walk from the center of town. From P. Umberto, follow V. Mirabello along the water until reaching the intersection with the stoplight. Turn left here, then take your first right on V. Indipendenza. Continue uphill, taking the first left on a branch of the main road. The hotel is around the corner from the grocery store. Twelve rooms come tastefully furnished with wooden furniture and paintings, all with TV, phone, large bath, and view. (☎0789 72 73 28. Breakfast included. Reservation required July-Aug. Singles €43-55; doubles €60-82; triples €70-110. V.) Up V. Indipendenza before you turn left for Archipelago, **Hotel La Conchiglia ❹**, V. Indipendenza, 3, has seven comfortable rooms that offer superb amenities, including air-conditioning, bath, TV, phone, microwave and minifridge. (☎0789 72 80 26. Breakfast included. Singles €40-60; doubles €80-100. AmEx/MC/V.)

Pick up lunch at the **Comiti** supermarket, V. Amendola, 6, at the intersection with V. Italia. (☎0789 73 90 05. Open M-Sa 8:30am-1:30pm and 5:15-8:15pm, Su 9am-1pm. MC/V.) Young and hip locals and tourists flock to **Garden Bar ❸**, V. Garibaldi, 61, for its tasty, varied cuisine, friendly owner Spike, and couches at the tables upstairs. Try the *bruschetta* (€1.50-4) for a small snack. (☎0787 73 88 25. Pizza €3.50-7.50. *Primi* €5-13, *secondi* €5-20. Cover €1.50. Open daily 11:30am-3pm and 5-11pm. MC/V.)

🌊 🏝 BEACHES AND ISLANDS

The islands surrounding La Maddalena are paradises of uninhabited natural beauty. Their national park status protects them from development and curbs the activity of tourists who bathe in the sparkling coves. Some claim that these waters, radiating in brilliant shades of green and blue, are the clearest in the world. Some spots have been closed off altogether, including the forested island **Budelli** and its beach, **Spiaggia Rossa**. Fortunately, the nearby island **Razzoli** has equally magnificent swimming holes, and sightseers can still set out to islands like **Santa Maria,** with its long, white sand cove, by boat. Santa Maria's **lighthouse,** a 20min. stroll from the beach down a labeled trail, looks out over the surrounding islands, including nearby **Spargi.** The waters in Spargi's **Cala Verde** bay shimmer in stunning shades of green. On Spargi's western side, lovers canoodle on the shores of the pristine **Cala dell'Amore.** Around **Cala Corsara,** windswept rock formations reward the adventurous with spectacular vistas. Without a private yacht or powerboat, the only way to explore the archipelago is on a full-day **boat tour** on what are affectionately termed "spaghetti boats" for their afternoon pasta lunches. Companies like ▓**Delfino Bianco di Ulisse** (☎347 36 63 628 or 0789 73 86 66) send ticketsellers to the docks of Palau mornings and evenings. Packing up to 100 people, the cruises are fun and informative, as guides point out the garish or whimsical rock formations along the way. Tours cost €30-35 and typically include a pasta lunch and two or three 2hr. stops at beaches along the way, often at Spargi's Cala Corsara and **Cala Santa Maria,** including a picture-only stop at Spiaggia Rossa. Most boats leave between 10 and 11am and return between 5 and 6pm. Purchase tickets one day ahead; tours are usually less crowded on weekends.

Buses run from La Maddalena to Caprera's Punta Rossa (6 per day 9:42am-1:15pm, last return 6:40pm), giving travelers access to beaches along the eastern peninsula. Catch buses at the port for Caprera or the Northern Coast of La Maddalena island. Sunbathers fill the shores of **Spiaggia del Relitto,** where a wide strip of white sand and expansive swimming cove have made it one of Caprera's largest and most popular beaches. To reach it, follow the main road through Caprera to Punta Rossa and turn left on the dirt path after the beach Due Mare, following it for 1km. Visitors can rent chairs and umbrellas or explore the rugged coastline in paddle boats and kayaks, available along the beach daily 9am-7pm. If Caprera doesn't satiate the quest for the perfect panorama, bike or motor along La Maddalena's **Panoramica dei Colmi,** about 25km of paved road circling the island. The road passes by marvelous sea views and attractive beach destinations, including **Cala Lunga** and the watersport-friendly **Cala Spalmatore.**

SANTA TERESA DI GALLURA ☎0789

Perched on a hilltop, it is not immediately clear to new arrivals that Santa Teresa (pop. 4000) is in fact near water. But as soon as you crest the hill in the middle of town, the sight of the strikingly blue sea is breathtaking. Santa Teresa is a lovely launching point for exploring coves, inlets, and the Capo Testa, a peninsula of wind-sculpted granite with magnificent beaches. Santa Teresa boasts its own sandy beach, Rena Bianca, from which the hazy shores of Corsica are visible.

▐ TRANSPORTATION

ARST buses (☎0789 55 30 00) depart from V. Eleonora d'Arborea, in the parking lot across the street from the port office, and run to: Olbia (1¾hr., 6 per day to town and airport 6:10am-8:50pm, €3.72); Palau (40min., 12 per day 6:10am-8:50pm, €1.76); Sassari (3hr., 5 per day 5:15am-7:15pm, €5.83). Buy tickets at **Baby Bar** on V. Nazionale, 100m from the bus stop, or on board. **Saremar** (☎0789 75 41 56) runs **ferries** to Bonifacio, Corsica (1hr., 8-10 per day 8am-8:30pm, €9-12 including port tax for Corsica). Tickets are available at the office on V. del Porto. Open daily 9am-12:30pm and 2-10:30pm.) For a **taxi**, call ☎0789 75 42 37, 0789 75 44 07, or 0789 74 10 24. **Car rentals** are available from **Hertz** on V. Nazionale, 58. (☎0789 75 41 27; www.gulpimmobiliare.it). Open M-Sa 9am-1pm and 4-7:30pm. Cash only.) **Scooters** and **bikes** can also be rented from **Global Noleggio**, on P. San Vittorio (☎0789 75 50 80; www.globalinformation.it). Single- or double-seat motor scooters €40-47 per day, mountain bikes €10 per day. Open daily 9am-1pm, 3-8pm, and 9:30pm-midnight. AmEx/MC/V.) If motors aren't for you, go **horseback riding** with a horse from **Li Nibbari**, Localita da Testa. (☎337 81 71 89. Guided excursions €16 per hr.)

▐▌ ORIENTATION AND PRACTICAL INFORMATION

The ARST bus stop is at the far end of the parking lot that is across the street from the post office. Facing the port office, turn right, head to the intersection, and turn right on **Via Nazionale.** Head for the church at the end of the street, in **Piazza San Vittorio,** and turn right again to reach **Piazza Vittorio Emanuele.** The tourist office is on the opposite side of the *piazza*, on the 2nd level.

Tourist Office: P. V. Emanuele, 24 (☎0789 75 41 27). Assists with accommodations and rooms for rent. Ask about boat, horse, and moped rentals, as well as information about nearby archaeological attractions. Open June-Sept. M-Sa 8:30am-1pm and 3:30-7:30pm, Su 9am-noon and 5-7pm; Oct.-May M-Sa 8am-1pm and 3:30-6:30pm.

Boat Tours: Consorzio delle Bocche, P. V. Emanuele, 16 (☎0789 75 51 12), offers tours of the archipelago. Full-day tour daily 9:15am-5pm. Lunch included. €40, ages 4-12 €20. Office open daily 9am-1pm and 6pm-12:30am.

Emergency: ☎113. **Ambulance:** ☎118.

Medical Clinic: ☎0789 75 40 79. On V. Carlo Felice. Open 24hr.

Internet Access: Happy Phone, V. Imbriani, 1 (☎0789 75 43 17), off P. della Liberta. 4 computers; there's usually a wait. €1 per 10min., €5 per hr. Open M-Sa 9am-1pm, 4-8pm, and 9:30pm-midnight, Su 10am-1pm and 4-8pm.

Post Office: V. d'Arborea (☎0789 73 53 24), near the bus stop. Open M-F 8:05am-12:45pm, Sa 8am-12:30pm. **Postal Code:** 07028.

▐ ACCOMMODATIONS

▧ **Hotel Moderno,** V. Umberto, 39 (☎0789 75 42 33; www.modernoweb.it), centrally located off V. Nazionale. 16 comfortable rooms with patterned bedspreads, bath, A/C, and balcony. Friendly staff. Hallways display Sardinian artifacts and crafts. Buffet breakfast included. Open Apr.-Sept. Singles €38-60; doubles €62-105. MC/V. ❸

Hotel Bellavista, V. Sonnino, 8 (☎/fax 0789 75 41 62), heading toward the ocean, take your 2nd left off P. Liberta on V. Sonnino. Close to the beach. Airy rooms all have tiled bath; many have balcony with sea view. Breakfast €5. Singles €35-40; doubles €50-60. Higher-range prices are for rooms with terrace and view. MC/V. ❸

Pensione Scano, V. Lazio, 4 (☎0789 75 44 47). Small, bright rooms with trim furniture share large baths. Breakfast included. Rooms €31-78, depending on season, number of people, location of bath, and if there are meals included; call for details. MC/V. ❸

🔆 FOOD

Shops line V. Aniscara, off P. V. Emanuele. A fruit and clothing **market** by the bus station opens Thursday morning and runs until the early evening. The **SISA** supermarket, on V. Nazionale next to Banco di Sardegna, has picnic supplies. (Open M-Sa 8am-1pm and 4:30-8pm, Su 9am-noon. MC/V.)

▨ Papè Satan, V. Lamarmora, 22 (☎0789 75 50 48). Look for the sign off V. Nazionale. Neapolitan family cooks pizza in a traditional brick oven in the internal courtyard. Try the rich *pizza alla Papè Satan* with cream, butter, mozzarella, and prosciutto (€7.50) or the *quattro stagioni* (€8). Cover €2. Open daily noon-3pm and 7pm-midnight. ❷

Ristorante Azzurra, V. del Porto, 19 (☎0789 75 47 89). Friendly staff serves delicious fish and homemade pasta like *tagliatelle* with clams, tuna, eggs, and tomatoes (€8.50). *Primi* €7-13, *secondi* €6-16. Open Tu-Su noon-2pm and 7-11:30pm. AmEx/MC/V. ❸

Da Thomas, V. Val d'Aosta, 22 (☎0789 75 51 33). Enjoy fresh fish and a menu full of shellfish treats on a relaxed outdoor patio, away from touristy city center. *Primi* €6-14, *secondi* €7-14. Open daily 12:30-3pm and 7-11pm. AmEx/MC/V. ❸

Marlin, V. Garibaldi, 4 (☎0789 75 46 97). An *enoteca* with a posh feel but very reasonably priced dishes. Unique entrees like the cocoa *tagliatelle* with lobster (€12). *Primi* €7-9. Fish €10-12. Open daily 11am-3pm and 7-11pm. ❸

👁 🅲 SIGHTS AND BEACHES

Long before tourists discovered it, Santa Teresa was home to **Lu Brandali,** one of the largest and least disturbed prehistorical villages in the region. Follow V. Nazionale past the end of town, then turn right on an unlabeled dirt road across from the **Nonna SISA** supermarket. From here, a narrow path leads to a massive Sardinian **Tomba di Giganti,** communal village graves used between the 14th and 10th centuries BC. Due to their enormous dimensions and stone construction, the tombs were believed in later years to hold legendary giants. Overgrown trails wind uphill past the old village dwellings and a pair of towers before culminating at the ruins of a *nuraghe*. The village is not very well labeled, so stop by the tourist office for historical information on the site.

V. XX Settembre, off P. V. Emanuele, leads toward the sea. As the road forks, bear left and continue past Hotel Miramar to reach **Piazza Libertà.** The Argonese **Tower of Longonsardo** (c. 1358-1577), on the ruins of an ancient *nuraghe*, is framed by a stunning sea backdrop. Corsica's shore is visible through the mist. (Open daily 10am-12:30pm and 4:30-7pm. €1.) Facing the tower, take a left and wind down the street. Then walk down the stairs to reach **Spiaggia Rena Bianca,** a popular white-sand beach in a swimming cove. (Chair rental €6, with umbrella €12. Paddle boats €10 per hr., kayaks €5-8 per hr. Open daily 8am-7pm. Cash only.)

Some of the town's most notable attractions lie 3km away, at the rugged peninsula **Capo Testa.** Take the **Sardabus** from the post office (10min.; 5 per day; €0.67, round-trip €1.24) or bike (about 1hr. walking) along **Via Capo Testa,** off

V. Tibula from V. Nazionale. If you're walking, take the opportunity to get off the busy highway and see some gorgeous vistas by walking through the wooden gates on the right of the street as you head toward Capo Testa; this Ente Forest of Sardinia has trails for people and horses that wind through brush and boulders and crest onto views of the coastline that are truly breathtaking. The bus stops at **Spiaggia Rena di Ponente,** where two seas meet to form long parallel beaches ideal for water sports. (Chair rental €6. Umbrella €6. Single canoes €5 per hr., doubles €8 per hr.; windsurfers €12 per hr.) Keep walking up the street that runs between the two beaches, then take a left into an opening in the rocks (about a 25min. walk—asking for directions along the way will likely be essential) to reach the remote and stunning ◪**Valley de la Luna.** Once an international hippie community, it is now home to some 20 dread locked hangers-on who live in rock dwellings in the sides of the valley and hang out on the beach. The valley holds abandoned fire rings, rock paintings, and carved posts, and is ringed by granite trails great for exploring.

OLBIA ☎0789

As the closest port to the mainland, Olbia (pop. 41,000) is a major transportation hub that benefits from the thousands of tourists who come through the port and airport daily. Located a short distance from the Golfo Aranci, Olbia provides a good, if expensive, base for visiting other more interesting locations. Take a quick stroll past the shops and restaurants, then head elsewhere before you wonder where your money went.

▐ TRANSPORTATION

Flights: Local bus #2 runs from **Olbia Costa Smeralda Airport** to the city center (€0.55).

Trains: FS (☎0789 22 477) on V. Pala, just off C. Umberto. Service to: **Golfo Aranci** (30min., 7 per day, €1.85), **Sassari** (2hr., 4 per day, €5.90) with connections to **Alghero, Cagliari, Oristano,** and **Porto Torres** (2¼hr., 2:08pm, €7.05). Buy tickets from machine in lobby or from *biglietteria,* open 6:05am-12:30pm and 1:50-8:15pm.

Buses: ARST station, C. Umberto, 64 (☎0789 21 197), follow C. Umberto across the train tracks and continue straight for about 10min. The station is on the left, with the *biglietteria* in the building's side entrance. To: **Palau** (1hr., 14 per day 4:20am-11:15pm, €2.58); **Porto Cervo** (1hr., 5 per day 6:25am-4pm, €2.70); **Santa Teresa di Gallura** (2hr., 7 per day 6:45am-8:15pm, €3.72); and **Sassari** (3hr., 6:15am and 8:05pm, €7.64). Buy tickets at the ticket office in the station. **Sun Lines,** V. Pozzo, 23 (☎0789 50 885), the airport (☎348 26 09 881), and Stazione Marittima (☎0789 20 80 82), run a shuttle service to Porto Cervo and Palau from the airport, Stazione Marittima, and P. Crispi (4 per day, €12). **Local buses** have 3 useful lines: Line 1 goes through the city center to V. Veneto and V. A. Moro, Line 2 from the airport to the city center and suburban outskirts, and Line 9 from the Stazione Marittima to the city center and train station.

Ferries: Tirrenia (☎0789 24 691), in Stazione Marittima.

Taxi: At the airport (☎0789 69 150) and in the city center (☎0789 22 718).

Car Rental: Avis, V. Ghiberti, 14 (☎0789 53 960) off V. Aldo Moro. 21+. Open daily 8am-11pm. AmEx/MC/V. Many rental companies also have airport offices.

⚔️ 🔋 ORIENTATION AND PRACTICAL INFORMATION

Ferries arrive at **Stazione Marittima,** 1km east of the city center on **Viale Isola Bianca.** ARST buses run from Stazione Marittima to the **ARST station** on **Corso Umberto,** Olbia's main street, as well as **Piazza Margherita. Viale Regina Elena** shoots off P. Margherita and leads to **Piazza Crispi.** On the other side of P. Margherita is **Via Porto Romano,** which winds across the train tracks and enter the suburban landscape of **Viale Aldo Moro,** lined with everyday shops and snack bars.

Tourist Office: V. Piro, 1 (☎0789 21 453), just off C. Umberto. Helpful, English-speaking staff provides free **maps** and information on accommodations and transportation. Open M-F 8:30am-2pm and 3:30-6pm, Sa 8:30am-2pm.

Currency Exchange: Banca Intesa, across C. Umberto from the ARST station, has an **ATM.** Open M-F 8:30am-1:30pm and 2:45-4:15pm, Sa 8:30am-noon. Several other banks and ATMs around the town center.

Pharmacy, C. Umberto, 134 (☎0789 21 310). Open M-Sa 9am-1pm and 5pm-8:15pm.

Hospital: Vle. Aldo Moro (☎0789 55 22 00).

Emergency: ☎113. **Carabinieri:** ☎0789 21 221. **Ambulance:** ☎0789 55 22 01.

Internet Access: 🖪InterSmeraldo, V. Porto Romano, 8/B (☎0789 25 366). 9 fast computers in an air-conditioned room, with bean-bag chairs in the back and DSL ports for laptops. Helpful and friendly English-speaking staff. Fax and copy service available. €2.50 per 30min., €5 per 1hr. Open M-Sa 10am-11pm, Su 5-11pm. Cash only.

Post Office: V. Bari, 7 (☎0789 20 74 00). Take V. Acquedotto from C. Umberto to the intersection of V. Acquedotto and V. Bari. Open M-Sa 8am-1pm. **Postal Code:** 07026.

🔣 🔲 ACCOMMODATIONS AND FOOD

Olbia is lacking in budget accommodations. Your best bet is to inquire about *agriturismi* options at the tourist office. Nevertheless, for those who can afford it, Olbia does have some very comfortable establishments. With a homey restaurant on the first floor, **Hotel Terranova ❹,** V. Garibaldi, 3, lets recently renovated rooms with air-conditioning, bath, and TV. (☎0789 22 395. Breakfast included. Wheelchair accessible. Singles €40-60; doubles €60-80. AmEx/MC/V.) **Hotel Gallura ❸,** C. Umberto, 145, decorated with roosters and other rustic touches, offers rooms with plaid bedding, air-conditioning, TV, telephone, and bright baths. The restaurant downstairs is renowned as the best in Olbia, but is outside most reasonable budgets. Guests at the hotel, however, get a taste at the included breakfast. (☎0789 24 629 or 0789 24 648. Singles €35-50; doubles €65-95. AmEx/MC/V.) **Hotel Cavour ❹,** V. Cavour, 22, in the heart of Olbia, has 21 bright rooms with air-conditioning, bath, and fridge. (☎0789 20 40 33. Singles €50-65; doubles €75-90; triples €100-120; quads €110-140. AmEx/MC/V.)

Many restaurants along C. Umberto advertise overpriced tourist menus and cater to a mostly foreign crowd. Head down the little side streets for a less expensive, more authentic meal. The **Super Pan** supermarket, P.Crispi, 2, is perfect for stocking up on supplies. Go to the end of V. Regina Elena, take a left and walk through P. Crispi; you will see the signs from the *piazza.* (☎0789 26 382. Open M-Sa 8:30am-9pm, Su 8:30am-1:30pm.) 🖪Gelateria Smeralda ❶, C. Umberto, 124, has the best *gelato* in town. Try the purple local specialty *mirto* (myrtle) or the prickly pear for a change of pace. (☎0789 26 443. Cones €1-3. Open M-Sa 4pm-midnight. Cash only.) ■**Antica Trattoria ❷**, V. G. Pala, 6, serves massive portions of hearty Sardinian specialties to hordes of hungry visitors and locals—be sure to get a reservation in order to sample the dozens of delicacies offered in the spectacular *antipasto* bar. (☎0789 24 053. *Primi* €6.20-7.80. Meats €6.20, fish €7.80, *antipasto* buffet sliding scale from €4. Open daily 7:30pm-midnight.) Just off C. Umberto, **Pizzeria Il Pomodoro ❷**, V. Sassari, 10, serves pizzas at reasonable prices. Try the *San Felice* (with salmon and shrimp) for €8. (☎0789 28 880. Pizza €3.10-8. Cover €1.50. Open M and W-Su 7:30-11:30pm. AmEx/MC/V.) Set in an old-fashioned stone house, **Da Paolo ❸**, V. Cavour, 17, other entrance at V. Garibaldi, 18, serves delicious victuals like the Sardinian specialties *culurgiones* (cheese and potato dumplings; €6.50) or *zuppa gallurese* (bread with cheese soaked in broth; €6.50) in a lively family atmosphere. Browse the restaurant-owned shop next door for some Sardinian products. (☎0789 21 675. *Primi* €6.50-10, *secondi* €6.50-14. Open M-Sa 12:30-2:30pm and 7-11pm, Su 7:30-11pm. AmEx/MC/V.)

ORISTANO ☎0783

In the 7th century, the inhabitants of Tharros repelled invasion after invasion until a band of merciless Moorish pirates forced them to abandon their homes. With nowhere else to go, they set up camp around nearby Oristano (pop. 30,000), which soon became an independent commercial port under Eleanora of Arborea, one of Sardinia's most important saints. Today, the city is also a base for exploring the nearby Sinis Peninsula and its enticing Phoenician and Roman ruins at Tharros, the awe-inspiring arch at S'Archittu, and the beaches of Is Aruttas.

▐ TRANSPORTATION

Trains: In P. Ungheria, 1km from the town center (☎0783 89 20 21). Ticket counter open 6:20am-8:15pm. **Luggage storage** available. To: **Cagliari** (1-2hr., 16 per day 4:50am-9:24pm, €4.55); **Macomer** (1hr., 10 per day 5:40am-9:25pm, €2.90); **Olbia** (2½hr., 2 per day 1:20pm and 7:48pm, €8.85) via **Ozieri, Chilivani,** or **Macomer.** To get to **Sassari,** connect via Macomer or Chivilani.

Buses: PANI, V. Lombardia, 30 (☎0783 21 22 68). Ticket office inside Bar Blu, on V. Lombaridia. Open daily 7am-10pm. To: **Cagliari** (1½hr., 4 per day 8:55am-9:34pm, €5.84); **Nuoro** (2hr., 4 per day 7:05am-7:50pm, €5.84); **Sassari** (2¼hr., 4 per day 7:05am-7:50pm, €7.18). **ARST,** on V. Cagliari 182, with 2nd entrance on C. V. Emanuele, has local service (☎0783 71 185 or 800 86 50 42). Ticket office open daily 7:30am-2pm and 4-6pm. To: **Cagliari** (2hr., 7:10am and 2:10pm, €5.94); **Bosa** via Cugaieri 2 hr., 4 per day, €8.47); **Putzu Idu** (dir.: Su Pallosu; 50min., 7 per day 7am-6:18pm, €1.76); **San Giovanni di Sinis** (July-Oct.; dir.: Is Aruttas; 40min.; 5 per day 9am-7:05pm, last return 7:45pm; €1.45); **Santa Caterina** (dir.: Scano Montiferro; 40min., 8 per day 7:50am-7:05pm, €1.76).

Taxis: At P. Roma (☎0783 70 280) and at the train station (☎0783 74 328). Available 7am-1pm and 3-8:30pm. For 24hr. service, call ☎336 81 35 85.

Car Rental: Avis, V. Liguria, 17 (☎0783 31 06 38). 25+. Open M-F 8:30am-1pm and 4-7:30pm, Sa 9am-noon. AmEx/MC/V.

Scooter Rental: Marco Moto, V. Cagliari, 99/101 (☎0783 31 00 36). Bikes €8.50 per day, scooters €30-75 per day. Insurance and helmet included. Open M-F 8:30am-1pm and 4-8pm, Sa 8:30am-1pm. AmEx/MC/V.

Bike Rental: Ciclosport Cabella, V. Busachi, 2/4 (☎/fax 0783 72 714). Large selection of beautiful mountain and road bikes. Extremely knowledgeable staff. Open M-F 9am-1pm, Sa 9am-1pm and 5-8pm. Bikes €30-60 per day. AmEx/MC/V.

✈ ☎ ORIENTATION AND PRACTICAL INFORMATION

To get to the city center from the **train station,** follow **Via Vittorio Veneto,** the street farthest to the right, to **Piazza Mariano.** Then take **Via Mazzini** to **Piazza Roma,** the heart of the city. From the **ARST bus station,** take the exit nearest the ticket office and turn left. Continue past the *duomo* and head straight to **Via De Castro,** which spills into P. Roma. From the **PANI bus station** on **Via Lombardia** on the other side of town, face Blu Bar and turn right. At the end of the street, turn right on **Via Tirso,** left on **Via Cagliari,** and left on **Via Tharros,** which leads to P. Roma.

Tourist Office: Pro Loco, V. Ciutadella de Minorca, 8 (☎/fax 0783 70 621). **Maps** and info on local festivals. Open M-F 9am-12:30pm and 4:30-8pm, Sa 9am-noon. **EPT, P.** Eleonora, 19 (☎0783 36 831). Info on Oristano and province, lodgings, events, sights, and excursions. Open M-Th 9am-1pm and 4-6:30pm, F 9am-1pm.

Currency Exchange: Banca Nazionale del Lavoro, Banca di Napoli, Credito Italiano, and **ATMs** are in P. Roma. All open M-F 8:20am-1:20pm and 3-4:30pm, Sa 8:20-11:50am.

Luggage Storage: In the train station. €1.55 per day. Open daily 6am-7:30pm. Also at ARST station. €1.55 per day. Open daily 6am-7:50pm.

Emergency: ☎113. **First Aid/Medical Clinic:** ☎0783 743 33. **Ambulance:** ☎118.

Pharmacy: V. Umberto, 49/51 (☎0783 603 38). Open M-F 9am-1pm and 5-10pm.

Hospital: ☎0783 31 71. On V. Fondazione Rockefeller.

Post Office: V. Mariano, 4 (☎0783 36 80 15). **Currency exchange** and fax available. Open M-F 8am-6:50pm, Sa 8am-1:15pm. **Postal Code:** 09170.

⌂ ACCOMMODATIONS AND CAMPING

Oristano caters primarily to travelers on their way to the beach, and low competition makes for high prices. For info on attractive *agriturismi* and B&Bs, ask at the tourist office or call the **Posidonia Society,** V. Umberto, 66, in Riola, 10km from Oristano. (☎0783 41 16 60; www.sardegnaturismo.net. Open daily 9am-1pm and 4-8pm.)

ISA, P. Mariano, 50 (☎/fax 0783 36 01 01). From ARST station, take exit nearest to the ticket office, turn left, then right on V. V. Emanuele. Walk through P. D'Arborea and adjoining P. Martini, then follow V. Lamarmora to the end. Turn right, then immediately left, and follow signs. Hotel with luxurious Sardinian floors (made from the spines of fish) and oriental rugs. All rooms have bath, A/C, TV, phone, and minibar; some have balcony. Breakfast included. Singles €50; doubles €85; triples €100. AmEx/MC/V. ●

Piccolo Hotel, V. Martignano, 19 (☎0783 71 500). From the ARST station, take exit nearest to ticket office, turn right and continue across P. Mannu. Head down the street to the left and take 1st left. Turn right at the end. Small hotel on a quiet street in the historical center. 18 rooms with bath, some with TV and balcony. Singles €32; doubles €53. Cash only. ●

Antonella Bed and Breakfast, V. Sardegna, 140 (☎0783 73 863). From P. Roma, turn right off V. Tirso on V. Sardegna. About a 10min. walk down V. Sardegna. 3 huge rooms on the outskirts of the historical center share a balcony and clean bath. Kitchen facilities available. Breakfast included. Singles €25; doubles €45. Cash only. ●

Marina di Torregrande, V. Stella Maris (☎/fax 0783 222 28), 150m from the beach and 100m out of Torre Grande toward Oristano (7km). Orange local buses leave from V. Cagliari in front of ARST station (10min., 2 per hr. 7:30am-12:30am, €0.80). Facilities include bar and market with fresh produce. Free parking and hot showers. Open May-Sept. €5.50 per person, €2.60-3.50 per child, €6.60-9.10 per tent. Bungalows with bath €65. Electricity €1.60. Cash only. ●

▐ FOOD

The **Euro-Drink** market, P. Roma, 22, sells inexpensive basics and Sardinian products like *mirto* and *seadas*. (Open M-Sa 8am-2pm and 5-9pm. MC/V.) A **SISA** supermarket is at V. Amiscora, 26. (Open M-Sa 8am-8pm. MC/V.)

▨ Ristorante Craf da Banana, V. De Castro, 34 (☎0783 706 69). Slightly more expensive than other restaurants near the center, but far more stylish, with low-arched brick ceilings and fine cuisine, featuring a delicious *ravioli della casa* with a meaty wild boar-and-mushroom sauce (€7), and piglet, donkey, or kid cooked just to order. *Primi* €8, *secondi* €8-13. Open M-Sa 1-3pm and 8-11pm. Reserve ahead. AmEx/MC/V. ❸

Trattoria Da Gino, V. Tirso, 13 (☎0783 71 428). Locals love the cozy dining room and family feel. Menu features selections of spaghetti, ravioli, fettuccine, *gnocchi,* and *risotti. Primi* €4-10, *secondi* €7.50-12. Open M-Sa 12:30-3pm and 8-11pm. MC/V. ❸

Pizzeria La Grotta, V. Diego Contini, 3 (☎0783 30 02 06), off P. Roma. A bright restaurant serving the best brick-oven pizza in town. The dining room is large and loud even at the beginning of the dinner hour; there is also an indoor smoking section, enclosed from the main restaurant. A popular favorite is the *pizza alla carciofi freschi e bottarga* (with artichoke hearts and fish eggs; €7.50). Pizza €2.80-8.20. Cover €1.50. Open daily 7:30pm-12:30am. AmEx/MC/V. ❷

Ristorante Il Faro, V. Bellini, 25 (☎0783 700 02; www.ristoranteilfaro.net). As dad and son chat with customers at this elegant family-owned restaurant, mom cooks up unique renditions of Sardinian specialties like *pecora* (lamb) with potatoes and onions (€16) with the highest-quality ingredients, though such innovation doesn't come cheap. *Primi* €13-15, seafood *secondi* €15-30. 4-course *menù* €45. Cover €3. Service 15%. Open M-Sa 12:45-2:45pm and 8-10pm. Reserve ahead. AmEx/MC/V. ❺

◉ ♫ SIGHTS AND ENTERTAINMENT

The whimsical **Chiesa di San Francesco,** complete with two small brightly tiled domes, is the largest *duomo* in Sardinia. First built in 1250, it was heavily restructured in the 19th century, leaving little of the original interior intact. A notable remnant is the gruesome wooden crucifix with the emaciated and tortured body of Christ. Constructed by a 16th-century Catalán teacher, the cross was once attributed to Nicodemus; it was said that such a vivid depiction could only have been captured by an eyewitness. The sacristy houses a 16th-century polyptych, *St. Francis Receiving the Stigmata* and Nino Pisano's 14th-century marble statue of San Basilio. (In P. E. d'Arborea at the end of V. de Castro. Open daily. Mass Su 9am. Free.) Once a fortified entrance to the medieval city, the 13th-century **Tower of San Mariano II** dominates P. Roma. On summer evenings, young *Oristanesi* gather in this *piazza* and the adjoining C. Umberto to flirt, sip Ichnusa (Sardinian beer) and chatter away on their *telefonini.* The collection of Nuraghic, Punic, Phoenician, and Roman artifacts at **Antiquarium Arborense** was unearthed at Tharros, and includes urns, cups, and earthenware of all shapes and sizes, some dating as far back as 5000 BC. Also on display is a tabletop model of the ancient port of Tharros. (In P. Corrias, near P. E. d'Aborea. ☎0783 79 12 62. Wheelchair accessible. Open M, W, and F-Sa 9am-2pm and 3-8pm, Tu and Th 9am-2pm and 3-11pm. €3, students and seniors €1, children under 14 €1.50.) In its synthesis of Lombard and Pisan influences, the 12th-century **Basilica of Santa Giusta** is typically Sardinian. (V. Manzoni, 2, on the road to Cagliari, 3km out of town. ☎0783 35 92 05. Open daily 7:30am-12:30pm and 4-7:30pm. Free.) To get there, take the ARST bus (dir.: Arborea; 5min.; every hr. 6:15am-8:05pm, last return 9:30pm; €0.67) and get off at the first stop. To arrange vineyard and gastronomic tours, hikes, and tours of the Sinis Peninsula, contact the **Posidonia Society.**

BOSA
☎ 0785

Glowing with cheery pastels, Bosa is half medieval village, half Riviera vacation spot. This unique little town sits by the Temo River, a dazzling sight both by day and by night. Though the *centro storico* is a generally sleepy place, the newer Bosa Marina 1km away boasts beautiful beaches, an assortment of seaside bars, and a hostel. If arriving from Oristano, be sure to look out the window as you travel; at the small hill-towns along the way.

TRANSPORTATION. Buses run from Bosa to **Piazza Palmiro Togliatti** in Bosa Marina (5min., 22 per day, €0.67). Additionally, buses from Alghero or Oristano often continue to Bosa Marina. **ARST buses** run from Bosa to **Oristano** (1½hr., 6 per day 5:10am-4:20pm, €4.44), Alghero (8am and 5:40pm), Olbia (6:15 and 6:30pm); and Sassari (2hr., 6:20am and 10:45pm, €4.44). Buy tickets at the *tabaccheria*, V. Alghero, 7A. **FDS buses** run to Alghero (1½hr., 6:35am and 3:40pm, €5) and **Nuoro** (1¾hr., 4 per day 6:06am-7:31pm, €5.10) Buy tickets at the FDS office in P. Zanetti. (Open in summer daily 5:30-8:30am, 9:30am-1pm, and 1:05-3:20pm; in winter 5:30-8:30am and 9:30am-7:35pm.) For a **taxi**, call ☎ 336 81 18 00. To **rent cars, scooters,** or **bikes,** stop by **Euroservice**, V. Azuni, 23. (☎ 0785 37 34 79.) 25+ for car or scooter. Cars from €80 per day; scooters €18-44 per day; bikes €10 per day. Insurance included. Open M-F 9am-10pm and 5-8pm.)

ORIENTATION AND PRACTICAL INFORMATION. Bosa, the city proper, lies across the **River Temo** from **Bosa Marina.** Buses stop in Bosa's **Piazza Angelico Zanetti,** from which **Via Azzuni** leads to **Piazza Gioberti** at the base of the *centro storico*. The **Pro Loco Tourist Office**, V. Azuni, 5, the intersection of V. Francesco Romagna and V. Azuni, provides **maps** and information on both the town and surroundings. (☎ 0785 37 61 07; www.infobosa.it. Open M-F 9:30am-12:30pm, Tu and Th also 6-8pm, Sa 9am-noon.) The **tourist office** for Bosa Marina is on the Lungomare about 5min. after the right turn off the main bridge. (Open M-F 8:30am-12:30pm and 3:30-11pm.) For **currency exchange** and a 24hr. **ATM,** head to **Unicredit Banca,** at the corner of V. Lamarmora and V. Giovanni XXIII. (☎ 0785 37 31 18. Open M-F 8:20am-1:20pm and 2:35-4:05pm, Sa 8:20am-12:45pm.) In case of **emergency,** call ☎ 113, the **Red Cross** ☎ 0785 37 38 18, or the **carabinieri** ☎ 0785 37 31 16. The **hospital** and **guardia medica** can be reached at ☎ 0785 37 31 07. **Internet Web Copy,** P. IV Novembre, 12, has five computers with fast connection (€6 per hr.) and **fax** services. (☎ 0785 37 20 49. Open M-Sa 9am-1pm and 5-9pm.) The **post office,** V. Pischedda, 1, also has currency exchange. (☎ 0785 37 54 55. Open M-F 8:15am-6:30pm, Sa 8:15am-12:45pm.) **Postal Code:** 08013.

ACCOMMODATIONS AND FOOD. Bosa Marina is home to a well-run **Youth Hostel (HI) ❶,** V. Sardegna, 1. After you cross the bridge from Bosa Centro, take a right on the *lungomare*. V. Sardegna is about 5min. down, on your left. Close to the beach, the hostel has clean rooms, a bar open until midnight, and a nice staff. (☎/fax 0785 37 50 09. Breakfast €3. Dinner €10.33. Reception 7:30-9am and 3:30pm-midnight. 6- to 8-bed dorms €10.33. Sheets €1.50 and hot water €1.50. Doubles available by reservation. HI members only. Cash only.) Also in Bosa Marina, the friendly **Hotel Al Gabbano ❹,** on Vle. Mediterraneo, offers large, comfortable rooms with simple wood furniture directly across from the beach, all with bath, TV, air-conditioning, phone, and minifridge, and most with balcony. (☎ 0785 37 41 23; fax 0785 37 41 09. Restaurant downstairs. Beach chair and umbrella included. Singles €45-64.50; doubles €61.50-81.50. Higher prices include breakfast. Full pension also available. AmEx/MC/V.) **Albergo Perry Clan ❷,** V. Alghero, 3, in Bosa, offers 12 simple, lovely rooms with TV, bath and A/C. From the bus stop, follow V. D. Manin and take first right on V. Giovanni XXIII; the hotel is on the left after P. Dante Alighieri. (☎ 0785 37 30 74. Singles €25; doubles €40. Cash only.)

SARDINIA

Head to **SISA** supermarket, P. Gioberti, 13, for fresh produce and groceries. (☎0785 37 34 23. Open M-Sa 8am-1pm and 5:30-8:30pm.) Couched in a medieval building in the *centro storico*, **Ristorante Borgo Sant'Ignazio ❷**, V. S. Ignazio, 33, serves traditional cuisine like lobster in *salsa bosana* (with onions and tomatoes; €9) and *azada di gattucio* (€8), a relative of shark. (☎0785 37 46 62. *Primi* €6-10, *secondi* €8-14. Open in summer daily 1-3pm and 7:30-11pm. AmEx/MC/V.) **Sa Pischedda ❷**, V. Roma, 8, has a garden patio on the other side of the river and prepares fantastic *razza alla bosana* (garlicky sautéed flat fish) and brick-oven pizza. (☎0785 37 30 65. Pizza €5.90-11, dinner only. *Primi* €8-9, *secondi* €4 per 100g. Open daily 1-3pm and 8pm-midnight. AmEx/MC/V.)

 SIGHTS AND BEACHES. Bosa's historical **Quartiere Sa Costa** doesn't allow cars. The town's panoramic **Castello Malaspina** is a short hike uphill through the *centro storico;* take the flowery staircase or the broad V. di Castello to see the castle that dates from 1112 and still holds the early 14th-century **Chiesa Nostra Signora Regnos Altos.** (☎333 54 45 675. Castle and church open daily 9:30am-1:30pm and 5:30-8:30pm. €2, under 12 €1.) Bosa's principal museum, **Casa Deriu,** C. V. Emanuele II, 59, exhibits the original furnishings, tapestries, and family portraits from the wealthy Deriu family's home. The 3rd floor holds a collection of ceramics, prints, and paintings by Bosano Melkiorre Melis, a leader in the applied and plastic arts. (Open Tu-Su 11:30-1pm and 6:30-11pm. €3, children €1.50.)

A long stretch of sandy beach filled with local families awaits in Bosa Marina, where bars line the *lungomare* and surround the **Aragonese Tower.** (☎0785 37 70 43. Open July through August as a Contemporary Art Museum 10am-12:30pm and 5-8:30pm.) The **Bosa Diving Center** (☎0785 37 56 49; www.bosadiving.it), V. Colombo, 2, in Bosa Marina, offers snorkeling, scuba diving (day and night dives), and boat tours to nearby grottoes and beaches. Call for more info.

NUORO   ☎0784

Though set against a dramatic mountain backdrop, the architecture of this provincial capital is a mix of the Spanish-influenced buildings characteristic of other Sardinian towns and post-WWII block-style apartment complexes. The town is known for its cultural value, boasting Sardinia's contemporary art museum, the Museo Arte Nuoro (MAN), and the only government-commissioned ethnographic museum. It's also heralded for its proximity to the breathtaking Monte Ortobene, a breathtaking viewpoint for vistas that reach all the way to the ocean.

> **TIP**
> **S.O.S.** Buses stop running at 8:30pm and taxis are few and far between. If you are planning to be out past this time and are staying outside the city center, avoid getting stranded and arrange for transportation home before you leave.

◪ TRANSPORTATION

Trains: ☎0784 301 15. On V. Lamarmora in P. Stazione. Buy tickets M-Sa 7:30am-7pm. To **Cagliari** (3½-5hr., 6 per day 5:45am-6:51pm, €10.80) via **Macomer.**

Buses: The following bus companies serve Nuoro:

ARST (☎0784 29 41 73). Buses stop at the ARST station on V. Toscana between V. Sardegna and V. Santa Barbara. Tickets available at the bar in the ARST station (open M-Sa 6:30am-9pm), at Il Gusto Macelleria next door, and at bars along the street. To: **Cagliari** (2:05 and 7:10pm, €9.50); **Dorgali** (1hr., 6 per day 6:53am-7pm, €2.01); **Olbia** (7 per day 5:30am-8:50pm, €7.64); **Oliena** (30min., 13 per day 6:53am-7:45pm, €0.80); **Orgosolo** (30min.; 8 per day 5:50am-6:30pm, last return 7:40pm; €1.45).

PANI, V. B. Sassari, 15 (☎0784 36 856). Walk up V. Stazione and follow it to the right. Ticket office open 9am-noon, 5-7:30pm, and 30min. before each departure. Buses to: **Cagliari** (3½hr., 4 per day 6:52am-7:31pm, €11.31) and **Sassari** (2½hr., 6 per day 5:52am-7:31pm, €6.77).

F. Deplano (☎0784 29 50 30) runs buses from the ARST station to the **Olbia airport** (1½hr., 5 per day 4:15am- 4:45pm, €9.30) and to the **Alghero airport** (2¾hr.; 3 per day 3:20am, 11:25am, 4:20pm; €12.39). Buses are scheduled around plane arrivals and departures.

Public Transportation: Buy tickets (€0.57) for the local buses at newsstands, *tabaccherie*, or in the train station. **Bus #4** runs from P. V. Emanuele through the center of town to the train station and the hospital (3 per hr.), while **E6** runs in the opposite direction, stopping at the train station on its way through town to P. V. Emanuele. **Bus 9** runs to the top of M. Ortobene.

Taxis: Fadda Taxi (☎380 73 73 366) At night it can be a very long wait, so call ahead.

Car Rental: Autonoleggio Maggiore, Vle. Monadtir, 116 (☎070 27 36 92; fax 070 20 80 536). Affiliated with National Car Rental. €72.64 per day. 23+. Open M-F 8:30am-1pm and 3:30-7pm, Sa 8am-1pm. AmEx/MC/V.

ORIENTATION AND PRACTICAL INFORMATION

From the ARST station, turn right on **Viale Sardegna.** When you reach **Piazza Sardegna,** take a right on **Via Lamarmora** and follow it to **Piazza delle Grazie** and the center of town. To get to the **tourist office** from P. delle Grazie, turn left and follow **Via IV Novembre** uphill to **Piazza Italia.** Facing the PANI bus stop, turn left and take **Via B. Sassari** to P. Italia and the tourist office. **Via Roma** leads from P. Italia to **Piazza San Giovanni** and the town's social hub, **Piazza Vittorio Emanuele. Corso G. Garibaldi** is a major street with shops and cafes that runs out of P. V. Emanuele.

The enthusiastic staff at the **EPT Tourist Office,** P. Italia, 19, has brochures and hiking info. (☎0784 32 307; www.enteturismo.nuoro.it. Open in summer daily 8:30am-2pm and 2:30-7:30pm.) In an **emergency,** call ☎113, an **ambulance** at ☎118, or the **carabinieri** at ☎112. For a 24hr. **medical clinic,** call (☎0784 24 02 49). The **Ospedale San Francesco** (☎0784 24 02 37) is on the highway to Bitti. **Internet Access** is available at **Informatica 2000,** C. Garibaldi, 156. (☎0784 37 289; fax 0784 23 50 87. €1 per 10min., €2.50 per 30min., €5 per hr. Open in summer M-F 9am-1:30pm and 4:30-8pm, Sa 9am-1:30pm.) The **post office** is at P. Crispi, 8, off V. Dante. (☎0784 24 52 20. Open M-F 8am-6:50pm, Sa 8am-1:15pm.) **Currency exchange** is also available. **Postal Code:** 08100.

ACCOMMODATIONS

Inexpensive hotels are rare in Nuoro and campgrounds are in distant towns; if you plan to stay in the area, consider B&Bs close to town or Monte Ortobene, or head to the smaller hamlets in the hills. ☒**Casa Solotti ❸,** in Località Monte Ortobene, has five large rooms that share two bathrooms and a terrace with a mountain view. Welcoming multilingual owners serve homemade jam, yogurt, and *pasta sfoglie* for breakfast. They also lead excursions to the island's interior in the winter and spring. (☎328 60 28 975 or 0784 33 54; www.casasolotti.it. Call for free pickup from town. Singles €30; doubles €52, with bath €60. Cash only.) **Hotel Sandalia ❹,** V. Einaudi, 14, along the road to Cagliari and Sassari, is a 20min. walk from the center. From the ARST station, go as far as V. Lamarmora and turn left; the hotel is at the top of the hill and marked with a large marquee on the roof. All rooms are modern and come with bath, A/C, TV, and phone; many have a mountain view. (☎/fax 0784 38 353. Singles €54; doubles €74; triples €78; quads €82. AmEx/MC/V.)

FOOD

A quality bakery, **Antico Panifico,** V. Ferraciu, 71, off P. delle Grazie, sells hot rolls fresh from its wood-burning oven, a Sardinian *pane carasau,* and scrumptious *panzerotti* (from €1.75) filled with cheese, tomato, and a choice of eggplant, mushroom, or ham. (Open M-Sa 8am-1:30pm and 5-8pm.)

> **Canne Al Vento,** V. Biasi, 123 (☎0784 20 17 62). High class and low prices in this remote restaurant. Guests dine on classic *culurgiones* (ravioli stuffed with potatoes, cheese, and mint; €7) or heaping platters of *arrosto misto* (mixed grilled meats; €10). *Primi* €5.25-9, *secondi* €5.25-12. The espresso (€0.70) is out of this world. Open M-Sa 12:30-3pm and 8-10:30pm. AmEx/MC/V. ❷

> **Ristorante Tascusi,** V. Apromonte, 15 (☎0784 37 287). The owner cooks at this local favorite. Try the *malloreddus al sugo di cinghiale* (pasta in wild boar sauce; €5.25). *Menù* includes *primo, secondo, contorno,* and 0.5L of wine (€10). *Primi* €4.65-8, *secondi* €6-13. Open M-Sa 12:30-3pm and 8pm-midnight. MC/V. ❶

> **Da Giovanni,** V. IV Novembre, 9, 2nd fl. (☎0784 305 62). Don't miss this humble local favorite. Try the *scaloppa alla vernaccia* (beef in white wine sauce; €8). *Primi* €8, *secondi* €8-11. Open M-F noon-3pm and 7:30-11pm, Sa noon-4pm. AmEx/MC/V. ❷

SIGHTS

All the cool kids gravitate toward P. V. Emanuele—nicknamed *giardini*—to sit, talk, and smoke in the evenings; folks of all ages flock to the bars on C. Garibaldi in the evenings to take their *passegiatte* and enjoy a beer and a smoke.

MUSEO DELLA VITA E DELLE TRADIZIONI POPULARI. Sardinia's largest ethnographic museum contains an extensive collection of traditional costumes, hand-woven rugs, musical instruments, sweets, and jewelry from around the island. The pieces are arranged in a series of stucco houses circling a flowered courtyard, a reconstruction of a typical Sardinian village. One house contains carnival masks shaped like devils, donkeys, pigs, cows, and goats; don't miss the creepy Mamuthone costumes in the main building. *(V. Antonio Mereu, 56. ☎0784 25 60 35. Open Oct.-June daily 9am-1pm and 3-7pm; July-Sept. 9am-8pm. €3, students €1, under 18 or over 60 free.)*

MUSEO ARTE NUORO. Affectionately termed the "MAN," this striking white building contains a collection of 20th-century Sardinian art that uses both traditional and contemporary themes—a welcome change from the Nuraghic bronzes that crowd Sardinia's other museums. The middle two floors maintain a permanent collection of works by 20th-century Sardinian painters, while the first and 4th floors display rotating exhibits by modern artists. *(V. S. Satta, 15. ☎0784 25 21 10. Open Tu-Su 10am-1pm and 4:30-8:30pm. €3, students under 25 €2, under 18 or over 60 free.)*

MONTE ORTOBENE. A moving bronze *Christ the Redeemer*, a statue of the town's symbol, beckons hikers to the peak of this hill, where a shady park and dynamic views await. Follow a 50m trail from the tourist office to the bronze Il Redentore, dating from 1905. From the bus stop on Monte Ortobene, walk 20m down the road to see Monte Corrasi, which dwarfs the neighboring town of Oliena. *(Take the orange ATP bus #8 from P. V. Emanuele 7km to the summit (15 per day 8:15am-8pm, last return 8:15pm; €0.55). Or hike the 4.5km trail Il Solitudine; start behind Chiesa della Solitudine at the beginning of V. Ortobene and follow the red and white blazes marked "Trail 101.")*

▶ DAYTRIP FROM NUORO

ORGOSOLO

Take an ARST bus (40min.; 8 per day 5:50am-6:30pm, last return 7:40pm; €1.45) from the ARST station in Nuoro.

The bus ride alone merits a trip to picturesque **Orgosolo,** but the town itself is known for its ◪**murals,** which range in style from Picasso-like Cubism to contemporary advertisement art. The murals cover the buildings along C. Repubblica and its surrounding alleyways and attract artists from around the globe. The Milanese anarchist group Gruppo Dioniso created the first mural in 1969, and Francesco del Casino, a teacher from Siena, reinvented the mural-painting as an ongoing project in 1975. His works focus on social and political issues, including imperialism, fascism, and commercialism. Artists make new murals focused on modern themes like terrorism and Sardinian independence; one commemorates the terrorist attacks on the World Trade Center on Sept. 11th, 2001.

The town **tourist office,** P. Caduti in Guerra, next to the 2nd bus stop, distributes city **maps** and information on the murals. (Open in summer daily 7am-7pm.) Although there's not much to see besides the murals, those who choose to stay should check out the cozy **Petit Hotel ❷,** V. Mannu, 9, off C. Repubblica. Backtrack from the bus stop at the small park (keeping the police station to the right), then head up the incline on the left and follow the signs. Eighteen quiet rooms all have bath, dark wood furniture, and balconies. (☎/fax 0784 40 20 09. Breakfast €5. Singles €25; doubles €45; triples €57; quads €67. AmEx/MC/V.)

To eat a traditional meal in the mountains, contact **Cultura e Ambiente,** a local organization that operates excursions into the hills and organizes lunches in a field behind its restaurant, **Supramonte ❸,** in Località Sarthu Thithu, 3km uphill from town. Busloads of tourists come to devour smoked meats, cheese, fresh produce, and pastries off wooden platters. (☎0784 40 10 15 or 349 17 75 872; www.supramonte.net. Conducted for groups, but individuals may call ahead to join. Transportation provided on request. Lunch €18. Call for group rates.) The group also runs the clean, panoramic **Camping Supramonte ❶.** (€10 per person; bungalows with bath €23. Hot showers free. AmEx/MC/V.)

DORGALI   ☎0784

Nestled in mountains and ringed by pastures, pint-sized Dorgali offers visitors relaxation and quiet among friendly locals. Since the tourism boom hit Sardinia in the 60s, travelers have trekked to Dorgali to admire the ceramic, weaving, and woodworking shops that line its main street. Though roads connect it to nearby Cala Gonone and archaeological sights, Dorgali's farmers and artisans maintain the isolated town's isolated charm.

▣❷ TRANSPORTATION AND PRACTICAL INFORMATION. ARST buses stop at V. Lamarmora, 59, across from the *carabinieri,* and at the intersection of V. Lamarmora and C. Umberto. Buy tickets at the bar at the intersection of V. Lamarmora and C. Umberto. The schedule is posted at the tourist office. Buses run to: Cala Gonone (20min., 10 per day 6:20am-7:45pm, €0.67); Nuoro (45min., 9 per day 6:05am-7:50pm, €2.53); and Olbia (3hr., 2 per day 6:35am and 5:25pm, €7.64). **Via Lamarmora,** which runs uphill from the bus stop, and **Corso Umberto** (perpendicular to V. Lamarmora) are the major streets. **Via Roma** descends to **Viale Kennedy,** which runs along the bottom of town. The ■ **Pro Loco Tourist Office,** V. Lamarmora, 108, offers detailed info on Dorgali, Cala Gonone, and surrounding attractions. (☎0784 962 43. Open M-F May-Sept. 9am-1pm and 4-8pm; Oct.-Apr. 9am-1pm and 3:30-7pm.) **Currency exchange** and **ATMs** are at **Banca Intesa** (open M-F 8:30am-1:30pm and 2:45-4:15pm, Sa 8:30-noon), at the intersection of V. Lamarmora and V. Fleming, and at the post office. In case of **emergency,** call ☎113, the **carabinieri** (☎0784 961 14; open 8am-8pm), an **ambulance** at ☎118, or contact the **medical clinic** (☎0784 965 21; open M-F 10pm-8am, Sa-Su 24hr.). **Farmacia Mondula,** V. Lamarmora, 55, at the intersection with V. Sardegna, posts the after-hours rotation. (Open M-Tu and Th-Su 8:30am-1pm and 4:30-8pm.) The hospital, **Ospedale Civile San Francesco** (☎0784 24 02 37), is in Nuoro, on the highway toward Bitti. The **post office** is at the corner of V. Lamarmora and V. Ciusa, across the street from the bus stop. (☎0784 94 712. Open M-F 8am-noon.) **Postal Code:** 08020.

⌐⌐ ACCOMMODATIONS AND FOOD. Accommodations in Dorgali are generally less expensive than those in neighboring beach resorts. Ask the tourist office for a list of *agriturismi.* Surrounded by gardens and fruit trees, ■**Il Querceto ④,** V. Lamarmora, 4, 10min. downhill from the town center, is reminiscent of a countryside retreat. The front entrance and restaurant feature rotating exhibitions by local artists; the 20 enormous rooms all have tiled bath, A/C, satellite TV, and large balcony. (☎0784 96 509; www.ilquerceto.com. Breakfast included. Singles €42-58; doubles €64-90; call for information on larger rooms or partial pension. AmEx/MC/V.) Dorgali's best deal, **Bed and Breakfast ❷,** V. Azzuni, 5, keeps four rooms, all with bath, in the town center. TV room, kitchen, and terrace make the place even more comfortable. (☎/fax 0784 96 335. Breakfast included. Singles €25; doubles €45. Cash only.) Follow the signs off V. Lamarmora to the family-managed **Hotel S'Adde ❸,** V. Concordia, 38, which keeps attractive rooms with wood paneling, terrace, bath, A/C, and phone. (☎/fax 0784 94 44 12. Breakfast €6. Wheelchair accessible. Parking available. Singles €35-45; doubles €56-60; triples €75-80. AmEx/MC/V.) Restaurant downstairs is tasty and reasonably priced (*primi* around €7).

Locals crowd the lunch tables at ■**Ristorante Colibri ❸,** V. Gramsci, 14. From V. Lamarmora take V. Cerere, which becomes V. Gramsci, to the intersection with V. Flores, to chat over plates of scrumptious game and the local specialty *penne alla dorgalese* (with hot pork sauce; €6.50) or boar with rosemary seasoning. (☎0784 960 54. *Primi* €6.50-7, *secondi* €10.50-11. Cover €2. Open July-Aug. daily 1-3pm and 7-10pm; in winter closed Su. Cash only.) For a small town, Dorgali has no shortage of snack bars, but the brick-oven pizzas at **Il Giardino ❶,** V. E. Fermi, on the road to Cala Gonone, are a slice above the rest. Try the delicious *giardino,* laden with grilled veggies (€7), a bountiful salad (€7), or an international selection of beers (from €2). The house tiramisu (€3) is the best dessert in town. (☎0784 942 57. Pizza €6-8. *Primi* €6-9, *secondi* €8-16. Open M and W-Su noon-3pm and 7pm-midnight. Wheelchair accessible. AmEx/MC/V.) **Deiana Dolci Sardi ❶,** V. Africa, 3, serves handmade Sardinian sweets. Take V. Cavalotti off of V. Lamarmora to P. Francetta. (☎0784 95 096. Pastries €7.50-22 per kg, most around €8. Open M-Sa 8am-1pm and 4-8pm. Cash only.) Dorgali is also known for its red wine, which is heavy, and very flavorful. Ask for a sample at the **Enoteca di Elena Pira,** V. La Marmora, 96 (☎0784 96 574. D.O.C Dorgalese wine €10-12, other bottles €3.90-12. Open 8:30am-1pm and 3:30-9pm.)

⌐ SHOPPING. Dorgali's craft stores are at the heart of its appeal. Tourists wander the tiny streets observing artists weave, mold, and bake their wares. Stores display the handmade *filigree* jewelry, *tappeti* (wool and cotton weavings), carvings, and pastries along V. Lamarmora and its side streets; many showrooms are next door to the owner's workshop. Serafina Senette and her mother weave beautiful *tappeti* at **Il Tapetto di Serafina Senette,** P. G. Asproni, 22. (☎0784 95 202. Open daily 8:30am-1pm and 4:30-8pm. Cash only.) At **Ceramica Loddo,** V. Lamarmora, 110, owners sell their ceramics, handcrafted and painted in attractive original designs. (☎0784 96 771. Open M-Sa 9:30am-1pm and 4-8pm; Aug. also open Su. MC/V.)

CALA GONONE ☎0784

Nestled on the sea and surrounded on three sides by mountains, Cala Gonone was once only accessible by boat. Now a tunnel connects this town to Dorgali, though the difference between the two is remarkable. As you emerge from the tunnel, a vast expanse of hazy blue grey is the ocean in the distance. As people continue to discover the profound beauty of this spot, Cala Gonone is quickly becoming one of Sardinia's most popular tourist destinations, with mountains to scale, archaeological wonders to explore, a postcard-perfect harbor sheltered by limestone cliffs, and secluded sandy beaches—including the famed Cala Luna.

TRANSPORTATION AND PRACTICAL INFORMATION. Buses depart from the tourist office, at the intersection of Vle. Del Bue Marino and Vle. C. Colombo. **ARST buses** run to Dorgali (20min., 10 per day 6:40am-8:10pm, €0.67), where bus service to all other cities begins. Buy tickets at Bar La Pinetta on Vle. C. Colombo. Vle. C. Colombo leads downhill to the harbor; **Lungomare Palmesare** and **Lungomare S'Abbe Durche** run along the seafront. The **tourist office,** on Vle. del Bue Marino, offers info on accommodations and boat schedules. (☎0784 93 696. Open daily Apr.-June and Sept. 9am-1pm and 3:30-7pm; July-Aug. 9am-11pm.) An **ATM** is outside the yellow building in the center of the port. In case of **emergency,** call ☎113, the **medical clinic** at ☎0784 934 66, or the **carabinieri** at ☎0784 961 14. An **Internet** point is at Vle. C. Colombo, 5. (☎0784 92 00 15. €3 per 15min., €6.50 per hr. Open M-Sa 10am-1pm and 5-11pm. Cash only.) The **post office,** at the corner of Viale C. Colombo and V. Cala Luna, has **currency exchange.** (Open M-Sa 8:15am-1:15pm, last day of the month 8:15am-noon.) **Postal Code:** 08020.

ACCOMMODATIONS AND FOOD. One of Cala Gonone's oldest hotels, **Hotel Miramare ❹,** P. Giardini, 12, looms large over the town, right in the center of the harbor. Amenities include a rooftop solarium, balconies with loungechairs and ocean views, baths, A/C, Internet, TV, and phone. (☎0784 931 40; www.htlmiramare.it. Singles €40-67; doubles €70-120. Half pension €54-82; full pension €64-92. AmEx/MC/V.) The simple **Piccolo Hotel ❹,** V. Cristoforo Colombo, 32, is an excellent value, with 13 bright rooms, clean baths, and balconies. (☎0784 93 235 or 0784 93 232. Breakfast €2.50. Singles €43; doubles €58. Extra bed 30%. Cash only.) **Camping Villaggio Calagonone ❶,** V. Calloddi, 1, just off Vle. C. Colombo, is set back from the harbor in a mountain-ringed pine grove. Site amenities include a restaurant, pizzeria, market, bar, and recreational facilities. (☎0784 93 165; www.campingcalagonone.it. Reception daily 8am-8pm. Gates open 7am-11pm for cars. Adults €12-17.50, children ages 2-12 €6-9. Tent, parking, and hot showers free. Campers for 2 €30-50, with toilet €34-59; for 4 €52-88/54-92. Bungalows for 4 with shower €57-123. Chalets with 2-4 beds €44-200. Electricity €2-4. MC/V.)

Most places along V. C. Colombo and the *lungomare* serve decent fare; there is a **SISA** supermarket on the corner of V. Cala Luna and V. C. Colombo. Next to the post office, **Ristorante Self-Service L'Anphora ❶,** V. Cala Luna, is a cafeteria-style restaurant offering a huge variety of dishes, including fresh sea bass baked with mushrooms (☎0784 93 067. Pizza €2.50-2.70. *Panini* from €1.60. *Primi* €6-9, *sec-*

ondi €4.50-12. Takeout available. Open in summer daily 8:30am-11pm. AmEx/MC/
V.) **Il Pescatore ❸,** V. Acqua Dolce, 7, serves flavorful favorites like mixed *antipasti* (€12 per person) and *spaghetti allo scoglio.* (☎0784 831 74. *Primi* €8-10,
secondi €9-18. Open daily 12:30-2:30pm and 7:30-11pm. MC/V.)

◪▨ **BEACHES AND OUTDOORS.** Cala Gonone is ideally positioned to allow
access to both stunning beaches and adventure-sport venues. V. Bue Marino
leads 3km along the waterfront, passing long stretches of beach with clear water,
pebbly sand, and a shallow base before arriving at the resplendent **Cala Fuili.**
▨**Cala Luna,** famed for its crystal clear waters and tropical backdrop, is accessible
by boat or foot. Sheltered by limestone cliffs, the isolated cove has maintained its
pristine beauty despite the boatloads of tourists that visit daily. To reach Cala
Luna, hike a strenuous 1½hr. on the 4km trail that departs from Cala Fuili. Alternatively, **Consorzio Trasporti Marittimi** sells ferry tickets to Cala Luna at its white
booth on the port. (☎0784 93 305; ticket booth 0784 92 00 51. 8 per day 9am-5pm,
last return 6:30pm; adult round-trip €8.50-16, ages 4-12 €4.50-8.) Consorzio also
runs ferries to the elusive **Bue Marino.** The most famous of the deep grottoes
carved into the mountainside between Cala Fuili and Cala Luna, Marino is accessible only by sea. (Ferry fees include guided tour. Bue Marino: adult round-trip
€13-18, ages 4-12 €8. Bue Marino and Cala Luna: adults €18-25, ages 4-12 €11-
15.) Tour guides lead visitors through cave chambers that conceal natural curiosities, including the dripping stalactites of the "Lamp Room," and the "Mirrors
Room," in which a large pool of water reflects off the cave walls in a rainbow of
colors, owing to variances in mineral composition. (30min. tours offered in Italian, English, and French. 8 per day, 10 in Aug.; 9:30am-5:30pm; €7.)

    Prima Sardegna, V. Lungomare Palmasera, 32, rents cars (€55-72 per day), moun-
tain bikes (€16-21), and single and double kayaks (€24/42). Its guides also lead
excursions by boat, bike, or foot to natural and archaeological sites for €30-160
per person, depending on trip and duration. (☎0784 93 367 or 333 57 62 185;
www.primasardegna.com. Open daily 9am-1pm and 4-8pm. AmEx/MC/V.) **Dolmen
Servizi Turistici,** V. Vasco de Gama, 18, arranges tours, and rents mountain bikes
and scooters at comparable prices. (☎347 06 85 604 or 347 88 16 640; www.sarde-
gnadascoprire.it. Info booth at port. Office open daily 9am-1pm and 4-8pm. Info
booth open daily 8:30am-11pm. AmEx/MC/V.) Many booths along the port provide
private daily boat rentals. People interested in **scuba diving** should head to **Argo-
nauta Diving Club,** V. dei Lecci, 10, behind the campground. (☎0784 93 046;
www.argonauta.it.) Also serving tourists' marine interests is **Dimensione Mare,** on
V. C. Colombo (☎338 82 51 08; www.dimensionemare.com.)

APPENDIX

LOCAL CONDITIONS

TEMPERATURE AND CLIMATE

°CELSIUS	-5	0	5	10	15	20	25	30	35	40
°FAHRENHEIT	23	32	41	50	59	68	77	86	95	104

To convert from °C to °F, multiply by 1.8 and add 32. For a rough approximation, double the Celsius and add 25. To convert from °F to °C, subtract 32 and multiply by 0.55. For an approximation, subtract 25 from Fahrenheit and divide by two.

AVERAGE TEMPERATURE AND PRECIPITATION											
	JANUARY			APRIL			JULY			OCTOBER		
	°C	°F	cm/in.	°C	°F	cm/in.	°C	°F	cm/in.	°C	°F	cm/in.
Florence	10/2	50/35	7.3/2.9	19/8	66/46	7.8/3.0	31/17	87/62	4.0/1.6	21/10	69/50	8.8/3.5
Milan	6/-4	42/25	6.4/2.5	17/5	63/40	8.2/2.7	28/15	82/59	6.8/2.7	18/6	63/43	9.9/3.9
Rome	14/3	56/38	2.5/1.0	19/7	66/45	2.1/0.8	30/17	86/62	0.5/0.2	22/11	73/52	3.6/1.4
Venice	6/-1	42/31	5.8/2.3	16/8	61/46	6.4/2.5	27/18	81/63	6.3/2.5	18/9	64/48	6.9/2.7

TIME ZONES

Italy is 1hr. ahead of Greenwich Mean Time (GMT), 6hr. ahead of US Eastern Standard Time (EST), 9hr. ahead of Pacific Standard Time (PST), 9hr. behind Sydney, and 11hr. behind Auckland. From the last Sunday in March to the last Sunday in September, Italy switches to Daylight Savings Time and is 2hr. ahead of GMT but still 6hr. ahead of EST.

MEASUREMENTS

Italy uses the metric system. Below is a conversion chart for the English system

ENGLISH TO METRIC	METRIC TO ENGLISH
1 inch (in.) = 2.54cm	1 centimeter (cm) = 0.39 in.
1 foot (ft.) = 0.30m	1 meter (m) = 3.28 ft.
1 yard (yd.) = 0.914m	1 meter (m) = 1.09 yd.
1 mile (mi.) = 1.61km	1 kilometer (km) = 0.62 mi.
1 ounce (oz.) = 28.35g	1 gram (g) = 0.035 oz.
1 pound (lb.) = 0.454kg	1 kilogram (kg) = 2.202 lb.
1 fluid ounce (fl. oz.) = 29.57ml	1 milliliter (mL) = 0.034 fl. oz.
1 gallon (gal.) = 3.785L	1 liter (L) = 0.264 gal.
1 acre (ac.) = 0.405ha	1 hectare (ha) = 2.47 ac.
1 square mile (sq. mi.) = 2.59 sq. km	1 square kilometer (sq. km) = 0.386 sq. mi.

ABBREVIATIONS

ABBREVIATIONS	
Corso	C.
Contrada	Cda.
Di, Del, Dei, Della, Delle	d.
Locanda	Loc.
Piazza	P.
Piazzale	Ple.

ABBREVIATIONS	
Porta	Pta.
San, Santo, Santa	S.
Strada	Str.
Via	V.
Viale	Vle.
Vicolo	Vco.

DISTANCES AND TRAIN TRAVEL TIMES

	Bari	Bologna	Bolzano	Florence	Genoa	Milan	Naples	Rome	Turin	Trieste	Venice
Bari		6hr.	11hr.	7hr.	10½hr.	8½hr.	4½hr.	5hr.	10hr.	10½hr.	8½hr.
Bologna	681		3½hr.	1hr.	3hr.	2hr.	5hr.	3hr.	3½hr.	4hr.	2hr.
Bolzano	950	291		5hr.	5hr.	3½hr.	10hr.	7hr.	5½hr.	5½hr.	3½hr.
Florence	784	106	397		4hr.	3hr.	4hr.	2hr.	5hr.	5hr.	3hr.
Genoa	996	285	399	268		2hr.	7½hr.	5hr.	1½hr.	7hr.	5hr.
Milan	899	218	276	324	156		6½hr.	5hr.	1½hr.	5hr.	3hr.
Naples	322	640	931	534	758	858		2hr.	9hr.	9hr.	7hr.
Rome	482	408	90	302	526	626	232		7hr.	6½hr.	5hr.
Turin	1019	338	408	442	174	139	932	702		7hr.	5hr.
Trieste	995	308	338	414	336	420	948	715	551		2hr.
Venice	806	269	225	265	387	284	899	567	165	165	

THE ITALIAN LANGUAGE

PRONUNCIATION

VOWELS

There are seven vowel sounds in standard Italian. **A, i,** and **u** each have one pronunciation. **E** and **o** each have two slightly different pronunciations, one open and one closed, depending on the vowel's placement in the word, the stress, and the regional accent. Below are approximate pronunciations.

VOWEL PHONOLOGY	
a	"a" as in father (casa)
e: closed e: open	"ey" as in grey (sera) "eh" as in wet (sette)
i	"ee" as in cheese (vino)
o: closed o: open	"o" as in bone (sono) "aw" as in ought (bocca)
u	"oo" as in moon (gusto)

CONSONANTS

C and G: Before **a, o,** or **u,** c and g are hard, as in *candy* and *goose* or as in the Italian *colore* (koh-LOHR-eh; color), or *gatto* (GAHT-toh; cat). Italians soften c and g into **ch** and **j** sounds, respectively, when followed by **i** or **e,** as in English *cheese* and *jeep* or Italian *cibo* (CHEE-boh; goodbye), and *gelato* (jeh-LAH-toh; ice cream).

Ch and Gh: H returns **c** and **g** to their "hard" sounds in front of **i** or **e** (see above): *chianti* (ky-AHN-tee), the Tuscan wine, and *spaghetti* (spah-GEHT-tee), the pasta.

Gn and Gli: Pronounce **gn** like the **ni** in *onion,* thus *bagno* (bath) is "BAHN-yoh." Gli is like the **lli** in *million,* so *sbagliato* (wrong) is said "zbal-YAH-toh."

Sc and Sch: When followed by **a, o,** or **u,** sc is pronounced as **sk.** *Scusi* (excuse me) yields "SKOO-zee." When followed by an **e** or **i,** sc is pronounced **sh** as in *sciopero* (SHOH-pair-oh; strike). **H** returns **c** to its hard sound (sk) before **i** or **e,** as in *pesche* (PEHS-keh; peaches), not to be confused with *pesce* (PEH-sheh; fish).

Double consonants: When you see a double consonant, stress the preceding vowel; failing to do so can lead to confusion. For example, *penne all'arrabbiata* is "short pasta in a spicy red sauce," whereas *pene all'arrabbiata* means "penis in a spicy red sauce."

STRESS

In Italian, the stress generally falls on the penultimate, or next-to-last, syllable. An accent indicates when it falls on the last syllable like *città* (cheet-TAH).

GENDER AND PLURALS

Italian nouns fall into two genders, masculine and feminine. The singular masculine ending is usually **o,** as in *duomo,* and the feminine is usually **a,** as in *donna.* Words ending in an **a** in the singular (usually feminine) end with an **e** in the plural; *mela* (MEH-lah; apple), becomes *mele* (MEH-leh). Words ending in an **o** in the singular usually end with an **i** in the plural; words ending with **o** or **e** take an **i** in the plural: *conto* (KOHN-toh; bill), is *conti* (KOHN-tee), and *cane* (KAH-neh; dog), becomes *cani* (KAH-nee). Words with a final accent, like *città* and *caffè,* and words that end in consonants, like *bar* and *sport,* do not change in the plural. Adjectives agree with their noun in gender and number. They are formed by adding the gender and number ending to the root.

ARTICLES

In Italian, the gender and number of a noun determine the article that precedes it. **Definite articles** are **il, lo, la, l', i, gli,** and **le.** For all singular nouns beginning with a vowel, *l'* is the appropriate article: *l'arte* (the art). *Il* is used for masculine singular nouns that do not begin with a vowel, z, or *s impura* (s+any consonant), which are preceded by the article *lo:* il gatto (the cat), *lo zio* (the uncle), *lo stivale* (the boot). The article *la* is used with feminine singular nouns beginning with a consonant: *la capra* (the goat). In the plural, *le* precedes all feminine nouns (*le scarpe;* the shoes) and *gli* is used with masculine nouns beginning with a vowel, *z,* or *s impura* (*gli stivali,* the boots; *gli aerei,* the airplanes). The article **i** is used for all other masculine plural nouns: *i libri* (the books). **Indefinite articles** are **un, uno, una,** and **un'.** *Un* and *uno* behave like *il* and *lo,* respectively, except that *un* can precede a masculine noun beginning with a vowel: *un gatto* (a cat), *un uomo* (a man), *uno stivale* (a boot). For feminine nouns, *un'* is used before vowels and *una* is used everywhere else: *un'edicola* (a newsstand), *una ragazza* (a girl).

PHRASEBOOK

NUMBERS			
1	uno	15	quindici
2	due	16	seidici
3	tré	17	diciassette
4	quattro	18	diciotto
5	cinque	19	dicianove
6	sei	20	venti
7	sette	30	trenta
8	otto	40	quaranta
9	nove	50	cinquanta
10	dieci	60	sessanta
11	undici	70	settanta
12	dodici	80	ottanta
13	tredici	90	novanta
14	quattordici	100	cento

MONTHS*			
January	gennaio	July	luglio
February	febbraio	August	agosto
March	marzo	September	settembre
April	aprile	October	ottobre
May	maggio	November	novembre
June	giugno	December	dicembre

DAYS OF THE WEEK*	
Monday	lunedì
Tuesday	martedì
Wednesday	mercoledì
Thursday	giovedì
Friday	venerdì
Saturday	sabato
Sunday	domenica

*Note: In Italian, days of the week and months are not capitalized unless they come at the beginning of the sentence. Also, *domenica*, the Italian word for Sunday, is the only day of the week that is of the feminine gender.

GENERAL		
ENGLISH	**ITALIAN**	**PRONUNCIATION**
Hi/bye (informal)	Ciao	chow
Good day/Hello	Buongiorno	bwohn-JOHR-noh
Good evening	Buonasera	BWOH-nah-SEH-rah
Good night	Buonanotte	BWOH-nah-NOHT-teh
Goodbye	Arrivederci/ArrivederLa (formal)	ah-ree-veh-DEHR-chee/ah-ree-veh-DEHR-lah
Please	Per favore/Per piacere	pehr fah-VOH-reh/pehr pyah-CHEH-reh

Thank you	Grazie	GRAHT-see-yeh
How are you?	Come stai/Come sta (formal)?	COH-meh STA-ee/stah
I am well	Sto bene	stoh BEH-neh
You're welcome/May I help you?/Please	Prego	PREH-goh
Excuse me	Scusi	SKOO-zee
I'm sorry	Mi dispiace	mee dees-PYAH-cheh
My name is...	Mi chiamo...	mee kee-YAH-moh
What's your name?	Come ti chiami? Come si ama Lei? (formal)	COH-meh tee kee-YAH-mee/ COH-meh see kee-YAH-mah lay
Yes/No/Maybe	Sì/No/Forse	see/no/FOHR-seh
I don't know	Non lo so	nohn loh soh
Could you repeat that?	Potrebbe ripetere?	poh-TREHB-beh ree-PEH-teh-reh
What does this mean?	Cosa vuol dire questo?	COH-za vwohl DEE-reh KWEH-stoh
I understand	Ho capito	oh kah-PEE-toh
I don't understand	Non capisco	nohn kah-PEES-koh
Do you speak English?	Parla inglese?	PAR-lah een-GLEH-zeh
Could you help me?	Potrebbe aiutarmi?	poh-TREHB-beh ah-yoo-TAHR-mee
How do you say...?	Come si dice...?	KOH-meh see DEE-cheh
What do you call this in Italian?	Come si chiama questo in italiano?	KOH-meh see kee-YAH-mah KWEH-stoh een ee-tahl-YAH-no
this/that	questo/quello	KWEH-sto/KWEHL-loh
more/less	più/meno	pyoo/MEH-noh

TIME		
At what time...?	A che ora...?	ah keh OHR-ah
What time is it?	Che ore sono?	keh OHR-eh SOH-noh
It's noon/midnight	È mezzogiorno/mezzanotte	eh MEHD-zoh-DJOHR-noh/MEHD-zah-NOT-eh
now	adesso/ora	ah-DEHS-so/OH-rah
take me now	prendi mi adesso	PREN-dee mee ah-DEHS-so
tomorrow	domani	doh-MAH-nee
today	oggi	OHJ-jee
yesterday	ieri	ee-YEH-ree
right away	subito	SU-bee-toh
soon	fra poco/presto	frah POH-koh/ PREH-stoh
after	dopo	DOH-poh
before	prima	PREE-mah
late/later	tardi/più tardi	TAHR-dee/pyoo TAHR-dee
early	presto	PREHS-toh
late (after scheduled arrival time)	in ritardo	een ree-TAHR-doh
daily	quotidiano	kwoh-tee-dee-AH-no
weekly	settimanale	seht-tee-mah-NAH-leh
monthly	mensile	mehn-SEE-leh
vacation	le ferie	leh FEH-ree-eh

DIRECTIONS AND TRANSPORTATION		
Where is...?	Dov'è...?	doh-VEH
How do you get to...?	Come si arriva a...?	KOH-meh see ahr-REE-vah ah
Do you stop at...?	Si ferma...?	SEE FEHR-mah
...at the center of town	in centro	een CHEHN-troh

...at the consulate	al consolato	ahl kohn-so-LAH-toh
...at the hospital	all'ospedale	AH-los-peh-DAH-leh
...the station	la stazione	lah staht-zee-YOH-neh
near/far	vicino/lontano	vee-CHEE-noh/lohn-TAH-noh
turn left/right	gira a sinistra/destra	JEE-rah ah see-NEE-strah/DEH-strah
straight ahead	sempre diritto	SEHM-preh DREET-toh
here	qui/qua	kwee/kwah
there	lì/là	lee/lah
the street address	l'indirizzo	leen-dee-REET-soh
the telephone	il telefono	eel teh-LEH-foh-noh
street	strada, via, viale, vico, vicolo, corso	STRAH-dah, VEE-ah, vee-AH-leh, VEE-koh, VEE-koh-loh, KOHR-soh
large, open square	piazzale	pee-yah-TZAH-leh
stairway	scalinata	scah-lee-NAH-tah
beach	spiaggia	spee-YAH-geeah
river	fiume	fee-YOO-meh
toilet, WC	gabinetto	gah-bee-NEH-toh
What time does the... leave?	A che ora parte...?	ah keh OHR-ah PAHR-teh
From where does the... leave?	Da dove parte...?	dah DOH-veh PAHR-teh
...the (city) bus	...l'autobus	LAOW-toh-boos
...the (intercity) bus	...il pullman	eel POOL-mahn
...the ferry	...il traghetto	eel tra-GHEHT-toh
...hydrofoil	...l'aliscafo	LA-lee-scah-foh
...the plane	...l'aereo	lah-EHR-reh-oh
...the train	...il treno	eel TREH-noh
the ticket office	la biglietteria	lah beel-yeht-teh-RI-ah
How much does it cost?	Quanto costa?	KWAN-toh CO-stah
I would like to buy...	Vorrei comprare...	voy-RAY com-PRAH-reh
...a ticket	...un biglietto	...oon beel-YEHT-toh
...a pass (bus, etc.)	...una tessera	OO-nah TEHS-seh-rah
one-way	solo andata	SO-lo ahn-DAH-tah
round-trip	andata e ritorno	ahn-DAH-tah eh ree-TOHR-noh
reduced price	ridotto	ree-DOHT-toh
student discount	lo sconto studentesco	loh SKOHN-toh stoo-dehn-TEHS-koh
The train is late	Il treno è in ritardo	eel TRAY-no eh een ree-TAHR-doh
the track/train platform	il binario	eel bee-NAH-ree-oh
the flight	il volo	eel VOH-loh
the reservation	la prenotazione	la preh-no-taht-see-YOH-neh
the entrance/the exit	l'ingresso/l'uscita	leen-GREH-so/loo-SHEE-tah
I need to get off here	Devo scendere qui	DEH-vo SHEN-der-eh qwee

EMERGENCY

I lost my passport/wallet	Ho perso il passaporto/portafoglio	oh PEHR-soh eel pahs-sah-POHR-toh/por-ta-FOH-lee-oh
I've been robbed	Sono stato derubato/a	SOH-noh STAH-toh deh-roo-BAH-toh/tah
Wait!	Aspetta!	ahs-PEHT-tah
Stop!	Ferma!	FEHR-mah
Help!	Aiuto!	ah-YOO-toh

Leave me alone!	Lasciami stare!/Mollami!	LAH-shah-mee STAH-reh/MOH-lah MEE
Don't touch me!	Non mi toccare!	NOHN mee tohk-KAH-reh
Go back to where you came from!	Vai a quel paese!	VAH-ee ah KWEL pa-EH-zeh
I'm calling the police!	Telefono alla polizia!	tehl-LEH-foh-noh ah-lah poh-leet-SEE-ah
military police	carabinieri	CAH-rah-been-YEH-ree
Go away, moron!	Vattene, cretino!	VAH-teh-neh creh-TEE-noh

MEDICAL		
I have... allergies	Ho... delle allergie	OH... DEHL-leh ahl-lair-JEE-eh
...a cold	...un raffreddore	oon rahf-freh-DOH-reh
...a cough	...una tosse	OO-nah TOHS-seh
...the flu	...l'influenza	linn-floo-ENT-sah
...a fever	...una febbre	OO-nah FEHB-breh
...a headache	...mal di testa	mahl dee TEHS-tah
My foot/arm/booty hurts	Mi fa male il piede/braccio/culo	mee fah MAH-le eel PYEHD-deh/BRAH-cho/COO-loh
I'm on the Pill	Prendo la pillola	PREHN-doh lah PEE-loh-lah
(3 months) pregnant	incinta (da tre mesi)	een-CHEEN-tah (dah TREH MEH-zee)

RESTAURANTS		
food	il cibo	eel CHEE-boh
wine bar	l'enoteca	len-oh-TEK-ah
breakfast	la colazione	lah coh-laht-see-YO-neh
lunch	il pranzo	eel PRAHND-zoh
dinner	la cena	lah CHEH-nah
coffee	il caffè	eel kah-FEH
appetizer	l'antipasto	lahn-tee-PAH-stoh
first course	il primo	eel PREE-moh
second course	il secondo	eel seh-COHN-doh
side dish	il contorno	eel cohn-TOHR-noh
dessert	il dolce	eel DOHL-cheh
bottle	la bottiglia	lah boh-TEEL-yah
waiter/waitress	il/la cameriere/a	eel/lah kah-meh-ree-EH-reh/rah
the bill	il conto	eel COHN-toh
cover charge	il coperto	eel koh-PEHR-toh
tip	la mancia	lah MAHN-chee-yah

HOTEL AND HOSTEL RESERVATIONS		
hotel/hostel	albergo/ostello	al-BEHR-goh/os-TEHL-loh
Could I reserve a single room/double room (for the second of August)?	Potrei prenotare una camera singola/doppia (per il due agosto)?	poh-TREH-ee preh-noh-TAH-reh oo-nah CAH-meh-rah SEEN-goh-lah/DOH-pee-yah (pehr eel DOO-eh ah-GOH-stoh)
Is there a bed available tonight?	C'è un posto libero stasera?	cheh oon POHS-toe LEE-ber-oh sta-SER-ah
with bath/shower	con bagno/doccia	kohn BAHN-yo/DOH-cha
Is there a cheaper room without a bath/shower?	C'è una stanza più economica senza bagno/doccia?	cheh oo-nah STAN-zah pyoo eko-NOM-ika sen-zah BAHN-yo/DOH-cha
open/closed	aperto/chiuso	ah-PEHR-toh/KYOO-zoh
sheets	i lenzuoli	ee lehn-SUO-lee
the blanket	la coperta	lah koh-PEHR-tah
the bed	il letto	eel LEHT-toh

APPENDIX

heating	il riscaldamento	eel ree-skahl-dah-MEHN-toh
How much is the room?	Quanto costa la camera?	KWAHN-toh KOHS-ta lah KAM-eh-rah
I will arrive (at 2:30pm)	Arriverò (alle due e mezzo)	ah-ree-veh-ROH (ah-leh DOO-eh MED-zoh)
We're closed during August	Chiudiamo ad agosto	kyu-dee-AH-moh ahd ah-GOH-stoh
We're full	Siamo al completo	See-YAH-moh ahl cohm-PLAY-toh
We don't take telephone reservations	Non si fanno le prenotazioni per telefono	nohn see FAHN-noh leh preh-noh-tat-see-YOH-nee pair teh-LEH-foh-noh
You'll have to send a deposit/check	Bisogna mandare un anticipo/un assegno	bee-ZOHN-yah mahn-DAH-reh oon ahn-TEE-chee-poh/oon ahs-SEHN-yoh
What is that funny smell?	Che cos'è quest'odore strano?	keh kohz-EH kwest-oh-DOOR-eh STRAH-noh?

AMORE		
I have a boyfriend/girl-friend	Ho un ragazzo/una ragazza	Oh oon rah-GAHT-soh/oo-nah rah-GAHT-sah
Let's get a room	Prendiamo una camera	Prehn-DYAH-moh oo-nah CAH-meh-rah
Voluptuous!	Volutuoso/a!	VOL-oot-oo-OH-zhoh/zhah
To be enamoured of	Essere innamorato/a di	Eh-seh-reh een-am-mo-rah-to/ta dee
Just a kiss	Solo un bacio	SOH-loh oon BAH-chee-oh
Are you single?	Sei celibe?	SEY CHEH-lee-beh
You're cute	Sei carino/a (bello/a)	SEY cah-REEN-oh/ah (BEHL-loh/lah)
I love you, I swear	Ti amo, te lo giuro	Tee AH-moh, teh loh DJOO-roh
I'm married	Sono sposato/a	Soh-noh spo-ZA-to/ta
You're quite a babe	Sei proprio un figo/una figa	SEY PROH-pree-yo oon FEE-goh/oona FEE-gah
Give me pleasure	Fa mi godere	Fah mee go-DEHR-ay
I only have safe sex	Pratico solo sesso sicuro	PRAH-tee-coh sohl-oh SEHS-so see-COO-roh
Leave her alone, she's mine	Lasciala stare, è mia	LAH-shyah-lah STAH-reh, eh mee-ah
Leave right now!	Vai via subito!	Vai VEE-ah SOO-beet-oh
I'll never forget you	Non ti dimenticherò mai	Nohn tee dee-men-tee-ker-OH mah-ee
The profound mystery of what you just said sets my soul on fire	Il profondo mistero di ciò che sta dicendo mi infuoca il cuore	Eel pro-FUN-doh mee-EH-row dee CHEE-oh kay stah dee-CEN-doh mee een-FWOH-cah eel ku-WOR-ay
Not if you're the last man on earth	Neacnhe se lei fosse l'unico uomo sulla terra	nay-AHN-kay say FOH-say LOO-nee-koh WOH-moh soo-LAH TAY-rah.

AT THE BAR		
May I buy you a drink?	Posso offrirle qualcosa da bere?	POHS-soh ohf-FREER-leh kwahl-COH-zah dah Beh-reh
a beer	una birra	OO-nah BEER-rah
glass of wine	bicchiere di vino	bee-KYE-reh dee VEE-noh
liter of wine	litro di vino	LEE-troh di VEE-noh
I'm drunk	Sono ubriaco/a	SOH-noh oo-BRYAH-coh/cah
Let's go!	Andiamo!	Ahn-dee-AH-moh
I don't drink	Non bevo	nohn BEH-voh
Cheers!	Cin cin!	cheen cheen
Do you have a light?	Mi fai accendere?	mee fah-ee ah-CHEN-deh-reh
No thank you, I don't smoke	No grazie, non fumo	noh GRAH-zyeh nohn FOO-moh
I was here first!	C'ero io prima!	CHEH-roh EE-oh PREE-mah
Do you believe in aliens?	Credi negli extraterrestri?	CREH-dee neh-lyee ehx-trah-teh-REH-stree
I feel like throwing up	Mi viene di vomitare	mee VYE-neh dee voh-mee-TAH-reh

MENU READER

PRIMI (FIRST COURSES)	
pasta aglio e olio	garlic and olive oil
pasta all'amatriciana	in a tangy tomato sauce with onions and bacon
pasta all'arabbiata	in a spicy tomato sauce
pasta alla bolognese	in a meat sauce
pasta alla boscaiola	egg pasta, served in a mushroom sauce with peas and cream
pasta alla carbonara	in a creamy sauce with egg, cured bacon, and cheese
pasta alla pizzaiola	tomato-based sauce with olive oil and red peppers
pasta alla puttanesca	in a tomato sauce with olives, capers, and anchovies
gnocchi ("NYAW-kee")	potato dumplings
ravioli	square-shaped and often stuffed with cheese or vegetables
tagliatelle	thin and flat, these are the northern version of fettuccini
polenta	deep fried cornmeal
risotto	rice dish, comes in nearly as many flavors as pasta sauce

PIZZA	
alla capriciosa	with ham, egg, artichoke, and more
con rucola (rughetta)	with arugula (rocket for Brits)
marinara	with red sauce and no cheese
margherita	plain ol' tomato, mozzarella, and basil
pepperoni	bell pepper
polpette	meatballs
quattro formaggi	with four cheeses
quattro stagioni	four seasons; a different topping for each quarter of the pizza, usually mushrooms, *prosciutto crudo*, artichoke, and tomato

SECONDI (SECOND COURSES)	
animelle alla griglia	grilled sweetbreads
asino	donkey (served in Sicily and Sardinia)
bistecca	steak
cavallo (sfilacci)	horse (a delicacy throughout the South and Sardinia)
coniglio	rabbit
cotoletta	breaded veal cutlet with cheese
cozze	mussels
gamberi	prawns
granchi	crab
manzo	beef
osso buco	braised veal shank
polpo	octopus
prosciutto	smoked ham, available cured *(crudo)* or cooked *(cotto)*
salsiccia	sausage
saltimbocca alla romana	slices of veal and ham cooked together and topped with cheese
seppia	cuttlefish, usually served grilled in its own ink
speck	smoked raw ham, lean but surrounded by a layer of fat
tonno	tuna
trippa	tripe (chopped, sautéed cow intestines, usually in a tomato sauce)
vitello	veal
vongole	clams

APPENDIX

CONTORNI (SIDE DISHES)	
broccoletti	broccoli florets
cavolo	cabbage
cipolla	onion
fagioli	beans (usually white)
fagiolini	green beans
funghi	mushrooms
insalata caprese	tomatoes with mozzarella cheese and basil, drizzled with olive oil
insalata mista	mixed green salad
lattuga	lettuce
melanzana	eggplant
tartufi	truffles

ANTIPASTI (APPETIZERS)	
bresaola	thinly sliced dried beef, served with olive oil, lemon, and *parmigiano*
bruschetta	crisp slices of garlic-rubbed, baked bread, often with raw tomatoes
carpaccio	extremely thin slices of lean, raw beef
crostini	small pieces of toasted bread usually served with chicken liver or mozzarella and anchovies, though other toppings abound
fiori di zucca	zucchini flowers filled with cheese, battered, and lightly fried
suppli	fried rice ball filled with tomato, meat, and cheese

FRUTTA (FRUIT)	
arancia	orange
ciliegia	cherry
fragola	strawberry
lampone	raspberry
pesca	peach
prugna	plum
uva	grape

DOLCI (DESSERTS)	
gelato	Italian-style ice cream
granita	ice-based fruit or coffee slushee
macedonia	fruit salad
panna cotta	flan
sfogliatelle	sugar-coated layers of crunchy pastry with ricotta
tiramisù	marscapone, eggs, and lady fingers dipped in *espresso*

PREPARATION	
al dente	firm to the bite (pasta)
al forno	baked
al vino	in wine sauce
al sangue	rare
fritta/o	fried
ben cotta/o	well done
cruda/o	raw
fresca/o	fresh
fritta/o	fried
non troppo cotta/o	medium rare
piccante	spicy
ripieno	stuffed

INDEX

ABOUT LET'S GO

NOT YOUR PARENTS' TRAVEL GUIDE

At Let's Go, we see every trip as the chance of a lifetime. If your dream is to grab a machete and forge through the jungles of Brazil, we can take you there. If you'd rather bask in the Riviera sun at a beachside cafe, we'll set you a table. We write for readers who know that there's more to travel than sharing double deckers with tourists and who believe that travel can change both themselves and the world—whether they plan to spend six days in London or six months in Latin America. We'll show you just how far your money can go, and prove that the greatest limitation on your adventures is not your wallet, but your imagination.

BEYOND THE TOURIST EXPERIENCE

To help you gain a deeper connection with the places you travel, our fearless researchers scour the globe to give you the heads-up on both world-renowned and off-the-beaten-track attractions, sights, and destinations. They engage with the local culture, only to emerge with the freshest insights on everything from local festivals to regional cuisine. We've also opened our pages to respected writers and scholars to hear their takes on the countries and regions we cover, and asked travelers who have worked, studied, or volunteered abroad to contribute first-person accounts of their experiences. In addition, we increased our coverage of responsible travel and expanded each guide's Beyond Tourism chapter to share more ideas about how to give back while on the road.

FORTY-SIX YEARS OF WISDOM

Let's Go got its start in 1960, when a group of creative and well-traveled students compiled their experience and advice into a 20-page mimeographed pamphlet, which they gave to travelers on charter flights to Europe. Four and a half decades later, we've expanded to cover six continents and all kinds of travel—while retaining our founders' adventurous attitude toward the world. Laced with witty prose and total candor, our guides are still researched and written entirely by students on shoestring budgets, experienced travelers who know that train strikes, stolen luggage, food poisoning, and marriage proposals are all part of a day's work.

THE LET'S GO COMMUNITY

More than just a travel guide company, Let's Go is a community. Our small staff comes together because of our shared passion for travel and our desire to help other travelers see the world the way it was meant to be seen. We love it when our readers become part of the Let's Go community as well—when you travel, drop us a postcard (67 Mt. Auburn St., Cambridge, MA 02138, USA), send us an e-mail (feedback@letsgo.com), or post on our forum (http://www.letsgo.com/connect/forum) to tell us about your adventures and discoveries.

For more information, visit us online: www.letsgo.com.

MAP APPENDIX

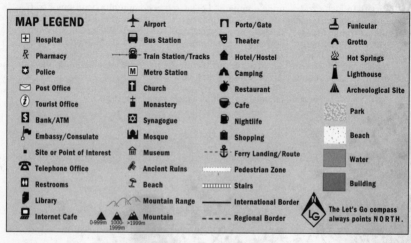

MAP LEGEND

✈ Airport	⛩ Porto/Gate	🚠 Funicular
⊞ Hospital	🚌 Bus Station	🎭 Theater	⌒ Grotto
℞ Pharmacy	🚂 Train Station/Tracks	🏨 Hotel/Hostel	♨ Hot Springs
✪ Police	Ⓜ Metro Station	⛺ Camping	🗼 Lighthouse
✉ Post Office	✝ Church	🍎 Restaurant	🔺 Archeological Site
ⓘ Tourist Office	✞ Monastery	☕ Cafe	Park
🏦 Bank/ATM	✡ Synagogue	Nightlife	Beach
Embassy/Consulate	☪ Mosque	🛍 Shopping	Water
■ Site or Point of Interest	🏛 Museum	⚓ Ferry Landing/Route	Building
☎ Telephone Office	Ancient Ruins	Pedestrian Zone	
⊞ Restrooms	Beach	Stairs	
Library	Mountain Range	International Border	
Internet Cafe	Mountain 0-999m 1000-1999m >1999m	Regional Border	The Let's Go compass always points NORTH.